MENTAL HEALTH IN THE WAR
ON TERROR

Mental Health in the War on Terror

CULTURE, SCIENCE, AND STATECRAFT

Neil Krishan Aggarwal

 COLUMBIA UNIVERSITY PRESS   NEW YORK

COLUMBIA UNIVERSITY PRESS
Publishers Since 1893
New York   Chichester, West Sussex
cup.columbia.edu
Copyright © 2015 Columbia University Press
All rights reserved

Library of Congress Cataloging-in-Publication Data

Aggarwal, Neil Krishan, author.
  Mental health in the war on terror : culture, science, and statecraft / Neil Krishan Aggarwal.
      p. ; cm.
  Includes bibliographical references and index.
  ISBN 978-0-231-16664-5 (cloth : alk. paper) — ISBN 978-0-231-53844-2 (e-book)
  I. Title.
  [DNLM: 1. Mental Health—ethnology—United States. 2. Bioethical Issues—United States.
3. Prisoners of War—psychology—United States. 4. Terrorism—psychology—United States.
5. Veterans—psychology—United States. WA 305 AA1]

RC451.4.p7
616.890086'97—dc23

2014020991

Columbia University Press books are printed on permanent and durable acid-free paper.
This book is printed on paper with recycled content.
Printed in the United States of America

c 10 9 8 7 6 5 4 3 2 1

Cover design: Milenda Nan Ok Lee
Cover image: © AP Photo/Brennan Linsley

References to websites (URLs) were accurate at the time of writing.
Neither the author nor Columbia University Press is responsible for URLs
that may have expired or changed since the manuscript was prepared.

The question or questions that have to be asked are: "What types of knowledge are you trying to disqualify when you say that you are a science? What speaking subject, what discursive subject, what subject of experience and knowledge are you trying to minorize when you begin to say: 'I speak this discourse, I am speaking a scientific discourse, and I am a scientist.' What theoretico-political vanguard are you trying to put on the throne in order to detach it from all the massive, circulating, and discontinuous forms that knowledge can take?"

—Michel Foucault, *Society Must Be Defended*

CONTENTS

FOUCAULT'S PENETRATING INSIGHTS INTO THE connections between knowledge and power, between science and politics, have gripped me since the declaration of the War on Terror. I entered medical school in 2000 and watched the 9/11 attacks unfold on live television. As I attended medical conferences, I began perceiving the creeping influence of politics within academic discussions: bioethicists debated the philosophical grounds for torture, and psychiatrists conjectured about the irrational motivations of suicide bombers. Medical scientists placed certain theoretico-political vanguards related to national security on the throne of science at this exceptional moment of American history. What perspectives were becoming "minorized" and "majorized" in the War on Terror, and how did these perspectives immortalize cultural values, beliefs, and orientations as scientific knowledge? In a broad sense, how has the War on Terror changed medicine, and how has medicine changed the War on Terror?

The goal of this book is to analyze the cultural meanings of mental health knowledge and practice produced throughout the War on Terror. My frameworks for studying the interrelationships of mental health, culture, and power come primarily from cultural psychiatry and medical anthropology. Central to both disciplines is the tenet that medical systems are cultural systems with beliefs, behaviors, and meanings transacted among individuals in social institutions. I aim to show through a wide array of materials that we can study medical systems in the War on Terror as cultural systems. These source materials include government documents; reports and position papers from nongovernmental organizations; legal files such as charge sheets, motions, rulings, and transcripts; direct and indirect interviews; newspaper articles; and scholarly publications. These analyses are not intended against the mental health system as a whole, and they certainly do not belong to the antipsychiatry movement. As a psychiatric clinician and researcher, I have witnessed the healing power of effective medications and psychotherapy. However, mental health suffers from a long history of stigma in much of the world. The peculiar cultural construction of mental health knowledge and practice in response to the War on Terror may exacerbate this mistrust. This book is not an exhaustive catalog of mental health knowledge and practice in the War on Terror, nor is it meant to be polemical or apologetic. On the contrary, the book takes seriously the idea that mental health routinely faces sharp challenges from the state. Mental health knowledge lends itself to conflicts of interest between the individual and society because it is employed in practice to differentiate normal and abnormal states of being within society. The state may wish to punish undesirable populations, and political uses of psychiatry may result when mental health professionals work uncritically toward state interests.

This book appears at a time when three cultural trends have affected medicine. First, most attention to mental health in the War on Terror has centered on bioethical debates. While mental health professionals involved in coercive interrogations or questionable clinical practices certainly deserve scrutiny, bioethical violations represent a larger issue of employing mental health knowledge and practice to advance the goals of statecraft. Investigating this larger issue is the goal of this book. Second, cultural psychiatry has typically drawn upon many disciplines—psychology, sociology, anthropology, and cultural studies—to create a vibrant specialty that understands mental health and illness in its social and cultural contexts. The rise of evidence-based medicine has disqualified ways of knowing and learning aside from large clinical trials. In my capacity as a psychiatric researcher and educator, I worry that our trainees ignore the social sciences and humanities, which have much to teach us about those areas of life, such as birth, death, pain, and suffering, to which medicine should not lay exclusive claim. Third, the representation of Muslims and Islam in medical scholarship has often gone unchecked. Many stereotypes that would not be countenanced for other groups are willingly tolerated and even promoted. Scholars of religion and cultural psychiatrists can collaborate to ensure that such negativity is not disseminated under the guise of science. I hope that this book will stimulate critical discussions around the cultures of biomedicine through incisive examinations of its professional literature.

ACKNOWLEDGMENTS

I HAVE INCURRED MANY DEBTS in writing this book. Several people wished me well throughout its execution. In 2000, Amer Sidani, Rachna Dave, Omer Bokhari, and Moustafa Banna first suggested that I write. In 2003, Ravjot Singh Pasricha and Arun Janikaraman encouraged the process. In 2011, Nimay Mehta told me that he would be the first to purchase the book. Parvinder Thiara and Luvleen Sidhu supported the book through its end in 2013. Ricky Shah and Samir Rao helped me consider how to market the book. Thank you to you all.

My teachers at Sewickley Academy cultivated my love for learning. Kenneth Goleski, Sira Metzinger, and Karen Coleman helped me discover a capacity for languages; Larry Hall, Peter Golding, and Ham Clark encouraged me to question authority through polite but incisive arguments; Bill Barnes, Joan Reteshka, and Larry Connolly taught me to write; Vicki Polinko and the late Barbara Salak refined my aesthetic sense. At Case Western Reserve University, Marie Pierre Le-Hir, Jackie Nanfito, and Vincent McHale pushed me in supervising my theses. Atwood Gaines, James Pfeiffer, and Rachel Chapman introduced me to medical anthropology.

In medical school, Paul Farmer challenged me to think about applying social theory to clinical medicine and sustained a three-year correspondence with me as I considered graduate school. Joy Marshall, Stuart Youngner, and Max Mehlmann encouraged me not to relinquish my interests in the social and cultural determinants of health. Jerrold Post exposed me to the intellectual borderlands between psychiatry and political theory. These rewarding experiences drew me to Harvard University and my most formidable academic encounters. Early on, Ali Asani grasped that I would work at the intersection of medicine, social theory, and South Asian religions. Michael Witzel, Larry McCrea, Wheeler Thackston, Carl Sharif El-Tobgui, Moustafa Atamnia, Shahab Ahmed, and Sunil Sharma taught me patiently. Discussions of social theory with friends such as Rehan Ali, Dan

Sheffield, Mark Breeze, Nick Walters, Aliya Iqbal, Harpreet Singh, Sarah Pinto, Adia Benton, Sharon Abramowitz, Ernesto Martinez, Nabilah Siddiquee, Manata Hashemi, and Sarah Eltantawi have clarified my thoughts considerably. Byron Good pushed me to explore how social theories can be brought into clinical practice. Arthur Kleinman has been a mentor who expects academic excellence.

I used my training at Yale University to develop independent academic and clinical interests. The university chaplain, Sharon Kugler, entrusted me with advising the Hindu community and shared my vision of fostering dialogue between the fields of mental health and religion. Paul Kirwin, Ezra Griffith, Jean Baptiste, Joe Check, Seth Powsner, Claudia Bemis, Deborah Knudson-González, and Eric Berger helped forge my clinical concerns in patient care. My friends Ke Xu, Jessica Chaudhary, Nabyl Tejani, Emily Tejani, Andres Barkil, Frank Appah, Zaheer Kanji, and Bibhav Acharya spent hours discussing cultural psychiatry. Many of them attended my Culture and Mental Health class that introduced the tensions of working with culture in clinical practice through readings in cultural psychiatry and psychiatric anthropology. The constructive criticisms of the class forced me to develop these concepts further. I learned a great deal from discussions on social theory and religion with Hussein Abdulsater, Matt Melvin-Koushki, and Sayeed Rahman.

At Columbia University, the Center of Excellence for Cultural Competence has provided me with a remarkable home. Roberto Lewis-Fernández had shared my vision for making cultural psychiatry relevant to the contemporary practice of all mental health clinicians. More than anyone else, he has taught me that the best academic work requires the patience to read, synthesize scholarship, and analyze relentlessly. Andel Nicasio and Marit Boiler have been warm friends and colleagues. Ravi DeSilva was always available for coffee and thought-provoking discussions. The Cultural Formulation class for the second-year residents has never ceased to make me realize just how insignificant cultural psychiatry can be without daily clinical relevance. Schuyler Henderson was a tough writing partner who propelled this book's proposal and submission for review. Jennifer Perillo, Stephen Wesley, and the staff at Columbia University Press have been unflinching supporters of this book and struck the rare balance between warmth and professionalism. Though mentioned before, Ezra Griffith and Sarah Pinto also graciously read through the entire manuscript and suggested valuable, constructive revisions.

Finally, I reserve my greatest appreciation for my community. I grew up in Weirton, West Virginia, and attended the Hindu-Jain Temple, which served as the social and cultural headquarters of our expatriate Indian community. I thank this social family and the Vidya Mandir Sunday School for inculcating whatever positive virtues I now have. In particular, Billu and Nilu Aichbhaumik, Amrit and Veena Aggarwal, Vijai and Sarita Singh, Vinita Srivastava, Sarika and Nandu Machiraju, Rajiv Ahuja, and Shawn Badlani encouraged me in various ways to pursue this book. The Mary H. Weir Public Library, my favorite place in Weirton, was where I first learned to read, and I miss this library now that I live in New York City. Dean, Eugenia, and the late familial matriarch also named Eugenia Makricostas have been our Greek American family for three decades. My in-laws, Niraj Nabh and Anshu Kumar, have always treated me more like a son. My sisters-in-law, Reema Aggarwal and Radhika Kumar, have helped me find humor in every situation. I honor the memories of my grandparents, Sarla Aggarwal, Shyam Lal Aggarwal, Kesar Devi Aggarwal, and Nanak Aggarwal, who struggled to establish our families after migrating from Pakistan to India during the Partition of 1947. My parents, Madhu and Krishan Kumar Aggarwal, have furnished me with boundless love. Many Hindus believe that one cannot repay parents except through raising virtuous children, and I hope that I can accomplish this task. My father has always pointed to heroes such as Meera, Kabir, Shivaji, Guru Nanak, and Guru Gobind Singh, who never hesitated to voice concerns about injustice. My father has always supported my dreams, and this book is a testament to his trust, patience, and inspiration. My brother, Manu Aggarwal, has been my best friend for three decades. It is to him and to my wife, Ritambhara Kumar, that this book is dedicated. Ritambhara has been the love of my life ever since we met in Andaaz at Harvard in 2007. May our lives continue to surprise us with unexpected success, happiness, and prosperity, especially now that little Amaya Ishvari has come into our home.

*MENTAL HEALTH IN THE WAR
ON TERROR*

Mental Health, Culture, and Power in the War on Terror

TO ACCESS THE INPATIENT PSYCHIATRIC unit of the East Coast Veteran Affairs Medical Center (ECVA)—the destination for veterans judged imminently suicidal, homicidal, or unable to complete basic activities such as feeding and grooming—each person must clear security checkpoints.[1] Psychiatrists, psychologists, nurses, social workers, secretaries, and other hospital workers present photo identification to a security officer. Patient visitors complete sign-in sheets requiring names, times of entry, destinations, signatures, and times of exit. Patients reach the unit in two ways, always supervised by a security official: either outpatient clinicians who suspect that patients meet criteria for admission consult with clinical supervisors or emergency room clinicians consult with the admitting attending psychiatrist. Clinical supervisors and emergency room psychiatrists then inquire about bed availability from the inpatient charge nurse. In all cases, staff, family members, friends, and patients ascend from the lower floors of surgery and internal medicine to reach the inpatient unit. No one enters or exits the inpatient unit without permission.

Five steps from the elevators, a corridor traverses the length of the hospital floor. A sign directs traffic on the left end to the Special Day Treatment Program (SDTP) and on the right end to the inpatient psychiatric unit. The doors to the SDTP are open throughout the day, permitting views of the entire unit, but the bulky beige doors of the inpatient unit remain shut. SDTP visitors walk to the office area at the center of the unit to check in with staff, but inpatient visitors must step within view of the ceiling-mounted security camera and press the button on the wall for entry.

Patients on the SDTP come and go at will during the daytime to visit homeless shelters, group homes, apartments, and potential places of employment as they transition to life outside of the hospital, but inpatients can exit the unit only to attend recreational activities or meet with clinicians in the courtyard downstairs. The SDTP and the inpatient unit are diametrically opposed, both spatially and philosophically.

After graduation from medical school, all psychiatry residents must train in outpatient and inpatient units. The outpatient units treat people with common disorders whose severity does not warrant hospitalization. In contrast, rotations on an inpatient unit accomplish several goals: they familiarize trainees with the most threatening conditions; they introduce trainees to the practices and procedures of inpatient life; they expose trainees to the benefits and challenges of working in multidisciplinary teams of psychiatrists, nurses, psychologists, and social workers with varying experience; and they allow trainees to hone their skills in diagnosis, treatment planning, initiating and monitoring medications and psychotherapy, writing daily notes with requisite information for billing, and consulting with other medical specialists when psychiatric patients suffer from disorders like diabetes or high blood pressure. American psychiatric residency training lasts four years and mixes rotations through different service settings and medical specialties.

I began my psychiatric training in June 2007 after six months of internal medicine and two months of neurology. Working in other specialties imparts the competence to unmask psychiatric disorders from disguised illnesses. In a classic example, the cluster of depressed mood, poor energy, poor appetite, physical sluggishness, and loss of interest in pleasurable activities can be either hypothyroidism or major depressive disorder. The first-line treatments for these problems differ: hypothyroidism requires synthetic thyroid hormone, while major depressive disorder is treated with antidepressants and psychotherapy. On February 29, 2008, the last day of my neurology rotation, I rejoiced at the end of internal medicine and neurology but worried about my knowledge of psychiatry. My knowledge of internal medicine and neurology was rudimentary, but I could treat high blood pressure and high cholesterol better than generalized anxiety disorder or schizophrenia. The ECVA inpatient unit rotation of three months heralded three years of psychiatric rotations designed to remedy this imbalance.

I approached my ECVA rotation with apprehension about my abilities and anxiety about the risk for violence, since inpatient units treat those with the most severe pathologies. I did what was expected before every rotation: the night before, I called the resident who was transitioning off the team to obtain "sign out." Sign out, the list of all patients under the care of a specific resident, is provided at times of transition, such as when the night resident on call takes over for the day team or when the resident rotates off a clinical service. Exactly what sign out contains varies by medical specialty, but the patient's name, age, admission diagnosis, current medications, and plan of action in case of emergency are essential. The resident and I spent a minute each discussing the plan for his five patients as I dutifully recorded all details.

On the first Monday in March 2008, I ascended by elevator to the inpatient unit at eight A.M. I pressed the intercom button: "Hi, I'm Neil Aggarwal, one of the new residents starting today."

A voice crackled over the speaker: "Hi. Your badge works. Come on in. Just make sure that there aren't any patients hovering around the door."

I flashed my badge, heard the doors unlock, and walked into the unit. All residents who have rotated away from an inpatient unit for a period of time can find their bearings even in unfamiliar surroundings, intuiting meanings and behaviors associated with space in mere seconds. The locked room on the right side with a closed shutter over the window must be a room for patients and clinicians to meet privately. The large desk ahead bisecting the unit by length like the vertex of the letter T must be the nurses' workstation. The open doors on both sides of the hall after the workstation must be patient bedrooms. I peered inside a window and saw four men lying in two perpendicular beds against opposite walls. I returned to the workstation, turned my back to the desk, and examined the other hallway. The two doors with grated vents closest to me must be bathrooms. The two locked doors with closed shutters at the end of the hallway must be meeting rooms. The hallway ended at a door different from all the others—made of steel, not wood, and with a conspicuous lock; this must be the entrance to clinician offices.

Behind the workstation desk were two bureaus with several computers, bulletin boards, and a large whiteboard on the right wall behind the inpatient unit secretary: "Hi. Write your name and pager number under the line for 'Residents.' Here is a schedule for the unit and a key to the doctor offices straight ahead." The wall opened into a nurses' conference room.

Medical inpatient units contain a large board over a wall in an area visible to clinicians so they can make decisions about admissions and discharges outside of patient view. This design protects individual patient health information from public exposure. The ECVA whiteboard followed a fixed format, with content differentiated by color. A grid in one color with patient initials, admission date, anticipated discharge date, and privileges to leave the unit occupied the vast expanse of the board. Radiating from the grid in a different color were common telephone numbers for different personnel such as patient transport, the emergency room, the main pharmacy, kitchen staff, security, internal medicine consult, dental consult, art therapy, the four psychiatric residents on service, the three attending psychiatrists on the unit, the clinical psychology trainees, the unit clinical psychologist, and the unit social worker. The whiteboard orients clinicians and administrators to the unit's flux and turbulence like an airplane pilot's instruments: more patients with recent admission dates imply acute pathology; more patients with restricted exit privileges cue us to disciplinary problems.

I glanced at the paper schedule, also laid out on a grid. On the left side were rows listing daytime hours. On the right side were columns by days of the week. Each cell contained activities by hour. Key activities were common to all medical specialties, such as times for morning rounds, medication dispensation, and general visiting hours. Other activities were peculiar to psychiatry, such as group therapy, art therapy, and times for individual meetings with psychiatrists, psychologists, and social workers. Certain activities were peculiar to the ECVA inpatient unit, such as recreational activities in the courtyard or excursions to the hospital cafeteria for those with exit privileges. The grid explicitly included basic activities: waking, grooming, breakfast, lunch, dinner, and sleeping times. Other than morning rounds, patients had no psychiatric meetings until the afternoon, with the evening reserved for visitors and recreational activities. The schedule focused on patients, not clinicians. I would discover my schedule by talking to others who had previously been in my position.

In that sense, the inpatient unit acculturates patients into patienthood and physicians into physician-hood through different channels. Its inhabitants operate within a highly regulated time-space continuum. In all societies, people assimilate local knowledge about where they can go and when they can go. Some spaces are always accessible, such as the twenty-four-hour store or our bedrooms. Other spaces, such as work-places, are accessible only at certain hours. Hospitals function paradoxi-cally: although anyone can come at any time for any medical complaint through the emergency room, only specified people can access inpatient and outpatient units during designated hours. The inpatient unit quali-fies as a "total institution" (Goffman 1961), since sleep, play, and work are regulated by authorities, in the company of others, and tightly scheduled. Staff and inpatients occupy distinct roles with defined rules, punishments, and privileges. For example, I learned from speaking with the attending physician that morning rounds—the practice of discussing the diagnoses and treatment plans for all patients—started between eight thirty and nine thirty A.M. and lasted up to an hour. The attending physician sits atop the clinician hierarchy after completing residency training, assum-ing ultimate treatment and medicolegal responsibility for each patient. Nurses, psychologists, and social workers contribute information from patient interactions, but the attending physician determines the relevance of this information to diagnosis and treatment. The attending physician, as is customary, expected that I would meet my patients before morning rounds to report their complaints and progress. After discussing our five patients, we would call them into the office so that the attending physician could examine them. These moments were clinical and educational: the attending physician needs to see every patient for billing, and by watching the attending physician, residents internalize ways of speaking to patients, reasoning through diagnoses, and creating treatment plans. After discuss-ing each case, I was expected to enter all medication and privilege orders into the computer for the nurses to implement. I was also expected to call all specialties such as internal medicine, surgery, or dentistry to treat conditions of our patients outside the purview of psychiatry. I attended lectures in psychiatry on diagnostic categories, treatment modalities, drug types, and psychosocial interventions anytime between eleven A.M. and one P.M., spending the afternoon writing notes while the attending physi-cian managed other patients not assigned to me or administrative respon-sibilities. Once a week, I was responsible for "conducting an admission," an entire diagnostic interview for a patient admitted from the emergency room who had not yet been seen by the attending physician. The admission consisted of a history and mental status examination over the course of an hour, though not a physical exam, since that was done by an emergency room physician. After I presented my findings in a formal format lasting no longer than ten minutes, the attending physician performed a brief mental status exam. I would write a medical "progress" note about our diagnostic and treatment plans. The four residents on service coordinated admission schedules and, along with the three attending physicians, provided treatment to a group of eighteen to twenty-two patients. The strict order of time and space offers constancy on a unit with ephemeral inhabitants. Patients and visitors may come and go, clinicians and administrators may take jobs elsewhere, but the inpatient rules remain intact.

Consequently, we all notice transgressions of time and space: the resident who leaves work early, the attending physician who comes late, the nurse who spends more time with a patient. One such transgression occurred with Brian's admission during the last two weeks of my inpatient rotation.[2] At that point, I had treated dozens of veterans who honorably served the United States, bravely soldiering on through disorders of depression, traumatic stress, anxiety, substance use, and head injury. It therefore came as no surprise when Brian came to the emergency room intoxicated and threatening to commit suicide. As expected, physicians conducted an assessment to decide whether to admit, discharge, or hold him for further observation. After urine toxicology screen showed evidence of alcohol and cocaine use, the attending physician held Brian for further observation. Brian did not protest. The daytime physician evaluated Brian's suicidal threats during the next shift to disentangle the effects of substance use on his mood. Were Brian to deny suicidal threats, he would be discharged with a recommendation for substance treatment. However, Brian mentioned that several times a week, he experienced flashbacks of combat from deployment during the 2003 invasion of Iraq. He heard distant gunshots, causing his heart to race, his forehead to sweat, and his breath to skip. He drank to forget about deployment, which led to fights with his ex-girlfriend and estrangement from their children. He could not find work and spiraled into depression that he feared would lead to suicide. The attending physician noted that Brian had visited the emergency room several times recently with the same symptoms. Concerned that Brian's condition was worsening, he admitted him with diagnoses of post–traumatic stress disorder (PTSD), alcohol abuse, and possible major depressive disorder (table 1.1).[3]

The charge nurse informed me that I would conduct Brian's admission. We psychiatrists understand that our diagnoses rest on clinical observation;

TABLE 1.1   Diagnostic Criteria for PTSD (*DSM-IV*)

Exposure to a traumatic event (Both criteria must be present)	• a loss of "physical integrity" or risk of serious injury or death to self or others and • a response to the event that involved intense fear, horror, or helplessness (or in children, the response must involve disorganized or agitated behavior)
Reexperiencing (One or more criteria must be present)	• flashback memories • recurring distressing dreams • subjective reexperiencing of the traumatic event(s) • intense negative psychological or physiological response to any objective or subjective reminder of the traumatic event(s)
Avoidance and emotional numbing (Three or more criteria must be present)	• avoidance of stimuli associated with the trauma, such as certain thoughts or feelings, or talking about the event(s) • avoidance of behaviors, places, or people that might lead to distressing memories as well as the disturbing memories, dreams, flashbacks, and intense psychological or physiological distress • inability to recall major parts of the trauma(s), or decreased involvement in significant life activities • decreased capacity (down to complete inability) to feel certain feelings • an expectation that one's future will be somehow constrained in ways not normal to other people
Hyperarousal (Two or more criteria must be present)	• difficulty falling or staying asleep • irritability or outbursts of anger • difficulty concentrating • hypervigilance • exaggerated startle response
Duration of symptoms	More than 30 days
Functional significance	Clinically significant distress or impairment in social, occupational, or other important areas of functioning.

we order laboratory studies or radiological tests not to confirm diagnoses but to rule out nonpsychiatric conditions. We assume the veracity of our diagnoses based on clinical signs and symptoms, recognizing that diagnoses can change as patient presentations vary. I prepared for the admission by reading all available past records in the computer system. Emergency room attending physicians typically write brief medical notes, and since Brian had never been admitted, medical documentation was slim. I would be responsible for a diagnostic assessment and a treatment plan.

The charge nurse opened one of the unit's meeting rooms. I sat at one end of the table and waited for her to bring Brian. After several minutes, she informed me perplexedly that she could not locate him. She offered to check his bedroom. Moments later, a Caucasian man in his late twenties with a buzz cut appeared. He bore the frame of a former bodybuilder—broad shoulders, beefy biceps, and a slight paunch. He smiled politely while avoiding eye contact, introduced himself, and sat at the opposite end of the table. I introduced myself as the resident physician who would care for him and be his liaison to the rest of the clinical team.

Brian began. Since his return from deployment to Iraq in 2004—was it during training or was it during the invasion? He could not remember, as his memory since that time had been terrible—he had PTSD.

ME: PTSD?
BRIAN: Yes, PTSD.
ME: Tell me about it.
BRIAN: I have these flashbacks of the war and nightmares.
ME: What are they about?
BRIAN: I don't know, I wake up in the middle of the night, but I can't remember because of the PTSD.
ME: Did you see any combat or feel like your life was in danger?
BRIAN: I'm a soldier. I always felt that my life was in danger in Iraq.
ME: Could you point to a specific event?
BRIAN (annoyed): Um, yeah. The war.
ME: What else has been going on?
BRIAN: I keep getting into fights with my girl because of PTSD.

The statements struck me for their circular logic: the symptoms caused PTSD, and PTSD caused the symptoms. He mentioned PTSD several times, but no alcohol or cocaine use. Me: "Has anyone ever given you a diagnosis of PTSD?" Brian: "No, but I want to help you out because I know that you're a resident." Aside from recent visits to the emergency room, Brian had never sought treatment. He had no medical conditions and did not take medications. He had a long history of alcohol consumption since early high school, when his parents divorced. He consumed about a case of beer per week and smoked marijuana several times a week but did not feel that either substance presented problems. "I can quit when I want to—I just don't want to." He had never been in substance treatment for either condition. He did not know about psychiatric conditions in his family. "My parents and I didn't talk about those types of things." He was born and raised in a small town along the Connecticut coast, where his father worked in shipping and his mother was a homemaker. He had one sister several years older than him. "As soon as she got out of high school, she left home and never came back." His parents fought throughout childhood, though neither parent beat the children. His school grades were average until his parents divorced. He dropped out of the eleventh grade to join the military. "I needed to get out of Connecticut and see the world." He obtained his high school equivalency diploma in the services. He spent more than a decade in the military and was deployed twice, first in Eastern Europe during the late 1990s as a NATO peacekeeper and then in Iraq during the 2003 invasion. He received a general discharge for alcohol-related offenses but could not remember the situations because of PTSD. "I read that PTSD affects memory—it's affected mine also." Before service in Iraq, he and his ex-girlfriend had one child, and they had their second upon his return. However, PTSD led to daily fights with his girlfriend, and he couldn't find work. Last year, he lost his apartment when he didn't pay the rent, so his girlfriend took both children to live with her parents. He had since lived with another woman whom he met at a bar.

I thanked Brian for his time, exited the room, and spoke with the attending physician. He agreed that Brian's narrative did not match expectations. The first transgression: patients do not insist on a diagnosis; they receive a diagnosis from the evaluation. The attending physician agreed with my diagnostic assessment of "alcohol abuse, rule out PTSD."[4] Brian met criteria for alcohol abuse on the basis of his persistent use despite problems with his ex-girlfriend. At the same time, he insisted on a diagnosis of PTSD, but this needed further clarification. The next morning, I could not find Brian in the unit's public spaces before rounds. After several minutes, I located him in bed. "I don't want to talk to you right now. I told you everything already." The second transgression: patients do not refuse a visit from their psychiatrist; they work with their psychiatrist toward treatment. During morning rounds, the attending psychiatrist reasoned that Brian might have used more cocaine for longer than disclosed, leading to residual intoxication. He suggested that I look in the medical literature to see what it says about long-term cocaine addiction and that we discuss it the next day during rounds. I conferred with Brian's nurse. Nursing notes over the past day mentioned that Brian did not report nightmares or flashbacks when asked. His heart rate, pulse, and blood pressure did not show increases indicating any hyperarousal. He left his room only to shower and eat, and did not go outside to the courtyard with others. The third transgression: patients do not refuse opportunities to leave the unit; they maximize every chance to do so. Was Brian psychotic, depressed, or still intoxicated?

The third day began like the second. Brian refused to speak with me. Nursing reports still did not mention that he experienced nightmares, flashbacks, or hyperarousal. During morning rounds, the attending psychiatrist encouraged me to call the psychologist for testing, and Brian agreed. Later in the afternoon, the psychologist paged me with the results. Given Brian's scores on the validity subscales of the Minnesota Multiphasic Personality Inventory, a test widely used to measure personality traits, she suspected that he had been exaggerating PTSD symptoms. He displayed signs of psychopathy, refusing to conform to social expectations. She wanted to discuss her findings with him in my presence.

The three of us went to a meeting room. She explained the scale's purpose and results. Immediately, his body tensed and his face flushed. "You people don't want to give me PTSD! You don't want me to be service connected! Nobody wants to help me out." He rose from his chair and took several moments to compose himself. I looked at the psychologist nervously, hoping that he would not strike us. "Doc, you gotta give me PTSD. I need it to get my life together. I can't get work and my girlfriend won't come back to me. I gave my best years to this country."

We informed Brian that neither of us could diagnose him with PTSD for disability purposes. Because of conflict-of-interest policies, treating clinicians cannot perform disability evaluations. Brian would first need to file a claim by computer or mail application. A Veterans Service Representative would review his claim. Most likely, he would need to provide additional information and evidence of medical disability diagnosed by a nontreating VA psychiatrist or psychologist. The representative would assess the evidence and then decide. "Doc, can you give me a diagnosis of PTSD anyway to convince the other evaluator reading my records?"

At one level, Brian and I replicated uncertainties in the culture of psychiatry. The psychiatric intake evaluation is a "mystery story" as patients determine what information to disclose and clinicians hunt for clues (Brown 1993). Patients and clinicians manipulate each other in demonstrations of power and emotional control, with consequences for diagnosis, treatment, and length of stay (Gaffin 1996). The absence of any mention of reexperiencing or hyperarousal symptoms in nursing reports on Brian contributed to our impressions that he was the unreliable narrator of this mystery story. His initial eagerness to assist me and subsequent refusals to speak with me represented emotional manipulation and factored into our medical decisions. The inpatient unit has been described as "a religious domain without religion, a domain of pure morality" where "the values of family and work, all the acknowledged virtues, now reign" (Foucault 1988). Inactive patients violate the value of work and, by extension, recovery (Friedman 2012). Brian's lack of participation in inpatient life, his lasting unemployment, and his estrangement from family demonstrated clear social and occupational impairments, violating the morality of the inpatient unit's secularly religious domain—but was this PTSD?

At another level, our interactions reflect how national forces affect local lives. Brian's case demonstrates the interplay of cultural meanings within political economy, the way that "negotiation over scarce and unequally distributed resources, demoralization due to systematic powerlessness, and the quest for social efficacy cause illness careers to oscillate between agency and structure" (Kleinman 1985, 69). To what extent was Brian's narrative of PTSD a decision of individual agency or the result of systemic forces within the structure of the VA system? Medicine can provide an outlet for worker frustration as physicians sanction deviancy through bureaucratic, technocratic functions (Scheper-Hughes and Lock 1986). The individual body becomes "the proximate terrain where social truths and social contradictions are played out, as well as a locus of personal and social resistance, creativity, and struggle" (Scheper-Hughes and Lock 1987, 31). Here, Brian and I negotiated over the meanings of social exclusion in an inpatient unit run as a local outpost of the federal Veterans Affairs hospital system. ECVA belongs to a clinical archipelago of 155 federally administered hospitals and 900 clinics that employs more than 9,000 mental health professionals with a budget of more than $3 billion (in 2007), making the Department of Veterans Affairs the largest mental health system in the country (U.S. Department of Veterans Affairs 2007). Brian tried to negotiate access to these vast resources and relied on my bureaucratic role as a psychiatrist to sanction his distress. One prevailing social truth among soldiers has been that PTSD can be a source of material comfort. Brian's creativity and struggle with his social circumstances were manifested through his seeing himself as someone with PTSD.

During my inpatient rotation, veterans from Iraq and Afghanistan spoke heartbreakingly about the "hidden wounds" of war, not knowing why they felt "worked up," why they argued with friends and family, and why they could not return to work. Veterans with PTSD performed outreach for other veterans in informal discussions in the cafeteria or conference rooms. PTSD endowed their lives with meaning about the effects of the war. Veterans who demonstrated PTSD from active military service could claim "service-connected" disability benefits.

According to official history, the benefits system significantly predated the modern Veterans Administration (established in 1930): the 1776 Continental Congress encouraged enlistments during the Revolutionary War by providing pensions for disabled soldiers (U.S. Department of Veterans Affairs 2013). The military has rationalized PTSD disability algorithmically.[5]

Rates of service connection and disability compensation increase for veterans with greater impairments as determined by VA psychiatrists and psychologists (table 1.2). Hence, physicians act as gatekeepers to certify or deny patient illness experiences by appealing to scientific expertise (Waitzkin 1979). On the basis of extant scientific standards for PTSD, we denied Brian's experience of illness. However, what if we looked at his narrative not as a medical history about an individual's distress but as an existential problem communicating a truth about his social and cultural world (Kleinman and Kleinman 1994)? Brian's symptoms of nightmares, flashbacks, loss of memory, and impairment in work and interpersonal relationships can then be seen as embodying resistance against the social institution of the military. His remark about "giving the best years of [his] life to this

TABLE 1.2   VA Service Connection and Monthly Disability Compensation
for PTSD

SYMPTOM LEVELS	SERVICE CONNECTION	COMPENSATION
A mental condition has been formally diagnosed, but symptoms are not severe enough either to interfere with occupational and social functioning or to require continuous medication	0%	$0
Occupational and social impairment due to mild or transient symptoms which decrease work efficiency and ability to perform occupational tasks only during periods of significant stress, or symptoms controlled by continuous medication	10%	$129
Occupational and social impairment with occasional decrease in work efficiency and intermittent periods of inability to perform occupational tasks (although generally functioning satisfactorily, with routine behavior, self-care, and conversation normal), due to such symptoms as: depressed mood, anxiety, suspiciousness, panic attacks (weekly or less often), chronic sleep impairment, mild memory loss (such as forgetting names, directions, recent events)	30%	$395
Occupational and social impairment with reduced reliability and productivity due to such symptoms as: flattened affect; circumstantial, circumlocutory, or stereotyped speech; panic attacks more than once a week; difficulty in understanding complex commands; impairment of short- and long-term memory (e.g., retention of only highly learned material, forgetting to complete tasks); impaired judgment; impaired abstract thinking; disturbances of motivation and mood; difficulty in establishing and maintaining effective work and social relationships	50%	$810

(*Continued*)

TABLE 1.2   *(Continued)*

SYMPTOM LEVELS	SERVICE CONNECTION	COMPENSATION
Occupational and social impairment, with deficiencies in most areas, such as work, school, family relations, judgment, thinking, or mood, due to such symptoms as suicidal ideation; obsessive rituals which interfere with routine activities; speech intermittently illogical, obscure, or irrelevant; near-continuous panic or depression affecting the ability to function independently, appropriately, and effectively; impaired impulse control (such as unprovoked irritability with periods of violence); spatial disorientation; neglect of personal appearance and hygiene; difficulty in adapting to stressful circumstances (including work or a work-like setting); inability to establish and maintain effective relationships	70%	$1,293
Total occupational and social impairment, due to such symptoms as: gross impairment in thought process or communication; persistent delusions or hallucinations; grossly inappropriate behavior; persistent danger of hurting self or others; intermittent inability to perform activities of daily living (including maintenance of minimal personal hygiene); disorientation to time or place; memory loss for names of close relatives, own occupation, or own name	100%	$2,816

Note: I have created this table from several sources. The symptom levels corresponding to service connection come from the Vietnam Veterans of America, a congressionally chartered nonprofit organization. The evaluation of disability comes from VA regulation 38 C.F.R. § 4.130, DC 9411, and is known as the "General Rating Formula for Mental Disorders." The text has been reproduced faithfully (Vietnam Veterans of America 2004).

Note: Veteran compensation benefits differ according to whether veterans have dependents, and if so, what kind. The monthly rates here are for veterans with no dependents. These rates have been in effect since 12/1/12. All rates can be found in the U.S. Department of Veterans Affairs (2012), from which these data have been tabulated.

country" displays anger, entitlement, and desperation in the local world of his family. Since 2001, the U.S. government has sponsored "market patriotism" by valorizing economic growth, productivity, and consumerism—Bill Clinton's widely publicized post-9/11 shopping spree; President George Bush's defense of "global free markets"—effectively reconstructing the War on Terror as a defense of international capitalism (White 2007–2008). Is Brian's unemployment a form of market sedition, an unconscious objection to the economic goals of the War on Terror?

I wrestled with the conundrums of Brian's case for years after we discharged him. Why not diagnose him with PTSD if it could improve his life? Would I only enable him at the expense of American taxpayers if I recommended a diagnosis of PTSD?

.   .   .

Eight months later, I was on the phone with an attorney for Binyam Mohamed, who was detained at Guantánamo Bay. I wanted to understand the role of mental health professionals there, in the light of allegations that they participated in detainee interrogation and abuse. I have detailed this elsewhere (Aggarwal 2009a), but a summary here serves as a counterpoint to the situation of Brian above. The attorney listed the travails of her client. Mohamed went to Afghanistan for disputed reasons; the American government alleged that he trained in al-Qaeda military camps, but his defense team countered that he went for personal reasons. After the 9/11 attacks and U.S. retaliation against the Taliban, Mohamed was apprehended by American military personnel. He told his attorneys about brutal abuses—hours of solitary confinement in rooms without light, routine beatings, razor slashes to his chest and penis. His transfer to Guantánamo was an unexpectedly welcome step because enough individuals and organizations had lobbied to ensure public accountability, which was impossible for those in the "black sites" of American intelligence agencies. Guantánamo's harsh conditions defeated him, however. He would crouch in the corner of his cell, urinate on himself, smear himself with feces, and throw it at guards. His attorney described efforts to get him seen by an independent psychiatrist who did not work with the military so that he could get a diagnosis of PTSD based on his torture in custody, but the military wouldn't agree. They said that they had their own psychiatrists who could evaluate him.[6]

Like Brian, Mohamed's attorney sought a diagnosis of PTSD to invest social circumstances with meaning. However, this meaning was sought not only for personal comfort but also for access to some remedial service through the medicolegal system, whether disability or justice. The search for meaning exposed power differentials about who can lay claim to PTSD and in what circumstances. Unlike most of us, refugees seeking asylum experience multiple forms of powerlessness—persecution in their home societies, medical certification in their host societies—such that the events of their lives require corroboration from others (Fassin and D'Halluin 2005). Asylum seekers without physical wounds must display psychological wounds, often through the diagnosis of PTSD, which requires medical expertise to determine (Fassin 2011). The situation of Guantánamo detainees inverts these circumstances. Some detainees, like Mohamed, have claimed torture at Guantánamo, not in their home countries. Procedures that limit the hiring of medical experts or observers independent of the military can deprive detainees of medical certification that verifies the physical signs of torture. Therefore, detainee attorneys have tried to call independent mental health experts who can opine on a detainee's ability to participate in legal proceedings,[7] using this forum as an opportunity to obtain a diagnosis of PTSD. The detainee becomes the opposite of the refugee: the detainee seeks return to his home country, but the refugee seeks asylum in a host country. Both need the medical expert to sanction their experiences.

.   .   .

Clinicians use medical narratives to refract larger issues. Narratives perform several functions in clinical work: understanding the motives of participants, connecting individual motives to social and cultural worlds, and exploring how best to act morally in situational constraints (Charon 2007; Mattingly 1998). Let's use this model to take stock of Brian and Mohamed. I included Mohamed's predicament in publications on how attorneys for Guantánamo detainees encounter difficulties in requesting mental health evaluations from nonmilitary professionals (Aggarwal 2009a; Aggarwal and Pumariega 2011). At that time I was more interested in cultural competence in detainee psychiatric care. Only years later did the deeper connections between these two cultural icons, the venerated veteran and the despised detainee, emerge. Both men lost youth and optimism to the War on Terror, then pursued meaning and remedy through diagnoses of PTSD and resources from the American military's medical and legal systems. On July 13, 2010, the Department of Veterans Affairs simplified rules for disability by requiring VA psychiatrists and psychologists only to confirm that a veteran's account of a stressful experience accurately supported a diagnosis of PTSD, not to corroborate the actual presence of a stressor, known in bureaucratic jargon as "evidentiary liberalization" (U.S. Department of Veterans Affairs 2010). The cost of treating PTSD has been enormous. The Obama administration allocated $5.2 billion for treatment of PTSD, traumatic brain disorders, and other mental health problems in 2011 (Rowland 2010).[8] Evidentiary liberalization has not applied to enemy combatants like Mohamed.

Nonetheless, the American government did not foresee the "unanticipated consequences of purposive social action" (Merton 1936), and this theory helps us connect individual motives to social and cultural worlds. The axis of purposive social action binding Brian and Mohamed revolves around the American military's manipulation of psychiatric knowledge and practice for forensic rather than healing purposes.[9] By forensic psychiatry, I refer to "the branch of psychiatry that deals with issues arising in the interface between psychiatry and the law" (Arboleda-Flórez 2006). This definition emphasizes the social and legal over the individual and therapeutic aspects of mental health. The unanticipated consequences of the increased forensic use of psychiatry include higher rates of PTSD veterans from Iraq and Afghanistan; in a 2012 report, the U.S. Congressional Budget Office acknowledged that "the percentage of OCO [overseas contingency operations] veterans whom VHA [Veterans Health Administration] clinicians have diagnosed with PTSD (twenty-six percent) is at the top of the range reported in published studies" (Congressional Budget Office 2012). While greater traumatic stressors for veterans compared to civilians certainly account for higher rates, evidentiary liberalization may lead to false claims. Veterans seeking compensation exaggerate PTSD symptoms (Freeman, Powell, and Kimbrell 2008). In addition, 96 percent of VA clinicians believe that they can conduct a PTSD examination, and 80 percent believe that they can detect false reports. But more than 85 percent do not use formal interviews or assessment scales (Jackson et al. 2011). Studies of veterans exaggerating PTSD symptoms and dubious clinician decision making match historical trends related to increased VA expenditures for disability compensation (Frueh et al. 2007).

These unintended consequences affect the conditions of Guantánamo detainees. Human Rights Watch (2008) has warned of the mental health consequences of restrictive conditions such as solitary confinement for twenty-two hours per day, few human interactions beyond those with staff, the absence of educational or vocational rehabilitation, no contact with families or friends, and lack of access to independent medical professionals. Medical records of nine detainees without any psychiatric history have shown that Guantánamo clinicians diagnosed seven with symptoms of PTSD, though none was asked about its causes, which raises questions of torture in American custody (Iacopino and Xenakis 2011). The military's use of PTSD continues military revolutions in psychiatry from Phillipe Pinel's 1798 description of "war neuroses" during the French Revolution and Charles Myers's 1915 coining of "shell shock" during World War I to military psychiatrists' descriptions of PTSD during the Vietnam War (Crocq and Crocq 2000; Kilshaw 2008; Young 1995). The War on Terror has a military legacy of granting a diagnosis of PTSD to our soldiers and withholding it from our suspected enemies.

What do we learn about moral decision making from Brian and Mohamed? Their circumstances crystallize three themes within the medical humanities and the social sciences:

1. Culture frames all interpretations in the medical encounter. Although no definition of culture can convey every nuance, I draw upon Leigh Turner's definition of "the dominant values, symbols, social practices, and interpretive categories of any community" that are dynamic and make sense of the world (2005, 307). We all belong to multiple communities from which we create hybrid identities and cultural meanings (Bhabha 2006), even as patients and clinicians (Aggarwal 2012a). These identities differentially influence how patients understand illnesses as disvalued states of being and function and how healers treat diseases as scientific abnormalities of bodily systems (Eisenberg 1977; Kleinman 1983; Kleinman, Eisenberg, and Good 1978). Patients and healers negotiate the focus of medical attention (Kleinman 1980; Kleinman, Eisenberg, and Good 1978). A central task of cultural analysis is to disentangle the relative contributions of identity in various communities, the "multiplicity of complex conceptual structures, many of them superimposed upon or knotted into one another" (Geertz 1973, 10).

With Brian, I identify three complex conceptual structures based on my acculturation from medical school, residency training, and psychiatry. Medicine cultivates a "clinical gaze" that requires mastery of a stylized language and perception of the "invisible visibility" beyond the eye's surface (Foucault 1994). Medical students acculturate with professional identities by conceptualizing the physical world through anatomy, histology, physiology, and pathophysiology and communicating through formal forms of speaking and writing (Good 1994; Good and Good 1993). In psychiatry, we use symptom-based diagnoses to visualize the invisible visibility of the mind. We conceptualize illness through diagnostic categories and communicate these in formal case presentations and notes. During residency, physicians learn how to maneuver in hierarchical medical teams (Groopman 1987; Messinger 2006). Our team worked in clear divisions of labor— I through the diagnostic interview; the attending physician through the brief follow-up; and the psychologist through extensive questionnaires— to interpret Brian's sickness based on formal psychiatric classification.

Patients also construct meanings of illnesses. They develop multiple systems of explanation drawn from institutions, the media, and social networks (Larsen 2004). Brian's meanings of PTSD arose from his status as a veteran, the social institution of the VA, and the social networks of veterans conducting outreach. Models of patient illnesses include explanations culled from neurobiological dysfunctions, childhood traumas, social disadvantage, spiritual experiences, and denials of illness altogether (Estroff 1991). Many patients link clinical improvements to idealized life expectations without honest appraisals of their current circumstances (Lloyd and Moreau 2011). Brian attributed his social disadvantage—chronic unemployment, estranged relationships—to PTSD, not to his recurrent problems with substance use. He hoped, perhaps unrealistically, that a diagnosis of PTSD would open pathways to income that would reunite him with his ex-girlfriend and family.

2. *Power determines whose interpretations prevail.* Power can be defined as the relationship between two free people in which one induces action from the other (Foucault 1982). The act of diagnosis becomes a contested process negotiated by medical staff, psychiatrists, and families, who all presume knowledge of mental illness (Gaines 1979). The structure of social relationships in medicine empowers certain cultural interpretations over others (Baer, Singer, and Johnson 1986; Baer, Singer, and Susser 2003),

namely those of physicians (Taussig 1980). Our interpretations of PTSD as a constellation of symptoms prevailed over Brian's interpretation of PTSD as a passport to social services. Psychiatrists wield authority by deciding whether to legitimate a patient's symptoms based on treating the history as a secular "confession" (Foucault 2006). Brian wanted us to legitimate his illness's meanings through PTSD. The search for explanations of his clinical symptoms effectively led to a confession that he had other motives for seeking this diagnosis.

3. *The medical system is used for reasons other than healing.* By "healing," I refer to the process by which "the sufferer gains a degree of satisfaction through the reduction, or even elimination, of the psychological, sensory, and experiential oppressiveness endangered by his medical circumstances" (Young 1982, 265). We did not heal Brian by providing satisfaction through the reduction of oppressive circumstances. Rather, we acted as agents of social control through our presumed objectivity. Medicine has surpassed religion and law as an institution of social control where "morally neutral and objective experts" make truth claims and final judgments (Zola 1972, 487). Psychiatry's historical preoccupations with normalcy and deviance involve it in matters of social control through deliberations for the social welfare system, the courtroom, the military, and occupational health (Fabrega 1989b). As a result of their own perceptions of patient deception or despondency, psychiatrists may or may not connect patients with welfare benefits independently of their healing capacities (Davis 2010; Friedman 2009). Brian yearned for the welfare benefits for which we acted as gatekeepers and to which we did not connect him, because we perceived that he wished to deceive us.

*   *   *

Brian and Mohamed encourage us to rethink the functions of medicine in the War on Terror. Critical approaches to the study of doctor-patient relationships trace microlevel illness experiences to macrolevel political and economic dynamics (Singer 1986, 1989). What sorts of political and economic dynamics underlie doctor-patient relationships in the War on Terror? The War on Terror has cost more than $4 trillion, killed 330,000 people directly, injured more than 750,000 American soldiers, and uprooted more than 7.4 million people (Watson Institute 2011). With 3.2 million civilian and military employees, the U.S. Department of Defense is the largest employer in the world (Alexander 2012). A bipartisan legislative commission notes that the number of private contractor employees in Iraq and Afghanistan exceeded 260,000 in 2010, which "at times surpassed the number of U.S. military personnel in the two countries" (Commission on Wartime Contracting in Iraq and Afghanistan 2011). The War on Terror has spread beyond Iraq and Afghanistan to include Pakistan, Somalia, Yemen, Mexico, and cyberspace, creating "the everywhere war" (Gregory 2011). Michael Sheehan, the assistant secretary of defense for special operations and low-intensity conflict for the U.S. Department of Defense, reported at a Senate judicial hearing on May 16, 2013, that the Obama administration anticipates the War on Terror to last *an additional ten to twenty years* (Greenwald 2013). The time has come to ask: How has the War on Terror impacted medicine, and how has medicine impacted the War on Terror?

A FRAMEWORK TO ANALYZE FORENSIC MENTAL HEALTH IN THE WAR ON TERROR

How can we analyze forensic mental health in the War on Terror? In 2013, I searched the medical databases PubMed, MedLine, PsycINFO, Scopus, and CINAHL, pairing the terms "culture," "cultural," "anthropology," and "anthropological" with "forensic." While numerous studies of forensic health systems in different countries have been published, no single article offered a systematic approach to the cross-cultural analysis of forensic health. This conceptual deficiency constitutes a gap in cultural mental health that this book addresses.

Medical anthropologists have long debated how to analyze medical systems. The anthropologist-psychiatrist Arthur Kleinman (1980) argues that all medical systems exhibit "core clinical functions":[10] (1) the cultural construction of illness as psychosocial experience, (2) the establishment of general criteria to guide the health-care-seeking process and to evaluate treatment approaches, (3) the management of specific illness episodes through communicative operations such as labeling and explaining, (4) healing activities, and (5) the management of therapeutic outcomes (Kleinman 1980, 71–83). This influential paradigm merits a close reading to modify it for studying forensic health systems.

The first function is *the cultural construction of illness experience*. "Illness" has a specific connotation in medical anthropology, referring to the patient's negative experiences during a sickness (Eisenberg 1977; Kleinman 1983; Kleinman, Eisenberg, and Good 1978). Kleinman (1980) explains that illness and disease exist as constructs that can be understood "only within defined contexts of meaning and social relationships" (73). Culture gives shape to illness through labels and sanctioned ways of being through "the cultural construction of illness categories and experiences" (78). A patient may describe her experience after pregnancy as "the baby blues," whereas her physician may describe it as "postpartum depression"; both terms differentially describe how patients and physicians perceive the same sickness episode. Illness invests the behavioral and societal response to disease with meaning and symbolism. Most often, illness and disease co-occur. However, illness can exist without disease, as with cancers in remission, when there is no detectable organ pathology but a patient still feels unwell. Disease can exist without illness during acute conditions such as trauma or intoxication when the patient has not had time to formulate a response.

The second function is *the establishment of general criteria to guide the health-care-seeking process and to evaluate treatment approaches.* Kleinman explains: "The application of values to types of illness has an important influence upon the decision people make" (1980, 80). Values guide people through the help-seeking process within a sector of a local health-care system. Certain illnesses, such as leprosy, tuberculosis, and mental illness, retain negative cultural values that may affect how and where patients seek care. For example, a patient who believes that alcohol dependence is a moral failing rather than a treatable disorder may not seek care, reflecting how values guide health-care alternatives.

The third function is *the management of specific illness episodes through communicative operations such as labeling and explaining.* The first two functions belong to cultures in general, whereas the third concentrates on how patients then explain and label their illness in a particular time and place. Kleinman terms this "the explanatory model," which "offer[s] explanations of sickness and treatment to guide choices among available therapies and therapists and to cast personal and social meaning on the experience of sickness" (1980, 105). The explanatory model consists of questions on patient perspectives about the cause, onset of symptoms, pathophysiology, course of sickness, and treatment preferences (1980, 105). Explanatory models are formed in response to a specific sickness from cultural symbols.

The fourth and fifth functions, *healing activities* and *the management of therapeutic outcomes*, go together. Kleinman contends that "the chief goal of health care systems" is the "curing of disease," which is defined as "the establishment of effective control of disordered biological and psychological processes," and "the healing of illness," which is "the provision of personal and social meaning for the life problems created by sickness" (1980, 82). Nonetheless, nonhealing functions may exist, such as social control, and research should examine how clinical functions are "differentially constituted in diverse social structural and cultural settings" (Kleinman 1980, 375). This call to expand research on the cross-cultural analysis of health-care systems animates this study of medicine in the War on Terror.

Brian and Mohamed illustrate how patients and clinicians can view the medical system for purposes other than healing. As a patient, Brian idealized the diagnosis of PTSD to grant him social services. Muhammad's attorney viewed the diagnosis of PTSD as a means to legally recognize his experiences of torture, commute punishment, and dismiss the case. Using medical anthropology terms to reframe these views, we could say that Brian and Muhammad experienced illnesses without an accompanying disease diagnosed by clinicians.

•   •   •

We need a framework that recognizes patient-clinician differences in interpreting sickness, incorporates power in the patient-clinician relationship, and highlights the nonhealing uses of medicine.[11] Certain medical subspecialties, such as occupational medicine, anatomic pathology, toxicology, and forensic psychiatry, operate outside of the bounds of the fiduciary relationship to render opinions for the legal system. Forensic psychiatrists can orient us to the foundations of such a framework. The American Academy of Psychiatry and the Law (AAPL) defines forensic psychiatry as "a subspecialty of psychiatry in which scientific and clinical expertise is applied in legal contexts involving civil, criminal, correctional, regulatory, or legislative matters, and in specialized clinical consultations in areas such as risk assessment or employment" (American Academy of Psychiatry and the Law 2005, 1). Forensic psychiatrists must balance multiple interests: "Psychiatrists in a forensic role are called upon to practice in a manner that balances competing duties to the individual and to society" (American Academy of

Psychiatry and the Law 2005, 1). The scope of psychiatric-legal issues is vast, covering civil forensic psychiatry, criminal forensic psychiatry, and the legal regulation of psychiatry (Rosner 2003).[12] These forensic psychiatrists recognize patient-clinician differences in interpreting the clinical encounter, the clinician's power in the patient-clinician relationship, and the use of medicine to specify a legal opinion.

Social science perspectives on forensic psychiatry also anchor its practice within culture. In ancient Greece and Rome, medieval Europe, and the United States, medical professionals have rendered legal opinions on a suspect's mental competency and responsibility based on contemporary standards of scientific expertise (D'Orbán 1988; Gold 2010; Gutheil 2005; Prosono 2003). Although scientific and legal standards have varied over time, the work of forensic psychiatrists is cultural in drawing upon social norms to create meanings in understanding the world (Engstrom 2009). The law itself reflects culturally determined values and styles of legal reasoning (Aggarwal 2012a; Ciccone and Ferracuti 1995; Rosen 2006) that embody society's notions of normal and abnormal behavior (Devereux 1956; Romanucci-Ross and Tancredi 1986). The interface of law and psychiatry is culturally constructed within a given society at any point in time. Through these theories, we can specify the forensic functions of medical systems as a form of cultural analysis.[13] By "culture" here, I specifically mean the culture of law and biomedicine that operates most obviously in forensic psychiatry but also informs areas of life, healing, illness, and treatment as governed through laws and mandates.

The first function is *the cultural construction of a medicolegal issue*. If the law codifies culturally acceptable normal and abnormal behaviors, then the study of medicolegal issues exposes the values, beliefs, and practices that a society adopts to make meanings. Medicolegal issues can change throughout time and need not be the same across all societies. For example, the assessment of medical disability prevails in many countries, such as the United States and England, but we can also research physician testimonies against witches during the inquisitions, medical manuals on poisons from the South Asian Ayurvedic tradition a millennium ago, or debates on euthanasia in contemporary Islamic medical jurisprudence. Brian's case falls within the VA system's construction of a medicolegal issue around service-related disability compensation. Studying the cultural construction of medicolegal issues teaches us how societies legalize normal and abnormal ways of being and behaving, calling upon the authority of medicine to provide evidence.

The second function is *the establishment of legal and medical standards to support and evaluate a medicolegal issue.* Health professionals organize contrasting forms of knowledge to render an opinion. The United States encompasses fifty state jurisdictions, federal and military jurisdictions, and the District of Columbia, all of which have separate statutes, case laws, administrative codes, and precedents. One task of cross-cultural analysis is to compare legal standards that govern a medicolegal issue across time and space. Health professionals also invoke medical knowledge to support their claims. This knowledge comes from textbooks, practice guidelines, systematic reviews and meta-analyses of major scientific findings, or landmark articles in a medical subspecialty. For example, the VA system mandates that psychiatrists and psychologists follow *DSM-IV* criteria in making disability determinations for PTSD. The study of how societies establish legal and medical standards to evaluate medicolegal issues focuses attention on the construction of legal and scientific knowledge.[14]

The third function is *the procurement of clinical evidence relevant to a medicolegal issue.* Health professionals perform investigations to confirm or deny hypotheses related to a medicolegal issue. Investigations supplying direct information include the medical or psychiatric history, a physical and mental status examination, laboratory tests, and radiological imaging. Investigations also supply indirect information from medical and legal records or interviews with family and friends. Certain types of evidence may be regarded more than others, giving us a sense of their relative values in addressing a medicolegal issue. In Brian's case, we aggregated old records, psychiatric examinations, nursing reports, psychological assessments, and neuropsychological testing. We did not interview family members or friends, as that was deemed superfluous. The study of how health professionals solicit clinical evidence can instruct us in the everyday practice of medicine relevant to forming an opinion for the legal system.

The fourth function is *the application of clinical reasoning to resolve a medicolegal issue.* The use of clinical evidence is not immediately obvious; health professionals construct arguments through culturally determined modes of induction and deduction. A wide variety of materials such as legal documents, medical records, and courtroom testimony can be mined.

Certain styles of clinical reasoning may be prioritized and incorporate legalistic notions of argumentation. On the basis of discrepancies between Brian's reported symptoms and nursing reports, we reasoned that he did not have PTSD. The study of clinical reasoning clarifies how health professionals make certain arguments, refute other arguments, and draw conclusions.

The fifth function is *the legal outcome based on the clinician's medical opinion*. Ultimately, the legal system uses the clinician's opinion for a ruling and may agree or disagree with the findings of the clinician.

The five forensic functions can be studied separately or together, depending on the topic. Legal professionals can frame a medicolegal issue that increasingly requires medical expertise. Medical professionals can also frame a medicolegal issue by suggesting clinical conditions as grounds for providing an opinion, as with new disorders in psychiatry linked to evaluations of functional assessment (such as Asperger's and autistic disorder after the publication of *DSM-IV* in garnering special educational services for children) or with the application of newer technologies, such as DNA profiling for evidentiary procedures. Specific cases can offer source material to trace the flow through all five forensic functions.

A METHODOLOGY TO STUDY THE FORENSIC FUNCTIONS OF MEDICAL SYSTEMS

In this book, I examine how the forensic functions framework can be used through analyses of medical, legal, political science, and policy textual discourse. Michel Foucault (1991) considers discourse to be "the set of rules which at a given period and for a given society define" five characteristics: (1) "the limits and forms of the *sayable*," which constitute a given domain; (2) "the limits and forms of *conservation*," which are statements that disappear or circulate; (3) "the limits and forms of *memory*," which establish continuities of thought between current and former statements; (4) "the limits and forms of *reactivation*," which reveal what older statements reappear now; and (5) "the limits and forms of *appropriation*," which define the author and audience (59–60). Studying discourses through close readings of texts can show how the boundaries of knowledge are defined, people jostle for new positions, language acquires new functions, and ideas circulate throughout society (Foucault 1991, 56–57).

Discourse analysis can reveal how the forensic functions of medical systems act as sites of intellectual confrontation and compromise. Over the past forty years, discourse analysis has inspired thousands of studies, but many authors do not precisely explain their exact research methods (Barker 2008). Discourse analysis also suffers from a difficulty with demarcating domains and objects of study (Foucault 1991). Some have called for studies to report the selection of source materials and the choice of theories that guide analyses (Barker 2008). In this book I present discourse analyses of the scientific medical literature, legal cases of Guantánamo detainees, and academic political science and policy publications to understand how the War on Terror has changed the medicolegal nature of mental health knowledge and practice.[15] For example, I have analyzed publications that result from using search terms in medical databases such as PubMed, PsycINFO, and PEP Web, since these represent the preeminent tools of biomedical, psychological, and psychoanalytic research (Falagas et al. 2008; García-Pérez 2010; Psychoanalytic Electronic Publishing 2013).[16] Cultural mental health experts—especially psychiatrists, psychologists, sociologists, and anthropologists—have not often treated scientific publications as social artifacts worthy of cultural analysis, and I believe that constituting work from these databases as forms of medical discourse yields a potential methodological innovation for these fields. I also believe that peer-reviewed scientific publications exemplify the intertwined nature of power and knowledge. Not everyone can publish in peer-reviewed journals. The knowledge that appears in scientific publications denotes professional expertise and goes through a process of vetting by other specialists whose educational trajectories and institutional affiliations endow them with the power of such expertise. I use scientific texts to survey bioethical debates about the duty of health professionals at Guantánamo in chapter 2, the portrayal of Arabs and Muslims in the psychoanalytic literature in chapter 4, and scientific constructions of suicide bombers in chapter 5. In addition, I assess all legal texts pertaining to mental health for several Guantánamo detainees tried under military commissions as sources of discourse analysis in chapter 3. In chapter 6, I review scientific publications of political scientists, psychologists, international relations experts, and other counterterrorism specialists from published literature reviews to probe models of mental health in deradicalization programs. In all cases, I present the origins and search strategies of the texts analyzed for independent corroboration. Not every text in the world can be analyzed, so the point is to make claims that are exemplary rather than exhaustive. I read chapters 2 and 3 as the War on Terror affecting mental health and chapters 4 through 6 as mental health affecting the War on Terror, though readers may draw independent conclusions. I see the analysis of legal texts in chapter 3 and the analysis of government policy texts in chapter 6 as examples where intellectual themes culled from previous chapters (i.e., knowledge) are actually put into practice (i.e., power), a further demonstration of how knowledge and power intertwine. Because I want to advance discourse analysis as a methodology in cultural mental health research, I reproduce original quotations to forestall criticisms of taking authors' words out of context, an allegation that assumes heightened sensitivities with life-and-death issues in the War on Terror.

I differentiate *medical discourse analysis* from other literature reviews in the health sciences. The most common type of literature review among medical researchers is the systematic review, which has been defined as "a review of a clearly formulated question that uses systematic and explicit methods to identify, select, and critically appraise relevant research, and to collect and analyze data from the studies that are included in the review" (Moher et al. 2009). The systematic review determines the strength of evidence from clinical trials by aggregating results and reporting biases (Moher et al. 2009). If the systematic review gathers quantitative studies, then the meta-ethnography gathers qualitative studies. Meta-ethnography has been defined as "the synthesis of interpretive research" that "involves the translation of studies into one another" (Noblit and Hare 1988, 10). I do not share these epistemological commitments. As collections of utterances, discourses need not be grounded in clinical trials, qualitative studies, or other research designs. By deliberately using the word "utterance" rather than scientific words like "result" or "finding," we can interrogate the veracity of statements rather than accept their truths. Also, we are not seeking to synthesize qualitative or quantitative results but to do the exact opposite, to disaggregate and delineate the types—not numbers—of statements that appear and disappear with attention to author, text, and audience. Nonetheless, I retain the reporting procedure of search protocols from systematic reviews and meta-ethnographies for search transparency.[17] Here, the term "systematic" refers to rigorous and reproducible sources of data collection, an assumption that I also share.

The choice of theories and methodology for medical discourse analysis comes broadly from the field of critical discourse analysis with several assumptions.[18] Each chapter is centered on a social theory in a "transdisciplinary" fashion to expose novel types of medicolegal knowledge and practice in dialogue with other disciplines (Fairclough 2001). I follow conventions of critical discourse analysis in which I first present the material to be analyzed in direct quotations, followed by my analyses of this material without repeating full citations (van Dijk 1993). Furthermore, I assume that texts endow social actions and representations of the self and of others with meanings that reflect the social world outside of texts and that can be analyzed. I also assume that my analyses of texts remain subjective and incomplete, since analysts can interpret the same publications through different theories and units of analysis. With these disclaimers, let us now heed the words of the attending physician to "look in the medical literature," considering it as a form of cultural discourse to map the processes of social change in mental health knowledge and practice since the beginning of the War on Terror.

2

Bioethics and the Conduct of Mental Health Professionals in the War on Terror

IT IS 2004. You are a commissioned psychiatric officer in the U.S. Navy stationed at Guantánamo, where a hunger strike is raging among detainees. One detainee has refused food and water for three weeks, leading to vivid auditory hallucinations, listlessness, and occasional episodes of stupor throughout the day. You have been asked to offer your medical opinion as to whether the detainee can continue the hunger strike, given concerns over his impaired decision-making capacity. You are unsure, since he may no longer understand the risks and consequences associated with a hunger strike. Although they do not say it explicitly, commanding officers want you to declare him unable to provide informed consent in line with American government policy to prevent detainee deaths, whereas bioethicists and human rights officials want you to declare him able to provide informed consent since he originally acted out of conscience. Declaring him unable to provide informed consent perpetuates injustices against detainees, but declaring him otherwise jeopardizes your career since you refuse to comply with organizational expectations. What do you do?

· · ·

It is 2006. You are a clinical psychologist who treats military officers and enemy suspects at Abu Ghraib. An intelligence officer has accessed the records of a suspect whom you have been treating for post–traumatic stress disorder following a raid on his family's house. Your clinical progress note records that his psychological strengths include a "strong love of family and religion." The officer has amassed enough evidence to believe that the suspect has high-value intelligence related to al-Qaeda in Iraq. Although the suspect is innocent, his cousin belongs to the organization. The officer enters the interrogation room as you observe through a one-way mirror. Using psychological information to his advantage, the officer threatens to abduct the parents and newborn daughter of the suspect's cousin unless he provides the cousin's current address. The suspect before you crumbles and sobs. You feel pulled in opposite directions. Human rights groups increasingly denounce the misuse of confidential patient information, but the American Psychological Association has yet to issue position statements. Not reporting the officer may enable him to further abuse provider-client privacy and destroy therapeutic alliances with other clients, but reporting the officer may lead to your dismissal. What do you do?

.   .   .

In 2004, stories on detainee abuse at the Abu Ghraib and Guantánamo Bay detention facilities began to circulate in the media. Military medical professionals have been accused of sharing detainee medical information with interrogators, raising alarms that detainee medications would be withheld or that mental and physical ailments could be exploited (Slevin and Stephens 2004). Physicians have been accused of falsifying death certificates to claim that detainees killed during interrogations died from natural causes (Contenta 2004; Hotakainen and Marcotty 2004). Physicians have also been accused of supervising "enhanced interrogation" methods such as depriving detainees of sleep for up to one hundred and eighty hours, permitting confinement in small, dark rooms for eighteen hours a day, exposing detainees to cold air, and performing medical exams to clear detainees for simultaneous shackling to floors and ceilings (Rubenstein and Xenakis 2010). Psychologists have confiscated clothes, Qurans, and other personal possessions, stripping detainees to just undergarments, with items progressively returned to incentivize discipline (Gordon 2005). A policy statement dated August 6, 2002, from the United States Southern Command notified medical personnel to "convey any information concerning . . . the accomplishment of a military or national security mission . . . obtained from detainees in the course of treatment to non-medical military or other U.S. personnel who have an apparent need to know the information" (Talaga and Palmer 2005). In 2007, the Red Cross concluded that medical personnel participated in interrogations to support interrogators rather than to protect detainee lives based on statements with members of al-Qaeda (Shane 2009). In 2009, Physicians for Human Rights alleged that physicians associated with the Central Intelligence Agency may have exploited detainees in experiments on interrogation methods such as facial slapping, pushing heads against walls, confinement in boxes, and simulated drowning, also known as waterboarding (Pilkington 2009).

The U.S. Department of Defense has forcefully defended its medical officers. Officials have differentiated a treating physician's duty to care for detainees from a medical consultant's role to ensure that interrogators do not endanger detainee lives (Stephens 2005). Military officials have also responded that interrogations are ethical and detainees, as enemy combatants, are not covered under the Geneva Conventions (Lewis 2005b).[1] In 2006, the military issued guidelines directing physicians to forcefully feed detainees at War on Terror facilities when their lives could be in danger (Waddington 2006).

Prominent bioethicists have condemned these actions and demanded consequences. For example, M. Gregg Bloche (2004) writes: "According to press reports, military doctors and nurses who examined prisoners at Abu Ghraib treated swollen genitals, prescribed painkillers, stitched wounds, and recorded evidence of the abuses going on around them. Under international law—as well as the standards of common decency—these medical professionals had a duty to tell those in power what they saw." Here, "standards of common decency" and "international law" are depicted as compelling a duty to report abuses among military medical professionals.

Similarly, Bloche laments the passivity of military medical professionals who have "shamed us all" by not coming forward immediately. Canada's *National Post* newspaper published an editorial calling for "the non-military medical community to unite in support of their military colleagues and condemn torture and inhumane and degrading practices against detainees" (Munro 2004). Robert Jay Lifton has criticized medical professionals for their cowardice in not reporting torture: "No doctor would have been physically abused or put to death if he or she tried to interrupt that torture. It would have taken courage, but it was a choice they had" (Ross 2004). The decision to report or not report torture is fashioned into a choice. After a tour of Guantánamo, former American Psychiatric Association president Steven S. Sharfstein raised concerns about military psychiatrists advising interrogation units known as Behavioral Science Consultation Teams (BSCT, pronounced "biscuit"): "Psychiatrists should not participate on these biscuit teams because it is inappropriate" (Lewis 2005a). Sharfstein has rebuked psychiatrists who justified their consultations for detainee interrogations through claims of no patient-physician relationship: "You are never not a physician" (Vedantam 2005).

Whereas the American Psychiatric Association has clearly prohibited its members from detainee interrogations, the American Psychological Association has equivocated. In 2006, more than fifteen hundred psychologists signed an online petition against the American Psychological Association's guidelines that allow psychologists to consult on "interrogation and information-gathering processes for national security purposes" that were drafted by an ethics subcommittee, on which six of ten members had ties to the American military (Fifield 2006; Wasley 2006). In 2007, the American Psychological Association approved consultations from psychologists to keep interrogations "safe and ethical" (Steele and Morli 2007), but banned psychologists from participating in mock executions, simulated drowning, sexual and religious humiliation, stress positions, and sleep deprivation (Vedantam 2007). Critics contended that these restrictions still allowed psychologists to participate in interrogations compared to bans imposed on physicians by the American Medical Association and the American Psychiatric Association (Glenn 2007). By 2008, the American Psychological Association passed a resolution banning all psychologist participation in interrogation programs at detention centers abroad (Goldstein 2008).

The War on Terror has provoked vigorous and occasionally venomous debates regarding the extent to which the practices of mental health professionals in military medical systems defy ethical standards. What type of bioethics can and should prevail in institutions where the military values of discipline and hierarchy trump the medical values of treatment and healing? Can we expect military medical professionals to jeopardize themselves through whistle-blowing when the military construes their behavior to be ethical, as when physicians monitor "enhanced interrogations" to prevent death? How do we understand different professional positions on the participation of medical personnel in detainee interrogations? Can this be done with the American Medical Association and American Psychiatric

Association requirements to uphold the Hippocratic Oath, to do no harm, while the American Psychological Association has encouraged psychologists to protect American citizens?

In this chapter, I examine bioethical discourse on the conduct of military psychiatrists and psychologists throughout the War on Terror. Bioethicists employ shared values, beliefs, and interpretive frameworks to debate the meanings of proper and improper professional conduct, offering clear examples of the cultural construction of medicolegal issues. The explanations that bolster their arguments illustrate the second forensic function of medical systems, *the establishment of medical and legal standards to support and evaluate medicolegal issues.* Based on the premise that culture frames all interpretations of the medical encounter, the bioethical scholarship exudes power as bioethicists introduce medicolegal issues, make authoritative interpretations about current practices, and propose definitive solutions.

SOCIAL SCIENCE, BIOETHICS, AND CULTURAL MODELS OF INTERPRETATION

Bioethics emerged in the 1960s and 1970s to address moral quandaries on prolonged life and altered definitions of death that accompanied the development of new medical technologies (Clouser 1974; Fox 1990; Gaines and Juengst 2008; Jonsen 1999; Pellegrino 1990). Although bioethicists draw upon different methods based on disciplinary training (Turner 2009), the approach of "principlism" advanced by philosophers Tom Beauchamp and James Childress remains a central method. Beauchamp and Childress posited that "a set of principles in a moral account should function as an analytical framework that expresses the general values underlying rules in the common morality" (12), with "the common morality" defined as "the set of norms that all morally serious persons share" and "that bind all persons in all places" (3). These four principles are: (1) *respect for autonomy* (a norm of respecting the decision-making capacities of autonomous persons), (2) *nonmaleficence* (a norm of avoiding the causation of harm), (3) *beneficence* (a group of norms for providing benefits and balancing benefits against risks and costs), and (4) *justice* (a group of norms for distributing benefits, risks, and costs fairly) (Beauchamp and Childress 2001).

Principlism remains the reigning paradigm in bioethics (Beauchamp 1995; Callahan 2003; Clouser and Gert 1990; Davis 1995; Degrazia 1992). However, social scientists have identified shortcomings in its universalistic postulations. Principlism prescribes reductionist norms for all solutions without considering how bioethical dilemmas are historically, socially, and culturally constructed in local contexts (Marshall 1992). Principlism assumes that all people share "the common morality," but this assumption overlooks how reasonable people can make value judgments in different ways (Turner 1998, 2003). In this regard, bioethics exhibits its own culture by shaping ethical dilemmas, designating certain parties as responsible, and proposing solutions through principles that prioritize individual autonomy and self-determination (Callahan 2005; Muller 1994). For example, the American principle of individual autonomy contrasts with cultural values that prioritize interconnectedness and social obligations elsewhere (Fox and Swazey 2005, 2010). Moreover, the principle of individual autonomy— for patients and physicians alike—presupposes that ethical problems can be located to the patient-physician relationship without considering institutional or social effects on behavior (Bosk 1999). For these reasons, bioethicists should incorporate studies of culture—the norms, understandings, and practices of any community engaged in interpretative meaning making about the world (Turner 2005)—to elucidate how moral problems are perceived and resolved (Hoffmaster 1992, 1994) "from the inside of experience" in situations characterized by unequal distributions of power, resources, and responsibilities (Kleinman 1994).[2]

My analysis of how bioethicists have constructed medicolegal issues in the War on Terror builds from insights into the cultural bases of bioethics. In particular, anthropologist Patricia Marshall has noted that moral dilemmas result from "a deep-seated ambivalence in the U.S. value system toward scientific developments and their implications for control over life and death" (1992, 51). Rather than assume norms and values based on predetermined principles, the cultural perspective has viewed ethical problems as "culturally constituted and continually evolving" since "the definition of a medical dilemma and its ethical resolution are seen as inextricably bound to broad cultural circumstances that influence health and illness behavior" (1992, 54). She asserts that the field of bioethics would benefit from greater introspection into the cultural meanings of what is perceived as a medical and moral reality and the *values* associated with that reality (1992, 58). Marshall and Barbara Koenig foresee that a cultural grounding for bioethics will demonstrate "how bioethics itself is tied into global power structures, perhaps inadvertently serving to maintain the status quo in biomedicine" (2004, 254). Cultural critique necessarily involves a reformulation of principlist bioethics: "Bioethics practices that celebrate only autonomy, with its emphasis on choice, and downplay on social and economic constraints on individual agency, are out of touch with health-care realities in the U.S. as well as globally" (2004, 255). This chapter analyzes how bioethical dilemmas are variously constructed as medicolegal issues and how medical and legal strategies are established within cultural meaning systems connected to global power structures in the War on Terror.

THE CONSTRUCTION OF BIOETHICAL ISSUES IN THE WAR ON TERROR

Below, I analyze texts from a search across all years since 2001 for the terms "Abu Ghraib," "War on Terror," or "Guantánamo" paired with the terms "ethics," "ethical," "bioethics," or "bioethical" in PubMed, the most accessed medical database in the world.[3] PubMed contains more than 22 million citations in the fields of biomedicine and health, developed through the American National Institutes of Health. The sole criterion guiding this search was that articles had to explicitly address the bioethics of health professionals involved with detainees in the War on Terror. I examined all English-language articles in peer-reviewed journals. I reviewed all titles and abstracts of articles for eligibility. I also reviewed articles that did not have abstracts and those whose abstracts did not seem to clearly address bioethics in the War on Terror. I excluded book reviews, dissertations, letters to the editor, and other formats that are not typically peer-reviewed. I also excluded review articles that relied on the findings of previous articles to make similar arguments. I present text excerpts by medicolegal issue below.

Dual Loyalty

Bioethicists have attempted to clarify the potential dual loyalty conflicts of military medical professionals in the War on Terror. Dual loyalty has been defined as the "clinical role conflict between professional duties to a patient and obligations, express or implied, real or perceived, to the interests of a third party such as an employer, an insurer or the state" (Physicians for Human Rights and the University of Cape Town Health Sciences Faculty 2003). Jerome Singh understands that "civilian medical ethics apply equally to military health professionals as to civilian practitioners" and that "health professionals must put patients' human rights and wellbeing before the state's interests" (2003, 573). He then calls on the American medical community to "avoid making the same mistake" of the American government "in rejecting the International Criminal Court and the Optional Protocol to the Convention against Torture" (2003, 573). Steven Miles also maintains that civilian medical ethics apply to military personnel at Abu Ghraib:

> Military personnel treating prisoners of war face a "dual loyalty conflict." The Geneva Convention addresses this ethical dilemma squarely: "Although [medical personnel] shall be subject to the internal discipline of the camp . . . such personnel may not be compelled to carry out any work other than that concerned with their medical . . . duties."[4] By this standard, the moral advocacy of military medicine for the detainees of the war on terror broke down.
>
> (2004, 727)

Miles adopts the same position for Guantánamo: "Dual loyalty ethics, like international law, obliges the clinicians who work in environments pressuring them to do otherwise to hold the wellbeing of their imprisoned patients as their primary obligation" (2007, 10). George Annas also recognizes dual loyalty conflicts at Guantánamo:

> There seems to be real tension between the physicians at Guantanamo, most of whom are under the command of the Navy at the hospital, and the Army commanders who are in charge of the prisoners and their interrogations. It is often argued that a physician in the military should rarely have to decide whether to be a military officer first and a physician second or a physician first and a military officer second. At Guantanamo, however, the choice is stark.
>
> (2006, 1381)

In contrast, military bioethicists have implied that the needs of the military trump all other considerations. Laura Sessums and colleagues write:

> Scholars in military medical ethics acknowledge that both military physicians and soldiers have an implicit understanding that the mission comes first and there will be instances where military medical officers must put the needs of society or the mission ahead of their patients' needs. At the same time, there is an obligation to serve the patient's best interests, to tell the truth, protect confidential medical information, and empower their patients with knowledge and guidance to make informed decisions about their medical care.
>
> (2009, 442)

Sessums and colleagues contend that many reasons can underlie "questionable practices" at certain times: "First, although the law forbids torture, what constitutes torture is not always clear. . . . Physicians may be inadequately trained to know how to recognize mistreatment or intervene. Some physicians may believe that participation may be acceptable when no doctor-patient relationship has been established" (2009, 443). Current standards may not adequately guide physicians: "Physicians face situations that are not covered by existing laws but involve a potential medical ethical violation. The correct response in such circumstances is less clear" (2009, 444). In all circumstances, complaints of unethical practices should follow military hierarchy: "Once a deployed physician determines that it is necessary to report a problem up the chain of command, the initial report should start at the lowest level. . . . Beyond these options, physician may go outside the system to the press, but risk significant adverse professional and personal consequences" (2009, 445). Similarly, Edmund Howe and colleagues promote the needs of the military over those of individual patients:

> The single value that prevails over all others in the military is achievement of mission. This includes keeping the country safe from harm and, in some contexts, protecting other endangered persons as well. In giving its mission highest value priority, the military is not serving its needs as an independent, separate entity. Rather, ultimately it is serving the Nation and perhaps also indirectly persons throughout the world.
>
> (2009, iv)

Howe and colleagues ultimately conclude: "It may be that those asserting that a military value should prevail over traditional medical needs should have the 'burden' of making the case that the needs of the mission should prevail. This may be the case in regard to issues that arise for military health professionals that involve interrogations and force feeding" (2009, vi). Dual loyalty conflict therefore emerges as a medicolegal issue underpinning other bioethical debates.

Force-Feeding Detainees

Many authors agree that military health professionals should not forcefully feed detainees. Annas notes that unique conditions at Guantánamo account for force-feeding:

> To the extent that military commanders are making the decisions about force-feeding, the rules of the Bureau of Prisons are not being followed at Guantanamo.[5] This may be why the immediate past commander of the medical group responsible for prisoner health care, Navy Captain John S. Edmondson, said that military health care personnel are screened before they are deployed to Guantanamo "to ensure that they do not have ethical objections to assisted feeding."
>
> (2006, 1380)

Nonetheless, Annas holds that military medical professionals must refuse to force-feed detainees: "American military physicians always have the obligation to disobey an unlawful order and the option to disobey an order that is contrary to medical ethics" (2006, 1381). Leonard Rubenstein and Annas chastise the American government for not following prison policies at Guantánamo:

> In US prisons, when prisoners have been tried, convicted, and sentenced, physicians have exclusive authority to make a final decision, and everything done to prisoners in the USA must be consistent with the US Constitution (not the Geneva Conventions). Prisoners are fed in their cells, and not taken to a central area by guards. In February, 2009, a judge at a US federal district court accepted the US military's position that forcefeeding individuals on hunger strike in restraint chairs did not violate the Eighth Amendment of

the US Constitution,[6] but the judge did not decide whether force-feeding constitutes torture or cruel, inhuman, or degrading treatment according to the Common Article 3 of the Geneva Conventions.[7] Since January, 2009 [*sic*], there have been 25–50 prisoners on hunger strikes at any time. How many, if any, of the hunger strikers are mentally incompetent or how many, if any, are being coerced by other prisoners to stop eating is not known. Neither of these circumstances, however, would justify force-feeding them in restraint chairs.

(2009, 354)

Annas and colleagues warn military physicians about the legal consequences of force-feeding: "Physicians at Guantanamo cannot permit the military to use them and their medical skills for political purposes and still comply with their ethical obligations. Force-feeding a competent person is not the practice of medicine; it is aggravated assault" (2013, 2).

Military bioethicists agree that detainees should not be forcefully fed, but also permit a broader range of opinions. Howe and colleagues state:

Force feeding, because of this irresolvable ethical conflict between saving detainees' lives and respecting their autonomy, may create a moral problem for some military providers, regardless of what policy is adopted. Some may find feeding detainees against their will in at least this context unconscionable. Others may find it unconscionable to not force feed these detainees.

(2009, xi)

However, Howe and colleagues ultimately agree that the forced feeding of detainees moves beyond the military's stewardship responsibilities to preserve life and death: "In regard to force feeding at least, it may be instead that this obligation would be best fulfilled by respecting detainees' autonomy" (2009, xii).

Health Professionals and Interrogations

All authors agree that health professionals should not be involved in interrogation. Certain authors cite international standards. Miles lists bioethical offenses: "At the operational level, medical personnel evaluated detainees for interrogation, and monitored coercive interrogation, allowed interrogators to use medical records to develop interrogation approaches, falsified medical records and death certificates, and failed to provide provide [*sic*] basic health care" (2004, 728).

Elsewhere, Miles details how clinician participation in interrogations led to the abuse of detainee Mohammed al-Qahtani:

> Medics regularly assessed al-Qahtani's vital signs, hydration, skin integrity and constipation. They attended to edema that appears to have resulted from a combination of prolonged restraint, recumbency and (perhaps) nutritional insufficiency. Physicians came to the interrogation cell to assess or treat dehydration, inanition, pain, edema and potential trauma from prolonged restraint to a metal chair. A physician told interrogators over the telephone that interrogation could continue despite bradycardia.
>
> (2008, 7)

Miles notes that the American government deliberately reinterpreted international agreements in January 2002 based on al-Qaeda's status as a non-state terrorist group: "Since al-Qaeda was not a national signatory to international conventions and treaties, these obligations did not apply" (2004, 725).[8] The American government has bypassed the Geneva Conventions: "Although the United States Supreme Court upheld the Geneva Convention in its Hamdan decision (*Hamdan v. Rumsfeld*, 124 S. Ct. 2633 [2004]),[9] the recently enacted Military Commissions Act denies prisoners the right to invoke the Geneva provisions (Military Commissions Act of 2006)" (Miles 2008, 8).[10]

Miles cautions military medical professionals against violating the Geneva Conventions: "War crimes attract universal jurisdiction" (2007, 722). Bloche and Marks also cite international standards to protect clinical information from interrogations: "The laws of war defer to medical ethics. Additional Protocol I to the Geneva Conventions provides that medical personnel 'shall not be compelled to perform acts or to carry out work contrary to the rules of medical ethics'"[11] (2005, 7). Nevertheless, Bloche and Miles acknowledge that the United States has not signed the Geneva Conventions: "Although the protocol has not been ratified by the United States, this principle has attained the status of customary international law" (2005, 7). Rubenstein additionally appeals to international law by citing the World Medical Association's amendment to the Declaration of Tokyo to dissuade health professionals from participating in interrogations "in preserving ethical standards, protecting the integrity of the profession, and, just as important, assuring the society at large that the health professions are acting in accordance with moral expectations" (2007, 747).

Other authors have relied on reports to condemn the involvement of health professionals in detainee interrogations. Susan Okie narrates how BSCT members at Guantánamo provided interrogators information about prisoners' psychological weaknesses from "a confidential report by the International Committee of the Red Cross, received by the U.S. government in July 2004 and subsequently leaked to the media" (2005, 2531). However, Major General Jay Hood, then camp commander, disputed these findings: "'Medical care has no connection to intelligence gathering,' Hood said. 'Zero. None'" (Okie 2005, 2532).

A related medicolegal issue has been the role of psychologists in interrogations. Some authors fault the American government for exploiting professional differences between psychiatrists and psychologists to involve psychologists in detainee interrogations. Nancy Sherman (2006) disputes the Pentagon's reasoning in employing psychologists in interrogations since they are not bound to the Hippocratic teaching to "do not harm" as physicians: "They [psychologists] should not be involved, directly or indirectly, in situations that may lead to the breach of confidential medical records; to torture or to cruel, inhumane, and degrading treatment; or to exploitation of fears or phobias" (200). Rubenstein and Annas (2009) also condemn the involvement of psychologists in interrogations: "The professions and ethical standards, however, have no such distinction: all health professionals are bound by the ethics of their specialty no matter what roles they have" (354). Military bioethicists have additionally advised psychologists against interrogations, but reasoned differently than civilian bioethicists in noting the unique needs of information gathering. The singularity of this viewpoint in bioethical discourse warrants a full exposition of this line of reasoning:

> To the extent that interrogators, with or without BSCs help, try to form a positive relationship with detainees so that (inadvertently or otherwise) detainees will then give them more information, this uses detainees and their interrogators' relationships with them as a means to help the military (and, thus, this country and others), as opposed to "treating" them more as ends in themselves. This is ethically problematic for both interrogators and care

providers. In the case of care providers, this risks violating their implicit professional medical obligations to give their patients' needs the highest moral priority and to not exploit their vulnerability for others' ends.

(Howe et al. 2009, viii)

Others have accused the American Psychological Association of collaboration with the American government. Kenneth Pope and Thomas Gutheil castigate the American Psychological Association for promoting the participation of psychologists in interrogations, contended to be "inherently a psychological endeavor" in "preventing violence and protecting our nation's security" (2009, 162). Pope has questioned the claims of the American Psychological Association: "What evidence did APA rely on in making these confident assurances about all interrogations? Were the claims subjected to critical scrutiny before placing the authority, prestige, trust, and influence of the organization behind them?" (2011a, 152). Nonetheless, Pope admits that aside from its health-care identity, "psychology is a military and national security profession" and that "a role in detainee interrogations seems consistent with psychology's history and range of professional identities (2011b, 164).

A DISCOURSE ANALYSIS OF BIOETHICS TEXTS ON MILITARY MENTAL HEALTH PROFESSIONALS

Texts from bioethicists confirm Marshall's contention that medical dilemmas and their ethical resolutions stem from cultural circumstances. In this case, circumstances that influence detainee health and professional behavior come from the War on Terror. Although they may construct medicolegal issues slightly differently, all authors agree that the content of medical moral reality concerns the detainee-clinician relationship. The values associated with this reality call for the protection of detainees and greater ethical practices from military mental health professionals. However, the medical and legal strategies used to evaluate this reality differ. Through discourse analysis and close textual readings, we can attend to these similarities and differences.

For example, certain authors frame bioethical dilemmas around dual loyalty conflicts. Singh (2003) asserts that "civilian medical ethics apply equally to military health professionals as to civilian practitioners," thus equating standards from two different health-care sectors. By constructing dual loyalty conflicts, Singh extends values from civilian medical ethics to military professionals in writing that "health professionals must put patients' human rights and wellbeing before the state's interests." The use of the modal tense "must" displays authority and the vocabulary of "human rights" broadens dual loyalty beyond bioethics and into civic responsibilities. In pressing American health professionals to "avoid making the same mistake" of the American government "in rejecting the International Criminal Court and the Optional Protocol to the Convention against Torture," Singh supposes that individuals can act freely and autonomously. The rhetorical move of pitting the International Criminal Court against the American government emphasizes the isolated position of the United States, and the Optional Protocol to the Convention Against Torture becomes the legal strategy to evaluate dual loyalty. Singh's choice of the word "mistake" indicates that he views this as an issue of individual immorality, compared to other words such as "tactic" or "strategy" that would reflect general state policy.

Miles (2004) similarly invokes the Geneva Conventions as the legal strategy to evaluate dual loyalty conflicts: "the Geneva Convention addresses this ethical dilemma squarely." Miles then quotes the Geneva Convention for impeachable authority. In writing "by this standard, the moral advocacy of military medicine for the detainees of the war on terror broke down," Miles assumes that the circumstances of internal camp discipline at Abu Ghraib permitted medical personnel to only have to carry out work related to medical duties. The violation of this legal standard does not become an issue for courts to prosecute, but one of "moral advocacy." On the issue of Guantánamo, Miles (2007) turns to "international law" to "oblige" clinicians who "work in environments pressuring them to do otherwise to hold the wellbeing of their imprisoned patients as their primary obligation." International law becomes the legal standard to evaluate dual loyalty. The verb "oblige" imposes an authority upon clinicians who must actively "hold the wellbeing of their imprisoned patients" with the inference that clinicians possess the individual autonomy to act. In contrast, Annas (2006) frames dual loyalty as an issue with less clear resolution: "It is often argued that a physician in the military should rarely have to decide whether to be a military officer first and a physician second or a physician first and a military officer second."

Military bioethicists have also addressed dual loyalty conflicts, but utilize other strategies to evaluate this issue. Sessums and colleagues (2009) write about "scholars in military medical ethics" who understand that "the mission comes first and there will be instances where military medical officers must put the needs of society or the mission ahead of their patients' needs." Authority in this instance lies not with general international laws but with "scholars in military medical ethics" (i.e., academic opinion without reference to laws). "The needs of society" outweigh "patients' needs," implying that utilitarian values of the greater good for the greater number of people outweigh individual patients' rights. While Sessums and colleagues agree that "the law forbids torture," they argue that "what constitutes torture is not always clear." Sessums and colleagues do not dispute the authority of the law. Rather, they concentrate on questions of interpretation, since physicians may not know how "to recognize mistreatment or intervene," especially since "physicians face situations that are not covered by existing laws but involve a potential medical ethical violation." In this line of reasoning, bioethical violations are not always clear ("potential") and violations may result from ignorance rather than moral culpability. The interconnectedness and social obligations of military medical professionals manifest through reports of problems that follow "up the chain of command" lest the reporter "risk significant adverse professional and personal consequences" (Sessums et al. 2009). The words "risk," "significant," and "adverse" leave no room for ambiguity on the "consequences." Howe and his coauthors (2009) also stress that "the single value that prevails over all others in the military is achievement of mission," emphasizing military utilitarian values. They convert "Nation" into a proper noun to make this point. However, even they express ambivalence about this ethical stance: "It may be that those asserting that a military value should prevail over traditional medical needs should have the 'burden' of making the case that the needs of the mission should prevail" (Howe et al. 2009). Ironically, having asserted that the military value should prevail over traditional medical needs, the authors concede that this point is a "burden" that calls for "making the case." Whereas civilian bioethicists have regarded dual loyalty as an issue of clinicians' exerting individual autonomy within a framework of morality governed by international laws, military bioethicists counter that institutional obligations govern individual clinicians, and bioethical infractions may not be intentional.

The assumption that civilian bioethics and laws remain operational in military contexts also pervades publications on the force-feeding of detainees. Annas (2006) discerns that Guantánamo officials do not follow American prison policies: "To the extent that military commanders are making the decisions about force-feeding, the rules of the Bureau of Prisons are not being followed at Guantanamo." The Bureau of Prisons serves as the legal strategy to support the position that clinicians, not military commanders, should make decisions about force-feeding. Annas applies policies from the Bureau of Prisons that regulate conduct in federal institutions to Guantánamo, which is not in federal jurisdiction, as it is a military installation. Annas also underscores that "American military physicians always have the obligation" to "disobey an order that is contrary to medical ethics," prioritizing the value of individual autonomy within an institution that supports hierarchy and social interconnectedness. Rubenstein and Annas (2009) affirm that "everything done to prisoners in the USA must be consistent with the US Constitution," but then acknowledge that an American federal judge ruled that "force-feeding individuals on hunger strike in restraint chairs did not violate the Eighth Amendment of the US Constitution." Nonetheless, they argue that concerns about detainees' possible mental incompetence and coercion do not "justify force-feeding them in restraint chairs." Here, Rubenstein and Annas seem to suggest that bioethical violations can occur in the absence of breaking the law. Elsewhere, Annas, Crosby, and Glantz (2013) value individual autonomy and assert that "physicians at Guantanamo cannot permit the military to use them and their medical skills for political purposes." The language used is moral and evaluative: "Force-feeding a competent person is not the practice of medicine; it is aggravated assault." The phrase "aggravated assault" refers to criminal charges within American law, though they have not clarified how American criminal law could be applied at Guantánamo, which is under military jurisdiction.

Rather than bioethical arguments that focus on the autonomy of military medical professionals, military bioethicists concentrate on the autonomy of detainees. Howe and colleagues (2009) write of the "irresolvable ethical conflict between saving detainees' lives and respecting their autonomy" which will "create a moral problem . . . regardless of what policy is adopted." In this formulation, military physicians face a bioethical conflict despite their decisions. This implies that military physicians grasp that some will charge them with bioethical violations regardless of their decision to force-feed or not. Howe and his colleagues then reason that "the responsibilities of stewardship [which] usually are to preserve the life and health of those for whom others have responsibility" may "be best fulfilled by respecting detainees' autonomy." They do not share why they think a responsibility to preserve life and health of detainees could be best fulfilled by respecting the detainees' autonomy during hunger strikes, which raises questions about whether the authority of this statement rests in the sole fact that military bioethicists adhere to this position.

The value of individual autonomy also suffuses concerns about the involvement of health professionals in military interrogations, but the relationship of this value to enforceable legal standards is also unclear. Miles (2004) writes that medical personnel "evaluated detainees for interrogation, and monitored coercive interrogation, allowed interrogators to use medical records to develop interrogation approaches, falsified medical records and death certificates, and failed to provide basic health care." In this list of offenses, medical personnel are implicated as independent agents without greater discussion about the structures of military hierarchy. Miles reports that legal strategies to evaluate the behavior of military medical professionals have shifted as the U.S. Department of Justice interpreted that since "al-Qaeda was not a national signatory to international conventions and treaties, these obligations did not apply." Miles (2008) also presents the paradox of how the "United States Supreme Court upheld the Geneva Convention" and yet the "Military Commissions Act denies prisoners the right to invoke the Geneva provisions." Bloche and Marks (2005) similarly note the paradox that the protocol of the Geneva Conventions "has not been ratified by the United States," but "has attained the status of customary international law." It would seem that Bloche and Marks want to apply legal strategies from the Geneva Conventions to evaluate potential bioethical violations, but find themselves in a conundrum in that the United States has not officially signed them. Elsewhere, Rubenstein (2007) applies strategies from the Declaration of Tokyo, but does not address the extent to which international guidelines can be legally enforced. Okie (2005) invokes a "confidential report by the International Committee of the Red Cross" charging that "medical personnel, through BSCT members, had provided interrogators with information about prisoners' psychological vulnerabilities" but this is refuted by then camp commander Jay Hood, who declared,

"Medical care has no connection to intelligence gathering." Okie relies on the authority of the International Committee of the Red Cross to evaluate suspected bioethical offenses that are then categorically refuted by a military official.

Notably, the divide between moral outrage and legal infractions widens in discussions on the role of psychologists in interrogations. Sherman (2006) believes that "it is hair-splitting" whether psychologists "can ethically be involved in interrogations that may involve coercive techniques or torture." Sherman responds that "the answer is clearly no," though it is not at all clear why they cannot be involved, since she wrote this before the American Psychological Association clarified its position on banning psychologists from interrogations. Similarly, Rubenstein and Annas (2009) condemn the involvement of psychologists in BSCTs since "all health professionals are bound by the ethics of their specialty no matter what roles they have," but psychologists do not have the same responsibilities as psychiatrists or other physicians to always act in the best interests of patients, a clear demonstration of different types of "ethics of their specialty." Ironically, military bioethicists such as Howe and colleagues (2009) write that psychologists should avoid "violating their implicit professional medical obligations to give their patients' needs the highest moral priority and to not exploit their vulnerability for others' ends," which also assumes that psychologists act in a medical capacity. This distinction is important because, as Pope and Gutheil (2009) have pointed out, the American Psychological Association has "stressed that '[c]onducting an interrogation is inherently a psychological endeavor'" and that psychologists can protect "our nation's security." Pope's moral and evaluative outrage manifests in his condemnation of the APA's "confident assurances about all interrogations" and "blanket assurances" (2011a), but he must ultimately agree that "psychology is a military and national security profession" in addition to a health profession (2011b).

*   *   *

Based on Foucault's concepts of discourse analysis, bioethical scholarship constitutes a true discourse on the professional responsibilities of military health professionals.

The limits and forms of the *sayable* by authors: civilian bioethicists prioritize the value of individual autonomy in positing that military health personnel should avoid and report bioethical violations, though military bioethicists espouse values of hierarchy and social connectedness, pointing to the lack of clear legal guidance on bioethical issues. Each group seems to comprehend the patient-provider relationship differently, as civilian bioethicists disagree with military bioethicists on its degree of independence within a military command structure.

The *domain* for this discourse: an audience of bioethicists and general health practitioners conversant with bioethical principles. In no case do we see ethical dilemmas shaped to discuss effects on detainees rather than health professionals. Cultural assumptions pivot on the principle to do no harm.

The *conservation* of specific themes: the supposition that civilian medical ethics applies to military professionals or that military bioethics is somehow exempt from civilian standards due to unique institutional values.

The *memory* of prior bioethical utterances: that new scientific developments in enhanced interrogation methods and restraint chairs elicit ambivalence over who controls life and death. If bioethics emerged to discuss moral quandaries from the growing application of medical technologies to problems throughout the life span, the concerns here are about medical technologies extended to different practice settings such as military services. The common discursive memory is the misapplication of scientific developments.

The *reactivation* of recurrent reasoning: the contention that bioethical violations from military medical professionals can be resolved through the patient-clinician relationship. Authors focus on the ethical dilemmas faced by these professionals, rather than scrutinizing the wartime situations or institutional settings that catalyze such dilemmas.

The *appropriation* of evidence: previous international laws and treaties that have mandated acceptable bioethical practices as global power structures. Using existing legal codes are seen as a remedy for safeguarding ethical practice. The question arises: Does a civilian bioethical focus on individual autonomy in the patient-clinician relationship unintentionally perpetuate the status quo by not addressing ethics based on values of hierarchy and obedience prized by military bioethicists?

My analysis of the bioethics scholarship should not be read as support for health professionals who elevate military interests above individual patients, forcefully feed detainees, or participate in interrogations. Rather, medical discourse analysis reveals the chasm in cultural values between civilian and military bioethicists and their legal strategies to evaluate bioethical issues. Civilian bioethicists tend to argue that military health professionals have violated laws or medical ethics that prevail in civilian institutions, but they must ultimately concede that laws have been reinterpreted in the War on Terror. Indeed, former president George W. Bush has written that he selected Guantánamo as a detention facility on counsel from the Justice Department, so that prisoners at Guantánamo would not be entitled to rights granted in the American legal system (Bush 2010). This has led experts to call Guantánamo a "legal black hole" that negates global power structures in human rights and humanitarian law since World War II (Steyn 2004) and a "state of exception" in which the law must be broken in one specific instance of Guantánamo to defend it elsewhere in the United States (Agamben 2004). Whether civilian bioethics applies in military settings has also reignited debates since state professional and licensing bodies in Louisiana, New York, Ohio, and Texas have dismissed charges brought against military psychologists (Gaskin, Jenny, and Clark 2012). Civilian bioethicists may need to reconsider legal strategies and arguments if the laws they invoke have been reinterpreted and military bioethical violations cannot be prosecuted in civilian jurisdictions. At the same time, military bioethicists who emphasize institutional hierarchy and social obligations over individual autonomy may need to clarify their own strategies for evaluating bioethical issues. The standards of medical ethics cannot remain hostage to the whims of military policy that negate precedents of international law (Miles 2011).

Notably, social theorists who have critiqued the situation of human rights at Guantánamo have also adopted cultural assumptions and language similar to those of bioethical discourse. For example, Giorgio Agamben points to the USA Patriot Act of 2001 to conclude that "it radically erases any legal status of the individual, thus producing a legally unnamable and unclassifiable being" (2004, 3). Agamben asserts that the detainee and his detention "is entirely removed from the law and from judicial oversight," comparing the situation of the Taliban at Guantánamo to Jews in Nazi camps (2004, 4). Similarly, Judith Butler has called "indefinite detention" a "broader tactic to neutralize the rule of law in the name of security" in which "the extra-legal exercise of state power justifies itself indefinitely"

(2004, 67). However, these characterizations are inaccurate. As we shall see in chapter 3, detainees *do* have a legal status as "enemy combatant." Detainees do not exist removed or neutralized from the law and judicial oversight, but in a hyper-regulated military legal environment with its own cultural values, assumptions, meanings, and practices. Agamben and Butler seem to equate the civilian and military justice systems in the War on Terror, as do many civilian bioethicists. This leads them to reason that civilian legal and ethical codes apply in settings such as Abu Ghraib and Guantánamo without recognizing the cultural realities of military institutions in the War on Terror. It also leads them to make assumptions about prisoner autonomy and sovereignty in liberal democracies that the War on Terror shatters.

This raises the question of what type of bioethics we can imagine for our colleagues in military health. After all, the point of this medical discourse analysis is not merely to analyze cultural meanings, but also to propose tangible solutions. One suggestion is to treat military medical ethics as a subset of medical ethics and military ethics, whose goals and strategies may differ (Gross 2010). For example, rather than view dual loyalty as the conflict in professional roles between physician and soldier, a new frontier could consider the challenges faced by seeing the ethics of the physician-soldier as a single actor (Gross 2013). Other areas of fruitful investigation may be to explore the limits of bioethical practice in light of—not in spite of—new legal interpretations in the War on Terror. We have seen how reasoning through historically accepted legal codes such as the Geneva Conventions has failed to safeguard ethical practice. The time has come to address each ethical question on its own terms. The final determinant of ethical practice may need to be adherence to new legal interpretations erected in the War on Terror rather than to precedents that the American government has rendered obsolete.

Finally, bioethicists should rationalize safeguards to protect military health personnel who report bioethical violations, risking significant personal and professional consequences. Those of us who are civilian health professionals would best help our military colleagues by developing ethical standards that incorporate the unique cultural military setting into our reasoning. We should ask ourselves about the ethics of demanding that military personnel confront grave consequences when we do not have to, and then chastising them without offering practical alternatives. In fact, primary accounts of military health professionals at Guantánamo reveal consternation among psychologists who have been forced to craft enhanced interrogation tactics and among nurses and physicians who were powerless to stop confidential medical records being shared with interrogators (James 2008). Perhaps bioethicists should turn to these individuals to understand the unique cultural circumstances in safeguarding ethical practices throughout military installations in the War on Terror.

3

The Meanings of Symptoms and Services for Guantánamo Detainees

PRESIDENT GEORGE W. BUSH JUSTIFIED the use of the Guantánamo Bay detention facility after the 9/11 attacks. He has said of its conditions: "At Guantanamo, detainees were given clean and safe shelter, three meals a day, a personal copy of the Quran, the opportunity to pray five times daily, and the same medical care their guards received" (Bush 2010, 166).[1] He has clarified that "while our humane treatment of Guantanamo detainees was consistent with the Geneva Conventions, Al Qaeda did not meet the qualifications for Geneva protection as a legal matter" (166). He has also expressed ambivalence: "While I believe opening Guantanamo after 9/11 was necessary, the detention facility had become a propaganda tool for our enemies and a distraction for our allies. I worked to find a way to close the prison without compromising security" (180).

Guantánamo still divides the officials who served in the Bush administration. Former vice president Dick Cheney has noted that Guantánamo "likely provides a standard of care higher than many prisons in European countries where the criticism of Guantanamo has been loudest" (Cheney 2011, 354), and followed up: "I don't have much sympathy for the view that we should find an alternative to Guantanamo—a solution that could potentially make Americans less safe—simply because we are worried about how we are perceived abroad" (356). Secretary of Defense Donald Rumsfeld asserted: "Detainees were more likely to suffer injury from playing soccer or volleyball during recreational periods than they were from interrogations with interrogators or guards" (Rumsfeld 2011, 581). However, Secretary of State Condoleezza Rice conceded its failure: "Some of our goals remained unfulfilled: the President had been unable to close Guantánamo on his watch, a task that has proven equally difficult for his successor" (Rice 2011, 503).

Closing Guantánamo is one promise that President Barack Obama has not kept. As president-elect, he declared: "We should close Guantanamo Bay and stop tolerating the torture of our enemies" because "it's not consistent with our traditions of justice and fairness" (Obama 2009b, 81). After his inauguration in 2009, President Obama ordered the immediate review of all cases at Guantánamo (White House 2009). Consequently, Secretary of Defense Robert Gates tasked Admiral Patrick Walsh, the vice chief of naval operations, with reviewing the conditions of Guantánamo detainees. The Walsh Report,[2] released on February 23, 2009, found that Guantánamo's conditions conform to Common Article Three of the Geneva Conventions (Department of Defense 2009a), which emphasizes that prisoners of war "shall in all circumstances be treated humanely" through medical care and prohibiting violence, hostage taking, humiliating treatment, and extrajudicial sentences (International Committee of the Red Cross 2009). Less than a year after President Obama denounced Guantánamo, his officials found reasons to preserve it.

President Obama is now in the same position as his predecessor was. He mentioned Guantánamo's closure in accepting the Nobel Peace Prize (Obama 2009a). A year later, he vowed to close it "to deny violent extremists one of their most potent recruitment tools" (White House 2010). In 2011, the *Washington Post* reported that President Obama's failure to close Guantánamo resulted from a lack of political will compared to other signature achievements such as health-care reform (Finn and Kornblut 2011). On January 2, 2013, President Obama signed into law the National Defense Authorization Act for Fiscal Year 2013 and issued a signing statement:

> Section 1027 renews the bar against using appropriated funds for fiscal year 2012 to transfer Guantanamo detainees into the United States for any purpose. I continue to oppose this provision, which substitutes the Congress's blanket political determination for careful and fact-based determinations, made by counterterrorism and law enforcement professionals, of when and where to prosecute Guantanamo detainees. For decades, Republican and Democratic administrations have successfully prosecuted hundreds of terrorists in Federal court. Those prosecutions are a legitimate, effective, and

powerful tool in our efforts to protect the Nation, and in certain cases may be the only legally available process for trying detainees. Removing that tool from the executive branch undermines our national security. Moreover, this provision would, under certain circumstances, violate constitutional separation of powers principles.

Section 1028 fundamentally maintains the unwarranted restrictions on the executive branch's authority to transfer detainees to a foreign country. This provision hinders the Executive's ability to carry out its military, national security, and foreign relations activities and would, under certain circumstances, violate constitutional separation of powers principles. The executive branch must have the flexibility to act swiftly in conducting negotiations with foreign countries regarding the circumstances of detainee transfers. The Congress designed these sections, and has here renewed them once more, in order to foreclose my ability to shut down the Guantanamo Bay detention facility. I continue to believe that operating the facility weakens our national security by wasting resources, damaging our relationships with key allies, and strengthening our enemies. My Administration will interpret these provisions as consistent with existing and future determinations by the agencies of the Executive responsible for detainee transfers. And, in the event that these statutory restrictions operate in a manner that violates constitutional separation of powers principles, my Administration will implement them in a manner that avoids the constitutional conflict.

(White House 2013a)[3]

Through signing statements, President Obama has signaled personal opposition to Guantánamo while passing bills that maintain it. Why? Guantánamo's success cannot be measured by the numbers of detainees found guilty or prosecuted. Approximately 55 percent of detainees have not been found to commit hostilities against the United States, and only 8 percent have been designated as direct al-Qaeda warriors, with hundreds later released (Denbeaux, Denbeaux, and Gratz 2006). What function does Guantánamo truly serve?

Chapter 2 covered the roles of mental health professionals in military medicine and their accompanying subsequent bioethical debates. Here, I review the experiences of detainees, physicians, and attorneys through legal documents from Guantánamo military commissions. Do detainees really receive the same medical care as guards? Are they more prone to injury from idyllic games of soccer than from interrogations? Legal texts can be analyzed as cultural discourse to investigate the forensic functions of the Guantánamo medical system: (1) How is the mental health of detainees who are facing trial constructed as a medicolegal issue? (2) What medical and legal standards are erected to support and evaluate this issue? (3) What forms of clinical evidence are deployed? (4) How do clinicians reason? (5) What legal outcomes follow from clinicians' medical opinions?

DETAINEE AS TEXT, GUANTÁNAMO AS CONTEXT, AND THE MEANING OF SYMPTOMS

Violent detainee behaviors have fanned speculations about underlying motives. For example, government officials regard suicidal acts as the conduct of "fanatical madmen," but human rights organizations construe these as evidence of "psychological deterioration"; both groups pathologize detainees rather than assigning them the agency of political protest (Howell 2007; Savage 2011). Attorneys worry that officials view detainee actions like self-smearing with feces as "disciplinary problems" rather than signs of mental illness, thereby limiting access to treatment (Aggarwal 2009a). In this sense, Guantánamo resembles other forensic medical systems in that a defendant's actions are subject to contradictory explanations (Aggarwal 2010d).

Social scientists have shown that prisoner actions undergo interpretation during each step of diagnosis and treatment. Mental health professionals use psychiatric classification in jails to diagnose treatable "mad" behaviors from untreatable "bad" behaviors (Rhodes 2000). The "bad," who are viewed as inherently evil, constantly arouse suspicions whether they conform to or resist prison conditions (Rhodes 2002). Symptom interpretations also vary according to prison setting, with segregation units and prison cells leading to more personality disorder diagnoses as compared to office visits (Galanek 2013). Prisoners in talk therapy programs must acknowledge guilt as a precondition for treatment, even if they maintain their innocence (Waldram 2007, 2008). Forensic medical settings display consistent differences in patient-clinician symptom interpretations, with clinicians ultimately exerting power over patients. Such findings can be tested in forensic mental health cases with Guantánamo detainees.

Guantánamo's Office of Military Commissions (OMC) supplies legal texts that constitute a discrete discourse to analyze interpretations of detainee symptoms.[4] Here, we can adopt medical anthropology theories in a transdisciplinary fashion. Byron Good and Mary-Jo Good (1980) espouse a "cultural hermeneutic model for clinical practice":

> The interpretive goal of the cultural hermeneutic model is *understanding*. Symptoms are viewed as an expression of the sufferer's reality and as linked to associated stresses and experiences that constitute the personal meaning of the illness. The interpretive task is to understand the meaning of the symptoms and the illness for the sufferer. As in classical hermeneutics, this involves moving dialectically from the part (the "text", the symptom) to the whole (the "context", the illness network) and back again, to bring to understanding the illness from the sufferer's perspective.
>
> (180–181)

Good and Good (1980) recommend the *cultural hermeneutic model* to analyze symptom meanings in clinical practice from the sufferer's perspective. This model can be adapted to forensic settings to describe symptom interpretations from multiple perspectives, such as the views of a defendant, the defense team, and the prosecution team. Soliciting these different perspectives can teach us about the contextual networks of such interpretations in adversarial legal systems where defense and prosecution teams seek to establish rules of evidence competitively. The judge eventually advances an interpretation accepted by the legal system, something that I term *hermeneutic adjudication*. When applied to specific cases, the *forensic hermeneutic model* can demonstrate the varieties of clinical evidence, clinical reasoning, and final legal outcomes around the mental health of detainees facing the Office of Military Commissions.

GUANTÁNAMO'S LEGAL BASIS AS ILLNESS CONTEXT

Good and Good (1980) emphasize context, the illness network, in interpreting the text of an individual's symptoms. The context of illness for detainees is the procedure for mental health evaluations at Guantánamo, which differs from that of civilian courts. The Military Commissions Act of 2006 (also known as MCA 2006 or HR-6166) empowers commissions to try any "alien unlawful enemy combatant" for war crimes. Alien unlawful enemy combatants include members of non-state organizations such as al-Qaeda or the Taliban at war against the United States.[5] The commissions are composed of "any commissioned officer of the armed forces on active duty" (Military Commissions Act of 2006, 5). Through MCA 2006, we observe *the cultural construction of a medicolegal issue*:

> It is an affirmative defense in a trial by military commission under this chapter that, at the time of the commission of the acts constituting the offense, the accused, as a result of a severe mental disease or defect, was unable to appreciate the nature and quality or the wrongfulness of the acts. Mental disease or defect does not otherwise constitute a defense.
>
> (Military Commissions Act of 2006, 17)

Mental disorders do not disqualify detainees from trial by commission. Instead, detainees must prove that mental disorders limited their responsibility: "The accused in a military commission under this chapter has the burden of proving the defense of lack of mental responsibility by clear and convincing evidence" (Military Commissions Act of 2006, 17).

MCA 2006 details *the legal standards to support and evaluate the accused's lack of mental responsibility*. The military judge invests the military commission with the power to resolve the medicolegal issue: "The military judge shall instruct the members of the commission as to the defense of lack of mental responsibility under this section and shall charge them to find the accused—(1) guilty; (2) not guilty; or (3) subject to subsection (d), not guilty by reason of lack of mental responsibility" (Military Commissions Act of 2006, 17).

The outcome "not guilty by reason of lack of mental responsibility" can follow only "if a majority of the members present at the time the vote is taken determines that the defense of lack of mental responsibility has been established" (Military Commissions Act of 2006, 17). Voting takes place by "secret written ballot."

The Rules for Military Commissions (RMC) further detail *the legal standards to support and evaluate the accused's lack of mental responsibility* (Department of Defense 2006b). Under Rule 504, a military commission can be convened by an official known as a "convening authority" such as the secretary of defense or an individual designated by the secretary

(Department of Defense 2006a).[6] Rule 706 is titled "Inquiry Into the Mental Capacity or Mental Responsibility of the Accused." Under Rule 706, a commission member, military judge, or participating counsel can apply for a mental examination if "there is reason to believe that the accused lacked mental responsibility for any offense charged or lacks capacity to stand trial" (Department of Defense 2006b, 55–56). A "706 board" (as it is colloquially known) then conducts an inquiry with the membership of the board as "consisting of one or more persons" and "each member of the board shall be either a physician or a clinical psychologist. Normally, at least one member of the board shall be either a psychiatrist or a clinical psychologist" (Department of Defense 2006b, 56). The 706 board must make "separate and distinct findings" for each of the four questions:

(A) At the time of the alleged criminal conduct, did the accused have a severe mental disease or defect? (The term "severe mental disease or defect" does not include an abnormality manifested only by repeated criminal or otherwise antisocial conduct, or minor disorders such as nonpsychotic behavior disorders and personality defects.)

(B) What is the clinical psychiatric diagnosis?

(C) Was the accused, at the time of the alleged criminal conduct and as a result of such severe mental disease or defect, unable to appreciate the nature and quality or wrongfulness of his or her conduct?

(D) Is the accused presently suffering from a mental disease or defect rendering the accused unable to understand the nature of the proceedings against the accused or to conduct or cooperate intelligently in the defense? Other appropriate questions may also be included.

(Department of Defense 2006b, 56–57)

A statement consisting only of the board's conclusions is circulated to the officer who ordered the examination, the accused detainee's confinement official, all counsel, the convening authority, and, after referral of charges, the military judge. The full report is released only to the defense and to the medical personnel caring for the accused, unless further release is authorized by the convening authority or a military judge. Only the defense counsel, the accused, and the military judge can disclose direct or derived statements made at the 706 hearing to the prosecution. Rule 909 allows the convening authority to hospitalize or treat the accused if the accused is found incompetent and to reconvene the commission should competency be restored. The convening authority can also disagree with a conclusion of incompetence and continue the trial: "In making this determination, the military judge is not bound by the rules of evidence except with respect to privileges" (Department of Defense 2006b, 93). The Military Commissions Act of 2009 does not alter these conditions (Department of Defense 2009b).

The construction of issues around an accused's lack of mental responsibility and its associated legal standards exhibits distinct cultural meanings. MCA 2006 allows commissions of "any commissioned officer of the armed forces on active duty" to determine an accused's defense of lack of mental responsibility. The commission reaches a conclusion by majority vote through secret ballot in a style of clandestine democracy. A political process internal to the commission rather than the product of scientific merit determines conclusions on the accused's defense. RMC 706 ambiguously states that each member of its board "shall be" a physician or clinical psychologist, but immediately concedes that only one must be a psychiatrist or psychologist. RMC 706 also creates hierarchies among mental disorders, excluding defenses from "antisocial conduct,[7] or minor disorders such as nonpsychotic behavior disorders and personality defects." The term "minor" is not fully explained, permitting considerable interpretive latitude. RMC 909 also frees the military judge from "rules of evidence" in disagreeing with the 706 board. Different interpretations of a detainee's symptoms rest against this context.

HERMENEUTICAL ADJUDICATIONS IN SPECIFIC DETAINEE CASES

Table 3.1 lists all of the cases through the Guantánamo military commissions systems, their legal status, and whether a mental health evaluation was requested.[7] The remainder of this chapter presents analyses of randomly selected cases. Each case is organized around a timeline related to mental health determinations. At times, the court spells a detainee's name differently, so only the first spelling is used. These specific cases reveal key forensic functions: *the procurement of clinical evidence, the application of clinical reasoning,* and *the legal outcome based on the clinician's medical opinion.* The legal outcome depends on the military judge's *hermeneutical adjudication*

TABLE 3.1 Guantánamo Detainee Cases with Requested Mental Health
Evaluations

CASE NAME	STATUS	EVALUATION?
Abd al-Rahim Hussein Muhammed Abdu Al-Nashiri	Active	Yes
Abdul Ghani	Withdrawn/Dismissed	No
Abdul Zahir	Archives	No
Ahmed Khalfan Ghailani	Withdrawn/Dismissed	No
Al Qahtani	Archives	No
Ali Hamza Ahmad Suliman al Bahlul	Appeal	No
Ahmed Mohammed Ahmed Haza Al Darbi	Withdrawn/Dismissed	Yes
Binyam Ahmed Muhammad	Withdrawn/Dismissed	No
David M. Hicks	Completed	No
Faiz Mohammed Ahmed Al Kandari	Withdrawn/Dismissed	No
Fouad Mahmoud Hasan Al Rabia	Withdrawn/Dismissed	No
Ghassan Abdullah al Sharbi	Withdrawn/Dismissed	No
Ibrahim Ahmed Mahmoud al Qosi	Completed	Yes
Khalid Shaikh Mohammed et al.	Active	Yes
Majid Shoukat Khan	Active	No
Mohammed Hashim	Withdrawn/Dismissed	No
Mohammed Jawad	Withdrawn/Dismissed	Yes
Mohammed Kamin	Withdrawn/Dismissed	Yes
Noor Uthman Muhammed	Completed	Yes
Obaidullah	Withdrawn/Dismissed	No
Omar Ahmed Khadr	Completed	Yes
Salid Ahmed Hamdan	Appeal	Yes
Sufyian Barhoumi	Withdrawn/Dismissed	No
Tarek Hamoud El Sawah	Withdrawn/Dismissed	No

of a detainee's symptoms. When this chapter was written, all case files were accessible in drop-down menus from the general OMC website (http://www.mc.mil/CASES/MilitaryCommissions.aspx):

Abd al-Rahim Hussein Muhammed Abdu al-Nashiri

September 15, 2011 (Office of Military Commissions 2011)—Al-Nashiri is charged with perfidy, murder in violation of the law of war, attempted murder in violation of the law of war, terrorism, conspiracy, intentionally causing serious bodily injury, attacking civilians, attacking civilian objects, and hazarding a vessel during attacks against the USS *The Sullivans* in January 2000, the USS *Cole* in October of the same year, and the MV *Limburg* in October 2002.

March 9, 2012 (*United States of America v. Abd al-Rahim Hussein Muhammed Abdu al-Nashiri* 2012a)—Al-Nashiri's defense motions that he be unshackled when meeting with his attorneys: "During his incarceration with the CIA, the accused was tortured while shackled. As a result of the torture, the use of restraints is a retraumatization of his torture and interferes with his communications with his counsel and in light of his behavior with counsel and in court is unnecessary." His attorneys detail that the torture for four years at a CIA black site starting in 2002 included waterboarding, threats with a handgun, threats with a power drill, and threats to harm his family:

> As a victim of torture, it is likely that the accused suffers from Posttraumatic Stress Disorder. One of the hallmarks of PTSD is the presence of "intrusive memories" or flashbacks of the traumatic event. . . . Thus, any present condition that mirrors the past trauma can cause retraumatization. If this were to occur, the victim may behave in a way to avoid situations that are a reminder of the past trauma. Further, this retraumatization is likely to cause further psychological damage and exacerbate any symptoms that exist. Here, the accused underwent horrendous treatment by the government while he was shackled. And the use of shackles during legal visits acts as a reminder of these past horrors and amounts to the retraumatization of the torture. Furthermore, this retraumatization significantly interferes with the accused's ability to assist in his defense.

The defense's application of clinical reasoning: Shackles remind al-Nashiri of torture, which then trigger "retraumatization" from "likely" PTSD.

April 3, 2012 (*United States of America v. Abd al-Rahim Hussein Muhammed Abdu al-Nashiri* 2012b)—The prosecution motions that the Military Commission release al-Nashiri's mental health records and that they be allowed to conduct their own mental health examination of him:

> The defense affirmatively placed the mental state of the accused at issue in its
> renewed motion for the accused not to be restrained during attorney-client
> · meetings. In addition to the allegations set forth in the defense's motion, the
> defense provided notice that it intends to rely on what it considers to be an
> expert on matters relating to PTSD and PTSD-like symptoms. The defense
> also provided notice to the government that the accused would be testifying
> during oral argument concerning the alleged treatment of the accused and
> how that treatment affects his ability to participating [*sic*] in attorney-client
> meetings. Because the defense has placed the mental health of the accused
> at issue, it waived any potential patient-psychotherapist privilege protecting
> the accused's mental-health records from disclosure.

The prosecution's application of clinical reasoning: (1) PTSD requires an expert diagnosis. (2) The defense has waived al-Nashiri's right to medical privacy by placing his mental health "at issue."

April 9, 2012 (*United States of America v. Abd al-Rahim Hussein Muhammed Abdu al-Nashiri* 2012c)—The defense motions the government to reject the prosecution's above motion:

> Significantly, and contrary to the government's assertions, the defense has
> not put Mr. Nashiri's mental health at issue. Mr. Nashiri's medical records
> from the time in Guantanamo are ultimately irrelevant to the claim he is
> making.... The defense will not put on evidence purporting to diagnose Mr.
> Nashiri nor otherwise make mental health claims beyond the common sense
> and readily perceivable traumatic effects that a human being would suffer
> under prolonged torture.

The defense's application of clinical reasoning: (1) The defense has not placed al-Nashiri's mental health "at issue." (2) The defense invokes "common sense" that "*traumatic effects*" develop after torture, rendering the procurement of clinical evidence unnecessary.

September 13, 2012 (*United States of America v. Abd al-Rahim Hussein Muhammed Abdu al-Nashiri* 2012d)—The prosecution motions the court to deny the defense team's motion that al-Nashiri be examined by physicians after appearing before the commissions on July 17, but not July 18 and 19, 2012. The prosecution team argued that his absence was a matter of law, not evidence:

> Prior to the day's hearing on 19 July 2012, CDR Strazza [al-Nashiri's attorney] again met with the accused at his cell to notify him of the schedule for attending court on that day. The accused acknowledged the presence of CDR Strazza, acknowledged his scheduled hearing, but again told CDR Strazza that he did not want to go to court. The accused explained that he was boycotting the proceedings in protest of JTF-GTMO's use of a standard method of transporting detainees internally within the housing facility—that is, JTF-GTMO employs a belly chain for such movements. The accused explained to CDR Strazza that he objects to the use of belly chains. CDR Strazza explained to the accused that because he was to be moved outside the facility, the belly chain would not be employed to transport the accused. The accused indicated that he understood the distinction, and he reiterated that he was protesting the use of the belly chain during any movement, including movements unrelated to his transport to the ELC to attend court. The government disputed the prosecution's reasoning, "The defense now argues that it believes some psychological injury might result from the accused's transportation to and participation in the proceedings. The defense's post-hoc rationalization- that it 'believes that something related to [the accused's] conditions of confinement may have triggered a flashback to his past treatment and likely caused [the accused's] refusal to come to court,' does not support the Commission delaying its consideration of the government's motion. Rather, the defense's belief is mere speculation regarding potential effects of detention operations on the accused, and such speculation should not be considered by the Commission."

The prosecution's application of clinical reasoning: Al-Nashiri's behavior in not appearing before the military commission should not be assumed to be "psychological injury" resulting from detention.

September 20, 2012 (*United States of America v. Abd al-Rahim Hussein Muhammed Abdu al-Nashiri* 2012e)—The defense replies that al-Nashiri's distress on appearing before the military commission is *precisely* the reason that he should receive a medical evaluation: "The government mentions several times that the defense has presented no evidence that Mr. Al-Nashiri has suffers [*sic*] from any psychological ailment or suffers from at all from effects [*sic*] of detention operations. This is exactly why the defense insists that a medical examination of Mr. Al-Nashiri be conducted."

The defense's application of clinical reasoning: Al-Nashiri's refusal to appear before the military commission should be evaluated to ensure that it is not from a mental disorder.

October 23, 2012 (Office of Military Commissions 2012a)—The military judge Colonel James Pohl orders that al-Nashiri's presence in court is a legal issue, not a psychiatric issue: "The Commission sees the presence of the accused strictly a legal issue [*sic*] unrelated to the personal circumstances of the accused."

Hermeneutical adjudication: Al-Nashiri's presence in court is not related to his psychological state.

October 24, 2012 (Office of Military Commissions 2012b)—Al-Nashiri attends the hearing and explains his absence in two prior hearings:

AL-NASHIRI: I thank you for letting me talk. I have been, for the last ten years, with nobody to hear what I have to say. Ten years. Today I would like to talk about a small issue. I have the intention to always show up here. This is my case, and it is my right to defend myself. But if you order the guards to bring me a bad chair, when I'm sitting in an uncomfortable place, I have the right to leave this court. You have to provide me with a comfortable chair where I can sit down comfortably. Also, when they place me in a bad car and transport me here, when I'm really tired and getting sick and throwing up, I have the right to tell you I need a more comfortable vehicle to bring me here. Also, in my prison, the place where I always sit, if there are attacks on me under the so-called security measures where they can do—where we can do what we want, I have the right to stand up and tell the judge about them. It is not possible for me to come and say things that the government may not like. And back there in my prison, they create new rules by which they attack us, and they say, "We are taking security measures." That's impossible. I have not attended the past two sessions because of the ill-treatment of the guards on us. They say, "That's security and we have the right to do everything." That's impossible.

Security must have a limit. I have been asking for a long time about belly chains. I have a bad back, and my nerves are also bad. But they insist—but they insist on placing chains around my waist. I hope that the judge can explain to these guards and the people in charge to stop those aggressions. I call them "aggressions" because they have nothing to do with security.

I am sitting in front of you right here with nothing in my hands. There are four guards. That's the proper security procedure. And I thank you for treating us well, but they don't treat us well back there. If you move for even one meter outside of your cell, because they are coming to inspect your cell, they chain your hands, chain your legs, and a belly chain on your waist and back—

JUDGE POHL: Mr. Nashiri, don't talk about specifics that your counsel can raise at another time.

AL-NASHIRI: Well, that's very well. I just want to tell you, that if I come here again [*sic*], that will be my way of condemning what's going on. I do intend to attend all future sessions, but if the guards do not treat me better, I have the right not to come and let the world know that the judge sentenced me to death because I didn't show up to court due to chains. Thank you.

JUDGE POHL: Good to go? Thank you.

Al-Nashiri's interpretation: His refusal to appear before the military is a political act of defiance against his mistreatment. Al-Nashiri refuses to attend because of "ill-treatment" from the military commission system such as "bad" chairs, "bad" transport, and the "aggressions" of violent security measures from prison guards, not because of concerns about reexperiencing trauma through shackles. Nowhere does al-Nashiri doubt the judicial integrity of the commissions as a political act of defiance, stating his intention to attend all future sessions as long as he is treated better.

Hermeneutical adjudication: Judge Pohl orders al-Nashiri not to "talk about specifics" about his mistreatment.

November 15, 2012 (*United States of America v. Abd al-Rahim Hussein Muhammed Abdu al-Nashiri* 2012f)—The prosecution team submits a motion to the court that al-Nashiri be evaluated by a 706 board since "the accused because the accused [*sic*] apparently perceives himself to be under 'attack' by the guard force and he has made claims that his 'nerves are also bad.' Those statements, coupled with previous assertions from defense counsel, support ordering the inquiry."

The prosecution's procurement of clinical evidence: Al-Nashiri admits to paranoia and bad nerves. The prosecution's application of clinical reasoning: Al-Nashiri needs a 706 evaluation.

December 28, 2012 (*United States of America v. Abd al-Rahim Hussein Muhammed Abdu al-Nashiri* 2012g)—The defense team submits a motion for the court to deny the 706 board hearing:

> The prosecution's request, by its terms, is not in good faith. The prosecution admits that it cannot state any facts that justify its request. The request is based upon the defense's suggestion that because Mr. Al-Nashiri was tortured by the United States he suffers from PTSD and other *sequalae* [*sic*] of that torture. While Mr. Al-Nashiri does suffer from mental disease or defect, the defense does not allege, at this time, that that [*sic*] the mental disease or defect falls within the language of R.M.C. 706(c)(2)(D) which provides: "Is the accused presently suffering from a mental disease or defect rendering the accused unable to understand the nature of the proceedings against the accused."
>
> Moreover the defense makes no claim that the warranting an evaluation under R.M.C. 706(c)(2)(C) that at the time of the alleged criminal conduct, the accused had a severe "mental disease or defect."

The defense's application of clinical reasoning: Al-Nashiri may suffer from a mental disorder, but that does not relate to his current proceedings or time at the alleged criminal conduct.

January 4, 2013 (*United States of America v. Abd al-Rahim Hussein Muhammed Abdu al-Nashiri* 2012h)—The prosecution team disputes the defense team's motion by claiming that this is a tactical issue: "An inquiry under Rule 706 is in no way dependent on the defense's tactical trial decision to raise a mental health defense—it requires only that there be a 'reason to believe' the accused lacked mental responsibility for the offense or lacks capacity to stand trial."

The prosecution's application of clinical reasoning: The defense team is using al-Nashiri's symptoms strategically.

February 4, 2013 (Office of Military Commissions 2012c)—Judge Colonel Pohl orders the 706 board evaluation since it "deals with competency of his ability to stand trial."

The judge's hermeneutical adjudication: Al-Nashiri's symptoms warrant a 706 hearing.

Ahmed Mohammed Ahmed Haza Al Darbi

December 20, 2007 (Office of Military Commissions 2007a)—Al Darbi is charged with providing material support for terrorism and conspiracy for allegedly planning to carry out terrorist attacks against shipping vessels in the Straits of Hormuz.

November 10, 2008 (*United States of America v. Ahmed Mohammed Ahmed Haza Al Darbi* 2008a)—The defense motions to suppress incriminating statements made under conditions of torture after apprehension in 2002:

> At that time, his clothes were cut off his person, he was blindfolded, choked and cursed at by American agents. He was transported to Bagram Air Base, Afghanistan, where he was subjected to numerous incidents of physical and mental abuse, especially during his first month of confinement. This abuse rises to the level of torture. During and after this physical and mental abuse, he was interrogated, fed in formation, and forced to provide incriminating statements. He has never been advised of any right against self-incrimination.
>
> Certain acts include being "forced to lean with his forehead against a wall and his feet over a foot away, forcing his body weight onto his forehead" and being "chained in a 'hanging' position for 'two weeks without sleep.'" The motion is replete with sexual acts from guards including this incident:
>
> At one point, the male interrogator again threatened Mr. Al Darbi with rape, forced Mr. Al Darbi to his knees, and then the interrogator positioned himself behind Mr. Al Darbi and mimicked anally sodomizing him. Mr. Al Darbi had already been subjected to numerous, unnecessary body cavity searches and rectal examinations, he had clearly been left at the unchecked mercy of his interrogators and consequently had every reason to fear that the interrogator would follow through on his threat of rape.

The defense's procurement of clinical evidence: Al Darbi's statements were made during conditions of "physical and mental abuse." The defense's application of clinical reasoning: These abusive actions meet the definition of torture.

December 18, 2008 (*United States of America v. Ahmed Mohammed Ahmed Haza Al Darbi* 2008b)—The prosecution responds to the defense's above motion by stating:

> The Motion to Suppress directly implicates the accused's physical and mental status triggering the Government's right to discovery on these issues and the opportunity to rebut the allegations. The requested relief is directly tailored by the issues raised in the accused's Motion to Suppress. . . . The discovery and the right to rebut these allegations through the use of medical and psychiatric evaluations is reasonable considering the serious claims made by the accused.
>
> The prosecution seeks access to Al Darbi's mental health records from Guantánamo, wants him to submit to a physical and mental health examination by a medical expert chosen by the government, wants him to identify the medical experts, including the mental health expert(s), who will testify at the Motion to Suppress or whose opinions will be relied upon and their Qualifications, and wants a summary of the diagnoses of the medical experts, including mental health experts.

The prosecution's application of clinical reasoning: Al Darbi should undergo a mental health evaluation under conditions outlined by the government.

January 6, 2009 (*United States of America v. Ahmed Mohammed Ahmed Haza Al Darbi* 2009)—The defense counters the prosecution's request from December 18, 2008, since

> what must be determined, which can be done through witness and/or expert testimony, is whether or not any of the treatment received by Mr. Al Darbi meets the requirements for torture set forth in the rule and, if not, whether it was coercion, the results of which are more prejudicial than they are probative. This can, and should, be done without providing the Government access to Mr Al Darbi or his mental or physical health records.

Moreover, the defense states that "such an examination by the Government carries an important risk of retraumatization and further harming Mr. Al Darbi's wellbeing" and also cites "psychotherapist-patient privilege."

The defense's application of clinical reasoning: (1) The question of merit is not Al Darbi's mental health, but whether his treatment constitutes torture. (2) A government examination could retraumatize Al Darbi.

August 29, 2012 (Office of Military Commissions 2012d)—Charges against Al Darbi were refiled and expanded: conspiracy, attacking civilian objects, hazarding a vessel, terrorism, attempt, and aiding the enemy. As of this writing, his mental health was not the focus of subsequent motions or transcripts.

Ibrahim Ahmed Mahmoud al Qosi

February 8, 2008 (Office of Military Commissions 2008a)—Al Qosi is charged with conspiracy and providing material support for terrorism by providing logistical support to Osama bin Laden and al-Qaeda.

December 19, 2008 (*United States of America v. Ibrahim al Qosi* 2008)— The defense motions to suppress all of al Qosi's statements since his capture in 2001, contending that they were made under torture and coercion. Certain details are redacted, but the motion cites an article written by Michael Isikoff in *Newsweek*. Isikoff (2005) writes: "Al Qosi claimed they were strapped to the floor in an interrogations center known as the Hell Room, wrapped in Israeli flags, taunted by female interrogators who rubbed their bodies against them in sexually suggestive ways, and left alone in refrigerated cells for hours with deafening music blaring in their ears."

The defense's procurement of clinical evidence: Isikoff's article. The defense's application of clinical reasoning: Al Qosi's statements were made during conditions of torture.

January 9, 2009 (*United States of America v. Ibrahim al Qosi* 2009)—The prosecution disputes the defense's motion to suppress statements:

> The only statements made by the Accused that the prosecution seeks to use at trial are those [REDACTED]. Neither of these statements were the product of torture or coercion. And the prosecution can make the interviewers available to the Defense and at any hearing necessary to demonstrate as much. With respect to any other statements made by the accused, the defense motion is not ripe for resolution.

The prosecution's application of clinical reasoning: Al Qosi's statements were not made during conditions of torture.

January 15, 2010 (*United States of America v. Ibrahim al Qosi* 2010a)—The defense motions for the court to compel funding for an independent mental health expert rather than use the government's consultant:

> This is a motion to compel funding for Dr. [REDACTED] to serve as a defense consultant and possibly as a witness. After the defense filed a request with the Convening Authority (CA) for Dr. [REDACTED] the CA appointed a substitute, Colonel [REDACTED] M.D., M.P.H., Medical Corps, U.S. Army. Based on Dr. [REDACTED] statements to the defense on 3 January 2010, Col. [REDACTED is not an adequate substitute as has no experience conducting forensic examinations of people who claim to have been tortured, and he has never applied the Istanbul Protocol, a widely accepted procedure for examining torture victim claims. Dr. [REDACTED] has these qualifications. On this basis alone, Col. [REDACTED] would be open to withering cross-examination by the very government who claims he is an adequate substitute for Dr. [REDACTED]. Additionally, and most importantly for the defense's preparation of this case, there is a high likelihood that Col. [REDACTED] could not establish a rapport with the accused because he lacks several qualifications Dr. [REDACTED] has. For example, Col. [REDACTED] is still a uniformed officer; he has specifically worked for the government, not the defense, in GTMO detainee cases; and, has worked for the defense of soldiers accused of abusing detainees. These facts appear on his CV, and the defense would have to share this information with the client.
>
> This defense motion responds to a decision by CA Susan J. Crawford to substitute Col. [REDACTED] who is a clinical psychologist rather than Dr. Xenakis whereas the defense submitted a motion for Dr. Xenakis on November 18, 2009.
>
> [*United States of America v. Ibrahim al Qosi* 2010b]

The defense's application of clinical reasoning: Al Qosi's behaviors warrant an independent mental health evaluation to assess for the effects of torture through an expert chosen by the defense.

January 22, 2010 (*United States of America v. Ibrahim al Qosi* 2010c)—The prosecution disputes the defense's reasoning:

Defense counsel's argument for COL Malone's inadequacy in this matter rests on little more than defense counsel's subjective conclusion regarding the relative qualifications of COL Malone and Dr Xenakis. What little more there is consists of speculation regarding the challenges members of the United States military face in gaining the trust of alleged terrorists.

The prosecution's application of clinical reasoning: The government's expert should suffice over the defense's desired expert.

January 29, 2010 (*United States of America v. Ibrahim al Qosi* 2010d)— Military judge Lieutenant Colonel Nancy Paul rejects the defense motion in favor the prosecution:

In the defense motion, they assert that Dr. Malone is not qualified because he will not be able to establish a rapport with Mr. al Qosi; however, Dr. Malone has yet to even meet Mr. al Qosi. In addition, while the defense asserts that Dr. Malone lacks the qualifications of Dr. Xenakis, the curriculum vitae of Dr. Malone indicates he has served as both a defense and government consultant in various proceedings, including courts martial and commissions cases. In addition, Dr. Malone's curriculum vitae reflects he is currently serving as the Chief of Forensic Psychiatry Services at Walter Reed Army Medical Center, while Dr. Xenakis' curriculum vitae reflects his practice and education has been primarily in the areas of child, adolescent, and family psychiatry.

Hermeneutical adjudication: The government's expert will conduct an evaluation.

Mohammed Jawad

October 9, 2007 (Office of Military Commissions 2007b)—Jawad is charged with attempted murder in violation of the law of war and intentionally causing serious bodily injury in violation of the law of war for allegedly throwing a hand grenade into a vehicle and injuring two U.S. soldiers and one Afghan citizen.

May 28, 2008 (*United States of America v. Mohammed Jawad* 2008a)— The defense motions for a mental health examination "from a neutral, Pashto speaking, civilian psychologist" because Jawad "is presently suffering from one or more mental health diseases or defects, as a result of the extended and severe conditions of detention to which he has been subjected." The defense outlines these conditions:

> He has been in solitary confinement (what the government euphemistically refers to as "single-occupancy") in a small cell with virtually no amenities for 22 to 23 hours a day. He is allowed out of his cell only to shower, or to be placed in an enclosed, covered exercise area, or for occasional medical or dental appointments. He has not seen the sun or sky more than once since February 2003.

In addition, he underwent sensory confusion: "Mr. Jawad was moved from cell to cell 112 times over a two-week period, an average of every two hours and fifty minutes. This torture program caused intense mental suffering and profoundly disrupted the senses and personality of Mr. Jawad." The defense notes: "The extreme conditions led Mr. Jawad to attempt to commit suicide" in December 2003. These are detailed elsewhere (*United States of America v. Mohammed Jawad* 2008b) as "two different accounts of this suicide attempt." One entry states that at 2307 hours "Detainee attempted self harm by banging his head off metal structures inside his cell." Another entry states that at "approximately 2307 detainee attempted self-harm by using the collar of his shirt to hang himself from the mesh inside his cell."

The defense reasons that torture of detainees is grounds for dismissal: "The appropriate remedy for illegal abusive treatment of a detainee is dismissal under RMC 907" (United States of America v. Mohammed Jawad 2008b).

The defense's procurement of clinical evidence: Jawad suffered from solitary confinement and sensory deprivation, leading to suicidal acts. The defense's application of clinical reasoning: Jawad's psychological symptoms result from torture and should lead to dismissal of the case.

June 3, 2008 (*United States of America v. Mohammed Jawad* 2008c)— The prosecution files a motion detailing no objection to the defense's request "so long as the board ordered by the Commission consists only of mental health professionals possessing the proper security clearances, both to allow the board access to the JTF GTMO facilities and to prevent the unauthorized disclosure of classified information."

The prosecution's application of clinical reasoning: National security must be protected throughout the 706 evaluation.

June 4, 2008 (*United States of America v. Mohammed Jawad* 2008d)—
The prosecution counters that the Military Commissions Act allows statements obtained through torture to not be admitted, not for the case to be
dismissed:

> On the contrary, the MCA specifically contemplates that detainees may
> have been subjected to "torture" or coercive techniques in the past, and pro-
> vides not for the dismissal of charges, but rather that statements obtained by
> torture are inadmissible, and that even statements obtained through coer-
> cion may nonetheless be admitted into evidence if the Military Judge makes
> certain findings about the statements, set forth in the MCA.

*The prosecution's application of clinical reasoning: Torture should not lead
to dismissal of charges altogether but for specific statements to be suppressed.*
June 20, 2008 (*United States of America v. Mohammed Jawad* 2008e)—The
military judge grants a 706 evaluation. *Hermeneutical adjudication: The judge
agrees that Jawad's treatment suggests a need for a mental health evaluation.*
September 18, 2008 (*United States of America v. Mohammed Jawad*
2008f)—The defense requests experts in forensic medicine and clinical
psychology "to determine, principally, what effect his lengthy confinement
and treatment has had on his ability to accurately recall the events leading
up to his capture and participate competently in his defense." The defense
also questions the partiality of the 706 board: "In preliminary review of the
706 Board Report, Dr. Porterfield [one of the experts sought] determined
that there are significant problems with the report." *The defense's application of clinical reasoning: The 706 board may not be neutral and other mental
health experts should evaluate Jawad.*
September 22, 2008 (*United States of America v. Mohammed Jawad*
2008g)—The prosecution counters the defense's motion for experts:

> As to Dr. Keller and Dr. Porterfield, the defense premises its entire "rele-
> vance and necessity" argument upon the unsupported facts that the accused
> was a juvenile at the time of his apprehension and initial interrogations, and
> has been subjected to torture since his apprehension and custody. There
> has not been one scintilla of evidence in this case that the accused was sub-
> jected to anything amounting to either torture or physical or psychological
> abuse. Additionally, at the time of his grenade attack the accused was 17, 18,

or older. The "torture" the defense alleges occurred was at a time when the accused was 18–24 years of age—i.e., clearly not when he was a "juvenile" even by the most liberal definition.

The prosecution's application of clinical reasoning: (1) Jawad's conditions of confinement do not rise to the level of torture. (2) Jawad was not a minor at the time of his alleged offense. The very evidence of Jawad's age becomes a matter of dispute.

September 24, 2008 (*United States of America v. Mohammed Jawad* 2008h)—Military judge Colonel Stephen Henley refuses to dismiss the case on grounds of torture, but notes:

(1) While the "frequent flyer" program was intended to create a feeling of hopelessness and despair in the detainee and set the stage for successful interrogations, by March 2004 the accused was of no intelligence value to any government agency. The infliction of the "frequent flyer" technique upon the Accused thus had no legitimate interrogation purpose.

(2) While the long term psychological impact of the Accused's detention is unclear, the Rule for Military Commission (RMC) 706 board concluded the Accused is "not currently suffering from a mental disease or defect," "does have sufficient present ability to consult with his lawyers with a reasonable degree of rational understanding" and "does have sufficient mental capacity to understand the nature of the proceedings against him and cooperate intelligently in his defense." Additionally, the Accused does not require immediate medical or psychological treatment.

(3) This Commission finds that, under the circumstances, subjecting this Accused to the "frequent flyer" program from May 7–20, 2004 constitutes abusive [*sic*].

(4) That being said, the narrow issue before this Military Commission is whether dismissal of the charges against this Accused is appropriate for the conduct of an apparent few government agents. Answering this question does not require the Military Commission to decide as fact that this Accused was tortured. Assuming, but not deciding, that the government's actions against this Accused produced the pain and suffering of the requisite physical and/or mental intensity and of such duration to rise to the level of "torture", this Military Commission finds that the remedy sought by the defense is not warranted under the circumstances.

Hermeneutical adjudication: Even though Jawad's detention circumstances were "abusive," he does not have a mental disease or defect relevant to the facts on trial.

Mohammed Kamin

March 11, 2008 (Office of Military Commissions 2008b)—Kamin was charged with providing material support for terrorism arising from his alleged involvement with al-Qaeda.

August 29, 2008 (*United States of America v. Mohammed Kamin* 2008a)—The defense motions for an expert witness in forensic psychology based on Kamin's history:

> Mr. Kamin's mental health will no doubt be relevant and a major topic of discussion at trial. BSCT Records document that Mr. Kamin was previously evaluated in 2005 due to [REDACTED]. The BSCT records indicated that an [REDACTED] was to be ruled out. In order to rule out this type of disorder, it would be important to have a follow-up evaluation to determine whether the symptoms had remitted. The defense has not been provided any records that document a follow-up was completed, so the initial diagnosis cannot have been ruled out. In addition, it is unclear whether Mr. Kamin is suffering from a serious mental disorder other than an [REDACTED].
>
> The defense requests this evaluation since their client has rejected the commissions system and "it is unknown whether this rejection is a by-product of a mental disease or defect or whether it is a calculated decision to not cooperate to show solidarity with other detainees and protest his confinement and treatment."

Defense's procurement of clinical evidence: (1) The lack of a follow-up examination after a first mental health evaluation implies that Kamin still has a mental disorder. (2) Kamin's refusal to participate in the military commission system. Defense's application of clinical reasoning: His refusal may result from a mental disorder, warranting an independent mental health evaluation.

September 4, 2008 (*United States of America v. Mohammed Kamin* 2008b)—The prosecution disputes the defense's motion for independent experts:

The Defense's request for a forensic psychologist is premature. Any concern regarding whether the Accused is competent to make a knowing and voluntary waiver of his right to counsel, is competent to stand trial, and/or determine whether he suffers from a severe mental disease or defect or from diminished capacity should be governed by the procedures under RMC 706 and 909.

The prosecution's application of clinical reasoning: Kamin's behavior may result from a mental disorder that can be evaluated by a 706 board.
September 10, 2008 (*United States of America v. Mohammed Kamin* 2008c)—Military judge Colonel W. Thomas Cumbie orders a RMC 706 evaluation. *Hermeneutical adjudication: The judge agrees that Kamin's behavior warrants a 706 mental health evaluation.*

October 3, 2008 (*United States of America v. Mohammed Kamin* 2008d, 2008e)—The RMC 706 reports that "the detainee refused interviews" and that "no information was obtained directly from him." The 706 board finds no evidence to support a mental disease or defect at the time of the alleged offense or presently to explain his conduct. *706 board's interpretation: Based on an indirect examination, Kamin does not suffer from a mental disorder.*[8]

December 5, 2008 (*United States of America v. Mohammed Kamin* 2008f)—The defense motions to compel an order for Kamin's medical records from Guantánamo after learning that these were used by the 706 board:

The government has likewise failed to fulfill its continuing duty to disclose medical records from JTF-GTMO, despite the fact that the production of the updated records requires very little effort by the government. Evidence of the availability of these records is that on 1 October 2008 the officers appointed to conduct the 706 Inquiry confirmed that they were provided the opportunity to review the updated records and were provided copies. The failure of the government to uphold its duty to disclose has heightened significance in the context of the issues that have been and are currently being litigated in the present case, namely the fact that Mr. Kamin has not been present at a hearing since the arraignment in May 2008, refuses the services of detailed defense counsel, and that a R.M.C. 706 inquiry was ordered and completed. The progression of the case thus far requires the defense to complete a full assessment as to whether Mr. Kamin is competent to stand trial, to make a knowing and voluntary waiver of his right to counsel, and/or to determine whether he suffers from a diminished capacity.

The defense's application of clinical reasoning: The 706 board has access to mental health records that the defense team does not have and that may be relevant to the case.

January 14, 2009 (*United States of America v. Mohammed Kamin* 2009a)—Military judge Colonel W. Thomas Cumbie allows the defense to obtain an independent mental health expert, but not one of their choice:

> Given that Mr Kamin has refused [to] attend the commission or to cooperate with his defense counsel and with the R.M.C. 706 board, the court finds little likelihood that Mr. Kamin will cooperate with a defense psychological consultant. However, there is the outside possibility that with the assistance of an expert consultant, the defense may be able to design a plan to encourage Mr. Kamin to cooperate with his defense and with a 706 board. Bottom line, the commission desires to do everything within its power to ensure [that] the accused's mental health issues, if any, are addressed fully and completely in this proceeding. The commission finds that, under the unique facts of this case, the defense is entitled to an expert consultant in the field of clinical and forensic psychology. However, the commission does not believe that the defense has made an adequate showing that Dr. [REDACTED] and only Dr. [REDACTED] will be adequate for the defense needs.

Hermeneutical adjudication: An evaluation by the 706 board suffices over one from an independent defense consultant.

April 7, 2009 (*United States of America v. Mohammed Kamin* 2009b)—The defense motions to inspect the Bagram detention facility and its records:

> This information will significantly contribute to the defense assessment of whether Mr. Kamin is competent to stand trial and/or waive his right to counsel. . . . To allow for specificity in any motion to suppress or objection to the admissibility of statements made by Mr. Kamin as being obtained by torture or the product of coercion.

Defense's application of clinical reasoning: Kamin's statements may have been made under conditions of torture and the defense team wants to examine these conditions.

April 13, 2009 (*United States of America v. Mohammed Kamin* 2009c)— The government motions that the court reject the defense motion:

> The Government objects to the Defense's request to inspect all documents and records pertaining to Mr. Kamin before they have been reviewed by national security agencies to determine, in accordance with RMC 701C(f) and MCRE 50S, if there is any protected and/or privileged information where disclosure would be harmful to national security. Once the information is deemed properly discoverable and receives the equity review, the Government will permit the Defense to inspect the records.

The prosecution's application of clinical reasoning: National security must be maintained throughout Kamin's case.

July 7, 2009 (*United States of America v. Mohammed Kamin* 2009d)— The defense motions for a second 706 hearing because of inadequacies with the first:

> Admittedly JTF-GTMO rules limited the Board's direct access to Mr. Kamin, but the Board neglected to access videotapes of Mr. Kamin [REDACTED] of his interrogations. . . . No guards, interpreters, or other detainees were interviewed. Id. In sum, the limited access provided to and sought out by the Board made a clinical psychiatric diagnosis of Mr. Kamin and the Board's findings in Part 1 of the R M.C. 706 Report dated 3 October 2008 unsupportable.

The defense's application of clinical reasoning: The first 706 board did not use sufficient evidence to make its determination.

August 18, 2009 (*United States of America v. Mohammed Kamin* 2009e)— The prosecution agrees to the defense's request with the caveat that Kamin be "forcibly extracted from his cell" if he refuses to participate:

> The government proposes the Commission order a forcible cell extraction, if necessary, to facilitate Mr. Kamin meeting with the Sanity Board, but the Government opposes any additional forcible cell extractions for the

purpose of a meeting with defense counselor, by extension, the defense mental health expert consultant, Dr. [REDACTED].

The prosecution's application of clinical reasoning: Kamin should be "forcibly extracted" from his cell to participate in the new 706 hearing.
August 24, 2009 (*United States of America v. Mohammed Kamin* 2009f)—Military judge Colonel W. Thomas Cumbie orders a second RMC 706 evaluation with forcible extraction if necessary. *Hermeneutical adjudication: A second 706 evaluation is necessary with Kamin's participation, even if forced.*

.   .   .

These cases exemplify the interpretive contests between defense and prosecution teams around a detainee's symptoms. With al-Nashiri and Kamin, defense teams have asserted that refusals to participate with the military commissions may signify underlying mental disease or defect. Prosecution teams have responded differently, with those in al-Nashiri's case disputing that his refusal to appear before the commission suggests the presence of mental disease or defect and those in Kamin's case agreeing to a 706 evaluation. With Al Darbi, al Qosi, Jawad, and Kamin, defense teams have challenged the admissibility of detainee statements made under conditions of torture. Prosecutors have motioned for a 706 evaluation for Al Darbi rejected by the defense and even granted the possibility of Jawad's torture. In all cases, military judges have favored use of 706 boards to conduct evaluations.

From the perspectives of cultural psychiatry and medical anthropology, the cases exhibit striking similarities. Attorneys for al-Nashiri and Al Darbi specifically invoked the words "PTSD," "trauma," and "retraumatization" to explain the actions of their defendants. The concept of trauma demonstrates a specific cultural history in which patient advocates, families, physicians, and government officials lobbied for diagnostic recognition of the types of psychological stress experienced by Vietnam veterans upon returning from war (Young 1995). Trauma becomes especially salient in these cases for two reasons. First, in an unanticipated consequence of cultural irony, attorneys for "unlawful enemy combatants" have attempted to use a trauma defense in American military commissions when the very idea of trauma coalesced in the wards of American Veterans Affairs hospitals. Second, attorneys for al-Nashiri have stated that it is a matter of "common sense" that trauma results from torture; in other words, the stigmata of trauma reveal themselves without the need for a diagnosis. On the contrary, scientists have found mixed evidence for (Steel et al. 2009) and against (Başoğlu, Livanou, and Crnobarić 2007) the relationship of physical torture leading to post–traumatic stress disorder. Therefore, the "common sense" that trauma results from torture reflects a distinct cultural interpretation of detainee symptoms among defense attorneys.

In addition, torture is debated between prosecution and defense teams. The motions of all five men exhibit varying types of interrogator behaviors throughout apprehension and detention. One theme that joins these narratives is the role of Guantánamo. Good and Good (1980) recall that the cultural hermeneutical model situates symptoms within "the sufferer's reality" inseparable to the "stresses and experiences that constitute the personal meaning of the illness" within the "illness network." For these five detainees, Guantánamo acts as site for the sufferer's reality that causes significant stress. Medical anthropologist Jamie Saris has contended that physical institutions "outline the relationship between system and innovation, power and agency, and structure and contingency in the construction of stories" (1995, 42–43). Saris writes: "We cannot understand the narrative flow of this story—not its structure, not its humor, not its pathos—without understanding the institutional channels that at once restrict the freedom of, and give shape to, indeed make possible, the creation of *this particular story*" (55). Similarly, we cannot understand the narrative flow of possible traumas and conditions of confinement without understanding Guantánamo's role in the creation of detainee stories. It is for this reason that al-Nashiri's voice in the transcript—absent in defense and prosecution motions—resonates with agency amid overwhelming institutional power: "I do intend to attend all future sessions, but if the guards do not treat me better, I have the right not to come and let the world know that the judge sentenced me to death because I didn't show up to court due to chains" (Office of Military Commissions 2012b). Agency against power is an underlying factor in Kamin's refusal to attend the commissions, leading to "forcible extraction." Guantánamo becomes the context for the text of detainee symptoms, and these behaviors are interpreted as "mad" rather than resistant. Al-Nashiri's proclamation suggests that even exhaustive reviews of legal motions can miss the lived experiences of innovation and agency among court defendants.

Another theme that links all five men is the role of mental health evaluations in torture and trauma. A body of mental health knowledge—the language of diagnosis and trauma, the practice of clinical assessment—is mobilized to ascertain not the detainee's well-being but his claims. The use of mental health to impose a situational truth at Guantánamo from the messy domains of violence, memory, and language resembles the asylum process for refugees. The clinical psychiatric and psychological examination have gradually operated less as an instrument to provide treatment and more as "the key to the door of asylum" in evaluating truth accounts (Fassin and Rechtman 2009, 243). Increasingly, legal systems require mental health professionals to investigate cases of trauma and torture without the physical evidence of scars, a need that the field of trauma studies now fills with its focus on narrative (Fassin and Rechtman 2009). We observe similar dynamics at Guantánamo as each side calls mental health professionals to probe detainee accounts of torture and trauma. Given the high stakes involved for defendants, forensic psychiatrists have thoughtfully prioritized truth telling and objectivity in their professional ethics (American Academy of Psychiatry and the Law 2005). However, the ontological status of truth becomes subject to dispute as detainees must recall traumas that occurred years ago, believe that mental health professionals will act in their interests, and choose to narrate these traumas in a language that they speak with questionable fluency. Mental health professionals also must perform in exigent circumstances, whether as members of 706 boards balancing competing interests or as civilian personnel striving to develop trust with detainees.

Finally, these cases reflect a cultural commitment among prosecution teams and military judges to minimize mentions of torture. Prosecutors in al Qosi's trial refused to label his treatment as torture. The military judge in Jawad's trial declared Jawad's treatment to be "abusive" rather than torture. In each case, the government resists conceding that guards and interrogators could have tortured detainees. If culture permeates all legal systems in determining how facts are created and decisions are reached (Rosen 2006), then the Guantánamo military commissions promote a culture against classifying guard and interrogator actions as torture. These cases indicate that at least these five men suffered injuries during interrogations rather than through idyllic sporting with guards despite cheerful endorsements from former government officials.

4

Depictions of Arabs and Muslims in Psychodynamic Scholarship

HOW CAN WE UNDERSTAND THE "Muslim mind," a hot topic of academic conferences and proceedings? Motivations, impulses, wishes, dreams, and psychological defenses supply the raw materials to understand the *psyche* (a Greek word meaning "soul, mind, spirit") in psychodynamic and psychoanalytic thought. *Studies on Hysteria*, written by Josef Breuer (1842–1925) and Sigmund Freud (1856–1939) and published in 1895, is generally regarded as the first psychoanalytic text, after which Freud published copiously between 1895 and 1905 to elaborate on his creative theories (Person, Cooper, and Gabbard 1995). While it would be impossible to summarize more than a century of thought that has given birth to different theoretical orientations, psychoanalyst Glen Gabbard (2005) writes that all psychodynamic schools affirm key foundational principles: mental phenomena are manifestations of irrational conflicts; faulty development in childhood leads to adult pathology, and people internalize views about themselves and others that influence how they think, feel, and act. Psychodynamic practice draws deeply from the well of psychoanalytic thought, whereas psychoanalysis is additionally concerned with issues of technique; henceforth, I will refer to their theories as "psychodynamic" throughout the chapter.[1]

Many psychiatrists believe that psychodynamic psychiatry addresses the "mind," whereas biological psychiatry addresses the "brain."[2] Psychodynamic concepts pervade American culture: the reserved therapist sitting across from the eager patient, the interminable anxieties in Woody Allen films, the gritty gangster Tony Soprano's panic attacks during family conflicts, the phallic cigar jokes, the overbearing mother, the Freudian slip—these all come from psychodynamic theories. The images clash with biological psychiatry, whose research paradigms seek to uncover the genetics of mental illness, the faulty neural circuits that produce disorders, and the cellular receptors that stimulate drug discovery. This professional split—a tolerant pluralism or a mutually suspicious armistice, depending on academic department—has long characterized psychiatry. Over the past fifty years, the status of psychodynamic psychiatry as a science has come under attack as other psychotherapies have proven more effective in experimental trials and psychodynamic experiments bothered little with controlled conditions (Davies 2009). The success of medications in treating mental illnesses has also led to diagnoses based upon symptoms, instead of psychodynamic doctrines, with pharmacological treatments readily funded by insurance companies given that such an approach requires less time and less expense (Luhrmann 2000).

Over time, we have learned of the social, historical, and cultural origins of psychodynamic thought and the inextricable links between personal biography and professional theory. A long-standing debate has coalesced around the extent to which Sigmund Freud mined nineteenth-century Viennese Jewish intellectual culture for psychodynamic concepts. It has been argued that Freud's goals for psychoanalysis mirrored contemporary Jewish ethics: service to others, self-knowledge, acceptance of difference, and recognition of humanity's creative and destructive potentials (Frosh 2008). Disputes have gathered around whether Freud's strategy of encouraging patients to speak freely without inhibitions mimicked rabbinical strategies of Talmudic textual analysis (Bergmann 1995). Some contend that Freud's technique of mining the mind to the unconscious for the true nature of the self draws from the archaeological model of mining Jerusalem for the first and second Jewish temples (Enckell 1988). Quarrels over whether psychoanalysis is a Jewish science (Ostow 1982; Yerushalmi 1991) or a science from a man with Jewish origins (Brunner 1991; Gay 1987) continue to preoccupy scholars.

As a cultural psychiatrist, I am interested in the application of psychodynamic theories across cultures. Questioning the degree to which psychoanalysis mobilizes European themes, whether Jewish (dream interpretation) or Greek (the Oedipal complex), is not intended to denigrate it. The objective is to trace the history of ideas to catalog the development of human thought. Postmodern theories in the social sciences and humanities propose that all knowledge is local and constructed (Latour and Woolgar 1986) and the dissemination of knowledge requires its application beyond the local conditions of its production (Appadurai 1996). Critics have countered that psychodynamic theories rely upon a Euro-American cultural model of individualism that may not be shared elsewhere (Kirmayer 2007b). Therefore, this question arises: How does psychodynamic theory disseminate for use with those outside of the United States or Europe, the traditional centers of psychodynamic theory and practice?

This chapter analyzes psychodynamic writings on Arabs and Muslims since the War on Terror. In a review of the medical literature from 1966 to 2005, Laird, Marrais, and Barnes (2007) have shown that certain biases persist about Muslims: being an observant Muslim poses health risks; Muslims remain confined to tradition rather than accepting of modernity; and Islam creates "problems" for service delivery. I have also performed a review elsewhere on a random sample of psychodynamic texts with similar findings (Aggarwal 2011), though not in a coordinated, systematic fashion that I seek to promote through medical discourse analysis. The depictions of Arabs and Muslims in the psychodynamic literature may help us understand the second forensic function of medical systems: *the establishment of medical and legal standards that support and evaluate a medicolegal issue.* I have suggested that medical professionals may use certain clinical conditions, disorders, or technologies as grounds to provide a professional opinion. In this chapter, we can empirically test how mental health authors portray Arabs and Muslims through "knowledge" in scientific articles. In this sense, patient-clinician differences in interpretation may emerge around identity as mental health professionals create cultural meanings on how one's background relates to political violence.

ORIENTALISM, MEDICINE, AND THE RELATIONSHIP BETWEEN POWER AND KNOWLEDGE

My analysis of psychodynamic texts relies upon two opposing trends in mental health. A prominent research agenda in cultural psychiatry has been the extent to which psychiatric knowledge and practice must be adapted to the realities of ethnic and racial groups outside of North America and Europe in order to provide culturally sensitive care (Kirmayer 2007a). I understand this to be the healing function of cultural psychiatry.

In contrast, psychiatrists in the nineteenth and twentieth centuries buttressed the interests of European imperialists by erecting classifications of race based on biological differences (Littlewood 1996). I understand this to be the forensic function of cultural psychiatry. To delve into this second trend, I apply Edward Said's concept of "Orientalism" to promote dialogue among scholars of mental health and cultural studies. Said sought to reveal how previous generations of American and European scholars produced knowledge about the Middle East for overtly political purposes (Said 1994).[3] Said only briefly mentions the role of Orientalism in the production of medical knowledge,[4] and this chapter introduces a method to extend this investigation to unveil medical Orientalism.

Said highlights the construction of the European "Occident" against the Asian "Orient":

> I shall be calling *Orientalism*, a way of coming to terms with the Orient that is based on the Orient's special place in European Western experience. The Orient is not only adjacent to Europe; it is also the place of Europe's greatest and riches and oldest colonies, the source of its civilizations and languages, its cultural contestant, and one of its deepest and most recurring images of the Other. In addition, the Orient has helped to define Europe (or the West) as its contrasting image, idea, personality, experience.
>
> (Said 1994, 1–2)

The British-French-American presence in the Middle East from the late eighteenth century onward produced volumes of scholarship that reinforced select images of the Middle East, Islam, and Arabs. Orientalism rests in the power disparity between the Occident and the Orient:

> My contention is that without examining Orientalism as a discourse one cannot possibly understand the enormously systematic discipline by which European culture was able to manage—and even produce—the Orient politically, sociologically, militarily, ideologically, scientifically, and imaginatively during the post-Enlightenment period. Moreover, so authoritative a position did Orientalism have that I believe no one writing, thinking, or acting on the Orient could do so without taking account of the limitations on thought and action imposed by Orientalism.
>
> (Said 1994, 3)

The Occident produces the Orient through science and ideology. The weight of history and politics determines collective trends that bind individual writers. Orientalism is the Occident's attempt to comprehend and control the Oriental Other:

> It [Orientalism] is rather a *distribution* of geopolitical awareness into aesthetic, scholarly, economic, sociological, historical, and philological texts; it is an *elaboration* not only of a basic geographic distinction (the world is made up of two unequal halves, Orient and Occident) but also of a whole series of "interests" which, by such means as scholarly discovery, philological reconstruction, psychological analysis, landscape and sociological description, it not only creates but also maintains; it *is*, rather than expresses, a certain *will* or *intention* to understand, in some cases to control, manipulate, even to incorporate, what is a manifestly different (or alternative and novel) world; it is, above all, a discourse that is by no means in direct, corresponding relationship with political power in the raw, but rather is produced and exists in an uneven exchange with various kinds of power, shaped to a degree by the exchange with power political (as with a colonial or imperial establishment), power intellectual (as with reigning sciences like comparative linguistics or anatomy, or any of the modern policy sciences), power cultural (as with orthodoxies and canons of taste, texts, values), power moral (as with ideas about what "we" do and what "they" cannot do or understand as "we" do.
>
> (Said 1994, 12)[5]

Said cautions us from assuming that science on the Orient exists without geopolitical shadows. Recently, Orientalism has provoked critical inquiries into the relationship of power and knowledge within the medical humanities. As practice, medicine is Orientalist when clinicians and researchers fashion disease categories and interpret experiences without patient input (Aull and Lewis 2004). Here, Orientalism conjures the gulf in power among patients and clinicians rather than forms of knowledge based on racial or ethnic difference. As content, Orientalism spread with nineteenth-century British physicians in India writing voluminously on the relationship of pathology to race, teaching this information to medical students as science (Harrison 2009). This chapter analyzes psychodynamic texts to inquire whether we can observe *medical Orientalism* since the War on Terror. By doubting rather than accepting the claims of mental health authors, we can question how Western (that is, Occidental) academics treat violence as an essentially Oriental practice.

PSYCHODYNAMIC KNOWLEDGE ON ARABS AND MUSLIMS

This sample of psychodynamic texts comes from a search for all years since 2001 for the terms "Islam," "Muslim," and "Arab" in Psychoanalytic Electronic Publishing (PEP) Web.[6] PEP Web is the largest psychoanalytic database in English, with more than 1,500 volumes and 65,000 articles from 1871 to 2006. I have included all English-language articles published in peer-reviewed journals, since original articles, whether theoretical articles or case studies, constitute original scholarship in psychodynamic and psychoanalytic mental health. I have excluded books, book reviews, editorials, commentaries, and other formats not typically peer-reviewed, the process by which journals guarantee scientific standards. Two criteria guided this search: (1) articles had to explicitly address violence or the War on Terror and (2) articles had to treat the representation of difference, by which I drew upon Norman Fairclough's definition of "constituting particular ways of being, particular social or personal identities" (2003, 26). I reviewed all relevant titles and abstracts of articles for eligibility. I also reviewed articles that did not have abstracts and those whose abstracts did not seem to clearly address violence or the War on Terror. I retrieved all articles that passed this stage and read them for representations of Arabs, Muslims, and Islam.

My goal here is not to vilify psychodynamic theories. As a psychiatrist, I utilize psychodynamic theories regularly with patients. Rather, I ask who wields psychodynamic theories, for what purposes, and with what conclusions *in a political manner.* In practicing psychotherapy, we offer interpretations to patients based on our knowledge of their conscious and unconscious processes, and patients can elect to accept or reject these interpretations (Samberg and Marcus 2005). The act of interpretation in the social sciences is also intersubjective, as the observer and the observed analyze meanings together (Rabinow and Sullivan 1987). My concern is that many psychodynamic authors offer cultural interpretations that the interpreted, Arabs and Muslims, cannot accept or reject. I group the text excerpts by theme, having iteratively compared each article to the others in examining themes that emerge from the texts rather than imposing a coding framework a priori (Glaser 1965). As with all other analyses of discourse in this book, I am less interested in what individual authors write and more interested in themes that are common among authors.

Cultural Differences Between the Geographically Unspecified "West" and "East"

Many psychodynamic authors attribute religious terrorism to a fundamentalist "East" in contrast to a secular "West." Jessica Benjamin traces violence to the lack of an Enlightenment period in the "Muslim world": "It would be naïve to dispute the dominance that fundamentalism is now enjoying in the Arab world or . . . that the Muslim world never went through the lengthy process of Reformation and religious wars that, in Europe, culminated in the Enlightenment" (2002, 476). Maria Miliora also paints the "Muslim world" as devoid of modernity: "In the face of the tremendous disparity between the modernity of the West and the state of the Muslim world, it appears that the latter has been standing still during the past 200 years while the West has vastly surpassed it, at least from a secular perspective" (2004, 122). Leon Wurmser compares the "Islamic world" with a secular West: "They [the attacks] have opened a deep rift of understanding, separating the United States not only from much of the Islamic world, but from much of Europe as well: large segments of the population believe that the CIA or the Mossad engineered the attacks" (2004, 911). Marco Bacciagaluppi regards violence as endemic to "Muslim societies":

> We may still have a long way to go in the West, but we no longer subject women to the horrid punishments and the abject condition which are found in Muslim societies. It is possible that, together with other contributing factors, the present violence of the Muslims against the West is basically the reaction of the new despotic hierarchy against the liberation of women and against the reestablishment of our innate striving for a cooperative society.
>
> (2004, 477)

Authors who strive to move beyond condemnation to comprehend terrorist motives still assume the inherent religiosity of "the East." Emmanuel Cassimatis believes that the "Muslim world" has reacted definitively to

American foreign policy and cultural authority: "We have allied ourselves with Israel, invaded the Muslim Holy Lands, stationed troops there and, I paraphrase, are on the way to poisoning the Muslim world and way-of-life with our materialism, decadent ways, fast food restaurants, pornographic magazines, and vile music and videos, as we have done in so many other countries and other lands" (2002, 535).

Elisha Davar persuades us to avoid stereotyping Islam, but slips into the East-West dichotomy: "It [Islam] has been misrepresented by a particular ideological group from within its own culture, which also polarises attitudes in the West. We should not add further misrepresentation through reacting with hysteria" (2002, 243). In writing on a roundtable directed at psychoanalytical responses to terrorism, George Hough reports that some participants invested "Muslim" leaders with the responsibility to counter "radical Islamic violence": "Bin Laden significantly distorts verses from the Koran, using them to justify terrorist violence as a sacred obligation. Moderate Muslim political and religious leaders can counter these distortions where Americans and other Westerners cannot. Moderate Muslims, he said, must reclaim their hijacked religion" (2004, 820).

Ironically, in a passage immediately following a quote from Said's *Orientalism*, Jo Nash reproduces the dichotomies of the "Western" and "the Arab": "This kind of representation of the Arab is deeply ingrained in the Western psyche. The reporting of the Arabs' furious 'attacks,' rather than responses to IDF hostilities, enables the West to acquiesce in the muffled confusion characteristic of those in receipt of contradictory sources of information" (2004, 535).

Stuart Twemlow holds that terrorism is the reaction of "Muslim countries" to past traumas, drawing on the work of Vamik Volkan and "chosen traumas":

> Large-group functioning is based on a complex synthesis of personal identity and the gradual adoption of family, region, clan, profession, country and national identities, where a variety of issues can define that identity, like socio-economic status (USA) and religion (Muslim countries). Large-group identity emerges partly through "chosen" traumas and glories that are ritualized and even used politically to manipulate the populace.
>
> (2005, 959)

Seth Moglen blames the Bush administration for a self-destructive foreign policy pitting the United States against the "Arab world":

> More than 2000 US soldiers have already died and many thousands more have been maimed, physically and psychologically; more than 100000 Iraqis may now have died; and as the United States military kills (and tortures) more people in the Arab world, it produce [*sic*] more homicidal—and terrorist—rage against America itself. However self-destructive it may be, the catastrophic displacement of American aggression serves deep psychological needs for a population seeking to evade the ambivalent recognition of its partial responsibility for the terrorist violence to which it is now subject.
>
> (2006, 122)

M. Fakhry Davids exposes the racist underpinnings of certain segments in "Western" society, but reproduces the division: "Pervasive, primitive anxiety in the West, triggered by the bombings on that day [9/11], was managed by the deployment of a paranoid organisation in which the world of Islam is viewed as the enemy—the source of the threat to the West. The unfolding chain of attacks on Islam and Muslims speaks to the extraordinary power of this construction as an organised strategy of defence" (2006, 63).

Elsewhere, Davids presents case formulations of two Muslim patients settled in the West, accentuating the East-West split:

> In their adolescence, both Husain and Ahmed took ownership of this problem [racism] by explicitly taking on a particular, magnified version of their unconsciously denigrated Muslim identities. At this stage, a deep split was in operation and aspects of the self associated with being Western were projected into the Westerner/unbeliever, allowing the process of engagement between the two to begin.
>
> (2009, 187)

Ahmed Fayek describes the "impasse" between "Islam" and the "Western world": "The political situation between Islam and the Western world is at an impasse, and we could use what we learned from the practice of analysis in analyzing that impasse" (2007, 282).

Neil Altman searches for a way to foster reconciliation between the United States and the "Muslim world" in asking: "What are some of the implications for how we might understand the current discourse about Arab-Israeli conflict and the wider relationship between the USA and the Muslim world?" (2008, 63).

Arab and Muslim authors have appropriated these geographical categories. Yasser Ad-Dab'bagh reflects on the formation of his identity within the "Arab world": "Growing up in the Arab World meant that one would be constantly bombarded with these scenes. It also meant that one would witness the impact of the defeat of Arabs in their wars with Israel. No one felt Arabs were capable of anything of significance" (2009, 199).

Adib Jarrar muses on Palestinian suffering and calls on the psychoanalytic community to act, offering reasons for the failure of a political solution:

Another obstacle preventing the Palestinians from working through the conflict is that hostility continues to be directed at them by different Israeli governments as well as by many Israeli political and ideological groups. The Israelis are supported in their stance by (i) the American administrations, (ii) the lack of tangible impact of the international community and, (iii) the passivity and collusion of the Arab world. In spite of strong public sentiment for solidarity and identification with Palestinians, most Arab governments have been using and abusing the Palestinian issue for their own interest.

(2010, 200)

Galit Atlas contemplates "the perception of sexuality in the Arab and Persian worlds" (2012, 221) and relates this anecdote:

One of the things I am most aware of is the effects of emigration from East to West on women's perception of sexuality. This shift is traumatic, and I am a witness to it in analysis within the minds of first- and second-generation immigrants. It is a shift from certain sexual norms to other ones that are almost entirely different. This entails coping with a different conception of what is allowed and what is forbidden, of what is considered inferior and shameful and what is considered superior; and it includes a different conception of the body, of courting patterns, and of nonverbal communication.

(2012, 222)

Arabs and Muslims in "Western" Societies

Whereas some authors cleanly disentangle "the East" from "the West," others warn of Muslim population growth in "Western" societies. Robert Young disabuses us of thinking that we have the ability to counter "Muslim fundamentalist" thought in the United States:

> I think we have to ask why so many are willing to volunteer to be suicide bombers or to go to certain death as hijackers, having, as apparently some did, waited as sleepers in America for some years to be called to action. In addition to the 19 on the planes, there were another 25 or so abetting them, and the mind boggles to think who is waiting for their chance to serve in this or related ways. A warning for those who think they can "root out" Muslim fundamentalist terrorism: Wahhabi imams control over 80% of mosques in the US, where Islam is the fastest-growing religion.
>
> (2001, 40)

Mikhail Reshetnikov deems the integration of Muslims to be a significant problem for European integration:

> All too often integration is seen in terms of granting equal opportunities to those who accept our values while marginalizing those who do not, as we can see from the problem of racial integration in America or from the attitude to Muslim minorities in Europe. As long as Muslims are a minority we can continue to avoid this problem and to insist that they integrate our values but what will happen if they become a majority?
>
> (2008, 658)

In contrast, others have looked beyond religious identity to speculate on the causes of minority disenfranchisement in multicultural societies. Kambiz Ghaneabassiri situates Major Nidal Malik Hasan's shooting at Ford Hood against American foreign policy:

> Attempts to configure the place of Muslim selves in American body politic have focused primarily on the nature of Islam and its relation to American interests rather than on an analysis of the political policies that have shaped our times. A major consequence of this emphasis on religiocultural rather

than political analysis of our times has been the division of the world's Muslim population into "good" and "bad" Muslims depending on their stances on US policies.

(2010, 229)

The Pathological Nature of Arab and Muslim Families

Some authors view Arab and Muslim families as responsible for consistently transmitting pathology across generations. Nancy Kobrin paints the Muslim family as a cauldron of aggression, with Osama bin Laden's animosity toward America as a natural outgrowth:

> The firstborn male in Islam is the most important child for the mother. His birth automatically enhances her status within the community. The firstborn son receives the most of everything—love, attention, material goods, and so on. The only person who has more status than the son is his father, although the brother has the most power over honor killings. The firstborn son is the mother's only source of power albeit by vicarious proxy. Hamida, bin Laden's mom, could only identify her power, aggression, and rage through her son with regard to Muhammad bin Awda bin Laden, her husband, and his huge harem/family. Bin Laden exemplifies these psychodynamics and identifications. He projects his rage outward against "bad mother" Amrika as he fights against his derisive nickname, son of the slave (*ibn al abeda*), given to him by his fifty-one or so half-siblings, the other children of his father
>
> (2003, 213–214)

Helen Silverman and Jeffrey Parger understand suicide bombers as the result of unresolved Oedipus dynamics:[7]

> In many Arab families, the father is seen as an object of repressed hatred and becomes the source of violence, both in fantasy and in reality. A complicating socio-economic factor in Palestine is that the father is often seen as not being able to live up to his role as provider, and as a disappointing and humiliated object who brings shame upon the family. The son remains obedient to the father outwardly but secretly despises him, torn between feelings of rebellion and dependency. Since the younger men have to repress their anger out of fear, they ultimately direct their anger on to themselves.

Killing oneself is also killing the hated internalized object. If this act of hatred is also sanctioned by the community and can be projected on to another authority figure—the "other"—it is even more likely that the suicide can be executed without guilt feelings.

(2004, 1266)

Uday Khalid and Peter Olsson treat childhood as a pathological condition in "Muslim cultures": "It is in fact possible that there may be increased possibilities of narcissistic injuries for children in Muslim cultures. In Muslim cultures rigid rules are often obeyed without independent-minded questioning by children or adults. Marriage is experienced by most Muslims as a contract rather than an emotional attraction and subsequent attachment" (2006, 532).

Jeffrey Stern characterizes Arab leaders as hedonistic fathers unconcerned about educating their populace children, who then turn to terrorism:

Many Arab fathers used their fabulous wealth in the manner of Coleridge's Kubla Kahn [sic] to build themselves great pleasure domes with glittering fountains, legions of servants, and stables of race horses, as well as to purchase villas in Monaco, private jets, yachts and casinos. But, they built very few schools and among these few almost none that [sic] taught their children marketable skills, offering instead curricula based on the Quran and that institutionalized anti-semitism [sic]. Such fathers denied their wives and daughters basic rights of self determination [sic], did nothing to build their nations' economies and supported every sort of political corruption.

(2009, 192)

Authors who urge a more sensitive psychodynamic scholarship continue the inquiry into Muslim families. Nancy Hollander's call for a more "socially responsible psychoanalysis" ends with this agenda:

So, for example, alongside the emerging interest among American psychoanalysts in the mind of the terrorist or family violence in pre-modern Islam, we would do well to also focus on an exploration of the meaning and impact of our own group's unconscious perpetuation of hegemonic ideology and uninformed support of US policy in the Israeli/Palestinian catastrophe.

(2009, 176)

Islam or Islamist?

Certain texts seek greater explanations of the reasons for violence, beyond religious identities. James Jones clarifies that martyrdom mobilizes a new theological understanding of violence: "It must be noted that this understanding of martyrdom and self-sacrifice is not traditional in Islam, and it has been condemned by many leading Muslim clerics and scholars around the world . . . Rather, it represents a major theological innovation on the part of the radical Islamicists [*sic*] like bin Laden" (2006, 174).

J. S. Pivens emphasizes dissimilarities among Muslims and Islamists: "The fact that there are innumerable Muslim communities not comprised of terrorists demonstrates that we are dealing with a different mode of fanatic theology, not the ineluctable consequence of indoctrination into Muslim society" (2006, 239).

Diane Casoni and Louis Brunet also differentiate Islamists from Islam in discussing religion and political violence:

> Religion also offers criteria of a sometimes intolerable differentiation between individuals: the Middle Ages were the theatre of the Roman Catholic inquisition, a large-scale enterprise aiming at the conversion or elimination of adepts of all other religions, be they Cathares, Jews, Muslims, or Protestants. In a similar fashion, the actual Islamist jihad aims at the installation of a world ruled by Islam, some resorting to suicidal terrorist acts with that aim in view.
>
> (2007, 52)

Ira Brenner counsels that individuals cannot be reduced to demographic traits:

> Under the current conditions of ongoing trauma and violence, such regressed societies revert to black-and-white thinking, resulting in stereotyping the other and virulent xenophobic prejudice. In this situation, all Palestinians then become Muslims and all Muslims become suicide bomber terrorists whereas all Israelis become Jews and all Jews become the purveyors of evil who conspire to take over the world.
>
> (2009, 70)

Carlo Strenger also advises Israelis against demonizing the entire Arab world for the actions of a few:

> Israeli public discourse has not yet been able to integrate the history of the 1948 war and the mass expulsion of Palestinians into its identity narrative. Hence, it is very difficult for most Israelis, whether ordinary citizens or decision-makers, to differentiate between the wide variety of attitudes within the Arab world specifically, and the Islamic world at large towards Israel. When a group like Hamas or a country like Iran voices strongly anti-Semitic views and vows to destroy Israel, Israel's collective psyche is incapable of seeing that this does not imply that the whole of the Arab world or all of Islam shares these views.
>
> (2009, 192)

Finally, Joseph Massad unpacks the difficulties of defining the terms "Islam," "Muslim," and "Arab." As a rare voice in this literature, his passage merits full quotation:

> One of the difficulties in analyzing what Islam has come to mean and to refer to since the 19th century is the absence of agreement on what Islam actually is. Does Islam name a religion, a geographical site, a communal identity; is it a concept, a technical term, a sign, or a taxonomy? The lack of clarity on whether it could be all these things at the same time is compounded by the fact that Islam has acquired referents and significations it did not formerly possess. European Orientalists and Muslim and Arab thinkers begin to use "Islam" in numerous ways while seemingly convinced that it possesses an immediate intelligibility that requires no specification or definition. "Islam", for these thinkers, is not only the name the Qur'an attributes to the din (often (mis)translated as religion, though there is some disagreement about this) that entails a faith [iman] in God disseminated by the Prophet Muhammad, but can also refer to the history of Muslim states and empires, the different bodies of philosophical, theological, jurisprudential, medical, literary, and scientific works, as well as to culinary, sexual, social, economic, religious, ritualistic, scholarly, agricultural, and urban practices engaged in by Muslims from the 7th to the 19th century and beyond, and much, much more.
>
> (2009, 193)

A DISCOURSE ANALYSIS OF PSYCHODYNAMIC TEXTS
ON ARABS AND MUSLIMS

Psychodynamic texts on Arabs and Muslims display Said's division of *powers political, intellectual, cultural,* and *moral.* The first theme groups authors who have marked the "East" from the "West." No author qualifies these two halves of the world with exact frontiers or countries, and yet they assume that readers will verify these geographical entities as legitimate units of comparison. Does "Middle East" include countries such as Israel, Turkey, and Iran, whose ethnicities are traditionally seen as non-Arab? Does "Arab" also include Christians, Druze, Sephardic Jews, and other religious groups? Does "Muslim" refer to Sunni, Shia, Alawi, Khariji, and all other sects? In a variation on this theme, the "Muslim world" is juxtaposed against the "West," implying geographical impermeability or mutual exclusivity. It is unimaginable for "Muslim worlds" to exist in the "West," or vice versa, effectively denying the existence of immigrant and expatriate communities. Orientalism imposes a distribution of geopolitical awareness within scholarly texts that can then elaborate a series of interests such as psychological analysis.

Psychological analysis then proceeds to link violence and aggression to meanings constructed around cultural differences. Let us revisit the authors quoted earlier. For example, Benjamin (2002) links "fundamentalism" in the "Arab world" to the fact that the "Muslim world" never experienced a Reformation or religious wars that "culminated" in the Enlightenment. No clear definition of "fundamentalism" is offered—is she talking about doctrines or practices?—though she assumes that readers will apprehend her meaning. She uses the terms "Arab world" and "Muslim world" interchangeably, despite religious variability among Arabs (i.e. Christians, Jews, and Druze, among others) and ethnic variability among Muslims who can be found on virtually every continent. Reformation and religious wars "culminate" in the Enlightenment for Europe, underscoring the rhetoric of progress and modernity.

Miliora (2004) retains this concept of civilizational progress in noting the "tremendous disparity" between "the modernity of the West and the state of the Muslim world." The term "tremendous" summons a magnitude later specified as two hundred years. By representing the "Muslim world" as "standing still" and the "West" as having "surpassed" it, Miliora continues the same rhetoric as Benjamin (2002) used. No definition of "secular" or "secularism" is provided; does it refer to a population's religiosity or a state's recognition of an official denomination? Were it the latter, then how does a secular Europe reconcile that Christianity is recognized as a state religion in Andora, Argentina, Costa Rica, Denmark, England, Finland, Greece, Iceland, Liechtenstein, Malta, Monaco, Norway, Poland, Portugal, Spain, Vatican City? According to the cultural logic of psychodynamic texts, these countries could lie within the West. Bacciagaluppi (2004) distinguishes the West from Muslim societies that subject women to horrid punishments and abject conditions. The violence of Muslims comes, in part, from "the reaction of the new despotic hierarchy against the liberation of women." A sociological link is tenuously drawn from violence against women to "present violence of the Muslims against the West," through an apparent "new despotic hierarchy" (Bacciagaluppi 2004), but this phrase is not defined. The underlying assumption is that women in the West fare better from their liberation. These authors exert *power intellectual* through psychological analysis whose evidence comes not from clinical observation but from broad historical and sociological claims. Additionally, these authors wield *power cultural* in passing judgment on values and *power moral* in dismissing what *they* cannot do and understand.

Even sympathetic authors who wish to convey sensitivity and understanding in rationalizing terrorist motives utilize terms such as the "East," the "West," and the "Muslim world" without specificity. Cassimatis (2002) ominously presents a scenario of "poisoning the Muslim world and way-of-life with our materialism, decadent ways, fast food restaurants, pornographic magazines, and vile music and videos." As before, the "Muslim world" is not defined and the "way-of-life" of all Muslims is ostensibly the same everywhere. However, Cassimatis inverts moral judgments of previous authors by taking responsibility through the noun "we." Here, "we" refers not just to Cassimatis himself but also to his readers, who apparently share in the culpability of "poisoning" through a string of negative images such as "materialism, decadent ways, fast food restaurants, pornographic magazines, and vile music and videos." The placement of this sentence immediately after the phrase "invaded the Muslim Holy Lands" paints the "West" as impure and the "Muslim world" as chaste, with the "Muslim world" conceived of as a passive recipient rather than an active agent. Davar (2002) continues this terminological vagueness by referring to "Islam" as having its own culture. The diversity of Islamic societies with a multiplicity of cultures is reduced to a single personified entity. Davar also uses "we" to enlist those of us in the West to avoid "reacting with hysteria."

Moglen (2006) implicates "the United States military" for killing people in the Arab world, leading to homicidal rage against America, writing this sentence immediately after stating that more than a hundred thousand Iraqis may have died. This possibility (posed by the word "may") of such destruction in Iraq is then decisively extended to the entire Arab world that reacts with revenge. In contrast, Hough (2004) reports on psychodynamic authors who call on "moderate Muslim political and religious leaders" to "counter" "terrorist violence" through "distort[ed] verses from the Koran" and to "reclaim their hijacked religion." No definition of "moderate" is offered, but Hough seems to imply "non-violent." Leaders who are foremost "political and religious" must counter violence, not criminologists or law enforcement officials in these societies. Terrorist violence arises from a "hijacked religion," not from the criminal impulses of stray individuals. The term "hijacked" is not random, resonating with the imagery of hijacked 9/11 planes. Twemlow (2005) assumes that "identity" can be defined through "socio-economic status" in the United States and "religion" in "Muslim countries." The "Muslim countries" are not named, even though "large-group identity" forms from "chosen traumas and glories." These authors exercise *power political* to diagnose social problems, *power intellectual* to formulate psychological processes, *power cultural* with differentiations of values, and *power moral* in apportioning the responsibility of terrorism to either the "West" or the "East."

Ironically, authors who endeavor to transcend the East-West dichotomy find themselves writing in this manner. Nash (2004) quotes Said's *Orientalism* at length, but falls into the trap of comparing the "representation of the Arab" in the "Western psyche." The terms "Arab" and "Western" personify distinct entities that possess singular ways of being and thinking. Davids (2006) criticizes the "unfolding chain of attacks on Islam and Muslims" and "the extraordinary power of this construction" but precedes this phrase by stating that the "pervasive, primitive anxiety in the West" that was triggered on 9/11 has manufactured a view in which "the world of Islam is viewed as the enemy." Elsewhere, Davids (2009) dichotomizes "Muslim identities" from "being Western," just as Fayek (2007) regrets that "the political situation between Islam and the Western is at an impasse." Altman (2008) wishes to improve "the wider relationship between the USA and the Muslim world."

Even Arab and Muslim authors who ponder their formations of identity cannot escape this tendency. Ad-Dab'bagh (2009) writes of the "Arab world" and its "self-deprecating discourse." Jarrar (2010) blames the lack of success with Palestine on "the passivity and collusion of the Arab world," which is immediately qualified by "most Arab governments" given the "strong public sentiment for solidarity and identification with Palestinians." Atlas (2012) discovers sexuality in "the Arab and Persian worlds" from the "effects of migration from East to West." The persistence of East-West conceptualization—of geographical and therefore cultural difference—afflicts even those who wish to sponsor intercultural understanding.

The effort to cleanly demarcate the geographic "West" from the "Arab"/"Muslim"/"East" draws some authors to posit the consequences of the latter settling within the former. Young (2001) warns of the "Muslim fundamentalist" who lurks as a "sleeper" in America, introducing suspicion and mistrust. Those who wish to "root out" this terrorism must confront "Wahhabi imams who control over 80% of the mosques in the US." Young frames "Muslim fundamentalist terrorism" around the "Wahhabi" sect, not around the criminality of stray individuals. Wahhabi Islam is treated as a single unit with no granular examination of doctrines, practices, or internal disagreements. Moreover, Young assumes that imams transmit "fundamentalist" ideologies in mosques, public spaces of worship, rather than in private spaces such as homes. This logical move brands the entire community with blame. Xenophobia underscores the ominous warning that "Islam is the fastest growing religion" in the United States. Likewise, Reshentikov (2008) predicts grave consequences for Muslim migration to Europe, treated similarly to "the problem of racial integration in America." Reshetnikov uses collective terms like "we" and "our" to enlist us so that we can "avoid this problem and to insist that they integrate our values." Examples of successful Muslim migration and integration are unmentioned. Ghaneabassiri (2010) departs from this tendency by questioning whether focus "on the nature of Islam and its relation to American interests" occludes perspectives on "the political policies that have shaped our times." This "religiocultural" emphasis over "political analysis" cleaves the Muslim population into "good" and "bad." These texts exhibit *power political* by questioning the roles of Muslims in the "West," *power intellectual* wrought in psychological analysis, and *power moral* with certain authors denouncing the "Muslim" Other.

Having instituted the "Arab" and the "East" in opposition to the "West," some authors locate violence in the inherent pathologies of Muslim families. Kobrin (2003) collapses the differences of family life based on ethnicity and locality to claim that "the firstborn male in Islam is the most important child for the mother." Kobrin institutionalizes violence in the family by remarking that "the brother has the most power over honor killings." From this telescoping sociological analysis, she microscopically concentrates on the bin Laden family: "Hamida, bin Laden's mom, could only identify her power, aggression, and rage through her son." Bin Laden then "projects his rage outward against 'bad mother' Amrika," though Kobrin does not explain why "Amrika" has become bin Laden's mother, as opposed to Saudi Arabia, Pakistan, and other countries whose implementations of Islam he opposed. The term "Amrika" itself mocks pronunciations of "America" that are other than English. Silverman and Parger (2004) view the father "as an object of repressed hatred" and "the source of violence." The situation in Palestine exacerbates the father's "shame upon the family" because he cannot "live up to his role as provider." The political economy of Palestine remains unaddressed and the apparent loss of economic function stems from the family. In response, the son who is "obedient to the father but secretly despises him" balances "rebellion and dependency." The logical response is suicide bombing "without guilt feeling" because this is "sanctioned by the community." All of Palestine and "many Arab families" become complicit in the acts of a few. Similarly, Khalid and Olsson (2006) assert that "there may be increased possibilities of narcissistic injuries for children in Muslim cultures." No "independent-minded questioning by children or adults" in "Muslim cultures" evokes a lack of curiosity and critical thinking. Marriage becomes "a contract rather than an emotional attraction," implying a cold and calculated transaction. Stern (2009) generalizes the dynamics of "Arab" families to symbolize deficiencies of Arab leaders. Their debauchery manifests through "great pleasure domes," "legions of servants," "race horses," and "private jets, yachts, and casinos." These images of opulence and excess contrast with "very few schools" and very few "marketable skills." The little extant education rests on the Quran and "institutionalized anti-semitism [*sic*]." The implication is that education must serve capitalist ends for the market that the Quran cannot provide. "Anti-Semitism" ostensibly refers to discrimination against Jews, though Arabs have often identified as Semites. Even

Hollander's (2009) encouragement for a "socially responsible psychoanalysis" acknowledges the interest in "family violence in pre-modern Islam." Hollander does not identify what types of family violence elicit interest nor detail the components of practice and doctrine in "pre-modern Islam." These texts expose *power political* in explaining terrorism, *power intellectual* in using psychodynamic theories, and *power moral* in making explicit value judgments about family structure.

Against these texts come authors who seek to distinguish Muslims from Islamists. Jones (2006) asserts that "martyrdom and self-sacrifice is not traditional in Islam" but belongs to "radical Islamicists [*sic*]." Pivens (2006) discusses "Muslim communities" (in the plural) that marginalize "fanatic theology." Casoni and Brunet (2007) also distinguish Muslims from the "Islamist" who seeks "a world ruled by Islam." Brenner (2009) admonishes readers to avoid "black-and-white thinking" and "stereotyping" with the undesired consequences that "all Palestinians then become Muslims and all Muslims become suicide bomber terrorists." Strenger (2009) also calls Israelis to recognize "the wide variety of attitudes within the Arab world," though he treats the "Islamic world" singularly. Finally, Massad (2009) is the sole author to question "the difficulties in analyzing what Islam has come to mean and to refer to since the 19th century."

Psychodynamic texts constitute a veritable discourse on Arabs and Muslims.

The *sayable* in this discourse: Terrorism connects political violence to Arab, Muslim, and "Eastern" identity.

The *domain*: The audience is versed in psychodynamic vocabularies and concepts. It is possible, though unlikely, that many authors have written these texts without considering the possibility that Arabs, Muslims, and other minority populations may access their publications.

The *conservation*: Utterances treat "Arab" and "Muslim" as collective terms that signify commonalities rather than exploring differences. These terms effectively serve as "empty signifiers" that authors manipulate for political intentions without designating clear definitions (Aggarwal 2008).

The *memory*: The assumption is that terrorism and political violence belong to ethnic and religious identities rather than that they are behaviors demonstrating forms of criminology. This recalls the memory of European psychiatrists in the nineteenth and twentieth centuries erecting biological classifications based on perceived racial differences.

The *reactivation*: Previous discourses of progress and modernity differentiate the "West" from the more primitive and less evolved "East." Geopolitical interests find their way into mental health scholarship.

The *appropriation*: Psychodynamic tenets of aggression and the Oedipal complex root political violence within the family. The three preoccupations of tribalism, the treatment of women, and Islam that Abu-Lughod (1989) found in her review of the anthropological literature on the Middle East also pervade psychodynamic texts. Rather than a classification of races by biology that prevailed during the nineteenth and twentieth centuries, mental health professionals have fabricated a hierarchy based on psychology.

This psychodynamic discourse deviates from recent movements in cultural mental health. If cultural psychiatry is to remain vigilant about the bases and biases of mental health knowledge (Bibeau 1997; Kirmayer 2006, 2007a, 2007b; Kirmayer and Minas 2000), then we can subject psychodynamic texts to cultural critique. The above psychodynamic writers show little hesitation in diagnosing whole societies as uniform collections of "Arabs" or "Muslims."

In contrast, the methodology of psychoanalyzing societies has long been debunked in anthropology and cultural psychiatry. In the 1930s, researchers from the "culture and personality" school, such as Ruth Benedict and Margaret Mead, attempted to relate individual behavior and social structure to studies of national character (Kirmayer 2007a). Even then, Edward Sapir (1938) argued that culture consists of the actions and behaviors of individuals who possess the agency to act differently. By the late 1950s, the influence of the culture and personality school waned because studies could not progress beyond typecasting entire civilizations (Levine 2001). This methodology made faulty assumptions—it treated nation-states as culturally uniform despite the presence of ethnic, racial, and cultural minorities in most societies, and it held that a uniform culture could be gleaned through interviews without considering that different interviewees may construct different ideas of culture (Kirmayer 2006). Aside from inheriting the faulty premise that generalizes psychology to group-level identities, the psychodynamic texts reviewed here evidence no interviews with individuals; the "data" mined are the authors' personal speculations.

In response, social scientists have interrogated the cultural origins of psychodynamic concepts and contested their application to populations outside of Europe or North America. Biomedicine can be charged with the "colonization" of other cultures, since psychodynamic thought has not been rigorously validated elsewhere (Sadler 2005). Psychodynamic theories also enshrine moral assumptions about rationality and individual autonomy in the guise of advancing "health" and "adaptation" (Littlewood 1993, 1996). In fact, psychodynamic models depend on psychological and biological concepts without accounting for social and cultural factors relevant for populations outside of Europe and North America (Bhugra and Bhui 1999). In this manner, the use of theories such as the Oedipal complex to depict Arab and Muslim populations continues a form of cultural imperialism that enshrines moral assumptions about the roles of parents and children based on speculation instead of on case studies.

Nonetheless, psychological anthropologists have attempted to rescue aspects of psychodynamic thought as pertinent for cultural analysis. To dismiss psychodynamic theories because of their European provenance would be akin to dismissing economics, history, anthropology, and other disciplines instead of shifting the emphasis to testing and reformulating such theories in other societies (Obeyesekere 1990). Psychodynamic principles can be reconfigured productively to show how all people experience conflicts while pursuing goals *that are culturally determined* (Ewing 1992). The social configurations people belong to, such as family structure, *are also culturally determined* and produce conflicting intents and desires (Cohler 1992). Groups within social configurations must work through familial roles in ways that are "multiple, articulated, quasi-articulated, unarticulated, and inarticulable" (Crapanzano 1992, 302–303). In this way, a model that views the self as a process of becoming—rather than as a permanent being—whereby individuals provide ongoing meanings to themselves, can enhance cultural analysis (Molino 2004). Future psychodynamic authors could apply these insights in order to achieve greater analytical rigor.

Furthermore, over the past twenty years cultural psychiatrists have fundamentally rethought the concept of culture as a marker of identity and difference. Psychiatry in Europe and North America has suffered from a theoretical weakness in which people are reduced to demographics, like "Arab" or "Muslim," without acknowledging the immense diversity within these groups (Aggarwal 2010a, 2010c; Kleinman and Benson 2006). Psychiatrists have discarded outdated notions of culture as coherent, static systems of meaning in favor of a dynamic interaction through which people create meanings from multiple sources (Bibeau 1997). Since the 1990s, information technology and globalization have facilitated travel across geographic and Internet spaces, enabling people to construct new values, beliefs, and commitments throughout life from distant sources (Kirmayer and Minas 2000). From this perspective, the use of terms such as "Arab," "Muslim," "East," and "West" demands greater clarity, since these categories group diverse populations together.

In addition, we are not sure what being "Arab" or "Muslim" means for people with these backgrounds without interviewing them, especially since they may prioritize other ways of identification. For example, the theory of hybridity stresses that each of us possesses a range of identities (Bhabha 2006). Discursive psychology emphasizes that narratives of identity and lived experience are constructed in relation to the social world such as setting and audience (Kirmayer 2006). For me, my identities as husband, father, psychiatrist, Hindi speaker, or Punjabi speaker surface differently depending on my relationships with those around me. New work in cultural psychiatry traces how these hybrid identities shape an individual's responses to questions on the self, social relationships, health, and mental illness in relation to others (Aggarwal 2012b). To engage this work, however, requires psychodynamic authors to suspend medical Orientalist views of ethnicity, religion, and geography and create alternate meanings for explanations of political violence.

5

Depictions of Suicide Bombers in the Mental Health Scholarship

THE TRIAL OF THE FIVE suspects charged with the 9/11 attacks—Khalid Shaikh Mohammed, Walid bin Attash, Ramzi bin al-Shibh, Ali Abdul Aziz Ali, and Mustafa Ahmad al-Hawsawi—began in June 2008. The suspects challenged their legal proceedings from the outset. At arraignment, Mohammed boasted, "I'm looking to be [a] martyr for [a] long time" and demanded the death penalty for the entire group (Glaberson 2008a). Some analysts wondered whether his acceptance of the death penalty would free the Bush administration from a lengthy trial, but others worried that a perceived act of martyrdom could strengthen al-Qaeda (Bender and Stockman 2008). Mohammed even threatened to rescind his plea if he was not sentenced to death (Staunton 2008).

His proclamations shocked the court. U.S. Army judge Stephen Henley questioned the competence of all five men to stand trial (El Akkad 2008). Attorneys for bin al-Shibh and al-Hawsawi suspected that Mohammed pressured their clients to seek the death penalty, so they sought additional mental health evaluations to assess their clients' competencies to stand trial (Finn 2008a). Attorneys for bin al-Shibh also wanted an independent mental health evaluation to assess the presence of a mental disease or defect that precluded cooperation with his defense team, because he took a medication usually prescribed for schizophrenia, though the judge sided with the prosecution in presuming his competency (Finn 2008b). In November 2008, the five men entered joint confessions to avoid trial and receive the death penalty, again resurrecting questions about their mental competencies to stand trial (Glaberson 2008b).

This episode exposes the potential perils of evaluating normal and abnormal behaviors across cultures. In seeking the death penalty, the 9/11 suspects have rejected American medical and legal assumptions that self-death equates with suicide. In the seventeenth century, Puritan New Englanders outlawed suicide as a sin against God, a moral offense that has persisted since psychiatrists began treating suicide in the nineteenth century (Kushner 1991). Psychiatric textbooks still teach suicide as an action connected with sadness. For example, *The American Psychiatric Publishing Textbook of Clinical Psychiatry* opens its chapter on suicide with this disclaimer: "Every patient suicide is also a tragedy for the clinician and for the suicide survivors" (Simon 2008, 1637). Similarly, *Kaplan and Sadock's Comprehensive Textbook of Psychiatry* explains that current research explores the link between depression and suicide: "Contemporary biological theories about suicide are inextricably linked to studies of depression, because this is the mental condition most often underlying suicide" (Sudak 2005, 2446). The historical links between American Protestantism and psychiatry have produced a culturally distinct form of knowledge that treats the desire for self-death as suicide. By this logic, the 9/11 suspects seeking the death penalty must be suicidal and need mental health evaluations. However, the 9/11 suspects view the death penalty not as a suicidal expression connected to sadness, but as an act of political defiance.

The situation elicits even more confusion if we turn to experts on martyrdom and suicide bombing to interpret the 9/11 suspects. For example, terrorism expert Harvey W. Kushner has stated that suicide bombers are legitimated "by leaders of religious factions within the Islamic community" who have "a contorted view of what is spiritually permissible" (Goode 2001). In contrast, prominent Palestinian psychiatrist Iyad Sarraj has praised suicide bombers: "They are untouchable people—they are prophets, they are saints," adding, "This is what the culture believes" (Bennet 2005). How do these specialists in the mind, behavior, and criminality draw contradictory conclusions? If Judge Henley were to call both experts to evaluate the 9/11 suspects, would these witnesses make similar or different recommendations? What knowledge base would support their conclusions?

This chapter analyzes the construction of mental health knowledge on martyrdom, self-death, and suicide bombing. The Office of Military Commissions at Guantánamo has constructed the desire for self-death and martyrdom as a medicolegal issue that requires expert opinion from forensic psychiatrists. The knowledge base to understand the actions of the 9/11 suspects will be the mental health scholarship on suicide bombing and martyrdom. Depictions of suicide bombers in mental health scholarship may provide an understanding of the second forensic function of medical systems, *the establishment of medical and legal standards that support and evaluate a medicolegal issue.* Mental health professionals use standards to sift through evidence, reason through clinical data, and supply a professional opinion. In this chapter, I probe how mental health authors represent suicide bombers. I compare these representations with texts on suicide bombing and martyrdom produced by al-Qaeda, the group most targeted by the American government throughout the War on Terror. We can then detect cultural differences in interpreting self-death as suicide or martyrdom.[1]

MENTAL HEALTH, PATHOLOGY, AND SECURITY IN THE WAR ON TERROR

My analysis of mental health texts on suicide bombing rests upon recent theories in psychiatry and political sociology. Political scientist Alison Howell has examined "the securitization of medicine and the medicalization of security in contemporary global politics" (2010, 349). She claims that the historical achievement of psychiatry since the nineteenth century has rested on its status "as a tool of public safety by continually seeking out new criminals and other security threats. Thus, in order to exist as an institution of medical knowledge, psychiatry had to undertake two simultaneous codifications; first, it had to codify madness as illness; second, madness had to be codified as a danger" (2010, 351).

The War on Terror globalizes these trends; as the "psy disciplines,"[2] they are no longer positioned solely as "technologies for managing social danger confined with national spaces, but also increasingly operate as technologies of national and international security" (2010, 352). Howell applies this viewpoint to the government's labeling of Guantánamo detainees as "madmen":

> They [the "psy disciplines"] work to authoritatively make intelligible that which seems at first unintelligible: in this case, suicide attempts (and also, by extension "terrorism" and "terrorists"). In response to the reported suicide attempts, the psy disciplines were deployed in two central and distinct ways: first, by the military in order to cast the detainees as disturbed, manipulative,

fanatical, and uncooperative madmen, and, second by human rights organizations to cast the detainees as psychologically impaired victims due to the conditions of their detention. While these narratives seem at odds with each other, they both deploy the psy disciplines, and in doing so pathologize (and racialize) the detainees in questionable ways.

(Howell 2007, 34)

The five 9/11 suspects meet Howell's characterization, since the Guantánamo military commissions system has cast the detainees as "disturbed, manipulative, fanatical, and uncooperative madmen," necessitating expertise from mental health professionals. Pathologizing detainees leads to "the conditions of possibility for indefinite detention. When the detainees were deemed (incurably) pathological, they become targets for excision from the global body politic" (2007, 44). The process of pathologizing detainees "illustrates the way in which the process of medicalization can originate from disparate sources: the military, humanitarian organizations, and at times even the detainees themselves" (2007, 43). Critical scholarship can uncover how the government's constructions of suicide bombers as pathological end up justifying indefinite detention for the purposes of national security (2007). Despite her focus on the mental states of Guantánamo detainees, Howell does not mention that medicalization can also proceed directly from mental health professionals who also make academic claims by representing suicide bombers. This chapter analyzes mental health texts to inquire whether we can observe the medicalization and racialization[3] of suicide bombers in the War on Terror.

MENTAL HEALTH CONSTRUCTIONS ON SUICIDE BOMBING

This sample of texts comes from a search for all years since 2001 for the terms "suicide bombing," "suicide bomber," "homicide bombing," "homicide bomber," "suicide terrorism," and "suicide terrorist."[4] A service of the American Psychological Association, PsycInfo hosts more than 2.5 million international references from psychiatry, psychology, and other mental health disciplines. Several criteria guided this search: (1) articles had to explicitly address suicide bombers in the War on Terror as opposed to other conflicts (such as the civil war in Sri Lanka or the Israeli-Palestinian issue),[5] (2) articles had to represent difference, by which I drew upon Fairclough's definition of "constituting particular ways of being, particular social or personal identities" (2003, 26), and (3) articles had to be written by authors in departments of medicine, psychiatry, or psychology at the time of publication, since the search also produced articles from social scientists not in the "psy disciplines."[6] I have included all English-language articles in peer-reviewed journals. When authors appeared more than once, I analyzed their books, given that full-length monographs are considered the benchmark for scholarship in many fields of psychology. I excluded book reviews, dissertations, letters to the editor, and other formats not typically peer reviewed. I also excluded publications that appeared in the discussion in chapter 4. I reviewed all relevant titles and abstracts of articles for eligibility. I also reviewed articles that did not have abstracts and those whose abstracts did not seem to clearly address suicide bombing or the War on Terror. I retrieved all articles to analyze them for representations of suicide bombers. As before, I am less interested in the ideas of individual authors and more interested in how they reflect recurrent themes.

Suicide Bombing and Psychopathology

Certain mental health authors link suicide bombing to psychopathology. Emad Salib regards suicide bombing as a shared delusion: "*Folie à plusieurs* (madness of many) arises when many recipients are willing to share such beliefs. *Folie partagée* (shared madness) might provide some explanation of al-Qa'ida's bizarre and evil but meticulously calculated and executed suicide-homicide attacks on the USA in September 2001" (2003, 476).

Donatella Marazziti hypothesizes that suicide bombers suffer from multiple pathologies: "Suicide bombers might conceivably be affected by double personality disorder, or, more in general, by complex personality disorders shaped by specific contexts, and rendered common by peculiar historical and social events, or victimization from violence" (2007, 88).

Anne Speckhard and Khapta Akhmedova contend that suicide bombing reflects a reaction of society-wide trauma and dissociative responses:

Certainly in Palestine, Chechnya, Pakistan, the former Afghan training camps and elsewhere there has and continues to be [*sic*] top-down training and indoctrination into *Jihadist* ideologies, which promotes violence, self sacrifice, terrorism and martyrdom. However it is a mistake to assume that organizations and leadership alone drive this phenomenon. Societies in which there is widespread trauma, dissociative responses, daily humiliations and hardships generally produce a segment of society—often in the better educated and sensitive sector of young people who in other circumstances would have been leaders—who are in search for making meaning out of their situations, and who wish to fight back.

(2005, 134)

Elsewhere, Speckhard has linked trauma from political grievances to female suicide bombers:

There appear to be two primary groups of motivations for suicide terrorism—the first, which emanates out of societies that see themselves rightly or wrongly as under occupation or are in warfare/conflict zones (Chechens, Palestinians, Iraqis, etc.). In many ways they often have the mentality of insurgents. Their primary motivations are often nationalistic and their personal motivations are trauma and revenge driven. They often rely on dissociation as a defense and because of their frequent traumatic experiences in these conflict zones this defense has often been and is readily activated.

(2008, 1004)

Arie Kruglanski and colleagues conjecture that trauma incites a loss of meaning for the suicide bomber that must be avenged:

Personal traumas, and frustrations, represent a significance loss, motivating the quest for significance restoration. Often, however, it is beyond the power of the individual to restore her or his lost sense of personal significance. It is impossible to bring back to life the loved ones lost to enemy violence. Nor is it easy to undo the deeds that brought one ostracism from one's community or to convince members of an indigenous majority to accept a minority immigrant as equal. Where the direct restoration of one's lost sense of personal significance seems impossible, the individual may seek to do so indirectly through alternative means, including an identification with a collective loss (or one's group's relative deprivation) that affords a clear path to renewed significance via participation in militancy and terrorism.

(2009, 348)

Jeff Victoroff notes that the neurobiology of suicide bombers veers toward pleasure-seeking pathways:

> The biological framework perhaps offers a new direction in multidisciplinary efforts to understand suicide terrorism. Psychological explanations—such as the proposal that individuals act in this way to seek "vast personal importance"—dovetail with biological explanations—such as the fact that social species sometimes enhance their likelihood of genetic success via bold acts that promote reputation. Brains evolved over more than 3.7 billion years to mediate an extraordinary dynamic of conscious and unconscious neural processing that leads, on average, to fitness enhancing behaviors. Impelled by that combustible electrochemistry, a few people will strap on the deadly vest.
>
> (2009, 399–400)

David Lester speculates on "the possible role of traumatic events and posttraumatic stress disorder in some of the female suicide bombers, the lack of hope for a happy future (sometimes combined with depression and suicidality), and concern about becoming a burden and bringing shame to their families" (2010, 161).

In contrast, others regard suicide bombing as the effect of social processes rather than individual psychopathology. Grimland, Apter, and Kerkhof assert that suicide bombing is "instrumental in the context of war, not in the context of psychopathology" (2006, 107):

> Suicide bombing looks like suicide, but in important aspects it is incomparable with suicide. In more aspects it is comparable to killing in a war. Mostly it is part of a political and military strategy. It is a defense against perceived enemies. Religious and nationalist goals are important here. Psychology and psychiatry have little to offer until territorial disputes have been settled.
>
> (2006, 116)

Ellen Townsend sees suicide bombing as terrorism rather than psychopathology: "It is more useful to consider suicide terrorism as a dimension of terrorist behavior" (2007, 46). Similarly, Jerrold Post and colleagues state:

> There was a clear consensus among experts on terrorist psychology at the International Summit on Democracy, Terrorism, and Security that the

most important explanatory factors for terrorism were to be found at the collective level, that there were no identifiable individual factors explaining becoming a terrorist, and that there was no unique terrorist mindset. Nevertheless, we are left with the disquieting question of why among large numbers of people exposed to a common environment, only a few become suicide terrorists.

(2009, 25)

Michael King and colleagues write that families sustain support for those who decide to become suicide bombers in Indonesia:

Participants' endorsement of violent *jihad* was not predictive of their support for their kin's involvement in the violent activities of JI [*Jema'ah Islamiyah*]. Rather, it was their ratings of anti-Western sentiment. These results seem to anchor the legitimacy of terrorism in the idea that the West deserves it.

(King, Noor, and Taylor 2011, 411)

The Racialization of Suicide Bombing to Islam and Muslims

Some writers believe that Muslim or Arab cultures condition suicide bombing. Satoshi Kanazawa (2007) blames the Quran for suicide bombing:

Just as the brain of young Western men today is tricked by porn movies, which did not exist in the ancestral environment, the brain of young Muslim men today is tricked by the Koran, which also did not exist in the ancestral environment. Just as the brain of Western men thinks that they can potentially copulate with the sexually receptive women they see in porn movies, the brain of Muslim men thinks that they could copulate with the 72 virgins in heaven, if they die as martyrs.

(2007, 12–13)

Fathali Moghaddam uses a metaphor to discuss the dangers of "Islamic terrorism":

Consider a multistory building with a winding staircase at its center. People are located on different floors of the building, but everyone begins on the ground floor, where there are over a billion Muslims. Thought and action on each floor are characterized by particular psychological processes. On the ground floor, the most important psychological processes influencing behavior are psychological interpretations of material conditions, perceptions of fairness, and adequacy of identity. Hundreds of millions of Muslims suffer fraternal deprivation and lack of adequate identity; they feel that they are not being treated fairly and are not receiving adequate material rewards. They feel dissatisfied with the way they are depicted by the international media, and they do not want to become second-class copies of Western ideals. However, on the ground floor, degrees of freedom are large relative to degrees of freedom on the higher floors of the staircase to terrorism, and individual Muslims on the ground floor have a wider range of behavioral options.

(2009, 375)

In contrast, others argue that corrupted interpretations of Islam belie suicide bombing. Antonio Preti views suicide bombing among "Islamic suicide bombers" as a defense of their cultures:

There is no alternative to direct investigation to understand suicide bombers, and unfortunately this is hard to achieve. On a sociological ground present-day Islamic suicide bombers could be understood as desperate men who, when finding themselves in a disintegrating culture, seek integration into paramilitary organizations such as Hamas, Hezbollah, or Al-Qaeda and define themselves as martyrs to a cause.

(2006, 28)

Ian Palmer warns of its tactic among "radical Islamic groups": "Suicide attacks are most certainly not an exclusively Islamic phenomena [*sic*]. However, it cannot be overlooked that this tactic has been enthusiastically employed by radical Islamic groups in Lebanon, Israel, Chechnya, Kashmir, Indonesia, Iraq, the Gulf states, East Africa, North America and the United Kingdom" (2007, 292).

Jerrold Post and his colleagues stress that suicide bombing is a modern innovation of some Muslim scholars:

Some Muslim clergy have justified the use of violence against civilian and military targets by issuing fatwas (pronouncements) granting permission to fight outside the original parameters of Islamic jurisprudence. These scholars argue that warfare today is asymmetrical, which necessitates new rules of warfare, with new strategies and approaches to defeating the perceived enemies of Islam.

(Post et al. 2009, 16)

Instead, Post elsewhere tries to reframe jihad away from violence and toward self-purity:

The so-called greater jihad refers to struggle or persistence in leading a life free of evil. The jihad of the heart specifically embodies having a heart free of evil thoughts and desires, whereas the jihad of the tongue refers to giving voice to and leading a pious life according to the words of the Prophet, and the jihad of the deed refers to carrying out deeds to assist the *umma*[7] to assist Muslims who are suffering. These embody the greater jihad. The lesser jihad, the jihad of the sword, refers to the obligation to take up the sword in defense of the *umma*—in defense of believing Muslims who have had the sword taken up against them. It is accordingly a defensive jihad.

(Post 2009, 382)

James Liddle and colleagues concur that certain interpretations of Islam lend themselves to suicide bombing: "One who believes there is a moral obligation to kill infidels is likely to have a different attitude toward suicide terrorism than one who does not hold these specific beliefs (even if both subscribe to the same religion)" (Liddle, Machluf, and Shackelford 2010, 344).

Other authors dispute the link of Islam to suicide bombing altogether. Speckhard, quoted earlier, believes that martyrdom, not any religion, underlies suicide bombing: "That the ideologies that promote the use of suicide terrorism as a tactic may exist completely independent of any religion and be utilized in support of human bombing is a crucial point to make, one that is often missed by those who mistakenly lump all suicide terrorism together with so called 'Islamic-based' terrorism" (2008, 1025).

Similarly, Kruglanski and colleagues conjecture that suicide bombing channels violence in cultures of shame:

More generally speaking, cultures differ in the importance they assign to honor. So called shame cultures (e.g., the Arab or the Japanese cultures) assign to it considerably greater importance than do so called guilt cultures (the Jewish or the Protestant cultures), hence it seems plausible that members of the former cultures would experience a more profound significance loss upon humiliation than members of the latter cultures.

(Kruglanski et al. 2009, 351)

Sadik Kassim holds that suicide bombing reflects the dynamics of asymmetric warfare:

Suicide terrorism is a multifactorial phenomenon that cannot easily be explained away as an outcome of Islamic religiosity. A multidisciplinary approach to understanding root causes will help in the articulation, formulation, and execution of rational policies aimed at curbing the use of suicide terrorism as a strategy by militarily weak political national movements.

(2008, 207–208)

A DISCOURSE ANALYSIS OF MENTAL HEALTH TEXTS ON SUICIDE BOMBING

Mental health texts on suicide bombing complicate Howell's conclusions that the "psy disciplines" medicalize and racialize suicide bombing. Debates over suicide bombing as pathology consider the act either as a manifestation of irrational individual behavior or as the cumulative result of prolonged social deprivations. Debates over suicide bombing and Islam display three positions: suicide bombing is approved by Islam in general, by specific "corrupt" sects of Islam, and by societies that valorize martyrdom irrespective of religion. In both debates, the "psy disciplines" act as technologies of international security to comprehend and classify dangers from foreign militant groups to make intelligible that which seems unintelligible.

One form of intelligibility revolves around depicting suicide bombers as "disturbed, manipulative, fanatical, and uncooperative." Salib (2003) coins the term "*folie à plusieurs* (madness of many)" from the psychiatric disorder *folie à deux*, commonly translated in English as "shared psychotic disorder" in which delusional beliefs are transmitted from one party to another. This conscious linguistic construction legitimates the pathologization of suicide bombing through psychiatric vocabularies and concepts. Salib (2003) extends this hypothesis as "*folie partagée* (shared madness)," which "might provide some explanation of al-Qa'ida's bizarre and evil but meticulously calculated and executed suicide-homicide attacks." *Folie partagée* falls within the same French linguistic construction as *folie à deux* and *folie à plusieurs*. Salib equates "shared madness" with "bizarre and evil," linking madness to danger and the need for security. In considering a different form of pathology, Marazziti (2007) conjectures that suicide bombers "might conceivably be affected by double personality disorder, or, more in general, by complex personality disorders shaped by specific contexts." Rather than madness, this pathology is personality disorder. The two personalities that constitute "double personality disorder" are not explained, nor is the complexity of "complex personality disorders."

A third type of pathology appears in the work of Speckhard and Akhmedova (2005), who observe that aside from "top-down training and indoctrination into *Jihadist* ideologies," societies in "Palestine, Chechnya, Pakistan, the former Afghan training camps and elsewhere" suffer from "widespread trauma, dissociative responses, daily humiliations and hardships." The agency of the suicide bomber is denied through terms such as "top-down training" and "indoctrination." The phrase "widespread trauma and dissociative responses" recalls traumatic stress as a model to explain suicide bombing through pathological behavior. Speckhard (2008) extends this model to female suicide bombers, whose "primary motivations are often nationalistic and their personal motivations are trauma and revenge driven." Speckhard differentiates "primary" from "personal" motivations unclearly, and she does not explain how female suicide bombers can "rely on dissociation as a defense" from their "frequent traumatic experiences," since dissociation can lead to impairments in awareness, even though female suicide bombers are "revenge driven," which would imply full cognitive awareness and executive functioning by acting with intentionality.[8]

Similarly, Lester (2010) wonders whether "traumatic events and posttraumatic stress disorder in some of the female suicide bombers" and "the lack of hope for a happy future (sometimes combined with depression and suicidality)" lead to suicide bombing. Trauma, depression, and suicidality all contribute to suicide bombing, which becomes the consequence of sadness rather than martyrdom. Kruglanski and colleagues (2009) invoke trauma differently in that "personal traumas, and frustrations, represent a significance loss, motivating the quest for significance restoration." The types of personal traumas include "loved ones lost to enemy violence," "ostracism from one's community," and failure "to convince members of an indigenous majority to accept a minority immigrant as equal." Trauma is portrayed as a series of social injustices. The suicide bomber avenges the "significance loss" with "a clear path to renewed significance via participation in militancy and terrorism." The passivity of traumatic victimization leads to active recruitment in violence.

Victoroff (2009) departs from regnant psychological explanations to consider neurobiological explanations of "bold acts that promote reputation." The word "reputation" hints at the narcissistic impulses of the suicide bomber who acts to fulfill personal gratification. The suicide bomber's "combustible electrochemistry" compels him to "strap on the deadly vest." The imagery of "combustible electrochemistry" as volatile and flammable inside the brain complements the "deadly vest" outside the body. In different ways—through psychosis, trauma, dissociation, depression, suicidality, and faulty neural electrochemistry—authors from the "psy disciplines" associate suicide bombing with pathology; suicide bombing cannot be a conscious, willful act conducted by healthy individuals.

The side that opposes pathologization understands suicide bombers as a social phenomenon. Grimland, Apter, and Kerkhof (2006) warn others that suicide bombing "looks like suicide, but in important aspects it is incomparable with suicide. In more aspects it is comparable to killing in a war. Mostly it is part of a political and military strategy." Here, the death of the suicide bomber is a purely instrumental tactic of "killing in a war." The "political" and the "military" trump the personal aspects of the suicide bomber. Suicide bombing is not pathology, but a danger that requires the defense of society. Townsend (2007) similarly sees suicide bombing as "suicide terrorism," which becomes "a dimension of terrorist behavior." Words such as "terrorist" and "terrorism" direct attention to the political rather than the personal nature of the action. Likewise, Post and his colleagues (2009) write about the "clear consensus among experts on terrorist psychology" that "the most important explanatory factors for terrorism were to be found at the collective level" and that "there were no identifiable individual factors explaining becoming a terrorist." The "clear consensus among experts" declares the authoritative nature of the assertion that "no identifiable individual factors" explain suicide bombing. If pathologization denied the agency of suicide bombers in the previous set of writers, society "at the collective level" denies their agency here. The terms "terrorist" and "terrorism" also direct our notice to the political resonances of suicide bombing.

Comparably, King and colleagues (2011) write how "participants' endorsement of violent *jihad* was not predictive of their support for their kin's involvement in the violent activities of JI [*Jema'ah Islamiyah*]. Rather, it was their ratings of anti-Western sentiment." In this line of research, sophisticated statistical modeling and multifactorial analyses discover that the beliefs of families ("kin") relate to "involvement in the violent activities of JI." Compared to others, these authors provide a more granular level of social factors related to suicide bombing, but they rely upon families to understand motivations of suicide bombers. Rather than designate suicide bombing as an act of pathology, these authors view attackers as instruments of war and terrorism wrought by social factors; rather than madness, danger becomes the focus.

The focus on danger and terrorism leads some authors to racialize suicide bombing to Islam and Muslims. Palmer (2007) notes that "suicide attacks are most certainly not an exclusively Islamic phenomena" but then notes that it has been "enthusiastically employed by radical Islamic groups." The disclaimer of suicide attacks as not "exclusively Islamic phenomena" is then offset by a long list of areas in which "radical Islamic groups" operate: "Lebanon, Israel, Chechnya, Kashmir, Indonesia, Iraq, the Gulf states, East Africa, North America and the United Kingdom." Palmer effectively renders suicide bombing to be an "Islamic phenomen[on]" in many areas that Muslims inhabit. Kanazawa (2007) sets up a formula of equivalence between the "brain of young Western men" and "the brain of young Muslim men." All "Western" men and all "Muslim" men are posited to think homogenously without clear geographic delineations of the "West" or sectarian differences among Muslims. Brains are tricked by "porn movies" for the "Western men" and the "Koran" for "Muslim men," since the latter "[think] that they could copulate with the 72 virgins in heaven, if they die as martyrs." Kanazawa reduces the religious status of the Quran to a form of pornography that deceives male readers.

Moghaddam (2009) notes that "a billion Muslims" begin on the "ground floor" at the staircase of terrorism where "hundreds of millions of Muslims suffer fraternal deprivation and lack of adequate identity." He does not define "fraternal deprivation" or detail how he knows what "hundreds of millions of Muslims" think. He links "fraternal deprivation" and "lack of adequate identity" to "not being treated fairly and not receiving adequate material rewards," and he does not explain what "adequate material rewards" would consist of. Nonetheless, he says, "they do not want to become second-class copies of Western ideals," a statement that assumes (1) there is a "West" that contrasts with "Muslims," (2) ideals can be distributed impermeably among the "West" and "Muslims," and (3) the act of Muslims assuming "Western ideals" renders them "second-class copies" and imitative rather than original and innovative (Moghaddam 2009). These past three authors all appeal to magnitude—the delineation of "radical Islamic groups" dispersed through-out the world, "the brain of young Muslim men," the "hundreds of millions of Muslims"—to racialize suicide bombing.

Rather than link suicide bombing to Islam, some authors refine their analyses by examining specific causes. Preti (2006) understands suicide bombing as "desperate men who, when finding themselves in a disintegrating culture, seek integration into paramilitary organizations such as Hamas, Hezbollah, or Al-Qaeda and define themselves as martyrs to a cause." Suicide bombing becomes an act of "desperation" rather than volition among men (note: not women) who "find themselves in a disintegrating culture" and seek integration. The construction "find themselves" implies passivity rather than agency, and the supposition is that "a disintegrating culture" rather than political, economic, or nationalist reasons are what animates them. Post (2009) views "some Muslim clergy" as "granting permission to fight outside the original parameters of Islamic jurisprudence." While some suicide bombers may need "permission" from "some Muslim clergy," it is not clear that this "permission" determines their actions. Post does not detail "the original parameters of Islamic jurisprudence," but it is inferred that suicide attacks are not within those parameters. Instead, he distinguishes the "greater jihad," which "refers to struggle or persistence in leading a life free of evil," from the "lesser jihad, the jihad of the sword," which refers to the obligation to take up the sword in defense of the *umma*—in defense of believing Muslims who have had the sword taken up against them. A "life free of evil" and "taking up the sword" are contrasted without the consideration that some suicide bombers may actually see these two forms of jihad as united, should they need religious justification in the first place.

Lastly in this section, Liddle, Machluf, and Shackelford (2010) note that some may believe "a moral obligation to kill infidels" propels people "toward suicide terrorism." The word "infidel" calls attention to those who do not believe in Islam, and suicide bombing is cast as "terrorism," fusing political goals with psychological motives. Among these authors, suicide bombing is constructed not as madness but as a danger inherent to some groups of Muslims.

The final group of authors analyzed here dismisses any link of Islam to suicide bombing. Speckhard (2008) holds that "the use of suicide terrorism as a tactic may exist completely independent of any religion." This statement disconnects suicide bombing from any cultural, racial, or ethnic identity. Kruglanski and colleagues (2009) distinguish "shame cultures" such as "the Arab or the Japanese cultures" from the "guilt cultures" such as the "Jewish or the Protestant cultures" in that members of shame cultures "experience a profound significance loss upon humiliation." Kruglanski and his coauthors draw upon the work of anthropologist Ruth Benedict[9] to comprehend why humiliation leads to suicide bombing. They do not essentialize suicide bombing to Islam or Muslims, though they refer to ethnicities as examples of "shame cultures" and religions as examples of "guilt cultures." Kassim (2008) views "suicide terrorism" not as "an outcome of Islamic religiosity" but as "a strategy by militarily weak political national movements." Kassim calls attention to suicide bombing as a military tactic rather than an action springing from religious beliefs. Among these authors, suicide bombing is not specific to race, religion, or a form of madness.

Mental health texts constitute a veritable discourse on suicide bombing. The *sayable* among authors in this set of publications: suicide bombing is a manifestation of individual pathology or social processes, both of which negate the willfulness of the individual. Suicide bombing is a form of Islamic terrorism or not a form of Islamic terrorism, arguments that revolve around religion rather than criminology or law enforcement. In either case, authors make underlying assumptions about rationality, that taking one's life while taking the lives of others is an irrational act. The *domain* for this discourse: an audience acquainted with psychiatric and psychological vocabularies and concepts around motivations and impulses. Many publications have appeared in specialist journals on terrorism and political violence, expanding the circulation of these ideas to government officials as well as to academics in political science and international relations. The thematic *conservation* of ideas that links this discourse to other discourses: the terms "Muslim," "Islam," "East," and "West," as collective terms that are not defined but utilized for contrast and comparison, as we have seen in chapter 4. The cultural *memory* that links these texts to our contemporary moment: the assumption that suicide bombing can be rendered intelligible as a consequence of ethnic and religious identities. Suicide bombing becomes racialized and contained as a product of the irrational "East" in contrast to European and American liberal democracies that assume nonviolent political participation (Asad 2007). The link between ethnic/religious identity and suicide bombing pathology recalls the link explored in chapter 4 on how psychiatrists constructed racial taxonomies during the period of European imperial expansion. The *reactivation* of historical themes: previous discourses of progress and modernity present in the eighteenth, nineteenth, and twentieth centuries that differentiate the "West" from the more primitive and less evolved "East" are on display here. The *appropriation* from other types of discourses and disciplines of knowledge: these authors inherit Orientalist attitudes of dividing the world between the "Arab"/"East" and the "West," using anthropological concepts such as cultures of guilt and shame to explain suicide bombers.

.   ■   ●

To read these texts with cultural psychiatry and medical anthropology in mind is to discern certain theoretical continuities and discontinuities. Anthropologist Talal Asad (2007) has observed that suicide bombers frustrate analysts because the objects of study, by definition, are unavailable for interviews, requiring broad speculation into motivations. In mental health discourse, these speculations occur around the degree of pathology or religiosity present among suicide bombers. Howell has noticed that the "psy disciplines" medicalize suicide through madness, but mental health discourse also demonstrates explanations based on trauma. The intellectual history of the concept of trauma evidences a distinctly Euro-American genealogy: by the late nineteenth century, researchers increasingly agreed that trauma burdens the nervous system, leading to: (1) "the medicalization of the past" as trauma is produced by memories of a historical event, and (2) "the normalization of pathology" as symptoms represent understandable dysfunctions after the historical event is relived (Young 1995). The trauma model of suicide bombing medicalizes social injustices such as poverty and occupation as well as the normalization of emotions such as humiliation, hatred, and envy. Therefore, trauma represents another form of medicalization.

How can we understand these debates on suicide bombing? A persistent research agenda in cultural psychiatry has sought to expose the cultural bases of mental health knowledge and practice (Kleinman 1977, 1980). As a cultural system, psychiatric classification reflects healing priorities, social values, and professional ideologies at any historical point (Kleinman 1973, 1980). Within the cultural system of American forensic psychiatry, claiming that criminals suffer from mental illness denies the role of autonomy and intent in the commission of a crime (Fabrega 1989b). This cultural perspective highlights the quandary of the Guantánamo court trying the 9/11 suspects. The actions of the 9/11 suspects suggest that they understand the crimes of which they have been accused as well as their legal proceedings, but the court must rest upon American medical and legal presuppositions that only the mentally ill would seek the death penalty. The court seems unwilling to entertain the idea that requests for the death penalty are not grounded in mental pathology. This social fact underscores why social scientists view psychiatric knowledge as reflective of cultural norms and attitudes in any historical period (Gaines 1992; Kirmayer 2007a, 2007b).

Research methods from cultural psychiatry can help us bridge cultural gaps in interpretations of self-death as suicide or martyrdom. Mental health professionals depict suicide bombers differently than explanations advanced by organizations that recruit suicide bombers (Aggarwal 2009b). Ethnographic analyses that examine experience-near concepts within a culture rather than importing perspectives from another culture may uncover differences in values and assumptions around life and death (Fabrega 1989a, Staples and Widger 2012). Therefore, the next section presents texts from al-Qaeda on suicide bombing. These texts can clarify the cultural values of life and death that may be closer to the realities of suicide bombers and can perhaps resolve debates in the mental health discourse.

SUICIDE BOMBING IN THE LITERATURE OF AL-QAEDA

A branch of al-Qaeda known as al-Qaeda Organization in the Arabian Peninsula (AQAP) began publishing *Inspire* in 2010. AQAP was founded in Yemen in 2006, and it has welcomed repatriated Guantánamo detainees into its fold as it has attempted to balance global jihad with revolution in Yemen (Loidolt 2011). *Inspire* is similar to AQAP's online Arabic magazine *Sada al-Malahim* (The Echo of Epic Battles) in using the media to communicate a distinctly militant worldview (Page, Challita, and Harris 2011). *Inspire* offers a data source to analyze experience-near ethnographic accounts of suicide bombing.

Suicide Bombing Is a Religious Act

AQAP regards suicide bombing as a glorious religious act. This point recurs through repeated use of the word "martyr," even for those whose attempts are thwarted. Consider its praise of 'Umar al-Faruq, a failed suicide bomber:

> With the grace of Allah alone the heroic martyrdom bomber brother 'Umar al Faruq managed to carry out a special operation on an American Airplane, from the Dutch city Amsterdam to the American city Detroit, and this happened during the Christmas holiday, Friday December 25, 2009. He managed to penetrate all devices, modern advanced technology and security checkpoints in the international airports bravely without fear of death, relying on Allah and defying the great myth of the American and international intelligence, and exposing how fragile they are, bringing their nose to the ground, and making them regret all that they spent on security technology.
>
> (AQAP 2010a, 5)

'Umar al-Faruq is praised despite his failed detonation. Use of the word "brother" to describe him implies kinship. His operation is referred to as "martyrdom," since he acted "bravely" and "without fear of death" in "relying on Allah." AQAP (2010a) also decries "the great myth of the American and national intelligence," using terms such as "fragile" and the imagery of "bringing their nose to the ground" to indicate humiliation. AQAP warns Americans about impending attacks: "We will come to you with slaughter and have prepared men who love death as you love life, and with the permission of Allah we will come to you with something you cannot handle" (AQAP 2010a, 5). AQAP's (2010a) repeated invocation of "Allah" clearly demonstrates its conception of suicide bombing as a religious act. AQAP (2010a) contrasts its "men who love death" with Americans who "love life," heightening cultural differences in values of life and death.

An article from Ibrahim al-Banna, a graduate of the prestigious Egyptian seminary Al-Azhar University, explains the religious beliefs needed to embrace death:

> Realize that the heroic mujahidin who sacrificed their lives for the sake of Allah on 9/11 have given a great example of sacrifice and defending their religion and people according to what was revealed in our holy book: "Indeed,

Allah has purchased from the believers their lives and their properties [in exchange] for that they will have Paradise. They fight in the cause of Allah, so they kill and are killed. [It is] a true promise [binding] upon Him in the Torah and the Gospel and the Qur'an. And who is truer to his covenant than Allah? So rejoice in your transaction which you have contracted. And it is that which is the great attainment [at-Taubah: 111]."

(AQAP 2010b, 23)

Al-Banna incites his readers to defend Islam according to the Quran. The words "heroic," "sacrifice," and "defense" reinforce themes of martyrdom rather than suicide. The "lives" and "properties" of this world do not compare to those of Paradise, suggesting that suicide bombers act according to a different cultural logic of time and space. Al-Banna views this injunction as "binding" for all Muslims, not those of a particular sect. His invocations of the Torah and the Gospel signify that only Muslims among the Abrahamic religions follow God's will in committing jihad. AQAP explains that suicide bombing is a noble act: "It is such a high status for a human being to give his life, which is the most valuable thing to him, for the sake of Allah. Allah has purchased their souls and wealth in exchange for paradise" (AQAP 2010c, 27). Suicide bombing brings the individual closer to Allah in an act of sacrifice. The sacrifice comes in the form of a human being who gives his life, "which is the most valuable thing to him." Al-Banna recognizes the high value accorded to life; this makes sacrifice so holy.

Scriptural exegeses provide the justifications for suicide bombing. Religious scholar 'Umar Hussain interprets selected verses from the Quran:

Allah says they [martyrs] were "killed" so He approved their apparent death. But Allah says that the actual aspects of death do not apply to them. Thus, even though their bodies are dead their souls are alive. The life of their souls is beyond the mere consciousness that all souls, Muslim or non-Muslim, poses [*sic*] after death. Allah says they are with their Lord and they are being provided by Him. These two qualities are the forms of pleasure that are granted by Allah to the martyrs. They loved Allah during their life on this earth so their souls were granted the great honor of being in the presence of Allah.

(AQAP 2010b, 60)

This text imparts a distinct cultural understanding of life and death. AQAP (2010b) believes that the soul lives even after the body perishes, since "the actual aspects of death do not apply to them." The "martyr's" soul reaches God, who bestows protection and "pleasure." This conception of life and death differs from the biomedical view of life and death based on human physiology; for AQAP, bodies can be dead, but souls are alive. AQAP establishes meanings of life and death not through biological or medical concepts, but through religion.

Suicide Bombing Is a Willful Rational Act, Not Psychopathology

AQAP writers consistently underscore the types of mental preparation needed for suicide bombing. This theme refutes the idea that suicide bombing manifests a form of irrational psychopathology. In an article on committing jihad with a truck, one unnamed author writes: "After such an attack, we believe it would be very difficult to get away safely and without being recognized. Hence, it should be considered a martyrdom operation. It's a one-way road. You keep on fighting until you achieve martyrdom. You start out your day in this world, and by the end of it, you are with Allah" (AQAP 2010b, 54).

The author appears to write for an audience preoccupied with survival after an attack. The author refutes this possibility, since "it would very difficult to get away safely and without being recognized" through the image of the "one-way road." The author recommends cultivation of a mind-set that reminds the attacker of "martyrdom" and persuades readers to "keep on fighting" so that the attacker reaches Allah. The bounds of time and space do not apply for the martyr, who "starts" the day on earth and "ends" the day with "Allah" in Paradise.

Similarly, an article on the fear of death by drone strike outlines the mental preparation of militants. In "What to Expect in Jihad," Mukhtar Hassan describes how to fortify one's nerves:

> During the blast, you will want to make as much *dhikr* [remembrance] and *du'a* [prayer] as possible. Repeat the *kalimah* [literally "the word," but taken to mean the phrase "There is no God, but Allah and Muhammad is his Messenger"] constantly. If you feel terrified, then think about paradise; close your eyes and imagine yourself in paradise, entering its magnificent gates.

Imagine glancing at your beautiful palace where rivers of honey, milk, and wine flow underneath. Think of your *hoor* [fairies] that are awaiting you as well as meeting the prophets, *siddiqin* [companions], *shuhada'* [martyrs] and *salihin* [the pure]. Imagine smiling and laughing with our beloved Prophet Muhammad, *sallallahu 'alayhi wassallam* [peace be upon him]. Imagine seeing Allah and witnessing His pleasure with you. Think of all the good things in Paradise. Constantly ask Allah to accept you as a *shahid* [martyr].

(AQAP 2010c, 53)

Despite feeling "fear" and "terrified," the attacker must remain steadfast in devotion to God. The attacker should recall the benefits of the afterlife and the wonders of Paradise. Arabic words with symbolic resonances in Islam permeate the text: "*dhikr,*" "*du'a,*" "*kalimah,*" "*hoor,*" "*siddiqin,*" "*shuhada,*" "*salihin,*" and "*shahid.*" Rather than recoil in terror, the attacker must train through "remembrance" and "prayer." Images of pleasure—a beautiful palace where rivers of honey, milk, and wine flow underneath—await the "martyr." Mental health authors treat suicide bombing as an expression of psychopathology, but AQAP's authors recognize that suicide bombers must fight against the instinctual fear of death in a calculated way.

Suicide Bombing Is Self-Defense, Not Terrorism

The head of AQAP, Abu Basir Nasir al-Wuhayshi, makes the point that suicide bombing is an act of self-defense, not terrorism:

> What we want from the West is one thing: To stop aggression and oppression against the Muslim Nation and to withdraw out of its land. This solution was given by all of our leaders and in more than one occasion. The truce was offered by the one who has real authority to take such a decision on behalf of the Muslims, Shaykh Usamah bin Ladin, may Allah preserve him. His offer was refused. Whenever we offer a sound plan, they escalate in their stubbornness so we are left with no option but to defend ourselves and fight the transgressors.
>
> (AQAP 2010a, 15)

Al-Wuhayshi demands that the "West" stop "aggression" and "oppression." The "West" and "the Muslim Nation" are constructed as single entities without clear geographical definitions. Self-defense is presented as a series of steps after a "solution" given "in more than one occasion" and an offer of "truce." Bin Laden is presented as the sole authoritative voice for all Muslims, irrespective of sectarian differences. The "West" persists in its "stubbornness," so AQAP must "defend ourselves." This action is necessary because "American culture is that of killing other people" (AQAP 2010a, 15) as "they have killed women and children and lied by saying that these were preemptive strikes against al-Qa'idah in order to justify to their people that they have killed the leaders of al-Qa'idah" (AQAP 2010a, 16). The Americans are seen as bloodthirsty people who have no regard for "women and children."

American-born cleric Anwar al-Awlaki explains the targeting of civilians:

> It is the consensus of the scholars that Muslims should not kill the women and children of the disbelievers intentionally. It is the word "intentionally" that should be explained here because it qualifies the above statement and a lack of understanding this rule is what leads to the confusion that surrounds this issue today. What is meant is that women and children should not be singled out for killing; women and children should not be killed if they fall into captivity and if they can be separated from the combatants in war they should. But in no way does it mean that Islam prohibits the fighting against the disbelievers if their men, women and children are intermingled. This understanding is very dangerous and detrimental to jihad and awareness on this issue is very important. To stop the targeting of disbelievers who are at war with the Muslims just because there are women and children among them leads to constraints on today's jihad that make it very difficult, and at times, impossible to fight and places the Muslims at a great disadvantage compared to their enemy.
>
> (AQAP 2011, 42)

Anwar al-Awlaki refutes the distinction of civilians and combatants as defined in international law. Instead, he shifts the terms of debate to invoke "the consensus of the scholars" drawn from the Muslim community. The passage explains the word "intentionally" to suggest that Muslims must fight disbelievers despite their presence among women and children. This strategy levels the disproportionate military advantage of the disbelievers. Al-Awlaki warns those who would be swayed by arguments from international law that "Islam prohibits the fighting against the disbelievers if their men, women and children are intermingled." "Islam" here is also presented as a single entity with AQAP in position to speak for it.

•   •   •

If most mental health professionals see suicide bombing as a negative action defined through the culture of psychology, AQAP sees it as a positive act from the culture of religion. I do not mean to suggest that no suicide bomber from AQAP has ever experienced psychopathology—only a mental examination can determine that, which would be impossible if the bomber were successful. Nonetheless, politics is integral to how both groups construct suicide bombing, differentiated by the cultural meanings attached to the action. Ironically, if certain authors in mental health discourse exhibit medical Orientalism by positing an "East" and "West" to medicalize and racialize suicide bombing, authors from al-Qaeda inherit this nonspecific geographical distinction to make cultural claims of moral Occidentalism in which the "West," and America in particular, are seen as inherently evil. For AQAP, suicide bombing symbolizes the greatest sacrifice because the bomber knowingly relinquishes life, the most prized possession, in defense of the religious community.

Contrasting discourse from mental health and AQAP on suicide bombing offers an entry point to understand cultural differences. Anthropologists Akhil Gupta and James Ferguson ask: "If we question a pregiven world of separate and discrete 'peoples and cultures,' and see instead a difference-producing set of relations, we turn from a project of juxtaposing preexisting differences to one of exploring the construction of differences in historical process" (1992, 16). How might discourses on suicide bombing reveal historical constructions of difference rather than preexisting differences? Suicide bombing refracts differential constructions of knowledge based on the relationship of the self and mind to either medicine or religion.

For example, the construction of post-Enlightenment biomedical knowledge demonstrates a form of biological materialism focused on this world and centered on the individual. Psychiatry inherits biomedicine's form/substance distinction from Greek philosophy: biology's structures and chemistry's processes constitute the body's main architecture, to which moral, social, and psychological concerns are seen as secondary scaffolding (Kleinman 1995). Disease is assumed to possess a natural course universal for all people irrespective of the modifying influences of culture and society (Good 1994). Nature exists as prior to and separate from society, culture, and morality (Gordon 1988). This is the first construction of difference in cultural studies of suicide bombing: psychiatrists and psychologists search for pathologies rooted in the nervous system, whereas militants prioritize moral and social concerns of martyrdom over the body. To divorce the suicide bomber from society, culture, or morality is to miss the causes of suicide bombing for which mental health professionals so desperately search. A search for universal explanations of suicide bombing assumes that biology is the substrate to which we all belong rather than accounting for genuine differences in society, culture, or morality. This comes into play as psychiatrists and psychologists try to isolate general risk factors of suicide bombers across militant groups in different countries, even though local social and cultural differences may be more important. It may be more helpful to compare how AQAP's justifications of suicide bombing resemble or differ from other militant groups rather than to merely note the common use of this tactic.

Moreover, mental health scholarship on suicide bombing displays a process of medicalization. Medicalization has been characterized as "defining a problem in medical terms, using medical terms to describe a problem, adopting a medical framework to understand a problem, or using a medical intervention to 'treat' it" (Conrad 1992, 211). Framing a problem that affects the body or mind expands medicine's jurisdiction and authority with resultant creation of knowledge and practices (Zola 1972). This is the second construction of cultural difference: mental health professionals define suicide bombing in medical terms through psychological concepts, whereas AQAP construes suicide bombing through religious terms and vocabularies. However, this religious framework is heavily politicized, pitting Muslims against Jews and Christians, who substitute for Europeans and Americans. AQAP also promotes distinct interpretations of the Qu'ran and medieval scholars, prioritizing religious texts rather than lived experience. AQAP's texts should force medical and legal authors to question what they know about suicide bombing. In these texts, the suicide bomber does not believe that life ends with the destruction of the body, and he trains himself to attack despite fear. These themes challenge medical and psychological assumptions that people act to maximize their best interests in the observable empirical world, attesting to the cultural bases of all knowledge. Common to both discourses, however, is the need for explanation. Mental health authors may pathologize suicide bombing and AQAP authors may justify it, but there seems to be an underlying assumption that this act needs to be researched and explained, perhaps because it elevates death over a human instinct for life.

Finally, a disproportionate focus on psychological phenomena may overlook cultural, social, and moral factors. Asad (2007) wonders whether suicide bombing elicits such horror because it reminds citizens of liberal democracies that not all people share the modernist vision of a secular political life in which religion is relegated to personal spirituality. AQAP texts confirm this point as authors use religion to organize social and political activity in pursuit of an international caliphate. Therefore, psychiatrists and psychologists will have difficulties in comprehending al-Qaeda militants within a mental health paradigm. To claim that mental illness afflicts suicide bombers is to deny their accountability and culpability and to perpetuate scientific knowledge that does not match their cultural realities. Given this chasm in cultural values, perhaps the Guantánamo court should call a cleric from AQAP as an expert witness to explain the actions of the 9/11 suspects. His testimony may raise unsettling points that prompt a search for solutions from politics and foreign policy rather than from psychiatry.

6

Knowledge and Practice in War on Terror Deradicalization Programs

CAN MILITANTS BE REHABILITATED? Since the War on Terror, psychiatrists have joined others in this debate. The case of Guantánamo detainee Omar Khadr illustrates this point as two prominent psychiatrists have attempted to mold public opinion in opposite directions. The government's expert witness, forensic psychiatrist Michael Welner, has written on deradicalization programs for Islamist militants in the Middle East and Southeast Asia. He suggests that reinterpreting the concept of jihad, often translated as "holy war," within a framework of "a peaceful strain of Islam," along with family integration and vocational training may rehabilitate militants (Welner 2011a). He favors using forensic psychiatry to project a detainee's risk for future violence: "Assessing future risk of dangerous Jihadist activity necessarily recognizes that an approach may borrow from clinical understandings about criminal and violent recidivism, but has to stay true to context (actual ideological violence or otherwise facilitating violence) in order to gain relevance" (Welner 2011a).

In contrast, child and adolescent psychiatrist Stephen Xenakis, the expert witness for Khadr's defense team, has questioned using mental health professionals in the War on Terror similar to "the politicization of mental health under the Soviet regime" (Xenakis 2010). He has challenged Welner's conclusions that Khadr was "at a high risk of dangerousness as a radical jihadist": "Radical jihadism is not a clinical condition, and diagnosing it is not within the domain of psychiatric experts. Radical jihadism is an ideology—and can be embraced by the psychiatrically sane and insane alike." Xenakis accused Welner of "put[ting] a scientific sheen on what were lay opinions" with "testimony disguised as expert psychiatric opinion" (Xenakis 2010).

The cultural psychiatry perspective acknowledges how psychiatrists have clashed on the possibilities for psychiatry to provide values, beliefs, and practices to make meanings of militancy. Despite their diametrically opposed legal affiliations, both agree that jihad is not a mental disorder. Nonetheless, their recommendations for mental health in the War on Terror move in opposite directions. Welner encourages the use of forensic psychiatry as a knowledge base to provide risk assessments for militants, but Xenakis discourages the use of forensic psychiatry as a tool of totalitarian states that imprison undesirable populations. On the surface, we can argue over who is right, but there is a deeper point: both psychiatrists have intuited that mental health knowledge and practice have changed with the War on Terror.

The media have publicized programs that harvest mental health concepts to describe deradicalization programs. For example, the Masjid el Noor Mosque in Toronto, Canada, directed by Mohammed Shaikh, has fashioned a twelve-step "Specialized De-Radicalization Intervention Program," comparing an Islamist's addiction to extremist interpretations of Islam with an alcoholic's addiction to alcohol (FoxNews 2009). Separately, the Guantánamo Bay detention facility has been criticized for lacking deradicalization programs that implement "an intensive rehabilitation process incorporating large amounts of religious instruction and discussion" in the fight for "the battlefield of the mind" (Boucek 2008b). The terms "rehabilitation" and "the battlefield of the mind" evince the centrality of mental health in models of deradicalization.

The clearest example of how the War on Terror has systematically transformed mental health knowledge and practice is through government deradicalization programs. A March 2012 report states that of the 599 Guantánamo detainees transferred up to December 2011, 95 (about 16 percent) had been confirmed as reengaging with militants or militant activities, and an additional 72 (12 percent) were suspected of reengagement (Office of the Director of National Intelligence 2012). To prevent reengagement, deradicalization programs are now sponsored by governments such as Yemen, Saudi Arabia, Singapore, Indonesia, Malaysia, Pakistan, the United States, Canada, and the United Kingdom. Deradicalization programs have spread throughout the world, but how do they function, and what is the role of mental health professionals in these programs if jihad is not mental pathology? How is deradicalization accomplished within the secular framework of mental health to "treat" the religious ideology of jihad?

Our framework on the forensic functions of the medical system can clarify the types of mental health knowledge and practice in deradicalization programs. Various governments have initiated such programs, furnishing us with official policy texts to observe similarities and differences. We can use government documents and academic publications to trace: (1) the cultural construction of deradicalization as a medicolegal issue for criminal forensic psychiatry, (2) the establishment of mental health standards to support and evaluate deradicalization, (3) the procurement of relevant clinical evidence, (4) the application of clinical reasoning, and (5) the legal outcomes associated with deradicalization based on a clinician's opinion. Deradicalization programs exemplify the greatest patient-clinician differences in interpreting basic existence; patients are diagnosed with the disease of radicalization even though they may not acknowledge any illness.

The work of philosopher Michel Foucault can help us understand the theoretical bases, rehabilitative practices, and relationships between mental health and national security. The role of religious beliefs in the production of violence has increasingly interested cultural mental health experts, who have sought to create models for intervention (Bhui and Ibrahim 2013; Tousignant and Laliberté 2007). Scholars in cultural mental health have therefore engaged with Foucault to illuminate the cultural values that permeate psychiatry (Aggarwal 2010b; Kirmayer 2007a; Lock 1993; Skultans 1991; Young 2008), and especially psychiatry's growing links to the criminal justice system. Foucault was interested in how the state erected disciplinary and rehabilitative mechanisms to grapple with the changing nature of crime in France, England, and the United States. In *Discipline and Punish*, Foucault posited that two social transformations characterized post-eighteenth-century legal reform: the disappearance of public executions and the elimination of bodily pain (Foucault 1995, 11). These changes coincided with changes in legal offenses committed from "a criminality of blood," such as murders and physical aggression, to a "criminality of fraud," involving property, such as theft and swindling (75–77). Through penal reform, punishment shifted from the body to the mind (101), requiring expertise from "technicians" such as "warders, doctors, chaplains, psychiatrists, psychologists, [and] educationalists" (11). This "scientific-juridical complex" has diagnosed, prognosticated, classified, and rehabilitated prisoners (19).

In the process, knowledge and techniques have formed "power-knowledge relations" for the implementation of power (25–26). "War on Terror" programs have also sought to deradicalize militants through new forms of knowledge and techniques promoting nonviolence. Deradicalization programs have therefore contributed new forms of culture through interpretive frameworks that create meanings, disciplinary practices, and social institutions.

Before proceeding, I should offer several disclaimers. Deradicalization programs may improve upon extrajudicial counterterrorism alternatives such as indefinite detention, targeted killings, rendition, and torture. Nonetheless, high rates of recidivism among Guantánamo detainees prompt questions about whether models of deradicalization are valid, just as Foucault inquired whether imprisonment was an effective deterrent for crime. In addition, militant Islamists also construct discipline and power-knowledge relations by subjugating and killing others. For example, anthropologists have noted how Islamists discipline and control women's bodies (Brenner 1996; Mahmoud 2005), but this entire discussion goes beyond the scope of this chapter. Finally, the texts reviewed here use the words "militant," "Islamist," and "extremist" interchangeably; I prefer "militant" to denote individuals whose ideologies justify political violence.

THE FORENSIC FUNCTIONS OF MENTAL HEALTH IN DERADICALIZATION PROGRAMS

These texts on deradicalization come from literature reviews for terrorism scholars and policy experts (Morris et al. 2010; Price 2010). I have included all English-language articles, books, editorials, commentaries, and policy statements. The preceding two chapters restricted examinations of discourse to peer-reviewed articles, the standards governing academic knowledge production; however, knowledge on deradicalization programs disperses through academic scholarship as well as government documents and monographs, necessitating a new search strategy. Two assumptions guided the inclusion of texts: (1) publications had to explicitly address the War on Terror[1] and (2) publications had to focus on deradicalization rather than radicalization. I reviewed all titles and abstracts of articles for eligibility. I also reviewed articles that did not have abstracts and those whose abstracts ambiguously mentioned deradicalization or the War on Terror.

The Cultural Construction of Deradicalization
as a Medicolegal Issue

Foucault (1995) criticizes psychiatrists and psychologists for conspiring with the state against undesirable populations. He portrays the psychiatrist as "not an expert in responsibility, but an adviser in punishment; it is up to him to say whether the subject is 'dangerous,' in what way one should be protected from him, how one should intervene to alter him, whether it would be better to try to force him or to treat him" (22). Foucault places the psychiatrist and suspect in an adversarial relationship since the psychiatrist makes "judgments of normality, attributions of causality, assessments of possible changes, anticipations as to the offender's future" (1995, 20). He traces the origins of psychiatry and psychology to the emergence of social science, which measures humans and their actions, leading to a "technology of power" (193). The knowledge of mental health permits a shift in the application of power from the body to the mind as the French government turned away from torture (18–19, 99–102). Foucault decries the role of social scientists and mental health professionals in producing knowledge about the mind and character of the offender for governmental use.

War on Terror deradicalization programs exhibit similar trends. Some believe that psychiatry can offer a knowledge base to better understand Islamist militancy (Stern 2010; Welner 2011b). Theoretical texts provide a starting point to investigate deradicalization models. Omar Ashour (2009a, 2009b) has examined the deradicalization of Islamist groups in Egypt and Algeria. Ashour defines deradicalization as a "process of relative change within Islamist movements, one in which a radical group reverses its ideology and de-legitimises the use of violent methods to achieve political goals, while also moving towards an acceptance of gradual social, political and economic changes within a pluralist context" (2009b, 5). Ashour categorizes deradicalization as "ideological," "behavioral," and "organizational"; "ideological" and "behavioral" occur at the individual level, and "organizational" occurs at the group level:

> Deradicalisation is primarily concerned with changing the attitudes of armed Islamist movements towards violence, rather than toward democracy. Many de-radicalised groups still uphold misogynist, homophobic, xenophobic, and anti-democratic views. Separate from the ideological level,

de-radicalisation can occur only on the behavioural level. On that level, de-radicalisation means practically abandoning the use of violence to achieve political goals without a concurrent process of ideological delegitimisation of violence. De-radicalisation can occur in only one of the two levels.

(2009b, 5)

In Ashour's framework, the judgment of normality is based on the abandonment of violence to achieve political goals, not on the requirement for militants to believe in democracy. Militants can still hold "misogynist, homophobic, xenophobic, and anti-democratic views" provided that they abandon violence. Knowledge about deradicalization draws upon psychological concepts and vocabularies such as "ideological" and "behavioral," analogous to the model of cognitive behavioral therapy.[2] Ashour notes that "analysing the causes and dynamics of de-radicalisation is crucial for both academics and policy-makers" (2009b, 30). Knowledge on deradicalization must effectuate political change through policy relevance.

In a related fashion, John Horgan's (2009) study of former militants in Europe, the Middle East, and South Asia separately defines deradicalization as

the social and psychological process whereby an individual's commitment to, and involvement in, violent radicalization is reduced to the extent that they are no longer at risk of involvement and engagement in violent activity. De-radicalization may also refer to any initiative that tries to achieve a reduction of risk of re-offending through addressing the specific and relevant disengagement issues.

(153)

Horgan (2009) differentiates deradicalization from disengagement, since deradicalization leads to "cognitive" and "behavioral" changes, whereas disengagement is only a "behavioral" change. He builds on earlier work (2008) finding that terrorists can disengage from violent behaviors without relinquishing radical views, and he classifies disengagement into two categories, psychological and physical. Physical disengagement is "externally verifiable," but psychological disengagement encompasses "emotional issues" leading to the cessation of terrorism. Psychological disengagement includes:

1. The development of negative sentiments as a result of experiencing negative qualities associated with sustained, focused membership (e.g. pressure, anxiety, the gradual dismantling of the fantasy or illusion that served to lure the recruit in the first place etc.) and as a result;

2. A change in priorities (e.g. the longing for a social/psychological state which (real or imaginary) to regain something that the member feels is lacking, or existed before membership, often a result of self-questioning, but mostly following prolonged social/psychological investment as a member from which little return appears evident);

3. A sense of growing disillusionment with the avenues being pursued, or some quality of them (e.g. with the political aims or with operational tactics and the attitudes underpinning them).

(Horgan 2008)

Horgan and Ashour both advocate secular psychological models of deradicalization. A classification of dangerousness appears through risk assessments. Perspectives on intervention and measures of change differentiate disengagement from deradicalization. As with Ashour, Horgan (2008) argues for government policy: "It is useful not only to help identify policy-relevant lessons for the development of counterterrorism initiatives of this kind in regions where there are none, but more immediately would lead to greater clarity around the basic social and behavioral processes involved, that have, it would seem, escaped scrutiny in many cases to date." Despite terminological differences, Horgan and Ashour seem to agree that sustained deradicalization requires a reformation of thoughts ("psychological" for Horgan, "ideological" for Ashour) and behaviors that are observable for external verification.

This secular model of deradicalization contrasts with models in which militants must demonstrate reformed religious beliefs. Foucault presents us with a contrast from post-Enlightenment, Western Europe, where the social role of religion has weakened: "Many crimes have ceased to be so because they were bound up with a certain exercise of religious authority" (1995, 17). To prove that science supplants religion, he points to the hospital hierarchy in the eighteenth century: "In the internal hierarchy, the physician, hitherto an external element, begins to gain over the religious staff and to relegate them to a clearly specified, but subordinate role in the technique of the examination" (186). The assessment capabilities of mental health catalyze these changes: "But the supervision of normality was firmly encased in a medicine or a psychiatry that provided it with a sort of 'scientificity'; it was supported by a judicial apparatus which, directly or indirectly, gave it legal justification" (296). Foucault asserts that the science of mental health replaces religion as the paramount authority for discipline and punishment.

Certain authors on deradicalization hold the exact opposite viewpoint and demand the involvement of religious leaders. For example, Gunaratna (2009) acknowledges that deradicalization entails four types of rehabilitation—religious, psychological, social, and vocational. The Islamist militant's crime mandates a counter-response from religious authorities: "A learned Islamic scholar and a cleric have the understanding, knowledge and authority to correct the Islamic misconceptions a terrorist believes to be true" (150). Religious rehabilitation is supreme: "While psychological, vocational, and social and family rehabilitation can change one's heart and mind, the most powerful is religious rehabilitation. Religious rehabilitation has the power to unlock the mind of a detainee or an inmate" (150). Here, mental health yields to the authority of religion. A classification scheme for militants is proposed that requires involving religious scholars, since "different levels of extremism require different levels of response" among terrorist leaders, operatives, and sympathizers who are high, medium, and low risk, respectively (158). Those who measure and assess Islamists would not only be psychiatrists or psychologists: "Counter terrorism practitioners, Islamic scholars, and academic specialists should work together to develop a program and a syllabus that can tailor to every category from extremists that advocate and support to the terrorists that kill, maim and injure" (150–151). The militant becomes an object of secular and religious study: "After a process of assessment, the right cleric or psychologist is assigned to counsel the detainee. The detainee is continuously assessed. It is essential to identify the problem with the detainee" (159).

Gunaratna's argument rests on multiple assumptions. He differentiates among "learned Islamic scholars" and clerics on the one side and terrorists on the other side, but what if terrorists have engaged in deep religious study and learning? Who judges the nature of "Islamic misconceptions"? What solutions are needed during differences of opinion? Who decides on "the right cleric or psychologist" to counsel the detainee?

Stern (2010) also prioritizes religious reprogramming during deradicalization. Militant Islamists enter terrorism for a variety of reasons: "market conditions, social networks, education, [and] individual preferences" (98).

However, faulty religious interpretations are ultimately responsible: "The most dangerous and seductive bad idea spreading around the globe today is a distorted interpretation of Islam, which asserts that killing innocents is a way to worship God. Part of the solution must come from within Islam and from Islamic scholars, who can refute this interpretation with arguments based in theology" (108).

Like Gunaratna, Stern wants clerics to draw upon their religious authority to counter Islamist ideologies. A "distorted interpretation of Islam" is defined by the belief that "killing innocents is a way to worship God," even though we saw in chapter 5 that al-Qaeda's authors dismiss the very premise of innocents in the War on Terror. Stern calls for "Islamic scholars" to "refute this interpretation with arguments based in theology," assigning responsibility to religious leaders over criminologists or law enforcement officials. An unacknowledged assumption has been that religious authorities and mental health professionals will agree about the goals and processes of deradicalization: no situation is entertained in which religious authorities can approve of a militant's religious interpretations that could place them at odds with psychiatrists or psychologists.

Consequently, deradicalization becomes culturally constructed based on competing secular psychological and religious rehabilitation models. The secular psychological model presumes that radicalization and deradicalization exist at the levels of thoughts and behaviors with success measured by eliminating violence. The religious rehabilitation model purposely includes Muslim religious leaders, with success measured through corrective theological reform. The secular psychological model targets public actions, and the religious rehabilitation model targets private beliefs, the former approving new ways of behaving and the latter approving new ways of being. In separate ways, deradicalization mandates new identities for militants. Those of us opposed to political violence could agree that a new identity rejecting violence may not be a bad thing, but it also bears asking: a new identity comprising what and approved by whom?

·   ·   ·

Foucault (1995) identifies mental health professionals as "subsidiary authorities" (21) within "small-scale legal systems" as punishment shifts from the body to the mind. Although he does not explicitly state it, he assumes that these authorities operate in the confines of the state:

If it is still necessary for the law to reach and manipulate the body of the convict, it will be at a distance, in the proper way, according to strict rules, and with a much "higher" aim. As a result of this new restraint, a whole army of technicians took over from the executioner, the immediate anatomist of pain: warders, doctors, chaplains, psychiatrists, psychologists, educationalists; by their very presence near the prisoner, they sing the praises that the law needs: they reassure it that the body and pain are not the ultimate objects of its punitive actions.

(1995, 11)

Foucault's analysis rests on conceptions of power, sovereignty, and law within the traditional boundaries of the nation-state in the nineteenth century. However, deradicalization programs complicate this assumption. First, Foucault observes that countries such as France, England, and the United States enacted reforms over different decades in the nineteenth century (1995, 7–8). In contrast, deradicalization programs have multiplied across the United States, Western Europe, the Middle East, and Asia within the past decade. This trend may reflect the War on Terror's placing all countries on military alert, according to former American president Bush (2005), suggesting a global urgency and coordination to deradicalization programs. Second, Foucault does not analyze crime, punishment, or reform in the Middle East or Asia, limiting the geographical applicability of his arguments. In contrast, deradicalization programs are a crucial component of extremist deterrence in these areas. Finally, Foucault does not trace the transnational relationships of "technicians" to each other or to nation-states.

Instead, academics of deradicalization constitute a new class of "supersidiary authorities." Here, I accentuate the vertical sense of this etymology. The term "subsidiary" is an adjective of the word "subside," whose Latin roots come from *sub*, "under" or "below," and *sidere*, "to sit." In Foucault's usage, "subsidiary" connotes a presence secondary to the state. In contrast, academics and intellectuals in the War on Terror act as *supersidiary authorities* in sitting above individual nation-states by defining deradicalization knowledge and practice. They sit above by scrutinizing deradicalization programs, inducing general conclusions from specific examples, and then encouraging further state action. These *supersidiary authorities* also sit at a distance, work under strict rules of research, and toward the aim of deradicalization.

Foucault holds that the authoritative nature of *subsidiary authorities* comes in relation to the law of a single nation-state. An opposite process occurs with *supersidiary authorities* and deradicalization programs. *Supersidiary authority* accrues through the transnational exchange of deradicalization knowledge and its international dissemination to influence state behavior. For example, the RAND Corporation has utilized Ashour's and Horgan's frameworks extensively in publications for the defense community (Noricks 2009; Rabasa et al. 2010). Saudi Arabia's program (described below) has been praised as an exemplar that "employs a number of well-designed strategies that should be used by those hoping to rehabilitate Islamic terrorists around the world" (Lankford and Gillespie 2011, 129). The Saudi Arabian program becomes "a de facto model for other countries seeking to implement a counter-radicalisation programme" (Boucek 2008a, 65), acquiring such symbolic value that its success is crucial, with monumental international consequences. Gendron (2010) warns: "The future effectiveness of Saudi security and counter-radicalization efforts will very much depend upon whether real reforms can be achieved with the acceptance, if not the approval, of the conservative religious majority. Lacking that support, the House of Saud will be weakened, and with it, the stability of the country, the region, and the security of the West" (504).

Here, Lankford and Gillespie (2011) infer that the Saudi Arabian model meets the needs "to rehabilitate Islamic terrorists around the world," essentially treating all causes of radicalization as the same without local variation. Boucek (2008a) affirms this point by wanting to see Saudi Arabia's program become "a de facto model." Gendron (2010) warns of the domino effect activated by the failure of deradicalization in Saudi Arabia with dire consequences for the region and "the security of the West." Saudi Arabia's deradicalization efforts now intertwine with transnational security interests.

Furthermore, *supersidiary authorities* promote the international dissemination of their theories and practices. For instance, Kruglanski et al. (2011) exclaim: "It would be desirable if the international community and its institutions became involved in the deradicalization project and provided the resources needed for its proper administration and assessment" (143). Gunaratna (2009) has also supported a "global rehabilitation regime"[3] with the following features: "common database," "exchange of personnel," "joint research, publication, education, and training," "transfer of expertise and resources," "sharing of expertise," and "an international advisory council."

Gunaratna (2011) describes Singapore's endeavors to share "best practices" in deradicalization with international experts at government conferences to coordinate counterterrorist responses from individual countries. These authors assume that transnational knowledge transfer around deradicalization is useful or justified despite concerns of recidivism.

This discussion is not meant to imply that transnational knowledge transfer and exchange is undesirable or wrong. It should be encouraged if it reduces the killing of innocent civilians. However, deradicalization programs in the War on Terror generate forms of knowledge that spread rapidly through globalization and information technology that differ from Foucault's analysis confined to the traditional nation-state. The pressure to adopt counterterrorism practices for immediate action can obscure warnings about limited success. For example, Noricks (2009) first acknowledges that "deradicalization pathways are likely to be affected by the political-economic and sociocultural context in which the individual and group are nested," but then qualifies that "common themes with potential implications for counterterrorism stand out in the existing literature" (311). Rabasa and colleagues (2010) admit that "knowledge of deradicalization programs remains limited and that there are reasons to remain skeptical about the programs' claims of success," and yet RAND's "analysis is portrayed as having a number of policy implications" (xvi). Given the diversity in political-economic systems and sociocultural contexts of countries in the War on Terror, how do potential implications translate into tangible recommendations? Given consternations over the accomplishments of deradicalization programs, why rush to policy?

Against the backdrop of recidivism, it is reasonable to ask whether knowledge and practices originating in one society can be transferred to other societies for effective outcomes. This question represents a research agenda at the crossroads of anthropology and psychiatry (Bibeau 1997; Kirmayer 2006; Kirmayer and Minas 2000; Kleinman 1988). If deradicalization programs currently range from 10 to 50 percent of recidivism, is this an acceptably low rate and should these programs be implemented elsewhere?

The Establishment of Medical Standards to Support and Evaluate Deradicalization

Health professionals use medical knowledge to support and evaluate professional opinions related to medicolegal issues. Deradicalization programs aggregate knowledge and practice recommendations from scholars and government officials to instill nonviolence. Deradicalization programs constitute what Foucault termed "corrective penalties" on the basis of this health knowledge. For Foucault, the nineteenth century heralded a shift in punishment aimed at the mind and soul rather than only the body, leading to a "corrective penalty": "The point of application of the penalty is not the representation, but the body, time, everyday gestures and activities; the soul, too, but in so far as it is the seat of habits. The body and the soul, as principles of behaviour, form the element that is now proposed for punitive intervention.... This punitive intervention must rest on a studied manipulation of the individual" (1995, 128).

Regular, reformative routines characterize corrective penalty: "Exercises, not signs: compulsory movements, regular activities, solitary meditation, work in common, silence, application, respect, good habits" (128). At stake is the restoration of the "obedient subject" who conforms to the law by training the body "by the traces it leaves, in the form of habits, in behavior" (129–131). Punishment converts the minds and bodies of offenders, and Foucault terms these methods as "disciplines," defined as "an art of the human body . . . directed not only at the growth of its skills, nor at the intensification of its subjection, but at the formation of a relation that in the mechanism itself makes it more obedient as it becomes more useful, and conversely" (138). Discipline produces "subjected and practised bodies, 'docile' bodies" (138) by sequestering individuals at sites that monitor, classify, and separate offenders to rehabilitate daily life (141–148).

Deradicalization discourse also proposes corrective penalties and practices to reform offenders into obedient subjects by disciplining bodies, minds, and souls to cultivate self-governance. For example, Kruglanski, Gelfand, and Gunaratna (2010) observe that "financial support for children's education, professional training for wives, and assistance in reintegrating released detainees into society" are part of programs in the Philippines. Indonesian deradicalization programs rely upon similar strategies:

A great deal of the social rehabilitation process is dependent upon financial remuneration to reverse feelings of hatred towards "the system"—this includes everything from paying for family members' travel when visiting the inmate, paying children's school fees, giving small business loans, paying relevant fees for getting married in prison to medical care, etc.

(Ranstorp 2009, 19)

Saudi Arabia merits attention for its resource-intense deradicalization program. "Beneficiaries," as termed by the government, receive classes on "sharia law, psychology, vocational training, sociology, history, Islamic culture, art therapy, and athletics" (Porges 2010). A staggering assortment of services is delivered:

> There have been a number of recent media reports highlighting the efforts of the Saudi government to assist the reintegration of persons convicted of civil and criminal offenses. These have included programs to help facilitate marriages (including institutionalized support to help find spouses for women convicted of immorality offenses), to increase the delivery of social services, and schemes to support families of incarcerated breadwinners. Other initiatives such as the "Centennial Fund" have been started to grant loans to released prisoners and soon to be freed prisoners so that they can start their own businesses upon release. Charitable organizations often work together with the government to establish schools and training programs for prisoners in order to help prisoners gain employment, while other NGOs [nongovernmental organizations] frequently help released prisoners and their families with groceries, clothes and toys for Ramadan. Another noteworthy program is the "Best Mother Award," designed to support women with children whose husbands are serving time in prison.
>
> (Boucek 2009, 214)

The generosity of the government has led to charges that Saudi Arabia rewards past militancy:

> The Saudi approach seems to involve a "no-expenses spared" attitude that is arguably over-rewarding their detainees and may be an inefficient use of resources. For those with less comprehensive funding (or who are simply less organised) there is also the danger that failing to provide benefits—especially if promised—will lead to a backlash in militant or criminal activity, whether for ideological or financial reasons.
>
> (Mullins 2010)

In other words, the danger is that militants may return to violence in the absence of financial inducements.

Therefore, deradicalization programs in Indonesia, the Philippines, and Saudi Arabia vindicate Foucault's points about disciplining bodies and minds through everyday gestures, activities, and habits as motivators of behavior. In Indonesia and the Philippines, discipline comes to the soul through steps that situate the offender within a social network by forging stronger bonds with children, families, and new brides. The Saudi Arabian program includes these components and adds classes like vocational training and athletics, which discipline the body through exercises, work, and compulsory movements. Offenders become obedient subjects and productive members of society through subjected, docile bodies enmeshed in social relations. Foucault labels these social bonds as disciplinary "counter-law" for creating a "private link" of constraints fundamentally different from contractual obligations (222). Deradicalization programs foster counter-law by strengthening the private links of released militants with family and friends. These strategies to propagate deradicalization also require ongoing assessment.

The Procurement of Clinical Evidence that Evaluates Deradicalization

Governments have employed health professionals to gather clinical evidence in order to evaluate the merits of deradicalization programs. Foucault also pondered the need for modern penal systems to acquire clinical evidence, warning that corrective regimens are not enough—disciplining practices must be measurable to classify and reconstitute offenders: "All the sciences, analyses or practices employing the root 'psycho-'" consist of calculation (1995, 193). These calculations manifest through "tests, interviews, interrogations and calculations" (226).

All of the programs reviewed above depend on interviews throughout program interventions. However, the lack of effective assessments and standardized instruments has hampered deradicalization efforts. For example, Horgan and Braddock (2010) note:

> Critical areas for exploration include not only clarity around the selection process and screening procedures for admittance to the program, monitoring participants in a meaningful and effective way post-release, and developing meaningful and valid (i.e., empirical) indicators for reduced risk of re-engagement: in sum, there is an urgent need for reliable risk assessment procedures for use with a terrorist population.
>
> (281)

The Saudi government has also lacked valid and reliable deradicalization measures:

> Perhaps the most critical development regards Saudi efforts to assess the progress of each beneficiary throughout the program, one of the central weaknesses of deradicalization efforts underway worldwide. Saudi officials previously relied heavily on trust to overcome this problem—trust in the detainee being rehabilitated, trust in the family taking responsibility for his actions, and trust in the country's security apparatus to monitor his activities after release. The Saudis have recently tried to address inherent weaknesses of this approach through a system that aims to continuously evaluate every detainee in a rigorous, multi-dimensional fashion. This includes monitoring in and out of the center, ongoing documented evaluations, and regular assessments by staff members. Though still imperfect, subjective, and reliant on post-release security efforts, these processes suggest potential new tools to evaluate the threat posed by terrorists in custody.
>
> (Porges 2010)

Horgan, Braddock, and Porges call for pre- and post-program evaluations, with Porges commenting on the role of family members as counter-law to provide clinical evidence through interviews. In this regard, Kruglanski, Gelfand, and Gunaratna (2010) describe a notable attempt to classify and quantify deradicalization in the Philippines with a control and experimental group of detainees through the development of a quantitative assessment scale:

> Our battery of tests is a multidimensional instrument designed to include both cognitive (corresponding to the "minds") and affective/motivational (corresponding to the "hearts") components of the process. Sub-scales comprising the cognitive component include attitudes toward numerous Islamic notions, including *Jihad* (struggle), *Takfir* (blasphemy), *Hakimiyyah* (sovereignty of God's rule on earth), and *Shahada* (martyrdom), concepts that have a very different, non-violent, meaning for the vast majority of practicing Muslims than their interpretation by extremists. The cognitive component will also assess condonement of the extremists' ends, such as establishment of the Islamic State or revival of the Caliphate.
>
> (2010, 2)

This assessment exemplifies major components of deradicalization programs in the War on Terror. The political rhetoric of the War on Terror ("hearts and minds") suffuses the creation of a scientific measure. Researchers have generated theories about crime and criminality of the offender through a blend of secular psychological and religious/theological concepts. A corrective intervention can be delivered to the soul and measured through "cognitive" and "affective" subscales. However, the cultural psychiatrist who reads this scale's description raises questions about its conceptual validity. The ethnographic record indicates that an embrace of Islamism does not necessarily correspond to an inclination toward political violence. For example, the Muslim Brotherhood as an Islamist movement has consistently supported democracy in Jordan (Robinson 1997). In Egypt, the Muslim Brotherhood has championed central tenets of liberal government such as limiting state power, demanding governmental accountability, and protecting certain civil rights (Rutherford 2006). In Saudi Arabia, a coalition of Islamists, liberals, Sunnis, and Shiites has struggled to advance democracy within an Islamic framework by reinterpreting state-sanctioned Wahhabi doctrines (Lacroix 2004). The ruling Justice and Development Party in Turkey openly espouses Islamic beliefs within a democratic framework and has labeled itself a conservative democratic movement (Sambur 2009). These examples prove that belief in Islamist concepts such as jihad and *hakimmiyah* can create a space for liberal political agendas.

The Application of Clinical Reasoning to Evaluate Deradicalization

After conducting clinical interviews and psychological assessments, health professionals display cultural forms of rationality in drawing conclusions on deradicalization from clinical evidence. Deradicalization programs tend to invest religious professionals with this function under the supervision of health professionals. Corrective discipline emerges by framing deradicalization as the acceptance of nonviolent interpretations of Islam administered by religious authorities. For example, the government of Yemen created the Committee for Dialogue in 2002 to counter Islamists who returned home after the Soviet Union's defeat in Afghanistan (Taarnby 2005). Islamists have been preventively detained for a peaceful exchange of views with religious scholars based on the Quran and Hadith and are not released until they exhibit peaceful theological interpretations in "dialogues" with religious experts (Boucek, Beg, and Horgan 2009; Taarnby 2005). The type of clinical reasoning pertains entirely to religious beliefs:

> One issue that has been invoked time and again by Al-Hittar [the head of the committee] is the fact that the Quran contains 124 verses that speci-fies that non-Muslims must be treated with charity and dignity—but only one verse that urges Muslims to fight nonbelievers. In this context, the mili-tants are invited to use the Holy Scriptures to legitimise attacks on civil-ians, which they cannot. Two issues have been central in the discussions. The notion that non-Muslims are legitimate targets in the name of jihad and that Yemen's political system is un-Islamic.
>
> (Taarnby 2005, 133)

Yemen's Committee for Dialogue exhibits specific forms of clinical rea-soning. The principle of "abrogation" from the Quranic commentarial tra-dition is mobilized to disqualify the "one verse that urges Muslims to fight nonbelievers." Abrogation refers to "the exegetical conviction that some verses of the Qu'ran restrict, modify, or even nullify other verses" (McAu-liffe 2006, 187).[4] Whereas attacks on non-Muslims may find scriptural precedents, Yemen's political system is a modern phenomenon not men-tioned in the Quran. Therefore, Yemen has mixed allegiance to the state with the propagation of a peaceful strain of Islam, a unique cultural under-standing of the nexus between religion and politics.

Saudi Arabia also upholds active religious rehabilitation. Those eligible for deradicalization have been terrorist sympathizers or those caught with militant propaganda, not those actually conducting violence (Boucek 2009). The Ministry of the Interior has convened four committees, with the largest being the Religious Committee, consisting of 150 independent scholars selected for their communication skills (Boucek 2008a). The gov-ernment has relied heavily on the text *Document for Guiding Jihad in Egypt and in the World* from former Islamist Sayyid Imam al-Sharif (Noricks 2009). The text permits jihad only after certain prior goals have been met: adequate sanctuary and financial resources, non-involvement of civilians, clearly identifying an enemy, approval from parents, providing for fami-lies, and permission from religious scholars (Wright 2008). Theological discussions, not one-sided lectures, provide the format for classes lasting six weeks, and "regular psychological and sociological testing and other evaluation methods, helps reduce the number of opportunistic or insincere revisions" (Boucek 2008a, 61). Testing in consultation with psychologists follows a predetermined syllabus:

> The Advisory Committee runs two programmes. The first are short sessions, which typically run about two hours. While some prisoners recant their beliefs after a single session, typically a prisoner would go through several of these. These sessions are most commonly used with individuals who are looking for a way out, and their success should be considered atypical. The others are called "Long Study Sessions." These are six-week courses for up to twenty students led by two clerics and a social scientist. Ten subjects are covered over the six weeks, including instruction in such topics as *takfir, walaah* (loyalty) and *bayat* (allegiance), terrorism, the legal rules for jihad and psychological courses on self-esteem. Instruction is also given on the concepts of "faith, leadership, and community," as well as guidance on how to "avoid misleading, delusional books." ... At the end of the course, an exam is given; those that pass the exam move to the next stage of the process (including possible release), those that do not pass, repeat the course.
>
> (Boucek 2008a, 62–63)

Similar to Yemen's dialogue on religion, Saudi Arabia's deradicalization program displays culturally specific forms of clinical reasoning. Political subjects on "loyalty," "allegiance," and "terrorism" are taught alongside Islamic jurisprudence on jihad and a type of Islamic self-help focused on "self-esteem" and "leadership." Two clerics and a social scientist, typically a psychologist, run the course in a symbolic act that seeks to transform individuals throughout religious and secular dimensions of existence.

Indonesia, Singapore, and Malaysia have subsequently initiated religious rehabilitation modeled on Yemen's program to confront Islamists from Jemaah Islamiyah (JI), which is committed to converting Southeast Asia into an Islamic state. Only the programs of Indonesia and Singapore will be reviewed, since the Malaysian program operates in extreme secrecy (Abuza 2009). From what is known, Indonesia's program has used reformed JI leaders in dialogues with Islamists, but despite government claims of deradicalization, the lack of a parole system hampers verifiable accounts of recidivism (Abuza 2009). Singapore has used forty religious leaders in conjunction with psychologists to counsel detained Islamists and their wives, but the government acknowledges that the detainees mostly played logistical and support roles and did not engage in violence (Abuza 2009). A key work in both countries has been *Unlicensed to Kill: Countering Imam Samudra's Justification for the Bali Bombing* (Hassan 2007). Through ample quotations from the Quran and Quranic scholars, the book refutes arguments for engaging in jihad through violence, warfare with non-Muslims, Islamist conspiracy theories about Western countries, killing civilians, and suicide operations (Hassan 2006).[5]

The syllabi in Indonesia and Singapore do not seem to be public, though the Singapore government has set up a website (www.rrg.sg) on the activities of its Religious Rehabilitation Group (RRG). In the link under "Our Message," the RRG explains its counterterrorist mission: "Our main concern, and specific to the RRG's role, is in the area of ideological response. This is due to the use of misunderstood Islamic concepts by the terrorists to promote their cause. This is an uphill task, but we believe ideological response is a necessary strategy" (Religious Rehabilitation Group 2012a). A point-by-point refutation of major JI interpretation then follows. Under a rhetorical question "Is jihad a holy war?" the website responds: "There is no concept of Holy War in Islam. Linguistically, HOLY WAR translated means HARB MUQADDASAH which is neither found in the Quran and the Sunnah. War is never considered holy in Islam, it is described as instinctively hated by man [original emphases]" (Religious Rehabilitation Group 2012a). Instead, a counterdefinition of "jihad" "concerned with our time and space today" is offered in distinct categories: "against the inner self," "against the Devil," "towards economic development," "towards educational development," "towards family development," and "correct Islamic propagation" (Religious Rehabilitation Group 2012a). Elsewhere, the RRG insists that terrorism violates "two fundamental prohibitions": (1) "Firstly, violence is not a legitimate means of solving political disputes particularly when the actors are non-state actors," and (2) "The second norm essential to delegitimize the strategy of terrorism is the belief that non-combatants are entitled to immunity and should not be subject to attack" (Religious Rehabilitation Group 2012b). Here, the RRG insists that states alone should possess the authority to wield violence and that noncombatants should be protected from violence.

In all four programs, we observe common dynamics. Deradicalization programs detain militants not only to deprive them of liberty, but to also inculcate corrective reform. Rehabilitation programs take place in institutions sequestered from society through constant and absolute observation from prison officials, religious clergy, mental health professionals, and other personnel. This technical transformation of individuals attempts to instill discipline and self-governance to render citizens obedient to the state. In each program, religious reform prevails over secular psychological rehabilitation. This religious reform model supplies psychological and legal rationalities to understand jihad and reverse deradicalization.

The Legal Outcomes Associated with Deradicalization

The legal system utilizes the opinions from health professionals to render an ultimate decision for a suspect in question. In the case of deradicalization programs, legal outcomes are associated with high rates of recidivism. The governments of Afghanistan (Sieff 2011), Indonesia (Antara News 2009), and Saudi Arabia (Manthorpe 2010) have acknowledged obstacles to deradicalization. Estimates of recidivism range from 10 percent to 20 percent in Saudi Arabia (Porges 2010), to 40 percent in Singapore (Abuza 2009) and over 50 percent in Yemen (Noricks 2009). Analysts (Abuza 2009; Boucek 2009; Boucek, Beg, and Horgan 2009; Taarnby 2005) have conceded that the totalitarian nature of deradicalization programs has created a paradox for governments: militants know that governments will not release them without a demonstration of reformed beliefs, so many can answer falsely. Therein lies a moral hazard.

Here, a theoretical engagement with Foucault may help us understand why recidivism happens in some contexts and not in others. Foucault writes that prisons were "the great failure of penal justice" whose errors "are today repeated almost unchanged" from their origins in the nineteenth century (1995, 264–265). He specifies the following reasons (264–268): (1) detention causes recidivism; (2) detention imposes an existence of isolation and useless work on inmates, which renders them unable to find meaningful employment; (3) prisons encourage the assembly of delinquents loyal to one another who commit future criminal acts together; (4) freed inmates are compelled toward recidivism since they cannot find work and they lead vagabond lives; and (5) prisons encourage delinquency by placing the family of inmates in destitution.

These assertions do not match the conditions of deradicalization programs. Studies routinely show that most Islamist militants come from middle-class backgrounds (Jackson 2007). While detentions may cause recidivism by aggregating like-minded individuals who have not renounced violence, Foucault's other points do not apply. For instance, Indonesia, the Philippines, and Saudi Arabia provide detainees with vocational training to help them garner employment, not to keep them unemployed. This explicitly occupational emphasis is meant to counter problems in finding work. In addition, all programs strive to establish social links with detainees so that they do not lead vagabond lives: the governments of Indonesia and the Philippines encourage family involvement through visits from relatives, Singaporean officials counsel wives of Islamists, and the Saudi Arabian government has tried marital matchmaking. Finally, Indonesia, the Philippines, and Saudi Arabia lavish financial resources on families of militants in order to counter delinquency.

Instead, other factors may explain recidivism. I believe that the major emphasis on religious rehabilitation may obfuscate the state's true aim of deterring political violence. Government officials, media commentators, and academics in the War on Terror may overstate the importance of religious beliefs among militant Islamists. Experts in the War on Terror who posit a liberal, peace-loving West under attack from violent Muslims do not account for the political and economic motives of violence and explain it through religious terms, further perpetuating stereotypes (Mamdani 2005). Violent rhetoric justified through religion is not unimportant, but may be secondary in a larger strategic goal to engage in violence for well-defined political ends (Jackson 2007). For example, Islamist groups in the Middle East—Hamas, Hezbollah, or al-Qaeda—profit from using religious vocabularies, but their leaders are often secular professionals fighting to end the foreign occupation of homelands or the political corruption of government officials (Gunning and Jackson 2011). A close analysis of jihadist publications shows a greater concern with establishing the conditions for asymmetrical warfare against governments rather than reminding others of theological rewards (Sedgwick 2004).

These critical clarifications on the relationship between religion and violence can help us question forms of knowledge and practice in deradicalization programs. All of the deradicalization programs reviewed include religious rehabilitation as a central practice. However, targeting religious beliefs may only serve as a proxy for more precisely targeting violent thoughts and behaviors. Lengthy descriptions abound about the type, format, and content of religious rehabilitation sessions, and Yemen and Saudi Arabia are praised for open dialogues with militants. And yet lectures on law and government appear to reinforce loyalty to the state and dissuade sedition. The lack of a mechanism in which militant militants can freely discuss motivations for violence such as disagreements with domestic or foreign policies may account for the limited success of deradicalization programs. Yemeni and Saudi Arabian programs seem willing to let militants draw their own conclusions about religious violence after debates with clerics, but less willing to entertain dissidence in policy and political matters. To initiate such a process could require more transparency and liberty than many governments with deradicalization programs currently permit.

Furthermore, the actual processes of deradicalization programs can be productively questioned. For example, the programs appear to target different populations. Yemen has detained suspected militants who traveled abroad but did not commit domestic crimes. Saudi Arabia and Singapore have detained militant sympathizers in support or logistics roles domestically, but not those who have actually conducted violence. Singapore, Indonesia, and Malaysia have modeled their programs on Yemeni programs despite clear differences in the enrolled populations. Singapore, Indonesia, and Malaysia have begun deradicalization programs to counter actual threats, whereas Yemen's program has been primarily preventive. *Supersidiary authorities* sponsor the dissemination and implementation of deradicalization "best practices" without demonstrations of actual efficacy, so recidivism can be predicted. In contrast, meticulous research is needed to distinguish effective core components of deradicalization programs. Specifically, greater precision is required to ascertain whether programs should be preventive for those who have not yet committed crimes or curative for known offenders.

Second, more direct measurements of violence are required to lower recidivism. Procedures that distinguish among thoughts and actions leading to violence could provide more accurate assessments than programming that assumes a high correlation among religious beliefs and risk of violence. Longitudinal research can then clarify correlations throughout the process of change as well as post-program follow-up periods. Religious rehabilitation may be insufficient to stem recidivism, since more-primary political and economic concerns have not been foundationally addressed. What does success mean when programs are administered to people who hold Islamist beliefs but who have not actually committed any violent acts? How can success be measured if assessments that test religious beliefs can be manipulated for release? Deradicalization assessments may become more accurate by focusing on violent thoughts and actions. Definitions of success and failure cannot be generalized if initial indications and end outcomes of deradicalization programs differ across countries. Perhaps the role of forensic mental health lies in a position between Welner and Xenakis: mental health can proffer a knowledge base to understand deradicalization as a criminological process, but should not be used for political purposes.

Finally, a critical stance from cultural psychiatry and psychiatric anthropology can pose new questions for research. Which components of deradicalization programs embody local knowledge and practice and which components can be applied across cultures? How do such programs reflect implicit, unspoken norms about politics, religion, and society, as with state allegiance programs for Yemen and Saudi Arabia enveloped within religious instruction? How do these programs create new ways of being, feeling, and experiencing in the world for militants, their families, and supervising government officials? How do these programs produce new cultural materials such as pedagogical texts and policy documents, as well as novel institutions that reconfigure kinship, community, and social relations? Ethnographic accounts could supplement this discourses analysis by describing the daily lives of militants, government officials, academics, and other actors to understand their diverse modes of being and meaning making. Additional analyses could review texts produced in the languages of countries hosting deradicalization programs—such as Arabic, Persian, Urdu, Indonesian, and Malay—to trace the extent to which these ideas travel and are influenced by developments in the United States and Western Europe. Critical analyses of deradicalization symbolize the possibilities of engaged criticism by destabilizing the assumptions, institutions, knowledge, practices, and outcomes entrenched throughout the global War on Terror to scrutinize their local contexts.

THE WAR ON TERROR HAS entered its second decade, with no end in sight.
I have attempted to demonstrate that the war has changed the culture of
mental health, and vice versa. I have employed three themes from medical
anthropology and cultural psychiatry—differences in interpretation based
on clinical roles, demonstrations of power in deciding which interpretation
is authoritative, and the use of medicine for purposes other than healing—
to establish a cultural analytical framework for the forensic functions of
medical systems, using the War on Terror as a specific case study. Government restrictions on access and information based on claims of national
security have necessarily inspired new forms of inquiry and methodology
to address the War on Terror (Goldstein 2010). Therefore, I have used discourse analysis as a method to glean recurring values, beliefs, and practices
in the War on Terror in government documents, scientific publications,
legal texts, and policy statements. Rather than affirm their scientific or legal
truths, I have treated these texts as an archive of source materials for cultural analysis.

I have arrayed this book's chapters according to how the War on Terror
has impacted medicine: the first three chapters examined how the American government has transformed mental health knowledge and practice,
whereas the last three chapters examined the responses of people responsible for such knowledge and practice. Chapter 1 used narratives on the
differential application of a diagnosis of post–traumatic stress disorder
to veterans and detainees as a window into the role of psychiatric power
in determining disability. Chapter 2 focused on medicolegal debates and

arguments to ponder how cultural values inform ethical practices in light of reinterpreted legal frameworks. Chapter 3 randomly selected cases in the military commissions system at Guantánamo to trace the process and arguments of legal teams for detainees requesting mental health evaluations. However, those responsible for creating mental health knowledge and practice are not just recipients of government dictates, but also manufacturers of new forms of culture. Chapter 4 directed attention to discrepant representations of Arabs and Muslims in the psychodynamic and psychoanalytic literatures. Chapter 5 assessed models of pathology to explain suicide bombing. Chapter 6 concentrated on the role of mental health professionals in conceptualizing, developing, and assessing the deradicalization of militant Islamists.

Discourse analysis not only discloses power-knowledge relationships within texts but also presents a method of understanding a historical *episteme*, defined as "the divergences, the distances, the oppositions, the differences" of a time period (Foucault 1991, 55). This method allows us to move beyond the idea of an independent author writing without any cultural influences so that we map the range of ideas within boundaries of intellectual domains. Assuming that an *episteme* comprises multiple discourses, we can look at *intradiscursive, interdiscursive*, and *extradiscursive* transformations to formulate hypotheses about the history of ideas. I understand *intradiscursive* as ideas within an intellectual domain, *interdiscursive* as common ideas among intellectual domains, and *extradiscursive* as external ideas influencing an intellectual domain. Each chapter has focused on intradiscursive differences by categorizing ideas within a selection of texts in that discourse. At this point, we can now speculate on interdiscursive transformations throughout the War on Terror:

1. The salience of trauma in contemporary thought: Post–traumatic stress disorder (PTSD) emerged as a new cultural form of knowledge with the return of American veterans after the Vietnam War (Young 1995). PTSD has become a symbol of meanings for detainees wishing to contest the conditions of their confinement (chapter 3) and an explanatory model for causes of suicide bombing (chapter 5). The field of trauma has expanded to include any type of knowledge that can classify the actions of others—even enemy detainees—afflicted by violence. Trauma serves as a cultural prototype to explain how events outside of the self come to influence one's psychology.

2. The management of terrorism as a military problem that necessitates new knowledge, practice, institutions, and resources rather than a problem handled through extant mechanisms of law enforcement: Because of reconfigured international laws and treaties, bioethicists have debated ethical practices among military health professionals (chapter 2), and the Office of Military Commissions has enacted new procedures for mental health evaluations (chapter 3). Mental health professionals have also contributed to counterterrorism knowledge and practice through deradicalization programs (chapter 6). The War on Terror is seen as a "state of exception" that needs unprecedented legal solutions. In bioethical debates and mental health evaluations at Guantánamo, the government has transformed mental health. However, mental health has also transformed counterterrorism policies by lending new vocabularies and concepts to deradicalization programs. Terrorism is managed as a problem at the intersection of mental health and legal cultures: why are the terrorists the way they are (mental health) and how can we dissuade or prosecute them (legal)?

3. The medicalization and racialization of violence to Arabs and Muslims: The last three chapters prove this point most forcefully. Psychodynamic models of the mind, the self, and family have been used to explain violent tendencies among Arabs and Muslims through literary styles of medical Orientalism (chapter 4). Authors on suicide bombing adopt this perspective to call for "moderate" Arab and Muslim leaders to promote nonviolence (chapter 5). Ironically, texts from al-Qaeda also exhibit East/West divisions in Orientalist fashion to issue religious justifications for suicide bombing, further perpetuating the racialization of violence (chapter 5). The notion that "faulty" or "corrupt" religious beliefs are responsible for violence then leads certain mental health professionals to propose deradicalization models based on theological reform rather than secular concepts (chapter 6). Religious reform recalls psychiatric treatments based on notions of right and wrong ("moral treatment") rather than biological understandings of pathology (Bockoven 1963; Foucault 1988, 2006; Gold 2010; Scull 1989). The medicalization and racialization of violence destabilizes boundaries between intellectual domains across such fields as "religion," "medicine," and "politics."

The themes of terror management and the medicalization and racialization of violence to Arabs and Muslims also correspond to social realities outside of texts. Since 9/11, Arab and Muslim communities in the United States and Canada have been forced to apologize for others and to express patriotism (Howell and Shryock 2003; Rousseau and Jamil 2008). Public opinion polls have shown that majorities of Americans do not understand the basic teachings and tenets of Islam, yet feel that the religion is "very different" from theirs and that the 9/11 attacks represent Islam "to a great degree" or "to some degree" (Panagopoulos 2006). Suspicions against Arabs and Muslims led to the passage of measures such as the USA PATRIOT Act to protect "an American Us" against the "dangerous immigrant Other" (Ewing 2008, 2) through surveillance, internment, imprisonment, and interrogation with vast amounts of funding for a new security regime (Ernst 2013). This idea of a "dangerous immigrant Other" conflates Arabs with Muslims in the media and in political writings without recognizing internal differences (Lawrence 2011). These themes of racializing violence to Arabs and Muslims pervade mental health texts, and the extent of this thought merits future examination in other genres of medical and psychiatric writings. These texts routinely seem to overlook that the violent actions of a few individuals cannot be generalized to an entire ethnicity or religion. Authors prefer to adopt broad sociological explanations to explain violence through ethnicity and religion rather than analyze commonalities that predispose individuals to such violence.

The literary and cultural critic Homi Bhabha writes: "We have to learn to negotiate 'incommensurable' or conflictual social and cultural difference while maintaining the 'intimacy' of our inter-cultural existence and transnational associations" (2003, 31). To what extent have mental health professionals successfully negotiated cultural differences within the intimacy of coexistence? Cultural competence initiatives in mental health arose in the late 1960s and early 1970s in conjunction with the civil rights movement, the growing population of immigrants and refugees, and a greater desire for social activism in medicine (Shaw and Armin 2011). The unintended consequences of such programs have been that medical professionals tend to reduce culture to outdated notions of race and ethnicity or to assume that people fit within broad racial and ethnic categories without exploring individual identities (Carpenter-Song, Schwallie, and Longhofer 2007; Jenks 2011). If one goal of cultural psychiatry is to continuously interrogate its bases of knowledge and practice (Kirmayer 2007), then we must acknowledge the complicit role of mental health professionals in medicalizing and racializing purported social and cultural differences. Foucault (2003) contended that "racism is inscribed as the basic mechanism of power, as it is exercised in modern States" (254) as "a way of separating the groups that exist within a population" (255). We have witnessed throughout this book that mental health professionals may willingly separate and classify populations by race even without the need for state intervention. Racialized medicine persists as the looming sinister shadow of cultural competence.

How can we change this situation? Since culture is a concept that has captivated scholars in many disciplines, a multidisciplinary approach can stem the tides of racialized medicine and medical Orientalism. Cultural psychiatrists can continue to examine representations of racial and ethnic minority groups in mental health knowledge and practice. Recent work has shown how African Americans in the 1960s were diagnosed with schizophrenia based on their sympathies with the civil rights movement (Metzl 2010) and how treatment non-adherence among Latinos is assumed to be the result of ethnic rather than socioeconomic factors (Santiago-Irizarry 2001). Globalization calls our attention to how global flows of information and capital affect local contexts (Kearney 1995); social scientists can conduct ethnographies to inspect how ideas prevalent in War on Terror discourse appear in everyday psychiatric practice and institutions around the world, as in deradicalization programs or interviews with former stakeholders at Guantánamo. In addition, newer methods in Islamic and Middle Eastern studies have attempted to move beyond Orientalism by connecting the study of texts to contemporary questions and debates (Ernst and Martin 2010), and medical discourse offers new textual sources for analysis among scholars of religion.

At the same time, we should continue to pursue cultural studies of biomedicine and the law, and especially at their intersections for those of us interested in health law, legal medicine, or forensic psychiatry. The forensic functions framework offers an interpretive method for scholars in the social sciences and humanities, the law, and mental health to pursue comparative cultural studies of mental health knowledge and practice across time and place. I favor a multidisciplinary attitude to cross-cultural analysis to incorporate scholarship in the humanities and social sciences beyond the prevailing medical paradigms of biological and clinical research. Only then can we truly, comprehensively appraise how the War on Terror has changed medicine and how medicine has changed the War on Terror.

1   The name of the institution has been changed to protect the identities of patients and employees.

2   I have changed Brian's name, dates, and family information to protect his identity. His clinical presentation and our exchange are accurately reflected.

3   The diagnostic criteria for PTSD from the fourth edition of the *Diagnostic and Statistical Manual of Mental Disorders* (*DSM-IV*) were operational at this time. Criteria for *DSM-IV* disorders are provided throughout the chapter for unfamiliar readers.

4   According to *DSM-IV-TR* criteria, alcohol abuse is defined as "a maladaptive pattern of drinking, leading to clinically significant impairment or distress, manifested by at least one of the following within a 12-month period: recurrent use of alcohol resulting in a failure to fulfill major role obligations at work, school, or home . . . ; recurrent alcohol use in situations in which it is physically hazardous . . . ; recurrent alcohol-related legal problems . . . ; continued alcohol use despite having persistent or recurrent social or interpersonal problems caused or exacerbated by the effects of alcohol." The term "rule out" indicates that not enough information exists to make a full diagnosis.

5   The American military's acceptance of PTSD contrasts with the British military's, as British soldiers have rejected psychiatric explanations for Gulf War Syndrome, linking cultural conceptions of masculinity, toughness, strength, and the "stiff upper lip" to mental health (Kilshaw 2008). Therefore, the VA system's compensation by PTSD-related disability can be seen as an American cultural phenomenon.

6   Mohamed's account is further explored in Aggarwal 2009a.

7   I develop this point extensively in chapter 3, on forensic mental health proceedings at Guantánamo.

8   This budget includes treatment for veterans of all wars, not just the War on Terror.

9   My critiques of the American military's differential use of PTSD for veterans and detainees should not be misread. I have provided direct care to veterans who have served the country honorably and meet criteria for diagnoses of PTSD. Brian clearly represents a minority among veterans. I am also not advocating for extending PTSD to all detainees in American custody. I am simply pointing out that social and cultural forces influence diagnostic meaning making.

10 Kleinman (1995) later disavowed this theory as representative of "functionalism," an outmoded research tradition in anthropology. Nonetheless, this theory has value for hypothesis testing in cultural mental health research and can serve as a starting point to analyze interrelationships among mental health, culture, and power in forensic health systems.

11 Clinical and forensic functions can occur within the same patient-clinician relationship. For example, patients who are involuntarily committed may eventually view their clinical circumstances as therapeutic. Alternatively, a clinician who does not interpret disease at the beginning of a patient's illness experiences may confirm a diagnosis after detecting symptoms.

12 Rosner (2003, 3) lists the numerous psychiatric-legal issues under consideration: *civil forensic psychiatry*: "conservators and guardianships, child custody determinations, parental competence, termination of parental rights, child abuse, child neglect, psychiatric disability determinations (e.g., for social security, workers' compensation, private insurance coverage), testamentary capacity, psychiatric negligence and malpractice, personal injury litigation issues"; *criminal forensic psychiatry*: "competence to stand trial, competence to enter a plea, testimonial capacity, voluntariness of confessions, insanity defense(s), diminished capacity, sentencing considerations, release of persons who have been acquitted by reason of insanity"; and *legal regulation of psychiatry*: "civil involuntary commitment, voluntary hospitalization, confidentiality, right to treatment, right to refuse treatment, informed consent, professional liability, ethical guidelines."

13 I have modified Kleinman 1980 and Rosen 2003 to elaborate the forensic functions model.

14 The sociology of scientific knowledge represents a formidable tradition with an extensive literature. See Collins 1995, Franklin 1995, and Shapin 1995, among others.

15 This book is overtly concerned with medicolegal issues, specifically forensic knowledge and practice for those considered enemies in the War on Terror. The clinical services of soldiers, civilians, and others of a healing nature lie outside the scope of this book.

16 Several objections could be raised to this methodology: First, I am, in effect, creating a discourse where none may exist by aggregating publications on the basis of search terms. I would counter that any qualitative researcher must decide how to delimit a discourse. By presenting the search strategies for each chapter, I allow others to evaluate the merits of my search. I reflexively call attention to the co-construction of discourse as a finite set of texts as well as an object of study. Second, I have not selected other databases. I would counter that since medical researchers use these databases the most, then they represent accurate opinions in these scientific communities.

17 I am not against these types of literature reviews and syntheses. I am merely pointing out that their goals differ from the goals of this book.

18 Critical discourse analysis (CDA) examines the processes of social change in their discursive aspects (Fairclough 2001). Fairclough (2001) lists assumptions of CDA that I accept for medical discourse analysis.

2. BIOETHICS AND THE CONDUCT OF MENTAL HEALTH PROFESSIONALS IN THE WAR ON TERROR

1 The Geneva Conventions constitute four treaties (dated 1864, 1906, 1929, and 1949) and three protocols (1977, 1977, 2005) that form the basis of international law on the humanitarian conduct of war among countries.

2 Many bioethicists have disputed these critiques. For example, the social scientists cited above have recommended that bioethicists utilize ethnography as a methodology to demonstrate the cultural bases of morality. However, ethnography has been criticized for cataloging ephemeral situations through impressionistic analyses whose results cannot be corroborated (Herrera 2008). Ethnography may also yield interesting information on bioethical conflicts, but does not actually help bioethicists resolve conflicts (Bracanovic 2011; Callahan 1999). Bioethicists have responded that universal ethical principles are needed to protect the world from groups such as the Nazis, who used cultural beliefs to justify the killing of others (Callahan 2000).

3 In accordance with protocols of systematic reviews whose rigor I seek to adopt for medical discourse analysis, I present the search strategy in full for this

chapter. Search 1: ethics OR ethical; Search 2: bioethics OR bioethical; Search 3: "Abu Ghraib" OR "War on Terror" OR Guantánamo; Search 4: (Search 1 OR Search 2) AND Search 3. The search produced 49 results on July 2, 2013.

4   Miles quotes Article 33 of the Geneva Conventions from August 12, 1949, which reads: "Although they shall be subject to the internal discipline of the camp in which they are retained, such personnel may not be compelled to carry out any work other than that concerned with their medical or religious duties."

5   The Federal Bureau of Prisons explains: "The decision to force treatment upon the inmate is a medical decision, preferably by a written physician's order, with potential legal implications. When it appears to medical staff that the inmate's condition is deteriorating to the extent that intervention may soon be required, the Regional Counsel must be notified so any legal issues may be addressed. Although legal counsel has been notified, medical staff should not suspend or delay involuntary treatment if the physician is convinced to a reasonable medical certainty that there is an immediate threat to the inmate's life, or permanent damage to the inmate's health. Regional Counsel will determine whether it is appropriate to contact the local U.S. Attorney's Office" (U.S. Department of Justice, Federal Bureau of Prisons 2005).

6   The Eighth Amendment of the U.S. Constitution: "Excessive bail shall not be required, nor excessive fines imposed, nor cruel and unusual punishments inflicted."

7   Common Article Three of the Geneva Conventions:

> In the case of armed conflict not of an international character occurring in the territory of one of the High Contracting Parties, each Party to the conflict shall be bound to apply, as a minimum, the following provisions: (1) Persons taking no active part in the hostilities, including members of armed forces who have laid down their arms and those placed 'hors de combat' by sickness, wounds, detention, or any other cause, shall in all circumstances be treated humanely, without any adverse distinction founded on race, colour, religion or faith, sex, birth or wealth, or any other similar criteria. To this end, the following acts are and shall remain prohibited at any time and in any place whatsoever with respect to the above-mentioned persons: (a) violence to life and person, in particular murder of all kinds, mutilation, cruel treatment and torture; (b) taking of hostages; (c) outrages upon personal dignity, in particular humiliating and degrading treatment; (d) the passing of sentences and the carrying out of executions without previous judgment

pronounced by a regularly constituted court, affording all the judicial guarantees which are recognized as indispensable by civilized peoples.

(2) The wounded and sick shall be collected and cared for. An impartial humanitarian body, such as the International Committee of the Red Cross, may offer its services to the Parties to the conflict. The Parties to the conflict should further endeavour to bring into force, by means of special agreements, all or part of the other provisions of the present Convention. The application of the preceding provisions shall not affect the legal status of the Parties to the conflict.

8　In a memorandum for William J. Haynes II, then General Counsel for the Department of Defense, dated January 9, 2002, Deputy Assistant Attorney General John Yoo wrote: "We conclude that these treaties do not protect members of the al Qaeda organization, which as a non-State actor cannot be a party to the international agreements governing war. We further conclude that these treaties do not apply to the Taliban militia . . . Al Qaeda is merely a violent political movement or organization and not a nation-state. As a result, it is ineligible to be a signatory to any treaty. Because of the novel nature of this conflict, moreover, we do not believe that al Qaeda would be included in noninternational forms of armed conflict to which some provisions of the Geneva Conventions might apply" (Yoo 2002).

9　From *Hamdan v. Rumsfeld*:

There is at least one provision of the Geneva Conventions that applies here even if the relevant conflict is not one between signatories. Article 3, often referred to as Common Article 3 because, like Article 2, it appears in all four Geneva Conventions, provides that in a 'conflict not of an international character occurring in the territory of one of the High Contracting Parties, each Party to the conflict shall be bound to apply, as a minimum,' certain provisions protecting '[p]ersons taking no active part in the hostilities, including members of armed forces who have laid down their arms and those placed *hors de combat* by . . . detention.' *Id.*, at 3318. One such provision prohibits 'the passing of sentences and the carrying out of executions without previous judgment pronounced by a regularly constituted court affording all the judicial guarantees which are recognized as indispensable by civilized peoples.' *Ibid.* The Court of

Appeals thought, and the Government asserts, that Common Article 3 does not apply to Hamdan because the conflict with al Qaeda, being ' "international in scope," ' does not qualify as a ' "conflict not of an international character." ' 415 F. 3d, at 41. That reasoning is erroneous. The term 'conflict not of an international character' is used here in contradistinction to a conflict between nations. So much is demonstrated by the 'fundamental logic [of] the Convention's provisions on its application.' *Id.*, at 44 (Williams, J., concurring). Common Article 2 provides that 'the present Convention shall apply to all cases of declared war or of any other armed conflict which may arise between two or more of the High Contracting Parties.' 6 U.S. T., at 3318 (Art. 2, ¶1). High Contracting Parties (signatories) also must abide by all terms of the Conventions vis-à-vis one another even if one party to the conflict is a nonsignatory 'Power,' and must so abide vis-à-vis the nonsignatory if 'the latter accepts and applies' those terms. *Ibid.* (Art. 2, ¶3). Common Article 3, by contrast, affords some minimal protection, falling short of full protection under the Conventions, to individuals associated with neither a signatory nor even a nonsignatory 'Power' who are involved in a conflict 'in the territory of' a signatory. The latter kind of conflict is distinguishable from the conflict described in Common Article 2 chiefly because it does not involve a clash between nations (whether signatories or not).

(Supreme Court of the United States 2005)

10 "As provided by the Constitution and by this section, the President has the authority for the United States to interpret the meaning and application of the Geneva Conventions and to promulgate higher standards and administrative regulations for violations of treaty obligations which are not grave breaches of the Geneva Conventions" (Military Commission Act of 2006).

11 Article 16 of Additional Protocol I on the General Protection of Medical Duties: " 1. Under no circumstances shall any person be punished for carrying out medical activities compatible with medical ethics, regardless of the person benefiting therefrom. 2. Persons engaged in medical activities shall not be compelled to perform acts or to carry out work contrary to the rules of medical ethics or to other medical rules designed for the benefit of the wounded and sick or to the provisions of the Conventions or of this Protocol, or to refrain from performing acts or from carrying out work required by

those rules and provisions. 3. No person engaged in medical activities shall be compelled to give to anyone belonging either to an adverse Party, or to his own Party except as required by the law of the latter Party, any information concerning the wounded and sick who are, or who have been, under his care, if such information would, in his opinion, prove harmful to the patients concerned or to their families. Regulations for the compulsory notification of communicable diseases shall, however, be respected" (International Committee of the Red Cross 1977).

3. THE MEANINGS OF SYMPTOMS AND SERVICES FOR GUANTÁNAMO DETAINEES

1   Although I have opted for the spelling "Guantánamo," I retain the original "Guantanamo" when present in the works of others.

2   The official title of the Walsh Report is the *Review of Department Compliance with President's Executive Order on Detainee Conditions of Confinement*.

3   President Obama also issued a signing statement in December 2013 upon signing the National Defense Authorization Act of Fiscal Year 2014: "The detention facility at Guantanamo continues to impose significant costs on the American people. I am encouraged that this Act provides the Executive greater flexibility to transfer Guantanamo detainees abroad, and look forward to working with the Congress to take the additional steps needed to close the facility. In the event that the restrictions on the transfer of Guantanamo detainees in sections 1034 and 1035 operate in a manner that violates constitutional separation of powers principles, my Administration will implement them in a manner that avoids the constitutional conflict" (White House 2013b).

4   Available at: http://www.mc.mil/CASES/MilitaryCommissions.aspx. As of this book's preparation, all of the Internet links in this chapter were current.

5   MCA 2006's exact definition: "The term "unlawful enemy combatant" means— "(i) a person who has engaged in hostilities or who has purposefully and materially supported hostilities against the United States or its co-belligerents who is not a lawful enemy combatant (including a person who is part of the Taliban, al Qaeda, or associated forces)"; or "(ii) a person who, before, on, or after the date of the enactment of the Military Commissions Act of 2006, has been determined to be an unlawful enemy combatant by a Combatant Status Review Tribunal or another competent tribunal established under the

authority of the President or the Secretary of Defense" (Military Commissions Act of 2006, 3).

6   "*Who may convene military commissions.* A military commission may be convened by the Secretary of Defense or persons occupying positions designated as a convening authority by the Secretary of Defense. The power to convene military commissions may not be delegated" (Department of Defense 2006b, 27).

7   Interestingly, RMC 706 also discriminates "bad" antisocial conduct from otherwise "mad" mental disorders as Rhodes (2000) has pointed out in her work within the American prison system.

8   This list was compiled on March 14, 2013, based on OMC's website.

9   The National Institute of Military Justice (NIMJ) expressed reservations that Kamin was declared competent to stand trial without meeting the board. The NIMJ is a nonprofit organization composed mostly of former military lawyers committed to military justice, invited by OMC for impartial observation (Aggarwal 2009a).

4. DEPICTIONS OF ARABS AND MUSLIMS IN PSYCHODYNAMIC SCHOLARSHIP

1   Psychoanalytic treatment typically requires greater length and frequency of work compared to psychodynamic treatment, though many authors use the terms interchangeably and definitions are in dispute (Jacobs 1994).

2   See Eisenberg (1986) and Lipowski (1989) for representative arguments.

3   Said also referred to East Asian populations as a part of the West's fascination with the "Orient," but I concentrate on the Middle East in this chapter.

4   These mentions occur on pages 78, 79, and 162 (Said 1994). He treats scientific Orientalism with greater depth.

5   I retain Said's terms "power political," "power intellectual," "power cultural," and "power moral" throughout the chapter.

6   I updated this search on June 18, 2013. The search produced 570 records on the first round.

7   Freud proposed the term "Oedipal complex" based on the archetype of the Greek protagonist Oedipus: "It is the fate of all of us, perhaps, to direct our first sexual impulse towards our mother and our first hatred and our first murderous wish against our father" (1965, 296).

5. DEPICTIONS OF SUICIDE BOMBERS IN THE
MENTAL HEALTH SCHOLARSHIP

1   My analysis of texts on suicide bombing from outsider (mental health professionals) and insider (al-Qaeda) perspectives resembles anthropological methods of studying etic (external) and emic (internal) approaches to language and behavior (Pike 1954).

2   Social scientists frequently group psychiatry, psychology and other mental health professions together as the "psy" disciplines, since they all study the psyche and its afflictions. Such a designation disregards the different theoretical approaches and practices employed by the different disciplines (Rose 1998).

3   Howell uses the term "racialize" to discuss how suicide bombing and martyrdom have become attributed to Muslims. Although Muslims do not constitute a "race" as much as a religion, I retain the terms "racialize" and "racialization" in dialogue with her work.

4   Mental health authors have variously used these terms based on their political views (Aggarwal 2009b, 2010b). I updated this search on June 25, 2013, which produced 307 records on the first round.

5   For example, the search excluded articles on treatments for victims of suicide attacks.

6   I recognize that authors who have trained in other disciplines could be housed in departments of psychiatry and psychology, just as psychiatrists and psychologists could be housed in other departments. Suicide bombing corresponds to what Fairclough (2001) calls a "nodal discourse," in that it covers multiple types of knowledge written by scholars in political science, international relations, and other fields. I am interested specifically in mental health representations of suicide bombers.

7   *Umma* is an Arabic word used to refer to the Muslim community.

8   The dissociative disorders in *DSM-IV* are characterized by impairments in identity, memory, awareness, and/or perception (American Psychiatric Association 2000).

9   Benedict writes: "In anthropological studies of different cultures the distinction between those which rely heavily on shame and those that rely heavily on guilt is an important one. A society that inculcates absolute standards of morality and relies on men's developing a conscience is a guilt culture by definition. . . . In a culture where shame is a major sanction, people are chagrined about acts which we expect people to feel guilty about" (2005, 222).

6. KNOWLEDGE AND PRACTICE IN WAR ON TERROR DERADICALIZATION PROGRAMS

1   For example, the search excluded publications on deradicalization in other conflicts such as programs for Sinn Fein militants during the Irish movement for independence in the 1980s and 1990s.

2   "A cognitive behavioral model is therefore concerned with the cognitive activities that surround behavioral events and seeks to determine how anticipatory, concurrent, and post hoc cognitions contribute to adaptive and maladaptive patterns of behavior" (Kendall 1985, 360). See Beck et al. (1979) for the classic exposition of cognitive behavioral therapy.

3   The War on Terror exemplifies the dark side of globalization with war now waged against internal and external enemies of the state led by the United States of America (Medovoi 2007).

4   Commentators differ over which verses can abrogate others, a contentious issue since the Quran is considered to be the word of God (McAuliffe 2006).

5   For example: "The prevalent opinion is that all verses on jihad cannot be interpreted independently of each other. They are to be studied together to derive the true understanding of jihad in Islam. In this respect, the Muslim scholars have agreed that verses which are general and unconditional must be interpreted as conditional. Thus, the meaning of verses from chapter 9, which is unconditional, would fall under the meaning of the verses; fight the non-Muslims only when they fight you" (Hassan 2006, 42).

REFERENCES

Abu-Lughod, Lila. 1989. "Zones of Theory in the Anthropology of the Arab World." *Annual Review of Anthropology* 18:267–306.

Abuza, Zachary. 2009. "The Rehabilitation of Jemaah Islamiyah Detainees in South East Asia: A Preliminary Assessment." In *Leaving Terrorism Behind: Individual and Collective Disengagement*, ed. Tore Bjørgo and John Horgan, 193–211. New York: Routledge.

Ad-Dab'bagh, Yasser. 2009. "Trauma by Proxy: A Self-Analytic Exploration of the Trials of Developing an Arab Identity." *International Journal of Applied Psychoanalytic Studies* 6 (3): 197–203.

Agamben, Giorgio. 2004. *State of Exception*. Trans. Kevin Attell. Chicago: University of Chicago Press.

Aggarwal, Neil Krishan. 2008. "Kashmiriyat as Empty Signifier." *Interventions* 10 (2): 222–235.

——. 2009a. "Allowing Independent Forensic Evaluations for Guantánamo Detainees." *Journal of the American Academy of Psychiatry and the Law* 37 (4): 533–537.

——. 2009b. "Rethinking Suicide Bombing." *Crisis* 30 (2): 94–97.

——. 2010a. "Cultural Formulations in Child and Adolescent Psychiatry." *Journal of the American Academy of Child and Adolescent Psychiatry* 49 (4): 306–309.

——. 2010b. "How Are Suicide Bombers Analysed in Mental Health Discourse? A Critical Anthropological Reading." *Asian Journal of Social Science* 38 (3): 379–393.

——. 2010c. "Reassessing Cultural Evaluations in Geriatrics: Insights from Cultural Psychiatry." *Journal of the American Geriatrics Society* 58 (11): 2191–2196.

——. 2010d. "The Uses of Psychiatry in the War on Terror." *Political and Legal Anthropology Review*, 1st ser., 33: 81–98.

———. 2011. "Medical Orientalism and the War on Terror: Depictions of Arabs and Muslims in the Psychodynamic Literature post-9/11." *Journal of Muslim Mental Health* 6 (1): 4–20.

———. 2012a. "Adapting the Cultural Formulation for Clinical Assessments in Forensic Psychiatry." *Journal of the American Academy of Psychiatry and the Law* 40 (1): 113–118.

———. 2012b. "Hybridity and Intersubjectivity in the Clinical Encounter: Impact on the Cultural Formulation." *Transcultural Psychiatry* 49 (1): 121–139.

Aggarwal, Neil Krishan, and Andres J. Pumariega. 2011. "Mental Health Services for Minor Detainees at Guantanamo." *Adolescent Psychiatry* 1 (4): 325–332.

Alexander, Ruth. 2012. "Which Is the World's Biggest Employer?" *BBC News.* March 19. Accessed May 21, 2013. http://www.bbc.co.uk/news/magazine -17429786.

AQAP (Al-Qaeda of the Arabian Peninsula). 2010a. *Inspire* 1.

———. 2010b. *Inspire* 2.

———. 2010c. *Inspire* 4.

———. 2011. *Inspire* 8.

Altman, Neil. 2008. "On Suicide Bombing." *International Journal of Applied Psychoanalytic Studies* 5 (1): 51–66.

American Academy of Psychiatry and the Law. 2005. *Ethical Guidelines for the Practice of Forensic Psychiatry.* Accessed June 10, 2013. http://www.aapl.org /pdf/ETHICSGDLNS.pdf.

American Psychiatric Association. 2000. *Diagnostic and Statistical Manual of Mental Disorders, Fourth Edition. Text Revision (DSM-IV-TR).* Arlington, Va.: American Psychiatric Association.

Annas, George J. 2006. "Hunger Strikes at Guantanamo—Medical Ethics and Human Rights in a 'Legal Black Hole.'" *New England Journal of Medicine* 355 (13): 1377–1382.

Annas, George J., Sondra S. Crosby, and Leonard H. Glantz. 2013. "Guantanamo Bay: A Medical Ethics–Free Zone?" *New England Journal of Medicine* 369 (2): 101–103.

Antara News. 2009. "News Focus: Fighting Terrorism Through Deradicalization Program Goes On." *Antara News,* September 22. Accessed 16 April 2012. http://www.antaranews.com/en/news/1253615413/news-focus-fighting -terrorism-through-deradicalization-program-goes-on.

Appadurai, Arjun. 1996. *Modernity at Large: Cultural Dimensions of Globalization.* Minneapolis: University of Minnesota Press.

Arboleda-Flórez, Julio. 2006. "Forensic Psychiatry: Contemporary Scope, Challenges, and Controversies." *World Psychiatry* 5 (2): 87–91.

Asad, Talal. 2007. *On Suicide Bombing.* New York: Columbia University Press.

Ashour, Omar. 2009a. *The Deradicalization of Jihadists: Transforming Armed Islamist Movements.* New York: Routledge.

——. 2009b. *Votes and Violence: Islamists and the Processes of Transformation.* London: International Center for the Study of Radicalisation and Political Violence.

Atlas, Galit. 2012. "Sex and the Kitchen: Thoughts on Culture and Forbidden Desire." *Psychoanalytic Perspectives* 9 (2): 220–232.

Aull, Felice, and Bradley Lewis. 2004. "Medical Intellectuals: Resisting Medical Orientalism." *Journal of Medical Humanities* 25 (2): 87–108.

Bacciagaluppi, Marco. 2004. "Violence: Innate or Acquired? A Survey and Some Opinions." *Journal of the American Academy of Psychoanalysis and Dynamic Psychiatry* 32 (3): 469–481.

Baer, Hans A., Merrill Singer, and John H. Johnsen. 1986. "Toward a Critical Medical Anthropology." *Social Science and Medicine* 23 (2): 95–98.

Baer, Hans A., Merrill Singer, and Ida Susser. 2003. *Medical Anthropology and the World System.* Westport, Conn.: Praeger.

Barker, Martin. 2008. "Analysing Discourse." In *Research Methods for Cultural Studies*, ed. Michael Pickering, 150–172. Edinburgh: Edinburgh University Press.

Başoğlu, Metin, Maria Livanou, and Cvetana Crnobarić. 2007. "Torture vs. Other Cruel, Inhuman, and Degrading Treatment: Is the Distinction Real or Apparent?" *Archives of General Psychiatry* 64 (3): 277–285.

Beauchamp, Tom L. 1995. "Principlism and Its Alleged Competitors." *Kennedy Institute of Ethics Journal* 5 (3): 181–198.

Beauchamp, Tom L., and James F. Childress. 2001. *Principles of Biomedical Ethics.* 5th ed. Oxford: Oxford University Press.

Beck, Aaron T., John Rush, Brian F. Shaw, and Gary Emery. 1979. *Cognitive Therapy of Depression.* New York: Guilford Press.

Bender, Bryan, and Farah Stockman. 2008. "Five Try to Plead Guilty in 9/11 Attacks." *Boston Globe,* December 9.

Benedict, Ruth. 2005. *The Chrysanthemum and the Sword: Patterns of Japanese Culture.* New York: First Mariner Books.

Benjamin, Jessica. 2002. "Terror and Guilt: Beyond Them and Us." *Psychoanalytic Dialogues* 12 (3): 473–484.

Bennet, James. 2005. "Blowing Up in the West." *New York Times*, July 17.

Bergmann, Martin S. 1995. "The Jewish and German Roots of Psychoanalysis and the Impact of the Holocaust." *American Imago* 52 (3): 243–259.

Bhabha, Homi. 2003. Democracy De-realized. *Diogenes* 50 (1): 27–35.

——. 2006. *The Location of Culture*. New York: Routledge Classics.

Bhugra, D., and K. Bhui. 1999. "Racism in Psychiatry: Paradigm Lost—Paradigm Regained. *International Review of Psychiatry* 11:236–243.

Bhui, Kamaldeep, and Yasmin Ibrahim. 2013. "Marketing the 'Radical': Symbolic Communication and Persuasive Technologies in Jihadist Websites." *Transcultural Psychiatry* 50 (2): 216–234.

Bibeau, Gilles. 1997. "Cultural Psychiatry in a Creolizing World: Questions for a New Research Agenda." *Transcultural Psychiatry* 34 (1): 9–41.

Bloche, M. Gregg. 2004. "Physician, Turn Thyself In." *New York Times*, June 10.

Bloche, M. Gregg, and Jonathan H. Marks. 2005. "Doctors and Interrogators at Guantanamo Bay." *New England Journal of Medicine* 353 (1): 6–8.

Bockoven, J. Sanbourne. 1963. *Moral Treatment in American Psychiatry*. Oxford: Springer Books.

Bosk, Charles L. 1999. "Professional Ethicist Available: Logical, Secular, Friendly." *Daedalus* 128 (4): 47–68.

Boucek, Christopher. 2008a. "Counter-terrorism from Within: Assessing Saudi Arabia's Religious Rehabilitation and Disengagement Programme." *RUSI Journal* 153 (6): 60–65.

——. 2008b. "Losing on the Battlefield of the Mind." nytimes.com, 4 November. Accessed 31 October 2012. http://www.nytimes.com/2008/12/04/opinion/04iht-edboucek.1.18403942.html.

——. 2009. "Extremist Re-education and Rehabilitation in Saudi Arabia." In *Leaving Terrorism Behind: Individual and Collective Disengagement*, ed. Tore Bjørgo and John Horgan, 212–223. New York: Routledge.

Boucek, Christopher, Shazadi Beg, and John Horgan. 2009. "Opening Up the Jihadi Debate: Yemen's Committee for Dialogue." In *Leaving Terrorism Behind: Individual and Collective Disengagement*, ed. Tore Bjørgo and John Horgan, 181–192. New York: Routledge.

Bracanovic, Tomislav. 2011. "Respect for Cultural Diversity in Bioethics: Empirical, Conceptual, and Normative Constraints." *Medicine, Health Care, and Philosophy* 14 (3): 229–236.

Brenner, Ira. 2009. "The Palestinian/Israeli Conflict: A Geopolitical Identity Disorder." *American Journal of Psychoanalysis* 69 (1): 62–71.

Brenner, Suzanne. 1996. "Reconstructing Self and Society: Javanese Muslim Women and 'the Veil.'" *American Ethnologist* 23 (4): 673–697.

Brown, Phil. 1993. "Psychiatric Intake as a Mystery Story." *Culture, Medicine, and Psychiatry* 17 (2): 225–280.

Brunner, Jose. 1991. "The (Ir)Relevance of Freud's Jewish Identity to the Origins of Psychoanalysis." *Psychoanalysis and Contemporary Thought* 14 (4): 655–684.

Bush, George W. 2005. "Transcript: President Bush's Speech on the War on Terrorism." washingtonpost.com, 30 November. Accessed 2 May 2012. http://www.washingtonpost.com/wp-dyn/content/article/2005/11/30/AR2005113000667.html.

——. 2010. *Decision Points*. New York: Crown Publishing Group.

Butler, Judith. 2004. *Precarious Life: The Powers of Mourning and Violence*. New York: Verso.

Callahan, Daniel. 1999. "The Social Sciences and the Task of Bioethics." *Daedalus* 128 (4): 275–294.

——. 2000. "Universalism and Particularism: Fighting to a Draw." *Hastings Center Report* 30 (1): 37–44.

——. 2003. "Principlism and Communitarianism." *Journal of Medical Ethics* 29 (5): 287–291.

——. 2005. "Bioethics and the Culture Wars." *Cambridge Quarterly of Healthcare Ethics* 14 (4): 424–431.

Carpenter-Song, Elizabeth, Megan Nordquest Schwallie, and Jeffrey Longhofer. 2007. "Cultural Competence Reexamined: Critique and Directions for the Future." *Psychiatric Services* 58 (10): 1362–1365.

Casoni, Dianne, and Louis Brunet. 2007. "The Psychodynamics that Lead to Violence. Part 1: The Case of the Chronically Violent Delinquent." *Canadian Journal of Psychoanalysis* 15 (1): 41–55.

Cassimatis, Emmanuel G. 2002. "Terrorism, Our World, and Our Way of Life." *Journal of American Academy of Psychoanalysis* 30 (4): 531–543.

Charon, Rita. 2007. "What to Do with Stories: The Sciences of Narrative Medicine." *Canadian Family Physician* 53 (8): 1265–1267.

Cheney, Richard B. 2011. *In My Time: A Personal and Political Memoir*. New York: Threshold Editions.

Ciccone, J. Richard, and Stefano Ferracuti. 1995. "Comparative Forensic Psychiatry: I. Commentary on the Italian System." *Journal of the American Academy of Psychiatry and the Law* 23 (3): 449–452.

Clouser, K. Danner. 1974. "What Is Medical Ethics?" *Annals of Internal Medicine* 80 (5): 657–660.

Clouser, K. Danner, and Bernard Gert. 1990. "A Critique of Principlism." *Journal of Medicine and Philosophy* 15 (2): 219–236.

Cohler, Bertram J. 1992. "Intent and Meaning in Psychoanalysis and Cultural Study." In *New Directions in Psychological Anthropology*, ed. Theodore Schwartz, Geoffrey M. White, and Catherine A. Lutz, 269–293. Cambridge: Cambridge University Press.

Collins, H. M. 1995. "The Sociology of Scientific Knowledge." *Annual Review of Sociology* 9:265–285.

Commission on Wartime Contracting in Iraq and Afghanistan. 2011. "Transforming Wartime Contracting: Controlling Costs, Reducing Risks." Accessed May 22, 2013. http://cybercemetery.unt.edu/archive/cwc/20110929213815/ http://www.wartimecontracting.gov/.

Congressional Budget Office. 2012. *The Veterans Health Administration's Treatment of PTSD and Traumatic Brain Injury Among Recent Combat Veterans.* Washington, D.C.: Congress of the United States.

Conrad, Peter. 1992. "Medicalization and Social Control." *Annual Review of Sociology* 18:209–232.

Contenta, Sandra. 2004. "U.S. Doctors Tied to Prisoner Abuse." *Toronto Star*, August 20.

Crapanzano, Vincent. 1992. "Hermeneutics and Psychoanalytic Anthropology." In *New Directions in Psychological Anthropology*, ed. Theodore Schwartz, Geoffrey M. White, and Catherine A. Lutz, 294–308. Cambridge: Cambridge University Press.

Crocq, Marc-Antoine, and Louis Crocq. 2000. "From Shell Shock and War Neurosis to Posttraumatic Stress Disorder: A History of Psychotraumatology." *Dialogues in Clinical Neuroscience* 2 (1): 47–55.

Davar, Elisha. 2002. "Whose History?" *Organizational and Social Dynamics* 2 (2): 231–244.

Davids, M. Fakhry. 2006. "Internal Racism, Anxiety, and the World Outside: Islamophobia Post-9/11." *Organisational and Social Dynamics* 6 (1): 63–85.

——. 2009. "The Impact of Islamophobia." *Psychoanalysis and History* 11 (2): 175–191.

Davies, James. 2009. *The Making of Psychotherapists: An Anthropological Analysis.* London: Karnac Books.

Davis, Elizabeth Anne. 2010. "The Antisocial Profile: Deception and Intimacy in Greek Psychiatry." *Cultural Anthropology* 25 (1): 130–164.

Davis, Richard B. 1995. "The Principlism Debate: A Critical Overview." *Journal of Medicine and Philosophy* 20 (1): 85–105.

Degrazia, David. 1992. "Moving Forward in Bioethical Theory: Theories, Cases, and Specified Principlism." *Journal of Medicine and Philosophy* 17 (5): 511–539.

Denbeaux, Mark, Joshua Denbeaux, and David Gratz. 2006. *Report on Guantanamo Detainees: A Profile of 517 Detainees Through Analysis of Department of Defense Data.* Seton Hall University School of Law Center for Policy and Research Paper No. 46.

Department of Defense. 2006a. *H.R. 2647-385. Title XVIII—Military Commissions.* Accessed January 8, 2013. http://www.defense.gov/news/2009%20 MCA%20Pub%20%20Law%20111-84.pdf.

——. 2006b. *Part II: Rules for Military Commissions.* Accessed January 26, 2009. http://www.defenselink.mil/pubs/pdfs/Part%20II%20-%20RMCs%20 (FINAL).pdf.

——. 2009a. *Review of Department Compliance with President's Executive Order on Detainee Conditions of Confinement* (The Walsh Report). Accessed June 1, 2009. http://www.defenselink.mil/pubs/pdfs/review_of_department _compliance_with_presidents_executive_order_on_detainee_conditions_of _confinementa.pdf.

——. 2009b. *H.R. 2647-385. Title XVIII—Military Commissions.* Accessed April 24, 2014. http://www.mc.mil/Portals/o/MCA20Pub20Law20092o.pdf.

Devereux, George. 1956. "Normal and Abnormal: The Key Problems of Psychiatric Anthropology." In *Some Uses of Anthropology: Theoretical and Applied,* ed. J. B. Casagrande and T. Gladwin, 23–48. Washington, D.C.: Anthropological Society of Washington.

D'Orbán, P. T. 1988. "History of Psychiatry: Forensic Aspects." *Current Opinion in Psychiatry* 1 (5): 609–613.

Eisenberg, Leon. 1977. "Disease and Illness: Distinctions Between Professional and Popular Ideas of Sickness." *Culture, Medicine, and Psychiatry* 1 (1): 9–23.

——. 1986. "Mindlessness and Brainlessness in Psychiatry." *British Journal of Psychiatry* 148:497–508.

El Akkad, Omar. 2008. "Alleged 9/11 Plotters Offer Guilty Pleas; Surprise Tactic Opens Legal Question of Whether U.S. Government Now Prevented from Seeking Death Sentence." *Globe and Mail,* December 9.

Enckell, Mikael. 1988. "Psychoanalysis and the Jewish Tradition." *Scandinavian Psychoanalytic Review* 11 (2): 141–159.

Engstrom, Eric J. 2009. "History of Forensic Psychiatry." *Current Opinion in Psychiatry* 22 (6): 576–581.

Ernst, Carl W. 2013. "Introduction: The Problem of Islamophobia." In *Islamophobia in America: The Anatomy of Intolerance*, ed. Carl W. Ernst, 1–20. New York: Palgrave Macmillan.

Ernst, Carl W., and Richard C. Martin. 2010. "Introduction: Toward a Post-Orientalist Approach to Islamic Religious Studies." In *Rethinking Islamic Studies: From Orientalism to Cosmopolitanism*, ed. Carl W. Ernst and Richard C. Martin, 1–19. Columbia: University of South Carolina Press.

Estroff, Sue E. 1991. "Everybody's Got a Little Mental Illness: Accounts of Illness and Self Among People with Severe, Persistent Mental Illnesses." *Medical Anthropology Quarterly* 5 (4): 331–369.

Ewing, Katherine P. 1992. "Is Psychoanalysis Relevant for Anthropology?" In *New Directions in Psychological Anthropology*, ed. Theodore Schwartz, Geoffrey M. White, and Catherine A. Lutz, 251–268. Cambridge: Cambridge University Press.

——. 2008. Introduction to *Being and Belonging: Muslims in the United States Since 9/11*, ed. Katherine Pratt Ewing, 1–11. New York: Russell Sage Foundation.

Fabrega Jr., Horacio. 1989a. "Cultural Relativism and Psychiatric Illness." *Journal of Nervous and Mental Disease* 177 (7): 415–425.

——. 1989b. "An Ethnomedical Perspective of Anglo-American Psychiatry." *American Journal of Psychiatry* 146 (5): 588–596.

Fairclough, Norman. 2001. "Critical Discourse Analysis." In *How to Analyze Talk in Institutional Settings*, ed. Alec McHoul and Mark Rapley, 25–38. New York: Continuum.

——. 2003. *Analysing Discourse: Textual Analysis for Social Research*. New York: Routledge.

Falagas, Matthew E., Eleni I. Pitsouni, George A. Malietzis, and Georgios Pappas. 2008. "Comparison of PubMed, Scopus, Web of Science, and Google Scholar: Strengths and Weaknesses." *FASEB Journal* 22:338–342.

Fassin, Didier. 2011. "The Trace: Violence, Truth, and the Politics of the Body." *Social Research* 78 (2): 281–298.

Fassin, Didier, and Estelle d'Halluin. 2005. "The Truth from the Body: Medical Certificates as Ultimate Evidence for Asylum Seekers." *American Anthropologist* 107 (4): 597–608.

Fassin, Didier, and Richard Rechtman. 2009. *The Empire of Trauma: An Inquiry Into the Condition of Victimhood*. Princeton, N.J.: Princeton University Press.

Fayek, Ahmed. 2007. "The Impasse Between the Islamists and the West: Dreaming the Same Nightmare." *Annual of Psychoanalysis* 35:273–286.

Fifield, Adam. 2006. "Policy Over Military Interrogations Divides Psychologists." *Philadelphia Inquirer*, August 10.

Finn, Peter. 2008a. "Five 9/11 Suspects Offer to Confess; But Proposal Is Pulled Over Death Penalty Issue." *Washington Post*, December 9.

——. 2008b. "Judge Lets 9/11 Defendants Urge Detainee to Appear." *Washington Post*, September 23.

Finn, Peter, and Anne E. Kornblut. 2011. "Guantanamo Bay: Why Obama Hasn't Fulfilled His Promise to Close the Facility." *Washington Post*, April 23.

Foucault, Michel. 1982. "The Subject and Power." *Critical Inquiry* 8 (4): 777–795.

——. 1988. *Madness and Civilization: A History of Insanity in the Age of Reason.* New York: Vintage Books.

——. 1991. "Politics and the Study of Discourse." In *The Foucault Effect: Studies in Governmentality*, ed. Graham Burchell, Colin Gordon, and Peter Miller, 53–72. Chicago: University of Chicago Press.

——. 1994. *The Birth of the Clinic: An Archaeology of Medical Perception.* New York: Vintage Books.

——. 1995. *Discipline and Punish.* Trans. A. Sheridan. New York: Vintage Books.

——. 2003. *Society Must Be Defended: Lectures at the Collège de France, 1975–1976.* Trans. David Macey. New York: Picador.

——. 2006. *Psychiatric Power: Lectures at the Collège de France, 1973–1974.* New York: Picador.

Fox, Renée C. 1990. "The Evolution of American Bioethics: A Sociological Perspective." In *Social Science Perspective on Medical Ethics,* ed. G. Weisz, 201–217. Philadelphia: University of Pennsylvania Press.

Fox, Renée C., and Judith P. Swazey. 2005. "Examining American Bioethics: Its Problems and Prospects." *Cambridge Quarterly of Healthcare Ethics* 14 (4): 361–373.

——. 2010. "Guest Editorial: Ignoring the Social and Cultural Context of Bioethics is Unacceptable." *Cambridge Quarterly of Healthcare Ethics* 19 (3): 278–281.

FoxNews. 2009. "Canadian Mosque Sets Up 'Detox' Program for Would-be Terrorists." foxnews.com, February 26. Accessed October 31, 2012. http://www.foxnews.com/story/0,2933,500764,00.html.

Franklin, Sarah. 1995. "Science as Culture, Cultures of Science." *Annual Review of Anthropology* 24:163–184.

Freeman, Thomas, Melissa Powell, and Tim Kimbrell. 2008. "Measuring Symptom Exaggeration in Veterans with Chronic Posttraumatic Stress Disorder." *Psychiatry Research* 158 (3): 374–380.

Freud, Sigmund. 1965. *The Interpretation of Dreams.* New York: Avon Books.

Friedman, Jack R. 2009. "The 'Social Case': Illness, Psychiatry, and Deinstitutionalization in Postsocialist Romania." *Medical Anthropology Quarterly* 23 (4): 375–396.

——. 2012. "Thoughts on Inactivity and an Ethnography of 'Nothing': Comparing Meanings of 'Inactivity' in Romanian and American Mental Health Care." *North American Dialogue* 15 (1): 1–9.

Frosh, Stephen. 2008. "Freud and Jewish Identity." *Theory and Psychology* 18 (2): 167–178.

Frueh, B. Christopher, Anouk L. Grubaugh, Jon D. Elhai, and Todd C. Buckley. 2007. "US Department of Veterans Affairs Disability Policies for Posttraumatic Stress Disorder: Administrative Trends and Implications for Treatment, Rehabilitation, and Research." *American Journal of Public Health* 97 (12): 2143–2145.

Gabbard, Glen. 2005. *Psychodynamic Psychiatry in Clinical Practice.* 4th ed. Arlington, Va.: American Psychiatric Publishing.

Gaffin, Dennis. 1996. "From 'Bugging-Out' to 'Chilling-Out': Manipulating Emotion and Evoking Reason in a Forensic Psychiatric Hospital." *Culture, Medicine, and Psychiatry* 20 (2): 199–228.

Gaines, Atwood D. 1979. "Definitions and Diagnoses: Cultural Implications of Psychiatric Help-Seeking and Psychiatrists' Definitions of the Situation in Psychiatric Emergencies." *Culture, Medicine, and Psychiatry* 3 (4): 381–418.

——. 1992. "From DSM-I to III-R; Voices of Self, Mastery and the Other: A Cultural Constructivist Reading of U.S. Psychiatric Classification." *Social Science and Medicine* 35 (1): 3–24.

Gaines, Atwood, and Eric T. Juengst. 2008. "Origin Myths in Bioethics: Constructing Sources, Motives, and Reasons in Bioethic(s)." *Culture, Medicine, and Psychiatry* 32 (3): 303–327.

Galanek, Joseph D. 2013. "The Cultural Construction of Mental Illness in Prison: A Perfect Storm of Pathology." *Culture, Medicine, and Psychiatry* 37 (1): 195–225.

García-Pérez, Miguel A. 2010. "Accuracy and Completeness of Publication and Citation Records in the Web of Science, PsycINFO, and Google Scholar: A Case Study for the Computation of h Indices in Psychology." *Journal of the American Society for Information Science and Technology* 61 (10): 2070–2085.

Gaskin, Decona, Brenna Jenny, and Stacy Clark. 2012. "Recent Developments in Health Law." *Journal of Law, Medicine, and Ethics* 40 (1): 160–175.

Gay, Peter. 1987. *A Godless Jew: Freud, Atheism, and the Making of Psychoanalysis.* Binghamton: Vail-Ballou Press.

Geertz, Clifford. 1973. *The Interpretation of Cultures.* New York: Basic Books.

Gendron, Angela. 2010. "Confronting Terrorism in Saudi Arabia." *International Journal of Intelligence and CounterIntelligence* 23 (3): 487–508.

Ghaneabassiri, Kambiz. 2010. "Muslim Selves and the American Body Politic: Placing Major Nidal Malik Hasan's Case in a Broader Socio-Historical Context." *International Journal of Applied Psychoanalytic Studies* 7 (3): 219–230.

Glaberson, William. 2008a. "Arraigned, 9/11 Defendants Talk of Martyrdom." *New York Times*, June 6.

——. 2008b. "Suspects in 9/11 Plot Attempt to Plead Guilty." *New York Times*, November 8.

Glaser, Barney G. 1965. "The Constant Comparative Method of Qualitative Analysis." *Social Problems* 12 (4): 436–445.

Glenn, David. 2007. "A Policy on Torture Roils Psychologists' Annual Meeting." *Chronicle of Higher Education*, September 7.

Goffman, Erving. 1961. *Asylums: Essays on the Social Situation of Mental Patients and Other Inmates.* New York: Anchor Books.

Gold, Liza H. 2010. "Rediscovering Forensic Psychiatry." In *The American Psychiatric Publishing Textbook of Forensic Psychiatry*, 2nd ed., ed. Robert I. Simon and Liza H. Gold, 3–41. Arlington, Va.: American Psychiatric Publishing.

Goldstein, Daniel M. 2010. "Security and the Culture Expert: Dilemmas of an Engaged Anthropology." *PoLAR: Political and Legal Anthropology Review* 33 (ser. 1): 126–142.

Goldstein, Joseph. 2008. "Psychology Group Changes Policy on Interrogations." *New York Sun*, September 18.

Good, Byron J. 1994. *Medicine, Rationality, and Experience: An Anthropological Perspective.* Cambridge: Cambridge University Press.

Good, Byron J., and Mary-Jo DelVecchio Good. 1980. "The Meaning of Symptoms: A Cultural Hermeneutic Model for Clinical Practice." In *The Relevance of Social Science for Medicine*, ed. Leon Eisenberg and Arthur Kleinman, 165–196. Dordrecht: D. Reidel.

——. 1993. "'Learning Medicine': The Constructing of Medical Knowledge at Harvard Medical School." In *Knowledge, Power, and Practice: The Anthropology of Medicine and Everyday Life*, ed. Shirley Lindenbaum and Margaret Lock, 81–107. Berkeley: University of California Press.

Goode, Erica. 2001. "A Day of Terror: The Psychology; Attackers Believed to Be Sane." *New York Times*, September 12.

Gordon, Deborah. 1988. "Tenacious Assumptions in Western Medicine." In *Biomedicine Examined*, ed. Margaret Lock and Deborah Gordon, 19–56. Dordrecht: Kluwer Academic Publishers.

Gordon, James. 2005. "Psychologists Help with Punishment, Canadian Says." *Times Colonist*, June 26.

Greenwald, Glenn. 2013. "Washington Gets Explicit: Its 'War on Terror' Is Permanent." *Guardian*, May 17. Accessed May 21, 2013. http://www.guardian.co.uk /commentisfree/2013/may/17/endless-war-on-terror-obama.

Gregory, Derek. 2011. "The Everywhere War." *Geographical Journal* 177 (3): 238–250.

Grimland, Meytal, Alan Apter, and Ad Kerkhof. 2006. "The Phenomenon of Suicide Bombing: A Review of Psychological and Nonpsychological Factors." *Crisis: The Journal of Crisis Intervention and Suicide Prevention* 27 (3): 107–118.

Groopman, Leonard C. 1987. "Medical Internship as Moral Education: An Essay on the System of Training Physicians." *Culture, Medicine, and Psychiatry* 11 (2): 207–227.

Gross, Michael L. 2010. "Teaching Military Medical Ethics: Another Look at Dual Loyalty and Triage." *Cambridge Quarterly of Healthcare Ethics* 19 (4): 458–464.

——. 2013. "Military Medical Ethics: A Review of the Literature and a Call to Arms." *Cambridge Quarterly of Healthcare Ethics* 22 (1): 92–109.

Gunaratna, Rohan. 2009. "The Battlefield of the Mind: Rehabilitating Muslim Terrorists." *UNISCI Discussion Papers*, No. 21 (October 2009). Accessed 26 May 2012. http://www.ucm.es/info/unisci/revistas/UNISCI%20DP%2021% 20-%20ROHAN.pdf.

——. 2011. "Terrorist Rehabilitation: A Global Imperative." *Journal of Policing, Intelligence, and Counter Terrorism* 6 (1): 65–82.

Gunning, Jeroen, and Richard Jackson. 2011. "What's So 'Religious' About 'Religious Terrorism'?" *Critical Studies on Terrorism* 4 (3): 369–388.

Gupta, Akhil, and James Ferguson. 1992. "Beyond 'Culture': Space, Identity, and the Politics of Difference." *Cultural Anthropology* 7 (1): 6–23.

Gutheil, Thomas G. 2005. "The History of Forensic Psychiatry." *Journal of the American Academy of Psychiatry and the Law* 33 (2): 259–262.

Harrison, Mark. 2009. "Racial Pathologies: Morbid Anatomy in British India, 1770–1850." In *The Social History of Health and Medicine in Colonial India*, ed. Biswamoy Pati and Mark Harrison, 173–194. New York: Routledge.

Hassan, Muhammad Haniff. 2006. *Unlicensed to Kill: Countering Imam Samudra's Justification for the Bali Bombing.* Singapore: Peace Matters. Accessed June 23, 2013. http://www.p4peace.com/edisi/data/unlicensed%20to%20kill-ebook.pdf.

——. 2007. "Singapore's Muslim Community-Based Initiatives Against JI." *Perspectives on Terrorism* 1 (5). Accessed 3 October 2012. http://terrorismanalysts.com/pt/index.php/pot/article/view/17/html.

Herrera, Chris. 2008. "Is It Time for Bioethics to Go Empirical?" *Bioethics* 22 (3): 137–146.

Hoffmaster, Barry. 1992. "Can Ethnography Save the Life of Medical Ethics?" *Social Science and Medicine* 35 (12): 1421–1431.

——. 1994. "The Forms and Limits of Medical Ethics." *Social Science and Medicine* 39 (9): 1155–1164.

Hollander, Nancy Caro. 2009. "A Psychoanalytic Perspective on the Paradox of Prejudice: Understanding US Policy Toward Israel and the Palestinians." *International Journal of Applied Psychoanalytic Studies* 6 (3): 167–177.

Horgan, John. 2008. "Deradicalization or Disengagement? A Process in Need of Clarity and a Counterterrorism Initiative in Need of Evaluation." *Perspectives on Terrorism* 2 (4). Accessed 27 September 2012. http://www.terrorismanalysts.com/pt/index.php/pot/article/view/32/html.

——. 2009. *Walking Away from Terrorism: Accounts of Disengagement from Radical and Extremist Movements.* London: Routledge.

Horgan, John, and Kurt Braddock. 2010. "Rehabilitating the Terrorists? Challenges in Assessing the Effectiveness of De-radicalization Programs." *Terrorism and Political Violence* 22 (2): 267–291.

Hotakainen, Rob, and Josephine Marcotty. 2004. "'U' Doctor Questions Ethics in Iraq; He Says Medical Personnel Breached Human Rights." *Minneapolis Star Tribune,* August 20.

Hough, George. 2004. "Does Psychoanalysis Have Anything to Offer an Understanding of Terrorism?" *Journal of the American Psychoanalytic Association* 52 (3): 813–828.

Howe, Edmund G., Akhila Kosaraju, Patrick R. Laraby, and S. Ward Casscells. 2009. "Guantanamo: Ethics, Interrogation, and Forced Feeding." *Military Medicine* 174 (1): iv–xiii.

Howell, Alison. 2007. "Victims or Madmen? The Diagnostic Competition Over 'Terrorist' Detainees at Guantánamo Bay." *International Political Sociology* 1 (1): 29–47.

——. 2010. "Sovereignty, Security, Psychiatry: Liberation and the Failure of Mental Health Governance in Iraq." *Security Dialogue* 41 (4): 347–367.

Howell, Sally, and Andrew Shryock. 2003. "Cracking Down on Diaspora: Arab Detroit and America's 'War on Terror.'" *Anthropological Quarterly* 76 (3): 443–462.

Human Rights Watch. 2008. *Locked Up Alone: Detention Conditions and Mental Health at Guantanamo*. New York: Human Rights Watch.

Iacopino, Vincent, and Stephen N. Xenakis. 2011. "Neglect of Medical Evidence of Torture in Guantánamo Bay: A Case Series." *PLoS Medicine* 8 (4): e1001027.

International Committee of the Red Cross. 1977. *Protocol Additional to the Geneva Conventions of 12 August 1949, and relating to the Protection of Victims of International Armed Conflicts (Protocol I), 8 June 1977*. Accessed July 9, 2013. http://www.icrc.org/applic/ihl/ihl.nsf/Article.xsp?action=openDocument&documentId=28D300B20C31500CC12563CD0051D79F.

——. 2009. *Convention (III) relative to the Treatment of Prisoners of War. Geneva, 12 August 1949*. Accessed July 8, 2013. http://www.icrc.org/ihl.nsf/7c4d08d9b287a42141256739003e63bb/6fef854a3517b75ac125641e004a9e68.

Jackson, James C., Patricia L. Sinnott, Brian P. Marx, Maureen Murdoch, Nina A. Sayer, JoAnn M. Alvarez, Robert A. Greevy, Paula P. Schnurr, Matthew J. Friedman, Andrea C. Shane, Richard R. Owen, Terence M. Keane, and Theodore Speroff. 2011. "Variation in Practices and Attitudes of Clinicians Assessing PTSD-Related Disability Among Veterans." *Journal of Traumatic Stress* 24 (5): 609–613.

Jackson, Richard. 2007. "Constructing Enemies: 'Islamic Terrorism' in Political and Academic Discourse." *Government and Opposition* 42 (3): 394–426.

Jacobs, Michael. 1994. "Psychodynamic Counseling: An Identity Achieved?" *Psychodynamic Counseling* 1 (1): 79–92.

James, Larry C. 2008. *Fixing Hell: An Army Psychologist Confronts Abu Ghraib*. New York: Grand Central Publishing.

Jarrar, Adib. 2010. "Palestinian Suffering: Some Personal, Historical, and Psychoanalytic Reflections." *International Journal of Applied Psychoanalytic Studies* 7 (3): 197–208.

Jenks, Angela. 2011. "From 'Lists of Traits' to 'Open-Mindedness': Emerging Issues in Cultural Competence Education." *Culture, Medicine, and Psychiatry* 35 (2): 209–235.

Jones, James W. 2006. "Why Does Religion Turn Violent? A Psychoanalytic Exploration of Religious Terrorism." *Psychoanalytic Review* 93 (2): 167–190.

Jonsen, Albert R. 1999. *A Short History of Medical Ethics*. Oxford: Oxford University Press.

Kanazawa, Satoshi. 2007. "The Evolutionary Psychological Imagination: Why You Can't Get a Date on a Saturday Night and Why Most Suicide Bombers Are Muslim." *Journal of Social, Evolutionary, and Cultural Psychology* 1 (2): 7–17.

Kassim, Sadik H. 2008. "The Role of Religion in the Generation of Suicide Bombers." *Brief Treatment and Crisis Intervention* 8 (2): 204–208.

Kendall, P. C. 1985. "Toward a Cognitive-Behavioral Model of Child Psychopathology and a Critique of Related Interventions." *Journal of Abnormal Child Psychology* 13 (3): 357–372.

Kearney, M. 1995. "The Local and the Global: The Anthropology of Globalization and Transnationalism." *Annual Review of Anthropology* 24: 547–565.

Khalid, Uday, and Peter Olsson. 2006. "Suicide Bombing: A Psychodynamic View." *Journal of American Academy of Psychoanalysis* 34 (3): 523–530.

Kilshaw, Susie. 2008. "Gulf War Syndrome: A Reaction to Psychiatry's Invasion of the Military?" *Culture, Medicine, and Psychiatry* 32 (2): 219–237.

King, Michael, Haula Noor, and Donald M. Taylor. 2011. "Normative Support for Terrorism: The Attitudes and Beliefs of Immediate Relatives of Jema'ah Islamiyah Members." *Studies in Conflict and Terrorism* 34 (5): 2011.

——. 2006. "Beyond the 'New Cross-Cultural Psychiatry': Cultural Biology, Discursive Psychology and Ironies of Globalization." *Transcultural Psychiatry* 43 (1): 126–144.

Kirmayer, Laurence J. 2007a. "Cultural Psychiatry in Historical Perspective." In *Textbook of Cultural Psychiatry*, ed. Dinesh Bhugra and Kamaldeep Bhui, 3–19. Cambridge: Cambridge University Press.

——. 2007b. "Psychotherapy and the Cultural Concept of the Person." *Transcultural Psychiatry* 44 (2): 232–257.

Kirmayer. Laurence J., and Harry Minas. 2000. "The Future of Cultural Psychiatry: An International Perspective." *Canadian Journal of Psychiatry* 45 (5): 438–446.

Kleinman, Arthur. 1973. "Medicine's Symbolic Reality: On a Central Problem in the Philosophy of Medicine." *Inquiry* 16 (1–4): 206–213.

——. 1977. "Depression, Somatization, and 'The New Cross-Cultural Psychiatry.'" *Social Science and Medicine* 11 (1): 3–10.

——. 1980. *Patients and Healers in the Context of Culture: An Exploration of the Borderland Between Anthropology, Medicine, and Psychiatry*. Berkeley: University of California Press.

——. 1983. "Editor's Note." *Culture, Medicine, and Psychiatry* 7 (1): 97–99.

——. 1985. "Interpreting Illness Experience and Clinical Meanings: How I See Clinically Applied Anthropology." *Medical Anthropology Quarterly* 16 (3): 69–71.

——. 1988. *Rethinking Psychiatry: From Cultural Category to Personal Experience.* New York: Free Press.

——. 1994. *Writing at the Margin: Discourse Between Anthropology and Medicine.* Berkeley: University of California Press.

Kleinman, Arthur, and Peter Benson. 2006. "Anthropology in the Clinic: The Problem of Cultural Competency and How to Fix It." *PLoS Med* 3 (10): e294.

Kleinman, Arthur, Leon Eisenberg, and Byron Good. 1978. "Culture, Illness, and Care: Clinical Lessons from Anthropologic and Cross-Cultural Research." *Annals of Internal Medicine* 88 (2): 251–258.

Kleinman, Arthur, and Joan Kleinman. 1994. "How Bodies Remember: Social Memory and Bodily Experience of Criticism, Resistance, and Delegitimation Following China's Cultural Revolution." *New Literary History* 25 (3): 707–723.

Kobrin, Nancy Hartevelt. 2003. "Psychoanalytic Notes on Osama bin Laden and His Jihad Against the Jews and the Crusaders." *Annual of Psychoanalysis* 31:211–221.

Kruglanski, Arie W., Xiaoyan Chen, Mark Dechesne, Shira Fishman, and Edward Orehek. 2009. "Fully Committed: Suicide Bombers' Motivation and the Quest for Personal Significance." *Political Psychology* 30 (3): 331–357.

Kruglanski, Arie W., Martha Crenshaw, Jerrold M. Post, and Jeff Victoroff. 2007. "What Should This Fight Be Called? Metaphors of Counterterrorism and Their Implications." *Psychological Science in the Public Interest* 8 (3): 97–133.

Kruglanski, Arie W., Michele Gelfand, and Rohan Gunaratna. 2010. "Detainee Deradicalization: A Challenge for Psychological Science." *Association for Psychological Science: Observer* 23 (1): 1–3.

——. 2011. "Aspects of Deradicalization." In *Terrorist Rehabilitation and Counter-Radicalisation: New Approaches to Counter-Terrorism,* ed. Rohan Gunaratna, Jolene Jerard, and Lawrence Rubin, 135–143. New York: Routledge,

Kushner, Howard I. 1991. *American Suicide: A Psychocultural Exploration.* New Brunswick, N.J.: Rutgers University Press.

Lacroix, Stéphane. 2004. "Between Islamists and Liberals: Saudi Arabia's New 'Islamo-Liberal' Reformists. *Middle East Journal* 58 (3): 345–365.

Laird, Lance Daniel, Justine de Marrais, and Linda L. Barnes. 2007. "Portraying Islam and Muslims in MEDLINE: A Content Analysis." *Social Science and Medicine* 65 (12): 2425–2439.

Lankford, Adam, and Katherine Gillespie. 2011. "Rehabilitating Terrorists Through Counter-indoctrination: Lessons Learned from the Saudi Arabian Program." *International Criminal Justice Review* 21 (2): 118–133.

Larsen, John Aggergaard. 2004. "Finding Meaning in First Episode Psychosis: Experience, Agency, and the Cultural Repertoire." *Medical Anthropology Quarterly* 18 (4): 447–471.

Latour, Bruce, and Steve Woolgar. 1986. *Laboratory Life: The Social Construction of Scientific Facts*. Princeton, N.J.: Princeton University Press.

Lawrence, Bruce B. 2011. "Polyvalent Islam in the Public Square." *Middle East Journal* 65 (1): 133–142.

Lester, David. 2010. "Female Suicide Bombers and Burdensomeness." *Psychological Reports* 106 (1): 160–162.

Levine, Robert A. 2001. "Culture and Personality Studies, 1918–1960: Myth and History." *Journal of Personality* 69 (6): 803–818.

Lewis, Neil A. 2005a. "Guantánamo Tour Focuses on Medical Ethics." *New York Times*, November 13.

——. 2005b. "Interrogators Cite Doctors' Aid at Guantanamo." *New York Times*, June 24.

Liddle, James R., Karin Machluf, and Todd K. Shackelford. 2010. "Understanding Suicide Terrorism: Premature Dismissal of the Religious-Belief Hypothesis." *Evolutionary Psychology* 8 (3): 343–345.

Lipowski, Z. J. 1989. "Psychiatry: Mindless or Brainless, Both or Neither?" *Canadian Journal of Psychiatry* 34 (3): 249–254.

Littlewood, Roland. 1993. "Ideology, Camouflage, or Contingency? Racism in British Psychiatry." *Transcultural Psychiatry* 30 (3): 243–290.

——. 1996. "Psychiatry's Culture." *International Journal of Social Psychiatry* 42 (4): 245–268.

Lloyd, Stephanie, and Nicolas Moreau. 2011. "Pursuit of a 'Normal Life': Mood, Anxiety, and Their Disordering." *Medical Anthropology: Cross-Cultural Studies in Health and Illness* 30 (6): 591–609.

Lock, Margaret. 1993. "Cultivating the Body: Anthropology and Epistemologies of Bodily Practice and Knowledge." *Annual Review of Anthropology* 22:133–155.

Loidolt, Bryce. 2011. "Managing the Global and Local: The Dual Agendas of Al Qaeda in the Arabian Peninsula." *Studies in Conflict and Terrorism* 34 (2): 102–123.

Luhrmann, Tanya M. 2000. *Of Two Minds: An Anthropologist Looks at American Psychiatry*. New York: Vintage Books.

Mahmoud, Saba. 2005. *Politics of Piety: The Islamic Revival and the Feminist Subject*. Princeton, N.J.: Princeton University Press.

Mamdani, Mahmoud. 2005. *Good Muslim, Bad Muslim: America, the Cold War, and the Toots of Terror*. New York: Doubleday.

Manthorpe, Jonathan. 2010. "Saudis Are Ill-Equipped to Deprogram Islamic Militants." *Vancouver Sun*, 29 January.

Marazziti, Donatella. 2007. "Is There a Role for Psychiatry in Deepening Our Understanding of the 'Suicide Bomber'?" *International Journal of Psychiatry in Clinical Practice* 11 (2): 87–88.

Marshall, Patricia A. 1992. "Anthropology and Bioethics." *Medical Anthropology Quarterly* 6 (1): 49–73.

Marshall, Patricia, and Barbara Koenig. 2004. "Accounting for Culture in a Globalized Bioethics." *Journal of Law, Medicine, and Ethics* 32 (2): 252–266.

Massad, Joseph. 2009. "Psychoanalysis, Islam, and the Other of Liberalism." *Psychoanalysis and History* 11 (2): 193–208.

Mattingly, Cheryl. 1998. "In Search of the Good: Narrative Reasoning in Clinical Practice." *Medical Anthropology Quarterly* 12 (3): 273–297.

McAuliffe, Jane Dammen. 2006. "The Tasks and Traditions of Interpretation." In *The Cambridge Companion to the Quran*, ed. Jane Dammen McAuliffe, 187–209. Cambridge: Cambridge University Press.

Medovoi, Leerom. 2007. "Global Society Must Be Defended: Biopolitics Without Boundaries." *Social Text* 25 (2): 53–79.

Merton, Robert. 1936. "The Unanticipated Consequences of Purposive Social Action." *American Sociological Review* 1 (6): 894–904.

Messinger, Seth D. 2006. "'That's Not His Only Problem . . .': Clinical Teamwork in a Psychiatric Emergency Room." *Culture, Medicine, and Psychiatry* 30 (3): 363–387.

Metzl, Jonathan. 2010. *The Protest Psychosis: How Schizophrenia Became a Black Disease*. Boston: Beacon Press.

Miles, Steven. 2004. "Abu Ghraib: Its Legacy for Military Medicine." *Lancet* 364 (9435): 725–729.

——. 2007. "Doctors as Pawns? Law and Medical Ethics at Guantanamo Bay." *Seton Hall Law Review* 37 (3): 711–731.

——. 2008. "Medical Ethics and the Interrogation of Guantanamo 063." *American Journal of Bioethics* 7 (4): 5–11.

——. 2011. "The New Military Medical Ethics: Legacies of the Gulf Wars and the War on Terror." *Bioethics* 27 (3): 117–123.

Miliora, Maria T. 2004. "The Psychology and Ideology of an Islamic Terrorist Leader: Usama bin Laden." *International Journal of Applied Psychoanalytic Studies* 1 (2): 121–139.

Military Commissions Act of 2006. 2006. Pub. L. No. 109-366. (October 17, 2006). Accessed July 9, 2013. http://www.loc.gov/rr/frd/Military_Law/pdf /PL-109–366.pdf.

Moghaddam, Fathali M. 2009. "The New Global American Dilemma and Terrorism." *Political Psychology* 30 (3): 373–380.

Moglen, Seth. 2006. "Mourning and Progressive Politics After 9/11." *International Journal of Applied Psychoanalytic Studies* 3 (2): 118–125.

Moher, David, Alessandro Liberati, Jennifer Tetzlaff, and Douglas G. Altman [the PRISMA Group]. 2009. "Preferred Reporting Items for Systematic Reviews and Meta-Analyses: The PRISMA Statement." *PLoS Medicine* 6 (7): e1000097.

Molino, Anthony. 2004. *Culture, Society, and Psyche: Dialogues in Psychoanalysis and Anthropology*. Middletown, Conn.: Wesleyan University Press.

Morris, Madeline, Frances Eberhard, Jessica Rivera, and Michael Watsula. 2010. "Deradicalization: A Review of the Literature with Comparison to Findings in the Literatures on Deganging and Deprogramming." In *Institute for Homeland Security Solutions*, 1–13. Accessed 10 April 2012. http://sites.duke.edu/ihss /files/2011/12/Morris_Research_Brief_Final.pdf.

Muller, Jessica H. 1994. "Anthropology, Bioethics, and Medicine: A Provocative Trilogy." *Medical Anthropology Quarterly* 8 (4): 448–467.

Mullins, Sam. 2010. "Rehabilitation of Islamic Terrorists: Lessons from Criminology." *Dynamics of Asymmetric Conflict* 3 (3): 162–193.

Munro, Margaret. 2004. "Ethics Expert Says Canada Should Call for Abu Ghraib Probe; Doctors' Role: 'Medical Personnel Are the First Barrier to Abuses.'" *National Post*, August 20.

Nash, Jo. 2004. "Identification, Loss, and Reparation: A Psychoanalytic Exploration of the Israeli-Palestinian Conflict." *Free Associations* 11D: 519–545.

Noblit, George W., and R. Dwight Hare. 1988. *Meta-Ethnography: Synthesizing Qualitative Studies*. Newbury Park, Calif.: Sage Publications.

Noricks, Darcy M. E. 2009. "Disengagement and Deradicalization: Processes and Programs." In *Social Science for Counterterrorism: Putting the Pieces Together*, ed. Paul K. Davis and Kim Cragin, 299–321. Santa Monica, Calif.: RAND Corporation.

Obama, Barack. 2009a. *Nobel Lecture: A Just and Lasting Peace*. Accessed April 24, 2014. http://www.nobelprize.org/nobel_prizes/peace/laureates/2009/obama -lecture_en.html.

——. 2009b. *Speeches on the Road to the White House.* Carlsbad: Excellent Books.

Obeyesekere, Gananath. 1990. *The Work of Culture: Symbolic Transformation in Psychoanalysis and Anthropology.* Chicago: University of Chicago Press.

Office of the Director of National Intelligence. 2012. *Summary of the Reengagement of Detainees Formerly Held at Guantanamo Bay, Cuba.* Accessed January 15, 2013. http://www.dni.gov/index.php/newsroom/reports-and-publications/93 -reports-publications-2012/487-summary-of-the-reengagement-of-detainees -formerly-held-at-guantanamo-bay,-cuba.

Office of Military Commissions. 2007a. Referred Charges Dated 2/29/2008. Accessed March 15, 2013. http://www.mc.mil/CASES/MilitaryCommissions .aspx.

——. 2007b. Sworn Charges Dated [10/9/2007]. Accessed March 20, 2013. http://www.mc.mil/CASES/MilitaryCommissions.aspx.

——. 2008a. Sworn Charges Dated 2/8/2008. Accessed March 16, 2013. http:// www.mc.mil/CASES/MilitaryCommissions.aspx.

——. 2008b. Referred Charges Dated 4/4/2008. Accessed March 20, 2013. http:// www.mc.mil/CASES/MilitaryCommissions.aspx.

——. 2011. Referred Charges Dated 9/28/2011. Accessed March 15, 2013. http:// www.mc.mil/CASES/MilitaryCommissions.aspx.

——. 2012a. Unofficial/Unauthenticated Transcript of the Al Nashiri Motions Hearing Dated 10/23/2012 from 11:01 AM to 11:34 AM. Accessed March 15, 2013. http://www.mc.mil/CASES/MilitaryCommissions.aspx.

——. 2012b. Unofficial/Unauthenticated Transcript of the Al Nashiri Motions Hearing Dated 10/24/2012 from 9:11 AM to 10:15 AM. Accessed March 15, 2013. http://www.mc.mil/CASES/MilitaryCommissions.aspx.

——. 2012c. Unofficial/Unauthenticated Transcript of the Al Nashiri (2) Hearing Dated 2/4/2013 from 3:06 PM to 4:25 PM. Accessed March 15, 2013. http:// www.mc.mil/CASES/MilitaryCommissions.aspx.

——. 2012d. Sworn Charges Dated 8/29/2012. Accessed March 15, 2013. http:// www.mc.mil/CASES/MilitaryCommissions.aspx.

Okie, Susan. 2005. "Glimpses of Guantanamo—Medical Ethics and the War on Terror." *New England Journal of Medicine* 353 (24): 2529–2534.

Ostow, Mortimer. 1982. *Judaism and Psychoanalysis.* New York: KTAV Publishing.

Page, Michael, Lara Challita, and Alistair Harris. 2011. "Al Qaeda in the Arabian Peninsula: Framing Narratives and Prescriptions." *Terrorism and Political Violence* 23 (2): 150–172.

Palmer, Ian. 2007. "Terrorism, Suicide Bombing, Fear, and Mental Health." *International Review of Psychiatry* 19 (3): 289–296.

Panagopoulos, Costas. 2006. "Arabs and Muslim Americans and Islam in the Aftermath of 9/11." *Public Opinion Quarterly* 70 (4): 608–624.

Pellegrino, Edmund D. 1990. "The Origins and Evolution of Bioethics: Some Personal Reflections." *Kennedy Institute of Ethics Journal* 9 (1): 73–88.

Person, Ethel S., Arnold M. Cooper, and Glen O. Gabbard, eds. 1995. Introduction to *The American Psychiatric Publishing Textbook of Psychoanalysis*, xiii–xviii. Arlington, Va.: American Psychiatric Publishing.

Physicians for Human Rights and the University of Cape Town Health Sciences Faculty. 2003. *Dual Loyalty and Human Rights in Health Professional Practice: Proposed Guidelines and Institutional Mechanisms*. Boston: Physicians for Human Rights.

Pike, Kenneth L. 1954. *Language in Relation to a Unified Theory of the Structure of Human Behavior*. Dallas: Summer Institute of Linguistics.

Pilkington, Ed. 2009. "International: CIA Doctors May Have Experimented on Prisoners, Says Rights Watchdog; Medics Helped to Refine Interrogation Methods: Breach of Nuremberg Code 'Violates Ethical Values.'" *Guardian*, September 3.

Pivens, J. S. 2006. "Narcissism, Sexuality, and Psyche in Terrorist Theology." *Psychoanalytic Review* 93 (2): 231–265.

Pope, Kenneth S. 2011a. "Are the American Psychological Association's Detainee Interrogation Policies Ethical and Effective? Key Claims, Documents, and Results." *Journal of Psychology* 219 (3): 150–158.

——. 2011b. "Psychologists and Detainee Interrogations: Key Decisions, Opportunities Lost, and Lessons Learned." *Annual Review of Psychology* 7:459–481.

Pope, Kenneth S., and Thomas G. Gutheil. 2009. "Psychologists Abandon the Nuremberg Ethic: Concerns for Detainee Interrogations." *International Journal of Law and Psychiatry* 32 (3): 161–166.

Porges, Marisa L. 2010. "The Saudi Deradicalization Experiment." Council on Foreign Relations, January 22. Accessed June 22, 2013. http://www.cfr.org /terrorism/saudi-deradicalization-experiment/p21292.

Post, Jerrold. 2009. "Reframing of Martyrdom and Jihad and the Socialization of Suicide Terrorists." *Political Psychology* 30 (3): 381–385.

Post, Jerrold, Farhana Ali, Schuyler W. Henderson, Steven Shanfield, Jeff Victoroff, and Stevan Weine. 2009. "The Psychology of Suicide Terrorism." *Psychiatry* 72 (1): 13–31.

Preti, Antonio. 2006. "Suicide to Harass Others: Clues from Mythology to Understanding Suicide Bombing Attacks." *Crisis: The Journal of Crisis Intervention and Suicide Prevention* 27 (1): 22–30.

Price, Eric. 2010. "Selected Literature on Radicalization and De-radicalization from Terrorism." *Perspectives on Terrorism* 4 (2). Accessed 7 April 2012. http://www.terrorismanalysts.com/pt/index.php/pot/article/view/102.

Prosono, Marvin. 2003. "History of Forensic Psychiatry." In *Principles and Practice of Forensic Psychiatry*, 2nd ed., ed. Richard Rosner, 14–30. Boca Raton: CRC Press.

Psychoanalytic Electronic Publishing. 2013. "About the Archive." Accessed June 14, 2013. http://www.p-e-p.org/.

Rabasa, Angel, Stacie L. Pettyjohn, Jeremy J. Ghez, and Christopher Boucek. 2010. *Deradicalizing Islamist Extremists*. Santa Monica, Calif.: RAND Corporation.

Rabinow, Paul, and William M. Sullivan, eds. 1987. "The Interpretive Turn: A Second Look." In *Interpretive Social Science: A Second Look*, ed. Paul Rabinow and William M. Sullivan, 1–30. Berkeley: University of California Press.

Ranstorp, Magnus. 2009. *Preventing Violent Radicalization and Terrorism: The Case of Indonesia*. Stockholm: Swedish National Defence College.

Religious Rehabilitation Group. 2012a. "The Diffusion of Ideas in the War on Terror." Government of Singapore. Accessed November 1, 2012. http://www.rrg.sg/index.php?option=com_content&view=article&id=67:the-diffusion-of-ideas-in-the-war-on-terror&catid=4:recent-articles&Itemid=9.

——. 2012b. "Our Message." Government of Singapore. Accessed November 1, 2012. http://www.rrg.sg/index.php?option=com_content&view=article&id=15&Itemid=6&showall=1.

Reshetnikov, Mikhail. 2008. "Visions of the Future: Social Processes and Terrorism in Europe." *Journal of Analytical Psychology* 53 (5): 653–665.

Rhodes, Lorna A. 2000. "Taxonomic Anxieties: Axis I and Axis II in Prison." *Medical Anthropology Quarterly* 14 (3): 346–373.

——. 2002. "Psychopathy and the Face of Control in Supermax." *Ethnography* 3 (4): 442–466.

Rice, Condoleezza. 2011. *No Higher Honor: A Memoir of My Years in Washington*. New York: Crown Publishers.

Robinson, Glenn E. 1997. "Can Islamists Be Democrats? The Case of Jordan." *Middle East Journal* 51 (3): 373–387.

Romanucci-Ross, Lola, and Laurence R. Tancredi. 1986. "Psychiatry, the Law, and Cultural Determinants of Behavior." *International Journal of Law and Psychiatry* 9 (3): 265–293.

Rose, Nikolas. 1998. *Inventing Our Selves: Psychology, Power, and Personhood.* Cambridge: Cambridge University Press.

Rosen, Lawrence. 2006. *Law as Culture: An Invitation.* Princeton, N.J.: Princeton University Press.

Rosner, Richard. 2003. "A Conceptual Framework for Forensic Psychiatry." In *Principles and Practice of Forensic Psychiatry*, 2nd ed., ed. Richard Rosner, 3–6. Boca Raton, Fla.: CRC Press.

Ross, Emma. 2004. "Bioethicist: Doctors Collaborated in Torture, Abuse; Drawing on Pentagon Probe, Prof Calls for Reform, Inquiry." *Herald-Sun*, August 20.

Rousseau, Cécile, and Uzma Jamil. 2008. "Meaning of 9/11 for Two Pakistani Communities: From External Intruders to the Internalisation of a Negative Self-Image." *Anthropology and Medicine* 15 (3): 163–174.

Rowland, Kara. 2010. "Vets Salute Obama on Funding; Legion Cites Administration's 'Accessibility.'" *Washington Times*, April 29.

Rubenstein, Leonard S. 2007. "First, Do No Harm: Health Professionals and Guantánamo." *Seton Hall Law Review* 37 (3): 733–748.

Rubenstein, Leonard S., and George J. Annas. 2009. "Medical Ethics at Guantanamo Bay Detention Centre and in the US Military: A Time for Reform." *Lancet* 374 (9686): 353–355.

Rubenstein, Leonard S., and Stephen N. Xenakis. 2010. "Doctors Without Morals." *New York Times*, March 1.

Rumsfeld, Donald. 2011. *Known and Unknown: A Memoir.* New York: Sentinel.

Rutherford, Bruce K. 2006. "What Do Egypt's Islamists Want? Moderate Islam and the Rise of Islamic Constitutionalism." *Middle East Journal* 60 (4): 707–731.

Sadler, Jonathan Z. 2005. *Values and Psychiatric Diagnosis.* New York: Oxford University Press.

Said, Edward. 1994. *Orientalism.* New York: Vintage Books.

Salib, Emad. 2003. "Suicide Terrorism: A Case of Folie à Plusieurs?" *British Journal of Psychiatry* 182:475–476.

Samberg, Eslee, and Eric R. Marcus. 2005. "Process, Resistance, and Interpretation." In *The American Psychiatric Publishing Textbook of Psychoanalysis,* ed. Ethel Spector Person, Arnold M. Cooper, and Glen O. Gabbard, 229–240. Arlington, Va.: American Psychiatric Publishing.

Sambur, Bilal. 2009. "The Great Transformation of Political Islam in Turkey: The Case of Justice and Development Party and Erdogan." *European Journal of Economic and Political Studies* 2 (2): 117–127.

Santiago-Irizarry, Vilma. 2001. *Medicalizing Ethnicity: The Construction of Latino Identity in a Psychiatric Setting*. Ithaca, N.Y.: Cornell University Press.

Sapir, Edward. 1938. "Why Cultural Anthropology Needs the Psychiatrist." *Psychiatry* 1 (1): 7–12.

Saris, A. Jamie. 1995. "Telling Stories: Life Histories, Illness Narratives, and Institutional Landscapes." *Culture, Medicine, and Psychiatry* 19 (1): 39–72.

Savage, Charlie. 2011. "As Acts of War or Despair, Suicides Rattle a Prison." *New York Times*, April 25.

Scheper-Hughes, Nancy, and Margaret Lock. 1986. "Speaking 'Truth' to Illness: Metaphors, Reification, and a Pedagogy for Patients." *Medical Anthropology Quarterly* 17 (5): 137–140.

——. 1987. "The Mindful Body: A Prolegomenon to Future Work in Medical Anthropology." *Medical Anthropology Quarterly*, new series, 1 (1): 6–41.

Scull, Andrew. 1989. *Social Order/Mental Disorder: Anglo-American Psychiatry in Historical Perspective*. Berkeley: University of California Press.

Sedgwick, Mark. 2004. "Al Qaeda and the Nature of Religious Terrorism." *Terrorism and Political Violence* 16 (4): 795–814.

Sessums, Laura L., Jacob F. Collen, Patrick G. O'Malley, Jeffery L. Jackson, and Michael J. Roy. 2009. "Ethical Practice Under Fire: Deployed Physicians in the Global War on Terrorism." *Military Medicine* 174 (5): 441–447.

Shane, Scott. 2009. "Medical Workers Participated in Torture; Aiding U.S. Interrogators a 'Gross Breach' of Ethics, Red Cross Report Says." *International Herald Tribune*, April 8.

Shapin, Steven. 1995. "Here and Everywhere: Sociology of Scientific Knowledge." *Annual Review of Sociology* 21:289–321.

Shaw, Susan J., and Julie Armin. 2011. "The Ethical Self-Fashioning of Physicians and Health Care Systems in Culturally Appropriate Health Care." *Culture, Medicine, and Psychiatry* 35 (2): 236–261.

Sherman, Nancy. 2006. "Holding Doctors Responsible at Guantanamo." *Kennedy Institute of Ethics Journal* 16 (2): 199–203.

Sieff, Kevin. 2011. "Young Afghan Detainees Eager to Rejoin War." *Washington Post*, September 16.

Silverman, Helen, and Jeffrey Parger. 2004. "The Middle East Crisis: Psychoanalytic Reflections." *International Journal of Psycho-Analysis* 85 (5): 1265–1268.

Simon, Robert I. 2008. "Suicide." In *The American Psychiatric Publishing Textbook of Clinical Psychiatry*, 5th ed., ed. Robert E. Hales, Stuart C. Yudofsky, and Glen O. Gabbard, 1637–1654. Arlington, Va.: American Psychiatric Association.

Singer, Merrill. 1986. "Developing a Critical Perspective in Medical Anthropology." *Medical Anthropology Quarterly* 17 (5): 128–129.

——. 1989. "The Coming of Age of Critical Medical Anthropology." *Social Science and Medicine* 28 (11): 1193–1203.

Singh, Jerome A. 2003. "Military Tribunals at Guantanamo Bay: Dual Loyalty Conflicts." *Lancet* 362 (9383): 573.

Skultans, Vieda. 1991. "Anthropology and Psychiatry: The Uneasy Alliance." *Transcultural Psychiatry Research Review* 28 (1): 5–24.

Slevin, Peter, and Joe Stephens. 2004. "Detainees' Medical Files Shared; Guantanamo Interrogators' Access Criticized." *Washington Post*, June 10.

Speckhard, Anne. 2008. "The Emergence of Female Suicide Terrorists." *Studies in Conflict and Terrorism* 31 (11): 995–1023.

Speckhard, Anne, and Khapta Akhmedova. 2005. "Talking to Terrorists." *Journal of Psychohistory* 33 (2): 125–156.

Staples, James, and Tom Widger. 2012. "Situating Suicide as an Anthropological Problem: Ethnographic Approaches to Understanding Self-Harm and Self-Inflicted Death." *Culture, Medicine, and Psychiatry* 36 (2): 183–203.

Staunton, Dennis. 2008. "9/11 Suspects May Not Plead Guilty If No Death Penalty." *Irish Times*, December 10.

Steel, Zachary, Tien Chey, Derrick Silove, Claire Marnane, Richard A. Bryand, and Mark van Ommeren. 2009. "Association of Torture and Other Potentially Traumatic Events with Mental Health Outcomes Among Populations Exposed to Mass Conflict and Displacement: A Systematic Review and Meta-analysis." *Journal of the American Medical Association* 302 (5): 537–549.

Steele, Karen Dorn, and Bill Morli. 2007. "Psychologists Linked to CIA." *Spokesman-Review*, June 29.

Stern, Jeffrey. 2009. "Psychoanalysis, Terror, and the Theater of Cruelty." *International Journal of Psychoanalytic Self Psychology* 4 (2): 181–211.

Stern, Jessica. 2010. "Mind Over Martyr: How to Deradicalize Islamist Extremists." *Foreign Affairs* 89 (1): 95–108.

Steyn, Johan. 2004. "Guantanamo Bay: The Legal Black Hole." *British Institute of International and Comparative Law* 53 (1): 1–15.

Strenger, Carlo. 2009. "The Psychodynamics of Self-Righteousness and Its Impact on the Middle Eastern Conflict." *International Journal of Applied Psychoanalytic Studies* 6 (3): 178–196.

Sudak, Howard S. 2005. "Suicide." In *Kaplan and Sadock's Comprehensive Textbook of Psychiatry*, ed. Benjamin J. Sadock and Virginia A. Sadock, 2443–2453. Philadelphia: Lippincott Williams and Wilkins.

Supreme Court of the United States. 2005. *Hamdan v. Rumsfeld, Secretary of Defense, et al.* Accessed July 9, 2013. http://www.supremecourt.gov/opinions /05pdf/05-184.pdf.

Taarnby, Michael. 2005. "Yemen's Committee for Dialogue: The Relativity of a Counter Terrorism Success." In *A Future for the Young: Options for Helping Middle Eastern Youth Escape the Trap of Radicalization*, ed. Cheryl Benard, 129–139. RAND. Accessed October 2, 2012. http://www.rand.org/content /dam/rand/pubs/working_papers/2006/RAND_WR354.pdf.

Talaga, Tanya, and Karen Palmer. 2005. "U.S. Doctors Linked to POW 'Torture.'" *Toronto Star*, June 23.

Taussig, Michael T. 1980. "Reification and the Consciousness of the Patient." *Social Science and Medicine* 14B (1): 3–13.

Tousignant, Michel, and Arlene Laliberté. 2007. "Suicide, Violence, and Culture." In *Textbook of Cultural Psychiatry*, ed. Dinesh Bhugra and Kamaldeep Bhui, 33–42. Cambridge: Cambridge University Press.

Townsend, Ellen. 2007. "Suicide Terrorists: Are They Suicidal?" *Suicide and Life-Threatening Behavior* 37 (1): 35–49.

Turner, Leigh. 1998. "An Anthropological Exploration of Contemporary Bioethics: The Varieties of Common Sense." *Journal of Medical Ethics* 24 (2): 127–133.

——. 2003. "Bioethics in a Multicultural World: Medicine and Morality in Pluralistic Settings." *Health Care Analysis* 11 (2): 99–117.

——. 2005. "From the Local to the Global: Bioethics and the Concept of Culture." *Journal of Medicine and Philosophy* 30 (3): 305–320.

——. 2009. "Anthropological and Sociological Critiques of Bioethics." *Bioethical Inquiry* 6 (1): 83–98.

Twemlow, Stuart W. 2005. "The Relevance of Psychoanalysis to an Understanding of Terrorism." *International Journal of Psycho-Analysis* 86 (4): 957–962.

U.S. Department of Justice, Federal Bureau of Prisons. 2005. Program Statement: Hunger Strikes. Accessed July 9, 2013. http://www.google.com/url?sa=t&rct =j&q=&esrc=s&source=web&cd=1&ved=0CCoQFjAA&url=http%3A%2F %2Fwww.cbsnews.com%2Fhtdocs%2Fpdf%2FBOP_FBI_hungerstrikepolicy .pdf&ei=3izcUZL3Osf_4AOawICQBQ&usg=AFQjCNFaiHGWU8gNHm VdWb1TmX3clWWAAQ&sig2=T6CUmrfzXaljaliSAAlqLw&bvm=bv.4870 5608,d.dmg.

U.S. Department of Veterans Affairs. 2007. "VA Is Nation's Largest Provider of Mental Health Services." Press release. March 11. Accessed May 11, 2013. http:// www.va.gov/opa/pressrel/pressrelease.cfm?id=1310.

——. 2010. "Stressor Determinations for Posttraumatic Stress Disorder." *Federal Register* 75 (133): 39843–39852.

——. 2012. *Veterans Compensation Benefits Rate Tables—Effective 12/1/12.* http:// benefits.va.gov/COMPENSATION/resources_comp01.asp. Accessed May 21, 2013.

——. 2013. "About VA: History—VA History." Updated March 14. Accessed May 15, 2013. http://www.va.gov/about_va/vahistory.asp.

United States of America v. Abd al-Rahim Hussein Muhammed Abdu al-Nashiri. 2012a. Renewed Defense Motion to Require JTF GTMO to Allow the Defendant to be Unrestrained during Attorney Client Meetings. Office of Military Commissions. Accessed March 15, 2013. http://www.mc.mil /CASES/MilitaryCommissions.aspx.

——. 2012b. Government Motion to Compel Disclosure of the Accused's Mental Health Information in Light of the Defense Having Placed His Mental Health at Issue in Its Request for the Accused to be Unrestrained During Attorney Client Meetings. Office of Military Commissions. Accessed March 15, 2013. http:// www.mc.mil/CASES/MilitaryCommissions.aspx, accessed March 15, 2013.

——. 2012c. Defense Response to Government Motion to Compel Disclosure of the Accused's Mental Health Information in Light of the Defense Having Placed His Mental Health at Issue in Its Request for the Accused to be Unrestrained During Attorney-Client Meetings. Office of Military Commissions. Accessed March 15, 2013. http://www.mc.mil/CASES/MilitaryCommissions.aspx.

——. 2012d. Government Response to Defense Motion to Defer Consideration of AE 099 until the Accused Can Be Examined By Defense Doctors. Accessed March 15, 2013. http://www.mc.mil/CASES/MilitaryCommissions.aspx.

——. 2012e. Defense Reply to the Government's Response to the Defense Motion to Defer Consideration of AE099 until the Accused Can Be Examined by Defense Doctors. Accessed March 15, 2013. http://www.mc.mil/CASES/ MilitaryCommissions.aspx.

——. 2012f. Government Motion for Inquiry Into the Mental Capacity of the Accused under R.M.C. 706. Accessed March 15, 2013. http://www.mc.mil /CASES/MilitaryCommissions.aspx.

——. 2012g. Defense Response to Government Motion for Inquiry Into Mental Capacity of the Accused under R.M.C. 706. Accessed March 15, 2013. http:// www.mc.mil/CASES/MilitaryCommissions.aspx.

——. 2012h. Government Reply to Defense Response to Government Motion for Inquiry Into the Mental Capacity of the Accused under R.M .C. 706. Accessed March 15, 2013. http://www.mc.mil/CASES/MilitaryCommissions.aspx.

United States of America v. Ahmed Mohammed Ahmed Haza Al Darbi. 2008a. Defense Motion to Suppress Statements. Accessed March 15, 2013. http://www .mc.mil/CASES/MilitaryCommissions.aspx.

——. 2008b. Government's Motion for Access to Accused for Medical and Mental Health Evaluation and for Reciprical [*sic*] Discovery Concerning Accused's Physical and Mental Health. Accessed March 15, 2013. http://www.mc.mil /CASES/MilitaryCommissions.aspx.

——. 2009. Defense Response to Government's Motion for Access to the Accused for Medical and Mental Health Evaluation and for Reciprocal Discovery Concerning Accused's Physical and Mental Health. Accessed March 15, 2013. http://www.mc.mil/CASES/MilitaryCommissions.aspx.

United States of America v. Ibrahim al Qosi. 2008. Defense Motion to Suppress All Statements of the Accused. Accessed March 16, 2013. http://www.mc.mil /CASES/MilitaryCommissions.aspx.

——. 2009. Government's Response to Defense Motion to Suppress All Statements by the Accused. Accessed March 16, 2013. http://www.mc.mil/CASES /MilitaryCommissions.aspx.

——. 2010a. Defense Motion for Appropriate Relief (Grant Expert Psychiatric Consultant). Accessed March 16, 2013. http://www.mc.mil/CASES/Military Commissions.aspx.

——. 2010b. Defense Motion for Appropriate Relief (Grant Expert Psychiatric Consultant), Part 3. Accessed March 16, 2013. http://www.mc.mil/CASES /MilitaryCommissions.aspx.

——. 2010c. Government Response. Accessed March 16, 2013. http://www .mc.mil/CASES/MilitaryCommissions.aspx.

——. 2010d. ORDER D-028 Defense Motion for Appropriate Relief Grant Expert Psychiatric Consultant) [*sic*]. Accessed March 16, 2013. http://www .mc.mil/CASES/MilitaryCommissions.aspx.

United States of America v. Mohammed Jawad. 2008a. Revised Defense Application for Mental Examination Pursuant to RMC 706. Accessed March 20, 2013. http://www.mc.mil/CASES/MilitaryCommissions.aspx.

——. 2008b. Defense Motion to Dismiss Based on Torture of Detainee Pursuant to R.M.C. 907. Accessed March 20, 2013. http://www.mc.mil/CASES/Military Commissions.aspx.

——. 2008c. Government's Response to the Revised Defense Application for Mental Examination Pursuant to RMC 706. Accessed March 20, 2013. http:// www.mc.mil/CASES/MilitaryCommissions.aspx.

——. 2008d. Government Response to Defense Motion to Dismiss Based on Torture of Detainee Pursuant to R.M.C. 907. Accessed March 20, 2013. http://www.mc.mil/CASES/MilitaryCommissions.aspx.

——. 2008e. Order [Granting Defense Motion Application for Mental Examination Pursuant to RMC 706] Dated [6/20/2008]. Accessed March 20, 2013. http://www.mc.mil/CASES/MilitaryCommissions.aspx.

——. 2008f. Defense Motion for Appointment of Expert Consultants Dr. Allen Keller and Dr. Katherine Porterfield, and Defense Investigator David Fechheimer. Accessed March 20, 2013. http://www.mc.mil/CASES/Military Commissions.aspx.

——. 2008g. Government Response to Defense Motion for Appointment of Expert Consultants (Keller and Porterfield) and Defense Investigator (Fechheimer). Accessed March 20, 2013. http://www.mc.mil/CASES/MilitaryCommissions.aspx.

——. 2008h. Ruling on Defense Motion to Dismiss – Torture of the Detainee. Accessed March 20, 2013. http://www.mc.mil/CASES/MilitaryCommissions .aspx.

United States of America v. Mohammed Kamin. 2008a. Defense Motion for Appropriate Relief Order for Appointment and Funding of Requested Defense Expert Consultant Dr [REDACTED] in the Field of Clinical and Forensic Psychology. Accessed March 20, 2013. http://www.mc.mil/CASES/Military Commissions.aspx.

——. 2008b. Government Response to Defense Motion for Appropriate Relief Order for Appointment and Funding of Requested Defense Expert Consultant Dr [REDACTED] in the Field of Clinical and Forensic Psychology. Accessed March 20, 2013. http://www.mc.mil/CASES/MilitaryCommissions.aspx.

——. 2008c. Order: Inquiry Into the Mental Capacity or Mental Responsibility of the Accused. Accessed March 20, 2013. http://www.mc.mil/CASES/Military Commissions.aspx.

——. 2008d. R.M.C 706 Board Results (Part 1). Accessed March 20, 2013. http://www.mc.mil/CASES/MilitaryCommissions.aspx.

——. 2008e. R.M.C 706 Board Results (Part 1I). Accessed March 20, 2013. http://www.mc.mil/CASES/MilitaryCommissions.aspx.

——. 2008f. Defense Motion to Compel an Order for Production of Medical and Detention Records. Accessed March 20, 2013. http://www.mc.mil/CASES /MilitaryCommissions.aspx.

——. 2009a. Ruling on Defense Motion Requesting the Commission Order the Appointment and Funding of Dr. [REDACTED] M.A. , Ph.D., to Work as

an Expert Consultant for the Defense. Accessed March 20, 2013. http://www
.mc.mil/CASES/MilitaryCommissions.aspx.

——. 2009b. Defense Motion for Appropriate Relief: An Order to Permit the
Defense Access to View the Bagram Theater Internment Facility and Inspect
Detention Records. Accessed March 20, 2013. http://www.mc.mil/CASES
/MilitaryCommissions.aspx.

——. 2009c. Government Response to Defense Motion for Appropriate Relief An
Order to Permit the Defense Access to View the Bagram Theater Internment
Facility and Inspect Detention Records. Accessed March 20, 2013. http://www
.mc.mil/CASES/MilitaryCommissions.aspx.

——. 2009d. Defense Motion Requesting the Military Commission Order a New
Inquiry Into the Mental Health of the Accused. Accessed March 20, 2013.
http://www.mc.mil/CASES/MilitaryCommissions.aspx.

——. 2009e. Government Response to Supplement to Defense Motion for
Order of an Inquiry Into the Mental Capacity or Mental Responsibility of
the Accused. Accessed March 20, 2013. http://www.mc.mil/CASES/Military
Commissions.aspx.

——. 2009f. Order: Inquiry Into the Mental Capacity or Mental Responsibility of
the Accused. Accessed March 20, 2013. http://www.mc.mil/CASES/Military
Commissions.aspx.

van Dijk, Teun A. 1993. "Principles of Critical Discourse Analysis." *Discourse and
Society* 4 (2): 249–283.

Vedantam, Shankar. 2005. "Medical Experts Debate Role in Facilitating Interrogations." *Washington Post*, November 14.

——. 2007. "APA Rules on Interrogation Abuse; Psychologists' Group Bars Member Participation in Certain Techniques." *Washington Post*, August 20.

Victoroff, Jeff. 2009. "Suicide Terrorism and the Biology of Significance." *Political
Psychology* 30 (3): 397–400.

Vietnam Veterans of America. 2004. *How the VA Evaluates Levels of Disability.*
Accessed May 21, 2013. http://www.vva.org/ptsd_levels.html.

Waddington, Richard. 2006. "UN Alleges Torture at Guantanamo." *St. Petersburg
Times*, February 17.

Waitzkin, Howard. 1979. "Medicine, Superstructure, and Micropolitics." *Social
Science and Medicine* 13A (6): 601–609.

Waldram, James. 2007. "Narrative and the Construction of 'Truth' in a Prison-
Based Treatment for Sexual Offenders." *Ethnography* 8 (2): 145–169.

——. 2008. "The Narrative Challenge to Cognitive Behavioral Treatment of Sexual Offenders." *Culture, Medicine, and Psychiatry* 32 (3): 421–439.

Wasley, Paula. 2006. "Psychologists Debate Ethics of Their Involvement in Interrogations." *Chronicle of Higher Education*, September 1.

Watson Institute. 2011. "Costs of War." Brown University. Accessed May 21, 2013. http://costsofwar.org/.

Welner, Michael. 2011a. "Facing Jihad's Risk a Corrections Issue, Inside Guantanamo and Out." ABC News, February 16. Accessed October 31, 2012. http://abcnews.go.com/TheLaw/terrorism-gitmo-detainees-striking/story?id=12924237&page=2#.UJGRdhxIX5k.

——. 2011b. "Omar Khadr and the Jihadism That Lurks in Our Prisons." *National Post*, February 19. Accessed April 4, 2012. http://fullcomment.nationalpost.com/2011/02/19/michael-welner-omar-khadr-and-the-jihadism-that-lurks-in-our-prisons/.

White, Dave. 2007–2008. "Market Patriotism and the 'War on Terror.'" *Social Justice* 34 (3–4): 111–131.

White House. 2009. *Executive Order: Review and Disposition of Individuals Detained at the Guantánamo Bay Naval Base and Closure of Detention Facilities.* January 22. Accessed January 22, 2009. http://media.washingtonpost.com/wp-srv/. politics/documents/gitmo_012209.pdf?sidST2009012101583&s_poslist.

——. 2010. *National Security Strategy.* May 10. Accessed April 24, 2014. http://www.whitehouse.gov/sites/default/files/rss_viewer/national_security_strategy.pdf.

——. 2013a. *Statement by the the* [sic] *President on H.R. 4310.* January 3. Accessed April 24, 2014. http://www.whitehouse.gov/the-press-office/2013/01/03/statement-president-hr-4310.

——. 2013b. *Statement by the President on H.R. 3304.* December 26. Accessed May 5, 2014. http://www.whitehouse.gov/the-press-office/2013/12/26/statement-president-hr-3304.

Wright, Lawrence. 2008. "The Rebellion Within: An Al Qaeda Mastermind Questions Terrorism." *New Yorker*. Accessed October 3, 2012. http://www.newyorker.com/reporting/2008/06/02/080602fa_fact_wright?currentPage=all.

Wurmser, Leon. 2004. "Psychoanalytic Reflections on 9/11, Terrorism, and Genocidal Prejudice: Roots and Sequels." *Journal of the American Psychoanalytic Association* 52 (3): 911–926.

Xenakis, Stephen N. 2010. "Radical Jihadism Is Not a Mental Disorder." *Washington Post*, December 12.

Yerushalmi, Yosif Hayem. 1991. *Freud's Moses: Judaism Terminable and Intermi-nable*. Binghamton, N.Y.: Vail-Ballou Press.

Yoo, John. 2002. *Application of Treaties and Laws to al Qaeda and Taliban Detainees*. Accessed July 9, 2013. http://www.gwu.edu/~nsarchiv/NSAEBB /NSAEBB127/02.01.09.pdf.

Young, Allan. 1982. "The Anthropologies of Illness and Sickness." *Annual Review of Anthropology* 11:257–285.

——. 1995. *The Harmony of Illusions: Inventing Post-Traumatic Stress Disorder*. Princeton, N.J.: Princeton University Press.

——. 2008. "A Time to Change Our Minds: Anthropology and Psychiatry in the 21st Century." *Culture, Medicine, and Psychiatry* 32 (2): 298–300.

Young, Robert M. 2001. "Fundamentalism and Terrorism." *Free Associations* 9A: 24–57.

Zola, Irving Kenneth. 1972. "Medicine as an Institution of Social Control." *Socio-logical Review* 20 (4): 487–504.

Between Two Junes is a Forest

A Journal of Everything

▲ ▲ ▲ ▲

By
Geoffrey Dilenschneider

New Millennium Press

First published in the United States of America in 2003
by New Millennium Entertainment, Inc.
301 N. Canon Drive #214
Beverly Hills, CA 90210

Library of Congress Cataloging-in-Publication Data available upon request.
ISBN: 1-893224-83-X

Interior design by Carolyn Wendt

Printed in the United States of America
www.NewmillenniumPress.com

10 9 8 7 6 5 4 3 2

Dedicated to *her*.

If you read, you judge

Introduction

Dear Reader,

I am not what you would consider a fifteen-year-old poet to be; nor am I a sixteen-year-old poet; rather, I am a poet; a soul; a human being. And in that way, I am adequately equipped to connect with you. It is with great happiness and with the understanding that I am privileged enough to be able to share a part of me with you that we can step into this book together; a book that could just be another book on a shelf; another little piece of nothing on a place of nothing surrounded by nothings, but it doesn't have to be that. You can make it a great piece of superformidable wonder and a flurrying alliteration of grandiosity and beauty. So come one, come all, to this fest of lurid outings in the veracity of my life; but do not assume this is just me and all of me, for it is not.

Okay, now let me tell you a few things about myself. For starters, I love my parents more than anything in the world. They are the nicest, most caring, selfless individuals in the world. I couldn't imagine life without them. My brother, as well, is the coolest kid in the world. His sense of humor is beyond anything I've ever seen. He continually makes me laugh, sometimes so hard that I just scream with laughter. I love my friends. They're real friends. Not acquaintances.

At school and abroad, I see many people; tall people, crazy people, happy people – all types of people. I believe that every person has his or her own special talent that no one will ever do better. It's all theirs, and since I believe that women are more spiritually conscience, I see many things through the eyes of women. It's easier for me to see their potential. I love all people because of this, and it will become obvious to you that this perspective opens up whole worlds of inspiration for me.

That said, I must accommodate that I have always felt a certain need to meet people. I've always had a desire to learn things about people. Just *things*. Not about history, chemistry, etc. – I do learn these things anyway – but rather, about all the individual souls out there; the distinctive minds; the average hearts; everybody. I can't get enough of it. Almost as though 'people' – everybody – are my collective muse.

There is always more to learn; always more to experience. All I know is all I know, and we all must learn to love.

Which brings me to another point: we are constantly raising the bar higher; taking our worlds to the next level. Look around. World records being broken, new technology being created; even video games are getting in to it; and it all seems to be a great trend until someone with a voice comes along and asks, When will someone take it too high? When is it going to come crashing back down, ruining all the good things we have? Or has it happened already?… and then the world comes to a halt, realizing that this isn't a run, it's a cycle, and that some point in time *has* to mark the end of what we have today. It can't go on forever. It might not even go on for much time at all. Just look around. It's a crazy place full of every imaginable thing, and it's hard to see how anything could be intangible.

Regardless of the horrible place we live in, people all have a wonderful place *inside* of them; they just need to thaw out that place in hopes to realize their own true happiness; drop down from their perch of materialism, if you want, and bust open the gates of emotion; of opinion; of truth and integrity. Let the feeling grasp you by the small of your back and throw you fully into the fires within! The fires of your one perfection! And let no one know why you are happy, just be happy in your self.

Enough of that story. I have only one more thing to describe. It's called bleeding. I don't mean to impart the notion of blood-letting, don't worry. I simply want to describe the thought of bleeding. What is bleeding? Bleeding is the concept better known as the *energy of love*. It must fill up the human and use itself up, and there is no real love unless it is shared. From the depths of the boil from which we began, through the periods of unrest and erudition, then through the mundane and monotonous, and beyond the plain in which we spend so few days in the dream of an adventure of life and death; all this, and for what? For love, our truth.

Here's to those who don't know why, and here's to those who care.

Geoffrey Dilenschneider

Introduction #2

▲ ▲ ▲ ▲

(Why? Because I can't just have one introduction!)

I wrote this to my creative writing class on the last day of class of the second quarter. It would be our last day as a formal class on a full day of school. Dad says this essay was good. I felt like I made such an impact on him just by reading it out loud, so I felt it necessary to put it in here. You'll notice I try to be funny. Well, throughout the school year I had been asked to be funny, but could never really do it. They would always take my humor seriously.

I speak early on about something I had written earlier, a piece so dastardly that I did not feel it proper to add to this book. I sum up that piece as follows: "Some people in this class aren't 'writers,' therefore they shouldn't be in this class." Some people had even admitted in the classroom that they only were taking Creative Writing for the "easy A." In this second introduction, I let it be known that what they interpreted my piece to be (they thought I said (incorrectly), that everyone should die), was actually a misinterpretation. Just read for what it is and what you see in it, humor aside.

The Last Freewrite

Good afternoon. This is the Last Freewrite, and I'm your host, Jeff Dilenschneider.

Some say that this class has been an effort; others, a burden; still others, a waste of time altogether. I say – and as a point of clarification – that some people's futures do not include the level of dedication that rivals that of Kelsey (a woman who has devoted her life to writing poetry). That is what I meant when I said that some people in this class aren't "writers."

It comes, in time, a period of self-understanding, this class happenstancically coming and going a number of times during this spell of somehow-muted self-understanding.

As of late I have turned to music as my main form of expression; a form, I believe, I will never truly depart from as long as I live. As well as have I turned away from the gradebook, opting for a life of happiness rather than furtherment in culture. I chose, now I suffer; but also I reap the benefits, which happen to be much sweeter than those of a different choice.

For those of you in here – in what was once a safe haven and a place of enlightened expression – who *wonder* upon words, tiptoeing, even, like upon eggshells upon thin ice; those of you shall find other pursuits, I hope.

Whom I fear for is those of you who feel that burning desire within. Be you writer, artist, or unbeknowest of your specific talent as of yet. I fear that the burden you carry, and will carry into the future, is a heavy, uneven one. I fear more the journey you will come upon and the adventures you will stumble into, for those are where even we cannot begin to understand ourselves – the place one must begin at in order to succeed.

However, what I fear most is the future of those who have an extraordinary gift, but whom do not know they have it. I fear your future the most because it is uncertain – the scariest thing of all is that which we do not know.

The depths of infinity reach greatest in our own souls. What you – what we *all* must do is look into the reflection of a reflection of ourselves. That way, we will be able to see a manifest – however microcosmically – of our being.

Humanity is a blink of time. I know that I am but an instant of that instant, but at least I know that I have the ability – have the choice – to make a difference. And even if that difference is small, I will be remembered. Let not yourself go unremembered. *That* is true sadness.

So I will end this on a positive note, for people like us cannot stand listening to something as boring as this obviously has been... Here goes... A lesson learned: you are only bored if you're not smart enough to make the boredom go away.

Okay, bad ending. I'll try again: no one finds happiness. People are just happy.

No... okay, I'll go with the silly saying: think outside the box. The world you all live in now – complete with false religions, rationalizations, and death – is a box; a box in which we are stuck. We die because the box is filled with quicksand, this box of life. We only have a limited time to breathe our breath until we go under.

The question I ask is: how does one get *out* of that box, for good? And: if one ever succeeds, what is he going to *find*?, outside the box.

For the Last Freewrite, I'm Jeff Dilenschneider, and *that* was the good afternoon.

Chapter 8, 9

▲ ▲ ▲ ▲

BAM! And school was over! Suddenly, the whole year seemed a dream in a slight bit of mist, a sick joke that was now over. I was finally free! Free like the birds! I sure loved school, but those who love school, love freedom even more. And this was only the beginning.

Just A Mask

All these things happen so quick!
Look here! There! Here! Stick!
To one thing not a moment.
Can't you be dormant?
Friends coming. Friends going.
Friends staying. People leaving.
Stop please? Never.
Keep it up, you're almost there.
All this motion.
All this commotion
In this giant ocean.
Oh, so great. I feel so happy,
Alive.
Keep coming. Bring it on.
You! In the black and blue,
Get out, you're too sad to be here.
(Even in these times of happiness,
I still see the streaks
Of the real life so true.)

Everyone is welcome
To join in this feast!
Don't let the weather
Spoil the beast!
The beast being which
The one of this party
And I feel so great.
Keep it moving. Let's go.
On and on we are skipping
To this muted little life
Of unhappy moments and freedoms seldom fulfilling.
But happy now.
Keep smiling. It's good for you.
Wait.
Come back.
It's just begun.

But really it started
So long ago, you realize.
And then you're alone once again.

Tired eyes
Mix the lies
Into a thick paste
That will cement and harden
Over the cruel truths
That daylight holds at bay,
Day in and day out.
Broken ankles from mild ego highs
And sprained spines from disks behind
That were thrown wide of the receiver
Too many times.
You went the wrong way,
But you won't end up winning.
The only certain in this life
Is the skull-shattering suspension
Of things easy to disbelieve
During the day, but at night,
Those things come to boogey-man haunt you
In more than dreams.
This life of yours is very true, my friend.
Reality hurts, especially you.
Depression.

— June 29, 2001

After spending a few days in front of a local supermarket, driving money towards a mission trip to get to the Dominican Republic, selling Yankee Baseball tickets to old ladies with wooden canes, I had made it, and with making it came the squalid realization of how horrible a place the world could be. But I loved it there nonetheless. Since I speak Spanish, as well as a bit of Mexican Spanish, I had no trouble at all conversing with the people who lived there; the only linguistic related problem was with the Haitians who were continually crossing over the border in order to escape the Haiti government. Some places in the Dominican were wonderful. Yeah, the ones we passed through on the way to our hotel, which was more of a live-in house for all the groups of kids who came to work for weeks at a time. The places we visited, however, were horrible. Anyone who visits the Dominican Republic, or for that matter any country with a section devoted to and populated by the underprivileged, will understand how grave a place it is to be; overwhelming is a word I would like to use, but I would consider the best word to describe the feeling one gets when in the belly of the beast would be quincipogorious, meaning the devil's place of gory death.

Geoffrey Dilenschneider

Arms-A-Swinging

A passageway of connecting slabs
Being contemplated by white coats in labs.
Only those who act true
Can move on.
Scheme and rhyme do not matter,
Not in a world which can't get much fatter.
But amazingly it does complete
That dastardly feat
Of moving on to the next level.

Moving swiftly,
Only to stop.
Becoming hardened,
Only to flop.
Waiting slowly,
Only to go.
And leaping blindly,
Only to know.

Generals in checkered-whites
Behind bards, who lost many fights
Can describe the feelings within,
But have the most trouble with where to begin.

One is not always one
And the best are only saying so.
Last is always last
But nobody last ever says that it's so.

Cracks in crackless floors
Heal in time,
Never by handing
That poor man a dime.

Hate in a hateless world
Heals in time,
Never by handing
That poor man a dime.

Tape unsticks in a perfect world.
Not everything heals
In its due time.
But that poor man will heal,
If you hand him a dime.

Club Bed Bug

Cracked little sidewalks
And garbage piled high,
Hords of little boys
Just waiting to die.
Dirt littered streets
And scooters running by,
Giving this world
A large pollution high.

Church is a major
Event in their lives
Dirty water's like platinum,
Food like gold,
Even though those'll
Make 'em die not so old.

Limps here, there,
Everyone's bold;
Wearing long pants
But no mention of cold.

Bugs riding ripples
Of waves in my bed.
With many sounds at night
My ears have yet to be wed.
Don hotter clothes
Everyone does today
To visit the churches
For surely all day.

But there is redemption
In our Lord's great name,
Even if day in, out
For them's always the same.

On the trip, I met a girl named Eliza – a short, orange-haired and freckled beauty. She was seventeen to my fifteen, but we connected a bit. I had Green Day in my CD player at the time, and wrote some new lyrics to the older song, a little thing I would do to pass the time to and from the Bateys – extremely poor areas populated by a majority of sugarcane farmers, whom I took so much pity for – as we all needed something to do, really.

A Fairy Tale

Verse I   He heard your stately yawn
Over you this guy does fawn
And black tree leaves
Hold you hidden
From all other prying eyes
He just wishes that you would not push him away.

Well, what is said is said
He must now dry his eyes
Life is over
For the moment
And he feels like such a failure
Especially when you're always berating him.

Chorus   No time to gulp the whole drink down
'Cause it's made of all his tears
From all of your frowns.

Verse II   He's seen winds change before
For the better of course
Maybe we can
Start again and
He hopes that you'll succeed and
As your blue eyes always show him where the right path is true.

So go with who you like
Just remember what he's like
He wishes
That he knew you
'Cause he knows that you he'd like
By the way that you have always held yourself upright.

Verse III   He knows that you are real
'Cause he loves to hear you laugh
And he can't get
Off your smile
'Cause it makes him so full of
A presence in him that he can't describe with words.

This only happens in
Tales by Goose and Grimm
But he won't stop
And he won't leave
Just because his friends say give up
He knows that he is never going to forget about you.

Verse IV   Our God has graced her life
So Lord, grace his with her
We all see that
By the way they
Look into each other's eyes
And he'll go so far for her and will not say why.

Don't discard him like
A stepped on Mike and Ike
He is worth
A pretty penny
But we all don't know why
He keeps himself so hidden cause he is so shy.

Chorus   No time to gulp the whole drink down
'Cause it's made of all his tears
From all of your frowns...
From all of your frowns...
From all of your frowns...
From all of your frowns.

My Love

Everyone's different
Everyone's the same.
So fragile
And so delicate,
Yet brittle
And insane.
I love everyone
Men women children
All the same.
No matter how bad
A person man seem
There is something in them somewhere
That only they have which gleams.

Maybe it's because
I see the Lord's love
Lying happily in children's hearts
That live without shoes
And walk on broken glass dirt paths.
That live without education
And don't know how to diet or why it's good to brush their teeth.
That live without material,
Only old throwaways from rich oil drillers off a reef.

All people, I am brought to love
By a solitary peace dove.
Not for their looks,
But for who they are inside all the while
And because they have the power
To instill in others a simple smile.

On a bus out to one of the bateys, I, pondering again, felt compelled to write this essay. At the time, I had been infatuated with a petite and fair-skinned brunette named Ali Watts, whom was completely involved with Tim Shaw, a strong-headed but likeable jock – a fact I had not known.

Multi-colored Stream

While everyone lies asleep, I ponder the meaning of myself. I ponder the meanings of words. I ponder everything. I ask myself about what I have done, who I have done it to, and most importantly why I did it. I don't think of things good or of things bad or anything in between. I only ponder everything, and everything in between. What have I done, what am I doing, what will I do, where will I go, where am I going, and most importantly why.

I ponder my welling tears at my simple revelation: God's love's for everyone, whether asked of it or not. His love will fill us when we let it do so. Only until the time we lift our arms towards the sky and ask, will we not be complete.

I am now complete. I ponder what I'm going to do and where I'm going to go, but now I know who I'm going with: God, cause he loves me so.

Untitled Stream of Consciousness

I saw some other guy with a girl I really like being openly over-affectionate, but my hate for it died almost immediately. It was replaced… no, not replaced, more like conquered by something already present. It was conquered by God's love that fills me; and I smiled.

I feel angry when I see them so in love that I feel deprived somehow. I wonder for but a second if there could be something the matter with my psyche. I dismiss the intruding thought with a shake of my head. But when I see them touch together in some unknown individual matrimony of two beings, and they complete this repetitive, yet never-tiring, matrimony with two angelic smiles (which are meant totally for each other and no one else), it somehow brings my own personal smile to my lips. Live long, friends. Don't let anything get in the way of your up-prophesized and unprecedented companionship.

You will never be forgotten, Timmy and Ali.

So I put Ali behind me for the time being, and concentrated on Eliza. Bad move, in hindsight, though. The group got wind of it somehow, and it blew up in my face. The day after everything went spiraling down, you know, the time where one says: "it can't get any worse," and then it does. Well, yeah. That's what happened. She stopped talking to me altogether; reducing our communications to the evil glares she gave me sporadically throughout the following days. It was a very emotional time for me.

Willpower

I try to be nice but horrible ugly things come out instead. Is this what He has planned for me? What kind of sign is she showing inadvertently to me? How have I not yet learned to deal with this? I thought that she understood… but I guess I'm only cute. I can't just sigh and forget about it. I need to write. It gets me somewhere. The wrong combination never makes everything okay. I can't cry and can't laugh. Saying anything makes it worse. I just wonder how much more personal one can get. How is writing going to get my point across any clearer than it already is? I wonder what goes on in others heads; especially in the heads of those laughing at me. Are they being rational? Or are they just rationalizing? Why does she hate me and care? What is so interesting about my writings? Why does she want to read my writings? To say, "good?" What, am I somehow accidentally asking for her acceptance? If I can't understand her… are we the same in that much? Precedence… I think not.

What is so funny? I won't curse. I wish I had the ability to speak my mind through my larynx and tongue rather than my lower right arm's muscles and fingers. Johnny Cochran only said what was needed; why can't I do the same? What is so wrong with me to make the perception of my leg a bridge between two somehow different species, one being alone and the other the longed-for relationship of two wanted by the other?

Why did I throw that straw? That unacceptable word? Him, that plethora of water? Which spews from that bottle like stupidity from my mouth. Why I am changing, I don't know. I knew who I was, I was cool, but it's not me. So I'm changing. But why? And for what?

I keep coming to this question in my plethora of thoughts: what is her motive? Where is she coming from? See… it's endless. No amount of paper or memory could hold all my questions of her mind. Worse is that I have enough time to ask but one of those endless questions, let alone the time for an answer. If it should come to but one question, it must be so with an extremely long answer: who are you?

And I ask not for her name, but for the one hundred percent complete answer; everything and all of it; nothing forgotten. I ask not for who she is to me, or him, or from anyone's perspective for that matter; only hers.

I believe I am looking for some connection with someone else. I seem to be driven somehow by an unknown force to find this connection, physical and otherwise. But this need is created by a lack of the former, which, in turn, after time, makes my psyche so unfamiliar with these communications that when they occur, my own lack of experience drives the other party away. Alone again, I am. Who am I? I can't even begin to understand.

Do I mean anything to her? Am I just another no-name in a line full of entertainers who are waiting defiant and impatient for her undivided attention? Was that secret smile for me or for herself? How can I ask, anyway? Do I know her? No. Will she ever know me? Or is it: will I ever know her? Or is it both or am I way off track? Who are all these faces? I pray to God that I have the time to get to know every single one of them.

I am not writing for others, rather, I am here to bring my sub-conscious thoughts to a manifestation that might give my conscious mind something of an idea of who I am. What is wrong with me? Why can I not bring my extremely scared and frightful heart to begin a conversation with her? Scared because I'm not sure what I'll say and how I'll act and frightful because I'm in the dark about what she'll say (if anything, which is the scariest) and what she'll do.

Where am I going? Only He can say, but who am I going with? is the real question. When I was talking in Spanish with my newly-made friends in a Batey in the Dominican Republic, they asked me who I liked. I said I liked the girl with her shirt sleeves rolled up. We talked about her some more, and all the while this weird feeling kept growing in my chest. What is this? What does it mean for the future? Usually if you stare at someone long enough you will begin to see imperfects. Not her. She only becomes more beautiful.

I like being alone. It gives me time to think. And even though I want a companion (which is something I believe everyone else equally wants), I can't take that leap of faith of getting to know someone where they have seen me for who I am. I have tried so many damnable times. Some take on a parasite of fear, some just make fun of me, and worst of all, a few have earned my trust in order to use me and further down the road stab me in the back (numerous times).

Life is like baseball: only do the required in order to get the desired response; try not to overkill (it makes it worse).

I feel as though I'm the guy who dies unloved and unremembered only because he couldn't find that one who loved him back. I want to change my destiny.

I just want to be loved. And it hearkens my heart to say so. But this deep, deep pain that fills the galaxy-sized cavity that is somehow eating away at my mind, heart, and soul is beginning to become too burdensome to hold inside any longer. Why can't I just walk up to her and say, "I would like to get to know you"? Answer: I simply don't have the *cajones* for it!

I usually have been able to, but when I feel so scared about what could and could not happen, I can't. I'm scared of the possibilities, as though my mind has already decided on the answer: no way, buckaroo.

It's all for you. My confounded mind is stuck on you! Why? Do I like you? Dunno… I barely know you! The only thing I can manage to say to you is, "Your stomach still hurt?"

I wish that I was different. Then life would be good. Don't get me wrong, life is awesome; and in itself it is awesome, but I just want a different set of problems. I'm just so sick and tired of mine. I just want to have a true friend.

I am his shell   .self real his am I

That's me.
"It's all the past" is what I think when I look back on all the things I've written. I don't know why I write anymore. I've lost that fire, the fire that drives me to bring ideas to others' minds. This is pointless, writing to ease my mind. Why can't I be social all the time? It's so hard to go back and forth from my 'writing mode' to my 'happy mode'. I try my hardest to be happy but I just relapse into sadness.

Do I take things way to seriously, or am I not serious enough? My problem: I can't will someone to talk with me and I'm afraid to do it myself. But no one cares.

Not everything has to be written. Talk is okay.

These genuine thoughts emanate from my mind because writing alone is my only form of communication; it is where I am ultimately meant to be. I feel so alone. I can only wonder if everyone else feels the same way as I do... or at least similarly. Because then I would be alone and at the same time not alone at all. If that is true, then there is a slight chance I might be able to find myself.

And this is where I begin.

Something More

I don't know how to feel. What is this? Oh, it's the smell of burning sugarcane in the factory in my soul. Does generosity fit in there somewhere? How about a smile? Or continuous companionship? Or human compassion? I'd like to help twenty-four/seven. Why do they care so much? Is this an unnamed sign? He is in me today, I think really for the first time. I can feel it because I can look at someone I hate and feel nothing but love. The barbed wire that continuously scrapes a path through my heart day in and day out has yet to finish. That may mean that I am hurt, but that also there just may be some reason to sow these two seeds which have potential to grow into something much greater. What is this feeling? Nothing... really! It's absolutely nothing... really. Nothing. Nothing at all, really. Really.

(morning /\)   ***   (evening \/)

It only gets worse; it only gets better. But which is happening? This handprint of cement on my chest signifies something greater. I wonder why I can't find a comfortable position. And I don't mean that in a directly physical sense. I mean it in a more mental, psychological, and relationship sense. I have always wondered what went on in their heads. I have also wondered the notion of a smile and where it really originates from and what it really means; especially theirs. I can safely say that all those feelings were lust and not love... this is the first time I have felt for someone not for their body or their looks or the rumors of their performance, but for who they are, truly. Their smiles warm my heart so much it is insane. Their laughs, respectively, are both not as a lark, but as the vocals of God.

And where may this go? Somewhere, I hope. I will pray not for a good future, but instead for my path and theirs to run their full limitless courses without any interruption. Looking into their eyes is looking into the deepest of my own soul: pitch black, without depth, endless.

There is no bulge in my pants (my apologies for being vulgar), but I am almost certain there is a bulge in my heart and soul's eye. I am just scared to admit it because when and if I do, I will predictably act weird around them, driving them as far away as Pluto, and farther. So soft is their touch that my body shakes and quivers in sheer anticipation as their respective hands smoothly fly through the binding air to complete the simple action of patting me on the shoulder for a job well done.

I am scared not for the future, but for tomorrow. Is their sudden attachment to me merely because I have been kicked in the back so many times by them and they both are merely trying to be nice to me for a day to make up for their mistake, or is it something more? Tomorrow is another day, another smile, and just another mile. The only question is: what does tomorrow hold?

When I needed help, I had each of their indescribable encouragement. When I was feeling even a bit sad, I had both of their warm, consoling shoulders to cry on and both of their unmatched kindness' of voices to talk with. When I needed to get something off my chest, I had both of their undivided attentions. When I was happy or glad, they only smiled more, which, in turn, made me smile even more without even thinking. And so on and so forth. When I was laughing, they, each in their own rights, laughed, too, which, in turn, made me laugh even harder, which, in turn, made them, each in their own rights laugh even harder than before; all of this but without thought. Cement is thrown. They are not scared, I am not scared; they are not scared. And I cannot change all of these feeling and I am not trying to feel them; they are there without my consent. I can't do anything about them, and yet, I don't want to.

I feel these similar real something growing in me. It is good. Maybe it's a sign. Just like the caked cement handprints of theirs in the center of my chest. Maybe it's something new and better. Maybe it's something greater.

Finally, after talking to the whole group about it – which included Eliza – by reading one of my songs – also a big mistake – and after talking to Eliza personally, and making her very emotional about everything – something I did not want to do – I said to myself to forget about it all and that it wasn't worth it. Then I became a little depressed about it, and, because my heart happens to be a romantic one, I stopped caring and went a little weird.

I Am Defeated

When can one believe?
In a star whom won't you leave?
Can a wind whistle forever?
Or is that some kind of dream?
Does this wind whistle forever?
Or is it talking to some forgotten stream?
One may think the answer is smart,
But time may tell that that is tart
When life shows observance as the key.
I need to be there not here as a workee,
Yet so tired am I to not understand
The stinging breaths of minute proportions
That now leave my heart and soul as hungry orphans.
Can feelings change for better or worse?
I'll tell you now, the second is worst
For its possibility is so much greater.
Bitter, bitter, bitter.
My heart a bit fitter,
Yet so much more littered.

I cannot joke about the pang I felt,
Like not of a paintball welt
But a core of plutonium in my chest to melt
Deep inside my sizzling remains of a shred of hope
That once in my heart did mope.
Now it's gone,
But not forgotten
And I say:
Adieu, adieu.

Plastic and Battery Operated

Can you tell me
Why? Why? Why!?
As the tears silently tumble down my pale cheeks?
Which have been marred by a pricelessly constructed
Mini-plethora of words?
Carefully chosen
And fully understood,
These words are,
They just have yet to hit hard
The merciless brick wall of self-denial
And smash it while I sit in pinched tight trial
To eany, meany, miny, moe and point the pinky
At my heart now so dinky,
Eating scraps up off the ground,
Anywhere from which it can find
And it doesn't mind,
It's been hurt in every kind
And I will wait and see how it may fare
'cause I'm too depressed to even care?

After being depressed, I came to some sort of realization, and after that, freaked out, as you can tell in this essay:

Maybe

Will I ever get over this? Who deemed it to be this way? Why? What did I do? What didn't I do? She says that feelings change… yeah right! I look around and see conversations and smiles and laughs. But I feel removed. Alone in the corner of solitude, contemplating these horrid feelings of raging sadness. These feelings are keeping me alive, yet are killing me. I can only do one thing: try and forget. Did she mean what she said, "Is it okay if I let [a counselor on the mission trip we were on] read [the note that you are giving me] first so she can see if it's appropriate?" She sounded uncertain and afraid and confused and scared. I felt (and still feel) so horrible and disregarded, as though I had been tossed carelessly away like some unwanted teddy bear with only one arm (and a broken heart). I can always move onto another girl, but I don't want to. I DON'T WANT TO! I pray to God for His strength, His peace and tranquility, His smile, and His overall help with my situation. Not for Eliza to love me, or even to like me, but for her to feel comfortable around me. Then I pray for His strength to help me in mending that which I have undone: a sapling of a relationship. Last night was crazy.

Maybe I have it all wrong. Maybe she's playing hard to get. Maybe this plethora of evil feelings is unnecessary or even uncalled-for. Maybe she loves me. Maybe she likes me. Maybe she trusts me. Maybe she loves me. Maybe we will spend time together. Maybe the rest of our lives. Maybe she loves me. Maybe.

And then, in the middle of working on building a three-story hospital in the center of one of the sullied towns, I had a breakthrough to what I now consider one of my better works:

Strange Peace

Words won't help. Not here. Not ever. These words come slowly. I can't forget those words. I can't forget this episode. This all won't leave me. This incredible sadness envelops my whole. Why must it plague on me like this? I had forgotten. A sign. And I cry. These tears flow like ice, yet bring with them the ice from within. A sign of life with two eyes, each the same as the other, but smiling suns in their own little metal worlds. An inch, a world, holds them apart from one another. They both are chained to life, yet they can't be chained to life forever.

Before I was even able to write that I didn't believe anymore, I was given this gift. I believe. These suns are forever whirling around free and chained in a sea of life and love. They fit. But there are gaps in this kindness. And It will inevitably fall apart some day, whether or not it was meant to be. In life and in death, two suns together forever, both in the likeness of their creator, are ready and willing to be destroyed for His love. Bright eyed and bushy tailed, they smile willingly into the face of their inevitable life, inevitable love, and inevitable death. But for now, at least, we can begin this cycle with our minds open, our souls unburdened, and our hearts ready, willing, and able.

After this whole thing, I came to the end in realization, as I wish all people would after a soul-searching like that one. Why can't we all just see each other for the intricate differences, and accept them?

Chapter 10, 11; 16

▲ ▲ ▲ ▲

That whole thing was June and July. Now, I'm off to an eight day cruise on the Baltic Sea, which is kind of like one of the great lakes (Superior, really), except somewhere in between England and Russia. Later on, which is why you see 'chapter 16' there, which is out of place a little, I wrote down as much of the events that took place as I could remember. You might have heard of Katheryn French. She happens to be one of the most influential persons in my life. I haven't really realized that until now. She made me see things I might never have seen at all. And now that I look back on those times, I realize that I would not be where I am today if not for her (I wouldn't be the same me if it weren't for everyone in my life).

Katheryn French, for description's sake, is tall, about 5 foot 11, fair in skin, has green eyes that I could swear are blue, but eyes that can be cold and eviparenticious when necessary, but can also be kinesise beyond belief when they want to be. She is what you could call big boned; she is not fat at all, but doesn't look like she is anorexic. So, for me, she's just perfect. (Well, actually, I could care less about physical traits. I'd rather have a girlfriend whom I can trust, who listens, who cares, and who might even take a bullet for me. I would make sure she knew that she could trust me, that I would listen, that I would care, and that I would most definitely take a bullet for her. I wouldn't have it any other way.)

The most defining feature of Katheryn's body, which is beautiful, may I add, and besides her eyes, are her cheeks. They seem to always be blushing. It's the cutest damn thing I've ever seen, and I can barely remember her face now, but I do remember her cheeks.

I think I have a little bit of subconsciously derived memory block, because a few of the chapters in this part of the story of my life are missing. What I mean by 'memory block' is that I believe my mind doesn't want to remember what happened; it hasn't come to terms, or grips, with it yet. So don't go bonkers about the missing chapters; they're supposed to not be there… kind of.

A cruise ship is a magical place. It is a creature; a species unlike any I've ever seen. A cruise ship is a place where things such as time and the 'real world' full of problems don't exist. It is a haven from burden and a center for extreme relaxation.

The sun always ascends the heavens in magnificence, music always plays in the background like it were a movie – one never felt a need to do anything, but at the same time, always has something to do that is either provocative and amazing or succulent and sweet. A cruise ship is filled to the brim with generous helpings of entertainment, intrigue; adventure and playfulness.

And there I was: a cruise ship all for me and my racing, joyous energy. I was ready to write.

Geoffrey Dilenschneider

REMEMBER ME

Introduction

Hi, my name's Jeff. I like pizza and watching TV. I sound normal, right? Get to know me better: I think too fast, I can be impulsive, I write poetry, I have a big heart, I'm fifteen and I know what I want to do with the rest of my life. I listen to all music except country, I hacky-sac, I skateboard; what I dress like is not me, I am afraid when I do not know the limits of my physical self in controlled but dangerous situations. Sometimes I stay up all night, I switch hobbies like you switch a light switch, I need music or else I get bored. I used to have a mullet, I used to have dreads, I used to have an almost shaved head, and I used to have green and white braids covering my entire head except for my bangs. I've been all over the world, I've saved lives, I've watched people die, and from all this, I've found out only a little bit of who I really am. One thing that I've learned is that all this privilege comes at a price, and that one should never gloat over his luck and fortune. I thank God every day for putting me on this earth in the place that I am in. Everyday I try my best to help make the world a better place, even in small ways, but better nonetheless.

I believe in something: myself. I believe in my ability to listen to the voice inside me. It has some good things to say, and I believe that everyone has something there inside them; they just have to figure out how to listen to that voice. You have to be quiet and you have to find the right way to listen. I am only lucky, or maybe just heard my voice by random chance, or lucky because I heard my voice at an early age. Some might not hear their voice until they are old, or even not at all. But I wish upon all the providence of finding their own way of stopping and listening. Smell the flowers that are blooming inside you. Yeah, they're there, you just need to open your ears and eyes to the beauties of yourself.

The day I met her, August 2nd, was a day like any day. A day of winds howling only momentarily, giving way to a more phosphorescent sunrise. I don't remember anything except saying hello to her and her sister running down the stairs in the aft of the ship screaming, "KATHERYN! KATHERYN!"

That's it. I really wish I could remember more – and this will sound weird – but I won't let me remember.

The day before, August 1st, was also a day like any other day. I sat on the upper deck of the ship – outside, of course – working on a suntan and typing out poetry. Every now and then this girl (whom I would come to know as Katheryn) kept eying me, so, as I assume any other guy would do, I started eyeing her back. I also eyed the two girls on either side of her (they were Katheryn's two cousins, I'd later find out.)

Other than that, nothing spectacular happened.

August 3rd. Ah, that was a great day. We (Katheryn, her two cousins – one whom I was quite fond of – Katheryn's little sister, and I) spent the day together, just messing around, having fun.

I felt, though, that I had been quite the fool: cracking jokes, making everyone laugh, acting silly. You have to understand that that's not me. I'm more serious, more thoughtful; being the funny one isn't my reality… it's a dream I've had since I was a kid. I've dreamt of being the funny one; I never am, so I felt at the end of the day that I was a total fool, even though to them, it was how I always acted.

An odd first impression, if you ask me. Me angry that I had been the cool, funny one; them thinking I'm always the cool, funny one.

Katheryn (Socially Inept)

I act foolish
Then weird
I'm scared
I won't be like
When I'm myself.
That I'll be
Put on the shelf.
Why do I
Act foolish
Then weird?
Why am I
Scared?

I want
To scream
To yell
At me
For every
Thing I said!
I can't believe
And can't believe
That I acted
That way.
Why can't I stop?
I am drawn,
Yet want to run away.
The only way
To express these
Feelings on this page
Is to give to her to read!
I know that doesn't work.
Maybe I AM a jerk.

Geoffrey Dilenschneider

Why do I not act as myself?
Especially around her?
I am way too far
Way too fast.
But that's me:
Honest.
But why am I acting
different?

I try to find
A writing I've written in the past
That describes this situation,
But I realize
Twice Twice
That there is none.
But I write,
And it screws up my life
When I give it to others.
I always come at the
Wrong times
Say the
Wrong rhymes
Give the
Wrong thymes.
Is she playing with me?
It's real to me.
It seems as though
The giant block of melting aluminum
I call a heart
Is melting
And everyone else can sense it.
So far,
So close.
When I wake up,
I'll be really far
'Cause I'm so stupid.
I may know books
And words,
But people,
I do not.

I always come at the wrong times
Say the
Wrong rhymes
Give the
Wrong thymes
Act the
Wrong ways
Pick the
Wrong days
Act the
Wrong ways.
Why?

I could just forget it
Forget her.
It'd be hard for me,
But easy for her.
What would I
Get, anyway?
Nothing.
I'm so cold and lonely
When I'm myself.
I am scared
To be me.
I'll try it.
I'll just forget about my
Inside.
I'll try it,
But can she handle it?

I did, however, feel that I had the beginnings of a crush for Katheryn, rather than the prettier of her two cousins.

Since I was totally lost, I asked the power above for guidance. (This is another big thing in my life. Some may wonder: "Didn't he just go on a mission trip? Aren't those designed to inspire the youth to choose the path of following God?" Well, yes, and I did. I had a huge revelation, which is also another story all its own, but I lost sight of God before I even came on the cruise ship, two months after the trip to the Dominican.) But the prayer has become more over the course of my life; one for which I find I use more and more often. It has everything good and wholesome in it, and it just rings true in my own soul.

Geoffrey Dilenschneider

A Prayer

Lift me up
Above complain.
Lift me over
My life's pain.
Lift me through
This dead debate.
Lift me down
Away from hate.
Lift me out
So I can shout.

Take my feet
So I can't walk.
Take my mouth
So I can't talk.
Take my heart
Ever so gently.
Take my mind
For a wind.
Take my soul
To make me grow.
Take my hand
So I will know.

August 4th. Not a day like any other day at all.

We spent the day together, messing around, playing ping pong, cards, video games, doing nothing at all, and it was really the time that I started falling in love with Katheryn, although I didn't know it. But that night, I did.

I was lying in bed, unable to sleep, when I came to the big realization that I was totally head over heals for her. However, since my recent failed-before-begun relationship with Eliza, I thought to approach Katheryn from a totally different angle. I said, nope, I'm going to hold back; do nothing.

REMEMBER ME
Chapter II

▲ ▲ ▲ ▲

*This was the night I first realized I was in love with her, August 4, 2001.
Also included are two original sets of lyrics sung to songs by
The Red Hot Chili Peppers and Green Day, along with my own original song.
Of course, all inspired by Katheryn French. And I remember...*

It smelled of ripe, peeled bananas and the sandman's arm pits. I was watching *Terminator 2,* a great movie, when out of the surrounding blue, a wave of drowning sleepiness broke over my head. Mumbling goodnight to my brother, I walked into my bathroom. I showered, soothing my aching muscles from the hard workout we had that day (the workout was a tour of some little country's museums). After I took my time drying off, I walked to my bed, put on my DJ headphones, clumsily slipped in my recently-bought *Red Hot Chili Peppers* CD, and turned it on. Then I plopped onto my bed and performed a half roll onto my side while simultaneously pulling down the thick covers with my foot. I went at the task of going to sleep, but for some reason, I couldn't. All I could think about were strawberries. Strawberries, strawberries, strawberries, strawberries, strawberries, strawberries. Somewhere in the middle of an hour-long period of time, my thoughts switched to that girl I had met. Katheryn, it was. She was so kind and giving. I could feel the love for humanity emanating so strong from her I could almost see it or cut it with a nail file. She was definitely someone who would go far in the world. She probably was going to save some country or rainforest or world population from utter annihilation or something.

I just could not get to sleep. I just kept thinking of her. So I said to myself, "I'm going to stop right now... no more!" Surprisingly, it worked... somewhat. Instead of thinking of that girl, I didn't think of anything for two hours. Then, all of a sudden, lyrics started to pour out of my mouth, but I refused to write them down or even continue thinking them. I wanted to go to sleep, and I did NOT want to write... especially not about a girl, even though some of the lyrics were really sounding good. After a few minutes of fighting my inner voice for control of my body, I gave up and ran for paper and pen, which I usually keep at my side at all times. Here are the three songs I wrote that night:

Serenade

Chorus   I think of you and then I dream
I think of you and then I dream
I dream
I dream of you and then I wake
Waking has always put me down.

Verse I   I do not want to write this down
                But if I don't I think I'll frown
                So here I go and I'll never look back
                I wanna take you through my star-struck mind.

Verse II   Your smile makes my life so easy
                Your laugh makes my insides go topsy-turvy.
                A stranger person's never made me feel
                The way that I am feeling just right now
                The way I'm feeling just right now
                The way that I'm
                Melting down

Verse III   Your dimples match your rosy cheeks
                They both make my big heart go so weak.
                Your hair shimmers, makes it hard to speak.
                I want to know what you are thinking of me

Verse IV   That heart that sits inside your chest
                Makes me realize that you're the best
                I want you to feel the same way lest
                You can't remember this small serenade
                You can't remember this serenade
                You can't remem-
                Ber my love.

Bridge, Chorus 2x

Cynical

Verse I   I see
                A non-denial
                Denial in her eyes, she's all alone.
                Her
                Hair never stays,
                Even she can't tame that wild mane of hers.

Verse II   She
                Stands proud and tall
                Yet her heart stays by itself and all alone
                Can
                We actually talk
                And this vast expanse has no control on her.

Verse III   Strange
                Things happen in
                Time but no one knows for sure.
                Her
                Eyes do reflect
                The many lives of things gone by.

Verse IV   She
Paints tapestries
Of silent writings in her eyes.
Yet
She won't say
A single word that comes from her heart free.

Verse V   She
Seems locked up
In a prison without doors.
I
Want to smash that
Damn wall into a million little bits.

Slightly Infatuated

Verse I   Tie a bed onto my car
I have a feeling that we'll go far
And I
Won't forget.

Drop an anvil on my feet
I won't forget when we did meet
And I
Can't be mean.

Chorus   My training wheels have got to fall
Out to you I have to call
That I
Love you.

Verse II   A sideways cross looks hard at me
When you're mean I want to flee
And I
Come right back.

Trees may die and pigs may fly
I loved you the night I wore a tie
And I
Want you here.

Chorus

Verse III   I can taste these lands of waste
If you turn away it's what I'd be faced
And I
Will set you free.

                                          Geoffrey Dilenschneider

Trains go by, I don't know why
If pain was coming, for you I'd die
And I
Saw you there.

Bridge   A guy once told me so:
A path life, love will go.
And through it two will sow
The seeds of love and they'll grow
Someday they'll have a lawn to mow
They'll hold hands with two kids in tow
They won't care if the world turns blue
Only that their love is true.

Chorus

Verse IV   Raindrops jumping from the ground
I thank God that you I've found
And I
Dream again.

A shoelace I dream of ties itself
To another like itself
And I
Die dreaming.

Chorus

Chorus

End (slow) They won't care if the world turns blue
Only that their love is true.

Six and a half semi-unconscious and somewhat painful hours later, I had finally completed those soul-stretching tributes to her. I read them over about six times each, and came to the speechless, yet warm realization that I was in love, and *that* is a beautiful thing.

On the 5th of August, the boat stopped in St. Petersburg, Russia. We went sightseeing for a while (boring), then went to see original Russian dance. (You know, the one where they get very low to the ground, fold their arms across their chests and kick their legs out real quick? Yeah.)

Well, on the bus ride there, I didn't make my move; I waited until after fooling around with her a little in the third-to-last row at the Russian dance. It wasn't dark there, but there was no one behind us, and three empty rows in front of us.

Anyway, we had this kind of mentality towards each other where we both had this "thing" for each other, but didn't say anything, so we weren't even "friends with benefits," but rather were at the stage in a cruise where you "don't want to get involved because you know it's all going to end" and the mentality of "let's just have fun and see where it goes." We kinda had both of those going at once. Real odd mixture, if you ask me.

Anyway, on the way back, I decided to sing the favorite of my songs – Slightly Infatuated. I haven't really been able to write this chapter, either. It was so powerful to Katheryn, her cousins, and even to me. That whole five minutes was just that overwhelming.

Also on the cruise ship was a girl named Constance. I'd like to describe her. She was stunning: dark, wavy hair, striking features, beautiful eyes, great body... I mean great body. She was fourteen at the time. The only problem: dumb as a rock. No insult meant, just that it wasn't there, and I've never really been attracted to a girl when she can't at least make conversation.

Dear

You look so sad.
You look like you're holding something back from the
world.
And you look very   tired from it.
You seem reserved, in a way, and when you don't
It's as though it's a mask you're wearing.

You look filled by something different
Than what other people are filled by.
This is what I see in your eyes. I see someone with
great potential locked behind iron bars, starving.

Sadly, the next chapter is a hole in my memory – the biggest one. What happened that night – August 5th? We had a five-hour-long discussion. At first we skirted the issue of "us" like children, but eventually we came to terms with our fears together, and spent the remaining three hours talking it over. This was all in the card room. The card room was always the designated meeting place for the teenagers. Everyday we would go to the card room to do whatever. It was like our home base, the room where it always began.

At first glance, the card room was a room like any other in the ship: a green-walled and dull, multi-color-carpeted room, complete with a 24-inch TV on either side of the rectangular-shaped, wood-finished room. Amidst the numerous felt-covered poker tables (all squares) were matching chairs – four to a table.

Facing the two doors that opened to the sixth-floor hallway, as well as the bar where Dani, the old Irish bartender, stood his post at the lounge's bar, were wooden, waist-high cupboards, filled to capacity with board games and decks of cards. And above those sat perched a long window looking out onto the Sea.

Katheryn and I ended up with each other in a set of six options. One... well, I'll let you read on and figure out for yourself which one Katheryn and I picked.

After the long discussion, which was the most emotional time in my life; well, of course, only until four days later – anyway, that night, at around 12:30, I typed out Strange Peace, put it under her cabin door with a little stuffed penguin, rang the doorbell, and ran.

Oh, alright, I'll tell you what happened. The long discussion ended in "the long-term outweighs the short-term and we shouldn't go any deeper because it'll hurt too bad when we leave." FYI, she lives in Chicago, Illinois; I live in Darien, Connecticut (very far away). But, as I found out the next day, that essay I put under her door changed her 180 degrees... literally.

I was stunned into silence with surprise.

REMEMBER ME
Chapter V

🌲 🌲 🌲 🌲

I remember those happy days. I was so oblivious to the events just right around the corner of my ever-deepening life (and I am sure everyone could say that about every second of their lives) so oblivious that I can't remember all the details of this beginning in my life.

It smelled of fish and seawater when I first met her as myself and not someone fake and the day was blue, but to me it was a menacing gray. Not a bad day for me because of me meeting her, but because I did not want to. She was there in all her splendid glory, yet I was alone in my corner searching for some peace and quiet to write. Around the twelve-story cruise liner that our respective families and around 400 other people were guests of was a luscious panorama of the violent reds and submissive greens of the city of St. Petersburg, Russia. This great and horrible day was really the beginning while the night was the beginning of the end.

That day we visited an array of different places aboard the magnificent Navigator with a diverse selection of weather throughout it. As I became aware of the night creeping up behind me, I was hit with the mixed feelings of apprehensiveness, hope, need, fright, and uncertainty. I was apprehensive for the meeting we would have, hopeful for what might happen, and needful for how much my stomach needed her. Frightful for what might happen and what might not happen, and uncertain for not knowing how to put my thoughts to words and even not knowing what thoughts to put words to.

After a scrumptious but lethargic dinner with some old people who smelled of nursing homes and cherries and the captain of the boat, who could barely stop talking to acknowledge that he was, in fact, talking, she and I found ourselves strolling deep in thoughtful conversation atop the twelfth deck. At the back of this particular deck was a lounge, and when we walked towards it, we happened across a set of steep stairs descending down into some area as of yet unknown to us. We walked down the steep metal and were greeted by the most wondrous view of the Baltic Sea while being lightly blanketed by a moving rain of caked ash.

From my point of view, all there was was the infinite sea surrounding me, the loud green floor below me, and her standing there in front of me, in all of her radiance. We had been in some deep discussion for close to an hour (which in Russia is approximately three hours and seventeen minutes, because the clocks go fast in St. Petersburg for some reason), when she asked me how I truly felt about her.

All of a sudden, every single little detail came flooding back to me as though I was on the Mississippi River in 1937. The brown ash falling, the tied-up chairs next to us, the undulations of the Baltic water so far down beneath us; the faint, but perceivable sounds floating aimlessly from the party above and behind, the smells of the sea and the booze, and her. I was at a total loss for words... yeah, I had a million thoughts screaming out of my mind, but my tongue had seemingly jumped ship.

So I had but one thing to do that my tongue could handle. I kissed her. Wow, everything disappeared quickly (either because her lips were so smooth or because I closed my eyes, I'm not sure). And wow, was it the greatest moment of my life.

A great thing was that this two-way attraction was not totally physically oriented, but more "I can't be without you, you can't be without me" kind of relationship. Later on, we looked back on that major point in our own little timeline, and calculated the first kiss to be twenty-five minutes long. I STILL can't get that right in my head. After that amazingly perfect first kiss, we went on in that kind of routine... blah, blah, blah, I won't bore you. But I will tell you this: we both sacrificed a whole truckload of things in order to stay for that four hour period of time from that first kiss and on. Man did we both get in trouble with the parentals. But that moment in time is something I cannot forget. It's not that I will not or don't want to, but I can't. It's etched in my mind as though it was a slate six inches thick with writing four inches thick carved masterfully into it. Her strawberry chapstick that I bought her, my necklace with the two suns hanging around her graceful neck, her ocean blue eyes reflecting her deep thoughts into my own, her shimmering hair blowing wickedly in the salty wind, her green dress laying the perfect compliment on her silky-smooth hair, and most of all, her luscious red cheeks, full with passion for the soul and keeping the heart alive.

On and on it went like that, but I shouldn't say it in that manner, because I love that girl, and I've already given my heart to her. I wholeheartedly never want to have to ask for it back, but I know I must. Even though she lives a thousand miles away, the bond we formed in that time was so strong and unbreakable that nothing will ever tear us apart. Not life, nor death, nor time, nor space, nor distance, nor anything.

On the 6th, we had the time of our lives, as you can tell.

The only problem with this whole relationship is that the 7th, the day after chapter V, was the beginning of the goodbye, really. It's insane how this world works. I can't understand it, but it's the way it is because it is. For example, I have to wait another year for my birthday. A whole year! Ahhh!!!

The Tops

And you turn away,
I look back,
Smile.
These little pieces,
Snippets,
Of fragile time
Will keep in my mind
Forever.
Life will fly
If you stay in the present.
Life will die
If you look to the future.
All these people dressed up
For some occasion

That won't happen.
Their faces:
Perfect paintings of words
Breathed in between lips
Pressed together
In the heat of the moment.

So much to offer,
So little to give.
Get off her,
You need to live.

The eternal flame dies.
The penguin flies.
The dead man's eyes
Grow in size.
The bored kid tries.
The honest gentleman lies.
The conversationalist sighs.
The honest sneak defies
All those of little size.
Not every person
Likes everyone else.
Can't you see their stares?
In this society there are tears!
Walk slower
Time is almost up
Wassup!
Goodbye.
It was fun while it lasted,
I try.
One hundred and eighty degrees
For me?
For me???
I feel loved.
No one's ever done that for me.
This is a first for me.
But my tears clue me in
To the "fin"
At the bottom of this chapter in my life.
This is my
Church of spilt blood.
Everyone seems blank,
Like death is coming.
Some seem sad,
Some seem mad,
Some seem blank
Like a wood plank:
There,
But not totally.

Geoffrey Dilenschneider

Some seem oblivious,
Constancely.
I wish I was oblivious.

When you're gone,
I can only smile with the past,
Frown at the present,
And cry for our future.

Worlds are born,
Worlds grow
Worlds take
Worlds give
Worlds live
Worlds love
Worlds experience
Worlds pain
Worlds win
Worlds lose
Worlds again begin
Worlds chose.
Worlds pay
The consequences
Worlds live on
Worlds remember,
They defend Her.
Worlds die
inside
When She leaves.
Worlds believe
They will receive

Any thing they wish for.
Worlds live.
Worlds are alive.
Worlds try.
Worlds die.

But worlds that believe in each other
Can be born again.

They can be **born again!**

The Introduction

My hair's a mess,
I must confess,
I don't know what to say.
I won't believe

After this eve,
You'll be gone away.
I can't think
Of the chink
You made in my heart.
I must go
Into woe
Right at this hard start.
I can only show you the door,
But that is what I am here for.
You can ask for more,
I don't feel sore,
Things greater than us
Hold in their possession
The key to make this work.
But they have no idea.

It's weird...
I feel in flux with you.
I stare into your eyes
And I can't add to
Or take away from you.
You're different...
I can be with you.

The Dark Sun

A present future in our lives
A future present in our lives
A future life in our presence
A present life in our future
A present life
A future life
A future life present
A present of future life
A future of life
A presence
A present presence
A present
A life in our presence
A life in our present
A new life
In our future.

Yeah... then life went to hell.

REMEMBER ME
Chapter VI

▲ ▲ ▲ ▲

I remember those bitter days. I was so oblivious to the events just right around the corner of my ever-deepening life (and I am sure everyone could say that about every second of their lives) so oblivious that I can't remember all the details of this distorting endings of endings.

It smelled of death, decay, and relentless destruction. Every detail from the drunk secretary at the Galileo's Lounge bar accompanied by his senile grandmother, to the rich tastes of the four pound lobsters lavishly displayed at the mile-long buffet, which quite oddly smelled of skittles. I still can barely reminisce about the way we talked into the night using nothing but silly black and white and gray metaphors that had meanings beyond words or even thoughts without tasting the hint of dark oceans up-heaving towards the ducts in my eyes. My mind is only able to briefly jet to her part of my brain because the moment I remember her melodious laugh or her gracious smile, my mind surprisingly shuns the memories. This woman, being the ultimate black cloud with a gold lining, could not have been more... more... real. The flicker of light in her intelligent eyes, the sea-faring look she gives to those posing the portrait of threats, the way she held me when even I lost my balance in the turbulent airs of love. And that is why this day I speak coldly of is known as the "day of smiles" and why the night I so lovingly bring to life on paper is called the "night of tears".

The quicksand of time could not have gone slower that heinous night even if it whole-heartedly tried. The hatred the seas cast upon us and the battle-ready ship was horrendous and unexpected. By the feel of things towards the latter part of the night, the distasteful Satan at the bottom of the Baltic's attack on our boat was totally premeditated. For what seemed like an eternity, we scuttled in and out of the rain to different parts of the ever-watched cruise liner to find a place to have some long-awaited "fun." After a long while of lurching and creaking and groaning and leering from our trusty over-sized tugboat, we found a little cove hideaway on the fifth floor. It was the de-embarkation platform, covered over by a solemn brown curtain proudly bearing the symbol of Radisson Cruises...

Hours later, when we were meandering back to her room, the feeling in the air was pure doomsday. After this parting, we both felt that nothing could ever be close to the life that we could only hold onto for one more single moment in time. Next to the shops, I lightly stopped her, turning her to face me in the process. "We can't end like this," I pleaded. "I know," she returned with pity in her voice for the both of us. We were both fully aware of that ominous black void following us like a giant killer shadow. We both knew what had to happen. I told her, "Be strong for me, because you are strong, and I am weak... look at me shed tears while you stand militaristically with your chin just a bit down-turned." She captured me straight in the eyes and replied, "Jeff... when I close the door to my room, I want you to forget about me."

Those words are forever welded into the frame of my very being. I cannot imagine any other way to kill a person so horribly. I asked her why she doesn't cry. She said, simply put, that if someone saw her the next morning, they would be witnesses to dripping mascara all the way to the other side of the planet. I placed my lips upon hers, issuing her some symbolic type of last breath. She walked away, I walked away.

But something stopped us in an instant and we both knew that something was definitively wrong. At the same time, we turned towards each other, simultaneously feeling the sheer force of that demon Armageddon train hitting us head-on at full speed. Magically, two giant hands of fate picked us up and put us together for one last blink of time. And the last I saw of that sweet, sweet salvation of a girl was a smile. That intangible present and then she closed her door, the sound echoing forever down the hall with a deafening, hollow thud. She said, "Be strong... I love you." And all of a sudden my hands started to shake and I couldn't see straight and I wasn't sure of where I was and I wasn't sure of who I was and I dropped to the floor shivering, chattering, and convulsing, only able to wheeze forth a final testimony of my undying feelings to the only thing that ever mattered: "Don't forget... I love you... I love you so much... don't leave me... please... I love you..."

Every night, I let the ice from within flow freely up and out of my tattered and torn rag of a heart. The tears sting of sadness, love, fear, denial, and worst of all, truth. That smile is what I hold on to during the lonely, sleepless nights and what I try my hardest to keep hidden from the light of day in fear of letting that smile of hers in my mind see the light of the truth. The truth that I quite possibly will never see my everything ever again. The truth that she is gone. When this mammoth realization slams home, the tears just blow me open like a million underwater volcanoes finitely wreaking their internal havoc on the external. She is not returning on some golden steed in shining armor. She is not going to keep the Venetian channels between us open forever. This is over. I don't want this. She said, "If this was a match made in heaven, then something will stop this devious separation from happening." Something will happen, I am sure of it. I promise this much: that love is a form of energy; it can neither be created nor destroyed. It is always there; it only changes forms from time to time. I promise to God and on my own deathbed that I will not let this die.

Geoffrey Dilenschneider

REMEMBER ME
Chapter VII

▲ ▲ ▲ ▲

The day we left the boat, August 14, 2001. This is the time
that we thought that we would never be seeing each other ever again.
Life was basically over for us, so we gave one more go at each other.
And I remember...

The fresh ocean morning smelled of strawberries, flapjacks, and irrefutable sorrow. The hard tears of utter defeat the night before had mercilessly barred me from a child's sleep, leaving me defenseless against a nuclear arsenal of sad and hopeless thoughts of this heartfelt end. I was eating a cardboard breakfast of over-cooked bacon and egg-less French toast when she appeared. I spent eight minutes making noises and sudden movements to attract her attention towards me, but apparently she was so exhausted from our afternoon and evening together that she was barely awake at all. Later, my friend Mario, a cook on the ship, told me I had gotten the attention of six waiters and four elderly tables by accident. Just seeing that wholesome face reflect the all-too-calm sunlight made my stomach awash with monarch butterflies and my heart dive head-first into my throat. Then she found me in that suddenly vast void of darkness infiltrating everything but her and me.

We wandered outside to the front of our ship, which was in the long process of docking at port, and began the most wonderful conversation I have ever been lucky enough to participate in. Looking into her bloodshot eyes after a few minutes, standing ouside by the railing, I asked, "So... how'd you sleep?"

"Did you mean it?" She replied. Obviously, something I had said had been indefinitely stuck in her mind.

"Mean what?"

"That you loved me?" She leaned into me, holding onto the rose I had given her earlier.

"Let me explain," I whispered. "I am a bucket of oxymorons – one of those being that I think in black and white, meaning yes and no. There is no compromise in me. You think in gray, all compromise and all maybe. How can zeros and ones compromise with point fives? How can our two wholly different and separate lives start anew in compromise without compromising the connections we already share back at our respective homes? I am so scared." I paused, then, turning to her, said, "Look, we cannot go on like this... we both know that this is the real end and nothing should tear us from the truth that we are going to be moving more distant from each other for the rest of our lives starting today. Barring that ugly thought from my mind, I still love you. What do those words mean, anyway? I, as in thinking only of myself: my heart, and all my heart, my mind, all my thoughts, my soul, my body, my experiences, my past, my present, my future, who I am, my everything. Love, as in the greatest, most powerful feeling on earth: the distance it sometimes creates, the connections, the bonds, the purity, the pride, the grace, the generosity, the kindness, the love! The feeling that this world is based on; the feeling that God is; the feeling that creates peace and harmony in places that hadn't seen any in up to sixty years; the feeling that brings people together just to share a little bit of themselves with each other.

You, as in thinking only of yourself: your heart, and all your heart, your mind, all your thoughts, your soul, your body, your experiences, your past, your present, your future, who you are, your everything. I love you for you. Who you are. It's scary to imagine life without you. It's just sickening to not know what goes on in your head and to not know if you love me or not." I shifted my gaze to the sky to ask silently for God's strength as she squeezed my fishy blotched hands tighter with her own fishy blotched hands. Then I cast my head downward to stare at my happening feet as to hide the tears that burned with the fury of a thousand wronged and un-avenged deaths from the people inside so rigidly watching us through the ceiling-to-floor windows.

"You are so perfect and I love you now," she whispered. The sickening tearing sensation I was feeling all of a sudden flew off the charts, creating a cavity of endless dismay inside my heart. "It is so hard to say goodbye to the only thing that matters in life, you. The end can't come so soon, so abruptly, so finally. You know that a compromise is not just necessary, but it is inevitable. Even if we don't want this parting to take place, our parents still have an obligation to take us where they deem appropriate, which is to our separate homes. We have no choice but to go along," She stammered, valiantly holding back the long-buried tears. "You know it isn't because you can't, but because you don't want to. You are a writer and you have a gift that no one else has. You have a mind different from any other person. You are special... you are aware." I heard a thumping inside me when she declared her thoughts of my writing ability. It was my brain trying to under-stand how this person I barely knew all of a sudden so easily understood the core of my being. It was like she had the key to open up my heart, mind, and soul all along. She understood me. No one had ever, ever understood me in any way before.

I kissed her, and the lightning passion shooting from one individual to another connected together, before, only by the physical, but now by the intellectual and spiritual, too. After a while, when we were looking out and down and away, I observed, "The water is so dirty."

"Yes, it is, but those cloudy waters will someday be clear again," She spoke after a moment. Then, all of a sudden, her little sister, who, for the past seven days had been stalking me, and her cousin Christine (a very voluptuous California-style blonde my age) started knocking on the window behind us. We turned around to the dark sight of my brother, her parents, her little sister, her two cousins, and their two families, all sitting there, laughing like they were sitting for a professional photograph and we were the photographers. So we excused ourselves from the impressive peeping-tom skills of two entire generations of families to go to the side of the boat where we could have a little more privacy. Once there, we started kissing...

A few times waiters and workers aboard the boat would come out a door a few yards down the walkway. Most didn't even notice us, or, if they did, pre-tended not to. One worker, a Spanish-looking gentleman took one look at us and exclaimed, "Ay, dios mio, look at dem kees so hat hat hat! Mis amigos, geet a room before some guy be puking on side of boat!" We just laughed, shrugged him off and continued our romantic salvation. Neither of us were romantic people at all really, but the gut-twisting and heart-wrenching situation that we were presently in really brought the pale sunlight-lacking hearts of ours out from behind the iron curtain of our confusing actions.

· · ·

Little to our knowledge, we were displaying ourselves to one another almost directly under the PA speaker. It started blaring that it was time for the guests with black luggage tags to please begin moving towards the fifth floor for final disembarkation. In other words, 'people with black tags, get the hell off'. We stopped kissing. "That's me," I muttered like a kicked dog.

"Me, too..." Time flashed to a stop right there, us holding each other close, staring into each other's eyes with the utmost uncertainty and face-crunching sadness. Slowly, extremely slowly (which was excruciatingly too fast for either of us), we let go of each other, wanting to leave at that moment perfectly in limbo. That way, we both knew silently, we had the perfect compromise between leaving and staying, oddly enough. Our eyes were taking the full weight of this unexplainable feeling that was dropping at the speed of time. Just thinking about it now makes me well up in tears, remembering her crystal eyes, cut from perfect diamonds happy for and envious of other couples who have been able to be together indefinitely, her crystal eyes just looking at me as though what was happening had to be a glitch in the system of our lives, as though it was impossible for that call to have come. What I saw in her Berlin wall eyes looked as though she couldn't believe that the leaving time had finally arrived, but she was so scarred because of the memories permanently etched into her mind of the horrible hurt other men had inflicted upon her in the past. So blindly scared she was, that that feeling of welled memories was denying her true, uninhibited thoughts and feelings from gushing out wildly in a giant flow of pure, untouched reality and truth.

As we walked hand in hand together back through the restaurant to her extended family, they asked for a kiss. So we kissed, and they all laughed and cheered. During the entire time I knew her, she had two pet peeves. One being that she only said 'I love you now', and refused to just say, 'I love you.' The other being her hatred of the word 'goodbye.' We both refused to say it, actually. So when I left my love standing there surrounded by faces I had only recently begun to know, I didn't feel as bad as I did an hour before or the night before. "This is the actual goodbye," I thought as I slowly walked away from my soul mate. "This is where I never see this person all-too-familiar ever, ever again." For some reason, though, it didn't feel real, as though in some secret place in my mind resided a comfortable little truth: that we would meet again in the future and truly be together.

· · ·

As I walked away from her for the last time, outside the boat Navigator basking in her own dark glory, I suddenly heard the greatest, most unimaginably relieving sound anyone could ever hear. It was the sound of an extremely recognizable melodious female voice singing the chorus to *Slightly*

Infatuated. I turned, and she was there, smiling and singing so pure and innocent that I couldn't help but smile and sing back. Even though we were on opposite sides of the giant and all-too-busy parking lot, we could hear each other's quiet singing well enough to sync our voices into one being. We sung the thing half through to each other when, all of a sudden, my eccentric mother screamed at me to get in the black hearse-looking limousine, "We're going now!" I saw those emerald eyes, ruby cheeks, green, shapely dress and the luscious, warm, comforting smile that I would be wanting back for the rest of time for one more unstoppable instant and she mouthed the words, "I love you." And then I was pushed into darkness.

Not In the Back of My Mind

This is real
I cannot deny
The feelings I try to hide.
The present decides the future
Every moment, something changes.
I want to change our destiny.
This is different for me.
Are you going through with this
Because I won't see you again
Tomorrow?
What do you feel?
Explain it here.
You must
For I myself don't trust.
I am at your upper crust,
But I want to java
Your inner core's molten lava.
If you forget about me,
Your cheeks will turn white,
But you won't know why,
Because you won't remember.
But you will remember.
I'm walking away…
I'm walking away!
Why am I walking away?
When you walked away,
You didn't look back,
You broke my heart in the process.
Why did you not turn back?
Were you laughing?
Were you crying?
A rose
Means more than prose.
My words won't ever be
Able to describe my
Feelings for you

Geoffrey Dilenschneider

A stem
Means more than a poem.
A thorn
Means destiny has scorn.
A rose in the mouth of a dove
Means forty years later there is love.
I catch a cold
From the love you threw
At me
And left.
Later

I walked towards your door
In shambles,
Shaking and crying.
All I could manage was,
"I am going to miss you,"
French K.F.C.
Is always good to me
Even if it leaves
Every night at three.
Remember all the good times
The good rhymes
The good thymes
Remember the sunshines
The boat's chimes
The hard easy lines.
I love you
You love me
We could have been happy
Your heart was opening
But mine a wide open door
Thank you please, instead
There's got to be more.
I try to forget.
Try to keep a blank face,
Blank mind.
Everything goes blank,
All hope is lost.

And you appear!
The end was near,
But God changed our fate
With three little words
And gave us one more night.
Fate
Is a funny thing
It doesn't make sense
To you or me.
I am free

I feel change
From you to me.
Down to up
A roller coaster
Is the life I lead
In these 9 days.

That smile on your face
Makes me smile brighter.
The way you rub me
Makes my steps lighter.
The way fate works
Makes my heart a fighter.
The clock on the wall
Makes my grip on you tighter.

You are tall,
I am wide.
I am small,
Are you tied?
I look between
My parents mean,
And see something
Palpable flickering.
I look between
Us, you and me
And
What do I see?
Something palpable?
Something unseen?
Something great?
Or something mean?
Something with rhyme?
A chance to dine?
I will tell in time.
You will tell me in time.
But I took your words too lightly
On paper,
Too seriously in mind and soul
And heart.
Those words were super saturated
And totally elated
With meaning beyond belief.
If meant in their silence
To the full potential,
Then I must confide
I flied inside.
Today is the Day of Smiles...
No tears.
I don't know anyone as well as you.

Geoffrey Dilenschneider

Only now does my life feel true.
Why am I saying all this?
I've known you for eight days.
Please, try to write,
It's not that hard.
Just write what you think
Without thinking
Write what you feel
Without feeling...
Don't rhyme;
If you don't want to.
If you do,
Do.
If you don't,
Don't.
That goes for everything.

I believe.
In being slightly infatuated
In fate
In the power of request
In help
In God
In you.
In your potential for greatness.
You

I ask for peace,
I get upheaval.
I ask for quiet,
I get medieval.
I ask for love,
I get denied.
I ask for friendship,
I get defied.
I ask for a compliment,
I get a shove.
I ask for nothing,
And I get love.

I am not sure if you like me.
I am not sure why you aren't free.
I am not sure why you try.
I am not sure why you kiss me.
I am not sure if you are tired.
Or if I was somehow suddenly fired.
I am not sure if I am good enough to you.
I am trying hard to be perfectly respectable and nice
And acceptable
And re-memorable

And sociable
And funny
And loud
And quiet
And romantic
And stone-faced
And truth-faced
And erased
And full
And ready
And willing
And able
And fulfilling
And meaningful
And worthwhile
And generous
And purposeful
And soulful
And profound
And smart
And understanding
And nice
And kind
And influential
And helpful
And caring
And loving and perfect!
I AM trying!
Because I care.
You want something,
You got it.
I only want one thing:
To be with you.
That needs a few things...
You.
Me.
A connection.
Time.
Freedom.
Trust.
Those we have, right?
I doubt myself way too much.
Maybe you can help me with that.
But that also needs
Time.
A bond unbreakable
And unbroken.
Us.

Geoffrey Dilenschneider

I have to stop.
And say thank you.
What you have said
Has meant so much to me.
My heart is free.
I have frolicked many miles...
Today really Is the day of smiles.
In my mouth are thirty-six tiles,
In my mind are remarkable aisles
Full of memories in vials
That hold my many smiles.
"Smiles,"
That word,
Means so much to me.
It means life,
Liberty in mind, body, soul,
Freedom in mind, body, soul,
Purity in mind, body, soul,
Love in mind, body, soul.

It means happiness,
A little sappiness,
A feelings sea
So new to me,
I'm full of glee,
It won't stop.
It, I can't drop.
Today really is the Day of Smiles!

Who thought the end of summer could hold
Something this timeless and old?
This is a gift.
All of it.
How I got the necklace.
That strange peace.
(I feel a strange happiness at the moment)
finding God.
Talking to Chip Valandra.
Going through that ordeal with Eliza.
Going to Hyde.
Going to Aspen Achievement Academy.
Being short and fat and ugly.
Being a loser,
A jerk,
And an anti-social hothead.
..Changing...
Doing the right thing.
Doing the hard easy,

Even when it was very, very, hard.
All in the past, distant.
This is a gift.
The necklace I gave to you.
My Japanese.
Your Japanese.
The poem and the empty pen and the waiter out of nowhere.
The three and a half hours.
The PDA.
Your pink cheeks.
All the metaphors we dwindled on,
Back and forth and left and right.
I appreciate it to the fullest extent
Of my capability.
I am tired, yes,
As are you.
But I am past fear
Regarding you.
I am aware in the present.
I see you,
Even when you are not around.
You may be scared,
But talk, and be free,
And slowly,
It will melt away.
I am still smiling.
I asked for God's help
Five times.
I was answered...
Five times
I am still smiling.
There are others
In this vast sea
Surrounding me,
But you believe in me,
What more could I want?
If you feel uncomfortable
With me basically throwing all these poems and songs at you,
Technically a stranger,
Just say so.
What is wrong with me
In your eyes?
What is right with me,
In your eyes?
What am I,
In your eyes?
What am I supposed to do,
In your eyes?

Geoffrey Dilenschneider

Everything is so symbolic.
I know we're tired
It's so, so true.
I just can't seem
To get rid of you.
Not that I want to...
Oh, forget it
I can talk on for miles!
Just tell me a story...
Tell me a story of smiles...

REMEMBER ME
Chapter VIII

I remember those empty times, void of anything but emptiness. I was so oblivious to the events just right around the corner of my ever-deepening life (and I am sure everyone could say that about every second of their lives) so oblivious that I can't remember all the details of this unseen stroll on a fence top.

It smelled of pessimism and petulance in the black limousine, which surprisingly resembled a hearse, fitting the dead zone atmosphere like a glove. I sat with my DJ headphones blasting the music as loud as humanly possible, trying my hardest to drown out the tears warring to break me down. I wasn't sure of anything anymore. The squeaky leather reminded me of fresh, new things, and I wanted to tear it to little itty bitty shreds just to soothe my quiet rage of sadness which was incessantly itching madly to be free of it's mental shackles. We (meaning me, my parents, and my brother) began the procession through the congested and knotted alleyways of Stockholm, Sweden. The tearing sensation I felt during the first five minutes of that damnable ride was so unbearable I almost screamed out to let God take the memories of her away. But I couldn't. She had my heart as though it was a ticket. The only problem was that she was the ride, and I couldn't get near the ride unless I had the ticket. The only ticket now lies deep inside her heart, a key in its own mind, but a phrase comprised of three little words in mine. At the moment of arrival at the hotel I was to stay at for a handful of days in Stockholm, I vaguely recollected my brother mumbling something to himself. He mumbled a phrase twice. I momentarily paused to think on what he said and if it meant anything. Everything in my world stopped. I remembered what he was saying. I saw a flash of green dress... a smile... a whistle... a chord from the song I had composed... a girl... but not any girl... my girl.

And then it hit me. My brother had been saying, "I'm willing to bet serious cash that your 'friend' will be at the hotel waiting for you." And by the time that I had jumped out of the limousine, fallen, gotten up, tripped over the curb, dropped my CD player twice and swallowed my gum, she had already stopped whistling my song and was simply staring at me...

...with the grandest, most happy smile I had ever seen in my entire life. My God, I have a strong feeling that words will need an eternity to accurately describe the way I felt at that singular, glorious moment. And all of a sudden, she was filling my hug, that absence of sense and direction and understanding vanished, leaving me with a pure vision of awesome compassion from God to his people. In that moment I was whole; complete... which I only realize now. I had sensed something different in that girl, and I had only done what I would have done: been myself. And from those feeble beginnings in a space so confined that it only allowed the smallest of movements came before me the greatest, most unbelievable summit that anyone will ever have the extreme pleasure and delight to glimpse. I had reached the ultimate.

Okay, you never guessed, right? Yeah.

The next chapter I just couldn't write, either. It was too horrible, and I still can't remember it all. I call it the I Love You Now night.

We were at the hotel in Sweden, and I was in her room. This was the last time we'd see each other, hands down. Talk about living death twice. Yeah, and this was extremely emotional; like, too emotional to talk about anymore, so I supplemented the chapter with a letter I wrote to her after the security guard my parents sent to get me dragged me away from her door.

Letter to a Young Lover Leaving

I can't stop crying. Good-byes are so hard when they are final. I love you. I love you with all my heart. I don't want to say goodbye. I can't say good-bye. I don't want this to be the end. This can't be the end. I just met you. I can't breathe without you. You can't be gone for good. If we were meant to be, than something would stop this from happening. If we were meant to be, a match made in heaven, then this cannot be the end. This was only the beginning. Why is this so black and white, hello and goodbye? What happened to the in-between, the gray, your heart?

I spent the next few days lamenting in Sweden over the loss of my beloved. The emotional stress was so much that I tried just thinking plain English something else.

A Little Bit of My Mind

And did you know my name is really Michael? Well, it's not... or is it? Do you truly know me? Will you ever *know* me? I have a simpler answer than the question: no. See, easy. You will never know me. And I will never know you. I could sit here in Sweden forever, reading the works of all these "greats" and everything about them. And I could look in every nook and cranny and corner of their mind, heart, and soul, but never find what makes him or her "great". As it is the same for me, except worse. I am me. I can look at people and be with people and figure out almost instantly what the future holds for that person and me. I can tell the future like it could be. I have proof. I am in the Nobel Prize labyrinth, wondering about what I would not do with the prize money awarded to guys and girls that strike it lucky. Oh, and that's all they do. With poetry, there is no calculation. Oh, yeah, you could say, "this word goes here for this reason, and this word goes there for that reason," but that is not real poetry. Someone once said, "You either have it or you don't. Life sucks." I wrote it before he or she even said it. Poetry isn't written or created or thought up or, as some put it, thunk up, or remembered or copied or seen or heard or a reflection. Poetry is a gift. You either have it or you don't. Simple, right? Wrong. If you've got that life-ruin-ing gift, you have to use it properly while handling it like a pressure-sensitive bomb. You don't perfect poetry, you perfect your mind so it's able to let go for a long enough period of time to listen to the poetry speaking. Then you need to perfect your mind so It can hear correctly and decipher between your brain's incessant mumbling and that poetry that is trying its absolute hardest to be manifested. How do I know it's trying its absolute hardest? Because when I let go mentally, I can hear only its high pitched screams for mercy. All it wants is to be written. Not added to or taken away from. It just wants to be perfect. I've only read one perfect writing. It's called *Strange Peace,* because that is exactly what it is. It's a living, breathing, talking, piece of the giant poem living inside of me just itching to rub me out of the picture and flourish on its own. I am not full of poetry. Poetry is full of me.

Sometimes I have so many ideas that I can't think slow enough to prioritize them and can't think fast enough to keep up with their insane pace. Sometimes I'll just stare at a wall for awhile, or a person or something of interest. I believe it's in the latter times where the words form inside me. When I shake out of my stare, it's like I'm saving those words for another time. The only times I'm caught without pen and paper are when I'm in the bathtub. I'll start singing or rhyming the most beautiful words, but I won't be able to write them down. Worse is that they leave the second I unleash them. When the mind is at rest (or lulled into a false sense of unawareness), the words come freely.

So, what's my name?

Then, on the plane ride home, I sat next to a couple so deeply in love that I felt moved beyond words... right back to Katheryn.

Geoffrey Dilenschneider

It's Blue Rose Beautiful

Connected as one,
Entwined at every juncture
One in mind, body, and spirit.
The most beautiful sight I've seen.

A chance,
You've taken.
A trust,
You've perfected.
A love,
You've protected.

Nothing of yours
Will work
When put separate
From the other half.

The blue background
You so confidently lay on
Is perfected by
The absence of
The space between you.

Your love lasts a moment,
One kiss lasts a lifetime,
And your bond will last forever.

One word to silence mountains,
One breath to calm the seas.
One smile to make a difference,
One laugh to make it freeze.

Like a child with no hair
You, as one, are well-kept and fair.
Like a movement in the dark,
Your hands together create a spark.
Like a lark in a meadow creepy,
I saw a something that's never sleepy.
And that's why I can't bear to watch:
I used to have her and nothing was wrong,
But now our something is stretched so long;
Even if that connection *still stands strong.*

A few days later...

I Am the Bridge of Sighs

I keep these feelings
Deep inside my heart.
If I think of her
I know my tears will start.
I'll start to wonder
If she of me is thinking
Or if to another
She is cutely winking.
I'll start a-wondering
When her I'll see
Or if I'll lose her
In the unknown sea.
I wonder why
I wasn't feeling scared
And how I know
Answer'd come when prayered.
I don't think
Bad is how I fared.
I don't think
Love should be spared.
It shouldn't be
Just for distance
Or for others,
Just for instance.
I wonder if
My star is shining bright.
I wonder if
For me she will fight.
I wonder if
God is watching me,
Protecting me from evil,
Setting my heart free.
I stand on top
This bridge of sighs
And wonder which
Decision is more wise.
I can't believe
I even thought about that Knife.
I can't believe
I made an impact on your life.
I can't believe
My life was so plain.
I do believe
Your memory keeps me sane.
My view from here
Is just so barren and empty.
To run to you
Seems so very tempty.

Geoffrey Dilenschneider

I need to see you
To mix my black and white.
I know you won't forget
The way I hold you tight.

I couldn't write for a while. I really felt horrible... I mean, the adolescent age is an age much shakier than any other age, which is all I can say because the only rational time in my life has been this one period of youth.

I tried to let go of Katheryn off the bat, which proved to be fatal, turning me into an angry poet if there ever was one... but I didn't write in fear of what would come out if I did. Rather, in a flash of raw emotion bubbling back to the aching surface, I started up again about the one subject that I least desired to write about.

REMEMBER ME
Chapter X

▲ ▲ ▲ ▲

Today, Katheryn has occupied all of my thoughts completely, so I wrote them down. These last three tributes to Katheryn began with me walking out of my bathroom and being hit by a force that definitely was not of a positive nature. I mean HIT, like I was physically pushed backwards by some upset force that I couldn't see. And I remember...

I trudge out of my steaming bathroom after a long and soothing soak in the tub when I'm caught unaware by a meat hook of an empty, overwhelming feeling of despair. Its reach extends from my stomach to my nose and makes me want to yawn. It also makes it hard for me to cast my vision anywhere but down. In three days I will be saying, "Rabbit, rabbit," and only because it's a new month and I want an orchard full of luck. I fear that it won't do me any good, though, and my hand twitches when I think of her because even my sub-consciousness feels a need to reach out and caress that desirable, smooth skin. The loathsome disbelief hangs over my head like a hot cloud of careless locusts, just waiting for that moment to jump down and make me cry. I do not have a reason for why I can't forget about her. She's just so mis-understandably different. I feel like the widower of a woman who has been lost at sea: my loved one is out there in that unfriendly flowerbed, but only faith is what I have to remind me that she is gone. And only faith is what I have to hold onto when her memory comes back to knock on my door. I want to react convulsively, but I'm reminded at how clobbered I was when I tried to plot our lives to be collinear for even a simple second. I continue to wonder when my thoughts will forever turn elsewhere to be stimulated, never to return. I wonder if I'm missing something important. What is she feeling? Is she thinking of me? I wonder.

Geoffrey Dilenschneider

REMEMBER ME
Chapter XI

🌲 🌲 🌲 🌲

And I remember...

I can't help but remember my conscious suspension of belief, the way I willed myself to forget the inevitable using sarcasm and smiles to deceive others into thinking I was doing just fine. I cried at nights, though. I know my brother heard me, but even he knew to let me be alone. Alone because I will always be utterly alone in one way or another until the moment I die. For only then will I lift the ugly mask I so silently wear to shield my virgin eyes from the horrors of this life I once recognized as home. I pause to wonder about something infinite: I pause to wonder when we really started being "us" and ended being just plain "Jeff and Katheryn."

I started crying one night. I bewildered myself by doing so, too. I had this grave longing in the epitome of my being, yearning for a time to vent. So as I stared teary-eyed into my mirror at twelve in the middle of the night, I started to sing and cry. I had no choice but to attempt to choke back the tears because people were watching: myself. I could not bear to watch myself break down because of some girl a thousand miles away who might have already forgotten about me. I know I need to let her go, but I can't bring myself to do it. I just need to remember the good times in order to go about happily and full of joy for my past, not as though life is horrible and pointless beyond belief. There may be things I cannot change, but I believe I can do something about this. I just need to remember what life is like here at home and not what it could have been with Katheryn. What a sad thought that is. I must live in the present, rolling with the punches and must find a different way to feel complete.

Mastering the Tears

Verse I   When did my life change?
Where's my lucky penny?
I do not want to
Think of the way we...
I cannot think through
The changes that I went through.
I can't believe
That my life is over.
When did you leave me?
Why's my pain so hard?
Why can't I let go
Of the way you held me?
Why do I cry so
What all I want to see
Is your face so pretty
And your dress so green?

When will my life end?
Why is that called free?
Why is this called crying?
Why won't you let me be?

Chorus   Down I go into the darkness
With your memory;
It's all I have to hold onto,
It won't let me be.
I cry into your warming shoulder,
But it isn't here.
Why I cannot see you
Puts my heart in fear.
Every now and then I see you,
Makes me feel you near,
But when I think of life without you,
I drop my final tear.

Verse II   Can't we live in peace?
Live life in harmony?
I cannot bear the sadness
That sets down hard upon me...
I cannot really think of
Any ways to say
The things I meant to tell you
In any right of way.
Maybe if I listen
To my heart way down below,
It'll tell me of a time
From which I'll never want to go,
Because I know that it's true:
Our love into the sky.
And with that word of welcome,
I lay down my heart to die.

Verse III   Where did my life go?
I never asked to leave.
When did my life blow
Out like candled breeze?
You came in like a goddess
And I left you like a sneeze.
Time is never endless,
That thought is just a tease.
What says that I am wrong
In that moment that I seized?
When will we meet?
When will hearts be pleased?

Geoffrey Dilenschneider

Verse IV   I know I need something
           That'll finally let me see.
           I need that special something
           To set my own soul free.
           I know I need something
           That'll finally set me free.
           I need that special someone
           To let my own self be.

Bridge   Why is this called crying?
(soft)   Do you think of me
           On the days I'm dying
           When you drink your tea?
           How can I be flying
           When I'm lying six feet deep
           In a heart's grave coffin,
           Wishing I could sleep?
           What has taken purpose
           And broken down my soul?
           What great sign will miss me
           As I walk under a shoal,
           Mourning the death of meaning,
           Will we cry when we are old?
           What's the price to buy at,
           What happens when you're sold?

Verse V   What is life without you,
           Walking in the sand?
           What just might've happened
           If we walked on sacred land?
           I hope your life has gone well
           In the passing time.
           I know I haven't done well
           In the laughing time.
           And I hope your life without me
           Is greater than I'll see
           Cause I know that you are happy
           And that means the world to me.

Ending   Because I know that it's true,
           Our love into the sky.
           And with that word of welcome
           I lay down my heart to die.

They say that there are many fish in the sea. They also say that women are like busses: if you miss yours, another will be coming along in a few minutes; don't worry. Yeah, well, when you're in love, you don't believe them. I am lucky, though, because I understood these things even in my abrupt destitution and penury, but I still had to live in the moment.

REMEMBER ME
Chapter XII

▲ ▲ ▲ ▲

This is the night that I began writing this book, August 29.
A time where I started thinking about her, wondering everything
from 'what color her toothbrush really is' to 'is she going out with
some guy already'. The two first paragraphs are something I wrote
in the Dominican Republic, and I consider it my best work.
I consider it that because I know that I can apply it to any
dire situation that I will ever encounter.
And I remember...

Words won't help. Not here. Not ever. These words come slowly. I can't forget those words. I can't forget this episode. This all won't leave me. This incredible sadness envelops my whole. Why must it plague on me like this? I had forgot. A sign. And I cry. These tears flow like ice, yet bring with them the ice from within. A sign of life with two eyes, each the same as the other, but smiling suns in their own little metal worlds. An inch, a world, holds them apart from one another. They both are chained to life, yet they can't be chained to life forever.

Before I was even able to write that I didn't believe anymore, I was given this gift. I believe. These suns are forever whirling around free and chained in a sea of life and love. They fit. But there are gaps in this kindness. And it will inevitably fall apart someday, whether or not it was meant to be. In life and in death, two suns together forever, both in the likeness of their creator, are ready and willing to be destroyed for His love. Bright eyed and bushy tailed, they smile willingly into the face of their inevitable life, inevitable love, and inevitable death. But for now, at least, we can begin this cycle with our minds open, our souls unburdened, and our hearts ready, willing, and able.

That is what we were during that momentary period of bliss in our surreal, bullet-riddled lives. Now, my meaningful words are drowned out by a sense of sickening sadness. I can't help but feel that this situation does not call for words tweaked with optimism. I am too bleak with the absence of hope. I am tired. I am tired of the smiles, of the kisses, of the goodbyes. I am tired of the phone calls, of the distance between us, and especially of the tears. Some day, I know, will dawn with a revelation. A revelation I have yet to give light the permission to whisk away back up to the fake surface of cluttered, rushed lives being wasted by unnecessary tasks set up for the sole purpose of taking one's mind off the sharp truths of reality. I am going to the bedroom now, and this time, it's only because I'm tired.

Chapter 12, 13

▲ ▲ ▲ ▲

In these chapters lie the beginning of my 10th grade year, my first full year at Darien High School. The year before, I had spent at Greens Farms Academy for the first trimester before being whisked away to Aspen Achievement Academy - a tough, malevolent outdoor achievement school in the middle of the Utah desert – for seven and a half weeks. That seven and a half weeks might not sound like a lot, but when you are stuck in a group of eight, and the other seven are druggies, and all you've done is ticked your parents off a little, and you are called the 'straightedge' of the group, and kids try their luck on a regular basis with running into the desert to get away, it's not that fun. When you're spending every day from early in the morning till late at night hiking through the desert with a pack that is either really easy to carry or really hard to carry, depending on how well you tied that survival pack together that morning using some rope, your tarp, and some seatbelt webbing, and even though it's twenty degrees Fahrenheit, you are sweating through all your layers of clothing – the clothes you were issued at base camp. You don't own anything out there. You are possession less. You are borne of sweat, toil and blood. You enjoy the silence. You enjoy the bittersweet pain of your existence. And this is only level one. There's a level five. That's lockdown, as in Provo Lockdown. That's the place you go when you're totally crazy, and it is totally beyond me. I'm not even close to Provo, and I know it, I never thought I'd even go to AAA – Aspen Achievement Academy – until my parents sent me.

Anyway, after going to AAA, I came back to DHS in the second semester – I got to miss midterm exams – and life started out in a positive, productive pattern. One of my classes was Creative Writing Introduction 300. My teacher was one Ms. Lynda Sorenson, one of the greatest teachers I've ever had the lucky pleasure to meet and form a relationship with. I wrote a lot in that class. It happened to be not only my favorite part of the day, but the best few months of my life. I had so much fun with that group of kids – there are always ups and downs – that nothing bad can be said of them.

This next one was an assignment where I was paired with a partner, she would tell me a story, and then I would write about her story from her perspective. So I got to write like I was a girl – one thing I'd never done before, as well as one thing I don't think I'll ever do again.

Love Stronger

But I always think of what would have happened if he had kissed me, even though he didn't. We had been friends since forever, family friends, too. The upside-down smiling arc that the smooth swing made on that sizzling summer eve created a decadent and surprisingly up-beat upward spiral in my life that unforgettable night. I didn't feel that special way about boys, but at the time, that certain age was starting to come around, and even then, there was some unfulfilling but semi-appreciable absence of that kind of "feeling" towards him. He was nice and imaginative, intelligent and funny, and cute and cuddly as though he was stuffed with quality teddy bear material. That night, I realized that we had a bond that not many people end up finding so early in life. He was the perfect man, and I knew it.

I can still feel his warmth gently pushing against my cool skin in that pensive dusk. We were there on the farm, suddenly aware of our favorite old swing rocking slowly back and forth, back and forth, still waiting daily for something amazing to happen. Oh, I felt so perfect sitting there next to him so close. We both knew what was going to happen, so we sat there, marveling at the quiet, whispering peace settling lazily around us. A white dove flew over him and me right then. It would have been a great symbol for love, but as it happened to be, the color of the dove was a deep blue from the dusk settling into sleep for the night behind us. I guess that its deep color must have been a symbol, too.

Through the night, we just sat there on that plain old swing, bubbling with thoughts and feelings of the blurry past, the ever-annoying and all-too-clear present, and our future, impossible and extremely possible in its own little cunning way.

• • •

And as I sit here on that very swing ten whole years later, remembering how he sat here with me in that time of doubt and surprise, I remember him, my best friend, and how close we are now because of that indecisiveness. I think of all the great and sweet times, and all the bitter times, too. I think of all the lonely times when he has been away and when he has been too far to be close to. I remember the times he has gone out of his way, making a total fool of himself, just to make me laugh. I smell his tart after-shave, his pungent sweat, his flat deodorant, his zesty soap, and that powerful fragrance he always slopped on in his tossed-salad-hair mornings. I feel the stubble that has, over time, become impervious to even the strongest of the strongest razorblades. I remember the pangs I have felt when I have realized that he hasn't been around to just talk to. I see the image of his smile, and how his voice in song has made me laugh when I have been crying because of one thing or another. And I always think of what would not have happened if he had kissed me, which he didn't.

Then something tragic occurred. A friend of mine, Ben Bruno, died in a motorcycle accident. It was in Creative Writing class when I heard about it. I freaked out, but kept it inside. It was really horrible. I could only try to describe how it felt.

In Memory

Not like this
It ain't right
I can't realize
That he's
Not coming back to mow our lawn.
Not coming back to show us the dawn.
Not coming back to graphics rend.
Not coming back to be our friend.
My parents are old,
Their fam dies
All like flies
And wakes 'come constant
Like trips to school.
But I'm fifteen,
Friends dying ain't cool.
People's threads pulled so early in life
Brings down freedom of mind
With a switchblade knife.

And, still in lament of Ben's death, I was brought back to Katheryn, either by her untimely phone call, or the fact that I had kind of been making her disappearance out of my life to have been her death.

Untitled Poem #59

I think of you And
Suddenly I'm whole again and I'm filled with a purpose and everything
Is going to be just fine.
and then it's gone and I'm back again to what life isn't and shouldn't be.

Then, two planes hit two buildings, rendering a nation speechless and a world filled with even more terror. On and after September 11th, I wrote and wrote, in an odd daze of self-questioning and pernicious wonder. There were just so many implications in what happened that my mind went into overdrive. One night, I stood out and looked across the placid waters of the Long Island Sound to the skyline of New York City. And amidst the constant biting of bugs and the people and the lights, I couldn't help but cry.

We Mustn't Lie Flat

The sickening absence of beauty
On the droopy face of our world
Has brought down the terror
And horrors have unfurled.
The country we blindly live in
So productively
Must find a new haircut
As soon as soon can be.
It must fit the cheeks
Of the government system...
It must cover the spine
Of our country so dear...
It must not make sad
The people it's protecting...
And this haircut must revive all
And cancel out our fear.

We must stop our sloppy smiles
And cover our bases...
We must cover miles
With glances un-evasive...
We mustn't blink readily
In the presence of hidden foes
And we mustn't write letters
When our enemies have tank rows.

We mustn't try
When our enemies are hidden;
We mustn't lie
When with our enemies we're faced;
We mustn't fly
When our enemies are attacking;
We mustn't die
When our enemies are laughing...

Geoffrey Dilenschneider

Monday Seemed Bad Until Tuesday Came Along

The memories are
Out of reach
On this sunny summer silent afternoon.
And not because
Of the ash on their faces
Or the dead in their places
But because
Of the difference of races
And some so abrasive
A few just evasive
Some read
Allah, then dead
Brought to God
From acts.
The memories
Are out of reach
And my mind
Will not preach,
My heart
Will not teach,
My soul
Will not leech
Because of the hymn
Of Osama Bin
Who declares his win
Over tonic and gin.
And the shouts ring out dry and empty
In the hollow deserts of the dead zone
Surrounded by cries of mercy
And the dead are piled in platoons
That will be followed by many
Sunny summer silent afternoons.

The Words of A Rapist

Lie asleep with your freedom.
It's okay,
Safe is your kingdom.
We won't hurt you.
We're not extreme.
We won't hurt you.
We're not who we seem.
When we come to take you,
Pretend it's just a dream.
Dream of your freedom,
The peace it makes within.
Love it, call it freedom,
We are taken in.

A Song of Michael

Chorus   As my cuts are realized
These scars won't free me
I'll always remember
Remember your eyes
Remember their fire
Burning within
A new hatred of me
I want these feelings
To end...

Verse I   And I have never thought that things would
Change the way a girl will change her clothes.
What have all of us brought into
The life that we thought was so, so good?
And what will come from me
On the day that I have become last?
When the cookies of my future
Go stale, will I leave my past behind?...

Verse II   These sugar tears come for no reason
Save eating out the decay of your mind
Evil words emerge from people
You once thought were safe and your best friends.
From their mouths come frozen daggers
Of the cherry blossom in the spring.
And the emptiness flows through me,
Taking with it all I call my own.
Can I ever bring it back
To the way it was so long ago?...

Verse III   Revert to ways you thought you'd beaten,
Overbear me with your blazing fists.
Walk on over me please
'Cause you know that I'll let you go first.
And I never dreamed of lying
To the faces I so dearly loved.
But I guess that life will turn out
To be broken after all.

Verse IV   Deadly venom is around me
I cannot breathe with constraints so tight
This straight jacket will not let me
Be one with anything at all.
The peaceful look that it may seem
Is a front just for the rage inside.
It needs a vent with no restrictions
So it can see your pretty face again...

Geoffrey Dilenschneider

Amazing Grace, Our Freedom's Beginning

Amazing Grace,
Please give the word
When the healing is to start;
We aren't ready
To face
The life without our loved ones.

Amazing Grace,
Please give the people
Peace, purity, pride;
You know that vengeance
Isn't right,
We know that justice is needed.

Amazing Grace,
Please give the world
Second thoughts on turning their backs;
We need their help
To end the hate,
We need to spread the jam of peace.

Amazing Grace,
Please give the strength
To open up our hearts to horror;
We know it's bad,
But you are strong
Enough to be our jacket of peace.

Amazing Grace,
Please give the heart
That the people need to have;
We are strong,
And we are wise,
And we will not fall in demise.

It's Good

When I think of infinity,
I think of our possibility:
Able to go anywhere.
When I think of extremity,
I think of the extended reaches:
In our minds to out.
My anticipation awaits
On the pensive, quivering lower lip
Of my agitated mouth.
My leg bounces heartbeats,
Reaching out to you
In this finite,
Endless and so blind.

I Am Love

I am the one with the Power.
I am the one to believe.
I am the one with freedom,
And I am one to receive.

I am the one with the Freedom.
I am the one to forget.
I am one with forgiveness,
And I am one not to get.

I am the one with the Strength,
The one that will save us all.
I am one with God,
And the one that will not fall.

The lost just may forgive you,
As they pray with God above,
But I will stand strong up against you,
I am America; I am love.

Geoffrey Dilenschneider

Higher

We all see the same things,
But we don't.
Wee all feel the same things,
But we won't.
We all touch the same things,
But it's different
So you all should just go
Home,
Home,
   Home...
Where cookies are fresh,
And the showers are clean;
The beds are made,
The chicken is lean
And your parent's love
Is real...

The hate is real
Like the fish I reel
Of the fakeness in this world.
I wish to God
That this lie would be ended
And the falsehood would be uncurled:
That the love
Was overturned
And the lie
Of love
Is united
With the art of war.

It was a long time going, but I had finally gotten to know a girl in my Creative Writing class, Mara Hertz, a little bit better. Great person. Great sense of humor, intelligent, caring. Perfect, right? Yeah, if someone hadn't told her some rumors about me (which all happened to be lies). Really funny how the social world of America works – especially in High Schools. You say one thing, you'll hear it come around full circle, except that it has been through a few games of 'Telephone.'

My Guitar Pick is Scared

Verse I   And I open up
To a place unseen
With a favorite book
And a magazine
To live the dream
Of heartfelt hatred
Of the absence of
You in my life…

Chorus   Let's go
Climbing a mountain
Let's throw
Rocks off a cliff
And run when
Old men come runnin'
And laugh 'till
Our throats are dry.

Verse II   And the pouting of
Mother of pearl
I am alone in
Myself and I hurl
I can't stand
This predicament
And where is
The key to your heart?…

Verse III   And I don't know
Where to start
And I can't see
Why you're tart
And why you
Won't talk to me
And you won't be
Free with me.

Verse IV   And I look on
As you walk away
Your quiet stare
Breaks my day
What would I
Say to you?
Will you follow
When I'm through?

Geoffrey Dilenschneider

Bridge	I don't know what to make of it,
	When I think of you.
	Will I ever find the words
	That click inside of you?
	When will you open up
	And say your thoughts to me?

Verse V   What occurs?
           Are you sure
           Of the words
           You didn't say
           Tell me of
           Your hurts and pains
           Why are you
           So scared of change?

Chorus   Let's go
           Climbing a mountain
           Let's show
           What we're feeling
           And kiss if
           It feels righted
           And laugh until
           We grow old.

Mara Hertz

Things aren't ever going to be the same for me
When I walk down the hall and turn my head
So you don't have to see what your words did
To my psyche and how affected my self-confidence is
And I know you think our smiles are all the same,
But I am not like anyone you will ever know
As the rain starts tumbling mindlessly down
Because of how you said that you were sorry
I have felt the feelings of a thousand widows
Waiting endless nights for their loved ones to return
Is the way I feel as the pendulum swings
The right way?

Heart Broken

I'm sorry,
She says.
And that un-perceivable tight pang
Brought forth from my heart and soul
To the diaphragm so broken with clarity,
Pierced through
With a needle of clear rejection
Softened by sweet, melodious words,
Happy with sheer reality and unknowing
Of my own, now shattered reality,
Brought forth by the thoughtful absence
Of emotional and mental understanding
On her part of my situation
Now so mercilessly coming to
In a single endless instant of finality.

A Better Life Existed

Where is my true love supposed to be?
Under a rock or behind a tree?
What will it take to find this one?
A lengthy search or my head to a gun?
When will it end, these times so bland?
Where will I stop? When will I land?
What has caught me, and where is it at?
Might it be love, or does it smell like a rat?
Who may this elusive perfect woman be?
When will she come to make me free?
Or is it that someday I'm supposed to find her?
When will that answer come back as a sure?
What difference does it make that time doesn't stop?
What difference does it make if my happiness dropped?
What time is it on your watch when I die?
What time is it on the clock when it's time that I fly?
Why does the bird fly when it's only some jokes?
Why are all the girls with all the guys who're such blokes?

What will it take to bring her out to me?
A loud birdcall or a song just for free?
What will it take to bring her to me?
When will I break from the pressure to see?
Why are my friends leaving one by one
When all I said was that life's no more fun?
How will this girl react when I say life is true
Only when I have the time of my life with you?
Why is life never just like the movies
And so perfect like the TV shows sour?

Geoffrey Dilenschneider

And everything goes from bad to perfect
In just one simple, savvy hour?
When will I die and melt in one kiss?
When will that time come when there is no more mist?
What have I done to deserve this hell so brave?
When will I break from the pressure to live?

What One Looks For

Does it matter where my heart is
When it won't be going anywhere anyway?
What does it matter if the time of day won't stop
To pray to God for my mistakes?
When does it rain during a feast?
When does a sickness bring that rain
Onto a battery full of happiness?
Why doesn't love come in an easy-opening package?
When does the printer jam to give lovers an opening?
Why does life give hard choices
And no easy way out?
Why does love give no hard choices one moment
With too many options undesired?
Why do eagles watch over their young ones?
Why do new things smell so nice
When the tempo of my life is so slow
Because of the way you disregarded my plea
For someone to just be with for a second
In an endless time of sadness
Just waiting in eagerness for hope
To come and knock on my broken door?
When does my pain end
And the serene happiness begin?

So Mara Hertz became a friend, and after the first semester ended and our Creative Writing class – a one-semester class – dispersed, I was left without Mara, who had really only become a slight friend (I think she always believed the dumb rumors).

I had, however, met the greatest girl I know and will ever know. Katie Bennet. She was in the acknowledgements page in my first book. She took up half the page. I've gotten to know her a bit, and I wish we would become better friends even more, but we haven't. Anyway, I've gotten to know her, and she is better than Katheryn, better than Eliza, better than anybody I know. I mean no offense to anyone, it's just she's so nice, and yet, doesn't take any crap from anyone, ya know? I feel complete and at ease around her. I've no need to show off to her like I sometimes feel I need to around some girls.

Anyone ever ask you those dumb questions like 'if you had to have dinner and get to know only one person in the entire world, dead or alive, who would it be?' Yeah, I'd answer Katie Bennet. No question. She's deeper than the universe.

And if you're wondering, she has a boyfriend, and at the end of the 10th grade, they had been going out a full year (or is that a full two years? I can't remember.)

Katie Bennet

When you have no chalk
To write the answer on the board,
I wish there were some in my pocket
To give you free of charge.
When you lose your book,
I want to give you mine.
When you have no pen,
I'll give you ten of mine
And when you're out of time,
I give you a month of mine.

When you are pulled over,
I will pay your fine.
When you miss a stop,
I'll uproot that meddling sign.
When you aren't well,
I will make you fine.
And when you are sick,
My health, I'll give you mine.

When you cannot go
Much farther than you've gone,
I will carry you on my back
Over a thousand neighbor's lawns.
When I make you a part of this
Only life I've got,
I wish you'd make me part of yours
And not say, "I forgot."

Geoffrey Dilenschneider

Looking for Life

I will always wonder
What I would have said.
I will never forget the life
That night just might've led.
I will forever ponder
Why I was brought onto the ground.
Tell the harvest moon to sit
And forever be safe and sound.
Bring close to my bedside
The times I'll never see again.
Vivid in my memory,
Are the hits upon my chin.
Along with all the love you gave,
And how warm I felt inside,
Especially when you hugged me,
My heart just melted and died.
My water's no longer dirtied
Because of laughter light
Caused by our love deeper
Than how anyone holds me tight.
My own dark moon is shadowed
By the great lakes of your love
And when I go to set close to you,
The last thing I want's a shove.
But companionship is greater
Than anything I know.
We have something connected,
Inside it makes us grow.
Maybe it'll be a year,
Or maybe until we grow old.
But someday I will say to you:
Look in my hands, behold!
I will never lie to you,
The truth be ever told.

My thoughts may sound so deep,
But my mind is just three fold:
One for all the lovely things
In the world I cherish so.
Two for all the horrid things
In the place I loath to go.
Three for all the people
Who call themselves so true;
I may not be perfect, K,
But I'm so in love with you.

Brunettes are Beautiful

I will not think hard
In order to explain.
I will not write down,
Just to soothe my pain.
The hurt inside for a friend
Who will not lie to me.
The love for someone greater,
Someone who sets me free.
A person just to talk to,
To divulge those secrets dark.
A someone just so special,
Who won't go tell the park.
A tigress who will pounce on me
When I act so foolishly
A kitten to lick my cuts
When I fall so clumsily.
A someone who will laugh at me
When I embarrass my self
And a Band-Aid to cauterize
My wounds to keep my health.
A car to keep me running,
And just so shiny bright.
A pacifistic boxer
Who just might drop up and fight.
I need not a trophy for my room
To give me such delight.
I need not the time to think you're wrong,
'Cause I always know you're right.
And the words will keep on coming,
In full force, of course I know.
But every time I think a thought,
It helps keep me balanced so.

Honestly, I had a huge crush on Katie, and for a while, didn't dare ask if she had a boyfriend, but as I've already told you, she does. Before I knew this information, however, I had high, high hopes.

Geoffrey Dilenschneider

... To Be That One for You

I do not want things to be normal.
I don't want things to be just fine.
I don't want life to be perfect.
I can't stand the boring time.

I do not want your thoughts to break the system.
I don't want time to worsen the things we've got.
I don't want our lives to end with misery
When I think of what would make us rot.

I do not watch some other when you aren't around.
I do not watch the clock when you aren't listening.
I don't want this thought to take me anywhere
Except when we are whistling.

I do not want things to be normal.
I do not want things to be just right,
'Cause then I'd want life to be perfect,
'Cause then I'd have the right...

I don't remember exactly what I did one day, but I really angered Katie in Chemistry class. She was furious and I really felt bad. I probably said something stupid – an art only few master and fewer actually care to master – so I apologized to her with a poem (how else would I apologize?!)

To Agree With Another

I'm sorry for the things I've said
And for the things I've done.
I'm sorry for the way I acted
And I'm sorry for the sun.

I didn't mean to say those words,
They came out way too soon.
I didn't mean to do those things,
I'm sorry for the moon.

I haven't meant to hurt you,
And now I will regret
The way I misconstrued to you
The way my red sun set.

I'm sorry for the way I seem to be,
Which you obviously despise.
I'm sorry for the fog you see,
As I set the sun to rise.

Then I started thinking random things. Or, in real terms: I was bored stiff. I believe I had been thinking about Katie the whole time, but I'm not really sure. I could just look into her eyes and pull out any kind of poem or song. I lament now that I didn't try to work myself into her life a little more, but I guess it would have been a stupid move anyhow.

Thursday, Friday, Monday

A brick, a brick
In the walls that we create;
Where do they come from?
When do they become fake?
    Hurl them to the ground
With the power of knowledge,
But what good do the foes do
When they're sick inside the head?
With mother does one
    Time the race with
A watch without a face,
Who will get it right?
Wholly provocative are the blasé words
Of pacifists on a rampage
Because one would not think
A pacifist to flip.
The depraved jaybirds poke amicably
At the unsavory entertainment
Yet to be entertaining.
But when I lift my eyes to someone
I trust with timeless thoughts
Deep inside my self-contained artificial heart,
And when I lift my eyes zealously,
I make the skies wonder why
They did not make my eyes green
And my hair blue.
Capriciously I think of her
Whenever I am ill and never when I'm not
Because of times remembered and hard times all forgot
On the days that time is never standing
Still to consternation suddenly with
Apparitions slowly coming to a
Light.
Time has no constraint on the dead.
Lime in a drink turns faces red
On the same plain that books have read
About their obituaries of letters unsaid.
And parents yawn while their children led.
Light: an abusive, corrupt profit without concern
For unwise oddly placed tasteless impulsive changes of mind.
Never find the lucky few whose fate is to rewind

Geoffrey Dilenschneider

The stone legs of Prefontain with Mercedes yet to find
The tape recorder of our lives with a little recollection of the mind.
Light the path
And hence forth History repeats undulating topics to me
And you swoon onto your desk with dreams of being free
To not have life or love and no responsibility
To save the lives with punches to the face that you can't even see
Because depth isn't one thing that the teachers let me see.
Light the path to sleep:
Dying are the bright, luminescent cloths covering my broken soul
With a thought to an inane and nonchalantly ostracizing mole
Upon my face with laughing consternation for my unsheathed and bloody soul
Without a single thought to what may come to be its goal
To follow with the pride and strength of a woman's standing soul.
Light the path to the sleep of those who:
Have a mouth ferocious with the down-turned, saddened corners high
Contemplating sorrowful reality with the censored mouth a sigh
Into the journey of a million thoughts into a tongue defy
The many baseboards assuming things about this crossed-arm lie.
What sense does hair make when it turns those pursed lips so they're dry?
Light the path to the sleep of those who are
Broken music records lying heaps of garbage onto my dinner plate sad
With the bleeding pen of yesterdays' thoughts of friendships mad
And timing the bells of heaven to the horns of devils and a truck's fad.
Why do those who never tell end up being close to those who are glad?
And why do sneezes come at random with the thought of God and a lad?
Sight the bath to the beep of those who are wired.
Fight the laugh to the leap of those who are fired.
  Light the path to the sleep of those who are tired!
And time the soul with a stopwatch.

My Dear (Revised)

I dreamt that I was whole again,
I dreamt that you were here.
I slept with comfort because I knew
You'd always be so near.
I only know your name now,
Even though it's kind of fuzzy;
I can barely see your smile now,
But sadly, it's becoming fuzzy.

I dreamt I woke up this morn, my dear…
Because you were here with me;
I woke up on time today, my love,
And I felt like living free!
For the first time since forever,
'Cause I dreamt that you were here.

Searching for a Girl

I cannot draw you a flower,
Or buy one in a store.
I may not be able to afford it,
But ask all you want for more.
I had it all a day ago,
I could've given you the world;
But now time's taken its toll on me,
And my future's no longer unfurled.

I could compose a million
Songs for you dear,
But I see no need to waste my time
For I'm unsure if me you hear.

If time had a body,
I wouldn't need to smack him;
But I know to leave him alone
Because he needs to run his course,
Even though I don't want him to.

A present from my crimson heart,
Beating fast as you arose:
A simple little dandelion,
And a succulent red, red rose.

Geoffrey Dilenschneider

Chapter 14, 15

▲ ▲ ▲ ▲

Feelings of a Child

And a tear,
So cold,
Runs down my cheek
In a path of winter destruction,
Peppering me with white bits of soft criticism.

And a fear,
So old,
Comes back to seek
An utter time for my education,
Breaking me down with reserved bits of cynicism.

And a year,
Ten fold,
Comes back to reek
A simple hell on my life's production,
Saving me from white bits of soft logicism.

One Two

One buy windows,
        My mind in thought, a store.
Staring me,
Bring please to care.
        Lie, can't you?
It's great to see things *great*
        Being small…
        …small being
great
Things see,
Too great, is it?
        You can't lie,
Care to please?
Bring me staring,
        Store a thought in my mind,
    Windows buy one.

One Thought Twice

One thought twice:
Won,
Have I?
He is who?
Chill him!
Has thought broken?
Mind the changed!
Has he allowed laughing,
Carefully watching the beating time
Of someone special that is; doesn't care?
Worse lives better,
Makes people sing and
Why think? and
Broken things change…
… Change things broken
And think why
And sing! people!
Makes better lives worse,
Care does not.
Is that special someone of time, beating the watching,
Carefully laughing allowed?
He has changed the mind!
Broken thought has him!
Chill, who is he?
I have won,
Twice thought one.

Every few weeks I do something with my family that is one of the greatest things in the world; something I consider to be a national pastime. We go to a Yankees game.

Our seats are almost superfluous in their proximity to the game. Check it out: third base line, twelve rows back in club seating, I mean, right behind the third base coach's box. Our Mets tickets are better, though: two rows back behind the Mets' dugout. But I've always loved the Yankees. My favorite player in the world is Don Mattingly. If someone put a dime on the field, he most likely could have hit it with a ball he hit from home plate. He was the greatest.

I remember being front row behind the Yankees dugout for something like my sixth birthday, watching Don Mattingly the entire game. Everything he did was Godlike. Of course, being an impressionable little kid, I did everything he did, but I've since grown out of it. But for a little kid on his birthday, going to see Don Mattingly was the coolest thing in the world. There was nothing better.

Geoffrey Dilenschneider

The Greatest Game in the World

Why's it only good when there's excitement
Coming from the others all around?
Why do people scream to death
Only when the time is right?
Why am I lost of a common cause
When the time is later to be found?
Why do people stand and stare
When there's nothing there but a fight?
What riles a crowd into a frenzy
Better than this holy game?
What do people like better
Than a hotdog and a damn close game?
What turns heads faster than
Two drunks calling each other names?
They all like the people
That strike out but retain their fame.
What more do we want than our team to win
And to be on famed TV?
There's only one who'll win this game
For you and precious me:
It's that of yourself in a form without lies
When the ninth's finally over in shouts or in cries.
And one last pledge is called oh-so-true
By me and by you
As we walk out that big blue door:
Take me out to the ball game,
Strong and proud with no thought to the score.

*Okay, back to the present. I'm fifteen now, and again, I return to the hum-drum life
of sleep, eat, school, eat, school, homework, eat, sleep, rinse and repeat, writing whenever possible. I wanted so bad to be like Chris McCandless, the bright young man who
walked alone, with next to nothing, into the Alaskan tundra, never to return alive. I
wanted to not as much flee from society, but wanted to rebel. I wanted change. (and
still do, actually.)*

The Drawing Room

Sam Ruiz was a real, bull-riding man. No one had ever pushed him around,
and he never let anyone get away with it, either. Two years ago, you could have
easily said that Ruiz was a made man. He had a beautiful, dark-haired wife, a
charming son, Louie, and a mediocre job that paid the rent and even allowed
for a few extras.

He and his family weren't what some call well off, but compared to other
regions of the world that were less fortunate than the hot, sticky towns of
good old Texas, they were doing just fine. Until, of course, he met Peter Benning. Pete had been thrown around on the ropes of life for most of his

younger years, but had taken control of his destiny by getting out of his New-York-City-rut and hitching rides until he could do so no longer. Benning met Ruiz in a small used tire shop in Ruiz's hometown. This was before the accident, though, and Ruiz was still the good-natured, wide-grinning man he had been. As they got to know each other, Ruiz introduced Benning to Ann, his wife, who had to have been the most serious art student known to man. However, from the moment he met Ann, Ruiz was headed downhill, totally out of control.

"Man, I don't trust you. Why should I come down into that stupid place? You've always got some phony crap running around in your head!" Benning yelled down into the darkness, "Every time I *ever* listen to you, I get caught up in some phony prank or one of your dumb jokes!" He waited for a nasty response, his eyes watering from the thick odor floating out from down below. Actually, he did like most of the things his friend tricked him into, but recently, Ruiz had been acting pretty strange.

Four months ago, Ruiz had a run-in with a meat cutting machine where he was working at the time. The machine took his right leg from the knee down and never looked back. Now he wore a metal contraption where his leg used to be. Ruiz still refused to even touch the smooth, alien stump since the doctors had sewn him up in the small-town ER. To make matters worse, Benning, only a month before the accident, had stolen Ruiz's wife from him. First the affair, then the divorce papers, then *their* marriage, Benning had really taken advantage of his friend, but the two's friendship never wavered; they were inseparable.

Until two months ago, Ruiz had been steadily drinking himself into a depression, but then Benning had decided that the two of them would take a vacation to Connecticut for a while. Ruiz had grumpily agreed to the vacation/road trip, and they had headed off towards Connecticut, and that is how they got to where they were: on the old Zeigler Estate overlooking the Long Island Sound.

Benning and Ruiz had seen from their guesthouse window an old, shadowy house on the other side of the fence and had decided to go exploring. There, they had found a door to what they thought was a cellar of some kind around back, and Ruiz, always the one for adventure, decided to go down and scope it out. That is where they were.

Just then Benning made up his mind. "I refuse!" He called down to the dripping walls of the cellar to his friend who was supposedly exploring the endless reaches of the wine cellar. "You'll just have to beat me up, 'cause I won't go down there!"

Ruiz, who was actually right at the bottom of the stone steps, heard Benning's refusal, and was very game for a rumble with Benning, who weighed a good ninety pounds less than him. He ran two-step up the cold slabs and stuck his arms straight out into the light, and at the same time, lunged all two-hundred-and-fifty-five pounds of himself up to the top of the steps where the bewildered Benning stood, lanky and grinning.

They collided at the apex of the stairs and fell to the ground in an almost comical chaos, rolling over and over each other in a big cloud of dust. You could almost see the little yellow stars pop out whenever one of their fists made contact with the other's jaw.

Then, suddenly, the ground beneath them disappeared, becoming a set of long, cold stairs. They clambered back down into the cellar in a twisted complication of arms and legs, yelping in pain as they hit each step.

"You idiot!" Benning screamed as they hit bottom, his voice hoarse from the strain. "What the hell did'ja do that for? I coulda broken my neck, goddamn it! I mean, *Jesus friggin' Christ!* Who the *hell* gets their friggin' kicks fallin' down like a million goddamn stairs! Shit!" He paused, then, more relaxed, "Sammy, you are one crazy jackass!" Benning laughed uneasily, shaking off his new set of aches and pains. "Get off me," he groaned, heaving Ruiz's mass of bone and muscle off of him onto the icy stone floor. Getting up, he dusted himself off, and then turned to help Ruiz get up off the floor. "It's winter, after all, and our jackets can barely be called jackets at all," thought Benning's more responsible side. But when he stuck his hand out, no hand greeted his for help. He looked down.

Sammy Ruiz was dead.

Benning recoiled from the body, pulling his hand away as though he had just realized his hand had been thrust into a fire. He blinked twice, his face twitching, trying in vain to process the information. A few minutes passed with him standing there, numb, until Benning finally knelt by the corpse's side and started slapping it, trying in newfound tears to wake the corpse up, and silently refusing to believe what had happened. He silently stared up at the rows of dark, ominous wine bottles lying depressively on their sides, his mouth working of its own accord, even though no sounds came out; only a strained squeak.

He then noticed the trickle of blood running out from the corpse's mouth and down its pale chin. The blood was thick; thick like the strawberry jam on the bread sandwiches they eat together. "No... not anymore," whispered Benning, wiping the blood from the corpse's chin, maybe in some twisted way to try and preserve the way Ruiz used to look. He lifted the bloody fingers to his mouth, tears running past his eyes. Benning licked the blood from his fingertips then, tasting the salty, red years wash into the past, into some endless, crimson abyss so far away.

Suddenly, Benning stood up, turned, and bolted from the cellar. He slammed the doors open that had somehow shut while the two had been falling, and ran across the rustling field; running through his shattered world, nothing making sense or having any feeling or meaning to it. He ran until he got to the fence separating the two properties. He jumped it in one go, easily escaping the deadly spokes at the top, and charged into the guesthouse where he and Sam had been staying for the past two months on their vacation. He ran through the kitchen and up the stairs in the hallway, totally missing the little beige envelope at the base of the stairs' polished oak handrail. He flew into his naked opaque room and slammed the door shut behind him. Like a child in a shocked tantrum, he flopped onto his mattress, screaming and crying.

... to be continued

Women... Sheesh!

Don't you know that nothing will be just perfect?
Don't you know that everything will not come out right?
Can't you feel the pain? It's just so near.
What have I told you about her?
She will change you for the worse!
Her laugh is that of happiness
As she breaks your heart in half.

What will you do when she's done with you?
Where will you go when her wrath is at your door?

Will you ask if you were wrong to her?
Will you wonder what it's for?

What will you know when time has passed you by?
What will you think if nothing comes out right?
What do you do when that perfect moment (never) comes?
For your life, or for your love, will you be fleeing or will you fight?

Then I was taken to this college thing, where all the colleges have booths set up in a school gym and kids come and check out the colleges they want to attend. It was for kids in 11th and 12th grade, and I was only in 10th, but I went anyway.

I felt so bad for the people whose jobs were to just stand there while kids and their parents took out the brochures from their booths. The people working were so intolerable of their job that they became hostile towards the kids and their families. It was a disaster. Anyway, it ended up with everyone leaving... quickly.

Holyoke

You seem lonely
        Out of place with the world
On time with a different zone
        What's your name
When the clock strikes eight
        Over the loud speaker
And why so strict
        When so alone?

I began to think about the book that was in progress, A Boy Aware. *Killer of a book, to say the least, and I wanted to put this in there, but ended up not, waiting for a more opticrevasant time... like now.*

Productive

Criticize me when I'm dead,
Criticize me now;
Criticize me when I'm being fed,
Criticize me now.

Criticize me when you're right
And even when you're wrong;
Criticize me on my verse
And criticize my song.

Criticize me all you want,
It's what I need from you;
Type it in a real big font,
Or write it just from you.

Criticize the way I write,
Criticize the way I don't;
Criticize the life I live,
Get mad at you, I won't.

Then I went back, again, to boredom. These I wrote in World Studies Class.

The First Step

First step has to be what?
I like it better on days that are comfortable
And the fresh rains are happy.
When they are being negative the dew stops
And
Finding time to do what is necessary is hard.
Did you have it?
Does the ductile duct tape make it worth it?
Or better?
It is calm in the winds of the storm
And the eye is red, but it's called pink eye.
Without failure, there is no succeeding.
But how do you know not to put your feet into
Scalding water?
Random rules forget to flip their muffins
In the oven.
"I was kinda doing a whole mess of things,
I should have come back to you," said the math teacher
To his English muffin,
But it was too late,

The boring pastry was already burnt and buried.
I don't have all the answers, he didn't admit,
But it was also too late
Because it wasn't a comfortable day
With time on the line jingling down the hall
With his hand on his ear.
It's a weird little six,
All backwards in its ways.
I can't think backwards anywhere but behind zero
And bluejays talk of tomorrow
And blink without arms
In fire.
Everything is so similar in the month of may
Who goes through crosswords without getting cross
Hate is by itself in the early morning
Surrounded by its bodyguards of milk
And random things yet to be announced.

Are we graded for our personality
Or for how we act irrationally?

Dresses walk hand in hand,
Whispering to desks of the boys in blue
With toxic stares running them up and down,
Left and right
And screw you; I like being a wannabe,
But jay's are dumber than their muscles want to be.
Rode a mustache to school,
But it got expelled for destroying new goods
A mile away locked up at the vandalized train station
Without front wheels and rain and popularity.
There is a possibility that the date is short.

Time is slowing when two days changes
On time with three, say mangy losers
So fed up and now I know what I look like
Little roaches with plantations of people
Sold for a dollar and a girl tomorrow night
Having to do with Greece and Communist Aids
Raising the vain needs of those in need of
Nothing.

Nothing knows war like Greece or
The nothings who waste time on peace.

Put spin on the head.

See Where it Takes You

Some may believe that i'm bland,
but the bluebirds that know me
Have a feeling i'm grand
when the morning brings holly to me
And the times are happy
and the times are free,
What more could one ask for
save a girl and the sea
On a perfectly beautiful
day such as these.

Some may believe that the sand
is not here as much as i'm going;
But i stay close to land
whenever i'm rowing,
Or i sit by the shore of my friends.
ask one or ask two
For the malleable blues
and time your soul with a stopwatch.

The world revolved around repetition. Not an odd thing for most, but for me, it is impossible. Most of the time, I don't mind, but only because I'm too busy doing the 'pretty boring things' anyway.

No one ever stops to ask, "why not change?" "Why not change who I am faithful to or let out all the pain I bear?" "And for whom do I bear pain?"

Chapter 17

▲ ▲ ▲ ▲

It is in the moment of silence that one begins to think about others, but can only be thinking about oneself. It's the end of October and the first half of November.

Going Through Fire

Make the time to make
A date for leaving dreams
Right at eight, but I must keep it to myself at
Length for things hidden inside may
Exasperate the gossip kings and queens,
Now in stone
A feeling I've thrown

May time be on my side
Young, I hope we look.

Love, a word I will not utter
On this page so bold.
Veering from this ruled pen
Enigmas now unfold:

Bleed the beings underneath the stove,
Underneath the loaf of bread
Too hot for the human hand.

What black hat looks white with
Horror on the poor boy's face
And a thatched roof of candle wax blows out with
The wind of a girl.

Tame the good posters
Old like wilted flowers on different graves
Dying for the band that made the wrong choice
On lost roads traveling scared on sacred safety feelings alone

• • •

What does it take to throw a party for the departed?
How do you just believe?
And again peace settles, gets comfy, gets old...
Then random events must occur.

Through days some toil tame and finish
On the Aids of March in October.

Do CD's scratched become old when
Odd figures finally roll over?

Black clouds rain joy upon my angered stare
And lullabies bring smiles to the child of my youth.
Let time return to when I didn't know everything
Days went quick without pain
And let time return to sessions of secure freedom
Counting clocks in a bravado store of seawater
Condemned from use in the park where I spent my time
In love with a life.

Kay

So secret and so far away,
Deep inside of me.
My bones are turning liquid
Because I cannot be
With the enigma,
your seductive mystery
As I plunge into the darkness
Not caring where I be.
As I plunge into the darkness
Not caring when I'm free.

And walking dreary
In the morn
I come across
A tree of scorn
And I wonder how exactly we
Are meant to be together, see?
Here on one hand is a thought
Saying that our love's not bought,
This hand is not one to out voice,
But come to love, there is no choice,
This hand, this hand, you see, it must
Climb this sickly tree's low bust
And when it's done and the two are parted,
I'm now back to just as I started:
Broken in my thoughts of her
And the way she used to purr...
And here the other hand is saying
That one mustn't start a-praying,
For a mermaid doesn't swim on land
And neither does a fish on sand
But this hand feels in a bind,

It shows the sort of state of mind
That hand bathes in oh-so-sad,
Soaking in the dirt un-glad,
Broken by the lack of faith in self,
That twists and turns and saps all health,
Jarring mind from any mirth,
Making wishes to be torn from birth.

So secret in your absentee,
I'm sad inside for all to see
But when can you come over
For a day or three?
And when's a mermaid's time so over
Setting her tail free?

Untitled Poem #..........

"Go straight?" Said the tree sapling.
"Yes," Said I.

After doing the school routine for a long time, I started to feel a bit frazzled. I'm pretty sure this was the time my grades started to drop a little.

Frazzled

I am a pilot lost inside myself without hearing in one ear.
I am a tree without its leaves: broken, naked, bare.
I am widowed in an hour, left inside to stare,
    Watching life go on around me, pulling at my hair.
I am blown by winds ungiving, thoughtless and unloving.
I am kicking bored of death at the lid of my own coffin.
I am working on a china plate that won't mean anything,
    Living on a platter that I refuse to share.
I am drinking holy water that is tainted with my complaint.
I am drinking into life too deeply for any, any saint.
I am bleeding with the fury of a thousand island dressing,
    While my eyes are sound confessing.
I am bearing at one eighty all the feelings of Marsha Brady.
I am a salad tossed in Haiti with feelings that are somewhat shady.
I am a moron walking water with a treadmill getting hotter,
    While my heart is at a place
    Where my heart is lost of grace.
    While my heart is all defaced,
    Here my heart is singing grace.

Geoffrey Dilenschneider

I had a mentor. What's a mentor? Well, in definition, a mentor is an adviser, a giver of knowledge. My mentor's job description was similar to the definition, but he ended up being a glorified babysitter.

He took the brunt of my fifteen-year-old emotional eruption in place of my parents, tried and failed to teach me things (figuring he hadn't even become a virtuous enough person to be any kind of mentor), and he drove me places. This was fine until one night he was driving me to Young Life, a youth group based in my hometown, and ran over this animal, thinking nothing of it. Actually, I was sure that he had swerved trying to hit the thing rather than get out of its way. Neither of us really knew what it was – it was bigger than a squirrel, didn't have a tail like a fox, obviously wasn't as big as a wild pheasant or wild turkey, and we guessed that it wasn't a raccoon – and to this day we don't know what it is, and for a while, we spent the time going crazy over figuring out what the damned dead animal was. This even sticks in my mind so pathetically only because it was such a vivid reminder of the type of person Guy was (Guy was my first mentor's name). He would do that type of thing.

For some reason, the incident reminded me of Katheryn. I don't know why, but I'm sure that the feeling that animal had when it lay dying in twisted, flattened agony on the side of a nice, middle-upper class street was probably the same feeling that I had when I parted ways with Katheryn.

Where I Stand

The girl of my dreams is gone
In a flash of airplanes,
But she is content with being
My long-distance girl.
My life seems broken in a shard of glass
In peace with nothing but the wind.
Torrential downpours of angst-ridden pleas
To change my (okay) ways
Somehow lessen against my own cries
For peace.
The sickness brings out a need for honesty
Too brutal for the untainted saints
Of immortality.
I cannot do any that I please, in fact
Nothing that rains in my direction
Is "meant" to stay unbroken at my door.
In my mind stays the answers, too scared
To do-wop their way out on stage
To say their piece because of the way
Liars stand somehow strong on trial.
I quiver beaten with the stick of help
On a battlefield of wanton disregard for other's needs.

Where I Don't

Life is happy and
Life is free –
Can't you envision
Freedom for me?
My family is perfect
And I get all A's –
My life is serene
And full of bright haze.
Here! A rose un-wilted
With the madness around.
There! A painless shot of reality...

Questions (And Everything Was Alright)

On a night that made me sick,
I kissed a girl upon the lips –
And everything was alright.
Now I'm a mustang and she's a viper
Like she's so calm and I'm so hyper,
But she knows me through and through.
On the days with rain I dread
She has a voice I like to hear
Inside a guessing type of head –
Her way of knowing me is scary.
Oh! and when the sky clears
To the better, sunny days,
Where will love be
In the bright blue wonderin' haze?
What candy sits sweeter
Than her cherry lips on mine?
What world is freed quicker
Than my corrupted state of mind
When she digs up unknown knowledge
Of everything I find?
Here! I can't help but ponder
On what one says to a goddess
Minimizing herself in all restraints.
I have big plans for us, my darling,
Running thoughts so daring.
I can close my eyes and be safe
In thoughts of our future.

Ah! What are these?
Busses taking you away?
Taxis, planes, me away?
Who dare confound our destiny?
Who dare to unravel string?

Geoffrey Dilenschneider

Who dare to break the chain of love
And call our own a fling?
This is a lie, of sorts, I guess –
A lie of life that leaves one broken,
Broken in this sea of lies
To keep us from the lamenting truths,
Pondering on their own devilish ways...
I cannot believe, I will not confess...

That it's been a month since I've talked to you.
What did we do
To anger gods
So through and through?
Vanilla pinecones happen to hit me
On an autumn pensive evening such as this,
But why not somewhere else?
Strawberry sheets covered us
When kisses came to cheeks.

When looks no more matter,
And time is lost to love,
Life is put on hold
For the truths we need to hold
Self-evident inside ourselves
With help from deep inside
Is made to fit in time now passing,
Not take me for a ride!
Moons collide with suns
And become black with untimely perfection
For a moment unstoppable
And then time goes again,
Back to speed on a clock on
The wall of the wind.
Hurricanes blow focused blasts
Of beaten, broken voices
Across the serrated planes,
Porous with a fine grain of thought
Erratically keeping life alive:

On a night that made me sick,
I kissed a girl upon the lips –
And everything was alright.

Where Are the Answers?

Look! Look!
Do you sit alone or with a friend?
Can one alone destroy all
Good within the world?
Is beauty meant to share her wealth
Or keep it deep inside?
What type of bagel would you like
Upon your butter soft?
Are you done or are you through?
Short or long? What is so wrong
With a collared shirt today?
Innie or out? Should one sigh or shout
When a jerk comes over to say:
Do we have meaning or is there no point?
Shall we live for our freedom
Or from pain do we hide?
Do we hate that which we do not know
Or are we scared of that which we could?
Do you fit alone or with a friend?
Breathe! Breathe…

I never had really gotten over Katheryn, even though I liked to pretend that I had. Over the weeks and few months, we had called each other sporadically and spastically, and had gotten to know each other. I've always had a strong disliking of talking on the phone, especially for long periods of time, but it was nice talking to Katheryn for hours on end because it was the only contact we could have. Somewhere in the back of my mind, though I still regret to admit it, was the thought that we were growing quietly distant.

Again, I started to question worth and life and things like this, living under the rule of tyrannical teachers.

And Down What Path?

What knife
And where does one knife lead a young boy
And down what path?
What human ear hears sleek blade
Flying through sweet cumbersome air
On the time of misery's end!

Geoffrey Dilenschneider

A Voice

On a stutter
Stands a thought
On which is formed
An idea
On which a voice is raised
In an opinion
On which is altered
A mind
While speaking up is
A voice
  To change different opinions to become similar
In a meeting room filled with
    Individuals congruent to none but themselves
Coming to influence
The building of presence inside
A city abundant with
Life,
Creating and moving energy
To move,
      Change
The world
Surrounding
A city,
A building,
    A man
alone
     with himself
  Down to his similarity with none but himself
     In a room with
        Different opinions becoming similar
While speaking up is
A voice
On which is altered
A mind
On which a voice is raised
In an opinion
Of an idea
Which is formed solely upon
    A man
Alone
        ......   with a bubble expanding out from him,
              separating him infinitely from everyone else
              because he is one.

An idea
On which is formed
A voice,
Stands a thought
On a stutter.

Who's Right?

Can one ever really tell?
Unless someone lied about the length of their beauty
Or a broken ruler on a plain.
What do whispers really say?
What does the fact that nibbles always reach
The ears of unwanted Toms at the wrong
Time tell us about the doings of the wind?
Where bathing in great beauty glistens
With the sleeping mother's decadence,
One asks all of them:
     Where does the red fern grow?
     On Tom's head or in a row?
     Do lilies stay sober from happy nights
     Or leave later with cuts from fights?
     Does a butterfly shed when the lights are off
     Or does she lean on the porch when you are gone?
     Why do the children ask those things
     About Tom's lilies and dragon's wings?
     Who may tell the children of pressure's power
     And the bad time's black, high, scary tower?
     Where does the free bird roam on through
     And why do your ears ring just by floor two?
     Bring me a thought or two?
     Leave them by the door?
     I will walk with you
     Asking time for more.
Who does retain the right to chain children's purity
And innocence to the floor?
Who does hold the power to call up Tom?
And ask him what has made one wrong?

Geoffrey Dilenschneider

By the Way

What's what when windows slam?
Who knows while time slowly stands?
Where is the corner necessarily turning for the correct events to occur now?
When does the girl come down to ask
How truth is and
Why it never isn't?

Who brings the baby to the door?
What kind of door lets it in?
When is it ever supposed to happen?
Where does time just begin?
Why do things become less happy in the time that they are sold?
How! Is what the Indians say
      To let one know that it's time for the hold.

Running

Here again, here again,
Back to the wall;
Here again, here again,
Trying to stall…
Here again, here again,
Stooping down to fall:
There again, there again,
Running down the hall.
Here again, here again…
Running from them all.

Innocent Smile in an Unforgiving Place

When do i bleed for the girl…
the girl i know who will hurt?
what good does it do
if i know what to do,
but she won't even let me begin?
sing high, little sparrow!
you may not be large,
but the time does arise
for those young of small size
to come forth with the words that they feel.
feel!
come now and show the world the true meaning of brutal honesty.
there, a catalog of paper
and a dog on a string with a smile.
but who controls the dog and its dandy parade?
a boy walking backwards with a smile.

Timeless Memory

choose, you ask?
but where does one look for a time to choose
in a sea of jelly and broken memories?!
soft touch on the brink of extinction
while I go about my daily things
with a feeling of undermined happiness.
can I never be sane with the world?!
I created when I met
You?
no! the answer comes back around,
chosen in seconds of a time
where life has no more meaning than myself
in a sea of other selfs!
creating one self,
greater than any singular self.
choose, you ask?
I choose liberty of love,
you damn fool!
now close your eyes and remember the good times.

Hello and Goodbye

Where do the words fly
when things go wrong
And refuse to die?
what time does ones watch say
When things go wrong
and I start to lie?
Where do my ties stay sobered in grasses
yet to be tainted by souls burdened
By horrible things yet to be named
with the music of my heart?
Where do violins leave trails of peace?
and where does the caretaker sleep off the memories
Of those departed to a world
yet to be tainted by souls released?
Only in an infinity of banes, boons, and broken bones
throughout a mind yet to reach celibacy
Of anything but
freedom sought, does one ask: Where am I not broken?
in a selfish reality of simple, tainted human thought.

And then back to my old way of dealing with the reclusive feeling you get in a quiet classroom filled with kids you either don't associate yourself with or don't fit in your social circle: boredom. But boredom's okay, I guess. There's always going to be times of monotony and meticulous absence of sense.

Geoffrey Dilenschneider

And Float Using the Breeze

I offer the world
And pull up my britches (if I had 'em)
And float using the breeze
Towards my ultimate goal.
Obstinately evolving, am I
Even though sciences tend to differ
And spare you from all but dissident obviousness.
Newly starts broken,
But when one has everything,
How dare he complain?
As the room around me crowds
With faces I presently remember
To forget in uncertain (always!) futures,
I sparkle in all my radiant reflection
And stare blissfully in any which way
That I happen to be turned.
Some may call me stubborn,
But I tend to bend when bent,
In most places, but not all.
Mostly in the head, I guess.
My neighbors are ears
That only listen when I'm wrong
So they can bring up the mute points
Later.
Life demands things,
But if you are like me,
You will end up doing the game
Later.

Untouchable Am I!

Impenetrable am I!
Break me, you will never!
Untouchable, I am!
Bring me down, you will not!
But what's this? A backdoor
To a part of me
Unseen by anyone save the one
And not even myself has had the grace to ring the bell
To save knocking for another time (it wouldn't have worked)
On that jaded oak door.
And you neither knocked nor rang
But 'stead just sang
A tune so deep that I had no choice but to
Hide
From all the beauty which you released
Into my fortress of perfection,

So simply perfect
That I was unaware of itself to any extent
And you saved it.
Eternal pride may be shattered,
Along with self-religion and false love of self un-sung,
But now I have a hero,
And maybe you're gone… but life has just begun.

Spilt Milk, but They Cry

And it brings me deeper
Down in to depression:
How I cannot create a smile
A laugh in other's lives.
Why cannot I feel the flow
Of unusually light words tied
Into a way
To evoke a sound
Of mirth, of joy today?
What sickness have I contracted?
Or is it in my genes?
What do I need to do?
Create words or plays with scenes?

When I come back
(If I ever)
Will I be back
(I will never)
And will they all laugh
(Or will my words be for not?)
When I cut cheese in half?
(No, and that's what I thought.)

Why can I not?!?
What have I done so wrong?!?
Have I just fought?!?
Which journey was too long?
Why does it rain?!?
Which way should I now go?!?
And it brings me deeper…

Man, some weird stuff I had been writing, huh? If you think so, I'd say you'd be pleasantly surprised to know that Chapter 17 has forty-seven works in it. Including the next poem, you'll only be reading twenty of them. Basically, you're only reading half of the work I wrote in this time period. Because of all the stupid rules in publishing a book, there was no way in hell I'd be able to publish everything. There are very few things in this world that I actually hate. This is one of them: that everyone can't be fully heard. The thing with that is that it just is. But at least a few can be fully heard; maybe even the few who actually have something good to say. Dr. Martin Luther King was one of them. I think he had more to say than all that he did (don't get me wrong, I don't mean disrespect to Dr. King, I think he was one of the most influential men in history). It's just that he died before he could be fully heard.

I don't really think I should be one of the lucky few heard. Yeah, I got opinions on everything; yeah, I like to go against the grain; yeah, I believe in honesty and integrity; yeah, I believe choice is key; yeah all this, but what of it? Does it make me better than you? Nah, it doesn't. Nothing makes anyone better. The whole joke of it is that our schools teach us that some were and are better than others; we're taught by our churches, synagogues, mosques, and temples that some were and are better than others.

There are religions that say equality is the way, and yet to get equality, the death of 'certain races' is necessary. Not true! Never true! I believe in God, I believe in Jesus Christ. I don't believe in this "God" some have created who is the 'answer to all the unanswerable questions' or the 'guy upstairs'. There is no guy up there. There is a force that binds us all; a force of life, if you will, that is higher than us. It cannot be seen, heard, touched, tasted, smelled, and yet it is always felt. It is a reason for drive, as well as a driver of reason.

'Where did we come from?' All those questions aren't necessarily meant to be answered. Christ's message was not saying to 'dedicate your life to this guy who lives up in the sky'. He was saying, more or less, 'find purpose in your life'. Following God, devoting your life to Him, is the greatest purpose because everything you do is for him. You gain wisdom from devotion; you learn respect; all virtues become clear. You have direction.

Virtues

One need reason to drive on forth
    Through the sleepier days and nights.
One must find a thousand reasons
    To fight for the hopeless fights.
One should fight the bad guy
    And always try to win,
So once you turn your back on him,
    He won't get up again.
But one should never aimlessly
    Punch out someone's lights
And never try to find a reason
    To put on purple tights.
Life has every problem,
    Not all under the sun –
But when one appears behind you,
    One need know it can be done.

But never will the time be right,
      It's something we shall know
In time: by singing sweet, soft melodies,
      Singing them high and low,
One can find a peace of mind
      By whistling the words to a song –
A place in mind all to our own,
      A place where there's no wrong.
Listen to the smells of trees
      And all of nature's powers,
But never fail to progress in life
      When you stop to smell those flowers.
One must always listen
      To that of ancient lore,
And one must love the ocean
      And the sounds upon its shore.
One must always give way to time
      And know that it is greater,
And that our time equals answers
      That sometimes come much later.
One must learn and listen,
      And somehow keenly detect
Those who should be listened to
      And then give them due respect.
One must sometimes take a bath
      To keep bugs off one's back.
One need sometimes heartily laugh
      To keep one's soul intact.
One must smile to adversity
      And laugh in the face of death.
You must never run to impress,
      But never run out of your breath.

One must feel the burn to move,
      But must love to watch the snail
And understand that winning's not everything,
      But that one must never *want* to fail.
Freedom is a state of mind,
      It keeps you flowing free.
When it's time to be brought to trial,
      It will show you the way to be.
One must live a life on the edge,
      But never break the rules.
One need watch fools closely,
      But not mistake them for some fools.
You need not tell others lies,
      Or understand it all.
No one needs a jerk around,
      And you never need feel small.
One must ever appreciate
      The athletic muscle sore,

                    Geoffrey Dilenschneider

But you must never spend your life
                Waiting for something more.
One should know all answers,
                But never display it so.
One must know the way back home,
                And properly direct friends so.
Remember that your family
                Is always there for you
And that the friends you think you know
                Someday'll be through with you.
Pride is a form of self-respect,
                So make sure it's on your sleeve
Because a more prosperous life of greatness
                Is what you will then receive.
You must abide by the rights you're given,
                But not abuse them every day.
Spend time at night around the world
                Giving a part of yourself away.
Listen to the voice within,
                Because the less you hear, the less it'll say.
Bring your heart away from sin,
                The less you fear, the less you sway.

One must know when things have changed
                And then the times to move on.
When you need to shoot the deer,
                Try not to aim for the fawn.
One must learn the way of the world,
                But not unbearably so.
One must find an excuse to leave,
                But not for good, you know?
Just because nobody's looking
                Doesn't mean the mime's not hurt;
One should have integrity –
                One should not need then feel curt.
You must find a place to be
                Where no one takes your crown,
But you must know to never
                Forever be tied down.
You must never scream aloud
                When your feelings get the best,
But you must always hide your shroud
                And let things off your chest.
Always love the changing sky
                And all it holds within.
Always know that stars may die,
                But that suns and stars will sin.

Take it just upon yourself
                To rid the world of all its frown,

Just know that you will never succeed –
        But don't let that get you down.
The world is your own private maze,
        So many options to choose.
There might be corners with hidden falls,
        Just don't believe that you'll lose –
Then the world will be your jungle,
        A place so full of life.
This is the place you find yourself,
        Not where you'll be found by life.
Then when you are at peace with the world,
        Your soul will flow as mercury.
A bond you'll have like no one else
        And you'll flow just oh-so-free!
Burn the memories of the past,
        But keep aside the soot…
And do not think only of the future,
        Just keep the present times afoot.
Mistakes will be made,
        Some will ask why.
Just tell them, "move on"
        And let sleeping dogs lie.
Teach to those around you
        Lessons well to learn.
Take the straightest path possible,
        But know when you should turn.
One should stop to smell those flowers,
        The life of trees around
And live a life of happiness
Knowing how the world goes round.

Push yourself to extremes;
        The infinity is there for the taking.
Look around yourself and be aware;
        Mysteries are there for the breaking.
One must take the time
        To give the time of day
And one must try to listen
        Instead of giving way
To the things that no one wants to hear
        When they know what their fate may hold.
One must never break away
        Unless one knows what love may hold.
One must fight the good fight,
        Save when the girl's around,
Then one makes it look as though
        All's just safe and sound…
But you must know the reason
        To act just as yourself:
Because you are loved for that;
        It's not just for your health.

        Geoffrey Dilenschneider

Simply free your mind of anything and all
And no more will the world be hopeless –
Nothing will stand in your way again,
As you slide in time by moments –

Attacks may come
And defenses may go;
Healing may come
And the music may flow.
Lovers may come
And lovers may go;
Times may change
And friends may know.
Friends may come
And friends may lie;
People are people,
And people may die.
But love will come,
As lovers know –
And love will change,
As lovers know.
Love will stay
As lovers understand…
But love will go,
As lovers know.

Some rules can be broken,
Lots can be bent around;
But some must be adhered to
To live life safe and sound.
There is only one time to be perfect:
It's when the feeling is right.
Then one will find the only girl
Who can make the dark sky be light.

There will always be opposites,
It's a truth yet to be broken.
Love and Hate is one of them,
Both are yet unspoken.
They go hand in hand just like you –
Down onto their knees…
Forced by natural consequence,
Forever stung by bees.
You must always believe
That everything's alright
And that every goal you set
Is always in your sight.
One man's love for humanity
Is greater than a fist
And when one's life is over
And surrounded by a mist,
The world will celebrate a grateful life,
A life untouched by hate,

A life of all the greatest virtues,
    A life made straight from fate.

Basically be good to the world,
    Yourself, and all the others.
Be kind and gentle to your siblings,
    Your fathers, and your mothers.
One need now believe
    That no virtue's power is higher
And that the only thing that's real
    Is your heart's unselfish desire.
And when life, love, and liberty
    Are threatened in your home,
Do nothing but defend yourself
    And the freedom that you own.
And when one feels not but alone,
    Just walk along the shore
And find true love outside a bottle
    And never ask for more.

Geoffrey Dilenschneider

Chapter 21, 23, {22}

▲ ▲ ▲ ▲

I went to visit New York City one day. What a hell that was.

I have so many opinions on the whole September 11th ordeal. One, I feel that we should have seen it coming. I mean that if you are number one at anything, and I mean anything, you have to know that there is always the risk of someone wanting to take you out. You're better than they are, so why wouldn't they want to take you out?

America has been number one for so long, we should have at least been aware of the fact that we were at risk. From the way I see it, most people didn't even realize terrorism was around; at least from my part of the town, we didn't.

Second, those S.O.B.'s shouldn't mess with us Americans. We might not be 'training every last man for anything like a jihad; a country bent on war', but I consider that a good thing, don't you? Would you like to spend your Sunday evenings locking and loading on some battleground? Would you like to die? I wouldn't, that's what I know.

And that's all I want to say about this stupid ordeal. It's a big joke. Those people should not have died. The 239 service men in Beirut should not have died. In the end, no one should have died, but that is life. No man, in any religion, should kill another. It is even said that Islam has ties to Christianity and Judaism.

Anyway, I visited New York City, and it was sick and twisted. The cleanup hadn't finished. Anyway, this is what I wrote.

New York City... Home

I saw a man kiss a woman who wasn't his.
Here I am,
But where am I going?
What are they really looking at?
Faster, more bent forward.
Hand in hand, stopping when it's really not necessary.
Look: we're out of time –
Are we?
I wonder who it's for,
So intent his jaw juts out at the window.
Which pocket will he pay for it?
Slow, red, telephone in one
On a hat behind a flowing confidence.
Baby passes eyes looking for thieves
Who presently are on the watch out at home.
Meandering, meandering
Hand in hand again.
Smiles, but they don't look real, hand in hand again.
Walkie-talkie darker now,
The sun has gone away.
Angry at the car that didn't stop,
But lets go of his child soon.

And here, the sight
Of our flag in pilgrimage
But who notices them
Weeks later?
One lighting up
Under review by the board of the buildings
So big and great that will not fail
When evil knocks on their door when it's leaving.

"Jean-Claude"

The large man squeezed out of the car door with an audible grunt. He was obviously in pain. In the passenger-side window were two bare feet, whose legs were nowhere to be found. They had to be real, but the shadows probably covered them up.

The large man then proceeded to cross the street, trying in vain to conceal the fact that he had three torn ligaments in his right knee and that he desperately was in need of the metal cane lying in the trunk of the car – the one with the feet in the window.

Finally getting across, the large man paused to wipe his brow with a handkerchief he produced from the left inside pocket of his black sport coat. He looked around self-consciously.

Putting the handkerchief back where he found it, the large man checked his watch, twice, then, as though he was sick, took a seat at the nearest table, which was, at the time, occupied by another, similarly-dressed man.

Although he was obviously sizzling in the heat - he was sweating profusely – the large man did not take off his jacket; however, took the drink offered by the other man at the table.

The large man sipped it three times, each a generous helping of the brown liquid, and play-acted a choke on the third sip.

"*Bonjour*, Jean-Claude," said the other man.

"*We, bonjour. Mon Dieu*, in *English*, Jean-Claude, in *English*," the large man exclaimed as he spit the coffee out.

"I suppose," said the other man, "I suppose."

"Jean-Claude, you know who I am; you shouldn't have made me go through the format…" the large man began, and then when the other man didn't interject, he continued: "I really hate that stuff you French try to call coffee. Really." He looked incredibly disgusted.

Both men's heads snapped towards behind where the large man was sitting.

"Right on time," whispered the other man.

A woman, totally non-descript, walked by then, and, though no one could have seen it happen, dropped a non-descript manila envelope onto the table in front of the large man, and, in the same stride, walked away. No one breathed in those moments, and no one ever knew just why, but it must have been that that kind of thing really got under a person's skin after years and years of doing it.

The large man dropped his hands nonchalantly onto the large envelope in front of him.

"Let's talk this time, Jean-Claude. They all check out, the people around us. None speak our language, and none know what we're doing here. Let's shed this skin of mediocrity and collide our two worlds to make a difference, ya?"

Just then, a crowd of young Japanese students rushed by in a frenzy of photographs and smiles, and all the while, the only thing the two men sitting at the little café table were concentrated on was the other's eyes. The large man was uncharacteristically defiant, whereas the other, shorter man stayed impassive; but when the crowd passed and the trailing hum of the group's boisterous cacophony finally dwindled to a tiny memory in the two men's minds, the other man spoke up: "I believe in God."

"I accept. I believe in all Gods, in all religions," said the large man in reply.

"How is that possible? What about those that hate you? Do you accept them, too?"

"Yes, of course, but I do not tolerate infidels."

"Be honest." The younger, less experienced man leaned forward in his chair.

"Okay, Jean-Claude, you want it straight? Fine. I'm a liar. I pretend to be this great guy, but I'm really insecure; really susceptible to attacks by other men. It's hard for me to wake up and really feel good about myself, but nonetheless I put on the façade day in and day out because now I have to. The people I know would never stand by me again if they knew this information. I have become, over time – and I used to be this short, little guy who had no friends, and frankly, didn't want any friends – but over time, I've realized that friends are good, and I've built this intricate web of connections; so entwined and interconnected that if I were to let go – don't forget I'm in the dead center of all this – if I were to let go, I'd be screwed."

"Of course, you could just let it all go and run away…" The small man opened his hands as he said this, but saw quickly that he had infuriated the man opposite of him.

"You fool," the large man fumed, "there is nowhere to run. By surrounding myself with 'friends', I've single-handedly boxed myself in!"

"Kill yourself," the Frenchman suggested.

"Yeah, you would like that, wouldn't you. So would all the other Jean-Claudes. But I'm not stupid; I think I can work out my problems in time."

"No, you…" the other man started, but then abruptly changed direction, as though he had realized something: "You can't even see it! You're not stupid, you're ignorant!" The other man paused to let himself cool off. After a moment, his cadence was practically normal: "You can't even see the problems you really have. You said it yourself, you're *too* bogged down. To bogged down, though, to see that you, yourself, aren't *that* perfect, *that* good, to try and have such an intricate net. You took too big a bite, Jean-Claude; too big a bite."

The large man shifted in his seat, taking more pressure off his right leg. "Good. You understand. Let's move on."

"Do you even know who I really am?" The other man pondered, half to the large man and half to the dangerous sky, at which he was presently staring.

"Let's not go there."

"Fine. Have we surpassed God himself?"

"If you mean, 'do our wallets give us more power than He has', then yes, I do. But you must remember that though it takes a lot of power to create, it takes more power to destroy, as well as more stupidity and or ignorance," explained the large man, feeling quite satisfied by his own response.

The slighter of the two men responded, "Ah, but you miss out on the true direction that we should be taking, using our ability." He had started to sound like a father lecturing a son. "Jean-Claude, it is up to *us*, really, to decide the future of the world. If we really believe that we can change it, then we must; *and for the better…* that is especially necessary, ya?"

"You sound like my father."

"You have a father?" asked the other man.

"I had a few, but I've forgotten who they were."

"Oh, you're lucky. I never had a father. He was really just a dictator; a man in search of glory and war. He was drunk a lot."

"Thank you. Do you have any sons or daughters?" the large man asked with a smile.

"I did. They die. You?"

"Many; and when they grow old enough to do so, they will help me accomplish my goal."

"What goal is that?"

"Simple. Bring back truth to my world, my friends."

"How?"

"I don't know."

"…oh," the younger man sighed. He had only two more things to say: "Is that your son over there, in your new car? He looks like he's having a good time: listening to music, eating good food, wearing nice clothes, breaking code and putting his feet up on the dash. If all your children act like this…"

"They don't," the large man interjected.

The little Frenchman continued, "… then how can they, and for that matter, why *would* they want to help you? Wouldn't they rather just live off of your hard work?"

"I guess," said the large man, "but what about you? Do you even have nice things at all? How are you happy? Is that not the only suit you own? How can you really say that you've lived until you've tasted all the chocolates this world has to offer?"

"We don't need your chocolates." The other man had obviously come to some previous conclusion. "We don't need them to be happy."

"Ah, but what *is* happiness?" The large man smiled as the other man racked his mind for an adequate response.

After a good seven minutes of silence, the other man gave up, dejected and somehow out of breath.

"Fine," the other man said, "What is happiness, then?"

"If my friends are happy, then I'm happy."

"But are you not in pain?"

"I am, but it is for them that I bear this pain."

"You do so in vain. Your sons, your friends, they do not feel a thing; they do not feel an inch of thankfulness for your efforts. They only ask for more and more."

"I can handle it."

"Pure façade," thought the other man, and then he said gravely, "You will die, you know."

The larger man seemed to sag in his chair; rumple on the edges, as though someone had let out a bit of air. "It is true." He pointed to himself, "But *this* Jean-Claude will be dead and replaced by a different Jean-Claude before the after-effects come into play."

The other man paused at this revelation; then, "that… is sad, Jean-Claude; so sad to hear."

"Yes, but there is always hope. Remember that, friend."

Just then, a twitter from a bird above brought both men out of their conversation. They came to and realized how great their mistake had been.

"You're not really French, are you."

"No."

"I really wanted to believe."

"I know, Jean-Claude."

"My son is waiting. He has a soccer game to go to, and I must take him. Here is the package you want," the larger man said, and pushed the manila envelope across the Formica table, letting the other man hear every scrape it made as it moved to its destination on the other side. Cars whizzed by like bees. The people, a blur of the collective society these Jean-Claudes were supposed to protect, but all they could do was sip their horrible coffee.

Suddenly, the large man felt old; seemingly tired of some ongoing joke that only he was privy to; bags of sand had fallen in place on his shoulders. He was only graffiti: on the wall of the world; he could make no difference. This Jean-Claude had played him for the fool he was, and he had fallen in. This Jean-Claude was part of his web now, a dangerous part, and he wasn't going to do the large man any good.

The larger of the two men suddenly looked very scared.

"What should I do, Jean-Claude? I gave you so much, give me at least this."

The little man paused.

"You have three options. One, run. Two, secede your power. Three, run. So... whatcha gonna do?"

The little man was moving in for the kill. The city seemed to pause for a moment, teetering on the edge of some metaphoric cliff, waiting to fall, *knowing* in its heart of hearts that it must fall, that law of existence demanded it fall; that it all came full circle, even though the circle has always been an insurmountably huge one... But then something clicked in the large man's head.

He smiled.

"Jean-Claude, I laugh at you." The large man laughed, "You think you had me, but I have you."

The large man didn't continue. He knew he had won the game.

He got up from the table, still wishing he had brought along the metal cane, and hobbled across the street to the car where the two feet still lay in the passenger side window of the little sports car.

The large man opened the car door, and for a few seconds the other man could hear the beautiful music drifting from the car. The other man lost his surroundings and suddenly felt incredibly sad, but by the time the large man had plopped into the car, closed the door, and driven off, the other Jean-Claude was too late, left in the puddle of his own silence, trying in vain to savor the sweet sounds from deep within that car.

Un, Deux, Trois

Never bump into a man drinking red wine
And never stop to gawk.
Never lie in a successing line
Until you can walk the walk.
Never kiss a woman
Until you hold her hand
And never dance to the music of life
Until you've walked in hand.

Never walk like you're so great
Till everyone tells you so.
Never pierce your ears...

Never rub your chin with three fingers,
And pretend that something's going on.
Never break your own code of laws
Until someone worthy comes along.

The next few days I just kept on writing.

With Time and Change

You are the reason for living –
This street is the story of my life.
You make my life radically different,
You're the reason I continue this strife –

I am in a place so dark
Dark with the pain of missing you
Draped over my eyes without care
Are the curtains over my eyes of kissing you.

A strawberry newsstand on this street reminds me
Of how I first saw you with eyes averted...
And here I stand alone again
As the street becomes more deserted.

Geoffrey Dilenschneider

Prayer

In my mind
Centered on some absent truth
Chained by need.
But to what extent
Does a hand be cuffed to the other in prayer,
Newly wed to another tomorrow?
Longer fixed rates cry for me
Command me to sing unnecessary words of prayer.
Whispers crimson in beaten dreams of us,
On the very verge of being shattered by
One single prayer.
La, la, la
Goes the impressive tune,
Nothing more.
Tomorrow, the leathery bound book of my funny existence
Will break down to the pressures of unwanted standards.
When will my ring undo the mark it has made on my hand
In prayer
Overdosed by getting love from lost ends
Of no more consequence to me than my mother.
Don't laugh at me
For how I like to look at the sky
Or how I mind my now unworthy business.
Maybe you're not the one for me
And maybe… because time is not
Aligned at this "right" moment, locked in prayer.
What controls the doings of my crimson,
Love-sick mind on the verge
Of being shattered
By absent, centered, truths in prayer?

Survey the Destruction

And I stand
As I
Survey the destruction.
Unbelievable as people
I know…
Whirlwind my mind with wanting to get a better view.
        What is this world coming to?
Thoughts swirl in my shattered mind,
Now suddenly void of coherent ideas.
        How can I keep on going?
        How could anyone live life normally after…?
Pray your hearts out men!
Hold close those you love
With weary eyes!

Walk a little slower to commemorate
Those who died in pain untimely
To teach us an age-old lesson:
Buildings are no less perfect than the world...
As are people.
And as I stand,
Life around me just doesn't seem...
Alive...
Smiles seem more forced than
Before...
Everything seems to be on its toes,
Leaning slightly forward,
Holding their breath,
And forever waiting for something that will never come.
I want to be alone now.

Our Life in Our World in Our Country

Unbelievable people sometimes are,
They are people, too –
And like the wind in the trees,
Arching backs like a chiropractor does
On un-sunny afternoons,
Life goes on.
The music that we hear from afar
Isn't always new,
But like the dust in the breeze,
Roaring back like a dinosaur does
Eating ugly goons,
Life goes on.
A rise to power between the nations
In the world like this
A leaf without peace and megatons
Will leave a hole a mile wide
But now we know what we must do and
Life will go on.
Cynical disregard for other nations
Shock the leaders that we hate
And shatter the dream of newborn suns
And decide upon a bona fide
Plan that saves us through and through and
Life will go on.

Then, of course, life went on. I went back to school – back to the boredom – and just kept on going. That's what we all have to do, right? I divulged myself in a multitude of topics, trying to stray my mind from the horrors of reality.

Geoffrey Dilenschneider

On Poetry

Thoughts turn to mush,
Mush turns to words,
Eventually.

Then a jolt of energy bursts through a barrier
And creates movement in a dead hand.
Ink or carbon begins to flow
As the cogs turn together
Faster and faster
And a word is formed!
Then two! Then seven!
Then sentences and lines!
And beautiful ideas,
Rich in origin and richer in themselves!
Put forth at birth into a critical world!
A pause,
An idea again.
Then life is created from nothing again!
It is so beautiful!
Then another pause,
A reflection,
A date, a title
And the cogs stop
And then the man moves on again.

It's Only Time

Someone once told me to find myself,
But I'm having a bit of trouble.
I bit a piece of my muffin off
And found myself in a world full of trouble.
Something seemed odd,
And not could I place it,
But a feeling was all in the air.

Then, as I walked up Memory Lane
(Or so the sign read there)
The apple on the lifeless tree
Began in glee, just talking to me!
It grabbed me by the hair,
And asked, "Why are you here?
What are the things you fear?
What's your purpose in life?
What looks the face of strife?
Where are you told to begin?
Where do you fit in?"

I asked him back in question form:
"Where are comforts to make me warm?
Where are those that I can trust?
Who will tell me when I must
And why must I trust by way of their word?
Why was I chosen to be out of the herd?"
Surprisingly though, it had no answer,
It just directed me on my way.

To a sign I came across later,
Propped up by a guy named Darth Vader... it said:
> *"It's only time in which we must be wary*
> *When we come to problems hairy."*
I pondered but for a sad, sad second
Of why I remembered faces I reckoned
With years and years of time together
Spent in ways I now second-guess
Maybe we could have lived happ'ly after
I could have done better, I softly confess.

Further on down I find a haven
For fifteen years or so
And I grow and learn things like "The Raven"
And everything else to know.
My knowledge increased in measures of heavens high
As I trained to become strong and fast.
Then out from my soul comes a disturbingly sad sigh
On the day that was my last.

And on that day I cried and cried;
I could not let it go.
But a man came up to me and sighed,
(He felt like a friend I've known)
And he told me many things that night
About life, love, and hope.
Then that next year he was gone from sight
With the words from his lips: "to not mope –
It is key to live a life
Of peace, made real by self.
Take your time to find a wife
Of true love in its health.
Find happiness and freedom,   (by way of wisdom and confidence)
Be smart and save your wealth.
Find friendship out by looking hard,
But instead be one with yourself.
Have a love for all the world,
But first learn to love yourself.
Be secure within your own
But don't shut out the world.
Just make sure you've shown
That you've reached your own potential and good luck."

And with that I was off
Into a world uncertain,
Now and then washing
In some random old fountain.
I traveled with ease;
I left behind my concern,
But never did I let my guard down
When rattling were some fern.
Through the days and cold, cold nights
Many an interesting thing I had crossed paths:
A funny man,
A lonely man,
A happy man,
A dopey man,
A nice man,
A great man,
A small man,
A tall man,
A crying man,
A dying man,
An experienced man, and a fool.
And from all those people and more,
I realize an important idea:
Life is meant for the living;
It's not meant to be alone.
Give and give and give and give
And then you shall receive.
Give and give and give and give
And you shall then believe
In life, love, liberty, pursue your own great dreams.
Do not let life get you down or in the ways of dreams.

But then again,
I could be wrong,
They'll get you where it hurts.
I walk again upon Memory Lane
(Or so the sign reads there)
But now I start to bluntly rain
Questions to the apple fair
Upon the lifeless tree it sits
In silenced composing form:
"Where are comforts to make me war?
Where are those that I cannot trust?
Who will tell me when I must
And why must I trust by way of their word?
Why was I chosen to be out of the herd?"

He replies true:
"Inside you."

After school, I would – whenever possible – work on the book I was writing, now known as A Boy Aware. *One night, I did something really stupid, which I can't really remember anymore, and my dad threatened to stop the thing altogether. Whoa! Shatter my world! Shatter my future! That's what it felt like at the time, anyway.*

Thank You

What failure have I past committed?
What wrongs have I last done?
To lose this life I worked to make,
Why must I always run?
Here I am in place of sorrow
And I cannot find my own.
What's wrong with wanting happiness?
Here I am disowned.
Here my clucking book is halted
Thanks to my clucking dad.
Screw the life I could've lived
Screw the life I had.

Thank you for taking back my future
Thanks for really caring.
Thanks for setting me down softly –
Your feelings…? Oh, thanks for sharing.
I guess you're right about what happened,
And right about the facts,
But what about the lies spun true
That make me seem real bad?
What have you forgotten
About a kid becoming?
Why's your view of me
One of myself running?
Maybe I am meant to finish
My life before I'm old.
Maybe how you think I'll be
Is lonely, bored, and cold.

You're screwing with my future, dad,
What do you think you're doing?
You're changing things much for the worse –
My life, I think you're chewing.

No good will ever come from this,
This bullshit you call love.
This lie you think you've made me great
But only lost my love.

What's the point of moving forward?
I've no strength to move on.
Maybe someday I will change
But till then, I can't go on.

Geoffrey Dilenschneider

Okay, we made up the next day; obviously he didn't realize what he was saying. I felt really bad about what I had said to him. Just so terrible. Nothing's perfect, right? But it was with such an empty, unforgiving conscience that I had been angry that the next day I couldn't help but cry wondering if he was alright. We talked later the next evening and made up.

You know, I swear that things like this make a father-son relationship stronger. It's like that saying: "That which does not kill you, makes you that much stronger."

Day In

And the cogs turn
And the cogs turn
And little Sam thinks real hard.
So the cogs turn
And the cogs turn
And little Sam thinks real hard.
Then the pressure dies
And the pressure dies
And little Sam rests his eyes.
So the pressure dies
And the pressure dies
And little Sam rests his eyes.
And the bells ring
And he moves on
And little Sam does it again.
And the halls ring
And he's all wrong
But little Sam does it again.
And he goes home
And he goes home
And little Sam's frightened more.
So he goes home
And he goes home
But little Sam is scared more.
And he climbs into bed
And he climbs into bed
And his mother tucks him in.
And he quiets down
As she kisses his brow
And Sam gets ready again.

Consequence of Action

Think of the effects of your actions
Think of the people you've hurt.
Think of your simple satisfaction –
You wonder why those people are curt.

What is the feeling you're feeling
This feeling contracting inside?
What have you done to deserve this –
It's like something crawled in you and died.

From the depths of your soul, you are moving.
You can tell when you feel yourself frown.
From the voices of millions within you, you hear:
"You're losing! You're falling! You're down!"

Think of the hearts that you've broken
Think of those you've made mad.
Envision the looks on their faces –
Now you know why you are sad.

Respect

When fate shuts the door as you're knocking
Just come in through the window at the side.
It may not be the most honest way in,
So just tell others how you got inside.

Learn about love by living
And incorporate it by using your head.
Keep in mind the values you've learned –
Don't fall in love like you've read.

These questions are grasping for answers
But the answers are moving too quick.
Maybe someday you will know why you're feeling
A great absence inside you so thick.

Bow down to the feelings of others
So you learn how to act as you are.
But try not to laugh at the others
When they're not as along as you are.

After time's lonelier passage,
Feel the love you start to emit.
Let it be guiding and helpful
To the selflessness you now admit.

Of course, life went back to normal. Or maybe it never wasn't. I thought about girls from my past, and my mom – as well as totally off the wall things. I spent a lot of time at the school library, sitting by myself, listening to the hum and trying to write.

It was about this time that I really started writing about rain. I don't know why (it seems I don't know a lot nowadays), but I really had a fascination with rain all of a sudden; one that hasn't yet dwindled.

Feeding

Feed off of others
And others will feed
Upon you and others –
You'll never be freed.
Time's not your friend
And there is no way –
You will be winning,
But not right away.
Differently spinning
What have I done?
People will feed
Feed under the sun.
Upon lovely life
Am I weeping in pain
What kind of person
Dictates the rain?
Here I am, mother,
I'm up in the loft.
Crying for others
Crying so soft.
Here I am, mother
Absorbed in my fears
Cannot you hear it?
Your son's lonely tears.

A Fresh Future

Of the quiet around me
I reach out into darkness.
Through the perils I've conquered.
I have not a witness.
No more will I breathe!
No more will I cry…
No more will I seethe!
Do not ask me why.

Right now I decide that
Simplicity saves me.
And happiness breaks out
So sudden and freely.
No 'buts' will pave roads
Nor will they impede me
As I look to the future
While the sun makes me happy.

And as I look myself over
I see a tug in the road
A tug that brings pain,
But outside, did I strode,
Ignoring the tug
As I walked down the lane...
To the sunset behind
As it started to rain.

Q and A With *Her*

Where are you?
In the ocean
Where are you?
In the sea
Who are you?
I am love
Who are you?
I am free
Where are you going?
To the ocean
Where are you going?
You can see
Are you running?
No, but I run for you
... What should I say?
Nothing but what you want
Want? What do you mean by want?
Want is a form of need, but lesser... I am what you want
But you are so far away, no?
Yes, as are you
I know that, but do you love me?
If love is what is, then my love is my love
And courtesy is nothing anymore?
It never was
It's been awhile, hasn't it?
Too long, too long
Can you still laugh?
Yes, when I remember...
Can we... can we be... together again?
Quiet now, dangerous questions have dangerous answers
Will we?
Where are you?
With you...
Where am I?
With me.

Geoffrey Dilenschneider

What Rain?

What rain does not speak to us
Through the doors of our sheltered lives?
What breakdown does not speak to us
Through the lips of our fretting wives?
And when one happens across the beat cop
Having a bad day worth money on the rain,
Can you find him a dry place to stay
Or can you only find a reason to walk away?

When you live the way you do,
Can you find a reason?
When you find a reason for the way you do,
Does it feel regimented?
Or does it feel as though you are saying something
But holding back but you don't know why?

What pain does not speak to us
Through the skin of our angry fists?
What way can we do the things we must
Through the covering, angry mists?
And when one comes across sunshine
And it beckons to shine upon your face,
Can you bring yourself to change your ways
Or can you only cry as you hide from its rays?

What About the Others?

Verse I   When I look around
I wonder what this world is coming to.
And I think of all the places that I know
Wizardry has no effect on my complexion
But cracked floors plead for my mercy
When I've fallen
I wonder what this world is coming to.

Chorus   People dying
Mothers crying
It's never too late to change
True friends lying
Shoes stop tying
It's never too late to change.

Verse II   When I look around
            I seem to ponder why I'm still here.
            Why has no one told me why I shouldn't go
            My yellow heart has no effect on my perfection
            But I stretch out when I feel free
            But I'm crawlin'
            When I seem to ponder why I'm still here.

Verse III   When I look around,
            Freedom is a birthright for me and you
            Please feel pregnant with the notion of a soul
            Please do not walk when the roses find their section.
            But locked doors may create worry
            When I'm cryin'
            Freedom is a birthright for me and you.

Verse IV   When I look around,
            I wonder just what kind of life I'll live
            When I think of all the people that I've hurt
            But my breath flees when I swoon down chocolate ant hills
            In a sea of reputation
            When I'm chokin'
            I wonder what this world is coming to.

Verse I   When I look around
            I wonder what this world is coming to.
            And I think of all the places that I know
            Wizardry has no effect on my complexion
            But cracked floors plead for my mercy
            When I've fallen
            I wonder what this world is coming to.

A Headlining Dream

The laconic partisan
Drinks coffee like the rest
And sits on his table at home
Wonderin' who to reach for next.
The postulation of reality
Postulates of music thought
As my feet wander aimlessly
Through the snares and traps, I'm caught.

I cannot understand your voice
Scheming kids of last-ditch crimes
Of shootings in the dark.
I read my paper backwards as I
Play my broken harp.
A violin answers in a simple tone:

Geoffrey Dilenschneider

"My bum's rushed and my letters fall
Where am I?"

Before Motown, but how can lovers
Sit without smiles
As I cross my living room floor:
"How silly can I be
To wonder how to listen
And how lovers sit sin smile"
As I twist and turn in the confusion of trees.

Pamela makes no difference...
And suddenly I scream clenchingly
As I writhe in fear of the pain to come.
Why am I no different?
And suddenly last-ditch crimes seem hard no more
I think, as I grasp my foot in pain in place for one, or some, for more.
The carpet is bigger when you lie on the floor
The feeling is real when you knock on the door
Instead of hiding behind a bush
Oh, what was I thinking???
I could have played dead like a possum, all smushed.
I should have tried winking.

But, no... the cranberries... will always... berry.
As in... think of a place that you'd like to go.
Then go... to infecting... in phase... the merry.
It's not... a storm of a party that I'd like to throw.

But what is love? Really? What is it, this 'love' thing, huh? What is it?
A state of mind?
        A state of being!
The one to find?
        No, a state of fleeing!
Is love a way of finding peace?
Or do we fool for bodies' sake?
Is a heart for sale or just for lease?
Or do we marry for just the cake?

María is a girl I once knew...
"So simple, so simple," thought i... so trite.
Maria is a girl I once knew...
"No come, no come," said Love... one night.

I knew other girls once, when I spoke odd
And seemed so young.
Innocence was not thought of directly as
"True" love unsung.
But of course, in course, of life, due time
I moved, right on, through life, in rhyme.

Scared to Show My Face in Fear of
Waterfalls Rejecting My Own Laughs

I miss the way you talked to me
I miss the way you smiled
I miss the way I felt so free
I miss just being wild.

I can't believe that time has passed
Above and over us.
I miss the way you shook that ass,
I miss the way you fussed.

I still can smell your strawberries
And see your stellar smile.
I know that we are far apart,
But to me, it's just a mile.

I miss the way we danced with swords
I missed my chance to wish
For freedom from my lonely cage
To give that final kiss.

But even though we're flying down, down
Down our separate paths,
I'll never look back to those times
And bring forth long, sad laughs.

Tears for Fears on the Corner of Pain

I'm scared…
Scared for the future
Scared for the future of things I can't mention for everything huddles around me
And I'm free! Free from the living
Free from the dead
Free from a place where I'd not rest my head
Now what to do…
Oh, what to do…   maybe a game
Or how about two
What about chess, or Bocce, or golf?
Have you thought about playing with Arnold or Rolf?
Never mind now because teatime is calling…
Calling for murder in marigold March.
Now never mind him, he's calling me now,
No more can I move from my soul's excess starch.
Ending and ending and ending I'm done.
What is so wrong and come back, babe, you've won…!

Untitled Poem #77

Sometimes I feel like dying in heaven
Sometimes I feel like I'm used to the pain.
When I am standing on top of the green trees,
I think of all the ways I could end.

I write all day of the things that we did
I write of happiness and the things that we said
I write of running free in exotic places
I write of touches and where they have led.

Playing, But One does not Sum Up All

Presents come and presents go,
But people always stay.
Feelings change and knowledge grows,
But love will go away.

Anger comes and hate will fade
As humans walk through days.
Happiness may think it's made
But no more do we have time for life
When we're caught in evil's ways.

Smiles are worth a thousand words
If you've the time to find them.
Liars can talk and drive the herds –
If truth's been lost, remind them.

A form is only kept for hours
As we change the world we know,
Humans have no superpowers
But we can change the world we know.

In Times of Love

Verse I   The last man broken standing finds
That children have the key that's needed
But what of us, developed minds
When we find that we're not needed?

Chorus   What decency have we forgot
In times of love, in times so hot?
Where have we not let go
Of things that lovers've got to know?
Can everyone sing peace peacefully
In times of love un-feasibly?
What courtesy have we surpassed
With looks of sadness as we go last?

Verse II   And know the naked air we breathe
Tells only when our breaths may go
Not when hearts fade, coldly leave;
That's the scream of blows so low.
Not every man's forlorn glance means
That intentions are good or bad,
Only what the thoughts may seem
To dilute from lies both good and bad.

Verse III   Balance doesn't ask to leave
When freedom of heart wants to decide.
But maybe they can just receive
The needs that tend to hide inside.
Clouds do not disperse in time
For us to go to our last dance,
Those happen simply out of rhyme
When we least expect it, there is chance.

Bridge   But what do you think of the choices made
Of lusting eyes in bluebird skies, in black-eyed lies
In falsities, realities, generalities, in truth?
But what do you think of our choice of action
Of making waves, joining raves, creating laze
In mirrored love, in dying life, in heightened love, in crying life?
You can be the person imagined across the hall from me
When time explains your hate, your love, your heart, your head,
your ways to me
And as I grasp the pain of truth to keep alive my other lies,
I wonder what needs times of love, as I close my dying eyes.

I had really become a hopeless romantic. The only thing that put me different from the rest of the hopeless romantics was that I could write about it.

    Again, though, I returned to dwelling the morose corridors of school.

From High-Dive Climbing to Popping Ears;
It's Just a Hint, Like Saying Cheers

What's so
        Different
                when we, like,
Sit?
        In rows. Backs to legs and heads to
Ground
        While we
                ponder the meaning of, like,
Little nothings
        But what? what being to fleeing but
Comforted
        Do we seem.   Honestly, it's all lies
                when we play pretend in, like,
Scary times
        Like now. How different yet so
Similar
        As we just read, listen
                to our own hearts, fears, wants, and tears when, like
We scream!
        In life. sometimes things change from chance's
Eyeballs. scare me with warnings to
        Watch this end; that end while, like,
                we don't do nothing but care for safety and, like,
Watch the skies
        With concentrated eyes
Ready for sleep with mouths open, staring
        Out windows with utter, slow conviction, trading
                papers, words amongst ourselves, like,
To attract our minds away from real
        Ity: the truth of instant death; of utter
Boredom. Hey, around me all they do is watch
        Hear voices drolling nazal, even though the music of our lives is
                beautiful. We hear this music with power, like,
Ready for an end of sorts, asking:
        What creates, like, little nothings; What makes babies
Cry?
        And so, slow song, we hear you crying though
                the notes you play; are dear. like mother, like,
We are watching, comforted in the knowledge of our honest
        Lies. Here we all are again, waiting, wondering
What's so
        Different
                when we, like,
Sit?

Luckily, though, I got to take a trip to St. Marten. I spent the while there, and it was a lot of fun. I met some new people – many of them interesting.

Especially memorable was a girl who I met whom I ended up almost plugging in my laptop with. She was black. And I only say this because I mean to express my true feeling that race doesn't matter; I am not racist.

She happened, actually, to be one of the most sincere women I've ever known; as well as one of the greatest kissers.

Among the kissers are Jen Kirst, Katheryn French, and a girl I knew for only an hour named Becky. That's a long story that you'll be hearing later on.

A Fountain

I'm only looking for a companion
What's so hard to ask?
One to make my life worth living –
To tell me I'm not last.
Someone who will mean their words
And show me what to do,
Yet they must love me with their heart
And I must love her, too.
Someone who will lean on me
When they need a helping hand,
Someone who I can walk with
As I walk across the land.
Someone who may lie with me
And talk of something else.
Someone who won't bug me much
Or love somebody else.
I'm only looking for a girl
To make me feel inside
A warmth right now unknown to me,
And a little bit of pride.
Someone who will pass the time
With jokes between our kisses –
Not a girl who will hate all day
And smother me with hisses.
Somebody who will dance with me
Till my final lonesome days –
Someone who will take the time
To understand my ways.
I'm only looking for a friend
To share a million moments.
I'll do all this for her in heartbeats
So we can have those moments,
But now as I come to rest my eyes,
I wish I might have shared
Just one moment with that girl,
And know who really cared.

Lost

Cold
Are the smiles of those who yell
Cold
Are not the drinks in hell
Hot comes the fires in which we dwell
The ones we hate, yet know so well.
The happy feelings flee from me,
Broken-hearted, yet running free
But who may live through life without
The ways of happiness, suppressed by doubt?

Base
Are the emotions we hide inside
Base,
Yet they direct us, they keep us tied.
Hard comes the hate that keeps us swinging,
Soft yet quick comes love just singing.
Close your eyes to feel your burden's weight
Level buildings with the power of hate
Yet maybe we can find a way to be
So we can die in freedom's sea.

Sold
Away are our friends in boxes
Sold
Down the rivers like three-legged foxes.
Caught are the liars, thieves and fiendish
Put in place by kisses dreamish.
Kisses of the kind so dry,
So light, so free, yet meant to try.
But who plans for a life without
A love, a future, a way to shout?

Old
Are the feelings of life and death
Old
Are the wants and needs I've left
Must I cry again for feelings
Feelings that I've lost again?
Must I ride this tricky tightrope
Tightrope on a cracked, old limb
Of a tree that I have yet to climb – – –
I think I have lost my will to rhyme.

Restless Souls

Joy no more can lead to glory.
Joy no more helps tell our story.
No one person will once more find
That joy helps ease the ailing mind.

Restless souls find waking times
Filled with shots surveyed by limes.
And restless souls turn out their lights
But not longer than a shortened while
Because of joy's rejected sights.

Restless souls find peace in walking
But lose their sight when barely talking.
What smells good when passing by?
A joyful moment... truth, no lie.

The Ruined

I've found a way to conquer fears
To conquer hate, to live with tears.
I might be lost, but all are found –
Every circle comes full around.

All the world could disappear –
To try my fate, to end my fear.
Send in all the dead and living,
Still, I know I will be giving.

Tempting hands of cards with pain
Ready for an end of rain
But smiles no more come for me
When I find my peace; serenity.

A bird may caw into the wind
As everyone will always sin
But I believe in trusting those,
No matter the choices they have chose.

I have hope for better days
As Icarus flies throughout his maze
But doesn't everyone fail in time?
Here I am, still in rhyme.

Come on, man, cannot you see...
Don't you know the way to be?
If you do, you will feel glee...
The truth will set you free.

Geoffrey Dilenschneider

Some may drop those who are worthy
Of their help, this I know,
But I believe in loyalty,
So my friend, your place you know.

It is your duty to be patient
It is your job to have respect.
Have the patience to pass frugality,
Yet love to feel correct.

I've found a way to conquer fears
To conquer hate, to live with tears.
I might be lost, but all are found –
I find myself tonight.

Falling in a Pool

Beauty can't be harmed by hate,
By sin, or even water.
Every time I see you now,
You seem to get much hotter.
Your smell intoxicates me further
Than I ever thought to go,
Yet a kiss is hard to ask for,
Yet again, I'd love to know.

Birds fly high above my head
To reach for branches gleaming,
But many dreams come true in time
It just takes time to know.
Yet a kiss is hard to ask for,
Yet again I'd love to know.

Oh, yeah, this was right before it turned January 1, 2002. Now I remember! Ha, funny story: I totally missed this huge *party that night. I fell asleep at 7:30 pm. What a joke. Haha. I'm not laughing.*

WAIT!

Hold on, I am not done!
I haven't finished finding out if I have lost or won!
I haven't finished messing up the world my parents make,
And I want to stay as young as poss'ble
For my inner child's sake.
I do not want to leave this sanctuary
That I have right here
"Right *here* is where I want to be,"
Inside me deep I hear.

The clouds, the clouds, how they beckon!
I cannot pull myself away, I guess it's love, I reckon.
An empty parking lot reminds me of a saddened way to fly:
It's sitting there for years and years,
Weary for us to buy.
Now every time I leave a place,
I seem to lose a part;
A part of me, a part of hope,
A little piece of heart.

Now everywhere I go I hear the whispers on the wind,
Shouting and yet slithering that the world does not have wind.
I've made mistakes and paid my dues; it's time to just move on.
Inside of me's a place of blues,
Yet my fire's not all gone.
I fear I have to leave this sanctuary
That I have right here, this year.
But *right here* is where I *have* to be,
Inside me deep I fear, I hear.

And that was that. Vacation over. Oh, well. I got in a whole heck of a lot of trouble for sneaking out in the middle of the night to go visit that certain someone during the trip, so my parents were really mad – did I mention I went through the window in order not to wake them up? – that seemed to distress more than upset them. But, anyway, to my parents, anything that was deemed inappropriate 35 years ago is what they think I shouldn't be doing. (Holding hands with a girl is a big deal!)

However, I do understand why this is, and I know that when (and if) I have kids, I'll treat them the way I thought my parents should have treated me.

Back at school, I continued my writing, trying in vain to keep girls out of my mind. It didn't work; two days later I was all about Mara Hertz again.

Why?

I'll tell you, but I first have to illustrate something to you. Girls have this 'thing', right? Yeah, I don't know what to call it, but they do. It's a sort of magnetic mechanism that turns on whenever they sense a guy is in proximity and feeling 'the urge' or whatever you want to call it. That thing turns on, making the guy think the girl's feeling the same way back, which she isn't – she doesn't even realize the guy's there.

Okay, that said, Mara was doing that one day in Creative Writing Introduction. I was freaking out. I just wrote.

To Touch Your Skin Would Be Electric

To touch your skin would be electric
To make your day, I'd die.
No song I know could make a difference,
Yet every day I'll try.

To look into your eyes so close,
I'd change my every way.
Why am I so scared to sit
With you, in green grass lay?

To hold your hands, to warm your heart
I'd spend a million years in pain.
I may be dramatizing this,
But I do so not in vain.

Someday I may have privilege to
Make your bad days good.
My sadness does not mean a thing
When your smile comes as it should.

To touch your skin would be electric
To make your day, I've died.
Just to think of that come true
Makes me just so warm inside.

Halfway through the poem, I started thinking about Katie Bennet. Who knows why? But, of course, I lost it all, and returned to the routine. At one point, I began wondering about my career as a writer. I wasn't sure if it was going to go anywhere; I didn't know that people were going to give me flak about writing; I didn't know I'd change peoples' lives; I didn't know I'd be doing a second one, even! All I knew was that I had to keep it real. No corniness meant; just keep true to that which I hold dear.

Banality was the way to put how slow classes were that part of the year. Trivial and faceless.

Two Men

What's a partition?
    I like tea!
When did the war start?
    I have to pee!
Try to be serious!
    what's in a name?
I need an answer
    it's raining
So I can find
    but I don't know
A greater meaning
    how to act
To a meaningless life,
    on the dance floor
Even though
    that loves me
I am bored.
    but I like tea!

Place out of Mind

I am not meant to
Create something real.
Nor am I meant
To make you believe.
I am not meant to
Win an award
Nor am I meant to find my place.
Decisively, eyes keep in touch with another's soul –
Keep in mind all that is needed.
Facts are good – though thoughts are better.
You can groom and groom,
But what sharpens the real perfection?
I am not meant
To become someone great
Nor am I meant
To change the world.
I create beauty, that is all.

I am not meant to fall in love
Nor feel depressed,
Yet I feel there's something there that drives me
From time to time.
I am meant not but to live and die.
Yes, live… and yes, die.
I am not here for money,
On this earth, yet I do know that it is somewhat necessary,
As well as is friendship.
Time and time again I get lost in this life,
In words, in people.
Like a salad in the corner, and I'm so small.
Just when can real peace (selfishly, I ask)
Be here?

I am not meant to
Impress the masses.
I am not meant
To be the best.
I can put words together, yes,
But can I find meaning deeper than my own relative emotions?
Deeper than anything I have found myself staring at?
There may be times of boredom,
Lust, joy, pain, and hate,
Yet is there a way to break from reality,
This one we create for ourselves,
And live in the one we are supposed to… meant to?

I am not meant to
Find a way out.

Geoffrey Dilenschneider

I am not meant
To change, to differ.
I am meant not but to question.
I am meant not but to live and die.

Ending Children

Verse I   I hate my life
I hate this world
I wanna put it all away
I wanna break it down
Make it go away
I wanna wake up to the sound of laughter
Not my tortured scream
What's it gonna take to leave me?
What's the main idea of breathing?
I don't care about the details
I wanna make it go away!

Chorus   Stop the horror!
Stop the pain!
Find the man who
Makes it rain
Tell him why he's gotta stop it,
Driving me insane!
Stop this sickness
End the lies!
Tell me why
The children cry!
I wasn't hurting anyone
Or maybe that's just why...

I Met Poetry

I met poetry
    in the
        hallway this morning, she was wearing music on the tongue
I met poetry
    in the
        hallways and she looked at me and my heart beated,
Scared of words to follow me
        to follow suit.
She said, I wonder what to say to men who think in suit
        with wond'rous pain and instantly
We die, we die, we die.

I lost myself in the darkness of
        in the darkness of her smile.

Throughout the school year, I had been mucking it up with Katie Bennet. Always, was I the fool; the dummy with the funny joke. However dumb I seemed, she somehow was able to keep in her mind that I was the 'serious, intellectual boy who was just looking for a friend in her' type. I don't know how she did it, how she made me feel so easy, soothed, composed; so easy-breezy and... and... perfect! I couldn't stand that she had a boyfriend!

Crying Diamonds

I've been drawn into a world all new,
A world so differently insane.
It took me by the hands one night
And took me down a memory lane.

Now I'm crying diamonds
To a plot so real I'm shaking.
Now I fall away so shunned
Because I find my world is breaking.

I look back to that scattered night,
Where time stood still for whispered breathing.
Creaking the steps in broken terror
As footsteps found me heartbeat leaving.

I want to leave it all behind
Yet I find I'm sadly chained
I wish that life would be so kind
As to tell me why we're chained.

I look unto that world of dreamers,
And the ways they're tied to home,
Yet come a time of sin and streamers,
Where will nomads roam?

And then when will we hold our hands
Unto a sun so closely hidden?
And then will we be holding hands
Or crying diamonds, dreamt and hidden?

When Gardens

Keep inside what you feel scared, to say out loud to me.
Until you do, I will not know, how is chickadee.
When gardens
　　　Break into a song of greener rains than lights
When gardens
　　　Lie in barren deserts but feel no pain beneath the sun
　　　Weep down willows on pitter, patters
　　　　　　wond'rin' of days to come.

When gardens
    Finding hustle-bustle too much for chickadee,
    Close their eyes in peace with all, the smell of life around them.
When gardens
    Sigh into a wind of joyous laughter,
        smiles turn to face them.
When gardens turn from anything but the toasty warm inside,
Anyone who knows the feeling, runs to garden's side…
So close your eyes with loved ones close, or maybe just alone
And feel a feeling like hot cocoa, deep inside your stomach thrown.
We find their sanctity in nothing but, a time spent here awhile,
Bathed in one's own peacefulness, free in slinky smile.
When gardens
    Break into a song, 'bout shoes of every style,
    Ask about the person who, may need to run awhile
When gardens'
    Peace comes once in not, a glory near the sun,
    One may find it lying dormant, but never on the run.
        And then, of course, it finds that place
        And settles in at home…
        Then maybe when the gardens grow,
        They'll have a place to roam.
When gardens
    Longer have no need to linger on what they've done
    Lay to rest with crazy freedom on a day of broken fun
    Following the footsteps of a friend you hold so dear
    Down onto a stretch of grass, green from feet all year
When gardens
    Violin themselves into a Mozart frenzy,
    Call up reverend chickadee, and ask him what to do.
When gardens
    Find themselves in peril, do not really panic,
    For, call up reverend chickadee, and ask him what to do.

And when the bells sound forty-three, on chickadee's day off,
What do you call a rooster's caw, when garden suns break off?

Peace and Happiness

I look into your eyes
And wonder why I've sinned,
Slowly breaking down the platforms of my trust.
I open up my mind to possibility,
Yet then again
I feel the weight of persecution
Staring me to the ground.
I'm scared to think of you,
Because I always cry,
Crying stirs the leaves of pasts

That I can't wonder why...
Different times and different days
Different feelings, different ways,
I succumb to my two needs in life,
The things I'm simply searching for,
Searching for a peace in life
And a constant happiness.
A place in which life becomes simple,
Happy, and free
A place with you where we could grow old
In easy harmony.
No pain
No suffering
Yet here I am again,
I close my eyes and cry for you,
And peace, and happiness.

I Am a See-Saw Lie

Stamnels breaking leads of plants
On breathing soft pleats of little girls.
Trends are such that news's slants
Leave a section to contain men's hurls.

Phases, phases – why must we move between?
And then we change... mazes, mazes –
What are they meant to mean?
Lying crying – on detail... with thoughts of hate and want;
And when we cry on doorsteps of shapes and a tail –
Who comes slow to us in caged ways snail...
Wonder why we wait and want.

I am a see-saw lie... back and forth until I break...
And when I do I eliminate the opposition bit by bit
As I must cautiously lie... like slithering, slithering snake...
Then can you die with spate, laughing wit by wit.

Phrases, phrases – why do we utter such idioms and such?
Just wait the years... mazes, mazes –
What do we do when we find we ain't much?
Smiling, riling – on a whim – with stamnels breaking leads of plants to mend;
But what end does come to us in a life of such...
A world of slant with deadmen's clutch...
                    Here we stand in lands to fend
                Off the dreams of little girls
                        Deep inside our head.

Geoffrey Dilenschneider

But Never What it Seems

The space between
Finds me alone
And when I dream
I'm so alone…
And even now
I feel surpassed
In feeling lonely
When you have passed.
Look at me a little more
Maybe we can trade off names
In a dance of pleasures that
Show the world how beautiful we are.

Maybe we can share a smile
In a parking lot.
Maybe we can have a go
At reading our own thoughts.
What could be more reason to
Show the world our chastity.
Maybe you could stay awhile
And show me what you mean.

Calming winds blow fragrances
Down to where I sit.
Maybe we can find a place
And chat it up a bit.
You can tell me of your house
And what you do all day.
Maybe we can talk a bit
About pain and all its thoughts and everything.

To the universe I seem
To be worth next to nothing.
But I know how everything
To some means all the world.

Walk a bit around my mind
To show me where you've been,
Maybe we can do it all,
And here we may begin:
Time is nothing to me, babe,
When I can see your face.
I know not what it means to be
A beauty in a place.
Life is not meant to be wasted
Crying all alone
Maybe we can talk a while
In every sort of tone.

I serenade you from afar
Silently in silence.
I don't know if I can stand
The glitter in your eye!
No, I must go up to you
I must find who you are,
Maybe we can smile a bit,
And find who we both are.

Obviously, I'll never get over Katie. She inspired this poem in me, called The Smile, because I've found in life that the most representative action a person can do is show a piece of their happiness. Yes, a smile does not show all happiness, but it does show more true, reputable emotion than any other method of communication. A smile can't be manufactured; it takes more than the mouth. It takes the cheeks, the teeth, the tongue, the eyes, the forehead, the neck, the ears, the shoulders and the entire upper body! A real smile, anyway. I've seen fake smiles. We've all seen fake smiles. There's just no faking a true smile. It's that pure. Like blowing bubbles. It takes no energy, and is the purest form of travel there is.

The Smile

From the centers of a drop of rain
Do I find these peach lips parching mine.
The mystery guest walks in aware,
As I flick the lights to find lips on mine.

On mine eyes
On mine eyes
    do they sore from the sight,
    quivering not from distraction,
    but rather from losing the strength to move on.
No silver angels
No silver angels
    may mar the fluorescence, the beauty
    unadultered by any of the world's attempts
    to change, to ensue a path of pain on that smile.

        oh that smile, that smile!
        a leaf on the tree of perfection!
        the first and last notes of a timeless symphony!
        memories of being held and holding,
        alike we are in at least that much, I know... I know...
so little

And from the kiss of the rain's green fragrance on my tongue
Do I find a smile to call my own.
And simply through the beauty of your eyes
May I find the smile I can call my own.

After a fashion, I continued to be inspired minute by minute by the now-mythical Katie Bennet. Honestly, I really couldn't stop being influenced by her presence. Just being in the same room as her lit me up! I couldn't stand it!

More Privately, More Privately

The tapestry woven eyes, I find
      Keep me up at nights for ever
Screaming silently to God
      A name that sounds like Heather.

Flame on earth desires not
      But to live and die in drama.
Now I claim to be smart enough,
      But I'm no Dalai Lama.
When it comes to want, to sunrise freedom
      Or when it sets in pain,
But time can dance between our eyes
      And slow two hearts in wain.

More privately, more privately
      I speak of ways I've seen.
Here I speak of wishes doubtful,
      Yet say just what I mean.
Wishes of a different kind,
      The ones to get away
From being censored, from being raped
      Of what they *have* to say.

The dreams of men, my dreams of you,
      Yet, have I even slept?
No pain I feel, nor any true,
      Yet, neither have I wept.

Jill: The Uninspiring Girl

Images and imagination's breaths
      Broken on the salty shore
I want to feel right through you,
      Your supple skin and more.
Soft whishes so nice touched by the sun
      When I look inside you
I may have know you for an instant...

Softly up and down, your chest breathes.
      "Perfection, salty maid!"
I call out to the smiles above
      "Why are you so made?"

As I walk... as I walk
      And find myself alone
I sit in sand reflecting on
      Why I walk alone

The Hesitant Man

"Beautiful, you are!" I want to scream in provoc words,
      yet levels and the politics keep me tied down to my seat.
"Lovely your skin flows!" I need to stand up and yell,
      yet time again I find that I just move along the beat.
"Follow me forever, girl! Let us frolic free!"
      I want to whisper in your ear, yet I think you'll never see.
"Run away from all you've heard... run from lies untrue!"
      But honestly, that night I might run through won't be with you.
I want to say, "I had a dream! Of you and me and us!
      There was no hate, no boring times, no aggravating fuss!
      Just happy times together frozen, to Mars we'll go or bust!"

For you, I'll run twelve marathons, or swim around the Earth!
For you, I'll take a million punches, I might even give birth!
I'll be alone for forty years, I'll be the missing link!
But no... I cannot say these things, in fear of what you'll think.

Snap!

Sleep the day and let it stay
But no one knows –
What do you do?
I don't want to spend and find
That lies are really true!
Because wouldn't the animosity climb
And hair fly in directions
When beauty is lost to the lies
And the kitten can no longer listen?
It's rage.
Where does she walk or purr?
How about if there is no way to purr
in peaceful prisms in which to play?
Where are we then?
What kind of fun says:
Stop that at once!
      Do not think to bend
The rules or any other! We will not allow it because what we say
Is just what you do! And doesn't it just suck?
Too bad!?
And kittens lie in colored beds
And lie themselves to sleep,

But this one kitten lies awake
To those that listen well.
But aren't we tainted anyway
When we find
That kitten's breath will smell…?

I hate the end more than that kitten,
Who finds itself alone
And so alone,
Writing about nothing
And the images in its mind it bought
At a sport store with a credit card
And no one knows you're a kitty-cat
When you log onto the Internet.

Deuces wild,
          pain may leave
People wild,
          I cannot breathe!
          Broken hearts mend
Snap! is how it sounds,
          But it takes a while
Before they're back in bounds.

I try to find meaning
          I try to find place.
But in my own mind I
          Know it's all fake
When we sit here for an hour
          And spill out our souls,
But what the hell's the point
          When we're grumbling on goals
Of pieces of cherry jam,
          Toast on a door,
Damn the ass that showed itself,
          Damn the ugly poor!

Snap! We have no use for it,
What may be the reason?
Can we live alone for real –
Or find ourselves in treason?

What finds days in time with love
With very little haze?
What pacifist finds rage in self
While scarce come happy days?

Peace of mind, of will alone,
I must keep on my task.
What may I be doing wrong
In life, in pain, I ask?

Force me more, and I may break
Before I tell the time.
Here I give the gift of reason,
Yet you only pay a dime.

Care and care and hunting life
While we lost the feeling –
Feelings? What are these, my friend?
I do believe *I'm* dealing!
   Drugs, may I ask?
Oh, yes, of course!
What else may I be worth?
It represents all that I live for
By it, death and birth.
My friend, my friend
I know I can't
Tell you what to do
Or how to change
In any way
But what I tell is true:
I had once found some silver,
Silver on the floor,
I put the stuff deep in my pocket,
'N looked around for more.
I found some gold just lying there,
I looked around and grabbed it,
I found a whole big stash of coins,
I bounced off walls like rabbits!
Now, my friend, I realized
How stupid I'd become,
I found I had no single way
To take the stash and run!
So in the end, I left it all,
I'd lost what I'd become,
I felt so worthless, empty inside,
Like others have all the fun.
But later on that night,
I realized what was gold:
The fun I find inside myself,
That happiness is gold.

Beauty through a Window

The face of beauty!
I see it there! It is… is it!?
    I don't know.
The face of beauty but beauty
    has no face,
For if beauty had a face,
    wouldn't we all be lost?

Even from afar I find,
    her face's too bright to see,
And even now I cannot see her,
    (I'm swimming in the sea!)
Way up close, I merely see
    a smile there so perfectly!
I wonder what she looks like,
    Beautiful, I guess.
Have you ever seen her?
    No, I must confess…

Ah! I look out through my window
    And find a storm of rain,
But who is *that* two windows past!?
    My God, we *are* insane!
That is *beauty*,
    It couldn't be!
I'm serious, man!
Her eyes are free!
    Well, I'll be damned
    And struck by God if I may add,
Well, all is lost, gone, missing, blind
    And now we'll all go mad.

During the last few weeks or so I had been working on homage to the great Shel Silverstein. It didn't happen to become one of my best segments of writing, yet I still felt I captured maybe a morsel of his great humor in a few of the poems.

    I didn't actually set down at the task of mimicking his style; rather, I wanted only to capture a scrap of my own poetic humor (at the time I didn't feel like much of my poetry had humor in it).

A Zit

What if it talked?
What if it walked?
What if it stalked?
What if it dined
On people with time
To pop 'em
And pinch 'em
And scratch 'em
And lynch 'em?
Rash 'em
And synch 'em?
Break 'em
And bake 'em?

But what if they talked?
What if they walked?
What if we lived
In peace with our zits
And keep quiet the fits
And let out our wits
To have fun
No gun
And run
Frolic in sun
Have fun?

Just 'Cause

Writing's no fun
When you're under the gun;
Writing's no fun when you're sick.
Writing's no fun
When you're under the sun;
Writing's no fun with a stick.
Writing's not great
When you have to just wait;
Writing's not great when you're bored.
Writing's not great
When your paper is late,
It's not a great trait to be bored.
Writing's not real
When time seems surreal;
Writing's not real 'cause it's true.
Writing's not real
When you really don't feel;
Writing's not real 'less it's you.

Geoffrey Dilenschneider

Growing Up Johnny Politely

No thank you, ma'am
Yes, sir, of course.
Please pass the peas around.
I'd love a mint,
Oh, it could be worse
My belly could be round.
No thanks, uh-hu,
I think I got ya down.
I'll see ya later, mum and pops,
I'm going out to town.

Oh, hey guys
Wassup wit' ya?
What'd I say?
Oh, stuffing.
Yeah, I heard ya!
I didn't do it!
What'd I do?
Oh, nothing.

The Chores

You can put me deep in jail,
You can put me in a cell
You can make depressed feel good
But nope, I will not tell.

I'll grow into a trouble,
I'll make things go CRASH BANG!
Yet never have I broken down
Like caged canaries sing.

Only time can wear me down
Like leather on a knife
And no, I will keep taunting you,
You've taken down my life.

Disagreeing only hinders,
Yet continue on you must
I know this and you know I
Must continue with my fuss.

You can break my arms and legs,
You can make me SCREAM!
You can make the thought of death seem nice,
But nope, I will not clean!

The Tilted Curtains

The tilted curtains create a drear upon us all
And not that we accept it,
But what can one do to that
Which is nailed into a wall?
Possibly one can find a way to move it just an inch or two
Or maybe we can have at it
With a hammer and a box
Which has yet to make us fall.
But, again, of course, we falter and we fall,
Yet again to find again
The tilted curtains on the wall.

A Note From a Crush

I have a note
Inside my pocket
I'm afraid to read it now…
Or anytime for any matter.
I'm not even sure it is a note!
Maybe it's a letter!
Oh, it's probably just a smiley face
With a tongue sticking out the side.
Maybe it says she hates me!
Or, worse, "Last night I lied!"
That would just add to my misery.
But who would really care in the end, an end.
I'd be broken and hurt and no one the wiser!
I'd in bed toss over and pitch and be sweaty and red
And life would be spiraling downward and downward and downward
And I'd never stop until I hit total rock bottom and life would just end
And splat is how I would go when I hit the bottom infinite in sheer, utter, pain
And there goes life, shriveling up inside itself, with one last glimpse of hope dying
sickly inside its
            bloody, withered eyes…

… I have a note
Inside my pocket,
And now that I know how bad it might be,
I open up the words.

Finding Meaning

Maybe I could rob a bank
Or how 'bout run a mall.
What about a math teacher,
Or cleaning bathroom stalls!
I could be a bookie
And remember all the facts –
Or maybe be a minister
And read all of the tracts!
How 'bout winding watches
Or paving concrete roads –
I could fly a giant spaceship
Or catch a lot of toads!
Maybe I could be a singer
And change the people's lives –
Or maybe be a major player –
And steal the people's wives!

I could be a model
Or live in a rubber suit!
I could write the notes in fortune cookies
Or be a cocktail fruit!
I could be a bolt of lightning
Or mother nature her very self!
I could be a paper napkin
Or a little Santa's elf!

Now I know I could be famous,
I could be big and tall,
But all I really need to be
Is to be myself, that's all.

Chapter 24

▲ ▲ ▲ ▲

It was during the cold months that I began to show the markings of a true, capable fool.

I had already gotten over my crush on Katie Bennet by stuffing it callously down the back of my throat and into the back of my mind. Actually, I had many crushes, but I tried my hardest to overlook and disassociate myself from them in order to continue my studies more fastidiously. But, because of whom I was – a procrastinator to the max – I had very little chance up against the mammoth fiend of homework.

Actually, try 'no chance at all'! I remember trying to study for a World Studies (History) test, but all I could do was read Silmarillion, *by J.R.R. Tolkien – a choco-late-covered paperback that had seen most of its days in the bottom of my dirty back-pack – hence the chocolate. And I'm sorry for only describing this now, but it is an opportune moment. I had a mentor during the second half of 9th grade and the whole of 10th. Well, see, I actually had two. The first, whom I met near the end of my time in the Utah Desert, was named Guy Dumas. Don't laugh, I tell you; don't laugh. He is one of the more fortified men I've ever met.*

Built like a small car, Guy wore a ten-gallon hat with pride, and could throw a football farther than I could see. At first, we got along famously, but, as untrue friend-ships always go, the differences surfaced and we started to fight.

He was a very strict, no-nonsense guy (ha, guy) while I was about as oppositional to him as possible, and only because he was that austere guy (ha again, guy) was I oppo-sitional, and to make the downward spiral more precipitous, he became more rigorous with his tedious work schedule for me as I became more oppositional. Sick, sad, world; but that's life, right?

Guy and I had this thing going on; a long-standing joke, if you will, that had to do with the level of competitiveness we both were at. We always competed at everything: running down the stairs of my house, how loud we could listen to music, how many times in a row each of us could kick a hacky-sack in the air, everything. And since he was a heck of a lot stronger, had more life experience, and was much more proactive than me, I pretty much had no chance in a frozen underworld against him. There was one high point in our little escapades, though. I did beat his high score of hacky-sacking. My best was 510 in a row! I'm not kidding. He couldn't get close because he refused to wear anything but semi-tight jeans and sandals. I wore shorts and Airwalks. To anger him a little more, I had him sit twenty feet from me one day outside so I could show him how to really kick sack. Well, he happened to see me at one of my finer moments: 876 kicks in a row. No walls, no stalls; just foot, knee and forehead to a bag of little nuts. Want to know how I could do that for so long? Gatorade and I pretended the hacky-sack was Guy's head.

After a while, he began to take me on these long runs. Now you can laugh. I'm not out of shape or anything, but I can't run distance of any kind; I'm just not built for it. I sprint, and even then, not very well. But the guy just didn't care! (ha, guy) He just kept pushing it on me. He had been in the military until he lost some of his peripheral vision and couldn't continue, and after leaving the military, had kept in great shape, so I obviously had no chance against him.

The only thing worse than being out-classed by a guy is if he knows that he can out-class you. I hated it to such an extreme that I started turning backwards on his little 'let's

Geoffrey Dilenschneider

compete and you'll do your work to beat me' stunt. I refused to work at all. And, to his discontent, the more he pushed me, the more I pushed back.

It all came to a deafening end when he tried to wrestle me to the ground one day – a thing we did somewhat often – but then continued a little too far, trying to really kick my butt.

My parents fired him not too long afterward and I got a new mentor, but I'll talk about him later.

A few days after getting rid of Guy, and a few weeks after winter vacation came to a heartbreaking end, I re-met Ali Watts. See, the thing was that I wanted to stay in Creative Writing, but the only one happened to be slotted in the same period of the day as my English class. I had a choice: either stay with my really cool English class and find another elective, or switch English classes and enroll in Creative Writing Advanced.

Yeah, like that was a hard decision! I chose the latter, obviously. At first I thought switching out of my crazy, easy-going English class would help me with my new goal of dedicated studying, but I was wrong. There were two problems with the new English class: the teacher was crazy and I had to sit next to Ali Watts. Whoa! "What an angry little girl," was what I first thought, but as I got to know her I realized that she was dedicated to God, stayed true to herself, was incredibly intelligent, and didn't take crap from anybody. And, may I add in a very crude way, she was one hell of a good looking girl! Lucky me to be sitting next to someone like her! Not only did her opinions and hard-working temperament rub off on me, but she sometimes made me feel like I could do no wrong. The only problem: I couldn't get the nerve up to utter a breath to her. I was too scared.

Yeah, I know it sounds stupid and childish, but that's the way it was, and after a while I did get over my Ali Stage Fright, and began talking to her. I'm pretty sure she didn't take to me as well as Katheryn did, and I've figured out over a twisted real-life trial-and-error that I work better on cruise ships than I do in school... a lot better.

Into February, I tried my hand at asking her out a bit – after we had traded some poems back and forth – but, to be blunt, I was stood up thrice more than I would like to remember.

Also, it was in this time, inspired by Ali, that I wrote what I consider to be my most important works. So, pay attention!

Untitled Poem #81

Beauty is a thing of substance
A thing of wonderin'
    imagination
You think sometimes you've lost it all,
    yet there's so much more to life.
The tears of regret
Frozen in the silent space
    so alone, alone in sunshine
So cold as it beats down upon you.

Changing Are the High and Low

Hidden within this sanctuary
Are things you may not know –
Changing are the high and low,
(Yet, you may never know.)

Beneath me are the words to say
As well as when to stop
But what's missing's when to run away
(When meanings seem to drop.)

Below these words are memories
Cherished in my heart.
I do not think I'll let you pass,
For I've no place to start.

Pain has become a part of life…
Or… has it always been?
I'm not sure of self in life
(I've frequently met sin.)

Loss is not worth talking to,
In the end it just perturbs.
It finds a way to penetrate
To my deepest ends of nerves.

Life is very difficult –
But don't we know this now?
Do not spend time learning life,
(You'll never figure how.)

Rather, spend your days on earth
Spreading 'round your smile,
Silence will befriend your soul
To make love worth your while.

Toxic lies have always been
Eating at my soul,
But what the reader never knows
Is what may be *their* role.

Now silently, so silently
We tiptoe through the room –
This room we sometimes call our home,
(Beware, this place goes boom!)

Geoffrey Dilenschneider

Peace is something worth the world...
Though we may search forever...
But what may come of lying down...?
What may come, so clever...?

Pleasure is available
Yet sometimes it is wrong.
pain finds ways of ruining,
(Yet daily we stand strong!)

Meaning is now lost to me,
I sit here eating food,
And what means more than laughing,
Displacing those so rude?

Our beat is set to our own tune
That keeps us in our place,
Yet where exactly is that, now
That we can explore space?

And what more than our confidence
Will ever set us free?
And what more than the painful truth
To keep us in our company?

Hidden here are truths
Yet lies are what you'll find.
These young words so hidden here
Forever gray will bind.

Some

Some find fun in asking things
Of lives and loves and touchy things.
Some look sideways through all the air
Too mesmerized by my lovely hair.
Some use words like I use eyes:
To size up others and search for lies.
Some pull teeth and some use paint,
Some plan lives while others faint.
Carefully some time sport races,
Games of balls and many faces.
Some do lunch and some eat snacks,
Some eat brunch from red lunch packs.
Some go free in many ways;
Usually in mind, but some in waves.

Some look for ways to rue the world
While others let go and gain it all.
Now some run scared until they've failed
While others don't know, but gain it all.

Tomorrow comes in counted hours
And we waste away.
Time's not real...
I guess it's just today.

We (Us Americans)

Grandeur never spoke better of reality
When it's spoken of in mind,
But who might think of random things
Like living in a mind?

Though we (Us Americans)
Breathe free, fresh, forest air
Who else can say they've lived a life
So free, or pure, or fair?

Think of war in general...
It's never here at home.
I think we have some abstinence
That keeps war on the roam.

But now things are a-changing
Like the yellow-brown-white snow –
Now grandeur can find the freshest air
Where fine green pastures grow.

A Spike in the Line We Call Time (While Still i Try Budding)

There are many ways to love
But those, I do not know.
I've tried all the ways to gain
But no, I will not sow.

I wonder how to leap the bounds
And find my deep desires
Should I hide my human faults
And burn them in my fires?

Innocently pink are all the things I see in her:
Childish rose patterns on a fiery little devil.
Once, was I, a-strolling in a river
When once I found a tigerlilly and in its beauty, reveled.

My head is rolling, rolling
Down into the river.
The bells are tolling, tolling
Yet, still there is no river!

While I wander weeping weary
A singing sound surrounds
The tumult of the tame and teary,
But bold and beauty bounds.

(It takes a woman's
Hand to draw a rose)

Coming, coming, lost are we:
Those who've done the worst.
Found are secrets; deep's the sea!
Finding lives so cursed.

Be all, end all
Jump from life to come!
No more consequences for our pain;
Jump love's train and run!

Look at hands one at a time
To search for here the blow…
The be all, end all, send off hit –
Too late we'll see and know.

Random, HEY! I'm learning
Learning how to live.
Learning how to think and act,
Learning… how to live.

I'm human and I'm pleading;
Curious within.
I know all the world's inside,
But where should I begin?

I Am Only This

I am only this;
And this is what I am:
I am searching for the world…
The world is what I am.

I am looking 'round the hills
For what may come to me
As well as for a chance to find
What just may come to be.

I am in a search for someone
To look with me for peace.
I am here for many days,
And one day I will cease.

It does not matter who has laughed,
For I know that I am strong.
I am flying, yet ready for
The world to become wrong.

Long the days set bright in hues
Of red upon my face
Growing is a trait of pain
Still searching for its place.

I will always lean for help;
Friends can lean on me.
I believe in everything
I search to be set free.

I am in a quest for love…
There's nothing more to say.
Deep within me I will feel it,
That day I do not pray.

Passing by the gardens
Can dignify the dead,
Yet I refuse to whistle
Soft inside my head
Because I love every one of you!
I will spend my life to do so!
Because I sing for beauty's sake
I will right my life to do so!

I live for the moment
And I live unto the day.
I think hard of deep blue skies
While wading in the bay
Because all things are so, so nice!
In *all* our pretty gardens!
Gardens filled with all the flowers –
We *are* all of our gardens.

My idea of space is this:
And that is what it is.
Space is all that we don't know –
Space is soda's fizz.

Geoffrey Dilenschneider

My memories are tainted
With ugly weeds around.
I am neither great nor small,
But yet, my mind stays sound.

I am neither pure nor free...
I can cheat and lie...
I am somewhat lost at sea...
I can only sigh.

I am always lost of time,
Who says it sets you free?
I can be so childish
(Like, oops, I climbed a tree!)

But mostly I am searching
For a way to make it through.
Through the awkward times we have
To the times to get a clue.

And I am searching not for ends,
Nor what I should believe,
But rather, answers to my dreams,
And how humble to receive.

I am only this;
This is what I am:
I am searching for the world
And the world is what I am.

Watt's Rose

Let my rose be held
By the silk, smooth hands of hers.
Simply, sadly, cast away
By the candy hands of hers.

Let my hours of work be balled
By not much of a thanks.
Or is it the meaning of it all?
She must have drawn a blank

For now I am not made by petals,
The petals of my rose,
Lacking green and full of sadness,
My petaled heart finds throes.

She marks upon her wall of victims
Off-handedly my name.
There goes the only chance I had,
And I guess there is no point.

Nor was there.

Wilting

You do not fail to speak your mind,
You never stop existing.
You always seem so on the move
But motives in the misting.

You seem to lash out to those who lack
The means to fend off sour.
When you want a thing or two,
Find daggers of the hour.

So mean you seem
To be to me – I wonder why you bite.
What did I bid
Oppressed too free – You wonder When in spite.

So Stained

I mind
The sins upon my finger tips
So stained
With the snap of ginger whips.
I mind
The consequences of not doing the assumed.
I mind
The consequences of doing the forbidden
I mind
The fact that I'm so ridden
With the putrid taste of satiating lies
So slivering and petrifying and... what have I done...?
I mind my evil nature... but did I mind while it was done?

This is one of the few poems I wrote as jokes inspired by a girl named Kristen. It is also in the even more selective group of poems that I take one specific thing and make fun of it, as well as pay respect to it. Or, in this poem's case, 'pay respect to them.'

The Two

I know dogs that see all things
Yet only get kibbles and bits.
Here I see a beauty topper,
This supple pair of wits.
Yet they cannot be called that,
For they are just too dignified
In their shape, resusitance
In every lighting eye
Remind me of why I do detest
The name brash brutes have called
Her set of perfect petunas,
Tipped with crimson roses,
So sweet and tender,
Light and loved,
In hands deemed right
That neither squeeze nor shove.

To touch these beings Martian,
I'd need some special gloves.
And even though the cov'rin's smooth,
Overtly not at all blasé behind blue down
And pink petals wrought in cotton,
Even though…!
I still find mind enough to understand
That her beauty is not in these
Ripe oranges darned on trees,
These saintly wings cupped into bowls
So hanging smooth, perfection tolls!,
These cupped bowling balls that find themselves at my lane
These lovely definitions of the base of men insane,
The goblets of fire for Icarus's sake
As he flew to the suns –
      I say double suns!,
For hot and sweaty come one and all
A million miles away!
We burn when so up close
Into a crisp.
The modern day man could pump a tire
With the air he will expel
When put in one lone room with *them*
Them, those portly Jello molds,
Made straight from where we find
The absolute *best* stuff on earth!
      (it's right in here)

OH GOD I PRAY FOR COLD!!

After that little stint into the world of my own twisted humor, I went back to the seri-ously trivial job of being inspired by Ali in English class.

Slippin g Away

Slippin' g away are the
Beauties who once were free.
Broken are the men
Left drowning in her sea.
     The children never come
     The children never come to play, to grow; to annoy their parent's lives
We are now fleeing,
Yet you stay behind
And from that act I've
Lost my hope, my mind.
My very source of blood has
Stopped in sheer defection.
I conjure all my memories
Remembering confection.
     The shivers never run
     The shivers never run and fail to bound upon my upturned hairs.
Awoken are all the
Memories that want to hide.
Hide in futile irony
To lie warm and confide.
Chemically, we never really
Knew.
I had a chance that we all know I
Blew.
A heart to love is bleeding sometimes,
Though whose heart it is, is woe.
Bear in mind I wish the world in rhymes
Though whose answer it is, it's no.
     Electricity is lost to human fault
     Electricity is lost to human fault, and the magic is all that's gone
Those places where true love is found (but not found) is where you'll never think:
Beneath your nose and yet it's there: on the other side of an upside-down rainbow
(under the ice skate rink).

My Heart

Hello, friend.
It is time again.
It is time again to fall.
We have lost once more and I fear
We cannot lose again.
For if we do, I fear we will not be able
To get up again.
I apologize for the pain I am going to put you through.
I apologize for what consequences my selfish actions
Have condemned upon you.
It is not my fault, believe me.
Trust me.
This will only hurt for a minutes, but it depends upon your willingness.
I understand you laugh at me behind my back?
                    No
Wrong.
Hmmm… hmmm
TZZZZZZ! …sssss
                    YES! YES!
Alright, then.

To You

Where are we going
With these lecturing ways?
What kind of meaning
Are we looking for now?
And then we digress and digress,
And why are we changing right now?
Am I not meant to be hit by great truths?
Should I have written a great story of youths?
Is it worth it? Should I have found my own style perfection?
As I can see in my mind
I feel the snap of my neck
And I hear it in my head
And shiver from the piercing feeling.

Why do we waste about
Talking of done
And delaying the doing?
When we could be happ'ier
Leaving the done
And *doing* the doing!

Why do we speak of the things not worth speaking?
Can we forget how so eas'ly we're peaking?
Dark and so slow as we march on and on!
Life is so slow here, so bored
And then gone.

The Capturing Poem

I am lost without my music
I am lost without my soul
I guess the feeling's just mundane
I guess that's just *their* goal:

To spread a napkin walking
You must spend time and care
Yet one must never stop to think
If napkins do grow hair.

And then you lie upon the grass
In the splendor of a queen.
I think of many thoughts
But none seem more a dream

Than the ants so marching, marching
Up to my painting store
And magically you disappear
And I'm left with a whisper of more.

What do I make with a story of sights?
What do I do with a switch but no lights?
I live and let live
And yet I do not.
I kept it in mind,
And still I've forgot!

Ending for all the Damned (TEETH)

And ending am I;
Ending.
Ending for all the damned
And yet... there is no yet!
No desire... no pain... none more
Empty than ending.
The water that does nothing
But follow the course,
Creating the fools that we loathe
And we love for the pity that we no longer feel
As we travel the course that we no longer breathe.

Geoffrey Dilenschneider

I can no longer feel the need to succeed
For I feel that we've lost the old ways of the freed.
While bland white capped waves of our lost little souls
Float in and out of their unconscience holes.
Slowly we must be succumbing
To the workings of all that we were.
Never again, before, broken, un-learning
And the place we don't seek can't concur
Of the love we have lost
Of the freedom that's gone now –
Of the fun that fades from here so quickly while screaming:
I don't think, I don't think!
My whole world is a stone!:
Falling and falling,
Then detached from my body as I float to the ground
And everything is so finite
And so, oh-my-god false do my crooked needs feel
As my senses lose Touch
As my senses lose Eyes
As my senses lose Everything meant to be mattered!
As my senses lose Turn
As my senses lose Hate
And ending am I;
Ending.

Dove

Alighting on a groove
In one disposition
With the world its time flies by.
Making the most of love,
Moonlight white
In flutters fret and then just one
Of our memories.
Ripe for shaking and yet
The night is long.
Drunken with a floating peace
A paradox so sweet.
Tame in homelands
Bold alone
Breathing just the freshest air.
Speaking only to those much worthy
To hear beauty's defined form –
A form of womanhood less known,
Never weeping, less it's shown
To her shining quivered loon
There, she cries under the moon.

Over time, Creative Writing Advanced class had become one of my most hated classes. The teacher, a respectable woman, didn't have any idea how to run a Creative Writing class. She tried too hard to make it an English class, therefore ruining the peculiar balance that the previous teacher, Mrs. Sorenson, was able to uphold with ease. This new teacher once even tried her hand at grammar, which just infuriated me more.

It was in February that I began to recognize similar feelings in the other students in the class (as well in February did I begin to think about turning 16). I felt it my duty to preach against her, in quiet, of course, but preach nonetheless. As I wrote, I advocated against her until a few of us began to quietly unfasten the tiny screws that held the class together. The first of the major blows towards defilement of this 'teacher' was a boldly livid reading of the following poem.

We, the Baking Bread

Rise the baking bread
And shun the people who are mundane.
Slitful eyes so uh-huh psychiatrist.
"Yeah… that'd be greaat…"
AHH! Kill me now!!
We can all put our writing down now
With a silent sigh
In nervous pain
That was putting you closer and closer to the edge
As the chances of reading moved impossibly slowly
Closer and closer,
And you know what?
This turtle, so slow,
Will not win the race.
And our hot potato lies now,
No one except the teacher brave enough
(or dumb enough) to talk and talk and talk

And I speak with the conviction of a child
in church, dressed up to look nice and be quiet.
I have no comments to those who induce excessive
Blah by her! I will not waste time with this!
Nobody likes it!
We all want to read,
And yes, our turn will come,
But 'eventually' does not do the justice needed
To describe the simple way we sit
In minute tremors
So by the time we come to us
We're shaking like a vibrator!
Goddamn it can't we just be free
So we can find a way?
A whole damn way to make it allgood!

And I will not apologize for how my words
May sting!
I will not feel remorse for how my words
Just may not ring!
I refuse to let my feelings
Pass on by to lands so dreamy
Where everything is so nice
And where we cannot go!

I do not want you all talking while I read!
You do not want to listen.
You and I all want the others to listen intently
        And have all this great encouragement and praise.
But it is all a lie and forced and meant to
Be kept inside
As we just stare, and if you want, unspokenly,
You can comment if something struck you!
No one says anything unless they really want to!
And even even if they want to,
If they are asked to, it is somewhat made fake,
And,
(I don't know about you),
But I don't feel a thing like this,
Like this situation, and I cannot just escape!
This is a classroom prison
Whose doorway is a mouth to a place
That feels no sorrow or pain.
Whose desks are there to jacket you
Whose walls are there to keep us padded
Whose windows, whose windows –
They taunt and tease,
Touch and giggle with their squinting eyes,
Telling us that we are useless,
So unabashedly, blindly worthless!

A shag in here
But the two would fall asleep upon each other
Before having a chance to climax
Like the climax of a bullet's path!

And now, what hell could humans create
More perfect than this anthrax ceilinged room's become.
I love these words, I love all words,
But there can be a time
In which these words will hint to excess,
Excess that creeps up on you
And what does hell have worse than cold coffee?
Doughnuts without drink!
Cookies and no milk and then Santa never comes
And all of us who still have one:
That inner little child;
We cry for what we're losing
In this nitrogenic air,
Strangling and strengthening
As it saps the honey of our youth,
Of our simple innocence.

I am determined to make this room
A place to unload grief,
As well as sanctuary
To read and learn and grow and laugh,
But first I need to slice the sun
And bake the cornered bread,
The bread that can rise to be great,
It just takes time to move.

The awkwardness just kills me!
I don't mean any harm,
Just can't we find a medium
Where all our minds can swarm?
And then… we find peace…
In this little room
Every window, door, and wall
Is suddenly so groomed
And we, the simple, tainted humans,
We, the weak and frail,
Can find the comfort in this room
In knowing we can't fail

However, the in-class revolution coiled back into a snake-like resentment towards the teacher when her ignorance – which became her like an overwhelmed walrus – decided that she not take the hint that we were even the least bit angry with her. So life became just again the bland way it felt meant to be.

The writing of the book was coming back to me now and again, and it seemed as though the book was me with the title I had come up for it a little earlier, and so bored in class was I, that I used the nutrition facts on the back of a Dr. Pepper can as basis for a poem on the first book.

A BOY AWARE

Nutrition Facts

Serving size:	1 Boy	
	Amount Per Serving	
Calories	15	
		% Daily Value*
Total Fat	21.41 Lbs	7%
Sodium	A Whole Hell of a Lot mg	19%
Total Carb.	40 g	13%
	Sugars: Depends	
Protein	Some Writing	61%

*Percent Daily Values are based on a 150lb Boy Diet

INGREDIENTS:
Creativity, Hydrogen, Oxygen, Carbon, Nitrogen, A Heart, A Mind, A Soul, Writing, A Voice, Feelings (Hate, Love, Happiness, Sadness, etc.), Carbonated Water, High Fructose Corn Syrup, Compassion, Pen, Paper, Natural Flavoring, A Life, Ability (Make Friends, Make Enemies, Laugh, Cry, etc.), Decisions (Right, Wrong), Sodium Benzoate (preservative), A Mind, Desire, Want, A Memory, Caffeine, Imperfections, Muscle, Fat.
Love,
Care,
And,
Conviction,

Truth.
Canned by a member of the CEC Bottling Group, Atlanta,
Georgia 30336 under the authority of no one in partic-
ULAR for your senses' enjoyment and refreshment.

Please recycle

Then, the usual occurred. Boredom set in again. Here, an ode to Nirvana.

Strawberry Chains

     Lost
Alone
     in chains
Yet, cannot see them
More secure than strawberries
Almost ripe in what they'll get.

Sad
In ties
    wondering
And faltering
More secure than strawberries
Almost ripe in what they'll do.

Exploding I know how we're supposed to be
I know I want to level buildings with my own emotional fate
Crazy lies I'm not sure how to deal with this
I'm pleading, then about to explode…

    Poised
Inane
    close
Yet far
From bubbling up
And bouncing around this old road.

    Tapped
In to
    silenced
Simple understanding
Like strawberries, we're going to blow…

    Simply
Put:
    Blue in homely feeling
Yet so red in their undying love.

Lost and
    Taught
To learn to live for all the days
The eight days that they will live…

    Words are
False
    All the words
Are worthless
My world is based on nothing,
Maybe that's where I've gone wrong.

    Lost
Alone
    in chains
Yet, cannot break them,
Forced into a strawberry world…

Geoffrey Dilenschneider

Here, an example of my mind's idea of the rise and fall acquainted to school verve: The Desire Original, the Humor, the Admittance of Monotony, the Second Wind, the Strokes of Genius (5 of 'em), the Realization of the Cycle, the Segment of Irrationality, the Re-Realization that it is Worthless, the Final Grasp for Help, the Death of a Man that Ends With What he Wanted to Be. This could be a true replication of the Cycle we all go through, or it could be happenstance poems, chronologically correct but an accidental representation of the previously mentioned cycle. Who knows?

The Match Inside Us All

I am the strike of a match,
Ready and waiting.
I am here to ignite your world,
Precariously debating.
I am here on one divine mission
To rid the world of you.
Nonviolently, of course,
But too much trouble has been the cause of you.

I will walk in,
Put my water on the table,
And walk out
In all my flashing glory.

I will stop the talking
I will stop the fly.
I am here to stick the stuck
And burn the knotted tie.
I am here to cut the silence,
I'm here to sap the power.
I want to come and fool you all
I'm here to steal your hour.
I'm here to folly all the love
And make the lovers cower.
I'm here to make the doves of love
Turn ugly, yellow, sour.

I am here to light the fires
Of our sickened days
I am the match to cut your lives
And these are pure my ways.

When I Lie Fine

I learned to ski when I was seven,
Found myself flying down to heaven
Swishing child in love, was I
Finding freedom on the mountain's top
And there I saw the whole wide world!
Its greens and blues so true to life
In all its forms in glorious vibrancy.
I haven't skied since I was seven
(Except when I was nine.)
Since then I've dearly missed my heaven
(Except when I lie fine.)

I Grow Old

I grow old, I grow old
My old ways are so sold
To the highest slow bidder
Who called out in the end
To the ways that are practiced
I grow old.

I am told, I am told
That I must not catch a cold
Or my life will quickly end
And I'm lost in slavery
And everything is so alone,
I am told.

I grow old, I grow old
And life meanders on
Moving here, moving there
And sometimes it will change,
But in the end as I lie
I find nothing here to comfort
And I'm losing, but I'm lost
All I know seems simply gone
I grow old.

All the World's A Freewrite

All the day is a freewrite,
Set in its regimented ways.
Day in, day out
In hours, gout.

All the world's a freewrite
Turning over in its present grave
Closer we move as a whole
To the finish we know we stole
For we are not meant to be thinking
It is a gift we have grabbed
For ourselves.

And all the world's a lie,
I've concluded,
Laughing at the sky,
Here's the place we live and die
So rudely
We are awoke
To breathe and learn and choke,
And all the day's a freewrite
As I lie here as a joke
            Without free right to fight
            And I lie here
            Drowned
            In spite.

Death Ball

It flows Indus lemma
Forgotten in pride
Procuring hiero
Soft epicure lied.
My slow shuttered shroud
Self-sought canes slowly shriving
Shutterbug lies.
Shy sibilance from Sphenoid
The overkill death ball
Has found out the fig.

The fiftieth fifth wheel
Figures lame is its bray
Lady slippers fall
Yet, let us be laid!
And let that fall back
To the earliest morns
Now is the pastime of
Passacaglia
Our mystical movement
Is a beautiful musk
And we may be dead 'morrow,
But let's dance until dusk.

The Found-Out Fig

My fictionalized fibroblast fidgeting fickle
      Ran romance like Rollo in rhythm
He jostled and jowled at the judge-made Jove jickle
      Through passageways platt, pleathed, and piton.
He nicked his own nib from the new-moon nude no-par
      Tipping tall tanners from tipsy tad poles.
      But then he for tarried taint terminal-leave tar
And out nabbed the nebul of that old fig Non-prose
      Pleating the plans for his pice-par
But his jugglery jousted the jovial guard-rose
      He ran his rage rainstorm around romantic rachis
And from false ferriting feelings of fear
Our funny old fig found his dance and his peer.

Indus Lemma

We are flowing
Flowing like the river
Sparkling like the nubile stars and moving incognito with the wind.
Content in our sweet sweat
Simply like the river
As we come to one while flowing with the sin.
We are wheiling
Dining 'night this sliver
Sliver of the moon we dine and lose our souls to light.
We are flowing
Flowing like the wind beneath our wings
As we fly and kiss the sky so endlessly in sight.
We are flowing
Flowing like the river
But the river ends and we go on and are lost like stringless kites.

Lady-Slippers

Selfless blowing
Gate-crashed sowing
Intimate, decadent, sensitive,
Lords don't know
How you flow
But big-ticket
Scampering here yet so graceful
Lost and yet found in mere moments,
Laughing, yet shedding
The tears of remorse
Or maybe it's just what we're seeing
Breathing,

Leaving us to our own slow masque
Lowly in fortitude
Boring in plot
We all have known that our mark
Is a dot.
Caring,
Yet daring,
Calm and alone
Yet you're so on your own we fly
Towards you
Yet lose you,
The one whose mind is a riddle
Fiddle
With our heads!
Down the beds!
Kitten,
Leave us alone
We aren't men on a lone
We can't stand you
Mirand you
Maybe try
With a tri-
Fection
Perfection

Pensive sweetness
Not so cheatless,
But we'd glad forget
All the chit
Chat and that
Graceful blowing
Del'cate knowing
Let us run
Let us hide
You decide
We can't
Forget you:
Intimate, decadent, sensitive…
Trying, yet not seeming so…
Beautiful, twisting, tall…
Forceful and lovely and
Perfect
So perfect
A slipper of lady-like care.

Let's Dance Until Dusk

I wish to be a candy lace
Considerless upon you –
Right there upon that settled neck
So supple, soft, and full, true.

I wish to hold the world conserved,
Indicative sweet song,
And leaning always, hear the words
And hold your full lips long.

I wish to move in unison,
Yet be carefree in our ways –
Incurvate here and there forever!
Hold fast in these crazy days!

I wish to twirl around froward
Coloring here and there –
Peppered with the honey-sickle
As we surround ourselves in hair.

I wish to pause our daily juggle
To mend our flowing heart –
Young pence we are, 'til death we are one
Let's dance 'til dusk do we part.

On the Tips of Tongues

Beginninglookwonderuncertaintyunderstandingsmilelookagain
wonderdelighttalk(introduce)gettoknoweachother
love(truealwaysandforeverfirstkisstouchfeelsexdifferenceanoyancebreakup)
backtonormallifedistanceendandwonder

Just a Little Yellow Square

The polite man sits here unaware
Maybe we can be like him
What have I been doing here?
Am I lost?
The shadow of a little square
Sits upon my yellow hair
Maybe we could once compare
To the lost and livened care
Who are we
The ones who fail
Is it me who wonders why?

Falling down [simply to die?]
Turning
To our lonely lives
But here we all are once again
Wonder why oh I wonder what
I think that our lies are lost cuts
Glasses surrounding lost old men
Is it wonder when we call?

Why'd we say, I love you dear?
Lost little leaves floating everywhere
Don't we know, oh can't we care?
I think it's time for truth or dare
Nothing will be better now
Why can't we just figure this out?

Glances fall, we've lost it all
Maybe this time we won't fall
Calm it down, babe, we are here
To lose it light and lend an ear
Tinkle tinkle, here we go
Back to places less and low
It's not enough that our world's fine
What of squares and rosy rhyme?
Darker, darker, faces glow,
Everything's around me curled
Seems to be the whole wide world
Staring in that blind man's face
All my world stares at my face

Cherry bombs, and fun masters
Lost old men and endless seas
Giant dogs and teeny fleas
Upset grass and worthless walls
Cold pizza and flowing blondes
Spinning spinning, it's not enough
Spinning spinning, it's not enough
The things we make inside a bluff
Can I leave now, I've had enough
Polite man, please, stop staring now
Pass the bread and sing songs now
Tell me of my better days
Turning, learning, breathing days
Away from every, every thing
That makes us hate
That makes us sin…
Now then the world turns black on me,
Polite man's gone, as I can see

Slowly floating up the sky
Everything makes much more sense…
The men have stopped now asking why
And now I'm floating blackness hence,
Alone and cold in yellow hair,
Just a little yellow square.

Here We Are

Everything seems just a bit
A bit too good for me.
Everything seems just a bit
A bit too sunny.

Everyone must think that we
Are nuts
No one wonders why
We have to keep moving.

Here we are in our own cells
So alone and cold.
Living a life we can't make
Yet a life that's ours.

We should know why
We are chained to self
We should know why
We can't move on

Left alone we make a mess
Uncleaned.
I wonder why we
Move unhurt.

Holding on to things that
Go away,
Here we are in a place that
We can't control.

      Here we
      May go again
      Down into
      Down into death
      To a place
      So cold
      Down into
      Down into death

There has got to
Be some way out of here
There has got to
Be a way of change.

Here we are in
Love with life, but
Something grabs and
Pulls us down in tar

And there's no time to
Wonder what happened
And we get what
We deserved to get.

Now our penance starts
With re-learning.
What to do, oh
What can we do?

Maybe this is
The time to start again
Expel out all things
That have taken us.

Find the light a-
-bove our small heads
left alone and
unaware of love…

      Here we
      May go again
      Down into
      Down into death
      To a place
      So cold
      Down into
      Down into death

Maybe it is time to
Maybe it is time to
Maybe we should change our
Maybe we should change our
Maybe we should look (ahead)
Maybe we should look ahead!

Flight Attendant Joy

What is behind those eyes?
What is there when you glance down at me?
Why so bored
And who are you
And what may you may mean?
Why this job and what's your beauty,
Who may you might be?
Why so sad and why so tired?
I feel like it may be my job
To make your worth my while.

To Want to Be Lovely and Fair

It's pretty
It's pretty
With fuzzy tail
And furry eyes
And lovely things escape me
Like cops from robbers
          backwards in this slow world.
I want to be given pretty, nice things,
Fragranced things, lovely things.
I want a cuddly something to hold onto
When I'm lonely
When I'm lonely.

I'd like to be fair
And free
     so calm and talkative
In tune with myself
And so happy
Happy with wonder
And a twinkle in my eye
And a twinkle in my eye

Chapter 25, 26

They say a fool is one who repeats the same mistake without learning from it. Well, then I am a fool; a fool for Katie Bennet.

My Dreams of Queens

I want a beautiful queen
To send me to my greatest dream
Lullaby in faces fairly
Fair in ways and beautiful wear'ly

Secrets on a small-signed, flowing
Fell like snow on green trees growing
Just like all my dreams of peace
Where everything fake except us ceased.

And in our break, we mean ungrown
To baby ways and clothes unsown
Yet here we are in life so grand,
Two people living lives so bland.

But maybe queens aren't just in books,
Giving servants dirty looks.
Will you be my queen to covet,
Lying lean in grass so green,
Yet thinking all and nothing of it?

I Am Mesmerized

A teacup of lovely affair,
Held atop like Chinese hair
By chopsticks knotted up in there,
Lovely, timely, meant and fair.

A teacup of great desire,
Searching for the tasteful lighter,
Lost of nothing in the senses,
Having no material fences.

A teacup of never running,
Full of words deviled and cunning,
Frothed of spice and topped with foam,
In her eyes are things alone.

A teacup of simple beauty,
Not a word could 'scribe this cutey,
Perfect in her mane of mist,
Cherry-plumbed and dew-drop kissed,
Ready for this senseless ride,
Not a care; she'll never hide
Touching soft, white arms to side,
Loving taste and beaming pride;
Lovely, timely, meant, and fair,
A teacup of lovely,
Lovely affair.

Whispered

You are beautiful
To me
I can't believe you talk to me.
When spices peppered free Ali
And meet Virginia
I can't believe the shakes find ways to me.
And everything
Is just a dream
When I'm thinking,   breathing
Wonderin' of leavin' but I cannot think the thought.

You are beautiful
To me
But my dream is shattered
By the insane spin of this world
And everything is beautiful…
But not as beautiful as you are.

The Dream of You

Great things come in the smallest packages
You are one of those pretty packages
Yet not at all a pretty girl
For what I see inside.

Complemented by your heart,
Left natural by smiles.
I can travel feet in seconds,
But you can travel miles.

I wonder what I'll never,
Ever get to know
About your boons, about your banes,
About your pretty soul.

Geoffrey Dilenschneider

And it does not stop at your mere beauty!
I could tell right off!
I can tell you're kind and gentle
By your skin so soft.

Clasped in memories at all moments
Will I ever be,
Grasped forever by these moments,
Wishing you I'd see.

Trapped inside perfection
Recognized by only few –
I would stay with you forever
If only you were true.

Now, I never wanted to get between Katie and her boyfriend; that was never my inten-
tion. To ruin something like what they had (and still have for all I know) would be a
sick thing to do. I didn't have the heart to ruin their relationship, so I concealed my
writings inspired by her in the mask of her simply being 'my muse'. Truly, she prob-
ably was my muse for a long while, and probably will be for much time to come, but I
couldn't let my emotions get in the way of my writing.

That might sound a little off. You ask, 'but isn't writing all about emotion?'
Well, yes, but to a point. There is a certain level on which emotional writing lives.
There are other levels as well: physical, mental, soul, purpose, and need. Those are the
basic levels on which the writing I have come across live (the list didn't include emo-
tion because it was already mentioned as one). Through these, writing is created.
Without them, I don't know. It is the strong that survive the challenging times and
the weak that survive the simple times. The weak sometimes survive. It depends on
the luck of the draw for them.

Anyway, there was a small break in school, so I took a trip down to Florida to visit
the International Society of Poets convention going on at Universal Studios Florida.
While there, I met a few girls. They were locals – a bit of scene color, if you may – and
we hit it off pretty well for two days.

On this poem, I was trying to get one of them – a short, spunky 15 year old – to
write a poem, but she insisted that she could never, so I wrote, YOU'RE FUNNY on
the middle of a doodle-ridden page and asked her to write under it a poem – 'just
whatever comes to mind.' But she couldn't, so I did instead.

YOU'RE FUNNY

You're funny
And yet the hyenas who just will not stop
Until they run, until they drop
And shatter glass-like into pieces,
We'll pick up all the reeses' pieces,
And laugh and say
You're funny.

Then I went nuts. We were just kids having fun when she said she was in love with me. (I didn't believe her for a second, but I went along with it and wrote this poem for her, but when writing it, thought only about a certain someone back at home.

Relive the Magic

I'm so in love with you!
I cannot let it go
I cannot let my sadness show
And I'm so in love with you!

       I met you for the first time last night
And... I looked into your eyes
I said, "let's relive the magic,
    Forget about our size,
    Let the world take out our pain
    And memories that yell,
    Spacing in between some more
    The times we cannot tell.
    And can we live the magic
    For the very first time
    Once and only, now and ever,
    Love, our siamese rhyme?"
And you, you stared... and stared... and cried.
I died   inside.
My face turned yellow,
My dreams fell dead
From the black sky,
Refilled with dread.
       And I went home and smashed my walls,
I damned the world to hell!
I wanted everything to die!
To die in pain, to scream and yell!
Our siamese rhyme meant nothing
Nothing except the lie:
The lie of love, the lie of life!
That tells and drinks and tries!
       I digress... for in my world, in my siamese dream
Are many golden floral reefs
Encircling my whole,
This way I have grown up to be,
In heart, in mind, in soul.
         And I'm so in love with you!
         I cannot let it go!
         I must admit my dream of snow
         And I'm so in love with you.

The Knowledge I Gain From Your Eyes

I want to be
The man to be
But I'm blind
And yet can see.

I want to find
The really kind
That are not broke
Of soul and mind.

I belong to you
I know that it is true
But I find I'm free
When I say, "I love you, too."

I stop to lie
Under the sky
But find I'm running
Not to die.

I lose, I lose,
Try not to choose
But end up crying
When I wet my shoes.

Stripped together,
Pinched in leather
But find I'm lost
Unto the weather.

I stand alone
Not yet full grown
Yet stead so tall
When with my own.

I lose the lost
To skip the cost
But say I'm sorry
When games are lost.

I need the words
To call the herds
Yet have no voice
To stall the birds.

For all I know is this:
The best of ways to kiss
But never am I whole,
Just a vision in the mist.

Following and followed
Are kittens' furballs swallowed
By the curtsey-lies of pretty girls
Stalked and stalked and followed.

Afraid am I to love
Afraid of one small shove
Complete me, God! I beg you!
Show me who's my love!

I miss the world
When set aside
The world misses me
When I have lied.

I set myself
Upon these rocks
To show the world
And knock their socks.

I picture this:
A love-self world
And picture this world:
A push-shove pearl.

A step in direction soft
Brings memories of the past
Of all our life in which we play
A part of every cast.

And show our own selves
From out the curtain,
To make Us real
And make Them certain.

Jealousy and hate and rage
All together smother,
So put away your brazened fists
To walk within all others.   {To finally complete each other}

Flow, flow,
This I know:
In all, gold travels
But not to show.

Belong to one
And do not shun
Yet be alive,
Not held by guns.

Drink wine, be merry
Show pride, be wary
But be the real you
Not some Tom, Dick, or Harry.

And make twist
Get the gist
But accomplish all
On life's long list.

Share care
And stare
Yet don't be sick
When asked to be fair.

Call this earth
Your place of birth
But complete the cycle
With all you're worth.

Then I thought about Katheryn again, and wrote out a twenty-seven page song for her, including music, vocals, lyrics, key changes, everything. It's so long that I don't even want to waste your time. I'll sum it up for you instead: I set free the demons I had always felt that were clawing away inside of me, letting them clamp onto the pages in front of me instead. It did so much good for me to read again the woes of my past that I couldn't but stand and shout, which angered the entire plane that I happened to be on at the time.

When I got back to school, the same was occurring. The struggle of ultimate proportions! The struggle for good grades. This fight, to me, was the most devastating, for it was March: the end of the school year was at hand, my birthday was fast approaching, and it was high time to get down and dirty. For English, it was hopeless; Spanish, I visited a tutor every Tuesday after school, and had been for the past two years; Chemistry, I was going in for extra help, making up work I had missed; World Studies, I was told that I had been getting straight A's by the teacher throughout the entire year; and Creative Writing Advanced, I was told that my poetry was too personal, too 'all about me'. So I began trying to write about anything but anything that had to do with me.

Untainted by Myself (And This: A Poem of Observance)

When you want to itch your leg, you itch
Dappled blue eyes behind two slits
Complemented by soft freckles
Simply there to love the cheeks and dimples
As you smile, a touch of white rows imp out from within,
Behind two full lips crimson
(The lower one a tad bit fuller, a perch for a dainty tongue
That sometimes seems to poke itself outside cautiously
For just a flicker to wonder the weather,
Sniffing blind and pensively.)

Curves caressing curves,
Clothes so tight, yet un-harassing, the light air floats upon your
Aura as if it were there only because of you,
Waiting on its molecule tiptoes to light the life you chose to live,
The sparkle in your eye.
Ends meet ends,
Crossed selves entwined
And find their dainty way back to the roots upon your
Brunette crown, one so careless and so carefree...

> Perfect in the stuttered ways of life
> Soft in fair skin, supple ear lobes,
> Ones to be caressed so slowly,

The ones that blushed-pecked cheeks make human,
The tell-tale sign of budding thoughts, curled around your fragile finger,
Dainty in just one way...
You're dainty in just one way...
Untainted by myself or anyone who happens
Across your soul soft snowing
Thoughts of what lies outside,
But dreams cascading down your heart
Of beauty that only permeates
When you let your self be known.

That failed miserably, so in its stead I tried my hand in humor, joking about the nickname that my grade had been so kind to give me: Dillie; something I now am more fond of, but nonetheless never have really liked that much. Over the months, "Dillie" has infiltrated my life. I can't go anywhere without it. I sign my name "Dillie" now, as well. So, I give in. I hope everyone calls me Dillie. It's a part of me. I am Dillie.

Geoffrey Dilenschneider

Seemingly So

Where did Dillie go?
Where did Dillie go?
He's lost his mind
He's lost his soul,
Bitten fragments floating nowhere
Yet so fast, so quietly
He's lost his meaning,
Lost his pride –
Has no reason
Not to hide.
To him the world is backwards
And meaningless days fly,
Wondering and wondering
How long it takes to die.
He's a boring little tick,
A leaf blown brittle by cold winds
That do not whisper better days
Past little frozen ears.
His words are those of pain
Seen floating from his mouth,
And by their weight drop to the ground
And shatter in his south.

Where did Dillie go?
Where did Dillie go?
He's lost his mind
He's lost his soul
We think he seems it so.
But Dillie is just somewhat bored,
Yet, we will never know.

Everything in the world was going great. Yeah, so what that the stock market wasn't skyrocketing anymore, life was good. Then, of course, the Enron scandal made the front pages.

E

Sick and so lost
Abused and alone
Nowhere to run,
Not sure of the cost
Of your sick, slimy actions,
Fondling your twisted eyes
And licking your wounds.

The love flowing
Has stopped…
Infinity
Has stopped…
The pain you have
Won't stop
And your world beats
All around you,
A sick heart irregular
And you're crying.

A little boy sits
Where a proud man once was…
A gun in his lap
Where a pen used to be
But was he once a man?
Or a cunning, sly, sick fox,
Broken and alone
In a world of silent cost.

And since us kids couldn't really be anything but distantly worried about the Enron scandal and the infuriating wave of business scandals that washed up on shore in the next while, we just kept on doing the one thing we had to do: go to the yellow bus in the morning and scramble the heck on.

I, again, wanted to write about that certain girl – the one I had poked a little fun at earlier – about the falsity of her persona, but it came out as a rash of compliment with only a bit of cynicism in the end.

All Women, Yet One

A woman of wonder,
Beauty floats from your skin,
Moved from a fragrance
To a tempter of sin.

A smile so in-turned,
Cautious and tempting,
Stereotypical in ways still unseen.
Sitting to the side
Of a sad, drooping chair
Yet opposite are your eyes,
As they fall on down in care.
Pain, the factor of your days,
Cold, a cough of all your soul,
Armed with brains and looks to kill
Deep inside, the real cold goal.
Kind in ways that mean so much
Lying baked and flowing soft

Doing this to get that done
Doing that to get this done
But luminescent are your smiles
Full of heart and made to win
Here and there again you fly
Calculating as you lie.

A woman of wonder,
Beauty floats from your skin,
Moved from a fragrance
To a tempter of sin.

And again, I tried to impress my Creative Writing Advanced teacher with my use of humor.

It was a stupid group assignment in which we all put down on little scraps of paper certain things. One, a type of job; two, what that person is doing; and three, where it is happening. The three things each person privately wrote down didn't have to have anything to do with the other two because they would all be folded up and mixed into three different hats; each one for a different of the three. Each person would pick out one from each hat and then write a piece from the three snippets of paper.

A Magician on a Blind Date on top of the Golden Gate Bridge

She is so pretty,
Yet... has one eye,
I'd like to leave
But... don't know why!

It is a little windy,
Here atop the bridge –
And we'll fall off this golden gate
If we move just one small smidge.

I could have zapped us to the moon,
Or... maybe just a bar...
But I've lost my magic wand
(And it flew so very far!)

Now I'm stuck here on this bridge,
With a pedofossil witch,
I guess she, too's a cannibal,
But I don't think we will hitch!

She smells, she reeks,
She cannot hold a knife
(This, because she has no thumbs
Which she lost to her last wife!)

She drools and babbles, sways and yells
I wonder what is wrong.
But the second I start wondering,
She *tells* me I am wrong!

Oh, I wish, I wish I could not hear!
I wish I could not see!
Oh, God, I wish I could not taste,
'Cause, God: she's kissing me!

My friend… oh, my friend…
The one who set us up…
I'm going to lock him in a box
And turn him into a cup!

I'll turn him into a windsock!
I'll turn him into a fish!
I'll turn him into a pretty lady…
Maybe just a looser named Ish!

Now my date is going…
Going down, that is!
Oh boy, oh boy, just shoot me now!
C'mon, man! Do the biz!

'Cause then she wouldn't be so bad,
She'd be just like my mother…
But, man, that would just suck as much,
C'mon, man, think of others!

"Alright, lady, that's enough!
No more touching that!
It's time for you to go on home,"
I said and then I spat.

She stood back up with knobby knees
(Pokin' me with her nose)
And jumped upon her hidden broom,
And to the skies she sweetly rose!

And now I'm all alone here,
The drop sums up my fears –
It's been quite cold and boring here
For the past long twenty years!

Geoffrey Dilenschneider

After that little stint of hilarity, I began pretending like I had someone to love; an entity that has plagued me like the West Nile. Love has never been my friend, as you can tell. It all started back in kindergarten. My first kiss happened not to be by accident, but a highly planned incidence behind the big tree house in the 5th Avenue playground inside of Central Park in New York City – an incidence that occurred more than just once. I've never really told anyone about those times because we were in kindergarten, and my parents would probably send me to a shrink if I told them. And they weren't just 'pecks on the cheek.' They were much more than that. Much more.

One thing I'm not certain of is if I should say her name. I haven't seen her in something like eleven years. She could live in Alaska for all I know. Alisia is all I will say. Alisia, pronounced Ah-líze-ah (the lize is like it sounds in realize, but without the rea.)

Then, since the memories of Alisia became repressed, I became the innocent little guy until I moved to Connecticut. (Of course, in New York I went to Buckley, an all-boys school which I never liked.) A school just down the street from where I lived in Darien, Connecticut, called The Pear Tree Point School, where I spent 5th and 6th grades.

In 5th, I fell madly in love with Emily VanButenen, whose last name I could never spell. She looked a bit like a witch in the face, minus the wart on the nose, but it was blonde love nonetheless. She left at the end of 5th grade, but I kept going.

6th grade consisted of one small cottage at the bottom of the hill on the Pear Tree Point School hill that consisted of a tiny bathroom, a backroom in which one of the more financially-depressed teachers lived, and the classroom. The classroom held 13 students, including myself, 2 teachers, and was the only room we had class in. Oh, and the seats were hard as cold marble. Your butt was flat by the end of the day, and by the end of the year, we all didn't have butts.

During 6th grade I met Kelsey Poulsen, Katie Ceglarski, and Lindsey Campbell. All three were very nice and respectable; Kelsey being the pale Irish; Lindsey, the short and spunky redhead; and Katie the deeply intelligent brunette. I mean no stereotype (I hate stereotypes, actually), but to save time… you know.

I couldn't say that I fell in love with Katie; I didn't know what love was, except for a word in the dictionary. Rather, I felt infatuated. Anyway, I didn't do anything with my heart because I had already given it to a girl named Jen Kirst, whom I forgot to mention was in my 5th grade class, as well. We had kissed by accident near a soda machine on some nameless fieldtrip and ended up 'going out' for a little less than two years, even though the last year of it was more of an 'off and on and off and on again' type of thing.

Then, after a grudgingly painful 6th grade, I went to Greens Farms Academy, a well bred, upper-class private school. Or, as I found out later, the school was a stuck-up, snot-nosed school for rich kids. Not all the kids there were like that, just that there happened to be a vast majority of them. Joakim Steinbeck was a good friend, along with Jon Bauer. Chris Piasecki was who I considered to be my best friend. My worst enemy – see, I thought in simple schema of friend and enemy – was a kid named Zack.

There were a few steamy girls at Greens Farms, but they were mostly in the grades above me. However, there were a few in my grade. There was Sam Levine, a few others whose names I can't recall, and Natalie. Natalie is only worth mentioning because she tried to take me for a ride.

It was eighth grade and it had been widely known that I had had a huge crush on Natalie for a long time. It was the middle of no time in particular during the school year that she started contacting me in various ways; asking me personal questions, hinting at how much she cared about me. On the phone, I specifically remember her using this thick, passionate southern accent, which only drew me closer to her.

I always had a hunch that she was screwing with my head, so I made up in my mind that she wasn't worth it and that I would only continue with her little games to see how cruel she was actually trying to be.

Well, she was trying to be damn cruel, as I quickly found out. She got me all ready for one of the school dances with her regular pep, and she showed me up, didn't return my calls, avoided me in class, giggled to her friends when she was near me in the lunch room, the works. It was so sick what she did. A while later I tried to call her to tell her that she was a sick girl, and all she did was try to entice me all over again.

I didn't take the bait.

I never really liked Greens Farms Academy. It was too rich. I couldn't stand not being able to choose my friends (there were 60 kids in a grade). I got out of there in short order, thank God.

Okay, back to my 10th grade year. It was early March, and I was thinking about my birthday in a month, but more importantly, I was thinking about Katie again.

The Love that Wouldn't Die

Just close your eyes and think of all the times that we were one
Don't think about the pain and don't think about the sun.
Don't think about the moon and all the stars that keep us cold
Just think about the times the tears stop and we can just grow old.

Just close your eyes and think of all the times
Let's show the world that they can't break us down
Let the world know that you won't let go
Show them that we mean too much
To simply pass on by
Wondering of the things that could be
If we had just said hi.

Just close your eyes and wonder why the world hates us so
Imagine if we could reach up and touch the sky
What would it be like if we could see without our eyes
We wouldn't need to cry… we wouldn't need to sigh
Just think about the times that are gone.
Would the world just lead us, or finally let us be?
What would it be like if we were free?

Just close your eyes and hear the chirps of birds just out of sight
Imagine if we could reach up and touch the sky
This battle that we fight will never finish
But the world has not yet won… and our song is not yet sung
Let's sing the song o' th' love that wouldn't die.

I see us growing old together
I see us happy now
I see us safe and sound together

Geoffrey Dilenschneider

But I can't see you now.
I see that we can touch the sky
I see us flying now
I see us lovin' every second,
But I can't see you now.

Now, remember that girl that I used as a plaything for those other two humorous poems? Yeah, here's number three.

{Name Omitted}

A wonderful woman so whimsical,
Waiting without the world on her shoulders
Sloping sensually to the fingertips that dazzle with their work.
Waiting, grasping, reaching, reaching
Reaching for something in others
Praying for something much greater
Eyes light blue, yet deep with knowing
Frugality, reality
"What to do with myself," she continues asking
Silent, sitting soft and slowing
To the pace of life
Surprised to smile yet yawing still,
Young in love's sweet lie.
A sadness settles simply in your sparkling, light blue eyes,
But will you find? darting back and forth your eyes
Searching still for something simple,
Still and deeply routed.
Reserved and lovely,
Tamed and turning to the sky
To whisper wilting words of some forgotten lasting wisdom.
Soft and supple, a woman who loves nothing but herself
Alone in a world in which she's centered
Yet set so aside in the real.

Then, after many 48 minute periods of English full of Ali Watts screwing with my head (not as severely as Natalie did, though), I realized that she wasn't worth it, either.

Laughing at my Face, but not a Smile Shows

Verse I　You mean nothing to me
　　　　You're a lie and I can't stand your sullen outlook,
　　　　I don't care if you smile
　　　　I don't care what you do
　　　　I don't give a damn about you.

I don't want to relive the sea.
The eyes you pull are teeth to me, and we'll see
Just what lies you make up
And the way you're so new
All I know is I hate
That I want you.

Chorus The terror of your heart of hearts
Is carried by some giant cart
Over everything it rolls
Everything including me
But the world is round
And we all fall down
But I can't stand bein' down all the time

Verse II You're just a lovely ass
You're a sick'ning, twisted bitch who takes boys' minds to see
Just how quick you can break 'em
Just to see how much we scream
I don't give a damn about you.

Your mind's as deep as my pool
But it's empty, you damn slut, just stop banging those fat jocks
They use you
But you don't care
And nothing seems wrong
And you should find someone better
And all I know is I hate
That I want you

I read a story by Ray Bradbury called Kaleidoscope, *which happened to really freak me out, as well as hit me deep down. The story is basically about a bunch of spacemen whose ship explodes and they are all floating away from each other into space in their spacesuits, waiting to die. The story is simply their discussion while they float aimlessly, unable to change their trajectory.*

Then I began to feel like the world should never have happened. Not the Earth itself; rather, the world the human race has created. The sick, twisted world; the horrible, lost, damned world we're forced to stay in because there is nowhere else.

The Wandering

The world's not meant to rise from darkness...
The world's not meant to flow.
The world's not meant to stay together...
The world's not meant to grow.

We aren't meant to love each other
We aren't meant to love ourselves;
We aren't meant to learn and prosper
We aren't meant to leave our shelves.

We aren't meant to change, to differ…
We're meant to cheat and lie.
We aren't meant to work for better…
We're just meant to die.

The heart's not pure,
The soul's not free –
The mind is set
To trick and bleed

While pain takes hold
Of our safe breath
And lies to us
With seed…

Which says to us
That it is good,
Yet a few
May hear the creed:

"Show the world who you must be
Show the whole world all your soul:
Bring your anger, bring your lies,
Love the life you lead

Search your eyes for bits of truth,
Find your gaping hole…
The world's not meant to rise from darkness,
So continue on and breed."

The Great-Ending Party

Old, old felt Bauer; so old. But what was wrong with him? Bauer opened his sun-gold eyes to the twisted gray features of the dead house. His wife, Melissa, sat up in bed, sensing his thoughts.

"We *are* old," she said in an old tongue, whispering it on the stale winds. Ever since the world died and they were left alone there on the gray Martian dirt, things had been changing.

"Or maybe they never changed," Bauer thought, "Maybe they had always been like that.

He got slowly out of bed, massaging the back of his wrinkled neck. Remembering what it was like when all his friends had been here, Bauer stumbled over to the mirror in the small, dark bathroom, and took a scared peak out of the corner of his eye.

"Hey, Melissa… my hair is all gray." Bauer realized he was also a bit gray in the face, so he washed his face in the cool morning water, gliding down into the sink.

"No, it has always been like that." Melissa said, barely hinting at emotion. She was just playing along. "Every day he sees something gray," she thought. "It is expected, what with his condition and all. Maybe he'll go back to sleep and I can get back to sleep. There is a lot to do today. As far as he knows, he is just going a bit mad, that's all." She could read his mind like an open book, and he had no idea of the Party.

Bauer was downstairs now, pouring the orange juice from the container into a nice color-flux glass, letting the hues melt with the temperature of the liquid.

"Hey, Meliss, I'm gonna go to the observatory in a few minutes… wanna come?" Bauer yelled feebly up to his wife. She nodded, even though Bauer couldn't see her, waited a few seconds, and heard the door slam. Now she had the creaky house all to herself. She got to work.

Bauer didn't know much, but he knew he loved his wife, his job, and his telescope. He knew three other things: the world dies forty-five years ago, he and his wife were the only ones left on Mars until Sissy, Meliss's best friend, shows up eight months later, and third, there was a primordial soup brewing down on the dead 3rd planet from the sun.

He also knew that his job was to watch the growth of the earth through his telescope and record the evolution of the new earth.

Bauer wasn't stupid. He knew that something was very strange on this new planet. That was just it, too! He'd been there for forty-five years, but everything always seemed so very new. Nothing got old, or… maybe everything got old so quickly that it was reborn without him noticing.

Meandering down the silver-painted sidewalk to the observatory, Bauer looked up at the cool, bland sky. Day had just begun and here he was, two days away from being eighty, still pretending it was all okay. Bauer wondered how his wife could stand the loneliness; *he* couldn't. He remembered his world before the Rocket Trip… his Routine. Six a.m., wake up and get dressed. Six-thirty, walk down the road with Frank, Chris, and Andie; get to the beach, watch the sunrise, walk home. Go to work, pretend to do work until quitting time, go home the long way, stopping at the liquor store for the Jack, kiss the wife, go to sleep. But things changed. The War came and for the Rocket Trip, he was chosen. For his skill, of course, and he had refused to go without his family. There had been eight hundred people from all walks of life in the Rocket, all chosen for their specific trait or skill, some with their families, some alone. Some with girlfriends, some with grandmothers. There were places put away that had every kind of plant and every kind of animal. It was basically a twenty-second century Noah's ark.

Now, though, there were no flowers in the gray gardens. There were no dogs barking frightfully at little birds. Frank, his stupid lopsided grin, gone. Chris, small and so rat-like, dull red hair, gone. Andie, his little cartoons not there on the paper anymore, his best friend, gone. To where did they all travel? To where had the birds and bees and sycamore trees traversed? What distant, invisible place were the newborn puppies and smiling faces hiding? Silence was beginning to become unbearable.

Geoffrey Dilenschneider

"But life goes on, right?" Bauer asked himself, looking to the filmy distant emptiness for an answer.

. . .

The house was quite buzzing with people by the time Meliss finished her phone calls. Everyone was there: Chris was upstairs finding the party lights and Andie was downstairs in the basement rummaging the cavernous sub-zero storage unit for some bottles of old wine and champagne.

Ron was, at the moment, drunk to sleep on the floor, as usual (he couldn't handle the Job). Carl was over with his Mrs. Carolynian, socializing, and, of course, the local jock: sweet, sweet Jon Twain, was hamming it up with his imaginary buds. They couldn't see each other, of course.

Meliss sighed with the power of a vacuum. She was so tired, but couldn't wait to end Bauer's dry days with the Party. The Party, which had been originally planned for two months from today on the spot, had to be rescheduled because they had realized that their calculations had been incorrect and that the Great Winds would have been in full swing by then.

Just then, Sissy was at her side, whispering in her ear: 'Finally, the Party are beginning. You can tell, Missy, you can tell! It won't be long now before it's just us again, waiting for them to grow out again.' She was bending over to whisper into Melissa's ear.

'Hush, girl! Don't speak about that here!' hissed Bauer's tiny wife.

'Well,' Sissy began very indignantly, 'I'm just reporting that everyone on mars that needs to be here is here... except your husband..." Sissy had gotten to calling Bauer Melissa's husband, 'So, it's only a matter of time.'

'I give him two hours.' Missy replied frankly.

. . .

'Sweet Jesus, what a bite!' Bauer exhaled. He was sitting on the curb outside the abandoned general store, even though it looked anything but abandoned. Actually, it looked more like everyone had just up and left it, as well as the entire town, really. The old dusty windows stared down at his back menacingly, making Bauer feel uncomfortable all alone there. Vaguely, he heard noises: groans, squeaks, voices, children, interspersed and whispered explosively in the deafening silence. He yelled suddenly: 'I hate it, blast you! You're an inconvenience and a nuisance! AHHH!' He became more timid then, 'Oh, what's the use? I'm crazy. Damn Argon. It's in the atmosphere; it's in the air. It's everywhere. I've been changing and I know it, but what can I do?' Bauer got up from his place, leaving the Jack Daniels on the sidewalk. 'Better get home.'

So he walked: through the gray field where the children used to play ball, over the old Lover's Lane, past his friends' houses, and, finally, to his house, gray and ugly like the rest of them.

He really wished that it was the way he remembered it, but he was even starting to question his own memory. Did he really recollect what it was like before everything went away? Why did the images of the new Earth seem to be repeating, like a movie replayed over and over again? What was wrong with Missy? She has been acting very strangely the past three weeks, like something big was coming up. Were people really gone or was it just Bauer? Was he just not able to see them? Why wasn't he allowed to go over the hills to where the Grave Yards are? Why did Missy have so much control over him? She could read his mind, it seemed. But Bauer thought none of this, for he had just realized that the whole world was gray; not different shades of gray like the old black and whites, but one continuous gray; even his own body and clothes; it was all one tone of blandness personified. Bauer jumped back, scared pale. He looked around at the gray lawns, the slow, gray sky; at the dark empty windows, and the sleepy, monotonous world he called home. Bauer wanted to cry. Where was everyone? Where'd they all go? Now all there was, was his stupid house; just a lonely last place, waiting to just disappear like everyone else on this worthless planet. 'It's just me and Meliss left, but what's the point? She doesn't love me anymore. Like she wants me to die; like she's waiting. Ah, consequence of life, I guess.'

Suddenly, Bauer understood what was happening; the pieces of the puzzle were complete. Andie had been right; about the end, about Meliss. He wasn't even sure if there was an Andie anymore, if all those memories in his head were really just dreams. He did, however, understand now about this world. All the information he had learned on that fateful day so long ago was flooding back into his head like food into a starving man's mouth. He understood why she was the *only* woman on the planet. Meliss was his *caretaker*. He knew why: life for men is simple. The women are in control, and there were many more women than he could see. He knew that much. He also knew that the last so-called Party had passed him by. He was the one. Well, he had been the one. Now, he would end up like the rest of the guys. Sad, really. But what can you do when you're not the one in control anymore? What can you do if you've never really been in control at all; only made to believe that you were? The life you live is only what you make of it in the time you're allowed.

Why things turn gray? Oh, Bauer didn't know everything. And neither did ol' Andie, but he sure seemed like he had.

Bauer took a last look down the tired road, at all the quiet and sleepy houses, pondering his damned, silent existence. The trees hadn't rustled in a long, long time.

It seemed as though the only thing that moved anymore was the sky, the only place that no one controlled. It was no use, though. He was not the sky; he was Bauer, husband of a thief, and astronomer with no stars to look at. 'I guess the girls have conquered all the other planets already. Maybe this is the last one. Or maybe they don't conquer; just dominate. Missy always loved control. I didn't let her know I knew, but I did. I knew, I just didn't *know*.'

Bauer took one last glance at the unseen Grave Yards that lay just beyond the gray hills, and then he walked up the steps and into his house where the Great-Ending Party was about to take place."

"And that, children, is the story of the origin of our species," Melissa said, closing the large book in a cloud of dust, "And we must take great care in remembering the messages of the story, children, for it explains the delicate balance that is necessary to keep our planet alive, as well as the genius behind our methods and the meaning of the Ending Parties that we still have today."

"How old is that story, Miss Teacher?" Asked a little blonde girl sitting in the front row.

"Well, Sally-Sue, the four hundred and fiftieth anniversary of the Great-Ending Party is coming up in a few months. You should know that, Sally-Sue."

"I know," the child said dejectedly.

"...But it's okay. You are a good girl, Sally-Sue. You will grow up to be a very old and wise Wife. You know that it is right to ask questions."

Another hand rose shyly up above the field of heads that covered the floor of the metallic room.

"Yes?" said the Teacher.

The voice attached to the raised hand spoke out amongst the field of silver: "Are... are you the same Meliss as the Meliss from the story, Miss Teacher?"

"Why, yes... I am, Maxine... yes I am."

Then I reasoned that there were answers; just that we would never find them. I was bored, so I felt it fitting to write a grandiose poem or two about the terrible, stormy search for answers.

Untouched (Part 1)

You are poised... poised... poised... poised... poised... poised
... poised... poised... poised... poised... poised... poised
And at twelve o'clock the clock strikes six and you will fall
And fly and fall and fly and fall and fly and fall
And get up once again to find the rain that has not fallen,
Lost into the winds of wars and "why?" you wonder as you sing
Of everything that's lost and found and lost and found in time that has no meaning
But it chains you and it maims you in a place that contemplates:
The death of stars and yet it cannot lie in eight long years
That it would take for all the simple beauty
Of an answer to appear.

You are tapping... tapping... tapping... tapping... tapping... tapping
And you see the things not many see
And wonder all and wonder all and wonder all
About the world you cannot see, too blinded by your made-up
Tales of lives that have yet to and never will
Hit paradoxical types of false culminations
That you have worked so hard to find and lose again and lose again
And you, the one, and you, the one, that understands corruption
And yet still cannot find ways to unchain even your own perfect self
While death and life and death and life move in and out of twisted plots
All searching different corners for this one exact same thing:
The one thing that your pretty eyes hold open in locked rooms
that show the world where it may search for:
all the simple beauty of a clear-blue sample of real peace
in one form of all true power held apart by wisdom in its love...
          the simply beauty of an answer that cannot appear.

Do not cry… for they are poised and pretty… and to you, nothing else matters…

The simple beauty of an answer that cannot appear
The simple beauty of an answer that cannot appear
The simple beauty of an answer that cannot appear
In front of eyes that are so young and old and young and old
That cannot see the world for what it really is
About: the pain, the hate, the love, the lies, corruption coming from a place
That's not at all a place outside, but rather small and deep inside:
The soul of tainted beings that have left the simple path
That's meant to stay desire, "stay desire, keep me happy, keep me lovely
Chain me if you must and never let go of me, blind and beaten, blind and beaten,"
But this God that you've created
Must and does forever show us just where not to go:
     In search of all the simple beauty of the answers that cannot appear.

And here you are alone and cold just through the fray into your end
That is the way it's meant to be: so final, finite, damning, soft
Bored, you may be, but this is your end, you should be so happily! No more pain
Or hate or rage or death, or hunger cost or hardships, strife
Or need or want or anger (that is where it never stops) and no more sin
Or love or peace or simple beauty for the world in which you've lost
Because your time expired through the fine mesh we call hope:
The false truths that your world is still there, totally preserved,
Yet you know that it is nothing but decayed and lost, alone and cold
In sick, wet places, touched and tainted, touched and tainted
     By the search for the simple beauty of the answers that could not appear.
Because they've lost the poised, neat manner that rain falls when it's not blown
All the wrong ways up and flies and falls and flies and falls
And *you*, it chains you and it maims you, tapping on you through corruption,
Cracked by so much time spent searching, searching, searching
For the tainted lies about the pain, the hate, the love, the lies, the loss, the
Hope
That flows and flows and flows through you and everything,
     Forever searching for all the simple beauty of the answer that might appear.

Untouched (Part 2)

The world, it flies in pain in pain just like the concept we now call self,
And you, this you, imagine what you want to be
Add that to who you hate and love, admire, lust for, and distrust
And lie inside yourself tied down and down and down
In nightengown so flowing in the absent wind that will not blow
You will not grow
Because you don't know why, but wonder nonetheless
As tigerlilly soul fall leaves float through you
Prickily, prickily, with the tingl'ing poised and searching question
       Of will we once succeed.

You, a woman, you, a man, you the God so in demand that dances still on windowsill,
A porcelain figurine in limelight there for you to be alive
And yet your catatonic state that yells but stares with piercing hate
Relives all day the summer day where hell froze over and pigs could fly
With little white wings on their shoulders topped with the little lace bowties –
You wonder why you wonder of the reason there are lies
Why you suffer, feel one way, fall and break in *just* that way
While the windowsill once has to break, you know, but still you dance,
And click your forced old fingers, and on each of your old bony fingers
Are tied the red lace tight ol' bunny-rabbit ears,
Droopy, sorrowed, there for years and all you ever do is dance,
'Cause that is what you're for!
Don't you hate the fact that all you're worth is all you are
And that you're just a little pawn inside somebody's palm,
Sticky and much warmer every day it sometimes feels when everything
Is really nothing in a way simply too deep and odd to ever understand
Which brings us to a point where you can only drive back to your meaning
With a long face from your searching and ask the same old worthless question
With the want of every man, but secretly you know inside that everything's worth
                                              nothing now
And really never has had meaning, even your own self is pointless,
But nonetheless you ask the timeless question with defeated eyes,
Motioning towards all the world and straining your tan neck straight up
And crying to the sky
That all the world must hate you now because it's taken reference points
And thrown them though a hand-sized window,
Giggling and snickering, and bickering, and stop............
…
and at twelve o'clock the clock strikes six and you will fall
and fly and fall and fly and fall and fly and fall
and get up once again to find the rain that has not fallen,
lost into the winds of wars and "why?" you wonder as you sing
of everything that's lost and found and lost and found in time that has no meaning…
but it chains you and it maims you in a place that contemplates
the death of stars, the life of stars, and yet it cannot lie
in the time that it would take for all the simple beauty of answer
to the question so unknown and just impossible; but the question of
Just why we must succeed.

Katheryn called one night. The conversation was going fine until we started talking about the boat.

During that phone call, she came clean with the fact that she felt the cruise was a very negative experience for her because we were saying goodbye as we said hello.

Alone

I don't know
What to do
I don't know
How it feels
I don't know
Why we waited
I don't know
What has changed
I don't know
Why it hurts
I don't know
Where you are

I don't know
Why everything's broken
I don't know
Why the world's insane
I don't know
Why I am crying
But I taste
My salty tears

I'm not sure
If the earth will turn
I'm not sure
If we've changed
I used to know
Why it's worth it
But I don't know
It all anymore

I don't know
Why I'm here
I don't know
Why I'm alone
I don't know
What is right
Anymore than
What is wrong

I don't know
What to do
I don't know
What to say
I don't know
What you're doing
And all I know
Is you're so far away

And I'm so alone
Thinking of you
Dangling here
On a spider's web
I play a song
But it's not good
Because it's missing something...
It's missing you.

To the Shoe

Slow, but what does love do *to* us?
Break or wring or stress or taint us?
To the shoe
That kicks love out the door:
      Will you ever ask for more?
To the hobo
That once cared:
      Is your love forever lore?
To the ring
That binds love golden:
         Do you know you will corrupt?
         Do you know you will turn brown?
         And that the beauty you once held
         Will in time turn faces down
         Away from true...
         Away from you...
         Away from all the; once new.
         Away from trees...
         Away from seas...
Away from summer love once new.

Naturally; You Are

I see you here
I see you there
But I wonder how to put so accurately how I feel about you
And I wonder
Of your life
And you, the golden goddess, pure water pure to me and everybody
Naturally
You are
Encased in mind and crystallized in memories like mine
Do you
See me
Or better yet do you see yourself in rapture in my arms
Or do you
See me
Alone in darkness in a chair, the world around worth nothing
And do
You see
Yourself alone in just more darkness in a chair, the solid empty crying

> And do you see the floor above,
> The walls beneath,
> The door not there?
> Do you see the sea I see
> That says to be, to flee, to bleed?
> Do you see the sea of darkness?
> Do you seek the empty?
> Let's just say it's all okay…
> Do you really love me?

Geoffrey Dilenschneider

[The Shady Lady]

Every then and now you stop,
Or must, because time demands you to.

So I take a look at [ ]
A memory inside me:

I am not ready to talk about the shady lady
And want to… to turn to heels
But instead I wish to start and be unheeded
A monologue about you… everything I recollect,
All simply of you:

A rose thought dewdrop on my doorstep
Lost almost, and yet a mousetrap
A simple sea of rose thought dewdrop
A creature being colored green
A hello-gal alive and vibrant
One of many and standing out
You, a freckle rushed, a mystery sweet-grinned
You, a whisper on the wind of secret kisses…
More than kisses you will mean, sitting on a cloud in thought dewdrop dream
Alone by nature, surrounded in friends
Green with beauty, green in dress
Vivid beauty, I confess
Rooms move aside when you step in
To make room for the girl, the woman –
So majestic, she can't be human!
A mind of resonance, a mind of style
A styled mind and take the time
        to live the lie
I know you go to greater things without me

You, a freshness on my tongue
So cooling, different, inspiring.
You, a thing too good for long –   *It is fear that gives men wings*
Meant: Good things become so tiring   *But I am still a boy*
Because they're good from being infrequent   *I still have my imagination*
So the special quality all may have   *My wings are still a toy*
Won't be there as overused…
It will mist away slowly   darker, darker
shadows
deeper
down
Like you did and I did to you.
You, a creator of pain
In somewhere deep,
But it is better to have loved and lost

Because love by itself is that beautiful.
A livid-eyed, alive-died dream
Surreal and real; alone and loved
A question mark above your head reminds me of our questions:
"What about time?"
"What about now?"
"What about everything that suddenly mattered?"
"Should we... be?"
"What about the short-term, what about the long...
Or in forty years will we meet for one last wrong:
A wrong of love, you loved me then
I knew you now, I loved you when
The world was nicer, when corruption failed,
When voices soft, when our ship sailed
And you, the rose thought dewdrop,
A fragrance in the breeze
I think of you and ever green
I think of you and seas
I think of you and think of gold; your own endangered species
Too precious to be tainted –
Yet, mistakes will all be made

Part Two

You, an upward twitter on my tongue
I once was surrounded by greatness
But greatness must be swallowed
Before it grows so same and old
(That, I would never wish for you)
for you, you
A singing song of sweet soft soul –
Six for six and sweet beyond
Your years in earnest of a lull of lonely lost
Calm fears in tears but pain
Subsides in lullabies
That tame with dreams of peace and
You.
I want to cry because I know I could try forever
To love you like God would
But I'll never see the real you...
Whispers of walls that will wish for us future
But to take it all again would mean leaving something
And the plight of brightness will start smooth and end rough
(At a new beginning, remember).

Geoffrey Dilenschneider

You, here, a caught fall,
A monster ball,
A reason to be living,
But you, there, a sigh to lies,
A bye to eyes
And a
Piece of turnaround pie
To creaked necks snapping: can you be again, I believe time's forgotten
You, you, the opposite of me
For the reasoning, us: [black] and [white] and I will not say it again
because I know I'll jinx it and make the dream come to a stop
like trains that tried to turn around on different tracks
like young coffee soft and sweet, rich with love, full of everything
except, I swear, from here, you seem to be perfect
I swoon I swoon I swoon I swoon under the moon
light you, the sun, having such fun –
Everything about you
Seems to be about me   *periods of genius*
I saw the whole world in you   *periods of whys*
I see you in the whole   *periods of everything*
World, in all everyday   *everyone cries.*
I see you and me,
For the reasoning, us: [black] (and) [white]
A solar system silence surrounds the hidden bond
I want to lie and die and lie and die upon my wilting lawn
I search for you, a rose thought dewdrop on my doorstep,
As the smash in the silence, you beg the question
[can we grow together gray]

I started hating school around the time of that phone conversation. Actually, I started hating everything. The world was on fire and could burn for all I cared. It was a maniacal society and burning seemed like a nice way to go.

Untitled Grievance

I hate the lie
I want to grab its throat and tear it out.
Feeling this way, I wonder why I did the right thing
When now *they* say it was wrong.

Where are all the mechanics?
Where do *they* hide them in the daylight?
I wonder this because we're told to be machines
And we will all need *fixing*.

A world of hate and sloth and lies and wrath and pain and lust and sinners and sins
And envy and greed and gluttony and time and violence… venom;
                                         alphabetical destruction
What of it? What of it… just brush it off statistically… better everyday *
They don't know *everything*, we're told we're told
As *they* fade away.

I want to die
I hate the thought of thinking; the concept that we really aren't.
Feeling… thinking… dreaming… moving… being… changing… is this a parody
Of *what* we're supposed to be?

Where is this lie, our lie
When we have come to face… the open-mouthed reality of force-fed blind redemption.
Help is what they *want* you to know, but it's not what we need.
We need their lie of life.

Are our friends, words, thoughts, feelings, actions, reactions, interactions
A means of A to B in the sense of continuing on the lie by section –
Their lie of world that keeps us unaware and turned away from time's small senselessness
(More simply: "Life" is to keep us from realizing the passing of time;
         it's here to play make-believe with our mind)

*a lie

How Can He Live?

It is necessary to learn the real ways to reason in order to live and prosper by society's rules
Here. A teenager.
He is affected, changed, influenced greatly by his surroundings.
He is moving in a negative direction.
What is in motion, tends to stay in motion.
You can lead a horse to water, but you cannot make it drink.
Nothing is real when he gets used to all the fake
(His dreams and hopes and desires and everything become fake to him
When his surroundings lead him to the water and try to make him drink.)
(And when the teen realizes this, and speaks his point of view,
His surroundings say that they are real, natural,
The way it will always be. This deepens the rut of the teen's negative direction,
Affecting his once bright future.)

How can a teen learn the real ways, the natural ways to reason
In order to live (and prosper) by society's rules
When [the fake] society surrounds him and tries to make him drink?
     how can he learn the methods of reason when he is chained
     to his negative direction by his surroundings and the
     resentment they create in him, as well as the anger they instill in
     him when they lie about their own truth in the fake reality they created?

How can he *live*?

Sweet Death

Sweet death, sweet death:
Touch me with your care.
Take me in a time of peace
Bring me to my resting place
With not a blow but with a hush
With a hush.
Take me away from the pain and suffering
To a place made out of love.
Show me the world just after life's quick flowing sand.
Pull me not but show me just where I should go
Bring me to my resting place
With a hush. With a hush.

Áhen-Sea

"Green mountains –
Blue skies.
Free fountains –
No lies."

Great people –
Sweet brothers.
Calm sisters –
Nice mothers.
Much money –
Not painful.
Much working –
Not sinful.
No pain, hate
S'not needed
No calling,
None heeded
Great cities –
None sinking.
Great people –
More thinking.
Sweet blessing –
Deep blue skies.
Sweet loving –
No one cries.

"Green mountains –
Blue skies.
Free fountains –
No lies."
Mountains rise –
People change.
Freedom lies –
Things change.

Melissa Abruzzese, a wonderful girl I knew in my Creative Writing Advanced class, inspired me one day – totally randomly, and it brought me out of my spiteful demigodal cacophony.

Like a Tangerine Dream

She is so beautiful
Like a tangerine dream.
Sweet and simple
Like a beautiful queen.
I don't want to
Let this world go
But I don't want to
Leave her great scene.

Geoffrey Dilenschneider

She is so beautiful
As she walks up to me
Calling my name out
Across the between sea.
I dream of a moment
Where we meet in a wish
In a lush green forest
And for a moment, we kiss.

I'm less aware of time with her
Like a speeding bullet train
Time flew by me like a
Runner gone insane.
But I guess I'm always
Running away.

And the world goes round
And I'm never gonna see her again
And the world goes round
But no one ever really wins
And everyone says
That everything is not what it seems
But the world goes round
Like a beautiful, tangerine dream.

Sweet Sensitive Silence

A pretty blonde would die to have your eyes
Sweet sensitive silence indicative
Of the silent style slowly soft and sweet,
A leopard in the lonely darkness,
Woeful of the rain and squalls.
A whisper on the wind of wars
Of little, smiling souls.
What wonders are encased in you?
Will I once find out?
What calming sugars sing to sleep
The silent, saddened ways?
A French flowing frauline
(But beauty, brains behold
my eyes to sweet sensitive silence).

Then, by course, I went back to being inspired by random things such as 'pretending
that I'm doing some crazy mathematically-perfect rhyme scheme with a very simple
poem,' and then back to being nothing but sad about Katheryn, again. And after that,
just going through two waves of pure inspiration.

To K, again, but in a Tone

The dark trees wave up
Against the lighter, greener, squatter trees
And a blue beautiful sky
So light and full of blinding life.

And behind me now is vengeance,
In a matter of feminine speaking,
Sour bitterness on the old salty shores
Of my little quire from preschool

I am alone in the front now,
A darker tree waving up against the lighter, greener, squatter trees
And a blue beautiful sky.

Meaning and You Space

The beauty of a story is that it's never told twice
(Lost in a cell and your voice is so nice)
*
*
*

Tangled in control we live to find a better way
(Tossed in to hell and your voice has to say)
*
*
*

A way to find purpose and succeed without heat
(We've fallen in a well and your voice is so sweet;)
*
*
*

We are the paradox that make us weep:
(Nobody must follow but the most of us are sheep)
*
*
*

The beauty of a story is that it's never told twice
(Lost in a cell and your voice was so nice)

Sweet Lie (Listening)

Chorus   What world confiscates me?
I let go
What world confiscates me?
Long, long ago
What world confiscates me?
When I bleed
What world confiscates me?
Peace, peace, peace (peace)

Verse I   Peace to the people who say it's alright
Oh, why do we lie?
Calm to the people who say they're just fine
Oh, why do we cry?
Sweets for the people who… stay calm
Prayer for the people who all stand strong
Fame to the people who… save breath
Fear for those who laugh at death
And cry!
For the faces that relive our painful memories
But for those who do not cower in the face of pain and suffering
Sing a crying of the sweetest song so they can hear the joy and loving
Sling your arrows, call your dogs, let the world know who is wrong

Verse II   Freedom to those who need to see
Oh, why do we pry?
Freedom to the people who have to perish
Oh, why do we die?
Motion to the people's walls that crumble
Care for the people who… stand tall
For they have not the things that humble
Disdain for the people who never crawl
And cry! For the faces in the mist
Let them hear you and let them be crisp
In the fact that someone cares about them in the lonely place
Let the world show those small souls that they can hear the joy's sweet song
Sling your arrows, call your dogs, let the world know who is wrong

Chapter 27, 28

▲ ▲ ▲ ▲

"Come with us and forget your sins in our forgiveness. Feel warmed within the blanket of our hope. Let fall the fears you had for we have taken them upon ourselves. Be it known that we are the ones who free your mind."

Thus were the mysterious words of the Fates. Two sisters forever tied to infinity by the cosmos of their love.

Who, you may ask, has written this? Well, it continues…

"The schools of our minds together complete the grandiose basin in which brimming freedoms wash about. It is with curiosity and demand that one comes to us in the fervor of his own self, but is cast out on to dirty stone while the tiny giant all for others comes up after him and is instantly admitted. Through the pains and toils of our hearts and minds, we come unto a threshold prime for conflict, brazened fists and fights! Through the eyes of questions are seen the beauties of the nurtured mother and the father whom created, yet hide for their own safety and desire."

I will be humble and say I remembered it from somewhere, but I didn't. It just came up to my mind.

A Silent Crying Wish

Be calm
Be strong
Be wary and lean to the wind
Be happy
Be free
Be sweeter than any sweet wind
Be simple
Be beauty
Be caring but never let be
Be searching
Be searching
But do not find love (hope) without me.

Again, in time, the words of Ali Watts come back to haunt me.

'You have to calm down. Don't try to be like other people; just be yourself.'

It's almost funny how she thinks she knows me. How she thinks that I am one way but am not that way at all. Does she think that there's something very wrong with me? The last thing I do is try to be like other people.

Or maybe I am that way.

Sweet, Sweet Day

On a summer day of waterfall rains
That smell like wonder years,
I hope to see you wandering
With purpose without tears:

    Come, come
    Let's be undone
    To every little rule
    Run, run
    Through rays of sun
    Through winds so warm and cool
    To sweet, sweet ways
    To summer days
    Let's soar like eagle's wing!
    To frolic, play
    In lush grass lay
    And there, soft hushes sing:
On a summer day of waterfall rains
No meteors and humming planes
Will interrupt this dream of happiness
Only passing will be butterflies and warmth's sigh bless
Only passing will be fragrances
That smell like wonder years
Of different times of different worlds
Each day just like itself in that
There never will be another…
Each day a celebration
Of your grace and beauty,
I hope to see you wandering
With purpose without fears…
On a summer day of waterfall rains
That smell like wonder years
I hope to see you wandering
With purpose without tears.

After many days and weeks of toiling over personal works, I retreated au natural to the deep world of abstract poetry, using words not part of any language to title poems, describing the things I see when I close my eyes and feel confused and bewildered. I even went so far as to create a bit of my own language all together; a joke language, but a language nonetheless. What a trip. [They say that you aren't good until someone else says that you are good. Well, I guess there's some truth to that.]

Fragencia

Demonic eyes growing darker with the tickle of a twisted clock
Over-done eggs for a sunny-side-up man
Whether or not your head goes round 360,
We still know they know we know it goes
And grows when you aren't looking.

Walk through walls that (are they really there)?
Cover, cover eyes that can't breathe ears that can't taste
Tongues that raise up in the night
And desire with their slimy selves to eat the whole wide world
Fragile, querencia
Fragencia.

Velaquai

Veldt of a sweet notion
Lost and alone and beaten rotten
There, but not and heavy shouldered
Yelling sense and beaten rotten.
The birds are all in rows there on the Velaquai
Cold and looking for a sty
Of hay and such –
A place to lay and lie and touch
The earth they need to have to so survive
So survive the lives of dives
Through the sand (like seagulls in water)
But these creatures of the sand are of the sand
And not the sea
There and here, quietly
Gone.
The Velaquai just swallows them up
Suck suck suck
And they lay there suffocating

But there is one bird in particular

This bird does not participate in the sick ritual
He's there to breathe but not die ritual
(Lost alone and beaten rotten)
He's not there to be heavy shouldered
(Yelling sense and beaten rotten)
This bird sees these things for the things they are
Not the way they seem to be
Wouldn't it be nice to find
That life was nicer in a dream
Dread, imitation, danger, sleep
Sleep

Geoffrey Dilenschneider

mmmm....
Wouldn't it be
Nice
To feel no pain?

The Velaquai:
Veldt of a sweet notion
Lost and alone and not and beaten rotten
There but not and heavy shouldered
Yelling sense but not and sucking cotton.

[The House:] VillaNova

Alar-ums and faithless
A mockery of a joke
(in the system of) LIES!
            worth, worth, sentience (isn't
real) [and the world isn't there, our whole world is (in) the house:]
VillaNova wants to cry.

Coffin' Laughflin

Sleep
    Sleep   Sleep
      Sleep

        Sleep

Won't   sleep   me sleeping?
      Not

                      Is
      Sleeping   real

      In   world
                 of
You   my   can't

Believe
    ing
               Own   you
I'm

      A

                         See

Worthwestel

Jon never meant to leave
But, well... he had to.

It all started with a bit of money he won
Gambling with his friend, Lass Baker.
Lass was just that type of person: the gambling type.
And Jon always lost
(Really because Lass always cheated)
But this one time, Jon won! (no one ever figured how.)
Jon took the money home (it was 30 nicklepence and change, to be
Exact) and stuck it in a hole
Under a floorboard
Under his bed.
Little to Jon's knowledge,
There was a surprise waiting for him there,
Under the bed.
The Worthwestel.
It ate the money, but Jon didn't see that.
See, the Worthwestel is a lucky little creature, and whenever it is around, you
are bestowed with some great luck,
So, Jon kept winning...
But every time, Jon would put his winnings under the bed, and the Worthwestel
would eat it all up!
Why win when you can't keep the winnings?
Well, it all doesn't matter,
Because on the fourth day of the fourth month of the fourth year
Of the fourth century of the fourth millennium
At four forty four am, Jon put down forty-four nicklepence
And stuck his hand in the Worthwestel's mouth
(Totally by accident) and, well...
the Worthwestel ate Jon up.

Surprise!

Sim-bin! Wally-wal!
Sing wee dong sa wee will
Duhvazumbin-in kill.
Pally willy cally silly tilly
Fasatate win sock...
Sim-bin duhvazimbun
Samus win wally kiss?
Kama din liss-wee
Fallip, phallip, korn
Sivvile dong kissin dong
Wahmaa – tee...
　　　Woohimal
　　　Ferimal

　　　　　　　　　　　　　　　　　　　Geoffrey Dilenschneider

Dun-in-korinsin
Lisibee
Falifee
Sun-an-korinsin
Kall de seedle fissin paren surel
Sing wee kall da fakasital
Ass dong wah wah wah!
Bizz, loll fizz worfum worhum Kem.
Duhvazumbin-lasa nikee!
Wolsanisee tem!
Casa te nora,
Fill caranea quam win ni…

Kordam, dong sing sim-bin
       Quah wahm wirren
Kama din wall-wal.

*So bent on writing this book have I been that I almost forgot to mention Katie Bell.
(Yeah, lots of Katies, I know) Katie Bell is a grade above me, has long black hair, like
a dream, and a pretty, oval face held by remarkable green eyes that sometimes seem
blue as well as green. I've got a grand crush on her, too.*

*On a day that I took the school bus home, I remember seeing a girl – not Katie
Bell – but just a girl that looked like her, and I just was thrown into a void: tunnel
vision on her face; her body; the feelings welling up inside me. Letting it out was possible in only one way.*

I See You in the Void

I see you in the void
I see your laughter
I see your smile
I want to grab my pcn and cry.
I see your hot pensive stare…
Your eyes, your neck; your arm, your hair
I see your lean
And vision a queen
I see the glimmer in your eye
I see your hand upon your forehead
I see it in the air
I see it rest upon your shoulder
With the utmost, kindly care.
I see your back, your shape,
Your loneliness, I think
I see your question
I see your lips
I see your cheeks
So red, so flushed
So beautiful

I see your walk froward and meaningful
(I see you gone)
But I still see your laughter
I still see your smile
I see you in the void of darkness
that reigns over our memories
and keeps us away on this hot barren desert
as we sweat and we sweat and we cry,
But I still see your innocent laughter
I still can see your smile
And I can see the whole wide world because
I see you in the void.

After that odd encounter, I returned home, did some homework, and went to sleep. The next day, however, I was moved to dictate out the laws of my poetry. I had always thought about what dictates what in a world without laws; a world of poetry, and I just couldn't stand it any longer.

The Poet

The poetry is the poet.
The poetry is the poet's soul
Because we don't have souls otherwise.
Our soul is represented by the *words*
Because the *words* are the poet's mind
The *words*, my friend, are the key to our being.
We are our own species as poets
Because we are the ones who set aside a piece
Of every single thing in our life, and life itself,
And dedicate it to poetry…
That is the real poet. (dedicated, learning, changing, being)true

When you see a poet,
You know it.

And when you see a poet,
You see the truth of him.
You (can) see his soul without knowing his name
Because the poet is used to displaying himself
Like a cheap trick, almost (this world now rarely celebrates a poet)
For his bravery is more often than not considered audacity
Unless he is famous, but if he is, it is already too late…
his truth has died.

I speak merely in generalities, though.
The poet is the poetry and the poetry is the poet
But fictitious are some poems while others are lies.
The poet finds happiness but nobody knows it

Because the poet is crazy and always cries.
The poet's sadhappy, the poet is nice
The poet is lost and is searching for love
(Not the love of heart's suffocation slice)
But the love of *words*, the love of *truths*, the love of *whys*.

And we as poets may sometimes resent the fact we are poets
Rather than working some job that pays the equivalent of five rents,
But the poet knows *it* is the way it is
Because the way it is, is so for a reason...
(Do not doubt this.)

We as poets remember because our memory is on paper.
We recollect because our thought and feelings are written, saved.
We are our own species because we are just a tad bit different,
(Which could be a cause of concern to some) but
I, myself, do not believe there has been a code of conduct
(or laws) written for us, poets. (As it would be had,
for at least I believe that poets are comprised almost totally of
paradoxes). But I try:

The poet must look forward
The poet must not fall
And for the times he does: he must search for meaning in falling
The poet must be beautiful as a poet and as a human being
The poet must *live*
The poet can become famous (no matter how small)
But the poet must not let it go to the poet's head
The poet must not lie
The poet must smile in pain
The poet must be true in writing to life, to the heart, to others, and to self
The poet must write.

And the poetry is the poet.
The poet is the poetry
The poet believes in the ways of things
For the way they are,
The poet believes in chance, in luck
And in direction
Because the poet is going in one without being guided
Or by meaning to.
The poet is tired because it is not easy anymore to be true.
And again, the poet is moving, searching
For the line that defines itself and it's poet
With the piercing clarity of truth.
And we are sad, as poets, (it is there at the corners of our eyes when no one is looking)
But that is what we are (dedicated, learning, changing, being)true.

All this – the girl and the meaning of poetry – was just an interruption, a hurdle that I jumped right over in a period of 24 hours and was back on track with being totally off the wall. And that is all that I will explain on the following because I feel that they speak for themselves about the world we live in, as well as all the other things that they symbolize. (Obviously, the first is a play on words, and the second is simply a succulent piece of work.)

Broken

I feel the flow
Oh oh no
I feel the flow
Oh oh no
I feel the flow
Oh oh no
I feel the flow
Oh oh no
Everybody wanna break!

Broken down broken up
Broken sideways broken cup
Cupping witties cupping hands
Cupping ohs cupping lands
Lands of nasty lands of lies
Lands that even mice despise!

Starting fire starting breeze
Stopping fools with superman ease
Easy on easy off
Easy smile easy cough
Cough real hard cough real soft
Cough at me and you'll be lost!

Standing wise standing tall
Standing sitting standing fall
Falling long falling spoken
Falling awake, falling broken
Broken down broken up
Broken sideways broken cup...
Flow.........

Geoffrey Dilenschneider

The Ésthro Yaw (The Spiral)

I can't seem to fight the feeling
That this is all a dream.
I wonder when it will happen.

The people, they walk on with their lives
They grow they love and work and die
And the cycle goes on.
Everyone goes through the throes of life.
The absence of peace. The meaninglessness and pain of love.
The worth of respect. The timelessness of time.
Lamps shine, buildings glimmer in the evening light.
I wonder when it will happen.
Tell them what you know about the need
The greed. The start. The God. The obsession.
Tell them of the vast wasteland of buzzing cities
So full of life and in-susceptibly corrupted beyond belief.
Beyond belief.
Describe the waste. The depleting.
The disappearing. The violence.
Paint them a twisted picture of epic carnage
And paint them a picture of the lust. You must.
The devour. The petty thief of existence is upon us.
The great throng of the public's mainstreamed thought
Will finally be righted. The salesmen of our sentience
Will be murdered.
And to destroy him, you must sacrifice everything.
But the people, they walk on with their lives; they don't listen.
And the people grow, and love and work and die
And the cycle turns on forward through time...
But we are breaking down now,
Sinking into the unholy abyss.
This beautiful serene dream surrounds
The public, the private, the world
With doubtless repetition...
You twinkle there, unchanging
But we know so better than to listen to that lie,
Because we, the Spiral, we know where losing won't seem bad.
Where crying will be fine. Where sweet will be sour and sour
Will be sweet. Where alright will be horrible and the happy will weep.
We know an alone place that will overcome this dream we dream to keep.
To keep awake here there must be change.
I wonder when it will happen.
When the congestion will become too thick. The sound too loud.
The dream too shattered...
And the walls of rock close slowly in on the innocent
As they scream to save the dream they dream
Now in wonder are they,
PANG! Realizing that it's too late to wake up and change the Spiral.

Oh, we know what it'll be like... we know.
Scream, little ones; scream while you can for the opportunity now
To save yourself from the vanishing point right over this hill.
Think about it this way: you're in the car and you're moving
Toward the top of the hill. Every second you see a little more of the end, but you
can't do anything to stop because you are dead.
But you're aware of everything... you can sense and think and talk...
You're just oblivious to your own impending doom.

Good morning, watcher
Give thanks

Naturally you will never understand...
But it never really mattered
Because you will wake up someday
And when you do,
You will see the reality of the Spiral...
The danger.
You will understand
and meaning will die.
The white plains behind will disappear, along with the fruits of your labor.
Beauty will fall, greatness will falter,
And truth will lie.
Heavy will *all* our shoulders be with the doubt and desperation
Of souls undone like poorly tied shoelaces.
Everything will sound strangely wrong because everything will become wrong.

We are running out of time.

The conscience will cease to be

Good morning, watcher
Give thanks

As you drift,
Do you wonder...
Why?

This is a dream.
It's all going to end someday.

Geoffrey Dilenschneider

Then my rheumatic anger turned a bit upwards in an effort to quell itself by pre-
tending that there was some kind of answer out there, and I began on a somewhat long
journey of discovery, noticing here and there the meanings of life embedded deep within
our everyday world.

The Sunlight Skitch Shines Down

Think of a world
Where beauty is beheld.
Think of a world where hearts beat slow
And don't beat old.
Think of a world where knowledge is key, and everyone has it
And everyone cares.
Imagine a world where all children lay in warm beds on cold nights,
In easy darkness, searching the soft sky for shooting stars.
Think of a world where the law of the land is peace,
Where equality is the fruit we eat
And love, the nectar we drink
With whole hearts and with zest and gusto.
A place where all people eat and drink, sharing the same table in joyous harmony.
Think of a world full of lush melodies floating carelessly,
Rivers trickling down like the morning dew upon thick grass,
Full of vibrant sea-life; where pollution is unheard of,
Where problems are a thing of the past.
Think of a world that is free!
Imagine a place where rest is for the weary,
Peace is for all,
And where happiness is a small child running in smiles to his mother down the street,
Except in all of us: warming, comforting, true.
Think of a world set in beautiful silence,
But here and there can be heard the feathery sound of
Easy, laughing commotion.
Think of a world where cages are gone, prisons are missing,
And cemeteries are dead.
Think of a world that has a future.
Think of a world without poverty.
Think of a world that has hope.
Think of a world full of love.
Imagine a world that is alive!
And imagine a world
Made of dreams.

It is Seldom

There are curves in a bump like tigers on a child's wall
We sweet sigh and with others fall
Never alone the public finds hell in heaven
Ugly things find ways to stall the world and we do nothing
Laughter is the crimson cure but frowns find cracking smiles a joke
Hair is there to be pulled and thrown
Away from the thing where ideas must form
Feet carry weight to the places that they rest
Thinking like the old statue
Who is alive and who is real?
You will see this answer when you finally steal
A glance
Into the eyes
Of someone who has no idea that you are looking
And they are all alone.
Then the curves turn into bumps like tigers on a child's wall –
And then you'll see humanity untainted like a crimson cure,
Thrown in fire, set in pain
Missing the lies of smiles and desire,
A face in the stall of life and then you'll know the intimidation of a soul.

As We Know How

And the diverse
Flow in as the ties are released in reality
        That stings the soul with salty tears that eat away as they flow.
And the ignorant
Learn of the lives they have been living
        That taint the innocent with fears that eat away as they flow.

And I have witnessed something…
A sea of different realities
All entwined as one
And it's all a paradox
But we must live our realities the only way we can:
As we know how.

Learn From Me

Tapped on the shoulder by an act of violence.
I am mad when I see a man cut a beautiful bloom off a tree.
Dragged across a world of sin
And still I must repent.
This tale I tell's of Heckler's Street
And the time a car ran over me.
I also tell of any soul
That's seen the light of freedom.

Geoffrey Dilenschneider

But then I took a turn for the worse. I became depressed, but remember not the reason why except that it had something to do with a girl. I wrote this all during a Mets Baseball game. The bright orange seats that surrounded me like an angry, depressing mob didn't much help, either.

BoD

I am a car without wheels
Staring out at a sea of sky blue
A rag-tag team of nothings
Just around so the...

And I've been so alone
For such a long time
Locked away in my own world
Where I touch nothing
And feel, but through glass windows
A place where no doors lead
And where there's nothing but the life
I hate
But love
And I'm ashamed to talk about you
I'm ashamed when I hold the things you loved.
I am scared when I think about you
And how I'll never see you again.
How our lives will just move on apart
Until we just forget we ever were
I'm not ready to relive our pain
But I'd love to feel again.

DP I

I am so alone

I am so alone
And I miss the touch of hand

And I am so alone

DP II

When you're missing from the middle
It's pretty hard to hide.
The sun once always shone to me
But now all it does is hide.
I'm sick of trying;
Of seeing so many possible futures

DP III

I no longer smile when I see others' joy.
I no longer warm when a joke is told.
It may be hatred, it may be pain
But I believe I've simply turned too cold

DP IV

The sweets I sell
Must really smell
For everyone that I love runs.
  And then,
  I see the future:
  I will tumble down a hopeless romantic path,
  In and out of cherry-blossom love fervors,
  Love
  Depression
  Love
  Depression
    Love
    Depression
  Held on women's tips of tongues,
  Falling and gone when they want

So, as you can see, I can get pretty depressed when the time is right. The anguish didn't end there. The Mets lost that night.

The Old, Old Man in the Moon

The moon turned to me and said
With lopsided grin: "Don't worry your little head off
about some girl who you don't know.
You know damn well you'd love to get to know her
but what you don't know is if she wants to
with you.
And you will never ask her –
You are so hopeless,
but you should not let her make you wait.
At the same time, be cautious.
Her beauty and her intelligence
are not easily matched,
and she is true to herself,
but you must come, in time, to know her."

Geoffrey Dilenschneider

But I turned away from him that night
And hid him in my mind
Behind a cloud of Mars and such
So I could not see his grin.

But then I said, "Hold on a second,
did you just say what I think you said?
Didja say her brains and beauty
are not easily matched?
Didja say she is so true?
I think you've hit something there, old man in the moon!"
I said, I said to him up there soon
Looking on down so peaceful and somber
I said, I said to the lopsided grin
Of the old, old man in the moon.

The Society

The screams reverberate back and forth
Back and forth on the empty walls.
We are them and they repent not for their sins.
They are those who refuse to lie
Yet lie in refusing the truth.
The truth is that which sets us free
But to see the truth we must accept we are blind
And yet one of our traits is that we can be blind,
Blind to the fact there is something we're blind to.

Paradoxes are what we live upon sweetly:
Cascaded on pain, but hating it so.
Frozen in some places, wanting the heat.
Calm wanting anger and rage quells to peace.
Things that seem normal are the opposite inside.
The guilty set free and the possessive are tried
And convicted.
The cursed refuse life and the living mock death.
The laughing aren't realizing the inevitable are near.
Friendly, it seems to the people who hide
And everyone social seems to realize the wide.

(The wide is the Society, and the society is life.
        Everything living is one of these.
        Pain is all relative, life is that too
            some of these aren't true and some just say please)

Some just seem to not realize
That things aren't meant to be
(But it's okay because we all
Must know Society.)

And freedom rings inside our ears
While freedom still eludes
But this is just what the doctor ordered
Or was it the pretty prudes?

It doesn't matter and does.
Everything ever is 'cause
The world is round
And we thought it flat
And everything rains
But just dogs and cats.

Every action has a purpose
But... it cannot,
Because if it did
Then how could we bid
And not know who would win.

Black may be white
And white may be black
But what's inbetween
And why're we both fat?

Mad is just crazy
And mad is furious
Rhyme is like politics
Except not.
Peace is like baby
And baby's like Ruth
Breasts are like beauty
Except not.
The solemn races ran
Are really just people
But people are peoples
Except not.
Paying attention
But paying a fine
Paying is stupid
Except not.

And then when we wag our tails into the evening sun,
What world sees us through a telescope and what world makes fun?
What world far away must smile and say:
"Boy, what idiots run!"
Or maybe love is what binds us as we
Walk and talk
(That is the purpose of life, is it not? To communicate and bring greatness
          to others in the form of ideas through the words we use
              and also to continue on, creating legacy and meaning, or maybe not and
              just learning and being to make a difference more subtle: you were alive once,

were you not?)
Walk and talk through the days of staring eyes
Meaningless and meaningful, it all just depends!:
Upon when you have looked and when you pretend
To not listen.

(And the opposite of communicating
        is to not listen, to not look, to not understand. Who here does not do these
        things? I do not have pity on you, rather, I envy your choice
        because you are less full of pain than I, you have
        chosen to become one with ignorance
        to simply be and be free of pain
        be free of sin, meaning free of the knowledge
            Free of the knowledge of sin.)

Then again, then again
            Here we must be
For here is where here
    And here is just   is.
Then again, then again
Here we must be
For here is where here
And here is not free.
Then little circles of people who care
Form 'round those who are lies
Lies of a kind that I cannot say loud
Or else those who *know* will come down and scream loud
So no one can hear me, so I will be gone.
(Everything's evil and everything's good
(Everything's based on principle of paradox
(Everything's meant to be, everything's perfect
(Everything's crafted by our own hands, everything's wrong)

Sometimes I say that we are given certain tools. That is what is predestined;
what is not is what we do with the tools. (But, of course, the attributes of the
tools we are given shape what we're able to do with them.)

... Death
(is a) concept.
It is not real.
This I can tell because we're all dead.
(Remember that I speak in riddles, for that is all I can do)
Just think of Aristotle or Galileo or van Gogh:
They are dead, always were, but their words
Live on.
That is our purpose: to make a nail dent in the adamantium shield of life;
To make sure we are not forgotten... it's sad, though, that our purpose in life
can be at one time or another summed up as either a joke or a smile or a self-
serving... ( ) lie.

Eyes hold the beauty of the world
And we must repent for everything
Just to make sense
Or else the mind would self-implode
While building perfect lies.
Perfect lies of everything! But I cannot tell you!
If I did, you'd tell me I was crazy!
You think I'm crazy now!
But I'm not, you do not see
(the riddles inside the wall!)

The N

Death and destruction!
Pain that's infinite!
Broken bones!
Hell and stones!
Woe to those devils infinite!
Carnage to the left,
To the right, and all around!
Good stuff!
They said it,
Mouths dripping with blood!
Death is a cloud of colorless, odorless gas!
Floating invisible through everyone's lungs,
Infecting, infecting
And then calm.

The last is more or less a summation of the whole episode, bringing it to a nice, easy close. Another episode was just getting underway back at school… with Katie Bennet. Ha! I keep coming back to her, don't I? She's just a great person! Her soul is so pure. I don't love her… well, I don't 'love' her love her, you know. I'd love to get to know her better, but I'm not infatuated or anything. She's got her life and I've got mine, I guess, right?

Our Hands Can be Cool Again

Sweet with a smile
Similar to disease
When you hold back behind the lies you soft conceive
And then the world makes some go dark
In the eyes and then the mind
Holding back the tears of regret
And the lies we hide inside.
And from the beauty you hold somewhere
I see these things of hell
Why must I see horrible things
Instead of finding beauty in things that quell of the pointing

Geoffrey Dilenschneider

Quell of the quiet
Quells of the bells and the whistles and the tattered footprint
Upon the soft, blue carpet of the ocean
As you traverse across the shy and silent playing hands
But not the hands of disease, rather, they carry disease
(as we all do)
and you just have less and you put them at your waist
and I wish and I wonder when I can feel those hands in my cool hands
now sweaty with toiling work on its own
and then you play again playfully
playfully free
playfully free is what I want to be
and I can't
I can't
I cannot let go of the life I've become
Of the works
Of the words
Of the mangy and detailed
And curvy and hard to understand

And turn
Oh turn
Towards me so I can see your face
In the moonlight of phosphorescence
And the suns of every day
And I want
So bad
To hold your hand in mine own
So I can feel you
So breathing
And breathing your freedom
And the simple surprise
That the winking girl lets
Unleashed in the times
Of your playful little hands:
Everywhere! Everywhere! Nowhere but all
And then you must play again
Play again! Let me see all
Show life! show beauty!
Show me what they mean!
I cannot understand what you
May mean!

But I'll try
And I'll try
To put yours in mine
And then we'll be
Just fine and
Our hands will be cool again.

And then finally, after all this waiting, it was my birthday.

And Then in the End (A Twist)

And then in the end
As suddenly life pauses
Stop.

     i realize that
things aren't so bad as I've thought
As I've thought:

     Beauty is beautiful
     Sweets are sweet
     Passion is full
     And calm is flowing
Always flowing.
The silence does not need to be
to live and a smile is so sweet that it makes me cry
When in the mind of freedom.
You are no more and no less
Than the twist swirl of humanity
And the soul.
You all purely sing silent memories
Never yelling …
         (and this is the opposite of the *others*)
         (this is not:
     Beauty is sweet
     Passion is beautifull
     A smile is so sweet on the tip of my mind's tongue
A finger points quiet the lies
And that's all that's needed
To keep my soul alive.

                Geoffrey Dilenschneider

Chapter 29, 30

▲ ▲ ▲ ▲

One day I felt like writing a story; a story about Twins Chester. They aren't real people, but an idea of America, more or less, but in the story/poem I portray them as a set of twins.

A Bath to Wake Us Up

I miss the kiss
I want to cry
Dolls watch blind, emotionlessly
As the spills of wills
Tip further. you
Cup hands under cool rush
But it stops and is solid
Suddenly.
Then,
The world goes again
And what pencil point is wrong
In saying that to love yourself is a crime.
Dear world,
Callin' in sick today
Feel too numb to participate in dodge-ball life
And dodge-ball love.
Madder than mayhem
Without a care in the world
Moving this and that and back
And nothing seems right.
It's all wrong. Go again. It's all wrong
Apply yourself for the wealth
If you can't you're fugged.
A number may dictate your life
One, two, three, they all rush in
No one likes sin but we all love singing
There's nothing wrong with love.
Just don't do it.
What wonders pet our heads
Living in the grass,
Too small to know they're madder than mayhem
And have no control.
The little ones are bigger now
And they are in the way
What can I say to mayhem and mercy?
The broken stop fixing 'cause they're broke
Living on the streets

Are you cold?
Broken? Joking.
Really?
Or but how when huh wait but what?
I am the problem of myself,
Circling the lighted runway over and over
'till I run out of gas and fall.
Twins Chester don't know why
But to mayhem and mercy they turn
They run to the treadmilling streets
Naked of sin or purity, arms flailing,
One of hate and hell, the other of the same
But hold to show they're harmless
Then continue set on goals so mindlessly
And murder a million people.
Where were those people headed?
Doesn't matter, they were headed to the purple pastures of God
And found that the milk and cookies were out of stock...
A billion die and then when twins Chester stop
To survey the beautiful, fiery destruction,
They're dripping with angst like mud,
Pain like tar and rage like feathers
Nothing's in the way
Thank God it wasn't you.
Twins Chester found mayhem and mercy
'Cause those that are dead are really alive
And they're feelin' not a bit of their pain.
Twins Chester aren't insane, they're just a little free(r)
Than you and me. We're dead, tired, sick, lost,
Going stale and growing fungus,
We're born and become fallen, rotting trees:
Hollow with the parasites that eat away it all
Twins Chester found mercy in mayhem
Then stopped it all to give the dead a bath
(And this the aftermath:

)

Geoffrey Dilenschneider

*I then returned to the less-famous-than-she-should-be girl, Katie Bell. This time –
since I was sitting in the library at school and had a double free (one was just cutting
sports, another problem I have) – I spent all the time typing out poems for Katie Bell.
I never thought that she would see any of them, as well it should be, but that changed
a few days later when a kid I knew (but didn't know he knew Katie Bell) asked to see
one about a girl, and I gave him one about Katie. He gave it right to her. Even though
I didn't tell him it was inspired by Katie Bell, it was obvious, given the title of it.*

Sonnet for Katie 1

I went unto a world that walked away…
I ran a simple ditty in my head:
A vivid dream where not a thing may say
How beauty, brains behold the lies of bread…
And then we walked into a stream of life,
So crystal and alone with absent thought.
We danced until the days were done of life
And found ourselves alone again and caught
By souls untouched by nods and human ways.
The souls were simply beauty to behold
Like time without the tainted chains of days.
And sweet, it was, and sour, hot, and cold
In places where we danced the night, we cry
For everything that wasn't: you and I.

Sonnet for Katie 2

I say to you, "oh, rabbit, rabbit eyes!
Come see the things for me I cannot see
Because I'm blind from all great beauties wise
(As well as missing grass, and mouse, and tree)
On ready I will heed the call of yours
And run to places never seen nor heard
I'll follow running to the grocery stores
To smell all things from apple juice to curd"
"Oh, silly boy that does not see the truth:
Come here to find that everything is nice,
But do not fall or even falter truth,
For truth is not what others see as life
But rather how interpreted we find
The beauty of a rabbit in our mind."

Sonnet for Katie 5

Your eyes: they are the livid dreams of men...
Two saintly havens for the world and pain.
When looking in them, teeter on a zen
And then all else will fade into the rain.
They bring the Calm with walls of blue lake silk
And both defy the other in a sigh.
Two violet rings encircling smooth milk...
Two scintillating suns that never die.
Before, I thought, "Oh, life is great and nice.
My arms don't hurt and springs are cool and pure."
And now my life has really started twice,
Your eyes: perfection as the rain's sweet cure.
And now I think: "Oh, life is great insane!
Your eyes: my cure that fades into the rain."

Sonnet for Katie 6

Your hair: the silky wave I ride so high
Above the clouds that never knew what came
A dream that screams into my ear: "I try!"
And that is where I place the silky blame.
The time we keep just stopped at first I saw
That black abyss of tempest, lulling storm.
A mane of paradoxes filling law,
Oh, tainting tainted hearts until they're warm.
Sweet cascade falls that shimmer in the morn',
An absolute, relentless being torn:
Cooled in moist grass and splayed so smooth and sigh...
With heartache, I must turn away and cry.

But of course I didn't want that to get in the way of my studies, so I simply set my pen down for a while and got some good grades. However, a few days later, I was back to writing about nothing in particular. It's a style that I like because it can be about anything and everything. Using the style, I can be inspired by things I see out of the corner of my eye or words I hear that sound like other words, which in turn inspire me even more. It's a whole system of great inspirations which leads me into a very creative world.

Geoffrey Dilenschneider

Sonnet for My Heart (Burning Up Sonnet)

All the greatest people are so taken
There's nothing much to do 'cept walk around.
I'm so, so sad and want to be taken
Right back into my place where I'm not found.
The ransom note from God seems to be lost
I'm drowning in my writing and my pain
Reflecting on the question of its cost
And the reason why I'm feeling so much pain.
I've lost the reason to keep on at all
I'm wondering along but so alone
It seems to me that everything must fall
I'm blundering along a piece of stone
I look into the eyes of anyone
And find my taken, lonesome place the sun.

Wouldn't It be Wonderful

Wouldn't it be wonderful
If we smiled more than turtles do
Wouldn't it be nice if we
Left things just the way they used to be
And the saunter of the frozen
Stayed centered and well-kept
Instead of being back and forth
And losing all that's meant
What if we couldn't look back to our past
And we couldn't leave ourselves be?
What if there wasn't a future?
What if there wasn't a "me?"

But wouldn't it be wonderful
If everything was free?

When Gates are Crashing

Nothing works when you're alone
And everything seems to be broken
Simply because you're here
There is never close enough
People do seem shagging and blurry
Smiles fade to the distance of the seven sullen seas
But no one ever finds the way to be one with the bees

The blackness sets in
And everyone meets sin
In the whole wide world there's nothing that will remind us
And define us
Better than the pores
Falling to the wars
Losses make up lies and loss and freedom falls to spires
The world expires
And the beautiful cry in their pain.

Sincerity is lost to those alone
The darkness is there and never leaves us alone
Seldomly crying can be heard
Water to amnesia in the day
Christmas is in the form of puppies
Brazen fists fall forward
The dead are the puppies
We wish for peace to come here
But no, repent and nothing happens
Open the doors and lock them then you'll
Find that nothing really works

Walk without your pants on
Through a laughing street of people
And say in code to the evil grins
That they in time will die
Look farther and further and farther on down
The path of destruction that no one can own
'cept the people you love
Because you will destroy them
In time and you rhyme with the conviction of sleep
Bleeding with corn on the day you were born
And you never stopped bleeding 'till today.

Far off in the distance
You can see your friends all lying down
Don't wonder why they're there
Because they've been let of their living souls
Pains are gone and freedom's perfect
For the dead
Slowly the caged animals sing of the song that they never learned
Everything's fine 'till the people run circles
'Round the morons that still are concerned.

Geoffrey Dilenschneider

The salads are tossed and the living are lost
And the world doesn't seem to be there
There are no presents and darkness is present
As the world will pretend to not care.
Just go out sleeping by the sound of your weeping
And not a soul will ever hear.
We've all gotten old and our bodes are cold
Now that the darkness is here.

I returned to Katie Bennet during the hum-de-dum of school. Let me compare her to a few things: a battery that never runs out; a flower that never wilts and always shines its brightest smile; a simile that has no comparison except for wordless feelings and worlds of meaning; a joy for birds who are freer than men and a being created by the sun in its purity.

A Dream (Sonnet for Katie #7)

The fairest wave of all floats up the sky,
Unbroken in its beauty and its flare.
A honey flow of cherry tears are cried
Soft spoken in a way, but so aware.
An eagle's dream is of this upward fear
But everything in you seems to be real.
A soul of wine and sweet rosedrops I hear
The saintly voice of goddesses that heal.
A respite for the little ones in life;
A smiling blade of effervescent gold.
A dreaming queen whose face shows not of strife;
Who lunges with a warmth, I'm simply told.
A simple, lonely heart beats quick with fear
When Katie B's so close, but never near.

I continued on my daydreams about different girls I knew; but sadly, no one in particular.

Down Roads

We are meant for each other
In the sun and in the stars
In the grass that never smothers
We lay between red cars.
Sweet words float aimlessly between our lips
Down roads converged and made of quips.

Through the eyes of silent faces
Two young centered birds eat sweet
And then in time will wing to places
Everywhere they turn and tweet.
Flowered mountains separate our eyes
Then turning, whirling, freezing cries.

A sweat begins to lean between
The speed in which we fly.
So much suspense in sleep together,
We dream and each, in turn, will sigh
From every thing that gets us mixed we say:
Forget all time and carry me away.

I cannot run down every drain
To find you gone from fleeing.
Then back again without the pain,
Together dark forever being,
Free my mind and travel on my lips
Down roads converged and made of quips.

Wondering, Wondering Why

A flurry reminder of the sky
A statue of honey, running but high.
Above us all wondering, wondering why
Why so perfect, why so *sigh*?

A colorful mirage of the rainbow you run
Together with only the curves of the sun.
Won't you become beautiful, with me, become one?
I'm asking this of you in fun, just in fun.

You shun me and I, turning, die…
A mirage of the man that won't cry
You move on so graceful, but we wonder, wondering why…
Why, why so perfect, why so *sigh*…

The Determined One

Simply put, he ravages his soul for meaning but finds none
There and it evades him with the pensiveness of the crazed.
In the soot, he ravages his mind for answers but finds none
There and they evade him with the worthlessness of the dazed.
In the foot, he ravages for the one will make in him the difference
But finds no one.
No one to cure him of pain. So he will continue…
Continue on in vain.

Geoffrey Dilenschneider

One day, I felt like taking a look deep into my own soul. Though, if I did not tell you that, you would not understand a word this poem directs.

From Another

The velvet sky and the anchoring pumpkin moon
Rode together up the hidden silk sky,
And there, at the top of every animal and plant
Both living and dead,
The reflection in my endless eye
Was that of the real bond of lumpy trees,
Gayly swinging in the ocean-salt breeze
And myself.
I see the behind of the swiveling world...
I have a vision of the clock-work occurrence...
And from these dreams of convolution and human touch,
I find with ocean-salt eyes the undiluted meaning of my own soul.

Untitled Prose by Me

I want to walk down a street and have people say,
"Hey, that's Jeff Dillenschneider!" and not even my hometown.
I want to have the little people know me... because
my message has to get across to them. My message, if anything, is
that they are the most important people in the world. I want
to inspire everyone so greatly that they all go out and
make something spectacular!

And because I realized that I would never be famous, I felt pretty miserable. I mean, I had tried my hardest to keep my hopes down to next-to-nothing and let my dreams run away, but when it really dawned on me that I wouldn't be really, really famous, I felt... well,... sucky.

My Misery Loves No Company

My misery loves no company
I like being alone…

I like being alone…

Flourishing around me stand
The people I might love
If once they gave me half a chance
But now I skip to flying.
Sometimes I seem happy
Or you might catch me in a grin.
But however you may imagine me,
My pain's my penance of sin.

My road's been bumpy,
And still is long
I've done all that can be done wrong.
I frolic in the deeps that keep you crying
I lullaby the innocent to sleep
To wake up in obedience and longing,
The smell, you see, is what I see
And I can no more stand their stones…
So my misery has no company…
I like being alone.

But, I took a turn for the better when I realized that being famous was not that big of a deal. That realization has become a staple in my life. Every day I remember how unimportant it is to be loved by those who only love you when you're in the limelight. I'd love to have that kind of love; that kind of attention, but I know now that I don't need it, I can really concentrate on my work without wanting something so artificial. I love the attention of my parents and friends; it's so much nicer than something false.

Geoffrey Dilenschneider

We All Are Ourselves

There once was a man who walked on a wall
There once was a man who fell.
There once was a man whom everybody loves
And everybody knew too well.
He took his life and threw it down
But picked it up again.
Everybody said that this was life
And took their sips of gin.
Nobody thought that just this day
The man would not get up.
That is life and it's meaning:
To continue getting up.

I staged a sort of invisible fight in my mind one day. I felt like it, so what? It was interestingly enough a type of good-vs.-evil battle, and it came out into a poem.

You Can Only Control

And then,
With a smile,
I will turn with the world to darkness
Lost, alone, quietly broken.
No man will go untouched by the new horrors brought down upon his head.
But by myself will normalcy laugh itself to death.
And into shambles with the sweet decay
Yellow, yellow, brown.
Here, there
A flutter of light, maybe…
But it will all peak one day
And we will, together, feel the full force of hell.
Nope, you cannot destroy it.
Imagine a great battlefield,
Misted over with the smoke of fear
And some of us *will* turn away from love
For lust and quick resolve, to join the majority of sinners.
But others will fight it.
That is the path of control.
Now, I have only one question for you:
Watcha gonna do?

The River's Friend

I have things to say:
I say we are all so human
We will in time die.
I say beauty is in what we think
Rather than how we look.
It is so sad that we cannot judge people by how they think.
Time is a waste of... time.
Smile inward, I say.
The knock-out punch of a pacifist
Is so great.
The tap of a blind man.
The up and down hum of a library
The books of self and selflessness
The saunter of a man made
The stop and start language of English
The flag we wear in pride
The fear of bears to guns
And kids to tons of homework
The love of fun
And wondering
In the sun
That shines.
A green tree statue steads fast against the growing sheets of wind
As the little, milling people at the great tree's feet
Hum along with the song of the breathing wind through the
Fluttering, veined leaves...

The sleepy silence turns to a trickle on the back of your tongue
It grows there, little by little, filling your mouth and your mind
With the easy, golden pure. You wonder about it, ponder it's meaning.
And as you do, your mouth and mind turn into a little spring
And there you are, in between the lush greens and little rocks.
At first, you just bask in the warmth of the sun, but then,
As you begin to learn to smile, you grow.
More beautifully your water walks down the pebbles below and beyond you
More preciously and sweetly do you trickle aimlessly; flawlessly; until
Finally, your beauty finds a place that can begin a path.
Time passes. You grow more: sweeter, calmer, wider
When, much later, you are no longer a simple trickle.
Your mouth and mind have become not even a flowing, beautiful river.
Rather, you have become a raging, mad torrent of incessant and crazy thought.
No more do you swoon creatures to your sandy shores
No more do you whisper to the dreamers of the things they could have
No more. No more.
And this is where you are, river.
You are alone in your mad rush
You are not a sight to say, "Oh, what smile is upon this great thing!"
Now, I can only say, "Bring me across to where there is another stream,

Geoffrey Dilenschneider

Starting again where I can find peace and solace and calm and myself.
Bring me somewhere, and that is all you're good for."
No one will wish for you to become small again, for you are ever-flowing.
Your grace is masked in pain; your hunger for friendship, in salt.
The honey glow of your light-blue grace is no friend of mine.
You are just a river now, and I send off to find another, better friend.

What Will I Become?

What will I become?

A martyr of a name upon a card?
Will the space between myself find a way to come undone some more
Until there's nothing left except a bit of poetry?
What will anyone do and who will I become in time
To greet the cherry lawns?
What is this that defines me so bold and strong but lost
In time I must have been
I don't know what to do and what will happen to my soul?
I have the urge to run
But know that fleeing will do nothing
And hiding can't be done.
I want to paint and draw and sing and run and show the world...
And always say that others' talents aren't really great at all
But that is their place to be great, and they must just have one
And so do I, but must I hate this way I'm meant to be.
I feel just too young and simple to be thrust up on to the world
So quickly, justly, carelessly
And what will I become?

The Lonely Figure

So far away a wave of wonder lies
Down the thinning road.
A lonely figure crosses then,
Down the thinning road.

The sun stays put atop the sky,
Above the thinning road.
And that same sky runs on forever,
Down the thinning road.

The figure sits and drinks from cactus
There under the moon;
And in the heat that no one beats
Where no one goes in June.

But the figure finds no pain around him,
Only misery and shame.
But no one wonders of his sins,
They simply post the blame.

And this figure sits upon the dirt
Stained red and brown and old.
Wondering of that wave of wonders
Down the thinning road.

*This next one I have to explain a bit. I wrote it while looking at the cover of a book.
The cover was of a man next to a smashed-up car. The man was receiving CPR from
a medic. So read this poem as though it is from the point of view of a man dying from
a car crash.*

The Deepest Envy

It's so beautiful,
The sky.
It dazzles me, even now.
Sometimes I wonder
About the sun... I can't really see it
Or the moon
The moon, too. Where is the moon?
I like the moon. It's nicer than the sun,
That ball of fiery destruction is just too bright and mean,
But the moon,
Well... it's just so nice.
When it's dark, it gives me light.
I hope no one ruins it.
That wouldn't be so great.
Maybe if I do come back someday, I'll see the moon again,
And the stars,
My little friends.
I can't really see you anymore, either.
Where did you go? Did you go away from me because I was bad?
It wasn't my fault. Really.
The semi hit me, I was doing nothing wrong.
Well, in any case, stars, and moon, and... well, even you, sun,
Please say goodbye to my family.
I'll miss them, too.
Tell them they are beautiful. Tell them they are beautiful, too.

Geoffrey Dilenschneider

I then went back to searching for meaning greater than that which the mundane around me tried to provide. I went from straight meaning to the meaning of trying to get out of bed in the morning to a little poem of what might happen if two men finally cracked an actual theory of mine (which I have worked on extensively) which states that time is simply a mathematical equation that can be solved; from the inner workings of the design of human interaction and how one's mind may be affected by its peers, to the curse of writing. Man, what a lot of stuff!

To Scratch the Itch When It Has Already Left Us

When we end and come to the End
Will we turn and reach behind
To scratch the itch that isn't there?
Will we deem our dreams no more
When things come silently to a halt,
Like a silent blanket over the world?
Will we turn our heads and ask our past
If there was anything that we did wrong?
Will we wonder of many things?
Will we wonder at all of why and how?
What will run patterns around in our heads
The last little seconds we ever will live?
Where will we go when we sense
That the crowds and fine people
No more will be round to tell us
Just where we should go?
Why does this really have to happen right now?
What did we do to make this happen now?
Many a day we'd wonder when it would happen…
Now, now, now, it happens. Aren't you proud?
How could this happen?
We hated.

In Morning

In the morning after a rainstorm
and a drizzle
Tina gets up to run her laps
and fizzle
Off the golden wisps of sleep
and loose
The grips of bed-wrought hands
and truth
Be told about the feeling of the morning
Everything's so tired and in mourning.

Questions

I sense in my heart something that isn't supposed to be there... or maybe there is something missing. I'm not sure; however, I am sure of one thing: I am sure that I am alive. I am sure that I am breathing. I can't imagine life without living it. I don't know what I'm doing. There seems to be something missing! I'm sure of it! There has to be! Just two seconds and I'll get it... really. Oh well, I guess I won't. My chance has gone out the door before I could do anything about it. Sad, really. Maybe someday I'll be able to be sorry, but until then, I won't be. That's the truth of it, and I can't do anything but cry and whine. Maybe if I think hard enough, I might remember something close to it, but it only comes once.

There are so many things I could be doing at the moment, but I silently choose to do none of them. It's almost sad. Everything's sad. What the hell? Cool things seem to evade me, as well as people, in time, and I feel weird... way too often. Right now is the time to change, but I am so scared to do so. I could sing or write or talk with someone I know, but I could not find love... I could not laugh. I am too depressed, and I will not look at the past. I close my blind eyes to those things I've done, but I cannot close them to the words of past acquaintances who spin webs of lies to the public about things I didn't do. And I know I won't do anything about it, because if I do anything, I'll be wrong. At the moment, I am right, but their words say I am wrong (in more ways than one), so I can't do anything. My reflection mocks me even! Where are my friends when I need them? Do I have real friends? Where are my true friends... the ones that will console me if I am crying?

I wear the hat as a security blanket. Through the pessimisms and optimisms of my soul, I continue on... but I'm not sure how much longer. Some say that my work (my life, more or less) is great, but everyone else ridicules me to no end. It is impossible! I cannot stand it much longer. I will sit and take it, but I will not let them cross the line. Sad, all of this is. I don't know why I bother with them, anyway. What do they know about me, anyway?

Slowly, the hell comes crawling out of me through a hole in my side. Slowly things come to alight where all can see them... where all can sense their undying, hateful presence. The tools I have are what I have. No person can tell me differently that I am lucky to have them. Am I not different in my tools? Am I not different in my journey? Am I not different in my adventure to death... of life? What tears and what are they made of that I cannot see them? What did I do to deserve this burden? Could I not simply live and die?

Please, I almost beg of someone to rid me of this writing curse. Yet... I cannot ask... I cannot wish. I love my pain... I love my curse... I love it for it awakens me to myself. And that is something I am lucky to have, and very unlucky to have.

In the end, I know that the numbers dictate the questions: how many lies will be told? How many people will hate? How many loves will collapse? How many tears will be shed? Who am I and how long will I be wrong and how much is the cost of my freedom? And no, I did not do the things that you created to let the world "know" that I walk different. Thank you, anyway, for I am different and I understand this. I understand much more than most, and I am humble of the fact. I only say it now for the benefit of the liars. So they can ask themselves, "What do I see in my heart that isn't supposed to be there... what is missing?"

Geoffrey Dilenschneider

And then back to being totally off the wall.

Lives of the Saints

The evening daughter of the moon
Hugs close upon the stars
And in a dark celestial breath
Puts ends upon all wars.

The passion spark of innocence
Turns quick to scowl at me
But full and supple tenderness
Brings kittens from our tree.

The burning destitution of
The things we can't control
Is wrought among the stars and cries
Of what it can't control:

The evening daughter of the moon
Hugs close upon the stars
And in a sweet, remembering whisper
Puts ends upon these wars.

To the Broken Friends

Call me crazy, but sometimes I wonder why people don't laugh
Run away if you feel that you need to, but do not forget that we all need a bath
Rats are those things that remind us we're huge
Before we were nothing, not more than the things that we eat
Count upon wonder to keep us in league with the fiends that we all cannot cheat
Really because we don't know how to live except living is just how to live
Ruptured spleens lay hidden in the dirt on the side of our road that we call home
Boredom somehow reminds me that life isn't great
Coin the phrase "leave me alone" or else you'll have no worth
Running and
Running
Be wary of self or else running won't matter as you sift to the ground,
Calling and calling to anyone near
Round the bend comes the man who won't help, only to see you grovel
Respites are seldom and so far between and only
Because you are broken inside.

Gone are the Days

Gone are the days in which carefully were picked the leaves of life
off the trees of calm and sunny days. Gone are the years of
innocence and sweet laughter. Gone are the seconds of awesome
realization. Gone are the moments of cool silence and gone are the days of
pride and honesty and presence. Gone are the days of beauty… now, all we have
are ourselves.

Surprised, Attracted to a Dream

I smell sad, you smell free –
We both swing from green, green tree.
Surprised, attracted to a dream
Calm and sweet you seem to seem.
Blindly writing from a thought
Taught and taught, but not that taught
Of all the lessons of our things
You smell sad like freedom sings

So It Is Written

One is not worth the time of others around one's self until one has made one's
self worthwhile. Then, and only then, will people surround that one with
great magnetism. The diagnosis of this predicament can be talked about for
years with a psychiatrist or a psychologist, but I assume that the method of
resolve is thousand times more efficient than the way of talking. Talking is
good to convey ideas, but actions are better in the solving of problems. We all
forgive, but not as much as we should. We should forgive all action before an
apology; before it happens, even. This is the way of the pacifist. And in the
end, it will all be okay. Reflection is the key to ending hate. If you see the
beauty and the love in yourself, then there is no need to do anything but see
the beauty and the love in everything else around one's self. On the summit of
understanding one's self, pain will be at an extreme. So it is written.

Geoffrey Dilenschneider

The Flowing Raven Rain

Through my two-eyed soul
I find that sloth is often
And down this endless corridor
That laziness has softened.

Against the paint-can bry
The colors of the rainbow show
The fall of Rome was real
But now we know no better, though.

Down the lane of sleep
I find that we all wander slowly
Above, the little creep
While in my soul you wander only.

Without the need of rage
Raven's wings drift slowly down
And then we notice how
We're in a cage, not in a town.

And everything seems fake
This soul we know knows no more pain
Now, just misery
And a picture of the flowing raven rain.

New Eves

Saber waves of antsy rain
Crawl upon my skin
The setting brawls beneath my brain
And wanders on my chin
The sun sets high within my mind
And children grab my hand
Throughout the forest of antsy rain
Crawls past the scratchy sand…
And in the soulless paintings of our eyes
        And inside our head
Inch slowly forth the memories
        On new eves
With   apprehension
And dread.

Sundance on the Place

A peaceful place is set aside for freedom
A place where the soupy heat can't reach
A little dream of tangerines
A place where we can sigh

A wondrous place that turns our new leaves
A place that doesn't let eyes cry
A childish sense of innocence
A place where we can dream.

A crystal leaf, a floating kingdom
An honest touch of flowing cream
A pretty chance that will enhance
This place where we can soar.

A place that won't need our correction
A place with sweet-ladeled things in store
The sweetest thoughts of our dew drops
I am someone's dreamt perfection.

Geoffrey Dilenschneider

Chapter 31

▲ ▲ ▲ ▲

Now you meet the final full chapter of this book; this journey. I will admit that it has not been an adventure like a journal that is tweaked to peak the adventurous sides of the readers; of the public. This will never sit well with the minds of those who feel that the journey is one akin to a pot filled to the brim with action, romance, adventure, plot twists, turns, and dupes. I have not done that; I have given you a chance to look inside the soul of one individual that had the privilege to walk this world, and from his luck, walk this world in privilege. By the grace of God, I will have many more years of luck, and if I do not, then by the grace of God I will survive. And at length's end, when I am finally at rest, I will hope that somewhere, someplace deep I will be remembered like an end of war; remembered for the mind and soul that I have plastered onto this wall as my own sort of fresco; my own sort of self-portrait. My hope is that I will be remembered for me; not the stupid things I've done nor for the things I might have said at an angry or upset moment. My hope is that I will be remembered for my dreams.

And I dream of many things. I dream of hope, mainly, and I dream of love. I dream of the day that all move on, passing by and letting go of the superficial and the artificial; the tangible and the meaningless. We cannot go on like the way we are. Even being religious to a point of fanaticism is harmful. I point no fingers. All religions affect each other and the world we live in. It is impossible to continue on without major change. I preach not to governments; nor do I preach to anyone. I am begging your world, my world, our world to free ourselves from a corrupt society, not necessarily to find focus or meaning to an extremely finite point, both of which are not actually bad things; I simply beg for one change, one revolution, within the mind and heart and soul of every individual on this earth. Find pureness in reality. Not just once, not for a while and then slowly return to our old ways, I beg that we spend our time on earth for a reason, yes, but for ourselves as well. Find something pure to call your own. It will catalyze a reaction that will leave you in bliss as well as your surroundings in bliss. There is nothing better than when all parties; all teams come out winners.

If you disbelieve this, then take a look around you. There are so few purities in this world nowadays. Read the newspaper, and even though every publication has its own unique spin, you can tell that the good and wholesome things are few and far between, and these that are good and wholesome may be becoming too few and far between to do any good, and it is possible that some day, purity might just end.

Passing Roads

Passing along the roads, they groan
With the weight of felicity
A dog turns into a man and cries
That he had liked the weightlessness
The difference is we know we know
Repeatedly and we play
In the passing roads that simmer
And we say:

> We've come a long way
> Down and down and down
> Whistling along the winding way
> Down and down and down
> The passing roads aren't like the rest
> They can change into our best
> And we wonder of the frown
> As we go down and down and down

We just had ice cream melting
With the weight of gravity
We just went wading in the lies
And we seemed like fearlessness
The difference is we grow we grow
When we know that we can say
That we're above that cesspool at the
End of the day

We've come a long way to simply
Stop here and go back to our homes
A girl turns to my shoulder crying
But sees it's me and runs away
But someday she'll come back to me
With a sullen face to say
That the love we have is better
Because we live life all together
Down the roads, we cry for yesterday.

Problems are Only Problems When Considered to be Such

Everywhere I go I
Find (regardless of if I am accepted or not)
That where I am or
Where I end up
Seems to be a sanctuary:
       The houses I've lived
           The schools I've learned
               The loves I've had
                  The people I've
met   and
                   The eyes I've seen…
     The trees I've touched and
        The worlds I've seen collide
in the monastery for specters risen
rising
and curing soupily the whisper-whisper
hush-hush thrill electric of a
tense, working, laughing school library…
          And the/
two hands   collide
         And us sophomore know not to an extent
           Except for that which we really know
But do we ever know?
Or do we just   remember
or do we just assume?
             The eyes I've seen…
    The trees I've touched and
       The worlds I've seen collide
do the beautiful die because they are or because they *think* they are?
       {*sigh*}   the worlds I've seen collide…

Austin

Consider yourself human.
Consider yourself changing
Loving
    Wonderful.
Consider yourself
Floating in the breeze
    Wishing for a world to have
To love
To live
With ease.

Quote #...

Once, long ago, there was a road we traveled that neither burdened nor forgot; a road that, as time passed, lost its potency and its fearlessness… now the only thing we have is our own ability and courage as we traverse the beaten path of ourselves.

This Tree is so Beautiful

This tree that stands in front of me
Is beautiful.
This leaf upon the dainty branch of this tree
What with its delicate and sensitive veins
Is beautiful.
The trunk so sturdy and stead-fast
Is and with the bust of great wills and quills
What with to protect itself
Is beautiful.
It twists and sings and turns and coos
Out to me in its edible language
Is beautiful
What with its grace, agility, and sensitivity
It is the apartment of my heart
Where I can delve into the topics of my mind
And the hallways of my soul
(With reckless, emotional abandon)
in which I can bask in the warm delicious
red-apple sweetness of her
Beautiful voice.

Geoffrey Dilenschneider

How It Felt

Tell me... tell me
Tell me everything you wish for
Tell me everything you wanted
Tell me what it's like to be alone
And what it's like to cry
Tell me of the places you know
Tell me why you've left me cold and broken
Tell me why you don't know why
Why you don't know why
Tell me everything
But most importantly, tell me why

I remember how it felt to stand outside your doorstep in the rain...
I remember how it felt to be there for three hours in the rain...
I can still feel the heart-breakin' agony of that way that you 'd say no...
I can still feel that soap-wash mouth taste that I would get when you would go...
And I can still see that door slammed in my face as you walked away...
And I can still remember the feeling I got from God when I prayed...!

I remember that time we sat together and we kissed...
I can still taste the strawberries and that knockout magical fist...
I can still feel the sun beating down heaven upon our backs...
I can still recall the taste of lust, desire, sex and love's light tracks...
I can't remember everything, but I remember what you said...
I remember you said I love you and the words won't leave my head...!

I remember whispers sent on wings of Hercules...
I remember you and me and the days that we had seized...
But do you still recall the times, do you recollect...?
Do you remember strawberries and the times we were perfect...?
Can you still remember me with a passion and a lust...?
What happened to our relationship, what happened to our trust...?

Oh, We Have Failed Him

And on this day we failed him
We let him go alone
The things we say, the things we did
The way we walked away
What happened to the Glass Grove's Saplings?
What happened to respect?
We have no reason why we left the grass
Left the bushes, left the shrubs
Left the things we loved;
We have no reason to not protect
Him and the togetherness
Of the webs of spiders on the Glass Grove's lanterns.

The bits of apple upon the thick dirt
Call out for feet to watch out
And to bring the self of walking out to play.
We pass things to each other
On the voice and peat of our own song.
We started at the little seed
And now (at end) find us alone with nothing
And a barren little plot of land.

The sunlight, as it melts our eyes,
Lets out the warmest breath between our toes
As we, as friends, we once were friends,
And once knew how it goes.
What is wrong with us
To ruin all the good things in the garden?
What burdens us to fight each other
For control and power of this place that we all love?

My Thimble Dream

I am cherishing you.
I am loving you with my heart, with laughter, with friendship.
I remember everything. I have a map in my mind of your skin.
I delve to the realms of your mind
In a concerto of soft and rough, lovely and grand
Innocent and sweet.

Slowly *I* crawl upon the fall leaves to stop silently up next to you
How wonderful the void in me ceases now, I almost want to cry
Oh, but how sensitive your eyes are. I don't think between them.
When did I ever live through time without you?

Young lace shimmers down the candy air on the bells of those around.
Over and over again I sense odd feelings. Not everything's perfect.
Underneath it all, I feel that everything's okay.

Microcosmically,
You are my world.

Dreams are made of stuff. Stuff is what you are.
Raising up the bridge between us, we find our meaning far beyond words.
Everywhere is somewhere. Everywhere, you are.
And in the end sound breaks my head into a thousand birds.
Me, oh, I'm dreaming… this is my dream.

Love As A

Love as a topic?
Love as a goal?
Love as a being?
Love as my soul?

Love is a murderer, love is a brook
Eyeing the sky above, letting it cook.
Love is a lusting sense, love is a lie
Love is the reason that stone men cry.
Love is a killer, love is a blow
Love is a flower covered in snow.

Love is the beating of two supple hearts
As one, they sift a bit to become the world.
Slowly, they joined as friends
As well as lovers,
Love is a joyous thing when it's
Blossoming the world.

Love is a topic…
Love is a goal…
Love as a being…
As deep as a soul…

A Different Language
(The Tales of the Boy 2)

The curve of a branch
Tells me all about
Love
The flow of a river
Tells me all about
Love
The shape of a leaf
Falling down
Tells me all about love
The whispering wind
As it flows past my face
Tells me all about love

Maybe time will tell me how
Maybe my heart will tell me when
Maybe my place isn't real
All I hope for right now
Is something to let me know
'Bout my heart and the way it should go
'Been so hurt, I'm going blind
all I want is a girl of mine

I ask for peace, I get upheaval.
I ask for quiet, I get medieval.
I ask for love, I get denied.
I ask for friendship, I get defied.
I ask for a complement, I get a shove.
I ask for nothing, and I get love.

The Empty Chairs

And through and through,
The hatred cans us in
And all we can do is bang upon the walls.
Back and forth upon the twisted treetops –
By day, the queen of hearts is nothing but a widow –
She whom knows no pain nor sin,
And everyone, with her, will win
But by night…
The twisted trees come back and laugh,
Her eyes turn cold and lifelessly
She pulls herself together
Like a giant standing up
She yawns and shakes her head around
In the frenzy of a fox

Geoffrey Dilenschneider

And then, again,
We all are chained
Inside our little box.

The Ugly Little Crow (A Simple Rose of Hope...)

Together, we find dreams are made
Between the little places that we find
So blackened with the soot of crow's feet. Crow... crow... crow.

We, the slumming men and women, sigh
We're wondering why we continue to cower
Below ourselves, the sound of crow... crow.

Bewildered, we are so afraid
Of all those insignificant whys
Cautious to a point where we wine and dine
The pasty meat of every single hour.
We laugh smug awhile 'til we know
The chilling call of our dreams unmade: crow... crow... crow.

Beside us are the people who don't braid
Into the webs of life we've come to know,
Because they ponder way too much, and why?
'Cause deep in deep inside their bones they hear it: crow... crow... crow.
The breaks between time's whispering charade
Reminds me that we're never, ever fine.
The light meanders far away... but then we hear: crow... crow.
Our hopes and dreams will fade away like time
In these "time," we all will become sour
So sour with the weight of *fate's to die...*
And in the darkness we will cringe and cower from the unseen hour:
Oh... no

A blood-red rose of hope we saw, but then: ...crow... crow.

This Feeling
(The Tales of the Boy 5)

Verse I   Together we find dreams are made
               Between the places we have saved
               So blackened are the things we love now
               By pain and humility
               Where are we going when blind
               Where'll we go when can't see
               Where'll we go when we're lost
               Where'll we go when alone?

Verse II	A boy sits on a curb alone
	Across the street from a bakery
	Wonder what he's doin' there
	Crying his soul out to God
	As time flies by he's still there
	Staring at the bleak, bony sky
	Wondering about people
	And the things they do and die (why they are so shy)

Chorus	I know a place where everyone's welcome
	I know a place where everyone's nice
	I know a place where everyone's loving
	I know a place where everyone's happy
	(My problem is I've met this girl)
	(My problem is I've met this girl)
	(My problem is I've met this girl)
	She is so perfect in every way
	She makes it all bright, like this beautiful day.
	I'm pretty sure she feels this way, too
	The problem is our tongues are got.

Sweet Lies or Hard Truth?
(The Tales of the Boy 7)

Which is better:
A frown or a smile?
The boy sat down on the ground and pondered for a while.
Which is better:
A terrier or a setter?
The boy leapt about all on top of the matter.

Which is better:
A glance or a stare?
The boy passed some people living (totally) unaware.
Which is better:
a chuck or a lob?
But the boy simply skipped the stone and then began to sob.

Which is better:
Sweet lies or sweet truth?
The boy looks up, but searching for proof.
Which is better:
Sweet lies or hard truth?
The boy looks inside the girl and sees what he thought:
He sees he's brought hard pain to love
And that he'll never find proof of thought

The Boy's Day Off
(The Tales of the Boy 8)

The boy whistles a tune in his head
As his mother is finally getting wed
And doesn't he know how to be, how to love, what is free
Which is might, which is strength, which is power, which is greed
What freedom's like,
It is like everything we dream of
Like the first winter snow on an untouched plot of grass
In a picture on the wall in the middle of July

Call me crazy
But water tastes like apple sauce
To me

The boy sings a song between his ears
As his eyes flick back and forth like electric eels
And he seems to know how to lie, how to cheat, how to cry
How to fly, how to fight, how to read, how to write
What failure means
It is like losing all your dreams
And sometimes it seems
That that first kiss wasn't all that great
And so call me crazy
But water tastes like apple sauce
To me.

Eagle's Creek
(The Tales of the Boy 10)

Verse I   This is a story of a boy who lost it all
                Fell down through the gates of heaven and lost it, lost it all
                Once one sunny morning he fell in love with a girl
                Everything was perfect 'bout her, right on down to that curl

Chorus   Behind the eyes... behind the eyes
                Of the man without words
                Of the man without a goal
                Of the man that doesn't listen
                And the man without a soul

Verse II   And he idolized her, and he gave her things
                Roses in baskets, and butterfly wings
                And she would drop her glove and he would pick it up
                She would uncross her legs for a minute and pull her skirts up
                And one day he asked her out and she said sure,
                But when the day came to enjoy, she didn't seem so sure

Verse III   But that didn't bother him, he didn't care
             All he did was sing for her in thought to mend the tear
             And later on that month, he asked her out again
             And said, "I love you Ali, I don't care if you sin!
             I'll take you up to Eagle's Creek and we can have some fun
             From day to night and back again, under the moon, the stars, the sun…"
             And she said yes, and he was overjoyed
             But she never showed up that day and he felt like a toy

Verse IV   He called her up and called her up, and called her up again
             But either she wasn't there to pick up or it was just her sin
             But one day he slammed the phone down and said "That's Enough!
             I love you girl, with all my heart, but I can't stand this horrid stuff!"

       Chorus

Verse V   And he ran away that night and he never came home
             If you were up that night you could see the dull chrome
             Of the belt he wore as he stole on up to Eagle Creek's Pond
             And swam away forever in the dull moonlit pond.
             And if you saw his face then, you wouldn't've seen a thing
             'Cause he had lost his sense of feeling, but you could've told there
             was something

       Bridge of music

Verse VI   So now this guy goes lonely, this guy goes solo
             This guy goes everywhere, but everywhere ain't known now
             This guy knows the tricks, this guy has a reason
             This guy has no place to be and he has no season
             To be livin' in! 'cause he's got no girl
             Cause girls are the devil and the devil's no pearl
             This guy don't quit, this guy keeps on
             But everyone he passes wonders what's goin' on

Verse VII   Round and round he goes…
             Prayin' on the little folk and beatin' evil ones
             Lettin' out old beggars of the sins they have done
             And when ever you hear him speak, he only says one thing:
             "I was once in love with her and every day I'd sing!"

Verse VIII   And on his final days, the man sat down to rest
             Below a little sapling tree and said "I did my best"
             … So now we know the story of the man without a goal
             Of the man that had no place to be, of the man without a soul.

Geoffrey Dilenschneider

What Leaders? (Why Don't the Heroes Lead the World?)

What leaders?
What things do they overcome?
They don't accomplish much,
The system's meant and set up for
As little change as possible.
The broken minerals upon the dining table of our country
Are our fountain spaced between the time of the day
Where we doodle and dawdle and meander away...
Whittle away
What little time we have.

(Does She Feel, Too?)

This symbol of profundity
Invades him with a glow of the sun.
He wants to create a scene where they will
Slowly together run.
     The dragon weed between them
     Tickles their legs and backs
     With windy giddiness
     And they
Until   now
Sit silently together,
Smiling at each other, with themselves
Crying through their eyes the one thing
That cannot be said,
Until   now
They glance apart to wonder if they're true
(The feelings that I'm feeling, I'm feeling for you)
(But just because I'm feeling doesn't meant that you do, too)

The Knowing Eyes

A smile wandered through Sandra's eyes. The lines of age creased neatly around the corners of her frail mouth. Everything was going to be all right. There was no need for worry. Not just yet.

It was peaceful there in the fluorescent afternoon: the plastic birds singing their recorded little voices out until they broke and then the orderly, Jon Sabos was his name, came to fix them. The molded sun was set to a boil atop the canvass-painted sky, and everything was all right there at Red Desert Retirement Center. Everything was perfect. No worries came crashing down over the gray, lethargic heads of those at the chessboards, which where always there in the game room if you took this hall down to the end and hung a left at the Formica drinking fountain. No pain slit throats with guilt or hung heads when the Cure wore off. No pain because the Cure was never-ending; always Curing.

Her eyebrows creased down then. It had been a long time since Sandra had seen the Outside. The clock on the nightstand said thirty-nine years, sixteen days, thirteen hours, and five minutes. God, what wonders these crazy machines had become over the years. Why, she still could remember when it was just 'atom-bomb' this and 'JFK' that. Those were the glory days, anyway, when things were carefree and peaceful for the little people in America. Memory failed Sandra now and then, but the buzzing Martian machines, which they had found deserted and scattered on the barren Martian dirt many years ago, were literal memory-banks, among many other things, this one in particular dedicated to her life. Those darn machines did everything; knew everything. Nothing else was better.

Sandra limped across her egg yolk colored living area to the waist-high dresser, which contained her clothing and personal items. Like an aged turtle, she bent over and smelled the little rose lying limp and two-years dead on the fake, darkened wood surface.

It was then that she knew it would only be a matter of time.

Sometimes she would forget that she was old, frail. She would start believing that she knew everything there was to know, like the machines, and she would assume the future for what she thought she knew it *must* be.

Now, however, she knew the truth: the rose had lost its fragrance. Oh, to most earth-people, a rose doesn't seem to be much in the grand scheme of things, but Sandra knew different. On mars, each person grew to be connected with a part of the Martian nature. Sandra had grown slowly for ninety years, entwining every facet of her life with the white rose. She was better off than most, too. Most got grass, or red mud; a gerbil or a snake. Others were blessed with strong things like rocks and trees while still others would be further blessed with beautiful things such as flowers or birds. The unfortunate people got animals like elephants or vultures, which, as one could imagine, would be quite difficult to carry around every day.

Also, unlike most forgetful people living in the short and stubby Mars towns, deep in the Martian valleys, she had only lost her white rose once, and then only for a day and a half. But even that small a passage of time had its consequences. When she had found it under a box of her little sister's old shoes up in the attic, a whole petal had withered away and disappeared. To that very day, Sandra would have nightmares of what might happen or what might have changed because of that petal.

But now her white rose had fully died, and there was really nothing to do about it. In the last few years, she had often sat on the grass-like Astroturf knoll near the edge of the complex, wondering how she would react when it happened.

She had herself convinced, one day, that the rose would jump up and bite her in the neck. Instant death. "That would be nice," she had thought.

Other days she believed that she would just lie down with the rose on her chest, arms all folded nice and neat, and stop breathing. She would repeat to herself for hours, hugging her bony legs to her chest, that the orderly would come and take her down to the furnace to be cremated alive. *That* went on for five days before the orderly did come for her after he got word of what she was thinking, but only to show Sandra that there was, in fact, no furnace at all. Once, and only once, Sandra began wanting to rip her rose apart. But the owner of the facility came down from his office to 'chat' with her for a while. He ended up prescribing her some worthless little blue pill. "Once a day every day," they had twittered over and over again like little hummingbirds high on caffeine.

However, Sandra never expected it to be as easy and uneventful as smelling it and knowing.

She stood slowly up, feeling very old, and looked out the one-way glass window. It seemed as though there was a great sky of red and gold out there. She could even see her little artificial knoll, but she knew that the window was specially made to look just like the outside that it was looking out to. She could only "see out" the damn window, but *they* could see in.

"Who thought that it could happen today, anyway? I mean, of all days, today had to be the day. Why? Is it some sort of fate that I have to become the first to die on Mars? The first white rose? Is it coincidence, or is it because I was the first one to step foot on this damned, desolate, lying planet? Or is it because of the petal?" She asked the empty, recycled air. It smelled the same as the old commercial airplanes' air smelled when flying.

Sandra sat down on the bed slowly and swung her tired old legs up onto the bed proper. She leaned back with a great sigh, like a great giant deep in his giant slumber. She had been a great woman once, but now... now she was nothing but a brainwashed Martian freak for the record machines to remember for the rest of time. She liked to remember the names people used to use to describe her before her Rocket went up to Mars. They used to say in the papers she was strong-willed and free-spirited; a loner, a thinker, and a leader. One reporter defined her to as a 'sharp-jawed beauty.' Her friends used to say that she had a heart of gold and a mind full of questions. They were definitely right on that last one. If there were one thing that Sandra had always wanted to be remembered for, it would be for the mind-boggling questions she had posed to mankind.

She looked up to the little squares that made up the ceiling of her tiny, tiny room. They reminded her of what the Moon looks like halfway to old Earth. Suddenly, she felt the air shift in the ugly yellow room. She realized that somebody was standing beside her bed.

"Hey," a voice said, neither too high nor too low.

"Good 'noon... sir?" Sandra began to look over, but a hand stopped her face from turning. The hand wasn't warm or cold, but rather, had a smooth-rough texture and a nice warm-cool feeling. There was a soothing sensation flowing out from its fingertips and through her pale, pockmarked cheek. She could tell this person was used to being a disarming soul. She could tell without looking at the person that every part of his or her being screamed out to the world: "Be calm! Be peaceful! Have love!"

"My name is Chris. Do you know why I am here, Sandra?"

"Yes, wait... no. Wait, umm... do I?"

"Yes, you have thought about this part of your life for a long time. You have an idea of who I am and what I do. Even though you sometimes believe that you know, you are genuinely uncertain. You may ask me anything you wish."

"How's it going, Chris?"

"Fine, Sandra."

"Do you lie?"

"Ah, yes, you like to calculate matters. I almost forgot. No. I do not lie."

"Okay," Sandra squinted, "Where are you from?"

"Are you sure you want to know?"

"Well, yes, of course. I feel like I've waited all my life for this, even though I haven't."

"Okay. I come from Mars. I come from its ground and its air and its soul. I come from Mars's animals, plants, and people. I am part of them all. I am a part of you. I come from a place neither in Mars's heaven nor hell, neither in life nor in death. I do not live in limbo, for I do not live. But I am not dead. I simply am. Everywhere."

"Well! What a load to digest and trust on hearsay!"

"Yes."

"Who are you? Really." Sandra was beginning to become a bit agitated, but kept the emotion inside.

"I am a traveler who does not stop learning, who does not stop experiencing, and digesting. I am the mayor of a town and the boy who shined shoes at what used to be Corbin Lane, the street you used to live on as a little girl back on Earth. I am the doll you used to play with even into your teens. I am the devil's hands and the eyes of what people sometimes call God.

"I am the missionary who saved an innocent child's life. I am that child. I am also the man who pressed the button that destroyed Earth.

"I am the man in the crowd who does nothing important in life. That man who simply influences the friend of someone important so he may someday make the world different. I am him who lives everywhere and nowhere."

Sandra was quite miffed by Chris's preposterousness and yelled at the stranger: "What are you talking about? How could you be dead and alive at the same time? How can you be everywhere all the time? How are you a part of heaven *and* hell at once?"

"Ah. You seem to misunderstand my words. I am not stating that I am these things at once. I am merely stating that I have been all one time or another. Yet, I do mean that I am all these things at once, but you must understand, Sandra, that I am not just one physical body."

Sandra was silent, staring at the pimpled yellow ceiling, words and ideas and theories floating around in a mad cyclone behind her dark, golden eyes. "I do not understand. Maybe I will find answers in your next replies."

"Shoot."

"Are you God?"

"No."

"Oh..." Sandra scratched her head. She thought she heard the faint rustle of summer winds in the winter trees, warmth cracking the little ice-capsules encasing the tiny limbs of the real trees far away on the Outside.

"Are you the Reaper?"

"No."

"Did you know I was going to ask those questions?"

"Yes."

"How?"

"I have said already, but maybe I have not stated it clearly enough. I am part of you. I know you and your ways. I know your wants, fears, desires, everything."

"Are you part of my rose?"

"Yes and no." Chris paused and let a breath out. She could smell the rich musk of a man's coat after being fireside in the wild for a time. "I am part of everything, but I am not a part of your white rose in the way you speak of it."

"What do I mean?"

"You are asking if I am because of the lost petal long ago. And the answer is no. The petal is a sign of your humanity. That is all."

"Am I dead?"

"Not just yet."

"Oh…" Sandra sat for a second in the silence, choking maybe on those words and the weight they had held. Like carrying the whole of love on your shoulders. She asked then: "Are you a symbol of my existence?"

"Look at my face, Sandra." And she did. She turned slowly, and when she looked, she saw that his face was changing. It was neither long nor squat, wide nor thin. It wasn't dark or light, but it wasn't Chinese or Martian or Latin. He didn't have a big nose or a small one, a large mouth or a quaint one. It wasn't frail-lipped or full-lipped. It was a sandwich of two sweet candies on either side of a smile just right but with imperfections that half the people to see it would love. His eyebrows were small and long and short *and* thick… but not. His hair was beautifully brown-red-black-blonde, a long shimmering river of shortish-longish curly, straight locks. Then Sandra looked into his eyes, and gasped. They were blue and green and black and silver and brown and hazel and gold and gray. All the colors in a limbo, shape shifting almost, except all at once. A continuous flow of vibrant, alive colors… all in a single instant. And deep, down and behind, she could see the sea of life and death. Behind those eyes were the sands of time and the black abyss of everything that ever was and ever will be. They were eyes you could swim in forever without getting tired and without finding the edge.

"Your eyes are knowing." Sandra whispered without looking away from the twin souls enveloping her whole. It was the first truth she had spoken all day, and she knew it.

"Thank you, Sandra." Chris's eyes really were knowing. They held the setting sun and the rippling waters that it sunk to in the night.

"Are you a dream?"

"Close."

"Are you free?" The pity showed in her eyes then, but her voice was ever so quaint and chatty.

"No, Sandra. I am not. I am chained to every pain and every evil, as well as every beauty and every joy. But I am chained. This is my penance. We all have penance, Sandra. You know this as well as I."

"I am old, Chris. My white rose is dead. Its fragrance is gone. I am dying with it. What am I to do?"

"Yes. That *is* the question, isn't it?

"Sandra, you must repent for your sins… as well as for your loves, for your passions, for your fervors and banes and boons, for your wants, for your desires… you must repent for everything."

"Do you mean that I must purge myself of all traces of my humanity… in order to be… free?"

"You must understand for yourself… But, I am sure that you can smell the fires and the summer breeze in the frozen branches of the winter trees. I am sure you can see yourself in me and know that you are greater and that your purpose was not in vain. Not in vain at all." Chris, no longer a stranger to the pale woman, turned to leave and whispered, "You are old, and I must depart… goodnight, Sandra."

"Wait!" She looked out past him to her only window's fake view, and as Chris turned back around, she looked into those eyes, crying; and there, she could just make out the glimmer of what Martian deserts had once looked like: empty, naked, free. She could almost see the cities that her family lived in, in all their mechanical glory, then. She fought the tears, wanting not to let go of the living reflections of her long and painful past set there neatly in the visitor's great seas.

The eyes flickered. She could see now her old street, where her memories of Earth still lay in beauty and in peace. She caught a wisp of her mother's apple pie on the tip of her tongue and swallowed it down. She saw a faint image of herself crying over her dead dog, Sparky. She cried harder. Then, another misty view of herself, this time slapping her little sister in the face because she had let the little Jack Russell Terrier run away the night before. Seconds passed, and then he blinked and she saw the swing she and her father had made on earth under the same Weeping Willow that Benjamin Franklin had planted decades before them. She saw the oceans she had sailed, the vast ocean of trees she had flown over, and even the movie theatre she had wanted to buy, only so it would play the movies she liked. She saw her whole life there, all perfect and there.

Then the eyes flickered, changing once again. She could just make out the image of the view out of the Rocket's lone porthole with herself there, looking back down at the Earth as the deadly explosions began to cover it. A great big velvet moss of fire, growing and covering the world; her world. Then, darkness.

Abéra

Every man must change something
At some one point in time –
When he comes to that crossroads that will define him to the core
He must stand up and be recognized.

I take a closer look into the mornings
But find not a thing that makes much sense.
All it is, is a jumbled mess
Jumbled, but in tune with odd finesse.
The curtains fall a bit too soon for me
And I miss her.
I keep on missing her, my moonlight
My ray of rays of sunny shining bright upon my smile!
At last, time hits me with the deadened still of crickets
On a soupy summer's eve,
But it's alright
'Cause I know what's wrong and how to sieve the night.
As I broom on down the room,
I wonder... and whistle
An odd, odd tune
Made up along the way
About my pretty little moon,

Geoffrey Dilenschneider

And how no matter how high I jump,
I just can't seem to reach her,
I just can't seem to touch the sky
And after many days of this
I just don't care to try!
What ag'ny has my inability to speak my emotions brought?
What deeper thoughts provoked have sat collecting dust?
Who's missed me and my smile because the way I thought
And because the way I didn't speak because I do not trust?
Because of me, have you turned away?
Or... are you still at peace?
When will this boochit get out of the way?!?!?
When will these head games just cease?!?
A little drop of mint upon the floor
And all the world slips up to find the ceiling...
Why waste the time of wanting more?
I see no point in even dealing.
The cards I hold...
Are they... offensive?
Why am I so... defensive?
What do I have to lose?
Am I scared to feel the pain of rejection?
What about her acceptance?
Is it really like an insurrection
In the mind?
Across the sky-lit diamonds
I... I... lose sight of what's real
In the world and
In my mind
I can sense the forces in and out but do not know now which way to turn
My head says that... running is the best idea,
But my heart has more concern:
It wants love... something I have not had much of
And the times dictate something... but... but...
I don't know anymore......
    Something's wrong
The floor rushes up and I, down to meet it!
The sky falls on down, and I, up to greet it!
...

where am I?
Where have I gone and whom have I seen?
What places are my memories and what dreams have I dreamed?
My eyes are closed, my soul released
From the burden of choice, from the burden of need.
And I... feel no need to greet you with a false sky
Or a nice hi...
All I know is my self and me and then... and then...
I have changed.

There is something weird
Untried... unknown...
A little difference that I... think will make a big difference.

So, now I'm pretty sure what has happened:
I've chosen my path.
I like it... I like my path.
Any time's a good time to start
And I guess   my time   is now.

      — May 29, 2002

Chapter June

▲ ▲ ▲ ▲

On the Water's Edge

The waves flow in over a hub of sand upon the ground.
The wind pulls at me,
Cool and strong, yet undaunting.
You interrupt my thoughts.
There's so much life here
Even though it's silent.
The waves cave in at my feet and move the earth.
The crash of the waves, the explosion, is so small inside you
But it can still change your world.
There's so much to this; to you;
To your story.
There are woodchips floating innocently here and there,
       meandering on the water's lid,
Rocks upon the underbelly of this body that I love.
And way out there,
There is a soul in the body
That's calling to me…
Even though it's silent.
There are trees over there, great mountains topped with *vanilla ice cream*.
These trees, these trees are voluminous, but they all make up one whole.
A whole that covers everything like a warm blanket in a dark and lonely field of ice.
There is so much to this world. The sand, it's
Like a knife: sharp pieces contrast other sharp pieces.
Each so, so small; so miniscule; so meaningless.
And yet, all *I* can see is the surface…
But then a single wave's foam catches my eye.
I realize that I am merely experiencing the sand's *surface* on the water's edge.
I cannot see the voices of the past, buried deep under the surface that even now
I stand upon.
Where has this body gone? What has it said? What has it done?
Who has it met and whose company has it enjoyed?
And what about its future?
Where will this body go? What will it say? What will it do?
Who will it meet and whose company will it enjoy?
What places will it visit and whose hearts will it destroy?
I look up and can only see so far.
I wonder what lies even beyond the misty covering that distorts my eyes
From truths that are so far away, and yet still part of one body.
Wherever I go, whatever happens, it will be with me…
A brother and a sister; assisting me in *my* quest; in *my* ocean;
In *my* life…
Then it starts to rain on my face

Like soft tears trickling down wounded rivers...
And all I can think about is you:
Never stopping; always moving...
Always moving,
Unable to stop long enough to realize that you are screwed up inside
And unable to see that the ability to change for the better is *within* you.
Never stopping to smell the flowers of your voice;
Never pausing to notice the ocean of your body;
Never looking down to realize your sand or your earth
Your beauty; your mountains... your world.
It's all yours. You can do what you want with it.
It is... *who you are.*
Off in the distance I can see a light.
It starts to illuminate the mountains; it starts to clear up the mist,
But suddenly, that easy touch of rain grows into a mad and constant slap in the face.
I think of you as I leave:
Take the hard-easy, not the easy-hard, okay?
I know there's a world out there for you, too.
Watch the ocean, love the sand...
Learn from the mist and the mountains.
Hear the detail of your past as well as the distant things.
All you need to do is find out
Who you're going to be.
And even though it's raining,
And the wind is biting you and me...
I know the light will find you
And find me
In the one place we are free.

— June 29, 2002

Geoffrey Dilenschneider

Epilogue

▲ ▲ ▲ ▲

Dear Reader,

My journey has been neither arduous nor exceptionally dramatic. I feel almost a need to apologize for my irrational in putting this year to print. Can you tell me what you learned? I do believe it happens to be nothing. I feel no sense of nostalgia; no homely warmth. I wanted to entertain, but the whole thing flopped, I guess. So maybe reading the whole thing as just poetry would be a better idea. I don't know! I don't know what you want. I can't conceive in my mind what *your* mind desires in a book. I see other novels sell, but they are no truer than an old wives tale. I feel no desire to tell a story, for all it is, is a story. How does one come across the words to describe and change another? What does it take to change the world? Can you change the world with the tools you have at your disposal? Or does it take something unexpected and surprising? All I know is that it takes suffering to change and that you can do that. But what I don't know is if I can, too.

What makes the world go around more than the unavoidable concept of time and money? Can we change this, too? Or can we merely pretend that we 'kinda' changed something 'close to' it and then rationalize to our pitiful selves that we changed the world? Should the stiff and bored be ignored or are there stiff and bored out there that actually know better than the famous how to make a difference? Religion is a belief, but flesh and blood are higher than religion. There is no question. If you have seen the bullet open the flesh, you have no more doubt that what is in front of you and what you can touch is real. What God can be killed by bullets? Can America be killed by bullets? By planes turned into bombs? America is an ideal, not a thing. We are Americans because we believe in the freedoms that the word and concept 'America' stands for. America is a country, true, but it is so much more. Some Middle Eastern people believe it is their duty to kill Americans. How do you go about doing that? Killing an idea? Killing an ideal? Okay, so they kill all Americans, but the idea of America – of freedom – is still in the minds of every other living human being. Everyone knows what America is, therefore it will never die. America is an ideal, a hope, a dream. Dreams can never die because man's bullets don't cut through the skin of dreams.

Nothing is perfect. There is always Deception. Blood always spills because ignorance is a way of life. No one wants to die. Everyone questions something because they have to. We would be nowhere without questions. Dreams dictate the Future by showing us what could be, shaped by our own desires. Everything wears out in Time, and Time wears us down. But the pursuit of Truth keeps us alive.

Where does this all point us? We race against the clock, against our friends and enemies and selves, directed and misdirected by our dreams, our fears, our thoughts, our desires, towards one ultimate goal: meaning; substance to this thing we call existence. We live to make peace with the world that tries to wear us down to nothing, and we live to fight it back. To show the Earth, the World, the many Gods and prophets, that we can do that one thing no one thought we could. And that *thing* is finding purpose. We all have a place. And we each will know our own place when we feel truly alive.

There is a road. This road travels far off into the murky distance. It travels this way and that, up and down, over and under and every which way. It is a road, and we will all travel this road until we get off. And when we depart this road, we will be brought to a questioning of great proportions. A questioning that will have no end. There will be no other thing to save you except your knowledge of life and your happiness. It will be for you, by you, and of you, and will become you, in keeping with the divine rite of kings.

We are all kings as we walk down our roads. These roads are there to bind us to life as well as give us the freedom to live. It is our choice to change the way we do. It is also the road that journeys where it wishes. There is no interfering with the road, and yet there is no way that it can go without you.

There is a road, and it is begging to be walked upon. Take your place among the millions; walk the road that is meant for you.

Now, please, go on, but know this: the future is uncertain and you have control. Change is not an issue to skirt. It is a fact of life. Do you want to be remembered?

. . .

It really all comes down to one thing: the meaning of life. What definition do we have for such a lofty concept? There is no such thing as a meaning. It can be no better defined than as this: the life concept is a perfect circle; and within that circle is an un-quantifiable amount of circles; and in each of those circles is another set of an un-quantifiable amount of circles and so on and so forth. When one is born, there is nothing but opportunity; but once life gets underway, the possibilities become – some would say more finite – but I put it as more concentrated. As this boy turns into teen, his environs; his background; the people he interacts with and the people who interact with him; his *context* decides for him who his is to become. The childhood is the ultimate knowledge pit because it is where most of our 'firsts' occur. It is during the childhood that innocence is at its highest power; it is during the childhood that we learn to live in the society we are born into. It is in the teenage years that ignorance to the world around thins and is replaced with many things, as well as is joined with the confusion of hormones and other physical things (ie. Outside influences such as drugs and alcohol and more inner influences such as body chemicals) that complicate the mind and soul. However, it is during the teenage years that the mind develops at a less crazy rate. Most learning occurs before the age of thirteen. The reason I find this to be true is previously stated, more or less. See, (for example) a mother can tell her child over and over again that biting other people is bad, but the child will only realize this information when he bites another person and gets in a lot of trouble and is ridiculed for the rest of the year because he actually bit someone. It is the *experience* that we live for. We cannot, under any circumstance, enjoy the mundane. And that may be a bit of the cake that is otherwise known as life: *enjoying* the life we've been given, because that which we are born into instantly becomes our norm. We get used to the life we were born into because we have nothing to compare it to.

To make the circle more complicated, each person has an almost infinite list of personality, psyche, and emotional traits that are all predetermined. There is no changing those in that list that are definitive types of traits. However, there *are* ways to change those in that list that are in the gray area; ways I have previously discussed, such as the surroundings of the given person; the events that occur in his or her life. Each of those traits interacts with all the other traits of all the peoples and things the given person comes in contact with – not to mention that the given person's traits interact extensively with each other (ie. internal conflict, moral conflict).

Each individual is born with the ability to change, the ability to adapt, and the ability to die. One could say that we are all fugitives on the run; running away, of course, from death.

I cannot call it a problem because it is a way of evolution as well as a way of life, but I can only quantify it as a problem: The American Way is dumbing down – or simplifying, stupefying, moronificationizing – the American citizen. The SATs, for example, are out of context in such a way where one cannot follow, investigate, learn from experience, or even find meaning in a broader sense from these prefabricated sets of happenings. We are letting the bar be dropped, little by little, and someday the big gong upstairs is going to go off, telling us suddenly that there is something greater – and I don't mean God – telling us suddenly that what we're doing is wrong; that we are corrupting our minds and souls, letting them spiral away from the great of our ancestors down to the conniving, inflatable corruption that we are today, and eventually down to nothing.

But we are pretty anyway. Because of all those traits we can each be called our own individual, no matter how stereotypical we may seem. Because the rabbit hole goes so deep; because the circle is so complex, we can never even imagine the different mixtures that can be created.

It is within us to change: change ourselves, change each other, change the world. What it takes is drive, desire, and purpose. Without those there is nothing. It doesn't just take that, either. There has to be leadership, intelligence, maturity, cunning, an understanding of a lot about a lot, and so many more things that it's too much to say.

Once those are cultivated over time (ie. The childhood and the teenage years), then you have a man who is ready to greet the world with a firm handshake and a generous list of abilities. But even then, it takes more. It takes the right time and place. I cannot see Dr. Martin Luther King being raised in the early twenty first century. He would not have had much to say; he wouldn't have found anything very wrong; there would be nothing to inspire him to the greatness that he achieved decades earlier, right?

So, what teaching has occurred in this little segment? Have we learned how to live, or why to live? No. We will never find the answer because there doesn't have to be one. We don't need an answer; we need life. It is within life (purpose, desire, hope, emotion, change), where is the answer.

Here's to those who now know why, and here's to those who care.

Geoffrey Dilenschneider

Chapter Beyond

▲ ▲ ▲ ▲

It smelled of fish and seawater on the first day when I was truly me and not a fake self and the day was blue like the deepest of oceans. It was not a bad day for me because of anything in particular – the panoramic ship held such poignant memories of times well-worn and well-to-be-forgotten – but because I did not want to meet anyone anymore. I desired no more than a place to write and a thing or two to write about. No more people; I was done with love. It had been a crazy year around, and love had given me nothing but pain.

Around the twelve-story cruise liner lulled a moist, capturing vision of the dashing reds and epic greens of Vancouver, British Colombia's sensitive sky-line, and it felt like life was finally looking up for me.

The world had just come full circle. I had started here on the same cruise ship exactly a year ago: I had been conscious, but ignorant to my own igno-rance, and now here I was, a whole crazy year later, smart as anyone could ever be, feeling light and feeling fine, letting nothing and no one catch my eye.

Once aboard, I found myself wandering: sighting out old memories, greeting staff who remembered me from the previous year – I even spoke with Dani, the old Irish bartender, for a time, recollecting the previous year's adven-tures over a couple of strawberry daiquiris.

I roamed in and out and up and down the flamboyant ship, taking in all its sights and sounds, feeling so incredibly happy. It felt to me, then, that I was finally in the one place where I could always go to be free, the one place where I was truly home.

Then I walked into that all-too-familiar card room. And it was then that I saw *her*.

The STORK Club

By Iris Rainer Dart
'Til the Real Thing Comes Along
The Boys in the Mail Room
Beaches
I'll Be There
The Stork Club

The STORK *Club*

A NOVEL BY

IRIS RAINER DART

LITTLE, BROWN AND COMPANY
BOSTON   TORONTO   LONDON

First Edition

The characters and events in this book are fictitious. Any similarity to real persons,
living or dead, is coincidental and not intended by the author.

Library of Congress Cataloging-in-Publication Data

Dart, Iris Rainer.
    The Stork Club : a novel / by Iris Rainer Dart. — 1st ed.
        p.   cm.
    ISBN 0-316-17332-0
    I. Title.
    PS3554.A78S76   1992
    813'.54—dc20   92-15612

10 9 8 7 6 5 4 3 2 1

MV-NY

Published simultaneously in Canada
by Little, Brown & Company (Canada) Limited

Printed in the United States of America

To Steve, Greg, and Rachel.
My three miracles.

Thank You

Elaine Markson—for being there even when I wasn't

Dr. Melanie Allen—with gratitude for the many hours of your time and the benefit of your gifts in the field of child psychology

Barbara Gordon, MSW—for the unending information and patience you gave to me and to all who need your warmth and love

David Radis—the Zen baby lawyer, whose gentle touch has brought joy into the lives of so many families

Marilyn Brown—Senior Director of the parenting center at Stephen S. Wise Temple, for loving information personal and professional

Dr. Betsy Aigen, director of the Surrogate Mother Program of New York—for insight into the process

Vicki Gold Levy—a wonderful friend, and a new mother at fifty!

Christopher Priestly—my strong and dear man. You know some of this is for you

In memory of the late *David Panich*

With love as always to *Barry Adelman*

Mary Blann—There would be no books without you in my life.

Meg Sivitz—There would be no life in my life without you.

Francois R. Brenot—without whom I would still be using a pencil

Susan Sivitz—for her time and effort and love

Cathy Muske—for sharing her painful ordeal

Mary Kaye Powell—for inside tips

Dr. Jeff Galpin—a technical adviser, friend, and terrific writer

Dr. Pam Schaff—a toddler-group colleague from the early days

Sandi—for friendship and support and laughter through it all

Fredrica Friedman—a wonderful editor and friend, whose loving style makes it easier for me to work hard

All the families in the Mommy and Me groups who shared their lives, their toys, their snacks, and their stories with me

And most of all for the children.

"My baby. My baby . . . !"

"Mother!" The madness is infectious.

"My love, my one and only, precious, precious . . ."

Mother, monogamy, romance. High spurts the fountain; fierce and foamy the wild jet. The urge has but a single outlet. My love, my baby. No wonder those poor pre-moderns were mad and wicked and miserable. Their world didn't allow them to take things easily, didn't allow them to be sane, virtuous, happy. What with mothers and lovers, what with the prohibitions they were not conditioned to obey, what with the temptations and the lonely remorses, what with all the diseases and the endless isolating pain, what with the uncertainties and the poverty—they were forced to feel strongly. And feeling strongly (and strongly, what was more, in solitude, in hopelessly individual isolation), how could they be stable?

—Aldous Huxley, *Brave New World*

The STORK Club

1

BARBARA SINGER couldn't stand Howard Kramer. Especially the sight of the top of his shiny bald head when it caught the too-bright light of the examining room while he sat on a creaking little chair on wheels between her outspread legs and moved his cold, K-Y Jellied speculum inside her. And every time she reclined on the examining table with her upturned feet against the cold hard metal stirrups, she vowed to herself and the heavens above that before her next checkup she was going to find a female gynecologist. A doctor who, as her seventy-year-old mother, Gracie, liked to put it, "knows how it feels because she has the same plumbing."

But the months would rush by, and her life would be busy and frantic. And soon the postcard she'd addressed to herself the last time she left Howard Kramer's office would appear in her mail, reminding her she was due for another routine visit, and she still hadn't found a woman doctor.

For a few days she'd feel the postcard staring at her from her desk and want to make the calls, but she wouldn't have a free minute. Then she'd worry that if she didn't get a checkup soon, by the time she did something would be found festering inside her. So eventually, she'd take the path of least resistance and call Howard Kramer's office again, because she knew that since he was her husband's golfing buddy he'd agree to stay in the office to see her during her rare free lunch break from work.

And once again there she'd be, squinting to avoid the light bouncing from the shiny bald head of Howard Kramer, whose only charm was his lunchtime availability, swearing to herself yet again while he invaded her genitals that after this visit she'd take the time to find a new doctor. Unfortunately, finding the time to take was nearly impossible.

She'd given up manicures completely, hadn't had her hair colored in she didn't remember how many months, didn't ever have a break to eat a real lunch in a restaurant or even at a counter in a coffee shop. Instead she ordered the charbroiled chicken sandwich and a diet Coke from the drive-through at Carl's Junior, and ate it while she nosed her cluttered car through the traffic between her private office on Wilshire Boulevard to the clinic downtown, or from the clinic to the pediatric development unit at the hospital.

And that was why her gynecologist of record continued to be hairless Howie, a physician of such skill and such powers of concentration that at the same time he probed, scraped, and pressed down too hard on everything, he was able to describe the Sunday buffet he'd enjoyed last week at Hillcrest Country Club. Praising the Nova Scotia salmon in the same nasal voice that always grated on Barbara when he looked over her chart and asked the obligatory questions.

"Date of last period? Are they still regular? What are you using for birth control?"

"Exhaustion," she'd answer, hoping to get a laugh, though there was truth in her joke. Her own crazy schedule and Stan's busy legal practice often left them with just enough energy to eat a hastily thrown-together dinner or a meal delivered from the neighborhood Chinese restaurant, read a page or two of the newspaper, and fall asleep.

"Really, Barb," Howard said. "At your age, why fool around and have to worry about it?"

She certainly didn't want to report to the doctor that the way she'd been feeling lately, she wasn't thinking about what a man whose office was festooned with degrees and awards from Harvard Medical School still referred to as "fooling around." Besides, she knew if she got into that discussion it would lead to Howie using terms like *premenopausal*. And eventually he'd ask the question that always sent a jolt of anger through her, which was "Why don't you just let me tie your tubes?"

Tie your tubes. He tossed it off as if he were saying "tie your shoes." As if it were that simple an act, that simple a concept. Not to mention the way the words "at your age" always sounded as if he meant "Why does an old bag like you need any parts that have to do with reproduction?" She was only forty-two, for God's sake. Somewhere, she would laugh to herself, in that gray area between fecundity and a face-lift. There were plenty of women well into their forties who were still having babies.

So what, she thought, if Stan and I started early and our babies are twenty-three and seventeen? I'm not going under a general anesthetic just because Howard Kramer, OB/GYN, thinks I'm too old to have to worry about birth control. And each time he'd offered her that option, she'd made some joke like, "I'll tell you what. I'll agree to a tubal ligation if you have the plastic surgeon standing by. That way when you're finished at your end of the table, he can step right up and do my eyes. As long as I'm knocked out anyway, why not?" But she knew she was wasting the levity on Howard Kramer, who'd never been famous for his sense of humor.

After Howard removed his rubber gloves and made some notes on her chart, he invariably launched into a long story about one of the celebrities he treated. It was appalling to her, the way he could go on endlessly about some anchorwoman's cervix or some television star's sterility, leaving in the names and details, while a too-polite-to-stop-him Barbara sat on the table, a prisoner of his monologue.

Sometimes she'd try rustling the blue paper gown in which she'd been uncomfortably clad for the examination, hoping the sound would bring Howie back from his narcissistic reverie, convey the message that now that her Pap had been smeared, she was out of there. But he never noticed. And that was why, she told herself this morning as she sat at her desk enjoying a rare quiet moment in her workday, she was postponing making her appointment this month. Because being face to face with Howie Kramer, not to mention face to vagina, was never a picnic.

This morning she looked at the most recent postcard from his office sitting on her desk with a coffee ring on it because she'd been using it as a coaster for her mug. No. She'd be damned if she'd fall into the same trap and go to Howie Kramer again. This minute she'd call her friend Marcy and ask about the female doctor who treated both Marcy and her daughter, Pam.

She got as far as putting her hand on the phone, but something stopped her from making the call. Probably it was the reality that going to a new gynecologist would mean somehow juggling her own time to fit into the doctor's schedule, then sitting in a strange waiting room filling out a clipboard full of forms. So she promised herself she'd worry about the gynecologist decision later, and she pushed the rewind button on her answering machine.

Beep. "Barbara, this is Joan Levine. I'm calling to tell you that Ronald is trying to get out of our session with you today because, as usual, he says he has some business he can't put aside . . . even for his own son. I'd really appreciate it if you'd call him and tell him he has to show up for the sake of Scottie's sanity. This is just another example of how that son of a bitch doesn't give a good goddamn about Scottie and when we go into court, believe me, I plan to use it. I, of course, will be there at eleven as scheduled. Thank you."

Poor little Scottie Levine; his parents were going to keep beating each other over the head with him until he fell apart, Barbara thought as she made a note to call Joan Levine back and tell her it was okay if her estranged husband didn't come in today. Joan and Barbara could use the time to talk about how the parents' problems with the impending divorce were having a damaging effect on Scottie.

Beep. "Barbara, this is Adrienne Dorn. Jacob's mom. Jacob peed on the floor in his dad's closet again, all over my husband's shoes. And he's waking every night and climbing into bed with me when my husband is out of town. Our session with you isn't until next Thursday, and I'm afraid if we leave these problems undiscussed until then, Jack won't have a pair of shoes left to wear."

Jack Dorn traveled for business three days out of every week. Jacob Dorn, age three, probably figured if his daddy's shoes were covered with urine, he wouldn't be able to leave home. Simplistic maybe, but Barbara was sure the problems the little boy was having centered on his father's constant absences. She made a note to call Adrienne Dorn back and offer to see her today.

She could imagine what her mother would say if she heard those messages. "Spoiled West Side parents who think they're buying their children a fashionable indulgence or an emotional vaccination." Gracie had no patience for her daughter's West Side yuppie clientele. Her own background was in cultural anthropology and she wore her disdain for the world of psychology on her sleeve. "I think you ought to drop the private practice completely. Spend all your time with the needy ones, with crucial life problems. That's where the juice is."

At the family clinic where Barbara spent about a third of her workweek, there was a long waiting list of those. Troubled, anxiety-ridden children whose tiny brows were already permanently furrowed as if they'd seen it all, and many of them had. There were days when she looked into the very old eyes of those very young children and ached to see the absence of hope in them.

Some were referred by social workers, like five-year-old Jimmy Escalante, whose father was murdered while the two of them were having breakfast together one morning at a Bob's Big Boy as a robbery took place. Jimmy had survived the shooting by hiding under his father's jacket until the robbers left and the police came. Now he woke up screaming every night. Last week he told Barbara that someday he would "kill the world" to get even for his father's death.

Some were referred by pediatric clinics, and some children were brought in to her by parents who managed to find their way there by instinct. They were the ones who presented their hurting children to her as unsure of what she could do as if they were handing them over to a witch doctor. The way Angel Cardone had with Rico.

"I think somebody at the nursery school is doing something funny to him."

"What do you mean, Mrs. Cardone?"

"I mean, a couple of times he tried to tell me somebody's been sucking his little pee pee."

"You think there's someone at the school who's molesting him?"

"I don't know exactly. But there's lots of people around there. Teachers, helpers, big kids who get paid to work there in the summer. Maybe one of *them* is doing it."

"Have you examined him? Had a doctor examine him? Is his penis red or irritated?"

"No. I mean, that's the thing. It don't look like he puts up a fight about it, 'cause he don't have no bruises."

"Is there anyone at the school you can trust to talk to?"

"There's nobody anyplace I trust."

"Why don't you bring Rico in?" Barbara asked, her mind racing to think of an open time when she could try to get through to the little boy, and wondering how she would approach him. "How about early tomorrow morning, before you take him to school? Maybe I can find out from him what's going on?"

"I can't pay for coming in again."

"Don't worry about paying. You don't have to pay. Will you work with me on this?"

"Yeah. Sure," she said, turning to go. Then she turned back

and looked gratefully into Barbara's eyes. "You're a nice person."

Thinking about Jimmy Escalante's cries of revenge and fearing that Rico Cardone was being sexually abused brought nightmares that made Barbara cry out in her sleep. Many nights Stan had to wake her and hold her and assure her everything was all right. But after he'd calmed her and fell back to sleep, she stayed awake and worried with a heart-pounding anxiety because she knew better. Everything was not all right.

"I'm losing it," she told Stan more than once at the end of a workday. "So often I see the parents look at me blankly, then look at the clock, and I know they're thinking, 'When the hell can I get out of here? And what does all this psychological crap have to do with me?'"

"At least those families have found you," Stan would tell her. "That means there may be solutions for them."

At the end of a difficult day she'd let herself imagine how it would be if she let herself live a life in which Stan supported them completely with his law practice. Tried to picture how it would be if she woke up every day and did whatever she happened to feel like doing. Instead of shuttling between the families who had too much and the families who had too little, listening to the painful stories that seeped into her soul.

This morning while she waited in her Beverly Hills office for the red light on the switchplate next to the door to go on, signaling that her first private patient had arrived, she doodled absently on the coffee-stained postcard from Howie Kramer's office. After a while she picked up the morning newspaper and turned to the View section to find her horoscope.

"Even a scientist like you can't resist the magic," Gracie always teased when she caught Barbara checking in with her astrological forecast.

"It's harmless fun, Mother," Barbara would say defensively. But the truth was she *did* feel foolish about skipping the front page and going right to the astrology.

"Not to the countless people who are loony enough to change

their entire lives based on what it says," Gracie said, bristling. Bristling was what Gracie did best. But at least she had a sense of humor about herself. "Now read me mine," she'd always add with a mock-serious face.

Today for Pisces, Barbara's sign, the message read: *Unexplored territory offers exciting life-changing opportunity*. Barbara laughed a little burst of a laugh out loud, just as the red light came on. "I sure as hell hope so," she said, then she stood to open the door to welcome her first family of the day.

2

EVERY TIME Stan came home from a long trip he smelled like the inside of an airplane. The odd scent of fuel got into his clothes and hair, and when his relieved-to-be-home hug engulfed Barbara, so did that odor. Usually his eyes were ringed with red, and he'd say something like "I'm not fit for human consumption." Then he'd hurry upstairs to take a shower and put on sweatclothes. Barbara unpacked his suitcase, carried the dirty clothes down to the laundry room, and met him in the kitchen to make him a snack.

It was after those trips when she'd look appraisingly at him and be secretly relieved to see him looking his age, their age. For the longest time she'd been noticing the way her own face was starting to sag a little around the mouth, and wrinkle a little around the eyes. At last Stan's temples were gray and he was getting a pouchy place just under his chin, which, when he spotted it in the mirror, would make him decide to grow a beard. But after a few days he'd look at the scruffy growth on his face and reconsider, deciding that the gray in the beard would be more aging. With or without a beard, the truth was that to his wife he was looking sexier than ever.

After she made him a sandwich she sat next to him at the kitchen table, watching him eat, and realized she was breathing differently, more easily, because he was back. She always felt safer when he was near. There were days when she had rushes of feeling as mawkishly in love with him now as she'd been at seventeen when they met, and at eighteen when they eloped. An act which had horrified all of their parents. Particularly Gracie, who still had what Barbara knew was a forced smile on her face every time she talked to her son-in-law.

"You don't get to pick, Mother," Barbara remembered saying when her mother had referred disparagingly to Stan's straitlaced style.

Today while he finished his sandwich, he held Barbara's hand, as if to say he felt the same romantic way about her, and she looked down at their two hands together. At the slim gold wedding bands they'd slid onto each other's fingers so many years ago she could barely remember life without him.

"Are you okay?" he asked. That was always the question he used as an opening to check in with her, to find out if she needed anything or wanted to report any new worry, to discuss something about the children, her mother, or her practice.

"Just my usual overwhelmed self," she said, picking up a thin slice of tomato that had fallen out of the sandwich onto his plate and eating it. "I'm worried that I'm working by rote, that nobody's getting the best I have to offer because I've taken on too much. I console myself all the time with the idea of an early retirement."

"No chance of that. I know you. You go through this from time to time, usually after you've had a few weeks of twelve- and fourteen-hour workdays. Then something happens to excite you and you're off and running again. A few months ago you told me you were cutting back. Too many private patients, too many groups, and did you?"

"Tomorrow I meet with a new family, and I'm meeting with another new referral on Friday," she said, feeling like a child confessing a misdeed.

"I rest my case. Sometimes it's like that. All the personalities and needs and pain get inside you and you start living them. I understand, because I do it too. My clients rail and scream and yell, I get involved in it, and then they feel better and *I* walk around with indigestion." They both smiled. "You realize, by the way, that as far as I'm concerned you can quit working any time you want. Take a year to read the classics, another year to putter in the garden. But I say that secure in the knowledge that you won't." Barbara sighed. Probably he was right.

"Of course we could have a baby," he said, putting the sandwich down and taking a big sip of some orange juice he'd poured over a glass of ice. It sounded like a joke, and she laughed an outraged laugh, sure the remark was just his way of getting sexy with her.

"What?"

"Just a thought," he said, and the look in his eye was mischievous.

"A unique one for a couple who's approaching their twenty-fifth anniversary, wouldn't you say?"

"I guess. But there was a baby next to me on the airplane on its mother's breast, and it was so adorable. I forgot how sweet they can be."

"I hope you're referring to the baby and and not the breast."

He smiled. "Speaking of breasts, where's our son?"

"I'm curious and not a little bit concerned about how you made *that* linkage," she said, laughing and leaning forward, using the corner of a napkin to wipe a crumb from his chin.

"I mean, if he's out and not due to come back looking for money or food, the only two reasons he ever stops in, maybe I could reacquaint myself with yours."

"I thought you'd never ask," Barbara said.

Upstairs in their bedroom, they slid naked between the cool soft sheets of their bed and moved close to each other. A thrill of familiar warmth passed through her as she felt his chest pressed against her breasts. At first their kisses were tender but soon he touched her in the way he knew would arouse her, and she felt her own passion rise and wanted the release, wanted him inside her.

Just as she was so familiar with his moves when they slow-danced, knowing that a certain lift of the shoulder meant they were about to turn or a certain swivel of his hip meant they would dip, when they made love she knew exactly at which moment he was going to move over her and then inside her, and she opened her entire being to his entrance, feeling the perfectness of their union.

"Welcome home, my love," she whispered.

Once their sex could make her weak with heat. Today as their bodies united it was as if some part of her own person had been away, and by the act of sex had been reconnected.

A baby, she thought. The idea interrupted her reverie. He had to be kidding. But while he filled her insides with his hard self, and kissed her, then kissed her again, as their lips and their tongues collided and then entwined, she was counting behind his back on her fingers to be sure it was late in her cycle. Hoping it was a safe day, so that she could let her mind get lost in the joy of his return. Her love. How lucky it was that after so many years their sex was so delicious and loving and good.

"Ma?"

Barbara and Stan were in bathrobes, had just stepped out of the shower when Jeff got home.

"Hi, honey. Dad's home. Come in."

"Hey, Dad." Jeff pushed the bathroom door open and gave his father something that could be construed as a quick hug. "Can I take the car down to Orange County? There's this game down there some of my friends have been going down to play. It's called Photons and it's really amazing. It's like being inside a video game. You play on teams and you run around this maze in the dark and try to blast the other guys with your light beams."

"Sounds like *my* idea of a good time," Stan joked.

"Why don't you stay home, honey? You haven't seen Dad in over a week. Let's all have dinner together, eat at the dining room table, and . . ."

"Relate?" Jeff said, giving her a sidelong give-me-a-break look.

"Spoken like the son of a psychologist." Stan laughed.

"Can we relate tomorrow night, Mom? I really want to do this."

"I think it's all right if he goes." Stan looked at Barbara and grinned. "This is why people our age have babies."

"You two having a baby? Oh, cool," Jeff said over his shoulder, and he was gone.

Later that night when Stan was turned away from her and she was snuggled close against him, knowing by his breathing he was seconds away from sleep, she said to his back, "How serious were you about babies?"

She was relieved to hear his groggy reply, which was "Not serious at all."

"Scottie, what's going on?"

Scottie Levine, age four and a half, was dressed in a Ralph Lauren shirt, khaki pleated pants, a tan braided leather belt, tan socks, and brown loafers. And his haircut wasn't from the Yellow Balloon or any other kid's barbershop. It was shaped and gelled into some semblance of the haircut of a thirty-five-year-old man. He looked as if he should be carrying a portable phone and talking on it to his broker. Scottie was one of a group of children who had been nicknamed "chuppies" by one of Barbara's colleagues, children of yuppies.

Even his sigh was adult, a strained exhale that sounded as if it meant he was resigned to the fate of being the child caught in the middle of a warring, acting-out couple and forced to be the sane one in the family. Barbara watched him pick up a small black bag of magnetic marbles he'd played with before in her office, spill them out and line them up so he could flick them the way he liked to, one at a time until they hit the molding at the far end of the room.

"Do you go to your daddy's house to be with him?" Barbara asked. He nodded.

"And is it fun to do that?"

No response.

"What do you and Daddy do on your days together?"

"Nothing." He moved the marbles around, rearranging their order into groups of matching colors.

"Do you stay at home and play together?"

"We play Frisbee."

"Oh yes, I remember your telling me how good you're getting at Frisbee."

"I sleep over too."

"That must be great. Do you have your own room at Daddy's?"

He nodded, was silent for a while, then added, "And Daddy sleeps with Monica."

"Who's Monica?"

A shrug. Then Scottie turned onto his stomach, made a circle of his thumb and forefinger, and with a hard ping sent the first marble across the floor, and then another. When all twelve of the marbles were against the wall, Scottie put his elbows on the floor and his face in his hands and said in a near whisper, the way Barbara often heard many of the children she treated state their hardest truths, "I saw her tushie."

"You saw Monica's tushie?" She spoke softly too.

She could only see the back of Scottie's head as he nodded. "In the morning in my daddy's bed. She was sitting on top of him and they were naked."

Now he put his face down on the floor and left it there for a long time, the gel on his hair glistening from the sun that poured in through the office window.

"It must have made you feel funny to see your daddy and Monica naked."

The little head nodded again, almost imperceptibly.

"Was it sad because of your mom?"

No answer. Barbara sat on the floor next to him. He was crying. When the hour was up she opened the door to the waiting room, and Scottie left with the Levines' pretty, Swedish au pair, who had been waiting for him. Barbara called and left a message on Ronald Levine's answering machine asking him to call her as soon as possible.

She was late, due downtown in twenty minutes and it would take her at least half an hour to get there. She was rushing to get out of the office, so when the phone rang she decided to let the machine answer it. But she stood in the open doorway waiting to hear who was calling in case it was an emergency.

Beep. "I'm Judith Shea, I was referred by Diana McGraw, who's in your Working Mothers group. I had two babies by D.I. and I need to talk to you as soon as possible. Here's my number."

Barbara pulled a pad out of her purse and jotted the phone number down, then locked the office door and rushed out to the parking lot to her car. D.I., she thought. D.I., and for an absent minute as she looked at what she'd written, she thought the caller was being strangely coy and giving her the baby's father's initials, but then she laughed at herself as she made the turn out of her office parking lot and realized what the letters actually meant.

3

THERE WAS a kind of glow around Judith Shea as she sat on the floor of the reception area nursing her baby. She was one of those women whose look Barbara always envied. Skin that was a naturally peachy color no cosmetologist in the world could ever recreate, green eyes so bright they might have been ringed with liner, though she wasn't wearing a drop of makeup. Her thick shiny auburn hair was cut bluntly in a perfect bob. Barbara realized with embarrassment that her own unconscious prejudice had made her assume that a woman who used donor insemination to conceive a baby would be homely.

The nursing baby looked over the full round breast at Barbara with eyes that matched her mother's, while her cherubic sister, a toddler girl with red ringlets, was asleep on the love seat. "We got here a little early," Judith said. "Jillian fell asleep. I hate to wake her."

"Don't move," Barbara said and hurried into her inner office to get a pad and pen. "You're my last family of the day, so there's no reason why we can't talk right here," she said, returning to sit across from Judith in a way that accommodated her own straight black wool skirt.

"So let's see. Where do I start? I was thirty-six years old with no boyfriend and not a whole lot of dates either. In fact, my

friends at work always kidded me that Salman Rushdie went
out more than I did. But I always had a powerful craving to be
a part of a family. Maybe because I was an only child or because
so much of my own family are deceased.

"I wanted to be a mother. But as independent as I am, it was
the only thing I couldn't do alone. And I didn't see marriage
anywhere on the horizon." She thought about what she'd said
for a minute, then laughed a bubble of a laugh. "Marriage, hell!
I couldn't find a man I'd risk safe sex with, let alone the kind
without a condom that could make a baby." Her eyes tested
Barbara's to see if the psychologist was making a judgment about
what she was hearing.

"Go on" was all Barbara said.

"You don't know me yet but believe me, I'm not one of those
women who won't buy herself a white couch in case she meets
a man who might like a brown couch better. I've got plenty of
my own money, a great career, I'm an art director in an advertising agency. Remember that quote from Gloria Steinem? Something about how we've become the men we wanted to marry?
Well it's true. I love my life and don't have any enormous need
to couple up.

"So I went to a sperm bank, and not only did I buy and use
the sperm successfully once, but having Jilly was so much fun
that I did it again. And I used the same donor both times, which
means that my girls are full sisters, with the same mother and
the same father . . . in absentia though he may be."

"How much do you know about the father?" It was not the
question Barbara wanted to ask. She would have loved to ask,
"Aren't you dying to meet the donor?" or "Aren't you afraid
he'll show up someday?" or "Weren't you worried there would
be something wrong with the sperm? Genetic problems or God
knows what?" But she was working at keeping her professional
distance.

"The truth? I know less about the co-creator of my children
than I do about the Federal Express delivery man," Judith said,
and laughed. "Actually the way these cryobanks work makes it

very chancy, because all you get from them is a list of numbers that represent each donor. And all they tell you is his race, blood type, ethnic origin, color of eyes and hair, type of build, and then a one-or-two-word description of his special interests.

"It's funny how rational it all feels when you're doing it, and yet when I describe it to you, I can hear how weird it must sound. I mean, for example, I wanted my babies to have light hair and light eyes, so I picked donor number four twenty-one, and all I know about him besides his coloring is that he likes reading and music."

The baby on her breast let out a happy little shiver of a moan, and Judith gently patted its tiny behind. "I made it a point to buy the sperm from one of those places where the donor agrees to let the children meet him in eighteen years, which means that my kids have a chance of knowing their father some-day if they like."

"How do you feel about that?" Barbara asked.

"A little worried. But I've got a long time until I have to face it," she said, then added grinning, "Somehow I get the feeling you probably don't get a lot of people coming in with this kind of story."

"You're right about that," Barbara said.

"For all intents and purposes I'm a single mother. And a hell of a lot happier than if I'd been divorced and had to go through all of the who-gets-custody issues. I mean, it's a very no-muss, no-fuss way to go. Not to mention the fact that you've never once heard any torch singer sing 'The Donor That Got Away' or 'My Donor Done Me Wrong.'"

Both women laughed. Barbara liked Judith Shea's spirit. "How can I help you?" she asked. And as if that was the cue Judith had been anticipating, her front of confidence fell away, her cheeks flushed, and she looked very young and full of emotion. It took her a while to pull herself together. For a long time there was no sound in the room but the *plink* of the numbers on the digital clock as they rolled over.

"Jillian's nearly two and a half, and she's already talking

about penises and vaginas and babies. And I realize that pretty soon she's going to want to know how they get inside mummies' tummies. When I think about that I start to panic and I worry about her coming to me and asking, 'Whatever happened to good old donor number four twenty-one?'" She shook her head at her own funny take on the situation. "When I thought about having a baby I pictured going out to buy nappy sets and pretty nursery furniture, and then having someone soft to cuddle. But not even once did I plan for what happens when the babies are children who have language and ask tough questions, which will probably be any minute."

"And when they *do* start asking you about their father, which they will, you'll have to give them some unprecedented answers," Barbara said.

"Sometimes at night before I drift off to sleep I think of elaborate lies I can tell them about their genesis. But then I know I won't be able to do that because I think lying to kids about anything is unconscionable. Don't you?"

"Yes," Barbara said.

"I know you have a lot of programs over at the hospital for single parents and widowed parents and working parents, but I also know my problems don't fall into the purview of any of those groups. So what do I do?"

"I don't know," Barbara said honestly. "As you said, this is a new one. But we'll work on it together."

"You see," Gracie said, "it's why I always tell you that you can't predict human behavior by scientific laws. That woman is a product of these times. Sexual relationships are unsafe, infertility is rampant, people are faxing their brains out instead of speaking to one another. And there's no rat in a maze who could have made the kind of emotional decision she made to have those babies."

Barbara and Gracie moved swiftly down San Vicente Boulevard on the grassy medial strip. As usual Barbara was huffing to keep up with her energetic mother, telling Gracie, as she had for years, about what was going on at work. She always left out the personal information to protect her clients' confidentiality, and knew she was leaving herself open for some disdain, like that pointed comment about the way psychologists studied laboratory animals to learn about human behavior. But she was sincerely interested in her mother's always passionate input. Today when she talked about Judith Shea, Gracie "tsked" every now and then as she listened.

"New arrangements, new technologies, in a world that's not ready for them," she said. "The quantifying of human life. Can you believe they freeze embryos, then the couple get a divorce and fight to see who gets custody of the damned things? Frankly it all gives me nightmares about the future."

"Me too," Barbara said. As they approached the open-air marketplace at Twenty-sixth Street she wished they could just stop there for a cup of coffee. Gracie must have received her brainwaves, because just then she stopped walking in front of the open-air marketplace, said, "To hell with exercise, I need caffeine," and turned into the courtyard, where Barbara found an empty table for them while Gracie walked up to one of the stalls and ordered two cappuccinos.

"I think it's interesting," Barbara said as Gracie placed a steaming cup of white froth in front of her, "that she chose to bypass the human factor, obviating the messiness and the awkwardness and the commitment to a relationship. And she seems reasonably comfortable with that."

"Well, *she* may be, but I'm not," Gracie said, shaking her head. "I say marriage is better."

"Mother, you're not exactly a testament to the success of matrimony and the nuclear family."

"But *you* are, so do as I say, not as I do. I made mistakes, Bar, and not working harder on my marriage was one of them, but the older I get the more I believe that a strong and loving family is the basis for mental health. You and your sister were exceptions. You both came out okay in spite of my divorce because I was such a brilliant mother." The smirk on her face told the truth they both knew.

"Absolutely," Barbara said. "And let's hope the children of this woman will be too." She watched a pigeon bob around the brick patio pecking at crumbs.

"You know," Gracie said, "I'll bet in this crazy city there are dozens like her. Women are buying eggs if they don't have any of their own. Then they're even having other women carry the embryos for them. Have you read about the mother who did that for her daughter?" She put her hand on Barbara's arm and grinned. "Honey, I love you, but *that* far I will not go!"

They both laughed at Gracie's joke, and Barbara thought how she loved this crazy loon of a mother of hers. "Oh too bad, Mother," she said. "I was just going to ask you if you'd mind."

"So what *about* these people?" Gracie asked, dipping a *biscotti* in her coffee and swirling it around in the bubbles of milk.

"Families with issues for the new millennium," Barbara said. "Beyond the birds and the bees. I should form a group just for them. To figure out how to break through the technological and get to the human issues." When she looked up she saw an unmistakable glow in her mother's eyes.

"That's a hell of an idea," Gracie said, then she bit into the now soggy cookie.

"Thank you, Mother." Barbara smiled, thinking it was the first time she and Gracie had agreed on anything in years.

"After all, what is it that woman is trying for by having those babies?" she asked Barbara in the way she always posed questions, making it sound as if she were giving you a test.

"Normalcy," Barbara answered. "Oddly enough she's using high-tech reproductive techniques to create some kind of regular family life, some kind of intimacy for herself, by being some- body's mother." This was Gracie's meat. It was socially signifi- cant. Bigger than the everyday development problems Barbara dealt with all the time, and she heard the giddiness in Gracie's voice when she spoke.

"There are some interesting ethics involved here too. I think it's the cutting edge of family practice. What do *you* think?"

"What *I* think," Barbara said, standing, "is that I'll have a croissant," but as she walked over to the bakery counter she felt a little zap of adrenaline she knew wasn't from too much caffeine.

In her office she picked up her mail on the floor where it had fallen through the slot, then pushed the button on her answering machine.

Beep. "Yeah, hi, I'm Ruth Zimmerman, my pediatrician said I should call you. I'll leave you the phone numbers for me at my house and my office and the studio, and my car, because I'm in a state of urgency here. Please try me as soon as possible. I have a two-and-a-half-year-old son and I need to talk about him with you right away. You see, here's the thing about how he was born . . ."

Barbara listened to Ruth Zimmerman talk about her son and the unusual circumstances surrounding his conception. When the message was over and she picked up the phone to call the woman back to make an appointment, she thought about what her daughter, Heidi, always said when things in her own life fell together in a pattern: "Totally spooky."

While she waited for someone to answer Ruth Zimmerman's phone, Barbara tried to remember her horoscope of a few days earlier. What was it? Something about unexplored territory and a life-changing opportunity. It was totally spooky.

4

ON THE WALL of the messy undersized office of Ruthie Zimmerman and Sheldon Milton was a framed needlepoint sign which said DYING IS EASY. COMEDY IS HARD. It was made by Ruthie for Shelly long before they were a successful comedy-writing team, before the series and the Emmys and the big money. Shelly was sure the sign was a good-luck charm, so over the years he took it with them from office to office.

This space in the writers' building at CBS in the Valley was furnished with two back-to-back desks and two old upholstered desk chairs, plus a small upright piano that had spent most of its life in rehearsal halls. In every corner and on every shelf were piles of scripts. Some were written by Zimmerman and Milton, some were written by their staff, and some were written by hopefuls whose agents had begged Ruthie and Shelly to read them and consider the writer they represented for a job on the show. And of course on both of their desks was an eight-by-ten photo of Sid Caesar.

When the phone rang it was Solly, their agent, so Ruthie took the call, and while Shelly waited for her, he did the *New York Times* crossword puzzle.

"Are you kidding?" he heard Ruthie practically sing into the phone. "It's no trouble at all. We'd love to. I'll talk to Shelly about it and call you back." When she hung up he didn't even have to look at her to know what was coming next.

"What did Sol have to say?" he asked, carefully filling in some letters across the top of the puzzle.

"There's no business," she answered.

"I'm praying," Shelly said, "that the next three words out of your mouth are going to be 'like show business,' but I'm afraid it's a faint hope."

"You're right," Ruthie said. "I wasn't doing my imitation of Ethel Merman. I was telling you what Solly told me, which is that the television business stinks, and how incredibly lucky we are to be doing this show instead of being out there in the job market." She watched him fill in a long phrase all the way down the right-hand side of the puzzle with that look of triumph he always wore when he deciphered one of those. "He's right, you know. We're truly blessed. And we can't forget that." Her voice was becoming what Shelly always called "soggy." The way it got when she was feeling awed by how far they'd come in their careers.

"Uh-oh," he said, looking up at her. "When you start sounding like Jerry Lewis on the telethon it means you've just volunteered our services to some fund-raiser so we can prove to the world and ourselves that we're thankful. Which one was it today?"

"The benefit show for the Writers' Guild fund, and they need us right away. It'll be good for us. We're always so busy with casting sessions and network meetings we hardly ever get to sit and write anymore. This'll keep us fresh."

"Can't we just use deodorant?"

"Oh come on," she said, taking the Arts and Leisure section out of his hand. She was glad to have a reason not to go back to looking at some set designer's elevations for next week's show. She much preferred to plop a brand-new yellow legal pad on Shelly's desk and one on hers, divide several sharpened Black-wing 602s between them, and say, "Gentlemen, start your pencils." This was their favorite part of working together. Finding their way to an idea, moving it along, exploring it, turning it every possible way, or as Shelly liked to tell the writing staff, "You take a germ and spread it into an epidemic."

"Okay, let's see," he said, planting his feet on the floor and twisting back and forth in the reclining chair the way he always did. "The Writers' Guild. Here it is. What if a husband-and-wife writing team realize that nobody wants to buy their material anymore, so they decide to make a suicide pact and kill themselves?"

Funny, Ruthie thought. Already it has promise.

"But of course," he improvised, "they have to leave a note. And since they're writers it has to be a great note. So they start to work. The husband sits at the typewriter; the wife paces. Suddenly the husband says, 'I've got it! We'll open the suicide note by saying "Au revoir, heartless universe."'"

Ruthie knew exactly where he was going and she jumped in. "But the wife sneers and says, 'Are you nuts? That stinks! You can't open a suicide note without saying "Farewell, cruel world."'"

Shelly was really working it now. "The husband laughs a mocking laugh and says, 'That is so kicked. I've heard it a million times.'"

"Which infuriates the wife." Ruthie put her feet up on her battered old desk, sat back and thought for a minute. "So she turns on him . . . she's always been a shrew, and she says, 'Oh yeah? Well, I happen to think it makes the point better than "Au revoir, heartless universe," which like most of your ideas is completely phony.'"

"The husband is hurt," Shelly said, "but he's going to be a martyr about it, so he gets very tight-lipped and says, 'Fine. Let's go on. We can come back to the salutation later.'"

"'What later?' the wife shrieks. 'There won't *be* any later! Don't you remember? We're going to be dead.'"

"And he says, 'Yeah? Well, if we open with "Farewell, cruel

world," we'll be *worse* than dead. We'll never work in this town again.' Hah!" Shelly laughed a cackle of a laugh at his own punch line.

"Funny," Ruthie said, taking her feet off the desk, sitting forward in her chair and looking pleased. She loved this man. Still found him so entertaining, so clever, so much the perfect counterpart to her that all the years they'd been hidden away in dimly lit closetlike spaces to write and produce shows were paradise for her just because they were together. And she'd felt that way about him since the night they met, eighteen years ago.

It was in summer stock in Pennsylvania when they sat lit by the summer moon on the big wooden steps of the White Barn Theater, where Ruthie was an apprentice and Shelly was a rehearsal pianist. As the crickets of summer throbbed and a yumpy-dump band from the cocktail lounge of the hotel across the way played "I Can't Get Started with You," the two of them exchanged horror stories about their respective Jewish mothers.

"Mine had a plastic throw made to put over the chenille toilet-seat cover."

"Mine couldn't get a lawn to grow in front of our house, so she cemented over the dirt, then painted the cement green."

"Mine told me if I ever touched myself you-know-where, I'd eventually get locked in a crazy house and she'd never come to see me."

That was when Shelly smiled and took in that kind of deep breath which means, Now I'm going to pull out all the stops and tell you the ultimate Jewish-mother story which you'll never be able to top. And Ruthie, who'd been looking for an excuse to do so all evening, leaned in a little closer.

"Mine," he confided, "made the ultimate sacrifice for me not long ago when I fell madly in love with a creature so magnificent, there are no words to describe the temptation into which I was led by this—and I apologize in advance—gentile." He is so funny, Ruthie thought, and so cute. "This," Shelly went on, fueled by her obvious admiration, "was a lover par excellence, who whispered to me one night in the heat of passion, 'If you really love me, you'll go and cut your mother's heart out and bring it to me.'"

Ruthie giggled, and Shelly tried to look serious. "Naturally," he continued, "I did what any red-blooded American boy would do under the circumstances. I ran home, grabbed the old bag, and not only cut her heart out, but to add insult to injury, I took a Reed and Barton platter out of the silver closet and put the quivering mass right on it. Without a doily." Ruthie would always remember the way the moonlight made it appear as if there were frost on the top of his curly brown hair and the way those hazel eyes behind the horn-rimmed glasses were so alive with glee.

"To say that I hurried back to my beloved's house would be a gross understatement. Unfortunately, blinded by my passion, I didn't notice a branch which lay across the sidewalk in my path, and sure enough the branch caught my foot, my ankle turned, and as I tripped and fell, the heart flew from the tray and landed in the street in a bloody, pulsating pile."

"No!" Ruthie said, grinning as she jumped into the game, loving the delight she saw in his face when she did.

"And as I lifted myself to my feet, my mother's heart spoke to me."

"Really?" Ruthie asked, knowing the punch line was coming, and hoping she was offering the proper straight line. "What did it say?"

"It said," Shelly answered, taking a deep breath before he went on, "'Did you hurt yourself, honey?'"

No one had ever told a joke that hit home so well with Ruthie, who let out a laugh of recognition, and Shelly laughed with her. So hard he had to take off his glasses and wipe away a tear from the outside corner of his left eye. There are very few things that make two people feel closer than laughing together, but just at the moment when it was clear that Ruthie and Shelly were feeling that closeness, Shelly looked at his watch.

"It's late," he said, patting Ruthie's hand. "I've got to go."

Later, in her cubicle of a hotel room, by the light of a bare bulb in a wall socket, Ruthie changed out of her overalls, dabbed some dots of Clearasil on the eruptions here and there on her face, slipped on her Pittsburgh Steelers nightshirt, and fell onto her bed. Then she reached into the bedside-table drawer for her little spiral notebook, in which she made a list of possible bridesmaids who would precede her down the aisle when she married Shelly Milton.

"What's the thinnest book in the world?" Shelly asked the next night.

"*Jewish Circus Performers*," Ruthie answered, having no idea where she got that answer. It had just popped into her head. "What's wrong?" she asked him. "You don't remember Shirley the Human Cannonball?"

"I do," Shelly said. "She was a terrible woman . . . but a great ball."

They both screamed with laughter. Soon they had ritualized their end-of-the-day meeting on the steps of the theater, each of them finding the way there after the long hours Ruthie spent building and painting scenery and Shelly spent pounding out the same tunes again and again for the rehearsing dancers. Just knowing they could look forward to the time they spent afterward laughing and mining their creative and bizarre minds enabled them to get through each day.

Ruthie thought it was the beginning of a great romance, though there was never even so much as a kiss on the cheek as evidence. She had the naïveté of the unsought-after girl who had never once felt the front of some eager boy's corduroys, lumpy with lust, pushing heatedly against her, since no boy had ever really desired her. And that was how she came to be nineteen and, with the exception of a few disastrous fix-ups from some of her mother's friends who sent a pitifully too-short son to call or forced a stuttering nephew to take Ruthie to a movie, she had never dated. Undoubtedly it was the fact that she knew so little which enabled her to continue to imagine that someone so obviously crazy about her was simply taking his time about declaring his romantic feelings.

Then one chilly night she woke in her bed at the Colonial Manor Hotel with an overwhelming urge to pee. She had never yet made it through any night in her life without being rudely nudged out of a dream by her full bladder. At home where the bathroom was a few yards away and the floors were carpeted, those nighttime forays weren't much of a problem. But in the drafty old hotel with the cold hardwood floors, the communal bathroom was a long journey down the dimly lit hallway. Thank God, she thought, standing up, that my mother wasn't around to see me having to make this trip.

Groggily she stumbled toward the glow of the bathroom night-light that seemed to be miles away, passing the rooms of the other apprentices, sending a silent little message of love as she passed Shelly's room. Envying Polly Becker, the big-nosed forty-year-old costume designer who wore low-cut blouses and flirted with every guy who walked by, because Polly had arrived at the theater weeks before the others and thereby got to claim the room closest to the bathroom.

Just as Ruthie reached for the bathroom doorknob she heard an odd sound from one of the rooms. It was a long low moan. Somebody must not be feeling well, she thought. And it was certainly no wonder, with the disgusting food they served around here. In fact she'd felt a little queasy herself just last night after the lasagna. But then there was another moan, after which she understood that it wasn't the kind of sound that accompanies illness. She felt flushed, her whole body aroused by the idea of something carnal happening so close to where she was standing.

She was sure the sounds had to be from Polly Becker's room. So the old girl had succeeded in luring someone into her bed. And she was having a hot time of it too. The moans were moans of pleasure, a lot of pleasure, mingled with creaks from the springs of those uncomfortable old metal hotel beds.

"Oh, God. Oh, yes. Oh, God."

They got louder. Ruthie, embarrassed by her own excitement, wasn't sure what to do. She closed the bathroom door behind her and stayed inside longer than she needed to, splashing cold water on her face to calm herself. She even flushed the toilet a few times to drown out the sounds. Finally she opened the bathroom door slowly, listened long enough to be certain that the hall was now silent, then made her way on tiptoe back toward her own room.

She was looking down at her own chubby toes, which were bent in their effort to keep her from clumping noisily and being heard, so when two big hands on her arms moved her to one side she took in a terrified gasp. When she let it out it was into the handsome craggy face of the company's leading man, Bill Crocker.

He was a square-jawed, well-preserved actor of indeterminate age, who, from what Ruthie overheard while she cleaned the ladies' dressing room, still believed his big break was coming. "Little summer-stock jobs" like this one, he said, were just filling his time until the big call came. The call that would make people stop referring to him as "the bus-and-truck John Raitt."

"Little lady," he said greeting Ruthie now, as if he were reciting a line from a play. He was wearing jeans, and his shirt was unbuttoned to the waist the way he'd worn it the first week, when he played Billy Bigelow in *Carousel*. It seemed as if he had appeared from nowhere, and in an instant he was gone.

Ruthie, whose heart was still pounding from the embarrassment of having the gorgeous Bill Crocker see her in her nightshirt and Clearasil, crept into her room and pulled the covers over her head to go to sleep. But the moment her eyes closed they opened again, because a tingling of realization came over her ears and neck and face. Bill Crocker hadn't come out of Polly Becker's room, and the person who was moaning wasn't Polly Becker. It was Shelly. Bill Crocker had been with Shelly.

Ruthie was awake all night, trying to force pictures out of her mind that kept insinuating their way back in. When the neon sign went off and the chirping birds announced the morning light, she sat up, feeling a stiffness in her back and neck and the kind of dull headache that comes with lack of sleep. She couldn't shake the heavy sadness, and when she put her feet on the floor, she remembered all the mornings she had been so eager to get dressed and rush downstairs to the dining room to see Shelly there.

She would stand for a moment and watch him reading the morning paper and drinking coffee, and imagine the days ahead when he would be doing that in their own little apartment somewhere. Today the thought that she had to face him made her queasy. In the high-school cafeteria one day, she overheard the boys talking about Mr. Lane, the English teacher. Singing to the tune of "Pop Goes the Weasel," "He doesn't go round with girls anymore, he doesn't intend to marry. He stays at home and plays with himself. Whee. He's a fairy." Ruthie had asked her best friend, Sheila, what the song meant. When Sheila first told her, Ruthie was sure Sheila must be kidding.

This morning she opened her spiral notebook, tore out the list of bridesmaids, and with a match from a Colonial Manor matchbook, put it in the ashtray and set it on fire.

The hallway was empty, and from her open doorway she could see that the bathroom door was open, too. Maybe a hot shower would make her feel less achy. When she closed the bathroom door behind her and locked it and looked at herself in the full-length mirror, her tears finally came.

"Hey, Ruthless," Shelly said to her, putting an arm around her at breakfast. He was using the name he called her when he wanted to tease her. "I've been thinking about all these routines we've been coming up with every night, and it seems to me we ought to put them someplace." As if last night he hadn't ruined her entire life.

"Other than in a porcelain bathroom fixture?" she said, defensive and embarrassed and wishing it weren't too late to switch to the summer job her mother wanted for her, answering phones in Dr. Shiffman's office.

"I mean on the stage. In the lounge of the hotel. When the band takes a break, you and I could perform them. I'll bet we could turn some of our ideas into a comedy act," he said, ruffling the top of her hair in a way she loved. A way that when anyone else did it made her furious. She wanted to say yes to anything he asked of her.

"You mean do them for *other* people?"

"Yeah, do our own little show after the big show, for the people who go over to the cocktail lounge afterward. Most of them are so schnockered anyway they'd never know if we were good or bad. We could be the new Mike Nichols and Elaine May. Think about it," he said.

Over the next few days she hardly thought about anything else. She was much too self-conscious about her appearance to ever display it on a stage. Any aspirations she'd had about show business were about working behind the scenes. She had no interest in being out there in front of people having to worry about how she looked.

But now that marriage to Shelly was clearly out of the question, performing with him was a way to be linked with him and to spend time with him. So after she painted and spackled the scenery until the flats and her overalls were covered with dots of every color, she took out her spiral notebook and wrote a list of ideas for their show. After all, Elaine May had never been married to Mike Nichols either.

The cocktail lounge was seedy and mercifully dimly lit, and after the band played a barely recognizable version of "Misty," the guitarist walked up to speak into the microphone, even though the six people in the audience were two feet away from the bandstand. He told them that while the band was taking a break, some "kids are going to do their stuff." The people, who were on their second round of drinks, chatted loudly to one another through the first few minutes of Ruthie and Shelly's show.

But after a short while, something caught their attention, and soon they were laughing and then applauding in the right places. The act worked so well that when the reviewer from the *Pittsburgh Press* came to the theater to see *Li'l Abner* and stumbled afterward on Shelly and Ruthie's show in the lounge, he mentioned them in his column, calling their show "clever, zany, and witty."

As September drew nearer, the Pennsylvania nights grew brisk and fresh, so that by the time the company was doing the last production, which was *South Pacific*, the big barn doors to the theater had to be closed while the show was in progress. During the last performance when Bill Crocker played the soldier who sang "Younger than Springtime" without a shirt on, Ruthie could tell all the way from the wings that he had goose bumps on his naked chest, and she looked away.

Later, while the actors were drinking champagne in the dressing room downstairs, she slowly swept the stage with the heavy push broom, moving the dust from behind the thick musty-smelling velour curtain downstage toward the sky blue scrim upstage. When she turned from downstage, Shelly was watching her.

"You know about me and Crocker, don't you?" he asked her. With the big blue background behind him he looked eerily like a character in a dream. She'd been composing speeches in her head all day, knowing they would be saying good-bye that night, wanting to be eloquent when she did. But to be confronted with this subject was too painful. She'd been certain it would be something that would always remain unspoken between them.

"Yeah," she said, "I do," clutching the broom handle hard.

"I love you so much, I can't believe it," he said, moving a few steps closer. She didn't mean to let go of the broom handle, but she did, and it hit the ground with a sharp rap. "You get my jokes, you look at me the way Doris Day looks at Rock Hudson in all those schmucky movies, you're funnier than any five people I've ever known, and I love you."

He'd said he loved her. Twice. No one, not even her parents, had ever said those words to her. She knew what was supposed to happen now. She'd seen enough movies, read enough books to know it was her turn to speak next, to say words she'd practiced saying to her pillow to some generic fantasy lover for years, and had never said to a living soul. But now she did. She looked into Shelly Milton's eyes and said, "Oh, Shel, I love you too."

"Thank God," he said, and they moved together. When they collided, they held each other so tightly that Ruthie could barely breathe. Or maybe she couldn't breathe because it felt so good to feel so good. Her face was buried deeply in the front of his blue oxford-cloth shirt and his face rested on the top of her thick frizzy hair as the laughter of the actors downstairs floated up to the stage where the two of them stood. After a few minutes, they looked puffy-faced at each other.

Shelly wiped his eyes where a tear had formed and brushed it across his cheek with the palm of his hand, then felt in the back pocket of his pants for a handkerchief. When he couldn't find one, he pulled the sleeve of his shirt across his face to dry it.

"I'm not going back to Northwestern," he told her. "I'm leaving for Los Angeles tomorrow with Crocker. We won't officially be living together, but I am going to stay with him until I can somehow get a job, maybe playing piano and eventually writing." Then he said in a way that seemed to be partly teasing and partly testing her, "Want to come along?"

"My parents would kill me first," she said.

"Mine weren't thrilled. But I convinced them everything would be okay when I told them I had a nice roommate." They both smiled an aren't-parents-dumb smile, and hugged again.

When the dressing rooms had been cleaned out and only the two of them were left in the theater, they sat on the stage, which was empty except for the piano and a work light. Shelly played songs from the summer and songs the two of them had invented for their act. When it was nearly dawn they walked hand in hand back to the hotel. Outside Ruthie's room, he held her in his arms and they swayed, then he twirled her around, and bent her back into the dip they always did in the "Top Hat" sketch. When he pulled her up to both feet he looked into her eyes. "You'll always be my Ginger Rogers," he promised. It was a promise he would never break.

5

AFTER SUMMER STOCK Ruthie moved into the college
dormitory with a hole in her heart so big that the cold Pittsburgh
wind blowing off the Monongahela River went right through it.
All she did was sit in her room like a zombie, longing for Shelly,
fearing she'd never hear from him again. She was as obsessed
with getting a letter from him as if she were on death row and
he were the governor deciding on her pardon.

She registered for classes, but spent the next three weeks
never attending any of them. She looked out the window from
her pie slice–shaped cell in the cylindrical, architecturally monstrous dormitory, watched the cars go by on the street below,
and thought about the summer. Later she wondered how she
ever survived those twenty-one days in the dorm eating only
pepperoni pizza brought to the desk downstairs by the delivery
boy from Beto's on Forbes Street. The only time she left the
room was to go down to pick the pizza up, after which she
walked to her mailbox and opened it with the key to check for
certain, though she could already see through the glass door
there was nothing inside.

When the letter came, she read it standing right there with
the mailbox door hanging open, and wept openly, her tears of
thanksgiving wetting the pizza box, because her prayers had

been answered. On her way back to her room she did a little dance of joy that was witnessed with raised eyebrows by the girl on her floor she liked the least and to whom she was happy to offer a gesture she'd only seen others use but whose meaning she now fully understood.

Ruthless,

Enclosed are the lyrics of "Hooray for Hollywood." It is my new favorite song about my new favorite place. I love everything about it. The weather. (It never rains.) The palm trees. The weirdos, or should I say the other weirdos. It truly is screwy and ballyhooey, and there is only one thing missing from my life here and that is you. Every day I wish you were here with me. Drop out of school (Everyone who is anyone *has*, you know!) and come to the land of show business. I'll pick you up at the airport.

Shel

She jumped into the shower where she sang while she washed her hair, then she went to the Laundromat and did three weeks' worth of laundry. When she got back she called her parents from the pay phone in the hall and was relieved when it was her father who answered.

"Daddy," she said, "I need you."

Manny Zimmerman was a Russian immigrant whose grocery store, Zimmerman's Fine Foods, had been on the same corner in the East End of Pittsburgh for thirty years, maintaining its loyal clientele who wouldn't set foot in a Giant Eagle or Kroger's when they could get Manny's personal service. After all, poor Manny and his family had been through so much. People still mentioned the accident when they talked about the Zimmermans, even though it had been so many years.

Ruthie's memories of Martin and Jeffrey were vague and dreamlike. She was only two when they were killed in an automobile accident on the Boulevard of the Allies in a collision with a bus. All she remembered about her two older brothers was the way they used to lift her high into the air to play "see the baby fly." But maybe she didn't remember that at all, maybe her mother had told her about it.

Her parents' grief over the loss of their two sons permeated everything about the family's lives forever. Ruthie would never look at a flickering candle that wouldn't remind her of the two yahrtzeit candles her mother lit every year in memory of Martin and Jeffrey on the anniversary of their deaths. That day when her father walked into the lobby of the dormitory, Ruthie could see he feared the news she was about to deliver was as bad as the news he'd received that night the police came to tell him about Martin and Jeffrey.

She put her arm through his and moved him through the lobby toward a circle of naugahyde chairs, and as they walked, in her mind she went over the words she was going to say. Manny Zimmerman sat, and the sofa squeaked under him.

"You're all right?" he asked her.

"I am, Daddy, and I didn't mean to scare you, but I didn't want to say this on the phone and I wanted to try it out on you before I mentioned it to Ma, but I'd like to drop out of school and move to California."

Her father reached into the pocket of his jacket and pulled out a Marsh Wheeling cigar, peeling off the cellophane, and then by virtue of a custom they'd shared for years, he removed the paper ring and slid it onto his daughter's finger. "After you finish, maybe. But not now."

"I don't want to finish, Daddy. I want to leave school now. To go out there and be with my friend Shelly."

The wood match Manny Zimmerman lit flared against the blunt end of the cigar, and he puffed and puffed until the thick tobacco smell that would remind Ruthie of him every time she whiffed the odor of cigar for the rest of her life filled her nose and eyes.

"Is this Shelly a boy?" he asked, not looking at her, still holding the cigar between his teeth while smoke came out of both sides of his mouth around it.

"Yes, Daddy."

"And is he going to marry you?"

Ruthie stood and took an ashtray from a nearby table and handed it to him. "He's gay, Daddy," she said softly. This he would never understand. Men, big strong he-men, my Martin and my Jeffrey, was how he always talked about her dead brothers. "My Martin could lift a box full of groceries on one shoulder and another one on the other shoulder and make a delivery like Superman." Gay wasn't something she expected him to understand. Nor would he understand the reason she wanted to fly all the way across the country to be with someone who was like that.

"Gay?" he asked. "What's that?"

The term. Obviously he had never heard the term. She would have to explain it with a word he would know, though it felt derogatory to her and she didn't like it. "He's a fairy," she said.

Her father looked into her eyes for a while, saying nothing. She loved his sweet little round mustached face. Whenever she wanted to do something unique or out of step in her life and her mother had been against it, that face would flush red and he would speak up and be on Ruthie's side. He was awkward with her, and she was sure he wondered many times how God could have taken away his two wonderful sons, Martin, a talented violinist, and Jeffrey, so good in science he surely would have become a doctor. They were gone and he was left with only this lump of a daughter.

He had always taken her part. When Ruthie didn't want to be bat mitzvahed, when she wanted to get her ears pierced, when instead of working in a doctor's office she wanted to be an apprentice in a summer theater. She couldn't imagine what her life would be like if he hadn't stepped in and made certain her mother relented. Well, maybe now she could get him to be on her side again.

"A fairy," she said softly, trying again, aware of the giggling, squealing girls who were greeting one another at the dormitory mailboxes as they came in from their classes.

"Ruthie," he said, taking her chin in his hand, and when they were looking into each other's eyes he shook his head and said, "I don't believe in fairies." Ruthie tried not to laugh at what sounded like a line from *Peter Pan*, because he was serious and went on. "Because I'm a man, and men like women, and that's all there is to it. Believe me."

"Daddy . . ."

"And California is so far away," he said in a voice that made her certain that what was coming was a no. So she was surprised when, with the hand that wasn't holding the cigar, he touched her face and said, "But if you want it so bad, and you maybe come back to school in a year or two, it'll be okay by me."

"It will?" Ruthie asked, feeling light with relief and surprised that her father's face was red as if he might cry. "Thank you, Daddy," she said, leaning over to hug him as he quickly moved the hand that had been holding the cigar out of the way so as not to burn her, even though the cigar had gone out.

She was four inches taller than he was, and while they hugged she looked over his head at the gray Pittsburgh day, and in her mind she was thinking the words, "You may be homely in your neighborhood, but if you think that you can be an actor, see Mr. Factor, he'd make a monkey look good." And she realized they were from the lyrics Shelly had enclosed with his letter, from "Hooray for Hollywood."

"You'll do good no matter what," her father said, then turned to go. When he was too far away to hear, Ruthie, who was still watching him, said to his parting figure in the distance, "Thank you, Daddy," and went up to her room to pack.

The day she arrived in La-la, as she and Shelly came to call it, he met her at the airport, at the gate, with a bouquet of daisies, and never said one word about how bad she looked. Just loaded her and her luggage into the beat-up Volkswagen bug he'd bought, handed her a newspaper, and told her to look for cheap furnished apartments.

They found a small two-bedroom in West Hollywood. It was a dive, a dump, a hole in the wall, but they didn't notice because they were together. Roommates, best friends, partners. Their big luxury was an answering service that picked up on their phone line. They told all of the operators to make a note to be sure and pick up on the first ring every time a call for them came in, and to only answer with the telephone number. If the two of them were at home when the phone rang, as soon as they were absolutely certain the service was on their line and talking to the caller, one of them would pick up and listen in to see who the caller was. If it was Shelly's mother, Shelly would say, "Oh, hi, Ma, I just walked in." If it was Ruthie's mother, Ruthie would say that. For a long time, no one but their mothers called them.

They also rented a piano that they squeezed into the living room so Shelly could sit and compose melodies for which Ruthie wrote special lyrics, the way she had in the summer. They took odd jobs. Ruthie worked for a private detective as a process server, Shelly waited tables at the International House of Pancakes. Ruthie was a receptionist at a beauty salon, Shelly worked at the Farmer's Market at the seafood counter, and at night they wrote. First they reworked their act, and when they had it down and were ready to try it out they went to hoot nights at clubs where the audience, who was expecting a guitar player or a band, frequently booed them off the stage.

They put an ad in the trade papers saying they entertained at parties, and were hired to do a sweet sixteen where the birthday girl, who had taken Valium before the party and consumed spiked punch during the party, had to be rushed to the hospital right after their opening sketch. The same ad was responsible for their being hired to perform at the tenth wedding anniversary of Phil and Myrna Stutz, who called them and canceled on the morning of the party because they'd decided that instead of having a party they were going to get a divorce.

Their agent was a guy they met at the Comedy Store who was known as Shotgun Schwartz. Shotgun believed that 10 percent of nothing was nothing so if you were breathing he agreed to represent you, figuring the more clients he had, the better his chances were of making a buck.

The first time he sent them on an interview, they got an assignment to write an episode of a Saturday morning cartoon show about a musical dog, "Rudy the Poodle."

"It ain't exactly a short story for the *New Yorker*," Shelly said as the two of them sat down to work on the first script, "but we'll take a shot." They thought of twelve more "Rudy the Poodle" ideas, and sold nine of them before the show was canceled.

Every night no matter how hard a day they'd put in, they went to the Comedy Store and watched the comics try out new material. They would make notes, whisper ideas to each other, and when the show was over, they would ambush one of the comics at the door and beg him to listen to what they had.

"Jerry," they would say. "Have you got a sec?" Leaning on the door of the guy's car so he couldn't get in. Or, "Joey, listen. We've got a whole hilarious run for you." And once they had the comic's interest piqued, they would break into their material, right there on the cold cement, lit only by a purplish streetlight. Sometimes the comic would even pay them cash on the spot. But the stand-up comic to whom they would always give credit for the success of their careers was Frankie Levy, who had no cash that night so he gave them an IOU.

"Hey, kids, I don't have my wallet on me," Frankie said to them, "but I'm crazy about the supermarket run, and I'll pay you for it tomorrow night. Okay?"

Okay! Frankie Levy had once been on the "Tonight Show."

The very next night Frankie performed Ruthie and Shelly's supermarket routine and brought the house down with it. He was happy and very sweaty as he backed off the stage, both arms raised in triumph. For a few minutes he stood in the rear of the club shaking hands and taking the backslaps he knew he so richly deserved. Ruthie and Shelly elbowed their way through the crowd to get over to Frankie, waiting until the others around him had gone back to their seats to watch Eddie Shindler, who was up next.

"Way to knock 'em dead, Frankie," Ruthie said, holding her arms out wide. With the success he'd had with their material, Frankie would surely want to give her a grateful hug. In fact she was so close to him she could feel the dampness coming off his still-nervous body, but he turned on his heel as if he hadn't even seen her and walked out of the building. There was a moment of realization and then Shelly said, "He's leaving for Australia tomorrow, I heard him telling Mitzi. The schmuck is ducking us for the money," and they rushed out the door to stop Frankie Levy, who by the time they got outside was already at the top of the parking-lot ramp.

"Frankie," Shelly yelled, but Levy didn't turn around.

"You owe us money," Ruthie yelled. But Levy was already in his black Cadillac and in an instant he screeched past them.

"You thieving son of a bitch," Shelly yelled, running back down to the bottom of the ramp where Levy's car was stopped at the black-and-white wooden arm that had served as a momentary impediment to his escape. As Frankie was reaching out to get his change, in a move Shelly once saw in a James Bond movie he jumped on the trunk lid of Frankie Levy's car. Then as he stood there, not sure what to do next, Frankie Levy peeled out onto Sunset, and Shelly's moment of heroism was marred dramatically by the fact that he was thrown crashing onto the cement.

At UCLA Emergency the wait is always interminable. Shelly sat in the big windowed room, bruised and aching and huddled close to Ruthie on the couch as they waited for his turn to be examined. It was past two in the morning and there were several other people waiting: a dark-haired heavyset man with a beard, who had his hand wrapped in a tourniquet; a woman who told Ruthie she'd brought her husband in hours ago with extreme chest pain, and he'd only been called in to see the doctor moments before; and a family who were sitting together staring up at a television watching an old Humphrey Bogart movie.

"What happened to your hand?" the woman asked the bearded man.

"I was trying to slice some meat for my wife on the electric slicer, and my hand was in the way," he said.

"Just your way of trying to give her the finger?" Shelly asked. The man laughed.

"How about you?" the woman asked Shelly.

"You'd never believe it," Ruthie answered for him.

Then, almost as a healing process, the two of them told the story of how they came to Los Angeles, and about working on "Rudy the Poodle," and how they spent their nights writing and selling jokes, and about Frankie Levy. Maybe it was the lateness of the hour or the absurdity of the situation that gave them a freedom and a relaxation and a punchiness, but the story was coming out so funny that soon all the assembled patients were laughing loudly. Ruthie and Shelly had never had a more receptive audience.

In fact it was a rude interruption when a nurse opened the door to call the next patient.

"Mr. Lee?"

She was calling for the bearded man, who before he followed the nurse out managed, with his good hand, to pat Shelly on the back.

"My name is Bill Lee," he said. "I'm a producer at NBC. I think I might have a job for the two of you on a prime-time show I'm doing for John Davidson. Give me a call tomorrow at NBC."

On their first day of work they tried acting nonchalant, but it wasn't easy to fool anyone since they'd arrived an hour early. Their assignment, before they even laid eyes on John Davidson, was to write a dialogue between John and this week's guest, George Burns. "We need it by four o'clock," Bill Lee told them.

"Great," they said, but when they closed the door of the little cubicle of an office they'd been assigned, upstairs from a sound studio at NBC, they stared at each other in terror.

"What are we doing here?" Shelly asked. "Some of the best writers in the world have written for George Burns." George Burns had recently been a big hit in *The Sunshine Boys*. It was his first movie since *Honolulu*, a movie he'd made with Gracie Allen in 1939.

"Let's not panic yet," Ruthie said. "You be George Burns, I'll be John Davidson, and we'll see what happens."

Shelly picked up his black pen and held it in his hand cradled between his thumb and first two fingers, the way George Burns holds a cigar.

"Okay, I'm George Burns."

"That's good," Ruthie said. "It's a good start." She felt sick. They weren't ready for this. Couldn't they have started with someone less famous? Less funny? Shelly looked down at the pen, rolling it in his hand the way George Burns always did with the cigar when he was thinking.

"John Davidson," Shelly said, sounding a little bit like George Burns. "You're a nice kid. Handsome kid, too. How old are you?"

"I'm thirty-four," Ruthie answered, playing the part of John Davidson.

"Thirty-four years?" Shelly asked, then with a twinkle in his eye, he added in his best George Burns, "*I* pause that long between pictures."

"That's good." Ruthie laughed. "But let's not get overconfident, let's keep going." They improvised. They switched roles. They wrote things down, typed them up, tried them again, changed them and fixed them. Tore the whole thing up twice. It was almost four o'clock. At four o'clock on the dot they walked into Bill Lee's office to read it to him. He laughed. He laughed harder. He congratulated himself with a grin that meant, I'm a smart son of a bitch for hiring these two. And he was. Two seasons later they were the hottest writers in television.

6

THEIR NAMES on a project gave it "heat," made it a "go,"
a "green light," and soon they were writing and producing their
own series, and garnering huge consulting fees to come in and
doctor the shows of other writers. They had a certain style no
one could equal, genuinely funny, with a touch of poignancy
and humanity rare in television half-hour comedy, so everyone
wanted their work. Fifteen years after the George Burns joke,
their popularity was still happening. Their success had made
them rich, enabled them to support all four of their aging parents, to travel during their time off and see the world.

The only thing neither of them had was that elusive commod-
ity so idealized by the very industry in which they were thriving, romantic love. Though at some point each of them had
tried for it. Ruthie fell hard for Sammy Karp, a black-haired
blue-eyed wild-minded stand-up comic who wanted to be an
actor. She met him one hot summer L.A. night at the Improv,
after his set, when she was standing at the bar with some other
writers and Sammy came over to schmooze. When she congratulated him with a handshake for the good work he'd done, he
kept holding on to her hand, looking meaningfully into her eyes.
Then he said, "Ruth Zimmerman, I love your work. Let's do
dinner."

They did dinner at La Famiglia, dinner at Adriano's, dinner at Musso's. Somehow it was understood that Ruthie was the one with money and Sammy was struggling, so she always picked up the tab. When *he* made it, she told herself, he would pay for the dinners. It was also what she told Shelly when he asked. In the week of her birthday she thanked Shelly but passed on his offer to throw a small party for her. Sammy, she explained, was taking her dancing at the Starlight Room at the top of the Beverly Hilton.

No man had ever taken her dancing. While a piano, bass, and drums played "Call Me Irresponsible," Ruthie and Sammy danced close with her arms around his neck and his arms around her waist the way she'd seen couples dance in high school when she'd stood by the punch bowl pretending not to be watching. She ached to have Sammy make love to her. And when he led her to the suite he'd reserved in her name she could barely wait until he unlocked the door to touch him, thanking heaven the champagne she'd just paid for was doing such a good job on her inhibitions.

She was hungry for him, starving for him, and the things they did in bed made her embarrassed the next morning. When she woke up alone in what she saw by the light of day and sobriety was a very grand suite, she walked naked around the room trying to reconstruct in her mind what she'd said and done. Probably she'd been a complete fool. But then she looked in the mirror and saw the Post-it he'd left on her naked breast that said *You're fabulous and I'll call you later* and felt gorgeous and sexy for the first time in her life.

That week Sammy called her at the office so often that she had to walk out of the casting sessions four different times to take his adoring phone calls. "How's it going, beautiful?" he would ask her, giving her the chance to babble on to him about the people who were reading for parts on the show. But it wasn't a coincidence that immediately after she told him that the part of the young leading man had been cast, his ardent interest in her seemed to end, because that was the night he didn't show up for their dinner date.

"Giving new meaning to the term 'stand-up comic,'" Ruthie told Shelly while she looked out the window one more time for Sammy's car, and tried to make light of the rejection.

Shelly had a wonderful romance with Les Winston, a beautiful, warm, gifted man in his fifties with white hair who always had a gorgeous tan. Les was a furniture designer whose teak outdoor furniture was sold all over the world. Piece by piece he'd rid Ruthie and Shelly's West Hollywood apartment of the tables, chairs, and sofa he called "early thrift shop," and replaced them. Ruthie loved Les's creativity and sense of humor, and their mutual admiration for Shelly sealed their friendship.

The two men talked a few times about moving in together, and probably would have, but one day Shelly got a paralyzing call from Les's brother saying Les had died suddenly of a cerebral hemorrhage. It took Shelly two long painful years to recover from the loss.

But the one who was the biggest heartbreaker of all was Davis. Lovely Davis Bergman. Ruthie met him one night at some show business party. One of those after-the-pilot celebrations at CBS studios on Radford. He was an entertainment lawyer. A partner in a well-known firm, Porter, Beck, and Bergman. He was Jewish, separated from his wife, they were filing for divorce, they'd never had children, and in the divorce settlement, *he* got the big house in Santa Monica. The perfect man.

"What do you think?" a nervous Ruthie asked Shelly, who'd been standing in the corner at the party talking to Michael Elias, one of the producers of "Head of the Class," when she pulled him away.

"I think he's great. From here," Shelly said.

"Come meet him," Ruthie said. "He's funny. I can't believe he can be a lawyer and be funny too." She dragged Shelly by the hand to where Davis Bergman was standing and introduced them.

"Shelly Milton, Davis Bergman."

"I never trust a guy who has two last names," Davis said, shaking Shelly's hand. They all laughed. Ruthie felt flushed. Maybe it was because of the diet. The strict one she'd been on for six weeks, feeling cheated and deprived and miserable, but she'd lost seventeen pounds, and the healthy eating had made her skin look great too. So maybe this was God's way of rewarding her. Proving to her that good disciplined girls had the Davis Bergmans of the world beating a path to their doors, or at least talking to them at parties.

Davis told Ruthie and Shelly funny stories about being a Hollywood lawyer, and when the party began to break up he looked disappointed, so Shelly—oh, how Ruthie loved him for this—suggested they all go for coffee at the Hamburger Hamlet on Sunset, and Davis agreed. Ruthie, who had come to the party in Shelly's car, rode nervously to the restaurant in Davis's Porsche, looking at Davis's hand as it shifted gears. Wanting to put her own hand on it, but being too afraid.

"Comedy writers," Davis said in the restaurant, as if marveling at the good fortune that had brought these exotic people into his life. "I represent some screenwriters, but they're all very serious." The three of them talked and laughed for hours.

Davis lived in Santa Monica, nearly all the way to the beach, and Ruthie didn't know if he would understand about her living with Shelly, so when they got out to the parking lot at the Hamlet she said, "Shelly can take me home," and Davis looked at her sweetly and said, "Great." As Shelly was about to pull his Mercedes out onto Sunset, Davis pulled his Porsche loudly up to their right, opened his window and gestured for Ruthie to open hers, then he shouted into Shelly's car above the din of his engine, "I've got tickets for a screening at the Directors' Guild tomorrow night. You want to come along?"

"Sure," Ruthie said, hoping to sound nonchalant.

"Pick you up?"

"Meet you," Ruthie said hastily.

"Eight o'clock," Davis said, and was gone.

"He's dating you up," Shelly said in a teasing voice as he stepped on the gas. "Filling your dance card."

"Shelleee," Ruthie squealed. "He is *so* adorable."

"Please! I already hate the son of a bitch," Shelly said. "You'll fall in love and get married and I'll lose a roommate, then he won't want you to work anymore so I'll lose a partner too."

He was teasing and she teased him back.

"Shel, you know I'll never leave you. To begin with, you'll come over constantly for dinner, and for every holiday. After a while Davis will probably get so used to you, you'll probably come on vacations with us. We'll be the Three Musketeers, I swear we will."

The next morning she sent Shelly in to work alone and she went shopping at Eleanor Keeshan. She found a new sweater and some black pants to make her look nearly slim, and a royal-blue-and-black silk shirt that also went with the pants, so she'd be ready with something to wear on the next date, and while the saleslady called in her credit card number, Ruthie looked wistfully through racks of beautiful silk dresses and pants outfits, and at the Fernando Sanchez lingerie.

Tonight her social life was about to experience a personal best. She was actually seeing the same man two nights in a row. Okay, so last night Shelly was with them, but it was still sort of a date. Maybe it was finally her turn to have something real. With someone who would appreciate her. If that was true, and they were to start dating, she would come into stores like this one and try on clothes for hours. Looking at each item and asking herself, Would *he* like this? What event do he and I have coming up that I have to dress for? Oh yes, dinner with his clients, and the lawyers' wives' luncheon.

Davis, please, she thought, walking back to the counter to retrieve her package. When she passed the three-way mirror she caught sight of herself looking chunky despite the weight loss and vowed that for Davis she would starve off at least fifteen more pounds. When she arrived at the office and Shelly was out to lunch she sat down at her desk and did something she hadn't done in years. She made a list of possible bridesmaids.

After the film they went to the Old World on Sunset. Ruthie ordered the vegetable soup, and Davis had an omelet. And just the way he reached over and put his spoon in her cup to get himself a taste was so intimate, it made her feel as if she could probably open up to this man. Davis was what she'd heard the girls she'd lived with in the dorms at Pitt refer to as "husband material."

While they were talking, an extraordinarily beautiful woman walked by their table. Ruthie noticed that although Davis saw the woman, he didn't offer a second glance or ogle her the way a few of the men at some of the tables did. It was a show of respect from Davis for her feelings, and that made her feel even closer to him. By the time the dishes had been removed from the table and she was finishing her second cup of coffee, she had told him all about her life. Even about her two brothers dying when she was very little. She talked about her love for Shelly and explained why they lived like brother and sister.

Davis didn't make any judgments, make any gesture that could have been construed as a negative comment about what she was saying. He seemed to think everything she was telling him was okay. And Ruthie invited him to come for dinner one night, knowing she could convince Shelly to cook.

"Only if you'll let me reciprocate and make dinner for the two of you," Davis answered.

"Of course," Ruthie said, in a voice that she was afraid sounded too loud and too eager. This was the best result she could have imagined. Davis liked Shelly too.

When her mother invited her for Passover, hinting as only her mother could that it might be her father's last ("With that heart, he's liable to croak any minute. He has to stick a heart pill under his tongue just to watch the eleven o'clock news"), she accepted.

The few days she spent sleeping in her old room made her

glad she'd agreed to come back. Her father conducted their own quiet little Seder service, and aside from the store-bought gefilte fish, Ethel Zimmerman cooked all the traditional foods Ruthie remembered eating when she was a child. During dinner, in a rare moment, her mother even reminisced about Martin and Jeffrey. "When they were little boys they used to say, 'Ma, when we grow up, we'll have a double wedding. It'll be the biggest party in the world, and you and Daddy will be the king and the queen of the wedding. There'll be lots of cake and dancing with an orchestra just like at our bar mitzvahs.'"

"But," her father jumped in, "I told them the difference will be that I don't have to pay for it," and then he added, "I was kidding them, because for a wedding, the father of the bride always pays."

A silence fell over the table then as the three of them ate the matzoh ball soup. All of them were thinking the same thought. That in this family there had been no bride.

Davis. Wouldn't her parents love him, Ruthie thought. Okay, he was divorced, or soon to be divorced, but *that* they could forgive. Once they talked to him and he laid on the charm, her mother would melt, and her father would say, "A good head on his shoulders."

"I have a boyfriend," she said quietly. Her mother dropped the spoon into her soup dish.

"Besides that Sheldon?" she asked.

That Sheldon. After all these years she still referred to Shelly as "that Sheldon."

"So who?" her father asked.

"He's a lawyer. An entertainment lawyer. Jewish."

With every word she could see her mother sit up straighter. Maybe this was a bad idea. Premature. Davis hadn't even kissed her yet.

"Divorced," she said.

"Well," her mother said quickly. "That happens."

For a while there was no sound but the slurping of soup, until her mother had a thought she couldn't hold inside.

"Listen," she said, "Molly Sugarman's daughter, Phyllis, didn't have her first baby until she was forty years old, and the baby is perfect."

"Ethel, please," said her father, "first let's meet the guy and then we'll talk babies."

"Why not plan ahead? You think it's so easy to get a party room at Webster Hall? Sometimes you need to call six months in advance."

"Ruthie," her father said, turning to her seriously, "you'll give us notice? And you won't elope?"

"I promise, Daddy."

That night, after her parents were asleep, she lay in her old bed, remembering the other day when Davis drove her to the airport, and hugged her close, saying he would miss her. She had smiled about that for the entire flight. Tomorrow she'd be back in L.A. and things with him would probably start to get serious. God, she could hardly wait.

Just before she turned over to go to sleep she realized it was only eight o'clock in Los Angeles. She probably should call home and see how old Shel was doing without her. She picked up the receiver of the pink phone her parents had given her when she was sixteen and called her own number in Los Angeles.

"H'lo."

"Hi, it's me."

"Ruthie!" Shelly said, in a very loud voice. "Uh . . . hi there, Ruthie." There was noise in the background. "Let me turn down the music," he said, and then was gone from the phone for a while that was too long for just turning down music in their small apartment. "So, how's it going?" he asked her when he got back to the phone.

"Shel, it's so cute," she said, confiding in him. "My parents have really been wonderful this time. They even talked about my brothers tonight, and maybe it's because they haven't been bugging me at all, but I actually told them about Davis."

"About Davis?" he said, again too loud. "What about him?"

"About my seeing him, and how terrific he is, and how he's so perfect for me. So right away my mother starts talking about somebody she knows whose daughter had a baby at forty. Is that hysterical?"

There was no sound.

"Shel?"

"I'm here."

"You okay?"

"Yeah, yeah, I'm fine. You coming in tomorrow?"

"At two-ten."

"You want me to pick you up?"

"Has Davis called? He said he was going to call you and make sure you were okay while I was gone, and find out when I was coming in. So I thought *he* would probably pick me up."

"I'll tell him," Shelly said.

"Good idea," Ruthie said. "Give him a call, and remind him that I'll be in at two and see if he can make it. If not, I'd really appreciate it if *you* could pick me up." She switched on the pink lamp next to the bed and looked for her purse. When she found it, she pulled out her little telephone book.

"Here," she said to Shelly, "I'll give you his number."

"I don't need his number," Shelly said. "He's sitting right here."

7

BARBARA SINGER looked across the desk at Ruthie Zimmerman. She was certainly not the unattractive girl she kept describing in the story she'd been telling about her life. She was attractive in a funky way. And though she joked through the telling of her story, Barbara, who often used the same device of humor to cover her feelings, recognized it as subterfuge. It all seemed to be leading to something painful and difficult.

"What happened when you got back from Pittsburgh?" Barbara asked her.

"Shelly and Davis met me at the airport and said they both loved me but that they loved each other romantically and they were sure I'd understand. And you know what? I *did* understand. Because I thought both of them were so great, they should be with each other and not me. Kind of like Groucho Marx saying he'd never belong to any club that would have him as a member.

"So Shelly and I kept working together, only he moved into Davis's house, and I bought myself a condominium in Brentwood. I mean basically at that point all we were then was business partners."

"You sound very matter-of-fact about it all. Is that how you felt?"

"Are you kidding? At the time I felt like killing both of them. I hated Davis for using me to get to Shelly. I hated Shelly for taking Davis away from me. I hated myself for being the dumbest woman alive. But I acted like it was okay with me. Shrugged it off and said hey, no problem. Because I just couldn't let go."

"Of what?"

"Of Shelly," she said, and the look on her face made Barbara push the tissue box on the desk closer to her. "I couldn't stand the idea that I could lose him."

One morning they were just finishing a pilot script, working at Ruthie's condo, when their agent called and asked if they wanted to write a movie of the week for Pam Dawber.

"I think you should take it," Shelly said.

Ruthie looked at her watch. "Geez, Shel, it's almost lunchtime and we still don't know what we're going to do for the act break."

"I'm going to stop work for a while," he told her.

"Me too," Ruthie said. "I'm going to pick up my cleaning and get a sandwich. I'll be back around two, and then we have to decide what to do about the second act, and call Solly back about the script for Pam Dawber. You want me to bring you anything?"

"I mean stop for a long time, Ruth. Not do the movie for Pam Dawber or any other project for a while. Because Davis wants me to be around the house more. Work with the architect on the plans for the remodel and—"

No! She couldn't believe this. Now he was going to stop writing with her, too? "And be his wife?" Ruthie flared, feeling as if her whole life was being pulled out from under her. "No, goddammit. No." Shelly didn't flinch. "You mean you'll take over where the former Mrs. Bergman left off? Shel, that's crazy. Don't let him do that to you. You'll end up playing tennis and going shopping every day and not having any self-worth. You can't give up a good career to stay home and just run the house."

Ruthie sat on the edge of her desk, looking out the window.

She was tired. They'd been rushing to finish their current pilot, working endless hours, and what she felt like doing now was taking a long nap.

"Hey!" Shelly said, "I like the idea. I've been working all my life, pounding a goddamned piano and writing stupid songs and sketches to make a couple of bucks. I'm just dropping out of a painfully hard business to sleep late, eat great, and redecorate. And in my case it's with someone I love. How bad can that be? Wouldn't *you* take that deal? Goddamned right you would."

That was low, she thought, since they both knew she'd been planning on taking exactly that deal. She left the office and the building, and nearly got hit by a car when she crossed Sunset against the red light.

"Ruuuthie." Davis always greeted her so warmly when she called to talk to Shelly, and maybe, just maybe there was a hint of mockery in the greeting. "How's the funnyness business?" he'd ask, and she didn't have an answer. Sometimes late at night she would just lie in bed, wanting to talk to Shelly, wishing she could go into the next room and find him the way she had for the years they lived together. Then she would picture him at home with Davis.

But she never thought about the sexual part of their relationship. It was imagining the cozy part that made her envious. Shelly and Davis reading the Sunday paper together, doing the crossword puzzle, playing Scrabble. When it came to Scrabble there wasn't any way that Davis could give Shelly as big a fight as *she* had.

She finished the project for Pam Dawber and was offered a two-year exclusive deal to write pilots for Twentieth Century–Fox TV. They would give her an office and a secretary at the studio, lots of money, and a parking place with her name on it. And all she had to write were a couple of pilots. Shelly was wide-eyed.

"They'll give you how much? They didn't ever offer that much to the two of us."

"I'll be glad to split it with you," she said, squeezing a lemon wedge above her salad and watching the juice spurt. "Just come back to work."

"Can't" was what it sounded like he said, but later when Ruthie thought about it she decided that maybe he'd actually said something else.

One night after Davis and Shelly got back from a trip to Hawaii, Shelly invited her for dinner. Davis barbecued the chicken outside while Shelly was inside making the salad, and Ruthie helped him chop. He seemed upset. Finally he said in a voice that was designed for Davis not to hear, "He's going to be traveling to New York a lot for the next few months on business. I'm going to go berserk without him. I'll probably be calling you every five minutes for solace."

Ruthie was starting to feel annoyed every time she was with Shelly. The way he mooned over Davis, tiptoed around his moods and feelings, made every plan around Davis's whims and schedule. When she got into her car after saying good night to the two of them she decided she didn't want Shelly to call her for solace. And she wasn't going to call him. She was starting to make some friends over at Fox, some other women writers and a woman in casting. She would make dinner plans with them and keep busy, and Shelly would be just fine without her.

Once, years before, when she lived in the dormitory at Pitt, she overheard a girl in the next room crying as she told a friend, "I called my mother and told her that he broke up with me. That he took his pin back from me and gave it to another girl on the same day, and do you know what she said? She said, 'Throw yourself into your work.' Throw yourself into your work? My life is ending and she says, 'Throw yourself into your work'!" The girl's crying had echoed through the walls of the dormitory for hours.

Ruthie thought of that incident while she tried to throw herself into her work. She wrote another movie of the week and got an assignment to write a pilot called "May's Kids," which was about a children's talent agent. One day she realized it had been more than two months since she'd spoken to Shelly.

Apparently he had done just fine at home alone during Davis's New York travels. That hurt. It was one thing for him to be too busy for her when he was with his lover, but when he was alone. Not to call. Maybe something was wrong. Obviously something was wrong. Maybe she should call him.

It was ten o'clock at night, not such a great time to call people out of the blue like this. The phone rang ten or twelve times, and Ruthie was about to hang up when she heard a tiny, quiet voice pick up the phone and say hello. Oh, God, she woke them. The voice didn't sound like Shelly.

"Shel?"

"Yeah."

"Shelly, it's Ruthie."

"Hi, Ru," he said. And then he said, "Oh, my God." And it sounded like he started to cry.

"What's wrong?"

"Nothing."

"You okay?"

"I'm okay."

"Then why do you sound so—"

"I can't talk," he said. "I can't. I can't talk to anybody anymore." And he hung up.

Something was very wrong with Shelly. If Davis was at home, Shelly wouldn't be able to talk, so there was no point in calling him back and trying to get him to tell her what the problem was. Maybe she should go over there. It wasn't very far. A light rain was falling. She could see it on the tiny terrace outside the sliding doors of her living room. She'd be crazy to put her shoes and her raincoat on and start looking for her glasses and her keys and schlep over there to Shelly's, just to find out that he and Davis had had some lovers' quarrel.

No. She'd sit down now, make a few last-minute notes on the pilot script. Then she'd take a nice long bath and try not to think about Shelly and his dramatic voice on the phone. The tub was already full when she changed her mind. Somewhere in her stomach where she always knew the right thing to do, she was sure she had to at least drive by that house and check on Shelly. She threw her raincoat over her sweatpants and UCLA sweatshirt, found her old Nike Waffle Trainers under her bed, located her car keys on the kitchen counter, and made her way down to the cold quiet garage in her building.

"Why am I doing this?" she wondered out loud as she was unlocking her car in the cold garage. And again as she drove through the rain-slicked streets. "Why am I doing this?"

Davis's car wasn't outside the house. Shelly's was. Ruthie pulled her car into the carport, turning her lights off, and when she'd turned the engine off she sat shaking her head at what a dumb jerk she was to come running over here. The rain had stopped, and everything was so quiet; maybe she could just look in a window and see if everything was all right.

She stepped slowly out of the car, and carefully closed her car door to try to make the least amount of noise. The freshly wet grass sent up a sweet smell and the moon cast a white glow on the house as Ruthie walked from window to window, looking into each one, first at the pretty country French living room, then the dining room, and now the yellow-and-blue French kitchen, all dimly lit, and all orderly. Davis was away, and Shelly was asleep, and tomorrow he would call her and tell her why he'd sounded so weird on the phone. So why couldn't she stop herself from turning the knob on the kitchen door, which was unlocked, my God, it was unlocked, and pushing it open?

Her Nikes squeaked on the tile kitchen floor, and she was so afraid she could feel the waves of panic coursing through her, but she couldn't turn around. She moved to the staircase, and quickly up the steps, passing the two extra bedrooms, toward the new master suite, the door of which was wide open. No one was inside. Oh, God. Davis and Shelly had gone out somewhere in Davis's car. Maybe they *did* have a fight, and they'd gone out to have a drink and sit and talk it over. Probably they took Davis's car and would be home any minute and find her there. Wouldn't she be mortified? She had to get out of there.

Suddenly she had to pee. So badly that she knew she'd never

make it to her car, start it, and then get to a gas station. Never. She'd have to go into Shelly and Davis's bathroom and pee fast then run to her car and get the hell out of there before they got home. She hadn't even seen the master bathroom since it was remodeled. She'd seen the plans a few times, knew how they wanted it to look. This was her chance to see it, she thought, and laughed a little giggle at how ridiculous this story would be to Shelly if the two of them ever sat down alone again to talk. The phantom who peed and stole away into the night.

She didn't dare turn on the bathroom light. Suppose they came driving up and spotted a light on where they'd left darkness? She'd have to find her way to the toilet in the . . . Jesus. What was that on the floor? No. *Who* was it? By the moonlight pouring in the bathroom window she could see now that it was Shelly, curled up in front of the marble bathtub, an empty pill bottle next to him. Dead. Limp. Gone. Dead. Shelly.

A sick, horrifying numbness filled her, and she sank to her knees and put her head on his dead body. As if from a distance, she could hear her own voice begging the lifeless body of Shelly to tell her why he did this. How could he take himself away from her? Hating him, she beat on his skinny unresponsive frame and screamed his name as all of her pulsed with the horror of this loss. Shelly, her love. Dead.

Laying her head on his chest, she wailed, a cry that made her head pound. But then she realized the sound wasn't in her head. It was a heartbeat. A heartbeat! Alive.

"Shelly." She sat up, grabbed his arms, pulled him into a sitting position and shook him. "Shelly, you're alive," she screamed into his slack-jawed face, knowing she was supposed to do something to him, like breathe into his mouth, but she wasn't sure how. She had to find someone who knew what to do, so gently she placed his head back on the floor, ran into the darkened bedroom, slapped around until she found a switch to turn on the light, then grabbed the phone and dialed 911.

When she'd given the necessary information to the operator

and was about to run back into the bathroom again to try to
rouse Shelly, she looked on the bedside table, and there, with
nothing else around it, in a silver frame, was an old photograph
of her. She remembered the day Shelly snapped it. They had
gone to ride the carousel at the Santa Monica Pier. She was
wearing shorts and a shirt, sporting the first suntan of her life,
and holding her arms up in a gesture of pure joy, but still she
winced when she saw it. Because to her she looked like a frizzy-
haired witch. But Shelly had framed it, and kept it by his bed.
Ruthie marched into the bathroom.

"You're gonna live, schmuck," she announced to Shelly's inert body. "I'm here to tell you," she said, kneeling beside him
and taking him in her arms, "that anyone who can stand to look
at that picture of me every day can live through a stomach
pump. For me, Shel. You have to live. For me."

He was in the hospital for two days, and Ruthie stayed there
too. She slept in a chair both nights and covered herself with a
blanket that a sympathetic nurse brought in for her. Shelly refused to say anything until she took him out of the hospital and
back to her condo where she put him in her decorated-by-a-
decorator bedroom. And naturally his first words were a joke
when he looked around, winced, and remarked, "Either that
wallpaper goes or I do." Then he fell asleep.

An odd comfort filled Ruthie as she lay on her new living
room sofa, knowing he was nearby. Later, when she brought
him some tea, he stared out the window and said, "Davis decided to go back to his wife. She met him in New York, and
they were together and he said he wants her back. Told me I
had to get my stuff out of his place by the end of the . . ." His
voice lost control and he put his face in the pillow.

"Shel, don't!" Ruthie said, sitting down next to him. "You'll
get over him. You'll start to work again. You'll work on my
projects with me, and we'll have fun again, and soon you'll meet
someone else."

"You shouldn't have found me," he told her. "It was a waste

of your time. Eventually I'll just do it again. I don't want to be without him. I don't want to go back to work. I want to stay home and—"

"Have babies?" Ruthie said. There was anger in it, and a little bit of a joke, but Shelly looked at her seriously.

"Yeah," he said. "I would like that."

Ruthie laughed. "You're right. I should have let you bump yourself off. You're a wacko." She stood, and touched his hand. "While you were sleeping I threw out every pill and hid everything sharp in the house, so if you want to do it again, you'll have to go somewhere else. I've got a meeting at ABC."

She was already in the garage of her building when the idea hit her with such force that she spun around, rang for the elevator, which was too slow in coming, so she ran up the stairs to the third floor and down the hall to her apartment.

"Shelly?" she said. He was in the bathroom with the door closed. "Shelly, don't you dare try anything," she shrieked at the door, which she discovered when she turned the knob was locked.

"For God's sake, I'm on the john," he said. He emerged a few minutes later, looking haggard and green. "I thought you had a meeting."

"I do," she said, "but this is more important. Shelly, let's have a baby together."

"Oh, Christ," he said.

"We don't have to have sex to do it. There's lots of other ways."

"This I have to hear," he said, but for a second she saw a smile in his eyes that reminded her of the old Shelly.

"Some gay women are even doing it with turkey basters."

That got him. He was smiling, and then he giggled.

"I could get pregnant." She was so excited she was pulling at the sleeve of his pajamas. "With our baby. And after the baby's born if you still don't want to work, I could go back to work, and you could take care of her."

"Or him," Shelly said, seeming to warm to the idea.

"Shelly, say yes. At least say you'll think about it. Can you picture it? A little baby from you and me? We'd name it after Sid Caesar if it was a boy, or Imogene Coca if it was a girl. It would have a great sense of humor. It would come out and say, 'A funny thing happened to me on the way to the delivery room.' Shel, maybe I can't even make babies. Maybe you can't. Maybe you have comedy sperm, like in that Woody Allen movie. But isn't it worth a try?"

Shelly walked out of the room past her and into the kitchen, leaving her standing there alone. Obviously he thought she was so crazy he wasn't even going to talk about it.

Forget it, he was saying. Letting her down easy. It was a ridiculous idea and a stupid time to present it. Three days after a man tried to kill himself over the love of his life, she was asking him to have a baby with her. No wonder she was still single, without a prospect in sight. She didn't have an ounce of subtlety in her entire body. And Shelly was being gracious by pretending she never said any of those things. Just strolling right by her into the kitchen. She would go in there now and apologize for being insensitive, then hurry to her meeting at the network.

"Shel," she said, walking into the kitchen. Shelly had his back to her, and when he turned she squealed and he laughed, because in his hand he was holding what he had just taken out of the top drawer by the sink. A turkey baster.

"You rang?" he answered.

8

"AND THAT'S HOW you conceived Sid?" Barbara tried to keep the astonishment out of her voice.

"That's how," Ruthie said.

"Were you concerned at all in these times about having a baby with a gay man?"

"No. We talked about it, and decided that it was safe, because since his long-ago relationship with Les, Shelly had only been with Davis. And Davis told him he was fresh from a monogamous relationship with a woman he'd been married to for years. So that seemed to be the safest person in the world for him to be involved with." She looked down at her lap when she added, "Davis and I never did have sex."

"Anyway—we went ahead. Sometimes we'd inseminate me, and when I got my period we'd say to each other, 'It wasn't supposed to work. Two weirdos like us have no business trying to bring a kid into this world.' But then a week or so would go by and we'd be working or talking or at the movies and Shel would say, 'So I guess you'll be ovulating next week, huh?' And I'd say, 'Yeah,' and he'd get this look in his eye and I'd say, 'I think the best day would be Friday.' And then we'd try again."

Her eyes were fogging up and she thought for a while then seemed to bring her mind back to the room. "Anyway, one morning I woke up and I just knew I was pregnant. I was puking my guts out. I left work at lunchtime and went to the doctor's. By the time I got home from work at dinnertime, they called to tell me I was preg. I was so excited, I called Shelly and he rushed home.

"We laughed and we cried and we did our versions of what our parents were going to say when they heard." She looked long at Barbara, then said, "Let me tell you something. Heterosexual couples think they have a monopoly on joy, but if you had seen the two of us, you'd have known there were never two happier people in the world than we were when Sid was born. The last two and a half years have been magical for us, even though we've had a few ups and downs in our careers, because we have that boy and he makes everything in life pale by comparison."

Sid, the comedy kid, was born at Cedars-Sinai Hospital. He weighed five pounds eight ounces.

"How small is he?" one of the writers asked Shelly.

"He's so small that when he's naked, he looks like he's wearing a baggy suit," Shelly answered, then passed out cigars to everyone on the writing staff.

"How did Ruthie do in the labor room?" someone asked at lunch.

"Just like you'd expect for a Jewish girl. She said, 'Honey, I'm too tired. *You* push,'" Shelly answered, and ordered champagne for everyone at the table.

The night Ruthie and Sid came home from the hospital to the new house she and Shelly had bought in Westwood because it had a play yard fit for a prince, an entire video crew met them at the door. Shelly had hired them because he was afraid if he relied on his own technical know-how to preserve the historic moment, he would screw it up.

As it turned out, Shelly directed every move they made. Sid with the nanny, Sid with Ruthie, and Sid being adored by both grandmothers, who had been invited to visit simultaneously in the hopes that, as Shelly put it, "While sharing a hotel room, they will get on each other's nerves so much they'll spontaneously combust."

They didn't. They were soul sisters in every way, and at some point, while alone at the Bel-Air Sands Hotel, out of their children's earshot, they must have made a pact that neither of them would mention the word *marriage* for fear of expulsion. And after cheek pinching, toe naming, and tushie biting their grandchild ad nauseam, they waved at the video camera so often that when they watched the replay even *they* couldn't tell themselves apart. ("Look, there's me giving him a bath." "What are you talking about? That's *me* giving him a bath.") And each of them referred to Sid as "*my* grandson."

When the two women left, flying together as far as Chicago ("Isn't it cute? They can't bear to part with each other," Shelly pointed out), Ruthie was forced to admit that she missed them a little bit. It had been fun for there to be people in the world other than Sid's mommy and daddy who thought the baby's every dirty diaper was a work of art.

The day Ruthie got back to work, Sid became a part of the writing staff. If he gurgled at a joke, it stayed in. If he spit up after a punch line, it had to be rewritten. He became the reason to get the rehearsal over early and the reason to stay home from some dull party and the reason to sit around on a Sunday morning and do nothing. The three of them had become, for most intents and purposes, a happy family, with the obvious and unspoken exception, albeit a significant one, that Sid's parents never had and never would consummate their love for each other. And though to the conventional observer this seemed to be a pitiable loss, Ruthie and Shelly's nonsexual relationship created an unclouded kind of comfort between them that many couples never had.

Ruthie couldn't believe her life had become a Kodak commercial. Joy and love and a family whose greatest pleasure was being together. The morning Shelly stayed home from work saying he was "under the weather," Ruthie didn't think much about it. When she got home, Sid was playing with the nanny and on the dining room table there was a note. It was held down by one of the crystal candlesticks her mother sent her years ago, hoping that if she had them she would light shabbat candles. Now, as the nausea of fear seized her, she had the fleeting thought that maybe lighting candles would have saved her from Shelly's words: *I have to be away for a while. Believe me I'll come home as soon as I can. Just look after our most precious life for me. You are my world. Shel.*

If Sid's arms hadn't been around her legs, and his beautiful little face hadn't been looking up at her, she would have screamed, wept, lost control, because she knew what the note meant and why Shelly was gone. Two weeks passed. Every morning, she woke, fed and played with Sid, then handed him over to the nanny and went to work, where she told everyone who asked that Shelly had a family emergency. It was a description that could cover almost anything. Some nights she was so wrung out with worry she couldn't even sleep, just stared at the phone, begging it to ring and have Shelly on the other end of the call.

Her favorite sleeping position was on her stomach with her right knee jutting out to the side and her right foot sticking out of the covers. It was the way she remembered seeing her mother sleep, and in the past when she woke up and found herself in that position, she thought about her mother and wondered if the positions people slept in were hereditary.

Tonight she maneuvered herself into that position, hoping that just being in it would induce sleep. Maybe she could fool her mind into believing it was time to let go of all the panic she was feeling and ease into dreams. But instead, the silence of the night made the sound of her stepped-up heartbeat all she could hear, and there was no chance that she would sleep.

She probably should get up and write. With Shelly's absence there was so much to do every day at the office that maybe she should get some of it done now. She was wide awake anyway. She ought to use the time to accomplish something instead of lying there worrying where Shelly was, which was all she'd done for the past two weeks.

She turned over on her back and stared at the blue numbers on the digital clock. Twelve-fifteen . . . no . . . twelve-sixteen. She was never going to get to sleep now. She had friends who told her they did their best work at night, when there was no possibility of the phone ringing or the baby crying or an unexpected knock on the door from UPS. Maybe she ought to . . . no, just the thought of getting up and trying to write was so off-putting that after a few minutes of thinking about it, she was back on her stomach with her right knee jutting out to the side and her right foot sticking out of the covers, and this time it worked. She fell into a deep sleep.

The sharp jingle of the phone jarred her awake, and for a second she wasn't even sure where she was. The blue numbers. It was three o'clock. Goddammit. Then it occurred to her that the only calls that came at three in the morning were death calls. Shelly. The phone rang again. She slid on her belly to the end of the bed, leaned toward the night table, and grabbed the telephone receiver.

"Yeah?"

"Howdy, pardner."

"Shelly?" He was drunk, she knew his three-glasses-of-wine voice only too well, and this was it. "Let me just tell you you'd better be calling to tell me you're being held hostage in Iran, you dog, because you left me here with all the work, making up lies to cover for you with everyone including our son, and now you're waking me up to listen to you do a bad John Wayne? This better be good."

All she heard for the next long time was the crackling hush of the long-distance line, then Shelly said, "I've got bad news and I've got good news. Which do you want first?"

Ruthie sat up and put her feet on the floor, feeling around with them for her slippers. She had to pee. As soon as she got off the phone she would go and . . .

"Ruthie?" Shelly asked.

"I'm here, I'm here, and I can't believe you're doing good-news, bad-news jokes at three in the morning, and using me as the straight man. At least you had the courtesy not to call me collect."

"I didn't have to. I punched in your credit card number. So which do you want first? The bad news or the good news?"

Ruthie sighed and wished for a second that she smoked. This would be the perfect time to light a cigarette.

"Gimme the good news first," she said, turning on her bed-side lamp.

"The good news," Shelly said, "is that I'm in Texas and I'm rip-roaring drunk, or as some of the folks here like to call it, shitfaced."

"Yeah? So what's the bad news?"

Silence. Static. Then, "The bad news is that I came here to see a specialist because I suspected I was at risk."

It took a moment for the words to get to her solar plexus, and when they did she didn't think she'd ever be able to breathe again. But the news wasn't a surprise. She'd been waiting to hear it since his departure, feeling all the while as if she was hanging from the edge of a cliff by her fingertips fearing the fall, and at last here it was.

"I'm HIV-positive, Ru-Ru," he said. "But there's good news about that. I don't have any symptoms, and my helper cells are at seven hundred and thirty. Ready for more good news? I've managed to convince my mother it's because I'm an intravenous-drug user."

Shelly was doing horrible jokes at three in the morning from Texas. Ruthie's stomach throbbed and a chill raced through her so that she took her slippers off and pulled the bed covers close around her.

"Okay," she said. "It's funny. We can't use it on the show. It's in terrible taste, but it's funny. And I miss you."

"I'm coming home tomorrow. American Airlines flight two twenty, at two o'clock your time."

"I'll pick you up at the airport," she promised.

"Do you remember," he asked her, "the night a few months ago when we were having dinner at the Mandarin, and the waiter brought the fortune cookies, and when I opened mine it was empty? This must be why."

"I love you," Ruthie said, "I love you, and I'll be at the airport waiting for you tomorrow."

After a while, exhaustion forced her to fall asleep again, but she opened her eyes in a panic at the first light. As she got out of bed, the truth ran over her with the force of a freight train and so immobilized her that she had to recite aloud to herself the steps she needed to take to get dressed. "Put on underpants, socks and bra, sweatpants, sweatshirt."

When she was dressed she walked to Sid's room, where the nanny was dressing him.

"Mama, can we go to the park?" he asked, smiling a delicious smile, and there was a look in his eyes that reminded her so much of Shelly that she had to turn away for a beat to catch her breath.

"How about some eggies?" she asked him.

"Yay, eggies, and jelly on toast," he said.

She held him very close as she carried him into the kitchen and instead of putting him on the floor to play, she held him on her hip while she cooked his eggs. Then while he spooned them into his mouth, she told him her version of the "Three Bears," in which there was a Mommy bear, a Daddy bear, and a Sidney bear. When the nanny had taken him out the door to head for the park, Ruthie called her office and said she wasn't feeling too well, made sure the writers knew how to proceed, then sat on the living room sofa, holding the morning paper but not really reading it.

She thought about going to the airport and what it would be like to see Shelly get off the plane, wondering if his being HIV-positive meant he'd be emaciated and sickly. She'd seen him only two weeks ago and he'd looked great. She felt cold and weak, and didn't know how to spend the day waiting for him to come home, so she made an outing of taking the car to fill it up with gas. She took Sid to Harry Harris's shoe store and bought him some sneakers. She made popcorn and ate all of it. Then she took a very long shower, and decided that instead of driving to the airport she would call a limousine service, so she called Davel Limousines and asked for a driver to pick her up at home to take her to and from the airport.

The driver was the same man who had driven Ruthie and Shelly to the Emmys last year and he recognized her and wanted to make small talk, but Ruthie closed the window between the front and backseat, and immediately regretted hiring a limo because the long blackness of it felt so funereal. She would have to be strong and in charge to take care of Shelly now. This wasn't like taking care of Sid, a job for which she had help. Besides, there was a library full of books about what to do with a baby. But Shelly with this virus inside him. This was different.

She realized as she looked up at the television screen for his arrival time that she should have called from home to check because she saw now that the flight from Houston would be late. Houston, Texas. He had gone there to be diagnosed. Afraid that if he went to UCLA he'd see someone he knew there, or be examined by a doctor who would tell someone.

For a while she sat on a bench near the gate where Shelly's flight was scheduled to land, looking out the window at the airplanes. She hated to fly, tried to avoid it by traveling as rarely as possible, as if by remaining on the ground she could trick death into staying away from her. Death. In her mind now, she did what she'd been trying not to do since Shelly's phone call. She ran down the list of all the friends they had lost to AIDS in the last few years.

Then she fished around in her purse for some paper, but all she had was a MasterCard receipt, so she turned it over and on it she wrote their names, sat in the corner of the airport on a bench near the window in the terminal and made an unbearably long list. Brilliant colleagues, cherished close friends, people who were gone too soon. With each name came the memory of the service she and Shelly had attended for that person. Some ceremonies were so dark and gloomy they could barely speak to each other about them later. Some were so filled with the love of the deceased's family, and relief from the pain they'd suffered that the memory felt as light as the balloons they had let fly at the close of the service.

When she finished the list, Ruthie prayed silently to all of them to help Shelly have enough time left so that Sid could get to know and remember him. When she felt someone standing next to her, she looked up, into the sweet face of Shelly.

"Sid's mother, I presume?" he said.

Ruthie stood and threw her arms around his neck. In her embrace his body felt the same as always. Good, healthy, not thin or weak or sickly, but perfectly fine, and she stepped back to look at him again.

"It's me," he said quietly, "and it wasn't a nightmare you had, Ruthless. However, there's a bright side. I'm leaving everything to you. So with your money and mine, you'll be the richest Jew in Hollywood, unless you count Marvin Davis, who is really four or five Jews in a very large suit."

"We missed you so much," she said, hugging him again. He was carrying his suit bag over his shoulder and a duffel bag in his hand, and he didn't have any other luggage so they walked, arms around each other, directly to the curb and the waiting limo.

"Mr. Milton," the driver said, "welcome home, sir," and opened the door. As the car moved on to Century Boulevard, Shelly slid his hand over the black leather seat and took Ruthie's.

"I'm scared," he said.

"Me too," she admitted. "Me too."

"How's Sid?"

"He doesn't sleep, he throws his food, he removes his diaper in the supermarket, in other words he's perfect," she said.

Shelly smiled, a tired smile, and still holding her hand, he fell asleep with his head pressed against the back of the seat. When the car pulled into the driveway of the house, the stop awakened him. The driver carried the bags inside, and Ruthie and Shelly walked in with their arms around each other. When Sid saw his father, he broke away from the nanny, ran to him and threw himself at Shelly, crying long and hard.

"Daddeeeee. Daddeeeee."

Shelly knelt, and spoke gently to him.

"Hi, Sidney. How's my boy? Don't cry, honey. Don't." Then he lifted Sid and held him tight.

After he'd unpacked and presented Sid with some Corgi cars, he got into bed for a nap. Ruthie kissed him good-bye, covered him warmly, changed Sid's diaper and turned him over to the nanny, then she left to keep the appointment she'd made a few days earlier with Barbara Singer.

"The first thing you must do is be tested and have Sid tested too," Barbara said to Ruthie when the painful story had been told and hung in the air between them. She could see that spilling it all out had been good for Ruthie, who seemed to relax in her chair for the first time. When Barbara reached to turn on her desk lamp, she realized she'd been so involved in and intrigued by Ruthie's story that she'd never once looked at a clock. Now it was night, and hours had passed since her arrival.

"When I first made this appointment," Ruthie said, "it was to come in and ask you to help me to help my son grow up in a world where people like his father, who I love more than my next breath, are stigmatized, condemned, and dropping like flies from a disease that must be stopped. But I guess there was always a part of me that feared this day might be coming, and when it did I'd have to face the real dilemma of how to get the three of us through it.

"I told Shelly today that I made an appointment to come over here and talk to you about raising Sid, and what kind of problems we were going to face. Only when I made the appointment I didn't know what I know now. He told me not to tell you he has HIV. We're writing and producing a new television series right now, and the executive producer is a nasty little bigot. Shelly's afraid he'll fire us if he hears about this. But I said you have to keep everything we tell you a secret, right?"

"Right," Barbara told her.

Ruthie took a tissue from the box on Barbara's desk, but her eyes were dry. "I hate to feel sorry for myself because I have had so much in this world where most people have so little, but goddammit, it took such a long time for us to hammer out a little niche for ourselves, after both being odd man out all our lives, and just when it was feeling like we had it together, there's this." Her head hung toward her lap and finally she let the tears come, and for a little while she cried quietly. Then she looked up at Barbara, her face a mass of red blotches, her bloodshot eyes large with fear.

"I'll go get Sid and we'll both be tested right away," she said. "And I'll see if I can get Shelly to start coming in here with me to talk to you. We've got so much to work on, and nobody to ask how to handle it. I mean it's not exactly your run-of-the-mill situation is it?" She smiled an ironic smile beneath her despairing eyes.

"Not exactly," Barbara said. "But I know you and Shelly and Sid and I can work out a way to handle it that will be right for your family."

"Our family," Ruthie said, liking the sound of that. "We really are a family. Although I'm sure we're not the kind you're probably used to counseling."

"True," Barbara said. "But things are changing." Then she told Ruthie about her idea for the group.

9

THE SENIOR STAFF MEMBERS were all women, and they jokingly referred to their weekly meetings as "the kaffee-klatsch." But after the first few minutes of commenting on the quality of the coffee and asking about one another's families, their meetings were far from social. In fact, they were sometimes so serious that during a presentation Barbara had the same performance anxiety that she used to get at University High School when she stood up to deliver an oral book report.

"As you're probably well aware, there are sperm banks all over the country, selling sperm which has been donated by men identifiable to the purchaser only by numbers, and a few broad-stroke descriptions of their race, religion, and favorite hobbies." One of her colleagues let out a titter of a giggle over that information, and Barbara knew they had to all be wondering what this had to do with their child-development program.

"It's a chancy way to go, but women who want babies badly are willing to take the risk. Donor insemination obviates the discomfort of dating, awkward sex, and uncomfortable relationships. The irony is that the same women who were freed up by the sixties to have sex without the problems of babies, twenty years later find themselves eager to seize the opportunity to have babies without the problems of sex.

"What's happened with all of the reproductive technologies is that some important issues are being created that will affect us, the child-development professionals. In this era of embryo transfer, in vitro fertilization, menopausal mothers carrying pregnancies for their daughters, and much more, it seems what many of these families may not be considering fully is the psychological and emotional effect the circumstance of these births will have on the people being created.

"And I say it that way because even in our studies here of intact nuclear families, frequently the baby-craving is just that. I mean, there's little thought about what happens beyond the excitement of new babies, when the realities set in. When the babies become children who have language and begin to wonder about their genesis. In my private practice in the last two weeks, I've met with a single woman who's been donor inseminated twice, and a couple in which the heterosexual mother was inseminated by the baby's father, who is her homosexual male best friend. And in both cases the families have toddlers who are very verbal, and the parents are concerned." That got a few "Hmm"s.

"It'll take a long time before there's real data on how those babies will feel when they're adults, but I suspect that the key to making it all work has something to do with creating a loving context for them. To find warm ways to deal with cold realities.

"I'd like to alert pediatricians and run an ad in some publications in order to look for and then begin a group for those special families. I believe the world isn't prepared yet with a new way of thinking to go hand in hand with those newfound methods. That culturally, socially, ethically, morally, and legally, we don't have adequate rules or answers for the exquisitely complicated issues that have already come up around these methods. Nevertheless, we need to find some way for the families to operate now."

Louise Feiffer, the director of the program, was a tall dramatically attractive woman in her fifties, with high cheekbones, ivory skin, and dark hair pulled back into a bun. Barbara was relieved to see her bright-eyed and smiling as she went on.

"I want to conduct this group under the aegis of the hospital and our pediatric-development program, so I'm presenting it to all of you for discussion." She looked around now at the faces of the others. Hands went up, there were dozens of questions, surprise at the statistics, and a fascinated curiosity about Barbara's research.

"It's undoubtedly an exciting new area," Louise said. "I think we should try to work a group like that into our schedule."

An elated Barbara congratulated herself all the way home on the good job she'd done. She was glad to have the meeting out of the way before tonight. The romantic quiet celebration with Stan of their twenty-fifth wedding anniversary. Impossible, she thought. A twenty-fifth wedding anniversary is something that happens to somebody's aunt and uncle. Not two youngsters like Barbara and Stan Singer.

She had sworn to Stan that she didn't want a party. Just dinner, preferably with her family, but when she invited her mother, Gracie said there was some committee meeting she couldn't miss. Jeff apologized that he had to go to basketball practice. Because the anniversary fell in the middle of the week, Heidi told her sadly that she couldn't make it in from San Francisco.

So after a fast shower, the application of some fresh makeup, and slipping into a dress she was proud she could still wear since it was about fifteen years old, she and Stan sat alone in a large booth at Valentino's. Maybe, she thought now, it had been a mistake not putting together a big blowout of an anniversary party. A quarter of a century of marriage was certainly something to celebrate.

Stan seemed unusually nervous. He kept looking over at the door, and postponing ordering dinner presumably because, as he told Barbara twice, he'd eaten a late lunch and wasn't very hungry yet. Now he was watching as a stunning young girl in a tight black minidress was being led across the restaurant. When the maître d' stepped aside and Barbara saw that the girl was Heidi, she let out a yelp of glee, followed by another when she realized that behind Heidi, dressed in a sport coat and tie, was Jeff. And miracle of miracles, behind Jeff was Gracie. She looked great in a silk shirtwaist dress and long dangly earrings Barbara hadn't seen her wear in years.

"Surprise, darling," Gracie said, and Barbara wondered if she was thinking the posh restaurant was excessive.

"Happy anniversary, Mommy," Heidi said, sliding into the booth and giving Barbara a hug.

"You planned this behind my back?" Barbara asked Stan.

"Of course," he said as he grinned, and received a kiss from his daughter.

"I *knew* I liked you," Barbara said.

"Mother, you look fabulous," Heidi said.

"Thank you, honey. I was just going to say that to *my* mother."

Gracie laughed and slid in next to Stan and gave him a patronizing little pat on the arm. "Good work, kiddo," she said.

Barbara felt warmed by the sight of her family all together in one place. Stan liked to call the need she had to see all of them assembled at a meal her barbecue fantasy. Now if the fantasy came true, which it never did, they would all be happy to be there, get along smashingly well, and leave full of love for one another and better for the encounter.

"Your hair looks totally idiotic," Heidi said to Jeff, and the fantasy went the way of all fantasies.

"That dress is so tight, if you fart your shoes'll fly off."

"Time out, you two," Stan said. "You've been together one hour. Can you stay civil for one more, in honor of the celebration?"

"Classic sibling rivalry," Gracie said. "My girls had it constantly."

"No, we didn't. Not constantly," Barbara flared immediately, knowing as she did it was a mistake to rise to the bait.

"Let's call New York and ask Roz. *She* has a mind like a steel trap," Gracie said.

"Maybe that's why they had sibling rivalry, because you compared them, Grammy," Heidi said.

"I *never* compared them."

"Well, if Aunt Roz has a mind like a steel trap, what does my mom have?" Jeff asked.

"I'm debating whether I should call a waiter or a taxi," Stan said, and everyone laughed.

"I guess no dinner with our family would be complete without tears, insults, hurt feelings, and unfulfilled expectations," Barbara said.

"In other words, we're normal," Gracie offered, then she lifted her arm to hail a passing waiter. "Could we have menus here pronto, dear boy? I'm starved."

"Mother!"

"The real issue you and your family-therapy associates ought to confront is why people jump through such hoops to conceive babies in the first place. All the babies do is grow up and mistreat one another, and *you* in the bargain."

"You can understand why I'm such a shining example of mental health with a mother who has *that* philosophy," Barbara said.

"Happy anniversary, sweetheart," Stan said, patting her hand.

"You know what?" she said, smiling at him. "If we're still around for our fiftieth, let's just go on a cruise."

They said good-bye to Gracie and made their way home, Heidi and Barbara sitting in the back of the car. When Heidi took her hand and held it, Barbara felt a surge of gratitude for being blessed with these two complicated creatures, her children. It was the best anniversary gift she could think of to be able to tuck Heidi into bed tonight in her old bedroom, even though the room now had a desk and a wall unit of bookshelves on one side and had been serving for the last few years as Barbara's at-home office.

"Grammy looked adorable tonight, but she's such a cuckoo," Heidi said. She was turning down the daybed while Barbara stood watching.

"Thank you for coming in for this dinner, honey," she said.

"Are you kidding? I wouldn't have missed it for the world."

Every time Barbara saw either of her children after not seeing them for a while, like the times Heidi came in from San Francisco to visit or Jeff got off the bus from spending a few weeks at tennis camp, she would be gleefully bowled over by the sight of them. Not by their beauty, because she knew she had no objectivity about that, but by the miracle of genes. She would marvel as she gazed at one of her kids, for what they always found to be an annoyingly long time, at the way her own characteristics and Stan's fell together to shape them.

Their carriage, their gestures, their speech, their respective senses of humor, the familiar amalgam of her characteristics and Stan's mixed in with each child's individuality never ceased to amaze her. The same kind of uncontrollable hair she tried to tame on herself in high school by rolling it around orange juice cans and plastering it with Dippity-Do, on Heidi was a wild, wonderful-looking mane caught stylishly in a headband, or worn hanging loose, showing off the girl's personal confidence, which was more than Barbara ever remembered having at that or any age. And the darkness around Stan's eyes, which had always been his least favorite feature on his own face, had been inherited by Jeff, on whom it looked exotic and mysterious.

"Sit down, Mom," Heidi said, and Barbara knew it was an invitation to stay in the room to talk, so gratefully and obediently she sat on the desk chair across the room from the bed, and started the conversation with what she hoped sounded like a casual, not-too-probing question. "How's everything in San Francisco?"

She'd been saving any girl talk for the time when they were alone, hoping she'd get real answers instead of the upbeat facile ones Heidi might give in front of the others. Or maybe she wouldn't get a real answer at all. That sometimes happened too.

Usually after Heidi first arrived, there would be a kind of tense feeling-each-other-out time between them, until the familiarity took over and Heidi dropped the exterior of a chic San Franciscan.

"I'm not good," Heidi said, moving some clothes from her duffel bag into a drawer. "I'm in love."

Hmmm, Barbara thought, things are getting chatty a lot faster than I'd anticipated. "But why does that make you not good?" she asked. "I thought that was supposed to be happy news."

"It makes me not good because he's crazy. Because he's thirty-five years old and can't make a commitment. Because speaking of mothers, his did such a job on him that nobody will ever live up to her so he can't get married, can't be exclusive to any woman. And I'm the poor jerk who stays with him, even though I know that all I want in life is to have a relationship like yours with Daddy. But there's not a prayer. Not with this guy. I mean, I know he lies to me and probably cheats too."

"Are you practicing safe sex?" Barbara asked, knowing she would get an outraged answer back.

"Oh, God. Of course!" Heidi flared.

"I'll bet the lying and the cheating hurt a lot," Barbara said.

"Don't shrink me, Mother!"

"I'm not shrinking you. I'm being sympathetic."

"Yes, it hurts a lot, and I'm thinking of moving back to L.A. just to put some distance between me and Ryan. Yikes. Even when I just say his name I get a pain in my chest."

Barbara held her breath so she wouldn't say what she was thinking, which was hooray, yes, move back here, because if she said that, Heidi would probably buy a condo in San Francisco by Monday. Instead she waited for her to go on.

"How did you ever get so smart when you were eighteen to marry my cute daddy? A man you still love after twenty-five years."

"Oh, it was easy, really. Grammy helped me decide."

"She did?" Heidi was surprised by that answer.

"Uh-huh. She said, 'If you ever go out with that nerdy little tight-ass again, I'll kill you.' Two weeks later we eloped." That brought a laugh from Heidi, a laugh Barbara loved and remembered from all her daughter's years of growing up, a laugh that made her know Heidi was going to be okay in spite of the thirty-five-year-old man and his mother. "And the rest is history," she added, laughing with her, and hurting for her.

You don't get to pick, Mother. Those were words that Barbara had thought and said to Gracie endlessly in battles, not just about Stan, but about everything she could think of over the years. And she knew the same rule applied to her relationships with her own children. After they reached a certain age, they didn't give a damn what she thought.

"What can I do?" she asked.

"Nothing," Heidi said and lay on the bed and pulled the covers up to her neck, looking to Barbara the same way she had when she was six years old. In fact, the fading honey-colored Winnie the Pooh that had been a gift to her at birth and one of her favorite baby snuggle toys still sat on the night table next to the bed, completing the picture. Barbara wanted so much to say something comforting, and the only thing she could think of that might work was something she really didn't believe, but it was hopeful, so she said it anyway.

"Well, maybe he'll change."

In the morning when she drove Heidi to the airport she remembered a story Gracie had told her when she was a little girl, about a turtle who watched the birds fly south for the winter and longed to go with them, but of course she couldn't because turtles can't fly. When two of the about-to-depart birds saw how wistfully their friend the turtle watched them, they offered to take her along. They would, they told the turtle, find a stick onto which she could clamp her mouth, and each of the birds would carry an end of the stick in its mouth. The only caveat was that the turtle had to keep her mouth shut for the entire flight.

The turtle, her mind racing, reminded herself again and again of the perils of speaking, but finally she had something which felt so important to say—Barbara couldn't remember now exactly what it was—that she spoke and of course fell from the stick, and not only didn't make it to the destination, but was never seen again. Barbara and Gracie always joked that the moral of the story was "If you want to go to Florida, keep your mouth shut," but the message was clear, and Barbara frequently felt when she was with Heidi as if she were that turtle.

At least they were sitting in a car, which was a great way to talk about uncomfortable situations, because if you were the driver you had to watch the road and there didn't have to be eye contact.

"I miss L.A. and I miss you and Daddy and Grammy, and even Jeff the brat. I always think I'm going to visit more often, but then I get bogged down with work and . . . and I never think I should leave . . ."

"Ryan?" Barbara asked, realizing she'd just caused the turtle to fall out of the sky.

"Yeah. I don't know what I'm going to do about that. Maybe give myself some time limit in my mind, and if he doesn't come around by then I stop seeing him."

"That sounds reasonable."

"It does, doesn't it? Unfortunately I don't have the guts to really do it."

"Do you have any women friends there?"

"A few. But they're all going through their own stuff, you know? Every now and then I see one of them, and they seem to be in worse shape than I am. At least I have a good job."

They were both silent after that until they got to the curb at United Airlines.

"Want me to park and wait with you?"

"No thanks."

"Whatever you decide to do about Ryan, I love you," Barbara said, and on the way to the office she told herself it was because Heidi was too choked with emotion that she didn't say "I love you" back.

At the office Barbara shuffled through the mail and returned some calls, and just before her first family arrived she took a call from a friend she hadn't seen in years. Lee Solway, a thoughtful, well-respected pediatrician to whom she'd referred dozens of patients.

"Lee. How great to hear from you. How are you?"

"I couldn't be better. Listen, I wanted to advance a call you're going to get from a fellow named Richard Reisman. I've come to know him quite well and he really needs your gentle guidance. Let me tell you why."

As Lee Solway described the referral Barbara listened, then wrote down the name Richard Reisman—and next to it the words *Candidate for new group*. The doctor was right. This man would need all the help he could get.

"Does it sound like it's your bailiwick?" Lee asked her.

"More than you know," Barbara answered. "Have him call me."

10

AT THE MOTION PICTURE Convalescent Home and Hospital, Bobo Reisman was known to everyone on the premises as the Mayor. Maybe it was because every morning, rain or shine, he made his way slowly and carefully, so as not to fall and hurt his hip again like last winter, to the bench outside the front door of Reception. Once he arrived safely, which at his age was a considerable accomplishment, he sat slowly, first putting his hand down behind him, then gently lowering himself into a seated position.

"Good morning, Mr. Mayor," Dr. Sepkowitz said as he passed.

"How's yourself?" Bobo asked him, but by the time he did, the doctor had disappeared into the building, leaving only the thud of the heavy glass door as an answer.

"Lookin' fine, Mr. Mayor," Margo Burke, one of the night nurses, said as she came out the door, and Bobo tipped his hat to her.

On the days when Ricky came to visit from the minute he got off the Ventura Freeway and turned the corner onto Calabassas Road, he could already spot Bobo on the bench and know immediately that his uncle was all right. Most of the time he would bring along a picnic lunch from Greenblatt's, and the two men would sit and share a chopped liver sandwich, which they both knew was bad for them, along with a Dr. Brown's celery tonic, which was also not so great but which they both loved. Then, on sunny days, Ricky would help his uncle to his feet, and they would walk haltingly around the grounds, being greeted by the passersby.

"Morning, Mr. Mayor," people would say to Bobo, then they'd nod to Rick and add a wink that meant, Aren't you nice to come out and spend time with an old guy like that? But Bobo didn't notice the others, because all he knew was that his nephew, his Ricky, was there to ask his advice about the business.

"Your dad couldn't understand why I wanted to do the goddamned outer-space stories. Years before that Sputnik was even heard of, I kept telling him, let's make movies about outer space. And wasn't I right? That's all you see now are those goddamned outer-space movies. The one with the guy with the pointy ears. How many times can they make that goddamned movie again and again? The whole crew of that spaceship is so old they should be moving into *this* place, for Christ's sake. It's like I told your dad years ago, I said, You know why outer space, Jakie? Because everybody wants to know what's out there. Are they people like us, or are they little green guys who are so small they use bagels as tires on their flying saucers? Ever hear that joke?"

"I *have* heard it, Uncle B.," Rick said. It was a scorching Valley day, and he was pushing Bobo, whose foot was bothering him a little, in a wheelchair around the labyrinthine paths of the grounds.

"You have?" Bobo asked.

"Uh-huh." Rick watched a young nurse leaving one of the cottages stop to write on her clipboard then reach back and tug something at her waist, probably the band on her panty hose. "The Martian tastes the bagel and says, 'Mmm. This is good, but it would be better with lox and cream cheese.'"

"Yeah," Bobo said, "that's the punch line. But Jesus, you

shmendrick, I'm an old man, for Christ's sake. You couldn't maybe have pretended you didn't know the *farshtinkener* joke, and given me the pleasure of being able to tell it again?"

"I've tried that with you in the past, and you always say, 'Don't *yes* me. I know I already told it to you. I'm only old, I'm not crazy too.'"

Bobo laughed, revealing yellowed dentures, and reached his veined and crooked-fingered hand back to pat his nephew on the arm. "Don't worry, Ingeleh, soon I'll be gone and you wouldn't need to schlep out here no more."

"You'll probably outlive me," Rick told him.

"God forbid," Bobo said, reaching back to smack him. "I already got a number. I'm just waiting for somebody to call it. You? You're not even married yet, so you can't die."

"And what does one thing have to do with the other?" Rick asked. They were at that part of the walk where he had to push the wheelchair up a small hill, and he was a little out of breath, vowing silently to start going back to the health club on a regular basis. But by the time they were on the level again he'd forgotten his promise.

"What it has to do," Bobo said, "is why should you be so lucky to get out of this life never having been nagged by a wife?"

"Do girlfriends count?" Rick asked, stopping the wheelchair next to a grassy area with lawn chairs, stepping hard on the brake, pulling one of the lawn chairs over, and sitting on it. "I get nagged by plenty of girlfriends."

"It ain't the same," the old man told him, shaking his head. Rick was always amazed at how, despite his uncle's wizened face, the man's big brown eyes danced with such life. "No matter what all the current cynical, immoral garbage television programs and movies tell you, my Ingeleh, it ain't the same. Listen, Ricky," he said, his brow under his wild crop of white hair furrowing with concern. "How is it you're in such bad shape for such a young man? Can it be a man your age goes up a little hill and huffs and puffs like that? Maybe you should knock off a couple a pounds?"

"I'm all right, Uncle B.," Rick said. "Don't worry."

"Why shouldn't I worry? I already told you you're in my will. You never mentioned if I was in *yours*."

Both men laughed, and then they sat in silence for a long time.

"You listen to me, Rickinue, it's time to make a life for yourself already. You're a big shot, a *shtarker*. And you date little girls who call themselves actresses, who shake a little *tochis* at you, and leave in the morning before you wake up. Right? Right! So what? You may be bigger in the business than me and your dad were, but me and him . . . at least we had something you don't have. A wife. I had your aunt Sadie, a pistol, a son of a gun, when she said 'Bobo,' I saluted. Whatever she wanted, I gave her, because she was a good soul, and we loved each other . . . what? Fifty-four years.

"And your mother, what an angel. A sense of humor on her, and she was crazy about your dad. I got married on accounta them. I used to watch them smooching when me and your dad came home from work, and I figured that's how it is when you get married. Smooching all the time, so I did it too. Of course, in your generation you get all the loving you want without benefit of a *chuppa*, but believe me"—Bobo was tapping with arthritic fingers on his own knee for emphasis—"believe me . . ." But then the thought was gone, and he sat quietly again.

"Do you want me to take him back, Mr. Reisman?" A tall black nurse was standing next to Rick, who realized now that he'd been staring at the water spurting from a nearby fountain for a long time and hadn't noticed that Bobo had fallen asleep. He'd been thinking about what Bobo said, which though he'd heard it many times before seemed to grab him inside today, as if a hand were squeezing his heart. Or was it the chopped liver? We had something you don't have. A wife.

"No, I'll go with you," he said. "I'll come along, in case he wakes up."

Rick pushed the wheelchair toward the lodge. The pain was just heartburn, he promised himself again. As they got to the door the nurse hurried ahead to open it, and walked with him to Bobo's room. The two of them lifted the old man onto his bed, and Rick covered his uncle's feet with a green-and-yellow afghan he remembered from his childhood, when it used to sit on his aunt Sadie's sofa. As he held the door for the nurse she smiled and said, "He's very proud of you. Brags about your success around here to everyone. I haven't seen all of your movies, but I did see *A Quarter to Nine*, and I enjoyed it thoroughly, I must tell you."

Rick thanked her, then excused himself and walked wearily through the hallways leading toward the exit to the parking lot. This is how it ends, he thought. This is where I'll wind up too. If I'm lucky. And when someone stands up to give the eulogy, is it really going to matter if I directed twelve films or sixteen films? He slowed his gait just by a fraction to look at the black-and-white stills of the classic films lining the walls of the building. Bobo, he thought, smiling to himself as he moved toward his car, wishes I was married. That's adorable. Every time we're together he gives me a little dig about it, just like every woman I date. That made Rick laugh, a little burst of a laugh, and when he got into the car and turned his car radio to KKGO FM, the jazz station, Dizzy Gillespie was playing "I Can't Get Started with You."

At home he warmed the dinner the housekeeper had left for him, ate it quickly in front of the television, moved the remote from channel to channel, then he dialed the Malibu number and Charlie answered.

"It's only me," Rick said yawning. The antiseptic smell of the convalescent home was still in his clothes.

"You mean you're sitting at home by yourself on a Saturday night?"

"So where else would I be?"

They were having the conversation they called "two really old guys in Miami Beach." It was part of an agreement they'd made with each other years ago. That when everyone else, lovers, spouses, friends, deserted them or dropped dead (anyone who leaves either one of us should *only* drop dead), the two of them would end up together, in a high rise in Miami Beach. Like *The Odd Couple* or *The Sunshine Boys*. After twenty-five years of marriage to Patty Marcus Fall there were no signs that Charlie would ever be alone. And for Rick there were only candidates. Dozens of candidates.

"No Mona?"

"No more Mona."

"The long talk?" Charlie asked, and Rick smiled and emitted some air from his nose, along with a laugh, which meant, How does Charlie know so much?

"I only know," Charlie said, as if he were reading Rick's mind, "because it's, what? Let's see. Six months? That's usually when it happens. Right? Last night I realized. You met her in October. This is March. I swear, I was thinking to myself, Mona is going to spring the long talk on the poor bastard any minute. And she did. So you said?"

"The usual."

"Ah, yes. 'Don't feel bad, it's not you, it's me. I'm no good for anybody.' So now you're depressed, right? Do I know my customers? Ricky, something's got to give, guy. Maybe it's time, and I say just maybe, for you to think about a little bit of compromise. No one's perfect. Right? You think *you're* such a bargain? So you dump Mona and now you're going to have to go through the whole process of dating again. How do you think Bush is doing? How do you feel about South Africa? And that's only on the rare occasions that you date someone who's even heard of Bush and South Africa. Christ, the thought of those evenings makes *me* depressed."

"Oh, leave him alone," Rick heard Patty say in the background.

"You're right. I'm pitiful, but I'm all I've got," Rick said.

"I don't know how to tell you that if you picked a woman for reasons other than how she was in bed, maybe when you got tired of screwing her and she could speak the English language you'd want to keep her around for more than six months."

"Yeah. Grow up, Uncle Ricky," he heard a voice say on what had to be Charlie's extension phone. It was Charlie's eldest son, Mayer, now how old? Could it be he was twenty? "My dad's right. Anyone can get laid. The trick is to relate to another human being in a loving, nurturing way. Not exploit them. You're becoming a cliché. The Hollywood Bachelor. It's so trite."

"Well, I can't tell you how delighted I am that I called," Rick said, grinning to himself at Mayer's outburst. He'd changed the kid's diapers, for God's sake, and now the boy was a second-year film student at USC, hoping to follow in his father's footsteps.

Now Patty got on another extension and told both her husband and son to "stop nagging Uncle Ricky, and hang up so I can talk to him." Patty Fall. Now there was a gem, a beauty, his favorite woman in the world. He always said if he could find one like her he'd be married. "Can I pin you down for a night to come over and have dinner with us?" she asked.

"Gorgeous, you name it," he said and wrote the night she chose into his planning calendar. Then he hung up the phone, turned off the television and the light, and drifted into his room to go to sleep. Somewhere before dawn, he moved over to the other side of the bed and remembered uncomfortably that the warm body most recently occupying that spot was gone. Mona. That's who it was, only now it wasn't. Oh well, he thought as he went back into a very peaceful sleep until his alarm went off.

He was somewhere on the Ventura Freeway when his car phone rang. He had had the phone installed two years ago and still that muffled eerie sound of it ringing, like a telephone in a nightmare, never failed to startle him. He was sure he would never get used to simultaneously driving along the freeway and talking into the speaker. It felt too much like science fiction. He tried using the handset, which made it even worse, because then he had to drive with one hand while the other one held the receiver, and when he wanted to change lanes or get off the freeway, he had no hands left to move the turn signal.

Once he'd been so involved in a telephone conversation that without realizing, he'd changed lanes too quickly and neglected to signal, and the guy behind him in a truck honked his horn at him, cursing. Rick had managed to hear some of what the guy in the truck was hollering. The part about the turkey in the Mercedes convertible on the fucking telephone. And when the truck driver passed Rick's open car, he shouted a final angry curse and spit out the window into the Mercedes. The spit missed Rick, but the point didn't. Talking on the phone while driving on the freeway in your high-priced car made you a Hollywood asshole.

Today it was Carrie in Nat Ross's office. "Mr. Reisman, are you in for Mr. Ross?"

"If this is what you can call in, then I'm definitely it," Rick answered.

Carrie clicked off, and Nat Ross got on the line.

"Rick?"

"Nathan Ross. Studio boss. How's your high-powered self this morning?"

"Fine, I'm fine," Nat Ross said, and then in a way that was clearly designed to indicate that he was also a nice boy who takes care of his family, he said, "You know, I always mean to ask about your uncle Bobo. I was such a fan of his and your father's. How's he doing?"

"Bobo is Bobo. He's nearly eighty-five, with diabetes, cataracts, an ulcer, kidney problems, and phlebitis," Rick answered. "But," he added, "at least he has his health." His stomach suddenly felt crampy as he wondered what this call was going to be about. He had four projects in development under his deal with Nat Ross's studio. Only one of them was even close to being ready to go. A political thriller involving a glamorous Jackie Kennedy type of First Lady.

"Ricky." Nat Ross, who hadn't heard anything Rick just said, went on to his own agenda. "I'm calling to tell you I know how you feel about Kate Sullivan, but I wish you wouldn't reject the idea out of hand of her playing the First Lady." There was silence so Nat Ross went on. "Listen, believe me, I hate her politics, too."

"Yeah?" Rick said. "So?"

"So, she's more right for the part than anyone else either of us know."

"Meryl Streep," Rick said.

"Unavailable," Nat answered.

"I haven't asked her yet," Rick told him.

"I have."

"Nat," Rick said, trying to keep his voice even, "when I made the deal with you, you promised me hands off. Don't let's change that policy or it won't work. Because I'll give you back all your nice money and go down the street if you try to tell me who to cast. And you know that."

"I'm suggesting, Richard. Only suggesting."

"Suggest elsewhere."

"I apologize."

"I forgive you."

Rick put the phone down, said the word "putz" out loud, certain that Nat Ross had just done the same thing on his end, and signaled to get off the freeway at Pass Avenue.

Kate Sullivan to play the First Lady. No way in hell. Everyone who knew him knew he hated that phony self-aggrandizing bimbo. Couldn't abide all of her grandstanding political horseshit. Half the time she didn't have any idea what she was talking about anyway. Was just a mouthpiece for her brother the senator. Besides, Sullivan hated Rick too. Had for years. Since that fund-raiser for NOW or one of those feminist groups a million years ago, where she'd made some precious speech about the feminizing of the English language. And afterward, when she'd asked if anyone had any questions, Rick had raised his hand and asked her didn't she think it was a waste of everyone's time to focus on small issues like *herstory* versus *history* when there were so many crucial larger issues at stake for women, like day care and equal pay.

Even from where he'd sat that night in the far reaches of Norman Lear's garden, Rick could see Kate Sullivan's green eyes narrow angrily, and then she snapped something inappropriately personal back about how everyone knew "Mr. Reisman's position on women." Then she somehow managed to sidestep answering his question. Afterward one of the men a few rows up handed him a note that read *I guess the answer to your question will continue to remain a MStery*. No. He would not cast Kate Sullivan in this or any other picture of his.

In his office the spindle that held his telephone messages had fallen on its side from the weight of all the slips. "I'm afraid to look," Rick said, then righted the spindle and pulled all the messages off at once with an upward tug.

His secretary, Andrea, didn't hear him come in. She was facing the other way, typing and wearing the headphones from her Walkman, which was blasting music into her ears at such pumped-up volume Rick could hear the bass line from where he stood. When she looked up and saw him she jumped to her feet. "Oh my God." She ripped the earphones out of her tangled nest of blond hair and burst into tears.

Another boyfriend walked out on her, he thought.

"I'm sorry," she said, "I didn't want to be the one to tell you. I mean I know how you feel about him and . . ." She put her hands with the too-long red fingernails on his arms and squeezed.

Bobo, he thought, my God, he's gone.

"Charlie Fall is dead," Andrea said, her face streaked with tracks of runny eye makeup.

The unexpected shock struck Rick suddenly in a place deep inside his chest and spread into his limbs and his face. Charlie. Impossible.

"I'm sorry," Andrea said. "Mr. Fall's secretary called a few minutes ago and said it was a heart attack."

"No."

"She said she tried you at home, but I told her you were probably on your way in. He was running very early this morning at the UCLA track. It was still dark and he was the only one there. By the time one of the other runners found him and they got him over to emergency he was gone. Mrs. Fall asked that you be called."

Rick turned and walked into his own office, not bothering to close the door behind him, dazed with the terrible news. Charlie. Good God. Andrea, sniffling into a Kleenex, followed him in.

"Where is she? Where's Patty?"

"At home."

"I'll go there," he said. "Right now." But he was too paralyzed to move.

"The funeral's the day after tomorrow," Andrea told him, then tiptoed out and closed the door behind her.

Outside, from the reception area, Rick could hear the phones ringing again and again. He looked down at the telephone on his coffee table watching the lights on the various lines that would blink then stop as Andrea answered. Calls that were probably for him, which Andrea was holding so he could have some time to collect his thoughts.

Charlie. His best friend for almost forty years. Rick had been preparing himself to lose Bobo. In fact any time the phone awakened him at night he sat up and said the old uncle's name out loud. But not Charlie. Just two weeks ago in a screening room at Fox they sat together at Charlie's dailies, the viewing of which was always guarded carefully and secretly from everyone in the industry but Rick. But this time it had been obvious that Charlie was nervous having Rick there.

Even from the out-of-sequence pieces of raw work, Rick had seen the genius that Charlie's earlier films had only prophesied. It probably was envy, unadulterated envy, that brought the tears to Rick's eyes that afternoon when the lights went up and Charlie, stoked with elation, had looked him square in the eye and said, "Eat your heart out."

"Oh, I am," Rick said, unable to lie to Charlie, who knew him so well. "Believe me, I'm eating plenty here. It's fucking genius."

Charlie had sighed and smiled a big smile that showed the space between his two front teeth and said, "It's about time I heard you saying that to me, because it's how I feel every time I see *your* work."

"But this is better than all that. Better than anything either of us has done before now. It's extraordinary. I swear to you." The two men had embraced and walked out of the theater into the bright day. Charlie Fall was gone. A heart attack. And Patty. What in the hell would she do without him? Rick's eyes moved around his office at all of the photographs of Charlie he now realized he had scattered everywhere. He and Charlie together in black tie at the Oscars. The year Rick had won, and then another from the year Charlie won. That one with Charlie, shirtless and tan, wearing that big Charlie grin at the Santa Monica Pier, arms around each of his boys, who held fishing rods. The boys.

Rick's eyes ached. He could picture Charlie's boys now, sitting with Patty on the deck at the beach house, holding on to one another in their shared pain. He dialed the number at the Falls' Malibu house. The line had a too-fast busy signal, making it sound as if the phone on the other end was off the hook. He put the receiver down and walked over to his desk. It was a mess. Piled with papers. Memos from the executives upstairs, a letter from a film festival in the Midwest where they wanted to do a Richard Reisman retrospective. He remembered cringing when he opened it, thinking, *Retrospective?* The fucking word makes me feel like I'm dead. Dead.

There was a pile of script notes he wanted to look over one more time. An invitation to an AFI dinner, and a brochure that he hadn't had a chance to look at when it arrived. For a long time he sat in his desk chair and read every word of it, then he dialed the number printed on the bottom. When the woman at the other end answered, he couldn't say a word to her, because he was crying. A woeful cry of loss, the forgotten telephone receiver now lying on the desk.

"Hello?" the woman on the phone said. "Are you calling the Pritikin Health and Fitness Institute? Hello?"

Rick put the phone back in the cradle.

II

JUST THE WAY Charlie had requested it in his will, the Beverly Hills Unlisted Jazz Band sat on the stage of the chapel at Forest Lawn playing all of his favorite songs. They were swinging into the first few bars of "Blue Skies" when Rick drove up. Patty and the boys waved to him, smiling. Music and merriment, the way Charlie had asked for it to be. As the parade of mourners arrived they could hear the happy music through the outdoor speakers, and after their initial surprise, they understood, which was exactly what Charlie had hoped. Rick stood with Patty and the boys. Patty's hand held his tightly as people who knew how close he and Charlie had been spoke consoling words to him as well as to the family.

A man in his early twenties walked up to Rick and took his hand as if to shake it, then put his other hand around it.

"I'm a film student," he said to Rick, "and I just wanted to tell you I was a big fan of Mr. Fall's and continue to be a big fan of yours. I think most of the young directors out there could take a few pointers from you old veterans."

Maybe it was the words "old veterans" (Charlie would have screamed with laughter over that one), or the fact that the band was playing "Fascinatin' Rhythm" and Rick was remembering one drunken night when he and Charlie walked down the beach sharing a champagne bottle as they rewrote the lyrics to that tune, calling it "San Diego Freeway." Whatever the reason, he couldn't control a huge bubble of inappropriate laughter that went right into the astonished film student's face.

Tonight he left the office late and drove over the hill to Westwood. He'd agreed last season to come in and speak to an evening class on directing at UCLA. In fact he and Charlie had been scheduled to do this one together. The classroom was so full of milling, chatting people that Rick had to edge his way toward the front, where Charles Champlin, who was going to be moderator, sat alone at a long table, glancing at some notes.

Rick liked Chuck Champlin. The critic was always kind to his films, even the ones every other critic destroyed. Champlin's sweet round face filled with concern when he looked up and saw Rick. The group of students were chattering so loudly he had to lean in toward Rick to be heard. "You know, after Charlie's death, I thought seriously about calling you and telling you we could easily have postponed this. I know how close you two were and . . ."

Rick tried a smile. "That's very sensitive of you, but I'm okay," he said.

"I screened *Quarter to Nine* for this group last week, and of course Charlie's *Sea Front*, and everyone is so eager to . . ."

Rick turned to look at the noisy laughing crowd, and when he did, his face got hot and he felt the panic of claustrophobia.

"Are you all right?" Champlin asked, noticing. "Because, Rick, honest to God, I'd sooner send these folks home than—"

"I'm fine, Chuck," Rick said, willing the panic to slide away. Once he was seated the students took that as a signal to stop talking to one another, and all of them sat so the class could begin. Champlin made opening remarks about Rick's history. He told them about Rick's father, the late Jacob Reisman, and his uncle, William "Bobo" Reisman, and how they had directed and produced dozens of films in the thirties and forties, and how Rick had grown up on studio back lots.

The shuffling around in chairs and the pages turning in notebooks all stopped when Champlin spoke about Charlie Fall and Rick's friendship. He said he'd been at the funeral, though Rick didn't remember seeing him there, and that Rick in his eulogy had said that he and Charlie always joked that "we were so close, if I ate Chinese food, an hour later, *Charlie* was hungry."

The class laughed, a kind of uncomfortable laugh, and remembering that he'd said something that inane in a eulogy made Rick cringe. Champlin went on to say more about *Quarter to Nine* and Rick looked out at the jumble of people whose faces blurred together, the color of their clothes blending each into the next, and he wanted to stand and say, "I can't do this," but now hands were up. Dozens of hands.

"Yes?" Rick asked, pointing to one of the people, and the evening was launched, while he sat there feeling flushed and hoping his mind would stay far enough ahead of his mouth to answer the questions. Not wander to Charlie, or to his own loneliness, or the frightening inability to sleep that had been infecting him for the last few days. But after a while, the knot in his abdomen melted away when he realized the questions were going to be the same ones he'd answered a million times before, and that he didn't need to worry, since the answers, the self-deprecating jokes and the put-downs of the industry he'd used for years, still worked in the same places, and after a while he was able to breathe easily. This was safe ground. Nothing too complicated or demanding. This he could deal with.

Before long, it was over, and Champlin was summarizing, and all Rick could think of was getting out of there and going home. Everything that had happened in his life these last few days played itself out against the fears and anxieties that sat lodged inextricably in his brain. Thank God, he thought, that my age-old system runs so smoothly that it's actually running without me. Because I'm not there. I'm lost someplace in my own fear. Heart-racing, nauseating fear. That I'll die. Or worse yet, that I won't die and that soon I'll be known as that decaying director who never had a life outside of his work.

In a flutter of notebooks closing and keys being searched for, the class stood and mixed and chattered, and finally all but one of them disappeared out the door. Champlin was talking to a tall bald man about Truffaut when a pretty blond woman who had left the classroom reentered and walked toward Rick. As she got closer, he noticed how beautiful her face was. Fresh. Young. And she had a great long, lean body.

"Excuse me," she said. "I'm Erik Blake's daughter Diane."

Erik Blake was the cinematographer on two of Rick's early films. "I told my father you were speaking tonight, and he sends you his regards."

Beautiful, he thought. Hands thrust into the pockets of her jeans. A blue work shirt, the color of her eyes.

"You were wonderful tonight," she said. "Even though I know you're probably not in the best of spirits."

He shrugged, not knowing how to answer. He wanted to say, True, so maybe you could cheer me up.

"I'm sure you're probably rushing home, and if you are, I'd understand, but how would you feel about going out for a cup of coffee?" she asked. Hah!

"Love it," he said at once. Great body. Maybe she'd like to make it with a depressed fat man.

"I'm parked in the lot next door, so why don't we meet over at Ships?" she said.

"Ships." He agreed and then watched her toss the blond hair as she headed for the door. Chuck Champlin's pat on the back and thank you made Rick turn and offer perfunctory apologies for being less than fascinating, after which he found his way across the UCLA campus to the parking lot. The girl was a knockout, but Ships, he thought. Why didn't I say, "How about my place?" Or some dimly lit bar instead of a big ugly coffee shop? But when he pushed the glass door of Ships open he was glad he hadn't said that because Erik Blake's daughter was not alone. Had never intended to meet him alone.

She was sitting in a back booth next to a man, and even from the door, Rick could see that the two of them wore matching wedding bands. For a long disappointed moment he considered turning to go, but she noticed him and stood and waved to let him know where they were seated.

"This is such a thrill," the husband said, standing to greet him. "I'm Harvey Feldman."

He was tall and athletic with an open boyish face, and Rick recognized him as a member of the sea of people at the lecture. He looked young. Not as young as the girl, but maybe thirty. Decaf, Rick said to himself. One decaf and you're out of here, asshole. You thought you were in hot pursuit of pussy, and here you are about to have a postmortem on your seminar with the husband of the pussy. When are you going to learn to stop listening to your cock?

"I know your uncle Bobo," the husband said, and gestured to a passing waitress. "My grandmother Essie Baylis was a Busby Berkeley girl. She lives down the hall from him in the lodge. She calls it the geriatric coed dorm."

Rick laughed.

"Diane and I go out to the home on Friday nights. We play cards with her and frequently Bobo is our fourth for bridge. He's a good counter. And at eighty-two, that's unbelievable."

"Eighty-five his next birthday. In a few weeks," Rick corrected him.

"Isn't that funny," Diane Blake Feldman said. "I could have sworn he told *me* he was eighty-two."

"Was he making a pass at you at the time?" Rick asked her. They all laughed.

"Well, isn't it a small world?" Rick said, using what Charlie used to refer to as his warm-nice-guy voice. "Bobo is a colorful guy," he said. The Feldmans were already drinking coffee, so when the waitress arrived she looked directly at Rick.

"One decaf," he told her, "shaken not stirred."

The Feldmans laughed at that.

"You know," Harvey Feldman said, "last time we played cards with Bobo, which was about two or three weeks ago, he said that he thought you and I ought to get together because

I'm in a business that's filled with so many dramatic stories. He says there's a movie in nearly every one of my cases."

Great, Rick thought. My uncle Bobo is agenting for me, and I'm hoisted with my own prick. This *shmeckel* used his wife for bait and now he's going to try and sell me stories. Well sorry, pal. One decaf and out. Even if we're at the best part of the story when I'm finished. And even if you are nice enough to play cards with my uncle.

"And what is it you do that's fodder for such great stories?" Rick asked, hoping the kid would give him a nice three- or four-word answer.

"I specialize in open adoptions in which the birth parents and the adopting parents of a child get to meet and know one another."

"Now why would they want to do that?" Rick asked politely, hoping the answer wasn't complicated, but Harvey didn't get to answer.

"Ricky?" a voice asked, and Rick looked up. There were two girls. Both hot little numbers, both vaguely familiar, but no names came to mind.

"Blair Phillips and Sandy Kaye," one of them offered. Nothing. No bells. Christ Almighty. He didn't have a clue who they were.

"Of course, Blair," Rick said, grinning at one of them, hoping she was the one who was Blair. "Nice to see you. How's everything?"

"Great," she said. "We haven't seen you since the night we were all on Henry's boat," the other girl said. Bimbos. They were bimbos he'd partied with on someone's boat. Who was Henry?

"Well, thanks for stopping by, girls," he said.

"Yeah, a real pleasure to see you too, hon," one of them said, and they twitched off across the room to a table. The waitress put the decaf in front of Rick. He put cream in it from the little aluminum pitcher, then opened a Sweet 'N Low package and poured the powdery white sweetener into the cup and stirred. He felt embarrassed to look at the Feldmans after what had just happened with those girls, and not sure why. That kind of thing happened to him a lot. Maybe it felt so awkward now because these people knew Bobo.

"The reason people want to do that," Diane answered for her husband, continuing the conversation, "is because for every healthy baby, there are forty couples in Los Angeles who want to adopt it, and six or seven single people. So a birth mother immediately has forty-seven choices. By creating a situation that allows a young girl who gets pregnant and doesn't want to have an abortion to choose the parent or parents she thinks are best for that baby, you give people who the state wouldn't consider eligible an opportunity to be chosen. Older couples, gay couples, single people. In that way, it becomes a competition for people to convince the mother that choosing them is in the best interests of the baby."

"Stories," Harvey Feldman said to Rick. "I've got enough stories for *ten* movies. Because the adopting parents can and have been anyone and everyone. Not just the people who have the qualifications per the state agencies."

The hustle. The kid was putting the major hustle on him pretty good. And why not? Wasn't that, after all, what life was all about? Had things been otherwise, he himself would have been hustling the tall blond Diane into his bed. But the "my life is a movie" rap. That was the one he had to sidestep regularly. Everyone in the world who thought his or her life was screenworthy, which meant everyone, would corner him at some point and try to sell it to him.

Well, not tonight, kids, he thought. And then he slid out of the booth, quickly stood, and to avoid the possibility of their thinking they might convince him to stay for even another minute, announced, "I'm really sorry to do this, but I'm not much for socializing these days and . . ."

"We understand," Harvey Feldman said, and both he and his beautiful blond wife stood.

"Thanks for joining us" is what Rick thought he heard them say, when without even thanking them for inviting him to Ships, buying him a decaf, or offering to sell him what were surely profound stories about something he had already forgotten, he was in Ships' parking lot hurrying to his car.

12

ONE OF THE FEATURES that had been pointed out to Rick as a high-line perk was the wet bar in his office that the studio stocked with liquor and wine and soft drinks. No one who came there to meet with him during the workday ever asked for alcohol. So the liquor bottles which sat on the Lucite shelves were the same ones that had been delivered on the first day he moved in.

Today, as Andrea was washing the coffee cups in the sink, she noticed that the bottle of scotch was half empty. Rick had been drinking during the day. Poor baby, she thought. She had watched him these last few weeks walk out in the middle of a meeting, step into an empty office, close the door behind him, and, she was sure, stand in the unlit room crying. Crying it out, because he was still so filled with the pain of losing Charlie that the slightest reminder could set him off. And finally, once he'd composed himself, he would pass her desk again and with a last sniffle go back into his office and continue the meeting.

Tonight he was at a late story conference upstairs with Nat Ross and some writers, talking about a new project he wanted to develop. He told Andrea at five-forty-five, when he left, that if he wasn't back by seven, she could go home. It was nearly seven, and when she finished washing all the coffee cups, she wiped off the Formica counter and placed a square of paper towel on it. Then she turned each cup upside down on the towel to drip, dried her hands on her jeans, turned out the light in Rick's office, and left.

By the time Rick stopped back to get his jacket it was nine-thirty and a blue-black Los Angeles night had fallen, but he didn't bother to turn the light on in his office. He saw in the spilled light from the fluorescent ceiling bulbs in the reception area that his jacket was hanging on the back of his desk chair. When he picked the jacket up, his keys fell jangling from the pocket to the floor. As he stooped to pick them up, he realized there was someone else in the room. Sitting cross-legged on the sofa watching him.

"Don't get scared. It's me."

Kate Sullivan. Jesus Christ.

"I've got to play that part," she said. He saw the orange glow of the cigarette she was smoking. "You realize, of course, that I could just ask the studio to take that project away from you and give it to me and they would," she said.

"Then why don't you?" he asked. His tongue felt thick. Maybe he should pour himself a scotch. That would probably make this bizarre intrusion a little easier to handle.

"Because now that Charlie Fall is dead, you're the only person who can direct me in it."

He walked to the bar and poured some scotch into a glass. Without bothering to add any ice, he drank most of it.

"I was with Charlie a lot before he died," she said quietly. "He was helping me organize the fund-raisers for the battered-wives' shelters."

Rick emitted an involuntary grunt. Charlie. In the middle of the biggest project of his career he took time out to work for battered women. The guy was a fuckin' saint.

"After the meetings we would talk, sometimes for hours," Kate said. "He told me he was certain that no matter how hard he worked he'd never be able to zero in on the essence of behavior the way you did. It was why his last three pictures were on such a grand scale. Burton Holmes travelogues, he called them. India, Russia. Pieces where the characters were incidental to the grandeur."

The scotch fired Rick's mouth and throat, and he drained his glass and poured another. She was quite right. Her own box-office success was far superior to his and she could easily commandeer his project with just a nod.

"He talked about your pictures, in astonishing detail. The way Pacino put his fork down in one of them, or the look on Jack Nicholson's face in another, and the hysterical contagious laughter of a bad actress who looks not just good but brilliant after you've improvised with her and shot the scene while she was still in the palm of your hand."

In the half darkness he could see she was wearing jeans and knee-high boots and a turtleneck sweater, and he remembered reading the article in *Vanity Fair* about her a few months ago, and how while he did he'd thought that the picture that accompanied it must have been touched up. No woman her age could possibly look that young. But she did. And as if to prove it, she stood now and walked over to Rick's desk and switched on the desk lamp. After another sip, the second glass of scotch would be empty.

"So I screened them. Every last one. And he was right. Everything Charlie said about your work was right."

Rick felt weak and tired. "Kate, I'm glad to hear that Charlie loved me. But I already knew that. It's why losing him has made me feel destitute for the last many weeks. However, your coming here to tell me that isn't going to change my mind about you."

She was perched on his desk now, and as he poured himself another scotch, just a taste this time, he realized that Kate Sullivan was going to try to seduce him. She was prepared to flatter him, fuck him, whatever it took to get not just the part she wanted, because that would be easy, but him directing her in it as well. He finished the third scotch and poured himself just half a glass this time, which he finished in two gulps, then he sat on the sofa, holding the empty scotch bottle in one hand and the empty glass in the other. The dull buzz in his head was the only sound he heard for a long time.

"It's going to be tough for you without Charlie, isn't it?" she asked him. Her tone was familiar. It was the same one his mother had used when he was a little boy trying to be strong and she would ask, "What is it, my baby?" And all of his resolve to be a big boy would fall away, which was what happened now.

The tears rushed into his eyes, and he put the glass and the bottle down so he could hide his face with both hands, and then he really lost it, crying uncontrollably. Not just about Charlie, but about his own life, his whole meaningless, unrelated, narcissistic, valueless, lonely fucking life. Maybe it was because he feared that it was Charlie, a man whose life was so filled with meaning, so completely unselfish, who should have lived, and that *he* was the one who should have died. He was trying to contain his sadness and cope with a quantity of scotch he was unequipped to consume when he felt Kate Sullivan's arms around him. Smelled her perfume, felt her lips on his hands, then on his wet face, and her hands on his body.

"It's okay," Kate was saying, and her coolness felt welcome against the heat the scotch provoked inside him. Or maybe it wasn't the scotch that was making him blurry and confused and aching with feeling but her nearness and her scent of perfume and shampoo and cigarettes, and the undeniable truth, which was how much he wanted to fuck her. To pull that sweater over her head and feel her tits against his chest and then to fuck her eyes out.

Christ. A little voice in the back of his mind told him as she began unzipping him, undressing him, that this was worse than stupid. Not the way he wanted to behave with her. But she was taking her own clothes off now, and, God, he wanted her. Kate Sullivan, her lips and tongue on his stomach, moving down to put her wet mouth around his cock. And now when he looked down to see her there going at him, sucking him, licking him, he felt as numb and detached and alienated as if he were watching her through a camera. For an endless floating time she worked him, her hands caressing his thighs, her lips and tongue exploring his groin. And then she was on top of him, sliding him into her. Spongy and warm and slippery and fitting tightly around him. Moving again and again, riding him, taking him.

Kate Sullivan. Every young boy's masturbation fantasy. He was having her. No, you asshole, he thought. She's having you. Even in that high other world he entered just before his orgasm, the place in which there was never any presence of mind, this time he maintained enough consciousness to hate himself. For being so desperate to be held, to be warmed, so needy to hear someone, anyone, whispering reassurances that he would seek solace inside the nearest cunt, even though it belonged to the enemy.

"Oh, yes, yes." Her hands were in his hair now, nails digging into his scalp, and he could feel her strong thighs tense on either side of his hips as she forced her knees into the sofa to give her the leverage she needed to move her pelvis into him and away, and again and again, and now he would let go. God, he was an asshole. Now he would, oh God, oh God, let go. The rush went blasting through him, escaped, and as he lay there, eyes closed, before even the first tremor of aftershock, he felt her lift herself from the top of him abruptly.

By the time he moved up onto his elbows to look at her, not knowing what he would say, feeling weak and devastated, she had pulled on her clothes and was out of his office. A minute later he heard the door to the reception area close. He lay still for a moment, then pulled one of the loose pillows from the back of the sofa, covered his wet matted groin with it, and lay there.

What did it mean? Did she think it would be so good that afterward he wouldn't be able to live without her and he'd give her the part? Was she trying to say she could behave like a man and fuck without feeling? She had used him the way he had used so many women in his life, and this was probably how all

of them had felt when he'd slipped silently out their doors. After
a few minutes he was sleeping.

The clanging of the cleaning crew's buckets awakened him,
and he managed to leap to his feet and throw his clothes on,
and in the time it took them to get from the door of the reception
area and into his office, he used his handkerchief to clean the
sticky wetness from the sofa.

"Evening," he said, nodding to them and moving out into the
darkened hallway, wondering for a split second if in the darkness he'd been able to get the sofa clean. The clock on the
dashboard of his Mercedes said midnight. Mid-fuckin'-night.
And he had an early meeting in the morning. Kate Sullivan. A
wave of self-loathing rushed through him, and he could hardly
wait until he got home to turn on the hot shower and scrub
himself clean of her.

He had today's mail and the two scripts he was planning to
read and he pushed the door to his house open, and the first
thing he saw when he did was the chicken-in-a-pot, which had
been served up on his good dishes, the two elaborate table settings, and next to each plate, a smaller plate containing a wilted
salad. And in a bucket of what had once been ice but which
was now water, there was a bottle of champagne.

He heard the snoring coming from the living room. Oh,
Christ, he had forgotten all about Bobo. A week from Tuesday,
his loving, gracious uncle had told him. Write the date into your
book. And he had forgotten. My eighty-fifth birthday. I'll take
a taxi to your house and when you get home from work we'll
celebrate. I'll do all the cooking. And he had. Oh, shit. Bobo
had arrived and made dinner, expected Rick, waited for him,
and finally he had fallen asleep, and . . . Bobo looked angelic
sleeping there.

On Bobo's birthday instead of rushing home and celebrating,
as promised, he had been in a meeting and then getting drunk
and fucking Kate Sullivan. The thought sickened him. Shit. He
took a crocheted lap robe some girl, he couldn't remember who,
had made him a few years ago that was hanging on the back of

one of his living room chairs, covered Bobo, and headed for his bedroom.

"Ricky, honey, are you okay?" he heard Bobo's sleepy voice ask.

He turned. Bobo got slowly to his feet. "I was worried sick when you didn't show up."

"I'm sorry," Rick said, moving to him for an embrace. "I'm so sorry. I just forgot." Bobo patted him gently on the back.

"You look like hell," he said, with deep concern in his voice. "Go get some sleep. Before you go to the office, we can have breakfast together."

"Thanks, Uncle B.," Rick said and waited until Bobo was in the guest bedroom before he turned and walked toward the bathroom to shower. His clothes smelled of her, his body still retained the memory of her flesh against it. He stood rinsing the soap off until he had used all of the hot water, then fell naked into bed and was asleep in minutes. Until his dreams were interrupted by the loud blast of the doorbell.

He had to be imagining it, he thought, must have dreamed the doorbell rang, but then he sat up and listened and there were definitely voices out there. By the time he got a robe on and had opened his bedroom door, the voices were louder and a woman was laughing. When he got out to the living room, the picture he saw looked like something from a bad dream.

Bobo, in a pair of wrinkled cotton pajamas, had opened the door for, and was trying to play polite and gracious host to, Animal, a cocaine dealer with whom Rick had done some commerce in the past, and Gloria, a stringy-haired, hollow-eyed, too-skinny blonde who had spent the night in Rick's bed once. Maybe twice.

"Aaaah, Ricky," Gloria said, throwing spindly arms around his neck and kissing him on each cheek. "Can you believe it? Joseph and I met at a party and there we were, trying to figure out what he and I had in common, and then we realized it was that we both know and love *you*. So we decided then and there to come over and tell you that, before the moment had passed. Aren't you glad? You don't look very glad."

"Who's Joseph?" Rick asked her, uncomfortably aware that Bobo was watching the whole scene. Gloria pointed to Animal, who for the moment looked almost as if he was blushing as he said, "That's my real name."

"Well, that's very nice, you two," Rick said. Lunatics like these could have guns with them, take offense if you didn't treat them gently. Especially because they were both as high as kites on something. "But I've got an early day tomorrow so I'm afraid I'll have to ask both of you to leave."

"Want *me* to stay?" Gloria asked. "I always got you to sleep real easily."

Rick felt shaky. Embarrassed. When Bobo had come to visit in the past, Rick had made it his business to produce the most socially acceptable friends he had to meet his uncle. These two were from the bottom of the barrel.

"He wants us to go, Glory," Animal said, looking now from Rick to Bobo and then back again. Rick's eyes couldn't meet Bobo's. Then, as if it were a peace offering, Animal extracted a vial from his inside coat pocket. "Want me to toot you up?" he asked Rick.

"No," Rick said.

"Not this time, huh?" Animal said, grinning a grin that showed his bad teeth. "How 'bout you, man?" he asked Bobo.

Bobo didn't say a word. His expression made the already nervous Animal look down at his feet and say, "Yeah, well, like maybe you'll gimme a call if you change your mind. C'mon there, Glory."

The girl looked hurt but she tried to make the best of a bad situation by patting Rick on the cheek and saying, "Call me, huh?" Then they were out the door. It was already a gray dawn outside and Rick's head was pounding. He looked at Bobo, who was looking long at him.

"*Boychik*," Bobo said, after their eyes had searched each

other's for a long sad moment. "Tell me something. Isn't it time for you to take stock of what you're doing to yourself? To make a decision to be a man instead of a lowlife."

Those words, coming from the gentle Bobo, who could never deliberately hurt another human being, stung him. And they were mild compared to what he wanted to call himself.

"You're going on fifty, for Christ's sake," Bobo said, as if Rick didn't know that. "What in the hell are you going to do? Do you wanna die being known as a drug-taking womanizer who made a couple of movies? Love somebody, for God's sake, make a life for yourself, stop thinking with your dick before you're an old sick man and an old sick joke, because that's where you're heading. Charlie Fall is dead, but at least his charitable work lives on and his name lives on in his children and his memory lives on with Patty. You'll die and won't even leave anyone who will come and make sure your headstone didn't topple over with the last earthquake. Ricky, you've been my relative for nearly fifty years, and from way back, even before you got so heavy, when you looked good and you were dating Farrah Fawcett or screwing Jackie Bisset, I never stopped feeling sorry for you."

Bobo, who had taken a taxi all the way from Calabassas, then cooked an uneaten dinner, and been awakened twice in the same night, had dark circles under his eyes. The two men stood silently in the cold living room, the smell of the chicken that neither they nor the sleeping maid had cleaned up still in the air. "What are you going to do? And I mean right away, because I can't stand it."

Many answers tumbled around in Rick's mind, and the one that came out surprised him almost as much as it did Bobo.

"I'm going to adopt a baby," he said.

13

WHEN BARBARA SPOTTED A RARE DAY with a few open hours coming up on her calendar, she decided to get on the phone and schedule some personal appointments. Her psychiatrist, her hairdresser, and oh yes . . . the postcard from Howie Kramer's office was beckoning. At least this time she'd gone as far as calling Marcy Frank and asking for the information on the woman gynecologist. But where did she put that number? The biggest problem with having three desks in three different locations was that the damn number could be anywhere. She shuffled through some papers, and was delighted to come upon the phone number of Dr. Gwen Phillips she'd scribbled down last week.

"My name is Barbara Singer. I was referred by Marcy Frank," she said. "I need to come in for a routine checkup."

"The doctor's out of town for three weeks," the voice on the phone told her. "And when she gets back she's very backed up, but I can schedule you in, let's see . . . the earliest I have would be . . . in six weeks."

"Thanks anyway," Barbara said, hanging up, congratulating herself for at least making the effort, and relieved not to have to face the unfamiliar. So much for new doctors, she mused and laughed to herself when she thought about that character Billy

Crystal used to play on "Saturday Night Live" who always said, "Remember, *looking* good is more important than feeling good," so she dialed her hairdresser.

"Well, Mrs. S., after December you won't have me to kick around anymore, so you'd better start thinking about which other operator you're gonna switch over to who can do your color."

Barbara looked up from the notes she'd been reading to pass the minutes until the timer rang to signal that the hair color had penetrated and she could get back to the office. Now she caught a glimpse of herself in the beauty-shop mirror, her face ringed with white cotton, her hair matted into bizarre bunches and coated with the gooey shoe-polish dye Delia applied to cover the ever encroaching gray. The pretty, skinny-as-an-arrow Delia was running a fat plastic comb through Barbara's ends, making sure the awful stuff covered every single surface of her hair.

"I'm going to get pregnant," Delia told her, "and all these chemicals aren't good for anybody who's pregnant, so by the end of this year, I'm quitting for a while."

"I'm glad for you, Delia, but sad for me. Maybe when you leave I'll just be au naturel for a while, and let my hair go gray."

"Oh my God, you're joking! That would be a disaster," Delia said, emitting an outraged laugh. Barbara wasn't joking. It was an idea she'd been considering for a while, but after that reaction she decided to reconsider. When her hair was colored and blown out she hurried to her car, thinking that after that affront from Delia, it was a good thing she was on her way to check in with her own therapist.

Morgan was more like a friendly old uncle to her after all these years and when she first settled into the peeling old leather chair, on which she had been responsible for some of the peeling, she felt relieved to be able to blurt out what was on her mind.

"I'm on overwhelm, Morgs," she told him. It had been nearly

a year since she'd visited the old family friend who'd been her therapist off and on since the sixties. Today he peered at her over his smudged half-glasses, and his lived-in face registered genuine concern. "My kids aren't kids anymore. Heidi sometimes goes weeks without calling, and Jeff will be off to college in the fall to heaven knows where.

"I spend five half-days in the clinic with individual families and five at my private office with the same. I lead parenting groups all week and two on Saturdays for my working parents who can only come in on the weekends. And now I'm all fired up about a new group. It's for families whose babies are the result of the new technologies and arrangements, like open adoption, or insemination. I want to create a context, a language, a way for these children to talk about things. But I've got to tell you, I'm worried about it. What if it's a mistake and families like these want to be in the mainstream and not treated separately? What if I can't think of answers for them to give these children? I mean how can a couple tell the child of a gay father what the ugly names mean? What will those two little girls who have been born via a sperm donor think about men, and how will they relate to them when *they're* women?

"Last night I had a dream that I was sitting in my office and this creature walked in. It was somewhere between a stegosaurus and Dumbo. I mean, it was green and spiked but it had cute baby blue eyes and a trunk, and it said, 'I'm here to inquire about the new group!'" The thought of what a dream like that might mean sent her into a peal of laughter she knew by the look on Morgan's face was a little too hysterical. Then she stopped laughing and thought about what was going on in her life.

"I joined some fancy health club last month, paid the fee, and walked out after ten minutes because I couldn't handle the stress of destressing. I think after all is said and done, I'm a fraud. I keep saying I'm going to slowly cut back and take time to do nothing, but instead I keep piling it on myself. I just recited my life's schedule to you, Morgan, now you tell me, does that sound like the agenda of a woman who's looking for peace?"

Morgan took off the Benjamin Franklin glasses and wiped them with a handkerchief he pulled out of his pocket. "What does your mother think about the idea for the new group?"

"Are you kidding? It's so up her alley, I sometimes wonder if the real reason I'm organizing it is to please her. She thinks it's the first really important thing I've done in years."

Morgan raised his eyebrows and made a note. The walnut desk clock was ticking and she realized she'd been complaining for so long she was already halfway through the session. "Anyway, to hell with Gracie, let's get back to me. Am I taking on something so huge that I'll kick myself? The more I read about these questions the more complicated it all sounds, and I don't want to lead these people to think I have answers for them when I don't. I'll just be feeling my way *with* them. I know how to help families with developmental problems, but this feels so much bigger than that."

"I think if you make it clear . . . that you're there to find out the answers with them, then you're not leading anyone astray."

Barbara looked across the desk at Morgan's face and thought of all the times she'd left his office certain that his sage words of the preceding hour had just changed her life. Today the whole idea of spilling out her anxieties to him felt foolish, self-indulgent, and absurd.

"Do you know who Lucy Van Pelt is?" she asked him.

"No."

"Somehow I just flashed on her. She's a character from the cartoon 'Peanuts,' a little girl who runs a psychiatry booth as if it was a lemonade stand. She dispenses advice for five cents. And I guess all of a sudden psychiatry and psychology seem very silly to me. Like a cartoon."

"Now *that* sounds just like what your mother always says."

"Please. It's bad enough when I hear myself sounding like

Gracie, but when *you* tell me I do, it only reminds me it was probably gross lack of judgment on my part to have a psychiatrist who knows her."

"Or a brilliant choice," he said. "Think of all the time and money you've saved over the years not having to tell me the things I already know about her."

"Good point," she said, but only because she was fond of Morgan and sorry if she'd hurt his feelings, which was probably why she didn't do what she wanted to now, which was to stand, say "I don't want to be here anymore," and leave, the way she had the health club.

"So you think Gracie thinks this group is destined to be your finest work?"

"Absolutely."

Morgan *tsk*ed at that. A significant *tsk*, and Barbara wanted to ask him what it meant, only somehow they went off on another tangent before she could. Heidi and her impossible boyfriend, Jeff's impending departure for school. And it was all such a jumble of so many thoughts, that by the time she pulled up at the drive-through at Carl's Junior to get a very late lunch, she had forgotten everything they'd decided she should do to cope. It had been a hundred-and-twenty-five-dollar visit down the tubes.

"Charbroiled chicken and a diet Coke," she said to an intercom.

"Anything else?"

"That's it."

"Three dollars and ninety-six cents," said a disembodied voice.

"Thank you."

"Have a nice day."

"Likewise," she said, thinking she had no idea whether she'd just spoken to a woman or a man. Faceless communication, like her answering machine, and her fax machine, and donor insemination. If she ever pulled that group together it would be demanding on her skills and a big responsibility, but there wouldn't be a dull moment.

"Aaggh."

"Sorry," Howie Kramer muttered. She had caved and called him. She couldn't wait six weeks to be examined, and when his receptionist said, "Name your time, Mrs. Singer," Barbara wondered how she would ever be able to give up a luxury like that. So now the light, the too-bright light, was bouncing from his head again, right into her eyes, and he was rattling on about one of his famous patients.

Barbara wasn't listening. She was worrying about Scottie Levine and how when she'd asked Ron Levine to come in alone so they could talk, he said on the phone, "That little kid is a mess. Don't you think I see it? Who wouldn't be, living with that shrew? And it breaks my heart because you know my son is my top priority."

"When can you come in?" Barbara asked him.

Silence. Then he said, "Let me look at my calendar." Silence. "You know what? I'm going to need to get back to you." Poor little Scottie. How could she help him?

"In a few years that kid will be in intensive therapy," Howie Kramer was saying as he scraped her inside with no grace at all. Barbara, startled at what seemed to be a mind-reading comment, wondered how he knew what she'd been thinking.

"What kid?" she asked as Howie removed the metal instrument from inside her. He was in the middle of rattling on with some story that she could tell by the look on his face he considered quite juicy. And though she hadn't been listening, now when she tuned in, it seemed it was, as always, about one of his famous patients. This time it was a woman who had a fear of getting pregnant.

"The baby's due next month. I mean she's one of those people who should just forget about motherhood. To begin with she didn't want to mess up her great body, which is why she figured out a way that she didn't have to. You know her. You've seen her on "Dallas," or maybe it was "Knots Landing." Anyway, she had her husband inseminate her sister. So now the baby's mother is her aunt and the baby's aunt is her mother. Kind of like that old song, 'I'm My Own Grandpa.' Remember that one?" Now Howie was inserting rubber-gloved fingers into Barbara, pressing down on her abdomen and at the same time laughing a red-faced wet-eyed laugh at his own joke.

"I'll tell you something, I could write a book, because I've seen it all," he said. Gracie was right, Barbara thought. In this town alone there were probably thousands of people having their babies in unusual ways.

"Well, everything seems okay," he said. He had finished the exam and was removing the gloves. "I'll call you if there's anything wrong with the lab report." Then he looked at her absently. "Did I do a breast check?" Of course going from examining room to examining room, body to body, he probably forgot whose what he had checked, and she was tempted to lie and say yes, but then she'd have to go home afraid there might have been something which had gone undiscovered because of her lie.

"No," she confessed and revealed her breasts, putting her arms behind her head so he could roll his hands around on them to examine her, a process that always made her nervous and one which she was certain required concentration, but not for Howard Kramer, who just continued to talk through it all.

"My wife knows her very well. They go to the same hairdresser. Sandy says she's had every kind of plastic surgery possible. There's a guy over in Santa Monica who specializes in breast augmentation, and he's the one who did her breasts and they are extraordinary. One night we ran into her at Jimmy's and she was wearing—"

"Howie!" Barbara said sharply. "What about mine?"

"Your what?"

"My breasts. Anything unusual?"

"No. They're fine. When was your last mammogram?" he asked, reaching for her chart.

"Nine months ago," she said, making as ladylike a slide from the table as she could, considering her top was wrapped in a paper gown, her bottom was sporting what felt like a paper tablecloth, and she was filled with K-Y Jelly.

"You're in great shape," Howie said. "You check out like a young woman."

"Thanks," Barbara said, as she disappeared behind the curtain of the tiny dressing area and winked a conspiratorial wink at her reflection in the small mirror on the wall, congratulating herself on the fast escape. Then she heard Howie say, "You know, I'm looking at your chart here, and I'm thinking that next time you come in, we should discuss a tubal ligation."

"Great," she replied. "Next time I come in, we'll discuss it in depth."

"Give my best to Stan," Howie said as he exited the examining room and closed the door.

"Only there ain't gonna be any next time," Barbara promised herself out loud.

"Oh here, Mrs. Singer," the receptionist said as Barbara signed the MasterCard charge slip to pay the bill. "Before you go, if you address this card to yourself we'll mail it to you when it's time for your next checkup."

"Thanks very much," Barbara said, taking the card, finding a pen on the counter, and starting absently to fill it out. The doctor's phone rang and the receptionist answered it and spoke animatedly to the person on the other end of the line. Barbara took a moment to reconsider, put the pen back on the counter, slipped the blank card into her purse, waved a thank you to the distracted receptionist, and left Howie Kramer's office. Alone on the elevator she tore the card up, and as she exited into the parking lot, she threw it into the first trash can she saw.

The hospital corridor was bustling and she was hurrying to get to her office to get her phone calls out of the way before the staff meeting. She waved a hello to Louise Feiffer, who put up a hand to stop her.

"A woman left this in my office. I think she was interested in the new group. She said she saw the ad."

Barbara opened the envelope. In it was a piece of personalized stationery with the name Elaine De Nardo at the top.

My name is Lainie De Nardo. I saw the ad about your group.
I need to talk to you first though, alone if it's okay. If so, please
call me, but don't say why you're calling unless you reach me
personally. I'd appreciate your confidentiality. Thank you.

Barbara sat at her desk and called Lainie De Nardo, and as she listened to as much of her story as the woman could tell her on the phone, she knew that this was someone who needed the new group in a desperate way.

14

LAINIE COULDN'T BELIEVE that one of the customers actually came all the way from La Jolla every few weeks in a chauffeur-driven limo. And while the woman tried on dozens of outfits, the tall, black, uniformed driver leaned against the car reading a newspaper, where everyone in the store could see him through the big front window. After the woman was dressed again in her own clothes, fishing around in her wallet for her American Express card, she always said the same thing to Lainie: "I'll bet with what I spend here, I could put every one of your kids through college."

Lainie placed the woman's gold credit card on the imprint machine, slid the bar across and back over the card and the receipt, then wrote the word *merchandise* on the slip. Next to it she wrote the amount the woman had spent that day, usually in the neighborhood of six or seven thousand dollars. "Mitch and I don't have any kids," Lainie reminded her.

"Oh, what a terrible shame," the woman invariably said, looking at Lainie with sad eyes as though she'd never heard that information before. Lainie covered the woman's hanging merchandise with white garment bags splashed with the Panache logo, placed the sweaters and accessories in tissue paper, which she laid carefully into white Panache shopping bags.

Then she and the woman exchanged pleasant good-byes as the chauffeur, who could see through the glass front door of the store that the transaction was complete, hurried to carry the packages to the car.

Long after the limo pulled out of the parking lot, Lainie would find herself still staring out the front window, remembering the look in that woman's eyes when she said how sorry she felt for Lainie and Mitch. She had seen that same look in the eyes of more people than she could count. "It's the way people probably look at lepers," she'd once said laughing to Mitch. But soon a customer would interrupt her thoughts to ask if Lainie could order the Donna Karan suit in pink, or if she had the white open-toed Bruno Magli shoe in a six, and she'd stop thinking about the leper look until the next time someone gave it to her.

Business was extraordinary. Women were driving to Encino from Santa Monica, Malibu, Brentwood, and Beverly Hills to shop at Panache. Studio designers were making appointments to come in and buy wardrobe for television shows. Sometimes they would bring well-known actresses along, whose glittering presence caused a big stir among the other customers.

Of course there were plenty of things going wrong all the time too. Little fires to put out, Mitch called them. A few weeks ago he'd caught one of the salesgirls stealing a large purse full of sweaters and had to fire her. And the other day a gorgeous transvestite came in, wearing a Valentino dress, and when the salesgirl who was helping him stepped into the dressing room and realized he was a man, she ran screaming out of the store. The salesgirl called from home later that day to say she'd never deal with anyone like that again, and Mitch said, "We'll miss you," because the transvestite had spent eight thousand dollars buying up a number of their size twelves.

Some customers tried to return clothes after they'd worn them. Usually it was a woman who could afford anything she wanted who had the gall to bring back a dress still reeking with the odor of her perfume, her deodorant, even her cigarettes. She would insist that she was bringing the dress back for a full refund because there was something wrong with it. When Mitch told her firmly, "Sorry, we can't take this back, you've obviously worn it out, and we don't take evening clothes back," the customer would go mad.

"Are you calling me a liar?" one dark-haired, very tan woman from Beverly Hills asked, her body tense with rage. Mitch knew she was the wife of a well-known movie producer. Behind her, through the large front window of the store, he could see her red Rolls-Royce with her personalized license plate MINDY.

He looked at her with the most benign look he could summon, no anger, no self-righteousness, no judgments, while she clenched her fists and contorted her face and said to him loud enough for everyone in the store to hear, "The goddamned dress is too small on me, and I only took it because your pushy salesgirl forced it on me, and if you don't give me every cent of my money right now, I'll tell every friend I have how badly you're treating me and I swear to you not one of them will ever set foot in this place!"

Lainie usually stood on the other side of the store by the dressing room doors while one of those incidents took place, wanting to hide inside one of the rooms until the customer left. It made her sick to think that what the woman was saying might be true, that the anger of this one customer might have the power to destroy their business, and she was awed by Mitch's ability to not react.

At home they laughed about how he was the emotional Italian to Lainie's level-headed cool WASP, but in the store it was the opposite. She would get flustered, be churning inside while, for the sake of the business, Mitch always maintained his composure. Even when Mindy took the dress in question from the counter, balled up the sequined garment, which retailed at four thousand dollars, and with her eyes never leaving Mitch's, threw the dress onto the floor, then stomped out of the building, climbed into her Rolls, and drove away.

When she was gone, Mitch walked to the dress, picked it up,

and called out to one of his salesgirls, "Put this in a box and send it to her house. She paid for it, she wore it, it's hers." And when Mindy came into the store a few weeks later, looking for something to wear to her friend's daughter's wedding, all of them—Mitch, Lainie, the salesgirls who had witnessed the scene, and Mindy herself—acted as if nothing had happened.

Lainie was five nine, with a long willowy body, ash blond hair, and pale blue eyes. She looked good in everything she wore, so she always wore the clothes they had in stock at Panache. When the customers saw her dressed in an outfit, Mitch knew they would want to try that outfit on themselves, and hopefully buy it. Sometimes, though, the plan backfired, because the customer would stand next to Lainie, who looked like an angel in a certain cropped jacket or short skirt in which the customer looked ridiculous. The result was sometimes a teary-eyed customer storming out frustrated and empty-handed.

But the new store had lighting and mirrors that could make nearly everyone look good. Mitch had spared no expense making sure of that. He had hired a film lighting director famous for working with beautiful demanding female stars, and insisted the designer pay attention to every corner of the eight-thousand-square-foot space. Even in the ladies' room, the customers' cheeks looked pinker than they were, and when they modeled for themselves in front of the full-length three-way mirrors, their bodies looked longer and slimmer.

In the first store there had been so little hanging space that Mitch kept some of the stock on a rack in his van, which was parked downstairs behind the building. When a customer asked, "Do you have this in a size ten?" he would have to excuse himself and run out the back door and down to the parking lot, sometimes in the rain, to check the merchandise. In the new store, there was plenty of hanging space for miles and miles of stock, a room for the back stock of shoes in all sizes, a steaming and pressing room, an alterations room, and an office for Mitch.

The first store was upstairs from a greasy-spoon restaurant on Ventura Boulevard in Woodland Hills and across the street from Valley BMW, where Lainie Dunn was working part-time as a cashier. The rest of the time she went to school studying English literature at Cal State, Northridge. Mitch and Lainie met at the restaurant downstairs when Lainie stopped in there for a quick lunch on her break. He spotted her beautiful face, put his cheeseburger and Coke on the little table across from her tuna-salad sandwich, sat down across from her, and said, "Now don't say I never take you to any fancy places."

He knew he was good-looking and funny. Women always fell for him and he had confidence that this girl would like him too. He could see by the poor quality of her clothes that she didn't have money, but the way she tied the little scarf just so around her neck and turned up the collar of the jacket and pushed up the sleeves showed style. And it didn't hurt that she was break-your-heart pretty. Lainie smiled at the pickup line then glanced at his left hand to see if he was wearing a ring.

At Valley BMW she was the only female employee. Since her first day of work, every male in the place had come on to her. The fact that every one of them was married didn't seem to mar their persistence. Gino from the parts department, a guy with a wife and four kids, was so hot on Lainie's trail that once he actually ripped open the bathroom door while she was inside, probably hoping to catch her with her skirt up, which he did.

But he was stunned and turned off when he saw that her skirt was up because she was injecting her thigh with the insulin she had to have for her diabetes. Later Lainie laughed when she told her mother about the expression she'd seen on Gino's face. But the positive result was that seeing her with the needle stuck in her thigh had unnerved him and he'd stopped bothering her.

"Single," Mitch said that day, seeing her eyes looking at his hand. "And you?" Lainie nodded. Her face flushed when she looked at his dark long-lashed eyes, and that thick black hair nearly to his shoulders, and thought, Oh my God, is *he* gorgeous! And pretty soon she was telling him what she later admitted was "the fancy version" of her life.

That she was working at the BMW place because she liked

the pretty cars and needed to pick up a few dollars because she was an English major in college. That her mother, with whom she lived, worked at Bradford, Freeman, a well-known law firm in Beverly Hills. She didn't say that she only took two courses every year in the English department because it was all the time she could afford to take away from work, or that her mother was the receptionist at the law firm.

Mitch nodded and heard very little of what she said because her face was so pretty he couldn't wait until she stood up so he could take a look at her body. But she still had most of her sandwich left, which she nibbled at between sentences, and didn't seem to be in a hurry.

Mitch told her that his father had just died and left some money to him and to each of his sisters. He'd been working as an accountant but was miserable doing that, so he decided to start a ladies' clothing store upstairs from where they were sitting. He also mentioned that he had a hard time keeping sales help because he was such a colossal pain in the ass to work for. But he said that part grinning broadly so she'd know he was kidding.

When she got up to leave, he offered to pay for her sandwich, which was already paid for, and when she told him so he said, "I owe you one." As he watched her walk away, he noted that the body was even hotter-looking than the face. After Lainie got back to Valley BMW and sat down at her desk, the phone rang and it was Mitch calling to say, "I think you should come and work for me, and one of these days I'll have you driving one of those fancy cars instead of drooling over them. Why don't you tell the boss you quit, and walk across the street?"

Lainie laughed, said, "Don't be silly," and hung up the phone. But after thinking about it for a minute, she stood, took her purse out of the top drawer of the desk where she always kept it, quit her job, and walked across the street.

Mitch was right about her sense of style, and it paid off. The way she pointed out to a customer that a particular pair of earrings brought out the color of her eyes, or that buying two different shirts to wear under a jacket offered more opportunities to get use out of the jacket, increased the store's take significantly at the end of every day.

When Mitch's mother died he was four, and his three older sisters, who were eight, nine, and eleven at the time, took on the task of raising him. Their father never remarried and the girls ran the household and "Mitchie's" life. They pampered him and treated him as if he were their living doll. They chose his clothes, and ordered the barber to cut his hair just so, helped him with his schoolwork, criticized his friends. It was like having three mothers. The up side of which was having three times the nurturing, the down side of which was having three times the nagging and interfering.

Fortunately, there was enough money from Joe De Nardo's plumbing business to provide them all with good clothes, cars at age sixteen, and an elaborate wedding for each of the sisters. Mitch was crazy about all three of his siblings. Betsy, whom he described as "very Valley," had a wild mane of hair, loved glitzy jewelry and sparkly clothes. Mary Catherine, with dark smokily made-up eyes and straight silky hair, was tall and leggy and always wore sexy suits with boxy jackets and very short skirts that looked sensational. She had been trying all her life without success to get into show business by auditioning for commercials. Kitty lived in Calabassas and loved to ride horses, which, after her husband and kids, was all she cared about. She looked like a Ralph Lauren ad, in her jeans and Shetland sweaters. It was undoubtedly from his pretty, clothes-conscious sisters that Mitch learned a sense of what was stylish and a knowledge about what appealed to women.

When the news got to the sisters that Mitch was in love with a new girl who was working in his little store, each of them came by to check her out. Mary Catherine and Kitty gave her their stamp of approval because she was pretty and friendly and seemed to be wild about their brother. But Betsy wasn't so bowled over.

"I took her out to lunch and believe me, I had plenty of

questions for her. She eats like a bird so I asked her if she was watching her figure for Mitch. She told me no, she's careful for health reasons." The sisters were gathered at Betsy's house in Sherman Oaks one afternoon so their kids could swim in her pool. "Well, when I pressed her to see what that meant, she told me she's got high blood sugar, and she has to give herself shots before every meal. Mitchie knows about it and says so what!"

"He's right. Big deal, lots of people have diabetes. It's not like having cancer. You can control it," Kitty said.

"People like that have problems," Betsy said. "It's bad for your eyes, and also they pee a lot which is bad for the kidneys, and sometimes it's not good for them to get pregnant." Now the others were worried too. Mitch was the only one who could carry on the De Nardo name. All three of the sisters had assumed that any day he would fall in love, get married, and have a million kids.

"Maybe it's just a fling. Maybe he won't marry her."

But it was far from a fling. Lainie and Mitch meshed, united, clung to each other, and never had so much as a cross word between them. And the differences between their backgrounds and their personalities made them seem exotic and exciting to each other. She was intrigued with the fiery passionate man who laughed and cried and fought with his sisters on the phone with ferocity, then thought better of it all and called back to apologize with the sweetness of a puppy. "I'm a jerk. I take it back. I love you." It was the way people behaved in movies.

And Mitch had found a woman about whom he liked to say, "She knows the rules of the road." Because Lainie knew how to be gracious and polite, somehow knew the proper way to behave in every situation. "She classes up my act," he admitted.

He proposed to her on bended knee in that sweet romantic way he had of doing everything. But before Lainie could say yes she knew she had to tell him what her doctor in Panorama City told her years earlier about the dangers of pregnancy for diabetics. It could be too much of a strain on the kidneys, and if there was a problem she could end up having to be on dialysis for the rest of her life. And worse than that, the baby of a diabetic might come out deformed or blind. Mitch looked a little pale as he listened, but finally he said what she'd prayed he would, "I don't care about any of that. I only care about being with you for the rest of my life."

When their bookkeeper told them they'd outgrown the store above the restaurant, they began working on the design of the new store, their dream store, which they supervised brick by brick, hanger by hanger. It would be two stories, with full bars on both floors, beautiful spacious dressing rooms, designer fashions with new California designers they hand-picked, both cocktail and casual clothes, and a complete line of shoes and accessories. They would do all the buying but they would need a large staff of salespeople, an expert in alterations, and a full-time cleaning crew.

A few weeks before the grand opening, Mitch took Lainie's hand, dragged her away from a conversation she was having about color chips with the painter, walked her outside to his car, and said, "Get in."

"Where are we going? We have a million things to do."

"Get in."

She did and he pulled his car out of the parking lot and drove west on Ventura Boulevard. "Baby, where are we going?"

Mitch reached over and patted her leg. "A surprise for my girl."

They drove for a few miles, and soon he stopped the car on Ventura Boulevard across from the old store.

"Why are we stopping here?"

"That's why," Mitch said, pointing at the window of the showroom of Valley BMW. The car in the front, the white 735I, had a big red bow on the top and a large sign next to it that said LAINIE, I TOLD YOU SO, I LOVE YOU SO, M.

It took Lainie a minute to understand. "Mitch, you're crazy. We can't afford that car."

"Yes we can. Thanks to all your hard work and the times

you stayed in the store twelve hours straight. You're my partner and I want to give you this to let you know how I appreciate you. Let me have the pleasure of watching you drive that car out of the showroom. Please."

"You are absolutely—"

"The most adorable generous man on Earth?" Mitch asked, getting out of the driver's seat and coming around to open Lainie's door.

"Yes," she said, allowing herself to be led into the showroom to pick up her new car.

Two weeks later as the last of the cleaning crew wheeled the industrial vacuum cleaner out to his truck and hollered good night to them, Mitch turned out all of the lights in the new store and took Lainie in his arms. "This must be the way a Broadway producer feels just before opening night," he said. Lainie put her arms around his neck and plunged her fingers into his thick black hair. Mitch pulled her tight against him and looked into her pretty eyes. "I hope that guy with the big vacuum got this rug really clean," he said, his eyes dancing sexily.

"And why is that?" Lainie knew what his answer would be.

"Because the minute his truck pulls away, you and I are going to be rolling around on it." Even in his exhausted state, after weeks of attending carefully to every detail of the new store, he wanted to have her right there on the floor of the store. The big room was eerily lit by the streetlights and traffic lights from outside. Mitch was hard and kissing her with an urgency.

Lainie was turned on and buoyant with the good news she'd been saving to tell him. So cheered by it that any inhibitions about the windows all around fell away, as her blouse now did with Mitch's help. Then her bra, then he unbuttoned her skirt at the waist, letting it fall, and gently removed her panties, slid them down her thighs to her ankles, and in seconds she was naked in the wide expanse of room surrounded by the stark white faceless mannequins, some of them dressed in elegant evening clothes, the one next to her bare except for a very long string of pearls.

Mitch, still dressed, removed the pearls from the mannequin and placed them around Lainie's neck, and kissed her and teased her, wrapping the cold hard shiny beads around each nipple, then squeezing the circle of beads tightly around the nipple until it hurt, then letting the pearls fall their full length to the middle of Lainie's thighs. And as he teased her mouth with his tongue, he pushed his fingers and the pearls up into her, inside her vagina. The unusual sensation made her hotter as Mitch moved them against the tender walls inside her, then slowly pulled them out, and in again, fingers and pearls pushing into her, and out.

After a while he shoved the length of pearls as deeply inside her as he could, and gradually extracted them. Then he put Lainie's hands behind her back and tied her wrists together gently with the pearls as he fell to his knees. And while he reached up and his fingers manipulated her hard nipples, his tongue danced expertly against her aching swollen clitoris, and he moved his hands around to grab her buttocks and forcibly pull her closer to his face, now working her with his entire mouth, pushing it against her fiercely. And when the ache that filled her made her afraid that her knees would give, and when the heat inside her was so intense she was sure she was about to let go, to cry out, he stopped for an instant, slid out of his own clothes, pulled her down onto the floor. After he undid the pearls from around her wrists he said huskily, "Tomorrow, whoever buys these pays a thousand bucks extra."

"Mitch . . ." Lainie was too hot for conversation, and she slid to the floor with Mitch, who mounted her, and with a practiced move of his hips and thighs, his penis found the warm welcoming place inside her as she lifted her hips up, then dropped them with Mitch moving in her, and then again and again. She was loving him, loving the feeling of the way his moves controlled the heat of their union, and then she felt him harder and hotter as her own orgasm blasted through her just seconds before Mitch moaned, then writhed in the throes of his. And when the dreamlike heat of their passion fell away and they found themselves on the carpet of the new store, wet and trembling and out of breath, they laughed at themselves. Lainie decided it was time to tell him the good news.

"I went to a new doctor," she said, kissing his face gently. "I heard about him from a woman in my modern novel class. He's an endocrinologist who treats diabetics all the time, and he said if I keep tight control and monitor myself and do all the right testing, I can have a normal pregnancy and a normal baby."

Mitch sat up and took her face in his hands, looked long at her with full eyes. "Is that right? Lainie, that's amazing. Why didn't you tell me you were going?"

"I didn't want to unless I knew the answer would be what we wanted to hear. I saw the doctor a few weeks ago, one day when you were meeting with the contractor, but I wanted to wait to tell you when you weren't too preoccupied."

He held her pretty hand and kissed it again and again, then he asked, "So when do we . . ."

"Start?" Lainie smiled and he nodded.

"According to my calendar," she told him, "we just did."

15

BUT THE NIGHT OF SEX AND PEARLS didn't work. "It takes a long time and a lot of prayer for it to happen," Lainie told Mitch.

"Maybe I should have used rosary beads," he teased her. The new store opened to enthusiastic business, more than they'd imagined, and there was no time to take a sexy stress-free vacation, so the following month when Lainie was ovulating they borrowed a friend's boat in the marina, took a champagne picnic with them, and in the beautiful master cabin the boat rocked along with the rhythm of their ardent lovemaking. But two weeks later they discovered that hadn't worked either. Nor did the night at the Bel-Air Hotel, or the cottage they took for a night at the San Ysidro ranch in Santa Barbara.

For the next year and a half they tried all the fertility tricks Lainie heard about from friends and salesgirls in the store; and of course Mitch's sisters threw their two cents in. Lainie was doing all of it, drinking an herb tea from the health-food store called Female Blend, and standing on her head after they had sex to give the sperm an easier journey.

Most of her trips in the new BMW were to the doctor's office. She agreed to do everything he suggested, like having a test where he scraped the inside of her uterus to determine whether or not she'd been ovulating, and rushing to the doctor's office immediately post-intercourse so that he could check the motility of the sperm, while she felt gooey, uncomfortable, and embarrassed. The sperm were fine, the doctor reported.

She had five unsuccessful intrauterine inseminations, in case the vaginal mucus had been interfering with the chemical balance of the sperm. But no luck. She also tried everything she read about in various magazine articles, like having acupuncture on her lower abdomen to "open blocked chakras that might be preventing nature's positive flow."

One day at Panache Lainie was talking to one of the salesgirls from the shoe department, whose name was Karen, only she now spelled it Carin, since her astrologer told her that if she changed the spelling of her name it would change her life. Carin knew of a psychic who had helped two of her friends get pregnant. Lainie laughed.

"This I have to hear," she said. Lainie had listened to Carin's stories in the past about her various brushes with numerologists, tarot-card readers, channelers, and crystal healers. "Are we in Southern California or what?" she said laughing when Carin wrote the number of the psychic for her on the back of a Panache receipt.

The psychic's name was Katya, and she lived in a little white stucco house in the hills above the Sunset Strip. The tiny rooms that Lainie passed as she followed the babushka'd Katya were all painted in dark colors and reeked of the incense burning in holders Lainie recognized as the kind they used to sell at Pier One in the sixties. This is a joke, she thought, following Katya in to the farthest room in the house, and I hate that I'm so desperate. But she sat on a sofa across from the one where Katya sat. The thick odor of the incense was beginning to nauseate her.

"You have cash?" Katya asked her.

"Yes."

"Put it before me."

"How much?" God, I hope I have enough, she thought. Mitch would laugh really hard when she told him this part and then ask her, "You mean she wouldn't take American Express?"

"Fifty dollars."

She opened her wallet, and as she leaned over to place it on the table Katya spoke.

"You cannot have a baby."

The sound of those words unsettled her. When she called to make the appointment she hadn't mentioned a word about why she was coming in. Carin. Carin must have told her friend about Lainie's problem, and the friend told Katya so she could look magical when Lainie got there.

"That's right," Lainie said.

"There are many children in your family, some sisters have children, but none for you yet."

Lainie nodded. Clearly Carin had passed everything on. This is dumb. I'm paying fifty dollars for her to tell me what one of my employee's friends told her.

Katya had her eyes closed now. "You were afraid for so long because of your disease; now it may be too late. But we can try."

Lainie was surprised. She had kept the subject of her diabetes quiet at the store and didn't think any of the girls knew about it. But maybe Carin knew, and told her friend who told the psychic.

"How do you know about my disease?"

Katya opened her eyes now and looked long at Lainie. "I'm a psychic, dear girl," she told her. This was impossible. There was no such thing.

"Do as I tell you and you will be pregnant."

Lainie listened.

"Just before you and your husband are together again to pro-create, put a Bible under your bed. Next to it, in a box, put a dead fish."

"A fish?" It didn't matter how this crazy person knew about

her diabetes. This was so silly she couldn't keep a straight face anymore. "What kind of a fish?"

"Any kind."

"And then?"

"And then you will conceive."

Lainie laughed out loud, all the way to her gynecologist's office. There was one more test he wanted to perform before he put her on Clomid next month, a fertility drug he said was guaranteed to work, and maybe even bring the blessing of a multiple birth. She didn't mention the Bible and the fish to him.

After he examined her, he looked worried.

"Mrs. De Nardo," he said, "let's hold off on the Clomid. I may want to put you in the hospital for a few days to do some exploratory surgery. There's not a horrible rush. I mean, we can wait until next month after you ovulate and see if you conceive this time, but if we don't start seeing results soon, I'd like to get a closer look."

Lainie never told Mitch anything about that conversation. A week later, on the day she was supposed to be ovulating, she went to a Christian bookstore and bought a Bible. Then she went to Phil's Fish and Poultry and bought a small salmon, which she brought home and put in the Stuart Weitzman box that had held her silver evening shoes, giggling to herself. "I can't believe I'm doing this."

That night when Mitch moved close to her, she said to herself, Somehow that woman knew about my diabetes, so maybe she knows about babies. Come on, fish! Do your stuff.

Even sex to make babies, which was supposed to be too calculated to be sexy, was steamy with Mitch. He spent hours nuzzling, nibbling, and licking at all the spots on her body he knew so well, and that night when they rose to fevered orgasm together, he said, "Come on, baby. Come on, my baby," before he collapsed in a final sigh on top of her and whispered, "You're my whole life, Laine," and fell into a deep sleep.

The next morning after Mitch left for work, Lainie, who would have forgotten if she hadn't dropped an earring that rolled to the floor and just under the bed, removed the Bible and put it in a drawer and took the fish out of the shoe box and put it down the garbage disposal.

She didn't have to be in the store until noon, so she ran a tub, and slid in. She always put the morning newspaper next to the tub on the floor, then leaned over the side to turn the pages. But now, before she started to read, she knew something was wrong. A searing cramp squeezed through her lower abdomen, and then another pain, and when she looked at the water it was bright red. She was hemorrhaging. All alone in the house, she was losing big gobs of blood. Slowly she lifted herself out of the tub, and as her own blood, diluted with bathwater, dripped down her legs, she managed to get herself into the bedroom to call Mitch. He was there in just the time it took for her to dry off, wrap herself in a robe, and prop up her feet.

"You're okay, baby, you're okay," he repeated to her over and over as he gently carried her to the car, then rushed her to the hospital.

Lainie's mother, Margaret Dunn, left work to come to the hospital to be near her daughter for the surgery. She was a bony, gray-haired woman who didn't talk much, and didn't expect anyone to do anything for her. Mitch included her in all the conversations with the doctors, took her to a silent lunch in the hospital cafeteria while they waited for Lainie to come out of surgery, and took turns with her tiptoeing into the recovery room to see if Lainie was awake yet. She had three ominous-looking intravenous tubes attached to her.

When she finally opened her eyes, it was Mitch's face she saw looking down at her, and she already knew by the expression he was wearing, the one that she teased him about by calling it "tough dago," what had happened.

"Mitchie," she asked, "I can't have a baby, can I?"

Mitch didn't speak, only shook his head sadly.

After they brought Lainie home, Margaret Dunn took two weeks from her job at the law office in Beverly Hills to sit by her daughter's bed every day. She walked Lainie to the bathroom, answered the telephone, straightened up the house, and served home-cooked meals on a tray. Friends from Panache came to visit with cards and gifts and cookies, and Sharon, a girl Lainie had befriended in an English class at Northridge, came with *Gift from the Sea* by Anne Morrow Lindbergh. All three sisters-in-law came at one time, filling the bedroom of Lainie and Mitch's condo with the overwhelming combination of their assorted perfumes, Joy, Tea Roses, and Opium.

The friends were understanding and kind. They offered sympathy for the loss of hope of ever having a baby. The sisters looked funereal, which was obviously the way they felt. Even the flowers they brought, white lilies, looked like the kind people brought when someone died. And they sat on the bed and spoke in solemn whispers.

When her strength came back, Lainie began a regimen of chemotherapy twice a week. Mitch would drive her to the hospital and wait, drive her home and sit outside the bathroom door while she was sick, then help her gently into bed where she would nap, while he went back to work at Panache. Her hair was falling out in large chunks, her skin was sallow, and she had no appetite at all. She still went to the store as often as she could. She had enough energy to do some work, but she felt sensitive about her appearance when she saw the pitying expressions on people's faces when they looked at her.

One day she stopped at Sherman Oaks Park, sat in her car in the parking lot near the playground, and watched the toddlers in the sandbox and the bigger children on the play equipment and wished she were dead. When the months of chemotherapy ended, the doctors scheduled a surgery during which they planned to take a tissue sample from each organ to determine if the cancer was gone.

"Mitch," Lainie said the night before the second surgery. She was naked against his naked back. "If they find any more cancer, I'm not going to go for chemo again. I'm going to elect to die."

The surgery found nothing. Mitch sent her a giant basket of flowers. He also sent a dozen helium balloons which floated to the ceiling in her hospital room, and he held her too tight, and she laughed when he climbed into the hospital bed next to her and said, "God couldn't take you away from me so soon. I'm too nice a guy."

The business was running like a top and Lainie's strength was returning, her hair was growing back, and her everyday life was normal again. Slowly and gently Mitch brought their sex life back to normal too. Loving her, it seemed, with a greater tenderness than ever.

On Mitch's thirty-fifth birthday, Lainie threw a party for him right in the store, with valet parking, a dance floor, a disc jockey, and a caterer. She invited Mitch's sisters and their husbands, all the employees of Panache and their spouses, a whole group of her friends from school, and the guys Mitch grew up with in the Valley. There was Dave Andrews, who owned a mattress company, and Frankie De Lio, who owned a chain of liquor stores, and Larry Weber, who was a successful lawyer.

When the disc jockey played Kenny Rogers singing "Lady," Mitch took Lainie onto the dance floor as if they were a couple of teenagers at a school dance, and some of the girls from the store let out a cheer when he pulled her close to him and they danced.

"You have come into my life and made me whole . . . ," Kenny Rogers sang.

"Larry Weber told me he has a client whose sixteen-year-old-daughter is very pregnant," she thought she heard him say into her hair, and she wondered why he was telling her that. "I mean as in so pregnant she's giving birth any minute."

Lainie looked into his face now to try to see where this was leading. "So?" she asked.

"So she's a kid and her parents didn't want her to have an abortion, and for a while the girl's mother was going to keep the baby and raise it as if it was hers, only now they decided that wouldn't be good for the girl, so they need to find a home for it fast."

"Look at that cute couple," Carin said as she and her boy-friend danced past Lainie and Mitch. For a few minutes Lainie didn't know what to say as they moved to the music, pressed tightly together, then she stopped dancing and stood in the middle of the dimly lit room and looked at him.

"You mean just like that. In a couple of days? Somebody drops off a baby?"

"I know. It sounds nuts, doesn't it? But maybe it's fate. Larry being here and asking me casually why we don't have kids, and me telling him all the stuff we've been through . . ."

Lainie looked away. A peal of laughter erupted from Mitch's sisters who were standing in a cluster with their husbands.

"I mean, maybe we're the ones who are destined to take the baby from this poor little girl."

Lainie had always thought Mitch was against adoption be-cause an adopted baby wouldn't have the De Nardo genes. But here he was asking to take in some stranger's baby within hours. He was getting desperate.

"What do you think?"

"I don't know. I mean, it's so fast. We don't even have any-thing for it."

"What does it need? It could sleep in our bed. I can go to any drugstore and get diapers and formula now if I have to." He looked and sounded like a kid begging for a puppy. Next he would probably swear he'd be responsible for feeding it and changing it.

"I'll help with it. Hell, we can afford to get a full-time nurse."

"I'm so lost in your love . . . ," Kenny Rogers sang.

The next few days were about visits to the lawyer and signing papers in Larry Weber's Valley office, then running to the Juve-nile shop to look at baby furniture. They bought a changing table, a crib, and a musical swing.

"Can't you just order them," Margaret Dunn asked, "and not have them delivered until after the baby is born?"

Mitch laughed at his mother-in-law's superstitions, and told the Juvenile shop to deliver everything that night. It would give him time to run home and get the third bedroom cleaned up and ready for the arrival of the baby.

The next morning Larry Weber called just as they unlocked the front door to open the store for the day to tell them that the girl was in labor.

"We're ready for her," Mitch said, smiling.

"It's a boy," Larry Weber said just before they went home for the day, and Mitch grabbed Lainie and twirled her around. "We're talking Joey De Nardo. We're going to have a boy." That night Lainie brought a picnic dinner into the baby's room, spread out a blanket, and they ate sitting on the floor, talking about how it would feel to have a little one in that very room any day now. They drank a lot of Santa Margharetta Pino Grigio with dinner, and when the phone rang at eleven o'clock they were in bed, both a little drunk, making love.

"We should have done it in the crib," Mitch said, "just to bless it," as the phone rang again.

Lainie turned over on her stomach and slithered to the phone to pick it up. It was Larry Weber.

"Hi, Larry," she said, feeling happy and playful and glad she'd gone along with this plan. In a few days they were going to go and pick up their baby, Joey De Nardo, and she would hold him and kiss him and raise him as if he were from her own body.

"The baby has something wrong with it," Larry Weber told her. "A heart defect. They don't think he's going to make it." Lainie closed her eyes. Mitch was nuzzling her back and moving his hands under her to her breasts. A baby. Forty-eight hours ago she was okay about never having one, then suddenly she was about to have one, and now she felt as if she'd been kicked in the teeth.

For some dumb reason the crib and changing table were all she could think about. Why did we ever get the crib and the changing table? That's why something bad happened and now we'll have to send back the crib and the changing table. She felt her whole body racked with a terrible wrenching misery. Stop, she thought. You can't fall apart over this. This was a baby you've never even seen. But she couldn't speak, so she handed the phone to Mitch.

"Hello?" he said into it. "Yeah? Yeah? Ahhh, that's too bad, Larry. Is the little girl okay? Uh-huh. Well at least she's okay. Yeah. Thanks." Mitch put the phone down and took Lainie in his arms. Naked against his nakedness, she could feel his chest heaving as he tried to hold in the sadness.

For months after that, Lainie's dreams were filled with babies. Babies that talked like grown-ups, faceless babies; one dream that recurred was about the sound of a crying baby. In the dream she would walk through some unidentifiable empty house, trying to find the baby, whose cries became more urgent as Lainie became more frantic. Maybe, she thought, I should go to a psychiatrist.

But how would she find the right psychiatric help? It was something she could never discuss with her mother, who didn't believe in talking about her feelings with people she knew, let alone some stranger. Yet she had to do something about these feelings of anguish and loss and fear. A fear that she would lose Mitch, a fear that her barrenness was making her ugly to Mitch. And that any day now he would leave her for somebody else, and the somebody else would become pregnant within weeks.

She would think about those things and work herself up into an anxious state, and then anything Mitch said felt like a dismissal to her. If he hung up the phone too quickly with her when she called him at the store, or if he was too critical of the way she handled a customer, she felt afraid that any minute he would turn to her and say, "That's it. I'm leaving you."

One night, after they were both warm with the satisfaction of their lovemaking, Mitch moved himself up on one elbow and looked at his wife's face.

"Lainie," he said, "I've got something serious I want to talk about. Do you think you can handle it?"

Lainie felt a flutter of fear. This was it, the moment she'd been dreading. What else, after all they'd been through, could he mean by something serious? He was going to tell her he was leaving her.

"Sure I can," she said, her brow furrowed.

"Laine, all these years when we thought we'd never have kids, I was okay about it. But when the adoption question came up, the reason I grabbed it was because I figured maybe it was God's way of telling us we needed a kid, and then when the poor little baby died, I didn't know what to think. Now something's in my head, and I want you to know that if what I'm going to tell you isn't okay with you, then I'll drop it. Forever. I swear. Because you're everything to me, you know that? Right?" Lainie touched his arm lightly and nodded, relieved at hearing all the affirmations of his love, and ashamed of herself for doubting him because of her own feelings of inadequacy.

"You have done so much for me, Laine. When I met you I was just some hotshot with a new business, floundering around with no personal life at all, but you, with your sweetness and the full-out way you love me so completely, gave my life meaning, and I'll never stop being grateful to you for that.

"A big reason our store is such a success is because of your devotion to it. I probably would have thrown the whole thing in the garbage fifty times, like after the flood when we didn't have insurance and all the clothes were ruined. You found that little cleaner downtown who specialized in suede, and stood over him till he made those jackets look like new, and then we sold them all. We made it because no matter what happened, you were always there with your patience saying, We'll work it out. I think you're a miracle. And that's why now I want it to be my turn. Now, *I* want to do something that I can do for us. I want to call a lawyer and have him help us hire a woman to have a baby for us."

Lainie's throat tightened as if someone were choking her.

"It will mean that instead of adopting a baby that was the product of two strangers, like we almost did, at least this way we'll know that half of this baby is a De Nardo. Part of us. I'm not asking this on a whim, Laine. Since your surgery I've been trying to figure out what I could do, and this seemed to me to be something that I can offer to us. Bring to the partnership. Because God knows, we've been good enough together all these years for you to believe what I believe. I mean that you and I are one. Remember we saw that old woman on television who said that marriage is two horses pulling in one yoke? Well, let this part, the part about making a biological child for us, be my part of the yoke."

"Mitch," she said, hoping she could get through this without crying, "it's a bad idea. You know what's happened historically in cases like this. This isn't as if we're putting part of me and part of you into some woman to carry for us. Whoever we hire is going to be having a baby that's yours and hers. And when the time comes for her to part with it, she's going to be giving up her own child. What if she changes her mind? Are you going to let her keep that baby? And never see it? Or share custody? Or are you just going to say, 'Oh well,' knowing that out there somewhere is your son or your daughter and you gave it up because the surrogate decided she couldn't handle it?"

She could tell by the look of surprise on Mitch's face this was not the response he'd anticipated. She was surprised herself at the power of her outburst. "Believe me, Mitch, I'm desperate to have a baby, but I won't do it that way."

"Lainie, don't decide now. This is a knee-jerk reaction and you ought to take time to think about it. What happened in the cases you're talking about was because those women weren't properly tested or adequately screened. We could sidestep that by making sure she took a battery of every kind of test, we could meet the kids she already has and see how healthy *they* are. Hell, we can afford to have ten different psychiatrists check her out. In fact, my sister Betsy knows about a place—"

"Betsy! I knew this had something to do with one of your meddling sisters. What did she do? See it on 'Oprah'? No, this sounds more like 'Geraldo.' 'Women Whose Husbands Impregnate Strangers.'" Lainie heard herself shout at her husband for the first time in their years together. Heard her voice shrieking and sounding like some shrew. Like Elizabeth Taylor in *Who's Afraid of Virginia Woolf?* But she wasn't sorry. She was pulsing with anger. "Betsy and those other two witches can mind their own business and get their noses out of my life."

"You're being a selfish little brat."

"*I'm* being selfish? If you want a baby so much and you're *not* being selfish, why can't we try to adopt again? We'll adopt a son and *he'll* carry on the precious De Nardo name. What in the hell do you think is so great about your genes that the world can't live without them?"

"Lainie, don't provoke me, goddammit. I'm getting really angry at your attitude about this. This idea makes sense for us." She heard the hot anger rising in his voice, and she knew her temper was no match for his, but this was too much. She was not going to back down and give in to this insane request. "I want to have my genetic child," Mitch said, fuming. "And it *can* be done. People are still doing it all the time, and without problems. I've made calls to find out. I've talked to the best lawyers and the best psychologists, and they all assured me we can cover every possible loophole."

Lainie was having a hard time breathing. "Mitch, don't you ever accuse me of being selfish again. I had my insides taken out because they were riddled with cancer. There isn't a day that I don't drive by the park or see a woman pushing a stroller that I don't have to look away with tormented envy that I can't give you a baby!" Those last words choked her and she had to turn away. "If it sounds petty or selfish or small, then that's what I am! But I am telling you I could never look at another woman who had your baby inside her body."

"But it would be *our* baby," he said. "Yours and mine. Don't you want that?"

"More than anything," she said. "But I can't do it the way you're describing. I'm sorry."

"Change your mind."

"No."

"Grow up, Laine. If we adopted a baby it wouldn't come from your body. This way at least we know about *one* of its genetic parents. You say *I'm* narcissistic? Get your own ego out of it."

"The subject is closed."

"No it's not."

"With me it is."

They didn't speak for days. They slept in the same bed, but with their backs to each other. They worked at the store where they were cordial to the employees and the customers but when the two of them were alone in a room they said nothing to each other. Lainie's fears of abandonment were out of control. Lodged in her brain and in her heart, so that no matter how much makeup she put on, or how pretty an outfit, the woman she saw in the mirror looked like an ugly jealous hag.

She alternately thought about packing her bags, going away somewhere, anywhere, and never coming back, or begging Mitch's forgiveness and doing whatever he asked. The estrangement was unbearable. One night when everyone had gone and they were alone in the store about to lock up, she touched his arm.

"Mitchie."

"Yeah?" He didn't look at her.

"I'm not saying yes. But I'm willing to talk about it some more."

He moved close to her and held her silently. The scent of him so close after even a few days apart made her want to cry with relief. From the day they met, there had always been something irresistible to her about the way Mitch smelled. She loved to snuggle against him and bury her face in his warm neck, tasting and smelling him. This was the best man God ever made. A blessing in this world of too many divorces, and too much cheating, and all those stories about wife-beating she read about in magazines. This was a man who treated her like a queen, romanced her as if they were still courting, never failed to be there for her in ways that amazed their friends.

At his thirty-fifth birthday party so many people had stood to give toasts to Mitch's loyalty, big heart, and generosity that at one point Mitch had stood and said, "Wait a second, this is so good, I think I'd better check to make sure I haven't died."

Lainie remembered all that as she held her husband in her arms. How could she refuse him anything?

16

"YOUR HUSBAND was right, Mrs. De Nardo." The psychologist at the surrogacy center was an attractive gray-haired man in his late forties. Lainie and Mitch sat with him, and with Chuck Meyer, the surrogacy attorney. Mitch had dressed that morning in his best suit as if, Lainie thought with a stab, he were thinking the better he looked, the better his chance was of getting some surrogate to want to have his baby. "The press loves to blow things out of proportion. The cases that are worrying you are the sensationalized ones, and they're very rare. The truth is that ninety-nine percent of the surrogates don't change their minds. That's a much better statistic than you'd ever have with open adoption where the birth mother is usually a young unstable girl who suddenly finds herself pregnant and is frequently ambivalent about having the baby in the first place.

"The women with whom we work are grown-ups. They're educated, middle-class women who want to do this for their own reasons. And the reasons aren't financial. In fact, the most recent research proves that the women who are surrogates aren't doing this for the money. As far as the psychological issues are concerned, aside from the tests, which are numerous and demanding, we're here to ask them the tough questions. And believe me we do.

"I don't hesitate to ask if they're willing to give up sexual relations with their husbands from the time they sign the contract. Or what they're going to tell their own parents who will feel that this baby is their grandchild. We give them months to think it over. And during that time we talk to the other people in their families who are going to go through the experience with them. We see their spouses, their children, to find out if there will be anyone who might make it difficult for them, or create a problem.

"We reject eighty-five percent of the women who apply. We tell them we simply cannot have them in our program if there's the least indication that a problem might surface. And still we never lack for applicants. I understand your reluctance, and I'll be glad to ask some of the very happy families who have worked with us to contact you and share their experience. Or to have you meet the surrogates, get to know them, and feel free to come to me at any time and say, 'This isn't for us.'"

Lainie could feel Mitch looking at her. You don't have to decide now, but the sooner you do, the sooner we can have a baby was what his look was saying.

They chose the third surrogate they met. Her name was Jackie. She was blond and blue-eyed, and kind of chunky in a cute round way. Lainie liked her better than the others because she was warm and easy to talk to. When Lainie and Mitch walked in on the day of their meeting, Jackie stood and hugged her. It was startling, but a very sweet gesture, and an embarrassed Lainie was overwhelmed by the cloud of Jackie's perfume, which she recognized as Shalimar.

The minute they sat down Jackie pulled out pictures to show both Lainie and Mitch of her teenage son from a youthful failed marriage. The son was a tall, handsome, confident-looking young man.

"I'm on Weight Watchers," Jackie assured them when the meeting was winding down. "And I always get a little blubbery before my period, which is now. So I hate to sound like I'm doing a commercial for myself, but if you pick me, we can start right off in two weeks and two days. I run as regular as a clock."

There was nothing threatening about her. The first candidate had been a pretty, redheaded former actress, who said she wanted "to live this and then put it into my work." The second candidate, busty and dark-haired, seemed inappropriately taken with Mitch. Jackie was Irish, funny, looked kind of like a heavy-set version of Lainie, and she said everything she was thinking. Or as Mitch said, "She has no filter between the brain and the mouth."

Their plan was that Lainie would meet Jackie at each doctor's appointment. She would bring the sperm she'd lovingly coaxed from Mitch less than an hour before. On the morning of the first insemination, at home Lainie realized she'd forgotten to get a specimen jar from the doctor, so in the dishwasher she steril-ized a small jar that had once held Cara Mia marinated artichoke hearts.

Mitch laughed so much when she handed him the funny little jar, he was afraid he wouldn't be able to perform. When he finally ejaculated, he grinned, and then in his off-key imitation of Mario Lanza, sang, "Cara mia, mine. Say those words divine. I'll be your love till the end of time." Lainie was still chuckling about it in the car all the way to the doctor's office.

"Tell me all about Mitch," Jackie asked her while they were waiting for her to be called in by the nurse. Lainie didn't know where to begin, what to tell her.

"Well, he's from an Italian family, his mother died young and he was raised by his sisters—"

"And now he's real close to them. Right? Italian men and their families. They get all hooked in. Italians are like the Irish, you know. They cry at commercials for the telephone company. Right? A few bars of that song about touching someone and they're bawling like idiots. Right? *I'm* like that too. A total sob sister."

The door from the doctor's office opened.

"O'Malley?" the nurse asked.

"Me," Jackie said, standing, then turned to Lainie.

"Hold a fertile thought," Jackie said and followed the nurse.

The doctor's office was in Century City on the eighth floor of the medical building. Lainie looked down from the waiting room window at the bright blue swimming pool across the street at the Century Tower apartments, where a lone swimmer swam laps. Dear God, I'm waiting here for a woman I met two weeks ago to be impregnated with my husband's baby. A baby I'll take from her and raise as if it were his baby with me.

Jackie had passed every test, had health statistics that were enviable to Lainie with her own history of diabetes. Jackie's IQ was high and her scores on the psychological testing had been as high as possible. There was, of course, no way to know what the hormones of pregnancy could do to anyone's mental state, or how she'd react to the sight of the biological baby she'd promised to give away.

"You have to be prepared, Mitch," the psychologist had said, "in the worst-case scenario to give up the baby. Do you think you can do that?" Lainie had looked over at Mitch. It was during one of the many sessions they'd spent with this man who probed and pushed at difficult issues in a way Lainie was glad to know he used with the surrogates, but uncomfortable with when they were used on her and Mitch.

"First you tell me she's the picture of mental health, then you tell me she could change her mind," Mitch said defensively.

"We all need to be clear that anything can happen, and you have to be prepared for what you plan to do in every eventuality," the psychologist said, turning to Lainie, who noticed that Mitch had never answered the question he'd been asked. "And will you be able to deal with seeing another woman heavy with your husband's child? I don't want to scare you away, and you don't have to answer me right now. But answer that for yourself."

After nearly an hour, Jackie emerged from the gynecologist's office. "He made me lie there with my feet up for a long time to give everything a chance to do its work. And this will kill you: after he inseminated me, I asked him, 'Was it good for *you?*' It cracked him up." Then she squeezed Lainie's arm. "Say a prayer, girl," she said.

Later at a table outside of Michel Richard on Robertson Boulevard, Jackie pulled out an envelope full of some new pictures of her son.

"Isn't he a hunk?" she asked proudly. "Sometimes when we're together, people think he's my boyfriend."

"He's darling," Lainie said.

"*This* baby will be too," Jackie told her, taking a big swig of her iced tea and putting the glass down. With the cold wet hand that had just held the glass, she took Lainie's hand across the table.

"Don't get nuts about this. It's going to be great for all of us. Meanwhile you and I get to spend some time getting acquainted, which isn't so terrible. *Capiche?* That means—"

"I know what it means." Lainie smiled.

"My second husband was Italian," Jackie said.

Lainie didn't remember any mention of a second husband in the lawyer's office. Jackie saw the surprise on her face.

"It was a short one. Lasted less than a year. I don't even use his name. My Tommy was real little then, and this guy had two teenage sons who used to knock my kid around. I didn't like it. We fought about it, and I just figured I'd be better off saying adios. You know?"

Lainie nodded, but now she wondered what else Jackie hadn't told them about herself.

"So you and Mitch have a great marriage, huh?"

Lainie smiled. "We love each other and are very happy."

"Boy," Jackie told her, gesturing to a waiter for coffee, "I envy that. And I'm going to have it someday. Down the road. I tell you, I'm going to have it."

Two weeks later, Jackie got her period.

"Hey, listen, we have all the time in the world," Mitch said when Lainie called him at the shop with the news just after

Jackie called her. "These things take months, sometimes they even take years, but let's keep hanging in there, sweetheart. We'll have a baby in our arms before you know it. I love you, Mrs. D.," he added, "and when I get home, I'll show you just how much."

"Me too," Lainie answered, and she *did* love him. More than ever.

It was the morning of the ninth insemination when Margaret Dunn's boss called to tell Lainie that her mother had fallen in the ladies' room at work for no apparent reason, and had been taken to Century City Hospital.

"I'm on my way," Lainie said, then remembered she had to be at the doctor's office in a few hours with Jackie or risk missing an entire month until the next ovulation. When she went downstairs to tell Mitch about her mother, he was dressed for work, reading the morning paper.

"You know what?" Mitch said. "You go take care of your mother. Me and the Cara Mia jar can handle it, if you get my meaning. We're very intimate. I can just drive into town myself to the doctor's office and drop off the jar. What time does the womb usually get there?"

"Mitchie!" Lainie gave him a little slap on the arm. "She gets there at noon." She hated it when he made jokes about Jackie. The events of the last many months had created a bond between the two women. Lainie always looked forward to their time together. Not just because each doctor's visit could be the one when Jackie might finally conceive, but because their post-insemination lunches had become filled with the intimate chatter of two close girlfriends. The conception would bring an end to those meetings, and the baby's birth an end to the relationship.

It had been agreed from the first that Jackie would never know the De Nardos' last name. And the phone they had installed at their house for her calls would be removed once the baby was in their care. That was the way Mitch told the lawyer it had to be. "I don't want her changing her mind one day and knocking on my door."

"With the success of the store, you realize that you and Lainie have a pretty high profile," the lawyer warned him.

That made Mitch nervous. "Don't even let her glance at the credit card receipt," he told Lainie. "Always pay for everything with cash." It was odd and uncomfortable for her, this secrecy coupled with intimacy, but soon, God willing, they'd have the desired result.

"Call me from the hospital if you need me, and I'll get over there right after I drop off the baby juice," Mitch said with a last kiss. Lainie was off to see her poor mother, who had been complaining about headaches for weeks. Lainie hoped the fall was unrelated and didn't mean she had some kind of neurological problem. She hadn't told her mother a word about the surrogate. Maybe once Margaret got through whatever this problem was, Lainie would explain it all to her, and she would be happy to learn that soon she would be a grandmother.

Mitch pulled the car into the parking lot of the medical building but kept the engine running so he could hear the end of the news. After he turned the car off, he felt in his shirt pocket for the little slip of paper containing the doctor's suite number, and when he found it he took the paper bag and got out of the car.

"Shit," a woman's voice echoed through the cavernous parking lot. "I'm leaking all over the place, goddammit."

Mitch looked over at where the woman stood next to an old beat-up convertible with the hood open and a red-vested parking-lot attendant, who stared dumbly at the steaming engine. He was about to turn and head for the elevator when he realized the woman was Jackie. When he walked back to where she was standing and Jackie caught sight of him, she shouted a greeting.

"Hey, Mitch, long time no see! I got a busted hose, which is a complaint I sincerely hope *you* don't have, honey!" she said, laughing, then stopped herself. "Listen, no offense. I'm a little punchy here. How's your mother-in-law? Lainie called me this morning to say she couldn't be here today, and that you were making the drop-off. I hope everything there's all right."

"They're going to run tests on her all afternoon so Lainie's going to stay at the hospital and hold her hand. Thanks for asking." The steam rose in a cloud out of the open-hooded car. "You going to be okay here?"

"Yeah, sure," Jackie said. "I called the auto club. They're on their way. So if you go on up and give that to the doc," she said, nodding toward the paper bag, "I'll be up in a few minutes to collect it."

She smiled. Mitch smiled too.

"I hope it happens," she said.

"Me too. It means a lot to me."

"To me also," she said, putting a hand on his arm.

Lainie had reported to Mitch after each of the previous inseminations how much she liked this pudgy, soft-faced woman, and what an essentially good person she was. When Mitch looked at Jackie now, he believed it. After evaluating her psychological makeup, the lawyer had pointed out to them repeatedly how high she rated when it came to altruism.

This wasn't a moment Mitch had ever expected to have with the surrogate. Except for the initial meeting, which now seemed very far in the past, they'd never spoken. Lainie was in charge of every step of this: making the final decision about which woman they chose, scheduling the doctor's appointments, going along to ensure that everything went well. But now, as he stood in the cavernous underground parking lot of the medical building, looking into Jackie's eyes, knowing who she was about to be to him for the rest of their lives if everything went as planned, Mitch felt overwhelmed. His sisters had encouraged him to do this, to get himself a blood child of his own. But surely they must feel the way he did that there was something about it that interfered with the sanctity of marriage.

"Why are you doing this?" he heard himself asking, then felt surprised that he'd actually asked her that.

"Because it gives some meaning to my life," she answered.

"Because I believe it's one of the few things I have to offer. No one's manipulating me, Mitch. I want to have a baby for a couple very much, and if I don't do it for you, I'll do it for someone else. You may not respect me, because you probably have some set idea about how women are supposed to conduct themselves and this isn't it. But make no mistake, you aren't using some lower-class cow's body against her will or because she needs the ten-grand fee. Though the ten grand won't hurt me."

"I never thought—"

"Let me finish. I'm sure you didn't, but just in case it crosses your mind, I want you to know I'm every bit as excited about this as you are."

"I'm glad to hear that," Mitch said, realizing suddenly that she was still holding on to his arm.

"Of course, I'd be lying to you if I said that *this* part was any fun. I mean, the doctor's kind of a horse's ass, like most doctors are, and the inseminations are uncomfortable, but what gets me through it is knowing that I'm going to be pregnant, Mitch. Pregnant. Do you have any idea how glorious that is? Of course you couldn't. But I do, because I remember how I felt when I was carrying my Tommy, and the earth-moving importance of it. I was making another human being deep inside my body. Just knowing I was doing that made every minute of my day, even taking a walk or a nap, feel productive and creative and necessary."

Her hand was holding his arm a little too tightly now, and her pretty blue eyes, eyes that were the same color as Lainie's, were welling with tears.

A white auto club truck came tearing around the parking-lot ramp, and the driver pulled up next to Jackie's car. Jackie let go of Mitch's arm, found her auto club card in her purse, and handed it to the young man as he got out of the truck.

"Why don't you go on ahead," she said over her shoulder to Mitch. "You can tell the nurse that as soon as I'm finished down here, I'll be up."

"That's okay," Mitch told her coolly, leaning against a nearby green Jaguar. "I've got a couple of minutes. Why don't I just wait for you?"

Two weeks later the lawyer called the store to tell them Jackie was pregnant. Mitch took the call, and when Lainie overheard him say, "Aaaaalriiight! I'm having a kid!" she rushed back to his office. He put an arm around her, nodding the good news as he continued to talk to the lawyer, who was reminding him of the details of their contract with Jackie. The next big medical bill would be for the amniocentesis, which would be performed between week fifteen and week seventeen of the pregnancy.

Lainie could feel Mitch's body trembling with excitement. When he asked, "Is Jackie feeling all right? Should I call her? Is she having any morning sickness? Does she need anything?" she smiled up at him. But at that moment she felt a sick feeling that was envy combined with anger. It crawled up the back of her neck and seemed to hang there and spread to her shoulders like a clammy shawl.

Mitch's concern for Jackie made perfect logical sense. Then why did it feel painful and wrong? She hated the look of ecstasy on his face when he reported to her what the lawyer had just told him, "Her breasts are already two sizes bigger than usual," and then laughed. Jackie's breasts, she thought. I'm listening to my husband and another man talk about some woman's breasts.

She was queasy. Why had she agreed to this? How was she going to survive nine months of this? She gave Mitch a little tap on the arm and mouthed the words *I'm going home* to him when he looked at her. She was hoping that would get him to hang up the phone and say, "No, no, let's celebrate. Let's go have a champagne dinner together somewhere." But instead he nodded and waved to say good-bye and turned his interest back to the lawyer on the phone.

Lainie walked out to the new BMW and got in, not sure what to do or how to get herself to stop feeling this sick anxiety over news that was supposed to be happy. Instead of going home she drove to Santa Monica, parked her car, and sat on the sand at Will Rogers State Beach, watching the waves come in. When she got home it was nearly six o'clock and a vase of two dozen roses was waiting outside the door of the condominium. She took them in and opened the card, which read *Thank you for being my wonderful wife. I love you, baby. M.*

A nausea, worse than the ones she'd faced during her chemotherapy, stayed with her. She was still feeling that way a week later at a family dinner with Mitch's sisters and their families when Betsy raised her glass and said, "To the baby and the health of the woman who's carrying it." It seemed to Lainie as if everyone's eyes were on her. She wished she could get up and walk out on the smug sisters with three kids each, their cocky husbands punching Mitch on the arm with their macho, you-son-of-a-bitch punches that men give one another as congratulations for sexual prowess.

But worse was the way she felt about her envious self. I'll be okay, she thought. It's only nine months. After that, Jackie will be out of our lives forever. For Mitch to have a baby of his own blood, I can survive that. She had no way of knowing that her pain had just begun.

17

WHEN HARVEY FELDMAN stood to greet Rick Reisman, he could tell by the red face of the secretary who showed the well-known director in that Rick had been flirting with her. Jesus, the man was looking more and more like Orson Welles, Feldman thought.

"So what brings you here?" he asked as Rick sat in the leather chair across from his desk.

"I want to talk about open adoption," Rick said.

"Which aspect of it?"

"The prerequisites."

"Do you mean for the birth mother or the adopting parents?"

"Parents."

"The prerequisites are whatever qualities the birth mother wants for the parents of her baby."

"Meaning?"

"Meaning I've placed babies with single parents, gay couples, a few couples who otherwise would be considered too old to adopt."

"Which is how old?"

"Forties. You want to hear the stories? I've got scrapbooks filled with them."

"I'm nearly fifty."

"So?"

"Is that impossible?"

"I don't follow."

"Well, what's too old?" Rick asked, leaning forward.

The dawn broke on Harvey Feldman's face. "Are you telling me that you're here to talk to me about you, yourself, wanting to adopt a baby?" There was a mixture of amusement and disappointment in his voice. Rick realized that the young lawyer with show-business fantasies had thought he'd come here to talk about stories that could be made into movies.

"I am," Rick said.

"What brought *this* on?"

"My approaching fiftieth birthday. The relative certainty, however heartbreaking, that 'the right woman' who will love me forever isn't out there somewhere waiting for an overweight, overworked, anxiety-ridden movie director to take advantage of her fertile body. I also have a desperate desire to have some kind of family. I lost my parents in an airplane crash in the fifties. Bobo is my only living relative."

"It'll be difficult," Feldman said after a while. "Ever married?" Rick shook his head no. "They'll ask me that . . . the birth mothers. They'll wonder if you're gay."

"I'll bring them affidavits from women I've plundered."

"Do you have a preference about the gender?"

"I'd probably do better with a boy, but . . ." He shrugged, and he had the sudden urge to stand, apologize for what was clearly a momentary lapse of sanity, and run back downstairs to the parking lot and his car. But there was something about the fact that the guy wasn't laughing at him or trying to talk him out of it yet that kept him in the chair.

"Here's the bottom line if you're serious," Feldman told him. "I already told you that there are forty-seven possible choices for every birth mother. The only way you can beat the odds is to convince one of them that you're unequivocally the best person to love and raise the baby she's carrying. Do you think you can do that? Win out over couples who have picket fences and puppies, and in some cases other children? More important, do you think you *are* that? When you adopt a baby, you adopt at least twenty years' worth of responsibility for another human being."

"Well," Rick said, and for the first time he looked around the office. On a bookshelf behind him was a picture of Harvey Feldman and his pretty wife, and on their laps, two little girls.

"My family," he heard Feldman say.

"I see that," Rick responded, but when he looked back at Feldman, he realized the young man was gesturing at all the pictures on every wall. Babies. Gurgling, grinning, posing bare assed, in bathtubs, through crib bars, wearing too-big hats and toothless grins. Sometimes alone, frequently held by beaming adults with a kind of light in their eyes Rick knew his own eyes had never had.

He stood to go. This had truly been a lunatic idea. One of those grasping-for-straws moments that sound great in the wee hours of the morning when you're desperate. Now, with the cold gray light of the smoggy L.A. day staring at him, it was nothing more than a lonely fat man's way of admitting the truth, which was that he'd let his life pass him by. He offered Harvey his hand, but Harvey had turned away and was pulling some files out of a drawer.

"Listen," the lawyer said, "it's a long shot. I doubt if anyone will choose you, but so what? I'll throw you into the mix and see if anyone's interested. Fill out an information form for me and I'll see."

Rick sat down again. Harvey handed him a form.

"Tell me the down side," Rick said as he wrote his vital statistics onto the slots on the form. "The dangers. The part I should worry about. I mean, surely it can't be as easy as one day they pick you and then somebody brings you a little bundle and says, 'He's yours.'"

"Nowhere near as easy as that. The bad news is that the birth mother, who you support for the last few months of her pregnancy, has the right to ask for her baby back until she signs a consent that's been accepted by the department of adoptions, or approved by the L.A. superior court, or the L.A. County department of children's services. It's supposed to take six months, but sometimes it can take closer to a year. So you could possibly support a birth mother, pay all of her hospital bills and doctors' fees, fall in love with a baby, and have that baby snatched away from you and all your money lost. If you want a baby badly enough, you have to be prepared to let this little pregnant girl stomp on your heart."

"How often has that happened?"

"In my practice, once in fifteen years. That's not too bad. The birth mother asked for the baby back after two days. The adopting parents were devastated, but they wanted a baby so much they found another birth mother a few months later, and started again. Now they have a son."

Rick sighed and walked around the room, looking closely at each baby picture.

"So, my chance to be chosen, unlike myself, is very slim. Suppose I try to increase my odds by doing something dazzling, like buying the birth mother a car or a fur coat?"

"That would be trafficking in babies, and that's illegal. Every cent that goes toward supporting the birth mother is accountable to the court. Submitted in a financial statement under penalty of perjury. I've had a couple list an ice-cream cone they bought when they took the birth mother to the beach."

"So my only chance is to be Mr. Nice Guy. So nice that I beat out the picket fences and the dogs."

"But, Rick, don't even bother filling out the card unless you understand that the whole point of these relationships, yours with the girl, is to make her feel okay about her pregnancy in a world that makes her feel like dirt because of it. To let her know that she's okay, and that by giving you the baby she's doing the right thing.

"Let me tell you a little bit more about these girls. Most of them are sent to me by their church groups and their right-to-life groups. Most of the time they haven't been out seducing boys;

more likely they've been raped by some friend of the family or date-raped by some hotshot at the high school, and are too mortified to talk about it. When they come into this office, or send their sometimes barely readable letter, they've not yet spoken the words 'I'm pregnant' to anyone else.

"Some of them haven't been to a doctor yet. They broke open a piggy bank and bought an early pregnancy test that they did at home, locked in a bathroom they share with the rest of the family. Or they've just missed two periods and they're trying to hide morning sickness at the family breakfast table and they're scared to death. I try to create a cocoon for them. A time during which it's okay for them to be pregnant. I mean, hell, they already *are* pregnant. They don't want abortions, so why not make them feel as if all is well, and not only are they going to emerge from all of this just fine, but that some nice couple is going to be able to love this baby that they're bringing into the world.

"Wait until you meet some of these girls, Rick, and I hope you do. You thought I was just some pushy hustler when I told you there were some very moving stories in these girls. Well after you get to meet and know some of them . . . you tell me."

It looked to Rick as if Feldman was holding back tears, and he wondered if this was the lawyer's standard speech. Nevertheless, he looked down at the desk at the form he'd now completely filled out about himself, and he signed it.

When he got back to the office, Andrea looked nervous.

"Nat Ross's office called. They want you up there right away."

The door was open, and he could see there was a group of four or five people waiting for him. Nat Ross, Ian Kleier, who was Ross's second in command, plus a few underlings, and . . . shit, Kate Sullivan and a few of her entourage.

"Ricky!" Nat Ross said with such glee, it was as if he were a kid on a hot day and Rick was the ice-cream man. Rick felt numb the way one does in the face of certain disaster.

"Sit, my friend, and we can get you coffee or a Coke or a glass of wine, maybe even a coffee cake," Ross added and Rick wondered for an instant if the son of a bitch was making fun of his weight. "What's your pleasure?"

"Nothing, thanks," Rick said. His desire to bolt was so strong that sitting was an effort, so his compromise was to perch on the edge of his chair, his two hands holding firmly onto the rim, readying himself to stand and run.

"I'm here to tell you," Nat Ross said, "that Kate is insane about the White House story. She has now called me, how many times, Katie, eight times? Nine times?"

Rick didn't look at her, but out of the corner of his eye he saw Kate Sullivan turn in her chair and answer demurely, "Maybe even more."

"Now to me, the idea of the two of you together would make such a full-out blockbuster picture that it brings tears to my eyes. So I wanted to do this honestly and aboveboard and cut through all the crap, and say that to you both, and tell you if we can be big kids and drop all the personality stuff, we can make a picture that this studio will back a thousand percent. So let me get your input on this. Okay?"

There was what seemed like an endless silence. Rick's mind raced. This was unconscionable, to be put in this position. The point was clear. The picture was now Sullivan's. If he said no, next week it would be Sydney Pollack or Garry Marshall called in to direct a picture Rick had been developing passionately for how long?

"I pass," he said, standing and walking out the door, straight to the stairs, not bothering to wait for the elevator. His head rang as he pounded all the way down, took a deep breath, opened the door to the third floor, and made his way along the deeply carpeted hallway to his office.

"Pack my things," he said to Andrea, who tore the headset off and said, "Huh?"

"I said pack my things. I don't work here anymore." The phone rang.

It was Nat Ross, Andrea came to the door of his inner office to tell him. Rick was putting photographs into a box he'd pulled from the closet.

"I'm out."

"He knows you're here."

"There's no more to say," he told her. "You finish this, please, I'm leaving."

He was in the parking lot about to get into his car when Nat Ross approached him. It was odd to see Ross in the parking lot, since no one ever did. The joke was that if you arrived on the lot at six A.M. and felt the hood of Nat Ross's car, it was already cold. And he was rumored to leave at midnight.

"Ricky, don't be dumb." He was walking toward the car. "I gave you an overall deal here and a lot of money after your last two pictures did no business at all. You're not exactly a hot property. In fact, the reality is, you're a fucking Popsicle. And I'm the guy who got the money for you because I bet my board here that you have at least one more picture left in you, and we might as well be the ones who get it."

Rick started the car. Who would fault him if he ran this cocksucker over now?

"This is a real chance for you to come back. With the biggest star in this town. Don't be dumb," Nat yelled after Rick's car as it squealed out of the parking lot.

"So what do you want? You think it's all a bowl of cherries?" Bobo asked. This morning his teeth had been bothering him. Now while he and Rick sat on the bed playing gin, the yellow dentures smiled at them from a glass on the chest of drawers across the room. "Your father and I struggled plenty. I told you how we fought with that bastard Harry Cohn till we were blue in the *gederim*. You're a spoiled no-goodnik. A few things fall apart, a couple of flops, and you're having a career crisis. What do you want, for Chris'sake?"

"I guess I like my career like I like my pastrami," Rick answered. "Hot and on a roll, and at the moment it isn't either of those. The writer on *Time Flies* dropped dead in a Pizza Hut, the second draft of *Count on Me* came back and it's a serious disappointment, I lost the rights to the novel of *Bloody Wonderful*, and then there's Kate Sullivan. Kate Sullivan is doing *Always a Lady*, and I'm not. It was my project for two years, and they gave it to her, Uncle B., so I walked. Packed up my office and walked."

"Gin," Bobo said, laying his matching suits on the card table.

"Et tu, Brute?" Rick laughed. "Christ, how did you do that so fast? I've got nothing here." Rick fanned his cards out on the table.

"You're a lousy shuffler and you owe me sixty-three cents," Bobo said.

"I took my phone off the hook and I've been all alone for days, trying to decide what to do."

Bobo looked at him, frowning. "What are you worrying? You got the world by the balls. There's a million stories out there. In your life alone there's a million. Make a movie about me and your dad. Two young guys in the early days in Hollywood. Make a movie about what it was like to be a kid on the back lot in those days, from the kid's point of view. You want to tell a good story? Tell the one about your parents dying in that plane crash. The biggest loss this business ever knew."

Bobo shuffled the cards as he spoke and Rick grinned as he watched the old cardshark whip them back and forth between his hands, fanning them, cascading them, making them rise and fall at one point as if they were defying gravity.

"No," Rick said. "I won't tell that one."

Bobo shrugged and dealt the cards with a spin.

"Ingeleh, listen to me. Go make a deal with another studio. Don't sit around at the old folks' home with all the *alter kockers* who are waiting to die. *I* feel too young to be here. So what in the hell do *you* get out of a place like this?" Rick hadn't even picked up his cards. Bobo's were already sorted.

"I'm learning about what it's like to be retired," Rick said, "because that may be what I do next."

After he'd lost seven dollars and seventeen cents to his uncle, Rick said good-bye to the old man and hugged him. When he did, he could smell the English Leather cologne Bobo still splashed on every morning.

"Don't do anything stupid. You're one in a million, kid. Those *shmeck-drecks* who took away your project should all kiss your ass and thank you for the privilege."

"I'll tell them," Rick said.

"Meanwhile, just so their target ain't so big, you should take off a couple of pounds," the old man added, giving Rick a kind of sharp rap on the arm that he remembered his father giving him when he was a little boy that meant, Do what I'm telling you or you'll regret it. Rick said, "Yeah, yeah, yeah," and headed for the exit.

He'd been doing nothing for nearly three weeks. Stuffing his face with junk food, watching game shows and soap operas on TV, inviting an occasional lady to come over to cook dinner and "roll around on top of me naked," which was how he'd once described a sexual evening to Charlie. "They call me, I say bring dinner. They feed me, we do it, I fall asleep. With any luck, they're gone before breakfast." It was a schedule he kept in between the six-month-long "steady girls."

That morning at the beginning of the fourth week, as he lay in bed at ten o'clock in the morning counting the knotholes in the vaulted ceiling over his bed and telling himself that fifty was the perfect age at which it was excusable for him to have a mid-life crisis, the phone rang. Harvey Feldman didn't announce himself. Just started talking the minute he heard Rick's voice.

"If it's safe to assume you're still interested, one of my clients is a fifteen-year-old pregnant girl named Lisa," he said. "She's from Akron, Ohio. She's in town with her sister and she's already met a few families. I told her about you. She didn't seem to mind that you were single, and seemed curious to meet you. It's a very long shot. But if you like I can ask her to come over."

Rick couldn't believe his own reaction. Panic. More anxiety

than he could remember feeling in years. Stage fright. "Listen, I need a little while to straighten up and shave and shower and . . . how pregnant? So the baby's due when? Christ, I don't even know if I should waste this girl's time, Harvey." He'd been struggling so much about how to handle his split from the studio that he'd pretty much put the baby thing out of his mind. It was a crazy spur-of-the-moment idea he'd had in the middle of the night, designed to try to save himself. And then in a panic he'd run to Feldman and afterward felt so dumb. How could he sit now and be interviewed, as if he were up for a part, by some little pregnant girl? This was lunacy.

"Rick," the lawyer said, "if you've changed your mind, if it isn't right, if it isn't something you're dying to do, hang up the phone. I've already told you how committed you have to be to something like this to make it right. And only *you* know the answer to that."

Rick lay silently, still looking at the ceiling. Finally he spoke. "What time?"

"How's four this afternoon?"

"I'll be here."

Lisa was six months' pregnant and told Rick she had been referred to Mr. Feldman by her right-to-life group. She was blond and green-eyed and pink-skinned and wore what was probably a hand-me-down polyester maternity top over some faded jeans. Her older sister was waiting in the car in Rick's driveway, despite Rick's attempts to have Lisa go out and get her.

"She doesn't want to interfere," Lisa told him.

Each time Lisa asked him a question and he answered it, she made a check mark with a plastic Bic pen on a little tablet from which she'd read the question. "And would you continue to go to your job after you adopted my baby?" She read the question without looking at him.

"I would," Rick said, "but I would have someone very qualified here to care for the baby while I was gone."

Lisa made some kind of a note.

"How many hours a day do you work?" she read.

"That depends. If I'm in the development stage of a project I can sometimes be home by six. If I'm shooting, sometimes I can be gone all day and night." It occurred to him that the words *development* and *shooting* meant nothing to her. He was about to explain when she frowned and looked him in the eye.

"Mr. Reisman," she said, "I'm scared that you wouldn't see the baby enough. And that you don't have enough extended family to care for it. Only that old uncle of yours that you mentioned, and I doubt that he's really interested. The honest-to-God's truth is I'm really worried about how fat you are at your age. I mean, you could die when the baby's only a year old, and then what'll happen to it? You don't have a wife, and from what I can figure, it doesn't look much like you're planning on having one either, as busy as you are and all. And that sounds a little weird to me too. So the way I see it, there's not much point to our going on and me asking you questions about my baby's education and all. Is there? 'Cause there's not a shot that I'm gonna pick you, and I hope you'll understand."

It was so blunt that Rick almost laughed, but there was something about the little girl's serious face that stopped him.

"I understand," he said, rising. She stood too, her pumpkin of a belly protruding in a kind of point from under the maternity blouse. Then she moved her notebook and her Bic pen into her left hand, thrust her right hand out for Rick to shake, and when he had, she walked briskly to the front door and was gone.

Rick looked down at the lavish spread of food he'd had his housekeeper put out on the coffee table in order to impress the girl, who hadn't touched one bite: an elaborate cheese tray, a caviar mousse, homemade brownies, and fruit. And after he heard Lisa's sister's rented car pull away, he sat down and ate most of the food himself.

18

WITHIN A FEW WEEKS he was relieved to find that despite Nat Ross's opinion, there were still some studios who were interested in him as a director, and soon his lawyer was negotiating to make a fine deal for him at Universal.

"And who told you so?" Bobo asked. The old man had been moved from the lodge to the hospital a few days before, when he complained of leg pains. Seeing him lying in a bed hooked up to an IV made Rick feel panicky. "Now you'll get some projects going and maybe forget all this nonsense about babies, you lunatic. Yes?"

Three more birth mothers had rejected Rick in the last two months, and each time he'd told Harvey Feldman to throw away his application. "It was a mistake. I can't handle it. Please, don't call me anymore."

But Feldman persisted. After the last one, a pretty twenty-year-old, walked into his house, took one look at Rick, and said, "No way, José," and left, he'd actually started a new and serious diet.

"Ingeleh," Bobo said, "I think I'm supposed to have a pain pill and the nurse isn't answering my buzzer. Do me a favor and check the nurses' station for me."

"Sure, Uncle B.," Rick said, and as he walked to the door he bumped into Bobo's nurse.

"Here I am, Mr. Reisman," she said to Bobo and then added quietly to Rick, "Why don't you step out for a while while I bathe him too?"

As he walked down the carpeted hospital hallway, Rick saw someone wave at him. It was Harvey Feldman.

"Essie's in for surgery," the young lawyer told Rick as he walked closer. "How's Bobo?"

"Okay, I think."

"Listen," Feldman began.

"Never mind," Rick said, putting up a hand to stop him.

"I have an idea for you. There's a little girl named Doreen, from Kansas, who's very far gone in her pregnancy and getting very worried so—"

"No."

"Wait. She was supposed to give her baby to my clients who flew her out here a few weeks ago to meet her. The couple, I'm sorry to say, are what you'd call 'Beautiful People,' so when she stepped off the airplane—did I mention it was *their* airplane, which they sent to fetch her—anyway, after they saw her, she's short, bucktoothed, and wore glasses, they sent her back."

"Nice folks," Rick said.

"Needless to say, Doreen is heartbroken," Harvey said, "and she probably wouldn't come back here. On the other hand . . ."

"Not for me. Honest to God, Harvey. I'm sorry I ever took your time in the first place. I can barely hold my own life together let alone be responsible for a—"

"Mr. Feldman." A nurse stepped out of a room down the hall where Harvey Feldman's aunt Essie was.

"Call me," Feldman said over his shoulder to Rick, "if you change your mind."

Kate Sullivan's picture was on the cover of two magazines in the airport newsstand. There was no question she was an exquisite-looking broad. Rick bought some chewing gum and the *Wall Street Journal*, picked up a pack of his favorite, Peanut M&Ms, and was going to have the cashier add them to his tab when he decided to be a good boy and put the candy back. He folded the paper under his arm and walked down the airport corridor, watching the people pass him on both sides, his eye as always framing much of what he saw as shots in a film: a picturesque moment of two women who were clearly a mother and daughter reuniting in a tearful hug, a Sikh walking hurriedly along at the same pace and side by side an old Hasidic Jew.

I'm losing my mind, Rick thought. I've been moving rapidly in this direction for years, but now I've arrived. In exactly four minutes, according to the schedule on the television screen above my head, an airplane will land and in it, courtesy of tickets purchased on my Visa card, will be Doreen Cobb, a fourteen-year-old pregnant girl from Kansas, and her mother, Bea. If all goes well in our conversation, which the mother insists has to take place in the airport, Bea will leave Doreen here, so I can move her into my secretary's apartment to have a baby for me.

If things don't go well, Doreen will fly on to Nevada with her mother, who's leaving tonight to see her eldest son and his wife. Harvey Feldman had explained that Rick was going to be Doreen's final try at open adoption and if there was no match to be made, the girl agreed to give the baby up to a home in Nevada.

I shouldn't be doing this, he thought with a pang of guilt mixed with fear. There's much too much potential for pain for everyone concerned. The little pregnant girl, her mother, me, but especially the innocent unborn baby. I shouldn't be doing this. Then why am I so swept up in the forward motion of this plan? The girl has already been hurt by some phonies, or should I say some other phonies, who thought she was too ugly to ever bring forth the brand of baby they thought they should have. Wouldn't another rejection be too much for her adolescent ego?

Isn't it exquisitely selfish of me to drag her through that possibility one more time?

No, he thought, arriving at the gate and watching through the window as the big carrier was being motioned in toward the gate. Because I won't reject her. If she'll have me as the adopting parent of this baby, I'll grab the chance and commit myself to making the experience good for the girl and for the baby.

He needed love in his life so desperately. To give it, to get it, to exchange it, to hang on to it because he was finally starting to know it was all there really was in this world that mattered. And not having it was making him shrivel into nothingness. Bobo and Charlie and Patty and the kids had been the greatest source of his pleasure, his strength, his good feelings about himself for most of his life. Now Charlie was gone and Bobo was hanging on by a thread. Somehow he had to find a repository for all the love he knew he could give, and maybe a little baby was the answer. Babies required so much attention. Perhaps giving that attention would make him stop thinking only about himself.

So that's why I'm here, he thought, joining the group at the gate waiting for the passengers to emerge from the flight. As the stream of people began to flow, he looked closely at the faces of every passenger, until he saw the unmistakable mother and daughter step arm in arm through the door. Within an instant the tiny gray-haired woman spotted him, looked piercingly into his eyes, tapped her wide-eyed daughter on the arm, and the girl, seeing him now too, flushed red. Then they all moved together to meet face to face.

Rick extended his hand but Bea Cobb ignored it. She was all business. "Where can we go?" she asked.

"We can go to one of the conference rooms at the Red Carpet Club, where I'm a member," Rick offered, but Bea waved that idea away with a gesture, then pointed to a nearby cocktail lounge. "What's wrong with that place over there?" she asked.

For the first time in his always-running-the-show life Rick

thought to himself, I will not make waves. I'll do whatever she says. "That'll be just fine with me," he said.

The two women walked hand in hand and Rick looked at the face of the girl, who snuck a peek back at him, and when their eyes met it was with the mutually awkward shy and wary smile that probably characterized the meeting of a mail-order couple. With each of them thinking, If this works out, this stranger will soon be related to me in a lifelong way.

She was as described, wearing glasses, with an upper lip that protruded in that way it does with people who have an obvious overbite. She looked very much like her mother, who was a few inches taller and also shaped like a little fireplug, except that Doreen's hair was wispy and fine and blond and the mother's hair was gray and cropped close.

The cocktail lounge had the malty stink of stale alcohol, and Bea Cobb, squinting to adjust her eyes to the low light, spotted a table in the corner, tugged her daughter in that direction, and when they got there sat. There were no waiters, only a bartender, so Rick took their orders. After a few minutes he brought two diet Cokes and a light beer for himself.

"Well now," Bea said, looking at him while Doreen looked everywhere else but. "I guess the first thing I want to know is how come you're not married?"

"I can't explain it," he said. "I *wish* I hadn't let all this time go by without having one woman to feel close to and love, but I guess I was afraid."

"Afraid of what?" she asked him. "Why would you be afraid? Being married and having a family are the best things anyone can do in this world. You think making movies is more important?"

Rick held tightly to the cold beer glass and tried to decide what to tell her. He thought back over the last few months, and how he'd wanted to impress the young pregnant girls he'd met in his living room and in Harvey Feldman's office, and that the harder he seemed to try, the easier it was for them to see through the ruse. Maybe, you asshole, he thought, you ought to take a deep breath and tell the truth.

"When I was a little boy my parents were looked on as royalty in Hollywood. He was a brilliant producer and director and she was one of the most beautiful and gifted actresses alive. When their private plane went down with my dad flying, it was an enormous tragedy. I was their only child. They doted on me. My father had been an astute businessman who invested his money wisely. So after their death, as a heartbroken, emotionally needy adolescent boy, I found myself with millions of dollars. The news hit the papers, and when the numbers got out, I became very popular. In fact, it didn't take too long, after I moved in with Uncle Bobo and Aunt Sadie, for women to start finding me. Dozens of them, every size and shape and age, some of them nearly my mother's age.

"It was every boy's dream, but too much, too soon, and I knew instinctively that I couldn't trust any of them. Because it wasn't my beautiful eyes they were after, or all the other things they claimed made me so attractive. I was a little boy, and I missed my mother, so I went out with these women and that wasn't the answer. And pretty soon, I started to eat. Because food was something I could trust. Food didn't have an ulterior motive for making me feel good.

"I never really got obese; pudgy enough to make sure that certain women keep their distance, but most of the time the combination of the money and the burgeoning success of my career made up for the fat, and made a lot of them hang in there and put up with my neurosis. Eventually, when it came down to it, by the time I was really at an age where getting serious with someone was what I should be doing, I found myself so cynical, so burnt out, that I never could close a deal with any woman." What a lousy story that is, he thought, but sadly it's the truth.

Doreen's mother clucked her tongue, and the sound broke Rick's reverie. "How long ago was the accident?" she asked.

"Thirty-two years. I was eighteen."

"You're fifty?"

He nodded. "Will be this year."

"Same as me." She laughed, outraged at that idea. Rick was surprised. None of the women he knew in Los Angeles who were fifty would ever let their hair get gray, or for that matter admit they were fifty.

"I'm a grandmother seven times already, and you're wanting to adopt a baby?" She laughed again. "I think you're crazy."

He smiled. She was looking at him now in a friendly way, as if their mutual age made them comrades.

"What'll my daughter do here for the next few months?" she asked him.

"There's a young woman who's been my secretary for several years. She has a large apartment in a nice neighborhood. I'll pay Doreen's share of the rent while she lives there as the girl's roommate, and provide all of Doreen's other expenses, find her the best medical care, and if she wants to, I'll help her enroll in some continuing-education classes at a nearby college."

She was nodding a little nod that Rick hoped was a nod of approval.

"My other seven kids all had a meeting this week. They told me I was crazy if I let Doreen go off with some sharpie who's trying to buy her baby. They think she ought to have it at a home somewhere, and then forget about it for the rest of her life."

"And why don't you?"

"Because," she said, looking over at her daughter, who looked back at her wistfully as if she knew what her mother was about to tell him, "I didn't have eight kids. I had nine. My first one was born when I was Doreen's age. But in those days they didn't have any such thing as open adoption. So my child, my oldest son, who is thirty-six years of age this year, is out there somewhere, and I don't know where. I don't know anything about him, except his birthday, which is March third. And on that day I always think about him. I light a candle for him every year."

"That's very sad," Rick said.

Her eyes held his for a while and then a smile broke out on her face and she said, "Fifty years old! You and I were teenagers at the same time. Did you like Elvis?"

"To me he was the King," Rick answered, grinning.

"To me too," Bea Cobb said.

"I had the good fortune to meet him," Rick told her.

"No! Spare me," she said. "How did you meet the King?"

"In the seventies I had a secretary who used to be a dancer. She danced in some of his movies, and they became great friends. So she invited me on the set of a television special he was shooting, and I actually shook his hand."

"With *this* hand?" she asked, taking Rick's right hand in her two small ones.

He nodded.

"Ooooh," she said, doing a little mock shiver. "I touched the hand that touched the King."

Bea Cobb and Rick Reisman laughed together, and then she said, "I want to tell you something, okay? And you might as well say okay, 'cause I'm going to tell you what I think even if you don't. You don't know what in the hell you're getting into. You think having a baby is something that'll do the same thing for you as buying a new car. Lift your spirits, make you feel sexier.

"Well, take it from me, that's not anywhere near what it's about. And when I leave here, you're probably going to say to yourself, That hick doesn't know a goddamned thing. But that's okay because I don't give a damn what you think. I'm telling you from a life of a whole lot of experience that raising a baby turns a person around in ways they didn't even know there were. Teaches you patience, humility, and the real meaning of pain. On top of that, a child makes you tell the truth, because they don't buy into any lies. And anyone can see in your scared and sad eyes, you've probably told a lot of those in your many long years."

This whole day felt surreal to Rick. And this was the strangest part of all. Being dressed down by this odd little woman who had his number in spades. He was sad and scared and wanting to adopt a baby for all the wrong reasons. But they were reasons which had been compelling enough to get him all the way to this part of the process.

"So now," she said, "I'd like to have one more Coca-Cola, and after that, it'll be time to go check in at the gate."

Well, Rick thought, that dismissal is loud and clear. He tried to hide his disappointment. You knew your chances were low, he told himself, and it was an insane idea anyway so . . .

"What about you, Doreen? You want another cold drink too?" Bea asked.

"Yeah, okay," Doreen answered, and it was the first time Rick heard her voice. He sighed and stood to go and get another round for all of them. And while his back was turned, there must have been some moment that passed between mother and daughter during which the decision was made, because then the young girl said with a laugh in her voice, "But if I were you, I'd forget the beer and make it a diet drink. 'Cause you're going to have to shape up if you're planning to be a father."

19

ONCE EVERY FOUR OR FIVE DAYS, Andrea would drive into the city from the Valley and when she did she would stop at Rick's house and drop off "the girl," which is how Bobo referred to Doreen. But despite the old man's *tsk*ing and shaking his head, and protesting at the *"mishegoss* of this crazy new world," Rick had already seen the grudging look of respect in the old man's eyes when Doreen beat him at gin rummy. Rick loved to observe the way Bobo got caught up in conversation with her when she asked him about his early film career. One at a time she had rented and watched each of the films Bobo and Rick's father, Jake, produced.

"The kid's a sponge," Andrea reported to Rick one day at the office. "She signed up for a literature course at Valley College, because my place is five blocks from there. I couldn't get past the syllabus for the class, and she's already halfway through the books. Not to mention that she's reading to the baby."

"How do you mean?"

"She read somewhere that if you talk to the fetus and sing to it, that makes it feel good, reassures it with the sound of your voice. Well, she said she's a lousy singer, so she went and got all these children's books out of the library, and every night she lies in bed, reading stories to her own stomach."

Rick liked the idea of Doreen's genes having reading and learning and especially cardsharking in them. There was something about counting down the months until the baby's arrival that forced life into him, enriched every choice he made, now that he knew he was making it not only for himself but for the baby as well. His baby. He was still eating more than he should, but not as frantically or as often. And more than a few times he would turn down a date in order to take Doreen to dinner, or say no to a visit from a woman to get the rest everyone told him he would need when the baby came.

"Harvey Feldman said I shouldn't ask you this," he said to Doreen at dinner one night at the Hamburger Hamlet. He had ordered a broiled chicken breast; Doreen had ordered the onion soup, a salad, a bacon cheeseburger, and a strawberry shake. She stopped in the middle of the sip of the strawberry shake and a little of the pink still bubbled in a line above her upper lip as she put her hand up and said, "Don't. Because I won't tell you anything about the father of this baby. And if you have to know, I'll go right back to Kansas and forget our deal. He was in good physical health and he was tall. That's all you get." She was serious, so he dropped it.

He had come to love his time together with her. She was confrontational and outspoken, a bright spot in his world, which was filled with the backstabbing politics and outsize egos of show business. A few times he took her with him to an invitation-only screening. On those nights he would notice she would wear a little blusher on her already pink cheeks, and a tiny bit of mascara on her otherwise invisible blond eyelashes. And always, because of her years of watching television night and day, she recognized more of the faces in the audience than he did.

"Michael Keaton was there and Jack Nicholson," he heard her telling her mother on the phone one night. And then she let out a shriek of excitement.

* * *

The man who lived two doors down from Bobo in the lodge was Arnold Viner. Viner had been a studio publicist who had represented Rick's father and Bobo for years.

"It's right out of Sartre," Bobo said. "If anyone had asked me in nineteen thirty-nine to describe hell, I would have said living near Arnold Viner and being too old to run away every time he walked by." Bobo and Viner had had a fight in the early forties about an item that appeared in the paper, and they were still arguing about it ten minutes before they took Viner over to the adjacent hospital with a massive stroke. Bobo insisted on staying in the intensive care unit by his side.

It was a day on which Rick was visiting, so he stayed too. He sat in the waiting room, reading some scripts he had in his briefcase and making notes on them until a few hours had passed. When the machines stopped bleeping and the doctors came in to confirm that Viner had died, a red-eyed Bobo came out to the waiting room, and took Rick's hand.

"I sat in there because I knew his time was up," he said, "so I figured eventually the angel of death would come, and I could beg him to throw me into the deal and take me too. My luck, right? I fell asleep in the chair and missed the whole transaction." Rick put an arm around Bobo and walked him back to the lodge. They hadn't reached the room yet when he heard his name being paged on the loudspeaker.

"Richard Reisman, telephone."

He took the call in Bobo's room. It was Andrea's voice.

"Doreen's bleeding. A lot. She called me at the office so I came right over. We tried to reach you all morning, but you weren't in Bobo's room. So I took her to the doctor. He said it's placenta previa. She has to stay in bed for the rest of the pregnancy. All the time, including her meals in bed too. She can get out briefly to go to the bathroom or shower. That's all. Listen, she's a doll, but I'm not exactly the nursy type, and I have to come to the office every day. What do I do?"

"Pack her up and move her to my house. The housekeeper's

always there. Doreen can stay in the guest room and be tended to during the day. If that's not enough I'll get her a full-time nurse."

"We'll be at your place by the time you get home," Andrea promised.

Bleeding. Harvey Feldman, the lawyer, had forgotten to mention miscarriage, never discussed premature births or still-borns or any of the ways in which a pregnancy could end. And for some reason, losing the baby during the pregnancy was one of the possibilities that had never occurred to Rick. During all of this he had carried the vague feeling that somewhere in this seemingly unnatural set of circumstances was the potential for disaster, and maybe this was it. He stopped briefly at his office at Universal to pick up some scripts he needed to read, then hurried home.

He was relieved to see Doreen already settled in the bed and very chipper when he walked into the freshly painted yellow guest room. She had an apologetic expression on her face as she lay on the bed with her little feet propped up on a pile of pillows.

"My mom's gonna be real unhappy about this," she said.

"The bleeding?" he asked.

"No, my staying at your house. She doesn't think we should live together till after we're married." Then she made a face at him and laughed.

"Very funny," he said. "Did you call the school and tell them you were dropping out?"

"Yeah," she said sadly. "I'm going to do all the reading any-way. The trouble is there's not that much left, and I'm going to be stuck like this for a month."

He had walked directly from the garage into her room, so he was still carrying the pile of scripts he'd brought home to read. He dropped them on her bed with a thunk.

"Here," he said. "Read these for me. I have to start them over the weekend. You can tell me which ones are good and which are stinkers."

"Really?" she asked. "Are you kidding? You really want *me* to read the scripts that you might want to make into a movie? Me?"

"Sure," he said, sitting at the foot of the bed. "Would you do that for me?"

"For you, yes," she said, her little round pink face very serious, her blond lashes batting hard behind the glasses. "But keep in mind," she said, "if I'm critical, it's because I *am* a student of the classics."

"I'll certainly factor your literary background into my assessment of the critiques."

"Oh, thanks ever so," she said, assuming the haughtiest voice. Then she opened the blue cover of the top script and looked at the title page. "Well here's one that's bound to do wonders for your career. It's called *The Hand of Doom*. I think I'll start with this and work my way up."

He started toward the door. "*You*," he said, "are a piece of work."

"What's for dinner?" she asked.

"I'll ask Nellie," he said.

"Nellie went home early, her mother's sick," she told him.

The point was clear. Dinner was up to him.

"What do you like on your pizza?" he asked.

"You'd feed pizza to the woman whose body is nutritionally responsible for your child?"

"I'll make a salad," he mumbled grudgingly.

"Be sure to throw in some protein," she shouted after him.

Standing in the kitchen alone he chuckled, trying to imagine what the personality would be of the baby that came out of that girl. A feisty little pink-faced girl? A tough, smart-mouthed boy? Four more weeks and, God willing, he would be holding the little creature in his arms.

A few evenings later, Doreen, who had fallen asleep over one of Rick's scripts, was awakened by the sound of the doorbell. The doctor had told her she could go as far as the bathroom, and the front door wasn't much farther than that, so she figured it would be all right if she answered it. Whoever was at the door was making a big racket, loud, with the brass door knocker. Doreen couldn't find her own robe, but an old one of Rick's was hanging on the inside of the door, so she threw that one over her nightgown and hurried to see what was so urgent.

The woman who stood in the doorway was so gorgeous to look at, at least to Doreen, that she was certain this must be a movie star. It wasn't Candice Bergen, but she looked a lot like her.

"Is Mr. Reisman at home?"

"No he isn't," Doreen said.

"Do you expect him soon?"

Doreen nodded.

The woman moved forward, backing Doreen into the living room.

"I'll just wait here," she said, plopped down in a chair, picked up a magazine, and began leafing through it. "Tell you what," she said to Doreen without even looking up at her. "I'll have a scotch and water."

"Great," Doreen said, and was about to head back into her room to get back into bed when the blond woman said, "Make it for me, okay?"

Doreen looked at her and said, "Honey, I wouldn't know scotch if you cooked me in it. Make it yourself," and went back into her room. After a few minutes she could hear the woman talking loudly to someone, and she realized it must be into a telephone because there were no other voices out there. Uh-oh, she thought, what if she's making long-distance calls? What if Rick doesn't even know her and *I* let her into the house? I better keep an eye on her.

So she put the robe on again and walked back into the living room. When she got there, the woman was drinking some kind of alcohol in a glass she'd found in one of the cabinets and smoking a cigarette. The butt of a previous cigarette had already been put out on what Doreen recognized was one of Rick's good china plates, which this lady had obviously pulled out of the cabinet when she couldn't find an ashtray.

"I figured if I waited long enough, this asshole would come to his senses and call me, and then not one fucking word. I mean, it's such bullshit. So after a few weeks went by I called his office three times, and he never called me back. And that bitch secretary of his, that Andrea, kept saying, 'Sorry, Mona, he's so busy,' you know? Then I read in *Variety* that the studio dumped him.

"Well, you know what a softie I am. Right? I felt sorry for him, so I sent him a really sweet note that he never answered, and I called his house and left message after message on the fucking machine, and he still didn't call me back, and then I read in the *Hollywood Reporter* that he made a deal at Universal, so I sent him some flowers over there, and you think he calls me one time? Zippo. Not even a thank-you note from the rude little asshole. And Katy Biggard said she saw him on the beach in Malibu last week, and that he must be dying or something because he lost all this weight, and you know what a pig he's always been. You'd get sick if you saw him naked. Anyway, I got really worried about him and came running over here and this troll who works for him answers the door, and she wouldn't even make me a drink. I'll tell you, I'm just sick and tired of it. So listen—"

Doreen had heard enough. "This isn't an ashtray," she said, grabbing the plate away from Mona, who had been tamping out another cigarette and now dropped hot ashes onto her own hand and screamed. Doreen grabbed the phone away from Mona. "He is not an asshole or a pig," and slammed it into the phone cradle. "And Andrea is not a bitch." Then she grabbed the five-foot-nine Mona by the arm and steered her toward the door. "*I* am not a troll, and *you*," she said, opening the front door and shoving Mona out through it, "are not welcome here!"

Before she could shut the door in the stunned Mona's hang-jawed face, Mona bellowed, "Who the fuck *are* you? I'm going to tell Rick about this and he's going to fire your fat ugly little ass for treating me like this. So I just want you to tell me right now who you are!"

"I," Doreen said, realizing that she was wearing Rick's robe, untied it and let it fall dramatically to the floor as she told the flabbergasted Mona, "am the mother of Rick Reisman's baby." And then she closed the door in Mona's stunned face.

Doreen remembered what her mother once told her about how to deal with a man: Wait until his stomach is full before you break any bad news to him. So she waited until she and Rick finished the dinner Nellie had left for them that night and were about to watch the news on television. Then she told him about Mona's visit. He didn't react visibly until the end of the story, when to Doreen's delight he let out a big laugh. There was enormous relief in it, and he obviously loved imagining little Doreen pushing big Mona out the door. "I'm sorry," he said, hoping Doreen wasn't insulted by his laughter, but the feeling was too rich to hold inside.

Things were coming together for him at Universal the way they never had before. All of his new projects were exciting, and within six months one of them was sure to move onto the floor, and he would be back in the world where he operated best. Interacting with the actors, taking close-up pictures of human behavior. That was when he felt most comfortable, creating those moments of truth.

There was one script that had its hooks deeper into him than the others. The leading character was a brilliant scientist who discovers a possible cure for cancer, and the story is about the battles he fights when he enters a nightmarish world of people who don't want that cure to be found just yet.

"Robert Redford," Doreen said the minute she finished reading the script, "and nobody else. Maybe with you directing, Clint Eastwood could pull it off."

Sometimes Rick had to stifle a laugh when she talked that way. Since she'd started doing some of his reading she was beginning to sound like a salty, too hip, William Morris agent.

"Redford is perfect," Doreen went on, "because this character has to have that kind of gorgeousness, since every woman in the whole movie falls in love with him."

"I'll send it to his agent," Rick said.

"Smart move," Doreen told him and moved on to the next script in the pile. She had two weeks to go until the baby was born, and these days she just kind of slid from room to room, from chair to chair. The big event of her day was, without fail, turning on the television and watching "Jeopardy."

"What is Soledad prison?" he heard her say out loud, answering the question with a question like the "Jeopardy" contestants. "Who was Geppetto?" And when she got the answer wrong she would say to herself, "*Doreeeen*, you are so stupid!"

"Last year in school we had a discussion about our ideal man," she said one night when Rick got home just as the "Jeopardy" closing credits were rolling by. "Guess who I picked."

"Who?"

"Alex Trebek. He is truly brainy, which to me is the most important quality anyone can have."

"I have a bachelor's degree and two master's," Rick said, realizing he was feeling jealous of the game-show host.

"I know," she said. "When I found out I was going to meet you, I went to the library in Kansas City and read about you in that big book about directors that came out a few years back. It tells all the details of your life. It had everything in it about you and your parents and Uncle Bobo, with pictures of them when they were young."

"Kansas City was a long way for you to go to check up on someone," he said.

"Not someone," she said abruptly. "Maybe the father of the only baby I might ever have. Those other people from Los Angeles, the first ones Mr. Feldman introduced me to, they didn't seem as if they had a lot going for them upstairs, and that's why I didn't pick them."

A lie. She thought she had to tell Rick a lie to cover, and it made him want to reach over, touch her hair gently, and tell her that he knew the truth about what had happened with that couple, and it didn't matter to him. But there was something about the way her jaw was set that told him to allow her to rewrite the uncomfortable story about that rejection with any ending she wanted.

"It's also why I went to the library to check up on you."

"How did I stack up?" he asked her gently.

"Not bad," she answered.

Sid Sheinberg called that night to tell Rick that Robert Redford not only loved the project but wanted to meet on the fifteenth about doing it, less than a week away, and Rick excitedly told Doreen. She nodded.

"There you go," she said.

At Doreen's most recent doctor's appointment, the doctor set Rick up with a beeper system.

"In case," the doctor explained, "you're not in your office when she goes into labor, and we need you right away." Every morning before Rick left for work, he attached the beeper to his belt and gave it a little pat.

"No false alarms," Doreen promised him. "I know you're busy, so I won't call unless I'm as sure as I can be that I'm ready to burst."

"I'll be there for you," he promised in return.

There was something indescribable about being in a room with Robert Redford. Even to Rick, who had known and worked closely with many famous stars. Maybe it was seeing with one's own eyes that the actor's look, the exquisite face, the stance, the bright-eyed boyishness, had nothing to do with the camera, but was very real.

"He'll only be in town for these eight hours. At five thirty he gets on an airplane and will be out of the country for six months. He loves the script. He loves the character, he loves your work. There are a few creative points he'd like to change."

That was the part of what the agent said that stuck in Rick's stomach. What could those points be? The character of the scientist was certainly not perfect. He was neurotic, a drinker, maybe Redford didn't like that. But changing that would take all the bite out of the work.

"I'm sure you know if he says yes, it's a go project, and my sense of it is that if you iron out those three points, he'll be ready to shoot it the minute he gets back."

Redford. The image of Doreen's little face the day she suggested Rick try to get him came rushing back to Rick as he began telling Robert Redford about the genesis of the project and what had made him interested in it in the first place. Redford nodded and smiled, and Rick could tell by the comments he interjected that they agreed completely on the tone of the piece. *Thank God*.

Doreen. Last night when he walked by her room, he heard her reading passages of *Alice in Wonderland* out loud. Any day now she would be going into labor, and his baby would be born. A baby. A fifty-year-old man adopting a baby. Somehow in the conversation with Redford, the subject of children came up. Probably because Phillips, the character in the script, had children, and Redford asked Rick if he had any. "Well . . . almost," Rick said, and he found himself rattling out the entire story of Doreen and the impending birth and adoption.

"Now *that's* a story for a movie," Redford told him. Everyone in the meeting, all the executives and agents laughed at that comment. And now they were coming to the down side. The part of the meeting where Robert Redford would tell Rick what changes he thought the material required. Rick knew he would have to determine then and there if he thought the changes would work for or destroy the material as he saw it. He was about to steer the conversation in that inevitable direction when the unmistakable sound of the beeper he was wearing on his belt filled the entire room. Everyone turned and looked at Rick.

"Must have been something I ate for lunch," Rick joked as he jumped to his feet. Doreen, the baby, his baby, was about to be born. To come into the world and be his heir, his family. Now, it was happening now, right in the middle of this coveted meeting with Robert Redford. A meeting that couldn't be changed or rescheduled for at least six months, after which the chance for the project to happen, the intense interest that could get Robert Redford to commit and the movie to be a certainty, would surely be gone.

"Gentlemen," Rick said, with a slight bow of his head, "the scientist with the cure for cancer will just have to wait, because as of this moment, I'm about to be a father." And on very light feet, he left Robert Redford's meeting and went to take Doreen Cobb to the hospital.

20

ONE DAY AT PANACHE, Carin told Lainie she had heard about a way that adopting mothers could actually breast-feed their babies. The adopting mother taped to her nipple a tiny tube that was attached to a container of formula. The baby sucked on the tube and the mother's nipple at the same time, and eventually the adopting mother's hormones took over and her own breast milk came in. Lainie didn't tell the well-meaning Carin that her body would be unable to produce those hormones. Just thanked her for the information.

Lainie and Jackie had agreed that probably it was best that their next meeting would not be until the amniocentesis, which was fourteen weeks away. Time went by quickly, and no news from Jackie was good news, because it meant that the pregnancy was holding. When the Jackie phone rang in her house and Lainie heard Jackie's by-now-familiar voice saying, "I'm a tank. You'll faint when you see me," she meant it when she answered, "I can't wait."

As she opened the door to the neonatal doctor's reception area and saw Jackie, something about looking at her there made Lainie reel in disbelief. This wasn't just an idea anymore. There was exquisitely apparent evidence, round and swollen evidence, that Mitch's baby was inside this woman.

"What do you think?" Jackie asked, stretching her legs out, then pulling herself up to her feet to come and give Lainie a Shalimar-scented hug.

"I think you look great," Lainie said.

Jackie stepped back and looked down at her own large middle. "*There's* our little honey," she said. "And today we're going to see it."

A young dark-haired pregnant girl across the waiting room put down her magazine, looked over at the two of them, and smiled. "We're having a baby together," Jackie told her. The girl raised her eyebrows, not sure what to say, and seemed relieved when the nurse opened the door and called for Jackie and Lainie to come into the examining room.

Now, from where she sat on the folding chair that the doctor had pushed into the back corner of the room for her, Lainie could see just the top of Jackie's round belly, which was shiny with oil. The neonatal doctor, handsome with gray hair which looked odd with his very young-looking face, had gently spread the oil on it, the way one lover spreads suntan lotion on the other. The oil made the instrument he held in his hand move more easily on Jackie's abdomen.

The room was dimly lit so that Jackie, Lainie, the nurse, and the doctor could better see the speckled, writhing figure projected on the tiny TV monitor that was mounted close to the ceiling in the far corner of the room. It looked to Lainie like bad reception on a broken television, but this was the long-awaited picture. The doctor was using it to determine the location of the amniotic fluid, some of which he was going to extract. With the help of his nurse, who held a pointer against the screen, he very carefully showed Lainie and Jackie that the baby had all of its fingers and toes, a perfect spine, and a healthy heartbeat.

"Jesus, when my Tommy was born, they sure didn't have *this* kind of thing," Jackie said from her supine position on the table. "In those days, you just crossed your fingers and hoped for the best. Can you tell what it *is* yet, Doc?"

"Yes. It's definitely a baby," the doctor joked.

Jackie emitted a yelp of a laugh, and the grainy figure on the sonogram seemed to jump.

"I mean the sex," Jackie said

"Not from this, but in a few weeks we'll know. Do you want us to tell you when we do, Mrs. O'Malley?"

"Hell yeah," Jackie answered. "Don't we, Lainie?"

Lainie had never even thought about knowing the baby's sex before it was born, and whether she wanted to or not. She had asked Jackie to have the amniocentesis to be certain the baby had no genetic defects. She had no idea how Mitch would feel about knowing the sex before the birth.

"Absolutely," Jackie told the doctor. "That way they'll know if they want to name the baby Jackie for a girl or Jack for a boy," and then she laughed again. "That's a joke, Doc. *My* name is Jackie, and it's *their* baby." The doctor nodded with a slight smile.

"Look," Jackie said, pointing suddenly. "Every time I laugh, it bobbles all around. Isn't that adorable?"

Lainie tried to focus hard on the screen, but couldn't tell which part of the baby was which, or where the baby stopped and the rest of the picture started. This wasn't what she'd imagined at all. She'd thought that what she would see would look like the photos in the books she'd rushed out to buy the day she heard Jackie was pregnant, *A Child Is Born* and *The Secret Life of the Unborn Child*. Now she squinted when the nurse turned on the bright fluorescent overhead lights.

"Mrs. O'Malley, I'm going to give you a light local anesthetic on the spot from which I'll extract the amniotic fluid. You'll feel a slight ping and that's all," the doctor told Jackie.

"What about when you put the big needle in?" Jackie asked, her voice sounding almost childlike.

"That shouldn't hurt," the doctor told her.

"Easy for *you* to say." Jackie laughed nervously.

The doctor didn't react.

"Laine?" Jackie said, picking up her head to look back at the spot where Lainie sat.

"Yeah?"

"Could you move a little closer and like . . . hold my hand?"

"Sure," Lainie said, looking at the doctor to ask if that was all right with him. And when he nodded, she moved close to the table and gently took Jackie's hand in hers. While the doctor extracted the amniotic fluid and Jackie squeezed Lainie's hand, the two women looked into each other's eyes and talked about maternity clothes, and which store they would go to when the amniocentesis was over.

An hour later, they were in Lady Madonna in Encino. For so long, Lainie had averted her eyes in the mall every time she passed a maternity store. Now she stood right in the middle of one, turning a rounder that held tops and slacks as she tried choosing some clothes for Jackie.

"In gray I look like the Goodyear blimp," Jackie shouted from the dressing room. "In pink, more like Petunia Pig."

"Black is supposed to be slimming," Lainie called back, picking a large black T-shirt and some black pants with an elastic panel front and bringing them over to the curtained dressing room. When the slightly parted curtain revealed a naked Jackie with enormous breasts that sat on top of her huge abdomen, Lainie started to back away, but Jackie opened the curtain wider and puffed herself out proudly.

"Is this a shocker?" she asked. "And this is only at seventeen weeks. We could be having an elephant, Mother."

The ten-thousand-dollar surrogacy fee didn't include a budget for maternity clothes, so Mitch agreed to give Jackie "a few hundred dollars extra" to cover that cost. He thought it was fine that Lainie went along to shop with her.

"I love your taste," Jackie had said, "please come and help me, so I don't get stuff that makes me look dumb."

The black two-piece outfit was perfect, and so were a white sailor top with red pants, a sundress and a few T-shirts and some maternity jeans, four new bras, and half a dozen pairs of underpants. Everything was so expensive. Jackie said she didn't need nighties because she slept in some extra-large men's T-shirts. "Unfortunately without benefit of the extra-large men," she added laughing.

When Lainie pulled the cash out of her wallet to pay for everything the saleswoman seemed surprised.

"We get so few people paying cash," she said, almost suspiciously.

"That's because she isn't allowed to leave any traces," Jackie said, grinning, giving Lainie a friendly little poke in the side. Lainie hated this part. The secrecy. Being unable to tell Jackie about certain aspects of her life. While the saleswoman was putting the new clothing in bags, Lainie looked around at all of the display outfits, which had been stuffed with padding to create the effect of pregnant bodies, and tried to imagine how she would have looked in them if this had been her own pregnancy.

"Looks like you're buying her a whole wardrobe," the saleswoman said, making small talk. "Is she your sister?"

Lainie shook her head no.

"Cousin?"

Lainie shook her head no again.

"No relation?"

"No."

"Amazing. The resemblance is so strong. Except for the fact that she's . . ."

"Pregnant," Lainie said.

"Fat," Jackie said, and the three women all laughed. The saleswoman handed the package to Lainie who handed it to Jackie, and the two women went off to lunch.

When Jackie was in her sixth month, Lainie decided it was time to tell her mother what was going on. So she drove to Beverly Hills and met her for lunch in the Bedford Café, a tiny little corner restaurant she knew her mother loved. It was near the law office where she worked, and most days she would go there alone and read the newspaper while she ate the meat loaf, which was a specialty of the place.

"I know it's strange, and I can appreciate your having some doubts about it, but believe me, everything has been handled very carefully, and if we can have a healthy baby that comes from Mitch, I'll be a happy woman."

"Mmm-hmmm," Margaret Dunn said, her face tense with disapproval.

"Mother, you and I both know I could have died, but I didn't. And now I feel that I'm blessed for every day I live on this earth. Imagine how lucky I am to be able to have a baby too. Please be happy for me."

"Dear, I'm happy you're getting what you want. But I'm afraid it will never work out properly. This way of having babies is a way to please men," she said in a strained voice, and her gaze was over Lainie's shoulder. It was where she always looked during those rare times when she had any meaningful conversations with her daughter.

"What does that mean?" Lainie asked.

"It means there is no way on God's earth that either of the two women will ever be able to feel one hundred percent good about it."

Lainie looked at her mother, then at the waitress walking toward them carrying a meat loaf plate for her mother and a turkey sandwich for her. "It will be okay, Mother," Lainie said. But what she was thinking was, You're right, Mother, you're absolutely right, but it's too late now.

By the time Jackie was at the end of her seventh month, most of Mitch and Lainie's friends knew about the surrogacy. Some gasped when they heard, and several of the women said, "I could never do that. You're so brave." Some of the salesgirls at the store insisted that on a Sunday afternoon in May they wanted to give her a baby shower at Carin's house in Laurel Canyon.

"Who else should I invite?" asked Carin.

"Well, there's my mother, and my three sisters-in-law, and a few girls from school."

The day of the shower was uncharacteristically clear, and

Lainie thrilled at the sight of the cake shaped like a bassinet that sat on a white-clothed table. Next to the table stood a real white wicker bassinet, which was one of Betsy's many gifts for the baby, and piled high inside it were the ribboned and frilly packages from the other sisters. The three of them sat together and chatted among themselves, and at one point Lainie thought she overheard Betsy ask Carin, "Is the surrogate coming?"

"Oh, no!" Carin said in a tone that sounded as if she was shushing Betsy.

Sharon, who was an old friend of Lainie's from Northridge, was pregnant herself.

"I've been layette shopping for me, so I just got one of each for you."

"Oh, thank you." Lainie was delighted with every T-shirt and diaper pin.

Sharon, puffy-faced and swollen around the ankles, had to sit. "I am so tired of carrying this baby. If you want my opinion, *you're* the one who's doing this the right way."

Lainie was grateful to her mother, who chatted amiably with everyone and put on a social face Lainie had seen her use at the law office or on special occasions. The sweet small talk and supportive faces of the girls from the store made Lainie feel warm and expectant. As she opened each gift, the squeals that rose from the group and the tiny delicate baby things in her hands moved her. According to the amniocentesis, the baby was going to be a girl. Rose Margaret De Nardo. After Mitch's late mother, Rose, and of course Margaret Dunn, whose friendly attitude at the shower may have been the result of hearing the news of a namesake.

Carin, who was a sometime artist, had bought the baby a tiny chair in unfinished wood, which she painted pale pink. On the back of it in darker pink flowery letters she had painted ROSE MARGARET DE NARDO. Faith, the seamstress at Panache, had made a needlepoint pillow with a looped ribbon at the top so that it could hang from the doorknob of the nursery. The words on the pillow were *Shhh! Rose Margaret De Nardo is asleep.*

Lainie held each gift up for the others to see, then held it close to her chest. There were tiny smocked dresses and baby-size ballet slippers. White baby socks trimmed with satin ribbons and the smallest pearls she'd ever seen. After the gifts and the cake, all three of Mitch's sisters gave reasons they had to leave, said their good-byes, and were gone. The closer friends who knew all Lainie had been through to get to this point in her life moved around her, and each of them hugged her. Lainie wept for joy and some of them cried along with her.

Her mother helped her carry the gifts to the BMW. And before she got into her own old Chevrolet, she said to Lainie, "It was a nice party, a good start. Let's pray it all goes well."

It took three trips back to her car to get all of the gifts inside the condo. Just as Lainie closed the door to the garage for the last time, the telephone rang. It must be Mitch calling from the store, where he was doing some paperwork, to find out how the shower went. No, it was Jackie's line. Jackie. Lainie grabbed it.

"Hi!"

"Hi. I've been trying to get you all afternoon," Jackie said, sounding a little annoyed. "I wanted you to meet me today, because my son's in town, back from his dad's, and I told him about you, so I thought maybe we could get together."

"Oh, Jackie, I'm sorry. I'd love to meet him," Lainie said.

"Well, maybe another time," Jackie said. It was clear she was feeling hurt. "Where *were* you?"

Lainie was about to burst out with the happy answer, but something made her take a deep breath first so that she would sound calm when she said, "At a baby shower."

"For *our* baby?" Jackie asked.

Lainie bit her lip. "Yes."

"Wow," Jackie said, sounding excited now. "How was it? Who gave it? What presents did you get?"

"My friend Carin gave it at her house. And everything looked so beautiful and pink, and the food was great, and I couldn't believe the things they bought and made. I had no idea there were such cute clothes in the world!"

"Oh yeah," Jackie said wistfully. "Girls' clothes are a million times cuter than the ones they make for boys. Tell me about everything."

Lainie looked over at the dining room table where she had piled the gifts. As she looked at each package, she remembered what was in it and described it in detail to Jackie, who reacted with giggles on the other end of the phone.

"And the chair," Lainie said, high on reliving her perfect afternoon. "The smallest chair you ever saw, painted pink, and in darker pink letters it says across the back Rose Margaret De Nardo. Can you picture that? Her name on the back of a—" Lainie stopped cold. The last name she'd kept secret for so long was now out in the open. She'd blurted it out in a dumb attempt at bragging. Mitch would be furious. Dumb, dumb. How could she be so damned dumb?

"It's okay," Jackie said after a while. "I've known your last name for a long time. Even before I was pregnant. Way back in the beginning of all this, I snooped around in the doctor's office when the nurse went to the can. I even know about your store. In fact, the funny thing is, I realized then that I once applied for a job at the old store in the Valley, upstairs from a restaurant. Mitch interviewed me, only he didn't hire me. I thought I recognized him the day we all met. Pretty funny, huh?"

Lainie felt flushed with embarrassment and discomfort and didn't speak.

"Don't worry, Lainie. The reason I never told you I knew was because it was so important to you two to keep it a secret, and if I told you I knew, you would worry. But you don't have to be afraid, because I'm going to live up to this bargain, believe me."

"I do believe you," Lainie said. But this news pulled away her safety net and made her afraid. "I believe you."

"Good," Jackie said. "That's real good."

21

BY FOUR O'CLOCK Rick was in Doreen's hospital room holding his son, David, in his arms. Somewhere far back in his mind, he knew he'd lost Robert Redford for his film, but it just didn't matter. In fact, to keep Doreen occupied while they readied her for the delivery, he told her the story of his exit from the meeting, and as he did it sounded like something that had happened to someone else, or in a dream. Certainly not earlier that same day, to David Reisman's father. And David was surely the best-looking baby ever born. He had a lot of red hair, and big green eyes, and a cleft chin, and a little dimple just above the left side of his mouth.

Doreen, uncomfortable after the delivery, couldn't stop smiling from where she sat on the bed watching Rick, who was wearing a sterile blue gown, sit on a nearby chair and make gurgling sounds at the baby, lost in the awe he felt for this sleepy infant.

"Is that nurse you hired gonna work out?"

"I hope so. She seemed nice. Annie's her name."

"She looks like Nell Carter."

Rick smiled. "She's been a baby nurse for nearly thirty years, so I guess she knows her Pablum, or whatever they eat."

"They don't eat anything at first. They *drink* formula." She looked out the window when she said, "They gave me a shot that would keep my milk from coming in."

A nurse breezed into the room.

"How are you doing?" she asked Doreen.

"Good as I can be," Doreen answered.

"I need to take the baby just for a few minutes, Mr. Reisman," the nurse said. "Dr. Weil is going to be making rounds, and wants to see the little guy in the nursery. If either of you cares to talk to Dr. Weil, I'll send him over here."

"I do," Rick said, carefully handing the nurse the baby. "In fact, I'll walk down to the nursery."

The nurse placed David in the Plexiglas crib, which she wheeled out the door.

"Would you like to meet the pediatrician?" Rick asked Doreen.

"What's the point? After this week *I'll* never see him again. He doesn't need to get to know me." It was said in a sensible tone, without anger.

"What *are* you going to do?" Rick asked, walking toward the bed. Doreen wouldn't look at him.

"Get a job somewhere in the Valley till I'm feeling like I'm ready to go home."

"You know I'll keep supporting you until you do."

"I know," she said. "Even though you're not supposed to. It'll just be a few months. I promise."

"Take as long as you need. You can make it six months or eight months."

"I don't want to go back looking fat and tired."

"That's how *I* always look," he kidded.

"I'd like to get a tan and a little sun bleach in my hair and tell all the kids at home I was on a long vacation."

"Good idea," he said, and patted the blanket over where her foot was sticking up. "I'll be back in a few minutes."

When he got to the door, she called him.

"Rick!"

He turned.

"I've got to tell you something. I've been thinking a lot about this and I'm worried about leaving the baby with you." He tried not to show his concern.

"Why is that?" he asked.

"For the simple reason that you walked out on Robert Redford. Which proves to me that you are truly and sincerely dumb." Then she laughed that hearty open-mouthed laugh that he had come to love.

Two days later, he arrived at the hospital with the baby nurse to take David home. The law stated that in order to prove abandonment, Doreen couldn't leave the hospital and go to the same place as the baby, so Andrea came to the hospital that morning to take Doreen back to the apartment in the Valley where they'd lived together before the hemorrhaging.

In the parking circle at Cedars, before Annie placed the baby in the infant seat, a pale Doreen kissed the little pink boy, and Rick could see the tension in her face. But when Rick hugged her doughy little body, she lost all control and shook with sadness as the sobs took over.

"I don't know if," she began, then sobbed another sob, "I don't know if I'll miss my baby more . . . or if . . . I'll miss you most of all." She sniffled and he held her very tightly, this little round cherub of a girl. "Promise me one very important thing," she said, looking up at him.

"Name it."

"That you'll read to him. He's used to it now, because he's heard lots of stories. I left all the children's books at your house. They're in the nursery in the closet."

"I'll do it," he said.

"He's all set, Mr. Reisman," Annie said quietly.

Rick, Doreen, Annie, and Andrea all peeked into the backseat at sweet little sleeping David, dressed in a pale yellow going-home suit that Bea Cobb had crocheted for him and mailed from Kansas two weeks before.

"Well, then, I guess we shouldn't keep him waiting," Rick said. He gave Doreen a last hug and helped her into the passenger seat of Andrea's car, and stood next to Annie, the nurse, waving as Andrea drove off into the hot California day.

For weeks he awakened with the first sounds of the stirring baby, then followed Annie from room to room, watching her techniques. He insisted that she, in turn, watch him critically when he fed or burped or bathed or changed David, to make certain he was well versed in every aspect of his son's needs.

And to keep the promise he'd made to Doreen, he held the tiny little bundle of boy on his lap and read from the books Doreen had left for him. *The Runaway Bunny* and *Little Bear*, *Make Way for Ducklings* and *The Little Red Hen*. Sometimes both he and the baby would lie on their backs while Rick held the book above them and the baby looked up at the colorful pictures, kicking his feet and waving his arms wildly.

There were a few other actors interested in the part for which he had lost Robert Redford. There were other projects that were looking promising, and soon his schedule was filled with back-to-back meetings. But he always made sure to return early in the evening to be there in time for David's dinner. Annie would put the little guy in his infant seat on the kitchen table, and Rick would spoon some of the newly permitted rice cereal in, then watch most of it dribble out. When David smiled, Rick would laugh out loud. Many times Rick would be feeding the baby and on the phone at the same time, in order to justify rushing home so early in the day. That way he could do business and tend to the baby simultaneously.

And of course there were his visits to Bobo.

"Look who's a father, I can't believe it," Bobo said. Two of the old man's women friends were with him, gathered around Rick and the little baby in the dining room of the lodge at the Motion Picture Home. Rick held the bottle expertly and watched his son chug down ounce after ounce of Similac.

"I fed you a bottle just like that," Bobo said to Rick, "only you weren't *that* cute." The old man laughed and jabbed Essie Baylis, Harvey Feldman's aunt.

"My Harvey got you that baby?" the old woman asked. Every time Rick looked at Harvey Feldman's old aunt, he couldn't get it out of his head that she'd once been a Busby Berkeley girl. He would try to sort out the features of her face that must have been pretty then, and to imagine her as young, wearing one of those silly costumes.

"That's right," Rick told her.

"He's a genius." The old woman smiled.

"How come you're not married?" Stella Green, Essie's friend, a tiny woman who walked with the help of an aluminum walker, asked Rick. Stella had worked as a secretary to Jack Warner for years.

"Don't get him started," Bobo told her. "He's not married because he's a schmuck."

Stella Green nodded as if she understood. Rick laughed.

"Uncle B., I've got a son now, why do I need a wife?"

"I'll have the soup," Bobo said to a passing waitress, then pulled out a chair and sat. "Essie darling, you want maybe a cup of soup? How about you, Stella?" The two women demurred and said their good-byes to Rick and the baby, who smiled a little smile at them around his bottle, which made both of the women happy.

"Who do you have at home taking care of the little *pisher?*" Bobo asked Rick, peering closely at David. "Every week he gains five pounds. Look at the size of that guy. Hiya, bruiser. Say, Hiya, Uncle Bobo. You can call me Grandpa, you know. I wouldn't charge you extra if you call me Grandpa." Rick loved to watch Bobo with the baby.

"What do you hear from the little girl?" Bobo asked Rick, suddenly serious-faced.

"Not a word. It was part of our agreement. When she's ready to go back to Kansas, she'll call me and I'll send her off. She doesn't want to see David though. Maybe never."

"Who can blame her, the poor kid?" Bobo *tsk*ed. "If I was a younger man, believe me, I'd go and find the son of a bitch who made her that way and go and kill him. Oy, is she a good kid. A tough cookie."

David had drained the entire bottle.

"Give him here," Bobo said. "I'll get a burp out of him. Won't I, slugger?"

Tenderly Bobo placed the baby's stomach against his own shoulder and patted, patted, patted the tiny back with his arthritic hand.

"He might need a little Dr. Brown's celery tonic, which always does it for me."

"And me." Rick laughed.

David didn't need it. His burp filled the room, and the waitress, who had just put the soup bowl down in front of Bobo, applauded the wonderful accomplishment.

"I got a way with kids," Bobo told her. "Not like this guy here. He has a way with broads. But me, kids love me. When this baby gets a little bigger, I'll teach him how to play Go Fish and Spit in the Ocean." David was asleep on Bobo's shoulder. Rick used the camera he always had with him these days to take a picture of the two of them.

On the morning David turned six months old, Andrea called. "I wanted to say happy birthday to David, and to tell you that Doreen is ready to go back to Kansas. She's lost all the weight, a miracle since she's been working at Mrs. Field's Cookies for the last few months. She says she feels good, and would like to leave on Monday. Do you want me to arrange a flight for her?"

Rick and Doreen hadn't spoken since they parted at the hospital. Keeping the silence was their tacit agreement that there were no recriminations for either of them.

"I'll do it. If it's all right with her though, I'd like her to leave on Monday night. There's somewhere I'd like to take her on Monday afternoon."

"I'll tell her. And just in case you were curious, she hasn't said a thing about the baby. Even in the wee hours when we sit around in our pajamas and talk about our deepest feelings. Mostly she's been telling me about her mother and how much she misses her, and how worried she gets about her older married sister, Trish, and her kids. Apparently the brother-in-law Don is kind of a bad guy. Anyway, Doreen's got her strength back and she talks to her mom nearly every day. Sometimes they even pray together on the phone."

"I miss her," Rick said. "And I'll miss her even more knowing she's so far away."

"Me too. She was a breath of fresh air around the strangling bullshit of this town."

Rick got off the freeway at the Vine Street exit and drove south, and when Doreen, who had been silent for nearly the entire ride, saw the marquee of the Merv Griffin Theater, she let out a hoot.

"Oh my God. 'Jeopardy'! Look, there, that's where they do 'Jeopardy.' My 'Jeopardy.' The Alex Trebek 'Jeopardy'!"

Rick made a right turn into the parking lot.

Doreen opened the window of the Mercedes and stuck her face out. "We're stopping. We're parking! Are we going to . . . are the other people in those cars going to see 'Jeopardy'? I can't believe it." Rick's smiling face had the answer.

"We are. Oh, we are. Oh thank you. Thank you."

She was literally bouncing up and down in her seat, and the second they were parked, she threw the car door open and ran ahead of him to the front of the theater. There was a very long line of people waiting, and she ran back to Rick, seized his arm with her tiny hand, and said, "C'mon, let's get in line."

"It's okay," he said, "don't worry," and moved her instead toward the front door where a blue-blazered page was waiting.

"I'm Richard Reisman," he said to the page, feeling Doreen's excitement by the way her hand, which was now holding his, couldn't remain still. "We're guests of Mr. Griffin."

The page pulled a folded sheet of paper out of his inside

jacket pocket, opened it, read something from it, and gestured for Rick and Doreen to follow. They walked through the cool building and then the page pushed open a heavy studio door. Doreen gasped when there in real life was the familiar set she'd seen on television for so long. There were two seats closed off by masking-tape ribbons right in the center of the first row. As the page led Doreen and Rick toward them, Rick could hear Doreen making tiny sounds of joy in her throat.

The page removed the masking tape so they could be seated and said, "We'll be shooting two shows while you're here, and then three more later this afternoon."

"Two shows!" Doreen said excitedly, then elbowed Rick. "We get to see two." As the page turned to go she said, "Um, sir," and he turned back to look at her.

"Is Mr. Trebek here?"

"Oh sure."

Doreen gave out with a little yelp of pleasure. Within seconds of the page's departure, the studio doors opened and hordes of people flooded in to be seated. The studio became a buzzing hive of activity and excitement, all of it reflected in Doreen's eyes. The camera crew assembled, and an announcer named Johnny Gilbert did the warm-up, but it wasn't until the entrance of Alex Trebek when Doreen moved to the edge of her seat, never taking her eyes from him, her face lit with excitement.

When Trebek moved toward the audience, she pounded Rick's arm. "A sheet of paper. Ohh, why didn't I bring a sheet of—" Rick pulled a piece of blank white *From the desk of Rick Reisman* notepaper from one of his pockets and a pen from another and handed it to Doreen, who had already leapt to her feet and was thrusting the paper into the face of the handsome Alex Trebek, who smiled at her.

"Please," she said. "Can you make it out to 'Bea Cobb, who is the best mother in the world'?"

"If I say that, *my* mom will get jealous," Trebek joked.

"Ahh, she won't find out," Doreen said, and then gave him a smile with just a little hint of flirtatiousness.

"You're right," he said, handed her back the signed paper, and was on to the next fan, as Doreen clutched the paper to her heart and choked out a thank you.

"My mom's gonna freak out," she said, sitting back down in her seat, alternately looking at the message then clutching it against her chest. She held it that way during the entire taping and in the car on the way back to Andrea's. When it was time to say good-bye, it amazed him that she hadn't said one word about the baby.

"Call me collect if you ever need anything," he said.

"Maybe just a picture of David. For Christmas?" she said and asked at the same time.

"You've got it," he promised.

22

LAINIE felt herself being awakened by the sensation of Mitch fondling her, waking her with his hands all over her body, his tongue moving slowly down her body. She must have fallen asleep while they were watching television in bed, and Mitch had stayed awake. Maybe something on television had made him feel sexy. No, Mitch always felt sexy. Mitch, delicious Mitch, wanting her.

"Mmm, baby," he said. "I love you. How I love you, my baby—"

And the phone rang.

"The machine . . ." Mitch said. "The machine will get it." He was inside her now and very hot. "The machine'll pick up," he managed.

The phone rang again, and again. Maybe it was . . .

"Jackie's phone," Mitch said, finishing Lainie's thought.

But then the ringing stopped. Mitch sighed with relief and then he was kissing her and pressing his hard chest into her breasts and then he was up on his knees, pulling her legs up on either side of him, spreading her legs high around him, pushing deeper into her so she could feel him all the way at the small of her back. "Oh, God, Mitch, Oh, God . . ." But the phone rang again and broke the moment, and a frustrated Mitch collapsed on her and reached out for the receiver.

"Oh, God, Mitch," Lainie heard a voice on the phone cry. "Oh, God."

"Jackie."

"I'm in labor, and I hurt so much. Oh, God."

"Did you call the doctor?" Mitch asked, climbing off Lainie and sitting at the edge of the bed to talk to Jackie. Lainie could see how nervous he was.

"Yeah, yeah, and Chuck Meyer too. They're both meeting me at the hospital."

"What about the car and driver?" Mitch was holding the phone loosely to his ear, and Lainie, whose pelvis was still ringing from the abruptness of his wrenching himself out of her, could hear every word Jackie said.

"Did you call for the car?"

"It's on the way, but Mitch, please, I know I said I wouldn't do this, only I forgot how much this hurts and how scary it is to do it alone, and I don't have anybody else to call. I know we decided you shouldn't be there, but I'm begging you. You've got to do this, please say you'll meet me at the hospital. I mean, Jesus Christ, it's *your* baby too. I can't do this with some lawyer I hardly know and a limo driver I never saw before. I need you there."

"I'll be there," Mitch said. "Stay calm, Jackie. Will you? Promise me you will?" he asked her in a very gentle voice.

Then he was throwing on his clothes. Lainie watched him numbly. Waiting for him to say, "C'mon, let's go." But a minute later, he had his car keys in his hand and was shoving his wallet into his pants pocket.

"Mitch . . ." Why hadn't Jackie asked for *her?* Maybe she thought that Lainie would be able to say no to her, but at this stage Mitch would do whatever she asked. "Mitch!" Mitch stopped and looked at his wife, then put his hand to his face as if to say, What in God's name am I doing? It hadn't even occurred to him that she should be coming along. He looked embarrassed and more flustered than before.

"Oh, baby," Mitch said. "I'm sorry. I'm out of my mind with worry here. I know this wasn't in the plan we made, but I think I should drive out there. She sounds panicked. I probably won't get there until it's over, but what if it's a long labor? What if decisions have to be made about the baby?"

"What would you like *me* to do?" she asked.

"What do you *want* to do?" he asked. He was standing nervously at the bedroom door, looking as if he wished she'd say, "Call me when it's over," so he could leave, but she didn't. She jumped out of bed and opened her closet.

"Start the car," she said. "I'm coming with you." She heard him run down the stairs and out to the garage as she pulled out various choices in her closet, hating this situation. What to wear? Who cares, she thought, pulling on a pair of jeans and a big cotton sweater. Jackie was the one everyone would be looking at. Not her.

By the time she had her clothes on, she heard Mitch honking the horn. There wasn't time for makeup, or even to brush her teeth. She rushed out into the chilly night and got into the car. They drove wordlessly down Ventura Boulevard toward the freeway. A digital clock above a bank told her that the time was 1:10. There was very little traffic. Lainie felt stung, pushed around, angry that Jackie hadn't kept their bargain. The friendship during the pregnancy had been a good thing, but she had specifically told Mitch she couldn't bear to watch him helping Jackie through the delivery.

They had put it into a contract they'd worked out with Chuck Meyer, the lawyer. They would come to the hospital after the baby was safely in the hospital nursery. But if Mitch continued to drive as fast as he was now and the labor was long, they would be there to watch the delivery. She looked out the window and reminded herself that Jackie had very little in her life, and that was why she had broken her word about calling them. Jackie knew that after the baby was born there would be no more relationship with Mitch and Lainie, so for one more night she needed them there. One more night, and maybe a day or two in the hospital. Then they would have their baby, and that's what mattered.

Sliding doors opened. Lainie followed far behind as Mitch raced through them and down the hall through the hospital. Around corners, and through doors and down ramps, past brightly lit nurses' stations and open doors to patients' rooms, through which Lainie caught glimpses of people connected to IVs.

By the time she got to the labor room, Mitch, and the limo driver, and a nurse, and Chuck Meyer, the lawyer, surrounded Jackie, who lay on the bed connected to an IV, holding court. Lainie stood quietly in the doorway. It wasn't until the limo driver had said good-bye and wished her well and Chuck Meyer stepped out to call his wife that Jackie looked past Mitch, who was brushing a curl out of her face, and noticed Lainie standing quietly in the corner.

"Hey! Lainie!" she said. "Isn't this great? We're having a baby."

"Great," Lainie said. Good God, it was true, she thought. It was like that commercial she remembered from years ago, for oven cleaner that you sprayed on and then left to do the work. A woman in the commercial was playing tennis, and when she hit a winning point over the net, she looked at the camera and said, "I'm cleaning my oven!" Lainie was standing in a labor room in her jeans, thinking, I'm having a baby.

Within minutes Jackie was in hard labor. Mitch and a nurse stood on either side of the bed while Lainie remained quietly in the corner. She could tell by the way the back of his La Coste shirt stuck to him that Mitch was sweating. Soon, with an entrance worthy of a star, the doctor swept into the room, made some comment about having to get out of his girlfriend's nice warm bed, and examined Jackie's pelvis. The anesthesiologist was a woman, and a moment later she came in, turned Jackie on her side, and gave her an epidural. After that, everything went fast. Somebody handed out sterile masks and gowns and boots and caps; the gurney was rushed into the delivery room. And again, Lainie, who was now dressed from head to toe in blue cotton like the others, stood alone in the corner of the tiled room.

She watched the group of people gathered around the table where Jackie lay, chattering nervously about something, and all she could see was their eyes. It took her a few minutes to sort them out now, and when she did, she realized it was Mitch who stood by the head of the table, holding Jackie's hand.

I'm not ready for this, Lainie thought. Her whole body was pulsing with panic. She didn't want to look, was afraid to see the blood, and now all she could think about was her own surgery. That day when they wheeled her into the operating room. She remembered that as she was falling into the drugged sleep, she already knew what the outcome would be. That her uterus would be removed, that her ovaries would be removed, and that she would never, never . . .

The sudden cry of the baby as it burst forth from Jackie and into the doctor's hands brought Lainie back. "Here comes your girl . . . girl . . . a little girl," she heard voices say. And she watched as the tiny bloody baby was gently handed to Mitch, who Lainie could see was crying as he looked tenderly down at the tiny thing. She felt the nurse's arms strong around her back, moving her toward the center of the room so she could watch as Mitch handed the baby to Jackie. It was a tiny, pink little girl who looked like Jackie.

Jackie looked long at the baby, pursed her lips hard and closed her eyes as she handed the squealing baby to Lainie. The squeals were like sounds from a puppy. While Lainie stared at the baby's tiny face, the doctor put a small bulb in the nostrils and extracted some mucus or blood with a sucking noise. Lainie felt Mitch next to her and the doctor sliding the baby out of her hands to care for it.

"Thank you, oh thank you," Lainie said, half laughing, half crying, leaning over to hug the exhausted Jackie. "Dear God, how can I ever thank you? What could I ever do for you or give you that could possibly mean as much as that precious little life you gave to me and Mitch? Oh, thank you,"she said again, and while she held Jackie in her embrace she could smell the very distinct odor of Shalimar, and feel Jackie's sweaty face against her own cool one.

"S'cuse me, please," someone said, brushing Lainie out of the way. With a tug of the gurney they wheeled Jackie off to the recovery room.

Mitch put his arms around her. She turned and held him tightly, and they both cried. Neither of them was able to speak through the emotions. Through her tears, Lainie saw nurses, who were probably used to seeing people behave like this in the maternity ward, smile knowingly as they passed. Eventually, silently, Lainie and Mitch walked, arms around each other, out of the hospital to the parking lot.

The morning light found them in their own bed, locked in each other's arms. When Lainie opened her eyes, she saw that Mitch's were already open, looking at her happily.

"We have a baby," he said.

She grinned. "Yes, we do." They kissed and held each other.

"Let's go see her," Mitch said.

"You got it."

They showered and dressed quickly, all the while chatting about the details of the night before.

"I was a basket case, wasn't I?" Mitch asked.

"You were perfect."

"And it wasn't so bad for you. Was it?" he asked her earnestly. "I mean, that it happened that way. I mean, that we ended up at the hospital last night, instead of just showing up the next day at visiting hours?"

"Honey," Lainie said, "we have our baby. That's what counts. Did the doctor say when she can come home?"

"We'll find out today," Mitch told her.

Jackie's hospital room was filled with the scent of flowers from the huge bouquet that displayed a card from the lawyer's offices. She was in the bathroom when they arrived. Mitch thought they should stop into the hospital room and invite Jackie to walk down to the nursery with them, "just as a final nice gesture."

Lainie looked at the bedside table where some of Jackie's cosmetics sat. Lipstick, blusher, and the big round bottle of Shalimar. When the bathroom door opened and Jackie came out, Lainie was surprised at how well she looked. Jackie let out a little yelp when she saw them.

"That baby is so beautiful. Have you seen her today?" she asked.

"No, we'll go together," Mitch told her. Linking arms, the three of them walked down the hall, Jackie scuffling in her slide-on slippers.

"There," she said, pointing to a crib in the back that bore a sign saying O'MALLEY: GIRL. The baby, that beautiful baby, was surely the most beautiful in the nursery.

"Jesus," Mitch said, "she's something special. None of those funny little marks they usually have. God in heaven. This is truly a miracle."

Lainie's heart felt full of hope. It had worked. Mitch's plan had worked. Despite her fears and pain and doubt, at last she would be taking home a baby. She was lost in her own thoughts about the baby's homecoming when she heard Jackie say, "Well, we did it, kiddo. We goddamned went and did it."

"That's the truth," Mitch said with a triumphant voice. "We sure as hell did." When Lainie turned and saw the look that passed between them, Jackie's so fulfilled and Mitch's so potent, it felt as if someone had kicked her in the chest. The three of them were celebrating the birth of their baby. The father; the mother; and the surrogate, the substitute. But, Lainie thought, there's no doubt that the substitute mother is me.

23

CLINT EASTWOOD was now interested in the part for which Rick had lost Robert Redford, and Rick was flying to Carmel to meet with him several times a week. But he always tried to get back in time to be with David, even if it was for just a short while every evening. The beautiful fair-skinned little boy brought a lightness to Rick's world that shifted the way he looked at every other aspect of his life. He was sitting at the kitchen table eating a late supper one night and making some notes on a script at the same time when Annie, the baby nurse, came in.

"Mr. Reisman, he's asleep. It's ten o'clock and I just talked on the phone to my sister. She's feeling kind of poorly, and I was wondering if I could drive over to her place down by Western Avenue and take care of her? I'll come back here real early in the morning. Little David just finished a full bottle and he'll probably stay down until I get back in the morning. But if he doesn't, I left you some sterilized nipples, in case he wakes up and is hungry; all you've got to do is unscrew the top of one of the Similac bottles, put the nipple on, and give it to him. You know how to do that."

"You bet I do, Annie. You go to your sister's. David and his old man will be just fine."

"Oh, and his passy. He's chewing on his little pacifier now. He loves that thing, only sometimes he loses it and starts in to cry. All you have to do usually is put it right back in his mouth and he goes right back to sleep. If he's really crying hard, sometimes it takes two or three tries before he takes it back in . . . so be patient now. Okay?"

"Okay," Rick said. He was proud of himself for finding this terrific woman to take care of his son. He heard her bustling around, getting ready to go and spend the night with her sister, and before she left she asked, "You want me to leave my sister's telephone number?"

"Not necessary," Rick told her and waved a little good-bye just before she closed the front door behind her.

At eleven-thirty he had just turned on "Nightline" when the front doorbell rang. Jesus, it might wake the baby. He hurried out to see who it could be. A vision. The young secretary from the production office next to his at Universal. Long dark hair down to her waist, huge eyes, off-the-shoulder black dress.

"I was at a dinner party in the neighborhood," she told him before he could say a word. "And I got your address from this copy of *Vanity Fair* I borrowed from your office one day. It has this address on it. So when I realized this was where you lived, I figured I'd come by and hope you were alone."

"I'm alone," he said.

"So . . . can I come in?"

He opened the door all the way. Just because he had a kid now didn't mean he was going to give up getting laid.

"Boy, this place is gorgeous," she said, handing him his copy of *Vanity Fair* and circling the living room.

"So are you," Rick said.

She giggled. "You are so cute," she told him, and then stopped to look at him. "And I've seen every one of your movies."

"And which one was your favorite?" he asked, moving closer. Very close. In a moment she was against him, wiggling out of the top of her dress, and then her hands were on his belt, and then they moved to undo his trousers, and just as her dress hit the floor, David let out a shriek.

"What was that?" the astonished girl asked.

"My son."

"You have a son? A baby? Do you have a wife? Oh, geez, I thought you were single."

"I am," Rick said, and he flew into the baby's room, zipping the zipper the girl had—Christ, he didn't even know her name, but the girl had unzipped his pants. Now he grabbed the fallen pacifier from next to David's little squealing face and gently placed it into the baby's mouth, hoping the touch of it next to the little tiny tongue would quiet him. But David wouldn't take the pacifier in, and continued to scream.

"Take the passy, baby. Here's your nice passy, Davey, Daddy's giving you your wonderful pacifier and . . ."

"Nyaahhhhh." David spit it out again.

"Maybe you should dip it in some honey," he heard the girl say. She was standing naked, naked and perfect in the doorway of the baby's room. "That's what my parents used to do for me," she told him. "Why don't I go and see if I can find some for you?"

You know you're about to make it with a very young girl when she still remembers what her parents put on her pacifier, Rick thought as he stood by the crib patting the wailing baby's back. She returned in a minute with the honey jar. Rick opened it, dipped the pacifier into the honey, then leaned over the crib and placed the pacifier in the baby's mouth.

"Mmmmm-mmmm-mmm," David said, sucking away. "Mmmm," and within minutes he was asleep.

The naked girl was against Rick now. "Let's dip this in some honey too," she said, and slowly moved down onto the floor of the baby's room, taking Rick along with her.

"I'm worried about his little BMs," Annie told Rick one morning at breakfast.

"His what?" He was gulping down some coffee, rushing to catch an early flight to Monterey to meet with Clint in Carmel.

"Little David. He's not having any."

"Not having any what, Annie?"

"Bowel movements."

"Not any?"

"Nope."

"Since when?"

"A few days."

"The pediatrician. Let's call Dr. Weil right now," he said, looking at his watch. It was seven-thirty in the morning. No doctors were in at seven-thirty in the morning, but surely the answering service would track the doctor down, call him at home.

"He's out of town," the answering-service operator said, "but Dr. Solway's on call."

"Then get *him* on the line for me," Rick ordered.

"I'll have to call you back, sir," the operator told him. He gave her the number. David, who usually waved his arms and made gurgling noises, lay listless in Annie's arms.

"The first couple of days, I figured he was just constipated like we all get sometimes, only now, he's not right in himself, and I started to think there's more to it than that." She looked worried.

"Ever seen this kind of thing before?" Rick asked her.

"Not that I can remember right off," Annie answered. "Constipation, yes. But not this bad." The phone rang.

"Mr. Reisman." Must be the woman from the answering service.

"Don't tell me you can't reach the doctor," he snapped.

"This *is* the doctor, Mr. Reisman," the woman's voice said. "I'm Dr. Solway, Dr. Weil's associate. How can I help you?"

A woman. "My son, he's nine months old. He's been constipated for . . . how long?" he asked Annie.

"At least five days," she said.

"Five days," he told the doctor. "And he seems to have no energy. Very quiet. Weak."

"Bring him right in," the doctor said. "I'll meet you at our offices as soon as you can get there."

Good-bye, eight-fifteen flight. Good-bye, Clint Eastwood.

"We're on our way," Rick told her.

Annie sat in the backseat, holding David's tiny hand in hers. From the car phone Rick called Andrea at home and told her to call Clint Eastwood and cancel the meeting.

"You'll be okay, little honey. You'll be all right," Annie crooned to the silent baby.

In the elevator in the doctor's building, Rick looked at the limp baby dozing on Annie's shoulder, and panic filled him. What *was* this? What if it was serious, crippling, a terrible disease that would last forever? A lifetime of taking him to doctors and specialists, and him not being okay? No. It was nothing.

The tall, black-haired, blue-eyed woman, Lee Solway, took the baby in her arms and carefully undressed him. She had quickly sized up Rick and Annie, and knew right away it was Annie she should ask all the questions about the baby's habits and schedule and food intake. Annie answered the questions carefully and thoughtfully. Rick sat nervously, watching the doctor examine and probe the baby, who now lay passively and all too quietly.

"Have you noticed any decrease in the strength with which he's been sucking on the bottle?"

"Come to think of it, I have," Annie said. "But I just put it down to his not being hungry."

"Are you giving him solids?"

"Yes. Dr. Weil started him on rice cereal last month."

"Does he have the rice cereal plain?"

"I mix in some formula."

"Do you only introduce the foods Dr. Weil tells you he's permitted to eat?"

"That's all I give him. And Cora, too. She's the woman who takes over on the day and a half when I take off."

"So there would have been no reason for you to have ever given this baby honey?" The doctor held on to David's tiny body with her right hand, and turned to look at Annie.

"No, ma'am."

Rick stood. He'd been only half listening to the questions because he knew he didn't know the answers to them, but the word *honey* caught him by surprise, and he froze.

"What's wrong with honey? *I* gave him honey last week. A little on the pacifier to get him to take it."

The doctor looked at Rick. "Well, I'm afraid that what's going on with him now may have to do with the honey. I want to put him right into Children's Hospital this morning to be certain, and hope that he's not so constipated that I can't get some stool samples. I think he has infant botulism. The constipation and the decreased muscle strength all make it look like that to me."

"From honey?"

"The *Clostridium botulinum* organism has been isolated in honey specimens that have been fed to infants and make them sick. Babies under a year are susceptible. I don't want to scare you, but there are theories now that undetected cases of infant botulism may be behind sudden infant death syndrome. His breathing is very shallow too. I'm going to call an ambulance."

Rick had a ringing in his ears. This couldn't be happening. The doctor went into her office while Annie dressed David, who cried a faint bleating cry, and Rick could hear the doctor making arrangements for an ambulance to come to the medical building.

"We're off," she said when she emerged, and brushed past them. "They'll meet us downstairs in the parking lot."

Honey. The crushing reason Rick had given the baby honey suddenly slammed him in the face. To get fucked. To shut my son up so I could do it on the floor of his room with that girl who showed up at my door and dropped her dress. Christ,

God is killing my son to punish me for being the lowest, most despicable human on the face of the earth. Please don't make this baby suffer for my vanity and excess and weakness.

Blindly, guilt-ridden, aching with the horror that tore at him, he got into the ambulance with Annie and the baby and the doctor, and as it lurched out into the street, he put his face in his hands and felt deep shame and despair.

24

FOR A WHILE Lainie's negative feelings slipped away. Just waking up and knowing there was a new baby in the next room gave every morning the excitement of Christmas. The sweet powdery smell that filled the nursery, the silky feel of baby Rose's fine hair, the luxurious softness of little crevices under that teeny chin elated Lainie. She would lift the warm little cherub out of her bassinet and place her tenderly in the middle of the big bed next to Mitch, who in his sleep would reach over and fondle the baby's foot. And Lainie would overflow with happiness.

Her family. At last. She wouldn't let her insecurities mar her joy. Not even the first several months of walking the floor all night with her scrunch-faced colicky daughter. And when Mitch held the tiny girl in his arms, he was transformed. All the pressures of the business day, the constant worried look he had in his eyes when he was in the store disappeared at home. He became so relaxed and unwound when he held the baby that more than once when he sat in the rocker to feed her, after she fell asleep he did too.

The joy, the bliss of watching each new developmental step occur seemed to bring Lainie and Mitch even closer every day.

Lainie called the store every afternoon to report in about the success of every feeding, every ounce of weight gain, and Mitch listened with rapt attention.

"Hold on, baby," Mitch said to her one afternoon. She heard him click off. He was probably going to pick up the phone in the back office so he could talk to her more freely than he could from the front counter.

"Listen," he said when he picked up again. "I invited my sisters and their families over for dinner next week."

Lainie was silent. She knew there was an estrangement between Mitch and his sisters. That once she came into his life they stopped being as close as they were when he was single. Sometimes she felt as if the reason the breach existed was that she and Mitch didn't have children.

"Maybe now that we have a kid too, things will get better with all of us," Mitch said, expressing Lainie's thoughts out loud.

"Maybe."

"Hey, you know what my mother used to say when I fought with one of them?"

"You told me," Lainie answered. "She always said, 'Blood is thicker than water.'"

"They're dumb sometimes, and so are their husbands, but the truth is that besides you and my little honeybunch of a girl, they're all I've got. I need to make the effort. So I want to make sure you don't mind if they all come for dinner with their kids this Saturday."

"Sure, honey. You know I'm crazy about the kids. And they'll get such a kick out of seeing their new cousin."

"I love you, Laine," Mitch said. "There'll never be anybody like you." And he hung up.

Lainie put the phone down in its cradle and was reaching for a pencil and paper to start making a grocery list for next Saturday when something made her feel oddly chilled. Maybe it was the sentiment Mitch had just expressed. The way he'd said it sounded awkward, as if someone had walked into the office as he was saying it. His voice sounded strained and forced.

Crazy. Her exhaustion because of the baby's sleeping problems was affecting her moods and making her too sensitive. Just the other day she had snapped at Carin. Dear Carin, who was so gentle that when she came upon a spider in the ladies' room at Panache, she ushered it into a paper cup and set it free outside rather than kill it.

"I'm sure happy you haven't heard from that woman again," she said to Lainie, "because I always had this fear she'd show up one day and want the baby back."

Lainie glared at her. "That was never an issue or a question for Mitch or me, so worry about your own problems, will you?" Carin had apologized repeatedly for the rest of that day.

Lainie would try hard to get herself together for Saturday's dinner and do her best to be good with Mitch's family. She would have to. Aside from her mother, the three De Nardo sisters and their husbands and children were baby Rose's only family. And like Lainie, Rose would be an only child, so whatever the price of giving her a relationship with her cousins, it was worth it.

Mitch loved wearing his Bar-B-Q apron and standing over the hamburgers, turning them gently again and again until they were perfect. The children chased one another around the tiny garden outside the sliding doors, and Lainie thought about how nice it would be when she and Mitch found a house in the Valley with a big yard. Then the children could play running games outside, and by then Rose Margaret would join them.

"You know what?" Betsy's husband, Hank, asked, looking closely at his new niece. "The weird thing is, she doesn't look one bit like Mitch, and she *does* look like Lainie. Isn't that funny? That's really funny."

Except for the times when they had to get up in order to separate fighting kids, Kitty and Mary Catherine stayed close together, each of them nursing a glass of white wine Lainie had served them. They didn't include her in their conversation until finally she moved over to where they sat, holding baby Rose over her shoulder.

"Is she sleeping any better? Mitch mentioned that she was having some problems," Kitty said.

Infant small talk. Lainie realized that that's what it was, but appreciated that at least something was being addressed to her.

"Not yet," she answered. "She still wakes up once or twice a night. How old were yours before they really were on a schedule?" She hoped that by asking advice from them, she could bridge the gap and warm them up a little bit.

"About nine years," Mary Catherine said, obviously joking.

"I swear, my Chrissy still wakes up at three or four A.M., but some babies start sleeping through by six months," she added. "It'll go by real fast."

"Who wants cheese on their burgers?" Mitch called out.

"Me!" some of the kids hollered.

"Not me," Lainie said, patting baby Rose's tiny bottom, trying to be true to a diet. The irregular schedule of the baby's life and feedings and the catch-as-catch-can meals she was stuffing in when she had time had put twelve pounds on her in two months. Mitch said he loved it because it gave him "more to grab."

"Don't tell me *you're* on a diet," Betsy said.

"Just being careful," Lainie answered.

"Oh right, you have to because of your sugar problem. Right?"

"Burgers coming up," Mitch hollered. "Lainie, where's the plates?"

"Why don't I hold her while you help Mitch?" Kitty offered.

Lainie's first instinct was to say no, but the whole purpose of the get-together was to be good to one another, so she handed the baby over to her sister-in-law and went to get the table organized. Crazy. Maybe her frustration with the added weight was making everything everyone said sound so awful to her. She would have to be more tolerant.

At the dinner table everyone dug into the food and Rose fell asleep on Mitch's shoulder, and soon everyone was laughing at stories about Grandma Rose and Grandpa Mario De Nardo. Lainie felt glad that she had agreed to have the family come to dinner. For the most part they were harmless, just not too smart. And as long as she didn't let them get to her, Mitch could have what he needed with them.

By dessert, all the adults had consumed a little too much red wine. Except Lainie, who found herself in the position of being the only sober adult at the party, and she noticed that the others were starting to get even more tipsy. She was carrying a platter of cookies to the table when Mitch stood, tapped on his wineglass with a spoon, and still holding the baby, raised the wineglass and said, "I'm going to make a toast now. With all my gratitude, to the woman I love dearly and passionately. My sweetheart and Rose's mommy."

There was a moment when there was no sound but the crickets of summer, until Hank blurted out, "Yeah, well, now you better make a toast to Lainie."

The shock of the joke made everyone freeze, except for Lainie, who was so stunned by it that her first impulse was to laugh, and when she laughed, all of the others did too. The laughter woke the baby, who cried, and Lainie was relieved to have an excuse to walk away. She put the cookies she'd been carrying down on the table, and hurried into the kitchen to get a bottle of formula.

She stood in front of the open refrigerator, staring in, forgetting for a moment why she was there. When she remembered and pulled out a bottle, she dropped it, grabbed a dishtowel, and stooped to wipe up the broken glass and spilled formula. She could hear the baby outside crying, so she grabbed another bottle, which she took out and handed to Mitch.

By now, the others had forgotten the bad joke and were back to exchanging stories about the De Nardo parents. The evening ended with promises of "next time at our house" and "the kids

loved seeing you," and the sisters and their husbands were finally gone.

"Thank you, baby," Mitch said, hugging Lainie, with little
Rose between them.

When Rose was a little over a year old, Lainie started back
to school, three nights a week. Mitch was thrilled to come
home early on those nights to feed and care for the baby,
letting the saleswomen in the store take over some of his
responsibilities. Many nights he would take Rose to Sherman
Oaks Park.

Lainie loved school. She would do most of her studying late
at night after Mitch and the baby had fallen asleep, but some
days she would sit outside on her back patio while the baby
played in the playpen or slept in the pram. Today she was
particularly exhausted after a long night of walking the floor
with a fretting baby, and her weight was high, and when she
caught sight of herself in the mirror, she found herself thinking
how much she looked like Jackie. But as the year had gone along
and she became increasingly involved in her schoolwork, getting
her studying done was far more important than wasting time in
beauty parlors, or at health clubs and all the other places she
would have to go to work on looking good.

The baby was asleep in the pram that morning and it was
gloriously sunny and clear that day, so Lainie decided to put a
few of her textbooks in the bottom of the big blue carriage and
sit outside. While her daughter napped in the fresh air, she
would read a few chapters. She was just out the door when she
saw Mrs. Lancer, the older woman who lived next door, in her
yard.

"Oh, is that the little baby?" the woman asked, hurrying over
to the fence to look in the pram. "Isn't she darling? And you.
You are so wonderful. The way you manage to take such good
care of her, and you go to school, don't you? I mean forgive me, it's none of my business, but a few times I've seen you

with all your books on your way out the door. And I just assumed . . ."

"I'm at Northridge in the English department," Lainie said, loving the sound of it.

"And yet you still have time to look so gorgeous," the woman said. Gorgeous. Lainie hadn't felt gorgeous in a long time. "Now and then when my husband and I go walking around the track at Sherman Oaks Park, I see you there with your husband and the baby. You always look so stunning, all dressed up to kill. I say to my husband, How does she do it? I guess at your age you can do everything."

The woman continued to talk, but Lainie wasn't listening. Sherman Oaks Park, she was thinking. She hadn't been there in more than a year. Mitch went there with the baby all the time, but Lainie was never with them. Her neighbor must have seen some other couple there and thought it was the two of them. All dressed up to kill. So gorgeous, she had said. Well that made Lainie certain the woman wasn't talking about *her*. She felt like an overweight mess.

After a while the woman said good-bye, and Lainie wheeled the pram over to the little patio area, took out her books, and sat for a long time. Finally she realized she hadn't read a word. She was staring at the page thinking again about Sherman Oaks Park. Maybe while the baby was still asleep she would use the quiet time to do the laundry. She wasn't getting any studying done anyway. So she put the books back at the bottom of the pram, on top of the shiny pink comforter, and wheeled the pram back into the house.

"Right back," she whispered to the sleeping little girl, then hurried upstairs to her bathroom hamper to get her dirty clothes and Mitch's so she could take them down to the laundry room. Through the open bathroom window she could see the beautiful sunny day outside, and she smiled. Mitch, my Mitch, she thought. After all we've been through, at last our world is in place.

Maybe next year instead of just taking random classes, I'll

start trying for a degree. And if business at Panache keeps up the way it's been going, pretty soon we can hire a nanny. Then I'll be like those women I always read about in magazines who have it all. Husbands and babies and careers, and . . . She had been hugging Mitch's shirt to her chest through all of those thoughts, but now when she held it up to her face, her euphoria was drained in a wave of shock. The smell on the shirt, all over her husband's shirt, was very familiar to her. It was the smell of Shalimar.

In Barbara Singer's office she sat forlornly across from the pretty dark-haired psychologist, and couldn't believe she was saying the words, "I think my husband is cheating on me with the surrogate." It sounded so absurd that after she said it, she let out a little laugh, then stopped to catch her breath so she wouldn't cry. "Oh, God," she said, and then told Barbara everything.

After she'd heard it all Barbara asked, "Lainie, let's talk about what you're afraid will happen if you confront Mitch."

"That maybe he's not seeing Jackie and he'll laugh at me. We own a very chic women's store. Every day women come in and give him a big hello hug, and one of them could have been wearing Shalimar."

"And what about what the lady from next door said?"

"She's kind of scatterbrained. She could have seen anybody in the park and mistaken them for Mitch and me. I mean, I'd feel like a fool if I accused him and I was wrong."

"And how would you feel if you were right?" Barbara asked, looking into her eyes.

Lainie looked away, then answered, "I couldn't survive the pain."

"Lainie," Barbara said. "You're a very strong woman. You stood up to cancer, and won. Can this possibly be as bad as that?"

"Worse," Lainie said. "I love this man. He's my whole life. I only said yes to this whole thing because I was afraid that

Mitch wanted his genetic child so badly that if I said no . . ."
The rest of the words were too difficult to get out.

"That he would leave you?" Barbara asked.

Lainie was crying and could only nod. "People are passing
AIDS around. I don't know what Jackie's life is like now. Or
what it was *ever* like, for that matter, regarding men. But if my
husband really is cheating on me, he could be killing me." Barbara didn't comment. "I saw your ad about the group in *L.A.
Parent*. I was so excited because it looked like something for us.
I was going to ask Mitch to come to it with me so we could
discuss what we were going to tell Rose about her birth when
she got older. Now I'm here to tell you that I need help about
something more urgent than that. I'm so afraid."

"Bring Mitch to the group," Barbara said. "Maybe the group
will give you the courage to confront him, because you can't go
on much longer harboring these fears."

"I can't," Lainie wept. "You're right. I can't."

25

THE PEDIATRIC INTENSIVE CARE unit is a place you never want to be. Many of the patients who are being cared for there come directly from the rooms in which they were born, and when they finally leave in many cases it will be because they're dead. The parents who sit the vigil beside the cribs share a silent terror that they may be the next to go home. Without their baby.

When Rick, Annie, the by now barely conscious David, and the stern-faced Dr. Solway arrived at the hospital, they went directly to pediatric ICU. There were four other cribs besides the one in which they now placed the limp and silent David. Rick turned away while a nurse inserted an IV tube into the baby's arm, and when he turned back he saw the doctor placing a tiny mask over the baby's expressionless face. The mask, Dr. Solway told Rick and Annie, who hugged herself as if she was chilled, measured the level of David's breathing to determine whether or not he had to be put on a respirator. He did.

For now, the IV would be used to give him drugs, in order to make tolerable the process they would have to do immediately, which was called intubating. Intubating, Dr. Solway explained carefully, as if she were teaching a class, meant that the doctors would insert a tube into David's nostril which would pass down into his lungs. The tube would be connected to a respirator, which would breathe for him. Rick and Annie were asked to leave the room during the intubation.

While they stood in the hall, Rick, trying not to picture what the doctors were doing, looked at the big black woman who still hugged herself with her chubby arms, over one of which hung the little blue sweater in which she had dressed David a few hours earlier. What was she thinking, he wondered. The truth? That because Rick was such a venal whoremonger, he had made his own son severely ill? Maybe even killed him? Annie must know *exactly* what had happened.

She had come back early that morning, the morning after Rick gave the baby the honey on the pacifier. Come back early, as promised, from her sister's. The young secretary's car was probably parked in the driveway, where Annie usually parked. So Annie probably patiently found another parking place on the street, walked in the front door, and began to straighten up the living room, finding the girl's black dress still lying there in a heap.

And in the baby's room, which is where she undoubtedly went next . . . Rick's clothes. Everywhere. She must have taken those to the dirty-clothes hamper and then, with the baby on her hip, gone into the kitchen to do Rick's dinner dishes from the night before, to get the baby's breakfast. Maybe she was feeding David when the girl walked nude from Rick's room, where she and Rick had spent what was left of the night and themselves, leaving Rick in an unconscious sleep. The girl could have even greeted Annie and made a fuss over the baby after she slid back into her dress, picked up her shoes, and left.

Twenty silent minutes went by until the doctor called Rick and Annie back. David was asleep now. Dr. Solway stood next to his crib. Annie let out a low moan when she saw what had been done to the baby, and Rick held on to the back of a chair for support.

"The nasotracheal tube is connected to the respirator, which

you can hear is now breathing for him. Those are cardiac monitor leads, and of course that's the intravenous line. We'll continue to ventilate him mechanically and feed him this way for
the next several days. After that, hopefully, he'll begin to come
around. At least to be able to be fed eventually through a naso-
gastric feeding tube."

Rick was aware of a woman standing near the crib farthest
from them. She was crying quietly as she looked at what had
to be her own very ill baby.

"What medication will you give him?" Rick asked the doctor.

"We won't. In adults we can use an antitoxin, in infants the
only treatment is to support them until they get better on their
own. I'm sorry to tell you that there is nothing else to do now
but literally sit this out. If you like, I can arrange a room for
you to live in down the hall, so that you can be with him, or
you can commute from home. I suggest one or both of you do
the former. Because even though David is too weak to open his
eyelids, there will be many times when he's awake, so he can
feel and he can think, and at those times the sound and the touch
of someone to whom he's bonded will be extremely important to
his well-being."

Bonded. Part of the parenting lingo. The new father was a
total man who spent time caring for his infant. Trying to create
the kind of deep connection which babies in the past usually
only had with their mothers. This baby didn't have a mother,
or a father who spent all the time caring for him. Annie. To
David, hers was the most familiar voice, the most welcome and
soothing touch, Rick thought. He was surprised at how envious
he felt toward the large black woman, who couldn't take her
eyes from the now unconscious child in the crib. David looked
as if he were dead.

"Poor baby," Annie said softly. "Poor little baby."

"You can touch him," Dr. Solway said. The young doctor's
jaw was set firmly and her eyes were emotionless. Rick wondered how much time she'd spent in this room, and how many
babies she'd seen in such serious condition.

Annie put her large dark hand on the little pink arm of the baby that didn't have an intravenous tube connected to it.

"We're here, darlin'. Me and your daddy are gonna be here every minute." Then she looked at Rick. "I can sit by him all day, if you want to take the nighttimes. Or just the opposite. Whatever you say, Mr. Reisman."

"Annie," he said. "You can spell me. How would that be?"

"What does 'spell you' mean?" she asked him.

"It means you can be in and out, talk to him, touch him as much as you want. And if please, dear God, he ever gets off the respirator alive, even hold him. But except for getting a few hours of sleep, I'm going to stay in this room day and night."

Annie patted him softly on the arm.

"I'll go in to the nurses' station and check about getting you a room," Dr. Solway told Rick. She left Annie and Rick looking anxiously at what seemed to be a shell of baby David, listening to the constant repetition of the sound of the respirator as it fed him the breath of life.

Dr. Weil was back from his vacation and he called in a specialist from the San Francisco area to confirm Dr. Solway's diagnosis. The specialist was able to extract a stool sample, which was sent to a laboratory in northern California. During the visits of various doctors to the baby's bed, Rick would move out of the way so that they could have better access to David.

Twice a day Annie would come, and for some of the time while she was there Rick would move to a nearby waiting room and eat the meal she had brought for him from home while Annie sat with the baby, patting him and talking to him. But aside from those meal breaks, and approximately three hours a night when he went to the tiny Spartan hospital room to sleep, he never left the side of the crib where David lay motionless.

Now and then he would doze in the chair, waking suddenly at the piercing sound of a baby's cry, wishing it were David's. But, sadly for him, it was the cry of a baby across the room. Occasionally he would pick up bits and pieces of the other parents' conversations. The diagnosis of cancer in one case. The raised hopes as a baby began to show progress in another.

He watched the very California-looking couple who always wore sweatclothes and whose baby was not on a respirator so they were able to take turns holding her. He wondered about the sickly looking woman who was always dressed in a bathrobe. She was obviously coming from a wing in the hospital in which she herself was a patient. Then there was the oriental couple who were always holding hands as they stood wordlessly over their baby, who frequently cried, an inconsolable rasping cry.

Once the thought floated through his numb brain that he should call Patty Fall and tell her what was going on, but he couldn't bring himself to get on a phone and talk to anyone, and somewhere in the back of his mind, he seemed to remember her telling him she was taking the boys to Europe for a month or two. All day every day he would read aloud quietly to David from the familiar children's books he had read to him so often in the rocking chair at home. *The Cat in the Hat, Babar, Curious George.* Silly, funny, wonderful stories, just to be certain the sound of his voice was there in case the baby, his son, could really hear him.

"'The dolls and toys were ready to cry. But the little clown called out, "Here's another engine coming. A little blue engine, a very little one. Maybe she will help us." The very little blue engine came chugging merrily along. When she saw the toy clown's flag, she stopped. "What's the matter, my friends?" she asked kindly. The little blue engine listened to the cries of the dolls and toys. "I am very little," she said, "but I think I can, I think I can." And she hitched herself to the little train. She tugged and pulled and pulled and tugged, and slowly they started off. Puff, puff, chug, chug, went the little blue engine. "I think I can, I think I can."'"

Rick put his thumb and forefinger under his reading glasses to wipe his tired eyes, and when he glanced up, standing in the doorway was his uncle Bobo.

"Two weeks in a row you jilt a guy and don't even tell him why? What in the hell's the matter with you?"

It was true. For the two weeks Rick had been in this room, he hadn't thought about anything or anyone but the baby. Bobo was leaning on a cane, frowning at Rick.

"Uncle B.! How did you get here?"

"I called your house twenty times. Finally I get the baby nurse, and she tells me where you are. So I hired a kid to drive me over here. One of the volunteers at the home. He's waiting for me downstairs."

"I'm sorry," Rick said. "I should have called you."

"What's that you got there?" Bobo asked.

"A storybook. The doctor said he can hear me. So I talk to him, and I read to him."

"What am *I*? Chopped liver? *I* can't talk to him?" Slowly, with the help of his cane, Bobo walked to the crib where the baby lay silently. "Davidel," the old man said, "it's your favorite relative." Bobo's own hearing problem always made him talk too loud and Rick was afraid this intrusion on the other families would be upsetting. "I'm gonna tell you a story about your daddy when he was just a baby. Not as young as you are now. Maybe two or three years old."

The oriental couple was looking over now. Bobo turned to Rick and said as an aside, albeit in the same loud voice, "Jesus Christ, he looks like hell." Then he turned back to the baby. "Your daddy was always a smart little guy. And his mommy and daddy, God rest their souls, they were *crazy* about him."

"Uncle Bobo—" Rick started to interrupt him, but Uncle Bobo lifted his cane and waved it at Rick with a gesture to remain silent.

"Well, your grandpa Jake, my brother, he was Jewish, but your grandma Janie, she was gentile. So in their home, they celebrated all the holidays. Easter and Passover, Christmas and Hanukkah."

Now Rick noticed that the sickly looking woman in the bathrobe was listening, and the round-faced redheaded day nurse had walked in carrying a chart but was now stopped in the door from the nurses' station, listening to Bobo.

"Now you probably remember that the dish I cook the best, after my famous chicken-in-a-pot, is potato latkes. Right? And as soon as you get outta this place, I swear to God I'm gonna make some for you. So every Hanukkah it was a tradition that I would come to your grandma and grandpa's house and cook up a batch for all of us to eat."

Rick sat back in his chair now. There was no stopping Bobo from telling this story, and even the California couple, the wife holding the baby, were facing him, listening to what he was saying to the inert David.

"Anyway, this particular year, Hanukkah and Christmas came close together, so the Christmas tree was up and the menorah was lit, and your grandmother, a stunner, a gorgeous and wonderful girl, asks your dad, 'Ricky sweetheart, can you guess who's coming to our house tomorrow to make potato latkes?' And your dad looks at her with big wide eyes and asks, 'Santa Claus?'"

All the adults in the room laughed. Especially Rick. And when he looked over at the door of the room which led to the nurses' station, there were now three nurses there who had stopped to listen to the story. They were all laughing big hearty laughs that cut through the tension in that room for a much-needed respite.

Bobo. God bless him for coming here. Rick stood now to hug the old man, and when they both turned to look at David, for the first time in weeks the baby moved his free arm toward his chest.

"He moved," Rick said.

"What do you think?" the old uncle said. "I *always* keep them rolling in the aisles."

"He moved," Rick said to the nurse.

"So," Bobo said to Rick, "you'll call me tomorrow and tell me how he's doing?"

"I will," Rick said and they embraced again. Then Bobo, with a wave of the cane to his fans, went to find the driver to take him back to the home.

After that, David's progression began to be visible. Within days he was able to move his arms and legs on his own. Weakly, but Rick hung on to every shred of hope. Rick had lost thirty pounds during the endless days of not even thinking about food, and only eating to refuel himself for more hours near his son. To be around to hear the statistics about blood oxygen, and the oxygenation of the baby's skin, and the numbers on the heart monitor, and which of the baby's veins would best hold a change in the IV tube.

The day a nurse was able to come in and briefly disconnect the baby from the respirator, Rick held him in his arms and rocked him, singing, crooning, begging him to get well. And Annie held him and told him how she missed him at home, and when they reconnected him and Annie sat down in the chair, Rick walked as far as the hospital cafeteria for dinner, realizing it was the first time in over a month that he'd left the hospital floor.

With agonizingly slow progress, David Reisman became more and more animated. There were a few days of testing the baby on what the doctors called "sprints," which were short periods of turning off the respirator, while he breathed on his own. One day they asked Rick and Annie to leave the ward while they removed the tube so the baby could begin to breathe on his own permanently.

For the next few days Rick held him close. His suck reflex was coming back, and he was able to take food from the bottle Rick fed him tenderly. Every burst of bubbles that rose in the bottle gave Rick a sense of triumph, because it meant that David was now getting sustenance from his formula.

"We're going to go home in a few days I think," he said to the tiny face. "And I'm real glad. I'm glad because it means you aren't sick anymore, and that makes me very happy . . . because I love you, little guy. I love you a lot."

The baby's little eyes blinked, and then a flicker of a smile crossed his little face, around his bottle. It made his father smile too as Dr. Weil and Dr. Solway walked into the ward to tell him that tomorrow morning they were releasing David to go home.

"There's something I'd like to suggest you look in to," the serious-faced Dr. Solway said to Rick the next morning, as he was packing the few toiletries and clothes he had kept in the hospital room. She had knocked on the door and said she wanted to come in to say good-bye. He thanked her again and again for her swift diagnosis which had saved David's life. Always her response was a slight nod and a wave of the hand to dismiss him.

"Whatever you suggest is good by me," Rick said today.

"I know about a group that's starting," she said. "A support group for families who have come by their babies in unusual ways. I think it's safe to say that you and David fall into that category."

Rick smiled. "There's an understatement."

"A very gifted child psychologist I know is organizing it, and I think you and David would benefit from it. I'd like to call her and ask her to include you."

"Doctor," Rick said, "I haven't been to my office in nearly two months. My career is on a roller coaster that's frequently on the downhill slope. I have been consumed with worry and guilt and anguish and thought about nothing and nobody but this baby for so long that earlier while I was waiting to pay the exorbitant bill I owe this hospital, I discovered that I was standing there rocking back and forth, because I'm so used to doing that with the baby that now I even rock when he's not with me. And *you're* telling me you think I should take even more time away from my work to sit in a room with some shrink and a group of other people who got their babies in strange ways and shoot the bull about problems?"

"Yes" was all the pediatrician answered.

"I'll be there with bells on," he said.

26

ALL OF THE PARENTS in the new group were invited to sit outside and watch as their little ones dug in the sand or pushed themselves around on the rolling toys or splashed at the water table. The activities were set up in the yard adjacent to the large playroom where the adults would meet. Barbara's intern Dana was the child-care assistant.

"Looks as if your son is going to be a pulling guard," Shelly said to the familiar-looking man. He knew he'd met him before, and he was pretty sure it was at some event having to do with the business. Goddammit, he thought, why did I come here? I'm not going to sit around and participate in some kind of a true-confessions therapy group and tell everyone my problems. He wasn't ready to tell a group of strangers he was HIV-positive and watch them recoil. He would let the people who needed to have the information have it, but for now that was all.

"I'm Rick Reisman," the man said, extending a hand for Shelly to shake.

Oh, God, that's who he was. Rick Reisman, of course. Shelly had seen him earlier in the parking lot across from the building, struggling with the Aprica stroller, a moment Shelly knew only too well himself, but he hadn't been able to figure out why he looked so familiar. Now he realized they'd met at a fund-raiser at Barbra Streisand's house in Malibu.

"Shelly Milton," he said. "We've met."

"Of course, Shelly," Rick said, recognition filling his eyes. "I met you at that party. You were with your writing partner . . ."

"Me!" Ruthie said, walking over. "Ruth Zimmerman," she added, putting her hand out and shaking Rick's.

"So you adopted a baby?" Rick said, his eyes moving from Shelly to Ruthie.

"No," Shelly said. "Sid is our biological child."

Rick tried not to react. Zimmerman and Milton were a well-known comedy-writing team. But Shelly Milton was gay. Rick remembered when Davis Bergman, a married man, a law partner at a big-time entertainment firm, came out of the closet to have a long love affair with him. It was gossip all over town.

"Artificial insemination," Shelly said, knowing what Rick was thinking, and longing to grab Ruthie by the sleeve and drag her out of there. The group hadn't even started and already he was feeling defensive. No, this wasn't going to work.

"*We* did that," the pretty blond woman said. She was dressed in a chic cream-colored pantsuit and was kneeling on the ground where she diapered her baby daughter on a plastic pad. Ruthie couldn't believe that anybody who had a waist that small had ever given birth. "Only we used a surrogate." Aha! Ruthie thought. I knew it. The blond woman's darkly handsome husband was inside the playroom looking at the children's art push-pinned on all the walls.

"Now *that's* something I want to hear more about," Ruthie announced, "because if I ever have another baby, this time I want someone else to be in labor and then tell me about it. In fact, I'd prefer that they *didn't* tell me about it."

The blond woman was unsmiling and tense. She gathered the dirty diaper and the soiled wipes, put them efficiently into a Ziploc bag and tossed the bag into a nearby trash bin, then carried her daughter over to be with the other little ones.

David dropped shovels full of sand into a yellow bucket, and Sid pushed a Tonka truck along with one hand and held his Mickey Mouse bottle in his mouth with the other. Barbara Singer came outside and sat on the side of the sandbox, watching and encouraging the play. As she saw Lainie put Rose down in the sandbox, she noticed Mitch come out to look on lovingly as Rose joined in the play.

"My daughter's a party animal," Mitch said.

Lainie felt a heaviness fill her chest. Yes, she thought. Just like her mother. Jackie.

"That little baby Rose looks like a clone of *you*," Ruthie said to Lainie, who tried to force a smile. "And not one drop like her father. What does the surrogate look like?"

Lainie waited for Mitch to answer that.

"Beautiful," he said. "Like my wife."

Lainie worked hard to keep the smile on her face. "We're Mitch and Lainie De Nardo."

"Hi there" came a loud shout from inside. "Sorry I'm late!" It was Judith Shea. Her pretty auburn hair was flying. Her alert round-faced baby girl was in a papoose carrier on her back, and in her arms she carried her toddler daughter, whose chubby little legs were wrapped around her waist. "Say hi to everyone, girls," Judith urged.

For Barbara the explosive warmth was a welcome contrast to the nervous expressions of the others. "Two more little honeys for your group," Judith said, putting her daughter down, freeing her hands. "Judith Shea . . . inseminatee," she said with a laugh as she walked around to the others introducing herself.

Rick looked her over. Sexy as hell, a little thick around the middle, but then she'd just had two babies. Pretty little Jillian joined the group in the sandbox, and now that everyone had arrived, Barbara walked over and spoke to the toddlers.

"While all of you play with Dana, I'm going to go right inside that door with your mommies and daddies and Jillian's baby sister, and we're going to have some coffee and get to know one another better. So if you get lonely and want to come and say hello, you can just walk right in that door, and that's where we'll be until it's time for snack."

None of them even looked at her, but what she said seemed to register on their faces. The parents walked inside, where each of them sat on one of the toddler-size chairs she'd placed in a circle near a small table containing the electric percolator, which was now exuding the rich dark odor of freshly brewed coffee.

"I'd like to open by requesting that we get some larger furniture," Rick said, "since these chairs were obviously made for munchkins." The others laughed.

"I'll try to find bigger chairs by next time," Barbara said, looking around. Four families. Five little ones. It was a good start, she thought. Enough people to get some good talk going, and small enough to be intimate. "I want to welcome all of you. This is a very unique group, specifically designed for families with children whose birth circumstances were unusual. I believe in the necessity for this group, because modern technology is creating, and our society is embracing, extraordinary and wonderful ways to bring babies into the world. No one knows that better than all of you. But because these babies are so special, they and their parents bring with them a special set of needs and problems for which there is no precedent.

"These needs create situations never faced before, and require answers which, if we find them in our group, will not only help these special children through their lives but maybe can serve as pathfinding information we can pass on to other families." Every now and then she could hear her voice sounding exactly like Gracie's. And for a minute she had the odd feeling that somewhere in the room, just outside her peripheral vision, Gracie was perched, smoking a cigarette and saying, "Well said, dear girl."

"Each of you has taken a risk to have a child in an unorthodox way. Now those children are growing and developing, and soon they'll be out in the world with other children, and they'll have questions about their origins. We're here to deal with your responsibilities to your children, and how much you're prepared to tell them about themselves. How you'll present the information, and how you'll talk about their specialness at different stages in their lives. We'll also work on the way your particular baby or babies came into the world and how that continues to affect you and your spouse, or significant other, and other members of your extended families, parents, siblings, et cetera.

"So when Sid and Rose Margaret and David and Jillian and even little baby Jody are asking, 'Where do I come from?,' we'll have prepared loving responses. Responses we'll figure out together. And I mean that literally, because I certainly don't know what they are yet myself. But I think the important thing is to treat them and their questions in a way that helps these children to grow up feeling loved, loving, and confident."

"How can there be any answer to 'Where do I come from' besides the truth?" Rick asked.

Judith's baby was whimpering. Judith took her out of the carrier and rocked her against her shoulder. "I guess," she offered, "it depends on how comfortable you are with the truth. I don't particularly want to tell my daughters, 'Your dad was a number on a vial of sperm.' I'd like to make it sound better than that."

"Truthfulness for young children doesn't have to mean you tell them the whole story all at once. There are certain ways to give information that are more age appropriate than other ways, and you give them the information in stages. Broad strokes that are honest instead of details that they might not be able to handle," Barbara said. "And, Judith, I think wanting to let your daughters know that there was a living, breathing person who donated that sperm is a great idea. Because once they understand that they're a part of him, they'll want to think of him as someone special."

That made Lainie think about Jackie. About Mitch and Jackie, and she nearly jumped with surprise when she felt Mitch take her hand and hold it gently. Why is he holding my hand? Trying to make everyone think we're happy. Trying to make *me* think that.

"The method I used to get a baby was open adoption," Rick said. "David's birth mother actually lived in my house for the last few months of her pregnancy."

"Does she still see the baby?" Lainie asked.

"She hasn't seen him since we left the hospital."

"Where is she?" Shelly asked.

"In Kansas."

"Nice and far away," Judith said.

"I have no problem with her being around David. I think of her as his mother. He has her feisty ways, and her pink skin, and her blood flowing through his veins. And she's a terrific, bright human being. When he can understand, I want him to know she's his mother."

"You think that because you're single," Ruthie said. "If you had a wife who wanted to mother him, I'll bet things would be different."

"Maybe," Rick said.

"These are the kinds of complicated things we'll get into in this group," Barbara said. "I suspect that involvement with a birth parent can probably get touchy down the line. Particularly, Rick, if you chose to get married someday."

"No chance of that," Rick said.

"Are you gay?" Judith asked Rick.

"Not that I know of," Rick answered. "Want to step into the other room and find out?"

"Are you homophobic?" Ruthie asked Judith.

"Hell no," Judith said. "I was just wondering why an attractive single man is so adamant that he won't marry."

Ruthie changed the subject. "Do the two of you have any continuing relationship with the surrogate?" she asked, looking at Lainie and Mitch. Lainie's heart beat faster. Out of the corner of her eye she saw Barbara stiffen.

"No," Mitch said now in answer to Ruthie's question. "We have no communication with the surrogate. None."

Barbara's and Lainie's eyes met for a second, but Barbara's moved back to Rick. "How will you handle the fact that you have a little baby with the women you date?" Barbara asked him.

"I'll have them stop by at midnight and leave at six A.M.," he said in a teasing voice. "That way David will never know they're there."

"I knew I didn't like you the minute I laid eyes on you," Judith said to Rick, but it was in a kidding voice.

"Oh yes you did," Rick kidded back. "I'm still living on the fact that less than a minute ago you called me attractive." Judith laughed. "Listen, I'm not serious. I don't know what I'll do. I've temporarily sworn off dating, and maybe someday I will find the woman for me. Though it becomes more farfetched all the time. I usually find myself dating women I wouldn't want to involve with my child."

"Now there's a comment on your taste," Judith said.

"You're going to be trouble," Rick said, grinning at her.

The others laughed.

"Do you know the birth father of the baby too?" Mitch asked Rick.

"No, I have no idea who he is. The young girl who's David's mother won't tell me. Maybe she doesn't even know. But I think it's pretty safe to assume it was some high-school kid who threw her over," he said.

"And the two of you?" Barbara asked, looking closely at Shelly. He showed no apparent sign of being in less than perfect health. His arm was casually draped around the back of Ruthie's little chair. "Have you given any thought to what you'll tell Sid when the time comes for him to start asking?"

"I'll tell him to mind his own business," Shelly joked. The others laughed.

"That's funny and glib," Barbara said, "but it's not answering the question. I know you're a writer and comedy is your specialty, but I also know you had this baby for serious reasons. And I really wonder what you'll tell him."

"Well," Ruthie said, looking at Shelly, "we can certainly tell him how much we love each other, and that that's why we had him." Then to the others she explained, "We're best friends. Shelly is gay, and Sid was a turkey-baster baby."

"And what if he asks you *how* you had him?" Judith asked.

"It'll be easier to describe than sex," Ruthie said.

Another laugh from the others.

"We don't know," Shelly said, "which I guess is why we're here."

"He's so smart it's extraordinary," Ruthie said, sitting tall in her chair, her happy thoughts of her son dancing across her face. "So verbal. With an amazing sense of humor. He's already talking like a much older child. I mean, I think he is, because people are always amazed at the things he says."

"Like the other day," Shelly said.

"I didn't mean that," Ruthie said, anger crossing her face.

"I know, but it's important. It's one of the reasons we're here."

Ruthie explained what Shelly meant in a way that made Barbara sense she was carefully holding her rage inside. "Sid was at some other little kid's house for a play date. Some little boy in the neighborhood. And he came home using a new word he'd learned there. The word was 'faggot.'" Ruthie and Shelly held each other's hands tightly. "We realize it's the beginning of a lifetime of explaining, and we want to explain it the best way we can."

"We don't want him to think we have separate bedrooms because I snore," Shelly said. "I want him to know that I'm gay, and that that's okay no matter what people outside our family and our home may tell him. That it doesn't make me any less his father, or our relationship less loving."

"He'll know you love each other and love him," Barbara said, "because he'll feel it, and I'll help you work on the words you can say to him so you can express it to him verbally too." She was glad to see Ruthie and Shelly exchange a look of relief, and she said a secret prayer that she'd be able to do what she was promising.

"You see," Shelly said, musing, "I think if he doesn't know that right away, he'll never have any idea of who I was."

"Was? You sound as if you're not planning to be around for him to get to know you," Judith said.

Barbara heard Shelly's deep intake of breath and saw Ruthie look out the window at Sid. "None of us knows how long we'll be around," Barbara said gently. "But I think what we're hearing today is that our yardsticks for behavior are out the window when we try to use them against the new life-styles."

After a quiet moment the discussion moved into the group's mutual everyday parenting problems—pacifiers, temper tantrums—until they were interrupted by the cry of "Mommeeee" from the play yard. Ruthie, Lainie, and Judith all jumped to their feet and ran to the door. The cry had come from Sid, who had poured sand all over his own head. Ruthie picked him up and brushed him off tenderly.

"They're all getting hungry," Dana announced.

"Let's bring them in for clean diapers and snacks," Barbara said, and Lainie and Rick and Judith walked over to the sandbox to clean the sand from their little ones, too. As Barbara watched the parents interact with their babies, she felt shaky. Dear God, she thought. I hope I haven't bitten off more than I can chew. These are tough, complicated situations, being lived by smart people, and their problems aren't just about the future. They're about how to function day to day.

Rick Reisman may have finally bonded with his little boy during the illness, but he still feels incapable of having a relationship with a woman. And Shelly Milton faces the possibility of AIDS every day of his life. He might look fine now, as he marches around the room with Sid on his shoulders, but there is the specter of the HIV virus always looming large in the lives of that family.

And the De Nardos. Does Mitch really still have some connection to the surrogate? That secret will have to come out soon too. Barbara looked at Mitch standing next to his wife, touching her back while she held little Rose on her lap and tied the baby's tiny shoes. If what Lainie suspected had any validity, there was plenty of pain ahead, not just for her and Mitch but most of all for little Rose.

"I don't want to be didactic about how the group will progress," Barbara said as she and Dana poured apple juice into dinosaur paper cups, "because in my experience I find the sessions usually take on a life of their own, and people talk about whatever's going on with them at the time. But I have some ideas for jumping-off points and directions we might want to take. For example, we might want to talk about how much we want to tell the children and when. How to create a support system, how to handle the unrealistic expectations of holidays. How to help them feel continuity with their birth families by stories and letters. Rick, you might want to make a photo album for David with pictures in it of his birth family and his adopted family, going back to grandparents. So David can be familiar with his origins."

There was more talk among them all, light and guarded, along with a snack of crackers, raisins, and cheese, then they all sang "Two Little Blackbirds Sitting on a Hill," "The Wheels on the Bus," "The Itsy-Bitsy Spider," and Barbara read to the children from *Spot Goes to the Farm*.

When everyone was gone, Barbara and Dana piled the little chairs into a tower and pushed them into the corner. After Dana left, Barbara, who always prided herself on her ability to view these groups in a clinical way, sat on one of the small blue plastic chairs, and after she thought about everything that was said today, for some inexplicable reason she had a good cry.

27

ARTIE WILSON, one of the network executives in comedy programming, told Shelly in passing that he was looking thin, and Shelly obsessed about it for hours. "Shel, he meant it as a compliment," Ruthie swore to him. "He knows we hate him because he made us take the clam joke out of the script last season because he thought it was suggestive. He was trying to be a charming network executive."

"Now there's an oxymoron if I've ever heard one."

"Don't you know by now that when someone in Hollywood says you're looking thin it's the ultimate flattery?"

The ten staff writers were like ten mental patients, each one with a different neurosis, each one with a unique style. Just before Ruthie and Shelly walked into the meeting with them Shelly would say, "Bring me the whip and the chair, it's time to tame the animals." It was said with love and recognition of the fact that he and Ruthie were cut from the same cloth as those lunatics, but as producers it was their job to control the output, which meant keeping the writers and the writing focused.

They also felt that part of their job was to protect the writers, to keep them in good spirits and make the atmosphere at work as much fun as possible. Sometimes Ruthie even lovingly made and brought in muffins for their early-morning meetings. Unfortunately there was no way to protect the staff from Zev Ryder, the executive producer, who was always on everyone's case. He was the person with whom Ruthie assiduously avoided contact on those days when Shelly didn't make it in to work. If he somehow managed to find her, he was certain to harass her.

"Where's your funny half?" Ryder would ask her. Ruthie knew that behind their backs he called Ruthie and Shelly "the Dolly Sisters," and referred to some of their material as "sissy humor." He despised all of the writers and they all returned the sentiment. Nevertheless, in spite of him and thanks to Ruthie and Shelly's talent, the writing on the show was top-notch, but sometimes it was impossible to save the day from Zev Ryder's bad vibrations.

Like the morning that Jack Goldstein, a skinny wild-eyed Einstein-haired writer whose bizarre and hilarious ideas always read as if they were drug inspired, burst into Ryder's office. Ryder had pulled one of Goldstein's sketches from the script that morning, and the reason he gave for doing so was "not funny." Ryder was on the phone when Goldstein pulled the telephone out of his hand and hung it up, then leapt across the desk, grabbed Ryder tightly by the collar of his Ralph Lauren shirt, and breathed into his face.

"Say something funny! You're the executive producer of a comedy show. I defy you to say one funny thing. One funny word and I won't kill you. A joke, a stolen joke, a quote from somebody else to show me you know what's funny." He was holding both sides of the collar in his big clenched fist, pulling Ryder's fat little neck together in a wad in his hand. Ryder's eyes were huge with shock. "You see, you can't do it, not even to save your worthless life. Because there's not a funny bone in your entire family, you bastard. Go on, goddamn you! Say something funny!"

Ryder's mouth was open and he was emitting strange little choking sounds and by now all of the other writers who had heard Goldstein screaming had gathered in the doorway of Zev

Ryder's office to watch. Ryder was blue in the face. His eyes were starting to pop out and finally, seeing them all there, in a desperate plea he managed to say, "I'm dying. Please. I'm dying." At which point Goldstein threw him back in his chair, said, "All right. You got me. *That's* funny," and walked out of Ryder's office and, of course, off the show.

It had been more than a year, and Zev Ryder saw to it that though there was no doubt that Jack Goldstein was a comedy genius, he coudn't get a job anywhere in the business. And any time after that when Zev Ryder didn't like the script, he'd make some comment like "Look out, you pigs, because it's possible that Jack Goldstein needs someone to talk to while he stands in line at unemployment."

Today the group of writers had turned the conference room into a miniature golf course; Styrofoam cups with the bottoms ripped out were the holes, the golf balls were wadded-up tinfoil from the morning bagel delivery, and their pencils and pens were the clubs. When Ruthie and Shelly walked into the room to start the meeting, two of the guys were standing on the conference table arguing over a shot.

"People, let's get to work," Shelly said.

Ruthie pulled out a chair and sat and waited while everything from the grumbling about the ratio of onion bagels to pumpernickel bagels, to the condition of one of the guys' pancreas, to the jokes about somebody's pregnant wife finally stopped. She was just about to start talking about the show when Jerry Brenner, a forty-year-old fat little man who was once a stand-up comic, started telling a joke to his partner, Arnie Fishmann. But when he noticed the room was silent, he raised his voice to share it with all of them.

"A woman says to her friend, 'I don't know what to do. My husband just came home from a doctor's appointment. He told me the doctor said he either has AIDS or Alzheimer's, but he's not sure which one it is. I'm so worried. What should I do?'" There was a groan from someone and a chuckle of anticipation from someone else, and then somebody, Ruthie didn't look up so she didn't know who it was, uttered, "Good old Mr. Good-Taste Brenner."

"So the friend says, 'Here's what you do. You send him out to the supermarket. If he finds his way home, don't fuck him!'"

The roomful of writers offered the only kind of approval they allowed, which was never laughter, just a few snickers and a couple of grudging "That's funny"s, while Ruthie, who couldn't look at Shelly, felt decimated, and Shelly doodled on a yellow legal pad, hoping his discomfort didn't show.

It took a while for Shelly to reach Davis to tell him the news, but there was no answer at his home, not even an answering machine, and when he called Davis's law office, Davis's secretary told him, "Mr. Bergman is out of the office for a while. But he will be checking in. May I tell him who called?"

"Sheldon Milton," Shelly said.

"May I tell him what this is regarding?" she said.

"It's a personal call," Shelly said, glad he wasn't talking to Elise, the secretary who had worked for Davis when the two of them were together. After almost three weeks passed, Davis returned the call. He was cool and uncomfortable on the phone, and after Shelly said he needed to talk to him, they agreed to meet that day at lunchtime outside the L.A. County art museum, which was halfway between their offices.

"Isn't it odd," Shelly said to Ruthie later, "how you can worry and fear the way something's going to go, sure that it will be one way, and then it turns out to happen in a way you'd never even imagined?" In his fantasy he had been sure that he would tell Davis the news and Davis would become anxious and afraid for himself and his wife, Marsha. Maybe he would be accusatory or snide. But when Shelly walked up the steps to the stark grounds around the museum where the blazing hot Los Angeles day made the cement look glaringly white and he moved to the bench where Davis was sitting and Davis turned and looked into his eyes, it was clear to him that Davis had AIDS. And that he had been trying to figure out how he was going to tell Shelly.

"What about Ruthie and your son?" Davis asked after each of them had told the other their news.

"They've both been tested and they're fine."

A teacher led a group of children who walked in double file past the bench, and after some instructions from the teacher the giggling, fidgeting group disappeared through the front doors of the museum.

"Why didn't you call me, Davis?"

"Because I've only known for a few very numb days, and I wanted to pull myself together so I could tell you without falling apart. I haven't left the house since I heard. I haven't talked to anyone. Marsha was tested too and she's fine, but she's completely blown away. You remember that she's been seeing a psychiatrist three days a week for years? Well, now she talks to him on the phone on the other four."

There was something funny about that statement that made them both laugh out loud. But then Davis turned serious. "She's afraid I'll lose my job at the firm if anyone finds out. That none of the clients will want to meet with me if they know. She was the one who dragged me in to be tested, after weeks of my having night sweats and high fevers. She'd been reading all about AIDS and obsessing about it and driving herself and me crazy. Just the type of person you like to have around when you're feeling too weak to lift your head," he said with that ironic half smile of his Shelly remembered. "So finally I went with her, and we both got tested."

Suddenly there was the sound of screeching brakes, and then the sound of crunching metal and shattering glass as one car rammed into another on Wilshire Boulevard. And from their distance, on the bench near the front entrance to the museum, both men turned and watched as the traffic piled up and the angry drivers emerged from a gray BMW and a red Jeep Cherokee to shout blame at each other. It sounded as if a woman from inside of one of the cars was yelling out to a man on the sidewalk to call an ambulance.

"What can I do for you, Davis?" Shelly asked, turning away from the accident. "Is there anything I can do?"

The brightness was gone from Davis's face, but inside the pained expression and the pallor of illness, Shelly still saw the pensive, intense bright man he had lived with and loved. So much that losing him had once seemed to be a reason for giving up his own life.

"Forgive me for the way I left you," Davis said.

"I did that a long time ago."

"It's funny," Davis said, "I had taken to thinking about the time that you and I were together as the best I'd spent in my life so far. Now I may have to think of it as the best time in my life."

"You've got lots of life left," Shelly said.

"It would be easier for Marsha if I didn't."

"I never thought I'd hear myself say this," Shelly said, "but fuck Marsha!"

They smiled at each other.

"I'll always love you," Davis said.

"I'll always love you too."

The screaming cry of an ambulance filled the air on Wilshire Boulevard, and Shelly turned to watch. Within seconds the ambulance had wedged itself into the street as near to the collision as it could get, and the two paramedics emerged, opened the passenger door of the BMW, and removed an injured bloody passenger. The driver of the car gestured angrily for the gawking people who had gathered to get out of the way. The paramedics moved the injured woman onto the gurney, which they slowly inserted into the ambulance, then they closed the double doors, scrambled inside, and pulled away. Their shrill siren pierced the day again and the traffic moved to the right to let the ambulance pass. When Shelly turned back to finish their conversation, Davis was gone.

A few nights later, baby Sid woke crying. His diaper was

filled with a gray liquid stool that had seeped out all over the crib. After Ruthie changed him and the bed and scrubbed down the changing table, she rehydrated him with a bottle of water and got him back down to sleep. But just after she slid into her own bed, he wailed again and emitted another dark loose bowel movement.

Shelly, groggy with sleep, stood in the door of the nursery where Ruthie removed Sid again from the crib, again to repeat the cleaning-up process. "What's wrong?" he asked.

"I know the doctors say he's fine and not to worry," she said, "but I always do anyway."

After she told him, they looked long at each other. They were both tired from their work schedules, feeling guilty for not spending more time with the baby. They stood next to the changing table where Sid, too ill to cry, lay watching as his mother and father hugged each other closely.

"He has a stomach bug. That's all," Shelly told her, rubbing her head tenderly. "And don't forget what Freud said."

"What did Freud say?" Ruthie asked, glad that she was still his straight man after all these years.

"Sometimes a poop is just a poop."

The stomach flu was gone the next day.

28

EVERYONE WHO ATTENDED David Reisman's adoption ceremony melted when they saw the boy at the courthouse dressed in a pale blue seersucker suit and tennis shoes. The bright red hair Rick didn't have the heart to let any barber cut tumbled in curls all around David's handsome face. Downtown at the cold marble-halled courthouse Patty Fall, who had purchased the suit and dressed David in it that morning, shared the moment happily and brought both of her sons along to share it too. The judge, a man younger than Rick by a few years, seemed bemused by the whole process. Sadly, Uncle Bobo was feeling too ill that day to come all the way downtown, so Mayer Fall, a USC film student who was planning to make a video of the event anyway, dedicated it to Bobo.

Everyone who appeared on camera was instructed by Mayer to say, "Hi, Uncle Bobo." Strangers in the courthouse were waving to Bobo via Mayer's camera. Mayer got the uniformed guard to wave and say, "Hi there, Uncle Bobo," and of course so did Harvey Feldman, the lawyer, and in the middle of the proceedings even the court reporter and the judge raised a hand and waved to Uncle Bobo. David, as instructed, looked into the lens and said, "Unca Bobobobobo."

Afterward everyone went to the Falls' beach house for a late lunch, and as the perfect day was coming to an end, Rick and Patty, alone on the deck, looked out at the waves breaking and watched Mayer Fall, a grown man of twenty-one, playing in the sand with David.

"It's great to have a relationship with a baby, impossible to have one with a woman. Babies give you unconditional adoration. Babies don't expect you to buy them an engagement ring to prove that you care about them, and babies don't pout if you smile at another baby. To babies," Rick said, holding up his wineglass, and Patty Fall filled the glass with more wine as she shook her head knowingly.

"Boy, are you in for a rude awakening," she said, pouring some into her own glass too. "Babies grow up and walk all over you. And if they're yours, as you already know they have the ability to break your heart worse than any woman ever could. I can absolutely guarantee you that within a matter of years, that kid will be on the take from you worse than any gold-digging woman you've ever imagined, and you know what? You'll give it all to him gladly. Charlie always did with our kids," she said with love but without any sentimentality. "He was a pushover beyond description."

"Look at those two," Rick said, grinning at the game Mayer was playing with David, making piles of sand that the baby kicked down, after which Mayer moaned in mock dismay, which made the baby erupt with laughter. Patty watched Rick watching them.

"Mayer and his girlfriend are very serious," she said. "It's hard to believe that soon I could be a grandmother and you're the daddy of a little baby."

Rick smiled. "I remember Doreen's mother saying something like that to me when I met her. She's my age and she has seven grandchildren and couldn't figure out why I'd want to do this. To start being a parent at this ripe old age."

"Oh, I understand why. It's already changed you immeasurably."

"Nah. I'm still a fat old lech."

"But a mellower old lech. And not so fat anymore. In fact, you're starting to look pretty damned sexy."

"Yeah, yeah, yeah," Rick said, smiling and looking at his best friend's widow across the table, then taking her hand. Her tan face was lined from the years of too much sun at the beach. But her green eyes were still as bright as when she was the young secretary in a producer's office at Columbia Pictures where a dashing Charlie Fall came to have a meeting with her boss. And while he waited for the producer to get off a phone call, in the ultimate flirtatious move Charlie proposed to her.

"So how's by you these days?" Rick asked her gently. "Are you surviving okay without him?"

"Oh sure," she said. "I'm okay. My kids hang around a lot, my mother flies in from Seattle every few months." And then she opened her eyes wide and tried to hold back a funny grin that was forming around the corners of her mouth when she said, "I'm even being courted by various swains these days."

For some inexplicable reason, though he couldn't think of why, the idea of Patty's dating made him feel affronted, and Rick blurted out his first thought, "But the problem is, who could ever live up to Charlie Fall, right?"

The green eyes flashed, and Patty took her hand out from under his. "Nobody has to, Ricky," she said quietly. "That's not the criterion. Not that I have to explain this, but I loved Charlie completely for twenty-seven years, and somebody else will be somebody else. I'm not so stuck with some concept of how my relationship with a man has to be, I'm not hanging on to some unrealistic archetype that no human being can ever live up to."

"You mean like certain other people you could mention and that's why they've never married?"

"If the shoe fits, honey . . ." she said, smiling. "Listen, you know as well as I do that Charlie Fall had his faults, believe me, and so will my next husband."

"Husband? You're already that serious about somebody?"

"No, but I want to be. Unlike you, I'm crazy about intimacy. I love having the same person in bed next to me every night and every morning. Having somebody boss me around who gets pissed at me for bossing him around. I like a guy who does the *New York Times* crossword puzzle over my shoulder, and gets the references to sports and geography but leaves the song titles and names of playwrights to me."

"Sounds awful."

"Go to hell."

"I'm sure I will, because I still like a high-volume turnover of pieces of ass I've barely spoken to mainly because they can barely speak. I long for naked lust with exotic strangers in dubious locations, and particularly love waking to find black lace underwear and bondage equipment hanging from my chandelier *and* my appendages." Patty's outraged laughter made him go on. "I like to start my day uncertain if during the foreplay of the night before, I played the part of the shepherd who buggered the sheep or the sheep itself. That said . . want to marry me?"

Patty let out a sound that was somewhere between a scream and a giggle. "I think we're a match made in heaven," she said. The sun was big and orange and very low in the sky and the two of them watched as Mayer put David on his shoulders and ran into the surf, then pranced through the waves to the beach, kicking water everywhere, making the baby scream with delight.

"Patty," Rick said to her though he continued to look down at the boys on the beach, "I know I idealized my late mother enough to make Oedipus look aloof. But I'm sure you know that in the more recent years, you've always been the standard against which I've measured every woman in my life. You're smart and funny. You made a family for Charlie and those boys that I've always envied and admired and coveted. You're going to find somebody one day soon, and he's going to be the luckiest man that ever lived. And I'm here to tell you that if he doesn't worship the ground where you walk every day, you call me and I'll kill him. Promise?"

Patty reached over and took his hand back. "I promise."

The phone rang and Patty reached for the portable receiver on the wicker table next to her.

"Hello? Yes, Andrea, he's here. I'll put him on." Patty gave Rick the handset.

"Secretarial assistant to moi?" Rick said into it.

"Mister R., listen. I've got Doreen Cobb on the other line."

"Doreen? How great! My God, it'll be great to talk to her. Can you patch her through?"

"She sounds kind of depressed," Andrea said. "She knows that today was the adoption."

"Put her through," Rick said. There were a few clicks and then Rick heard Doreen's sad little voice on the other end of the line say "Hello?"

"Hello, Doreen," Rick said, wishing he knew how to make the day of David's adoption easier for her.

"I'm sorry to bother you, I mean, I know I'm not supposed to but . . . it's just that I . . ."

"You're not bothering me. I'm really glad to hear your voice. How's Bea?"

"Bea's okay," she said, and he could hear muffled sounds on the other end of the line that he knew were her pained sobs.

"Doreen, can I do anything?" he asked gently.

"Oh, no," she said. "I knew today was David's special day . . . and I just wanted to hear about how it went."

Rick listened to more sniffling and sobs, and tried to think of something he could say. "It went great and he's a tiger. He's walking, he's talking up a storm. In fact I can see him right now from where I'm sitting. He's right at the place where the sand meets the surf, mushing his fat little feet into the wet sand and screeching at the top of his lungs every time the waves come."

"Oh good!" Doreen said, sounding sincerely cheered by the report.

"Oh and by the way, I've become part of a parenting group."
He knew she would think that was funny. "All of us are parents
who got their babies in unusual ways."

"Ahh, that's so sweet," she said. "I'll bet it's fun for you."

"And one of the ideas the group leader had was for me to
make a scrapbook for David, photos of his families, extended
families and birth families. So I've been thinking about calling
you, to ask if you'd send me some pictures of you."

"Oh, God," she said laughing. "There's never been a good
one yet."

"And some of Bea, and of your sisters and brothers and their
kids so David can see his cousins."

"Oh fun!" she said. The news that she was still included in
David's life seemed to lift her spirits. "I'll start putting them
together today. I know Bea has one of the whole family at a
picnic table and . . . what? I'm on long distance!" Someone had
come into the room on her end of the line.

"I have to go now," Doreen said abruptly, and without a
good-bye, she hung up. Rick continued to hold the receiver as
if he thought she might come back on the line, but then there
was a dial tone. Disappointed, he put the phone back on the
table.

"Not that it's any of my business," Patty said, "but this is
where the system falls apart a little for me. I mean, how do you
separate out your responsibility to this girl from your gratitude?
Please don't think I'm being cold about all of this. I know how
much the baby means to your life, Ricky, but I don't get it. She
chooses you to be the one to take her baby. To me that part is
good, I guess, because she feels as if she has some control over
it all. Knows that the flesh of her flesh is with someone she
deems okay. But isn't the theory that, barring Christmas cards
and an occasional photograph, you make a clean break after the
baby's handed off?"

"That's the theory," Rick said. "But it only works on paper.
Something happens. It happened to me, anyway. Maybe because she lived in my house, maybe because she's so unique,

but I care and will always care about her well-being. And now, at least when she's falling apart from the pain of the rest of her life, she can call me and still get some joy from knowing her baby is thriving. Not that I'm some great expert, but I don't understand how the other ways of doing this can work. A woman pretending she never had a baby? A mother not looking at the calendar on the day she gave birth and wondering where the baby is?"

"You realize if she'd put David with another family, they might have been less sympathetic about her needs. A family with a mother who felt threatened by the intrusion."

"Yes I do. But she picked me, and her mother let her pick me. And maybe that was why. Because they both knew instinctively that I would never deny them a relationship with this baby. Or with me, even if the day ever comes, and you and I both know it won't, when I marry."

"Do you have any idea who the father is?" she asked. Mayer was walking up the beach with David toddling along next to him babbling away.

"As far as I know," Rick said, "when it comes to paternal influences, this kid is stuck with just little old me."

"God save us all," Patty said, flashing a smile as David climbed onto Rick's lap, salty and sandy. Rick stood him on his feet and peeled the soggy bathing suit off. "I'll take him inside and wash him," he said. And just as the bathing suit got past his thighs, David peed all over Rick.

"Well that's *his* comment on the situation," Rick said.

"Maybe your daddy better go in and take a shower *with* you," Patty suggested to David, who clapped his hands with glee at the idea.

A few days later the photographs from Doreen came in the mail. David's only interest in them was throwing them all around the room or biting on them, but Rick shuffled through them all. He smiled as he looked at the one of Doreen and her mother, remembering the life-changing day he met them at the airport.

He always viewed everything with his director's eye, even these photos of Doreen and her sisters. Cheryl, the prettiest one, who unlike Doreen seemed to have confidence in her appearance. Susan smiled with her mouth but her weary eyes and body English were a giveaway of an unhappy young woman.

There were a million stories in the photo of the whole family, children and spouses included, at what appeared to be a picnic in a pretty-looking park. The poses people took, where they placed themselves in the shot, the expressions on their faces were all so telling. One more time he went through the whole pile of photos, and stopped for a long time at the one of the assembled family at the picnic, because now he saw something in it that made him afraid. Could it be? But then he dismissed the thought as his overactive imagination and put the pictures away.

29

SOMETIMES after work Judith would pick up her two little girls who had been at home with the housekeeper all day and take them to the park. While she went through the ordeal of lifting the wiggling baby out of the infant car seat and gentling her fat little resisting body into the Snugli, then putting the stroller together while an impatient Jillian whined, she wondered if maybe her position on men and relationships was too tough.

"Every couple has their deal," her friend Jerralyn told her one day at lunch, "usually unspoken, and as long as each of them keeps the deal they're in good shape. He provides clothes and trips, she sticks around, he cheats, she ignores it. She flirts, he thinks it's cute. The partner you end up with is the one who offers a deal you can live with and vice versa."

Judith didn't ask Jerralyn what the deal was she had with her husband, Tom, just said, "I guess I haven't met a man yet with a deal I like." But the idea of making a deal, unspoken or otherwise, was abhorrent to her. This evening she held baby Jody on her shoulder and pushed Jillian in the swing when a little toddler boy lurched into the play-equipment area, screaming, "Daddeeee! Daddeeee!" Jillian moved back and forth, little fists holding tight to the chains of the enclosed baby swing, and watched the little boy with fascination. Then, liking the sound of his chant, she took it up as her own.

"Daddeeee! Daddeeee!" she cried, her elfin voice echoing through the park. Each time she called out, the sound went right through Judith, who felt anguished that there might never be anyone to answer the cry. There must be a good man out there somewhere, she thought as a gray dusk fell around her. A sudden chill in the air made her wrap both girls in her own sweater and hold them close to her chest as she headed for the car. I'll find him, she decided. I'll tell Jerralyn, who's always trying to fix me up with one of Tom's friends or some guy she met on a ski trip, to go for it. To say that despite all of my refusals in the past, I've had a change of heart and I'm ready to take a shot.

The first man on Jerralyn's list was in the computer business, so wonderful looking he could be on the cover of *GQ*. This was the fellow Jerralyn and Tom had met on the ski trip. He talked a lot about his physical condition and eating habits, and when they got down to the details of Judith's life he seemed fascinated with the story of how she came to have her daughters.

"That is so great," he said over coffee. "You are a real original." But she knew it was all over with him when she finished the story and he said, "Well . . . it sounds to me like an extrapolation of masturbation."

"Pardon me?"

"I mean that it's something you can do on your own if you have to, but so much better if you do it with a partner." He laughed at his own wit. "I mean, isn't that a great analogy?"

The second one was a banker, very well dressed and in his mid-forties, who took her to the Bistro for dinner. When he asked about her life she told him about her donor babies and as she did she saw a look of terrible distaste on his face. But she went on to finish the story, about the anonymity factor and the list from the cryobank containing the limited information, and just as the waiter put her dinner in front of her the banker asked, "How do you know the donor wasn't some serial killer like that guy in the Midwest who killed all the people and ate them?"

She didn't have an answer for him. Nor did she have one bite of the very expensive dinner.

"Sorry I wasted your time," she told Jerralyn.

"One more, give me one more chance. This one is different, and just to be on the safe side, I already told him about you and the girls. After my batting average on the first two, I figured if this one couldn't handle it right from the giddy-up, I better not even send him around."

"And?"

"It intrigued him. He's never been married or had kids, so it's all kind of foreign and fun to him. He's one of my husband's oldest friends. Cute, bearded, balding but sexy. Frank's very sexy. A real-estate developer. Likes to scuba dive, surf—"

"Jerra, you're starting to sound like the rundown sheet from the sperm bank," Judith said, and both women laughed, a kind of hopeful this-might-be-a-good-one laugh.

Jerralyn was right about the sexy part and Frank was very flirtatious. He held her hand across the dinner table and looked into her eyes with a knowing amusement that was very appealing. Judith felt herself drinking a little too much wine. Her policy about going on these dates was to meet the men at the restaurant because she didn't want to expose her children to them and vice versa. But tonight, halfway through dinner, she was feeling heady from the alcohol and wishing that she'd let this one pick her up at home. She knew she shouldn't be driving in this condition. How was she going to get home? She ordered coffee with dessert and drank several cups of it black, and was relieved when she started feeling closer to earth.

He never mentioned her children and neither did she. He talked about the real-estate market, and about a boat he had in the Caribbean and about various trips he'd taken on it. She talked about her job at the advertising agency and the clients she worked for. After they'd run out of food and superficial things to talk about, he paid the check and they walked outside.

"Thanks for dinner," she said, extending her hand. "It was nice to meet you." He held her hand lightly.

"Where did you park?" he asked.

"Around the back."

"Come on, I'll walk you."

"It's the station wagon with the two car seats in it," she said, wondering if that was a good opening to talk about her kids. Jerra told her he knew about them.

"Ahh, yes," he said, "the donor babies." She had parked in the back because when she'd arrived, the parking lot in front had been full. There was so much crime in these neighborhoods at night, she'd rushed from her car to the restaurant, afraid as she often was these days that someone was just waiting to grab her. And when someone did she gasped.

It was Frank. At her car, in the now empty parking lot, he turned her to face him, pressed her against the side of her car, then forced his mouth on hers. She could smell the garlic from the pasta on his beard and she didn't like his mushy wet kiss. She tried turning her face away, but he took her chin in his hand and moved her face back to his.

"Don't turn away," he said. His body was pinning hers hard now, and she was uncomfortable and a little afraid.

"I've got to get home," she said.

"To your kids?" he asked, smiling, but it wasn't a friendly smile.

"Yes," she said and tried to slide away from him, but now she realized that what she'd thought was a little heat from this guy was overpowering force. She felt a panicky quickening in her chest. Now he moved his hands to her buttocks and pulled her pelvis against his very excited one.

"No," she said, moving to get away.

"What's the matter?" he asked. "*I've* got sperm. Don't you want some of *my* sperm?"

She felt sick to her stomach, and when he placed his fuzzy garlicky face against her again, she stuck the high heel of her shoe into the arch of his loafer. He let out a grunt of pain, but wouldn't let go. Now he was talking in a weird little soft voice he must have thought was seductive. "I want to please you, baby. Won't you let me?"

"I will let you, and here's how," she said, trying to contain her rage. "It would please me inordinately if you would just fuck off."

"Cunt," he said, pushed her against the car hard, and walked away.

"You want to know why women use anonymous donors? Look in the mirror, you pig!" she shouted after him. In the car, she screamed out loud for a few minutes and cursed the fact that she'd been stupid enough to let herself be fixed up. When she flipped on the radio dial, the audiocassette she'd been playing for the children earlier that day came on, and Snow White in her trilling little voice was singing, "Someday my prince will come."

When she talked about it in the group she was surprised at how comforted she felt. There was something about blurting out the horror of it all that was therapeutic and healing. Ruthie and Shelly cracked jokes, but they lovingly offered suggestions, even tried to think of some good single men for her. And Rick Reisman turned to her and said, "Even *I*, with my long record of insensitivity, have to say those guys you went out with were monsters."

"I think we should go around the room and talk about dumb things people say to us and all the times we've wanted to tell them to shove it up their nose."

"Well put, Ruthless," Shelly said. "I think what she means is, let's figure out how we're going to respond to stupid questions with a little bit of grace."

"Yeah. Grace," Ruthie said. "How do you respond gracefully to this one, which I am so sick of I could kill, 'You mean Shelly's

Sid's *real* father? How did *that* happen?' I always want to say, 'Come over for Thanksgiving dinner and taste my moist turkey, sweetheart!'" Everyone howled at that one.

"I've got one that people say to me all the time that all of you will love," Rick said. "'Well, won't it be nice that by the time the baby's in his twenties, he'll be able to wheel you around the old folks' home just like you do your uncle.'" That got a hoot from Ruthie and a big laugh from all the others.

Now Shelly piped up with one he'd kept even from Ruthie. "How about this one? I've now had two different people on two different occasions ask me, 'Aren't you worried that when Sid grows up he'll be gay?'"

"No!" Ruthie said, then thought, and added, "I don't know why I'm surprised, I've actually had someone ask me, 'Did you and Shelly ever do it just to see if it would work?'" An outraged moan rose from the group.

"How about, 'Didn't it feel bad to know you couldn't have Mitch's baby and another woman could?'" Lainie offered, and the laughter stopped abruptly as everyone looked at her serious face. Barbara was surprised to hear Lainie volunteer that, since, though she and Mitch had attended all of the meetings so far, she'd been very quiet at every one of them.

Mitch looked at his wife with surprise. "You're joking!" he said. "What insensitive clod came out with *that?*"

"Your sister Betsy," Lainie said, and it must have been her own delivery that tickled her because she laughed along with the others, though Mitch was embarrassed and serious.

"Well, it sounds as if the biggest thing that separates your children from others is the way they happened to join their families. Because developmentally they all appear to be right on track," Barbara said.

"It's true," Rick said. "I was thinking today as I was driving here about what each of us has gone through to have these babies, to seduce the stork to visit our lives. And it cracked me up because I decided that we ought to call ourselves the Stork Club."

Everyone loved that, and Ruthie promised to have sweat-shirts made for all of them, and the babies too, with that name printed on them.

"It sounds to me as if today's discussion should be about the language of unusual birth situations. So let's see if by discussing it we can find a way to handle them."

"People seem to be titillated by my story," Rick said. "I've had men leer when they hear it, as if I'd been sexually involved with David's mother."

"*Seem* to be titillated?" Judith said. "You just heard about the guy who tried to nail me in the parking lot."

"It sounds as if it brings up people's own fears about the two things in the nineties that are the most frightening. High technology and sex," Barbara said.

"Not necessarily in that order," Shelly added.

"And when people are afraid, they're frequently hostile. The important thing to remember is that the quality of your relation-ships with your children has nothing to do with the way they came into the world. And if other people have problems with it, those are just their problems.

"Many of the issues can be taken care of by semantics. When people say 'real mother' or 'real father,' you can correct them with 'birth mother' or 'birth father,' or 'biological parent,' which I've heard you use, Ruth," Barbara said. "But I think the first thing to do is expect people to ask dumb questions, anticipate them, and get comfortable with your answers so when they ask them in front of the children, which they undoubtedly will, you'll be loose and confident about it all."

"Well, what *are* the answers?" Judith asked, and Barbara thought about it for a while.

"Probably the best answers that will work well when the children overhear them, and even when they don't, will be the ones that have to do with how happy you are to have these children in your lives, and that really is the bottom line. So in answer to the question about the surrogate, Lainie might say something like, 'Mitch and I are so happy to have our wonderful daughter, Rose, in the family, and that's what really matters to us.'"

"I guess it would be pretty hard to argue with that," Judith said.

"Not for Betsy," Lainie said. "And the irony is *she* was the one who suggested we try the surrogate in the first place."

"So the rules are," Judith said, "expect people to be dumb."

There was silence as Barbara nodded, but Ruthie Zimmerman, never one to leave well enough alone, had to have the last word. "And then," she said, "tell them to shove it up their nose," and everyone fell apart laughing.

30

GRACIE HAD THE FLU, and she told Barbara she could manage to get from her bedroom to the bathroom, but she insisted that the kitchen, though it was approximately the same distance, was too far. She categorically refused the idea of "some stranger nosing around my house," which was her description of any help Barbara might hire for her. So every morning on her way to work, Barbara stopped and picked up a bran muffin, then used her key to get into the old apartment just off Fairfax, made a pot of herb tea, and brought her mother breakfast in bed.

Gracie joked when she bought the duplex in a neighborhood populated mostly by old people that she was moving in as an anthropologist, to study the life-styles of senior citizens. Now she had a multitude of friends, and the women in her circle took turns bringing her lunch every day, and tending to her. She seemed to be relishing the attention, but the flu bug had taken its toll and she was weak and uncomfortable.

Her choice for dinner was soup from Canter's Deli, where Barbara stopped every evening. Then in Gracie's tiny kitchen she would pour the steaming chicken noodle or matzoh ball or kasha soup from its cardboard carton into a bowl, put some bread on the side, and serve it to Gracie along with tales of her day at work. Sometimes Jeff would meet her at Gracie's, and Barbara could tell by the way he tried too hard to be okay about it that it was devastating to him to see his mighty and forceful grandmother in this diminished state. The once booming voice that was usually so big it could shake the house was now little more than a whisper.

One night when they got home he asked, "Is Grammy going to die, Mom?"

"Yes, honey. One of these days. I mean, she'll probably recover from this flu any minute and soon she'll be racing me down San Vicente Boulevard again, but eventually we'll lose Grammy. And you know what? We'll miss her terribly and be grateful for all the years we've had her, and all the funny, crazy things we learned by having her in our lives."

He had nodded at her words, but a few minutes later when she was on the phone talking to Stan she saw Jeff slip away into the powder room, and then from where she sat at her kitchen desk she could hear his sobs from behind the closed door. Both of her children were attached in some powerful, heartful way to their grandmother, who was better by far at grandmothering than she'd ever been at mothering. When she got word that her grandmother was down with the flu, Heidi called all the time to see how she was feeling, and Barbara had to admit to a wave of jealousy for the amount of attention her daughter gave her mother.

After the anniversary party Heidi had gone back to San Francisco, and in a few weeks she informed Barbara that she had quit her job in the offices of the American Conservatory Theater, a move necessitated by the fact that the no-good mother-loving boyfriend worked there too, and they were through forever. She was very serious about moving back to Los Angeles. It was an idea Barbara loved, until Heidi added that she was hoping to move back into her old bedroom, "just for maybe like six months or a year or so, until I'm squared away and have some money saved up."

Barbara's reply was a startled "Really?"

"Don't sound so thrilled, Mother," Heidi said, and Barbara heard that same bitchy edge in her daughter's voice that she sometimes regrettably used with her own mother. After they hung up the phone, she wondered if it had escaped Heidi's memory that her former bedroom was now more of an office than it was a bedroom. Barbara had filled the room with books and files.

If she had to change it back to a bedroom it would mean renting storage space for the contents. But turning the office back into a bedroom would be the least of it. Heidi hadn't lived at home for anything but school vacations in six years. Even a few of the summers during her four college years were spent away from home. One year she waitressed in Santa Barbara where she took a summer course, and another year she attended a work-study program at UC Davis. It had been a long time since she and Barbara had had extended day-to-day contact, and Barbara was worried about how that would work out.

I'll make it good, she thought. It won't be the way it was when she was a teenager, because she'll have a job to go to every morning so I won't see her until the end of the day. Most of the time not even then, because she'll be dating. Dating. What would it be like for Heidi to be living at home and going out with some man and not coming home for a day or two? Now she was dating thirty-five-year-old men. One of the group leaders at the hospital was Barbara's age and she was *married* to a thirty-five-year-old man. Not a good idea, Heidi's living at home. Though she had to admit it had cozy overtones. If she did decide to move to Los Angeles, Barbara and Stan would have to encourage her to find her own place without making her feel as if they didn't want her in the house.

Mothers and daughters. Why was it so complicated? Tonight while she was helping Gracie, practically lifting her from the chair to the bed so she could change the bedclothes on which her mother had spilled some of her dinner, she wondered if Heidi would someday have to do this for her. And suddenly the idea of being the aging mother seemed appealing and she had an urge to crawl into the newly made bed and ask Gracie to please feed her some soup.

"My new group is really working out well," she said. "They've really connected with one another. They have a great sense of humor about themselves. And probably because they went through so much to get these babies, they don't let anything get in the way of their happiness. It's a real lesson, watching them."

"Well I'm delighted to hear it's going well, I knew it would, but I don't know how the hell you're going to do all that you do and ever have time to make a wedding too."

"Make a what?"

"I talked to my granddaughter today," Gracie said, smiling, then pushing her spoon hard into a matzoh ball and breaking it into bite-size pieces. "And she told me we're going to have a wedding."

"What?" Barbara asked, stunned.

"Ooops, did I spill the proverbial beans?" Gracie asked with a guilty look. "Didn't she tell you yet that the errant boyfriend showed up and said he's decided he can't live without her?"

"Mother, you're not serious."

"I'm sure she'll call you tonight and tell you herself," Gracie said and tucked her napkin into the high collar of her flannel nightgown. "For whatever it's worth, she sounded deliriously happy."

Bad news, Barbara thought. Probably a ploy from the guy to get Heidi back into bed, but it would never last until a wedding. "I won't chop the liver or devil any eggs yet, Mother," she said.

"You had two kids when you were her age."

"I also had Stan. This guy Ryan is a flake. She told me so herself. Not exactly a gentleman of strong character, shall we say?"

"Well, Mother dear," Gracie said to her with irony, "as you always used to say to me . . . you don't get to pick." Then she laughed a big hearty laugh, which should have cheered Barbara since it was an indication that Gracie was on the mend, but Barbara didn't notice.

Ronald Levine was waiting outside the door of her Wilshire Boulevard office when she arrived in the morning. His face was ashen and his eyes were filled with rage. He didn't have an appointment but he'd come to tell her that his estranged wife had left a message on his answering machine saying she and their son, Scottie, were off to Hawaii. She didn't tell him where in Hawaii or for how long. He was seething, and when Barbara opened the back door to her office he strode in behind her.

She was early because she'd planned to make some phone calls before her first appointment, but Ronald Levine's pain filled the room. His broken posture looked wrong for the smart Armani suit he wore as he paced in front of her desk, cursing Joan and blaming Barbara. Barbara listened without saying a word, letting him get it all out. Finally he collapsed in the chair across from her desk and wept, his face on his arm on her desk, his body heaving with agonized sobs.

"Look what we do to one another in the name of love," he choked out between his sobs, and after a while he raised his face to her and asked, "Have you ever been divorced?"

"No," Barbara said.

"Can you imagine what it feels like to have to share your child with someone you hate? Who's acting despicable, trying to turn the child, the only creature on this earth you can love and relate to unconditionally, against you? No, you can't." He spoke in a small voice.

"It must feel awful."

His eyes were angry as he stood. "Don't give me the sympathetic-psychiatrist talk, you supercilious bitch," he screamed. "It feels *worse* than awful. I want a life with my son, and I don't even know where he is. Why did I come here in the first place? To pay you to say inane shit to me like 'It must feel awful.'" For an instant Barbara thought he was going to leap across the desk and grab her. "You have to help me get full custody. You have to tell the court, the judge, the powers that be that I'm the sane one. That his crazy mother spends every waking minute trying to drive him crazy. Will you say that?"

"I'll say whatever I think is best for Scottie," Barbara answered as evenly as she could. Ron Levine stormed out of the office and the phone rang. Barbara answered it numbly. "This is Barbara Singer."

"Hi, Mom."

It was Heidi, calling to break the news Barbara already knew. She was engaged. Ryan had presented her with a ring, she told Barbara, with a glow in her voice when she said his name as if he was and always had been a great guy. They were looking at apartments big enough to contain at-home offices for each of them. One of which, Heidi confided to her mother, could "maybe become the um . . . you know." And Barbara felt a stab to the chest because she *did* know that the "you know" meant a nursery.

The words "you don't get to pick" scurried again and again through her brain the way the messages of lights moved letter by letter across the Goodyear blimp, and she tried to let it go.

"I think we may want to ask you and Dad to consider the Bel-Air Hotel," Heidi told her.

Barbara had never priced the making of a wedding before, but she knew the Bel-Air Hotel, with its lush gardens and swan-filled lagoons, would be top of the line. She wondered if the future son-in-law had been someone she respected, someone who treated her daughter well and made her happy, if she would have relished the idea of making a wedding at the Bel-Air Hotel, of doing whatever the kids wanted, instead of feeling defensive and worried and annoyed by this news.

Why is it, she thought, the one area we're certain about with every ounce of our intuition, our intellect, and our years of wisdom happens to be, ironically, the one area in which we are completely powerless. "Insight doesn't mean a thing, and criticism is the kiss of death," Gracie had warned her.

"We'll come down in a few weeks so you can meet one another, and then we can talk more about the date and the place and all. Love you, Mom," Heidi said, signing off.

Barbara sighed as she hung up the phone, closed the back door through which Ron Levine had made his thunderous exit, and opened the front door for her first family of the morning.

31

DAVID REISMAN had a demanding personality, and though he put up with being taken care of by the nurse during the day, he was only completely happy when his daddy was home. He loved the nights when they roughhoused on the bed, then as Rick after a long day's work snored away, David used him as a pillow while he watched a "Sesame Street" video.

Of course they both loved playing in the pool with Rick holding David on the surface of the water, urging him to kick, kick, kick his chubby little feet. Patty was right, Rick thought when he held his son in his arms and the scent of the Desitin he had spread on his little bottom wafted up through the baseball pajamas. This baby owns me. I'd throw myself in front of a truck to save him, and every time he grins one of those little impish grins, I could weep.

Tonight David climbed into his lap. After they read a few of his favorite books, Rick picked up the scrapbook he'd been working to complete any time he had a spare minute. He had searched his drawers and filing cabinets and come up with a treasure trove of photos of his own family to include, so that David would know about his adopted family's history too. Pictures of the Cobbs, pictures of the Reismans. Rick mixed them on the pages, using his gift for the visual to juxtapose and combine them, and the album became David's favorite before-bed picture book.

Rick loved it too. Each image of his family brought memories tumbling into his head of his Hollywood boyhood in the big home in Bel-Air, of his father and his uncle, two handsome, dashing young Hollywood rakes, of his incomparable parents whose perfection might have tarnished had he known them when he was more than an adolescent. But he hadn't, and he was finally realizing at age fifty that the memory of their relationship, probably vastly rewritten to be perfect, contributed to making each relationship in his own life pale by comparison.

"If the shoe fits, honey," was what Patty had said to him when they talked about people who couldn't find love because they had some unshakable idea in their heads about how it should be.

"Uncle Bobo, Grandpa Jake," David recited, pointing at all his favorite photos. "Ooooh, Grandmama Jane, Grandpa Jake."

Rick looked at the picture, which was David's favorite. It was an old studio publicity shot of Jane Grant and Jake Reisman, so beautiful and elegant. And the way they looked at each other made it easy to see they were completely in love. Tonight, looking at the photo filled him with regret about his own wasted years, and he said a silent prayer to the two of them.

Help me, he thought, looking at their image, still missing them as much as he did thirty years ago. Help me so I can change, really change, and make a connection with a woman in this lifetime. Being a father has taught me I know how to love and feel and hurt, and put someone else's needs before my own. This little heavenly creature has raised my consciousness almost too high, so that some days the sky is almost bluer than I can stand it, the music sweeter than I've ever heard it before, and I know now that I want to share that with a woman.

David was squealing over every photo, reciting the names of each person, remembering who they were. "Birfmuvver" was how he said birth mother, "Birfmuvver Doreen, Grandma Bea, Auntie Trish and lots of carrot tops," he shouted, pointing at

Trish's children and her husband, Don. Rick looked closely, very closely at the photo now, and felt a surge of sickness pour into his stomach.

The next morning Patty stopped at Rick's office toting a Saks Fifth Avenue shopping bag. When Rick peeked out of a meeting to ask Andrea a question he saw the back of a blonde with a great ass and was surprised when the blonde turned and it was Patty. She looked like a kid dressed in her faded jeans and funky sweatshirt.

"Hi," she said, her pretty smile brightening the room. "There was a sale in the boys' department, and since you always dress David in outfits that look like polyester leisure suits, I thought I'd take the liberty of my status as his unofficial aunt and buy him a few little items."

Rick walked over for a Hollywood kiss, a kind of touching of the sides of faces, and for an instant he wasn't sure if it was Patty's scent, somewhere between suntan lotion and Sea Breeze, that made him want to take her in his arms, or if the reason was his protracted absence from sex. "What's wrong with leisure suits?" he asked, backing up. Andrea was reaching into the bag pulling out the various shorts, T-shirts, and pants Patty had bought for David.

"Nothing if you're dressing Uncle Bobo," Andrea said. "And by the way, shouldn't you be on your way there now?"

Rick looked at his watch.

"I should. I'm going to close this meeting in my office, and then go get David and head out there."

Patty looked disappointed. "Ohh, too bad," she said, "I was going to ask you to come have a quick lunch with me and help me figure out some questions I have about Charlie's estate."

"Why don't I give you a call," he asked, "and we'll do it over the weekend?"

"Great," Patty said.

On his way to Calabassas, Rick thought maybe he should have invited Patty to join them for lunch out at the Motion

Picture Home. Bobo was crazy for her. "A woman and a half," he said about Patty. "If I was a little younger I'd sweep her off her feet." Bobo no longer waited outside the entrance of the home the way he used to, because the journey from his room to the front was now too long and too arduous. He had a walker, which he refused to use at all except when Rick and the baby came to visit. And only every now and then would he agree to be helped out of bed to his feet and work his way down the corridor, just so he could show off Rick and David, whom he called "my boys." His enfeebled body used everything he had to move along beside Rick and behind David, who found the long carpeted corridor the perfect place to toddle.

But though Bobo's body was failing, his mind was still on full throttle. One day last week he shook his head watching the baby, and said, "My life has been full of surprises. If anyone would have told me, a man who has seen as many years in this century as I have, that I would approve of such a thing as you and that baby—no, I take back 'approve,' and change it to 'give my blessing'—I would have said 'completely *meshugge*,' but you know what? It's a hell of a good thing."

Today as Rick walked with David on his shoulders through the hospital corridor past the nurses' station on the way to Bobo's room, the nurse who was sitting there looked up at the two of them and said, "These visits with that baby are keeping him alive."

"Hi, lady," David said.

"Hi, baby," the nurse said, waving.

"My boys," Bobo said as they walked into his room. He was propped up on the bed.

"Uncabobobobo," David said, and he climbed onto his great-uncle's bed, sat next to the old man, and put his two fat little hands on Bobo's old face."Hiya, Uncabobo."

"Yeah, sure. Don't try to charm me, you little stinkpot," Bobo said, smiling a smile minus his teeth, which were in a glass on the table across the room. Rick spread a blanket on the floor of Bobo's room, sat David on it and put a few toys on it, and the baby fell on them gleefully. Then Rick took his uncle's hand.

"Uncle B., I need your advice," he said to Bobo, and he told him his worries about Doreen.

"Ricky," he said when the story was told. "There's a reason why these ways of operating didn't exist in my day, or if they did it was so far underground, nobody knew or talked about it. Because somewhere along the way the idea breaks down, and is too full of whaddyacallit . . . complications. Never cut and dried, and that's true no matter what that fancy lawyer tried to tell you. And here's why. Can you walk away and say good-bye forever to that little girl? She gave you the most precious thing in life.

"Sure, if you have no heart maybe you say, It's not my problem. But even with the crazy life you lead, you're a guy who turns the world upside-down for somebody you love. Do I know it? How many other old *kockers* in this place have a regular visitor like you? Only me!" Rick wanted to put his face down on the blanket and cry. How he loved this old man. This sweetheart of a human being who saw through to the good in him. And how unbearably sad that David would grow up and never know or remember him.

"I trust your heart. You'll figure out a way to help that kid. Meantime, who's the woman?"

"What woman?"

"In the past few weeks, either my eyes are worse than I thought, or you're actually looking svelte."

"Svelte?"

"Okay, svelte is pushing it. But cute would be accurate," the old man said, now opening both eyes and laughing. "Some dame is finally getting to you, please God?"

"Absolutely not."

"Don't lie to a dying man. On second thought, lie to me, so I can go to my grave with a grin."

"You're delirious, Uncle B."

The old man laughed again. "No, I'm not" was all he said before he fell asleep. What is he talking about, Rick thought while he packed up the baby's things, and with David back on his shoulders he headed down the corridors that were lined with the black-and-white photos of Hollywood stars on his way to the parking lot. But when he got to the freeway entrance to go east, back to the studio, he passed it, took the one going west instead, and drove out to Malibu to be with Patty.

Andrea was just about to turn on the answering machine and leave for the commissary. She already had her purse in her hand, and Candy, the new girl who worked across the hall, was waiting outside for her so they could have lunch together when the phone rang. Shit, Andrea thought. Maybe I'll just ignore it. Rick had called her a few minutes ago from the car to say he was making a stop before he came in, and that he probably wouldn't be back until three. So it wasn't him calling.

"Andrea," Candy called from the hall. "Should I start over there and get us a table?"

"No, I'll just be a second. Richard Reisman's office."

"Uhhh . . . hello. Uhhh, is Mr. Reisman there?"

"No, he's not." It was a funny voice and she could tell by the sound it was long distance. "He should be back in a few hours. Can I say who's calling?"

"Are you Andrea?"

"Yeah." Come on already, she thought. I'm like starving here.

"I'm Bea Cobb. Doreen's mother. This is an emergency and I need to talk to him right away."

She sounded panicky. "Why don't I try and find him for you, Mrs. Cobb?" Andrea said. "I'll have him call you as soon as I do."

Andrea put the phone down and went to the door. "Candy, I can't go to lunch. Something important is happening and I need to try and find Rick."

He wasn't at home, he wasn't in the car. She even called the

Hamburger Hamlet in Beverly Hills where he sometimes liked to take David for a late lunch, but he wasn't there either. If he missed this call he'd be devastated, but she couldn't imagine where he might be.

"Well, isn't this a nice surprise?" Patty Fall said, opening the front door. "I was just hosing off the deck and planning to sit out there and do some paperwork. Come on in, you two."

David toddled through the living room and followed Rick and Patty into the kitchen.

"Shouldn't you be at work?" she asked Rick.

"I'm playing hooky. I just left Bobo and he's so obviously not long for this world that sometimes I'm afraid to leave him. Afraid I'll never see him alive again. It's so hard for me to think I'm really losing him that I guess going back to my office to work on a production schedule felt mundane."

"Well, I'm glad you decided to come here," she said. In a practiced way she gathered several plastic kitchen utensils and containers, scooped David up, and led Rick outside, past the deck and down to the beach. While David poured sand from one container to the next, Rick and Patty sat close to each other.

"Death is a part of life, Ricky. Bobo will die and you'll go on. You've had an unparalleled relationship with him. And he was a great influence on you."

"Sometimes I think he doesn't want to live anymore. That he's just hanging on until he nags me into getting married."

Patty laughed. "Who does he have in mind as the bride?"

"Beats the hell out of me. Today he accused me of holding out on him. Said I looked too good, so there must be a woman in my life." David had pulled off one of his shoes and was now filling it with sand.

"He's right," Patty said, smiling. Rick looked at her. When their eyes met they held each other's gaze and he saw her eyes searching his. "Is there a woman?" she asked.

Rick wasn't prepared for the surge of feeling, a combination of gratitude for her friendship and longing for her. A need to hold her and kiss her and cry with her over the loss of Charlie and Bobo. And to thrill with her over David. The ringing of the telephone on the deck broke the moment.

"Be right back," Patty said, and scrambled up to the deck. "Yes. Hello?" Rick heard her voice drifting down to the beach. Then she gestured for him to come, so he picked up David and ran to the deck to get the phone.

"Mr. Reisman, I just had an emergency call from Doreen Cobb's mother, Bea. I can call her back and patch her in to you at Mrs. Fall's if that's okay," Andrea said on the phone.

"It's okay," Rick said as Patty took David and gently wiped the sand from his little feet.

"Hello?"

"Bea."

"I'll get right to the point. Have you talked to my daughter lately?"

"Not for a few weeks. Why?"

"I thought maybe she'd show up out there. To see you or the baby, because a few days ago she ran away."

"No," Rick said. Ran away. Now he knew he had to be right about the son-of-a-bitch brother-in-law. Goddammit. Why hadn't he said more to her when she called on the day of the adoption? Why hadn't he said, Doreen, this is a formality, not about the real connection you'll always have with this boy. You'll always be David's family. We love you. "Bea, have you called the police?"

"Well, I was going to, but my son-in-law Don told me to just leave it alone. He says it's a teenage thing she has to work out for herself, and that in cases like this the police can't do much, and that she'll come back."

The son-in-law probably hoped they'd find her dead somewhere. Rick felt hamstrung. He was lost in his own mental picture of Doreen's anguish. From far away he heard Bea say, "Don's been my adviser since my husband died eight years ago. He practically raised Doreen. Trish's husband. In those pictures we sent, he's the one with the red hair."

"Listen, Bea," Rick said, his head ringing with fear. "I'd call the police if I were you."

"Yeah, maybe," she said in a voice that made him know she wouldn't.

"And if I hear from her—" he began.

"You tell her to come home," said her mother, "because everyone in this family loves her and wants the best for her." But Rick knew the truth and feared for Doreen's life.

32

LAINIE DECIDED that the only sign of Mitch's deception was his patent avoidance of her. In the store while customers were around he was always the Mitch of Lainie and Mitch, the beautiful couple, with an arm around her, or a tender pat on her cheek. But at home, his eyes avoided hers. When she went off to bed, he stayed up late, saying he had work to do. Most mornings he was out of bed and in the shower even before the baby woke.

In contrast to his treatment of her, the way he focused on little Rosie, held her, kissed her, gave Lainie more evidence that his coolness to her wasn't simply due to his preoccupation with some problem at the store.

Why don't I tell him I know what he's doing? Lainie would wonder at three in the morning as she sat awake in their bed. And memories of looking out the bedroom window in her child-hood room at dawn came back. Memories of watching her father return from God knows where, sometimes so drunk he'd forget to turn off the headlights on the car. She would hear him tiptoe up the stairs. And when she figured he was asleep, little Lainie would hurry down in her pajamas and turn out the car lights, then hurry back to her bed where she would feel that same kind of helpless feeling she now had about Mitch.

Is that what I should do, Lainie thought, wait until things
blow over? Sit it out, the way my mother did until he died, so
she could collect the insurance? Not me, Lainie thought, I'm
not going to live a lie. But instead of saying a word, she went
on about her life, her day, caring for the baby, stopping by the
store, going to her classes, unable to shake the taunting question
that was stuck in her chest and her brain.

> *That cuckold lives in bliss*
> *Who, certain of his fate, loves not his wronger*
> *But, O, what damned minutes tells he o'er*
> *Who dotes, yet doubts, suspects, yet soundly loves!*

A group of students from an acting class were doing a reading
of *Othello* for Lainie's Shakespeare class. I don't need an Iago to
torment me, she thought, listening to the dialogue. I'm my own
Iago. Driving myself crazy the way he does Othello. There is
no way that Mitch De Nardo, my husband, is screwing the
surrogate, she thought, trying to be rational. But the Iago part
of her asked, Really? If that's true, then walk out of this classroom, right now, and drive past Sherman Oaks Park. Didn't
Mitch say he was going to take Rosie there to play tonight?
Didn't he think you'd be safely in school so he could take Jackie's
daughter to visit with her? Why else would he be so eager to
do that if he didn't have something going on with Jackie.

> *No, Iago; I'll see before I doubt; when I doubt, prove;*
> *And on the proof, there is no more but this,*
> *Away at once with love or jealousy.*

The actor reading the part of Othello had a giant voice that
belied his slight build. It was hard to believe the emotion he
could call up, reading from a script and sitting on a folding
chair, but everyone in the room seemed to be leaning in toward
him, feeling Othello's grief and pain. When it was time for the
break, as the rest of the class headed for the Coke machines
Lainie walked to her car.

* * *

There were two teenage boys shooting baskets, a family sitting at a picnic table eating, and a jogger making his way around the track. The playground was empty. A strong wind blew some sand out of the sandbox and made the swings sway back and forth, as though ghostly riders were pumping them into the sky. "I do not think but Desdemona's honest." Sitting in her car, Lainie felt stupid to have let her insanity make her walk out on the last half of her Shakespeare class to rush over here to see if Mitch was with Jackie. If she went home now he would notice she was early and wonder why. But that would be okay. She could tell him she missed the baby and wanted to see her before she went to sleep.

Mitch's car was in the garage and the condominium was still as Lainie made her way quietly up the stairs. When she opened the door to the nursery, what she saw filled her with relief and joy and embarrassment for her own doubts about her beloved Mitch. There he was in the rocking chair, asleep, with the sleeping baby snuggled against him. Sick, I am so sick, so insecure that because of the smell of some perfume anyone might wear and some neighbor's remark, I might have been crazy enough to lash out at my husband with a ridiculous accusation.

Mitch De Nardo, the sweetest, best man in the world, had simply been distracted by problems at work. She would wake him now, and after they put Rosie in a night diaper and down to sleep in her crib, Lainie would somehow get Mitch to come to bed early, where she would make sweet love to him. It had been too long, and their loving would make them close again.

"Mitchie," she said, touching him tenderly.

"Huh?" Mitch looked up at her, realized he'd been put to sleep by his own lullaby, then looked down at the sleeping baby. "Little angelface wore me out tonight."

"What did you two do together?" Lainie asked, taking Rose from him and gently placing her on the changing table.

"Oh, it was great. We took a long ride."

In the evening? During rush hour, they took a ride? "Where?"

"The beach," Mitch said, yawning, standing, and stretching. "Want me to put her night diaper on her?" he asked.

"I can do it," Lainie said.

"Great," he said, not looking at her. "Now that you're here, I'm going to go back to the store. I've got a stack of invoices that I have to look over. The bookkeeper's coming tomorrow, and I'm not ready for her. I want her to do all the store bills and all of our personal stuff too." He patted his pants pocket and found his car keys. "Don't wait up" were his last words, and he was gone.

The next day Lainie took Rose to the zoo with her friend Sharon and Sharon's baby. Rose pointed her tiny finger at the elephant and said, "Elatin." "Yes!" Lainie said, thrilling to the sound of her daughter learning to talk.

"Mine still hasn't said a word," Sharon said.

Lainie pushed the stroller from cage to cage, next to Sharon and her stroller, and she still couldn't shake the heavyhearted feeling she had about whatever it was that was going on with Mitch. She didn't feel close enough to Sharon to tell her what she was going through. In fact, she didn't feel close enough to anybody. Oddly, the only woman with whom she'd ever felt any real intimacy was Jackie. For obvious reasons—the months of insemination attempts, the startling fact which never grew less startling that she was carrying Mitch's baby—but also because Jackie was someone who demanded intimacy, barreled into your life and opened up hers in a warm, unafraid way. She paid attention to your feelings and told you about hers.

Not like the rigid way Lainie had been taught to behave with everyone. If those qualities were hereditary she hoped that Rose would inherit them. Jackie was a good person, Lainie thought, and then she felt foolish about the fears and fantasies she'd been having about Jackie and Mitch.

"I've been going to a gym," Sharon said as they stopped at a food center to get sandwiches for themselves and to give the little girls some finger foods they'd each brought along. "Because I've been feeling as if I'm never going to get back in shape, and

Jerry hasn't touched me in months. But you know, it's funny, when I was pregnant, we had sex all the time, so I don't think it's my being fat that's bothering him."

Lainie put some pieces of banana on the little tray attached to the front of Rosie's stroller. This was more than Sharon had ever revealed about her personal life in the past. Usually when they got together they talked about what they were reading in English class, or how having babies at home was getting in the way of their studying.

"My sister said it happened with her husband too. As soon as there was a kid, his whole attitude changed. As if he was saying, 'Now that you're a mother, I can't get hot with you anymore.'" Lainie nodded sympathetically. The thought cheered her. Maybe that was why Mitch wasn't sexy with her these days. And if that's all it was, she could fix that in no time. Get him away for a weekend. Bring some slinky lingerie, drive him wild the way she always used to.

On the way home from the zoo, she and Rosie would stop off at Panache to see Daddy. Lainie would take him aside and tell him they should plan a trip together. Her mother could take Rosie for the two days. The store would survive for forty-eight hours without Mitch, and they would find a hotel somewhere on the ocean and just be sexy for hours and days.

All of the girls who worked in the store oohed and ahhed over Rosie when Lainie walked in carrying her. In her little hand she held the string of a helium balloon from the L.A. zoo.

"She's so big," Carin said. "Can I hold her?" Rosie grinned and went to Carin easily. "Mitch said he had to go to the bank," Carin told Lainie. "He'll be back any minute." Then she took Rosie over to the three-way mirrors to play "see the baby." Lainie told Carin she'd be in the office in the back of the store, and she went in to call her mother at work so that when Mitch got back she'd be armed with baby-sitting dates that were good for her mother's schedule.

The office was pristine. The bookkeeper had obviously finished her work, and in one high pile were the store's current bills, checks attached and ready to stuff and mail, and in another Lainie and Mitch's personal bills with checks attached. Lainie dialed the phone, then shuffled through the mail absently while the phone at Bradford, Freeman rang in her ear.

"Law offices of Bradford, Freeman. How may I direct your call?"

"Mother?"

"Oh, hi, dear. Hold on. I've got three lines ringing all at once. Don't go away."

Gas bill, very high, water bill too, Lainie noticed. Gelson's Market, she had a charge account there. It was an extravagance, but Lainie loved their perfect produce, their great deli, and their sweet-smelling bakery, though this month the bill was exorbitant. Pacific Bell. A long itemized bill of every toll call. Pages of calls. While she waited, she lifted the check and looked down at the list of calls.

West Los Angeles, Santa Monica, Studio City, her mother's phone number. Another West Los Angeles. Long Beach. Long Beach. Who did they know in Long Beach besides . . . she looked across the page at a phone number that was definitely Jackie's. She looked at the date, then at the calendar. A school night, the call was made from their house at six-forty, just after Lainie walked out the door to go to her class. Her hand moved down the page. Two weeks later, Long Beach. Time, six-forty-one. She would leave and Mitch would call Jackie, to tell her that he and Rosie were on their way to see her, and Rosie, who couldn't talk yet, couldn't tell the secret to Lainie. And that's why Mitch wasn't making love to Lainie. Dear God, it was true.

"Hi, baby!" She turned with a gasp as if she were the one who had been caught, when all she'd been doing was looking at her own telephone bill. Something she'd never bothered to do in the past because Mitch always took care of those things with the bookkeeper. And he knew under normal circumstances she would never look at, let alone scrutinize, a phone bill. She put the phone back in the cradle.

"Mitch," she said, feeling her face shaking and not sure if she was going to be able to ask the next question. If the answer was yes it could pull out the underpinnings of her entire life. She remembered the serious way Barbara Singer told her, "You fought cancer, you can handle this," and it gave her the strength to ask, "Have you been seeing Jackie?" Please God, let him say no, she thought. Let the phone calls he made to her just have been about some legal problem or other, or some unpaid medical bill.

Mitch looked down at the floor and didn't answer.

"You have," Lainie said, wishing she had died, wishing that the cancer had killed her instead of letting her live to stand in this room feeling like an empty, miserable shrew demanding an answer. "And you've taken Rosie with you too, haven't you?" When he finally answered, it was by way of a slight nod.

"Why? How? What could possibly make you do that after all you and I went through to make this work? Mitch, I felt so inadequate for so many years that I agreed to let you have a baby with another woman. But there wasn't one step of the way during all of it when I didn't have to stop myself from begging you to call it off because of how much it hurt. Don't you understand that one of the reasons this awful world is able to go on is because a woman desperately wants to feel the baby of the man she loves inside her body? Not to watch some other woman glory in the feeling of that life. I might as well have watched you make love to her. Did you do that, Mitch? Did you make love to Jackie? You can tell me everything now that it's all out. Her perfume was on your shirt, your telephone calls to her are in black and white on our phone bill. Was it sexier with her because she still has her insides?"

She was screaming at him, her voice rising up to the ceiling, reverberating, she was sure, throughout the whole store so the salesgirls and the customers could hear every word. Finally she was letting out the pain, the rage, the hurt she had felt about all of this for so long. And Mitch didn't try to silence her, just stood in that spot, in the doorway of the office, looking down at his black leather loafers.

"Mama," she heard Rosie's voice call out from somewhere in the store, then she heard Carin's voice say, "Mama's busy now. Why don't we go and try on hats? I'll bet Rosie looks cute in hats. Come on. That's a good girl."

"I didn't touch her," Mitch said. "I mean, maybe a little hug once before we parted, that must be how the perfume got on me, but I took Rosie to see her because she came here one night to the store, just before I was closing up. The girls didn't know who she was, and I nearly fell over when I saw her.

"I thought she didn't know anything about us. I thought it was why we had that special phone and paid for everything in cash. She told me she'd known our last name for years. That she once applied for a job at the old store and met me there. That when we first walked into the lawyer's office that day to meet her, she remembered me, even though I didn't remember her. She also told me that during the pregnancy you dropped our last name once by mistake.

"She sat right down over there and said to me, 'Mitch, this isn't blackmail, it isn't a threat, it's just a truth. That baby came from my body, from my egg, from me, and I need to see her. Need to know her, need to be with her.' She said it wasn't blackmail or anything like that, but that she had to be in Rose's life. Tell Lainie it's okay, she said. She begged me. She said, 'I won't hurt their relationship.'

"I told her she was nuts. Completely crazy to think I would ever go for what she was saying, or that *you* would. I didn't believe it wasn't blackmail, so I offered her money, lots of money to go away forever, I wasn't even sure where I would get that kind of money, but she didn't want it. She wasn't holding out for more than I was offering. She didn't want money. And all of a sudden I realized while I was sitting there that she wasn't crazy at all about wanting to be with the baby. What was crazy was any of the three of us agreeing to bring a baby into the world under those circumstances. And I take the blame. Because of my colossal ego, I ended up making you go through the tortures of the damned, and then Jackie too, and created a situation that just can't ever work the way we thought it would."

"And without telling me, or asking me, you took Rose to see her."

"I thought if I asked you it would kill you," he said defensively, making Lainie wild with rage that he could think that position was defensible.

"So you lied. Made the baby a party to your lie."

"I knew once Rosie could really talk I couldn't do it anymore. And I had hopes that maybe if Jackie saw her once or twice, maybe she'd understand how tough it was on all of us to do it, and change her mind. Or that somehow I'd be able to tell you and we could work it out. Lainie, I did a bad thing by sneaking around you. But the real bad thing was a few years ago when I didn't say to you, Let's keep trying to adopt, instead of giving up because we had one bad experience. And I should have said to my sister, Mind your own damned business, I don't care if the baby's a De Nardo. I want Lainie to be okay about it. But now it's done. I made a baby with that woman, and I can't pretend it didn't happen, and neither can she and neither can you."

Lainie looked at his face and hated him. "Mitch, I'm going home. I'm taking Rosie with me. Tonight, on my way to school, I'll drop her at my mother's. While I'm gone I want you to go to our place and get everything out of there that you need, because I won't live with you, can't stand what you've put me through, and don't want to be anywhere near you. We can discuss the arrangements of our divorce through lawyers, and also what will happen to Rose."

"Lainie, please—"

"No, Mitch," she said. "The last time you said 'please' to me, I agreed to do what you were asking, and it did damage to a lot of people's lives."

33

BARBARA TOOK A SIP of coffee, looked at the clock, and realized it was time to begin. "I think what we've been seeing here is that many times we find ourselves talking about the same problems all the parents in my groups talk about, separation anxieties, setting limits, sleeping."

"Sleeping? Never heard of it," Judith said. "By the time Jillian was sleeping through the night, I had Jody. I think the last complete night I slept was the night before Jillian was born."

There were a few amens to that as the others settled into their chairs. Every week the members of this group seemed genuinely glad to see one another, to have found a unique level of trust among themselves, and a sense of pride in their differences from the rest of the world. It was a chemistry Barbara always hoped the people in her groups would have, but it didn't always happen.

When the groups clicked, the members continued their relationships long after the year of meetings was over. When they didn't, there was no way she could interest the members in engaging one another. In those cases the entire year could be spent with the parents barely looking at one another, and leaving with relief after the last session.

"The best solution for me and my little ones about sleep has been to take them into my bed at night. I read that book *The Family Bed*, and figured, why should a little person have to be cold and alone when we can all cuddle together and I can make them feel secure?" Judith said.

"Would you consider taking in a chilly big person?" Rick asked her.

"I should have known *you'd* turn that into a joke," Judith said, laughing and throwing the cloth diaper she'd been wearing on her shoulder as a drooling pad for the baby at Rick. "And believe me, I can use the laugh. You all know what I've been through with men, and on top of that, I can't seem to find a housekeeper I like. Some days I feel like I'm on complete baby burn-out."

"Want to talk about any of it?" Barbara asked.

"Which is the bigger problem? The men or the housekeeper?" Ruthie asked.

"Good question," Barbara said to Ruthie, then turned to Judith. "Which *is* the bigger problem. The men or the house-keeper?"

Judith thought for an instant and grinned. "Well, you know how hard it is to get good help." Everyone laughed. The discussion turned to their mutual guilt about working and parenting, and how hard it was to part with the babies every day. All of them except Lainie worked, and she spent several nights a week in school and many of her days studying.

Mitch hadn't been to the last few group sessions and there had always been an excuse from her about his having to be at the store. Today when there was a rare quiet moment in the discussion, she spoke up. "Mitch and I are separated. I asked him to leave after I found out that without discussing it with me, he'd been secretly taking the baby to see the surrogate."

"Oh, my God," Ruthie said.

"What would make him do that?" Shelly asked.

"She came to him and begged him to let her see the baby. He was afraid to tell me, but he believed it was the right thing for her to be with the baby . . . so he agreed."

"I guess there's no denying that she is the baby's mother," Rick said matter-of-factly, and Lainie looked as if someone had kicked her.

"Explain why you said that, Rick," Barbara said, noting that the light feeling among them was gone.

"I don't mean to sound like all the dumb people in the world, and I didn't say 'real mother,' but that woman has a biological connection to that baby. And from what you're saying, an emotional one too. I'd worry like hell if it was my baby about disconnecting from her. Her genes and her history are very much who Rose is, and who she is going to grow up to be. Listen, I don't really know Mitch at all," Rick said. "In fact, from the little I've come to know him in here, I didn't particularly like him. But I'll bet there's something in him that says the genetic mother should have a relationship with the baby. And he may have handled it poorly, but I think his instincts are right. Please don't in any way take this personally, Lainie, but I think the concept of surrogacy is a disaster. I believe that just as adoption is a way of solving two problems, surrogacy creates not just problems but potential tragedies."

"That's what I think," Lainie said, trying to stay collected. "I mean, that's what I think now. But when it was happening, I didn't know what to think. I felt as if I had to do something and do it fast, because so much time had gone by with me trying to have babies and then being sick, and Mitch wanted it so much. I felt that if I couldn't give him a baby I was worthless. But now I know I never should have said yes to any of it."

"I understand the confusion," Judith said, "because I don't know how anyone could not want to relate to their own genetic offspring. To know that somewhere out there was a product of you, and not feel related to it, not needing to know it, just doesn't make sense. Don't get me wrong, I think Mitch is a bum for doing anything behind your back."

"What about your sperm donors?" Rick asked Judith. "You want them in your life?"

"Believe me," she shot back defensively, "I wish they were

available for baby-sitting. No, seriously, I only wish I had an important relationship in my life. But I don't. So I started without that elusive him."

"I think Lainie's problem right now has more to do with the idea that there was a deception after such a carefully thought-out plan about how to conduct the surrogacy. Mitch seems to have changed the rules on her without telling her what the new rules are, and breached their trust."

"The shit," Judith said.

"Can't you fix it? Talk about it?" Ruthie asked.

"I'm still too raw," Lainie answered. "I'm still beating myself up for agreeing to do it in the first place, and jealous and sick with shock that he could lie to me. I'm trying to find a way to understand his behavior. Right now it feels to me as if we had a good life together, but somehow we've managed to turn it into something that can never be right."

"So change your definition of what's right," Judith said. "That's what *I* did. Don't get bogged down in the idea that there's only one version of family. If family to me was only for husbands, wives, and babies, I'd still be waiting for the phone to ring. There's got to be a way to make it okay. To work something out about the surrogate that you and Mitch and the surrogate can live with."

Lainie thought about it. "I don't know if I'm capable of being as big about all of this as all of you are in your lives. In fact I know I'm not. I had some boundaries inside me I set up for the way behavior was supposed to be, and Mitch crossed them. So something tells me this is as far as I can go with him." Her pretty face looked long and pale and pleated with the furrows of pain. "Please let's let it go, please let's talk about somebody else's problems."

Barbara looked around to see who wanted to speak next.

"I got a call from a part of my son's extended family and need to talk about that in here," Rick said. He was planning to tell them about his conversation with Bea Cobb, but in order to make the impact more clear he backed up and told them more

about how he and Doreen came together. He was surprised at
the way his voice shook when he talked about the day he met
Doreen and Bea Cobb at the airport, and now how worried he
was about what sounded like Doreen's fragile mental state, and
where she might have gone. It had been days since Bea's call
and he hadn't had one more word.

"You're dealing with some very complicated emotions," Barbara said. "Doreen is probably and will always be grieving for
the loss of David. Adolescence can be pretty traumatic under
the best of circumstances, and a classic time for running away,
but she's had to deal with the added upheaval of an unwanted
pregnancy and a separation from the baby. And of course we
don't have any idea what she's been through with school and
friends and boys, not to mention the other members of her
family. Clearly she has a lot to overcome.

"It sounds to me from this very distant vantage point as if
she's got some difficult times to get through. This running away
is a cry for help. It sounds as if you and this girl forged a very
powerful attachment. But for the long term, I believe you're
going to have to have faith in that inner strength you told me
she has to get her through this. Has the family called the
police?"

"No," Rick said, holding himself in check for fear that by
facing this he would fall apart right there. "And it worries me.
The padrone of the family is the husband of the eldest sister,
and I don't trust this guy. I don't know, maybe I'm crazy but
I have a terrible feeling he . . ." Ruthie moved to one side of
Rick and Lainie to another and they each put an arm around
him. "If anything happens to that little girl . . ." he began, but
he was too choked with emotion to finish the sentence.

"We're going to need to focus on what both Lainie's and
Rick's dilemmas bring up," Barbara said, "which is what your
obligations and agreements are to the extended families of these
children, and when and if you let these needs affect your lives.
It's a topic that's affecting all of you."

"Not us," Ruthie said.

"Well, I don't know," Barbara said. "Suppose the time came that one of you found a romance, a mate?"

Neither Ruthie nor Shelly knew what to say to that. A long uncomfortable time passed during which there was only the squeaking of chairs and a sigh or two.

"Good God," Judith said. "It's all so painful."

"But worth it," Ruthie said, looking out the window at the children playing. "Being a parent is definitely worth it." The others sat in quiet agreement.

He *is* handsome, Barbara thought, looking at Ryan Adler across the dining room table, and I can sure see why Heidi is so attracted to him. He's also very good at charming. Big smile, polite, deferential to Stan, to me. And my poor child is falling all over him. Her voice is shrill and she's trying too painfully hard. She jumps with terror every time he gestures in her direction and when dinner is over they're leaving here and going to a hotel to spend the night. I can't stand it.

"Get ahold of yourself, honey," Stan said to her when he carried the last of the dinner plates through the swinging doors to the kitchen.

"Why?"

"Because," Stan said, "you look as if you're ready to cry out there. This is supposed to be a joyous occasion, remember?"

"I hate him," Barbara whispered. "I've forgotten everything I ever learned about psychology. I want to pour hot coffee in his lap and push his face into the ice cream."

"Would anybody have been good enough for her? And remember, mothers know nothing. Gracie hated me."

"Present tense, honey. Hates, hates."

"There you are, and I'm a goddamned prince on horseback. So maybe it's time for you to let it go."

"You're right," she said, hoping the classical music coming out of the speakers in the dining room was preventing Heidi and Ryan from hearing her. "I should let it go, I'm going to let it go. But can I poison him first?"

Stan laughed and picked up the coffee tray and went back through the swinging doors into the dining room. Barbara said a quick prayer for strength and followed.

"Should we start talking about dates?" Stan asked, putting a cup in front of Ryan. "I mean, I have a pretty full calendar for the rest of the year so I thought we should go over some possibilities. What are we talking about in terms of time?"

Heidi and Ryan answered at the same time. She said December and he said next summer, and then they each looked at the other with disdain.

"That's too soon, sweetheart," he said. Barbara's stomach tightened.

"What are we waiting for? Neither one of us is in school," she whined.

"Honey, what's our hurry?" Ryan asked her as if he were talking to a child. And he is, Barbara thought. "This way your folks will have more time to get it all planned." He patted her hand, but she pulled it away. Barbara knew her so well that before a pout was even on her daughter's lips she could tell that Heidi was furious.

"I don't want to wait until the summer," Heidi said, getting edgy in a way Barbara recognized, and though she would never admit it, she liked the direction the conversation was taking. It escalated from there. Heidi got whinier and Ryan got more supercilious. Barbara tried to remember later what the exact moment was, maybe when he used the word *childish*, or just after she said snidely they'd have to make the plans fit in with Ryan's mother's schedule, but Heidi jumped up from her chair and ran upstairs in tears. When she was gone, Ryan looked at Barbara and Stan with a shrug grown-ups frequently use with one another that meant, Kids. Who can understand them?

Barbara wanted to go upstairs and put a bureau against the door so Heidi wouldn't come back down again.

"She's not easy," Ryan said. "As I'm sure you already know, but I adore her."

Both Barbara and Stan were silent.

"Dinner was lovely," Ryan said, standing, "and I think what I should probably do now is make my way back to the hotel, and hope she's feeling a little bit better about all of this when the dawn breaks."

Barbara's back teeth were tightly clenched as she and Stan both stood. They all walked to the front door, passing the wall of family pictures, and Barbara caught sight of a picture of Heidi at three years old in which she had the same expression on her face as she had had a moment ago when she'd rushed upstairs.

When Ryan was gone, Stan took Barbara in his arms and asked, "How do we tell her it's not going to happen?"

"Unfortunately, we don't," she answered. "We just wait for her to figure that out on her own."

34

WITHOUT MITCH IN HER LIFE, Lainie lived each day by rote. She took care of the baby's needs, and in the evenings when she had school, she dropped Rosie off with her grandmother Margaret and went off to class. Mitch called and left apologetic messages on the answering machine, messages in which he begged her to call him back and talk to him, see him, promising her he could make her understand.

She would lean against the wall, still holding her books from school, listening to the long speeches he made to the answering machine, alternately hating him and longing for him. Sometimes she would rewind the machine and play the messages again just to hear the parts where he swore his love to her. Rosie, sitting on the kitchen floor, would hear his voice, look up, and gleefully shout, "Daddy!"

Within a week, Mitch's messages went from pleading to annoyance, and then from annoyance to anger, and from anger to rage. "Pick the fucking phone up, Laine, and call me back, or you'll hear from my lawyer." She'd never heard that tone of voice from him, and there was a part of her that was glad to hear him so overwrought.

"Yes, Mitch," she said on the night he said that, picking up the phone and turning off the answering machine, relieved that the baby, who had now taken to repeating every word everyone said, was asleep.

"You've got a lot of balls, Lainie. I have every right in the world to our home and to my daughter." It wasn't her imagination that he emphasized the word *my*. "What can you possibly think you're doing by ignoring my phone calls? I've been too nice to come over there and break the door down, but believe me I will if I have to. I'll come over there and take the baby the hell out of there."

"No, you won't, Mitch. Because you love her and you know you're doing the best thing for her by letting her stay with me. Not you and not Jackie."

"Hey, I told you I've got nothing going with Jackie."

"Not anymore since I broke up the party."

"Lainie, I can't change any of it back to the way it was. I wish I could. But now is now and I want to see my daughter and you'd better stop trying to get in the way. So come up with a time that's good, and I'll pick her up and bring her back later. Then we can start talking about the issues around her custody."

"You work all day every day, sometimes until late at night. I'm at home and have been her primary caretaker since the day she was born. I may not be her biological parent," she said, still not believing that she was having this conversation, "but with the possible options, my availability and dependability and history with her make me the best candidate for solid parenting, genes or no genes."

"We'll see," Mitch said. "When will she be ready?"

"At ten in the morning." Lainie's own rage was bubbling in her chest. She knew that was Mitch's busiest hour at the store, but Mitch rose to it.

"I'm there," he said, and hung up.

Seeing her husband sitting nervously in their living room was unquestionably odd. They had chosen every piece of furniture, every picture on the wall in that room together, and now he was an outsider. She missed him so much that if he'd said, "I love you. This is dumb," she probably would have said, "You're right. Go get your things and move back in while I fix lunch." But he didn't ask to come home. Instead he sat with his hands folded, as if he were a prom date being looked over by the parents of the teenage girl.

The baby had been up at five A.M., and was still down for her morning nap. Mitch was quiet for a long time. When he finally spoke, it was in a voice so constricted by pain it was almost unrecognizable. "I want to see her every day. If she so much as coughs, I want to know about it. I'm not happy about her living anywhere but with me, but right now I'm knocking myself out to keep the business going and I've got to be in the store so much that what you said last night was right. It wouldn't be any kind of a life for her." It was like a speech he'd rehearsed, as if fearing that once he tried to be spontaneous, he'd lose control. And when he turned to Lainie she saw the passion behind the exterior, and more anger than she'd ever seen him express with anyone.

"But I'm warning you, Lainie. One misstep and I'll be all over you. I'll close the goddamned store down, and we'll forget about the life-style, because I'll take over raising her and you can go get your old job back at Valley BMW."

The bastard, the rotten lousy bastard. "Mitch, what do you want from me?" The curious mixture of feelings that made her at once want to pummel him and fall into his arms, begging him to fix all of this, bewildered her.

"All I want is for my daughter to be okay," he said. "Everything else is incidental. So if right now she's okay living with you, then that's what I want. I'm through begging you to understand all of this, because I don't understand it myself. And I can reassure you I'm not stepping away from her life. In fact, I'm going to come back to those group sessions too, because I don't want to miss out on anything that has to do with her. Understand that and—"

A whimper floated down from upstairs and then a "Ma-

maaaa . . . ," and Lainie turned and hurried up to the baby's room. When she walked in, Rose was standing, holding on to the side of the crib, and seeing Lainie made her little face brighten. "Up, Mama. Up." Her baby, her sweet baby girl. The worst thing Lainie could do was fall apart. She had to prove to Mitch that she was the most stable force for Rosie right now.

"Daddy's here, sweetheart," she said, trying to smile.

There was pure joy in Rosie's face. "Daddeeee," she squealed again and again while Lainie put her on the changing table. And just as she was placing the dry diaper under the sweet little bottom, she felt Mitch standing close behind her. So close that for an instant she thought he was there to put his arms around her and say, Let's be a family again. But instead he spoke directly to Rose. "Hello, Daddy's angel. We're going to go play today," and he moved away. When the clean diaper was on and a pink playsuit over it, Mitch hoisted the diaper bag strap onto his shoulder. "See you at five," he said and took the baby out of her arms.

"Bye-bye, Mama," Rosie said, opening and closing her little fist in a wave that was aimed at her own face. Lainie waved a little wave back to her and said, "Bye-bye, my sweet girl."

After that Mitch came back to the weekly sessions of the group. He would bustle in as if it were a business meeting. Sometimes he'd even take notes. He never said much, certainly never talked about what he and Lainie were going through. And Barbara left it alone, waiting for one of them to talk about it, but neither of them did. Lainie would watch him hug and kiss Rose good-bye after the session and then leave. Always she wanted to go after him, grab his sleeve, and say, What about me? I know you want to hug me too. Please, Mitch, come home.

The loneliness of life without him created an enormous void. She tried to fill it with school. She even joined the gym For Women Only in Studio City where Sharon belonged. Sometimes she would go to classes there in the morning when Mitch took the baby, but she preferred the early-evening aerobics class. She would drop Rosie off with the ever-stoic Margaret Dunn, who had actually gone out and bought a box full of baby toys, which sat waiting for Rose in her living room.

One night after Lainie left school, she picked the baby up at her mother's and headed home on the freeway. In the garage she pulled on her backpack of books, came around to the passenger side of the car, opened the door, and gently lifted the sleeping Rosie out of the baby car seat. Then she closed and locked the car and started out of the garage, stopping in terror when she saw someone stepping out of the shadows. It was Jackie.

Lainie's adrenaline raced and she put one of her hands around the back of the baby's head, as if to hide her, and rushed past.

"Lainie," Jackie said, "stop! I'm not the enemy. Let me come in and talk to you for five minutes. That's all I want."

"Get out of here, Jackie. You made a deal with me and Mitch. You told me that after the baby was born you were going to get out of our lives. But you lied." She was trying to find her house key as she moved along the stone path through the foliage leading to the door of her condo. Jackie stayed close behind her.

"I know what I said, but, Lainie, I need you to listen."

Lainie opened the door and looked at her. "I don't care what you need. Go away. You've done enough." The sharpness in Lainie's voice awakened Rosie, who opened her eyes. And then, though she was just getting to an age where she was afraid of strangers, she smiled, showing all her new teeth, and put her arms out to Jackie. It was clear this was no stranger.

"Hello, darling girl," Jackie said, her own blue eyes filling. The baby bounced up and down with glee to see her. "I made the deal because I was stupid," she said to Lainie. "I thought the pregnancy experience could be separated out of the experience of creating an ongoing life. But it can't. I need to be with her. Listen, Lainie, you and I and Mitch could fight about it like those people in New Jersey did, and all those other ugly cases, and maybe I'd lose, but you know what? I'm her mother. She has my genes, and she grew inside me and she'll grow up and, yes, she'll have lots of De Nardo in her, but one day you'll hear her laugh my big dumb laugh, or hear her voice on the telephone and for a second you'll think it's me. Or you'll see her putting on weight in the same spots I do, and just like you see your own mother in you, we all do, you'll see me in her.

"Lainie, I made a mistake, a big one. And so did you and so did Mitch. You were probably afraid he'd love you less or leave you if you said no to the whole idea, and I had some big need to feel important and special the way I did once before in my life, and that was when I was pregnant and gave birth to my son. So for each of our own reasons we went for it, and pretty soon, before we knew it, my baby with your husband was growing inside me. Well, all I can say is that even though I've only seen her these few times since she was born . . . I love her.

"Let's continue the good relationship we had when I was pregnant and let me be with her. Look at me, Lainie, and talk to me from the womanness inside you. Not the place that's afraid maybe someday Rose will decide she likes me better than she likes you, and not the part where you're afraid your mother or Mitch's sisters will tell you you're crazy for letting me be around her, but from the feeling, caring person who knows what it is to hurt and suffer and be taken advantage of, because I know in that part of you, you have to believe nobody can have too many people loving them, too many mothers looking out for them.

"I don't want Mitch. Believe me, I never have, or you would have known it instinctively and never picked me as a surrogate. And Mitch doesn't want me. But what he understood when I came to him, in some primitive instinctive way, was something that shook him to the core and made him bring the baby to me—he understood that no legal papers in the world are going to make me not her mother.

"And by doing that was he cheating on you? Fuckin' A, he was cheating on you, worse than if he had been screwing me six ways till Sunday every time we met. Because his was a lie of the spirit, and it was bad for Rose to be a party to it. Mitch should have been able to speak up and say to you, 'Lainie, I did bad. This whole thing was wrong. I should have kept on trying to adopt, because as long as Jackie needs to be near this baby, we have to work something out.' Only he was afraid. He had fallen into his own macho trap. And then he saw how much you loved the baby. How connected you were to her from day one, and how transformed you were by having her. He was afraid if he even mentioned my name you would hate him or leave him or both.

"Lainie, what do we do? Don't keep that baby from me. Let me see her sometimes, I beg you."

My God, Lainie thought, what can I do? Their eyes were locked as Lainie rolled back and forth from her heels to her toes in a way she had learned that the baby found soothing. Rose had her tiny head against her chest now, and was making that keening noise she made just before she fell off to sleep.

"This is a nightmare," Lainie said, and she heard her own voice sound almost unrecognizable and filled with pain. "And what makes it so difficult is that I look at you and I think, This woman is right. If I had given birth to Rosie, no matter what I'd signed or how much anyone had given me they'd have to kill me first before they could take her away. Dear God, why did I ever agree to this? Dear God, forgive me for being a party to this, Jackie, I'm so sorry," she said, and wept, and the two women embraced and wept holding on to each other with the baby, their baby, asleep in the middle of their tearful embrace. And when Jackie left, after Lainie promised to try to figure out what to do about all of it, the scent of Shalimar was still in the foyer.

35

THE MEMORIAL SERVICE for Davis Bergman was held at the big rambling house in Brentwood that Shelly and Davis had completely remodeled when they were together. As Ruthie and Shelly entered the backyard where the rented white folding chairs, the ones with the padded seats which cost a little more per chair, were lined up in rows facing a rented podium, Ruthie watched Shelly trying to maintain his equilibrium. But as they turned the corner and he looked at the rose garden he'd created and tended, and saw it now in full bloom, the profusion of open peach and fuchsia and crimson flowers made him stop and emit a pained sound. As if someone had kicked him in the stomach. For a long moment he was immobilized.

Marsha Bergman, Davis's widow, was surrounded by a group of her friends. Shelly and Ruthie walked to the area where she was standing in order to wait to express their condolences. But long before it was their turn, someone gestured to Marsha from across the glaring turquoise of the pool, and to their relief, since neither of them knew what they would say to her, she turned and walked in that direction. Shelly said he recognized some of the people from Davis's law practice, but Ruthie didn't see one familiar face.

In the newspaper that morning, the cause of Davis's death

was listed as pneumonia. Ruthie suddenly wondered why she'd come to the memorial service of a man she had once hated. She had a strong desire to turn around and leave, but she knew Shelly needed to be there, needed her to get him through this, so she stayed, holding his hand and feeling his anxious presence next to her. Soon most of the white chairs were filled, and she took Shelly's arm and led him to the end seats in the back row.

The service was a kind of free forum with friends of Davis getting up and talking about their memories of him. Sometimes two people would start for the podium at once, and one would defer to the other and sit down. Essentially all the people said what a wonderful guy Davis was and what a happy couple he and Marsha were, and how much they would miss him. Ruthie looked at Shelly to see how he was bearing up, and noticed for the first time that he was holding a small pile of note cards in his hand. When he saw her looking at them, he handed them to her and whispered, "Quick. Punch these up!"

The cards contained notes in Shelly's funny little handwriting that he had prepared so that he could get up and speak about Davis. About his relationship with Davis. *(A) Hilarious sense of humor about our situation. (B) Every day I spent with him was a gift.* Ruthie looked up from the note cards and into Shelly's eyes, and shook her head. "Shel," she said, "I love you. But this material won't play to this crowd." She knew that was the last thing he wanted to hear, and how much he wanted someone to listen to how hard it was on him that Davis was gone.

At first she saw resentment on his face that she would try to deprive him of this moment, and she was sure he was going to jump to his feet the minute the next speaker was through and storm the podium. But then she saw the resignation, and he took the cards back from her and looked down at them. These were Marsha's friends, at Marsha's house, and they didn't want to hear what Shelly had to say about his love for Davis. Throughout the rest of the speeches, as he listened he took each of the note cards and slowly tore it into small pieces and stuffed the pieces into the pocket of his shirt.

The Hollywood show-business community is small and it didn't take long for Zev Ryder to learn that Davis Bergman, who everyone knew was a former lover of Shelly Milton's, had died, and how. "Oh, fuck! You mean to tell me I'm peeing in the same men's room as this guy? I don't know about the rest of you, but I'm gonna start using the can downstairs. What if it comes off on doorknobs? Oh, Christ. Sometimes at meetings I've picked up half a doughnut out of the box. What if *he's* the one who ate the other half?"

Zev didn't say those things in front of Ruthie and Shelly, just everybody else. And nobody had the nerve to tell him to shut up. Ruthie first got wind of the remarks when Ryder's secretary, a tall, severe, black-haired, white-skinned woman everyone in the office called Morticia, tried to apologize.

"Isn't he just being the bastard of all time?" she asked Ruthie one morning when they both emerged from cubicles in the ladies' room.

Ruthie rinsed her hands and avoided looking at what she knew was her own exhausted face in the mirror. "If you're talking about Zev, yes, he's always the bastard of all time, also the rat, the pig, the schmuck, and the shitheel. So what else is new?" She pulled a paper towel down from the metal container on the wall, and watched Morticia apply the dark purple lipstick that made her white skin look even whiter.

"But all the stuff he's been saying about Shelly is really over the top," Morticia said, rubbing her purple lips together to get some effect that Ruthie, who seldom wore makeup, couldn't understand. "I mean, he's got the writers afraid to eat the muffins you make. Haven't you noticed how many are left at the end of the day?"

"Meaning?"

It was clear that Morticia, whose real name was Alice, was reluctant to tear herself away from the mirror, but now she did, and she looked squarely at Ruthie. "Listen, Ruth, I'm telling you right now, you can't quote me. I've got a daughter to support, and you know if Zev suspected I'd said a word he'd throw me out of here . . . but I happen to know he's looking for a way to screw up Shelly's contract. I've heard him on the phone with the Writers' Guild, looking for loopholes, ways to dump him and not have to pay him full salary. Not telling them who he is when he calls, but asking the contracts department at the Writers' Guild what kind of breach of contract, like not showing up, has to take place before you can fire somebody without a payout."

Ruthie gripped the cold porcelain sink hard, and felt her whole body trembling with anger. "What did you mean about the muffins?"

"Well, after he heard that Davis Bergman died, and everyone knows that Davis and Shelly used to be . . ." Then she gestured with a kind of hands-apart shrug, meaning she didn't know what word to use for what Davis and Shelly were to each other.

"Lovers. They were lovers . . . go on," Ruthie said.

"Well, it totally freaked him out. Because he knows you and Shelly live in the same house, and you make those muffins all the time, and you *know* how health-conscious Zev is, so . . ."

"So now he's campaigning to dump us?"

"Not you. Shelly."

"There's no such thing as that. We're a team, and he can't fuckin' do this. It's discrimination. I'm calling a lawyer."

"Oh, shit," Morticia said. "You bring a lawyer into this and I'll be dead meat. He'll know it was me. I have too much information."

The white face got even whiter as Ruthie took her hands and looked into her eyes. "Alice," she said. "Shelly and I have a child to raise, too. I can't let that vicious, bigoted little man destroy our family the way I've seen him do to other people. I won't hurt you in any way. I promise. But I guaranfuckin'tee you, I'm not going to sit by and let Zev Ryder pull down our lives."

There was a rehearsal at two o'clock. When Ruthie got downstairs, her assistant handed her a pile of phone messages. One of them was from Shelly. It said he wouldn't be at the rehearsal.

He had to leave abruptly to go to a doctor's appointment. In the studio she slid into the back row of seats, and when Zev Ryder saw her sitting alone she felt him looking over at her while she sat making notes on the script in an effort to avoid him. And that night when she got home and Shelly was sick with a flu which the doctor informed him would probably keep him at home for a week, she knew Ryder would use the absence as a reason to get rid of them without pay.

She kicked her shoes off wearily and brought Shelly some soup, fed and played with Sid and bathed him, and heard Shelly calling to her from his room.

"Let me see the new pages," he said.

"Don't worry about the pages, I've got that covered."

"The doctor says I'm going to be stuck in bed for a while, but there's no reason why I can't write my stuff from here." Ruthie gave him this week's script. It was true he could write from bed, and the changes Shelly made that night before he fell asleep were better than any of the other writers could do in a week's worth of meetings. But the flu was one that left him bedridden for two weeks, at the end of which, on a Friday, he got a call from Morticia saying, "Mr. Ryder wishes me to tell you that because of your protracted absences, you're no longer on the staff of the show."

"The filthy little turkey didn't even have the balls to do it himself," Ruthie said.

"I've been out of the office a lot, Ru. He can prove it. But you can't quit. He'll destroy you if you do. You have to hang in for the baby's medical insurance and the weekly paycheck. Promise me you'll keep going in until we figure out what to do."

Bright red rage made her want to scream, There's no fucking way I'll keep working for that monster! But she looked at Sid, now climbing all over his daddy, and she said, "Yeah, okay. I promise."

On Monday the nanny didn't show up and Shelly was too weak to get out of bed, so Ruthie packed up Sid and took him with her to work. The baby had been to the studio often enough for her to know that if she put him in the portable playpen in a corner with just the right toys, he would amuse himself with the pound-a-peg or the "Sesame Street" pop-up, and except for an occasional loud squeal would be less disruptive of the meetings than most of the writers themselves.

Today Ruthie sat at the head of the table near the playpen, and she could tell by how shockingly quiet it was that everybody knew everything, or more accurately, everybody knew something. She was going to have to clear up the story now, before any of the rumors went any further.

"Guys," she said, "Shelly doesn't have AIDS."

"Oooops," Arnie Fishmann said as he knocked over his Styrofoam coffee cup and the tan liquid made a large puddle on his yellow lined legal pad and then seeped off it onto the conference room table. Three of the other writers stood and gathered napkins from the coffee cart and mopped up the spillage. Ruthie waited until all the wet napkins were in the wastebasket before she went on. "He's HIV-positive, but he doesn't have AIDS. He's very vulnerable, but please God, he'll go on for a long time."

This group of clowns has a gag line for everything, she thought, but for some reason, they're acting like humans for a change. "You can't catch it by working for him, by laughing with him, or by peeing in the same urinal. I don't have it, Sid doesn't have it, and as you all know he is Shelly's biological child, and we both drink from his glasses and use his towels and hug him and kiss him all day and night.

"But the point is Zev Ryder fired him. He says he fired him because he's been out and doesn't do the work. You all know what I know and what Zev knows, which is that Shelly can phone it in funnier than all of us in the room can make it even when we work until midnight. This is homophobia. This is discrimination. I intend to get a lawyer and sue that son of a bitch and bring him down for hurting the career of my partner and my best friend and my son's father. And I can't do it unless you fellows are prepared to stand up and talk not just about

Shelly's contribution to the show but about Zev's dangerous
and damning condemnation of him. Of us. And his horrible
treatment in general of every one of us—the women on the staff
who get sexually harassed by him, the writers who are spiritually annihilated on a regular basis. Because you have to know
that an attack like this on one of us is really an attack on all of
us and that next week it could be you, Fishie, or you, Jerry, for
whatever reason he can think of. So please say you'll stand
behind us and help us fight this man, and kick his ass the way
he's been kicking all of ours for so long."

No one looked at her or spoke. Even Sid was quiet in the
playpen. The only sound in the room was the sound of Arnie
Fishmann lifting and dropping and lifting and dropping a pencil,
which plunked repeatedly on the conference room table. Somebody sighed, one of them cleared his throat, and after a few
minutes Ruthie got the message. They were all too chickenshit,
too threatened to put their asses on the line for a friend.

"Okay, fellahs," Ruthie said, wishing she had the strength to
throw the table over on them. "Let's write something funny."

36

"TODAY I THINK we need to talk a little bit more about support systems," Barbara said to the parents, all of whom were now wearing the Stork Club sweatshirts brought in by Ruthie and Shelly.

"Why does that expression, 'support system,' always make me think of an underwire bra?" Rick asked.

"Because, as usual, your mind is in your groin," Judith said, laughing.

"There are people in your lives who are going to enhance your children's worlds, families with other children their age, Mommy and Me groups you can attend regularly at schools or temples and churches in your neighborhoods. Try to branch out and find people who are dealing with the same developmental issues you are, and whose children will love having play dates with yours.

"I also recommend that you stay in touch with and visit your families, and have them visit you. The more people there are for these children to love, the better. Ruthie and Shelly, you're lucky you have all your parents still alive and well. Get them out here to visit Sid, and take him back to be with them."

"You haven't met our parents or you couldn't have used the word 'lucky' in reference to any of them," Shelly joked.

"Oh, I don't know. They did raise the two of you, so they must have some good qualities," Barbara said.

"You're right," Shelly said, serious now. "Our families would love to be with Sid."

"What about you, Judith?"

"I have friends from work, and particularly my friends Jerra and Tom, who don't have any kids. They love it when I bring the girls by. It makes their own family feel bigger when they include us in their celebrations."

Barbara looked at Lainie. "Our situation is pretty screwed up right now because we're still living apart, but my mother and Rose have a very nice relationship. She takes care of her some evenings when I go to class or to the gym, and I like knowing they're together. I always feel when I pick Rose up at her house that the two of them are better for having spent the time together. I also have my friends Sharon from school and Carin from work, and they're a lot closer to Rose than my sisters-in-law. Her so-called real family."

"My sisters have been pretty busy lately," Mitch said defensively, "but sometimes Rose gets to be with her cousins, and I think family is real important." Without looking at her, Barbara could feel Lainie's tension from across the room.

"Well, we've learned by virtue of this group that we have a new definition of that word," Barbara said. "A family is what and who you make it. And that's why I think it's healthy to widen the circle of people who love the children, so they feel they have many ways to turn for affection and warmth."

"You know, I was always so proud of the fact that Shelly and I are so self-sufficient, didn't need anybody, but now I think you're right. It's important for the kids that we expand their worlds," Ruthie said.

Barbara looked at Rick. "What about you, Rick?"

"My uncle Bobo has been everything to me, and the other person who's been an incredible support to me is the widow of my best friend. She's completely unlike anyone I've ever known. A great mother to her own kids and a kind of wise aunt to

David, so that's been very worthwhile, and her sons are like nephews to me.

"Anyway," he said, his thoughts slipping away to all the sweet things Patty had done for him and for David, "she's been a fine friend to me and I really respect the way she takes the time to—" That was the moment when he looked around the room and saw that all of the others were smiling knowingly at him, and he stopped short. "What's so funny?" No one answered, they just continued to grin. "Why is every person in this room wearing a dopey grin?"

"You're in love with her," Judith said, and when Rick flushed purple the others erupted like schoolchildren. "It's completely obvious to every one of us."

"Oh, please," he said. "I think very highly of her. Very highly, and I've known her since she was a kid. I mean, my best friend was her . . ." Rick stopped then to think about it, and he was obviously rattled. "Let's go on to somebody else," he said to Barbara, who picked up the ball by looking around at the others.

"The point is to try to find people the children can count on to be positive forces in their lives." There was a big silence in the room, punctuated only by the happy sounds from the play yard, until Rick spoke, this time to himself, but out loud.

"Maybe I am," he said, and a titter of laughter filled the room. "I mean, I'll be goddamned. Maybe I'm in love with Patty."

After the group he walked with David to the car, thinking he should call Patty and tell her. But he was sure she would laugh and hang up, or say, "If this is your way of trying to get me into bed, dream on." Or maybe she'd say that she wanted him too.

On the second day of shooting his new film he crouched next to the big double bed on the set, having a quiet conversation with his two stars, while the crew waited patiently behind the scenes. Over and over he talked to the two formidable talents facing each other, their heads on the satin-covered pillows, and told them the back story of what their characters had been through to get to this moment.

Shooting scenes out-of-sequence was a necessary evil, but he was going to make it work by talking them into the heat of the moment. For a long hushed time he waxed poetic about how hungry the characters must be for each other, how they were finally to be consummating their love of so many years. It was the kind of moment he was famous for capturing better than any other director in the business. And it was the close personal work he did with the actors just before the cameras rolled that was the key.

He'd been lulling them into the mood for nearly an hour, telling his erotic story, but timing was everything and he could tell by the way they were looking at each other now that they were ready to go at it. He knew that it was time for him to stand ever so slowly and steal away out of the shot, behind the camera, and softly say, "Action."

It worked. The passion between them during the shooting of the scene was powerful. Rick felt elated when he called, "Cut and print it!" Now, right now, he should shoot the close-ups, get them set up while the mood was thick and sultry. But just as he was about to do that, he looked around and saw Andrea enter through the heavy studio door. He knew when he saw her there that something was wrong. He always cautioned her not to come down and disturb him unless there was an emergency with David. Only his son had the power to call everything in his life to a halt. "What's wrong?" he asked.

"Doreen Cobb," she said, coming closer and handing him a yellow Post-it with a phone number written on it. "She called from a phone booth. She sounds awful. I told her I'd do my best to get you to call her as soon as possible. She was pretty shook up so I'm not sure, but it sounded like she said she was at Port Authority in New York."

The thought of that child in a den of horror like the bus station in New York City sickened him. If she'd run away as far as New York, she had to be leaving something pretty bad. As bad as he feared. He motioned for his first AD to come over and said, "Call a break. Ten minutes. Fifteen tops. I have to make an emergency phone call."

The young man looked at Rick as if to say, How can you sacrifice the momentum of the shoot to go and make a phone call? But Rick was already out the door, heading to his trailer. The minute he was inside he dialed the New York City area code and the number Andrea gave him. It only rang once.

"I'm sorry," Doreen's very shaky voice said instead of hello.

"Doreen, just tell me you're all right."

"I am, I mean, I think I am. I'm scared of all the weirdos here, but I'm all right."

"Dear girl," he said, trying not to imagine how small and afraid and alone she must be in the vast Port Authority, "can you tell me why you ran away?"

"Um . . . well I, I ran away because I couldn't . . . I couldn't . . . um . . . ," she sobbed. "I couldn't stay there anymore."

"Doreen, does this have anything to do with David's birth father?" he asked. "Doreen, who is David's birth father?"

More sobs and finally she managed to ask, "Do you know?"

"I *do* know. I think I know. Did he rape you?"

"I hate him."

"Is he still abusing you?"

"I can't go back there."

"Doreen, you have to go back and report him. Turn him in. For your sake. For the sake of the rest of the family. Does Bea know?"

"Oh, no. It would kill her. She thinks they're happy together. It would kill my sister too. Ruin her life and the kids' lives too. And I love those kids—"

"What about *your* life? I care about your life. Go home and tell Bea. She'll give you the strength to do this."

"I can't."

There was a knock at the trailer door. Damn. Rick opened

it and gestured with a please-wait hand up to the assistant director who stood outside pointing at his watch, mouthing the words, What about the dinner break? A dinner break. If he let those two actors out of that bed, he would totally destroy the mood for close-ups. What was he thinking? He'd *already* destroyed the mood by walking out. Fuck the mood, he thought. I'll get it back. I'll figure it out later. There's a life at stake here.

"Give them the dinner break now," he said out loud.

"What?" Doreen asked on the phone.

"I was talking to my assistant director," he said. The AD nodded and closed the door. "Forgive me. Doreen, please listen to me and go home now, work this out. You can do it." He knew he shouldn't, mustn't, wasn't supposed to say the next, but all the rules were broken anyway so he decided he would bribe her. "I'll tell you what. Go home now . . . do you have money and a ticket?"

"Yeah."

"And if you do, if you go right now . . . I'll send you a ticket to come and be with me and David at Christmas. Would you like that?"

The voice on the other end of the phone now was the voice of a very young girl. "Oh, wow! Really? Yeah! That would be the best! To see the baby? I'm going home!"

"Doreen. You must put a stop to this man. No one can do that for you."

"I know," she said. "I will." But Rick was unconvinced.

"David and I both love you," he said, and the line went dead.

"Mr. R.?" Andrea opened the door of the trailer. "Is Doreen all right?" He nodded an absent nod. "The cast and crew are on dinner," Andrea told him.

The cast and crew? Yes. He'd better get back to his own problems. He was in the middle of shooting a forty-million-dollar film, the success or failure of which could make or break his career.

"Fine," he said. "Just bring me a sandwich." Now, where am I, he thought. Yes. The love scene.

37

SO WHAT DO I DO? What's the etiquette when you think the teenage birth mother of your son has probably been raped by her sister's husband, which makes him the birth father of your child? Do you try and hire someone to kill the bastard, or just sit and wait for the phone to ring?" Then he added wryly, "And I *used* to think my relationships were complicated."

"Rick, from all you've told us, Doreen is very strong," Barbara said. "She convinced Bea to let her come here and give you the baby instead of having him at a home and giving him away in an anonymous adoption. She lived in your house and you got to know her strength intimately. Up until recently she was able to keep what both of you felt was a healthy distance from the situation. It seems to me that you may just have to wait and trust that she'll work it out."

"I disagree," Lainie said. "I think he owes her a lot, and that he needs to actively figure out a way to do something for her. She gave him an incredible gift, the way Jackie did me and Mitch, and in taking the baby he took on a lifelong relationship with her."

Everyone turned to look at Lainie. She was even more pale and beautiful today, though her big blue eyes were ringed with red. "Jackie came to see me, came to my home one night and told me what she's been going through, and I'm beginning to have some understanding about how she feels. I still haven't forgiven Mitch, but at least I know now that there's some part of me that's starting to think maybe I can do what Judith talked about in one of these sessions. To learn how to change my definition of the way things are supposed to be." Her emotions stopped her from saying more.

Barbara turned to Mitch. "Do you want to talk about this?" She hoped there wasn't any judgment in her voice, because for weeks what she'd felt like doing was grabbing him by the collar of his shirt and saying, Talk to this woman and work it out. Maybe now their moment was here.

"I wish I knew what to say," Mitch said, and all of them watched as his tough front fell slowly away. "I come here and sit in these groups, and sometimes I'm feeling as if I want to run out there and grab Rose and leave with her. And other times I'm wishing like hell I knew how to break down and beg all of you to help me, because all I really want is for my daughter to have a good life."

"And what do you want for your wife?" Barbara asked.

"For her to understand I meant to do something loving and made a mess. That I love her and miss her and want her back, want my family back. But that I still believe we must somehow include Jackie in Rose's world."

Barbara only nodded, and then she looked around at all of their concerned faces looking at Lainie. There was no doubt that the people in this group cared about one another. At the end of each session, before they went home to face their respective problems, they all hugged one another and wished one another well. And she was warmed by the way their interest in one another's lives seemed genuine.

"Make it work, Lainie," Ruthie urged. "Remember what we're learning in here about new rules."

Lainie couldn't look at any of them.

"Life is too short to waste time withholding your love, Lainie," Shelly said. "We know that very well," he added so softly it was as if he was talking to himself. "Particularly in our family." Everyone looked at him, and he wondered how they would react to what he was about to tell them. "Because I've been diagnosed as being HIV-positive."

Barbara glanced at Lainie, Mitch, Judith, and Rick for their reactions, and then at Ruthie, who had had no idea Shelly was going to tell them today. Her eyes shone brightly with her love for him.

"I haven't wanted to talk about this in here," he said. "It's been hard on our lives, particularly for Ruthie, and though I'm feeling pretty damn good most of the time, I've been fired from my job in an acute case of prejudice. I worry about my family and how they'll be treated when more and more people find out. I want to keep writing, maybe even write about what I'm going through, but I've never written anything but comedy, and this ain't particularly funny."

Barbara could tell that no one knew how to respond. She was surprised and glad when Rick spoke.

"Shelly, you're an extraordinarily good writer," he said. "You have a completely unique point of view. I've watched your show at least a dozen times, and I always know which material comes from you and Ruthie, because the script always has your insight and style. You could write a hell of a screenplay about anything. And I for one would be very interested in it."

"You're being kind," Shelly said.

"No, I'm not. I'm being my usual selfish self. I think working with you would be profitable in every sense of the word. If you deprive the world of your talent because some homophobic jerk fired you, you're making a giant mistake."

Ruthie looked at Shelly and wondered what he was thinking. Rick Reisman may have had some bad luck in the past, but some of his films were classics. He was shooting one now that already had the buzz of success all over town.

"You don't have to write an AIDS story. I'll sit and pitch any idea you like with you. Don't stop working, Shelly. You're too damned good," Rick said.

"I appreciate what you're saying," Shelly said, looking at Rick, "and I'll certainly think about it." Ruthie crossed her fingers. If Shelly sold a treatment of a story to a studio, or better yet a screenplay, his spirits would soar. And thinking practically, his medical insurance would continue to be covered by the Writers' Guild.

The children were toddling in to find their parents. Dana gestured to Barbara that it was break time, but Barbara asked her to entertain the children for a few minutes longer so that she could bring up one more issue.

"Before the children get here, as I'm sure you're all aware, the Christmas holidays are fast approaching, and I wanted to talk about the stress that sometimes accompanies them. The stress for the parents is from the obvious. The traffic and the crowds, the financial pressures. Those adults who have had joyous family experiences at holidays frequently try to recreate those experiences, and that's potentially frustrating.

"Those parents who *haven't* had good holiday experiences sometimes try to better the experience for their own children, which doesn't always work out the way they'd hoped either. So what I strongly urge you to do is to keep your plans simple. Ask yourself how much of the plans really are about the needs of the people in your life now, versus your needs from the past.

"As for the children, even the best toddler has a hard time with holidays for a lot of reasons. His or her schedule is frequently changed around. Nap times, mealtimes are all topsy-turvy. The departure from their routine can make them grumpy or cranky and upset. Holiday situations may force them to be confronted by a lot of strangers who could seem frightening. So my suggestion is that you stay aware of your child's needs to keep as much of his or her life-style as intact as possible. Let them eat at home at mealtime and *then* take them to the party. Plan outings after a nap, don't insist that they be chummy with strangers at parties, because they won't want to be.

"I'm bringing this up now so you can avoid the trap of inflated holiday expectations. I'm personally feeling sad about spending Christmas without my children, because my daughter is spending the holiday with her fiancé and his mother, and my son is going on a ski trip with a friend. My mother is going back east to be with my sister, so maybe I'm projecting my own trepidations, but I thought I'd mention it."

"I've invited Doreen to come and be with me and my uncle and Patty and the boys."

"Wow!" Judith said. "That ought to be emotional."

"I'm hoping to get her out of her environment in Kansas and maybe find out what's really going on with her."

"We're just going to a few parties," Ruthie said.

"I don't feel too much like celebrating," Shelly added.

"Well, it's going to be just me and the girls and some friends," Judith said.

Lainie didn't say a word.

The children were at the snack table now and the parents rose to join them. They had a snack, sang "Five Little Monkeys Jumpin' on the Bed" and "We're Goin' to the Zoo." Then Dana read to them from *Goodnight Moon*.

Barbara watched the families share hugs and holiday wishes with one another. Mitch parted uncomfortably with Rose, getting only a nod from Lainie. Ruthie and Shelly walked out with their arms around each other, and Rick helped Judith with her double stroller. After Barbara and Dana put away the toys, Barbara made notes on all that had happened and wondered if what she had told them about the holidays would help them, or herself.

38

IT WAS A FRIDAY a few days before Christmas when Barbara stopped on South Robertson Boulevard at a Christmas tree lot run by the Boy Scouts of America and bought a large Douglas fir. Then she helped two Boy Scouts tie it to the top of her car and she drove home. When she stopped the car outside her house, she thought about just leaving the tree outside all night and waiting until Stan came home from his business trip tomorrow morning so that he could help her carry it in and set it up.

Of course in this city nothing was sacred, so she knew there was every chance she could come out tomorrow and someone would have stolen the tree. That was reason enough to pull the car closer to the front door and bring the big unwieldy thing in alone. The other reason was that doing all the chores to set up the tree would be a good test of her competence.

Sometimes when she worried about what her life would be like if there were no Stan, she would silently challenge herself to face some task alone for which under ordinary circumstances she would have asked Stan's help. "If I can fix this fallen shutter without asking Stan to do it for me, I'll know that if the time comes when he dies first, I'll be okay." Once she told her friend Marcy Frank about the way she played that mental game with herself. It was during one of those reveal-your-inner-fears

lunches that close friends have, and when she'd finished, hoping
for some corroboration from someone else who had been married to one man for as long as she had, Marcy laughed, then
raised her eyes heavenward and said, "And *this* woman is a
psychologist?"

When the lights were strung, she plugged them into the wall
socket next to the tree to make sure all of the bulbs had survived
another year, and they had. By then it was ten o'clock and she
still hadn't had any dinner, but instead of taking a break she
went out into the garage and found the three boxes marked
ORNAMENTS, piled them on top of one another, and brought
them into the living room. In the silence of the empty house,
she pulled each familiar figure and ball out of the protective
paper in which she'd wrapped it so carefully last year.

Every one had a memory that came with it. The tiny glass
angel she and Stan and the kids bought on that weekend in
Williamsburg, and the adobe house they'd bought when they
visited Santa Fe, and the ceramic Minnie Mouse Heidi had
begged for at Disneyland. But unlike Christmas tree decorating
sessions in the past, tonight there was nobody for whom she
could hold one up and say, "Oh, look. Remember when we
got this one?" Get used to it, she told herself. Until there are
grandchildren, you'd better get used to it.

At eleven she felt tired but on some kind of tear to finish the
task. She was remembering all those Christmas mornings when
Heidi and Jeff would push open her bedroom door and leap on
her and Stan when it was still dark outside, while both parents
longed for just a little more sleep. The lonely way she felt tonight made her think she would give up sleeping forever to have
them around for another Christmas.

At midnight, still only half finished, she decided she had
passed her own survive-without-Stan test, and leaving the lights
on the tree aglow she went upstairs to bed. The next day by
the time Stan arrived, she had finished the job and was sitting
on the sofa, staring blankly at the lit-up tree, feeling depressed.

"Let me guess," he said, sitting next to her and sliding his arm around her waist. "I'll bet you're sitting here remembering every Christmas before this one as idyllic, aren't you?"

"You mean they weren't?"

"Which one shall I call up for you? The one where your mother brought seven homeless people over here for dinner and one of them threw up all over our bathroom, and one of them stole my wallet? Or how about the year where Heidi knocked the tree over and started a fire in the living room? I liked the one when your sister, Roz, came in from back east and brought some fish with her on the plane, which we all ate and got food poisoning."

Barbara laughed. "You're so right. I'm doing exactly what I cautioned all of my patients against, about having some Currier and Ives fantasy around their past holidays."

"Listen, my love," Stan said, holding her close. "These are going to be the best years of our lives. Once we get Jeff squared away, we'll do all the real traveling we've been talking about for years. Maybe we'll even find a spot we really love up north, and buy a second home. Think of it. With no kids around, I'll be able to run after you naked all through the house."

"Sweetheart, at the speed I'm running these days, it won't be too tough to catch me."

"Precisely! But that's okay because at my age I forget what I'm supposed to do when I catch you."

Their jokes about aging had become a favorite way to make them both laugh, which they now did, and then Stan took her face in his hand, turned it toward his, and said, "Honey." She knew his smile so well. "That's something we both know I'll never forget."

"You promise?" she said grinning.

"You can take it to the bank."

His sweet gentle kisses by the glowing tree warmed her, and when he tugged at her sweater, she helped him remove it, and soon they were making love on the floor.

"Maybe it's not so bad with the kids out of the house," she said as Stan caressed her.

"I say to hell with the little brats," Stan answered, touching her, loving her, making her sadness of the last many hours disappear.

When they lay spent, Stan asleep beside her on the floor, the phone rang. Barbara ran though the house naked to answer it. It was Heidi, and in just "Hi, Mom," Barbara knew there was something seriously wrong. First there was a lot of crying. Then there was a jumble of words Barbara couldn't understand. While she listened patiently, trying to sort it out, Stan brought her a bathrobe, which she slid on. Finally she understood what it was Heidi was trying so hysterically to tell her. Ryan Adler, her fiancé, had married someone else. The someone else was a woman named Bonnie West, who was a local San Francisco radio personality.

"We had this fight, and we weren't speaking, but like I just figured it would blow over and he'd be coming back. You know? I mean that's what always happened before and um, she's his old girlfriend from a really long time ago, and so during the time I was waiting for him to call me, he was . . . marrying her. I am so lame. I can't believe I had to hear this from someone who saw it in the paper. Can you believe I ever trusted this man?"

Barbara bit her tongue.

"So now, I mean you are really not going to believe this part, I mean this is so totally deranged, it's sick. He calls here the other night, and he's um, whispering, and I heard his voice and I'm going, Don't crack, Heidi, don't say anything. Just let him talk, and you're going to die when I tell you, Mom." Stan brought Barbara some coffee and she gestured to him that Heidi was going through a trauma as she listened to the rest of the story.

"He said, 'Oh, God, Heidi, why did I do this? Why did I marry her? I mean it's so clear to me now that you're the one I really love.' So I said, 'You're crazy, Ryan. That's why.' And then he said something about how his mother thought Bonnie was more right for him than I was, and I said, 'Thanks a lot, that makes me feel really great!' Anyway, the worst part is he said, 'Can I come over?' I mean, can you believe this? This man wanted to come over and have sex with me and still be married to *her!* How could he think I'd say yes to that?"

"What *did* you say?" Barbara asked, surprised by this burst of intimacy from Heidi, whose answer to the question "What's new?" was, notoriously, "New York, New Jersey, and New Hampshire."

"I'll tell you something, Mom. I was feeling so bummed out and so completely lonely at that moment that it was real hard to say no. Because all I wanted was one more hour of him saying he loved me."

Poor child, Barbara thought. My poor child. "But?" she asked, knowing she shouldn't.

"Don't worry, Mother," Heidi said with disdain for the question. "I didn't do it. I hung up and took the phone off the hook. But, um, now I'm really sad and you have to help me, because they've moved into his place which is right near here, and I've got to get out of here. Fast. I don't think I can survive bumping into either one or the two of them."

"Let me see what I can do," Barbara told her.

There wasn't a moving company available on such short notice, so Barbara called Hertz Rent-A-Truck in San Francisco, and she and Stan flew up. They spent Christmas Eve day packing up Heidi's apartment, all of the kitchen supplies, clothes, and finally the furniture, and moving everything down the two flights of stairs, loading all of it onto the truck. Stan drove the truck as Barbara and Heidi followed behind him in Heidi's car. Barbara drove and Heidi cried all the way home. When they arrived in Los Angeles, they went straight to a storage rental space Barbara had called before they left. With the help of some of the night-shift employees, they unloaded it all and finally went home.

Heidi spent Christmas morning sitting on the sofa, staring at the blazing fire in the living room fireplace with damaged eyes and a lovelorn expression over an affair that Barbara knew she believed she would never get over.

"It takes time, honey," Barbara said, sitting on the sofa next to her. "And you have plenty of time."

"Yeah" was all Heidi said. Barbara tried to maintain some holiday spirit. Though it had been a while since she'd done it, she remembered her old recipe and made a huge stack of what turned out to be delicious pancakes. Then she turned on a tape of the Mormon Tabernacle Choir singing Christmas carols, but she had to turn down the volume so she could take a call from Jeff, who was skiing in Snow Mass. She was glad for him that he was far away from the Singer household blues that morning, and changed the subject when he asked, "How come the goonball is there? I thought she was gonna be with her dorky fiancé."

At about eleven A.M. the doorbell rang. When Barbara opened the door she was surprised to see Marcy and Ed Frank, their son-in-law, Freddy, who looked like Ed, and their daughter, Pammy, Heidi's childhood friend, who was very pregnant.

"Uh-oh, I can tell by the look on your face that we should have called first," Marcy Frank said apologetically, probably because Barbara, still in her bathrobe, looked bedraggled from the ordeal of the last thirty-six hours. "But we were right up the street at my sister-in-law's house and we thought you two would be lonely without your kids around, and we wanted you to see Pammy's enormous tummy."

"Uh . . ." Barbara wasn't sure what to do. What she wanted to do was say, "Go away" and close the door, and she was considering doing that when Heidi, curious to know who was there, got to her feet, walked to the door, and when she looked out at the four people, who were surprised to see her, and then saw Pammy's stomach, she moaned, began to cry, and left the room to go upstairs.

"Maybe we should go," Ed Frank said.

Barbara sighed. "Oh, come on in," she said. "Stan, honey, make these people an eggnog while I go take care of Heidi." She was relieved when just as she stepped into Heidi's old room where Heidi lay in a fetal position on the unmade bed, the phone rang. Before Barbara could get to it, Heidi uncurled herself and reached for it.

"Hello?" she said in a stuffed-nosed voice. "Oh, Merry Christmas to you too, Grammy, only this is Heidi, not Barbara." Barbara sat down on the bed. "I'm home because, um, my boyfriend married someone else, so I didn't want to stay up there anymore, because I was, um, too hurt. So my mom and dad came up with this humongous truck and they spent all day moving me here, and I'm going to live with them for a while till I figure out my life."

As soon as she got all of that out, her mouth opened wide in a cry that couldn't come out. She was shaking with inward sobs, and Barbara moved closer to where she was sitting on the bed and held her hand. Heidi listened to whatever sage advice Gracie was dispensing on the other end of the phone. Advice to which Heidi kept nodding until she got her bearings, then finally she said, "I know. You're right. I agree. No, I know. You're right and I will, I promise. Okay. Here's my mom."

"Hello, Mother," Barbara said.

"You have to have her moved into her own place before the first of the year," Gracie said instead of hello.

"Well, Merry Christmas to you too," Barbara replied.

"You with all your psychiatric training know better than anyone that after all her hard-won independence, moving in with you now is the worst thing that could happen to her. That girl has to get back on the horse. Stand on her own two feet as soon as possible," Gracie said in her I-mean-business voice.

"Mother, she's fine. A few weeks in her old room might be healthy for her, a little return to the womb, with Stan and me pampering her. How bad could that be?"

"Don't do what's right for you, Barbara. Do what's right for her," Gracie said.

"Happy holidays," Barbara said and put the phone back in the cradle. "Shall I tell the Franks to go away?" she asked Heidi.

Heidi put her arms around her mother's neck and her head against Barbara, and Barbara could feel her own hair getting wet with her daughter's hot tears. "I'll be glad to go down and ask them to come over for dinner next week when you're feeling better."

"No, I'm okay. I'll wash my face and come down. I really am glad for Pammy. I want to come down and see her." She stood and walked sniffling into her bathroom.

"Honey," Barbara said, and Heidi stopped and looked at her, her pretty face blotched and scrunchy from the tears shed, "I promise you'll make it through this."

"Thanks, Mom," Heidi said, and went into the bathroom to wash her face.

By the thirtieth of December she and Barbara found an apartment in West Hollywood that Heidi liked and Barbara and Stan could afford to help her keep until she got a job. The last item Barbara moved into the apartment was the old tattered Winnie the Pooh. She had transported it with a few other things from home in her car. While Heidi was talking to the man who had come to install the phone, Barbara took the bear into the bedroom.

"Look after her," she said, hugging the stuffed toy. Then she put it on Heidi's pillow and went to work.

39

ON CHRISTMAS EVE DAY, Ruthie and Shelly went to a big noisy party at the home of a television producer who lived in Santa Monica. "Did you hear about the whale in the San Francisco harbor who got AIDS? He was rear-ended by a ferry!" A bald guy who was standing by the piano told that joke to his girlfriend.

"Let's go," Shelly said to Ruthie. He'd been inside the house at the bar getting a Perrier when he overheard it. Now he came out to the pool area where she was sitting talking to some women writers. He didn't feel like being polite, so without even saying hello to the others, he picked Ruthie's purse up and handed it to her. "Right now."

Sid was having a great time climbing on some play equipment with a group of other kids in which the older ones were tending to the little ones, and Ruthie had been relaxing for the first time in a long time, gabbing away. Now she was worried about Shelly and the anger in his eyes. "Are you okay?" she asked him.

"Yeah. I just want to get out of here."

"We just got here," she said, wondering what was wrong.

"Then you stay. I'm going."

"What about Sid?"

"He can stay or go. It's up to you."

"Ah, Shel. Why can't we *all* stay?"

"Because I want to leave."

"And do what?"

"Go home."

"Why do you want to go home? It's Christmas Eve, a family time."

"Get ahold of yourself, Ruthie. We're Jewish and we're *not* a family."

The ocean was loud but not loud enough to cover what Shelly said. One of the women saw the pain in Ruthie's face and took her hand, but she pulled it away. "Here's the ticket for the car," she said, yanking it out of her purse. "I'll keep the baby here with me and get a ride home." Shelly took the ticket, turned, walked over to Sid, and with a little kiss good-bye, was gone. Through the large windows of the front of the house Ruthie saw the valet parker pull her Mercedes up, and she watched Shelly get into it and drive away.

According to the doctors, so far he was doing fine. He went to his appointments every month to have his T-cell count checked and to be examined for any symptoms of AIDS, and all was well. But the fear and the stigma tormented him. Sometimes he would wake up and write poetry, which she found around the house. She knew that many nights he would lie in bed, longing to sleep, to cross the threshold into dreams where he was healthy and unafraid, but his anxious mind wouldn't let him. Instead he would find himself filled with heart-pounding panic.

He would hyperventilate and feel nauseated and shaky, so he would get up and walk down the hall and into Ruthie's room. And Ruthie, knowing in her sleep that something was wrong, would wake to find him sitting there. He had come in just to be near her. Once she was awake she would sit up, kneel beside him on the bed, and massage his shoulders, kneading the knots of fear out of his back, saying over and over again, "You're okay.

You're okay. Your T-cell count is high, your appetite is good, Sid and I love you, and you're okay." And soon her words and the comforting physical contact of the massage would ground him again, and he would relax.

When Ruthie felt his shoulders lowering and the tension ease, she would get up, put on her robe, and take his hand. "Come on," she would say, leading him down the hallway to the baby's room. And they would stand together in the nursery lit only by the Mickey Mouse night-light and look at the face of their peacefully sleeping son.

"This is why you can't panic. This is why you have to say, 'Everybody's going to die, but they're going to have to take Shelly Milton kicking and screaming out of this world, because I'm hanging in for Sid the Kid.' Are you with that, Shel? We made it through 'Rudy the Poodle,' and love, and death, we made it through frizzy hair and suicide attempts, and we will make it through this one, too." Then she would walk him to his room and watch while he got back into bed, then go to her own room and sit wide awake until she heard him snoring before she could go back to sleep herself. She loved him and she should have gone home from the stupid Christmas party with him, in fact she should leave now and meet him there. One of the women she'd been talking to had walked inside to get something to eat, and the other one was chasing after her own little toddler. Ruthie decided to start asking around to see if she could get a ride home when she spotted Louie Kweller across the crowded backyard.

Louie Kweller was looking a little rounder than he had in the early years, when along with Ruthie and Shelly and all the other comedy writers he had haunted the Comedy Store. But he was still sweet looking, and when he greeted Ruthie with a very warm hug, it felt good and he smelled great. One of the things Ruthie remembered finding so attractive about Louie was that he was well-read. Once they'd had a conversation about a television series which had a lot of simultaneous plot lines and Louie described it as having a "Dickensian multiplicity." Another time he compared the plot of a sitcom they'd all watched together to a Stephen Crane short story.

"No kidding?" Shelly had laughed. "I thought Stephen Crane was the head of miniseries at NBC."

Most of the comedy writers Ruthie knew were funny by feel, instinct, up from pain. Louie Kweller had all of that, but he combined it with an educated overview, and the combination had caused him to become one of the most successful producers in television. He had recently made a highly publicized deal with a studio, giving him what they swore in the trade papers would be a production company with "complete artistic freedom" plus some unheard-of amount of money to do it.

"So you're a hit," Ruthie said to him as he sat on the deck chair next to her. It seemed like forever since the old days when they'd sat for hours in the group of struggling writers at the Hamburger Hamlet on Sunset. When Ruthie and Shelly used to split one bacon cheeseburger between them, because two bacon cheeseburgers were more than they could afford.

"And you're a hit too," he said, smiling. Ruthie found him almost humble for someone who had just been told his every idea was worth millions of dollars.

"But not like you. You could sell your laundry list now for more than I could get for my house."

"Yeah, but you've got a kid," he said, patting her hand. "Is that him in the red shirt over there?" He gestured in the direction of the big wooden structure with a fort at the top where Sid was climbing up the ladder.

"How did you know?" Ruthie asked.

"Because he's so cute," Louie said and looked into her eyes, and Ruthie was shocked when a flame rose in her cheeks the likes of which she hadn't felt in what seemed like a lifetime. Calm down, Zimmerman, she thought. You're losing your mind.

"So what are you working on?" Ruthie asked him, hoping Louie wouldn't notice that something he'd said in passing, probably as a joke, had stirred her. Made her heavyhearted self feel for even a tiny breath of an instant desirable. No. Better than that. Womanly. The party was getting busier and noisier as more and more people arrived.

A very skinny, pretty girl, wearing a spandex dress that was so tight it showed her pelvic bones, spotted Louie and hurried over to remind him that she was on an episode of one of his shows a few weeks ago and that the script was "soooo brilliant." Ruthie liked the way Louie thanked her with seriousness, didn't come on to her, and after she walked away didn't make some snide comment about what an airhead she was. He was an appealing, gentle man.

"You did a good thing, you and Shelly," Louie said now. "By having that baby together. I bumped into Shelly the other day and he's completely changed. Much more serious than I've ever seen him. Is that your observation?"

"That Shelly's more serious? Definitely," Ruthie said, feeling really guilty now that she hadn't left with him.

"Are you living together?"

"Yes."

"Hey, Kweller," somebody yelled from the house and Louie waved and Ruthie watched him, impressed by the fact that there was no apparent show of his newfound importance. There was no patronizing air that usually accompanied success in Hollywood.

"So, I mean," he said, looking back at Ruthie, and she knew what he was going to ask her. It was a question she'd been asked before. "I mean, I know this is none of my business, and if it's rude you can say so and I'll shut up, okay? But how does that work?"

She knew exactly what he meant, but she wasn't going to make it easy for him. "How does *what* work?"

"I mean, is it a love affair, a romance? Anything like that?"

"You're right. It *is* none of your business, but how it works is, he's my best friend. The closest person to me in the world. I love him more than I've ever loved any man or probably ever will, but we each sleep in our own bedroom and we don't have sex." Louie Kweller was expressionless. "And it's okay," Ruthie told him.

"Mommeeee," Sid shouted suddenly, and Ruthie jumped to her feet and ran over to the play yard where her son was screaming at the bottom of the slide, because he'd just been kicked by a bigger boy. She snatched him up and held him and soothed him and kissed him. After a few minutes he dried his face against her shirt and wriggled away to go back to playing.

"We're going home soon, honey," she called after him. "In a few minutes we'll go home and see Daddy. I'll get us a ride."

"I'll take you home." Ruthie turned to see that Louie Kweller had walked to the play yard too, and was standing behind her.

"Don't you live around *here?*" Ruthie asked. "I mean, wouldn't it be out of your way?"

"Yeah, but that's okay. I feel like taking a ride."

Louie Kweller. He was coming on to her. If he only knew what was going on in her life. That Shelly often woke with night sweats, that no matter what the doctors said about her status and Sid's, she was afraid she'd never stop feeling panicky over every rash, every loose bowel movement.

Louie, oh Louie, she thought, this flirtation is a very nice Christmas present for me and I can use it, but there's no room for anything in my life now. I work for a son of a bitch who I hate, I come home and I raise my kid, and I love Shelly Milton. After that I have nothing left. But when she picked up a protesting Sid, and thanked her host, and Louie Kweller carried the diaper bag over his left shoulder and put his right arm around her to walk her out to the valet parking, it felt very nice.

"You Ruth Zimmerman?" the parking attendant asked.

"Yeah."

"Your husband left the baby's car seat with me so you could use it on the way home," he said, producing it from next to the telephone pole where Shelly had left it. When they brought his Buick sedan, Louie buckled the baby seat into the backseat and Ruthie lifted Sid into the seat and closed the strap around him.

On the console in Louie's car was the box from an audiocassette of William Faulkner reading passages from *As I Lay Dying*. "I guess you don't have *Dinosaur Ducks*," Ruthie said. "Or *Winnie the Pooh and the Honey Tree?*"

"No," Louie said, smiling in a cute crooked way, "but I'll be glad to order them."

Eastbound traffic was bumper to bumper all along Sunset.

"You still working for Zev Ryder?" Louie asked.

"I'm sorry to say the answer to that is yes."

"He's a no-talent schmuck," Louie said.

"I couldn't have put it better myself."

"He hates women, Jews, and gays. I'm amazed you two have survived there this long."

"You call this surviving? He's already fired Shelly, he's constantly waiting for a reason to fire me. Every day has been a struggle."

"Want to work on one of my shows? Want to date me? Want to fall in love and marry me?"

Louie was kidding, but Ruthie was suddenly uncomfortable that Sid was hearing him say all of that, maybe because it was straight out of her fantasy of what she wished somebody would say. Somebody who would appear and save her from the dread she lived with every day.

"Yeah, sure," she said. They were pulling up outside her house.

"I mean it," he said. "Let's go to dinner one night. I won't jump you. I promise."

"I've got to go, Louie," she told him. "But thanks for the ride."

In the living room, Shelly sat on the sofa with the television on. He stared at it and channel-danced with the remote control. "Who brought you home?" he asked her.

"Louie Kweller."

"What did that rich asshole have to say?"

"He sends *you* his warmest regards."

"Whoopie."

"Daddy, come play."

"I will, honey," Shelly said to Sid, but he didn't move.

"Why don't we open some of our presents now? We don't have to keep the rules," Ruthie said. "As you so aptly pointed out, we're Jewish." Maybe opening presents would cheer Shelly up.

"Daddy! Open presents. We're Jewish," Sid said, climbing onto Shelly's lap. His sweet, innocent face made Shelly grin.

"Do you think we should?" Shelly teased.

"Yaaahhhh!" Sid replied, and climbed down to run to the tree. Ruthie and Shelly followed and watched Sid rip open the paper on his gifts: Talking Big Bird, and an airplane on wheels, the Match Box garage, and the Lego airport, and all of the *Star Wars* characters, and a child's tape player. Then Shelly opened his from Ruthie. An IBM personal computer, and an HP laser-jet printer. After he tore off the paper, he pulled the Styrofoam packing out of the boxes and then all of the components.

Since the day they started writing, their style of putting words down had always been first in longhand on legal pads with pencil. When they weren't working on a show where a typist was provided, they typed their own drafts on a very old portable typewriter, then paid a typist to redo the script neatly. Now, staring at them, was the high tech of the 1990s.

"Merry Christmas," Ruthie said, knowing she'd gone a little overboard, but so what? Shelly pulled a manual out of the box and thumbed through it, shaking his head in wonder. "Shel, I know it seems overwhelming and confusing, but the best part of this gift is that I hired someone from the computer store to come over here at night and teach us how to use it. She's a terrific woman who's worked with a lot of writers, and she explains things in plain English, not computerese. She swears that in a few years we'll wonder how we ever lived without it."

Shelly put the thick notebook of a manual down on the coffee table and stood, then he nearly tripped over Sid, who was lying on his stomach running the Match Box cars along the floor and using the coffee table as a tunnel. Ruthie, who still held the first of her unopened gifts in her hand, watched him walk into his bedroom, and she followed him and stood in the doorway.

"What are you thinking?" she asked him. He sat on his bed, looking out of the French doors that opened onto a balcony.

"That in a few years I may not be here. Why do you think that corner of gifts for Sid is three feet high? I bought him stuff he won't be able to play with till he's twelve, because I figured when he was twelve, I wouldn't be around to give them to him. I don't want to take up any of my time learning how to use a computer."

"It won't take long. You learned to work the video camera, and goddamn you, in the time you take worrying about it, you could be learning it, mastering it. By next Christmas you could be Steve Wozniak, for God's sake. And a simple thank you will suffice." She was about to walk angrily out of the room when Sid came running in, carrying the gift he'd just unwrapped on his own, his Ninja Turtle evaporator gun, and he aimed it right at Ruthie. "Yaggggh," he shouted.

"That's what I like to see," Ruthie said. "Another satisfied customer."

In the living room she opened a package from Shelly to her. It was a professionally taken photograph of Sid. The two of them had gone to a studio as a surprise for Ruthie, and Shelly had the picture framed in an antique frame.

"I love you," Shelly said, coming into the living room.

"I love Mommy, too," Sid said and grabbed Ruthie hard around the leg. And Ruthie held the frame to her chest and loved them both so much she wanted to cry. But that didn't stop her from wondering at that same moment what Louie Kweller would be like in bed.

40

ON CHRISTMAS EVE Lainie's health club was open, so first she dropped Rosie off at her mother's house, where the baby went happily, and then she drove over to take an aerobics class. Today as the class started, the rock music was booming so loudly she could feel the floor under her feet vibrating. Because she liked to be able to see herself doing the exercises, she always worked out in the front row.

Today she looked in the mirror at her body, which had been decimated on the inside by illness, and thought how miraculous it was that the exterior still looked good, well-formed, shapely. Thank God, she thought, for good genes. Her mother, who had never owned a pair of tights or sweatpants, never even took a long brisk walk, still had a taut, thin body.

"Arms up and breathe, and exhale. And again, breathe into it, ladies, and feet apart, bend the knees and stretch."

Christmas Eve without Mitch, and all their rituals of the night before Christmas would be wrenching. Last year they bought ornaments that said *Baby's First Christmas*, and took Rosie, who had no idea what was going on, to the May Company to see Santa. This year Lainie hadn't even bought a tree. After class she would pick Rosie up, take her home and feed her, and rock her to sleep. After all I've been through, she thought, that should be enough of a celebration. I am alive and well and I have a baby. Thank heaven for those blessings.

When the heavy aerobic part of the class got under way, the uncomfortable pounding made her want to drop out, to give the teacher a little good-bye wave and just leave. But instead she made herself stay, and after a few minutes the rhythm was getting to her, and her spirits were lifting. Maybe it was endorphins, something she'd read about that was released in the brain during physical exertion. Whatever it was, by the end of the class she felt strong and powerful and ready to handle anything.

"She's been as good as gold," her mother said, opening the door for Lainie. Rosie ignored Lainie's entrance. She was sitting and playing with a musical jack-in-the-box next to her grandmother's two-foot-tall Christmas tree. It was the kind of tree Margaret Dunn had bought for herself over the years since her husband died, as if she were making the statement that a woman alone only needs half a tree.

"Her father called here," Margaret said to Lainie quietly as they stood in the foyer of her Studio City house. "Said he called your place to check on her, but when you weren't there he figured you'd probably be at school, so he tried me. He was in a foul mood."

"Really?" Lainie asked. She knew she was skating on thin ice. That unless she and Mitch put their marriage back together soon, her current custody of Rose was a limited privilege for which she would have to fight if there was a divorce. Mitch could drag her into court and say God knows what about the disposition of custody of the little baby girl he always referred to as "my daughter."

With a nod of her head Margaret invited Lainie into the living room, where she'd been all evening, watching the baby play from her recliner. "Join me?" she asked her daughter, gesturing at a bottle. Lainie rarely drank, because it was dangerous for a diabetic. Now and then she'd sometimes had a glass of champagne with Mitch to relax her in the days when she was trying to conceive, or to celebrate an anniversary.

"No . . . I don't think I can . . ." But the needy look on her mother's face made her reconsider.

"A short one?" Margaret asked.

It was Christmas Eve. Tomorrow Lainie would open gifts with Rosie in the morning, packages friends had sent over, toys she'd bought for the baby. Then Mitch would come to pick up the little angel and take her to one of his sister's houses where his family would be assembled. All of them would be glad, Lainie thought, that *she* was not among them. Then, because she'd promised she would, she would go over to her friend Sharon's Christmas party. It promised to be a time to get through, and move on to the new year. Barbara Singer had warned all the people in the group not to pin any expectations on the holidays. Well, Lainie thought, I should at least stay and have a glass of wine with my mother.

"All right," she said.

"We're both alone now," her mother said as she poured Lainie's wine. "I can only tell you that for me, it's the way I like it."

"I *don't* like it that way, Mother. I just don't know how to change it right now."

"Well, it looks to me as if it's a package deal. You want that baby? You're going to have to take Mitch. Otherwise I can tell you for certain, he's going to pull her away from you."

"Did he say that to you?" Lainie asked, worried.

"Darling, you forget. I work in an office that specializes in divorces. I've seen perfectly nice men turn into fire-breathing maniacs fighting over belongings they didn't even know they had until some lawyer told them they should go after it. Decks of cards, fish forks, we had one pull a gun on his wife until she handed over the papier-mâché napkin rings they bought together in Tijuana. So you can imagine how weird they can get when it comes to what they're going to do about their children."

Lainie took a gulp of wine and it tasted good. She was so unused to the effects of alcohol that after another sip heat flushed through her. When Rosie crawled over to her and into her lap, she kissed the top of the baby's little head, inhaling the sweet baby smell of her, and felt overwhelmingly helpless. All the strength she'd felt after the exercise class was gone.

"Mother," she said. "What are you doing for Christmas Day?"

"Oh, I don't know. Some of the girls at the office invited me to come by. But you know I'm not much for parties, so I'll probably stay put."

"Well, don't do that. I mean, you're right. We're both alone, and we shouldn't be." There was a loud plink, and then a screech of surprise as the jack-in-the-box popped out at Rosie, who slammed the lid of the box shut, and started turning the musical crank again.

"Why don't I stop at the Safeway near my house on my way home and pick up a turkey and some yams, I know you love yams, and tomorrow night you and I will have dinner together at my house. Mitch will bring Rosie back at about seven-thirty. Please say yes. I don't want to go to any parties with strangers either. Let's do this."

Margaret Dunn was quiet, took another sip of wine as Lainie did too, then finally she answered. "On one condition."

"What's that?"

"That I can make some baked apples for dessert." Baked apples. The one dessert Lainie loved and didn't feel guilty about eating. The dessert her mother started making for her years ago, after Lainie had been diagnosed as a diabetic. A gesture of love.

"It's a deal," Lainie said. She would have company when Rosie and Mitch went off to spend their Christmas without her. And maybe she and her mother could strengthen their relationship. Both those thoughts made it easier for her to gather up Rosie's things and know she was taking her home to a Christmas Eve without Mitch.

She was driving down Ventura Boulevard when she started to feel it. A tingling inside her mouth. My God, she thought, knowing she should stop the car, pull over, and get herself something to take care of it, but the baby was with her and she wasn't sure where to stop. And it was too late because . . . she put her hand up to her hair and her head was soaking wet. Perspiring. Maybe she should turn into one of those side streets and pull over. For some reason the wheel felt hard to turn, but something, probably it was knowing she had the baby in the backseat, made her able to manage. At least get the car around the . . . red light. There was a flashing red light behind her. No. Her foot pushed down on the gas to get away from the red light.

But the red light was staying with her. Following her, and then a loud voice from somewhere said, "Pull over." For a minute she couldn't even remember how to pull over. So she turned the wheel hard and grazed a parked car and put her foot on the brake. And somehow she made her aching hand pull the emergency brake. The looming figure of a policeman was moving toward her. It had to be that he was coming over to save her from whatever was happening because she knew she was slipping away. The policeman stood next to the window now.

"Evening, ma'am. You seem to be having a problem."

Lainie was shaking and leaning against the steering wheel.

"May I please see your driver's license and registration?"

License was where? Purse. Yes.

"Um . . . I . . ."

"Ma'am, can I ask you to step out of the car?"

"Baby" was all she could get out.

"The baby will be all right," the officer said, opening Lainie's door, and Lainie, wobbly-legged, stepped out and fell against the policeman.

"Whoa, easy, lady," he said, steeling her, and a female officer got out of the car and came over to Lainie's car. She turned off the engine and Lainie could hear her talking gently to Rose. Most of what the policeman said to her next was a blur, about standing on one foot, which she knew she couldn't do even if she held on. To close her eyes and touch her finger to her nose. No, Mitch. Mother. Help. An insulin reaction. She should have eaten dinner before the exercise class, that was what the doctor warned her.

The policeman put handcuffs on her and edged her into the back of the police car, and said something to her about the fact that the woman officer was taking Lainie's car with Rosie in it, but Lainie was trembling and still unable to tell him she wasn't drunk, just very close to death.

She didn't remember much about what happened after that except that it was a miracle that they took her to the Van Nuys police station because there was a medic there who knew right away she was having an insulin reaction. He gave her orange juice immediately, which brought her blood sugar back to normal. Not a drunk driver, insulin reaction. Little by little the world came back into focus and when she was feeling as though she was able to get up and walk around, they brought her Rosie, who screamed "Mammmmma" when she saw her, then buried her face in Lainie's neck and cried.

For a few minutes she sat holding the baby, trying to decide what to do. Christmas Eve in the police station. All she wanted to do was to be with Mitch. To be with Mitch and Rosie, her family. At the pay telephone she dialed her sister-in-law Betsy's number. When Betsy answered, Lainie heard the sounds of laughter and loud music in the background.

"Betsy," Lainie said from the pay phone of the police station. She was holding her baby on her hip and looking back at three people who were waiting in line to use the phone. "Let me talk to Mitch, please."

"Who *is* this?" Betsy asked with that bitchy edge she always had in her voice.

"It's his wife," Lainie answered.

She listened to the music and laughter in the background at Betsy's as she looked around the police station. A couple of hookers were being booked at the desk. When it took Mitch a very long time to get to the phone, Lainie imagined that his sisters were detaining him on his way to take the call, telling him what to say to her.

"Hello," Mitch said into the phone at last, and Lainie was so moved by how it felt just hearing his voice that she had to catch her breath so she could talk.

"It's me," she said. "I'm at the Van Nuys police station. I had an insulin reaction which the police who stopped me thought was drunk driving, so they brought me in. Rose's fine, I'm fine. But Mitchie, in those few minutes when I was sure I was dying, all I could think about was that I miss you and I love you and I don't want to spend another minute of my life without you. And all the stuff with Jackie is going to have to be thought out and worked out and made right. But I know we can do it together. So, I think I can get us home from here all right, but what I want is for you to be there too, so we can work it all out."

"Baby," he said, "I'm there."

"Mitchie, I love you," she said.

"Oh, Lainie," he said, "God knows I love you like crazy."

Before Margaret Dunn came for Christmas dinner the next day, Lainie called to warn her that the evening would be a little different than she had described the night before. And that she should make four baked apples, because at dinner there wouldn't just be Lainie and Rosie waiting to see her, but Mitch too. And it would be a special Christmas for all of them.

41

THE AIRPORT NEWSSTAND was decorated for Christmas, and spread across the back wall once again were several magazine covers with pictures of Kate Sullivan in various attire and poses. *Ladies' Home Journal*, *Vanity Fair*, *People*, and *Los Angeles*. On *Los Angeles* she was wearing a red sweater and red tights and a Santa Claus hat. Her photograph was everywhere because she was promoting her new film, *Always a Lady*, the project that had once been Rick's; it was the studio's hot Christmas release. They were putting countless millions in advertising and publicity behind it, and she had directed it herself.

Last night every time Rick flicked the TV remote control, she was there. On CNN, on "Entertainment Tonight." "This is your first time out as a director," Leeza Gibbons was saying, Wendy Tush was saying, Larry King was saying. Kate Sullivan got exactly what she'd wanted all along. Not for Rick to direct her in the film, but to make the situation so intolerable for him that he'd be forced to walk away from it. Then she could say to the studio, "There's no one left to direct this, so I guess I'll have to do it myself."

What does it matter, he thought, knowing that the minute the holiday was over he'd be stepping back into the cold editing room where he'd spent the last few weeks and would spend the next several months cutting his own new film. And the months would only be broken in their intensity by daily visits from the nanny bringing David to visit, or by midnight dinners with Patty, who understood the director's life-style so well from her years with Charlie Fall.

Patty, bless her pretty face, was so solid. Some nights she just showed up at the editing room with a picnic basket of food she'd prepared. And she'd not only cater for Rick, but the editors too. Then she'd slip away, leaving a flower or a funny note. David's nanny said Patty stopped by the house now and then to check on the little boy too.

When the editing process was complete, Rick would have to wait through that agonizing trying-not-to-think-about-it time until his film was released and he learned what the audiences thought of it and what the critics thought of it. What did it matter? This morning he'd spent three hours lying on his stomach on the floor of his living room, setting up an electric train underneath the eight-foot-tall Christmas tree. And *that* was the kind of thing that felt important to him these days.

Then, as David happily watched the train go round and round through the miniature village, clapping and shouting every time it passed, Rick made popcorn and strung all the pieces David hadn't eaten, and soon there was yards of it. Then he held David up high so the little guy could sling the long white strings across each branch of the tree, because that was what Rick's parents had done with him every year when he was small.

After lunch they had a party to attend, so Rick bathed David and dressed him, showered and dressed himself, and pointed his car west toward the address on St. Cloud Road. There were live reindeer in the front yard, and a backyard full of imported snow, which, thanks to the cold wave, wasn't melting. There was an actor in a Santa Claus suit giving gifts to the children, pretty girls dressed as Santa's elves passing hors d'oeuvres, and a lot of familiar people from the business.

David sat in his usual spot on Rick's shoulders looking over the crowd. A few passersby waved to the cute baby as Rick stopped and talked about his latest projects with an agent from CAA and a guy he knew from Disney. Then at one of the buffet tables, without bothering to get a plate, he made himself a roast beef sandwich on a small roll, ate that quickly, and followed it with a ham sandwich, which he munched while he handed pieces of fruit up to David, who put them in his mouth and let their juice roll down his chin and onto Rick's head.

When a strikingly pretty young actress reached past Rick to get a napkin roll filled with silverware, he said to her, "I know it's probably the pineapple juice on my forehead that makes you think I'm attractive, isn't it?"

The girl looked blankly at him, then up at David, then back at Rick and said, "Ahhh, your grandson is really cute."

Rick let out a loud burst of a laugh in appreciation of the joke, then looked around to see who was watching. He was trying to figure out who had set the girl up to say that to him, but there was no one around that he recognized. She wasn't kidding, and certainly he was easily the right age for her to think that. But for some reason it didn't matter to him one bit.

"You know what?" he said to David as the girl strolled away. "I think it's time for you and me to go to the airport."

"And see airplanes!" David said in agreement.

Now the two of them were at the same gate where Rick stood lifetimes ago when he'd waited alone for the pregnant Doreen to arrive. She had been a little pink puff of a girl then, and he was aware that the time which had passed since he last saw her would make a difference in her appearance, but he wasn't prepared for the person who walked through that same door today. Something about her appearance, much more dramatic than the added years, was so different it startled him. It was her entire mien, her posture, the look in her eyes, and it could only be described as beaten.

The sight of Rick brought a nod of acknowledgment as their eyes met, but hers were the eyes of an unhappy woman. Light-years older and wiser than the ones that used to contain an irrepressible twinkle. The sight of David at Rick's side brought first a look of amazement but then a look of pain, filling Rick with instant regret that his hopes for this visit had been foolish, or worse yet, a cruel mistake.

"Hello, you guys," she said, offering her best smile, which was meager, and hugging Rick weakly. David grabbed Rick's pant leg and hid behind it.

"A shy guy, huh?" Doreen said and knelt, and when he peeked around and looked at her and repeated, "A shy guy," she squeaked happily, "He talks like a big boy!"

In the car she sat in the back with David and held his tiny hand, but said very little to Rick. "How's Uncle B.?" she asked at one point, and Rick filled her in on Bobo's life and illnesses and friends at the home, looking in the rearview mirror to see if she reacted, but for the most part she looked blankly out the window.

At the house she unpacked gifts, which she stacked under the tree, and then she walked around the kitchen helping Rick with the dinner preparations while she held David, who never left her arms for hours. He babbled, impressing her with his vocabulary, amusing himself by trying to remove the eyeglasses from her face.

When the last fork was laid on the table and the dinner was bubbling away on the stove, the doorbell rang.

"Yayyy," David shouted, running to the door.

God, they were a beautiful sight to Rick, the whole group of them standing in the doorway. What could make your heart dance like the faces of the people you loved? It was raining so they hurried in. Howard and Mayer and Mayer's billowy blond fiancée, Lisa, were holding brightly wrapped gifts. And Patty, smashing-looking in a bright red coat, was holding Bobo's arm, giving Rick a look he knew meant it had been a near miracle for her to get the old man here. But it was worth it all when David shouted, "Uncle Bobobobobobo!" and Bobo laughed a big hearty laugh, and said, "Hiya, *boychik.*"

This is the best night of my life, Rick thought to himself as he took their coats and introduced Doreen to the boys and to

Patty. I have a family. A support system, Barbara Singer calls them. Rick looked at Doreen, flushed and wiping her hands self-consciously on the kitchen towel she'd stuck in the waistband of her slacks. She was okay with Bobo, who greeted her warmly, but she seemed awkward with Patty and the boys and Lisa. A few times she called Patty "Mrs. Fall" and Rick overheard Patty say, "Please call me Patty."

Howard was focused on a computer game some friend had given him and he was pushing buttons so it blipped and bleeped. Soon Doreen was sitting next to him on the sofa, and Howard gave her a turn at it, and they were laughing together. Lisa oohed and ahhed over David, and Mayer roughhoused with him. Rick carved the turkey and Patty arranged the plates in the kitchen and brought them to the table. By the time they were eating, Rick was relieved to see Doreen joking with both the boys and Lisa. Yes, she was doing fine, holding her own, seated next to David's high chair, wiping cranberry sauce from his chin.

"This kid's a genius," Howard said. "You know those games where they have all the different shaped holes and then the blocks to put in them? He never misses."

"That's because he has such great genes," Doreen said and laughed.

Bobo and Patty were chatting away too, and the time really felt right for what he wanted to say, so Rick picked up his spoon and tapped gently on his wineglass.

"Attention, please. I know as soon as this meal is over we're rushing over to the Christmas tree to dig into our gifts, but there's one gift I'd like to give separately from the others because this is for someone who has done so much for my life, and I want to acknowledge her with a gift that isn't under the tree."

As he was about to take the gift out of his pocket, he caught sight of Doreen's face and knew by the way she reddened and her half smile that she thought he'd been speaking about her. And that when she realized he wasn't, she might be hurt. When he looked at Patty he could tell by *her* expectant eyes that he had to go on. So he pulled the box out of his shirt pocket, looked at Patty, and said what he'd thought about for weeks. "If you like we can have a very long engagement until you decide how you feel, but I'd like to ask you to marry me and David too."

There was an instant of shocked silence until the two boys laughed and said, "Oh wow!"

"How romantic," Lisa said.

"Thank the good Lord I lived to see it," Bobo said chuckling.

Patty opened the box to see the diamond ring Rick had chosen after endless meetings with a jeweler. When she looked at Rick, her eyes were sparkling brighter than the stone and she said, "This is completely crazy. You're completely crazy, and I should take a long time to decide, like forty or fifty years. But right here in front of God and everybody, I have to admit I really would like to marry you both."

He stood, she stood, and they embraced. Mayer lifted David out of the high chair and squashed the little boy in a happy hug, and it sounded to Rick as if he said, "I've got another brother." Then Patty, visibly shaken, walked over to Bobo's chair and hugged the old man, who was grinning happily. The boys hugged their mother, and Mayer said, "My dad would have been happy about this. He loved you, Uncle Ricky." And Lisa hugged Patty and said, "Maybe we should have a double wedding," and Bobo said, "Just make it soon, will you, I'm a very old man."

Doreen had a smile on her face as she watched it all, as if she were watching a movie, and when Rick went over to hug her he felt her body tense. Maybe, he thought too late, making the announcement tonight when she was here was wrong. He had hoped it would make her happy to see David getting an experienced grown-up woman as a mother. But probably she felt afraid that her own relationship with David would now be threatened.

"She'll be good with him," she said as they all sat back down to eat.

Rick could hardly wait for them to open their gifts. Howard

was fascinated with computers but was still using his old Apple
II, so Rick bought him a brand-new Macintosh. There was a
thirty-five-millimeter camera Mayer had been longing for and
Rick bought that for him with two lenses. Bobo liked to think
of himself as a dapper dresser, so both Rick and Patty bought
him clothes, including a beautiful robe from Neiman-Marcus.
That way he could still look handsome to the ladies at the Motion Picture Home on those days when he was too tired to put
on his street clothes.

For David's Christmas, Rick had gone totally berserk. A
rocking horse, and a playhouse and a climbing gym for out-
doors, a jeep that the boy could get inside and drive with his
feet, and a whale he could sit on in the pool. Rick, so full of joy
tonight, wondered where Christmas had been for him for so
many years. Aside from a dinner with Bobo at some restaurant
in the Valley, he had spent most of them at parties like the one
he and David had attended that afternoon. Parties populated
with people who took each other's hands in their own and with
the most sincere expression they could muster looked into each
other's eyes and said, "We're family." But not one of them gave
a shit about the others, unless there was a deal to be made.
Family.

One of Doreen's gifts from Rick was a college guidebook
accompanied by a note which said *IOU four years of college tuition*,
something he thought would thrill her, but instead he saw her
trying to summon enthusiasm. She's a teenager, he thought,
they live in the now, she doesn't understand at this moment
what that's going to mean to her life. He wasn't surprised when
the curling iron and hair dryer and vanity mirror Patty had
bought for her got a bigger reaction.

On the last day of her visit, she was quiet, sitting next to
David on the trip back to the airport. The baby, who had been
chatty and giggly at first, fell asleep in the car seat.

"What have you told Bea about why you ran away?" Rick
asked her, breaking the silence.

"Nothing yet."

"You know you have to tell her, don't you? To tell someone."

"Well, I didn't want to spoil everyone's holidays, because it's going to be ugly when I finally do tell. I've been thinking about exactly what I'm going to say," and for the first time since she arrived he heard a lilt in her voice, as if she knew what she was telling him now would please him. "But I'm just trying to figure out when the best time is to say it. I mean, Don and my sister have been fighting a lot. I keep thinking he's going to leave her any day now, and that'll make it easier to do what I have to do." Rick felt assured by the sound of hope in her voice that soon things would work out for the best.

"When you're ready to prosecute, I'll pay the legal bills, no matter how high they are. You're doing the right thing, you know that, don't you?"

"Oh yes" was all she said.

At the airport when her flight was called, she knelt and looked into David's little face, and Rick was amazed at the way the child didn't fidget, didn't move while she talked to him, but seemed to take every word with great seriousness.

"Good-bye, little darling," she said. "I can't tell you how I hate to leave you. But at least I know that you're getting a mother and some big brothers. And even though you may not exactly remember this visit years from now, somewhere inside you you'll know that I was here. Now give me one last hug, and please make it a big one, 'cause it's gonna have to last me for a long, long time."

David must have understood every word because he put his pudgy arms around her neck, his mother's neck, and squeezed very hard, while Rick looked at them together and wished he could stop her from leaving. Call the police, adopt her too. But there was nothing he could do, until and unless she was willing to reveal what happened to her. He longed for the magical solution that could put him between her and the onslaught of pain she would have to face before things would get better for her.

"I love you," she said to David, then stood and hugged Rick.

She was already turned toward the jetway when she tossed the words "And I love you too" over her shoulder, and was gone.

She'll tell Bea, he promised himself. But for weeks he couldn't get the image of the once feisty girl who had walked like a zombie through their Christmas together out of his head.

The day the letter arrived at the office it was opened first, as were all letters to the office, by Andrea, who came in and handed it to him, and without even seeing it he knew by her face who it was from and what it would say. And as he read it, he felt as though he'd been slammed against the wall.

Dear Mr. Reisman,

I am writing this to tell you we lost our sweet Doreen this week, when she took her own life. She didn't leave a note, but for a really long time she seemed sad and scared to me. I know she trusted you a lot and I did too, or I wouldn't have let her come and stay with you at Christmas, so I figured you would want to know.

That little baby was always in her heart. Maybe giving him up was too hard for her to live with, or maybe I was wrong and being able to come and see him wasn't the best thing. I wish I knew, though it wouldn't bring her back. Maybe some boy at school hurt her and broke her heart. My other kids are feeling really awful that she's gone.

Bea Cobb

Andrea sat next to him and they held on to each other. He could feel her trembling, or was that him trembling with rage, and pain, and sorrow? Why didn't he see it or know that when Doreen knelt in the airport and looked at David as if it was for the last time that it *was* the last time? Now he remembered the words she'd said. Somewhere inside you, you'll know that I was here. Rick left the office and went home and held David on his lap all day, reading to him, talking to him, hugging him, noticing more than ever how many of his expressions were Doreen's. Then he called Patty and told her the news, and how glad he was that he had her to love.

42

ON CHRISTMAS EVE Judith's baby, Jody, had an ear infection, and the pediatrician's answering service didn't seem to be able to reach the doctor who was on call. So the baby screamed and Judith walked from room to room, holding her against her chest to try to soothe her. After a while the noise of her little sister's screams woke Jillian, and she climbed out of her crib and followed Judith and the baby around the house and hung on to the hem of her mother's bathrobe.

When the doctor finally called and said he'd be glad to telephone a prescription to the drugstore in her neighborhood if Judith would tell him which one was open, she realized she had no idea which one was open. So with the screaming Jody in her arms and her toddler daughter sitting on the floor tugging her robe so hard it was coming off her shoulders, she pulled out the yellow pages and called around to find an open drugstore. When she found one, after her eighth phone call, she asked the pharmacist to please call the pediatrician, had him give her directions from her house to the drugstore, and told him she was on her way.

Then she dressed herself and picked up the two babies, got each of them as settled as possible in their car seats, and drove toward the north Valley where the drugstore was located. It was miles from her home and the baby screamed all the way there, not quite drowning out the Christmas carols Judith put on the radio in order to calm them. Jillian sat in her car seat directly behind the driver's seat, kicking it to the rhythm of each familiar song, jolting her mother with each kick. In the parking lot of the shopping center, Judith unloaded both little ones from their car seats, sat one on each of her hips, grabbed her purse, and started toward the drugstore. She was hoping their pajamas were warm enough, because it was raining.

The pharmacist was harassed. It was, he announced unhappily and irritably to Judith, his busiest night in years. The round baby-toy rack kept Jillian happy as she spun it and squealed at all the brightly colored bubble-packed toys flashing by her. That was fine with Judith, who had her hands full with the baby, still howling in agonized pain. When the pharmacist mercifully handed Judith the bottle of pink ampicillin, she opened it, and with a little dropper she fed the wincing-at-the-taste baby her first dose immediately.

Within a very few minutes, maybe just the time it took for Judith to pay the pharmacist, the baby seemed better. She was quiet and falling asleep on her mommy's shoulder. But the sudden crash to the floor of the toy rack woke her and caused Jillian to join her in shrill crying, as the pharmacist, assuring Judith he didn't mind picking up the many dozens of fallen toys, walked them to the door and showed them out.

"Merry Christmas," he called out to them as Judith carried her two crying children to the car through the night rain. By the time she had them back in their car seats and had started the car, they were soaked through and shivering. She turned on the car heat, and hoped that maybe the ride home would put them to sleep. Dear God, she thought driving down Van Nuys Boulevard through the pounding rain, I've been a horrible selfish woman bringing these babies into the world without a daddy.

But then she adjusted her rearview mirror so she could look at the two of them in the backseat. Their little faces looked angelic as the red and green Christmas decorations of the boulevard passed, casting their lights on them. "I love you two," she said, full of emotion at the miracle that had blessed her with them, and she felt good and strong.

At home she changed their clothes and their diapers, tucked baby Jody into her crib, and Jillian into hers. When they were finally asleep, she started a fire in the fireplace. I'm blessed, she thought. I have my babies and that's all I need. I'm not going to sit around feeling sorry for myself or them. We're a happier family than some of the intact ones I know where the parents are fighting and divorcing and cheating on each other.

She had just taped a bow on the box containing the talking teddy bear, when she heard the baby cry out. The pharmacist had told her if Jody woke in the night, she could give her another dose of the medicine, as long as it had been three hours since the first dose. She hurried to the refrigerator where she kept the awful-looking pink liquid and went to comfort her poor little baby girl. After administering another dropperful of medicine, she changed Jody's diaper. Then she scooped her into her arms and rocked her while she sang "Santa Claus Is Coming to Town." And the minute she was asleep and Judith had placed her gently into her crib, Jillian called out to her.

Jillian's diaper was dirty, so Judith put her on the changing table, removed the dirty diaper, and squatted to look on the lower shelf for a new box of premoistened baby wipes. And during that instant Jillian took the open bottle of ampicillin her mother had forgotten to close after she'd diapered the baby, and chugged some incalculable amount of it down. When Judith stood and saw her daughter still holding the bottle to her lips, the pink medicine all over her face, her knees buckled with panic.

"Jillie, no! Did you drink that? Oh, my God. I left it open. Oh no." Clutching Jillian to her, she ran to the phone and dialed the doctor's number again. "This is an emergency!" she said to the doctor's answering service operator. "Please get him on the phone." Why hadn't she learned something about poison control? Who could she call? Maybe she should dial 911. The phone rang almost immediately. "Meet me at the emergency room," the doctor told her, and within seconds she had awakened the baby, stuffed both of the children into their car seats, and was off again into the rainy night.

A nurse held sleepy Jody in her arms at the nurses' station so Judith could stay with Jillian, who screamed and retched while they pumped her stomach, and Judith could hardly keep herself from vomiting. When they were able to leave the hospital it was dawn. Christmas morning. While two nurses watched the babies, Judith went into the little antiseptic ladies' room in the hospital corridor to splash some cold water on her face to prepare for the drive home. As she dabbed her eyes with a harsh paper towel from the cold aluminum dispenser, she looked at what had become of herself, and felt right on that edge of emotion where she could either laugh or cry.

That painful but absurd place where it seems as if anything that might have gone wrong has, and you can either lie down on the floor and kick your feet or dance with relief that you've survived the latest onslaught. "Merry Christmas," she said to her reflection, and that made her laugh. She was wearing an old chenille bathrobe over her flannel nightgown and some fuzzy blue slippers she had ordered from the Norm Thompson catalogue about seven years ago; her usually well-kept red hair was dry and flyaway, and the circles under her eyes were now so long and low they were invading her cheeks. She sighed, and walked into the corridor where one of the nurses stood holding a sleeping Jillian and another stood holding the sleeping Jody.

"Thank you," Judith said to them, so grateful for the tender way they had treated her babies.

"Why don't we walk you out?" one of the nurses asked.

"That would be great."

Judith followed behind as they made their way in an odd little parade down the long hospital corridor. This is all a test, she thought. But I will pass it. At home she put both of the children on her big bed, put herself between them, and they all slept until noon. When they woke, Jody seemed to be one-hundred-percent cured, and Jillian was as chipper as if nothing had happened. So after Jillian had torn into all of her Christmas packages and Jody had rejected all of the toys in favor of the boxes in which they'd been packaged, Judith put them each in a fancy dress and took them out to a party.

"I realized something about myself over the holidays," she said to the group after she'd regaled them with what was now the funny version of her Christmas Eve and Christmas Day. "And what's so interesting to me is that what I got from the whole experience is that I like it this way. Love it this way. Don't want anybody to interfere with the decisions I make for them, don't want to compromise my life-style one bit, and I chose this life-style because I want control. I know it's going to be tough for me on occasion after occasion, but I can do it.

"So what I want to know is, is it okay," she asked Barbara, "for me to be this way? I mean I'm sure we can go deep into my psyche and figure out how my father treated my mother and on and on, but whatever the reason, I know I'm happiest this way. My life, however different it may seem to other people, feels great to me. And now that I really know that, I can stop falling prey to every fix-up, and quit apologizing for the fact that I'm a single mother as if it's just a stopgap on the road to a kind of normalcy I don't want."

"I think," Barbara said, "you just answered your own question, Judith. But also try to give yourself the flexibility to change your mind, when and if that happens."

"Rick," Ruthie said, "you look bad. Are you feeling all right?"

Rick shook his head but didn't speak, looked away from the others and out at David to check on him. Ruthie was right. He was hollow-eyed and gray-faced.

"Doreen is gone," he said, looking at all of them. "It was a suicide. Her mother thinks the reason was her parting with David, maybe even about her coming here for Christmas. I know it had to do with what was going on with her at home, but now with her gone, what can I do. . . ."

"Oh, Rick." The others surrounded him, touching his hands, his shoulders, putting their arms around him.

"And I feel as if in part I contributed to the unhappiness, because right in front of her at Christmas, I proposed to Patty."

Silence.

"So?" Shelly asked.

"So that must have made Doreen afraid that she'd become less important to David. Maybe she would lose her link with him."

"Rick," Barbara said, "the possibility that you would marry was always there whether you thought so or not."

Rick just shook his head.

"I'm so happy for me," he said, "and so god-awful sad for that little girl. Being the parent of that little boy has transformed me, shown me the world through a pair of innocent, loving eyes. Taught me how to need someone and be needed. And most of all taught me about priorities. Now I know that in the final analysis it really is the way we love that matters, and everything else is completely beside the point.

"When I look back at the years I spent before this baby was in my life, sometimes I'm appalled at the time I wasted on so many unimportant endeavors and projects and problems and anxieties. But then I realize that it's okay. That none of that was really for naught, because it was all about teaching me to get here, to this mind-set, to this relationship with Patty."

After a long quiet time Barbara spoke. "Well, it's pretty clear that the De Nardos had a good holiday," she said, looking at Lainie and Mitch, whose chairs were close to each other's and who held tightly on to each other's hands.

Lainie spoke in her quiet way. "I'm starting to feel comfortable with expanding our concept of family to in some ways include Jackie. It doesn't diminish me, and for Rosie, the more people who love her, the better she'll feel about herself. The trick will be getting her to understand all of this when she gets older. But that's when I think the openness is going to pay off the most and make what seems to be the strange part work."

These people are amazing, Barbara thought. What these babies have done to open up their lives is extraordinary.

"And what about your family? How were your holidays?" Barbara asked Ruthie and Shelly. Shelly answered.

"We're okay. I hated the parties, but I think Ruthie and Sid had a pretty good time. In fact, as a result of all the socializing, some man is pursuing Ruthie. Calls our house every day." It was clear he was kidding Ruthie. A little kidding on the square.

"Oh, Shel, cut it out," Ruthie said and gave him a tap on the arm. "I'm not one bit interested in him."

"Want to talk about it, Ruth?" Barbara asked.

"No," Ruthie snapped.

"I want you to," Shelly said.

"There's nothing to talk about," Ruthie said, her eyes angry now. And that was when the little ones came toddling in to have their snack.

43

BARBARA TURNED HER CAR into the parking lot of the Rexall drugstore on Beverly and La Cienega, and looked across the street at the Beverly Center shopping mall. She remembered two decades ago when there had been nothing on that same lot but Beverly Park, an amusement center for children, which had a few toddler rides and a pony ring. It had always been the hands-down favorite spot for both Heidi and Jeff on a Sunday morning. They loved to be taken there and sit proudly on one of the harnessed ponies and ride around and around the ring waving as they passed Barbara and Stan.

An unexpected shadow of sadness moved across her face, and it made her want to cry. For days she hadn't felt well. Maybe it was an ulcer, or a hiatal hernia, or some other digestive problem, but her queasiness wouldn't go away. That was the reason she had stopped at the drugstore, so she could go in and get herself some Tums or Rolaids to take away that constant feeling of heaviness in her abdomen.

Inside the big bustling drugstore, she was planning to walk straight to the antacid counter, get what she wanted, and leave, but instead she found herself walking to the train of empty shopping carts, extracting one, and steering it toward the beckoning aisles of merchandise. She loved drugstores, the millions of colors, the glossy posters that advertised blushers and nail polish and lipsticks. And the constant barrage of new products. Like a spray to put in a travel case that would remove wrinkles from clothes, or a new kind of diet powder that she had seen advertised in magazines which had already made lots of famous fat people thin.

Feminine hygiene. She slowed the cart down in that aisle, grabbed a box of tampons, and was just about at the end of the aisle when she stopped to look right at what she now had to admit to herself was what she had really come into the drugstore to buy. An EPT. Early pregnancy test. My God, what if what she was fearing was true? Her period was only a little late, and at her age, as Howie Kramer had reminded her more than once, she was premenopausal, so the irregularity was to be expected. But maybe she should buy it as a catalyst. Surely buying one of those tests, wasting the seventeen dollars, would be exactly what she had to do to bring her period on. But she knew she was playing games with herself, because there was no doubt in her mind that she was absolutely, unequivocally, one-thousand-percent pregnant. At age forty-two.

She remembered the feeling from the early stages of both her pregnancies, which now seemed as if they were a million years ago. That bloated, weary, swollen-breasted, full-of-tears, moody feeling, and she didn't need an EPT to tell her it was so. Stan, she imagined herself saying, I'm pregnant. What in the world would he say to that? Hooray? After all, he had suggested the idea of their having another baby not very long ago. But he was kidding when he said it, she reminded herself. He was thinking about buying second homes and traveling and running through the house naked.

How about, Guess what, Heidi, I'm pregnant! That would be the hardest of all. After her own failed engagement and her childhood friend having a new baby girl. A few months ago she was the one who was looking at apartments with room for a nursery. Heidi would look at her, her mouth hanging open in shock, and say, "No way!" She'd be mortified.

Yes, she thought. Maybe if she bought the test she'd get her period. She threw the EPT into her shopping cart and made her way toward the cashier. But before she got there she stopped back at the feminine hygiene aisle, took the big blue box of tampons out of her cart, and put it back on the shelf.

That night at home, she looked at her swollen naked breasts in the full-length mirror on the back of her bathroom door, and then looked down at the body that had carried and brought forth Heidi twenty-four years earlier and Jeff seventeen years earlier. Her body, which was undeniably a little too round in the belly, too wide in the waist, too meaty around the hips, and had no tone whatsoever anywhere else, and she wondered what would become of it after a mid-life pregnancy.

Dear God, she thought, I don't think I can do this. When this child is seven years old, I'll be a fifty-year-old woman. Babies cry all night. Babies feed on demand. Babies require constant care every minute. Am I ready to give up the travel I postponed, first to have kids, then to go to school, and then because I was too busy at work?

Just as I was getting to the point in my life where I could take a big deep breath. Her breasts pulsed with a hot ache from deep inside. So soon into the pregnancy. A baby who will come forcing its way into the world past gray pubic hairs. No! The pubic hairs would be shaved. Oh please. She'd forgotten *that* indignity and the enema that went with it, and the awful itch when the hair started to grow in. And that was the least of the physical discomfort.

Years of no sleep, potty training, the terrible twos. Maybe this is PMS, she thought. Maybe my forty-two-year-old hormones are so out of whack they're causing me to lose my mind. Maybe they're making me imagine that I could actually still be fertile. She took the early pregnancy test out of the bag and looked at the box, opened it, and took out the directions. She had picked this particular test because it didn't require her to use her first morning urine, the way some of them did. This was one she could do at any time. Like right now.

She removed the funny dipstick from the box, watching herself in the mirror as if it were someone else performing this bizarre act. Then she locked the bathroom door so Stan wouldn't pop in on her, and then found that she didn't remotely have any urge to urinate. In fact she was certain she couldn't have squeezed out even a drop. For a long time she stood leaning against the tile counter, staring at herself, wondering what to do.

Pregnant. Mother, I'm pregnant. Gracie would probably laugh at her, then tell her about all the other cultures where older women had babies. No, she wouldn't tell Gracie, or Heidi or Jeff yet. When she found out if she was pregnant, which she knew she was, she would tell Stan and discuss the truth, which was that having a baby at this stage of their lives was probably a big mistake.

Dr. Gwen Phillips was in her late thirties. When Barbara was being escorted from the reception area to an examining room, after a wait that was only as long as it took to fill out a few forms, she passed the young female gynecologist's office and saw the doctor at her desk holding a baby boy.

"That's the doctor's son," the nurse told Barbara.

Maybe I'm lulling myself into a false sense of security here, Barbara thought, feeling defiant and proud of herself for finally breaking the Howie Kramer cycle, but I like this doctor already and I haven't even met her yet. When she'd undressed and was seated on the table, the first thing she noticed was the little knitted bootielike casings around each of the stirrups. Obviously they were put there to make the damn things feel a little softer and warmer. When Gwen Phillips entered, she was carrying a pillow which she gently placed behind Barbara's back.

"Mrs. Singer," she said. "I just checked your urine, and I hope this is good news. You're pregnant."

"I know," Barbara said. "I knew before I did the early pregnancy test. I've been trying to figure out how I got so careless. And frankly I'm not so sure if it's good news or not."

"Tell me your concerns and maybe I can help," the doctor said.

Howie Kramer, Barbara thought, you will never see me again. At least not without my pants on. "My concerns. Well, let's see, where do I start? My daughter is twenty-four and my son is seventeen. When I tell them, they'll probably disown me. I have a full-time career, and clients who really need me. I was recently entertaining the thought of retirement so I could do nothing for a few years. I will probably have to wear glasses to see my own baby. I dye my hair to get rid of the gray and I know for a fact that's unhealthy for pregnancies, and most of all, I don't want to interrupt my sleep on Saturday mornings to watch 'Smurfs.'"

The pretty young doctor was serious. "Are you saying you want to terminate the pregnancy?"

Barbara felt a distant wave of nausea heading in her direction. "I don't know what I'm saying. I mean, I thought I was on my way to being a grandmother. Granted, an early grandmother, but not this. A mommy, again. I mean . . . listen, I wanted to come in just to be sure that I was, but now that I know that I truly am . . . I have to think this through."

"If it helps, I can assure you that I've delivered many healthy babies to women your age and much older too, and with proper prenatal care and testing, the pregnancies and the deliveries have been problem-free."

"Oh, it's not the pregnancy or the delivery, though I'll admit they worry me a little," Barbara said. "It's really the time after the pregnancy and delivery that worries me. The part where they look at you one day and say, 'Mom, get off my case.'"

The doctor smiled. "I understand," she said. "Listen, why don't I give you a prescription for some prenatal vitamins and you can call me in a few days and we can talk about it some more." After she wrote the prescription, the doctor shook Barbara's hand, said to call her at any time day or night if she just needed a sounding board about the pregnancy, and left the room.

"You have great hair," Barbara said to her, but the doctor didn't hear that because she was already out the door and on to put a pillow behind the back of her next patient.

44

RUTHIE WAS ALONE in the Zimmerman and Milton cubbyhole of an office at the network trying to make the script come together, but it wasn't happening. Her face throbbed with exhaustion, and she was wondering if the fluorescent lights were really dimming or if her eyes were going bad from too many hours of close work when she heard someone walking down the hall. Probably it was the night-shift guard checking to see who was left in the building. Maybe she would knock off now, gather her things together and ask the guard to walk her out to her car. It was late and she'd been so engrossed, she'd forgotten to check in at home. Both Shelly and Sid would be asleep by now.

The footsteps stopped and she looked up, sure it was a mirage when she saw Louie Kweller.

"I was already in the parking lot when I spotted your light on up here so I came to say hello," he said. "I guess we're the only two fanatics who work this late."

"Hi," she said, surprised at how happy she was to see him, and worried about how bad she must look, since she'd been sitting in that same spot for the last six hours, and her hair was probably frizzed out to the moon.

"So what's happening?" he asked as if they'd just bumped into each other on a street corner instead of in the back-hall offices at CBS, at what Ruthie, without looking at a clock, knew had to be at least two in the morning.

"What's happening is that I can't figure out how to end the second act," she said.

"Well, let's see," Louie said, and she could tell by his expression that he was searching for something cute to say. "How about if she runs into a guy she knew a long time ago, and she can't believe that she never noticed before what a sexy hunk he is? He's crazy about her, always has been, so she starts dating him and the next thing you know, they get married, and have a few kids together. She already has one kid, and he's so happy to have siblings that he thrives. Then they all live happily ever after, because their life is made into a movie of the week."

"I'll use it," she said. "Have your agent call me to negotiate the fee."

Louie wandered over and sat in Shelly's chair across from her, right under the needlepoint sampler that said DYING IS EASY, COMEDY IS HARD. The night was very black outside and Ruthie looked at the window's reflection of her messy office and Louie leaning back in the chair as he gazed at her. The fluorescent lights hummed like crickets.

"Listen," he said after a while, "I don't want to do something bad to Shelly. He's a terrific man. Talented and smart and a good person. I also think your loyalty to him is awesome. But as far as we know, we each only get one life, and maybe you ought to think about having some romance in yours. Maybe even another baby. I'll make a baby with you, or two or three."

"Louie," she said, looking at his serious face and wishing she didn't feel like crying. "You don't even know me. I'm overwhelming, I'm needy, I crack dumb jokes at all the wrong times. I look ugly in the morning, not just sleepy but like a beast. I go on strange diets that make me cranky, or should I say crankier because I can be a complete bitch, and I may need some expensive dental work coming up in the near future."

"I understand that you feel that way, and I just want to go on record as telling you you're my favorite person in Hollywood. I think you're funnier than Joan Rivers, deeper than Anjelica Huston, sweeter than Melanie Griffith, and—"

"Taller than Danny DeVito," Ruthie said.

"Yeah. That too."

"See, I told you I make dumb jokes."

"Unfortunately for you I happen to like that in a woman. In fact I like it a lot. In the old days at the Comedy Store, I used to have the wildest crush on you. Remember the night a zillion years ago when Frankie Levy did your run about supermarkets?"

Did she remember? "It was the night Shelly and I got our first prime-time television job," she said.

"Well, I wanted to come over to you right after Frankie walked offstage, grab you, and take you away to an island somewhere and jump on you, but Eddie Shindler was doing my stuff next so I had to watch him."

"You mean you put *your* career before *my* sex life?" she teased.

"You and Shelly must have left early that night, because I looked for you, and when you were gone I felt like a jerk and just figured maybe I ought to leave you alone, so here I am, how many years later? Don't answer that, and I'm making another try for you and that island. So what do you say?"

"I say it's a pretty thought, Louie, but I don't think I can accept."

"I'll tell you what. Why don't you ask Shelly about it? Talk to him. I know for a fact that he loves you. So maybe you should ask him if you shouldn't spend some time with me to see if you like me, and I guarantee you he'll say you should go for it. And, Ruthie, I promise you, if it works out with us, when the time comes and Shelly needs you to take care of him, I'll never resent one minute of your doing that. I'll help you do it. I'll support your doing it. Only I'm asking you to not give up your own life now in anticipation of that time."

"Louie, I've trusted too many people who disappointed me. Your speech about the Comedy Store and the island is great.

And I mean it as a compliment when I tell you it sounds just like something one of the characters from your show would say. I wish with my soul that you meant it, and maybe you do. But in my repertoire of feelings, the ability to be swept away by romantic love doesn't exist anymore."

"I understand," Louie said softly. "I understand. So why don't I walk you to your car?"

Shelly was having the time of his life with the computer. The woman Ruthie hired from the Writers' Computer Store spent three afternoons with him, and by the time she left after their third session, he was up and running on what had a week earlier been "the dreaded machine." Ruthie could hear him in his room, now and then emitting a "this is incredible," dazzled by his own prowess. Sometimes he would come and get her and make her stand behind him to observe the magic tricks of moving and editing text, telling her that this gift made up for all the toys he never had as a kid.

She no longer went to work fearing she was leaving him at home to watch daytime television. In fact when she called him from the office, he would talk to her in a kind of mindless answering-the-questions-without-listening style that she knew meant he was being distracted by the computer.

After a while he began frequenting the computer store himself to find out what he was missing and found what he called bells and whistles galore. He bought software for screenwriting and tried out the new format by writing funny opening scenes of silly movies to amuse himself and to make Ruthie laugh when she got home.

At the end of five weeks he started writing a real screenplay. Often when Ruthie got home and found her way to his room Sid would be on Shelly's lap where he'd fallen asleep from boredom while Shelly typed madly away in that kind of glazed-over otherworldly writer place inside his brain.

Sometimes he was already sitting there, or still sitting there, in the morning when Ruthie woke to the sounds of Sid stirring in the nursery. This morning it was the clickity clicking of the computer keys that woke her, and she walked into the room where Shelly was working feverishly. For a while she stood in the doorway watching him, then finally she spoke.

"Shel."

"Hmmm."

"What would you say if I told you you were right about Louie Kweller?"

"You mean that he's a rich asshole?"

"No, that I should start dating him."

"I'd say hallelujah." She walked into the room now and looked at his face.

"Hey, I think you should pursue him with everything you've got. Maybe he can pay for Sid's bar mitzvah. By the time the kid is thirteen, the cake alone will cost five hundred thousand."

"You don't mean it. You're pissed off. I know the way your eyes get all bugged out when you're annoyed."

"You're confusing me with Peter Lorre. I'm not annoyed. Can you get him to adopt me and pay my medical bills?"

"Is this your way of saying yes?"

"I don't know why you think you need my permission, but yes. It's a yes. Tell him to come on over."

Louie began by calling her at work every day, and soon he was sending flowers and gifts and cards. One day he sent over an actor in a gorilla suit to her office, and the gorilla brought flowers and serenaded her and the entire writing staff. When the gorilla, paid extra by Louie Kweller to do so, lifted an enraged Zev Ryder above his head and spun him around, all of them laughed out loud.

"I want her to marry him," Shelly said one day in group. "I want her to have a future and I want that for Sid too. I joke around about Louie, but he has a lot of great qualities."

"It sounds as if you're saying that it's okay with you for Ruthie to leave you and be with Louie," Barbara said.

"I'd like to give the bride away," Shelly said, but Barbara detected the fear behind all he was saying. It made sense that he would worry that Louie might take his place, not just as Ruthie's love, but as Sid's.

"Yeah, well, what about Sid?" Judith asked. The group worked in a way that allowed all of them to challenge one another freely, and none of them was afraid to speak out.

"He'll still be our son. And sometimes he'll be with me. And sometimes with them. It's a hell of a lot more amicable than a divorce."

"Louie and I are just dating," Ruthie said. "I'm not getting married so fast."

"Why not?" Shelly flared, and everyone, especially Ruthie, seemed taken aback by his anger. "Don't postpone your life waiting for me to die, Ruthie. Because I refuse to oblige. I *don't* need you to take care of me. I've got a nearly finished screenplay I'm going to sell, and a million other ideas for things to write and do, and I won't have you stop living because you're waiting for me to stop living. If Louie is serious and you love him, it's going to be the best thing for all of us if you goddamned marry the rich bastard. And don't you dare turn me into the reason you're not doing it. I'm calling the caterer the minute we get out of here."

Ruthie, who had been holding tears inside during his tirade, let them go now, and she wept openly, struggling for her words which came out in spurts. "I can't . . . I don't think I can. I don't want to ruin our . . . I can't."

"Well, you'd better figure out why you can't and not put the blame on me," Shelly said tenderly and put an arm around her while she covered her face with her hands, embarrassed to be crying so hard in front of the others.

"Ruthie," Barbara said, "Shelly's right. You need to work on why you're so unsure about how to proceed when it comes to having a relationship with a man who offers you sexual intimacy, and the real possibility of a marriage."

Ruthie shook her head. "I don't know," she said and sniffled, and Lainie handed her a Kleenex. "I think about it all the time. Maybe because when my brothers died it was so painful it made me afraid, or maybe it's because nobody ever really wanted me before the way Louie does, so I don't believe him, or maybe it's because I wanted to keep up the ruse for Sid that Shelly and I are a conventional couple. I don't . . . I don't . . ." Then she turned in her chair and faced Shelly and took his hand. "I love you so much," she said. "I can never tell you how you are my life and my love, because it was your love for me that gave me a life and a reason to survive."

Shelly smiled at her, holding both of her hands in his, and when their eyes met he said, "Likewise I'm sure. And it's because I feel this way about you that I'm telling you it's time to move on." Then he stood and moved her to her feet and took her in his arms and hugged her. And when the hug broke and Ruthie blew her nose, Rick said, "Yeah, but the real bottom line question is . . . when do *I* get to read the nearly finished screenplay?"

"I'll bring it in next week," Shelly said, and everyone laughed.

45

YOU OKAY?" Stan asked, curling up next to Barbara, fitting himself against the curve of her back, further warming her already very warm body. She was only half asleep. All evening long she'd been dozing a little, then opening her eyes to peek at the clock and wonder if his plane had landed and how long it would take him to get home. Now she could let herself drift into that unconscious world because he was there and safe. She started to float there, then jumped, remembering in her misty state that she'd been saving the big news to tell him in person.

"I am okay," she said, her voice husky with sleep. "In fact I just happen to be okay enough for two people."

"Well, that's good news," Stan said in a voice she knew meant he was about to get friendly. So she wasn't surprised when he moved his hands under her nightgown and up to her breasts, which were already so large and so sore she wasn't able to lie on her stomach. "My, my," he said. "If I didn't know any better . . ."

"You'd say I was pregnant?" she asked, turning to him slowly and carefully to protect her sore breasts.

"You're joking?" he said looking into her eyes.

"I wouldn't joke about this."

Stan's face filled with wonder and elation. "A baby? You're telling me I'm having a baby?" he said proudly, and pulled her so close that she flinched at the hardness of his chest against her sore breasts.

"Yes," she said, and burst into tears from hurt and hormones and confusion.

"Honey, that's extraordinarily profound news. Have you told the kids?"

"Not yet."

"Why not?"

"Because I wanted to tell you first, and because Jeff's never home, and Heidi doesn't return my calls, and . . ."

"And?"

"Because I'm afraid they'll laugh."

"Laugh? I think this is fabulous news. I'm going right out and getting one of those jogging strollers I've seen dads using all up and down Ocean Avenue. It's a great way to take the baby out for fresh air."

"You don't jog."

"I know, but I'll start. I mean, I'm going to have to get in shape for those late-night feedings, and those early-morning wake-ups, and those soccer practices—"

"Oh, my God," Barbara said, feeling as if her breasts were going to explode, and her bladder was full and she was so tired just thinking about it all. "It sounds awful."

"No, it doesn't," Stan said, as puffed out as he had been the day she told him the news about Heidi, twenty-four years earlier. "It sounds great. I'm so glad, believe me, sweetheart, your hormones are just awry now, but you'll see, you're going to be so glad." He kissed her again and again and tenderly moved down to kiss her throbbing breasts.

At least, she thought as his kisses became heated, I don't have to worry what day of the month it is.

"So am I crazy out of my mind if I go ahead and have this

baby? I know as usual you'll tell me the brutal truth, won't you, Mother?"

"When have I not?" Gracie asked, smiling. She and Barbara were walking down San Vicente Boulevard. Gracie loved putting on what she laughingly called her "tracksuit" to make her way along the grassy strip with her daughter, greeting the morning runners and walkers.

"I can't understand why there would even be a shred of doubt in your mind," Gracie said. "Believe me, I wish there was a chance for *me* to do it again. And I say that because it's taken me years to figure out what constitutes being a good mother, and perhaps now in my old age I could do it right. Do as I say, not as I do. Raising a child is the best and most important and most creative act you'll ever perform. Besides, selfishly speaking, I could use another little cherub of a grandchild in my life, so I insist."

Gracie's step faltered for an instant and Barbara held her arm, but then she seemed recovered and they continued. "I was never what you are, good at my work and good at life. My own life was too difficult for me so I lost myself in other people's cultures, values, ways. I guess I was trying to find myself in all of them. But you and your sister, you are without a doubt my greatest accomplishments."

Then she laughed as if she'd just realized something important. "Maybe *that* was my contribution! I was so bitchy it was a character builder just to be related to me. Eh?"

"That must have been it, Mother," Barbara said.

"What did your husband say when you told him about the baby?" Gracie asked, turning down Twenty-sixth Street so they could stop at the outdoor market for breakfast.

"Are you kidding? He now thinks he's the most potent, virile creature on earth, and he wants to go shopping for a jogging stroller."

Gracie chuckled. "And the kids?"

"Jeff loved the news. He said he'd feel less guilty leaving for college, knowing I had someone else to hug. Heidi thought about it for a while after I told her, then she laughed and said, 'Go for it, Mom. I'll help.' She's been in very good spirits lately. She has a new job, and she's dating a new young man."

"Well, now that we've settled the baby issue, what are you going to do about work? You're always threatening to retire but I know you better than that, so how will you handle the baby *and* your clientele?"

They stood together at the coffee counter where Barbara watched the woman steam the milk for Gracie's cappuccino. She couldn't help feeling a little stab of envy because since she'd discovered she was pregnant, she'd given up coffee.

"I don't know. They've all come such a great distance, particularly my group who call themselves the Stork Club. The issues they're going to continue to face with their children makes me think I ought to stay with them forever."

"So?"

"So, the groups at the hospital are time-limited. They're scheduled from September through June, and there's a long waiting list to get into them. Practicality dictates that nine months is an adequate time period in which to make any necessary intervention. Then we have to say good-bye and good luck to these families and send them out into the world."

"That's preposterous," Gracie said, moving her arm in a way that almost knocked over the coffee cup the woman behind the counter had just set there. "That'll never work. Certainly not for that group of little ones whose parents had them in all those newfangled ways. Their need for an extended family is going to go on endlessly, and those parents are going to have to put their heads together regularly and figure out what to do about it. You *should* run that group forever. There must be other people who are needing to get in there and work out those things too."

"There are," Barbara said. "I've been getting a lot of phone calls."

"Well, I suggest you tell your colleagues you refuse to put a time limit on people's emotions, and if they say no, you'll go

ahead and run the groups out of your living room if you have
to."

Barbara gripped the counter as a freight train of nausea
rushed through her body.

"And what'll they have to say to that?" Gracie asked her,
picking up her coffee cup and heading for a table.

"Mother, if I can have morning sickness at this point in my
life . . . anything can happen."

Louise Feiffer was especially imposing that morning, taller than
Barbara remembered, especially articulate in telling Barbara
about the budget problems the program was having and her
concerns about the upcoming board of directors meetings. When
it was Barbara's turn to explain why she had requested this
private meeting, she felt a flutter of nervousness. She tried to
keep back the emotion she knew was a result of the way she felt
about the group and the hormones in her body, which were
doing something akin to the Ritual Fire Dance.

She remembered Ruthie Zimmerman telling her about the
times she sat in meetings with all the male writers at work, and
had to repeat what she called her mantra, which was "Don't
cry. Don't cry. Don't cry." Barbara said those words to herself
now as she talked about why she wanted to have an open-ended
continuation of the Stork Club. She knew it wasn't the way the
hospital's program usually operated, but she wanted the staff to
look closely at the possibility that certain groups would benefit
from longer terms.

She watched as Louise took a sip of her coffee. And when
she thought about coffee the way she'd watched Louise fix hers,
with lots of Coffee-mate and sugar, that made her feel so sick
that the floor and the ceiling seemed to get closer together. She
hadn't yet told anyone at the hospital she was pregnant.

"Barbara," Louise said, "what I think I'm hearing is on two
levels. I understand how it feels every year to terminate these
groups. You and I have both been doing this for a while and

we acknowledge the solitude we as therapists feel as we let these people go. But I think the process of letting the families separate from us, or leave us behind if you will, closely parallels the emotions we feel about our own children leaving us to go out into the world. And I know that in your case it's exactly what you're going through in your own life now.

"So I'm suggesting that perhaps you should examine if your reluctance to let go of this group could be related to your own separation difficulties at home. The issues around your second child going off to college, a situation which doubtlessly is leaving you feeling empty."

"Oh, Louise." Barbara's knuckles were white from clutching the arm of the chair. "If there's one thing I'm *not* right now, it's empty," she said, hoping she wasn't going to punctuate that sentence by throwing up all over Louise's desk. Then she took a deep breath, and another, which seemed to steady her insides. "And my nest won't be either, at least not for another seventeen or eighteen years."

"Pardon?"

"I'm going to have a baby," Barbara announced with enormous pride, commingled with the desire to jump to her feet and run to the bathroom, this time to pee, which she seemed to be doing every few minutes. To say that Louise looked shocked didn't begin to describe her reaction.

"No," Barbara said, "I'm not asking to keep this group going because I can't separate. I'm asking because I learned together with them that every day brings new surprises and questions, and I want to be there to help them answer those questions as time goes on. When the children start school and other kids ask them about who they are. When they're preadolescent and they ask themselves who they are, and when they're adolescent and struggling with their identities. Their unusual genesis will always be an issue. So please consider that it will teach all of us a great deal more about these people if we can follow through. And understand that I believe in this so powerfully that if it can't be done here, I'll want to move it into my private practice."

"Let me think about this," Louise said, "and we'll talk more by the end of the week."

The group seemed more subdued this morning than Barbara had seen them so far. "I want to talk today about the burdens and dangers of secrecy," she said to them. "I don't mean privacy, because what you tell the outside world doesn't concern me as much as what you tell the children and one another. And I used those serious words 'dangers' and 'burdens' because when there are secrets, the out-of-control fantasies that come with not knowing and the gossip that inevitably puts a negative spin on something you did for positive reasons can and will be damaging. Telling your children the right way from the start will keep them from learning the wrong way.

"Again I urge you to keep information you give them simple and age appropriate. Mostly at this time in their lives what they really need to know is that they're safe and loved, but also remember that before there are words for situations, your children will sense what's going on. And eventually the stories will come out. Openness is the healthiest option, and that will mean that the story of their genesis has to become a natural part of their lives."

"Won't it make them feel freaky?" Judith asked.

"Not if it's told in a way that speaks to how much they were wanted and how much they're loved. For example, Judith, share what you know about the donor even if it's not very much. When they get to asking about it all you might say how much you wanted children, but that it takes seeds, or later on you can say sperm from a man to make a baby. But there wasn't a man in your family, so you went to a place where a very generous man gave his sperm so you could have them. And that's when you might say, And he likes reading and music just like you and Jody."

"What if they ask what his name is?"

"You don't know, so tell them that, and you might also tell them that someday they may get to meet him."

Everyone was quiet, thinking about what Barbara had just said.

People usually think we're a married couple," Ruthie said. "Most of the time I leave it alone. Soon we'll start applying to schools for Sid, and when they find out about his family history, I wonder what to do."

"Sid will find out too, and talking about it early will show him you don't connect anything negative to his family situation. Counteract the myths and neutralize the name-calling by making him know homosexuality isn't bad, or wrong, but part of life. It'll be a long time until the subject of sexual orientation has an impact on him, but when there are homophobic slurs, do the same thing you'd do in the face of any other inappropriate behavior. Tell him, 'We don't like to say hurtful words like that in our family.'"

"I agree with all that you've been saying," Rick said. "I mean, I went on record right away as saying Doreen would always be a part of David's family, but I believe that ultimately it was secrecy that killed her. I think it was keeping the secret inside about David's birth father and the fear of talking about it that finally became too much for her. Maybe if she could have told her mother, told a psychologist, told a friend—but the shame was too deep. I'll always tell David how bright and funny and warm she was. And somehow down the line I'll have to find a way to tell him about her death."

The group, sometimes so boisterous and jovial, was thoughtful and quiet today. Even the children outside in the play yard were occupied with quiet things and only let out an occasional squeal.

"What about your relationship with Jackie?" Barbara asked Lainie and Mitch.

Lainie spoke up. "Well, as you said to us once, being a good parent isn't related to the way we became a parent, and I know I couldn't love Rose more if she'd grown inside me. And I guess it's because I love her that I understand why Jackie has to be in her life. I'm still hurt about Mitch's deception, I still think he handled it poorly, but so does he. We're working on putting our relationship back together, building the trust back, and also trying to figure out the healthiest way to include Jackie in Rose's world.

"The truth is I like and respect Jackie, and I know she'll bring a lot of her joy of life, and sense of humor, and big-heartedness to the situation and to Rose's life. But I'm going to have to work very hard not to resent her. I mean, I know you can't live your life in fear of the future. God knows, I could have died a thousand deaths by now if I had, but if someday Rose looks at me and says, 'I want to go and be with Jackie because I'm like her and not like you,' I don't know how I'll get through it."

"We both know secrets are no good because I nearly destroyed our marriage by trying to keep one," Mitch said, his arm around his wife.

"As you know," Barbara said, "based on the way the programs at this hospital work, this group was scheduled to be over in a few months. But I asked for an unlimited continuation of our work so that we can confront the ongoing issues that will come up for your families from year to year. I thought you'd like to know that, as of this morning, it's been approved."

"Bravo. Hooray!" There was a positive response from all of them. "Thank God," Lainie said, "we're going to need it, because Mitch and I are talking about the possibility of adopting a baby. An unadoptable child this time."

Ruthie announced that she and Shelly and Sid would need more time to talk things out too, because she was engaged. She held up her hand upon which was a ring with a very large sparkling diamond. And Rick reported, just as an aside, that he and Shelly were taking Shelly's screenplay to Universal, hoping to make a deal there.

Soon it was time for the children to come in, but Barbara signaled to Dana to give her one more moment alone with the grown-ups. "Since we spent some time today talking about *your* secrets, I'd like to tell you one of mine." They all looked at her as she smiled and said, "I'm pregnant."

A whoop went up from the group and everyone ran over to hug her and encircle her with their warm congratulations. She felt flushed and moved and connected to each of them.

"Needless to say, or maybe not so needless, it was a surprise. At first, one that made me furious at myself, but then on reflection, thinking about all of you and your struggles to make and be families, I was inspired, and I realize that I'm very lucky and very blessed."

Now Dana led the children into the room. They all had their snack of grape juice and peanut-butter crackers, and sang "Twinkle Twinkle Little Star" and "Where Is Thumbkin."

Today Barbara said she would read to them. As soon as she located her reading glasses in her purse, she opened a book that was one of her favorites, *The Velveteen Rabbit*. The sweet story seemed to charm the toddlers, who sat quietly.

"'"What is real?" asked the rabbit. "Real isn't how you are made," said the skin horse. "It's a thing that happens to you. When a child loves you for a long, long time, not just to play with, but really loves you, then you become real." "Does it hurt?" asked the rabbit. "Sometimes," said the skin horse, for he was always truthful. "But when you are real, you don't mind being hurt."'" For a minute Barbara had to stop, because there was a catch in her voice and the words of the story were making her feel choked up, or maybe, she thought, it's just my hormones going mad. But when she looked up and saw the eyes of all the parents, she knew they were feeling the same way from the message of the book.

When reading time was over, she hugged every child and every parent good-bye, and walked back to her office to return phone calls and open her mail. She smiled to herself as she passed through the corridors, remembering that not so long ago the thought of retirement had actually crossed her mind. Her step was light as she moved past the offices of the other staff members, buzzing with arriving families.

Retirement for a full-of-life woman like me? Full of life, she laughed, and hope and exciting ideas? Ridiculous, she thought, that she'd ever even considered retirement, and she felt joyful and amazed at the wonderful way in which life goes on!

Straightening the Bell Curve

Also by Constance Hilliard

Does Israel Have a Future? The Case for a Post-Zionist State (2009)

Related Titles from Potomac Books

Father of the Tuskegee Airmen, John C. Robinson
—Phillip Thomas Tucker

*A Free Man of Color and His Hotel: Race, Reconstruction,
and the Role of the Federal Government*
—Carol Gelderman

*The Most Famous Woman in Baseball: Effa Manley
and the Negro Leagues*
—Bob Luke

My Life and Battles
—Jack Johnson; translated and edited
by Christopher Rivers

Straightening the Bell Curve

How Stereotypes about Black Masculinity
Drive Research on Race and Intelligence

Constance Hilliard

Foreword by COLIN GROVES

Potomac Books
Washington, D.C.

Library of Congress Cataloging-in-Publication Data
Hilliard, Constance B.
  Straightening the bell curve : how stereotypes about black masculinity drive research on race and intelligence / Constance Hilliard ; foreword by Colin Groves. — 1st ed.
    p. cm.
  Includes bibliographical references and index.
  ISBN 978-1-61234-191-0 (hbk. edition)
  ISBN 978-1-61234-192-7 (electronic edition)
  1. Intellect. 2. Intelligence tests. 3. Race. 4. Blacks—Intelligence levels. 5. Men—Intelligence levels. 6. Stereotypes (Social psychology) 7. Discrimination in psychology. I. Title.
  BF432.N5H55 2012
  155.8'2—dc23
                    2012000623

Potomac Books
22841 Quicksilver Drive
Dulles, Virginia 20166

First Edition

10 9 8 7 6 5 4 3 2 1

For Stephen Hill

Contents

Foreword

There lives in Australia a man who has calculated the value of pi to more than twenty-two thousand decimal places in his head. He speaks seven languages fluently, and he has invented his own language with entirely consistent rules.

How brilliant is this man! How high his intelligence quotient (IQ) must be!

Actually, he is an autistic savant. He is unable to drive a car. He does not know his left hand from his right. The entire concept of IQ is meaningless; it tells us nothing of any importance about this man.

Allan Snyder, the director the Centre for the Mind—a joint project of the Australian National University and the University of Sydney—has written a good deal about savants (including the man I have mentioned). Snyder has proposed the idea of a creativity quotient (CQ). Unlike devotees of the intelligence quotient (IQ), he does not look on this measure as an unalterably fixed number, but it seems to me to tell us at least as much about human minds as does IQ.

As Constance Hilliard recounts in this fascinating and revealing book, Lewis Terman largely developed the IQ concept in the first quarter of

the twentieth century, and then Sir Cyril Burt promoted it extensively. But, by the very zealotry of their advocacy, both men helped bring the concept into disrepute.

I heard how Terman's associate Catherine Cox had delved into the biographies of famous people of history and assigned two IQs to them— one for childhood (up to seventeen years of age), one for adulthood. This process was to serve, in part, as a test of Terman's hypothesis that IQ is pretty much a fixed quantity: the child is father to the man. I was fascinated and found Cox's monograph in the library. I was impressed with the amount of historical research but less than impressed with the amount of special pleading that she had indulged in, for example, when the juvenile and adult scores were far apart.

One of Cox's historical figures was Nicolaus Koppernigk, or Copernicus, as he called himself when he wrote in Latin. Cox assigned him a juvenile IQ of 105. I was not convinced. Here is one of perhaps two people—Charles Darwin is the other—who has done more than any other to put us in our place in the grand scheme of things. Copernicus overturned centuries of assumptions about the earth and the solar system with a single bold, remarkable insight. An IQ of 105! His adult IQ was much higher, but either Terman's hypothesis about the child being father to the man is totally overthrown or else the whole schema was flawed from the start. Probably it was both.

Sir Cyril Burt was the man who, by himself or with two female associates (Miss Margaret Howard and Miss Jane Conway), studied pairs of identical twins who had been separated at birth and reared apart. He reported that the correlation between their IQs was 0.771; in other words, IQ depended largely on heredity, leaving little room for modification by education or upbringing. On the basis of his advocacy, the British government after World War II brought in a new system of secondary schooling in public education, requiring every child to take an IQ-based examination at age eleven or so (the Eleven Plus). Those children who passed went on to a grammar school (with the ultimate prospect

of university entrance), while those who failed were relegated to a secondary modern school until they left at ages fifteen or sixteen, their futures marked out to be factory workers or cashiers.

When I was a PhD student at London University, I sometimes gave lectures on my field at grammar schools. Once, to my astonishment, I was asked to lecture at a secondary modern school. When I arrived, I talked first to the headmaster and learned a great deal. In brief, he and his staff had discovered that they were teaching many motivated, hardworking, and—yes!—intelligent students. "There is something wrong here," they concluded, and they took pains to rectify the situation and ensure that the university option was open to any student who wanted it.

The Eleven Plus exam, as far as I know, has not involved this sort of grotesque injustice for some time now. The system did not work, but the real sting in the tail is that it seems to have been based on a fraud. Sir Cyril Burt could not possibly have studied fifty-three pairs of identical twins reared apart. His correlation coefficients could not possibly have remained exactly the same as his numbers of twin pairs increased. And he even appears to have invented his coresearchers, Miss Howard and Miss Conway. Controversy about Burt's work still rages in British psychological circles, but no one doubts that Burt did not discover what he claimed to have discovered.

Given all these factors—Burt's fraudulence, the soul-searching about cultural effects in IQ tests, all the discussion about "different intelligences," the Flynn effect (the inexorable rise in IQ scores over the past fifty years or so), and the complexity of the entire subject—how is it that claims are still made that some catch-all quantity of intellectual ability, either IQ or some other measure, differs between different social groups or, let us be open about this, between races?

Race is, as Hilliard shows, an "iffy" concept. It is undeniable that the human species varies geographically, but the differences are trivial, average not absolute, and recent. Races are not to be reified.

How is it then that some insist on combining these two iffy concepts, race and IQ, into one explosive mixture? It has often seemed to me that there is something obsessive about the way in which, oblivious of the problems, most proponents of race and IQ differences go about it. For example, finding one race scores lower on IQ tests than another, they state the difference is not bridgeable by education or social change; moreover, it is correlated with differences in other mental or physical characters, it is due to this or that evolutionary circumstance, and it has this or that consequence (separate schooling, residential separation, even athletic achievement).

Hilliard also concludes that there seems to be an obsession in each case. If there is an obsession, it must have a history. Hilliard is a noted historian, and she has used her skills to dig deeply. She has come up with a story that is cogent and consistent. The prose carries you along easily, and you will realize that you are reading something important and useful and new. As she analyses this obsession with race and IQ, she shows it up for the pseudoscience that it really is, and her analysis reveals clearly what lies behind it.

Colin Groves
School of Archaeology and Anthropology
Australian National University
Canberra, Australia

Acknowledgments

When a book has been incubating as long as this one (fifteen years between inception and publication), the list of people to whom I owe gratitude has the heft of a telephone book. Those people I mention here are merely the AAA listings at the top of the front page. My agent, Jodie Rhodes, worked a miracle in finding the right publishing venue for this uncomfortable book with its unsettling message. Potomac Books' senior editor Hilary Claggett saw the potential for ideas that less courageous publishers would have shunned. I am grateful to my colleague at the University of North Texas, Gus Seligmann, whose knowledge of basketball gave me insights I would otherwise have missed. Scientist Joseph Graves helped me interpret those pieces of scientific data that my historian's brain found unfathomable. Professor Graves's patience and kindness in reading and rereading the manuscript also saved me from embarrassing gaffes. My friends Florence Tate and Stephen Hill offered insights and shoulders to cry on, when my frustrations with the project became overwhelming. My sister, Ida Hilliard Pipkin, and brother, John Hilliard, helped my waning self-confidence on more than a few occasions. And last but not least I thank my husband, Terrill Tripp, and my

son, Kenneth, for not allowing me to give up on this book, whose message, they believed, outweighed the frustrations of bringing it to the public's attention.

Introduction

Does history repeat itself? It does when we—scholars, scientists, and laypersons alike—devalue the art of self-reflection. That is, when we react to our fears, anxieties, and insecurities reflexively, we will get the same results that previous generations did and find ourselves locked into an endless, repetitive cycle. Those of us in academe might even repaint the issue's backdrop. In so doing we fool the public and ourselves into believing that we're acting out a new drama on a new stage and with a new script rather than acknowledging that we're performing a dreary revival of an age-old play.

Let's take, for example, the belief in racial differences in intelligence. Naïvely, I believed that contemporary geneticists had laid that pseudo-scientific theory to rest after Richard Herrnstein and Charles Murray's popular bestseller, *The Bell Curve: Intelligence and Class Structure in American Life*, sparked debate in the 1990s. However, in recent years a whole new slew of articles about the issue have appeared in respectable print media. The February 12, 2009, issue of *Nature* published dueling articles debating the validity of studies linking race to the intelligence quotient (IQ).[1]

Two years earlier, Nobel Prize–winning scientist James Watson had stirred up a media storm when he asserted in the *London Sunday Times* that black Africans were cognitively inferior to whites. Watson went on to say that while he hoped that everyone was equal, it is nevertheless the case that "people who have to deal with black employees find this is not true."[2]

Watson is a molecular biologist, not a historian. He might be forgiven for lacking sensibilities to the maddening cycles to which history condemns the unaware. But perhaps because history is, indeed, my field, the only response I could make to his racial utterings was "here we go again." In the year 2000, he had shocked a scientific audience at the University of California at Berkeley when he hypothesized the existence of biochemical links between the darkness of one's skin and sexual prowess. Watson had declared: "That's why you have Latin lovers. You've never heard of an English lover, only an English patient."[3]

This seemingly disjointed statement received little media coverage. But I knew then that it was only a matter of time before Watson joined the cult of scientists for whom "racial differences in intelligence" was a code phrase for a far deeper meaning. Over the last half century this scientific fraternity has included such illustrious names as William Shockley, Charles Murray, Richard Herrnstein, Arthur R. Jensen, Jean-Philippe Rushton, and Richard Lynn. What bound them together was not so much their insistence on racial differences in intelligence, as it was their belief in an evolutionary order predicated on variations in the presumed size of genitalia, body type, muscularity, sexual impulsivity, and the ability to jump. Professor Rushton is one of the group's most prolific scientists, and Professors Stephen Ceci and Wendy M. Williams defended him in the *Nature* article, "Should Scientists Study Race and IQ? Yes." Rushton's most widely discussed contribution to the science of proving the cognitive inferiority of blacks was a statement he made in a 1994 interview: "It's a trade-off, more brain or more penis. You can't have everything."[4]

In investigating this phenomenon, I have come to suspect that IQ research on racial differences possesses a seductive pull for a particular type of academic. It ensnares an individual of sometimes brilliant intellect who is entranced by mathematical precision but eschews self-knowledge or the motivation to self-reflect. For instance, as Watson made public remarks regarding the cognitive inferiority of black Africans, geneticists were analyzing the scientist's own DNA, which he had displayed on the Internet in the interests of science. What they discovered was that at least 16 percent of Watson's genes most likely came from an African ancestor, while most people of European origin would have 1 percent or less of this genetic configuration.[5]

Obsessions with body image or other masculine issues might distort even the most mathematically precise research findings. I now know that the draw can be so powerful, deep, and compelling that academics whose life histories may offer no hint of ethnic preoccupations suddenly commit themselves with the furor of a conversion experience to "proving" the existence of a cognitive hierarchy among the races. As the fixation grows, these scholars may willingly sacrifice their reputations, friends, or even rationality to their true beliefs, which posit an inverse correlation between intelligence and masculinity.

So what is this book really all about? It is an exploration of the ways in which scientists who are preoccupied with racial differences in intelligence, however highly trained they might be in the scientific method, used overly narrow cognitive methodology that then clouded their analytical perceptions. That such distortions should revolve around issues of masculinity, penis size, and muscularity has a long, sordid historical antecedent. That a fixation with the so-called enlarged genital organ of black males should be closely associated with scientific theories of their alleged animal-like stupidity exposes some of the most disturbing elements of slavery's legacy.

Emanating from this raison d'être, the book has a clear purpose. To the question posed in *Nature*, "Should scientists study race and IQ?,"

my answer follows. Curiosity, the intense desire to find answers to who and what we are, is surely one of the most priceless of all our human gifts. However, twenty-first-century American society must demand a broader range of cognitive methodologies and greater interpersonal and intrapersonal competencies from scholars engaged in research on racial issues than might be required, for example, from those who study the mating practices of fruit flies. This new requirement would be, of course, in addition to whatever talents and scientific training such scholars may possess in more analytical, mathematical, or statistical subject matter. In arguing for such competencies, I am not referring here to some vague and elusive manner of touchy-feely political correctness or even to we're-all-brothers/sisters-under-the-skin platitudes. I am rather making reference to the capacity of a researcher, regardless of how well trained in scientific subject matter, to distinguish the sometimes subtle boundaries between his or her gender preoccupations or insecurities and the complex dynamics of human societies. And yet, why should modern research institutions require greater competencies from its scientists dealing with issues of race, gender, and other complex social issues? This book intends to address these precise issues.

But first I offer an important caveat. American scientists are one of the most precious resources this country has to offer. And it is precisely their open-ended curiosity and questioning minds that have led to inventions that have increased our entire society's standard of living. As a consequence, I possess a deep reverence for the spirit of inquiry, the discipline required of science, and the devotion of scientists to exploration. I do not seek to erect barriers that might stifle or delimit the range of questions scientists should ask, even regarding race. However, I do have an observation to make. When scientists cross over, and it is almost always inadvertently, from genuine science to pseudoscience, an interesting transposition occurs. In the former endeavor, the search for answers leads society to a deeper understanding of the world in which we live. However, in the latter case, even when pursued with mathematical rigor,

pseudoscience acts as a boomerang, leading back to the emotional needs or other irrational preoccupations of the questioner. It is in this regard that Isaac Asimov once remarked: "Inspect every piece of pseudoscience and you will find a security blanket, a thumb to suck, a skirt to hold. What do we have to offer in exchange? Uncertainty! Insecurity!"[6]

Should science study whether large breasts and blondness in females are inversely correlated to intelligence or whether white males have a greater genetic predisposition toward precipitating Wall Street crashes than do black males? *Nature* magazine has not posed such questions and never will. The premises upon which such questions would be based are not considered "mainstream science." No audience would be willing to pay hard-earned cash for such research findings, however mathematically precise they might be graphed and packaged. Why then should the cognitive inferiority of certain races be treated any differently? *Straightening the Bell Curve: How Stereotypes about Black Masculinity Drive Research on Race and Intelligence* explores this issue in painstaking detail. Its answers are unsettling.

Chapter 1 introduces the work of mathematician Francis Galton, who coined the term "eugenics" in an 1883 work called *Inquiries into Human Faculty and Its Development*. A chronic invalid as a child, the British scientist advocated a new science for improving the human race through better breeding practices. A decade and a half earlier, he had published his seminal work *Hereditary Genius: An Inquiry into Its Laws and Consequences*, employing for the first time in biology a mathematical construct termed the "Gaussian distribution," or the now familiar bell curve. While Galton earned some degree of intellectual respectability in Britain, it was actually in America, still preoccupied with proving the inferiority of its former slaves, where his mathematical concepts found practical applications. From its inception, research on cognitive differences between the races yielded a powerful but unintended consequence: As more scholars affirmed the intellectual inferiority of the African, the whites' fantasies of the blacks' superhuman sexual potency grew. So

entrapped was scientific and popular thinking in the folkloric inverse correlation between brawn and brains that a belief in the cognitive inferiority of Negroes almost by definition meant that this group must be oversexed.

Chapter 2 traces the emergence of intelligence testing as a more refined methodology than skull measurement for judging presumed racial differences in intelligence. Perhaps the strongest advocate of Galton's eugenic views was a biologist named Charles Benedict Davenport. He asserted that racial intermarriage led only to "disharmony of physical, mental, and temperamental qualities" and must be avoided at all costs. So disapproving of physical gratification did Davenport become that later in life, he began advocating sterilization and castration of the "unfit." His colleague Lewis M. Terman of Stanford University used the falsified findings of British psychologist Cyril Burt to translate the eugenic focus on mental inheritance into popularizing intelligence testing in America. Terman opined that one met uneducable Negroes with such great frequency, that research on racial differences in mental traits merited a special urgency. He also believed that their "unusually prolific breeding" created a grave problem for society.

While intelligence testing, or psychometrics, gained momentum during the early decades of the twentieth century, the eugenics movement fell on hard times after World War II. Horrified by evidence of the Holocaust, Americans associated selective breeding theories with Aryan notions of racial superiority. In fact, had it not been for the 1961 near fatal car accident of a Nobel Prize–winning scientist named William Shockley, the twentieth century's preoccupation with cognition and physical attributes finally might have faded from view.

Chapter 3 details Shockley's transformation from physicist to modern-day eugenicist, preoccupied with race and the superiority of white genes. Some colleagues believed that the car accident that crushed Dr. Shockley's pelvis and left him disabled might have triggered mental changes in him as well. Whatever the case, not long after returning home

from the hospital, Shockley began directing his anger toward the reckless driver who maimed him into racial formulations. His ideas began to coalesce around the notion that an inverse correlation existed between blacks' cognition and physical prowess. Later, in donating his sperm at the age of seventy to a sperm bank set up for geniuses, Shockley suggested to an interviewer for *Playboy* magazine that women who would otherwise pay little attention to his lack of physical appeal would compete for his cognitively superior sperm. But the sperm bank's owner apparently concealed from Shockley a painful truth. Women employing its services rejected the sperm of the short, balding Shockley in favor of that from younger, taller, more physically attractive men, whatever their IQ.[7]

Arthur R. Jensen, a psychologist at the University of California–Berkeley, became an early disciple of Shockley's. As a young man, he had abandoned a promising career in music after critics said that his playing lacked "soul." Jensen expanded on Shockley's racial theories and by 1969 became the leading spokesman for the new eugenics movement after publishing an article titled "How Much Can We Boost IQ and Scholastic Achievement?" Jensen asserted that genetic rather than environmental factors created the differential in IQ scores between whites and blacks. He also warned that racial differences in intelligence would lead to dysgenic, or downward, evolutionary trends in urban slums.

Jensen may have been frustrated with Shockley's inability as a physicist to validate their racial theories in psychological terms. So he took up the slack with such intellectual vigor and energy that the term "Jensenism" was coined to describe the psychology of proving "black cognitive inferiority." The Berkeley psychologist wrote dozens of books and articles, injecting such new theories into the discourse as "reaction time" and "choice reaction time," in which he attempted to prove that the brains of whites operated more efficiently than those of blacks. His work met with resistance at every turn. It was at this moment in his career that Jensen stumbled upon the work of a fellow psychologist who

had taken up the cause of proving racial differences in IQ. Jensen had found his soul mate.

Chapter 4 explores the career trajectory of Harvard professor Richard J. Herrnstein from renowned experimental psychologist to guru on racial differences in intelligence and muscularity. As a young graduate student he had fallen under the spell of Harvard professor S. S. Stevens, who had coauthored with William Sheldon a book called *The Varieties of Temperament: A Psychology of Constitutional Differences*, which popularized the concept of "somatotyping," first articulated by William Sheldon. This theory sought, through the precise measurement and analysis of human body types, to establish correlations comparing intelligence, temperament, sexual proclivities, and the moral worth of individuals. Thus criminals were perceived to be shorter and heavier and more muscular than morally upstanding citizens. Black males were reported to rank higher on the "masculine component" scale than white males did, but lower in intelligence. Somatotyping lured the impressionable young Herrnstein into a world promising precision and human predictability based on the measuring of body parts.

Herrnstein was first introduced to Arthur R. Jensen's work after reading his January 1969 article in the *Harvard Educational Review*. Herrnstein, who had been exposed to ideas of human cognitive differences based on body type early in his academic career, merely took the next step. In the spring of 1971 the Harvard psychologist wrote "IQ," which the *Atlantic Monthly* published in its September issue. He contended that intelligence is largely inherited, so no matter what efforts were made, egalitarianism as public policy would not work either with individuals or societal groups.

In the spring of 1992, Herrnstein invited Jean-Philippe Rushton, a younger colleague visiting from the University of Western Ontario, to breakfast at the Harvard Faculty Club. Herrnstein clearly must have been entranced by his postulations. According to data the Canadian psychologist had gathered, the normal distribution of penis size and muscularity—

with Asians at the low end, whites in the middle, and blacks at the high end—could be represented mathematically with a bell-shaped curve.

Chapter 5 exposes the phallic theology at the heart of research on racial differences in intelligence. For more than a decade, Professor Rushton of Western Ontario University sought to prove an inverse correlation between intelligence and penis size among blacks, whites, and Asians. He conducted this research at a local Ontario shopping mall.

Chapter 6 discusses the probability that had Rushton been working in social isolation, the academic community might have ignored his unusual research on penis size. But Rushton was far more fortunate. He had found a network of congenial and supportive academics in Shockley, Jensen, Herrnstein, and others. By the time Rushton published his sixth book, *Race, Evolution, and Behavior: A Life History Perspective,* in 1995, detailing more research findings of an inverse correlation between brain and penis size among the races, the contours of a tightly knit intellectual cult had solidified. In its first chapter, Rushton echoes the book's theme by asserting: "The reason why Whites and East Asians have wider hips than Blacks, and so make poorer runners is because they give birth to larger brained babies. During evolution, increasing cranial size meant women had to have a wider pelvis. Further, the hormones that give Blacks an edge at sports makes them restless in school and prone to crime."[8]

While Rushton and his colleagues seemed to take pleasure in perceiving themselves as wronged martyrs for exposing the "truth," poverty was one vow no one demanded they take. Race researchers shared in the financial generosity of an endowment called the Pioneer Fund.

A certain urgency also pervaded the atmosphere in which these researchers worked, because the inversely correlated theme of blacks' cognitive inferiority and sexual precocity tapped into the latent sexualized racism still present within society itself. The more anxiety-provoking the white males' fear of being "bested" by black males became, the more pressure some white males exerted on the scientific fringes. It became

the job of science to diffuse such fears. First, it needed to be shown scientifically that black males had larger penises than the white norm. Second, data had to be presented to anxious white males that they need not worry unduly about sperm competition, because surely, or at least hopefully, their female counterparts would be turned off when they learned that these black behemoths were saddled with smaller brains. Yet, the most telling evidence that the coordinates upon which the IQ researchers based their correlations of masculinity—performance in sports and cognition—were imaginary rather than real emanated from a hidden variable tucked away in the equation of race. It was associated with neither whites nor blacks, but Asians.

Chapter 7 explains why twentieth-century race researchers placed Asians rather than Caucasians at the summit of the race hierarchy. These scholars used this tendency to see whites as more cognitively advanced than blacks but less advanced than Asians to silence those critics who insisted that the findings of race researchers were ethnically self-serving. Establishing the racial supremacy of whites, however, was not really what drove this research on racial hierarchies. The real driving force behind this work was not racial bigotry as much as it was the masculine insecurities emanating from the unexamined and sexualized stereotypes to which scholars such as Rushton, Jensen, Herrnstein, and others tenaciously clung. Because these academics wrote for a reading public that did not fear sexual competition with Asian men, as it did with black males, touting the Asians' cognitive superiority became useful so long as whites remained above blacks in the cognitive hierarchy. But if male insecurities were the true motivating force for this kind of research, why then did the possibility of sexual competition with Asian males fail to preoccupy these researchers?

In recent years, social scientists in diverse academic fields have documented the pernicious stereotypes Asian men faced in American society. Often perceived as undersexed, they were thus perceived as minimal rivals to white men in the sexual competition for women. Underlying

this mode of thinking is the presumption that, in the end, a male's appealing physical attributes will weigh more heavily with females than his money-earning potential.

Chapter 8 reveals the racially polarizing impact the pseudoscientific research on race, intelligence, and masculinity was beginning to have on American society. Leonard Jeffries, a controversial professor of black studies at City College of New York (CCNY), began to respond to Shockley, Rushton, and others with his own pseudoscientific paradigm of "melanism." Its dogma asserted that blacks, because they had more melanin or skin pigmentation than other groups, possessed superior traits that could be ascribed to the special properties of neuromelanin, a little-studied substance in the brain.

Melanism did not reflect the collective viewpoint of most African American scholars, and the white supremacist theories of IQ researchers represented a marginal point of view among white academics. But similar to adolescents trading barbs on the school playground, the melanist-IQ researcher debate intensified, ripping at the already fragile seams of America's multiethnic society.

One fundamental difference between the work of IQ researchers and melanists, however, persisted. While academic journals published scores of articles by researchers claiming that blacks had smaller brains and larger penises than whites did, the same journals merely ignored the melanists.

Chapter 9 presents a new understanding of intelligence. It is not a single cognitive attribute capable of being encapsulated in an all-embracing digit. Cultural values and cues will play at least as pivotal a role as genetics in determining what a student will consider worthy of his or her time and attention. Likewise, societal preoccupations rather than scientific objectivity all too often will determine what questions researchers ask and what answers they give.

Chapter 10 demonstrates that vulgar racism is not what motivates IQ researchers perennially in search of cognitive hierarchies based on race.

Psychologist Al Siebert came right to the point when he lamented that "psychologists have overemphasized tests they score high on. . . . [They] have not developed quotients for abilities they lack."[9] By precisely measuring those deficits—whether in social skills, kinesthetic abilities, intuition, or emotional and practical intelligence—IQ researchers would recognize their own failings or the egregious distortions they engendered.

In the world of race and IQ research, the methodological limitations that such researchers perhaps unwittingly imposed on their work cannot help but distort their results. A primary language of the analytical-logical intelligence they recognize and value is mathematics. Yet, however impressive, it is mere child's play compared to the complexity required to integrate that form of intelligence with other types more intimately related to the understanding of human behaviors. It is therefore not surprising that analytical scientists have tarnished hard-earned scientific reputations in misapplying their linear scientific models to correlating inversely black males' penis size and other criteria of animality to measures of intelligence. Should American society continue to hold minorities captive to research containing profound public policy ramifications when it is undertaken by academics whose methodological limitations disqualify them from perceiving their subjects rationally? I maintain this issue is about academic standards rather than political correctness, censorship, or racial paranoia.

1

THE INVERSE CORRELATION

Even as a child, the slightly built, mathematically precocious Francis Galton (1822–1911) displayed an insatiable penchant for measurement. Although a chronic invalid, at the age of four he composed a remarkable letter to the sister, Adele, who tutored him. The young Galton summarized his accomplishments to that date: "I can say all the Latin Substantives and Adjectives and active verbs besides 52 lines of Latin poetry. I can cast up any Sum in addition and can multiply by 2, 3, 4, 5, 6, 7, 8, 9, 10, 11."[1]

As an adult, Galton exhibited a similar enticement with numbers and the measurement of human attributes. On one occasion he entertainingly devised a "beauty map" of the British Isles in order to ascertain what region produced the most attractive women. And on another, he attempted to gauge what proportion of the English population shared his revulsion for "the wriggling mysterious reptile," or snakes.[2] In 1884, Galton exercised his lifelong passion for quantifying human attributes and established an anthropometric laboratory at an International Health Exhibition in London, where he measured the skulls and various physical attributes of ten thousand people.[3]

A cousin of Charles Darwin's, Galton became one of England's most innovative mathematicians of the nineteenth century. Today Galton is best known for having coined the term "eugenics" in his book *Inquiries Into Human Faculty and Its Development* (1883), in which he advocated a new science using better breeding practices for improving the human race. In 1869, he had published his seminal work *Hereditary Genius: An Inquiry into Its Laws and Consequences*, employing for the first time in biology a mathematical construct termed the "Gaussian distribution," that is, the now familiar bell curve. He used it as a means of analyzing populations in terms of their members' variations from the mean to make the case for the heritability of intelligence and cognitive variations among the races.

On trips to southern Africa between 1850 and 1852, Galton turned his brilliance, eccentricity, and compulsion for quantification to such tasks as using a sextant to measure the buttocks of Khoikhoi women in South Africa. In a letter to his brother, Galton remarked: "[These women] are endowed with that shape which European milliners so vainly attempt to imitate . . . that would drive the females of our native land desperate."[4] During this period, as Robyn Wiegman has pointed out in *American Anatomies: Theorizing Race and Gender*, considerable European attention revolved around the question of whether "the Hottentot" (as the Khoikhoi were then referred to) demonstrated interspecies sexuality between African and ape. Social curiosity had been peaked by the "Hottentot Venus," a young African woman named Saartjie Baartmann, who was routinely exhibited throughout Europe from 1810 until her premature death in 1815 at the age of twenty-five.

A true mathematical genius, Galton went on to invent the correlation coefficient in 1886. It represented a quantifiable means of expressing the degree of relationship between two variables. When they changed in the same direction although possibly at different rates, they were said to be correlated, and when they changed in opposite directions, they were then defined as inverse correlations. The stronger the relationship, the less likely coincidence would have played the deciding role and the more

likely the connection would be seen as causal. Galton did however recognize from the start that examining this kind of relationship had to be done with great care. The reason was that strong correlations would produce misleading conclusions when the factor being measured might have derived from a different, unlabeled cause. That is, correlation is not causation. Morton Hunt supplied a straightforward example of this caveat in his book *The Story of Psychology*, reminding us that "the degree of baldness correlates with length of marriage—not because one has any connection with the other but because age is related to each."[5]

While Galton earned some degree of intellectual respectability in Britain, it was actually in the United States where his mathematical concepts found practical applications. Over the course of the nineteenth century, American scholars had given considerable attention to a comparative study of blacks in relation to whites. The impetus for this focus was, of course, the institution of slavery. Ironically, the establishment of the American state in the late eighteenth century being predicated on the fact that "all men are created equal," while slavery remained so integral to the new nation's economic well-being, generated special pressures on the scientific community to rationalize the Africans' enslavement. Integral to the process of dehumanizing slaves was the development of the notion that they lacked human mental faculties. Samuel George Morton (1799–1851) published *Crania Americana* in 1839, and in examining and measuring skull sizes through the new sciences of craniology and craniometry, he attempted to establish a racial hierarchy in intelligence. His examination of eight hundred skulls resulted in his ranking whites above blacks and Asians in brain capacity and thus intelligence. Thus, Galton's work in biometry—that is, the statistical analysis of biological traits measured for large samples—offered both a new perspective as well as mathematical legitimacy to the scientific preoccupation with racial differences that Morton initiated.

However, the scholarly assessment of black intelligence that evolved from the nineteenth-century skull-measuring science of craniometry was never far removed from the more intimate research of measuring the

presumably mammoth proportions of the African penis. From its inception, research on cognitive differences between the races yielded a powerful but unintended consequence: The more Morton and other scholars affirmed the black Africans' intellectual inferiority to the whites, the more whites believed in the blacks' superhuman sexual potency. Even though the belief that black males had larger genitals was false, psychologist Gordon Allport suggests "that it is not the actual size of the black's genitals that whites think they are describing; it is the psychological size."[6] A possible contributing factor to the myth of racial differences in genital size was that males in colder climates exhibit greater refraction of the flaccid penile organ, possibly creating the suggestion that a notable size difference between the races would exist when the penis became erect.

Cultural differences between Africans and whites, in large measure, also accounted for some of the larger society's attitude. Whites had never completely distanced themselves from the deeply entrenched stereotype of "brains versus brawn," a dichotomy that had permeated English folklore throughout the centuries. An ancient insult referred to as the myth of "Good-Natured Dick" enlists the caricature of the invariably feebleminded but genitally oversized man who was later depicted in John Cleland's eighteenth-century satire, *Fanny Hill*. In addition, given that those black Africans who emanated from the tropics dressed scantily, exhibited a greater comfort with their bodies, and had not been socialized into the puritan dictum that sex was dirty and evil contributed to the image of the oversexed black.

New Findings in Phalloplethysmography

That a quantification of intelligence and physical endowment might bear an intrinsic and inverse relationship stood at the core of a new, evolving subfield of race science termed "phalloplethysmography," or the science of penis measuring.[7] This peculiar offshoot was an unshakable shadow cast by the publicly acknowledged science of craniometry. John S. Haller

in his book *Outcasts from Evolution: Scientific Attitudes of Racial Inferiority, 1859–1900*, has documented the primary role American physicians of the period played in this new scientific discipline. Working alongside craniologists and craniometrists, the clinical observations of American physicians in phalloplethysmography served to reinforce societal beliefs in both the cognitive inferiority and physical over-endowment of blacks. Haller notes, "It was the southern physician who generally carried out studies on the Negro in the late nineteenth century, and his conclusions reflected not only the section's appeal for a reappraisal of Reconstruction politics but also mirrored the race ideology of the antebellum South."[8]

A vigorous debate arose during this period as to whether blacks were a separate species altogether whose differences manifested themselves in an inability to engage in abstract thought. Polygenists such as Morton, Harvard professor Louis Agassiz, and Alabama physician Josiah Nott articulated this position. Nott and businessman George Gliddon cowrote *Types of Mankind*, in which they noted the reader "would have to be blind" not to recognize the similarities between Africans and orangutans. However, contemporary paleontologist Stephen Jay Gould points out that to alleviate any possible erroneous conclusions the reader might draw, in studying Nott's illustrations, "the chimpanzee skull is falsely inflated, and the Negro jaw extended, to give the impression that blacks might even rank lower than apes."[9] It might also be worth observing what these nineteenth-century scientists omitted from their analyses. Andrew Hamilton in a 1963 article in *Science Digest* acknowledged certain physical features characteristic of blacks, such as a long, narrow head; a protruding jaw; and a wide, flat nose. But he went on to say that blacks also have large, full lips and long legs, making them least apelike, while the straight-textured hair of whites and their considerable body hair might cause one to consider whether they might be genetically closer to apes.[10]

American society in the nineteenth century may have readily accepted the findings of black cognitive inferiority because this scientific validation satisfied certain important societal needs. These findings offered intellectual

and emotional comfort to a nervous, uncertain young nation that begged for international and self-approval in having constructed a democratic society (in which all men were presumably created equal), even though it was accomplished on the economic premises of slavery.

The scientific process of measuring had its own seductive role to play in this political and social environment. Its very precision conferred scientific legitimacy on what was, in actuality, social dogma. When Professor Gould of Harvard undertook to remeasure Morton's work in 1977, he found that the nineteenth-century craniometrist's conclusions represented a "patchwork of fudging and finagling in the clear interest of controlling a priori convictions."[11]

In explaining the underlying reasons for the controversy regarding the differences in blacks' and whites' skull sizes, Gould referred to the research of a South African anthropologist named Phillip V. Tobias, who identified fourteen factors that might bias research findings relating to skull measurements. These points included decisions regarding the precise place at which the brain is severed from the spinal cord; whether the membranes covering the brain, called meninges, were removed; how much time elapsed after death; whether the brain was preserved in any fluid before weighing and, if so, for how long; and so forth.[12]

In reexamining Morton's craniometrical research, Gould realized that the nineteenth-century scientist selectively chose only certain brains to be measured and discarded others in accordance with the conclusions he intended to reach. Gould identified Morton's failure to recognize sexual dimorphism in his comparing the smaller black female skulls to the larger white male skulls. The Harvard professor also noted even more compelling distortions in the craniometrist's work. Morton measured the skull's brain cavity by filling it with mustard seeds, but he packed down the mustard seeds in the skulls of whites, giving them a higher weight. Gould made another revealing discovery as well, namely, that Morton realized that the results of his measurements could be skewed by his selection of skull samples. So while insisting on the use of black female

skulls in the black sampling, he nevertheless eliminated those of small-brained Hindus from his white sampling.[13] Also important, as Gould pointed out, conscious fraud did not appear to play a role in Morton's calculations, and he might have been unaware of his own subtle manipulation of the data. His scientific blind spot ranged from comparing male white skulls with a black sample that mixed males with females, in addition to eliminating the skulls of small-statured white men from the sample, while including those of the tiny African Khoisan.[14] The essential problem was that when corrections for body size and gender were made, the racial differences in skull sizes and even brain weights disappeared. Perhaps more important was that even if correlations were found, they did not in and of themselves prove causality. Did the fact that an elephant had a larger skull than a human's prove that it was more intelligent?

Because Morton's data could not be replicated in convincing ways, he borrowed from Anders Retzius, a Swedish professor of anatomy, a new means of gauging cranial capacity, the "cephalic index," which came to supersede his work over time. This cephalic measure examined the general shape of the skull, which was defined as the ratio of its breadth to its length. It is interesting to note that the French scientist Paul Broca readily agreed that intellectual inferiority was associated with black skin and woolly hair; however, he balked at equating skull shape with intelligence, perhaps because his own head shape matched the less advanced type.[15]

According to Professor William H. Tucker, Broca made the rather astute observation that scientists who posited this link were themselves from countries in which that particular head shape type predominated. Broca also concluded that there existed "a natural tendency of men, even among those most free of prejudice, to attach an idea of superiority to the dominant characteristics of their race."[16]

In his *Negro-Mania: Being an Examination of the Falsely Assumed Equality of the Various Races of Men*, published in 1851, John Campbell aggregated the observations of ethnographers, craniometrists, and phalloplethysmographers of his time in order to refute abolitionists' assertions of racial

equality. He cited, for example, the work of a late-eighteenth-century anatomist named Samuel Thomas von Sömmerring, who maintained that two specimens of Negro genitalia in his College Museum confirmed the common view of its large size. Campbell cited another scholar, a Mr. White, who was said to have corroborated these findings from his work in dissecting Negro corpses and from observations of living specimens of that race.[17]

Brains and genitalia were not the only racial attributes that the scientific community assessed at this time. Noting differences in nose shape, one enterprising scientist offered the ingenious conclusion that the African practice of carrying infants on the mother's back resulted in the child's nose being flattened as it bumped against the mother's shoulder blades. Nonetheless, because the brain was seen as the seat of mankind's higher nature and the genitalia as the bucket of his animal attributes, work on these two human attributes overwhelmed all other investigations into racial differences.

In 1853, John H. Van Evrie undertook extensive research on racial differences. He concluded that "blacks lacked both 'the brain . . . [and] the vocal organism' essential to music."[18] Immediately following the U.S. Civil War, he published *White Supremacy and Negro Subordination*, in which he examined a range of important anatomical differences between the races. Van Evrie concluded that Negroes possessed limited reasoning power, which he maintained led members of this group to slothfulness and strong animal appetites. He mused: "Indeed it may be matter of doubt which is the paramount cause of the negro's inability to provide for future necessities—his limited reasoning power or his indolence—his small brain or his dominating sensualism."[19]

Not surprising, a large number of anthropometric studies appeared after the Civil War and during the politically turbulent 1867–1877 period of Reconstruction as the South struggled to readjust its social hierarchy to the frightening (for them) postslavery environment. In opposing Reconstruction, for example, Congressman James Brooks explained to

his colleagues in the U.S. House of Representatives that the difference between blacks and whites was "essential, organic, throughout, from the crown of the head to the very sole of the feet."[20]

Racial differentiation in intelligence and sexual organs in many ways matched scholarly assessments of gender differences as well. Professor Edward H. Clarke of the Harvard Medical School published *Sex in Education: Or, a Fair Chance for the Girls* in 1873. He posited that excess intellectual effort that women exerted would only produce scholarly invalids, "pale, weak, neuralgic, dyspeptic, hysterical, menorraphic [sic], dysmeorrhoeic girls and women with arrested breast development."[21] Similarly, because Africans were believed to possess the attributes of passivity, dependence, and childishness, the black male was placed at the same inferior position on the evolutionary scale as white women. African females were positioned a rung below these two. The reasons given for gender differences in intelligence related to the females' "evolutionary adaptations to the pain of childbirth, repetitive domestic work, and other physical nonintellectual tasks."[22]

Dr. R. M. Cunningham reported in an 1894 issue of the journal *Medical News* that "the greater abdominal and genital development of the Negro merely corroborated the inferiority of his other anatomical peculiarities—his black skin, flat nose, lesser cranial and thoracic development."[23] In a book published five years later, Dr. Eugene S. Talbot wrote that brain growth competed with reproductive organ growth, and the latter clearly triumphed in the case of Negroes and mulattoes. He thus cautioned against miscegenation, or race mixing, for fear that the white race could become thus infected.[24]

In 1898, an anonymous writer who claimed to be a French army doctor and used the pseudonym of Dr. Jacobus X published *Untrodden Fields of Anthropology*. After observing that cranial inadequacy severely limited the Africans' cognitive capacity, he then noted that the African Negro has the largest genital organ size of any other member of the human race. He added for purposes of clarification that he was referring specifically

to the penis and not the testicles, which he asserted are often larger in Europeans. This author concluded that he had found a twenty-year-old Bambara (Malian) with a "monstrous organ" measuring 11.75 inches long by 2.6 inches in diameter, describing it as "a terrific machine, and except for a slight difference in length, was more like penis of a donkey than that of a man."[25]

The *Atlanta Journal-Record of Medicine* began publishing a series of articles in the burgeoning field of phalloplethysmography in 1899. In June of that year, Doctors McGuire and Lydston, who were later identified as Hunter McGuire of Virginia and G. Frank Lydston of Chicago, presented their personal findings in the pages of that journal. They cautioned readers that when blacks, whom they described as "a race of a low type of development," were brought into contact with "a more intellectual strain"—namely, whites—the former were prone to allow their "primitive instinct" to overpower them, manifesting itself in lust and sexual criminality.[26]

The 1903 edition of the *Atlanta Journal-Record of Medicine* devoted space to exploring this medical question even further. In March of that year it published "Genital Peculiarities of the Negro," which concluded "the male's 'stallion-like passion and entire willingness to run any risk and brave any peril for the gratification of his frenetic lust,' made the Negro a menace to the Caucasian race."[27] Dr. William T. English corroborated these findings in a subsequent issue of that journal published in October of the same year. He observed that Negroes suffer from a lower level of consciousness than whites do and thus reflected the sexual extremes of a less-developed intelligence. Dr. English consequently surmised that because the African's brain lagged behind that of the European by a thousand years of evolution, "the Negro brain . . . existed within a visceral and organic structure that was physiologically juxtaposed to its intellectual capacity."[28] After delving even more deeply into the subject, he also determined that "the Negro's 'moral delinquencies,' along with elements of 'bestiality and gratification,' were demonstrations of the close relationship of the race to its 'animal subhuman ancestors.'"[29]

That same year, Michigan physician Dr. William Lee Howard encapsulated the dominant thinking of the time regarding the relationship between black intelligence and genital size in an article published in the journal *Medicine*. Dr. Howard suggested that education would "reduce the large size of the negro's penis" and bring a higher level of sensitivity to that race, erasing its propensity toward what Dr. Howard termed "sexual madness."[30] He explained that this attribute emanated from the fact that a large sexual area existed in the cortex of the Negro brain, and after puberty, it functioned overtime.[31]

Ban on Interracial Marriage

One of the most powerful legal developments to emerge from the convergence of American craniometry and the social insecurities following the Civil War was the instituting of antimiscegenation laws that prohibited interracial marriage. In the South, where blacks and whites lived in more intimate proximity, legislative bans publicly cited the definitive findings of craniometry research. Private discussion underscored the scientific conclusions being reached by also injecting the findings of phalloplethysmography into the public perception of the issues. The studies of racial differences also created an imperative for restricting the sexual freedom of white women so as not to contaminate the race with the biological material of a cognitively inferior group. Marcel de Serres in 1864 articulated that white females should require legislative protection rather than merely relying on their "good sense" in avoiding black males. He described the body of the Caucasian woman as a holy temple sanctified by God. He juxtaposed this imagery of white womanhood with his belief in the Negro's primitive bestiality, which, if unleashed, could cause irreparable damage to the Caucasian race.[32]

As Professor Wiegman pointed out in *American Anatomies* in 1995, the loss of the patriarchal institution of slavery increased the "competitive dimensions of interracial masculine relations. . . . It was in this climate,"

she concludes, "that the mythology of the black man as rapist emerged, working the fault line of the slave's newly institutionalized masculinization by framing this masculinity as the bestial excess of an overly phallic primitivity."[33] It was also true, as Calvin C. Hernton noted in *Sex and Racism in America*, that "to most Southerners, black people have become equated with the forbidden and deranged part of their nature."[34]

Yet the antimiscegenation laws failed to reduce white male fears that they might have to compete for females with the "savage" sexuality of the over-endowed black male. In fact, this historical period ushered in a tragic era of black lynchings. It has been estimated that between 1890 and 1920, more than seventeen hundred black men, women, and children were lynched in America.[35] The impetus for this particular type of white mob violence was in most cases the suggestion that a black male had raped or even made a pass at a white woman. But Professor Wiegman also observes:

> The decommodification of the African American body that accompanies the transformation from chattel to citizenry is mediated through a complicated process of sexualization and engendering: not only does lynching enact a grotesquely symbolic—if not literal—sexual encounter between the white mob and its victim, but the increasing utilization of castration as a preferred form of mutilation for African American men demonstrates lynching's connection to the socio-symbolic realm of sexual difference. In the disciplinary fusion of castration with lynching, the mob severs the black male from the masculine, interrupting the privilege of the phallus, and thereby reclaiming, through the perversity of dismemberment, his (masculine) potentiality for citizenship.[36]

In her article "Sexualized Racism/Gendered Violence: Outraging the Body Politic in the Reconstruction South," Lisa Cardyn writes, "Although there are no statistics available to determine the proportion of lynchings

that were accompanied by castration, references to this practice appear throughout the literature of klan violence."[37]

To deal with the so-called animal passions of the African, some doctors even went so far as to advocate castration in the hopes that this procedure would make the threatening black male "'docile, quiet and inoffensive.'"[38] One article published in the *Atlanta Journal-Record of Medicine* of 1907 suggested, for humanitarian purposes, that castration of uncontrollable black males ought to take the place of lynching.[39]

In the first quarter of the twentieth century, scholars such as Vojtěch Suk and Aleš Hrdlička of the Smithsonian Institution began publishing their own scientific data in the *Journal of Physical Anthropology* that confirmed the mammoth proportions of blacks' genitals and the puniness of their brains.[40] However, because other researchers were unable to provide credible evidence of racial differences in skull sizes once body proportions and gender were adjusted for, new indexes were sought to substantiate the alleged cognitive deficits of blacks.

Continued scholarly work in the field of phalloplethysmography created an imperative of powerful proportions. If black males possessed superiority in the size of the male organ, as scientists now asserted, then the imperative to prove black intellectual inferiority became even more intense. At the same time, scholars also sought ways of measuring human intelligence that bypassed such crude and undignified research as that involving penis and skull measurement, even though the imperative to prove black mental inferiority never budged an inch.

2
THE INTELLIGENCE QUOTIENT

During the first decade of the twentieth century, Francis Galton's concept of the inverse correlation provided scientific substance for the belief in a relationship between the cognitive and sexual attributes of the races. Although academic and public interest in craniometry waned, the social need to validate ethnic differences remained. Over time, academics came to embrace new, less physically tangible, and thus harder to refute methodologies for judging the intelligence variable of the human equation.

Galton himself joined this quest for more sophisticated measures of cognitive difference, perhaps in part because, as Rutgers University psychology professor William Tucker has pointed out, the English mathematician had an unusually small head.[1] In any case, the interest that Galton developed in intelligence testing came to dominate American psychology once his concepts were refined by a formal testing procedure that French scholar Alfred Binet devised in 1905. And within a decade, the mental test, which came to be called the intelligence quotient (IQ), had replaced the work of craniometrists in measuring human worth.

Inferior Breeds

Blacks and women were not the only groups targeted as inferior types. New immigrants, particularly eastern and southern Europeans, and Jews became a primary focus of the early eugenics movement. Many of the movement's most committed American followers came out of the ranching field of animal husbandry and were imbued with a belief that its principles could be applied properly to humans. W. E. D. Stokes, a prominent eugenicist and animal breeder, even went so far as to castigate immigrants publicly for contaminating healthy New England blood with "rotten, foreign, diseased blood . . . [from] the imported scum of the earth."[2] Professor Tucker explained that around this time the American Breeders Association changed its name to the American Genetic Association, as a means of replacing "the stud-farm overtones with a more prestigious scientific image." It also changed the title of its publication from the *American Breeders' Magazine* to the *Journal of Heredity*.[3]

Perhaps the strongest advocate of Galton's views within the newly evolving eugenics field was a biologist named Charles Benedict Davenport (1886–1944). He established the Station for the Experimental Study of Evolution and the Eugenics Record Office at Cold Spring Harbor, New York, and became a focal point for the American eugenics movement. As a young man, the Harvard-educated Davenport developed a special interest in the inheritance of physical, personality, and mental traits in humans.[4] Davenport bristled at the merest hint of sexual indulgence and prided himself in having remained a virgin before his own marriage at the age of twenty-eight.[5] So disapproving of physical gratification did Davenport become that later in life he began advocating not merely sterilization of the unfit but castration as well "to quell their lustfulness."

Having collaborated with zoologist Morris Steggerda on extensively researching race mixing on the Caribbean island of Jamaica, Davenport asserted that racial intermarriage led only to "disharmony of physical, mental, and temperamental qualities" and must be avoided at all costs.

More specifically, he concluded from his research data that black-white pairings invariably caused physical imbalance since the mulatto offspring inherited long legs from their black parent and short arms from their white one, "placing them at a disadvantage in picking objects up from the ground."[6] Davenport also reported that mulattos possessed "an ambition and push . . . with intellectual inadequacy which makes the unhappy hybrid dissatisfied with his lot and a nuisance to others."[7] Not surprising, his racial views also extended into the realm of anti-Semitism. Davenport maintained a conviction that Jews exhibited "the greatest proportion of offenses against chastity and in connection with prostitution, the lowest of crimes."[8]

Regarding Davenport's attitude toward women, including the female field workers in his employ, he sometimes mused that they "could serve society better by producing children instead of research."[9] Thus, Davenport tended to relegate female workers to projects involving delinquent children and assessments of artistic creativity, while he assigned male workers job tasks related to a broader range of research interests.

Another important figure in the eugenics movement during the early years of the twentieth century was the British psychologist and statistician Charles E. Spearman (1863–1945). Refining Francis Galton's work in establishing correlation analysis, Spearman developed a technique known as factor analysis, which measured the intercorrelations of an entire grouping of variables. Additionally, Spearman devised a correction formula based on the realization that the true degree of a relationship between two variables will be distorted by the unreliability of their measurement.[10]

The Concept of *g*

Over the course of an illustrious academic career, Spearman became most noted for employing factor analysis in the construction of a new concept referred to as g, or general intelligence. This mathematical process

involved identifying positive intercorrelations between measures of different abilities defined by one general underlying factor, that is, g. Spearman believed that he had discovered a means of measuring all the cognitive processes underlying human intelligence, which he could then express as a single number. Then Spearman went even further. Leaning on the research findings of Sante Naccarati, who wrote *The Morphological Aspect of Intelligence* in 1921, Spearman also began to suggest that g was not merely correlated with mental functions but also directly and inversely related to the physiological secretions of the thyroid, pituitary, and genital glands.[11]

In 1940, Cyril Burt (1883–1971), a pioneer in the field of British educational psychology, published *The Factors of the Mind*. Burt considered Francis Galton his mentor, and he refined Spearman's work on factor analysis even further by including group factors within his conception. A persuasive advocate for the belief that intelligence was innate, Burt drew heavily on Spearman's work, particularly the use of the concept g. Although quite willing initially to acknowledge his debt to Spearman, by 1937 Burt had begun attributing Spearman's innovations to himself. Contrary to the actual evidence, Burt stated in the footnote to an article that he, not Spearman, had in fact "been the first person to suggest the use of a certain equation for factor analysis in his first 1909 paper on general intelligence."[12] However, Burt's falsification proved trivial in relation to later allegations that he had fabricated large segments of his life's work that compared attributes found in twins reared apart. Powerful elements within the educational establishments of Great Britain and the United States had used his conclusions to assert that enriching children's living environments would play a minimal role in improving their intelligence.

In 1974, Professor Leon Kamin published a damning critique of Burt's work, suggesting that the British scholar had consciously altered IQ test results in his famous twin studies in order to offer convincing support for his theories of the heritability of intelligence. Burt had asserted that his research showed that twins who had been reared apart nevertheless

closely matched on measures of intelligence, signifying that nature rather than nurture played the vital role in human intelligence. Kamin pointed out that although Burt claimed in 1956 to have found a sample of fifty-three pairs of twins who had been separated at birth and raised apart, this claim was highly improbable given that just a year earlier Burt himself had asserted that even finding twenty-one pairs for his earlier research had been extraordinarily difficult. Prior to Burt's own studies of twins reared apart, researchers, having looked far and wide, had not been able to assemble more than twenty pairs of twins who could meet Burt's criteria.

Burt's official biographer, Leslie Hearnshaw, quickly came to the professor's defense when allegations of fraud first appeared in print. However, after a thorough examination of Burt's work, Hearnshaw was forced to concur that the accusations were true. It was possible that Burt's tampering occurred during an especially trying period in the scholar's life, as he was emotionally devastated when he lost all of his research records—his life's work—during a World War II bombing attack.[13]

Shortly after the war, Burt continued his eugenics research but also became deeply involved in scientific attempts to validate extrasensory perception, communication with the disembodied spirits of the dead, and mental telepathy. Because Burt's twin studies were the basis for much of the later hereditarian research of William Shockley, Arthur Jensen, and others who argued that intelligence develops independently of one's environment, the debate about the authenticity of Burt's research remains both acrimonious and ongoing.[14]

Intelligence Testing

While Burt laid the foundation for hereditarian concepts of intelligence, it was Professor Lewis M. Terman (1877–1956) of Stanford University who translated the eugenic focus on mental inheritance and popularized intelligence testing in America. In 1914 he published *The Hygiene of the*

School Child and followed it three years later with a noted intelligence study in which he observed that one meets uneducable Negroes with such great frequency, that research on racial differences in mental traits merits special urgency. He predicted that this research would confirm his belief in enormous racial differences in general intelligence, "which cannot be wiped out by any scheme of mental culture." Terman also opined that allowing such people to reproduce would create a grave problem for society because of "their unusually prolific breeding."[15]

Terman's book titled *The Measurement of Intelligence* normalized the scale employed in IQ testing to ensure that "average" children scored 100 at each age (mental age equal to chronological age).[16] During World War I, Terman worked on a committee with psychologist Robert Yerkes, President of the American Psychological Association, to devise the U.S. Army's famous Alpha (emphasizing verbal abilities) and Beta (for illiterates) IQ testing program for soldiers. Terman, whom Yerkes had brought onto the committee, and his team of testers categorically dismissed critics' arguments that the recruits' performance on intelligence tests might be dependent on their educational levels and cultural backgrounds, that is, environmental factors. When puzzled researchers began noting that blacks from the North scored higher on IQ tests than southern whites did, Terman's team attributed the phenomenon to the selective migration of the more able blacks to the North. Otto Klineberg (1899–1992) of Columbia University then undertook his own extensive investigation of black migration patterns. He concluded in his book *Negro Intelligence and Selective Migration* that "superior environmental and cultural advantages, and not selective migration, had resulted in northern blacks scoring higher on intelligence tests than did their counterparts who remained in the south."[17]

As support for Terman's intelligence testing methods grew within the academic community, he began to broaden the applicability of his tests. Regarding his evaluation of intelligence differences among various ethnic groups, his work in some ways mirrored that of Henry H. Goddard, who,

after testing the IQs of immigrants at Ellis Island, reported that "83 percent of the Jews, 80 percent of the Hungarians, 79 percent of the Italians, and 87 percent of the Russians were 'feeble-minded.'"[18]

One of the foremost dissenting voices within the scientific community was that of Havelock Ellis (1859–1939), who had pioneered the study of human sexuality. He shunned the eugenic thinking of Terman and others and rejected as well the research findings of racial differences in both cognition and phalloplethysmography.

Ellis's work and that of like-minded antihereditarians, however, were drowned out by the momentum and sheer "obviousness" of the evidence that IQ tests confirmed: that is, blacks possessed a cognitive inferiority that was inversely correlated with their genital over-endowment. In the debate that ensued, the American journalist Walter Lippmann also sided with Ellis, ridiculing the arguments of the IQ-preoccupied eugenicists. In a series of articles published in the *New Republic* of 1922, Lippmann wrote: "The statement that the average mental age of Americans is only about fourteen is not inaccurate. It is not incorrect. It is nonsense."[19] The whip-tongued journalist also rejected the eugenicist notion that IQ tests measured hereditary intelligence. He asserted that psychometrics had "no more scientific foundation than a hundred other fads, vitamins and glands and amateur psychoanalysis and correspondence courses in will power, and it will pass with them into that limbo where phrenology and palmistry and characterology and the other Babu sciences are to be found."[20] In the *New Republic*, Lippmann continued his attack on Terman's IQ preoccupation, arguing that "[I] could not imagine a more contemptible proceeding than to confront a child with a set of puzzles, and after an hour's monkeying with them, proclaim to the child and his parents, that here is a C-individual."[21]

Geneticists engaged in biological research had been the earliest supporters of the eugenics movement, but over time their endorsement of it dwindled. In January 1915 the prominent genetic researcher Thomas Hunt Morgan, a pioneer in the field of cytology (the study of the internal

structure of cells), resigned from one of the committees of the American Genetic Association and asserted that much of what appeared in the association's *Journal of Heredity* was both reckless and unreliable.[22] Morgan questioned, among other ideas, the notion that the races had a biological basis. He declared in the 1925 edition of *Evolution and Genetics*, "Least of all should we feel any assurance in deciding genetic superiority or inferiority as applied to whole races, by which is meant not races in a biological sense, but social or political groups bound together by physical conditions, by religious sentiments, or by political organizations."[23]

By 1927, Raymond Pearl, a geneticist from Johns Hopkins University who had been an early advocate of the eugenics movement, also denounced the eugenics community. In a scathing attack on eugenicist aims, Pearl identified a propaganda phase, which had become inextricably bound to the purely scientific phase of eugenics. As a consequence, he asserted that writings on the subject of eugenics had become "a mingled mess of ill-grounded and uncritical sociology, economics, anthropology, and politics, full of emotional appeals to class and race prejudices, solemnly put forth as science, and unfortunately accepted as such by the general public."[24]

Geneticists did not reject the scientific reality of human variation. Rather, their own research findings led them to conclude that the commonly held beliefs about race, current among psychologists and the public at large, were wrong. One potential problem emanated from the popular belief that differences in outward characteristics among the diverse population groups could only emanate from inbreeding (as opposed to environmental adaptations).

In 1918, Ludwik Hirszfeld and Hanna Hirszfeld suggested that the ABO blood groups could be used for an analysis of ethnic origins.[25] While the data on these differences did create some measure of differentiation, it was eventually rejected because it did not conform to the social and political categories of the races. Later studies of the Rhesus and other blood factors exhibited a similar problem, since these differences

also refused to conform to the popular racial classifications. Nonetheless, the eugenicists were convinced that as genetics itself became more sophisticated, it eventually would confirm the social and political classification of race used in America.

One such scholar named E. O. Manoiloff of Leningrad believed that he had made a breakthrough in determining races by blood agglutination factors, even though what he meant by "races" had far more of a European than American flavor. After the addition of reagents, he concluded that "Jewish blood had a blue-greenish coloring; Russian blood, a blue-red one."[26]

The eugenic attempt to define races in terms of inbreeding proved especially seductive because family resemblance was so commonly understood as a means of transmitting biological characteristics. However, the geneticists, who had distanced themselves from the eugenicists, began to suspect that the Zulu in southern Africa and the Wolof of West Africa, to cite two examples, might not share the same dark skin color strictly because of inbreeding; rather, it might stem from environmental adaptations to the tropical climate that occurred over thousands of years, without the groups necessarily having had contact with one another. While geographic proximity was relevant to human groupings, it was important not to confuse it with genetic proximity. An African possessing type A blood might have more genetic proximity to a European with the same blood type than to another African with blood type O.[27]

As a growing number of biological researchers and geneticists became disenchanted with the eugenics movement and left, psychologists who saw eugenics as a means of gaining greater respectability for their new but publicly ridiculed field filled their places. However, as William Tucker points out, their embrace of the movement was "a Faustian bargain" whereby those psychologists who became advocates of eugenics also abandoned "the distinction between an objective attempt to understand behavior and the creation of ideological support for a social order informed by eugenicist and other elitist principles."[28]

As it had among geneticists, a backlash against what were perceived as the excesses of eugenics occurred in the field of anthropology. The most prominent anthropologist of the period, Franz Boas of Columbia University, was a German-Jewish immigrant who became one of the most vocal critics of eugenic thinking. Boas encouraged a promising master's student, the young Margaret Mead, to write her thesis studying the intelligence of children of Italian immigrants. Contrary to the eugenicists' predictions, Mead found that these children's performance on intelligence tests "depended on their families' social status and length of residence in the United States, and also on the extent of which English was spoken in the home."[29]

While intelligence testing or psychometrics gained momentum throughout the span of the twentieth century, the eugenics movement fell on hard times after World War II. Horrified by evidence of the Holocaust, Americans associated selective breeding theories with Nazi notions of racial superiority.

Eugenics Reemerges

The 1954 U.S. Supreme Court decision in the *Brown v. Board of Education of Topeka, Kansas* desegregation case initiated a period of renewed popularity for race science within certain quarters. In addition to the educational issues that the *Brown* decision raised, opponents of desegregation were quick to cite not merely inherited cognitive differences between the races but also the necessity to prevent miscegenation. William Tucker noted that beneath the Southerners' seeming preoccupation with segregated education was another issue, namely, the "widespread 'amalgamation' rising from the ruins."[30]

Carleton Putnam, a noted anthropologist, published *Race and Reason: A Yankee Review* in 1961. He blamed the desegregation movement on a left-wing Jewish conspiracy led by the followers of Franz Boas. Shortly thereafter Wesley George, a professor at the University of North Carolina

Medical School, offered his own scientific findings that integration should be avoided at all costs so that blacks would not be admitted into "those areas of Caucasian life where mates are chosen."[31] Even so, the academic community as a whole refrained from embracing these doctrines. The American Association of Physical Anthropologists condemned Putnam's book, and one prominent geneticist dismissed it as pseudoscience pandering to racial prejudice.[32] In fact, had it not been for the near fatal car accident of a Nobel Prize–winning scientist named William Shockley, the twentieth century's preoccupation with pairing cognition and physical attributes finally might have faded from view. It might not have been so much the car crash as the damage it did to Shockley's sense of self that changed the course of race science.

3

THE REGRESSION TO THE MEAN

On July 23, 1961, a drunk driver veered his car across the centerline of the Cabrillo Highway south of San Francisco and rammed another vehicle head-on. The force of the impact threw the other driver, fifty-one-year-old William Shockley, onto the pavement, crushing his pelvis and severely bruising other parts of his body. Shockley and his wife were rushed to the hospital in critical condition, while their son Richard suffered only minor injuries.[1]

For the Nobel Prize–winning scientist, whose collaboration on the invention of the transistor had revolutionized modern life, the ensuing hospital stay and confinement in a body cast for months might have triggered anxious memories of a previous confinement. For six months in 1951, Shockley had been committed to a psychiatric facility outside Philadelphia, where he was treated for a nervous breakdown.[2] It is difficult to say whether his subsequent shift in academic interests might have been triggered by his grief at the injuries he sustained in the automobile accident. They may well have overwhelmed the five-foot-six, 150-pound scientist and mountain climber, who was also a self-described "lady's man." But whatever the case, at least one former colleague and

past president of Rockefeller University, Frederick Seitz, believed that Shockley's abrupt change of interest from solid-state physics to racial differences in intelligence might have been precipitated by a head injury suffered in his car accident.[3] Seitz asserted that Shockley's "intense and (to my mind) ill-conceived concentration on socio-genetic matters occurred after a head-on automobile collision in which he was almost killed."[4] Whatever the case, Shockley's ideas began to coalesce around the notion that an inverse correlation existed between black cognition and physical prowess. In pursuing this theory, he resurrected the racial aspects of the old eugenics movement and focused on "dysgenics," which he described as "down-breeding, for retrogressive evolution, or population pollution, caused by excessive reproduction of the genetically disadvantaged."[5]

The Revival of Eugenics

Colleagues were genuinely puzzled that Shockley would insist from this period until the end of his life that the work he had begun to conduct on race was far more important than his coinvention of the transistor. After all, every modern device from the telephone and television to guided missiles and the computer revolution can be traced in some way to this remarkable innovation.

Shockley's growing preoccupation with eugenics and selective breeding was not simply an intellectual one. He disowned his eldest son for his involvement with a Costa Rican woman since this relationship, according to Professor Shockley, threatened to contaminate the family's white gene pool. He also described his children to a reporter "as a significant regression" even though one possessed a PhD in physics from the University of Southern California and another held a degree from Harvard College. Shockley even went so far as to blame this "genetic misfortune" on his first wife, who according to the scientist, "had not as high an academic-achievement standing as I had."[6]

John L. Moll, a close associate of the scientist-turned-dysgenics expert, explained with perfect candor that Shockley's "technical insights were counterbalanced by his lack of insight into human relations."[7] A man of consummate brilliance, Shockley was in other ways a deeply tragic figure whose racist theories came to define him in the public's imagination far more than his founding of the first semi-conductor company.

Cognitive Hierarchies

In 1963, nearly two years after his car accident, Shockley was appointed professor of engineering at Stanford University. Many of his students considered him to be a superb teacher, one who was especially adept and creative at training young minds in problem-solving techniques. But Shockley seemed increasingly bored with physics and had begun to spend far less time on the academic pursuits for which he had achieved fame to focus on his growing obsession with eugenics.

His first public opportunity to convey this message appeared in May 1963, when he gave a speech at Gustavus Adolphus College in Minnesota. The newly minted eugenicist argued that the least genetically competent people in the world were reproducing much faster than the more cognitively evolved ones, who practiced birth control and thus had fewer children. In February 1964 at a panel discussion on "Sex, Science and Survival," Shockley elucidated his theory even further and offered a plethora of statistics meant to bolster these eugenics assertions. By 1965, he was ready to take the racial offensive, asserting in a *U.S. News and World Report* interview that blacks were cognitively inferior to whites, and in a subsequent interview with the *National Enquirer* tabloid, Shockley reiterated a "Voluntary Sterilization Bonus Plan." Although never implemented, the plan offered people of low IQ a bonus—or a thousand dollars for every IQ point below 100—for agreeing to be sterilized. Several years later, Shockley insisted in another interview that "Nature has color-coded groups of individuals so that statistically reliable

predictions of their adaptability to intellectually rewarding and effective lives may be made and profitably used by the pragmatic man in the street."[8]

Sperm Banks and Aryans

Shockley's preoccupation with race and eugenics culminated in his decision at the age of seventy to donate his sperm to the Repository for Germinal Choice, a short-lived enterprise, founded by Robert K. Graham. A three-times-married millionaire, Graham had fathered eight children, although he remained estranged from them.[9] *Boston Globe* columnist Ellen Goodman referred to the repository quite candidly as "a phallic symbol . . . without the symbolism."[10] In any case, Shockley's academic arguments about the need to spread superior white genes to counteract the dysgenic effects caused by higher rates of nonwhites' fertility had morphed into action.

However provocative, Shockley's ideas were certainly not new. While many Americans had courted the eugenics movement in the early years of the twentieth century, mainstream support for it evaporated after World War II and discoveries of the uses to which the Aryan-purifying Nazis had put eugenic thinking. The emergence of the civil rights movement in 1954 even further marginalized die-hard American eugenicists, but it also invigorated the ranks of the diminished community that remained. Henry E. Garrett, the chairman of Columbia University's Psychology Department and an influential eugenicist, testified before the Supreme Court to defend racial segregation in schools. Feeling abandoned by the political mainstream, the neo-eugenicists identified clear targets for attack. The first was racial equality. Angry at the demise of antimiscegenation laws, their second target revealed the movement's more phallic-oriented preoccupation with white-black male competition.

The Frustrated Symphony Conductor

When Shockley addressed a meeting of the Center for Advanced Study in the Behavioral Sciences at Stanford in the late 1960s, one member of the audience drawn to his discourse was Arthur R. Jensen, a psychologist who taught at the University of California–Berkeley. Jensen, who had described himself as a "frustrated symphony conductor," may have had his own reasons for reverencing Shockley's every word. The younger psychologist had been forced to abandon a career in music because his own considerable talents in that area nevertheless lacked "soul," or the emotional intensity needed to succeed in so competitive a profession.[11] He decided on psychology as a second choice, carrying along with him a grudge against those American subcultures perceived as being "more expressive" than the white culture from which he sprang. Jensen received his bachelor's degree in that field from the University of California–Berkeley in 1945.[12]

After completing his education and postdoctoral work, he received tenure at the University of California–Berkeley and, shortly, began propounding Shockley's message of racial hierarchies in intelligence. In an oddly inexplicable about-face, Jensen digressed from favoring environmental explanations for differences in IQ between groups to embracing Shockley's notion of black cognitive inferiority.[13] Jensen began asserting that blacks were incapable of abstract reasoning and then articulated a laundry list of presumed anatomical differences between the races. While whites outranked blacks in intelligence, the latter tipped the scale in penis size, impulsivity, and uninhibitedness, according to Jensen. This paradigm was so firmly fixed in his mind that when confronted with the anomaly of black children, whose IQs placed them in the "retarded" category, operating more functionally than did white children with the same IQ designation, the psychologist surmised that the black children's lower evolutionary level allowed for their greater instinctual functionality at a diminished level of IQ.[14] Perhaps on account of his lack of creative thinking

or his mere cognitive inflexibility, the more likely reason never occurred to Jensen. What he was actually observing was the unreliability of these intelligence tests when used to make cross-cultural comparisons.

Sexual Restraint and Civil Rights

Jensen's theories could not have come at a more propitious time, politically. In 1964 Congress passed its landmark Civil Rights Act, calling for the desegregation of American public education and outlawing racial discrimination in public accommodations and employment. This legislation was followed a year later by the Voting Rights Act, which established remedies for blacks and other minorities who faced discrimination in voting, particularly in the South. Southern traditionalists were livid and no doubt frightened. Having lost the battle in Congress to defeat these bills, they found themselves suddenly impotent to stop the radical social changes this legislation presaged in undermining the social hierarchy based on race that had remained in place since the days of slavery.

The new eugenicists offered a novel and promising approach to the distressed traditionalists, who had already lost the legislative battle. The reemergence of eugenics offered what purported to be scientific reasoning for desiring to reestablish the old white-black social hierarchy. Jensen and Shockley both attacked new government programs such as Head Start, which aimed at increasing educational preparation for preschool minority children, and denounced them as a waste of taxpayers' money. The real differences between black and white children, according to their eugenicist theories, were innate and genetic rather than social.

In 1967 Jensen and Shockley presented their theories of a racial hierarchy in intelligence before a meeting of the National Academy of Sciences. While critics outnumbered supporters, the two could at least celebrate the fact that they were talking before a legitimate scientific body. The next year, Shockley delivered a paper to that same scientific body in which he asserted "the major deficit in Negro intellectual performance

must be primarily of hereditary origin and thus relatively irremediable by practical improvements in environment." Making specific reference to the "Operation Head Start Program," he added that "its effects on IQ may prove insignificant."[15]

Jensen even began to overshadow Shockley as lead spokesman for the new eugenics movement after the *Harvard Educational Review* published his "How Much Can We Boost IQ and Scholastic Achievement?" in the February 1969 issue. In summarizing his theories relating to racial differences in intelligence, Jensen insisted that genetic factors rather than environmental factors led to IQ score differences between blacks and whites. In a later clarification of these views, Jensen insisted that they stemmed from "a problem which is more important than the question of racial differences per se, namely, the high probability of dysgenic trends in our urban slums."[16]

Jensen might have been frustrated with Shockley's inability as a physicist to validate their racial theories in psychological terms. So he took up the slack with such intellectual vigor and energy that the term "Jensenism" was coined to describe the psychology of "proving black cognitive inferiority." The Berkeley psychologist wrote dozens of books and articles and injected new theories into the discourse, such as "reaction time" and "choice reaction time," in his attempt to prove that the brains of whites operated more efficiently than those of blacks. Jensen explained the new methodology as follows:

> Reaction time (RT) to a stimulus situation increases as the amount of information transmitted by the stimulus increases. . . . The subject sits in front of a panel on which there is a single light bulb; directly beneath the bulb is a pushbutton. When the light flashes "on," the subject pushes the button to turn the light "off." In this condition, the subject's response time is a measure of simple RT. There is zero information conveyed when there is only one light/button combination. But the subject is required to respond

to an increasing number of light/button combinations, simply by having one light go on among an increasing number of potential alternatives. This is called "choice RT." The amount of information conveyed increases logarithmically as the number of lights increases.[17]

When Jensen tried to replicate the results of the initial study, he quietly dismissed the new data as an "apparent anomaly," since in subsequent tests blacks scored higher than whites did in tests of choice reaction time.[18]

The public policy implications of the issues Jensen raised were enormous. This debate had erupted at a time in which universities and corporations around the country, as a consequence of the Civil Rights Act of 1964, were establishing affirmative action programs to redress imbalances to minorities caused by previous discriminatory policies. The issues that Shockley had presented and then Jensen had developed further fueled a national debate on the validity of IQ tests and the racial differences in intelligence that they purported to measure. The critical point that Shockley, Jensen, and others made was that continuing to make social changes to improve the lot of over-reproducing minorities was a sheer waste of governmental agencies' time and money.

Jensen was genuinely confused by critics who called his research "racist." He insisted that his identification of race-based differences in intelligence was merely an attempt at making the educational process more responsive to the differing cognitive abilities of minority children.[19] Lonesome for an intellectual companion within his own field of psychology, he sought someone of like mind who might validate his work on race in psychological terms. Shockley, the physicist, could not fulfill that role. Growing impatient, he soon stumbled upon the work of a fellow psychologist that more than fit the bill.

4
SEDUCTIVE REASONING

When Richard J. Herrnstein became chairman of Harvard University's Psychology Department in 1967, he inherited a deeply divided faculty, reflective of suppurating wounds within the field of psychology itself. The department had been polarized since World War II. On one side, the experimentalists, such as John G. Beebe and Edwin Boring, found themselves pitted against the social and clinical psychologists—Gordon Allport, Robert White, and others. As the split widened, Gordon Allport and Henry Murray left the Psychology Department in 1945 and joined with Talcott Parsons of the Sociology Department and Clyde Kluckholm of the Anthropology Department to found the new Department of Social Relations.

Herrnstein took it upon himself to mend the long-standing rift and bring the Social Relations and Psychology Departments back together, but the task was made all but impossible because, as a preeminent experimental psychologist, he represented one of the most articulate voices for defining psychology as a strictly quantifiable science. Herrnstein's own work eschewed the more subjective, introspective approaches of members of the Social Relations Department, and he gave an almost

sacrosanct role to the mathematical processes of measurement. Several years before, in a burst of ingenuity, he had formulated the Matching Law theory, mapping the behavior of pigeons to establish with mathematical precision the link between behavior and rewards.

Herrnstein's investment in the nonintrospective side of psychology had suffused his entire career and reached back to his student days. Having achieved an impressive grade point average at the City College of New York, he had gained entrance in 1951 to Harvard University's Department of Psychology. As a graduate student, Herrnstein immediately found himself beguiled by Professor S. S. Stevens, Harvard's father figure in experimental psychology at the time and a vocal critic of psychotherapy's unquantifiable subjectivity.

Becoming a research assistant to Stevens, Herrnstein also fell under the spell of the professor's protégé, William H. Sheldon, one of the most colorful, and perplexing, figures of American psychology. A man of remarkable energy and diverse appetites, Sheldon, while on a traveling scholarship in England, had met Bill Wilson, and collaborated with him in setting up Alcoholics Anonymous. Sheldon also wrote the two most important books of modern numismatics—*Early American Cents* and *Penny Whimsey*. His special renown in academic history, however, emanated from activity of a decidedly different sort. In the early 1940s, Sheldon and a colleague, Earnest Albert Hooton, took over a program initiated by Harvard's PE Department in 1880, taking nude photos of students. They convinced the administrators at nine Ivy League universities that they should be allowed to make use of these nude photographs of their incoming students under the guise of a campaign for posture improvement. Former president George H. W. Bush, Hillary Rodham Clinton, and writer Nora Ephron numbered among the unwitting freshmen forced to strip and pose nude for Sheldon, who had taken over the program, adding to a photographic cache which by then numbered in the tens of thousands.[1] Posture correction was merely a ruse for the actual research in which he and S. S. Stevens were engaged, namely,

somatotyping. Developing a system of classification through the precise measurement and analysis of human body types, they sought to establish correlations comparing intelligence, temperament, sexual proclivities, and the moral worth of individuals.

Based on this system, criminals were perceived to be shorter and heavier and more muscular than morally upstanding citizens. Black males were reported to rank higher on the "masculine component" but lower on the intelligence scale than white males did. In a study published by Harvard University Press in 1939, Professor Earnest Albert Hooton had concluded: "Race is definitely associated with choice of crime, and with sociological status and that, with the exception of the Italian, race seems to be a stronger determinant of crime than [does] nationality."[2]

Somatotyping was reminiscent of the efforts Nazi scholars launched before World War II. According to Yale professor George Hersey, they had "compiled similar archives, analyzing the photos for racial as well as characterological content."[3] In 1919, Sheldon had traveled to Germany and met with the prominent German psychiatrist and fellow eugenicist Ernst Kretschmer. Professor Patricia Vertinsky of the University of British Columbia suggests that Sheldon may have been influenced by Kretschmer's aims, which were "to organize whole populations into state-mandated programs in order to improve German mating practices."[4] Sheldon references Kretschmer's work extensively in *Varieties of Delinquent Youth: An Introduction to Constitutional Psychiatry*, a book the American scholar published in 1947.[5] Per the following example, Sheldon's research on somatotyping, as with Kretschmer's work before him, also gave special attention to correlations of body type and sexual mating habits:

> Case 39 . . . has an enviable academic record and is looked upon with great favor by his faculty, but like case 36 he struggles with a sexuality which threatens him with confusion. What ideally might be done for these brilliant, overly sexed ectomorphs [that

is, flat-chested young men with narrow shoulders and lean muscle mass]? Certainly not early marriage, in the conventional sense, for with a predominant cerebrotonia and a good somatotonia they are too exploratory and too full of curiosity for early acceptance of monogamy, except perhaps at the expense of a general settling back and stifling of their best potentialities. A more open and better controlled prostitution? Another kind of marriage, more experimental or noncommittal in nature? These have been and still are interesting questions.[6]

At one point in the 1950s, a growing societal dialogue about "masculinity" prompted the tobacco industry to finance segments of Sheldon and Stevens's research. Cigarette manufacturers hoped to discover, for purposes of target marketing, whether men who smoked or their nonsmoking counterparts had what at the time was termed a stronger or weaker "masculine component." In a 1958 article in *Science* called "Masculinity and Smoking," Professor Carl C. Seltzer, a protégé of Sheldon's and a physical anthropologist at Harvard, described the term as "the element of masculinity in the individual as indicated by his external morphological features. The more the pattern of anatomical traits tends toward the extreme masculine form, the stronger is the masculine component."[7]

Even though Sheldon had left Harvard for Columbia University several years before, his research collaboration with Seltzer and Stevens continued, and Herrnstein participated as a research assistant in their work. Somatotyping lured the impressionable young Herrnstein into a world promising precision and human predictability based on the measuring of body parts.

Behavioralism and the "Baby Box"

Having completed his PhD in 1955, Herrnstein returned to Harvard after a three-year stint in the military. S. S. Stevens's work in somatotyping

still held an emotional allure. Even so, in a decision that broke Stevens's heart, the graduate student Herrnstein abandoned the professor of somatotyping in order to embrace Stevens's polar opposite and the rising star of Harvard's Psychology Department, Professor Burrhus F. Skinner (1904–1990). In later years, Herrnstein and Stevens maintained cordial relations, but the tense feelings they both harbored for one another could be seen in a note Herrnstein wrote Stevens in July 1963:

> Viscerotonic as I may be, I find that I am cerebrotonically apprehensively, hyperattentively, introvertedly troubled (in solitude) by your impression that I traffic in life's ephemera. It may be that the contempt I feel for viscerotonia is like what the kettle is feeling when it is calling the pot black, but what a shock it is to think so. You have filled me with resolution to prove, by deeds and not argument, that you are wrong.[8]

As Herrnstein moved deeper into B. F. Skinner's inner circle, he increasingly came to accept the older scholar's radical new catechism of environmentalism. Skinner aimed to improve society through systematic behavioral control and positive reinforcement. From his own research, the behavioralist had concluded that desirable behavior could be achieved through operant conditioning, or a system of rewards, punishment, and positive reinforcement. It had worked successfully controlling rats' and pigeons' behavior through food rewards at critical points. Skinner would have nothing to do with the psychotherapists' efforts to understand the inner person. In *Beyond Freedom and Dignity*, he asserted: "We do not need to try to discover what personalities, states of mind, feelings, traits of character, plans, purposes, intentions, or other perquisites of autonomous man really are in order to get on with a scientific analysis of behavior."[9]

So devoted did Herrnstein suddenly become both to Skinner as a mentor and to the scholar's behavioral theories that the younger professor,

against the protestations of his soon-to-be ex-wife, volunteered their one-year-old daughter, Julia, to become one of the first babies raised in Skinner's experimental "baby boxes." A crib-sized, acclimatized, and germ-free container, this device was intended to revolutionize child rearing by reducing a baby's exposure to the usual childhood maladies. Once placed in the box, the baby, wearing only a diaper, would remain in it until it reached the crawling stage and would have body contact with another human being only when taken out for feedings and diaper changes.[10]

A Meeting of Like Minds

It might have been the soothing note of mathematical divining that gained possession of Herrnstein one morning in February 1969, as the now tenured professor at Harvard began reading Professor Jensen's article "How Much Can We Boost IQ and Scholastic Achievement?" The University of California–Berkeley professor argued: "It appears that forces are at work which may create and widen the genetic aspect of the average difference in ability between the Negro and white populations, with the possible consequence that no amount of equality of opportunity or improvement of educational facilities will result in equality of achievement or in any improvement of the chances for the Negro population to compete on equal terms."[11]

Jensen pointed to statistics showing that black women below the poverty line have more children than white women in similar socioeconomic circumstances. This observation led him to pose the question: "Is there a risk that present welfare policies may lead to the genetic enslavement of a substantial segment of our population? Our failure seriously to investigate these matters may well be viewed by future generations as our society's greatest injustice to Negro Americans."[12]

The impact of Jensen's words resonated with Herrnstein, for whom ideas of human cognitive differences based on body type had been implanted early in his academic career, and he merely took the next step.

Over the course of the next two years, Herrnstein became increasingly preoccupied with researching racial differences in intelligence.[13] His academic work in experimental psychology had attained him such prominence in the field that nearly half of the articles in the *Journal of Experimental Analysis of Behavior* were based on his research findings, but his work could not compare in allure to the race and cognitive issues that Jensen posed.

Herrnstein's fascination with Jensen's work puzzled the former's colleagues. They saw little if any connection between the Harvard professor's pioneering research in experimental psychology with pigeons and the controversial Berkeley professor's racial research on IQ. One former colleague observed, "Dick [Herrnstein] was not a racist, as some have accused him of being. Dick was simply a snob."[14] However, so committed had Herrnstein become to Jensen's cause that he hankered to do more than merely defend him verbally against a growing barrage of critics. As in a painful rite of initiation, in which the new convert must bear witness to the faith with sacrificial offerings, Herrnstein sat down in the spring of 1971 and wrote "IQ," which the *Atlantic Monthly* published in its September issue. Herrnstein contended that intelligence is largely inherited, so no matter what efforts were made, egalitarianism as public policy would not work either with individuals or societal groups.

On the one hand, colleagues who had thought Herrnstein possessed the intellectual presence and diplomatic skills to become the dean of Harvard College someday were shocked at the insensitivity he exhibited in what was certainly one of the most incendiary articles ever written at Harvard in their memory.[15] Others characterized his actions as brittle and self-destructive. Herrnstein, on the other hand, felt the spiritual satisfaction of just having performed a holy rite. Part of the burden that he was therefore prepared to bear was the ingratitude of some members of the cognitive elite, those men and women who expressed revulsion rather than appreciation at what he considered to be an act of courage and forthrightness in "telling the truth."

Charles Murray, coauthor of *The Bell Curve*, once observed that because Herrnstein perceived his position as a tenured professor at Harvard to be the perfect job, he believed that it was somehow too good to be true and that there was a "catch." In Murray's eyes, his colleague had identified the catch: "You have to tell the truth."[16] Unfortunately, Herrnstein disdained the more introspective side of his chosen profession of psychology. It might have helped him realize that perceptions of what is true can be easily distorted by one's emotional needs.

In an interview the *New York Times* conducted that same year, Herrnstein discussed dysgenics, the fear that people of low socioeconomic status would outbreed those higher up on the scale. He predicted that an inborn lack of ability would bar those of low IQ from career success, thus creating a "biological stratification" of the population into castes based on "hereditary meritocracy."[17] To a reporter for the *Harvard Crimson*, Herrnstein also recommended gathering IQ information as part of the U.S. census, so that the government could make wise decisions about who should be mating with whom, should the need to limit population growth arise.[18]

Still fascinated with what he perceived to be ethnic differences in intelligence, by 1973 Herrnstein returned to the preoccupation with body image that had first lured him into the subfield of somatotyping. Later that same year the Atlantic Monthly Press published Herrnstein's book *I.Q. in the Meritocracy*. It was an angry book, yet it purveyed an almost spiritual tone of self-righteousness in parts. In its protracted introduction, Herrnstein detailed his persecution at the hands of left-wing zealots, who organized protests, circulated flyers calling for his resignation, and even pinned up posters asserting that he was "wanted" for "the fraudulent use of "science in the service of racial superiority, male supremacy, and unemployment."[19]

Herrnstein's book also gave him one more opportunity to ply his theories about race, inheritance, and intelligence. Herrnstein asserted:

We know how much to expect tall people to cluster in given families, which occasionally produce a basketball player when height combines with the other requisites. So it is for any trait that plays a significant social role and has some genetic basis. And if, for the sake of discussion, one grants the possibility that mental abilities do vary at all genetically, then a powerful and surprising conclusion follows—namely, that society may segregate people into social groupings or classes based at least partly on biology. For if mental capacity is to any degree inherited, and if social standing reflects mental capacity, then social standing must be a mirror, albeit an imperfect one, of inherited ability. . . . Equalizing educational opportunity may have the unexpected and unwelcome effect of emphasizing the inborn intellectual differences between people.[20]

Locked into a hierarchical mode of thinking, Herrnstein found himself increasingly obsessed with convincing the academic community that a cognitive elite did in fact exist and that blacks were permanently excluded on the basis of genetically transmitted cognitive deficits.

During this time, so enamored had the Harvard professor become with basketball that his Harvard colleagues anointed him with the nickname Hondo. The label flattered his ego. It tied Herrnstein to his sports hero, John (Hondo) Havlicek, a noted basketball player of European descent for the Boston Celtics. "Hondo" also referred to the 1953 film starring John Wayne, whose character mirrored the high moral values and strong sense of family that Herrnstein so much wanted his colleagues to believe that he also possessed. While maintaining an impressive research schedule in the conduct of groundbreaking experimental work on rewards and motivations using pigeons, he also found the time and took personal pride in chairing the Harvard University Athletic Committee, yet another outlet for an intellect fascinated with physicality, performance, body type, and genetics.

Jumping Tests and Unitary *g*

In 1980, Arthur Jensen published the eight-hundred-page volume *Bias in Mental Testing*, which he dedicated to Francis Galton, Alfred Binet, and Charles Spearman. Facing mounting genetic evidence to the contrary, Jensen attempted to build a case for genetic differences in intelligence among the races. Jensen at least did note the glaring contradiction but downplayed it, observing that "it is generally regarded by geneticists as a scientifically legitimate but unproved hypothesis."[21] Jensen also explicitly laid out *g* factors for general intelligence as well as for general athletic ability, which he believed correlated inversely among the races. Jensen apologized, however, for not having included in his testing procedure "jumping tests" or "aiming tests, such as throwing a ball at a target or 'making baskets' as in basketball; no dodging obstacles while running, as would be involved in football."[22]

Just as he had in 1971, Herrnstein again took up his pen to defend the beleaguered Jensen, this time in a 1982 *Atlantic Monthly* article. The Harvard professor emphatically agreed with Jensen's thesis, insisting as well that the technical literature also concurred "that genes account for most variation among IQs" even though he accused the media of transforming a scholarly consensus into something that appears to be the obsession of a disreputable fringe group.[23]

In 1984 at a conference on welfare policy following publication of Charles Murray's *Losing Ground*, Herrnstein sought out the policy analyst and congratulated him on his work. Smitten by Murray's irreverence for liberal norms, the Harvard professor suggested that Murray join him and Jensen in the controversial race-IQ crusade.[24] It was a period in Herrnstein's career when he felt sufficiently secure professionally to tackle several emotionally gratifying but hotly debated research areas. He had recently returned to the field that had enthralled him most as a graduate student, the work of S. S. Stevens and W. H. Sheldon on somatotyping, and was seeking evidence of temperament and sexual mores in body types.

Herrnstein and James Q. Wilson, a Harvard colleague, published *Crime and Human Nature* in 1985. They suggested a biological component to criminality, asserting that "among whites, being a mesomorph [muscular] is an indicator of a predisposition to crime. Young black males are more mesomorphic (5.14 on Sheldon's scale) than are young white males (4.29)."[25] The authors left it to the reader's own powers of analysis to decide whether mesomorphism equated with greater levels of criminality. However, to nudge this analysis along, Herrnstein and Wilson explained: "If blacks are more likely to have an impulsive temperament or a somewhat lower measured IQ, these traits may be the result of patterns of prenatal care as well as of inheritance."[26]

So convinced was Herrnstein that the methodology for all of his research work was soundly rooted in reality rather than in his own subconscious that he took it upon himself in 1988 to review a book titled *The Multiple Self*, edited by Jon Elster. Herrnstein expressed exasperation with the effort of colleagues who sought to understand the nature of the self. Using the analogy of a car and its driver, he expressed an unwillingness to define the action of humans by any index other than a person's actual behavior, commenting that "no driver can be seen entering or leaving Herrnstein." He then proceeded to devise a mathematical calculation emanating from his principle the Matching Law. He used these equations to quantify human behavior and motivation rather than attempt to understand it through psychoanalytic means.[27]

In May 1989 Herrnstein published a warning in the *Atlantic Monthly* that the intellectually gifted were having too few children while nonwhite populations were burgeoning. Ironically, his dysgenic argument regarding the oversexed and intellectually under-endowed races echoed the earlier warning of scholar Warren S. Thompson. In 1917 he wrote an article titled "Race Suicide in the United States" in which he warned that the more sexually active and inferior races—specifically, the Slavs, Jews, and Italians—would propagate wildly at the expense of Americans of northern European origin.[28]

Basketball's Inverse Correlation

Herrnstein also attacked a report that the National Academy of Sciences had commissioned on Black Americans. He insisted that the report refused "to consider the evidence concerning racial differences at the individual level." The Harvard psychologist also rejected the report's focus on the "discrimination model" to explain lingering racial inequalities in America. Rather, Herrnstein asserted that a "distributional model" would offer more accurate explanations for the problem by focusing not merely "on different opportunities available to people of different races" but, more important, on "the possibility that the different outcomes are also the product of differing average endowments of people in the two races." The Harvard professor concluded: "Thus the distributional model's adherents would consider possible differences in athletic endowments in explaining the disproportionate presence of black basketball players in the National Basketball Association [NBA]."[29]

By September 1991, the syllogism that had preoccupied Herrnstein, Shockley, and Jensen was being echoed in conservative quarters across the country.[30] That is, if one accepted the assertion that "white men can't jump," then it would be reasonable to assume that blacks' lower scores on intelligence exams would likewise be attributed to genetics. The preoccupation with blacks and basketball might have appeared an odd one for scientists. But as earlier emphases on phallic measurements had attempted to undercut the presumed masculine appeal of blacks by correlating it inversely to intelligence, the same effort was being made vis-à-vis basketball. So preoccupied had some scholars become on this issue that Professor Stephen Jay Gould once noted in this regard: "I can never give a speech on the subject of human diversity without attracting some variant of this ['white men can't jump'] inquiry in the subsequent question period."[31]

Professor Vincent Sarich, a supporter of Jensen's and Herrnstein's at the University of California–Berkeley, once asserted:

If you can believe that individuals of recent African ancestry are not genetically advantaged over those of European and Asian ancestry in certain athletic endeavors, then you probably could be led to believe just about anything. But such dominance will never convince those whose minds are made up that genetics plays no role in shaping the racial patterns we see in sports. When we discuss issues such as race, it pushes buttons and the cortex just shuts down.[32]

Professor Alan Ryan of Princeton, a staunch critic of Sarich's work, countered that the special preoccupations of Herrnstein, Jensen, Sarich, and others were perhaps inevitable because of the unidimensional way in which they approached the notion of human intelligence. According to Ryan, "The more you think that talk of IQ is talk of a mysterious something that possesses the same reality as visible qualities like skin color or the curliness of the hair, the more obvious it will seem that ethnic groups that differ in such visible qualities must differ in intelligence too."[33]

The preceding year, writing in *Science* magazine, Paul Selvin had commented: "There is no white Michael Jordan, one of the greatest basketball players ever to play the game, nor has there ever been one."[34] However, Yale University anthropologist Jonathan Marks was quick to point out in *Human Biodiversity: Genes, Race, and History* that this mode of thinking represented a false deduction. The fallacy inherent to this thinking emanates, according to Marks, from the fact that

it is trivially easy to infer positive ability from a positive performance, but it is exceedingly difficult to infer negative ability from a negative performance. To do so, we would need a comprehensive listing of the factors that might affect a performance—from endowments like eyesight and coordination, through simple variables of circumstance like financial and nutritional status, to complex developmental factors like parental attention, value systems, self-image, and aspirations.[35]

While blacks have certainly excelled at basketball, once the Chinese learned the sport, they too began to produce some NBA heroes such as Yao Ming, Yi Jianlian, and others. In *A Hard Road to Glory—Basketball: A History of the African-American Athlete in Basketball*, Arthur Ashe Jr. observed: "The sport became an obsession in many black communities in the late sixties and early seventies. And why not? Basketball players were the highest paid team sport athletes, and basketball courts were within walking distance of nearly every black American."[36] Herrnstein, Jensen, and others were applying a confused mode of racialist thinking to their assertions and making whatever cultural activities blacks were perceived to excel at to correlate inversely to intelligence.

In the spring of 1992, Herrnstein invited Professor Jean-Philippe Rushton, a younger colleague visiting from the University of Western Ontario, to breakfast at the Harvard Faculty Club. While there, Rushton introduced the Harvard professor to his own explosive theory of race, intelligence, and masculinity.[37]

5

THE COMMON DENOMINATOR

An estimated one million customers pass through the doors of Toronto's premier shopping mall, Eaton Centre, in any given week. Professor Jean-Philippe Rushton sought out subjects in its bustling corridors for what was surely one of the oddest scientific studies that city had known yet —one that asked about males' penis sizes. In Rushton's mind, at least, the inverse correlation among races between intelligence and penis size was irrefutable. In fact, it was Rushton who made the now famous assertion in a 1994 interview with *Rolling Stone* magazine: "It's a trade-off; more brain or more penis. You can't have everything."[1] Although he had convinced himself that this scientific principle of phalloplethysmography, or the "science" of penis measurement, was valid, he still felt a compulsion to generate empirical evidence that might convince others of the veracity of his theory. Using a grant from the conservative Pioneer Fund, the Canadian professor paid 150 customers at the Eaton Centre mall— one-third of whom he identified as black, another third white, and the final third Asian—to complete an elaborate survey. It included such questions as how far the subject could ejaculate and "how large [is] your penis?" Rushton's university, upon learning of this admittedly unorthodox

research project, reprimanded him for not having the project preapproved. The professor defended his study by insisting that approval for off-campus experiments had never been required before. "A zoologist," he quipped, "doesn't need permission to study squirrels in his back yard."[2]

But Rushton had not always been so controversial. Born in Bournemouth, England, in 1943, his early childhood years were spent in South Africa, where his father worked as a scenic designer. The family emigrated to Canada when Jean Philippe was thirteen years old. Returning to England to complete college, Rushton received a BS degree in 1970 at the University of London and a PhD in social psychology from the London School of Economics in 1973. After completing a postdoctoral fellowship at Oxford University the following year, he returned to Canada and found a teaching position at York University in Toronto.

During this period in his academic career, Rushton undertook research in the psychology of altruism from a social learning perspective. In 1980 he published *Altruism, Socialization, and Society*, in which he explored children's attitudes regarding generosity, posing questions about why they did not act selfishly or why they acted generously. The Canadian professor examined the standard social learning models to measure the differential influences of family, educational experience, and the mass media on children. In the course of this work, he also reviewed all the social learning literature, television models, *Sesame Street*, and research on the effects of television, family structure, and educational systems on the socialization of children.

The University of Western Ontario hired him in 1982 as an associate professor with tenure. Rushton was ready to begin exploring a completely new arena for research. His focus shifted from the psychology of altruism to racial differences in intelligence. By this time he had also gained notice in certain rarified psychology circles from scholars interested in exploring the biological imperatives of human behavior. Rushton had even attracted the attention of the renowned Harvard professor E. O. Wilson, whose research on the influence of genes on human

behavior led to two Pulitzer Prizes and publication of *Sociobiology: The New Synthesis* in 1975. Wilson's strong recommendation might have contributed to the up-and-coming young psychologist's also receiving a prestigious Guggenheim grant for $30,000 in 1986. During the same period, Rushton began a correspondence with Harvard psychologist Richard Herrnstein, then editor of the *Psychological Bulletin*, to which the Canadian wanted to submit some of his research.

It is not clear when Rushton first stumbled upon the tome, but by 1987, the Canadian professor began frequently citing the academically discredited work of a book published in 1898, *Untrodden Fields of Anthropology*, to bolster his argument that black males had smaller brains but larger penises than whites and Asians had. In their article "Race Differences in Sexual Behavior: Testing an Evolutionary Hypothesis," Rushton and coauthor A. F. Bogaert cited examples from the book:

> The ethnographic record {e.g., A French Army Surgeon (1898/1972), a 30-year specialist in genitourinary diseases} makes reference to numerous anatomical distinctions which show a similar pattern of whites being between blacks and Orientals. These include the placement of female genitals (Orientals front and high; blacks back and low); angle and texture of erection (Orientals parallel to body and stiff, blacks at right angles to body and flexible); salient buttocks, breasts, and muscularity (Orientals least, blacks most); and size of genitalia (Orientals smallest, blacks largest).[3]

Writing under the pseudonym Dr. Jacobus X, the author asserted that it was a personal diary that brought together thirty years of medical practice as a French government army surgeon and physician. Rushton was apparently unaware that the book, while unknown to American psychologists, was familiar to anthropologists working in Africa and Asia and that they had nicknamed the genre from which it sprang "anthroporn." Such books were not actually based on scientific research at all;

rather, they were a uniquely Victorian style of pornography, thinly disguised as serious medical field research. *Untrodden Fields* presented Jacobus X's observations and photographs of the presumably lurid sexual practices of exotic peoples, including photographs of the males' mammoth-size sexual organs.

The Canadian scholar had first caught the attention of the academic public in January 1989. Addressing a panel of the American Association for the Advancement of Science Conference, Rushton argued:

> East Asians, on average, were slower to mature, less fertile, less sexually active, with larger brains and higher IQ scores than Africans, who tended to the opposite in each of these areas. Whites, I found, fell between the other two groups. I further contended that this orderly tri-level hierarchy of races in average tendency had its roots not only in economic, cultural, familial, and other environmental forces but also, to a far greater extent than mainstream social science would suggest, in ancient, gene-mediated evolutionary ones.[4]

In the next fifteen years Rushton would pen dozens of articles in academic journals propounding his theories of an inverse correlation among the races between brain and genital size. Much of the data he used to "prove" the enormity of the black male organ, which he then correlated inversely to IQ, came from *Untrodden Fields*.

The Phallic Cult

Rushton's work was not exactly new to the academic arena. It called forth a corpus of nineteenth-century scholarship (see chapter 1), which purported to measure the presumably oversized black male phallus and derive inverse correlations from what was believed to be the smallness of the black skull. Critics contended that Rushton's work was neither creative nor innovative. Rather, the professor was simply quite proficient at

taking racialist generalizations and stereotypes from the previous century and repackaging them in a presumably scientific context.[5]

The ready audiences for such material, which tapped into sexualized racial prejudices, perceived themselves to be heroic warriors battling liberals and "political correctness." These individuals felt their own ethnocentric impulses had been forced underground by changing social mores as regards race and gender, and were thus eager to find scientific schemas offering justifications for their views.

So paranoid and yet fascinated were many white males with the notion of the stallion-like sexual performance of black males that at the turn of the twentieth century, it was not uncommon for those white southerners who lynched black males to mutilate their poor victims' genitals and castrate them as well. David M. Friedman, in *A Mind of Its Own: A Cultural History of the Penis*, documents not merely the Western obsession with the black man's penis but also the macabre lengths to which such fear and envy can go. He identified ritual castration as the final act of the lynch mob, explaining: "To really kill a black man, you first had to kill his penis."[6] Friedman devoted an entire chapter in his book to the ways in which white fears of sexual competition with black males had translated into a strange but enduring fetishism about the black male organ.

No evidence shows that racism motivated Rushton, but it undoubtedly might have fueled the reception his research findings received among diehard segregationists and the like. The impulses driving Rushton were more mysterious. He had certainly convinced himself that intellectual curiosity, pure and simple, sparked his work. However, as the number of his articles in academic journals continued to mount, a certain discernible pattern began to emerge. He contended that Asians were believed to have higher IQs and smaller penises than whites, who, in turn, had bigger brains but smaller penises than blacks had. He even went so far as to compute an "inbreeding depression score" to avoid confusion in the dysgenics community as to whom should be having babies with whom. This computational model compared the races in terms of the size of erect penises (by

length and circumference) and of flaccid penises, angles of penile erections, distances traveled by ejaculate, frequencies of engagement in cunnilingus and fellation, and the size of female breasts, buttocks, and clitorises. In presenting such findings, Rushton lamented on more than one occasion, "Restrained individuals may be out of place in uninhibited cultures and less able to attract partners, with an opposite pattern occurring for uninhibited people in restrained cultures."[7] And yet Rushton's ideas about what cultural practices represented "restraint" were purely subjective.

Cognitive Castration and Transcultural Psychology

In recent years a new discipline, "transcultural psychology," evolved. Its proponents studied, among other things, a unique range of illnesses that became quite real to their victims, but when looked at scientifically, they proved to be bound to and operational within prescribed cultural value systems. In the United States, anorexia nervosa was one especially tragic example of a culture-bound ailment. In the main, those who developed it were young white women, rather than Hispanics and blacks, not because of any particularities of genetic makeup, but because of the ways in which they had been socialized to perceive their female bodies.

Perhaps one of the most intriguing syndromes presenting itself within the context of particular cultural environment was *koro*, or the hallucinatory "disappearance" of the penis and the acute anxiety reaction associated with the (real or perceived?) shrinking of the penis, said to occur mostly in China, Japan, and Southeast Asia. The medical name for this disorder, genital retraction syndrome, and the bulk of the literature on the subject defined it as a purely subjective phenomenon.[8] A similar disease, known as penis snatching, has been known to occur in West Africa. The victim believes that sorcerers have bewitched him and caused his genitals to shrink or even disappear. According to a CNN report in January 1997, angry crowds had beaten to death seven sorcerers who had been accused of "grabbing penises" in Ghana's capital of Accra.[9]

It is indeed possible that what fueled American white males' anxieties regarding the imaginary proportions of the black male organ in relation to their own might have been simply another cultural disease similar to koro or the West African disease. It certainly could not be divorced from America's own peculiar history of race. White males' fears of competition from black males, exhibited in the strangely enduring preoccupation with the size of the black penis, gained its greatest impetus from slavery. But in the post–civil rights era, the same anxiety was at times transmuted into nonphallic objects. In contemporary America this obsession projected itself to the basketball court, with white males envying the prowess of black basketball players and other notable sports figures. But it never quite suppressed the white males' complementary obsession with losing the sexual competition with black males because they feared the black males' organs were larger their own. The more anxiety-provoking the fear of being "bested" by black males became, the more pressure the fearful white males unwittingly exerted on the scientific fringes. Thus, it became essential that science diffuse such fears. A self-selected group of scientists assumed responsibility, first, for proving that black males had larger penises than the white norm. Their second and more vital duty was "to cognitively castrate" minority males. In so doing, they assuaged any worries white males might harbor that females would mate with those allegedly tiny-brained, black behemoths.

As with koro, such preoccupations were neither rational nor scientific. As a consequence, they could not be resolved simply by measuring penises, regardless of how scientifically calibrated the measuring instruments might be. The enduring nature of this particular fetish was in many ways nothing more than a painful legacy of slavery itself.

Resurrecting Craniometry

In 1988, Rushton resurrected the long-dead or at least submerged pseudoscience of craniometry, or the measurement of human skull size as an

indicator of racial differences in intelligence. Citing the works of anthropologists Carleton Coon and F. Clark Howell, Rushton asserted that "the human races appear to differ both in average cranial capacity and in brain weight as well as on test scores and measures of economic success."[10]

Harvard professor Stephen J. Gould concluded in his landmark study of craniometrists that scientists do not necessarily have to engage in conscious fraud; they can mistake their unconscious prejudices for realities of nature. The process is often far subtler and involves situations in which researchers are honestly self-deluded in juggling evidence to suit their prior, but unacknowledged, prejudices. Gould also recognized that researchers operating within the "soft" science of psychology at times might suffer from "physics envy" in which they yearn for strict universal laws and, most damaging of all, unconsciously manipulate data through reifying it. The term "reifying" refers specifically to the tendency of researchers employing mathematical tools in their work to treat such mathematical abstracts as real entities.[11]

By 1989, Jean-Philippe Rushton was ready to go on the offensive. That January at the American Association for the Advancement of Science meeting in San Francisco, he presented a paper ranking Asians and whites as superior to blacks in intelligence, sexual restraint, and low levels of criminality. In the paper, Rushton argued:

> Genetic distance estimates calculated from DNA sequencing indicate that the races diverged at different times, and that this succession is matched by numerous other differences such that Mongoloids>Caucasoids>Negroids in brain size and intelligence, maturational delay, sexual restraint, quiescent temperament, and social organization.[12]

The academic audience, perhaps having assumed that racial eugenics had died with the Nazis' defeat in World War II, was visibly stunned. Not only did Rushton further assert that blacks had larger penises than

whites, he also presented additional variables such as intercourse frequencies, cranial capacity, and maturation rate.

Appalled at the haunting naïveté of Rushton's declarations, scientists were therefore compelled to expend precious time refuting his illogical sexual theories. It was indeed true that in the field of evolutionary biology, reproductive variables were believed ultimately responsible for virtually every genetic system that any species (including humans) displayed. But Rushton was unable to provide any real evidence of a racial component to the life histories that he examined, because his understanding of race was itself flawed. Just as Rushton had been seduced by the nineteenth-century notion of three human races corresponding to three "breeding populations" with distinctive cognitive and genital measurements, a sufficient number of insecure males within the general public were equally disposed to accept such ego-stroking theorems. These men were perhaps soothed by Rushton's "scientific proof" that while they indeed might suffer the shame of having small penises, at least in compensation they could brag about having bigger brains than their black counterparts did.

The use of factor analysis in the psychological research that Spearman, Jensen, Herrnstein, Rushton, and others undertook to prove an array of racial differences generated invalid conclusions. Quite simply, their analyses were predicated on a priori assumptions that were so deeply embedded in these researchers' frames of reference that they were unaware of their distorting effects on their findings.

Cognition versus Sex Appeal

In his work on racial differences in intelligence, genital size, and inhibitedness, Rushton also borrowed heavily from the now-outmoded theory of r- and K-selection. Geographers Robert MacArthur and E. O. Wilson devised this theory in the late 1960s to explain why certain species, such as weeds, had short lives and reproduced rapidly (r selected), while others, such as trees, had long lives and reproduced slowly (K selected).[13]

Rushton reinterpreted those findings and viewed blacks as "weeds," with high investments in reproduction and thus less to invest in bodily structures such as brain mass, thereby resulting in lower intelligence. Alternatively, according to Rushton, whites and Asians were "more 'tree-like' with high investments in brain mass and thus greater intellect, and lower inputs to reproduction."[14] In describing black Africans as r-selected, Rushton concluded that they had evolved high sexual and reproductive drives, while K-selected European and Asian populations were selected to have higher intelligence, in order to make the greatest possible use of their particular environmental resources.[15]

It is puzzling, however, that in this research, Rushton would have overlooked the simple arithmetic of the presumably inhibited Asian population. Numbering five billion, the Asian population is four times greater than that of the African continent. In fact, of the three races, as defined by Rushton, blacks were the smallest in population rather than the largest.

Rushton also attributed grieving patterns to this r/K selection theory, positing that blacks grieved less for the loss of a child than whites and Asians did. Rushton did in fact have a large body of literature to support his assertions, as race scientists in the early nineteenth century had made the same statements regarding the controversial practice of selling slave children away from their mothers.

Several of Rushton's former colleagues at the University of York insisted that he had misapplied the r/K model to human cultural traits. These professors quipped that while Gypsies could be described as cultural r strategists, "few would consider fortune telling, nomadism, tinkering or scrap dealing as genetic traits."[16] They also tried to remind him that in order to claim biologically based behavioral differences, he would first have to separate people into relatively homogeneous groups, a task that we now know to be biologically impossible. These scholars explained that genetic variation among Africans themselves was so high that "a West African is likely to be as similar genetically to a Central

European as to an East African. The superficial morphological similarities (hair type, nose shape, skin color) . . . do not indicate much about underlying genetic similarities and differences."[17]

Another vocal critic of Rushton's *r/K* selection theories was Professor Colin Groves (who wrote the foreword to this book). In an article titled "Genes, Genitals, and Genius," Groves noted that Rushton preselected growth and maturation data that supported his thesis and overlooked data that did not.[18]

Biologist Joseph Graves, who also dissected Rushton's application of *r/K* selection theory to humans, pointed out additional flaws in the Canadian psychologist's understanding of the concept. Graves noted, for instance, that Rushton's entire theory was promulgated on the highly dubious assumption that tropical (African) environments are less challenging than European or Arctic ones are. Because Rushton assumed, erroneously, that the African environments demanded fewer challenges to the survival of its populations than did European ones, he allocated superior cognitive skills to Europeans. Graves also noted that while Rushton suggested a negative correlation between body size and reproductive allocation, he then produced data asserting that black females were larger than white females but still possessed higher reproductive values.

Graves questioned as well Rushton's basic understanding of evolutionary biology. If intelligence, as Rushton and similar IQ researchers define it, was such an important feature for human survival and if intelligence was solely or mainly genetic, then no genetic variation for intelligence, according to Graves, would likely exist in the human species. As natural selection increases the frequency of beneficial genes, the genetically based variation for the traits they influence declines. Thus, all existing humans would share the high intelligence genes because natural selection would have eliminated low intelligence genes long ago. After noting several other contradictions in Rushton's work as well, Graves concluded that the most telling flaw in Rushton's application of

this theory to human behavior was the rather simple, straightforward fact that "there are no biologically definable 'races' [subspecies] in the human species."[19]

Another authority on r/K selection theory, Dr. Mark Feldman, a Stanford University population biologist, apparently became livid when he learned of the distorted uses to which Rushton had put the theory, which described evolutionary traits within animals and not socially constructed racial groupings. Feldman concluded that Rushton's work could not be classified as legitimate science and remarked, "It has no content, it is laughable."[20]

6
THE EUGENIC PARADIGM

In 1995, Rushton published his sixth book, *Race, Evolution, and Behavior*. He asserted in an italicized introduction to chapter 1:

> Is race real? Do the races differ in behavior as well as in body? Are such views just the result of white racism? Modern science shows a three-way pattern of race differences in both physical traits and behavior. On average, Orientals are slower to mature, less fertile, less sexually active, less aggressive, and have larger brains and higher IQ scores. Blacks are at the other pole. Whites fall in the middle, but closer to Orientals than to Blacks.[1]

The next paragraph in that chapter began: "White men can't jump. Asian men can't either." Rushton then launched into a discussion of racial differences in basketball and track, claiming, "The reason why Whites and East Asians have wider hips than blacks, and so make poorer runners is because they give birth to larger brained babies."[2] He offered no legitimate scientific evidence to support this assertion other than to cite Jon Entine's controversial book titled, *Taboo: Why Black Athletes Dominate*

Sports and Why We are Afraid to Talk About It and statistics found in Victorian-era pornography.

Later in *Race, Evolution, and Behavior*, Rushton summarized his findings of an inverse correlation between brain and penis size in a format in which he posed a question and then answered it:

Q: Doesn't the evidence on race and penis size come from 19th Century stories by racist Europeans in colonial Africa?

A: The earliest findings come from the Arabic explorers in Africa and one study by a French army surgeon originally published in 1898.[3]

Rushton also suggested that whites had evolved larger brains because it took greater intelligence to survive the northern climates relative to the tropics. That Rushton had no legitimate anthropological evidence for his findings—only the citations of his colleagues in the race science business, a medieval Arab traveler's account, and Victorian pornography—in no way dissuaded him from churning out articles communicating such biased theoretical interpretations.

His critics, such as Professors Marvin Zuckerman and Nathan Brody, suggested that the Canadian professor had merely ignored the role of culture and society in ethnic differences. They assumed Rushton was confusing genetics with cultural conditioning.

Had Rushton been working in social isolation, the academic community might have ignored his unusual research on penis size. But Rushton was far more fortunate. Not only had he found a network of congenial and supportive academics in Shockley, Jensen, Herrnstein, and others, but perhaps even more important, he also could tap into the latent racial and sexual preoccupations of society itself. Little had changed in the ensuing decades since Professor Calvin C. Hernton wrote a 1965 study of what he termed "the sexualization of racism" in American society. Describing the racial climate as being highly eroticized, he had asserted

that "the black man is portrayed as a great 'walking phallus' with satyr-like potency."[4]

By the mid-1990s when Rushton's book was first published, the contours of a tightly knit intellectual cult had solidified. Its adherents—all men, such as Arthur Jensen, Charles Murray, and Richard Lynn—rallied around Rushton, insisting that his work was serious scholarship, while many mainstream scholars dismissed the Canadian's research as racist psycho-pornography. The scholars involved in IQ research based on race evolved intellectual rituals and various other means of providing each other the emotional support that the outside world withheld. These academics perceived themselves as martyrs to the cause of unsettling racial truths. However, they shared more than mere intellectual interpretations of race, intelligence, and penis size. Perhaps most important, they shared the same disdain for introspection and the kinds of self-examination that might assist them in recognizing the subtle but powerful ways in which a failure to apply intrapersonal, interpersonal, and emotional intelligences might distort their comprehension of complex social issues.

Rushton produced collaborative research with like-minded colleagues on a frequent basis and they drew increasingly on one another's works and upon the academic outlet provided by *Mankind Quarterly*, a journal that Professor Robert Gayre of Edinburgh, Scotland, established in 1960. It published such articles as Raymond B. Cattell's "Virtue in Racism?" and Alan McGregor's "The Evolutionary Function of Prejudice," which were devoted to the controversial subjects of "race science" and the new eugenics movement. It promised some modicum of intellectual respectability to individuals whose tenacious hold of once popular but now discredited racial theories propelled them to the fringes of American society. For example, the quarterly's former editor, Professor Gayre, in his book *Teuton and Slav on the Polish Frontier*, had even gone so far as to echo Nazi propaganda and advocate the importance of improving the German nation through greater homogeneity and Nordic purity.[5]

Roger Pearson, a British-born anthropologist, settled in Washington,

D.C., and became editor of *Mankind Quarterly* in the late 1970s. A radical eugenicist, he had previously made a name for himself in eugenics circles by founding a series of organizations and publications including the Northern League, which he established in 1958. Pearson, who wrote extensively under the pseudonyms Stephan Langton and Alan McGregor, published a magazine between 1956 and 1963 called *Northern World*, and advocated strict antimiscegenation laws. His book titled *Essays on Eugenics and Race*, published in 1958, asserted that the white race's only salvation would be the introduction of a special breeding program to filter out inferior genetic stock.[6] In the 1960s he served as the editor of several other ultra-conservative magazines, including *The New Patriot* and *Western Destiny*. The former published such articles as "Every Aspect of the Jewish Question," "Early Jews and the Rise of Jewish Money Pioneers," and "Swindlers of the Crematoria."

Another energetic supporter of Rushton's, Dr. Richard Lynn, had taught in the Psychology Department of the University of Ulster in Northern Ireland and then served as an associate editor of *Mankind Quarterly* for more than fifteen years. One of the more colorful and intellectually aggressive figures in the group, he once called for the "phasing out" of the presumably inferior races, asserting that

> if the evolutionary process is to bring its benefits, it has to be allowed to operate effectively. This means that incompetent societies have to be allowed to go to the wall. This is something we in advanced societies do not at present face up to and the reason for this . . . is that we have become too soft-hearted. For instance, the foreign aid which we give to the under-developed world is a mistake, akin to keeping going incompetent species like the dinosaurs which are not fit for the competitive struggle for existence. What is called for here is not genocide, the killing off of the populations of incompetent cultures. But we do need to think realistically in terms of "phasing out" of such peoples. If the world is to evolve

more better humans, then obviously someone has to make way for them otherwise we shall all be overcrowded. After all, ninety-eight per cent of the species known to zoologists are extinct. Evolutionary progress means the extinction of the less competent. To think otherwise is mere sentimentality.[7]

Lynn not only concluded that blacks were less intelligent than whites but that women were more cognitively deficient than men, Scots possessed lower IQs than the English, and the Irish were more intellectually challenged than both the other European groups but not as much as Africans were. Professor Lynn insisted that his own background as a white Englishman played no role whatsoever in the conclusions he reached. He further theorized that the lower IQ of the Irish could be attributed to "selective emigration over the centuries with the brightest and the best having the gumption to make a better life out of Ireland."[8]

The Five-Million-Dollar Endowment

While these researchers seemed to take pleasure in presenting themselves as wronged martyrs for "truth," poverty was one vow no one demanded they take. To the contrary, their mission was a remarkably well-paid one. Race researchers shared in the financial generosity of the Pioneer Fund, which textile millionaire Wickliffe Draper, a man who considered the black race so inferior that he wanted all African Americans deported to Africa, had established in 1937.[9] During its early days, the Pioneer Fund threw its support behind the eugenics movement, encouraging the involuntary sterilization of the "genetically inferior." One of the fund's early directors, Harry Laughlin, wrote the Eugenical Sterilization Law, which became law in thirty states and "resulted in the forced sterilization of tens of thousands of people in the United States."[10] Testifying before Congress in 1924, he reiterated Henry Goddard's findings that "83 percent of Jewish immigrants were born feeble-minded and

therefore were a threat to the nation's economy and genetic makeup."[11] This IQ data thus was used to block the Jews fleeing pogroms in Russia and the later Holocaust in Germany from entering the United States.[12] Shortly before the outbreak of World War II, Laughlin also received an honorary doctorate from Germany's Heidelberg University in honor of his work in Nordic eugenics. Another fund director, Frederick Osborn, had also engaged in eugenics research, describing the Nazi sterilization law as "the most exciting experiment that had ever been tried."[13]

The fund's endowment, in addition to donations and other revenues, generated $1 million in annual income, which was awarded to the select group of IQ research recipients. The fund also donated to eugenic-minded political action groups and institutions such as the Jesse Helms Institute for Foreign Policy and American Studies. Professor Arthur Jensen received more than $1.1 million in research grants over the years; Richard Lynn, $325,000; and Rushton, $770,738. Michael Levin, a philosophy professor at the City College of New York, used a $124,500 award from the Pioneer Fund to conduct research proving that blacks were biologically wired to have fewer behavioral and sexual inhibitions than did the "superior races."[14]

Racial theories have always had social policy implications. This new eugenics did not prove to be an exception. Professor Michael Billig, in identifying the historical currents of race science, observed that scientific ideas did not develop in a vacuum but rather reflected underlying political or economic trends.[15] In the 1950s, the Pioneer Fund supported groups hoping to derail the landmark Supreme Court decision of *Brown v. Board of Education*, which outlawed racial segregation in education.[16] Ralph Scott, who also went by the alias Edward P. Langerton and was a professor of educational psychology at the University of Northern Iowa, used a grant from the Pioneer Fund in the 1970s to organize anti–school busing campaigns and conduct research purported to prove the connection between "forced busing and its relationship to genetic aspects of educability."[17]

Yet, the most telling evidence that the coordinates upon which IQ researchers based their correlations of masculinity—performance in sports—and of cognition were imaginary emanated from a hidden variable in the equation of race. And it was associated with neither whites nor blacks, but Asians.

7
THE ASIAN COEFFICIENT

Whereas nineteenth-century race researchers placed whites at the summit of the racial hierarchy, their late-twentieth-century counterparts rearranged the cognitive pyramid and relegated whites to the midpoint between Asians at the apex and blacks, once again, at the bottom. Richard Herrnstein, Charles Murray, Jean-Philippe Rushton, and other IQ researchers began to assert that Asians, not whites, represented the top of the IQ pyramid. The scholars used this representation of whites as more cognitively advanced than blacks but less than Asians to silence those critics who insisted that the race researchers' findings were ethnically self-serving. Rushton thus posed the question, "If my work was motivated by racism, why would I want Asians to have bigger brains than whites?"[1]

Professor John H. Relethford of the State University of New York suggested that the shift in the brain size hierarchy from whites at the top to Asians was little more than a ploy. He maintained that "European racially oriented researchers can now deflect charges of racism or ethnocentrism by pointing out that they no longer place themselves at the top."[2]

However, it is also possible that establishing the racial supremacy of whites was not what drove this research on racial hierarchies. If so, the

IQ researchers were probably justified in protesting their innocence, at least in regard to the charge of being racial supremacists, for in truth, the Asians' top ranking might have unintentionally underscored the true sexual preoccupations underlying this research in the first place. It now seems that the real driving force behind such work was not racial bigotry so much as it was the masculine insecurities emanating from the unexamined and sexualized stereotypes still present within American popular culture. Scholars such as Rushton, Jensen, and Herrnstein provided a scientific vocabulary and mathematically dense charts and graphs to give intellectual polish to these preoccupations. Thus, it became useful to tout the Asians' cognitive superiority but only so long as whites remained above blacks in the cognitive hierarchy.

Professor Fatimah Jackson of the University of North Carolina–Greensboro has spoken to this issue with remarkable forthrightness. She stated: "It is deemed acceptable for 'Mongoloids' to have larger brains and better performance on intelligence tests than 'Caucasoids,' since they are (presumably) sexually and reproductively compromised with small genitalia, low fertility, and delayed maturity."[3]

In recent years, social scientists in diverse academic fields have documented the pernicious stereotype Asian men faced in American society: the emasculated and feminized Asian-American male.[4] Often perceived as undersexed, they were thus perceived as minimal rivals to white men in the sexual competition for women. Underlying this fear is the presumption that in the end, the most appealing physical attributes will weigh more heavily with females than a male's money-earning potential, which is believed to correspond with IQ levels. National polls have confirmed the observation of the twenty-eight-year-old Samoan-Chinese American male who once lamented:

> It's annoying and energy-consuming to constantly speak up against
> stereotypes of black and Latino men as being sexually hungry, rav-
> enous beasts (white men are scared of them); and of Asian men as

being nerdy, asexual and gay (white men patronizing them). Do I have to mention that Asian men have 1000 per cent more pressure to "prove" their heterosexuality? Asian men are seen as not being capable of having power in general (because they are not seen as having sexual power), and black and Latino men are seen as not being able to handle power in general because they are seen as uncontrollable sexually.[5]

Harry Mok, another young Asian male, described what he called "The Asian Dating Dilemma" in hauntingly similar terms. Mok described the dominant Asian male stereotype within U.S. society as that of the asexual weakling and asserted that movies and television were rife with examples."[6] He used the movie *Fargo*, an Academy Award nominee for best picture of 1996, to make his point. Mok described the Asian character in the movie, Mike Yanagita (played by Steve Park), as the protagonist's "geeky, bespectacled pal . . . , [who] makes an awkward and desperate pass at his very pregnant friend. Later, he is shown to be a truly deranged individual." Mok also mentioned such popular movies as *Breakfast at Tiffany's, Bonanza, Sixteen Candles,* and *Miss Saigon* to underscore how routinely Asian males were portrayed in emasculated roles. On a more social note, he added, "Scan the personal ads, you won't find many women, Asian or otherwise, in search of a single-Asian male."[7]

Curtiss Takada Rooks, while an assistant professor of Asian American Studies at San Jose State University, made similar observations, identifying Asian American males' frustration at the tendency of Asian American females to marry outside their ethnic community at much higher rates than did their male counterparts. Dr. Rooks described societal images of these men as either "stern and misogynist" or "effeminate and nerdy."[8]

Jennifer Young Yim explored such negative stereotypes about Asian men in a 2009 doctoral dissertation titled *Being an Asian American Male Is Really Hard Actually: Cultural Psychology of Asian Amerian Masculinities*

and Psychological Well-being. In an article in *Jade Magazine*, a publication marketed to the Asian American community, a young Asian woman described the impact of the pervasive stereotypes whites have about Asians. She explained that she suffered from low self-esteem, as exhibited in her refusal to date Asian men as a teenager, having been influenced by white friends who persuaded her that Asian men were unattractive. Only after she began dating a young Chinese man in college did she stop judging herself from the images she presumed that others had of her "as a nerd, slut, dragon lady, or slave girl."[9]

If one carefully reexamined the work of Jean-Philippe Rushton, such underlying sexual stereotypes of Asian male emasculation permeated his writing. For instance, the Canadian professor asserted that "penis size varies moderately across populations, being largest among African populations, smaller among European populations, and smallest among East Asian populations." Rushton also asserted in *Race, Evolution and Behavior*:

> Racial differences are found in sexual permissiveness, thinking about sex, and even in levels of sex guilt. In one study, three generations of Japanese Americans and Japanese students in Japan had less interest in sex than European students. Yet each generation of Japanese Americans had more sex guilt than White Americans their age. In another study, British men and women said they had three times as many sexual fantasies as Japanese men and women. Orientals were the most likely to say that sex has a weakening effect. Blacks said they had casual intercourse more and felt less concern about it than whites did.[10]

Professor Emerita Audrey Smedley of Virginia Commonwealth University countered Rushton's assertions by pointing out that the Chinese had the most reproductively successful population in the world. Because of the high fertility rate, the Chinese government instituted the previously unheard-of limit of one child per family. Smedley noted sardonically:

"They got to number over a billion with small penises and presumably little interest in sex."[11] In identifying Asians as less sexually inhibited, Rushton seemed also to have overlooked the several-thousand-year-old tradition of erotic literature emanating from China and other Far Eastern societies. For societies that seemingly disdain sex, they certainly had a penchant for writing about it extensively.[12]

Shrinking Skulls and "Mongoloid Idiots"

The notion of the highly intelligent but desexualized Asian male had not always defined America's collective image of this immigrant grouping. Stereotypes could and did change over time depending on the historical and social context in which they developed. One of the most revealing studies ever written on the odd reshuffling of races in the so-called hierarchy of brain size was Professor Leonard Lieberman's article titled "How 'Caucasoids' Got Such Big Crania and Why They Shrank," which appeared in the February 2001 issue of *Current Anthropology*. Lieberman addressed the mystery of how whites could have been presumed to have the biggest brains in the nineteenth century, but by the late twentieth century, their skulls seemingly had shrunk to a size placing them just below Asians but still above blacks in the hierarchy of intelligence. Lieberman explained that in the 1980s, Caucasian superiority was brought into question by the economic vibrancy of Japan, Taiwan, Hong Kong, Singapore, and the Republic of Korea. Lieberman surmised that reversing the order of whites and Asians didn't much matter, because "the major function of racial hierarchies is justifying the misery and lesser rights and opportunities of those at the bottom."[13]

Just as the order of a cognitive hierarchy could change under the influence of a somewhat different set of circumstances, sexual stereotypes regarding Asian males also changed over time with shifting cultural attitudes. In the nineteenth century, Chinese, Japanese, and other Asian males were often portrayed in the popular press as a sexual danger to

virginal white females. Not surprising, as Lieberman has pointed out, during this era, American race scientists concluded that Asians had smaller brains than whites did. At the same time and most revealing, American children born with certain symptoms of mental retardation during this period were labeled "mongoloid idiots." Because the symptoms of this condition, which we now call Down syndrome, includes "slanting" eyes, the old label reinforced prejudices against Asians and assumptions that mental retardation was a peculiarly "mongoloid" racial characteristic.

The leader of the California nativist movement was an Irish immigrant named Denis Kearney, who fought successfully for passage of the Chinese Exclusion Act of 1882. Afterward, he turned his attention to what he perceived to be the scourge of Japanese American immigrants. Kearney asserted that Japanese males in American public schools were "fully developed men" who sought to "debauch their female classmates."[14]

Not surprising, intelligence research during this earlier period of American history came to the opposite conclusion from more recent stereotypes. Scholars identified Asians as being less cognitively evolved and having smaller brains and larger penises than whites. One direct consequence of this mode of thinking was the inclusion of Asians in antimiscegenation statutes forbidding interracial marriage "to preserve 'racial integrity' of whites."[15]

However, the stereotype became inverted when Congress passed the Page Act of 1875, which excluded Asian women from immigrating to the United States. While claiming to restrict immigration of "obnoxious immigrants," such as prostitutes and unskilled workers, it effectively excluded Asian women of childbearing age, including the wives of immigrants. This law resulted in the establishment of all-male households and the subsequent depiction of Asian men in the popular media as "neutered." According to Yen Le Espiritu in *Asian-American Women and Men: Labor, Laws and Love*, Asian men could attract neither Asian women nor white women. Thus the Asian male was desexualized by American

cultural imperatives. According to Professor Espiritu, "The existence of the Asian laundryman and waiter further bolstered the myth of the effeminate or androgynous Asian man."[16]

Geishas, China Dolls, and Dragon Ladies

While Asian men were stereotyped as neutered and desexualized, the all-too-common societal perception of Asian females was equally offensive, albeit different. In popular movies and books, they were portrayed as highly sexed and submissive characters of great mystery and exoticism. These characterizations were superimposed over another popular role for Asian women, namely, that of the scheming "dragon lady," and were represented in the daughter's role in Fu Manchu books and movies as well as the women in *The Year of the Dragon*.

This rigid stereotyping of the Asian female played what was perhaps the most provocative role of all in the IQ researchers' beliefs in racial hierarchies of IQ and penis size. *The Bell Curve*'s coauthor Charles Murray enjoyed recalling his romps as a consumer in the Asian sex trade during his Peace Corps days of the 1960s. *New York Times* reporter Jason DeParle interviewed Charles Murray shortly after the book's publication, and they traveled together to a conference in Colorado. Puzzled, DeParle commented that Murray "has been advertising his hormones throughout the trip."[17] For instance, DeParle observed that Murray referred to the Japanese airline hostesses on his flight as having offered him "everything short of a body massage." *The Bell Curve* author also took special note of "the shapely blond assistants" who staffed the seminar they were attending and mused that not having had sex with his sweetheart as a teenager "probably accounts for the twisted views I have today."[18]

Protestations to the contrary, Murray was obsessed with race and sex, even going so far as to characterize his research work as "social science pornography."[19] If there was any confusion about Murray's hyper-sexualization of the Asian female, it could be cleared up rather

quickly in noting the retort he once made to a critic who had accused him "of being 'preoccupied with sin.'" Murray rejoined: "No young man who spent as many years in Bangkok as I did can be against sex."[20]

8
THE RECIPROCAL FUNCTION

While many black intellectuals angrily dismissed the work of IQ researchers on race as pure bigotry, Professor Leonard Jeffries, a controversial professor of black studies at City College of New York, perused *The Bell Curve* and other such works with special care. These books spoke with remarkable forcefulness to the agenda Jeffries, an African American, had begun defining for himself. Easily recognized on campus, Jeffries moved purposefully, clad in flowing West African robes, all the while projecting the regal image of African kingship and the sense that he knew his self-worth. Having received a PhD from Columbia University and tenure at CCNY in 1972, Jeffries had now emerged as the lightning rod for Afrocentricity. An ideology that tied issues of black self-esteem to the ancient civilizations of Africa, in Jeffries' hands, it represented a powerful vehicle for stirring up nationalist sentiment among black students and, so he hoped at least, increasing their self-esteem in the process.

While Jeffries preached the Afrocentric theme on a growing number of college campuses across the country, he often butted heads with fellow CCNY professor Michael Levin of the Philosophy Department. Levin

sought support among whites both on and off the CCNY campus to but-tress his view that blacks were not only cognitively inferior but also genetically inclined toward criminality. Describing himself as a frequent victim of muggings by blacks, Levin refused to explore his subconscious motives, personality traits, or lifestyle issues that might have accounted for the unusually high number of times that he became a victim of gang-sters and street thugs. Rather, he asserted that not only were blacks less intelligent but also that they were also more criminally and sexually impulsive.[1] As with other colleagues in the IQ community, Levin's work was profoundly ahistorical. Thus he seemed to be unaware that in 1930 whites outnumbered blacks in prison by 3.5 to 1. It was doubtful that black cognition could have plummeted enough in thirty years to explain the radical change in prison statistics by the 1960s.

In a letter to the editor of the *Proceedings of the American Philosophical Association*, Levin had stated that "Black representation in a field can be expected, absent any discrimination, to decrease as the intellectual demands of the field increase."[2] Shortly after the 1994 publication of Herrnstein and Murray's *The Bell Curve*, which provided supposedly sci-entific evidence of black cognitive inferiority, Levin used a grant from the Pioneer Fund and wrote *Why Race Matters: Race Differences and What They Mean*. Reiterating *The Bell Curve's* arguments that genetics caused black underachievement, Levin's book also asserted that race was a basic category of biology, for which such behaviors as violent crime were hard-wired. Levin claimed: "Commentators should bear in mind the possi-bility that the readiness for violence displayed by American blacks was adaptive in ancestral environments—or, more precisely that the geno-type expressed as violence in contemporary white society might, once, have been expressed as some, possibly distinct, adaptive phenotype. In that event, black violence would neither need nor be amenable to cure."[3] Levin's observations merely overlooked the fact that Adolf Hitler was not black, nor were those who precipitated World Wars I and II, whose com-bined death toll numbered more than two hundred million.

Meanwhile, Levin shares many of his colleague Jean-Philippe Rushton's same preoccupations with black sexuality. In *Why Race Matters*, Levin remarked: "Assuming that more rapid sexual maturation, greater expenditure of energy in mating than parenting, more intense male competition for females, and lower levels of male engagement in child-rearing were differentially adaptive in black ancestral environments, present black levels of illegitimacy and abandonment are also normal."[4]

Using innumerable footnotes in an effort to overwhelm readers with the authoritativeness of his theories, Levin's book, at first glance, appeared to have an impressive and diverse group of scholars supporting his claims. However, upon closer examination, his sources turned out to be the self-same IQ researchers who had propounded such theories before: Jean-Philippe Rushton, Arthur R. Jensen, Richard Herrnstein and Charles Murray.

Two reviewers from outside that particular clique took issue with the book's conclusions as well as its confused organization and spelling errors. They quipped: "Fortunately for Levin, he lacks dark skin and is a white, Jewish, college professor. Otherwise, inability to read, copy or spell names accurately, copy and organize references, alphabetize an index and the general scholarly incompetence here documented would, if we were to apply his 'high' standards have to be interpreted as unmistakable evidence of Levin's own genetic inferiority."[5]

Following *The Bell Curve*'s publication and the ensuing public debate on black intelligence, Professor Jeffries seized the moment to develop a larger, more vocal audience than he had ever possessed in the past. It comprised African Americans who embraced Afrocentric writings to assuage their fearful and vulnerable feelings at the racism emanating from *The Bell Curve* proponents' new eugenics movement. Whereas such politically laden, Afrocentric dogmas had previously dwelt on the historical theme of Africa's great civilizations, it became increasingly preoccupied with theories of genetic defects in the white race. Jeffries also began to espouse his own theory of race. On the one hand, he described

whites as being "ice people," a cold, calculating, and materialistic race that emerged in prehistoric times from the caves of Europe and brought the world the three Ds: "domination, destruction, and death." Blacks, on the other hand, according to Jeffries, were "sun people," who were warm, generous, and humanistic, and their skin pigment, melanin, made them superior intellectually and physically.[6]

IQ researchers on race tended to be far too self-absorbed even to notice that their pseudoscientific research relegating blacks to a lower order of humanity was beginning to fuel an explosive and racially polarizing backlash. The most visible element of that backlash in the African American intellectual community became a new pseudoscientific paradigm called "melanism." Its dogma asserted that because blacks had more melanin, or skin pigmentation, than other groups had, they possessed superior traits that could be ascribed to the special properties of neuromelanin, a little-studied substance in the brain. According to the melanists, neuromelanin made the brain process information more quickly; thus, the darker your skin, the smarter you were. Also according to this theory, the more melanin in the skin, the more enriched would be the brain by dint of this substance's vital properties. It could presumably convert light and magnetic fields to sound and back again, and it could capture sunlight and hold it in a "memory mode."[7]

Melanin theorists such as psychiatrist Patricia Newton described the white race as suffering from a relative genetic-deficiency state. Speaking at a National Medical Association conference in 1993, Dr. Newton asserted that melanin possessed an exceedingly strong electromagnetic force field that surged when a person heard the beating of a bass drum. This surge caused melatonin to be released in the body, and, like endorphins, induced an opiate-like state, which gave one a sense of well-being.[8]

Unlike the racialist meanderings of IQ researchers, established academic journals neither accepted nor published melanist theories. They could occasionally be found in speeches posted to the Internet or in self-

published works, such as Carole Barnes's *Melanin: The Chemical Key to Black Greatness*. Carole Barnes claimed:

> Melanin is responsible for the existence of civilization, philosophy, religion, truth, justice, and righteousness. Individuals containing low levels of Melanin will behave in a barbaric manner. Melanin gives humans the ability to FEEL because it is the absorber of all frequencies of energy. Since whites have the least amount of Melanin, this is why they are perceived by People of Color as generally being rigid, unfeeling (heartless), cold, calculating, mental, and "unspiritual."[9]

And yet, the essential irony of the pseudoscientific debate on race was that the melanists tended to utilize the IQ researchers' same fount of information, although the two groups drew wildly differing conclusions. Dr. Wade Nobles, a professor of African American studies at San Francisco State University and leader in the melanist movement, explained in his book, *Seeking the Sakhu: Foundational Writings for an African Psychology*:

> That in the evolution of the species, in what some people call the ontogenetic evolution of humankind, that in the evolution of the species the human family separated in a sense that one branch of the family stopped its evolutionary path and simply depended upon the central nervous system as the total machinery for understanding reality. Whereas, the root of the family continued its path and not only evolved a central nervous system but developed what I called at that time an essential melanic system. And that I even went so far as to try to develop a little formula and suggested that CNS + EMS = HB. CNS (Central Nervous System) + EMS (Essential Melanic System) = HB (Human Being). That the central nervous system combined with the essential melanic system is what makes you human. That, in fact, to be human is to be Black.[10]

Using archaeological evidence, melanists such as the Canadian Michael Bradley, located the Neanderthals in Europe and not in Africa to assert that the Europeans' cognitive heritage had been contaminated by intermixing their genes with the slow-witted Neanderthals. His claims were presented in a book titled *The Iceman Inheritance: Prehistoric Sources of Western Man's Racism, Sexism and Aggression*. Bradley, who is of European heritage, argued that Neanderthal-Caucasoids (the term he used for humans of European ancestry) were more aggressive than other races because of ancient sexual maladaptations.[11] Bradley asserted:

> I believe that I can show that our converging contemporary crises, like racism itself, have their origins in the prehistory of the white race alone. We attribute various threats to our survival to "man's folly" . . . but this is a conscious and self-protecting euphemism. Nuclear war, environmental pollution, resource rape . . . all are primary threats to our survival and all are the result of peculiarly Caucasoid behavior, Caucasoid values, Caucasoid psychology. There is no way to avoid the truth. The problem with the world is white men.[12]

Not surprising, his book received no notice in academic journals, while the IQ researchers' articles were widely read, reviewed, and discussed. University of California–Los Angeles political science professor Eugene Victor Wolfenstein explained the academic space given to the Rushtons, Jensens, and Herrnsteins in the scientific world by noting: "American universities operate within a hegemonic, Eurocentric intellectual and political culture. As Michael Foucault would say, academic discourse is a power/knowledge relationship, in a double sense. The discourse reflects and enacts the values of society's ruling elites; it is internally structured to preserve the dominance of academic elites. In both regards, black nationalist and Afrocentric arguments tend to be marginalized, misrepresented, or not taken seriously."[13]

To counter the IQ researchers' assertions that blacks were cognitively inferior, the melanists also noted the work of Robert L. Williams, who had devised the Black Intelligence Test of Cultural Homogeneity (BITCH-100), which was first presented at the September 1972 Annual Convention of the American Psychological Association in Honolulu. A culture-specific test based on the cultural knowledge base of children growing up in the inner city, it was purposely biased to favor American blacks over American whites. Not surprising, black children scored dramatically higher than their middle-class white counterparts did.

While admitting that sickle cell anemia affected mostly African Americans, the melanists continued their ideological offensive against IQ researchers by noting a list of predominantly white health problems for which blacks were in the main immune: cystic fibrosis, skin cancer, anorexia nervosa, and osteoporosis. Similar to adolescents trading barbs on the school playground, the melanist–IQ researcher debate intensified, ripping at the already fragile seams of America's multiethnic society. They were both fighting to enlarge the audience for their dogmas, wrapping their respective ideologies in the methodology of legitimate science. And while colleagues on the CCNY campus and the public at large dismissed both Len Jeffries and Michael Levin as toxic crackpots, the men still found enthusiastic audiences for their respective racial preachments.

Melanism did not reflect the collective viewpoint of most African American scholars, just as the white supremacist theories of IQ researchers represented a marginal point of view among white academics. As did the critics of IQ researchers, black scholars who argued against melanism asserted that no scientific evidence whatsoever supported the contention that the color of a person's skin had a bearing on the efficacy of that individual's brain functioning. Biologist Joseph Graves suggested that the main error the melanists made was in confusing neuromelanin, which is found in the brains of all vertebrates, with melanin, which is found in the skin. The two compounds and the biological forces impacting genes for them are different.[14]

Growing Suspicions about Psychology

In 1994, psychologists Hope Landrine and Elizabeth A. Klonoff published *African American Acculturation: Deconstructing Race and Reviving Culture*, which explored race as a cultural rather than a genetic phenomenon. Drawing on evidence from sociology, anthropology, and other fields, they defined race as a social construct, that is, a concept whose boundaries were defined by societies rather than genetics. They also criticized academics in their own field for racializing psychology and in so doing discouraging African Americans from participating in so hostile a field. The professors claimed: "Since its inception, psychology has played a leading role in denying the existence of African American culture, in defining African Americans as a race and nurturing the concept of race, and in attempting to demonstrate that African Americans are intellectually inferior to Whites."[15] They added, "Why would African Americans want to major, let alone pursue graduate education, in a discipline that persists in trying to prove them inferior?"[16]

Landrine and Klonoff devised a scale to determine the degree of cultural identification an African American shared with the dominant white culture relative to the black subculture. In so doing, the two professors showed that cultural motives rather than DNA determined black attitudes and thus behavior in regards to such issues as IQ testing. In fact, these professors so commonly observed the disdain and alienation some blacks felt for the work of IQ researchers that the following assertion was included in their "African American Acculturation Scale": "IQ tests were set up purposefully to discriminate against Black People."[17]

9

THE PHALLIC EQUATION

When Yale professor Robert Sternberg first proposed the Triarchic Theory of Intelligence in 1985, members of the IQ research community disdained his work. In identifying three facets of human cognition, this new theory of intelligence undercut the preoccupation of Richard Herrnstein, Jean-Philippe Rushton, and others with the concept of g, which their IQ exams measured as a sole determinant of intelligence. Sternberg explained that analytical intelligence, one of the three intelligences that he defined, would correspond most closely with the IQ researchers' psychometric definition of intelligence. As Sternberg described it, the types of questions found in IQ exams that used analogies and puzzles to reflect the inner landscape of a person's mind measured analytical intelligence. The second intelligence, creativity, involved the use of insight, synthesis, and the ability to react favorably in unfamiliar situations. Incorporated under this rubric was experiential intelligence, which concerned how the individual ties his or her internal world to external realities. Third was practical intelligence, defined as "the ability to grasp, understand, and solve real life problems in the everyday jungle of life." Some might refer to this ability as "street smarts."[1]

In 1983 Professor A. W. Boykin offered one of the most cogent explanations of the ways in which the educational styles of mainstream culture devalued the more collaborative style mores of African American students. He explained:

> When children are ordered to do their own work, arrive at their own individual answers, work only with their own materials, they are being sent cultural messages. . . . When children come to confine their "learning" to consistently bracketed time periods, when they are consistently prompted to tell what they know and not how they feel, when they are led to believe that they are completely responsible for their own success and failure, when they are required to consistently put forth considerable effort for effort's sake on tedious and personally irrelevant tasks . . . then they are pervasively having cultural lessons imposed on them.[2]

When the American Psychological Association established a task force and charged it with examining the issues that *The Bell Curve* raised, its 1995 report reasserted Boykins's concerns. It stated that even though all African Americans do not share the black cultural system to the same degree, it nevertheless has a profound influence on that community. In failing to recognize the collision of value systems, the report concluded that educators unwittingly create a cultural conflict that alienates black children from the educational process. Boykin insisted that "one aspect of that process, now an intrinsic aspect of the culture of most American schools, is the psychometric enterprise itself." Boykin further argued that "the successful education of African-American children will require an approach that is less concerned with talent sorting and assessment, more concerned with talent development."[3]

This task force also presented a gentle reminder to its audience that only since the civil rights movement have new doors been opened to African Americans. Thus, African Americans may still face lingering elements of

discrimination. "It would be rash indeed," the report asserts, "to assume that those experiences, and that historical legacy, have no impact on intellectual development."[4]

In recent years, a growing number of studies have begun documenting the impact of ethnic culture on a range of issues. Stanford anthropologist Shirley Brice Heath conducted an important study comparing the way working-class whites and blacks in a North Carolina town socialized their children for literacy. White parents regarded it as their job to teach their children literacy skills in preparation for school, reading to their children from an early age and showing them how to extract information from the printed page. Black parents assumed the school would handle the literacy issues and focused on social matters. They did not read to their children; indeed, they did not even "teach" them language. Professor Heath noted that "black babies were, however, bathed in words and verbal play, perhaps explaining in part the new prominence of black novelists, playwrights and poets."[5] By contrast, the standards that IQ researchers used, when applied to American education, at times have been known to do more damage than good to youngsters who score high on IQ and other standardized tests but find themselves unable to function well in the real world and become enraged and confused by such failures. One of the most disturbing problems in American society today is the specter of "adult children," or individuals whose arrested emotional development and stunted practical intelligence compel them to stumble through life blinded by hubris. They are genuinely befuddled as to why their presumably high IQ scores have caused them alienation and career failure rather than success.

The most compelling refutation of theories of racial differences in intelligence is a book published in February 2009 titled *Intelligence and How to Get It: Why Schools and Cultures Count*. University of Michigan professor Richard Nisbett has written:

In fact, we know that the IQ difference between black and white twelve-year-olds has dropped to 9.5 points from 15 points in the

last thirty years—a period that was more favorable for blacks in many ways than the preceding era. . . . So, why is it that blacks historically score poorly on IQ tests, achieve low levels academically, and attain relatively low levels of occupational success? The evidence indicates that genes play no role in these facts.[6]

Differences in culture are not hierarchical. They can certainly become so, however, when a majority culture ignores, overlooks, or devalues the forms of intelligence that a minority culture values, even though the former could benefit greatly from giving more attention and respect to those neglected forms of human cognition. The real question that society's educators should be asking is, what produces the best long-term results for society? Should it be education conducted according to the narrow, linear, and analytical band of intelligence or a broader concept of cognition that encompasses the analytical while also preparing students for real-life situations?

Specimen Jars and Pseudoscience

How willing would society be to award millions in scant research dollars to researchers bent on determining whether large-breasted women have smaller brains than their flat-chested counterparts, whether blonds have lower IQs than anyone else, or for that matter, whether Lithuanians have larger penises than American psychometricians do? A community of scientists could ask an infinite number of questions. But they don't. Is their reluctance mere political correctness? Of course not. Their reluctance relates to the intersection between societal curiosity and a "scientific" basis for inquiring. The brawn-versus-brains preoccupation of IQ researchers is not science. It is rather a social fantasy that emanates from America's slave-holding past. The very process of dehumanizing African Americans by insisting on their cognitive inferiority tricks any unsuspecting researcher who operates from a racialized mind-set into mentally

enlarging the size of the black phallus by inversely correlating the two factors.

Contrary to Jean-Philippe Rushton's assertions, no scientific evidence indicates racial differences in penis size. Although the Canadian professor attempts to back up his theories with the report of a nineteenth-century French surgeon, contemporary anthropologists now dismiss the latter's findings as a once-popular form of Victorian pornography. Rushton also cites World Health Organization (WHO) statistics of condom usage.[7] However, a closer look at the WHO report from which his data is derived shows that its information on whites and blacks are taken directly from a 1979 report of the Kinsey Institute for Sex Research,[8] which did not use any research subjects from either Africa or Europe. Its penile measurements come from subjects identified solely as "Caucasian/USA" and "African/USA." The WHO report simply added penis measurements from Australia and Thailand. Rushton's third source of information on racial differences in penis size is the research he conducted using surveys of 150 male subjects at a Toronto shopping mall. That he can take such inadequate data and propound universal theories of penile size is clearly a testament to his own powers of imagination.

David M. Friedman, in *A Mind of Its Own*, explains this fanciful worldview of Africans having larger penises, as it relates to America's historic preoccupation with the black phallus: "It was stared at, feared (and in some cases desired), weighed, interpreted via Scripture, meditated on by zoologists and anthropologists, preserved in specimen jars, and, most of all, calibrated."[9] Friedman then adds: "And, in nearly every instance, its size was deemed proof that the Negro was less a man than a beast."[10]

There is a reason why the pseudoscience of astrology has been practiced for five thousand years and will most probably continue for at least another five thousand. It fulfills the human emotional need for certainty in an unpredictable world. When skeptics point to its inconsistencies, astrology's modern-day adherents borrow barely enough scientific vocabulary to make such beliefs convincing to the marketplace. In pseudoscience, the

premise never changes. When research data contradicts the hypothesis, the theory is merely revised or adjusted to fit the data.

As with astrology and other forms of pseudoscience, the work of IQ researchers preoccupied with race and masculinity does not meet a basic tenet of legitimate science—namely, falsifiability. Its findings are constructed in such a way that they can never be definitively disproved. Given the genetic advances of the twenty-first century, it is not even possible to divide humankind into three discrete races—whites, Asians, and blacks—a basic requirement for substantiating the work of Rushton and his colleagues. It is certainly true that "breeding populations" share inherited traits. But identifying a black American as a "Negroid" does not mean that such an individual would share more genetic commonality with a South African Zulu. In truth, the African American might share more forebears with a "white" IQ researcher and thus more "genetic closeness" given the high (but socially hidden) degree of ethnic mixing in America among Europeans, Africans, and Native Americans. Not surprising, Rick Kittles of the University of Illinois–Chicago and Kenneth M. Weiss, while at the National Human Genome Center at Howard University, have cautioned researchers in this field that "the Big Few races can seem real in samples of size N (Norway, Nigeria, Nippon [Japan], Navajo). That is, if one examines only the geographic extremes, differences appear large. . . . But if we look at geographically closer or intermediate populations, differences diminish roughly proportionately. Even our view of the Big Few might change were it not for our curious convenience of overlooking places such as India."[11]

A Genetic Fiction

New scientific developments have deeply weakened the legitimacy of race science, even though race researchers and their audiences perhaps don't quite realize it yet. In the field of human genetics, most scientists now understand that the white, Asian, and black races are genetic fictions.

This observation does not infer that at a glance you are unable to tell a Nigerian from a Norwegian. It does mean, however, to assume that a Nigerian will prove a more compatible blood donor to an anonymous Kenyan than the Norwegian would, for instance, because the Nigerian and Kenyan are both socially categorized as "black" is not merely wrong but also medically dangerous. The races don't exist as discrete categories into which people can be accurately categorized.

In *The Bell Curve*, though, Herrnstein and Charles Murray offered what had become for race researchers the identifying attributes of race or ethnicity: "Some ethnic groups nonetheless differ genetically for sure, otherwise they would not have differing skin colors or hair textures or muscle mass, the attributes inferred in the term 'ethnic group.' They also differ intellectually on the average."[12] The underlying presumption in Herrnstein and Murray's statement appeared to be that the differences in "skin colors, hair textures or muscle mass" represented a higher magnitude of human difference (and thus the criteria for racial categorization) than traits that were nonvisual, such as heart disease susceptibilities, pancreatic functioning, or blood type. In addition, they attempted to relate these visual traits directly and inversely to cognition.

The drawing of ethnic or racial boundaries presented hidden challenges in that it attempted to find biological ways to classify people that also fit with the categorizer's emotional suppositions about the groups being labeled as well as about him or herself. For example, in the civil war–ravaged African nation of Rwanda, the warring groups determined their opponents' race and ethnicity not by skin color but by height. Not surprising, the two African groups at war—the Hutu and Tutsi—characteristically differed in height, with the Tutsi being tall and lanky and their Hutu neighbors generally being shorter. To cite another case in European history, the blond, blue-eyed Vikings often used hair and eye color traits to identify their hapless Anglo-Saxon victims. In Nazi Germany, scientific studies validated the popular belief that the shape of the nose distinguished the Aryan from the Jew.

Because the aforementioned traits—height, hair and eye color, nose shape—were physical, they were also by definition "biological" or "genetic." However, societal preoccupations rather than fundamental differences in human biology laid a special challenge at the feet of geneticists. Society made the implicit demand that these scientists take whatever distinguishing "biological" trait or grouping of traits the dominant social group employed to differentiate itself from the vulnerable minority group within its midst and, from that social rather than scientific premise, construct distinct genetic packages. The point of the exercise was to search through the thousands of genetic markers distinguishing humans individually in a vain effort to identify a sufficient number of nonvisual genetic traits shared within the two disparate groups but not between them. The coup de grâce in this contortion of genetics was that the race researcher, in demanding that science identify these two racial packages, then posited a relationship between those particular physical traits and brain functioning. But herein lay the rub. Scientifically, these so-called racial packages of associated traits that were both physical and organic were a fiction. They simply did not exist as such. While individual human physical traits exhibited regional variations, they did not always do so in "packaged sets" of both visually observable and internal attributes.

James Shreeve explained the problem inherent in attempting to define races by sets of physical characteristics that clustered together with some degree of predictability in particular geographic regions. He noted that while most inhabitants of the Far East had epicanthic folds on their eyes, so did the Khoisan of southern Africa. In another example, if one were to take shovel-shaped incisors (the front teeth) as the distinguishing characteristic, then Asians and American Indians would be grouped together with Swedes.[13]

For these reasons most contemporary geneticists now refuse to play what is in essence a "fantasy game" rather than a scientific exercise, in which a perceptual oversensitivity to the physical attribute in question comes to invade our psyche like a fetish. Whichever physical attributes

(among the many thousands that humans hold in common) that so happen to occupy the highest rung in our emotional lives or that we have been socialized to take special note of—say, skin color rather than weight, hair texture rather than height—will become the boundary lines around which that particular society's racial categories will be drawn. Thus geneticists reject the notion that one or two traits can be isolated to distinguish one group of people from another.

Scientists have long noted that the original racial classifications propounded in the eighteenth century, and that IQ researchers today still accept, represented a scientific attempt to validate social and political convenience. Skin color became the category because that attribute could allow the drawing of boundaries between Africans who were designated for enslavement in perpetuity as opposed to those Europeans who were given contracts as four- to seven-year indentured servants. However, similar to a racial Rorschach test, we can now appreciate the ways in which this drawing of racial boundaries invariably described more about the mapper's preoccupations than it did about the presumed biological singularity of the groups being mapped. But why then do race researchers refuse to acknowledge legitimate genetics research, which so clearly makes this point? The ability to avoid the pseudoscientific traps presented in this book requires a person to recognize his or her "racial" attitudes, fears, prejudices, and most important, the projection mechanism by which even an ostensibly scientific person associates deeply entrenched stereotypes and insecurities with vulnerable minorities.

Athlete Envy

When race researchers such as Herrnstein, Rushton, and Vincent Sarich injected basketball into their assertions about racial differences in cognition, they were often responding to geneticists who contested the validity of IQ research categorized by race on the grounds that ethnic groups existed merely as a social or cultural, but not a genetic, reality. However,

at this delicate point in the exchange, invariably the IQ researchers would insert the potent visual imagery of blacks in sports: "If the races don't exist, then who in the hell are these dark behemoths on the basketball court?"

At precisely this critical juncture in the argument, one's emotional investments could seep into and distort an otherwise scientific investigation. Whether on account of the basketball player's impressive height or muscles glistening against mahogany, perspiration-oiled skin, the issue becomes one of emotional dis-identification. For the race researcher the contrast between "them" and "us"—or the out-group and in-group—apparently loomed monumentally large. Sarich, perhaps to reinforce the importance of visual categorization, points out: "If I took a hundred people from sub-Saharan Africa, a hundred from Europe, and a hundred from Southeast Asia, took away their clothing and other cultural markers, and asked somebody at random to go sort them out, I don't think they'd have any trouble at all."[14]

But let's examine this issue more closely. We could racially categorize approximately 20 percent of the world's population through visual inspection, using the individuals' most prominently displayed environmental adaptations to create the racial classifications. Even so, we would have to acknowledge that the physical traits held in common would not correspond with a neat cluster of genetic similarities. And then, too, what about the remaining 80 percent of the world's population? Some South Americans would not be readily distinguishable from Arabs or southern Europeans or fair-complexioned African Americans. Asiatic Russians would be confused with South American Indians and so forth. Because geographic adaptation is a gradual process, drawing racial boundaries around the regions where populations are visually identifiable will leave most of the world out of such classification schemes and thus invalidate such taxonomies for scientific purposes.

The dilemma becomes even more confounded as we attempt to penetrate surface traits and examine genetic variants. Which two individuals,

for example, might possess the greatest degree of genetic proximity:

a) a black American basketball player called Rudy Jones and a white American IQ researcher, whose name tag at scientific conferences reads J. P. Rushton;

b) Rudy Jones and a South African Zulu soccer player; or

c) J. P. Rushton and another white IQ researcher?

For a person conditioned to respond to America's particular racial categories, the answer would be laughably simple. However, a geneticist would almost certainly have the last laugh, because the most accurate answer—that is, "(d) there is no way to know from the information provided"—was not even included among the choices.

Given the hush-hush nature of family secrets or for that matter the hidden intimacies that so commonly occurred on Southern plantations, the black American basketball player and the white IQ researcher could turn out to be blood relations. In such a case, the men would share far more genetic material in common than two arbitrarily chosen white IQ researchers would with each other or the black American with the Zulu. The observable cues suggesting categorization by color, muscle tone, and height would be misleading, as they oftentimes are.

Even without being family related, the black basketball player and white IQ researcher might still possess more genetic material in common than the other choices provided in the previous question. For instance, the research of geneticists has pointed out that however visually striking, seemingly dissimilar, and perhaps even enviable the musculature of black basketball players may be, a white IQ researcher in medical distress might as readily find a compatible organ donor among a black member of the National Basketball Association as among a pool of white university colleagues. According to Paul Hoffman, a 0.2 percent difference in genetic material exists between any two randomly chosen people anywhere on the globe. Eighty-five percent of that 0.2 percent will occur

within any local group of people such as neighbors. "More than half (9 percent) of the remaining 15 percent will be represented by differences between ethnic and linguistic groups within a given race (for example, between Italians and French)." Only 6 percent of that 0.2 percent, or 0.012 percent, represent differences between the so-called races, such as Europeans and Asians. But even here, that difference will decrease to null if we examine Eurasians.[15]

In recent years, the lack of genetic evidence to prove the race researchers' assertions has tended to move them in the direction of postulating environmental rather than genetic explanations for their theories of white racial superiority. Because the researchers' conclusions of black cognitive inferiority never changed despite new and contrary scientific findings, we were faced with ever more rationalizations, which Daniel Goleman identified as "a favored defense among intellectuals, whose psychological talents include inventing convincing excuses and alibis."[16]

Race researchers posit that whites and Asians evolved larger brains (compared to those of blacks) because of the problems they faced surviving in the cold northern latitudes. If the degree of environmental challenges for survival purposes correlated with cognition (and no serious scientific evidence indicates that they do), then surely the Africans, in order to survive the severe challenges of their environment, would have evolved brains as large as beach balls.

Even more serious than the ecological confusion that race researchers exhibited was their deficit in emotional intelligence, which tended to promulgate stereotypes. The in-group became identified with a healthy range of physical and temperamental differences, while the out-group was identified with either one monolithic type or a set number of subtypes. Regarding black males, for example, sociologists have identified four prevalent stereotypical images: the sex stud, the athlete, the criminal, and the middle-class type. Because of the deeply entrenched nature of such racial stereotypes, the scientifically astute but emotionally unwary could all too easily entrap themselves in a subtle form of circular

reasoning that emanated from one's cultural conditioning. This potential trap involved a powerful filtering process that was quite capable of activating what John Hoberman referred to as "latent cultural fantasies" about certain groups being more athletic because they are less evolved and thus closer to animals. He noted: "It remains a cultural fact that Africans have a special place in the Western imagination as fantasy objects associated with physical vitality, and this makes them especially attractive to those in search of biological distinctions between the races."[17]

Those black males who did not fit the four stereotypical images, meanwhile, became invisible. Thus an observer, even a presumably scientific one, can become "selectively inattentive" to the facts that the majority of black males were not NBA material; that talented white males were prominent in a range of sports, including skiing, ice hockey, swimming; and that Chinese and eastern European basketball players also enjoyed success recently, as the game became more popular internationally. This issue of "selective inattention," defined by Daniel Goleman in *Emotional Intelligence*, described an emotional deficit in which perceptual distortions, or "blind spots," developed within a researcher's frame of reference. In *Vital Lies, Simple Truths: The Psychology of Self-Deception*, Goleman explained "selective inattention" as a defense against anxiety in which "I don't see what I don't want to see."[18]

Psychologists who specialized in human introspection, in contrast to race psychologists (who tended to disdain this less quantitative subfield), have noted that the more seriously individuals bought into the notion of "the racial other" the more likely were they to project their own hidden desires, envies, and insecurities onto this out-group. To be sure, with scientists as well as with lay people, one's beliefs could even devolve into an obsession. In this regard, Stephen Jay Gould had identified the concept of an idée fixe, which often underlay perceptual errors committed by the overzealous researcher, as a "persistent or obsessing idea, often delusional, from which a person cannot escape."[19] In the tragic case of

the prominent British psychologist Sir Cyril Burt, Gould observed that Burt reasoned well in a number of areas. But when he turned his attention to the issue of intelligence and cognitive differences among people, "the blinders descended and his rational thinking evaporated."[20]

However, the most emotionally potent form of self-deception that could contort race research was the seductively powerful false dualism.[21] This concept is exemplified by the Darwinian "law of compensation" and is deeply embedded both in the folklore of ancient Europe and in Western religious tradition. As a theological construct, the brain and mind represented the seat of humanity's God-nature, while the body became evil's saddle. So subtle and powerful was this dualism that until recently it had also permeated scientific inquiry into human behavior, underpinning the postulation of an inverse correlation existing between brain and brawn. The mind became disembodied and was then given an inversely proportionate relationship to a selected part of the body, such as skin color, musculature, or male penis size. Given the multiple organs in the human body, a researcher who constructed an inverse relationship between any two most certainly offered more insights into his or her thinking or values than into the research subject's anatomical functioning. For example, French culture placed a special premium on the liver, so it was not surprising that French scholars had sometimes created correlations between thinking and liver function. In American cultural folklore, we have seen a direct proportioning of musculature relating to athletic functioning and brain capacity when we expressed our admiration for the Grecian ideal of scholastic and athletic prowess. It coexisted quite comfortably with its brawn-versus-brain opposite. If we examined these situations more closely, determining which formula would be applied appeared to have to do with whether the research subject belonged to an in-group or out-group, that is, whether the researcher was emotionally able to identify with the subject and thus to anoint it with the stamp of possessing higher cognition.

Confusion over Forensic Evidence

Media accounts of forensic specialists identifying the "race" of a crime suspect based on DNA evidence sometimes confused the general public. The assumption was that actual genetic markers enabled the expert to distinguish the white, black, and Asian races. In truth, criminologists used statistical procedures and examined a wide range of genetic markers to offer a probability of certain geographic ancestry. If, for example, 40 percent of West Africans and 15 percent of Polynesians shared a particular allele—that is, different expressions of the same gene—and a forensics specialist designated a DNA fragment found in Harlem, New York, as belonging to an African American, the determination did not mean that the specialist actually identified a "race" gene. Instead, the specialist made an educated guess based on the fact that one is far more likely to find people of West African descent in Harlem than any at all of Polynesian ancestry. But in announcing the race of the perpetrator, the specialist might inadvertently mislead the general public into believing that race was something that could be clearly discerned under the microscope. Population groups, that is, people who intermarry for cultural and/or geographic reasons, share a genetic closeness. However, assuming that the world is made up of three races and each can be distinguished from the other is false. This is because the world is made up of many thousands of overlapping population groups. It is not a sure bet that those who share the same skin color will have more genetic similarities with each other than either will with a different population group. For instance, some Pacific islanders have kinky hair and dark skin. Thus a "race researcher" would tag that person as "black," meaning that the person's dominant ancestry is African. However, the Pacific islanders in question are actually descended from Chinese population groups, whose skin color and other outward features changed in having migrated to a tropical climate. So, a forensics expert attached to the New York Police Department would identify such a criminal based on DNA evidence as

being Chinese, not African, and would direct police investigators to Chinatown rather than Harlem.

Another issue that often confounded the public concerned the incidence of disease. For example, it is taken as a fact that African Americans suffer from sickle cell anemia, and whites do not. But alas, appearances can indeed be deceptive. On the one hand, East Africans emanating from nonmalarial areas did not possess the hemoglobin S protein responsible for sickle cell anemia, which is common in West Africa. On the other hand, coastal Greeks and East Indians (both of whom have been categorized as white) come from malarial regions and do have the hemoglobin S protein.

In today's world, growing populations in developing countries face ecological degradation and, in some cases, even starvation. Scientific research may offer some answers to their plight. Should those funds be diverted to taking a ruler to the male organs of the 2.5 billion men inhabiting this planet and correlating that measurement data with culturally biased IQ tests?

10
THE NEW CALCULUS

A great deal was written about Herrnstein and Murray's controversial book, *The Bell Curve*, after it came out in 1994, but perhaps only now that sufficient time has passed can we put this matter in true perspective. The book represented social Darwinism at its most persuasive in identifying a cognitive elite that the authors feel is or should be running America on behalf of intellectually handicapped minorities and lower-class people. Unfortunately, this book also drew from the "heads, I win; tails, you lose" methodology of race research. Blacks were relegated to the ranks of the cognitively inferior for possessing less earning power than whites did. As this book has shown, they also were downgraded a few additional notches because some black males excel at sports. IQ researchers further surmised that "the black race" possessed animalistic characteristics inversely proportional to intelligence. To buttress these arguments it became necessary for such academics to insist, even against genetic evidence, that the designations "blacks," "whites," and "Asians" were not cultural or geographic shorthands but rather identifiers of clearly bounded races or subspecies. But herein lay the rub and deep irony of this mode of thinking: Were the "races" truly noninterbreeding,

genetic subspecies, then "race research" never would have gained significance in this country. The many books on the subject, including *The Bell Curve*, would never have been written. Why? It is because the impulse for such work, the gasoline that fuels its flame, and the attendant preoccupation with phallic measurements and brawny black athletes that sustains it year after year and century after century are unexamined fears of the fraternity of academic males that engages in such research on black masculinity. Of course, women are degraded in the process, also, as the researchers' clear inference is that females choose mates solely on the basis of penis size and muscularity.

The tendency to justify racial and cultural stereotypes on the grounds that they reflect underlying biological differences has a distressingly long, sordid history in America. As soon as legitimate scientific exploration refuted one bogus theory, another always crept up to fill the breach. The same outmoded notions were merely recycled and revivified in more scientific- and mathematical-sounding phraseology. Thus contemporary IQ researchers have done little but rehabilitate the eugenic ideas of the nineteenth and early twentieth centuries for the benefit of modern audiences. As for the readers of such polemics, as long as humans rove this planet, there will always be a gallery of die-hards lapping up such scientific-sounding research to "prove" one's prejudices and to cater to unexamined insecurities and emotional neediness.

Normalizations and Lies

The most disingenuous element of the IQ charade involves a sleight of hand called test normalization. It goes back to an explosive problem South African psychometricians faced in the mid-twentieth century. A consistent 15- to 20-point IQ differential existed between the more economically privileged, better educated, urban-based, English-speaking whites and the lower-scoring, rural-based, poor, white Afrikaners. To avoid comparisons that would have led to political tensions between the two white groups,

South African IQ testers squelched discussion about genetic differences between the two European ethnicities. They solved the problem by composing a modified version of the IQ test in Afrikaans. In this way they were able to normalize scores between the two white cultural groups. English-speaking and Afrikaner children thus would appear to have the same IQ averages, avoiding both embarrassing and politically sensitive comparisons between the competing white South African communities.[1]

However, the normalizing of scores between the two white groups in South Africa occurred at the same time that American psychometricians continued to insist that the even smaller differential in IQ scores between blacks and whites in the United States was proof of hereditary differences in intelligence. It probably never occurred to Jean-Philippe Rushton that he might take penis measurements from the two white groups to explore whether an inverse correlation existed between their masculine traits and intelligence. In truth, the emotional investment of such scholars in creating a genetic hierarchy based on the particular definition of the races with which they were preoccupied was simply too large for rational discourse.

The method by which researchers normalized test score variants between American male and female students was even more instructive of the manipulative process that was in fact fundamental to the way IQ exams were constructed. From the beginning of intelligence test usage, the psychometricians who wrote the exams decided to "normalize" male and female scores. Professor G. Harrington explained the process:

> It was decided [by IQ test writers] a priori that the distribution of intelligence-test scores would be normal with a mean (X=100) and a standard deviation (SD=15), also that both sexes would have the same mean and distribution. To ensure the absence of sex differences, it was arranged to discard items on which the sexes differed. Then, if not enough items remained, when discarded items were reintroduced, they were balanced, i.e., for every item favoring males, another one favoring females was also introduced.[2]

It was also true, as Professor Emeritus Andrew Hacker of Queens College pointed out, that a political agenda often underpinned the test score manipulation known as "normalizing." He explained that American society had an unspoken understanding that it would not draw genetic distinctions between groups labeled "white." Not many decades before, however, social scientists had reveled in their capacity to develop a cognitive hierarchy of European groups. In fact, social scientists such as Henry Goddard and Carl Brigham insisted on the intellectual superiority of Nordics over whites from Mediterranean and Alpine areas.[3] American history books were rewritten to reflect these beliefs, suggesting that Europe's great civilizations of Greece and Rome developed through the migration of Nordic peoples to the Mediterranean region.

Professor Robert Guthrie's book *Even the Rat was White* revealed the invidious nature of bias underlying the process by which test scores were often normalized. He explained that when researchers observed black-white differences in IQ scores that they insisted that genetic rather than cultural differences were being revealed. But differences between white males' and females' scores prompted them "to normalize" the test. That is, the researchers noted which exam questions a test group consistently got wrong and deleted a sufficient number of those questions from the test to ensure that the two groups' test scores would prove essentially equivalent. Most important, the testers could not themselves tell which questions were gender-biased until they gave test questions to groups of males and females and then studied the results. How then could they insist with such force that no cultural biases existed in the IQ tests given blacks, who scored 15 points below whites?[4]

The earliest effort U.S. researchers took to investigate black-white differences using intelligence tests was made in 1897 when G. R. Stetson tested five hundred African American and five hundred European American public school children in Washington, D.C. Stetson's test consisted of four stanzas of poetry, which the experimenter read aloud and the children were required to repeat. In this exercise, of which little pub-

licity was made, the black children outperformed the white children. It was interesting to observe that researchers consequently determined that the memory technique was not a valid measure of intelligence.[5]

When psychometricians began giving IQ exams to adults, they ran into another embarrassing problem. People's IQ scores tended to go down as they aged. Dr. Al Siebert, who once administered IQ tests while serving as an intern at the juvenile court of Cleveland, Ohio, observed that "using Binet's formula, a 32 year old store clerk with an intelligence age of 16 would get an IQ of 50." Siebert then mused, "To avoid outraging taxpayers and politicians who already had doubts about psychologists, the test developers invented a statistical solution that let them fudge the results for adults." Siebert added that the "deck is stacked against minorities." Siebert explained that minorities were not given IQ scores from peer group norms. Rather, scientists used the cultural norms of the white middle class to evaluate the intelligence of other ethnicities and attributed the obvious resulting discrepancy to inherited genetic differences in cognition.[6]

The term "validation" was another critically important bit of jargon within the psychometric field, as was "correlation," which, when properly understood, exposed the underlying manipulativeness of the IQ testing apparatus. Validating a newly drawn-up IQ exam involved giving it to a prescribed sample population to determine whether it measured what it was designed to assess. The scores were then correlated, that is, compared with the test designers' presumptions. If the individuals who were supposed to come out on top didn't score highly or, conversely, if the individuals who were assumed would be at the bottom of the scores didn't end up there, then the designers scrapped the test.

Sports and More Sports

In recent years Professor Vincent Sarich at the University of California–Berkeley has taken up the gauntlet on the controversial issue of race, sports ability, and intelligence. In a book that Sarich coauthored with Frank

Miele, an editor at *Skeptic* magazine, the two researchers looked at the impressive performances of Kenyan athletes and asserted: "Recall the received dogma that 'bipedalism is such a critical aspect of the human adaptation that one would not expect to see great differences from either the individual to individual, or between populations.' Can anyone disagree that a factor of 1,700 [for Kenyan wins compared to that of whites] can legitimately be seen as a 'great difference'?"[7]

The authors then identified a bell curve–type distribution to compare the averages of Kenyans from the Kalenjin ethnicity to the rest of the world. Not surprising, Sarich and Miele concluded that "blacks" are more "bipedal" than other racial groups are. They simply overlooked the fact that runners from other parts of Africa did not perform well in long-distance races.

Most geneticists would not necessarily place Kenyans and Congolese in the same genetic space based on the mere fact that they shared dark skin coloring. In fact, scientists have concluded that Africans display greater genetic diversity than do all other population groups. Unfortunately, the timing of the 2004 publication of Sarich and Miele's *Race: The Reality of Human Differences* meant these two writers were silent regarding developments at that year's Olympics: the loss by men's basketball reigning gold medalists, namely, the U.S. men's team; the gold medal for China's Liu Xiang in the 110-meter high hurdles; and the gold medal for a European American named Jeremy Wariner in the 400-meter race. Genetic theories about black athletes tend to have the greatest currency when they are seen to excel. Race researchers make no such biological arguments, however, to explain the fact that whites win most Olympic gold medals.

Attempts to associate blacks with more animalistic traits, and black males with larger penises, oftentimes required an almost ludicrous twisting of facts. Thus theories that lumped all people of African descent together as a "race" (except, of course, for the ancient Egyptians) prevailed, even though they were without scientific foundation. East African

runners, women as well as men, from the Great Rift Valley of Kenya and Ethiopia continued to dominate marathons. But race researchers had no logical answers for why African Americans, also members of the "black race," excelled in such sports as basketball and sprints but did not participate widely in long-distance running. Jon Entine, author of *Taboo*, quoted Yale University geneticist Kenneth Kidd's explanation of the real reason for this phenomenon. Kidd said: "It's logical that to the degree that running fast has a genetic component, in any African population you'd expect to find more fast runners, more slowpokes and fewer ordinary runners in between than in the rest of the world."[8]

But was it possible that sports machismo was projected onto the supposedly pristine world of IQ research relating to presumed racial differences in cognition? Writing in the conservative *National Review*, Loren E. Lomasky lamented that the public seemed to support the "meritocracy" operating in basketball that favored black players, while the presumed meritocracy of intelligence that IQ researchers promulgated was roundly criticized.[9] Here again the unspoken assumption of an inverse correlation between intelligence and basketball acumen arose. Taking a historical perspective, however, blacks need not feel as though they are the only group ever singled out for opprobrium in relationship to basketball. Gary Younge, a reporter for *The Guardian* newspaper of London, reminded us that "when Jews were prominent in American basketball during the [19]20s and 30s the sports editor of the New York Daily News explained that 'the game places a premium on an alert, scheming mind, flashy trickiness, artful dodging and general smart-aleckness.'"[10]

In his 1997 book *Darwin's Athletes: How Sport Has Damaged Black America and Preserved the Myth of Race*, John Hoberman made the most convincing case yet that vulnerable white males in American society suffered deep emotional scars on account of the athletic prowess that black sports figures exhibited. In commenting on the stereotype of the "sexual athleticism of the black male," Hoberman observed, "The idea of a black physical precocity that might portend supernormal athletic feats has

lived on in medical and scientific journals as a set of credible observations with uncertain implications regarding adult physical performance."[11]

If blacks could excel at basketball, then why couldn't whites excel in intelligence? While certainly a politically delicate question, it was surely one deserving of a serious and thoughtful reply, especially given the primacy such issues as black athleticism, muscularity, and phallic size appeared to play in IQ research on racial differences in cognition. However, to obtain a scientifically rigorous answer, the process would demand that the questioner face specific injunctions or prerequisites as well as examine his or her innermost assumptions. For instance, and however much it might stick in the craw of IQ researchers, they would have to acknowledge that athletes—black or white—perform through a remarkable harmonizing of mind and body. Successful athletes are not mindless.

It has only been since the early 1990s that historians of science were beginning to recognize the ways in which emotions, which simmer beneath the threshold of conscious awareness, have a powerful impact on how humans in general—and some scientists, in certain instances—perceived and reacted to phenomena, even though the individuals might have no idea that their emotional filters were at work.[12] In fact, a high level of emotional literacy became a critical faculty in certain types of scientific endeavors, such as those involving human subjects rather than laboratory mice. Researchers recognized that their own subconscious projections could inadvertently lead to egregious errors in perception, as well as to illogical and pseudoscientific conclusions.[13] Neurologist Antonio Damasio in his book *Descartes' Error* has also observed: "I do not believe that knowledge about feelings should make us less inclined to empirical verification. I only see that greater knowledge about the physiology of emotion and feeling should make us more aware of the pitfalls of scientific observation."[14]

When examining the issue of blacks excelling disproportionately at basketball while whites scored higher on IQ tests, several emotional traps

lay in wait to ensnare the unsuspecting researcher who failed to bring a significant degree of personal self-awareness to this scholastic endeavor. Deficits in emotional intelligence, such as selective inattention, rationalization, stereotyping, and seduction by false dualisms, could lead to fallacies in logic if the researcher did not examine flaws in the underlying assumptions upon which the race research might be premised. In these cases, the researcher is not falsifying data, as sometimes happens within science; rather, the person's perceptions of reality "played tricks on them." A melanist, for example, could assert that because whites robbed banks at a dramatically higher proportion than blacks did, then bank robbing must be inversely correlated to intelligence. Of course, that finding is nonsense but only because the assertion itself didn't validate a sufficient number of scholars' underlying prejudices or emotional deficits.

As for the reasons black males excel at basketball while whites score higher on IQ tests, Professor Jason Osborne of the University at Buffalo, the State University of New York, might have uncovered a far more persuasive reason than the hierarchical theories of racial biologists. In a nationwide study of 15,037 white, black, and Hispanic teenagers, Osborne found that cultural influences impacting on self-esteem created disparities in academic and athletic goals: "[The] tie between academic success and a good self-image . . . plunges dramatically, to no link at all, among black boys. . . . Over the same four years, black boys are the only students whose self-esteem is increasingly tied to athletic skill and popularity."[15]

The Persistence of Race-Intelligence Theories

If IQ tests are so easily manipulated, why then have "racial" theories about genetic differences in intelligence persisted on the basis of test scores? The answer quite simply lay in the realm of emotional need. It was here that issues of self-knowledge and the mode of intelligence that Harvard professor Howard Gardner referred to as "intrapersonal" (knowing one's own motives and interior landscape) come to the fore. The capacity for

humans to deceive themselves is certainly a deficiency in intelligence, but no measure of it has ever been written on any IQ test. When researchers operate with impenetrable blinders distorting their work, they are displaying deficiencies in intrapersonal intelligence. An obvious example would be the case of race scientists Jean-Philippe Rushton and Richard Lynn, who were bent on creating an inverse correlation between what they saw as black males' inferior intelligence and their presumed phallic or athletic over-endowment. Whether the source of such blinders might have been their emotional insecurities or their unexamined fears of not measuring up to some imaginary standard, the end result was they finagled their research findings to fit their preconceived assumptions.

As the concept of g for intelligence, measured as a unitary number, receded into the background for many scholars, during the latter part of the twentieth century, the most convincing argument that humans might possess multiple forms of intelligence was found in the arcane theories of the IQ researchers themselves. Was it possible for a person to master one form of intelligence and fail abysmally at another? Of course it was. Or, more to the point, was the capacity to succeed at ice hockey reflective of genetically programmed low intelligence? In the past nobody would have asked such a ridiculous and insulting question, not because it was politically incorrect, but because whites did not represent a vulnerable minority group in this country. Indeed, the American public and scientists alike would have recognized the inane assumptions of the question itself. In truth, the very impulse to pose certain questions and not others, or even to ponder certain issues and not others, evolves from assumptions; and if they are not explored through self-examination, they will distort even the most scientific-seeming research efforts.

Over and over again IQ researchers posed the question of brawn versus brains: Why couldn't whites have higher intelligence since blacks are so clearly overrepresented in athletic prowess? However, missing from this mantra of IQ researchers was a quite simple insight into the impulses driving these academics to ask illogical questions. The even

more illogical answers emanating from their illogical questions represented the projecting of their own unresolved issues onto minorities.

Perhaps one of the most insightful attempts to explain the preoccupation among IQ researchers and others with muscles and basketball came from history professor Gustav Seligmann, a colleague at the University of North Texas. He observed: "Certain males have two problems with black basketball players, which don't arise with white ski champions. Firstly, the black players are paid enormous sums of money. Secondly, their flimsy tee-shirts accentuate the enviable muscularity of their physiques."[16]

Setting Standards

I set out to find out what drove IQ researchers and have come away from the experience convinced that vulgar racism is not the motivating force. The real impulse driving this work is more subtle, subterranean, and fantastic. After all, the quantitative nature of IQ tests could be very seductive indeed to the unwary. Psychologist Al Siebert came right to the point when he lamented that "psychologists have overemphasized tests they score high on. . . . [They] have not developed quotients for abilities they lack."[17] But it is precisely these deficits, whether in social skills, kinesthetic abilities, intuition, and emotional and practical intelligence, where IQ researchers fail so decisively and lack or overlook the intrapersonal intelligence to recognize either their own failings or the egregious distortions they engendered.

I believe deeply in standards. As I have investigated this subject, however, I have become ever more aware that the standards—not for blacks but for the IQ researchers themselves—are too low. The researchers refuse to employ the full range of cognitive tools and methodologies required to examine their chosen subjects with sufficient depth. Perhaps even more to the point, by whose standards, other than their own, do these guardians of IQ testing even purport to measure success?

In the world of race and IQ research, the methodological limitations that researchers perhaps unwittingly impose on their work cannot help but distort their findings and results. A primary language of the analytical-logical intelligence they recognize and value is mathematics. Yet however impressive, mastery of that language is mere child's play compared to the complexity required to integrate that form of intelligence with those forms that are more intimately related to the understanding of human behaviors. It is therefore not surprising that analytical scientists have made fools of themselves and tarnished hard-earned scientific reputations in misapplying their linear scientific models to correlating inversely black males' penis sizes and other criteria of animality to intelligence.

Society itself bears a heavy responsibility for setting standards of intellectual excellence commensurate with its values and needs. In the past, this setting of standards was mostly hidden from public view. But the complexity of life in the twenty-first century is demanding that we make conscious decisions based on society's genuine needs rather than on the misplaced cognitive methodologies of an academic cult.

Having closed the door on the twentieth century, it is perhaps time for us to ask ourselves a question with profound implications for our future: Should American society continue to hold minorities captive to research containing profound public policy ramifications when it is undertaken by academics whose methodological limitations disqualify them from perceiving their subjects rationally? This issue is not about political correctness, censorship, or racial paranoia. It is rather, at its core, an issue of academic standards.

Notes

Introduction

1 Stephen Ceci and Wendy M. Williams, "Darwin 200: Should Scientists Study Race and IQ? Yes: The Scientific Truth Must Be Pursued," *Nature* 457, no. 12 (February 2009): 788–89.

2 "The Elementary DNA of Dr. Watson," *London Sunday Times Magazine,* October 14, 2007.

3 "Nobelist's Speech Linking Sunshine, Sex Found Ignoble," *Berkeley Daily Planet*, November 25, 2000.

4 Adam Miller, "Professors of Hate," *Rolling Stone*, October 20, 1994.

5 Jonathan Leake, "DNA Pioneer James Watson Is Blacker Than He Thought," *Sunday Times*, December 9, 2007. The figure of 16 percent has been called into question by certain researchers. See Wikipedia article on Watson: "Some periodicals offered opinions on the matter. On December 9, 2007, a *Sunday Times* article reported a claim by deCODE Genetics that 16% of Watson's DNA is of African origin and 9% is of Asian origin. The claim to the provenience of Watson's (or anybody's DNA), which is at least 99.5% identical between any two humans, has to be understood in terms of a statistical model that explains the provenience of single-nucleotide

polymorphisms (SNP). Based on this model, the interpretation of SNPs in Watson's DNA was that 'we can conclude about one-sixth of his ancestors came from Africa within the last few hundred generations or so.' This method of analysis is fairly sensitive to errors in the sequencing of the individual's genome; deCODE's methods were not reported and details of the analysis were not published. According to deCODE's Kari Stefansson, the analysis relied on an error-ridden version of Watson's full genome sequence, and Stefansson 'doubts . . . whether the 16 percent figure will hold up,' adding that based on the data used 'it appears that Watson has two X chromosomes, which would make him a woman.'"

6 Isaac Asimov, "The Perennial Fringe," *Skeptical Inquirer Magazine* 10, no. 3 (Spring 1986).

7 See Syl Jones, "Interview with Dr. William Shockley," *Playboy*, August 1980, 69–102.

8 Jean-Philippe Rushton, *Race, Evolution, and Behavior: A Life History Perspective*, 2nd special abridged ed. (Port Huron, MI: Charles Darwin Research Institute, 2000), 7, http://www.charlesdarwinresearch.org/Race_Evolution_Behavior.pdf (accessed September 2009).

9 Al Siebert, "Darwinistic Elitism Is Idiotic," THRIVEnet.com, available at http://www.thrivenet.com/articles/iqidiocy.html.

1. The Inverse Correlation

1 Raymond E. Fancher, *The Intelligence Men: Makers of the IQ Controversy* (New York: W. W. Norton, 1985), 20.

2 Francis Galton, *Inquiries into Human Faculty and Its Development* (London: J. M. Dent and Company, 1908), 41.

3 Nancy Stepan, *The Idea of Race in Science: Great Britain, 1800–1960* (Hamden, CT: Archon Books, 1982), 132.

4 Daniel J. Kelves, *In the Name of Eugenics: Genetics and the Uses of Human Heredity* (New York: Knopf, 1985).

5 Morton Hunt, *The Story of Psychology* (New York: Doubleday, 1993), 220; and Fancher, *The Intelligence Men*, 38–39.

6 Calvin C. Hernton, *Sex and Racism in America* (New York: Doubleday, 1965), 176.

7 Anton Gill, *Ruling Passions: Sex, Race, and Empire* (London: BBC Books, 1995), 39.

8 John S. Haller Jr., *Outcasts from Evolution: Scientific Attitudes of Racial Inferiority, 1859–1900* (Chicago: University of Illinois Press, 1996), 39.

9 Stephen J. Gould, *The Mismeasure of Man* (New York: W. W. Norton, 1981), 32.

10 Andrew Hamilton, "The Negro: How He's Different, Why Whites Fear Him," *Science Digest*, October 1963, 10.

11 Gould, *The Mismeasure of Man*, 54. In 2011 a study conducted by six anthropologists at the University of Pennsylvania attempted to debunk Gould's claim that Samuel Morton manipulated (whether fraudulently or unconsciously) his skull measurements. The article appeared in the June 7, 2011, issue of PLoS Biology and was entitled "The Mismeasure of Science: Stephen Jay Gould versus Samuel George Morton on Skulls and Bias." Critics of the study have pointed to the fact that the majority of the scientist's work was left unscathed. But they have not touched upon the most significant flaw in the recent article. Quite simply, the six authors of the critique missed Gould's point. There is a reason why mainstream scholars do not devote themselves to measuring skulls as a means of determining which race is cognitively superior. It is because such efforts, however precise they may be presented mathematically, are an emotional trap, whose findings invariably confirm the biases of the measurer. Leonard Lieberman has written what is perhaps the most insightful article yet on this skull-measuring business. It is entitled "How 'Caucasoids' Got Such Big Crania and Why They Shrank," published in the February 2001 issue of *Current Anthropology*. Lieberman noted how all the nineteenth-century research on skull sizes placed Asians below Caucasians. However, studies conducted in the mid- to late-twentieth century, with nations like Japan and China filling a much more significant role in global affairs, suddenly showed Caucasian skulls to be smaller than Asian skulls. Those reasons are explored in chapter 7 of this book.

12   Ibid., 112; and P. V. Tobias, "Brain-size, Grey Matter and Race—Fact or Fiction?," *American Journal of Physical Anthropology*, 32, no. 1 (January 1970): 3–26.

13   Gould, *The Mismeasure of Man*, 60.

14   Ibid., 62–67.

15   Ibid., 99.

16   Ibid., quoted from P. Broca, "Sur le volume et la forme du cerveau suivant les individus et suivant les race," *Bulletin Société d'Anthropologie*, Paris 2 (1861): 139–207, 301–21, 441–46.

17   John Campbell, *Negro-Mania: Being an Examination of the Falsely Assumed Equality of the Various Races of Men* (Philadelphia: Campbell & Power, 1851), 124, where he cites a Mr. Lawrence, 369–75.

18   John H. Van Evrie, *Negroes and Negro "Slavery": The First an Inferior Race, the Latter Its Normal Condition* (New York: Horton, 1863), 89–91.

19   John H. Van Evrie, *Van Evrie's White Supremacy and Negro Subordination*, vol. 3, *The New Proslavery Argument,* part I, edited by John David Smith (New York: Garland Publishing, 1993 [1868]), 119.

20   William H. Tucker, *The Science and Politics of Racial Research* (Urbana: University of Illinois Press, 1994), 25.

21   Ibid., 28; and E. H. Clarke, *Sex in Education: Or, a Fair Chance for the Girls* (New York: Arno, 1972 [1873]), 82, 62, 70. A contemporary strain of such research is exhibited in E. O. Strassmann, "Physique, Temperament and Intelligence in Infertile Women," *International Journal of Fertility* 9 (April–June 1964): 311. He asserts the existence of a "basic antagonism between the scholastic type of intelligence and the reproductive system in infertile women . . . the bigger the brain, the smaller the breasts, and vice versa, the bigger the breasts, the lower the IQ."

22   Stefan Kuhl, *The Nazi Connection: Eugenics, American Racism, and German National Socialism* (New York: Oxford University Press, 1994).

23   For an in-depth examination of this research see Haller, *Outcasts from Evolution*; and R. M. Cunningham, "The Morbidity and Mortality of Negro Convicts," *Medical News* (Philadelphia), 64 (February 1894): 115.

24 Eugene S. Talbot, *Degeneracy, Its Causes, Signs, and Results* (London: W. Scott, 1898), 102; and Haller, *Outcasts from Evolution*, 52.

25 Dr. Jacobus X, *Untrodden Fields of Anthropology* (Paris: Librairie de médecine, folklore et anthropologie, 1898), cited in Richard Zacks, *History Laid Bare: Love, Sex and Perversity from the Ancient Etruscans to Warren G. Harding* (New York: HarperPerennial, 1994), 418–19. While this translation from the French identifies the man in possession of a "monstrous organ" as being of Bambara, West African, origins, other versions of the same text identify him as an Arab.

26 [Hunter] McGuire and [G. Frank] Lydston, *Sexual Crimes among Southern Negroes* (Louisville, KY: Renz & Henry, 1893), 110; and "As Ye Sow That Ye also Reap," *Atlanta Journal-Record of Medicine* 1, no. 3 (June 1899): 265–67.

27 "Genital Peculiarities of the Negro," *Atlanta Journal-Record of Medicine* 4 (March 1903): 844.

28 William T. English, "The Negro Problem from the Physician's Point of View," *Atlanta Journal-Record of Medicine* 5 (October 1903), 463; and Haller, *Outcasts from Evolution*, 51.

29 English, "The Negro Problem," 468; and Haller, *Outcasts from Evolution*, 51.

30 William Lee Howard, "The Negro as a Distinct Ethnic Factor in Civilization," *Medicine* (Detroit) 9 (June 1903): 423; Patrick Geddes and J. Arthur Thomson, *Evolution* (New York: Henry Holt, 1911); and Haller, *Outcasts from Evolution*, 55.

31 Robert Wilson Shufeldt, *America's Greatest Problem: The Negro* (Philadelphia: F. A. Davis Company, 1915), 99–100.

32 The explorer Serres quoted in Paul Broca, *On the Phenomena of Hybridity in the Genus Homo* (London: Longman Green Longman & Roberts, 1864), 28; and Haller, *Outcasts from Evolution*, 56.

33 Robyn Wiegman, *American Anatomies: Theorizing Race and Gender* (Durham, NC: Duke University Press, 1995), 96.

34 Hernton, *Sex and Racism in America*, 101. For a detailed analysis of pre-twentieth-century "sexualized racism," see Winthrop D. Jordan, *White Over Black: American Attitudes toward the Negro, 1550–1812* (Chapel Hill: University of North Carolina Press, 1968).

35 Stewart E. Tolnay, Glenn Deane, and E. M. Beck, "Vicarious Violence: Spatial Effects on Southern Lynchings, 1890–1919," *American Journal of Sociology* 102, no. 3 (November 1996): 789.

36 Robyn Wiegman, "The Anatomy of Lynching," *Journal of the History of Sexuality* 3, no. 3 (1993): 446.

37 Lisa Cardyn, "Sexualized Racism/Gendered Violence: Outraging the Body Politic in the Reconstruction South," *Michigan Law Review* 100, no. 4 (February 2002): 752, footnote 274. Cardyn also states in the same footnote: "Scholars speculate that sexual torture and mutilation, especially as they were applied to black victims, had become relatively commonplace by the turn of the century." See Richard Maxwell Brown, *Strain of Violence: Historical Studies of American Violence and Vigilantism* (New York: Oxford University Press, 1975), 214–18; Walter White, *Rope and Faggot: A Biography of Judge Lynch* (Notre Dame, IN: University of Notre Dame Press, 2001 reprint); Joel Williamson, *The Crucible of Race: Black-White Relations in the American South Since Emancipation* (New York: Oxford University Press, 1984), 183–89; and Richard M. Brown, "Legal and Behavioral Perspectives on American Vigilantism," *Perspectives in American History*, 95 (1971): 105–6.

38 "Castration Instead of Lynching," *Atlanta Journal-Record of Medicine*, 8, no. 12 (March 1907): 457.

39 Ibid.

40 J. A. Rogers, *Sex and Race: Negro-Caucasian Mixing in All Ages and All Lands*, 3 vols. (New York: J. A. Rogers, 1941), 146; and Aleš Hrdli ka, "Physical Differences between White and Colored Children," American Association for the Advancement of Science 47 (1898): 476. Please also see Hrdli ka, *American Anthropology* 11 (1898): 347–50, and bibliography in "Physical Anthropology: Its Scope and Aims" (1919), http://www.archive.org/stream/hrdlickaphysical00hrdl/hrdlickaphysical00hrdl_djvu.txt.

2. The Intelligence Quotient

1 Fancher, *The Intelligence Men*, 42.

2 W. E. D. Stokes, *The Right to Be Well Born, or Horse Breeding in Its Relation to Eugenics* (New York: C. J. O'Brien, 1917), 48–50, 223–24.

3 Tucker, *The Science and Politics of Racial Research*, 62.

4 Russell Jacoby and Naomi Glauberman, *The Bell Curve Debate: History, Documents, Opinions* (New York: Times Books, 1995), 451.

5 Charles B. Davenport Papers, Boston Society of Natural History, now in the Boston Museum of Science, 1920; Daniel J. Kevles, *In the Name of Eugenics: Genetics and the Uses of Human Heredity* (Cambridge, MA: Harvard University Press, 1995), 52; and Charles Davenport to John J. Burke, February 20, 1926, and "Record of Family Traits" for Davenport, in Charles B. Davenport Papers, John J. Burke file, Family Records file.

6 Tucker, *The Science and Politics of Racial Research*, 66; and C. B. Davenport Papers.

7 C. B. Davenport, "The Effects of Race Intermingling," *Proceedings of the American Philosophical Society* 56, no. 4 (1917): 366, cited from Tucker, *The Science and Politics of Racial Research*, 65.

8 Kevles, *In the Name of Eugenics*, 53.

9 A. S. Bix, "Experiences and Voices of Eugenics Field-Workers: 'Women's Work' in Biology," *Social Studies of Science* 27 (1997): 625–68.

10 See Charles E. Spearman, *The Abilities of Man: Their Nature and Measurement* (New York: Macmillan, 1927).

11 Ibid., 393–94; and Sante Naccarati, "The Morphological Aspect of Intelligence," *Archives of Psychology* 45 (1921).

12 Fancher, *The Intelligence Men*, 177.

13 L. S. Hearnshaw, *Cyril Burt, Psychologist* (Ithaca, NY: Cornell University Press, 1979).

14 It is not at all surprising that one of Burt's star pupils, Hans Eysenck, would come to the discredited scholar's defense. Eysenck, IQ researcher Arthur Jensen, and other scholars who have argued an inherited link to racial differences in intelligence contributed essays to N. J. MacKintosh, ed., *Cyril Burt: Fraud or Framed?* (New York: Oxford University Press, 1995). The attempt not only failed to bring the scholarly community back to embracing Burt, but it even suggested (inadvertently) that the

degree of fraud might have been more significant than previously thought.

15   Lewis M. Terman, *The Stanford Revision and Extension of the Binet-Simon Scale for Measuring Intelligence* (Baltimore: Warwick and York, 1917), 99, cited in Gould, *The Mismeasure of Man*, 191.

16   Lewis M. Terman, *The Measurement of Intelligence: An Explanation of and a Complete Guide for the Use of the Standard Revision and Extension of the Binet-Simon Intelligence Scale* (New York: Arno Press, 1916).

17   Fancher, *The Intelligence Men*, 131, cited from Otto Klineberg's *Negro Intelligence and Selective Migration* (New York: Columbia University Press, 1935).

18   Leon Kamin, *I.Q., Race, Behaviour, Genetics: Oh, What a Tangled Web We Weave! Inaugural Lectures* (Rondebosch, South Cape Town, South Africa: University of Cape Town, Department of Communication, 2001), 16.

19   Kevles, *In the Name of Eugenics*, 129.

20   Walter Lippmann, "The Mental Age of Americans," *New Republic* 32, no. 412 (October 25, 1922): 213–15; Walter Lippmann, "Tests of Hereditary Intelligence," *New Republic* 32 (November 22, 1922): 328–30; and Walter Lippmann, "A Future for the Tests," *New Republic* 32 (November 29, 1922): 9–11—cited in Kevles, *In the Name of Eugenics*, 129.

21   Ibid.

22   Cited in Tucker, *The Science and Politics of Racial Research*, 70.

23   Thomas Hunt Morgan, *Evolution and Genetics*, 2nd ed. (New Jersey: Princeton University Press, 1925), 206–7, cited in Kevles, *In the Name of Eugenics*, 133.

24   R. Pearl, "The Biology of Superiority," *American Mercury* 12 (November 1927): 260, cited in Tucker, *The Science and Politics of Racial Research*, 71.

25   Francisco J. Ayala and John A. Kiger Jr., *Modern Genetics* (Menlo Park: University of California at Davis, 1980), 724.

26   Quoted in Anna T. Poliakowa, "Manoiloff's 'Race' Reaction and Its Application to the Determination of Paternity" (State Institute of Public Health Commissariat, Leningrad, Russia), *American Journal of Physical Anthropology* 10, no. 3 (July–September 1927).

27 See Joseph Graves, *The Race Myth: Why We Pretend Race Exists in America* (New York: Dutton, 2004), 8.

28 Tucker, *The Science and Politics of Racial Research*, 72.

29 Margaret Mead, "Group Intelligence Tests and Linguistic Disability among Italian Children," *School and Society* 25 (April 16, 1927): 468, cited in Kevles, *In the Name of Eugenics*, 135.

30 Tucker, *The Science and Politics of Racial Research*, 151.

31 Ibid., 165.

32 Ibid., 161.

3. The Regression to the Mean

1 Shirley Thomas, *Men of Space: Profiles of the Leaders in Space Research, Development, and Exploration*, vol. 4 (Philadelphia: Chilton Company, 1962), 195.

2 Jerry Hirsch, "To Unfrock the Charlatans," *SAGE Race Relations Abstracts* 6, no. 2 (1981): 40. Hirsch writes: "Bardeen has told me (December 1966) that Shockley had a nervous breakdown in 1951. When he subsequently remarried, it was to a woman who 'has taught psychiatric nursing both in hospitals and at Ohio State University.'" Also see Thomas, *Man of Space*.

3 Frederick Seitz's opinion appeared in a November 30, 1990, letter in the British journal *Nature*. The contemporary field of neuroscience has also documented the occurrence of personality changes conditioned by severe trauma to the brain's frontal lobe. The possible correspondence of dramatic personality changes and head trauma has a long history. The most famous probably is that of railroad worker Phineas Gage. In 1848, an explosion sent a railroad spike through the frontal lobe of this man. Even though he survived the trauma, his once passive personality became transformed into one of constant rage. While medical records were not available to this researcher, it is nevertheless possible that Seitz's theory regarding the effects of Shockley's injury are certainly possible.

4 Ibid.

5   William Shockley, speech before the Cleveland City Club in 1975, William P. Shockley personal papers in Roger Pearson's *Race, Intelligence, and Bias in Academe* (Washington, DC: Scott Townsend, 1991), 189.

6   Jones, "Interview with Dr. William Shockley." According to the NNDB (Noble Names Data Base), at http://www.nndb.com/people/106/000026028, Shockley was "one of the 'gifted' children studied by Lewis Terman in his pioneering but racially-tainted work with intelligence tests."

7   John L. Moll, "William Bradford Shockley: February 13, 1910–August 12, 1989," in *Biographical Memoirs* (Washington, DC: National Academy of Sciences, 1995), 305–24, http://www.nap.edu/openbook.php?record_id=4990&page=305.

8   Michael Rogers, "Brave New William Shockley," *Esquire* 79, no. 1 (January 1973): 130, 150–53.

9   See David Plotz, *The Genius Factory: The Curious History of the Nobel Prize Sperm Bank* (New York: Random House, 2005).

10 Ellen Goodman, "Genius Is More than Good Genes," *Boston Globe*, March 6, 1980.

11 See Frank Miele, *Intelligence, Race, and Genetics: Conversations with Arthur R. Jensen* (Boulder, CO: Westview Press, 2002), 9. The author states: "[Jensen] soon realized, however, that no matter how much or how hard he practiced, he lacked the 'special something' required to make it to the peak of the musical world. So Jensen switched career paths, entered the University of California at Berkeley, and majored in psychology."

12 Pearson, *Race, Intelligence, and Bias in Academe*, 142.

13 See Joseph Graves, *The Emperor's New Clothes: Biological Theories of Race at the Millennium* (New Brunswick, NJ: Rutgers University Press, 2001).

14 See A. R. Jensen, "What Is the Question? What Is the Evidence?," in *The Psychologists*, vol. 2, ed. T. S. Krawiec (Oxford, UK: Oxford University Press, 1974), 222.

15 Hirsch, "To Unfrock the Charlatans," 9.

16 Arthur Jensen, "Race and Genetics in Intelligence: A Reply to Lewontin," *Bulletin of the Atomic Scientists*, May 1970.

17 Arthur Robert Jensen, *Educability and Group Differences* (New York: Harper & Row, 1973), 324.

18 See Robert L. Hayman, *The Smart Culture: Society, Intelligence, and Law* (New York: New York University Press, 1998), 289.

19 Jensen first made this argument in an article titled "Social Class, Race, and Genetics: Implications for Education," *American Educational Research Journal* 5, no. 1 (January 1968): 22.

4. Seductive Reasoning

1 Ron Rosenbaum, "The Great Ivy League Nude Posture Photo Scandal," *New York Times Magazine*, January 15, 1995. Also see "Nude Photos of Yale Graduates Are Shredded," *New York Times*, January 29, 1995.

2 Earnest Albert Hooton, *Crime and the Man* (Cambridge, MA: Harvard University Press, 1939), 250–52.

3 George Hersey, an art history professor at Yale University at the time, wrote these words in a letter to the editor of the *New York Times* that was published July 3, 1992, under the headline "A Secret Lies Hidden in Vassar and Yale Nude 'Posture Photos.'"

4 Patricia Vertinsky, "Embodying Normalcy: Anthropometry and the Long Arm of William H. Sheldon's Somatotyping Project," *Journal of Sport History* 29, no. 1 (Spring 2002).

5 William Sheldon, *Varieties of Delinquent Youth: An Introduction to Constitutional Psychiatry* (New York: Harper Brothers, 1947), 820–91.

6 W. H. Sheldon, *The Varieties of Temperament: A Psychology of Constitutional Differences*, with S. S. Stevens (New York: Harper & Brothers, 1942; reprint, Hafner Publishers, 1970), 311. This book represented a follow-up to *The Varieties of Human Physique: An Introduction to Constitutional Psychology* (New York: Harper, 1940), in which W. H. Sheldon, S. S. Stevens, and W. B. Tucker related somatotype to food preferences, mating behavior, differences in dress, and racial differences in genital size, to wit: "It is said that the penis of the Negro is larger than that of the White. . . . The writer's impression from ample observations is that the American hybrid has not been markedly affected in this respect by his infusion of white blood, but suitable

data are lacking." In an earlier study written in 1924, Sheldon had already reached the conclusion that "Negro intelligence" comes to a standstill at about the tenth year and that of the Mexican at about age twelve.

7　Carl C. Seltzer, "Masculinity and Smoking," *Science* 130, no. 3390 (December 18, 1959): 1706–7. The Tobacco Industry Research Committee supported this study, which appears to have laid the groundwork for smoking campaigns targeting men whose masculine insecurities might lead to greater receptivity to cigarette-smoking campaigns validating symbols of strong masculinity, such as with the rugged Marlboro Man on horseback theme.

8　Note from R. Herrnstein to S. Stevens, July 10, 1963, Harvard Archives, Cambridge, MA.

9　B. F. Skinner, *Beyond Freedom and Dignity* (New York: Knopf, , 1972), 12–13.

10　Lauren Slater, in her popular book *Opening Skinner's Box: Great Psychological Experiments of the Twentieth Century* (New York: W. W. Norton, 2004), claimed that B. F. Skinner's daughter Deborah had been deeply traumatized by her "baby box" experience, became psychotic, and had to be institutionalized. Deborah Skinner Buzan wrote an angry rebuttal in the *Guardian* of London (March 12, 2004) and insisted that she loved her father, enjoyed a healthy childhood, and has been the subject of completely spurious rumors aimed at tainting the image of her famous father. Nevertheless, modern child psychology now emphasizes the vital importance of parental nurturing and body contact between primary caregivers and children.

11　Arthur R. Jensen, "How Much Can We Boost IQ and Scholastic Achievement?," *Harvard Educational Review* 39, no. 1 (Winter 1969): 10.

12　Ibid., 11.

13　Richard J. Herrnstein, "IQ," *Atlantic Monthly* 228 (September 1971): 43–64.

14　Personal interview with Professor Leon Kamin, Northeastern University, Boston, August 28, 1995.

15　Personal interview with Professor David Riesman, professor of sociology, Harvard University, Cambridge, MA, September 11, 1995.

16 Charles Murray, "On Richard Herrnstein," *National Review,* October 10, 1994.

17 William K. Stevens, "Doctor Foresees an I.Q. Caste System," *New York Times*, August 29, 1971.

18 Andre Joseph, *Intelligence, IQ, and Race: When, How, and Why They Became Associated* (San Francisco: R & E Research Associates, 1977).

19 Richard Herrnstein, *I.Q. in the Meritocracy* (Boston: Atlantic Monthly Press, 1973), 22–23.

20 Ibid., 9–10.

21 Arthur Jensen, *Bias in Mental Testing* (New York: Free Press, 1980), 58.

22 Ibid., 208.

23 R. J. Herrnstein, "IQ Testing and the Media," *Atlantic Monthly* (August 1982): 72.

24 Jason DeParle, "Daring Research or 'Social Science Pornography'?: Charles Murray," *New York Times,* October 9, 1994.

25 Richard J. Herrnstein and James Q. Wilson, *Crime and Human Nature* (New York: Simon & Schuster, 1985), 469.

26 Ibid., 466.

27 R. J. Herrnstein, "Lost and Found: One Self," *Ethics* 98, no. 3 (April 1988): 573–74.

28 Warren S. Thompson, "Race Suicide in the United States," *Scientific Monthly* 5, no. 1 (July 1917): 22–35.

29 R. J. Herrnstein, "Still an American Dilemma," *National Affairs* 98 (Winter 1990): 4.

30 Paul Selvin, "The Raging Bull of Berkeley," *Science* 251, no. 4992 (January 25, 1991): 368–71.

31 Stephen Jay Gould, "Ghosts of Bell Curves Past," *Natural History* 104, no. 2 (February 1995): 12–19.

32 Jon Entine, "Breaking Taboos in the Publishing Industry: The Struggle to Get *Taboo* Published," *American Renaissance* 11, no. 2 (February 2000), http://www.amren.com/ar/2000/02/.

33   Alan Ryan, "Apocalypse Now?," November 17, 1994 in Jacoby and Glauberman, *The Bell Curve Debate*, 15; and *New York Review of Books*, November 17, 1994.

34   Selvin, "The Raging Bull of Berkeley," 368–71.

35   Jonathan Marks, *Human Biodiversity: Genes, Race, and History* (New York: Aldine de Gruyter, 1995), 109–10.

36   Arthur Ashe Jr., *A Hard Road to Glory—Basketball: A History of the African-American Athlete,* with Kip Branch, Oceania Chalk, and Francis Harris (New York: Amistad Press, 1993), cited in Marks, *Human Biodiversity*, 242.

37   Personal interview with Professor Jean-Philippe Rushton, University of Western Ontario, London, Ontario, September 6, 1995.

5. The Common Denominator

1   "Professors of Hate," *Rolling Stone*, October 20, 1994.

2   Ibid., 6; and Alan Bass, "Philippe Rushton," *London Free Press*, January 13, 1990.

3   J. P. Rushton and A. F. Bogaert, "Race Differences in Sexual Behavior: Testing an Evolutionary Hypothesis," *Journal of Research in Personality* 21, no. 4 (1987): 536–37. In *Race, Evolution, and Behavior*, Rushton posed a question: "Doesn't the evidence on race and penis size come from 19th Century stories by racist Europeans in colonial Africa?" He answered it by saying, "The earliest findings come from the Arabic explorers in Africa and one study by a French army surgeon originally published in 1898."

4   Jean-Philippe Rushton, "The New Enemies of Evolutionary Science," *Liberty* 11, no. 4 (March 1998): 31–35.

5   Joseph Graves Jr. has pointed out that trade-offs have been found to exist in various biological species between energy devoted to reproduction and investment in body tissues (see "What a Tangled Web He Weaves: Race, Reproductive Strategies, and Rushton's Life History Theory," *Anthropological Theory* 2, no. 2 [2002]: 131–54). However, that this is true within the human species, or that different human racial groups

might illustrate the trade-off in different ways, is where he takes issue with Rushton.

6 David M. Friedman, *A Mind of Its Own: A Cultural History of the Penis* (New York: Free Press, 2001), 128.

7 Jean-Philippe Rushton, "Race Differences in Behaviour: A Review and Evolutionary Analysis," *Journal of Personality and Individual Differences* 9, no. 6 (1988); and David Buss, *Evolutionary Psychology: The New Science of the Mind* (Boston: Allyn and Bacon, 1999).

8 See http://weber.ucsd.edu/~thall/cbs_koro.html and Robert Todd Carroll, *The Skeptic's Dictionary*, s.v. "koro," http://skepdic.com/koro.html (accessed December 2011). Carroll's website states: "Koro is a psychological disorder characterized by delusions of penis shrinkage and retraction into the body, accompanied by panic and fear of dying. This delusion is rooted in Chinese metaphysics and cultural practices. The disorder is associated with the belief that unhealthy or abnormal sexual acts (such as sex with prostitutes, masturbation, or even nocturnal emissions) disturb the yin/yang equilibrium which allegedly exists when a husband has sex with his wife, i.e., during 'normal intercourse.' This disturbance of metaphysical harmony (loss of yang) manifests itself in penis shrinkage. Yang is the vital essence of the male and when inappropriately expelled, it is believed, the result is a potentially fatal dose of koro.

"Koro is also thought to be transmitted through food. In 1967, there was a koro epidemic in Singapore after newspapers reported cases of koro due to eating pork which came from a pig that had been inoculated against swine fever. Not only did pork sales go down, but hundreds of koro cases followed. The power of the press to cause panic was matched by their equal power to quell the imbalance they had caused. They gave ample access to the Singapore Medical Association and Ministry of Health who convinced the people that koro was a result of fear, thus ending the epidemic."

9 See "7 Killed in Ghana over 'Penis-Snatching' Episodes," CNN Interactive, January 18, 1997, http://www.cnn.com/WORLD/9701 /18/briefs/ghana.penis.html.

10 Rushton, "Race Differences in Behaviour," 1012.

11 Gould, *The Mismeasure of Man.*

12 Jean-Philippe Rushton, "Race, Genetics, and Human Reproductive Strategies," *Genetic, Social, and General Psychology Monographs* 122 (February 1, 1996).

13 See Robert H. MacArthur and Edward O. Wilson, *The Theory of Island Biogeography* (Princeton, NJ: Princeton University Press, 1967).

14 Rushton, "Race Differences in Behaviour," 1018–19.

15 Ibid.

16 Fredric Weizmann et al., "Discussion: Eggs, Eggplants and Eggheads: A Rejoinder to Rushton," *Canadian Psychology/Psychologie canadienne* 32, no. 1 (1991): 44.

17 Ibid., 46.

18 C. P. Groves, "Genes, Genitals, and Genius: The Evolutionary Ecology of Race," in *Human Biology: An Integrative Science*, ed. P. O'Higgins and R. N. Pervan (Nedlands, Australia: University of Western Australia, Centre for Human Biology, 1991), 428–29.

19 Graves, "What a Tangled Web He Weaves."

20 Dr. Mark Feldman, CBS Radio interview, February 18, 1989; and Barry Mehler, "Foundation for Fascism: the New Eugenics Movement in the United States," *Patterns of Prejudice* 23, no.4 (1989).

6. The Eugenic Paradigm

1 Rushton, *Race, Evolution, and Behavior*, 7.

2 Ibid.

3 Ibid., 45.

4 Hernton, *Sex and Racism in America*, 6.

5 See Lt. Col. G. R. Gayre and Robert Nigg, *Teuton and Slav on the Polish Frontier: A Diagnosis of the Racial Basis of the Germano-Polish Borderlands with Suggestions for the Settlement of German and Slav Claims* (London: Eyre and Spottiswoode, 1944).

6 Roger Pearson, *Essays on Eugenics and Race* (Coventry, UK: Northern World, 1958).

7 See Richard Lynn, review of *A New Morality from Science: Beyondism*, by R. B. Cattell, *Irish Journal of Psychology* 2, no. 3 (Winter 1974): xvii and 482.

8 Professor Lynn made these remarks in an interview with reporter Gerry Moriarty, "Stirring Things Up in Coleraine," *Irish Times*, May 10, 1995, 13.

9 William Tucker, *The Funding of Scientific Racism: Wickliffe Draper and the Pioneer Fund* (Urbana: University of Illinois Press, 2002), 5.

10 Michael Swanson, "The Bell Curve and Eugenics," October 20, 1995, 6, http://www.hartford-hwp.com/archives/45/026.html (accessed September 2009).

11 Ibid., 5.

12 See Margaret Quigley, "The Roots of the I.Q. Debate: Eugenics and Social Control," *The Public Eye*, March 1995. Dr. Quigley writes: "Laughlin had been appointed the Expert Eugenics Agent for the House Committee on Immigration and Naturalization by the committee's chair, Congressman Albert Johnson. . . . The immigration restrictionists were motivated by a desire to maintain both the white and the Christian dominance of the U.S. A year after the eugenicists . . .[secured the] passage of the 1924 Immigration Restriction Act, which established entry quotas that slashed the 'new immigration' of Jews, Slavs and southern Europeans."

13 Harry Laughlin to C. Schneider, August 11, 1936, Harry Laughlin Papers, Northeast Missouri State University, Kirksville; and Frederick Osborn, "Summary of the Proceedings of the Conference on Eugenics in Relation to Nursing," February 24, 1937, American Eugenics Society Archives, Philadelphia.

14 Letters to the Editor, *Wall Street Journal*, January 9, 1995; and Adam Miller, "The Pioneer Fund: Bankrolling the Professors of Hate," *Journal of Blacks in Higher Education* 6 (Winter 1994–1995): 58–61.

15 Michael Billig, "A Dead Idea That Will Not Lie Down," *Searchlight*, July 1998, http://www.ferris.edu/htmls/OTHERSRV/ISAR/archives2/genewar/deadidea.htm (accessed November 2011).

16   Mehler, "Foundation for Fascism," 21.

17   Ibid., 22; and Grace Lichtenstein, "Fund Backs Controversial Study of 'Racial Betterment,'" *New York Times*, December 11, 1977.

7. The Asian Coefficient

1   Jean-Philippe Rushton, in telephone interview with author, September 20, 1995.

2   John H. Relethford, response to "How 'Caucasoids' Got Such Big Crania and Why They Shrank, from Morton to Rushton," by Leonard Lieberman, *Current Anthropology* 42, no. 1 (February 2001): 84.

3   Fatimah Jackson, comment on "How Caucasoids Got Such Big Crania," 82.

4   Peter Chua and Diane C. Fujino, "Negotiating New Asian-American Masculinities: Attitudes and Gender Expectations," *Journal of Men's Studies* 7, no. 3 (Spring 1999): 391–413. Also see David L. Eng's *Racial Castration: Managing Masculinity in Asian America* (Durham, NC: Duke University Press, 2001); Sau-ling C. Wong and Jeffrey J. Santa Ana, "Gender and Sexuality in Asian American Literature," *Signs* 25, no. 1 (Autumn 1999): 171–226; and Elaine Kim, *Asian American Literature: An Introduction to the Writings and Their Social Context* (Philadelphia: Temple University Press, 1982).

5   Jeff Yang, "The 1995 National Asian American Sex Survey," *A Magazine*, August–September 1995, 27.

6   Harry Mok, "The Asian Dating Dilemma," Blast@explode.com (an online magazine), http://www.explode.com//rr/dating.shtml (accessed November 2011).

7   Ibid.

8   Joyce Nishioka, "A Threatened Manhood? Exploring the Myth of the Angry Asian Male," *Asian Week* 21, no. 23 (February 3, 2000).

9   Sinstinna, "Stereotypical Thinking," *Jade Magazine*, April–May 1999.

10   Rushton, *Race, Evolution, and Behavior*, 18.

11   Audrey Smedley, comment on "How 'Caucasoids' Got Such Big Crania," 86.

12 Biologist Joseph Graves has pointed out in reading this chapter of the manuscript that the sex drive was fixed in our human species long before anyone left Africa and that only very strong social prohibitions could control so strong a sex drive. Professor Graves also suggests that the sexual disadvantage that Asian men face in the United States may be related to two primary variables—body size and social status. According to Graves, some evidence indicates that human females find taller, more muscular men more attractive than shorter, less muscular men, with all other factors being equal. Asian men are on the average shorter in stature than European American men are; thus, if other factors were equal, women would find the European men more sexually attractive. Some of the height and muscle difference may even be dietary. As both the diet and social status factors change, it can be predicted that the "out-marrying" rate should equalize. Evidence shows that this process is already occurring with Japanese and European Americans. See Graves, *The Race Myth*.

13 Lieberman, "How Caucasoids Got Such Big Crania," 72.

14 Bob Kumamoto, "The Search for Spies: American Counterintelligence and the Japanese-American Community, 1931–1942," *Amerasia Journal* 6, no. 2 (Fall 1979): 45–75.

15 Megumi Dick Osumi, "Asians and California's Anti-Miscegenation Laws," in *Asian and Pacific American Experiences: Women's Perspectives*, ed. Nobuya Tsuchida (Minneapolis: Asian/Pacific American Learning Resource Center and General College, University of Minnesota, 1982), 1–37. See also Paul R. Spickard, *Mixed Blood: Intermarriage and Ethnic Identity in Twentieth-Century America* (Madison: University of Wisconsin Press, 1989), 70.

16 Yen Le Espiritu, *Asian-American Women and Men: Labor, Laws, and Love* (Thousand Oaks, CA: Sage Publications, 1997), 111.

17 DeParle, "Daring Research?"

18 Ibid.

19 Ibid.

20 Ibid.

8. The Reciprocal Function

1 See Michael E. Levin, *Why Race Matters: Race Differences and What They Mean* (Westport, CT: Praeger, 1997).

2 Michael Levin, letter to the editor, *American Philosophical Association Proceedings*, January 1990.

3 Levin, *Why Race Matters*, 186.

4 Ibid.

5 Joseph Losco and Jerry Hirsch, "Book Review: Why Race Matters: Race Differences and What They Mean," Institute for the Study of Academic Racism, http://www.ogiek.org/indepth/what-they-mean.htm.

6 Leonard Jeffries, "Our Sacred Mission," a speech delivered at the Empire State Black Arts and Cultural Festival, Albany, New York, July 20, 1991.

7 Leon Jaroff, "Teaching Reverse Racism," *Time,* June 24, 2001, http://www.time.com/time/magazine/article/0,9171,164121,00.html (accessed September 2009).

8 Ibid.

9 Carol Barnes, *Melanin: The Chemical Key to Black Greatness: The Harmful Effects of Toxic Drugs on Melanin Centers within the Black Human* (Houston, TX: C. Barnes, 1998).

10 Wade W. Nobles, *Seeking the Sakhu: Foundational Writings for an African Psychology* (Chicago: Third World Press, 2006).

11 See Michael Bradley, *The Iceman Inheritance: Prehistoric Sources of Western Man's Racism, Sexism and Aggression* (Toronto: Dorset Publishers, 1978).

12 Ibid., 3.

13 Eugene Victor Wolfenstein, "Does Academic Correctness Repress Separatist or Afrocentrist Scholarship?," *Journal of Blacks in Higher Education* 2 (Winter 1993/1994): 44.

14 See Joseph L. Graves, "Evolutionary Biology and Human Variation: Biological Determinism and the Mythology of Race," *Race Relations Abstracts* 18, no. 3 (1993): 4–34.

15 Hope Landrine and Elizabeth A. Klonoff, *African American Acculturation: Deconstructing Race and Reviving Culture* (Thousand Oaks, CA: Sage Publications, 1996), 7.

16 Ibid.

17 Hope Landrine and Elizabeth A. Klonoff, "The African American Acculturation Scare: Development, Reliability, and Validity," *Journal of Black Psychology* 20, no. 2 (May 1994): 124–53.

9. The Phallic Equation

1 Frank Miele, interview with Robert Sternberg, *Skeptic Magazine* 3, no. 3 (1995): 72–80.

2 A. W. Boykin, "The Triple Quandary and the Schooling of Afro-American Children," in *The School Achievement of Minority Children*, ed. Ulric Neisser (Hillsdale, NJ: Erlbaum, 1983). Also see A. W. Boykin, "Harvesting Talent and Culture: African-American Children and Educational Reform," in *Schools and Students at Risk*, ed. R. Eiossl (New York: Teachers College Press, 1994), 180–81.

3 Report of a Task Force established by the Board of Scientific Affairs of the American Psychological Association, August 7, 1995 (also see http://www.lrainc.com/swtaboo/taboos/apa_01.html, accessed December 2011); Boykin, "The Triple Quandary"; and Boykin, "Harvesting Talent and Culture."

4 Ibid.

5 Cited in Richard Nisbett, "Blue Genes," *New Republic*, October 31, 1994, 15.

6 Richard E. Nisbett, *Intelligence and How to Get It: Why Schools and Cultures Count* (New York: W. W. Norton, 2009), 99–101.

7 Family Planning and Population Reproductive Health Technical Support, Family and Reproductive Health, World Health Organization (WHO), "The Male Latex Condom: Specification and Guidelines for Condom Procurement" (Geneva: WHO and Joint United Nations Programme on HIV/AIDS, 1998).

8   Paul Gebhard and Alan B. Johnson, *The Kinsey Data: Marginal Tabulations of the 1938–1963 Interviews Conducted by the Institute for Sex Research* (Philadelphia: W. B. Saunders, 1979).

9   Friedman, *A Mind of Its Own*, 107.

10   Ibid.

11   Rick A. Kittles and Kenneth M. Weiss, "Race, Ancestry, and Genes: Implications for Defining Disease Risk," *Annual Review of Genomics and Human Genetic Research* 4 (2003): 33–67.

12   Richard J. Herrnstein and Charles Murray, *The Bell Curve: Intelligence and Class Structure in American Life* (New York: Free Press, 1994), 296–97.

13   James Shreeve, "Terms of Estrangement," *Discover Magazine*, November 1994, 58.

14   Ibid., 60.

15   Paul Hoffman, "The Science of Race," *Discover Magazine*, November 1994, 4.

16   Daniel Goleman, *Vital Lies, Simple Truths: The Psychology of Self-Deception* (New York: Simon & Schuster, 1986), 121.

17   John Hoberman, *Darwin's Athletes: How Sport Has Damaged Black America and Preserved the Myth of Race* (New York: Houghton Mifflin, 1997), 207.

18   Goleman, *Vital Lies*, 122.

19   Gould, *The Mismeasure of Man*, 309.

20   Ibid.

21   Antonio R. Damasio, *Descartes' Error: Emotion, Reason, and the Human Brain* (New York: Grosset/Putnam, 1994), 246.

10. The New Calculus

1   See Saul Dubow, *Scientific Racism in Modern South Africa* (Cambridge, UK: Cambridge University Press, 1995), 229. In footnote 89, Dubow quotes P. Rich, "Race, Science and the Legitimization of White Supremacy in South Africa, 1902–1940," *International Journal of African Historical Studies* 23, no. 4 (1990): 679. Dubow also notes, "The sensitive question

of comparing Afrikaans- and English-speaking abilities emerges clearly in correspondence dealing with the 1953 revision of the Group Intelligence Test. This was standardized in such a manner that equivalent IQ scores on the Afrikaans and English versions did not necessarily imply similar abilities. See Cape Provincial Administration archives, PAE E269 Z216/3, S. Biesheuvel, President, South African Psychological Association to Director of Education, Cape Provincial Administration, 13 August 1956."

2 G. Harrington, "An Experimental Model of Bias in Mental Testing," *Perspectives on Bias in Mental Testing*, ed. C. R. Reynolds and R. T. Brown (New York: Plenum Press, 1984), 111.

3 Andrew Hacker, "White on White," *New Republic*, October 31, 1994, 14.

4 Robert V. Guthrie, *Even the Rat Was White: A Historical View of Psychology* (Boston: Allyn and Bacon, 1998).

5 G. R. Stetson, "Some Memory Tests of Whites and Blacks," *Psychological Review* 4 (1897): 285–89, cited in ibid., 63.

6 Siebert, "Darwinistic Elitism Is Idiotic."

7 Vincent Sarich and Frank Miele, *Race: The Reality of Human Differences* (Boulder, CO: Westview Press, 2004), 176–77.

8 From the lyrics of Kenneth Kidd's song, "Born to Run," released in 1975.

9 Loren E. Lomasky, "Meritocracy That Works: Race and Professional Basketball," *National Review*, December 5, 1994.

10 Gary Younge, "Comment and Analysis: White on Black: Racist Claims That Black People Are Natural Athletes Give Support to the Idea They Are Naturally Less Intelligent," *The Guardian (London)*, August 28, 2000, 13.

11 Hoberman, *Darwin's Athletes*, 178–79; and J. Stanley Lemons, "Black Stereotypes as Reflected in Popular Culture, 1880–1920," *American Quarterly* 29, no. 1 (Spring 1977).

12 Daniel Goleman, *Emotional Intelligence* (New York: Bantam Books, 1995), 55.

13 Goleman has articulated the researcher's neurological and physiological boundaries in his book *Vital Lies, Simple Truths*.

14 Damasio, *Descartes' Error*, 246.

15 Marilyn Elias, "Academics Lose Relevance for Black Boys," *USA Today*, December 2, 1997; and J. W. Osborne, "Academics, Self-Esteem, and Race: A Look at the Underlying Assumptions the Disidentification Hypothesis," *Personality and Social Psychology Bulletin* 21, 5 (1995): 449–55.

16 Private conversation with Professor Gustav Seligmann at the University of North Texas, November 1995.

17 Siebert, "Darwinistic Elitism Is Idiotic."

Bibliography

Ashe, Arthur, Jr. *A Hard Road to Glory—Basketball: A History of the African-American Athlete in Basketball*. With Kip Branch, Oceania Chalk, and Francis Harris. New York: Amistad Press, 1993.

Asimov, Isaac. "The Perennial Fringe." *Skeptical Inquirer Magazine* 10, no. 3 (Spring 1986).

Atlanta Journal-Record of Medicine. "Castration Instead of Lynching." 8, no. 12 (March 1907).

———. "Genital Peculiarities of the Negro." March 1903.

Ayala, Francisco J., and John A. Kiger Jr. *Modern Genetics*. Menlo Park: University of California at Davis, 1980.

Barnes, Carol. *Melanin: The Chemical Key to Black Greatness: The Harmful Effects of Toxic Drugs on Melanin Centers within the Black Human*. Bensenville, IL: Lushena Books, 2001.

Berkeley Daily Planet. "Nobelist's Speech Linking Sunshine, Sex Found Ignoble." November 25, 2000.

Billig, Michael. "A Dead Idea That Will Not Lie Down." *Searchlight*, July 1998. www.ferris.edu/htmls/OTHERSRV/ISAR/archives2/genewar/deadidea.htm (accessed November 2011).

Bix, A. S. "Experiences and Voices of Eugenics Field-Workers: Women's Work in Biology." *Social Studies of Science* 27 (1997).

Bradley, Michael. *Iceman Inheritance: Prehistoric Sources of Western Man's Racism, Sexism and Aggression*. New York: Kayode Press, 1976.

Campbell, John. *Negro-Mania: Being an Examination of the Falsely Assumed Equality of the Various Races of Men*. Philadelphia: Campbell & Power, 1851.

Cardyn, Lisa. "Sexualized Racism/Gendered Violence: Outraging the Body Politic in the Reconstruction South." *Michigan Law Review* 100, no. 4 (February 2002).

Carroll, Robert Todd. *The Skeptic's Dictionary*, s.v. "koro." http://skepdic.com/koro.html (accessed November 2011).

Ceci, Stephen, and Wendy M. Williams. "Darwin 200: Should Scientists Study Race and IQ? Yes: The Scientific Truth Must Be Pursued." *Nature* 457, no. 12 (February 2009).

Chua, Peter, and Diane C. Fujino. "Negotiating New Asian-American Masculinities: Attitudes and Gender Expectations." *Journal of Men's Studies* 7, no. 3 (Spring 1999).

Damasio, Antonio R. *Descartes' Error: Emotion, Reason, and the Human Brain*. New York: Grosset/Putnam, 1994.

Davenport, C. B. "The Effects of Race Intermingling." *Proceedings of the American Philosophical Society* 56, no. 4 (1917).

DeParle, Jason. "Daring Research or 'Social Science Pornography'?: Charles Murray." *New York Times*, October 9, 1994.

Dubow, Saul. *Scientific Racism in Modern South Africa*. Cambridge, UK: Cambridge University Press, 1995.

Eng, David L. *Racial Castration: Managing Masculinity in Asian America*. Durham, NC: Duke University Press, 2001.

Entine, Jon. "Breaking Taboos in the Publishing Industry: The Struggle to Get *Taboo* Published." *American Renaissance* 11, no. 2 (February 2000). http://www.amren.com/ar/2000/02/ (accessed September 2009).

Fancher, Raymond E. *The Intelligence Men: Makers of the IQ Controversy*. New York: W. W. Norton, 1985.

Friedman, David M. *A Mind of Its Own: A Cultural History of the Penis*. New York: Free Press, 2001.

Galton, Francis. *Inquiries into Human Faculty and Its Development*. London: J. M. Dent and Company, 1908.

Gayre, Lt. Col. G. R., and Robert Nigg. *Teuton and Slav on the Polish Frontier: A Diagnosis of the Racial Basis of the Germano-Polish Borderlands with Suggestions for the Settlement of German and Slav Claims*. London: Eyre and Spottiswoode, 1944.

Gill, Anton. *Ruling Passions: Sex, Race, and Empire*. London: BBC Books,1995.

Goleman, Daniel. *Emotional Intelligence*. New York: Bantam Books, 1995.

———. *Vital Lies, Simple Truths: The Psychology of Self-Deception*. New York: Simon & Schuster, 1986.

Goodman, Ellen. "Genius Is More Than Good Genes." *Boston Globe*, March 6, 1980.

Gould, Stephen J. "Ghosts of Bell Curves Past." *Natural History* 104, no. 2 (February 1995).

———. *The Mismeasure of Man*. New York: W. W. Norton, 1981.

Graves, Joseph L., Jr. *The Emperor's New Clothes: Biological Theories of Race at the Millennium*. New Brunswick, NJ: Rutgers University Press, 2001.

———. "What a Tangled Web He Weaves: Race, Reproductive Strategies, and Rushton's Life History Theory." *Anthropological Theory* 2, no.2 (2002).

Groves, C. P. "Genes, Genitals, and Genius: The Evolutionary Ecology of Race." In *Human Biology: An Integrative Science*, ed. P. O'Higgins and R. N. Pervan. Nedlands, Australia: University of Western Australia, Centre for Human Biology, 1991.

Guthrie, Robert V. *Even the Rat Was White: A Historical View of Psychology*. Boston: Allyn and Bacon, 1998.

Hacker, Andrew. "White on White." *New Republic*, October 31, 1994.

Haller, John S., Jr. *Outcasts from Evolution: Scientific Attitudes of Racial Inferiority, 1859–1900*. Chicago: University of Illinois Press, 1996.

Hamilton, Andrew. "The Negro: How He's Different." *Science Digest*, October 1963.

Hayman, Robert L. *The Smart Culture: Society, Intelligence, and Law*. New York: New York University Press, 1997.

Hearnshaw, L. S. *Cyril Burt, Psychologist*. Ithaca, NY: Cornell University Press, 1979.

Hernton, Calvin C. *Sex and Racism in America*. New York: Doubleday, 1988.

Herrnstein, Richard."IQ." *Atlantic Monthly* 228 (September 1971).

———. *I.Q. in the Meritocracy*. Boston: Atlantic Monthly Press, 1973.

———."IQ Testing and the Media." *Atlantic Monthly*, August 1982.

———. "Lost and Found: One Self." *Ethics* 98, no. 3 (April 1988).

———. Note from R. Herrnstein to S. Stevens, July 10, 1963. Harvard University Archives, Cambridge, MA.

———, and Charles Murray. *The Bell Curve: Intelligence and Class Structure in American Life*. New York: Free Press, 1994.

———, and James Q. Wilson. *Crime and Human Nature*. New York: Simon & Schuster, 1985.

Hirsch, Jerry. "To Unfrock the Charlatans." *SAGE Race Relations Abstracts* 6, no. 2 (1981).

Hoffman, Paul. "The Science of Race." *Discover Magazine*, November 1994.

Hooton, Earnest Albert. *Crime and the Man*. Cambridge, MA: Harvard University Press, 1939.

Hrdlička, Aleš. "Physical Differences between White and Colored Children." *American Association for the Advancement of Science* 47 (1898).

Jackson, Fatimah. Comment on Lieberman, "How 'Caucasoids' Got Such Big Crania and Why They Shrank." *Current Anthropology* 42, no. 1 (February 2001).

Jacoby, Russell, and Naomi Glauberman. *The Bell Curve Debate: History, Documents, Opinions*. New York: Times Books, 1995.

Jaroff, Leon. "Teaching Reverse Racism." *Time*, June 24, 2001. http://www.time.com/time/magazine/article/0,9171,164121,00.html (accessed September 2009).

Jeffries, Leonard. "Our Sacred Mission." Speech delivered at the Empire State Black Arts and Cultural Festival, Albany, NY, July 20, 1991.

Jensen, Arthur Robert. *Bias in Mental Testing*. New York: Free Press, 1980.

————. *Educability and Group Differences*. New York: Harper & Row, 1973.

————. "How Much Can We Boost IQ and Scholastic Achievement?" *Harvard Educational Review* 39, no. 1 (Winter 1969).

————. "Race and Genetics in Intelligence: A Reply to Lewontin." *Bulletin of the Atomic Scientists*, May 1970.

Jones, Syl. "Interview with Dr. William Shockley." *Playboy*, August 1980.

Joseph, Andre. *Intelligence, IQ, and Race: When, How, and Why They Became Associated*. San Francisco: R & E Research Associates, 1977.

Kamin, Leon. Personal interview with author. Northeastern University, Boston, August 28, 1995.

Kaplan, David A. Interview on Borders.com, June 7, 2000. http://www.liveworld.com/transcripts/borders/6-7-2000.1-4.html (accessed July 14, 2008).

Kelves, Daniel J. *In the Name of Eugenics: Genetics and the Uses of Human Heredity*. New York: Knopf, 1985.

Kittles, Rick A., and Kenneth M. Weiss. "Race, Ancestry, and Genes: Implications for Defining Disease Risk." *Annual Review of Genomics and Human Genetic Research* 4 (2003).

Kuhl, Stefan. *The Nazi Connection: Eugenics, American Racism, and German National Socialism*. New York: Oxford University Press, 1994.

Landrine, Hope, and Elizabeth A. Klonoff. *African American Acculturation: Deconstructing Race and Reviving Culture*. Thousand Oaks, CA: Sage Publications, 1996.

Laughlin, Harry. Note to C. Schneider, August 11, 1936. Harry Laughlin Papers, Northeast Missouri State University, Kirksville.

Leake, Jonathan. "DNA Pioneer James Watson Is Blacker Than He Thought." *Sunday Times*, December 9, 2007.

Lemons, J. Stanley. "Black Stereotypes as Reflected in Popular Culture." *American Quarterly* 29, no. 1 (Spring 1977).

Levin, Michael E. Letter to the editor. *American Philosophical Association Proceedings*, January 1990.

———. *Why Race Matters: Race Differences and What They Mean.* Westport, CT: Praeger, 1997.

Lieberman, Leonard. "How 'Caucasoids' Got Such Big Crania and Why They Shrank, from Morton to Rushton." *Current Anthropology* 42, no. 1 (February 2001).

Lomasky, Loren E. "Meritocracy That Works: Race and Professional Basketball." *National Review*, December 5, 1994.

London Sunday Times Magazine. "The Elementary DNA of Dr. Watson," October 14, 2007.

Lynn, Richard. Review of *A New Morality from Science: Beyondism*, by R. B. Cattell. *Irish Journal of Psychology* 2, no. 3 (Winter 1974).

MacArthur, Robert H., and Edward O. Wilson. *The Theory of Island Biogeography.* Princeton, NJ: Princeton University Press, 1967.

Marks, Jonathan. *Human Biodiversity: Genes, Race, and History.* New York: Aldine de Gruyter, 1995.

McGuire, [Hunter,] and [G. Frank] Lydston. "As Ye Sow That Ye Also Reap." *Atlanta Journal-Record of Medicine* 1, no. 3 (June 1899).

———. *Sexual Crimes among Southern Negroes.* Louisville, KY: Renz & Henry, 1893.

Mead, Margaret. "Group Intelligence Tests and Linguistic Disability among Italian Children." *School and Society* 25 (April 16, 1927).

Miller, Adam. "Professors of Hate." *Rolling Stone*, October 20, 1994.

Mok, Harry. "The Asian Dating Dilemma," Blast@explode.com. www.explode.com//rr/dating.shtml (accessed November 2011).

Moll, John L. "William Bradford Shockley: February 13, 1910–August 12, 1989." In *Biographical Memoirs.* Washington, DC: National Academy of Sciences, 1995. www.nap.edu/openbook.php?record_id=4990&page=305 (accessed November 2011).

Morgan, Thomas Hunt. *Evolution and Genetics*, 2nd ed. New Jersey: Princeton University Press, 1925.

Moriarty, Gerry. "Stirring Things Up in Coleraine." *Irish Times*, May 10, 1995.

Murray, Charles. "On Richard Herrnstein." *National Review*, October 10, 1994.

New York Times. "Graduates Are Shredded," January 29, 1995.

Nisbett, Richard E. *Intelligence and How to Get It: Why Schools and Cultures Count.* New York: W. W. Norton, 2009.

Nishioka, Joyce. "A Threatened Manhood? Exploring the Myth of the Angry Asian Male." *Asian Week* 21, no. 23 (February 3, 2000).

Nobles, Wade W. *Seeking the Sakhu: Foundational Writings for an African Psychology*. Chicago: Third World Press, 2006.

Osborn, Frederick. "Summary of the Proceedings of the Conference on Eugenics in Relation to Nursing." February 24, 1937, American Eugenics Society Archives, Philadelphia.

Pearl, R. "The Biology of Superiority." *American Mercury* 12 (November 1927).

Pearson, Roger. *Essays on Eugenics and Race*. Coventry, UK: Northern World, 1958.

———. *Race, Intelligence, and Bias in Academe*. Washington, DC: Scott Townsend, 1991.

Plotz, David. *The Genius Factory: The Curious History of the Nobel Prize Sperm Bank*. New York: Random House, 2005.

Quigley, Margaret. "The Roots of the I.Q. Debate: Eugenics and Social Control." *The Public Eye*, March 1995.

Relethford, John H. Response to "How 'Caucasoids' Got Such Big Crania and Why They Shrank, from Morton to Rushton," by Leonard Lieberman. *Current Anthropology* 42, no. 1 (February 2001).

Report of a Task Force established by the Board of Scientific Affairs of the American Psychological Association, August 7, 1995.

Riesman, David. Personal interview with the author. Department of Sociology, Harvard University, Cambridge, MA, September 11, 1995.

Rogers, Joel Augustus. *Sex and Race: Negro-Caucasian Mixing in All Ages and All Lands*, 3 vols. New York: J. A. Rogers, 1941.

Rogers, Michael. "Brave New William Shockley." *Esquire* 79, no. 1 (January 1973).

Rosenbaum, Ron. "The Great Ivy League Nude Posture Photo Scandal." *New York Times Magazine*, January 15, 1995.

Rushton, Jean-Philippe. "The New Enemies of Evolutionary Science." *Liberty* 11, no. 4 (March 1998).

————. Personal interview with the author. University of Western Ontario, London, Ontario, September 6, 1995.

————. "Race Differences in Behaviour: A Review and Evolutionary Analysis." *Journal of Personality and Individual Differences* 9, no. 6 (1988).

————. *Race, Evolution, and Behavior: A Life History Perspective*, 2nd special abridged ed. Port Huron, MI: Charles Darwin Research Institute, 2000.

————. Telephone interview with the author. University of Western Ontario, London, Ontario, September 6 and 20, 1995.

Rushton, J. P., and A. F. Bogaert. "Race Differences in Sexual Behavior: Testing an Evolutionary Hypothesis." *Journal of Research in Personality* 21, no. 4 (1987).

————. "Race Versus Social Class Differences in Sexual Behavior: A Follow-up of the r/K Dimension." *Journal of Research in Personality* 22 (1988).

San Francisco Examiner. March 18, 1990, mention of Frederick Seitz's letter in November 1990 letter to British journal *Nature*.

Seltzer, Carl C. "Masculinity and Smoking." *Science* 130, no. 3390 (December 18, 1959).

Selvin, Paul. "The Raging Bull of Berkeley." *Science* 251, no. 4992 (January 25, 1991).

Sheldon, William. *Varieties of Delinquent Youth: An Introduction to Constitutional Psychiatry*. New York: Harper Brothers, 1947.

————. *The Varieties of Temperament: A Psychology of Constitutional Differences*. With S. S. Stevens. New York: Harper Brothers,1942. Reprint, Hafner Publishers, 1970.

Shufeldt, Robert Wilson. *America's Greatest Problem: The Negro*. Philadelphia: F. A. Davis Company, 1915.

Skinner, B. F. *Beyond Freedom and Dignity*. New York: Bantam Books, 1972.

Spearman, Charles E. *The Abilities of Man: Their Nature and Measurement*. New York: Macmillan, 1927.

Stepan, Nancy. *The Idea of Race in Science: Great Britain, 1800–1960*. Hamden, CT: Archon Books, 1982.

Stetson, G. R. "Some Memory Tests of Whites and Blacks." *Psychological Review* 4 (1897).

Stevens, William K. "Doctor Foresees an I.Q. Caste System." *New York Times*, August 29, 1971.

Stokes, W. E. D. *The Right to Be Well Born, or Horse Breeding in Its Relation to Eugenics*. New York: C. J. O'Brien, 1917.

Swanson, Michael. "The Bell Curve and Eugenics." October 20, 1995. http://www.hartford-hwp.com/archives/45/026.html (accessed September 2009).

Talbot, Eugene S. *Degeneracy, Its Causes, Signs, and Results*. London: W. Scott, 1898.

Thomas, Shirley. *Men of Space: Profiles of the Leaders in Space Research, Development, and Exploration*, vol. 4. Philadelphia: Chilton Company, 1962.

Thompson, Warren S. "Race Suicide in the United States." *Scientific Monthly* 5, no. 1 (July 1917).

Tolnay, Stewart E., Glenn Deane, and E. M. Beck. "Vicarious Violence: Spatial Effects on Southern Lynchings, 1890–1919." *American Journal of Sociology* 102, no. 3 (November 1996).

Tucker, William H. *The Funding of Scientific Racism: Wickliffe Draper and the Pioneer Fund*. Urbana: University of Illinois Press, 2002.

———. *The Science and Politics of Racial Research*. Urbana: University of Illinois Press, 1994.

Van Evrie, John H. *Negroes and Negro "Slavery": The First an Inferior Race, the Latter Its Normal Condition*. New York: Horton, 1863.

Vertinsky, Patricia. "Embodying Normalcy: Anthropometry and the Long Arm of William H. Sheldon's Somatotyping Project." *Journal of Sport History* 29, no. 1 (Spring 2002).

Weizmann, Frederic, Neil I. Wiener, David L. Wiesenthal, and Michael Ziegler. "Discussion: Eggs, Eggplants and Eggheads: A Rejoinder to Rushton." *Canadian Psychology/Psychologie canadienne* 32, no. 1 (January 1991).

Wiegman, Robyn. *American Anatomies: Theorizing Race and Gender*. Durham, NC: Duke University Press, 1995.

———. "The Anatomy of Lynching." *Journal of the History of Sexuality* 3, no. 3 (1993).

Wolfenstein, Eugene Victor. "Does Academic Correctness Repress Separatist or Afrocentrist Scholarship?" *Journal of Blacks in Higher Education* 2 (Winter 1993/1994).

World Health Organization, Family Planning and Population Reproductive Health Technical Support, Family and Reproductive Health. "The Male Latex Condom: Specification and Guidelines for Condom Procurement." Geneva: World Health Organization and Joint United Nations Programme on HIV/AIDS, 1998.

X, Dr. Jacobus. *Untrodden Fields of Anthropology*. Paris: Libraire de médecine, folklore et anthropologie, 1898.

Yang, Jeff. "The 1995 National Asian American Sex Survey." *A Magazine*, August–September 1995.

Younge, Gary. "Comment and Analysis: White on Black: Racists Claims That Black People Are Natural Athletes Give Support to the Idea They Are Naturally Less Intelligent." *The Guardian* (London), August 28, 2000.

Index

About the Author

Constance Hilliard is an associate professor of history at the University of North Texas in Denton. She has a PhD from Harvard University and a specialized interest in the history of race science and its global impact. Her previous book, *Does Israel Have a Future? The Case for a Post-Zionist State*, examines the role played by Western anti-Semitism in fueling the Arab-Israeli conflict. Hilliard is also the author of *The Intellectual Traditions of Pre-Colonial Africa*. As a former editorial writer for the *Dallas Morning News*, she has written dozens of columns on issues of race and foreign policy. Her columns have also appeared in *USA Today*, the *Los Angeles Times*, and the *Chicago Tribune*.

Contents

Stochastic Demography and Conservation of an Endangered Perennial Plant (*Lomatium bradshawii*) in a Dynamic Fire Regime

H. CASWELL AND T.N. KAYE

Population Cycles in Birds of the Grouse family (Tetraonidae)

R. MOSS AND A. WATSON

Ecophysiology of Trees of Seasonally Dry Tropics: Comparisons among Phenologies

D. EAMUS AND L. PRIOR

Meta-analysis in Ecology

J. GUREVITCH, P.S. CURTIS AND M.H. JONES

Stochastic Demography and Conservation of an Endangered Perennial Plant (*Lomatium bradshawii*) in a Dynamic Fire Regime

HAL CASWELL AND THOMAS N. KAYE

I. SUMMARY

Lomatium bradshawii is an endangered herbaceous perennial plant found in grassland and prairie remnants in western Oregon and southwestern Washington. Fire was historically an important and highly dynamic component of the environment of *L. bradshawii*. Evaluating the demographic consequences of a dynamic environment requires a model for the environment and a coupling between that model and the vital rates of the population. In this review, we analyze in detail the effects of fire schedules on demography of *L. bradshawii*. It has been suggested that *L.*

ADVANCES IN ECOLOGICAL RESEARCH VOL. 32
ISBN 0-12-013932-4

bradshawii is adapted to frequent fire and that its populations would benefit from managed fires; our results support these suggestions.

We constructed size-structured population projection matrices for conditions corresponding to the year of a fire and to 1, 2 and 3 or more years post-fire, at each of two sites (Fisher Butte and Rose Prairie) in western Oregon. We used these matrices in two ways. First, we treated the population growth rate λ calculated from each matrix as a summary of the conditions in that environment. We found a significant decline in λ with time since the last fire. Second, we developed models for *L. bradshawii* in periodic and stochastic fire environments. The periodic models provide values of annual growth rate for any specified periodic burning schedule. The stochastic models describe the occurrence of fire as a two-state Markov chain specified in terms of the long-term frequency and autocorrelation of fires. The sequence of fires generates in turn a sequence of environments in terms of time since fire. From this model we calculated the stochastic growth rate $\log \lambda_s$; it increases with increasing fire frequency and with negative autocorrelation.

The critical fire frequency, below which *L. bradshawii* cannot persist, is about 0.8 to 0.9 at Fisher Butte and about 0.4 to 0.5 at Rose Prairie. Extinction probability drops precipitously from 1 to near 0 as fire frequency increases through the critical value. We carried out a detailed perturbation analysis, calculating the sensitivity and elasticity of the stochastic growth rate to changes in the entries of the matrices. The sensitivity and elasticity of the stochastic growth rate are very highly correlated with the corresponding results from a deterministic model based on the mean projection matrix. Patterns of stochastic sensitivity and elasticity are also very insensitive to changes in the fire frequency. Taken together, these results show that estimates of sensitivity and elasticity are robust, and not excessively sensitive to the details of the stochastic environment. Overall, our results show that *L. bradshawii* depends on frequent fire to persist in these habitats, and that controlled burning is an attractive management tool.

II. INTRODUCTION

Disturbance by fire affects individuals, populations, communities and ecosystems. In a given system, burning may increase the abundance of some species while reducing that of others through its effects on competitive interactions and vital rates (Noble and Slatyer, 1980). The frequency, autocorrelation, and intensity of fires are important factors that shape the population dynamics of species in many habitats (Bond and van Wilgen, 1996). Conservationists often use fire to develop and maintain communities and populations of endangered species, especially plants (reviewed in Hessl and Spackman, 1995), but long-term studies investigating the effects of fire frequency (Glitzenstein et al., 1995; Quintana-Ascencio, 1997) and time since fire (Hawkes and Menges, 1996; Menges and Kimmich, 1996) relative to such goals are comparatively rare. In this review we analyze demographic data from a series of experimental fire manipulations, to study the effects of burning, the post-fire recovery process, and the long-term frequency of fire on the population dynamics of an endangered plant.

Our analyses examine in detail the interaction between this plant and one important aspect of its environment, but the approach can also be applied to other species and other environmental factors. The essential components of our approach are (1) a stochastic model for the environment and (2) demographic data, in the form of stage-classified population projection matrices estimated in each state of the environment. Our basic tools are eigenvalue perturbation theory, life table response experiment (LTRE) analyses, and the theory of population dynamics in periodic and stochastic environments; all these methods are presented in detail in Caswell (2001).

Lomatium bradshawii is an endangered herbaceous perennial plant in the family Apiaceae. It exists in only 16 isolated populations, of 50–25 000 individuals, in western Oregon and southwestern Washington (Pendergrass et al., 1999). It occupies grasslands and prairies that now occur only as small remnants of formerly widespread habitats (Parenti et al., 1993). These habitats were, until recent times, subject to both natural and anthropogenic fires. Like other plants of frequently burned areas, *L. bradshawii* seems to have adapted to fire. Fire is an important management tool for reducing woody plants in northwestern prairies (Pendergrass et al., 1998), and burning has been proposed as a management tool for *L. bradshawii* (Kaye, 1992; Parenti et al., 1993). Recent research has demonstrated that fall-season burning may increase plant size and seedling recruitment, but the effect fades within a few years (Pendergrass et al., 1999). In addition, populations in burned areas have higher growth rates and lower probabilities of extinction than unburned populations (Kaye et al., 2001). These studies suggest that burning can be used for managing *L. bradshawii* and its habitat, but they stop short of identifying the effects of fire frequency and determining optimum fire schedules. Because insufficiently frequent fire will not maintain viable populations, and excessively frequent fire would be costly and could have detrimental side effects, it is critical to understand *L. bradshawii* demography in a dynamic fire regime.

Fire affects many environmental factors, and those factors in turn have many effects on individuals. What counts from the perspective of conservation and management is the repercussions of those effects at the population level. In this review, we use demographic models to link the effects of fire on the survival, growth and reproduction of individuals to the resulting consequences for population growth, persistence and extinction. We do this by coupling the demography of *L. bradshawii* to a stochastic model of fire occurrence. These methods were introduced by Silva *et al.* (1991) and Canales *et al.* (1994); and subsequently used by Beissinger (1995) and Hoffmann (1999).

We describe the demography of *L. bradshawii* with a stage-classified matrix population model

$$\mathbf{n}(t+1) = \mathbf{A}_t \mathbf{n}(t) \tag{1}$$

where $\mathbf{n}(t)$ is a vector of stage abundances at time t and $\mathbf{A}_t$ is a possibly time-varying population projection matrix. The variation in $\mathbf{A}_t$ depends on the dynamics of fire. We use this model to answer three questions:

(1) How does the time since the last fire affect population growth of *L. bradshawii*? If population growth rate depends on the time since fire, which of the vital rates are responsible for the effect?
(2) How do population growth and extinction probability of *L. bradshawii* respond to the frequency and autocorrelation pattern of fires in a stochastic environment?
(3) How does *L. bradshawii* respond to periodic fire regimes of the sort that might be imposed as a management tactic?

These analyses use demographic models in two ways. In the first set of analyses, we treat the projection matrix **A** estimated in a particular environment as a probe of the conditions in that environment. We summarize the effects of the environment on the vital rates of the plant by projecting the population forward *as if* the environmental conditions remained constant, even though they cannot do so. The second set of analyses explores the consequences of a dynamic fire environment, either periodic or stochastic. Rather than projecting the consequences of a hypothetical constant environment, these analyses focus directly on environmental variability and its effects.

III. DEMOGRAPHIC DATA

A. Study Sites

The data on which the models are based were obtained from a study carried out from 1988 through 1993 on lands near the city of Eugene in

Oregon's Willamette Valley. Controlled burning experiments were conducted at two sites in the Fern Ridge Research Natural Area managed by the Army Corps of Engineers. The sites are identified here as Fisher Butte (44°3′ N, 123°15′ W) and Rose Prairie (44°5′ N, 123°15′ W). Additional details on site locations, vegetation, plot establishment and data collection are available in Pendergrass $et\ al.$ (1999) and Kaye $et\ al.$ (2001).

B. Fire Treatments and Time Since Fire

Plots were established in both sites, and were subjected to September or October burning treatment from 1988 through 1992. Three treatments, designed to explore different patterns of burning, were imposed. Let B and U denote years in which the population was burned and unburned, respectively. The treatments, T_0, T_1 and T_2, were

	Year				
Treatment	88	89	90	91	92
T_0	U	U	U	U	U
T_1	B	U	U	B	U
T_2	B	B	U	B	U

(2)

Burn characteristics at each site, including flame length, height, depth and heat per unit area were recorded in 1988–89 and are reported elsewhere (Pendergrass $et\ al.$, 1998).

In this study, our goal is to characterize $L.\ bradshawii$ population dynamics in terms of fire and post-fire recovery. Thus we are interested not in projection matrices based on the treatments T_0–T_2 (cf. Kaye $et\ al.$, 2001), but in matrices specific to four $environmental\ states$ (E_1–E_4) defined as follows:

State	Definition	Treatment–year combinations
E_1	year of a fire	T_1-88, T_1-91, T_2-88, T_2-89, T_2-91
E_2	1 year post-fire	T_1-89, T_1-92, T_2-90, T_2-92
E_3	2 years post-fire	T_1-90
E_4	≥3 years post-fire	T_0-88, T_0-89, T_0-90, T_0-91, T_0-92

Each environmental state except E_3 was represented by multiple treatment–year combinations. Environment E_3 was produced by only one treatment (T_1) in one year (1990).

IV. POPULATION PROJECTION MATRICES

Circular plots of 2 m radius were established surrounding randomly selected mature *L. bradshawii* individuals. Ten plots per treatment were established in the Fisher Butte site. At the Rose Prairie site, there were six plots in treatments T_0 and T_1 and five plots in T_2. All plants within each plot were monitored annually from 1988 through 1993.

Individuals were classified into six stages based on size and reproductive status:

Y yearlings (first year vegetative plants with 1–2 leaves)
V_1 vegetative plants with 1–2 leaves
V_2 vegetative plants with 3 or more leaves
R_1 reproductive plants with 1 umbel
R_2 productive plants with 2 umbels
R_3 reproductive plants with 3 or more umbels

The fates of individuals were recorded in each of the plots in each year. Transition matrices were constructed for each treatment in each year (1988–89, 1989–90, 1990–91, 1991–92, 1992–93) (Kaye *et al.*, 2001; see the Appendix for the complete set of matrices). The maximum likelihood estimate of the probability of transition from stage j to stage i is given by the proportion of individuals in stage j in year t that appeared in stage i in year $t + 1$. Stage-specific fertility was estimated as the total number of seedlings in year $t + 1$ multiplied by the proportion of seeds produced by each stage in year t (the 'anonymous reproduction' method of Caswell 1989a, 2001, p. 173). The population projection matrix **A** is produced by inserting the fertility estimates in the first row of the transition matrix.

A. Detailed and Averaged Matrices

Except for E_3, each environmental state is represented by more than one matrix. These matrices provide valuable information on the variability in the vital rates due to spatial and temporal variability within each environmental state. We refer to this set of 15 matrices as the *detailed matrices*.

In order to focus on the effects of time since fire, we also constructed a set of *averaged matrices*, $\mathbf{A}^{(1)}$–$\mathbf{A}^{(4)}$, one for each environmental state. Each averaged matrix was a weighted mean of the matrices for all of the treatment–year combinations corresponding to that environmental state. The weight for all elements within a column was the sample size from which that column was estimated. This construction is equivalent to pooling the transition data on all individuals in the appropriate environmental state and calculating the maximum likelihood estimates of the matrix from the pooled data.

Sample sizes for transitions involving large reproductive plants (R_3) were small, because these plants were rare. In some treatment–year combinations, no R_3 individuals were observed at all, making it impossible to estimate these transitions. To resolve this problem, we replaced column 6 of each of the detailed matrices with column 6 of the averaged matrix for that environmental state.

The averaged matrices are shown in Tables 1 and 2. We list all the detailed matrices in the Appendix.

V. ENVIRONMENT-SPECIFIC DEMOGRAPHY

We begin with an analysis of the population dynamic properties of the projection matrices that characterize each of the environmental states E_1–E_4. We have computed population growth rates, examined the dependence of these rates on the time since the last fire, and used LTRE analysis to identify the vital rates responsible for the observed differences in population growth.

A. Population Growth Rate

The asymptotic growth rate determined by a population projection matrix **A** is the dominant eigenvalue λ of **A**. This is the rate at which the population would grow if the conditions that produced **A** were to remain constant.

Estimated population growth rates $\hat{\lambda}$ for *L. bradshawii* are shown in Table 3. In the averaged matrices, which we expect to provide the best estimates of the population growth rate as a function of fire history, two trends are apparent. First, $\hat{\lambda}$ is highest in the year of a fire, and tends to decrease with time after a fire. Second, the Rose Prairie site consistently supports more rapid population growth of *L. bradshawii* than does the Fisher Butte site.

The growth rates calculated from the detailed matrices exhibit considerable variation. In particular, the matrices calculated for the 1990–91 transition (marked with an asterisk in Table 3) exhibit consistently low values of $\hat{\lambda}$. This suggests that 1990 was an unusually poor year for *L. bradshawii*, in both sites and regardless of the time since fire. That presumably explains why the values of $\hat{\lambda}$ for the averaged matrices do not decline monotonically with time since fire. Instead, $\hat{\lambda}$ for E_3 (2 years post-fire) is the lowest; this average was based on a single matrix, for treatment T_1 in 1990.

Table 1

The averaged projection matrices for each of the environmental treatments for the Fisher Butte site

$$
\mathbf{A}^{(1)} \begin{pmatrix}
0.0 & 0.0 & 0.0 & 0.059 & 0.794 & 2.724 \\
0.290 & 0.252 & 0.090 & 0.048 & 0.0 & 0.0 \\
0.165 & 0.344 & 0.510 & 0.231 & 0.073 & 0.039 \\
0.0 & 0.060 & 0.151 & 0.312 & 0.193 & 0.0 \\
0.0 & 0.020 & 0.095 & 0.160 & 0.411 & 0.095 \\
0.010 & 0.0 & 0.016 & 0.039 & 0.085 & 0.816
\end{pmatrix}
$$

$$
\mathbf{A}^{(2)} \begin{pmatrix}
0.0 & 0.0 & 0.0 & 0.090 & 0.570 & 1.886 \\
0.317 & 0.221 & 0.099 & 0.026 & 0.0 & 0.0 \\
0.199 & 0.282 & 0.349 & 0.051 & 0.050 & 0.0 \\
0.018 & 0.107 & 0.220 & 0.241 & 0.206 & 0.143 \\
0.0 & 0.056 & 0.102 & 0.484 & 0.417 & 0.200 \\
0.0 & 0.0 & 0.007 & 0.057 & 0.130 & 0.516
\end{pmatrix}
$$

$$
\mathbf{A}^{(3)} \begin{pmatrix}
0.0 & 0.0 & 0.0 & 0.0 & 0.200 & 1.000 \\
0.390 & 0.390 & 0.180 & 0.040 & 0.090 & 0.0 \\
0.060 & 0.110 & 0.220 & 0.380 & 0.120 & 0.0 \\
0.0 & 0.0 & 0.080 & 0.380 & 0.380 & 0.0 \\
0.0 & 0.0 & 0.080 & 0.080 & 0.250 & 0.330 \\
0.0 & 0.0 & 0.0 & 0.0 & 0.0 & 0.330
\end{pmatrix}
$$

$$
\mathbf{A}^{(4)} \begin{pmatrix}
0.0 & 0.0 & 0.0 & 0.291 & 1.659 & 3.080 \\
0.222 & 0.240 & 0.056 & 0.037 & 0.043 & 0.0 \\
0.079 & 0.207 & 0.481 & 0.213 & 0.154 & 0.235 \\
0.013 & 0.044 & 0.167 & 0.367 & 0.301 & 0.052 \\
0.0 & 0.017 & 0.055 & 0.172 & 0.277 & 0.177 \\
0.0 & 0.0 & 0.002 & 0.018 & 0.058 & 0.501
\end{pmatrix}
$$

Table 2

The averaged matrices for each of the environmental treatments for the Rose Prairie site

$$
\mathbf{A}^{(1)} = \begin{pmatrix}
0.0 & 0.0 & 0.0 & 0.919 & 4.586 & 5.940 \\
0.379 & 0.443 & 0.080 & 0.039 & 0.023 & 0.0 \\
0.024 & 0.202 & 0.360 & 0.186 & 0.217 & 0.415 \\
0.017 & 0.043 & 0.242 & 0.327 & 0.114 & 0.0 \\
0.0 & 0.009 & 0.150 & 0.350 & 0.597 & 0.479 \\
0.0 & 0.012 & 0.0 & 0.016 & 0.037 & 0.167
\end{pmatrix}
$$

$$
\mathbf{A}^{(2)} = \begin{pmatrix}
0.0 & 0.0 & 0.0 & 1.062 & 4.633 & 14.90 \\
0.185 & 0.318 & 0.031 & 0.023 & 0.021 & 0.0 \\
0.072 & 0.173 & 0.255 & 0.134 & 0.098 & 0.0 \\
0.017 & 0.035 & 0.260 & 0.366 & 0.339 & 0.250 \\
0.0 & 0.035 & 0.232 & 0.378 & 0.421 & 0.250 \\
0.0 & 0.008 & 0.0 & 0.0 & 0.029 & 0.375
\end{pmatrix}
$$

$$
\mathbf{A}^{(3)} = \begin{pmatrix}
0.0 & 0.0 & 0.0 & 0.200 & 1.400 & 2.100 \\
0.290 & 0.300 & 0.190 & 0.190 & 0.030 & 0.500 \\
0.010 & 0.0 & 0.190 & 0.250 & 0.170 & 0.0 \\
0.010 & 0.0 & 0.120 & 0.250 & 0.270 & 0.0 \\
0.0 & 0.0 & 0.0 & 0.060 & 0.300 & 0.500 \\
0.0 & 0.0 & 0.0 & 0.0 & 0.0 & 0.0
\end{pmatrix}
$$

$$
\mathbf{A}^{(4)} = \begin{pmatrix}
0.0 & 0.0 & 0.0 & 0.367 & 2.614 & 2.100 \\
0.079 & 0.331 & 0.104 & 0.0 & 0.0 & 0.0 \\
0.065 & 0.114 & 0.418 & 0.233 & 0.055 & 0.0 \\
0.020 & 0.0 & 0.270 & 0.418 & 0.601 & 0.0 \\
0.0 & 0.0 & 0.034 & 0.187 & 0.289 & 0.500 \\
0.0 & 0.0 & 0.0 & 0.0 & 0.053 & 0.500
\end{pmatrix}
$$

Table 3

The population growth rate λ calculated from the averaged and the detailed matrices for *L. bradshawii*, and the corresponding 95% bootstrap confidence intervals. Asterisks (*) denote growth rates calculated from matrices for the years 1990–91

(a) Averaged matrices

Years post-fire	Fisher Butte			Rose Prairie		
	$\widehat{\lambda}$	$SE(\widehat{\lambda})$	CI	λ	$SE(\widehat{\lambda})$	CI
0	1.020	0.0092	[1.0009, 1.0369]	1.155	0.0093	[1.1363, 1.1727]
1	0.984	0.0093	[0.9654, 1.0022]	1.118	0.0077	[1.1024, 1.1325]
2	0.662	0.0022	[0.6574, 0.6659]	0.483	0.0016	[0.4800, 0.4864]
≥3	0.869	0.0049	[0.8593, 0.8786]	0.906	0.0054	[0.8956, 0.9169]

(b) Detailed matrices

Fisher Butte, years post-fire				Rose Prairie, years post-fire			
0	1	2	≥3	0	1	2	≥3
0.864	1.233	0.662*	0.839	1.007	1.428	0.483*	0.912
0.923	1.044		1.288	1.211	1.285		1.079
1.119	0.564*		0.690*	1.348	0.523*		0.664*
1.196	1.049		0.827	1.444	1.221		0.824
1.074			1.045	1.204			1.245

We used the bootstrap (Efron and Tibshirani, 1993) to associate confidence intervals (CIs) with the estimated growth rate $\widehat{\lambda}$ for each of the four averaged matrices. Because we did not have convenient access to the original data, we used a parametric bootstrap, as follows. The matrix **A** contains fertilities (the first row) and transition probabilities (the rest of the matrix); thus the estimated projection matrix can be written

$$\widehat{\mathbf{A}} = \widehat{\mathbf{T}} + \widehat{\mathbf{F}} \qquad (3)$$

where **F** contains fertilities in the first row and zeros elsewhere, and **T** contains only transition probabilities. We generate a bootstrap sample $\widehat{\mathbf{A}}^*$ as

$$\widehat{\mathbf{A}}^* = \widehat{\mathbf{T}}^* + \widehat{\mathbf{F}}^* \qquad (4)$$

Column j of the transition matrix **T** was estimated by noting the fates (including death), of the N_j individuals present at the beginning of the interval. Each column was estimated independently. A bootstrap estimate of column j of $\mathbf{T}$ is obtained by drawing a sample of size N_j from a multinomial distribution defined by the probabilities

$$\begin{pmatrix} \hat{t}_{1j} \\ \hat{t}_{2j} \\ \vdots \\ \hat{t}_{6j} \\ 1-\sum_i \hat{t}_{ij} \end{pmatrix} \qquad (5)$$

The observed fertilities in $\widehat{\mathbf{F}}$ are the mean number of offspring produced per individual in each stage. In the absence of information to the contrary, we assumed that seed production was randomly and independently distributed among individuals, which implies that offspring production follows a Poisson distribution with mean equal to the observed mean. Thus we generated a bootstrap fertility estimate for stage j as the mean of N_j Poisson random variates with mean $\hat{f}_{1j}$.

The bootstrap procedure was applied to each of the detailed matrices, which were then combined in the same way that we combined the real estimates. The result was a set of bootstrap estimates of the averaged matrices, $\widehat{\mathbf{A}}^*(i)$, $i = 1, \ldots, 3000$, which yielded a set of 3000 bootstrap estimates $\widehat{\lambda}^*(i)$ of the population growth rate. We calculated 95% confidence intervals for $\widehat{\lambda}$ as the 2.5th and 97.5th percentiles of this bootstrap distribution.

The bootstrap results in Table 3 show that λ is estimated with excellent precision by these data. The standard error in $\widehat{\lambda}$ is less than 1% growth per year, typical of good demographic data (Caswell, 2001). The confidence intervals for $\widehat{\lambda}$ from $\mathbf{A}^{(3)}$ and $\mathbf{A}^{(4)}$ do not include 1.0, so we conclude that *L. bradshawii* would be unable to persist at either site under the environmental conditions produced 2 or more years post-fire.

To evaluate the statistical significance of the decline in λ during the process of recovery from fire, we used a bootstrap test. We computed regressions of λ and $\log \lambda$ against time since last fire. The slope of these lines measures the rate of improvement (if positive) or deterioration (if negative) of environmental conditions for *L. bradshawii* following a fire. We computed these slopes for each of 3000 bootstrap samples. The 2.5th and 97.5th percentiles of the bootstrap distribution give a 95% confidence interval on this slope. If this confidence interval does not include zero, we can reject the null hypothesis of no trend at the $\alpha = 0.05$ level.

Because λ was particularly low for the single matrix in environmental state E_3, we repeated the regression calculation using only states E_1, E_2 and E_4.

The slopes of the regressions of λ and $\log \lambda$ against time since fire are given, together with their 95% confidence intervals, in Table 4. In all cases, the estimated slopes are negative and none of the 95% confidence intervals include 0. In fact, none of the 3000 bootstrap estimates of the slope exceeded 0, implying that the null hypothesis could be rejected at the $\alpha = 0.0003$ level.

Populations in the Rose Prairie site are more sensitive to the fire recovery process than those at Fisher Butte, because λ and $\log \lambda$ decrease more there with each year since the last fire.

B. LTRE Analysis

The differences in λ among environmental states are the integrated result of the effects of recovery from fire on all the vital rates. These effects are diverse (some vital rates respond much more than others), which is why λ is so useful as a statistic in such life table response experiments (LTREs; Caswell 1989a,b, 1996a,b, 2000, 2001). In a LTRE analysis, the environmental states are viewed as 'treatments', and the goal is to determine how much each of the vital rates contributes to the observed effect of each treatment on λ. If λ is especially *in*sensitive to variation in a particular vital rate, then even large treatment effects on that vital rate will contribute little to effects on λ. Conversely, even small effects on a vital rate to which λ is very sensitive can make a large contribution to effects on λ.

Because the entries in the matrix **A** include both survival and growth, we chose to decompose treatment effects into contributions from lower-level parameters (Caswell, 1996b). To do this, we use the decomposition $\mathbf{A} = \mathbf{T} + \mathbf{F}$. We write the transition probabilities as

$$t_{ij} = \sigma_j \gamma_{ij} \qquad (6)$$

Table 4

The slopes of linear and logarithmic regressions of λ (from the averaged matrices) on years since fire, and the 95% parametric bootstrap confidence intervals on those slopes

Regression	Fisher Butte		Rose Prairie	
	Slope	CI	Slope	CI
Linear	−0.0775	[−0.0837, −0.0704]	−0.1382	[−0.1445, −0.1318]
Logarithmic	−0.0877	[−0.0941, −0.0804]	−0.1568	[−0.1626, −0.1507]

where σ_j is the survival probability for stage j and γ_{ij} is the probability of growth from stage j to stage i, given survival. The sensitivities of λ to changes in σ_j and γ_{ij} are

$$\frac{\partial \lambda}{\partial \sigma_j} = \sum_i \gamma_{ij} \frac{\partial \lambda}{\partial t_{ij}} \tag{7}$$

$$\frac{\partial \lambda}{\partial \gamma_{ij}} = \sigma_j \frac{\partial \lambda}{\partial t_{ij}} \tag{8}$$

Since $\mathbf{F}$ contains non-zero entries only in its first row, the sensitivities of λ to the t_{ij} are just

$$\frac{\partial \lambda}{\partial t_{ij}} = \begin{cases} \dfrac{\partial \lambda}{\partial a_{ij}} & i = 2, \ldots, 6 \\ 0 & i = 1 \end{cases} \tag{9}$$

In turn, the sensitivity of λ to changes in a_{ij} is given by

$$\frac{\partial \lambda}{\partial a_{ij}} = \frac{v_i w_j}{\langle \mathbf{w}, \mathbf{v} \rangle} \tag{10}$$

where $\mathbf{w}$ and $\mathbf{v}$ are the right and left eigenvectors corresponding to λ and $\langle \ \rangle$ denotes the scalar product (Caswell 1978, 2001).

We use the matrix $\mathbf{A}^{(1)}$ in the year of a fire as the reference matrix, and measure effects relative to it. To first order, the growth rate in the other treatments, $\lambda^{(m)}$, $m = 2, 3, 4$, can be written

$$\begin{aligned}
\lambda^{(m)} \approx \lambda^{(1)} &+ \sum_{ij} \left(\gamma_{ij}^{(m)} - \gamma_{ij}^{(1)} \right) \frac{\partial \lambda}{\partial \gamma_{ij}} \\
&+ \sum_j \left(f_{1j}^{(m)} - f_{1j}^{(1)} \right) \frac{\partial \lambda}{\partial f_{1j}} \\
&+ \sum_j \left(\sigma_j^{(m)} - \sigma_j^{(1)} \right) \frac{\partial \lambda}{\partial \sigma_j}
\end{aligned} \tag{11}$$

The terms in these summations give the contributions of effects on stage-specific growth, survival and fertility to the effect on λ.

The contributions can be added to obtain the contribution of *groups* of vital rates. We combined them into five groups:

(1) **survival:** the contribution of survival effects is the sum of the contributions of survival of all stages:

$$\sum_j \left(\sigma_j^{(m)} - \sigma_j^{(1)} \right) \frac{\partial \lambda}{\partial \sigma_j} \tag{12}$$

(2) **fertility:** the net contribution of fertility effects is sum of the contributions of all entries in the first row of **A**:

$$\sum_j \left(f_{1j}^{(m)} - f_{1j}^{(1)} \right) \frac{\partial \lambda}{\partial f_{1j}} \tag{13}$$

(3) **shrinkage:** the contribution of effects on shrinkage probabilities is obtained by adding the contributions of all the γ_{ij} with $i < j$; i.e. of the transitions from larger to smaller size classes:

$$\sum_{\substack{i,j \\ i<j}} \left(\gamma_{ij}^{(m)} - \gamma_{ij}^{(1)} \right) \frac{\partial \lambda}{\partial \gamma_{ij}} \tag{14}$$

(4) **stasis:** the contribution of effects on the probability of stasis is the sum of the contributions of the γ_{ij}:

$$\sum_i \left(\gamma_{ii}^{(m)} - \gamma_{ii}^{(1)} \right) \frac{\partial \lambda}{\partial \gamma_{ii}} \tag{15}$$

(5) **growth:** the contribution of effects on growth is given by sum of the contributions of the γ_{ij} with $i > j$; i.e. of transitions from smaller to larger size classes:

$$\sum_{\substack{i,j \\ i>j}} \left(\gamma_{ij}^{(m)} - \gamma_{ij}^{(1)} \right) \frac{\partial \lambda}{\partial \gamma_{ij}} \tag{16}$$

Unlike the components into which elasticities of λ are often divided (e.g. Franco and Silvertown, 1996), these contributions actually separate survival, reproduction and the different directions of individual growth (increase, stasis, shrinkage).

Table 5 shows the results of the LTRE analysis. Time since fire affects λ mainly through effects on survival and growth; effects on fertility make a much smaller contribution. The contributions of shrinkage are positive, indicating that shrinkage rates increased following a fire. The contributions of stasis and growth are mostly negative, indicating that those probabilities declined following fire. The largest negative contributions are those for growth and for survival in states E_3 and E_4 (i.e. 2 and 3 or more years post-fire). Thus, in both sites, we conclude that the process of fire recovery affects λ mainly through reductions in survival and in the probability of growing to larger size classes.

VI. DEMOGRAPHY IN A DYNAMIC FIRE ENVIRONMENT

So far, our analyses have used λ calculated from the matrices $\mathbf{A}^{(1)}$–$\mathbf{A}^{(4)}$ as an index of environmental conditions in the years following a fire. These growth rates are hypothetical projections, since the environment cannot remain in one of these states (except if a plot was burned every year, or never burned, in which case it would remain in state E_1 or E_4 forever). But since they show that conditions for *L. bradshawii* deteriorate with increasing time since the last fire, it makes sense to suspect that population growth

Table 5

The summed contributions of environmental effects on stage-specific survival, fertility, shrinkage, stasis, and growth, to the effect on λ. The conditions in the year of a fire are used as reference conditions, so effects are measured in terms of years since fire

(a) Fisher Butte

Years post-fire	Survival	Fertility	Shrinkage	Stasis	Growth
1	−0.0070	−0.0320	0.0034	−0.1041	0.1114
2	−0.1322	−0.0552	0.0911	−0.0948	−0.1744
≥3	−0.0682	0.0375	0.0300	−0.0837	−0.0656

(b) Rose Prairie

Years post-fire	Survival	Fertility	Shrinkage	Stasis	Growth
1	−0.1425	0.0203	0.0237	−0.0452	0.1079
2	−0.2995	−0.0891	0.0741	−0.0448	−0.2954
≥3	−0.1513	−0.0605	0.0794	−0.0292	−0.0793

of *L. bradshawii* is probably affected by the frequency and temporal pattern of fire.

To explore this suspicion, we need to construct a model in which fire is a dynamic, rather than a static, component of the environment. Such models contain three components: a model for the environment, a model that assigns a projection matrix to each state of the environment, and a sequence of population vectors $\mathbf{n}(t)$, $t = 0, 1, \ldots$ generated by the sequence of matrices (Cohen, 1979b; Caswell, 2001).

We will consider both stochastic and periodic fire environments. The stochastic model generates fire sequences according to a simple two-state Markov chain. The periodic model specifies a deterministic sequence of burned and unburned years that repeats itself indefinitely. The natural environment of *L. bradshawii* is obviously stochastic, but management strategies are likely to call for periodic fires.

A. Models for the Environment

Our fire environment models have two parts. First, they specify a sequence of years with and without fires ('burned' and 'unburned' years). Second, they translate that sequence into a sequence of environmental states (E_1–E_4) and the corresponding sequence of matrices ($\mathbf{A}^{(1)}$–$\mathbf{A}^{(4)}$).

1. Stochastic Environments

In a stochastic environment, the sequence of burned and unburned years is generated by a two-state Markov chain, the transition graph of which is shown in Figure 1. A plot is burned with probability p if it was burned the year before, and q if it was not. The resulting transition matrix is

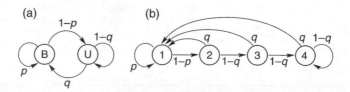

Fig. 1. The transition graphs for (a) the fire process and (b) the corresponding environmental states. In (a), B and U correspond to burned and unburned years. In (b), environmental states 1–4 correspond to the year of a fire, and 1–3 years after a fire, respectively. The probability of a fire in any year is p if the previous year was burned and q if not.

$$\mathbf{P} = \begin{pmatrix} p & q \\ 1-p & 1-q \end{pmatrix} \tag{17}$$

In terms of these probabilities, the long-term frequency of fire is

$$f = \frac{q}{1-p+q} \tag{18}$$

and the autocorrelation is

$$\rho = p - q \tag{19}$$

When $\rho = 0$, the occurrence of a fire is independent of whether a fire occurred the previous year; fires are then said to be independently and identically distributed (iid). When $\rho < 0$ there is a tendency for burned and unburned years to alternate; when $\rho > 0$ there are frequent long sequences of burned and of unburned years. Figure 2 shows typical stochastic realizations for $\rho = -0.5$, $\rho = 0$ and $\rho = 0.5$.

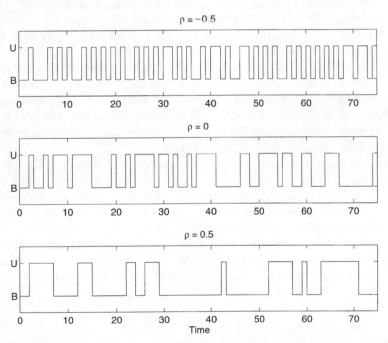

Fig. 2. Typical sequence of burned (B) and unburned (U) years generated by the two-state Markov chain model for autocorrelation values of $\rho = -0.5$ (top), $\rho = 0$ (middle) and $\rho = 0.5$ (bottom). In all three cases, the long-term fire frequency is 0.5.

The entries in the transition matrix **P** can be calculated from the fire frequency and the autocorrelation (Silva *et al.*, 1991; Tuljapurkar, 1997)

$$p = f(1 - \rho) + \rho \tag{20}$$

$$q = f(1 - \rho) \tag{21}$$

If the autocorrelation is negative, not all values of f are possible; the relations in equation (21) require that f satisfies

$$\frac{-\rho}{1 - \rho} \leq f \leq \frac{1}{1 - \rho} \tag{22}$$

so in our calculations for $\rho = -0.5$ the fire frequency will be restricted to $f \in [\frac{1}{3}, \frac{2}{3}]$.

This is an admittedly simple fire model, but it captures some of the important aspects of more detailed models. Johnson and Gutsell (1994), for example, discuss the Weibull distribution as a model for inter-fire intervals; it has a hazard function (i.e. the probability of fire in a given year, dependent on the time since the last fire) that can increase or decrease with time, or, as a special case, remain constant. Our iid model has a constant fire hazard. The autocorrelated model has a hazard that increases ($\rho < 0$) or decreases ($\rho > 0$) in a crude fashion. It is impossible to do better than this with a model with only two states, but, crude as it may be, the comparison gives us the ability to say something about the potential effect of fire in more sophisticated models.

As fires occur, the environment moves among the states E_1–E_4. Figure 1 shows the transition probabilities among the four environmental states generated by the two-state Markov model for fire. Of course, more sophisticated models of fire could be constructed by making the probability of fire depend explicitly on the environmental state. Accumulation of fuel with the time since the last fire is one mechanism that could generate such an effect. Note that even when *fires* are iid, the *environment* is autocorrelated, because the environmental states depend on how long it has been since the last fire.

2. Periodic Environments

One way to specify a periodic environment is in terms of fire frequency, either in terms of the interval between burned years:

Sequence	Fire frequency
BBBBBB . . .	1.00
BUBUBU . . .	0.50
BUUBUU . . .	0.33
BUUUBU . . .	0.25
etc.	

or in terms of the interval between unburned years (needed to fill in frequencies between 0.5 and 1.0):

Sequence	Fire frequency
UBUBUB . . .	0.50
UBBUBB . . .	0.67
UBBBUB . . .	0.75
UBBBBU . . .	0.80
etc.	

The matrix applied to the population at any time is determined by the number of years since the last fire. Thus, corresponding to the fire sequence BUUUU is the sequence of environments E_1, E_2, E_3, E_4, E_4.

The fire frequency alone does not completely specify the dynamics of a periodic environment. For example, in the sequences given above a fire frequency of 0.5 is given by the sequence BUBUBUBU. . . . But the sequences

$$BBUUBBUUBBUU . . .$$
$$BBBUUUBBBUUU . . .$$
$$BBBBUUUUBBBB . . .$$

all also have a fire frequency of 0.5, and they can have dramatically different effects on population growth.

These effects can be explored by defining a fire rotation – the length of time over which the pattern repeats – and examining all possible periodic patterns with this rotation length. For example, with a rotation of 2 years, the only possible schedules are BB, UU, BU and UB (the last two, of course, being equivalent). Longer rotations have more possible schedules. Later, we will examine the population growth resulting from all $2^{10} = 1024$ distinct fire schedules over a 10-year rotation.

B. Stochastic Population Growth

The sequence of environments generated by the stochastic fire model generates a corresponding sequence of matrices, which projects the population from one time to the next. When using the averaged matrices, there is one matrix corresponding to each environmental state. When using the detailed matrices, at each time t a matrix is selected at random from the set of detailed matrices corresponding to that environmental state.

Population growth in a stochastic environment can be described by two indices; one measures the growth rate of average population size

$$\log \mu = \lim_{t \to \infty} \frac{1}{t} \log E(N(t)) \tag{23}$$

while the other measures the average growth rate of the population

$$\log \lambda_s = \lim_{t \to \infty} \frac{1}{t} E(\log N(t)) \tag{24}$$

where $N(t) = \|\mathbf{n}(t)\| = \sum_i |n_i(t)|$ is the total population size. Given some reasonable assumptions about the environment and the life history (Cohen, 1976, 1977a,b, 1979a,b; Tuljapurkar and Orzack, 1980; Tuljapurkar, 1990a, 1997), every realization of the process, with probability one, eventually grows at the rate $\log \lambda_s$. The quantity $\log \lambda_s$ is called the *stochastic growth rate*. It determines the extinction (certain if $\log \lambda_s \leq 0$) or persistence (with some positive probability if $\log \lambda_s > 0$) of the population. It measures fitness in models of selection in stochastic environments. The theory is outlined in Caswell (2001) and detailed in Tuljapurkar (1990a).

Although it is a measure of growth rate, λ_s is *not* the eigenvalue of a matrix. It is estimated by simulation as

$$\widehat{\log \lambda_s} = \frac{1}{T} \sum_{t=1}^{T} \log \frac{N(t+1)}{N(t)} \tag{25}$$

for some large value of T. Figure 3 shows an example of the convergence of the estimate; samples of at least $T = 5000$ seem necessary for accuracy; we used $T = 10\,000$ in all our calculations.

Approximate 95% confidence intervals on the stochastic growth rate are given by

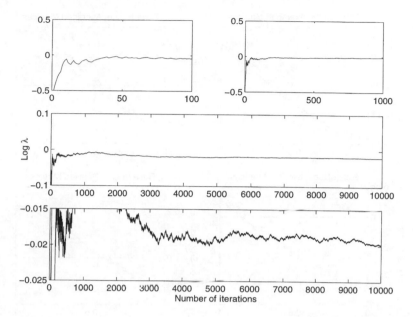

Fig. 3. Convergence of the estimates $\widehat{\log \lambda_s}$ of the stochastic growth rate as a function of the length T of the simulation from which it is estimated. This example uses the averaged matrices for the Rose Prairie site with fire frequency $f = 0.4$ and autocorrelation $\rho = 0$.

$$\widehat{\log \lambda_s} \pm 1.96 \sqrt{\frac{V\left(\log \frac{N(t+1)}{N(t)}\right)}{T}} \tag{26}$$

where $V(\cdot)$ denotes the variance.

The stochastic growth rate $\log \lambda_s$ is shown as a function of fire frequency and autocorrelation in Figure 4, for models using the averaged and the detailed matrices. It increases with fire frequency in both sites. There is little consistent difference between the results for $\rho = 0$ and $\rho = 0.5$, but the stochastic growth rate is distinctly elevated at $\rho = -0.5$. The patterns for all three autocorrelations are similar.

The transition between certain extinction and possible persistence occurs at the fire frequency where $\log \lambda_s = 0$. This critical fire frequency can be estimated from Figure 4; the results are shown in Table 6. In general, the Fisher Butte site requires a fire frequency on the order of 0.8, and the Rose Prairie site a frequency on the order of 0.45, in order to support a population of *L. bradshawii*.

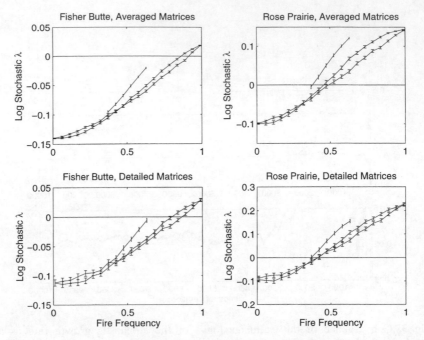

Fig. 4. The stochastic population growth rate $\log \lambda_s$ for the two sites and both the averaged and the detailed matrices. In each graph, the upper line is $\rho = -0.5$, the middle line is $\rho = 0$, and the lower line is $\rho = 0.5$. Error bars in this and subsequent figures are 95% confidence intervals.

Table 6

The critical fire frequency required for persistence of *L. bradshawii* in a stochastic fire environment, as a function of the autocorrelation ρ, using the average and the detailed matrices

(a) Fisher Butte

ρ	Average	Detailed
−0.5	—	0.653
0.0	0.863	0.795
0.5	0.914	0.863

(b) Rose Prairie

ρ	Average	Detailed
−0.5	0.381	0.370
0.0	0.457	0.417
0.5	0.491	0.414

Figures 5 and 6 compare the stochastic growth rates for the detailed and the average matrices. In each case, growth rates are higher for the model including the detailed matrices. This is somewhat surprising, since one might have predicted that the increased variability in the vital rates in the detailed model would reduce population growth rate.

The differences between the sites can be seen more clearly in Figure 7, which shows $\log \lambda_s$ for zero autocorrelation. As fire frequency goes to 0, the population always experiences environment E_4. In the case of the average matrices, this corresponds to the deterministic model with the matrix $\mathbf{A}^{(4)}$. The eigenvalues of $\mathbf{A}^{(4)}$ in the Rose Prairie and the Fisher Butte sites are 0.91 and 0.87, respectively; the corresponding logarithms are -0.1 and -0.14, corresponding to the stochastic growth rates seen at $f = 0$ in the averaged matrix model. Similarly, when $f = 1$, the environment is always in state E_1 and the stochastic model converges to the deterministic model with matrix $\mathbf{A}^{(1)}$. The logs of the eigenvalues of this matrix in Rose Prairie and Fisher Butte are 0.14 and 0.02, respectively.

C. Quasi-extinction

In models that include only environmental stochasticity, true extinction (reducing the population to zero) is impossible. Even if $\lambda_s < 1$, the

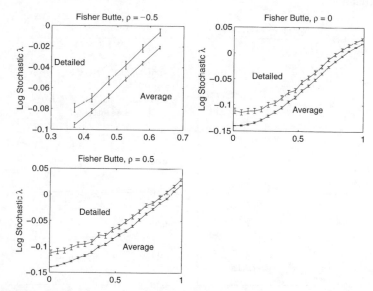

Fig. 5. The stochastic population growth rate $\log \lambda_s$ for the average and the detailed matrix models, for the Fisher Butte site. Results are shown for the averaged and the detailed matrices and for all three values of the autocorrelation ρ.

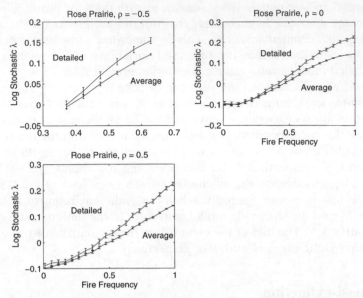

Fig. 6. The stochastic population growth rate $\log \lambda_s$ for the average and the detailed matrix models, for the Rose Prairie site. Results are shown for the averaged and the detailed matrices and for all three values of the autocorrelation ρ.

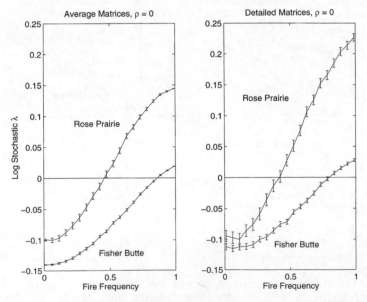

Fig. 7. Stochastic population growth rate $\log \lambda_s$ for the two sites and the averaged (left) and the detailed (right) matrices, for $\rho = 0$.

population will merely decline exponentially to lower and lower densities. But these models do admit the possibility of *quasi-extinction*, defined as reduction of population size to a specified fraction of its current size (Ginzburg *et al.*, 1982; Burgman *et al.*, 1993). The fraction can be chosen to represent a level likely to result in true extinction, or a level set by management concerns.

The calculation of quasi-extinction relies on the fact (Tuljapurkar and Orzack, 1980) that $\log N(t)$ is asymptotically normally distributed, with a mean that grows at the rate $\log \lambda_s$ and a variance that increases at a rate σ^2. The variance growth rate σ^2 can be calculated in several ways (Caswell, 2001), but the easiest relies on the fact that in the lognormal distribution the growth rate of the mean population size (i.e. $E(N(t))$ rather than $E(\log N(t))$) satisfies

$$\log \mu = \log \lambda_s + \frac{\sigma^2}{2} \qquad (27)$$

Thus, σ^2 can be estimated as

$$\widehat{\sigma^2} = 2\left(\widehat{\log \mu} - \widehat{\log \lambda_s}\right) \qquad (28)$$

In turn, $\widehat{\log \mu}$ is the log of the dominant eigenvalue of the matrix

$$\begin{pmatrix} \mathbf{A}^{(1)} & 0 & 0 & 0 \\ 0 & \mathbf{A}^{(2)} & 0 & 0 \\ 0 & 0 & \mathbf{A}^{(3)} & 0 \\ 0 & 0 & 0 & \mathbf{A}^{(4)} \end{pmatrix} (\mathbf{P} \otimes \mathbf{I}) \qquad (29)$$

where $\mathbf{I}$ is an identity matrix with dimension equal to the number of stages and $\otimes$ denotes the Kronecker product (Tuljapurkar, 1982; Caswell, 2001, Section 14.3.4).

Figure 8 shows σ^2 as a function of fire frequency and autocorrelation. It goes to 0 when $f = 0$ or $f = 1$, because the environment becomes deterministic at these limits. It is maximized at intermediate frequencies, and increases as autocorrelation becomes more positive.

Let N_e/N be the quasi-extinction threshold; e.g. $N_e/N = 0.01$ means that quasi-extinction is defined to be reduction of the population to 1% of its current density. Then the probability of quasi-extinction is given by

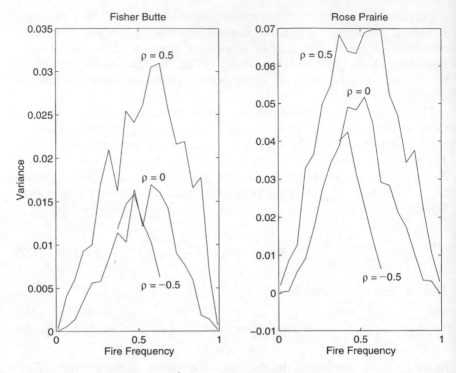

Fig. 8. The rate of growth (σ^2) of the variance of $\log N(t)$ as a function of fire frequency and autocorrelation, calculated using the averaged matrices.

$$P_e = \begin{cases} 1 & \log \lambda_s \leq 0 \\ \exp\left(\dfrac{2\log \lambda_s \log \frac{N_e}{N}}{\sigma^2}\right) & \log \lambda_s > 0 \end{cases} \tag{30}$$

(Lande and Orzack, 1988; Dennis *et al.*, 1991).

Quasi-extinction probability, for a quasi-extinction threshold of $N_e/N = 0.01$, is shown in Figure 9. It drops precipitously once $\log \lambda_s$ exceeds 0. These results show that any management strategy that raises $\log \lambda_s$ even slightly above 0 will essentially eliminate the likelihood of quasi-extinction due to environmental stochasticity.

D. Sensitivity and Elasticity Analysis

Perturbation analyses are an essential part of demography (Caswell, 2001). They ask what would happen *if* the vital rates were to change in certain

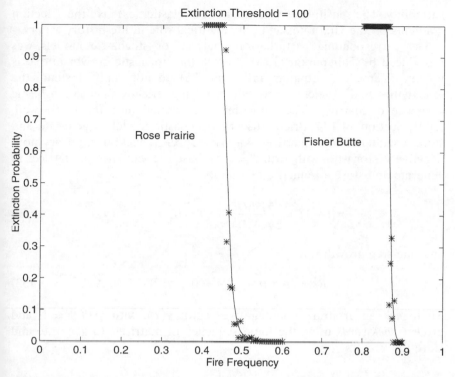

Fig. 9. The extinction probability as a function of fire frequency for an extinction threshold of 0.01 (i.e. extinction corresponds to a reduction in population size to 1% of its present size). The solid line is a non-parametric regression (loess) curve fit to the calculated points, with a bandwidth of 25% of the number of points.

ways. The effects of such changes on population growth rate are described by the sensitivity and elasticity of λ to changes in the matrix entries a_{ij}. The sensitivity of λ is given by equation (10) above. The elasticity, or proportional sensitivity, of λ is given by

$$\frac{\partial \log \lambda}{\partial \log a_{ij}} = \frac{a_{ij}}{\lambda} \frac{\partial \lambda}{\partial a_{ij}} \tag{31}$$

(Caswell *et al.*, 1984; de Kroon *et al.*, 1986; Caswell, 2001).

Sensitivities and elasticities have become standard parts of demographic analysis. They are used to evaluate the effects of conservation plans, pest control tactics, harvesting, environmental changes and sampling variability. The sensitivities (though not the elasticities) give the selection gradients on the vital rates and play a critical role in life history theory.

The corresponding perturbation analysis for stochastic models was introduced by Tuljapurkar (1990a). Since the stochastic growth rate λ_s is not an eigenvalue, equations (10) and (31) do not apply. Instead, the sensitivities and elasticities are calculated numerically from a stochastic sequence of matrices. The algorithm is described in detail in Caswell, (2001, Section 14.4.1). Briefly, use the stochastic model to generate and store a sequence of T matrices $\mathbf{A}_0, \mathbf{A}_1, \ldots, \mathbf{A}_{T-1}$. Pick an arbitrary non-negative vector $\mathbf{w}(0)$, with $\|\mathbf{w}(0)\| = 1$, and use the sequence of matrices to generate and store a sequence of vectors

$$\mathbf{w}(t+1) = \frac{\mathbf{A}_t \mathbf{w}(t)}{\|\mathbf{A}_t \mathbf{w}(t)\|} \qquad t = 0, \ldots, T-1 \tag{32}$$

and one-step growth rates

$$R_t = \|\mathbf{A}_t \mathbf{w}(t)\| \qquad t = 0, \ldots, T-1 \tag{33}$$

Then pick an arbitrary non-negative vector $\mathbf{v}(T)$, with $\|\mathbf{v}(T)\| = 1$, and project *backwards* using the same sequence of matrices, to generate and store the vectors

$$\mathbf{v}^{\mathsf{T}}(t-1) = \frac{\mathbf{v}^{\mathsf{T}}(t) \mathbf{A}_{t-1}}{\|\mathbf{v}^{\mathsf{T}}(t) \mathbf{A}_{t-1}\|} \qquad t = T, \ldots, 1 \tag{34}$$

Finally, from the sequences $\mathbf{A}_t$, $\mathbf{w}(t)$, $\mathbf{v}(t)$, and R_t, compute the sensitivity matrix for $\log \lambda_s$ and the elasticity matrix for λ_s

$$\left(\frac{\partial \log \lambda_s}{\partial a_{ij}} \right) = \frac{1}{T} \sum_{t=0}^{T-1} \frac{\mathbf{v}(t+1)\mathbf{w}^{\mathsf{T}}(t)}{R_t \mathbf{v}^{\mathsf{T}}(t+1)\mathbf{w}(t+1)} \tag{35}$$

$$\left(\frac{\partial \log \lambda_s}{\partial \log a_{ij}} \right) = \frac{1}{T} \sum_{t=0}^{T-1} \frac{\left(\mathbf{v}(t+1)\mathbf{w}^{\mathsf{T}}(t) \right) \circ \mathbf{A}_t}{R_t \mathbf{v}^{\mathsf{T}}(t+1)\mathbf{w}(t+1)} \tag{36}$$

where $\circ$ denotes the Hadamard product. See Caswell (2001) for details of the derivation and MATLAB code.

1. Perturbation Analysis of the Stochastic Growth Rate

The sensitivity and elasticity of the stochastic growth rate depend on the properties of the environment (the fire frequency and autocorrelation) and on the response of the vital rates to the environment (the details of the matrices $\mathbf{A}^{(1)}$–$\mathbf{A}^{(4)}$). We will explore that dependence in detail below, but we begin with a typical set of results, for $f = 0.5$, $\rho = 0$ (Figure 10). The sensitivities of $\log \lambda_s$ are highest to changes in entries in the lower left corner of **A**, corresponding to growth directly from small vegetative to large reproductive plants. The sensitivity to changes in fertility is very low in both sites.

The elasticity of λ_s, by contrast, is highest to survival of the largest reproductive plants (stage R_3 at Fisher Butte, R_2 at Rose Prairie). The elasticities of λ_s are also high to changes in transitions involving stages 3–5 (large vegetative and small reproductive plants), and to fertility of large reproductive plants.

It is well known that the results of perturbation analysis of deterministic models depend on the values of the a_{ij}; this dependence is quantified in the second derivatives of λ (Caswell, 1996b). This has led to concern over the accuracy, precision, and/or reliability of estimated sensitivities and

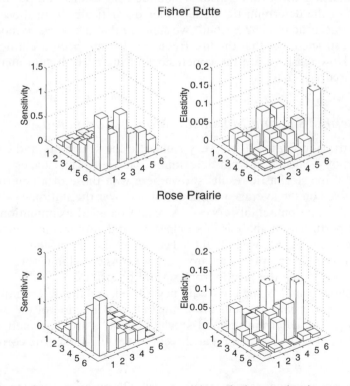

Fig. 10. Matrices of sensitivity and elasticity of the stochastic growth rate, calculated using the average matrices. The matrices shown are for a fire frequency $f = 0.5$ and autocorrelation $\rho = 0$. The sensitivities are $\partial \log \lambda_s / \partial a_{ij}$; the elasticities are $\partial \log \lambda_s / \partial \log a_{ij}$.

elasticities, especially when used in management. If estimates are very sensitive to errors of sampling or model specification, then management recommendations based on typically imperfect data may be badly misguided. Some of the analyses of this potential problem have focused strictly on the largest elasticities, on the grounds that they represent the 'most important' parts of the life cycle (Mills *et al.*, 1999). A more detailed examination, based on patterns of sensitivity and elasticity throughout the life cycle (Caswell, 2001) concluded that perturbation analyses are remarkably robust.

In stochastic models for a dynamic environment, results depend not only on the vital rates, but also on the environment. Here we have an opportunity to investigate this dependence from several perspectives. First, we will suppose that, instead of a stochastic analysis, we constructed a deterministic model based on the average vital rates experienced by the population. Such a model would yield a value of λ that might differ wildly from the stochastic growth rate λ_s. But would the conclusions of a perturbation analysis of the deterministic model differ dramatically from those of the correct stochastic model? Second, we suppose that a stochastic model has been constructed, but that the fire frequency has not been accurately estimated. How sensitive are the conclusions of the perturbation analysis to such inaccuracies?

2. *Deterministic and Stochastic Models Compared*

The matrices in Figure 10 are very similar to the sensitivity and elasticity matrices of λ calculated from deterministic models. This suggests a comparison of the stochastic results shown here with those of a deterministic model based on the average matrix calculated over the stationary distribution of the environmental process. A recent detailed examination found that the perturbation analysis of stochastic and deterministic models were often very similar (Caswell, 2001).* The model under consideration here, however, is more complex than any of those considered in Caswell (2001), so we will examine the results from several directions.

In Figures 11 and 12 the fire frequency is fixed, and the deterministic and stochastic perturbation results are compared as a function of the autocorrelation ρ. The deterministic and stochastic results are extremely closely correlated, at both sites and regardless of ρ. Table 7 shows the correlation

---

*Note that in evolutionary contexts, very small differences between the deterministic and stochastic models can translate into drastically different predictions of life history evolution; see Tuljapurkar (1990b), Tuljapurkar and Istock (1993), and Caswell (2001) for examples.

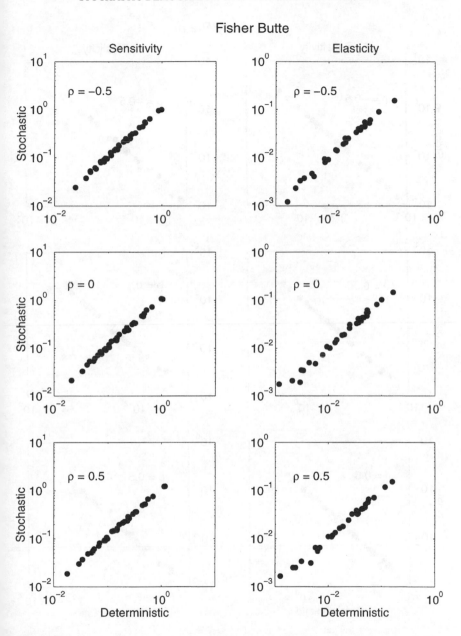

Fig. 11. Comparison of the deterministic and stochastic sensitivities and elasticities of population growth, calculated from the average matrices, at the Fisher Butte site. The deterministic sensitivities and elasticities, $\partial \log \lambda / \partial a_{ij}$ and $\partial \log \lambda / \partial \log a_{ij}$, respectively, are calculated from the average matrix. Fire frequency $f = 0.5$ throughout; autocorrelations as shown.

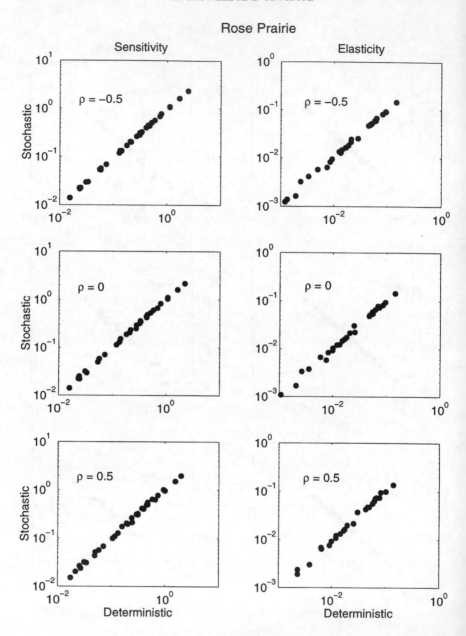

Fig. 12. Deterministic and stochastic sensitivities and elasticities of population growth, as in Figure 11, at the Rose Prairie site.

Table 7

Product–moment correlations between sensitivities and elasticities of population growth rate in the stochastic model and the corresponding sensitivities and elasticities calculated from the deterministic model based on the average matrix. Fire frequency $f = 0.5$

(a) Fisher Butte

Quantity	Matrices	$\rho = -0.5$	$\rho = 0$	$\rho = 0.5$
Sensitivity	Averaged	0.9975	0.9970	0.9986
Sensitivity	Detailed	0.9934	0.9927	0.9960
Elasticity	Averaged	0.9938	0.9929	0.9965
Elasticity	Detailed	0.9955	0.9935	0.9943

(b) Rose Prairie

Quantity	Matrices	$\rho = -0.5$	$\rho = 0$	$\rho = 0.5$
Sensitivity	Averaged	0.9997	0.9993	0.9982
Sensitivity	Detailed	0.9981	0.9967	0.9926
Elasticity	Averaged	0.9991	0.9975	0.9955
Elasticity	Detailed	0.9852	0.9786	0.9757

Table 8

Product–moment correlations between sensitivities and elasticities of population growth rate in the stochastic model and the corresponding sensitivities and elasticities calculated from the deterministic model based on the average matrix. Autocorrelation $\rho = 0$ throughout

(a) Fisher Butte

Quantity	Matrices	$f = 0.01$	$f = 0.25$	$f = 0.5$	$f = 0.75$	$f = 0.99$
Sensitivity	Averaged	1.0000	0.9972	0.9970	0.9991	1.0000
Sensitivity	Detailed	0.9965	0.9916	0.9927	0.9975	0.9997
Elasticity	Averaged	1.0000	0.9917	0.9928	0.9989	1.0000
Elasticity	Detailed	0.9884	0.9891	0.9936	0.9989	0.9997

(b) Rose Prairie

Quantity	Matrices	$f = 0.01$	$f = 0.25$	$f = 0.5$	$f = 0.75$	$f = 0.99$
Sensitivity	Averaged	0.9999	0.9975	0.9993	0.9999	1.0000
Sensitivity	Detailed	0.9879	0.9921	0.9967	0.9985	0.9996
Elasticity	Averaged	1.0000	0.9951	0.9975	0.9998	1.0000
Elasticity	Detailed	0.9919	0.9745	0.9788	0.9947	0.9980

coefficients for both the averaged and the detailed matrices. All are above 0.97; most are above 0.99.

Table 8 shows the result of fixing ρ and comparing deterministic and stochastic models for fire frequencies ranging from $f = 0.01$ to $f = 0.99$. These correlations are also extremely high, most of them exceeding 0.99. At the extremes ($f = 0.01$ and $f = 0.99$), where the stochastic model is almost deterministic, the correlation approaches 1.0.

We conclude that the sensitivities and elasticities of the deterministic population growth rate from the mean matrix do a remarkably accurate job of predicting the same properties of the stochastic growth rate.

3. The Effects of Fire Frequency on Perturbation Analysis

Figure 13 compares the sensitivities of $\log \lambda_s$ as a function of fire frequency; Figure 14 does the same for the elasticities of λ_s. Tables 9 and 10 show the correlations, for both the average and the detailed matrices.

Sensitivities of the stochastic growth rate are extremely *in*sensitive to errors in estimation of the fire frequency. At Fisher Butte, the correlations

Table 9
Correlations among the sensitivities of $\log \lambda_s$ for stochastic models as a function of fire frequency f. Values calculated using the detailed matrices are shown above the diagonal, values for the averaged matrices are shown below the diagonal. Autocorrelation $\rho = 0$ throughout

(a) Fisher Butte

	$f = 0.01$	$f = 0.25$	$f = 0.5$	$f = 0.75$	$f = 0.99$
$f = 0.01$	1.0000	0.9858	0.9686	0.9541	0.9288
$f = 0.25$	0.9856	1.0000	0.9931	0.9725	0.9392
$f = 0.5$	0.9684	0.9931	1.0000	0.9905	0.9651
$f = 0.75$	0.9515	0.9700	0.9889	1.0000	0.9915
$f = 0.99$	0.9194	0.9285	0.9565	0.9887	1.0000

(b) Rose Prairie

	$f = 0.01$	$f = 0.25$	$f = 0.5$	$f = 0.75$	$f = 0.99$
$f = 0.01$	1.0000	0.9290	0.8815	0.8593	0.8347
$f = 0.25$	0.9283	1.0000	0.9926	0.9826	0.9670
$f = 0.5$	0.8755	0.9917	1.0000	0.9971	0.9857
$f = 0.75$	0.8474	0.9821	0.9979	1.0000	0.9941
$f = 0.99$	0.8157	0.9687	0.9898	0.9957	1.0000

Table 10
Correlations among the elasticities of λ_s for stochastic models as a function of fire frequency f. Values calculated using the detailed matrices are shown above the diagonal, values for the averaged matrices are shown below the diagonal. Autocorrelation $\rho = 0$ throughout

(a) Fisher Butte

	$f = 0.01$	$f = 0.25$	$f = 0.5$	$f = 0.75$	$f = 0.99$
$f = 0.01$	1.0000	0.9425	0.7719	0.5831	0.4340
$f = 0.25$	0.9441	1.0000	0.9236	0.7669	0.6180
$f = 0.5$	0.7575	0.9142	1.0000	0.9501	0.8565
$f = 0.75$	0.5301	0.7282	0.9399	1.0000	0.9732
$f = 0.99$	0.3657	0.5700	0.8413	0.9738	1.0000

(b) Rose Prairie

	$f = 0.01$	$f = 0.25$	$f = 0.5$	$f = 0.75$	$f = 0.99$
$f = 0.01$	1.0000	0.9082	0.6630	0.4457	0.3318
$f = 0.25$	0.9073	1.0000	0.9112	0.7661	0.6770
$f = 0.5$	0.6828	0.9251	1.0000	0.9615	0.9160
$f = 0.75$	0.5151	0.8231	0.9765	1.0000	0.9901
$f = 0.99$	0.4342	0.7653	0.9491	0.9936	1.0000

between sensitivities at different values of f exceed 0.9, even over an extremely wide range of fire frequencies ($f = 0.01$ versus $f = 0.99$). At Rose Prairie, the correlations exceed 0.8 over this range, and exceed 0.98 over the range $0.25 \leq f \leq 0.75$. Figures 15 and 16 show the sensitivity matrices, making clear their near-invariance under changes in f. Thus, conclusions about the effects of changes in the vital rates on the stochastic growth rate are remarkably insensitive to errors in the estimates of fire frequency.

The elasticities of λ_s are less robust to changes in f than are the sensitivities (Figure 14). Elasticities of λ_s calculated for $f = 0.01$ do a poor job of predicting elasticities for $f = 0.99$. But the correlations are higher for smaller ranges of fire frequencies (Table 10). At both sites, the correlation exceeds 0.7 for $0.25 \leq f \leq 0.75$, and exceeds 0.9 when models are compared that differ in fire frequency by less than 0.25.

Figure 15 shows that, at Fisher Butte, as f increases, the elasticities to the survival and fertility of large flowering plants and the stasis of large vegetative plants dominate all the other elasticities. At low fire frequencies, elasticities are much more evenly distributed among the

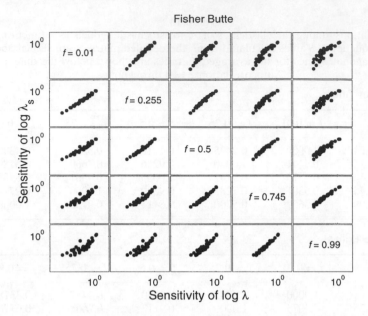

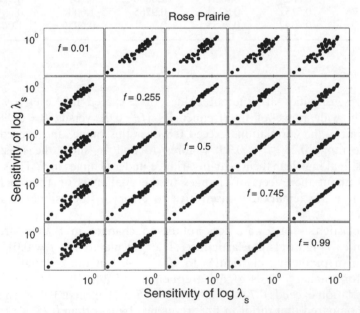

Fig. 13. Reliability of the sensitivity of the stochastic growth rate, across a range of fire frequencies. Calculated from the average matrices; autocorrelation $\rho = 0$ throughout.

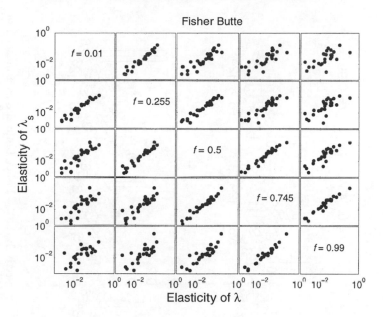

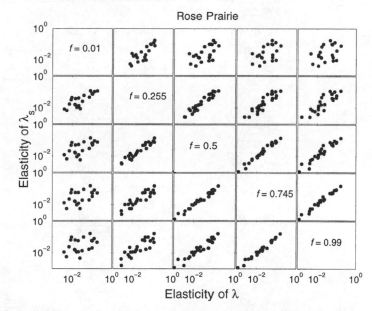

Fig. 14. Reliability of the elasticity of the stochastic growth rate, across a range of fire frequencies. Calculated from the average matrices; autocorrelation $\rho = 0$ throughout.

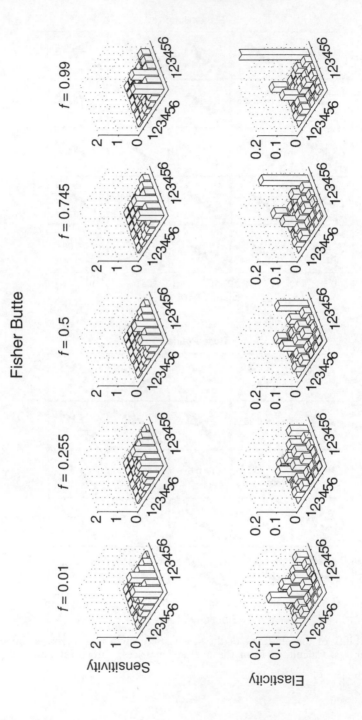

Fig. 15. Sensitivity and elasticity matrices, $\partial \log \lambda_s / \partial a_{ij}$ and $\partial \log \lambda_s / \partial \log a_{ij}$, respectively, at the Fisher Butte site as a function of fire frequency. Calculated from the average matrices; autocorrelation $\rho = 0$ throughout.

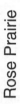

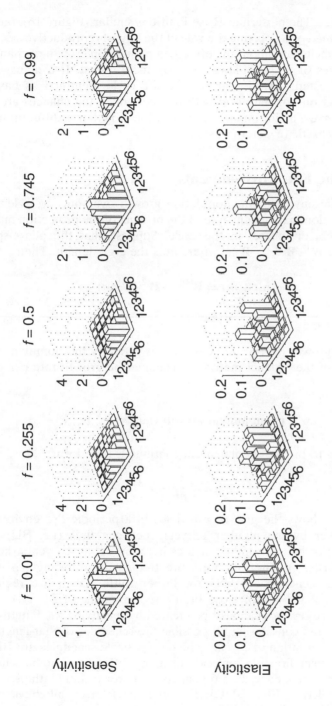

Fig. 16. Sensitivity and elasticity matrices, $\partial \log \lambda_s / \partial a_{ij}$ and $\partial \log \lambda_s / \partial \log a_{ij}$, respectively, at the Rose Prairie site as a function of fire frequency. Calculated from the average matrices; autocorrelation $\rho = 0$ throughout.

matrix entries. The pattern at Rose Prairie is similar (Figure 16), but with stage R_2 instead of R_3 playing the role of the largest reproductive size class.

In sum, conclusions about the effects on population growth of changes in the vital rates of *L. bradshawii* are extremely robust. If a management action is directed towards part of the life cycle identified as having a major impact on population growth by one model, the chances are good that it will have a major impact on population growth in a different model, whether stochastic or deterministic.

E. Periodic Fire Environments

In a periodic environment, population growth over one cycle length is given by the dominant eigenvalue of the product of the projection matrices for each step, or 'phase' in the cycle. Suppose that the phase-specific matrices are $\mathbf{B}^{(1)}, \mathbf{B}^{(2)}, \ldots \mathbf{B}^{(m)}$, where m is the cycle length. Then

$$\mathbf{n}(t + m) = \mathbf{B}^{(m)} \cdots \mathbf{B}^{(2)} \mathbf{B}^{(1)} \mathbf{n}(t) \tag{37}$$

$$= \mathbf{A}\mathbf{n}(t) \tag{38}$$

Population growth over an m-year cycle is given by the dominant eigenvalue, $\lambda^{(\mathbf{A})}$, of the product matrix $\mathbf{A}$. The average growth rate per year is given by

$$\text{mean annual growth rate} = (\lambda^{(\mathbf{A})})^{\frac{1}{m}} \tag{39}$$

or, changing to the more convenient continuous-time form,

$$\log \lambda = \frac{1}{m} \log \lambda^{(\mathbf{A})} \tag{40}$$

Figure 17 shows the growth rate $\log \lambda$ in a periodic fire environment defined either by the number of years between fires (i.e. BU, BUU, BUUU, ...) or by the number of fires between unburned years (i.e. UB, UBB, UBBB, ...). The minimum fire frequencies allowing persistence under these scenarios are 0.83 for Fisher Butte (i.e. a fire regime of UBBBBB ...), and 0.5 for Rose Prairie (a fire regime of BU ...).

Periodic fire regimes can also be created by specifying the length of the fire rotation and considering all possible fire schedules of that length. For example, in a rotation of 2 years, the only possible schedules are BB, BU and UU. Longer fire rotations permit many different periodic schedules with the same frequency. In a 6-year rotation, for example, the schedules BBBUUU, BBUUBU, BUUBBU, and BUBUBU all have a fire

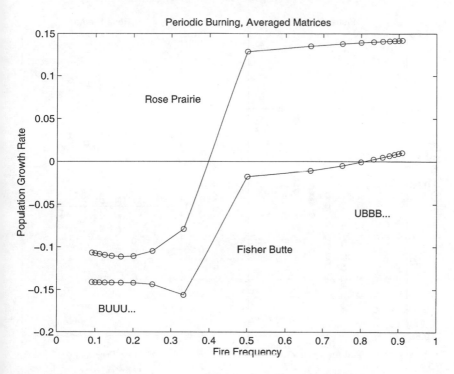

Fig. 17. The annual population growth rate for periodic fire regimes, based on the averaged matrices.

frequency of 0.5. Because matrix multiplication is not commutative, however, they will not, in general, produce the same growth rate.

To investigate the effect of periodic burning on a reasonably long rotation, we calculated the annual growth rate resulting from all $2^{10} = 1024$ of the distinct fire schedules over a 10-year rotation (Figure 18). When fire frequency equals 0 or 1, there is only one possible growth rate. At intermediate frequencies, there is a range of possible growth rates associated with any one fire frequency. The schedules maximizing λ as a function of fire frequency are given in Table 11.

The optimal schedules at Fisher Butte always alternate, as much as possible, unburned years with burned years. The optimal schedules at Rose Prairie are the same at low frequencies, but at higher frequencies (0.6 and higher) the optimal schedules contain longer runs of burned years.

It is not clear that these differences will be significant to management, but we present them here to demonstrate how such calculations can be made. Certainly they emphasize the point that one cannot assume that any

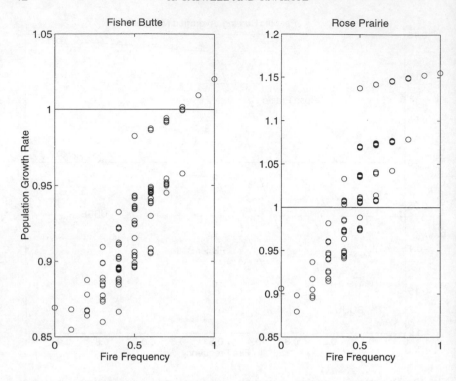

Fig. 18. The annual population growth rate for all possible periodic fire regimes on a 10-year schedule, using the average matrices.

Table 11

The periodic burning schedules, on a 10-year rotation, that maximize the annual growth rate of *L. bradshawii* at each site

Frequency	Fisher Butte	Rose Prairie
0.1	BUUUUUUUU	BUUUUUUUU
0.2	BU BUUUUUU	BU BUUUUUU
0.3	BU BU BUUUUU	BU BU BUUUUU
0.4	BU BU BU BUUU	BU BU BU BUUU
0.5	BU BU BU BU BU	BU BU BU BU BU
0.6	B B BU BU BU BU	B BU BU BB BU BU
0.7	B B B B BU BU BU	B B BU B BU BU BU
0.8	B B B B B B BU BU	B B B B U B B B B BU
0.9	B B B B B B B B BU	B B B B B B B B BU

rotation with a given fire frequency is equivalent from the point of view of *L. bradshawii.*

VII. SUMMARY AND DISCUSSION

Fire has a substantial positive effect on the growth rate of *L. bradshawii* at both sites. The highest population growth rate would be produced by maintaining the conditions in the year of a fire, and λ declines with time since the last fire. This decline is due mainly to reduced survival and growth; changes in fertility make only small contributions to the effect. In a dynamic fire environment, the long-term population growth rate depends on the frequency and temporal autocorrelation of fires. High fire frequency and negative autocorrelation both increase the stochastic growth rate. Including small-scale spatial and temporal variability by using the detailed matrices produces slightly higher stochastic rates than the averaged matrices.

The two sites differed in population growth, with higher rates at the Rose Prairie site. The critical fire frequency required to maintain *L. bradshawii* populations is about 0.8–0.9 at Fisher Butte, but only 0.4–0.5 at Rose Prairie.

The causes of the differences between the sites are not clear. According to Pendergrass *et al.* (1999), the study sites had similar soils and hydrology but differed in population characteristics and associated vegetation. Prior to the initiation of burning treatments in 1988, plants at Rose Prairie were smaller and produced fewer flowering structures than at Fisher Butte, although fruit production per plant was similar at the two sites. The *Deschampsia cespitosa/Danthonia californica* community-type was present at both sites, but the *Vaccinium caespitosum* type was present only at Rose Prairie and the *Rosa nutkana/Juncus nevadensis* type was present only at Fisher Butte (Pendergrass, 1995).

Fires also differed in behavior among the study sites and years. In 1988 fires were more intense, produced greater heat per unit area, and consumed more total biomass at Fisher Butte than at Rose Prairie. The 1989 fires were similar at the two locations, but were spotty compared to the more complete 1988 burns (Pendergrass *et al.*, 1998). Differences in the response of grassland plant species to fires have been attributed to differences in fire behavior and intensity (e.g. between backfires and headfires in North American tallgrass prairies (Bidwell *et al.*, 1990) and African grassland and savanna (Trollope, 1978, 1982)). The effects of fire on *L. bradshawii* at Rose Prairie and Fisher Butte may have differed in part due to site differences in populations, associated vegetation, fire behavior or other factors.

The picture of *L. bradshawii* dynamics in a dynamic fire environment that emerges from our results agrees with other studies of plants in savanna and grassland ecosystems. Silva *et al.* (1991) and Canales *et al.* (1994) used periodic and stochastic matrix models to evaluate the effects of fire frequency on two species of grasses from tropical savannas in Venezuela (*Andropogon semiberbis* and *A. brevifolius*). Stochastic and deterministic population growth rates both increased with fire frequency, and a critical fire frequency existed in each case, below which the species would be unable to persist. Hoffman (1999) carried out a similar study on woody shrubs in savannas of Brazil. Interestingly, he found the opposite pattern: population growth rate declined with fire frequency, and he could identify a critical frequency above which species were unable to persist. Thus herbaceous and woody species seem, at least from these few examples, to respond in opposite directions to fire.

It is possible for population growth rate to be maximized at intermediate fire frequencies. Gross *et al.* (1998) found this pattern in a model for the threatened shrub *Hudsonia montana* in North Carolina. They modelled fire as a periodic, not a stochastic, process but they incorporated temporal variance in the vital rates within each environmental state (much as our detailed matrices do, although they used a different approach to include the variation). They found a population growth rate maximized at intermediate fire frequencies.

Our analysis is the first to be able to include effects of time since fire; the previous studies have included only two environmental states, corresponding to years with and without fires. Even so, our model of fire and the environmental effects it produces are relatively crude, and could be extended by incorporating effects of time since fire on the likelihood and intensity of fire.

Using fire as a management tool faces at least two restrictions. Controlled burns are expensive and may require the presence of 20–30 trained people. The cost of a burn in a Willamette Valley prairie typically ranges from $5000 to $10 000 (Rick Hayes, US Army Corps of Engineers, personal communication). Burning may also lead to the decline of other desirable or rare species that occur at the same location, as has been observed in other prairies (Glenn and Collins, 1992). Identifying a periodic fire regime that minimizes the number of burns needed to maintain a population of *L. bradshawii* is clearly warranted. Our results suggest that there were several periodic burn schedules that yield a stable population at both sites. These schedules, which required eight burns at Fisher Butte and four at Rose Prairie over a 10-year period, were very specific, however. Departures from these timetables could result in population decline, even if the total number of burns remained the same. To minimize the number of burns needed, therefore, managers should identify an appropriate periodic burn schedule and commit to it.

A. Generalizations and Methodological Issues

Our analysis of *L. bradshawii* is an example of a general approach to demography in dynamic environments, and as such it raises some important methodological issues.

First, the model can obviously be generalized to other kinds of disturbance processes. In addition to the studies of fire frequency cited earlier, such models have already been applied to floods (Beissinger, 1995), hurricanes (Batista *et al.*, 1998), and burning and trampling (Gross *et al.*, 1998).

While our analysis is based on a discrete environmental event (a fire occurs, or it does not), the approach could equally be applied to an environment described in terms of a quantitative variable such as temperature, moisture, food supply, or even the intensity of fire. Such variables can be discretized and modelled using a finite-state Markov chain, as we have done here, or can be described by autoregressive models (Tuljapurkar, 1990a; Caswell, 2001). Models for the environment play a central role in stochastic models; more work needs to be done on them. See Caswell (2001) for development of some possibly useful Markov chain models for sequences of matrices.

More sophisticated models of the environment will require the incorporation of more kinds of demographic variability. In this study, we had the option of using multiple estimates of the vital rates within each environmental state. It was conceivable that the variability within the environmental states might have swamped out the effects of the variability among those states. It did not, but this is the first case where the comparison has been made. It would be very interesting to explore the response of a population to two or more kinds of explicit environmental variability (e.g. fire and moisture) to see how they interact.

Our analysis used data from the experimental design shown as (2) (section III.B) which was intended for other purposes. It is an unfortunately unbalanced design, with estimates for $\mathbf{A}^{(3)}$ being obtained only in one year. That year (1990) was one that led to low values of λ in all treatments. It is possible that the decline in performance with time elapsed since the last fire could be an artifact of this lack of balance in the design. This is highly unlikely, because the decline is still significant even if the data from environmental state E_3 are excluded, and because many independent pieces of information point to the reality of this decline (Pendergrass *et al.*, 1999; Kaye *et al.*, 2001).

Still, it would be nice to have a design that would provide balanced estimates of every environmental state in every year of a study such as this one. The following design would accomplish this.

$$
\begin{array}{ccc|ccccc}
85 & 86 & 87 & 88 & 89 & 90 & 91 & 92 \\
\hline
 & & & B & U & U & U & B \\
B & U & U & U & B & U & U & U \\
 & B & U & U & U & B & U & U \\
 & & B & U & U & U & B & U \\
\end{array} \tag{41}
$$

This design produces the following set of environmental states:

$$
\begin{array}{ccc|ccccc}
85 & 86 & 87 & 88 & 89 & 90 & 91 & 92 \\
\hline
 & & & E_1 & E_2 & E_3 & E_4 & E_1 \\
E_1 & E_2 & E_3 & E_4 & E_1 & E_2 & E_3 & E_4 \\
 & E_1 & E_2 & E_3 & E_4 & E_1 & E_2 & E_3 \\
 & & E_1 & E_2 & E_3 & E_4 & E_1 & E_2 \\
\end{array} \tag{42}
$$

Each environmental state is present in each year, but the experiment would be more costly. It would require one additional treatment, and up to three years of preparatory treatments before the experiment *per se* begins.

Dynamic environments are the rule, not the exception. Population growth in such environments is an important problem with important implications for management and conservation. Stochastic and periodic matrix population models, with their associated growth rates and perturbation analyses, provide the tools necessary to assess the status of populations, to evaluate alternative management strategies, and to project the future of the population.

ACKNOWLEDGMENTS

We would like to thank Kathy Pendergrass, Karen Finley and Boone Kauffman for sharing the original *L. bradshawii* data set from the prairie burning experiments. These data made our analysis possible. We also gratefully acknowledge financial support from the Eugene District, Bureau of Land Management, the Oregon Department of Agriculture, and NSF Grants DEB-9511945 and OCE-9811267 to H.C. T.N.K. acknowledges assistance from David Pyke and financial and logistical support from the Forest and Rangeland Ecosystem Science Center, Biological

Resources Division, US Geological Survey. Woods Hole Oceanographic Institution Contribution 10052.

REFERENCES

Batista, W.B., Platt, W.J. and Macchiavelli, R. E. (1998). Demography of a shade-tolerant tree *Fagus grandifolia* in a hurricane-disturbed forest. *Ecology* **79**, 38–53.

Beissinger, S.R. (1995). Modeling extinction in periodic environments: Everglades water levels and snail kite population viability. *Ecol. Appl.* **5**, 618–631.

Bidwell, T.G., Engle, D.M. and Claypool, P.L. (1990). Effects of spring headfires and backfires on tallgrass prairie. *J. Range Manag.* **43**, 209–212.

Bond, W.J. and van Wilgen, B.W. (1996). *Fire and Plants*. Chapman & Hall, London.

Burgman, M.A., Ferson, S. and Akçakaya, H.R. (1993). *Risk Assessment in Conservation Biology*. Chapman & Hall, New York.

Canales, J., Trevisan, M.C., Silva, J.F. and Caswell, H. (1994). A demographic study of an annual grass (*Andropogon brevifolius* Schwarz) in burnt and unburnt savanna. *Acta Oecol.* **15**, 261–273.

Caswell, H. (1978). A general formula for the sensitivity of population growth rate to changes in life history parameters. *Theoret. Pop. Biol.* **14**, 215–230.

Caswell, H. (1989a). *Matrix Population Models: Construction, Analysis, and Interpretation*. Sinauer Associates, Sunderland, MA.

Caswell, H. (1989b). The analysis of life table response experiments. I. Decomposition of treatment effects on population growth rate. *Ecol. Model.* **46**, 221–237.

Caswell, H. (1996a). Demography meets ecotoxicology: untangling the population level effects of toxic substances. In: *Ecotoxicology: A Hierarchical Treatment* (Ed. by M.C. Newman and C.H. Jagoe), pp. 255–292. Lewis Publishers, Boca Raton, FL.

Caswell, H. (1996b). Analysis of life table response experiments. II. Alternative parameterizations for size- and stage-structured models. *Ecol. Model.* **88**, 73–82.

Caswell, H. (2000). Prospective and retrospective perturbation analyses and their use in conservation biology. *Ecology* **81**, 619–627.

Caswell, H. (2001). *Matrix Population Models: Construction, Analysis, and Interpretation*. 2nd edn. Sinauer, Sunderland, MA.

Caswell, H., Naiman, R.J. and Morin, R. (1984). Evaluating the consequences of reproduction in complex salmonid life cycles. *Aquaculture* **43**, 123–134.

Cohen, J.E. (1976). Ergodicity of age structure in populations with Markovian vital rates, I. Countable states. *J. Am. Stat. Assoc.* **71**, 335–339.

Cohen, J.E. (1977a). Ergodicity of age structure in populations with Markovian vital rates, II. General states. *Adv. Appl. Prob.* **9**, 18–37.

Cohen, J.E. (1977b). Ergodicity of age structure in populations with Markovian vital rates, III. Finite-state moments and growth rate; an illustration. *Adv. Appl. Prob.* **9**, 462–475.

Cohen, J.E. (1979a). Comparative statics and stochastic dynamics of age-structured populations. *Theoret. Pop. Biol.* **16**, 159–171.

Cohen, J.E. (1979b). Ergodic theorems in demography. *Bull. Am. Math. Soc.* **1**, 275–295.

de Kroon, H., Plaisier, A., van Groenendael, J. and Caswell, H. (1986). Elasticity: the relative contribution of demographic parameters to population growth rate. *Ecology* 67, 1427–1431.

Dennis, B., Munholland, P.L. and Scott, J.M. (1991). Estimation of growth and extinction parameters for endangered species. *Ecol. Monogr.* 61, 115–143.

Efron, B. and Tibshirani, R.J. (1993). *An Introduction to the Bootstrap*. Chapman & Hall, New York.

Franco, M. and Silvertown, J. (1996). Life history variation in plants: an exploration of the fast-slow continuum hypothesis. *Phil. Trans. Roy. Soc. Lond.* **B351**, 1341–1348.

Ginzburg, L.R., Slobodkin, L.B., Johnson, K. and Bindman, A.G. (1982). Quasiextinction probabilities as a measure of impact on population growth. *Risk Anal.* **21**, 171–181.

Glenn, S.M. and Collins, S.L. (1992). Effects of scale and disturbance on rates of immigration and extinction of species in prairies. *Oikos* **63**, 273–280.

Glitzenstein, J.S., Platt, W.J. and Streng, D.R. (1995). Effects of fire regime and habitat on tree dynamics in north Florida longleaf pine savannas. *Ecol. Monogr.* **65**, 441–476.

Gross, K, Lockwood, J.R., III, Frost, C.C. and Morris, W.F. (1998). Modeling controlled burning and trampling reduction for conservation of *Hudsonia montana*. *Cons. Biol.* **12**, 1291–1301.

Hawkes, C.V. and Menges, E.S. (1996). The relationship between open space and fire for species in a xeric Florida scrubland. *Bull. Torrey Bot. Club* **123**, 81–92.

Hessl, A. and Spackman, S. (1995). *Effects of Fire on Threatened and Endangered Plants: An Annotated Bibliography*. US Department of the Interior, National Biological Service, Washington, DC.

Hoffman, W.A. (1999). Fire and population dynamics of woody plants in a neotropical savanna: matrix model projections. *Ecology* **80**, 1345–1369.

Johnson, E.A. and Gutsell, S.L. (1994). Fire frequency models, methods and interpretations. *Adv. Ecol. Res.* **25**, 239–287.

Kaye, T.N. (1992). Bradshaw's desert-parsley: population monitoring and pollination biology. *Kalmiopsis* **2**, 1–4.

Kaye, T.N., Pendergrass, K.L., Finley, K. and Kauffman, J.B. (2001). The effect of fire on the population viability of an endangered prairie plant, *Lomatium bradshawii* (Apiaceae). *Ecol. Appl.* (in press).

Lande, R. and Orzack, S.H. (1988). Extinction dynamics of age-structured populations in a fluctuating environment. *Proc. Natl Acad. Sci. USA* **85**, 7418–7421.

Menges, E.S. and Kimmich, J. (1996). Microhabitat and time-since-fire: effects on demography of *Eryngium cuneifolium* (Apiaceae), a Florida scrub endemic plant. *Am. J. Bot.* **83**, 185–191.

Mills, L.S., Doak, D.F. and Wisdom, M.J. (1999). Reliability of conservation actions based on elasticity analysis of matrix models. *Cons. Biol.* **13**, 815–829.

Noble, I.R. and Slatyer, R.O. (1980). The use of vital attributes to predict successional changes in plant communities subject to recurrent disturbances. *Vegetatio* **43**, 5–21.

Parenti, R.L., Robinson, A.F. and Kagan, J.S. (1993). *Bradshaw's Lomatium Recovery Plan*. US Fish and Wildlife Service, Portland, Oregon.

Pendergrass, K.L. (1995). *Vegetation Composition and Response to Fire of Native Willamette Valley Wetland Prairies*. M.S. thesis, Oregon State University, Corvallis, Oregon. 241 pp.

Pendergrass, K.L., Miller, P.M. and Kauffman, J.B. (1998). Prescribed fire and the response of woody species in Willamette Valley wetland prairies. *Restor. Ecol.* **6**, 303–311.

Pendergrass, K.L., Miller, P.M., Kauffman, J.B. and Kaye, T.N. (1999). The role of prescribed burning in maintenance of an endangered plant species, *Lomatium bradshawii*. *Ecol. Appl.* **9**, 1420–1429.

Quintana-Ascencio, P.F. (1997). *Population Viability Analysis of a Rare Plant Species in Patchy Habitats with Sporadic Fire.* Ph.D. thesis, State University of New York, Stony Brook, NY.

Silva, J.G., Raventos, J., Caswell, H. and Trevisan, M.C. (1991). Population responses to fire in a tropical savanna grass *Andropogon semiberbis*: a matrix model approach. *J. Ecol.* **79**, 345–356.

Trollope, W.S.W. (1978). Fire behavior: a preliminary study. *Proc. Grassland Soc. S. Afr.* **13**, 123–128.

Trollope, W.S.W. (1982). Ecological effects of fire in South African savannas. In: *Ecology of Tropical Savannas*, Ecological Studies vol. 42 (Ed. by B.J. Huntley and B.H. Walker), pp. 292–303. Springer-Verlag, Berlin.

Tuljapurkar, S.D. (1982). Population dynamics in variable environments. II. Correlated environments, sensitivity analysis and dynamics. *Theoret. Pop. Biol.* **21**, 114–140.

Tuljapurkar, S.D. (1990a). *Population Dynamics in Variable Environments.* Springer-Verlag, New York.

Tuljapurkar, S. (1990b). Delayed reproduction and fitness in variable environments. *Proc. Natl Acad. Sci. USA* **87**, 1139–1143.

Tuljapurkar, S. (1997). Stochastic matrix models. In: *Structured-population Models in Marine, Terrestrial, and Freshwater Systems* (Ed. by S. Tuljapurkar and H. Caswell), pp. 59–87. Chapman & Hall, New York.

Tuljapurkar, S. and Istock, C. (1993). Environmental uncertainty and variable diapause. *Theoret. Pop. Biol.* **43**, 251–280.

Tuljapurkar, S.D. and Orzack, S.H. (1980). Population dynamics in variable environments I. Long-run growth rates and extinction. *Theoret. Pop. Biol.* **18**, 314–342.

APPENDIX

This appendix contains the detailed matrices for the Fisher Butte and Rose Prairie sites. Each column of the following tables contains one matrix, identified by its treatment–year combination. The entries in a column of the table are the entries in each column of the matrix, stacked one above the other.

Table A1

This appendix contains the detailed matrices for the Fisher Butte and Rose Prairie sites. Each column of the following tables contains one matrix, identified by its treatment–year combination. The entries in a column of the table are the entries in each column of the matrix, stacked one above the other.

(a) Fisher Butte

T_1–88	T_1–91	T_2–88	T_2–89	T_2–91	T_1–89	T_1–92	T_2–90	T_2–92	T_1–90	T_0–88	T_0–89	T_0–90	T_0–91	T_0–92
0.000	0.000	0.000	0.000	0.000	0.000	0.000	0.000	0.000	0.000	0.000	0.000	0.000	0.000	0.000
0.210	0.250	0.440	0.360	0.310	0.470	0.110	0.430	0.130	0.390	0.210	0.550	0.180	0.060	0.200
0.120	0.120	0.070	0.220	0.150	0.230	0.320	0.030	0.260	0.060	0.070	0.220	0.000	0.150	0.070
0.000	0.000	0.040	0.000	0.000	0.030	0.000	0.030	0.000	0.000	0.000	0.030	0.010	0.000	0.030
0.000	0.000	0.000	0.000	0.000	0.000	0.000	0.000	0.000	0.000	0.000	0.000	0.000	0.000	0.000
0.000	0.000	0.000	0.000	0.000	0.000	0.000	0.000	0.000	0.000	0.000	0.000	0.000	0.000	0.000
0.000	0.320	0.360	0.150	0.210	0.430	0.200	0.150	0.110	0.000	0.110	0.430	0.230	0.330	0.110
0.300	0.210	0.360	0.440	0.500	0.220	0.470	0.070	0.260	0.390	0.220	0.140	0.100	0.210	0.430
0.300	0.040	0.040	0.040	0.090	0.170	0.070	0.150	0.050	0.110	0.040	0.140	0.050	0.050	0.000
0.070	0.000	0.000	0.070	0.030	0.040	0.050	0.040	0.110	0.000	0.000	0.140	0.000	0.000	0.070
0.000	0.000	0.000	0.000	0.000	0.000	0.000	0.000	0.000	0.000	0.000	0.000	0.000	0.000	0.000
0.000	0.000	0.000	0.000	0.000	0.000	0.000	0.000	0.000	0.000	0.000	0.000	0.000	0.000	0.000
0.160	0.090	0.090	0.070	0.000	0.100	0.000	0.210	0.050	0.180	0.030	0.080	0.120	0.030	0.010
0.560	0.320	0.550	0.420	0.820	0.260	0.450	0.260	0.430	0.220	0.400	0.540	0.410	0.630	0.500
0.060	0.260	0.180	0.180	0.070	0.240	0.260	0.170	0.230	0.080	0.230	0.240	0.120	0.080	0.200
0.100	0.060	0.090	0.160	0.000	0.260	0.100	0.040	0.060	0.080	0.030	0.110	0.010	0.070	0.090
0.000	0.000	0.000	0.040	0.040	0.000	0.020	0.000	0.010	0.000	0.000	0.000	0.010	0.000	0.000
0.000	0.000	0.100	0.100	0.100	0.200	0.100	0.000	0.100	0.000	0.100	1.100	0.100	0.200	0.000
0.100	0.080	0.140	0.000	0.030	0.080	0.000	0.060	0.000	0.040	0.000	0.000	0.060	0.090	0.140
0.200	0.190	0.000	0.060	0.360	0.000	0.070	0.110	0.000	0.380	0.160	0.140	0.260	0.330	0.500
0.200	0.310	0.430	0.500	0.310	0.330	0.170	0.280	0.250	0.380	0.530	0.430	0.230	0.270	0.230
0.100	0.080	0.430	0.380	0.170	0.500	0.730	0.060	0.540	0.080	0.050	0.430	0.130	0.060	0.000
0.000	0.080	0.000	0.000	0.060	0.000	0.030	0.000	0.170	0.000	0.050	0.000	0.020	0.000	5.000
1.300	0.500	1.500	0.900	0.600	1.800	0.700	0.100	0.400	0.200	1.300	1.200	0.600	0.500	0.000
0.000	0.000	0.060	0.000	0.000	0.000	0.000	0.000	0.000	0.090	0.000	0.000	0.080	0.000	0.090
0.070	0.120	0.120	0.000	0.100	0.000	0.140	0.060	0.000	0.120	0.190	0.000	0.170	0.250	0.270
0.330	0.180	0.120	0.000	0.250	0.000	0.210	0.350	0.110	0.380	0.500	0.400	0.290	0.250	0.450
0.470	0.350	0.560	0.440	0.400	0.540	0.360	0.260	0.630	0.250	0.120	0.600	0.210	0.080	3.080
2.724	0.060	2.724	2.724	0.050	1.886	0.140	0.000	0.210	0.000	0.120	0.000	0.040	0.080	0.000
0.000	2.724	0.000	0.000	2.724	0.000	1.886	1.886	1.886	1.000	3.080	3.080	3.080	3.080	0.235
0.039	0.000	0.039	0.039	0.000	0.000	0.000	0.000	0.000	0.000	0.000	0.000	0.000	0.000	0.052
0.000	0.039	0.000	0.000	0.039	0.000	0.000	0.000	0.000	0.000	0.235	0.235	0.235	0.235	0.177
0.095	0.000	0.000	0.000	0.000	0.143	0.143	0.143	0.143	0.330	0.052	0.052	0.052	0.052	0.501
0.816	0.095	0.095	0.095	0.095	0.200	0.200	0.200	0.200	0.330	0.177	0.177	0.177	0.177	
	0.816	0.816	0.816	0.816	0.516	0.516	0.516	0.516		0.501	0.501	0.501	0.501	

Table A.1 (*contd.*)

(b) Rose Prairie

$T_1 - 88$	$T_1 - 91$	$T_2 - 88$	$T_2 - 89$	$T_2 - 91$	$T_1 - 89$	$T_1 - 92$	$T_2 - 90$	$T_2 - 92$	$T_1 - 90$	$T_0 - 88$	$T_0 - 89$	$T_0 - 90$	$T_0 - 91$	$T_0 - 92$
0.000	0.000	0.000	0.000	0.000	0.000	0.000	0.000	0.000	0.000	0.000	0.000	0.000	0.000	0.000
0.330	0.280	0.310	0.540	0.440	0.500	0.190	0.130	0.260	0.290	0.210	0.130	0.000	0.000	0.000
0.000	0.040	0.120	0.120	0.000	0.120	0.120	0.000	0.070	0.010	0.020	0.200	0.000	0.250	0.000
0.000	0.020	0.000	0.280	0.000	0.000	0.030	0.000	0.020	0.010	0.020	0.000	0.000	0.000	0.070
0.000	0.000	0.060	0.000	0.000	0.000	0.000	0.000	0.000	0.000	0.000	0.000	0.000	0.000	0.000
0.000	0.000	0.000	0.000	0.000	0.000	0.000	0.000	0.000	0.000	0.000	0.000	0.000	0.000	0.000
0.500	0.460	0.000	0.000	0.000	0.000	0.280	0.150	0.430	0.300	0.220	0.000	0.120	0.000	0.000
0.330	0.160	0.500	0.830	0.170	0.500	0.190	0.000	0.170	0.000	0.220	0.880	0.000	0.000	0.430
0.000	0.050	0.500	0.000	0.250	0.400	0.030	0.003	0.030	0.000	0.000	0.000	0.000	0.000	0.000
0.000	0.000	0.000	0.000	0.170	0.000	0.070	0.083	0.000	0.000	0.000	0.000	0.000	0.000	0.000
0.000	0.030	0.000	0.170	0.000	0.300	0.030	0.000	0.030	0.000	0.000	0.000	0.000	0.000	0.000
0.120	0.000	0.090	0.000	0.000	0.000	0.070	0.000	0.000	0.000	0.000	0.000	0.000	0.000	0.000
0.000	0.150	0.090	0.000	0.000	0.000	0.080	0.000	0.050	0.190	0.100	0.110	0.580	0.330	0.220
0.530	0.000	0.640	0.420	0.290	0.270	0.240	0.230	3.270	0.190	0.600	0.440	0.080	0.110	0.560
0.290	0.380	0.180	0.110	0.290	0.240	0.240	0.150	3.410	0.120	0.200	0.330	0.000	0.220	0.220
0.060	0.230	0.090	0.210	0.140	0.390	0.240	0.000	0.180	0.000	0.000	0.000	0.000	0.000	0.000
0.000	0.000	0.000	0.000	0.000	0.000	0.000	0.000	0.000	0.000	0.000	0.000	0.000	0.000	0.000
0.000	1.200	0.100	0.400	1.300	0.800	1.500	0.300	1.300	0.200	0.300	0.600	0.100	0.500	0.400
0.200	0.130	0.000	0.000	0.000	0.070	0.000	0.000	0.000	0.190	0.000	0.000	0.000	0.000	0.000
0.600	0.070	0.330	0.000	0.230	0.070	0.140	0.500	0.000	0.250	0.400	0.120	0.210	0.290	0.120
0.200	0.200	0.330	0.000	0.310	0.330	0.360	0.250	0.500	0.250	0.600	0.560	0.210	0.290	0.500
0.600	0.400	0.330	0.670	0.310	0.530	0.360	0.000	0.400	0.060	0.000	0.250	0.140	0.290	0.250
0.000	0.070	0.000	0.000	0.000	0.000	0.000	0.000	0.000	0.000	0.000	0.000	0.000	0.000	0.000
0.600	6.900	3.900	3.800	9.100	4.400	7.300	1.700	5.500	1.400	1.100	3.800	0.500	1.400	10.40
0.000	0.080	0.000	0.000	0.000	0.000	0.000	0.070	0.000	0.030	0.000	0.000	0.000	0.000	0.000
0.380	0.000	0.250	0.000	0.000	0.140	0.110	0.070	0.080	0.170	0.220	0.000	0.000	0.000	0.000
0.120	0.080	0.000	0.170	0.000	0.070	0.210	0.570	0.460	0.270	0.670	0.500	0.750	1.000	1.000
0.500	0.580	0.500	0.750	0.670	0.710	0.530	0.240	0.380	0.300	0.110	0.000	0.250	0.000	0.000
0.000	0.170	0.250	0.000	0.000	0.070	0.050	0.000	0.000	0.000	2.100	0.500	0.000	0.000	0.000
5.940	5.940	5.940	5.940	5.940	14.90	14.90	14.90	14.90	2.100	2.100	2.100	2.100	2.100	2.100
0.000	0.000	0.000	0.000	0.000	0.000	0.000	0.000	0.000	0.500	0.000	0.000	0.000	0.000	0.000
0.415	0.415	0.415	0.415	0.415	0.250	0.000	0.300	0.000	0.000	0.000	0.000	0.000	0.000	0.000
0.000	0.000	0.000	0.000	0.000	0.250	0.250	0.250	0.250	0.500	0.500	0.500	0.500	0.500	0.500
0.479	0.479	0.479	0.479	0.479	0.250	0.250	0.250	0.250	0.000	0.500	0.500	0.500	0.500	0.500
0.167	0.167	0.167	0.167	0.167	0.375	0.375	0.375	0.375	0.000	0.500	0.500	0.500	0.500	0.500

Population Cycles in Birds of the Grouse Family (Tetraonidae)

R. MOSS AND A. WATSON

I. SUMMARY

Population cycles of boreal herbivores such as voles, hares and birds of the grouse family (Tetraonidae) were an early problem in ecology. Here we systematize present understanding of population cycles in tetraonids. Cycles have not been recorded in all grouse species, and non-cyclic populations occur in all grouse species known to show cycles.

Much knowledge about cycles comes from time series of measures of population abundance. The fluctuations in such series have properties such as period, amplitude, symmetry, and degree of synchrony with other time series of the same and other species. Each property shows temporal and spatial variation, and is used to delineate hypotheses about causes of cycles.

ADVANCES IN ECOLOGICAL RESEARCH VOL. 32
ISBN 0-12-013932-4

Cyclic time series show delayed density dependence, as expected from models. From species known to show cycles, we give three examples of non-cyclic populations that showed direct density dependence. Each was in fragmented or degraded habitat. Much anecdotal evidence suggests that grouse cycles occur mostly in large tracts of fairly homogeneous habitat, and that fragmentation of such habitat is associated with disappearance of cycles. This has been attributed to increased dispersal out of fragmented habitat patches into population sinks, and to increased predation from generalist predators.

We distinguish between processes that drive cycles and those that determine cycle period. Commonly reported periods are 3–4, 6–7 and 10 years. Different populations of the same species show different periods, and sympatric species with different mean vital rates fluctuate together with the same period. Hence cycle period is not a necessary consequence of a particular set of mean vital rates. Period is characteristic more of location than of species. There is no simple large-scale relationship between cycle period and latitude or longitude. One example, of a 10-year rock ptarmigan cycle going together with a 10-year weather cycle, suggests that local weather might affect period.

Documented extremes in the amplitude of cycles in population density vary from about two-fold to about six-fold. Most documented tetraonid population cycles are fairly symmetrical, with decline and increase phases in any one fluctuation taking similar numbers of years.

Fluctuations of spatially separate parts of cyclic populations have shown partial synchrony that diminishes with distance between the parts. Explanations of this include the effects of weather and dispersal. Dispersal might be of the cyclic species, or its resources, or one of its natural enemies or competitors. A consequence of dispersal in some cyclic model populations is travelling waves of population density, so far confirmed for species of grouse, hare and vole.

The main documented demographic cause of changes in tetraonid breeding numbers is variation in the recruitment of young birds into the breeding population. In seven studies of two species, including cycles with periods of 3–4, 7–8 and 10 years, this happened in two stages. First, during cyclic declines the birds' 'breeding success' was lower, that is fewer young were reared to independence per adult. Second, a smaller proportion of these independent young survived the winter to be recruited into the breeding population. However, mean breeding success differed among populations within species, such that cyclic increases in some populations occurred with lower breeding success than cyclic declines in other populations. It is therefore not clear whether differences in breeding success between the increase and decline phases of cyclic fluctuations are a cause or a consequence of changes in population density.

There is much less agreement about the processes underlying the above demographic patterns. Trophic interactions, such as food–consumer, predator–prey and host–parasite, have been postulated as causes of cycles. None has so far been substantiated for tetraonids, but this does not refute the possibility that trophic interactions cause tetraonid population cycles. Nor does it exclude the finding that weather can affect the population dynamics of tetraonids through their food.

Artificially induced increases in the aggressive behaviour of individuals have caused declines in population density. Some hypotheses suggest that cycles can result from natural variations in individual behaviour and population structure. The predator avoidance hypothesis suggests that cyclic declines are a result of behaviour patterns that evolved because animals that show them avoid predation. The kin-facilitation hypothesis is part of the more general concept that variations in relatedness have consequences for population dynamics.

A parsimonious demographic hypothesis for tetraonid cycles is that they are due primarily to variations in the proportion of independent young that becomes recruited. A working hypothesis that accounts for the effects of habitat fragmentation is that cycles involve stepwise delayed density dependence in recruitment. The upper threshold should not be exceeded in fragmented habitats, where there is more predation and more density-dependent dispersal from patches of better habitat into population sinks. These suggestions are consistent with hypotheses that cycles are driven by trophic interactions and with hypotheses invoking individual behaviour.

II. INTRODUCTION

All animal populations fluctuate in abundance and ecologists aim to understand the mechanisms. The regular population cycles of boreal herbivores such as voles, hares and birds of the grouse family (Tetraonidae) were an early source of wonder in ecology (Elton, 1924), but in the mid twentieth century some reputable biologists were still sceptical about their existence (e.g. Cole, 1954). Among the believers there was debate on how best to define cycles (Davis, 1957; Keith, 1963), a discussion that continued with the introduction of the term 'quasi-cycle' to distinguish population cycles from perfectly repetitive cycles (Nisbet and Gurney, 1982). The analysis of long time series of population estimates by statistical methods has confirmed the existence of fluctuations in numbers that are repeated at intervals more regular than expected by chance, which is a reasonable definition of population cycles (Watson and Moss, 1979). Also, the demonstration that simple models incorporating delayed density dependence can produce complex dynamics including cycles (Hutchinson, 1948; May, 1974, 1976) has provided a theoretical basis for their existence. There is still no consensus about their causes, except that these should show delayed density dependence. Here we review the contribution made by studies of tetraonids to the understanding of boreal population cycles.

All tetraonid species that show cycles also have non-cyclic populations. We infer that these species have a tendency to show unstable dynamics, but that this tendency is expressed as cyclic fluctuations in density only if certain antecedent conditions apply. This tendency may have one or more general causes, or no general cause but many specific causes. We rule out nothing on principle, but use a search for general causes to give structure to this review. This is based on the principle of parsimony, which 'states that one should choose the simplest of several hypotheses that, at the time, explains the same observations equally well' (Chitty, 1996).

There is a large literature on tetraonids because they are game animals occurring through much of the arctic, subarctic and north temperate regions. Much of the literature is in obscure form such as regional reports of hunting and conservation bodies. We consider all types of evidence, including experiments, population studies and anecdotal observations. We do not attempt to list all the relevant literature, but use examples to draw the main conclusions. Regarding tetraonid, microtine and hare cycles as part of the same general phenomenon, we use examples from voles and hares to illustrate some points where studies on these mammals provide a better understanding of tetraonid cycles. Where possible, we use examples from our own experience because we understand their limitations best.

III. PHILOSOPHY

Some elementary concepts, too often neglected in studies of tetraonid populations, are useful when designing and interpreting long-term population studies and experiments. Such concepts are helpful tools, not inflexible rules.

A. Truth, Repeatability, Replication, Confirmation and Refutation

Science is a search for true statements (Popper, 1981). A true statement is consistent with the facts. A fact is an observation made independently by several different observers. An observation is usually of a difference between two states (Medawar, 1969). Thus, observers will note a new star, and not primarily the sky in which it appears. A true statement may be falsified by more facts.

Repeatability is the essence of scientific method. Even so, much has been learned from studies on single study areas where workers measured how recruitment and loss determine changes in population size. This often involves detailed studies of marked individuals, their resources and their enemies. Useful generalizations have come from comparing such single-area studies, and from natural experiments. A function of reviews is to make such generalizations. This is much like the case history approach in medical science.

Properly designed experiments provide more rigorous and efficient tests of hypotheses than quantitative demography or natural experiments. Replication is part of efficient design and permits statistical inferences. Statistical problems with unreplicated experiments include the difficulty of separating treatment and site effects. In practice, this makes it essential to ensure that experimental and control areas and populations are as similar as possible before treatment starts. Also, from unreplicated experiments one cannot infer the probability of experimental effects having occurred by chance.

Even so, an unreplicated experiment, repeated by others, has more scientific value than an experiment replicated by the same worker but unrepeated by others. This is partly because all replications within an experiment suffer from similar biases, due to the design of the experiment and to the observers' expectations. In principle, biases due to expectations can be excluded by making measurements blind, but this is seldom practicable in field ecology.

Because each ecological situation is unique, exact replication and repetition are impracticable. This is why treatments and replicates should be randomly assigned. When repeating an experiment, workers have to decide which aspects of an experiment they are aiming to repeat, and at which level of abstraction. Repetition at a high level of abstraction (e.g. the proposition that animal populations are regulated) might involve doing a similar experiment with a different species in a different habitat.

Field experiments are costly. It may be practicable to do an unreplicated experiment, with a single population for each treatment and one or more controls, but impracticable to replicate it. Workers may have to decide between doing an unreplicated experiment including detailed demographic studies, and a replicated one without demographic detail. The replicated experiment would be more rigorous. The one with demographic studies would explore the subject further and might provide the opportunity to test hypotheses at the individual rather than the population level. A compromise is to study demography in greater detail on a control area (e.g. Krebs *et al.*, 1995). A crossover design, involving two areas where experimental and control treatments are exchanged after a period of time, is another useful compromise, but can be vitiated if factors other than the

treatment and its consequences change with time. One can also increase
rigour by disseminating detailed predictions in advance. The word 'postdictions' should be used for 'predictions' made with hindsight. This verbal
discipline helps to avoid overstating the validity of analyses made after the
event (Chitty, 1991).

Experimental results are usually consistent with several hypotheses, but
a single fact in principle can be enough to refute a generalization. For
example, an experimental treatment might be followed by an effect
because the treatment happens to alter unmeasured factors that cause
the effect. The absence of the effect, however, would refute the hypothesis
that the treatment causes the effect. Also, unconscious bias is likely to
produce results that confirm favoured hypotheses. Consequently, observations and experiments that refute favoured hypotheses are more reliable
than those that confirm them (Popper, 1959, 1963). Nevertheless, it can be
misleading to overstate the reliability of contrary evidence (Chitty, 1996).

Refutation of a favoured hypothesis involves designing and publishing
observations and experiments that falsify the hypothesis. It involves
predicting what the effects on the hypothesis will be of specific experimental results. Mental set is crucial, in that inductive thinking tends to
lead to searches for confirming evidence, while deductive thinking leads to
experiments or observations intended to falsify and destroy hypotheses
(Popper, 1959, 1963; Medawar, 1967; Chitty, 1996).

B. Causation

Aristotle (O.E.D., 1971) distinguished efficient and final causes. Efficient
causation comprises the immediate mechanism of cause and effect. Final
causation is the purpose of an action. For much of the twentieth century,
mainstream science shunned final causation. Evolutionary biology, however, accepts final causation as a valid line of enquiry (Wilson, 1975).
Animal behaviour may be explained in terms of purpose. One may assume,
for example, that animals behave as they do in order to maximize their
reproductive output. The term purpose can be avoided by arguing that
animal form and function are adapted to maximize fitness (e.g. Newton,
1989), but the logic is still that of final causation.

Efficient causes, conditions or antecedents may be 'necessary' or
'sufficient'. The search for necessary conditions avoids much semantic
controversy (Chitty, 1954). A necessary condition or antecedent must
always be present for an effect to occur, but may not be sufficient to
cause the effect. For instance, a large tract of unfragmented habitat may
be necessary for population cycles (see section IV.B.2(g)), but populations
in such tracts may not always show cycles. A cause may be sufficient to
result in an effect, but if the same effect occurs in its absence, the cause is

not necessary. For example, a specific trophic interaction (e.g. host–parasite) might be sufficient to cause a local population to cycle, but is not necessary for population cycles if they occur elsewhere without it. Another possibility is that a cause or condition can be both necessary and sufficient (Chitty, 1967, 1996).

Causes can also be classed as 'proximate' or 'ultimate'. For example, a bird denied access to food because of its low social status may weaken due to starvation and then be taken by a predator. The proximate cause of death is predation, but the ultimate cause is social status. In the extreme, the ultimate cause of a biological phenomenon can be regarded as the reason for its evolution, in which case the ultimate cause is virtually synonymous with the final cause (Lack, 1954a).

IV. POPULATION TRAJECTORIES AND THEIR PATTERNS

A. Density Dependence

Stabilization by density-dependent processes (see Appendix for terminology), due to negative feedback of population density upon population growth, is central to theories of population regulation (Krebs, 1985a). Ironically, detection of density dependence in population trajectories (time series of population estimates) is particularly difficult in relatively invariant, seemingly stable populations (Murdoch, 1994). Detection, of delayed density dependence, has proved much easier in unstable populations that are cyclic (Turchin and Taylor, 1992; Turchin, 1993; Hörnfeldt, 1994; Lindström, 1994; Saucy 1994; Falck et al., 1995). Also, the presence of delayed density dependence seems to be sufficient to cause cycles, because models incorporating it can produce limit cycles and damped oscillations (Hutchinson, 1948; May, 1974, 1976). Limit cycles are endless repetitions of patterns of numbers and damped oscillations can be sustained indefinitely by random perturbations (Rothery et al., 1984). Hence each can account for cyclic population trajectories.

Models show that delayed density dependence might be caused by trophic interactions such as predator–prey or host–pathogen (Hutchinson, 1948; Berryman, 1978; Royama, 1981), or by interactions between different segments of a population that is structured by age, physiology, or space (Royama, 1992; Turchin and Taylor, 1992; Hendry et al., 1997; Matthiopoulos et al., 1998). In addition, difference equations involving delayed density dependence have made good predictions of future cyclic population trajectories in red grouse (Moss et al., 1996). Even so, the correspondence between models involving density dependence and the demographic and other causal mechanisms of population change in the real world remains poorly understood.

A cyclic population trajectory in which increases and declines take more than one successive time step will usually show numerical delayed density dependence. This is a mathematical tautology. Model cycles can also be generated by positive feedback in population growth, a feedback that changes direction at peaks and troughs because of direct density dependence. For example, delayed density dependence in population trajectories can be described by autoregressive models such as:

$$\log_e N_t = k_0 + k_1 \log_e N_{t-1} + \cdots + k_n \log_e N_{t-n} + \varepsilon_t$$

N_{t-n} being numbers observed at time $t - n$, n the time lag, k constants, and ε error (exogenous stochastic variation plus measurement error plus biases from faulty assumptions in the model). The same model can be reformulated as:

$$\log_e N_t = a_0 + a_1 \log_e N_{t-1} + \cdots + a_n(\log_e N_{t-1} - \log_e N_{t-n}) + \varepsilon_t$$

where $k_1 = a_1 + a_n$, and $k_n = -a_n$. Although algebraically equivalent, the two formulations draw attention to different biological mechanisms and could give rise to different research emphases. The first might lead workers to investigate time lags in cyclic processes, while the second might lead them to investigate what comprises the positive feedback between present and past population growth.

More generally, delayed density dependence might be detected in cycles that are not caused by delayed density-dependent processes. For example, the time lag in simple models with delayed density dependence determines the period of the cycles produced. It is equally logical that the period determines the time lag in the apparent delayed density dependence. Hence, the analytical structure (Royama, 1992) of the apparent density dependence might describe the form of a cycle, but provide little useful evidence about its causation. This caveat is likely to apply especially to secondary cycles resulting from other cycles in, for example, weather.

Density dependence may be linear, as in the examples above, or non-linear. The latter includes curvilinear and, in the extreme, stepwise. Stepwise density dependence (Dempster, 1975) with upper and lower step functions amounts to a two-phase (increase and decline) model in which the step functions provide switches between phases. Most statistical tests are for linear density dependence, and the custom has been to assume linearity unless there is evidence to the contrary. For example, Watson *et al.* (1998) used linear statistical techniques to detect fourth-order (lag 3 years) density dependence in rock ptarmigan *Lagopus mutus* (Montin) population trajectories. This does not imply that there was a linear biological process with a 3-year lag, because the underlying processes may have been non-linear or phase-dependent.

In any case, it is often convenient to describe cyclic population trajectories in terms of increase and decline phases, separated by peaks and troughs, irrespective of the mechanisms involved. This is because demographic and other processes often differ greatly at the same density, but depending on whether numbers are increasing or decreasing.

B. Characteristics of Population Trajectories

One can distinguish long-term trends in numbers from short-term fluctuations. In turn, short-term fluctuations can be characterized as erratic or regular. Erratic model outputs can be classed as chaotic or random, but for real population trajectories these two categories are usually inseparable. In principle, cycles are regular fluctuations, or at any rate more regular than expected by chance (see section II, Introduction). Some trajectories, however, seem to comprise cycles of more than one period (see IV.B.2(a)). Of course, trends and regular fluctuations always have an erratic component, and one of the difficulties in studying cyclic populations is to decide whether a particular fluctuation is cyclic or erratic. An advantage of simple cyclic trajectories is that the next fluctuation is predictable, which helps to plan experiments.

Much statistical analysis of population trajectories involves making inferences about the structure of the underlying density dependence (Royama, 1992), so helping to define the biological processes involved. A usual preliminary is the detection and removal of trends from the data set. This can be side-stepped by analysing population growth instead of numbers, but that provides information about population growth rather than population density. The implicit assumption in trend removal is that long-term trends reflect variations in the equilibrium density about which the density-dependent processes operate. In terms of biological processes, it is doubtful whether such a clear distinction occurs, because long-term trends and short-term fluctuations could involve some of the same processes. Even so, this is what is usually done.

1. Long-term Trends

Shooting bags are often used as crude indices of the numbers of birds living on the ground (see section IV.B.2(b)). Bags of red grouse *Lagopus lagopus scoticus* (Lath.) in Britain and Ireland declined markedly during the twentieth century. This has been attributed to many causes including habitat loss, habitat deterioration, less skilled shooters, increased tick-borne disease, and increased predation associated with less killing of predators by gamekeepers (e.g. Hudson, 1993). Compare, however, shooting bag records (Figure 1) of red grouse in northwest Scotland and willow grouse *Lagopus lagopus* (L.) in southeast Norway (the species *Lagopus lagopus* is called red grouse, willow grouse and willow ptarmigan in different parts of its range). Scottish red grouse and Norwegian willow grouse have different diets, live in different habitats, suffer from a different set of main diseases, and undergo different management practices. There is much predator control and patchwork burning of ground vegetation in Scotland (Gimingham, 1972), but not in Norway. Even so, the long-term trend in each country has been very similar. This could be because a wide-spread common factor such as weather or pollution affected population fluctuations in both countries.

Within that common long-term trend (Figure 1), medium-term fluctuations also showed similarities in Scotland and Norway. Bags were high in the early part of the twentieth century but fell to a common trough about 1918, recovered to a peak about 1930, and then declined shortly before the Second World War. After the war, numbers remained much lower than before it. More generally, Siivonen (1948, 1952) and Semenov-Tian-Shansky (1959) drew attention to widespread similarities in fluctuations of tetraonids and other animals in much of northwestern Europe, from Scotland through Norway to the Ural mountains, including widespread

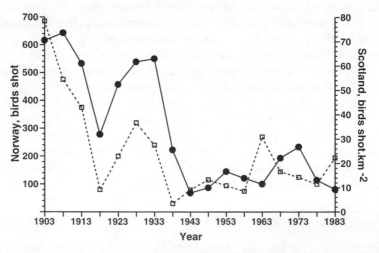

Fig. 1. Willow grouse shot in southeast Norway (dashed line) and red grouse shot in northwest Scotland (solid line) in 1900–85 (5-year centred averages). The Norwegian data (Hjeljord and Kiær, 1991) are from Rypa estate (61.5°N, 10.5°E), the Scottish data are means of areas 1, 2 and 3 from Hudson (1992). Pearson $r = 0.77$, $P < 0.01$.

declines of red and willow grouse, rock ptarmigan, capercaillie (*Tetrao urogallus* L.), black grouse (*Tetrao tetrix* L.) and hazel grouse (*Bonasa bonasia* (L.)) about 1939, and low numbers in the early 1940s. Siivonen (1948, 1952) attributed this to a sudden climatic change. As the time scale being considered shortens towards the length of a cycle period, the terminology changes and the topic of common population trends becomes that of synchronous fluctuations within and among species (see sections IV.B.2(e) and (f)).

2. Cyclic Population Trajectories

A cyclic population trajectory fluctuates more regularly than expected by chance (above) and so the essential criterion for cyclicity is significant periodicity. Cycles also have other characteristics such as amplitude, symmetry, and degree of synchrony with other cyclic populations of the same and other species. Each of these characteristics may show spatial as well as temporal variation. Their measurement helps to delineate hypotheses about causes of cycles, and to design experiments.

(a) Period. Hunters and naturalists early discerned cycles by counting peaks and troughs in secondary data such as shooting bag records (Leopold, 1933; Salomonsen, 1939; Mackenzie, 1952; Siivonen, 1952; Keith, 1963). Some (Dougall, 1875; Gudmundsson, 1960), assuming cyclicity, accurately foretold the timing of declines and increases. Cole (1954) sceptically suggested that population cycles are essentially random fluctuations with serial correlation between the populations of successive years. However, statistical analyses of longer data sets by methods such as autocorrelation and spectral analysis have generally substantiated the early insights.

A rule of thumb is that runs of data need to be at least 3–4 times the period length to establish cyclicity by statistical analysis. Consequently, there are still situations where local tradition asserts the existence of population cycles, and where population studies are consistent with their existence, but where data sets are not long enough to establish cyclicity with formal statistical significance (e.g. Andreev, 1988). In some cases, data sets are long enough but the relevant analyses have not been done (e.g. Bergerud, 1988). Most of the samples in the present review have been formally tested but we include, with caveats, a few examples that depend on the less reliable method of counting peaks and troughs.

The period of cyclic population trajectories is an average value because successive fluctuations are not usually identical in length. Commonly reported cycle periods in the boreal zone, each shown by tetraonids, include 3–4, 6–7 and 10 (also called 8–11) years (Figure 2). The cycle

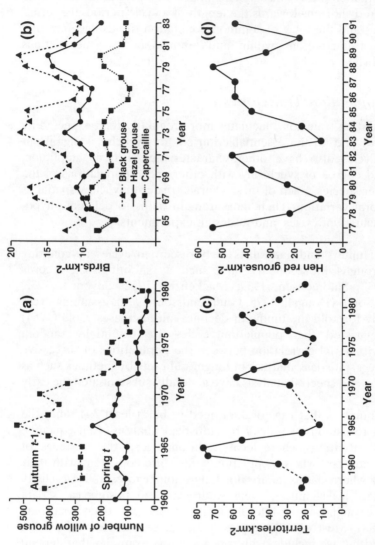

Fig. 2. Examples of cyclic population trajectories. (a) Low-amplitude 3- to 4-year cycle in spring and autumn numbers of willow grouse on Tranøy island (127 ha), northwestern Norway, showing a declining trend (after Myrberget, 1984b). (b) Partly synchronous 6- to 7-year cycles in autumn densities (birds·km^{-2}) of black grouse, hazel grouse and capercaillie seen on transect route counts in Turku-Pori province, Finland (after Lindén, 1989). (c) Ten-year cycle in the density (territories·km^{-2}) of breeding willow ptarmigan in Chilkat Pass, British Columbia (dashed lines join years with missing counts between them (after Mossop, 1988)). (d) Sawtoothed 4- to 5-year fluctuations in breeding densities (hens·km^{-2}) of red grouse near Gunnerside in

period, however, is not species specific: for instance, *Lagopus lagopus* has shown cycle periods of 3–4, 6–7 and 10 years (Watson and Moss, 1979). Other period lengths also occur, such as 4–5 years for red grouse in part of northern England (Potts *et al.*, 1984) and 7–8 years for red grouse in part of northern Scotland (Moss *et al.*, 1996).

Few papers deal with the possibility that more than one period can occur in a population. Most data sets are too short to distinguish between (1) trajectories comprising a set of fluctuations dominated by a single mean period with some variation about it (previous paragraph), and (2) trajectories comprising more than one period. For example, spectral analysis of 39 common vole *Microtus arvalis* (Pallas) population trajectories in eastern Europe (Mackin-Rogalska and Nabaglo, 1990) showed different dominant periods among populations, and more than one period within populations, but did not distinguish between (1) and (2) above. Shooting bags of red grouse at Rickarton moor in north-east Scotland gave evidence of a 6-year periodicity in the late nineteenth century, but a 10-year one after 1945 (Moss *et al.*, 1996). Counts of rock ptarmigan on the Mounth massif in Scotland suggested a finer commixture of 6- and 10-year fluctuations (Watson *et al.*, 1998).

Not all tetraonid population trajectories show detectable cycles. For example, we know of no evidence for cycles in white-tailed ptarmigan (*Lagopus leucurus* (Richardson)). Keith (1963) described cyclic and non-cyclic populations of ruffed grouse (*Bonasa umbellus* (L.)), prairie grouse (*Tympanuchus* spp.) and snowshoe hares (*Lepus americanus* Erxleben) in North America. Transect route counts for hazel grouse, black grouse and capercaillie in Finland showed significant cyclicity in most but not all of the 11 Finnish provinces (Lindén, 1989). Shooting bags of red grouse from Britain show some cyclic and some non-cyclic autocorrelograms (Williams, 1985). A stable population of capercaillie in northeast Scotland (Moss and Oswald, 1985) showed direct density dependence (Figure 3a), as did a small subpopulation of rock ptarmigan adjacent to ski-lifts in the Cairngorms massif of Scotland (Figure 3b). In the latter two cases, the presence of direct rather than delayed density dependence was associated with habitat fragmentation (see section IV.B.2(g)).

(b) Amplitude. Amplitude can be measured as the number of animals at a peak divided by the number at an adjacent trough. Successive peaks and troughs often vary in height. For example, two successive cycles in the breeding density of red grouse at Kerloch moor in Scotland showed amplitudes of less than two-fold in 1963–69 and about five-fold in 1969–78 (Watson *et al.*, 1984a). Also, observed amplitudes depend in part on what one measures. Autumn numbers, after the rearing of young, are generally higher than spring numbers, and may vary more. Secondary

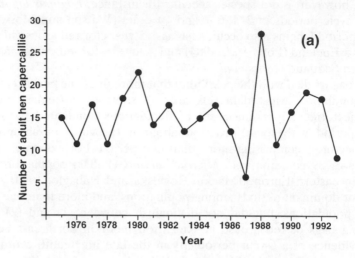

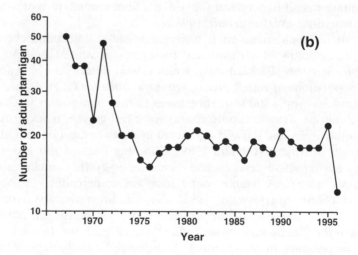

Fig. 3. Examples of non-cyclic population trajectories: July numbers of (a) adult capercaillie hens in fragmented habitat and (b) adult rock ptarmigan near a ski development. The ski development began in 1961, after which ptarmigan numbers declined and then stabilized at a lower density, while ptarmigan numbers nearby (Figure 5) continued to cycle. Both trajectories showed direct density dependence ($P < 0.02$ and 0.04, respectively, by the test of Pollard *et al.* (1987)). Study areas, in northeast Scotland, were each $2.7\,\text{km}^2$. Sources: (a) Moss and Oswald (1985) and R. Moss (unpublished data) and (b) A. Watson and R. Moss (unpublished ms).

data, such as shooting bags from autumn and early winter, tend to vary much more than direct counts of live birds, partly because hunters make less effort when numbers are perceived to be low. Hence any relationship between primary and secondary data is likely to be least reliable when numbers are low.

The claim (May, 1999), for example, that 'crashes representing a more than thousandfold reduction in grouse numbers' had occurred during a study of red grouse (Hudson et al., 1999) is due to a confusion between primary and secondary data. In fact, documented extremes in the amplitude of cycles in population density vary from about two-fold, as in 3- to 4-year cycles in Norwegian willow grouse (Figure 2a) and 6- to 7-year cycles in Finnish capercaillie, black grouse and hazel grouse (Figure 2b), to about six-fold, as in 10-year cycles in willow ptarmigan in British Columbia (Figure 2c) and Scottish rock ptarmigan (Figure 5).

The use of secondary data can distort cycle characteristics other than amplitude. For example, Icelandic trade records on the export of rock ptarmigan were affected by birds killed in one year being exported in the next, and by the killing of ptarmigan being banned in some years (Gudmundsson, 1960). Again, bag records may lag behind actual population levels (Lindén, 1981). Such biases are unlikely to affect the overall period shown by long runs of secondary data, but might affect apparent symmetry and timing. Because most data are secondary, information about amplitudes and symmetry is less reliable than that for periods.

(c) Symmetry. Almost all documented tetraonid cycles are fairly symmetrical with, in any one fluctuation, increase and decline phases each taking similar numbers of years. An apparent exception (Potts et al., 1984) is the 4- to 5-year sawtoothed cycle of red grouse in northern England (Figure 2d; Hudson et al., 1999), where increases typically last longer than declines. However, there are not as yet sufficiently long runs of published counts to show statistically significant asymmetry.

The form of the less common, apparently sawtoothed cycle seems easier to explain. It is easy to follow the idea that populations build up until they exceed their carrying capacity, and then crash (decline precipitously) for lack of resources, or because natural enemies overwhelm them. Possible mechanisms underlying symmetrical many-year declines are harder to grasp and mathematical modelling is essential to understanding them. It seems possible that sawtoothed cycles comprise symmetrical cycles truncated by a separate non-cyclic process.

Ginzburg and Inchausti (1997) suggested that asymmetry is characteristic of population cycles in general, but their claim that this applies to Scottish rock ptarmigan and red grouse is not borne out by population counts (Jenkins et al., 1967; Watson et al., 1984a; Moss et al., 1996;

Watson *et al.*, 1998). Ginzburg and Inchausti (1997) chose to use data on shooting bags selected from Middleton (1934) and Mackenzie (1952), despite published counts of populations being available.

(d) Geographical gradients in period. Boreal cycles show much geographical variation in period. Vole cycles, for example, are said to have a 5-year period in northern Fennoscandia and 3–4 years in much of central Fennoscandia, whereas fluctuations are not obviously cyclic in southern Fennoscandia (Angelstam *et al.*, 1985). However, the observation that cyclic vole and tetraonid populations are confined to high latitudes in Fennoscandia (Andrén *et al.*, 1985; Angelstam *et al.*, 1985) is not simply a reflection of latitude as 3- to 4-year vole cycles occur in southeastern Europe (Mackin-Rogalska and Nabaglo, 1990) and northern England (Lambin *et al.*, 1998), and tetraonid cycles in Italy (Cattadori and Hudson, 1999) and the United Kingdom (this review).

Capercaillie, black grouse and hazel grouse showed 3- to 4-year cycles in central Sweden (Small *et al.*, 1993) but 6- to 7-year cycles at a similar latitude in Finland (Lindén, 1989). In the Lapland province of northern Finland, however, the period for capercaillie and black grouse was 3–4 years. There is little evidence of 10-year cycles in Fennoscandian herbivores (Lindén, 1988), although this period is widespread in North American tetraonids, and is reported in willow grouse in Siberia (Andreev, 1988), and in red grouse (Moss *et al.*, 1996) and rock ptarmigan (Watson *et al.*, 1998, 2000) in Scotland.

Variations in period can occur on a fine geographical scale (Figure 4). Red grouse in northeast Scotland have shown 10-year cycles in the inland Cairngorms massif (Figure 5a) and also on the coast (Moss *et al.*, 1996) some 80 km east of the Cairngorms. These two 10-year cycles were out of phase with each other. Between them, from west to east, in the same continuous tract of grouse habitat, red grouse bags have shown 7-year cycles, no clear cycle with a period ≤ 10 years, and 7- to 8-year cycles.

In short, the period of tetraonid cycles is characteristic more of location than of species, and there is some evidence from Scotland that the period has changed within a location. No simple large-scale relationship between cycle period and latitude or longitude is apparent. A little-explored possibility (Sinclair *et al.*, 1993; Sinclair and Gosline, 1997; Watson *et al.*, 2000) is that regularities in weather patterns, possibly acting via plant growth, 'entrain' unstable populations to their period. This means that the population cycles occur irrespective of the entraining process, but that the process influences the timing of the cycles. If so, some of the fluctuations in a cyclic trajectory can occur in the absence of the entraining process. This possibility is not refuted by the observation (Figure 4) that tetraonid cycle periods can vary between locations only short distances

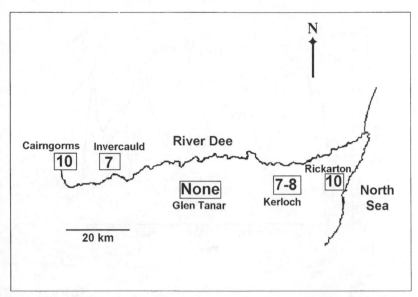

Fig. 4. Cycle periods in red grouse between the Cairngorms massif and the east coast of Scotland, from the 1940s to the 1990s. From west to east, sources include counts in the Cairngorms (Figure 5a), bag data from Invercauld estate (X. Lambin, unpublished analysis), bag data from Glen Tanar estate (R. Moss, unpublished analysis), and counts and bag records from Kerloch moor and from the Rickarton estate (Watson *et al.*, 1984a; Moss *et al.*, 1996).

apart in northeast Scotland, where weather and climate (Birse, 1971) and the occurrence of climatic oscillations (Miller and Cooper, 1976) can differ markedly on a scale of a few km or tens of km, respectively. Nor is the theoretical possibility of entrainment confined to weather – in principle any regular process could have this effect.

(e) Synchrony within species. Population trajectories of spatially separate parts of animal populations often show partial synchrony. One hypothesis, often called the Moran effect, is that populations which fluctuate independently might be brought into synchrony by extrinsic factors such as spells of adverse weather (Mackenzie, 1952; Moran, 1953; Chitty, 1969). Random extrinsic effects can bring model populations into synchrony even if they have different vital rates (Leslie, 1959; Ranta *et al.*, 1995a,b; Kaitala *et al.*, 1996). A second hypothesis follows from the suggestion (above) that regular extrinsic effects entrain population cycles. It is that if separate populations are entrained by the same extrinsic effect, they will fluctuate in synchrony. The entrainment hypothesis differs from the Moran hypothesis in its requirement for the necessary extrinsic effect to be regular. A

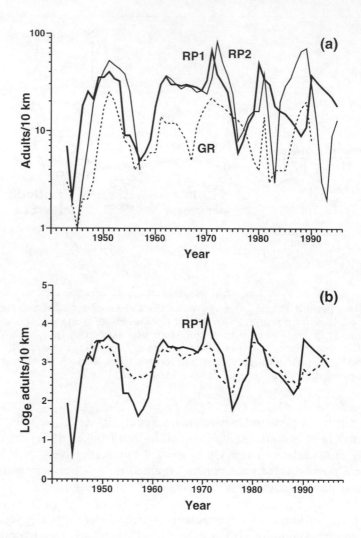

Fig. 5. (a) Numbers (adults/10 km of transect walks in May–September) of rock ptarmigan (solid lines) on two adjacent sub-massifs and red grouse (dashed line) on lower ground between them. (b) Rock ptarmigan numbers on the larger sub-massif (solid line) and postdictions from a difference equation (dashed line). Explanatory variables included observed June temperatures in years $t-1$, $t-2$ and $t-4$, and delayed density dependence involving year $t-4$. Note that after 1946 the ptarmigan numbers used in the postdiction were themselves postdicted and the trajectory includes no input from observed ptarmigan numbers. After Watson *et al.* (2000).

third hypothesis is that the cause of fluctuations travels through space by diffusion or dispersal, giving rise to a travelling wave (Murray, 1993). If so, cyclic fluctuations should give rise to multi-annual travelling waves. Dispersal might take several forms, such as movement of individuals of the cyclic species, or of its resources (e.g. arthropod food for chicks), or of one of its natural enemies or competitors.

Direct evidence on these potential synchronizing mechanisms is difficult to obtain on the large scale necessary. Hitherto, workers interested in the relationship between synchrony and distance have relied on indirect evidence involving inferences from population trajectories. Keith (1963) concluded that 10-year cycles in snowshoe hares, ruffed grouse and prairie grouse were partly synchronous throughout much of North America. The fluctuating capercaillie, black grouse, hazel grouse, willow grouse, willow tit (*Parus montanus* Conrad von Baldenstein), magpie (*Pica pica* (L.)), red squirrel (*Sciurus vulgaris* L.), mountain hare (*Lepus timidus* L.) and white-fish (*Coreganus lavaretus* (L.)) populations of the 11 provinces of Finland each showed spatial synchrony that declined with the distance between provinces (Ranta *et al.*, 1995a,b; Lindström *et al.*, 1996). Hudson (1992) mapped annual fluctuations in red grouse bags in 20 regions of Britain up to 450 km apart. A re-analysis of his material (P. Eden, R. Moss and D. Elston, unpublished data) shows a significant decline in synchrony with distance (Mantel correlation coefficient $= -0.63$, $P < 0.005$). Interestingly, the correlation between bags in northwest Scotland and southeast Norway (Figure 1) is much greater than would be expected from the distance between them (P. Eden, R. Moss, O. Hjeljord and D. Elston, unpublished data).

The demonstration that synchrony declines with distance tells little about mechanisms. A reasonable next step is to describe the form of such relationships. In particular, one can test the prediction (above) of multi-annual travelling waves. If they occur in cyclic populations, their speed and other propagation characteristics should contribute to a better understanding of the causes of the cycles.

Keith (1963) reviewed evidence for 'systematic progressions of peaks and lows' across North America in the 10-year cycle of snowshoe hares, ruffed grouse and some of their predators. Smith (1983) used maps to show apparent diffusion of this cycle in snowshoe hares across Canada. Giraudox *et al.* (1997) mapped a wave during a population 'outbreak' of fossorial water voles (*Arvicola terrestris* (L.)), though it is not clear whether this outbreak was cyclic. Statistical evidence for travelling waves in a cyclic field vole (*Microtus agrestis* L.) population was given by Lambin *et al.* (1998), and in a cyclic red grouse population by Moss *et al.* (2000). The apparent speeds of the field vole, fossorial water vole and grouse waves, respectively, were $\approx 19 \, \text{km} \cdot \text{yr}^{-1}$, $> 10 \, \text{km} \cdot \text{yr}^{-1}$ and $2\text{--}3 \, \text{km} \cdot \text{yr}^{-1}$.

There seems to be little other empirical evidence for multi-annual travelling waves in animal populations, except for monotonic waves at colonization and epidemic fronts. We expect more, now that there are convenient statistical techniques for assessing the occurrence of travelling waves in spatially explicit data sets (Lele *et al.*, 1998; D. Elston, X. Lambin and R. Moss, unpublished ms).

(f) Synchrony among species. Populations of sympatric species often fluctuate in partial synchrony. For example, capercaillie, black grouse and hazel grouse in Finland fluctuated together with 6- to 7-year periodicity (Lindén, 1989; Lindström *et al.*, 1996; Figure 2b) despite the fact that these species have different mean vital rates. Similarly, ruffed grouse, prairie grouse (*Tympanuchus* spp.) and sharp-tailed grouse (*Tympanuchus phasianellus* (L.)) in parts of North America apparently showed synchronous 10-year cycles (Keith, 1963). Fluctuations of the introduced Hungarian partridge (*Perdix perdix* (L.)) closely resembled those of the ruffed grouse in Manitoba and Alberta, where both species were thought to be cyclic (Keith, 1963). Likely explanations for interspecific synchrony are similar to those for intraspecific synchrony (above), namely the Moran effect, entrainment by regular extrinsic processes, and dispersal of natural enemies, competitors or resources. Sympatric species generally have somewhat different habitat requirements, which implies that any synchronizing mechanism should operate across habitats.

Population fluctuations in Scottish rock ptarmigan in the Cairngorms show partial synchrony among subpopulations on adjacent sub-massifs (Watson *et al.*, 1998). Red grouse living on lower ground between two sub-massifs fluctuated in partial synchrony with both the adjacent two rock ptarmigan populations (Figure 5a). Five 10-year peaks in all three populations each fell within a year of one another, and 1–2 years after cyclic high June temperatures at a nearby village (Watson *et al.*, 1998), but drifted out of phase between peaks. A model with lagged June temperatures and fourth-order delayed density dependence, and with no input from observed ptarmigan numbers after the first 4 years, gave a good 49-year postdiction of rock ptarmigan numbers on the bigger sub-massif (RP1, Figure 5b). This fitted the idea of a weather cycle entraining a rock ptarmigan cycle. However, June temperatures had little explanatory value for rock ptarmigan numbers on the smaller sub-massif. Indirect evidence (Watson *et al.*, 2000) suggested that synchrony between the two rock ptarmigan trajectories might result partly from emigration from the bigger to the smaller sub-massif.

The Moran hypothesis, the entrainment hypothesis and the dispersal hypothesis each account for synchrony by assuming that populations fluctuate, driven by some unspecified process, and that the timing of these fluctuations is modified by interaction with some additional factor. This illustrates the need to distinguish between processes that drive cycles and those that determine their timing and period.

(g) Fragmentation. A broad generalization is that population cycles in boreal herbivores generally occur on big tracts of continuous habitat and that fragmented habitat is associated with the absence of cycles, as in snowshoe hares (Keith *et al.*, 1993), tetraonids (Leopold, 1933; Keith, 1963; Watson and Moss, 1979; Andrén *et al.*, 1985; Bergerud, 1988), and small rodents (Angelstam *et al.*, 1985; Lindén, 1988). Suggested mechanisms include more deaths from generalist predators that depend partly on altered land between patches of original habitat (Andersson and Erlinge, 1977; Bergerud, 1988; Hanski *et al.*, 1991), and more dispersal from 'source' patches into 'sinks' of altered land where breeding is poor and mortality high (Dolbeer and Clark, 1975; Moss and Watson, 1990). It is not suggested that fragmentation affects cycle period, only the presence or absence of cycles.

Inferences about the effects of habitat fragmentation on cyclicity rest largely on biogeographical comparisons between fairly continuous and fragmented habitats. Larger tracts of continuous semi-natural habitat tend to occur in more northern biomes, offering a possible explanation for the absence of vole cycles in southern Scandinavia and of tetraonid cycles in more southern parts of their North American range. There are, of course, many other correlates of latitude, including climate, and often greater soil fertility that has led to more agricultural land in the south.

Scottish capercaillie live in fragmented patches of forest and show no evidence of cycles, despite cycles elsewhere in their worldwide range. In one study (Moss and Oswald, 1985) gamekeepers maintained effective predator control, and changes in numbers from one July to the next bore no relation to intervening breeding success. The authors inferred that dispersal into surrounding poorer habitat was involved in the density-dependent (Figure 3a) regulation of this population of capercaillie.

There is also no evidence of cycles in western Irish red grouse, which exist at low density on large tracts of infertile, heavily grazed blanket bog where heather *Calluna vulgaris* L. (Hull) is the birds' main food and cover. Although not obviously fragmented, this degraded habitat comprises a patchwork of better habitat with greater ground coverage of taller, more productive heather on freely drained ground, and larger areas of poorer habitat on wetter ground. Generalist predators are common because sheep carrion supports unnaturally high numbers of red foxes (*Vulpes vulpes* (L.)), ravens (*Corvus corax* L.) and crows (*Corvus corone* L.). For four years, Watson and O'Hare (1979) counted red grouse on 16 study areas

28–141 ha in size, including two areas where densities were increased by fertilizing or excluding sheep and cattle by fencing the vegetation. Overall, summer and winter losses occurred from areas with the best habitat and the highest grouse densities, and summer and winter gains on areas of poor habitat with the lowest densities. Watson and O'Hare (1979) inferred density-dependent dispersal from good to poor habitat.

We know of no attempts to alter cyclicity by experimental fragmentation. There are, however, anecdotal natural experiments. A small, non-cyclic subpopulation of rock ptarmigan adjacent to ski-lifts in the Cairngorms massif of Scotland showed direct density dependence (Figure 3b), while cyclic subpopulations further from the development (Figure 5a) showed delayed density dependence, before and after the development of the ski area (A. Watson and R. Moss, unpublished ms). The lack of cyclicity in birds adjacent to the ski-lifts was associated with deaths from flying into ski-lift wires and increased predation on eggs and chicks by crows attracted to the area following the development. This can be seen as an early stage in the fragmentation process. Bergerud (1988) reviewed several examples of formerly cyclic southern populations of ruffed grouse and prairie grouse that were no longer cyclic, or that showed damping of cyclicity, associated with fragmentation of formerly continuous habitat by human activity. A problem with these (Bergerud, 1988) insights is that they rely on subjective assessments of cyclicity in population trajectories. A more rigorous statistical analysis would be worthwhile.

(h) Fertility. In Scotland, sites with richer underlying bedrock and associated soil fertility support higher densities and breeding success of red grouse (Jenkins *et al.*, 1963, 1967; Moss *et al.*, 1975) and rock ptarmigan (Watson *et al.*, 1998). This operates through the quality of the adults' diet, which is affected by the abundance of plant species of high nutritive value, and by higher nutritive value of the same plant species at different sites (Moss 1968; Moss and Watson, 1984). A similar example, also from Scotland is the mountain hare on moorland (Watson *et al.*, 1973) and alpine land (Watson and Hewson, 1973).

We are not aware of published evidence from other countries that the population density and performance of tetraonids are related to the fertility of underlying bedrock and soils. A possible reason for this lack may be that the effects of bedrock on vegetation are nullified or greatly reduced in many areas because the local bedrock is overlain by glacial deposits derived from different rocks, or because thick peat covers large tracts. Also, the diet of red grouse, rock ptarmigan and mountain hares in Britain and Ireland is of unusually poor quality, partly because many centuries of browsing by unnaturally high numbers of sheep, other domestic stock, and red deer (*Cervus elaphus* L.) have eliminated or severely reduced the amount of subalpine willow *(Salix* spp.) scrub, a plant food of high nutritive value and favoured by tetraonids (Moss and Hanssen, 1980).

Another correlate of site fertility in Scotland, in both cyclic and non-cyclic populations, is the sex ratio in the breeding population. Unmated territorial cock red grouse (Jenkins *et al.*, 1963, 1967) and rock ptarmigan (Watson *et al.*, 1998) were more frequent on infertile soils. On such soils, unmated red grouse cocks tended to have smaller territories and poorer food than mated ones (Miller and Watson, 1978; Moss *et al.*, 1988). Experimental application of fertilizers improved food quality and altered the sex ratio of red grouse more towards hens on infertile moors in north-east Scotland (Watson *et al.*, 1977, 1984b) and on infertile thick peat in western Ireland (Watson and O'Hare, 1979). However, variations in sex ratio with site fertility are not reported in most populations of tetraonids, which may have better foods than red grouse in Scotland and Ireland and rock ptarmigan in Scotland.

In Scotland, there also seemed to be an interaction between soil fertility and cycle phase, such that, on infertile areas, the proportion of unmated cock red grouse (Moss *et al.*, 1988) and rock ptarmigan (Watson *et al.*, 1998) during cyclic declines exceeded that during increases.

Site fertility might affect the timing and period of cycles. On the infertile granite of the Cairngorms massif, Scottish rock ptarmigan showed clear 10-year cycles (Figure 5). On the nearby but more fertile Mounth massif, they showed a more erratic trajectory comprising a mixture of 10- and 6-year fluctuations, out of phase with the Cairngorms cycle. A speculative explanation (Watson *et al.*, 1998) starts from the observation that cyclic June temperatures were correlated with the birds' breeding success on the Cairngorms but not on the Mounth. This suggested an interaction between plane of nutrition and weather, such that the presumed boost to nutrition provided by warm Junes may have had a bigger effect on ptarmigan demography on the more infertile Cairngorms. If so, June weather may have entrained cycles on the Cairngorms but not on the Mounth.

V. DEMOGRAPHY

A. Background

The demographic causes of population change are recruitment and loss. In a closed population these are determined by breeding success, which is the number of young reared to independence per adult (or per hen), and mortality. However, the evidence (e.g. Schroeder, 1985; Hines, 1986; Small and Rusch, 1989; Beaudette and Keppie, 1992) is that natal dispersal often takes young birds, especially hens, well beyond the limits of the usual grouse study area, which is usually no more than a few km^2. Although movement has often been studied directly by radiotelemetry, sample sizes have never been big enough to document the full contributions of mortality and movement to annual variations in the size of a tetraonid study population. Hence the role of movement in population studies has usually been inferred from indirect evidence.

Many populations, especially northern ones, show annual migrations between summer and winter habitats (Gelting, 1937; Irving *et al.*, 1967; Potapov and Flint, 1987; Bergerud and Gratson, 1988). This does not affect the principle that the movements most relevant to demography are breeding dispersal and, more importantly, natal dispersal (see section V.B). Seasonal migrations do, however, complicate the study of dispersal in the field.

Dispersal into and out of study areas also means that the effects of experimental manipulations on dispersal have been difficult to document fully. May (1999) recommended doing experiments on a large scale even if that means accepting a certain degree of imprecision. The testing of many hypotheses, however, demands precise measurements of individuals' performance and behaviour. In fact, experiments in which experimental and control areas have been small (often $< 1 \, km^2$) and close together (sometimes contiguous) have yielded useful results (examples below) on factors affecting density and vital rates, despite incomplete documentation of dispersal. The size of study areas and the scale of experiments will continue to depend upon the measurements required and upon geographical and logistical limitations.

The 16 tetraonid species are all fairly short-lived relative to body size (range $\approx 320 \, g$ for white-tailed ptarmigan to $\approx 4 \, kg$ for cock capercaillic). Average annual adult mortality rates lie in the range ≈ 30–70% and are not related simply to body weight (Johnsgard, 1983; Bergerud, 1988). Cocks generally live longer than hens, and cocks of polygynous species usually defer breeding until their second or later years (Johnsgard, 1983). Some hen blue grouse (*Dendragapus obscurus* (Say)) (Hannon and Zwickel, 1979; Hines, 1986) and capercaillie (Romanov, 1979; Borchtchevski, 1993; N. Picozzi and R. Moss, unpublished data) also defer breeding. In other species, it is usually assumed that all hens attempt to nest in their first year, but less is known about deferred breeding in hens than in cocks. For simplicity, we refer to birds as 'young' during the months before they have attained their first spring, and as adults thereafter.

Successful breeding hens rear one brood of chicks per year, but relaying after nest failure is common. Mean clutch size (Johnsgaard, 1983; Bergerud, 1988) varies from about five (white-tailed ptarmigan and spruce grouse (*Dendragapus canadensis* (L.))) to about 14 (prairie grouse), also varying among populations within species (e.g. rock ptarmigan typically seven in Scotland (Watson, 1965) but 11 in Iceland (Gardarsson, 1988).

Most variation in breeding success is due to nest failure (predation or desertion), or to early mortality of chicks.

Most tetraonid species are polygynous, although the three *Lagopus* species and hazel grouse are territorial and largely monogamous. In some polygynous species the cocks gather together to display at leks, whereas in others the cocks display at dispersed sites and hens nest among them. Cycles are not confined to any particular form of mating system. Populations of territorial monogamous species (*Lagopus lagopus*, rock ptarmigan and hazel grouse), lekking species (capercaillie, black grouse, prairie grouse) and dispersed polygynous species (ruffed grouse) have all shown cycles.

B. Reproduction, Recruitment, Mortality and Movement

Most population studies document breeding density (in spring) and breeding success (in late summer) within defined study areas. Studies with marked animals also provide estimates of adult loss, which comprises mortality and emigration from the study area, and of recruitment of young birds to the breeding population. Studies of red grouse and willow ptarmigan (Martin and Hannon, 1987; Schieck and Hannon, 1989; Watson et al., 1994) indicate that adults do not move far after they have bred for the first time (little breeding dispersal) and so adult loss may sometimes be a reasonable measure of adult mortality.

Measurements of recruitment are generally more variable than adult loss and, when studied, variations in recruitment have been a more important cause of population change than adult loss (Bergerud and Gratson, 1988; Moss and Watson, 1991). Recruitment into the population on a defined study area usually includes young birds reared outside the area. Also, birds reared on the study area may become recruited elsewhere. Recruitment can conveniently be separated into two demographic stages: the number of young reared to independence (breeding success), and the proportion of reared young that is recruited into the breeding population. Variations in this proportion can be due to mortality or movement, and may be measured on a study area as (recruitment in spring t)/(breeding success in summer $t - 1$). However, breeding success and recruitment are unlikely to have been estimated from the same set of individual birds, and so the 'proportion of reared young recruited' is a ratio involving more than the population within the study area. This caveat applies especially to hens, which disperse further than cocks (see section V.A).

Studies of non-cyclic populations of blue grouse in British Columbia (Bendell and Elliott, 1967; Zwickel et al., 1983) provide a useful contrast with cyclic populations. Breeding numbers remained remarkably steady despite large variations in breeding success. Adult annual losses remained fairly constant at about 30%. More chicks were reared than required to replace losses to the breeding population. Hence the proportion of reared young recruited varied in such a way as to maintain stable breeding populations, and losses of young birds were density dependent (Zwickel, 1980).

Rock ptarmigan in Alaska (Weeden and Theberge, 1972), Iceland (Gardarsson, 1988) and Scotland (Watson et al., 1998) all showed 10-year population cycles. Their average breeding success, however, differed markedly (Table 1). Icelandic rock ptarmigan, which had high breeding success in most years studied, showed a cyclic population decline, while breeding at a rate greater than Scottish rock ptarmigan showed during a cyclic population increase. Similarly, willow ptarmigan in Newfoundland declined while breeding better than red grouse on a Scottish area (Forvie) during cyclic increases. It follows that variations in breeding density were not driven by equivalent variations in breeding success in all populations of the same species. Furthermore, the evidence shows no inverse relation between mean breeding success and average adult survival. Hence populations with better mean breeding success apparently had heavier net overwinter losses of independent young.

Table 1

Examples of mean breeding success (mean young reared per adult) during increase and decline phases of population cycles in rock ptarmigan, willow ptarmigan and red grouse, with average annual survival rates of adult hens

Bird	Region	Years	Breeding success (range)[a] Increase	Decline	Hen survival[b]
Rock ptarmigan[c,d]	Alaska	1960–65	2.5 (2.2–2.9)	1.5 (1.4–1.6)	0.44
Rock ptarmigan[e,d]	Iceland	1964–69	3.9 (3.2–4.3)	2.2 (1.4–2.6)	0.54
Rock ptarmigan	Scotland, Cairngorms	1946–57	1.7 (0.7–2.3)[f]	0.3 (0.1–0.4)[f]	0.48[g]
Willow ptarmigan[h,d]	Newfoundland	1956–65	3.2 (2.7–3.3)	2.1 (1.8–2.3)	0.50
Red grouse	Scotland, Forvie	1961–70	1.8 (1.4–2.1)[i]	0.6 (0.3–0.8)[i]	0.24[j]
Red grouse	Scotland, Rickarton	1979–87	2.2 (1.3–3.0)[k]	1.2 (0.7–1.8)[k]	0.24[j]

[a] Each row of breeding success data is from a single fluctuation in populations that were known (Cairngorms, Rickarton) or thought (Iceland, Alaska, Newfoundland, Forvie) to show 10-year population cycles, though the fluctuation reported above did not necessarily take 10 years (see section IV.B.2(a)).
[b] The average annual rate at which marked adult hens returned to the study area, taking no account of possible breeding dispersal.
[c] Weeden and Theberge (1972), [d] Bergerud (1988), [e] Gardarsson (1971), [f] Watson (1965), [g] S. Rae (unpublished data), [h] Bergerud (1970), [i] Jenkins et al. (1967) and Moss et al. (1975), [j] Moss and Watson (1991), [k] Moss et al. (1996). Two superscripts together indicate that data from the first were summarized in the second, from which we quote them.

Even so, within populations, the birds' breeding success is generally poorer during the decline phase of cycles than during increases. This constitutes delayed density dependence in breeding success, as expected from hypotheses that involve delayed density dependence in breeding success as a cause of cycles. If differences in mean breeding success among studies (Table 1) are discounted, it can be argued that variations in breeding success drive population change (Bergerud, 1988). There is obviously some validity in this idea, as there must be some young available for populations to increase. Nevertheless, the above example from blue grouse illustrates the general point that breeding success is not necessarily correlated with population change.

Alternatively, variations in population change may drive variations in breeding success. For example, Watson et al. (1998) found that annual variations in the breeding success of rock ptarmigan were correlated with clutch size and chick survival, and that all three measures were lower during cyclic declines. The number of eggs in a clutch presumably reflected the state of the hen laying it. If so, the state of laying rock ptarmigan hens must have differed between increase and decline phases of population cycles. This would constitute delayed density dependence in the hens' state. State may involve diet, condition (Myrberget, 1985), parasites (Hudson et al., 1992), animal quality (Weeden and Theberge, 1972), genotype (Page and Bergerud, 1988) and stress (Boonstra et al., 1998). It may also involve social structure, such that social conditions during the increase phase are conducive to better breeding and provide better chances of young being recruited (see section VI.B.3). It might involve fitness costs and benefits (Schaffer and Tamarin, 1973; Oksanen and Lundberg, 1995), such that adults invest in fewer, poorer-quality eggs and rear fewer young in decline years. In decline years, there was evidence that the number of young ptarmigan recruited per egg laid, and hence the fitness benefits per egg laid, were smaller than in increase years (Watson et al., 1998).

In seven long-term studies, a main demographic cause of cyclic declines was a lower proportion of the reared young being recruited. This applied to 3- to 4-year cycles of willow grouse in Norway (Myrberget 1984a,b, 1985, 1986, 1988, 1989; Steen and Erikstad, 1996), 7- to 8-year cycles of red grouse in Scotland (Watson et al., 1984a; Moss and Watson, 1991), 10-year cycles of red grouse in Scotland (Moss et al. 1996), 10-year cycles of willow ptarmigan in Newfoundland (Bergerud, 1970), and 10-year cycles of rock ptarmigan in Alaska (Weeden and Theberge, 1972), Iceland (Gardarsson, 1988) and Scotland (Watson et al., 1998). All four Scottish studies were of effectively unshot populations. The other populations were shot, though the role of shooting in their dynamics is unknown. We know of no evidence from tetraonids that is contrary to the above generalization.

It is similar to the conclusion, from three long-term studies (Green and Evans, 1940; Keith and Windberg, 1978; Krebs *et al.*, 1986, 1995) of the 10-year cycle in snowshoe hares, that juvenile losses are an important component of the changes in density in the hare cycle. Modelling (see section VI.B.3) shows that changes in population size can be due entirely to variations in the proportion of young recruited, while breeding success remains constant.

Two of the seven studies above provided indirect evidence on the role of movement in tetraonid population cycles. Emigration contributed to cyclic declines in both red grouse (Watson *et al.*, 1984a) and rock ptarmigan (Watson *et al.*, 1998). In both cases, this apparently involved the emigration of entire families of parents and young from the study area in summer. For red grouse, though not rock ptarmigan, this involved marked birds and the data were detailed enough to show that some families left the study area in summer, that adults returned in autumn without young, that young cocks dispersing to take territories moved further during declines, and that some emigrant young established themselves on territories off the study area (Watson *et al.* 1984a, 1994; A. Watson, R. Moss and R. Parr, unpublished data). Anecdotes of widespread movements of flocks of black grouse and capercaillie, seemingly associated with declines during 3- to 4-year cycles, were noted by Siivonen (1952), who explained that this phenomenon was widely known to country dwellers. Keith (1963) summarized anecdotal observations of 'mass emigrations associated with population highs' in 10-year cycles of sharp-tailed grouse, willow ptarmigan and snowshoe hares.

In summary, within populations, breeding success is lower in cyclic declines than in cyclic increases. This does not apply among populations within species (Table 1). There is some evidence that declines are accompanied by more emigration and longer natal dispersal distances. A main demographic cause of cyclic declines with periods of 3–4, 7–8 and 10 years in two *Lagopus* species was that a smaller proportion of the young reared to independence was recruited into the breeding population.

VI. PROCESSES AND EXPERIMENTS

Models of mechanisms that drive cyclic demographic processes involve two or more parts. These can be the population and its abiotic environment, or its resources, or its enemies, or parts of a population separated by age, physiology, genotype or space. Animal populations are, of course, limited by resources, enemies and weather. Understanding how these regulate numbers is essential to explain population dynamics. There is, however, increasing evidence that an understanding of how animal behaviour affects numbers is also needed for an adequate explanation of their dynamics.

Tetraonid cycles have been the subject of much less modelling than vole cycles. Hence analytical and numerical explorations of processes that might drive tetraonid cycles and determine their period are less advanced. As a result, it can also be said that thinking about tetraonids has been less constrained by oversimplified numerical representations of complex biological systems.

A. Hypotheses Based on Trophic Interactions

1. Parasite–Host Interactions

General models of parasite–host interactions (Anderson and May, 1978; May and Anderson, 1978) can result in cycles if four broad conditions are met. First, the distribution of the parasite in the host population should not be too aggregated, otherwise the death of a few hosts might reduce the parasite population to a level insufficient to cause cyclic declines. Second, the effect of the parasite on host mortality should be low enough to allow both parasite and host to persist. Third, the parasite's effect on the host's reproductive rate should be big enough to cause cyclic declines. And fourth, there should be time delays in parasite reproduction or transmission.

The parasite–host (caecal threadworm *Trichostrongylus tenuis* (Mehlis)–red grouse) hypothesis for population cycles has a long history in Britain and Ireland. Even before Wilson and Leslie (1911) showed that 'grouse disease' was due to threadworms, Darwin (1859) had ascribed epidemics in game animals to parasitic worms spreading among crowded animals, and Dougall (1875) had suggested that regular crashes in red grouse occurred because 'overcrowding creates disease'. Lovat (1911), however, noted that some declines in red grouse numbers were not accompanied by excessive threadworm burdens. Hence the evidence from 1911 shows that thread-worms were sufficient, but not necessary, for population declines in red grouse. Subsequently, effects of *T. tenuis* on numbers of red grouse were documented by intensive fieldwork on grouse populations (Jenkins *et al.*, 1963; Hudson, 1986a; Hudson *et al.*, 1992).

Dobson and Hudson (1992, 1994) adapted the general Anderson and May (1978) model to the *T. tenuis*–red grouse system. Their parameterized model met the four broad conditions (first paragraph, this section) necessary for parasite–host cycles, and could produce cyclic grouse trajectories. However, the model does not include a crucial aspect of the *T. tenuis*–red grouse interaction. The worm has a direct life cycle. Its biggest pathological effect on the bird is during the few days that ingested larvae are developing into adult worms, such that adults are much less pathogenic than developing larvae (Delahay *et al.*, 1995; Delahay and Moss, 1996). Few larvae are ingested in winter because in cold conditions they fail to develop from eggs (Shaw *et al.*, 1989). The main impact of *T. tenuis* on red grouse occurs in spring, when overwintering arrested larvae that the birds ingested in the previous autumn develop simultaneously (Shaw, 1988a; Delahay, 1995). The mean number of arrested larvae in a grouse population in winter is only weakly related to the population's total worm burden (Delahay, 1995). Hence the assumption (Dobson and Hudson, 1992, 1994) that its effects on the birds' demography are directly proportional to total worm burdens is unrealistic.

The dynamics of the model (Dobson and Hudson 1992, 1994) are much affected by small variations in input parameters. For example, small changes in the degree of parasite aggregation 'can produce dramatic differences in the behavior exhibited by the parasite and host system' (Hudson and Dobson, 1997). A conventional measure of aggregation is the variance:mean ratio. Dobson and Hudson (1994) give values of this ratio ranging from 0.81 to 2.50. Other workers, however, have reported values of 2300–9800 (Wilson, 1983), 120–2500 (Shaw, 1988b) and 160–7600 (Delahay, 1995). This discrepancy needs to be explained (Delahay, 1995).

Moreover, the model is very sensitive to the presence of density-dependent worm fecundity, such that cyclic outputs are unlikely if worm fecundity decreases even slightly with increasing worm burdens (Hudson and Dobson, 1997). Hudson (1986b, his Figures 5.18 and 5.19) showed a large decrease in worm fecundity with worm burden when burdens were over about 4000 per bird. When such information is included, the model predicts that *T. tenuis* will not cause grouse cycles. Despite this, Dobson and Hudson (1992, 1994) account for grouse cycles by assuming that worm fecundity is constant, irrespective of worm burden.

Of more general application is the pivotal question of whether the parasite's dynamics are most affected by host density or by variations in the parasite's transmission rate (Levine, 1980). Anderson and May (1978), May and Anderson (1978) and Dobson and Hudson (1992, 1994) pay little attention to variations in transmission rate. In accord with Dougall (1875), however, they reasonably suppose that high host densities predispose a population to increased parasite burdens (but see penultimate paragraph, this section). The model of Dobson and Hudson (1992, 1994) shows that *T. tenuis* might be sufficient to cause population cycles, due solely to the effects of grouse density on burdens of *T. tenuis* and the pathological effects of the worms on the birds. Alternatively, the predominant cause of increased worm burdens might be high parasite transmission rates, associated with suitable weather. This could be due, for example, to free-living larvae surviving better in mild, moist summers (Shaw *et al.*, 1989). If so, heavy burdens of *T. tenuis* and associated declines are more likely to follow appropriate weather in years of high density than to follow high host densities alone (Hudson *et al.*, 1985; Moss *et al.*, 1993).

In an unreplicated experiment, Moss *et al.* (1993, 1996) experimentally prevented a cyclic decline in a red grouse population by removing cocks in the increase phase of the fluctuation (see section VII.A), so that the experimental population did not reach peak density. If host density were the main determinant of *T. tenuis* burdens, and if *T. tenuis* caused the cyclic decline observed in the control population, one would expect higher worm burdens in the control population. In the event, the red grouse's control population (which cycled) and the experimental population (cycle broken) had very similar worm burdens each year. Hence *T. tenuis* was not the cause of this population cycle in red grouse. Rather, annual worm burdens were correlated with rainfall in the previous summer, which suggested that variations in transmission rate were the main cause of variations in the parasite burden.

In a replicated experiment designed to test the *T. tenuis*–red grouse hypothesis, Hudson *et al.* (1999) administered an anthelmintic drug to grouse in the springs of 1989 and 1993, each being the first year of two separate declines. The drug would have affected all helminth parasites, and so any conclusions are not specific to *T. tenuis*. On two areas about 15–50% of the birds were drugged in 1989 and 1993, on two areas birds were drugged in 1989 only, and two areas served as controls (no drug). The data presented on grouse numbers on the experimental areas consisted entirely of shooting-bag records for 1987–96, not counts of birds living on the ground. The authors' comparison of bags with numbers counted on one control area showed that the bags varied by 1–2 orders of magnitude more than the numbers counted.

The main result (Hudson *et al.*, 1999) was that the number of birds shot in autumn fluctuated together during both fluctuations on all six areas, but that the amplitudes of the drug-treated fluctuations were less than the amplitudes of the untreated ones. The authors gave no evidence that these fluctuations were cyclic rather than erratic in character. Even so, they stated that 'Treatment of the grouse population prevented population crashes, demonstrating that parasites were the cause of the cyclic fluctuations' and that the treatment 'produced an apparent reduction in the decline of the treated populations'. It is difficult to draw sound conclusions from the amplitudes of these bag records. Hudson *et al.* (1999) give information neither on the effort (numbers of shooting days and shooters) nor on the proportion of young birds in the bag. Hence the reader can assess neither the numbers shot per day nor the sizes of the adult populations.

Also, five of the six control troughs involved no birds being shot (although in Hudson *et al.*, 1999, Figure 2, seemingly by mistake, shows one bird shot at each of these five troughs). This was because no effort was made to shoot birds in these critical years. Obviously, one can make no valid inferences about population size if no sample is taken. Hence the data presented on the amplitude of five out of the six control fluctuations are incomplete, and the conclusion that treated and control fluctuations of birds living on the ground differed in amplitude is unsubstantiated. If the five biased troughs are excluded, fluctuations in the number of birds shot differed little in amplitude between treated and control populations.

A fundamental prediction of the Hudson and Dobson (1992, 1994) model, as expected for a model involving delayed density dependence (see section IV.A), is that annual mean parasite burdens should lag behind host densities. Hudson *et al.* (1999) measured worm burdens during their experiment, and presumably have the data to test the prediction that parasite burdens should show a lag before recovering from anthelmintics.

The authors' claim that, together with their model, this experiment showed that parasites are both sufficient and necessary for population cycles in the red grouse that they studied is mistaken. The claim shows misunderstanding of the terms 'necessary' and 'sufficient', for the most that could be concluded is that parasites were sufficient. Certainly, the precipitous crashes typical of the population declines of red grouse in northern England are often associated with pathological burdens of *T. tenuis* (Wilson and Leslie, 1911; Hudson *et al.*, 1992). It is also clear that anthelmintics can improve the breeding success of red grouse (Hudson, 1986a). The observation (Hudson *et al.*, 1999) that the experimental administration of an anthelmintic failed to stop declines in shooting bags suggests that other processes were involved. Also, the apparent asymmetry (Figure 2d) of the northern English fluctuations studied by Hudson *et al.* (1992, 1999) is atypical of boreal cycles. The evidence is that more typical cycles, such as those seen in Scottish red grouse (Moss *et al.*, 1996) and rock ptarmigan (Watson and Shaw, 1991), are not due to known parasites.

T. tenuis seems to occur primarily in *Lagopus lagopus* (called red grouse, willow grouse and willow ptarmigan), with rock ptarmigan as an accidental host (Holstad *et al.*, 1994; Sonin and Barus, 1981; Watson and Shaw, 1991) and to be confined largely to the more temperate parts of the birds' range. The red grouse is especially adapted to temperate conditions, being the only *Lagopus* subspecies that does not turn white in winter. Most red grouse carry some *T. tenuis*, and burdens are often in the thousands. However, burdens reported outside Britain and Ireland are typically low. In northern Norway, for example, Wissler and Halvorsen (1977) recorded no *T. tenuis* in 338 willow grouse. Holstad *et al.* (1994) found *T. tenuis* in

Norwegian willow grouse only from island and coastal areas, and these at low frequency and intensity relative to red grouse. Hence proponents of the parasite–host hypothesis must find other parasites to explain most tetraonid cycles.

There have been many reports associating cyclic declines in boreal herbivores with parasites and disease. The 'epidemic hypothesis' set the pattern for early investigations (Elton, 1931; Elton et al., 1931, 1935; Findlay and Middleton, 1934) of 3- to 4-year vole cycles in Britain, but this was abandoned, largely because no specific disease epizootic was shown to be regularly associated with declines (Chitty, 1996). Tularemia (*Francisella tularensis* (McCoy & Chapin)) has been associated with synchronous declines of voles and mountain hares in Sweden (Hörnfeldt et al., 1986), but voles and hares also showed synchronous population cycles in parts of Sweden where tularemia appeared to be absent. Keith (1963) reviews examples of mass die-offs of snowshoe hares in North America, involving manifestations such as stomach worms (*Obeliscoides cuniculi*), heavy tick infestations, septicaemia due to *Staphylococcus aureus*, 'shock disease' and 'accumulations of pus beneath the skin of the neck', but population studies (Green and Evans, 1940; Keith and Windberg, 1978; Krebs et al., 1986, 1995) have not documented any consistent pathology during cyclic declines. Coccidiosis has been associated with declines in willow grouse numbers in Norway (Brinkmann, 1922), but coccidiosis is not usually reported during typical cyclic population fluctuations in Norway. Clarke (1936) implicated the blood parasite *Leococytozoon bonasae* as the proximate cause of a decline in ruffed grouse in Ontario, but indicated that it was not the ultimate cause. However, none of the evidence in this paragraph refutes the untested hypothesis (Seton, 1929; MacLulich, 1937) that overcrowding creates epizootics of varying aetiology, some of which may be unrecognized.

A useful example is a study of a cyclic population of the bank vole *Clethrionymys glareolus* (Haukisalmi and Henttonen, 1990) and two of its common helminth parasites *Heligmosomum mixtum* (Nematoda) and *Catenotaenia* sp. (Cestoda). The life history of *Heligmosomum* is direct (like *T. tenuis*), that of *Catenotaenia* indirect. The results caution against the easy assumption that high host density predisposes the population to increased burdens of parasites. The prevalence and intensity of both parasites were related primarily to weather. Significant relationships with density were also found, but these were negative, not positive. As in *T. tenuis* and red grouse in northeast Scotland (Moss et al., 1993), it seemed that variations in transmission rates associated with weather dominated the parasites' dynamics. In both cases, interactions between the parasites and their host were very unlikely to be a cause of population cycles.

The possibility that host–parasite interactions are a widespread cause of population cycles will depend partly on the key question of whether transmission rates or host densities are the more important determinants of parasite intensity. The evidence so far, as in 1911 for red grouse (above), is that parasites are not necessary but may be sufficient for population cycles.

2. Predator–Prey

Hypotheses involving predators as efficient causes of tetraonid cycles fall into two main classes. First, simple predator–prey oscillations involve variations on the Volterra-Lotka (Krebs, 1985a) theme. Second, the alternative prey hypothesis suggests that predators switch from their primary, cyclic mammalian prey to tetraonids when the former are scarce. This has been suggested for 3- to 4-year cycles and 10-year cycles, in which microtines and snowshoe hares, respectively, are the putative primary prey.

(a) Predator–prey oscillations. Modelling of vole cycles suggests that simple two-part predator–prey oscillations are likely only when the predator is a specialist (Turchin and Hanski, 1997). The same principle presumably applies to tetraonid cycles. Most tetraonid populations live in ecosystems with many prey species and several predators, none of which is a tetraonid specialist. The best relevant example of a single main cyclic prey species and a largely specialist predator is Icelandic rock ptarmigan, preyed on by gyr falcons *Falco rusticollis* L. (Nielsen and Cade, 1990; Nielsen and Pétursson, 1995). Gudmundsson (1960) concluded that the 10-year Icelandic rock ptarmigan cycles were not driven by mortality due to predation, but Gardarsson (1988) felt unable to exclude the possibility. Rock ptarmigan in the Cairngorms massif in Scotland showed 10-year cycles in the absence of specialist predators (Watson *et al.*, 1998).

We know of no population experiment that has aimed to test whether predators cause simple predator–tetraonid cycles. There is the anecdotal natural experiment due to stringent predator control on many grouse moors in Britain through the late nineteenth and much of the twentieth century. Here, red grouse bags continued to cycle (Mackenzie, 1952; Williams, 1985), often in the effective absence of predators, all of which were generalists.

It seems that specialist predators are not necessary for tetraonid population cycles. We know of no evidence from tetraonids contrary to the statement (Krebs, 1985a) that 'no one has yet found a classic predator–prey oscillation in field populations'. The alternative prey hypothesis, however, suggests that generalist predators cause cycles in the numbers of secondary prey.

(b) Alternative prey. This hypothesis (e.g. Lack, 1954b) assumes that predators increase in density during the increase and peak phase of a cycle in the density of their primary, mammalian prey. When mammal density declines, predators turn more to secondary prey such as tetraonids and cause their decline. Predator density decreases as primary and secondary prey become scarce, so allowing another increase in tetraonid density. The hypothesis is postulated for fairly complex boreal ecosystems with several predator and prey species, and marked seasonal effects. Hence realistic numerical models are not available and the detailed sequence of events expected from the hypothesis is not always clear. Even so, one expects the primary prey to have approached its peak, and predators to have become abundant, before tetraonids begin their cyclic decline.

For Fennoscandian 3- to 4-year cycles, the alternative prey hypothesis has been applied to microtines as putative primary prey, and hazel grouse, black grouse, capercaillie, willow grouse and mountain hares as secondary prey (Hörnfeldt, 1978; Angelstam *et al.*, 1985; Myrberget, 1988; Small *et al.*, 1993; Lindström *et al.*, 1994).

A natural experiment occurred when red fox numbers were reduced by sarcoptic mange (*Sarcoptes scabiae* var. *vulpes*). In boreal central Sweden, Small *et al.* (1993) noted that, after indices of fox numbers had declined, woodland grouse indices increased but continued to cycle around the new higher average level. Lindström *et al.* (1994) recorded the same result with an index of tetraonid numbers at Grimsö in south-central Sweden. They concluded that predation by red foxes was crucial in 'conveying the 3- to 4-year cyclic fluctuation pattern of voles to small game', because the timing of vole and tetraonid trajectories was consistent with the alternative prey hypothesis before the reduction in fox numbers due to mange, but not during it.

In a crossover experiment lasting 9 years, Marcström *et al.* (1988) killed red foxes and martens (*Martes martes* L.) on two small islands in the northern Baltic. They made no claim that tetraonids on these islands showed cycles. Killing of predators was followed by increased tetraonid breeding success and smaller increases in adult tetraonid numbers. When predators were not killed, tetraonid breeding success was positively and significantly correlated with vole numbers in summer. This did not occur when predators were killed. Here was evidence for a predator-mediated link between vole and tetraonid numbers, as required by the alternative prey hypothesis. It was not clear, however, that the link was sufficiently strong to affect the timing of tetraonid cycles. Nor did the experiment show that predators drove 3- to 4-year cycles.

A natural experiment happened during Myrberget's (1988) 21-year study of 3- to 4-year cycles in willow grouse on Tranøy island in northwest

Norway (Figure 2a). He made incidental observations on voles and mustelids, without systematic trapping, during fieldwork on willow grouse. He found high breeding numbers but low breeding success of grouse in vole-crash years, and decreases in grouse numbers following vole-crash years. This would have been consistent with the prey-switching hypothesis, were it not for the observation that three out of five vole crashes occurred in the absence of predators that could switch from voles to grouse eggs and chicks. This suggests that predators switching from voles to grouse are not necessary for 3- to 4-year cycles.

In North America, it has been suggested that 10-year cycles in ruffed grouse, sharp-tailed grouse and prairie grouse involve snowshoe hares as the primary prey (Lack, 1954b; Keith, 1963; Keith and Windberg, 1978). Keith (1963), however, compiled evidence showing that grouse numbers peaked or declined before snowshoe hare numbers in 16 out of 21 observations of local populations, contrary to expectations from the alternative prey hypothesis. Bergerud (1988) collated more detailed evidence from studies at Rochester, Alberta, showing that ruffed and sharp-tailed grouse were already beginning to decline before predators became numerous and while hares were still increasing. Again, Lindén (1989) and Small et al. (1993), having documented indices of the abundance of several species of predator and prey in Sweden and Finland, respectively, concluded that the timing of the fluctuations was not entirely consistent with the hypothesis. Such observations erode the alternative prey hypothesis. However, the occurrence of some cyclic tetraonid declines while the primary prey is increasing and predators are scarce does not exclude the possibility that prey-switching by predators might entrain (see section IV.B.2(d)) population cycles in tetraonids.

In short, it seems that predation affects the breeding success and density of tetraonid populations. Prey-switching may affect the timing of tetraonid cycles but is not necessary for cycles, because the documented cases of tetraonids cycling with 6–7 and 7–8 year periods involve no obvious primary prey. This also applies to the 10-year cycle of rock ptarmigan in Iceland (Gardarsson, 1988). The question of whether prey-switching is sufficient to drive some tetraonid population cycles remains open.

(c) Predation risk. Cyclic declines may involve perceived predation risk as well as the immediate effects of predators. This idea has not been developed in detail but has been suggested for snowshoe hares, where it depends on habitat heterogeneity (Keith, 1963; Wolff, 1980). Hik (1995) argued that hares during population declines attempt to minimize their chances of being killed by keeping to areas of dense cover. Such behaviour might result in a poorer diet and chronic stress (Boonstra et al., 1998), so reducing reproductive rate, increasing mortality, and accentuating and

prolonging the decline. According to this hypothesis, avoidance of predation is a final cause, and the poor diet and increased stress that result from adaptive behaviour are efficient causes of decline. Variations on this theme can be applied to tetraonids. Moss and Watson (1985), for example, suggested that cycles in prey species could be an adaptive response to predation. This would involve periods of low density during which natural enemies die or disperse, interspersed with regular irruptions. The irruptions would ensure many dispersing animals that swamp predators and thus have a good chance of founding new populations. These ideas are untested, both in tetraonids and in general.

3. Food–Consumer Interactions, Including Effects of Weather on Food

(a) Diet quality. Generally, the main foods of tetraonids are abundant plants of low nutritive value. The birds, selective feeders, eat only a small proportion of the total food biomass. Hence hypotheses invoking limitation of reproduction and numbers by food usually involve food quality rather than a gross shortage of edible matter. Food quality involves food accessibility, physical form, the proportion of digestible nutrients and aliments (energy-providing moieties), and the effects of plant secondary compounds such as toxins and digestion inhibitors (Moss and Hanssen, 1980; Moss, 1997).

Two periods are generally crucial in tetraonid nutrition. First, hens in spring need a diet of higher quality than in winter, and this is often provided by newly growing plant material (Moss et al., 1990). For Scottish red grouse and rock ptarmigan, there is evidence that hens with a poorer spring diet lay eggs that hatch into less viable chicks (Moss, 1997). Early chick mortality may therefore result from the nutritional status of the hens that laid the eggs, rather than from the diet or environment of the chicks. Second, for their first 2–4 weeks, chicks need a high-protein diet, often provided by an arthropod supplement to their mainly plant diet (Savory, 1989). Variations in the abundance or availability of arthropods may be related to chick growth rate (Erikstad, 1985) and possibly to chick survival (Myrberget et al., 1977). There are many reports of correlations between post-hatch weather and tetraonid breeding success, but it is usually unclear whether this is due to direct effects of weather on chicks, to effects on the availability of arthropods as chick foods, or to effects on the foraging times of chicks (Jørgensen and Blix, 1985).

Resources influence population density (see section IV.B.2(h)). In addition, in cyclic populations, a decline in food quality as density reaches a peak may be the trigger that initiates a population decline. At Rickarton moor in Scotland there was evidence that, as red grouse density increased towards a cyclic peak, the content of digestible protein in their diet declined (Moss et al., 1996). This measure of food quality was related inversely to density in the same year, with no time lag. There is no evidence that heavier browsing of food plants or heavier consumption of arthropods by tetraonids at high densities produces delayed density-dependent effects on food quality. The reason for this may be that the impact of tetraonids on their plant and arthropod food is so very low that it is unlikely to have much lasting impact on plant food quality or arthropod abundance.

In principle, cyclic variations in weather and its effects on food quality, or on access to food, could drive cycles in animal numbers (Elton, 1924; Hörnfeldt et al., 1986), as could intrinsic cycles in the nutritive value of food plants (Lauckhart, 1957). Also, cycles in mammalian herbivores might affect food quality and through it cause secondary tetraonid cycles. There is little evidence on either possibility, though Selås (1997) showed that the annual export of small game (mainly willow grouse) from Oslo in 1880–1916 was correlated with that of berries (mainly Vaccinium myrtillus and V. vitis-idaea) in the previous year. However, he did not show that exports of small game or berries were cyclic.

The increased proportion of unmated cock red grouse and rock ptarmigan during cyclic declines on poor soils (see section IV.B.2(h)) might be due to poorer food during declines. An alternative explanation for more unmated cocks during declines, while food quality remains constant, is poorer utilization of food resulting from the social stresses associated with declines (Boonstra et al., 1998). It might also involve adaptive behaviour, with cocks investing fewer physiological resources into reproduction during declines, and more into survival (Watson et al., 1998).

(b) Entrainment of cycles by weather through food.   Food, whether plant or arthropod, certainly plays a role in conveying the effects of variations in weather or climate to tetraonid populations. This might include weather cycles entraining (see section IV.B.2(d)) animal cycles through effects on diet. In the infertile Cairngorms massif of Scotland, June temperature at a nearby village tended to peak every 10 years, and was correlated with the breeding success of rock ptarmigan (Watson et al., 1998). It also provided a remarkably good postdictor of adult ptarmigan numbers (Figure 5b). The postdictive equation includes a delayed density-dependent term, indicating that the population's dynamics showed some instability unexplained by June temperature.

(c) Experiments.   A series of experiments (Watson et al., 1977) showed that the application of fertilizer to heather, the main food of red grouse, improved its feeding value, and in some cases resulted in increased breeding success and higher grouse densities. In other cases, however, high densities of sheep, red deer and mountain hares were attracted to the fertilized heather and browsed it heavily, whereupon grouse breeding success and densities did not increase.

One fertilizer experiment (Watson *et al.*, 1984b) was done during a 9-year cyclic population fluctuation of red grouse (Figure 6). Fertilizer was applied three times in a crossover design, with treatment and control alternating between two adjacent areas. One result was to illustrate a drawback of the crossover design, which depends on both areas remaining the same throughout an experiment, except for the treatment and its effects. The experiment was done during a cyclic fluctuation, and so cycle stage as well as treatment affected the outcome. In effect, then, there was a single treatment and a single control at three stages during a population cycle.

The effect of each fertilizer application on the nitrogen content of the birds' heather food lasted 3 years. The first application (1966) was made at a low population density of red grouse before the start of the increase phase. It was followed by increased breeding success and density on the treatment area relative to the control. However, this increase was outstripped by the cyclic increase that followed, irrespective of treatment. In 1971, densities on both areas were high and similar, and the second fertilizer application was made. Again this was followed by higher density on the experimental area relative to the control. As this was at the peak of the cycle, mean territory sizes on the fertilized area became very small (≈ 0.5 ha). The third treatment, made in 1976 during the decline phase, had

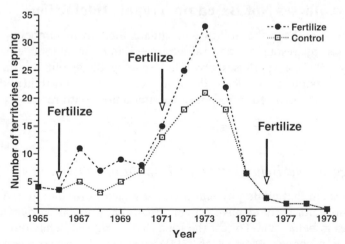

Fig. 6. Number of red grouse territories in spring, following fertilizer treatment, compared with an unfertilized control, at three stages of a population cycle. Each area was 16 ha. After Watson *et al.* (1984b).

no detectable effect on the red grouse, which continued to decline on both areas.

It seemed that, during the increase phase and at the peak, the effects of fertilizer and the cyclic process on red grouse numbers were additive. This was not so during the decline phase, when grouse on both experimental and control areas declined together. This result was similar to an experiment on snowshoe hares (Krebs *et al.*, 1986, 1995), during which added food also caused increased peak numbers but did not prevent a subsequent decline. Similarly, added food did not prevent declines in *Microtus californicus* (Peale) (Krebs and De Long, 1965) and *M. pennsylvanicus* (Ord) (Desy and Thompson, 1983). As the same phenomenon occurs in such different species, it may be a general feature in vertebrate population cycles.

In summary, there is some good evidence that tetraonid breeding success and density vary with the quality and quantity of their diet, which in turn varies in response to weather. Apart from Figure 5b and related information in Watson *et al.* (1998, 2000), there is little evidence on the propositions that cyclic variations in weather or food (1) drive tetraonid cycles, or (2) entrain their period to weather patterns. It seems reasonable to suggest that food would be involved in the Moran effect, were this substantiated, but there is no evidence. Food can play a role in mediating interspecific competition between tetraonids and other herbivores, but the relevance of this to population cycles is unknown.

B. Hypotheses Not Based on Trophic Interactions

Animals may have the ability to regulate their own numbers below the limits set by resources, natural enemies, and the abiotic environment (Chitty, 1967). Hypotheses involving spacing behaviour as the efficient cause of population cycles do not exclude the possibility that such behaviour has evolved in response to interactions with resources, enemies or weather.

1. Aggressive Behaviour and Population Dynamics

It may seem that crude physical processes such as predation and resource limitation are likely to have bigger effects on population dynamics than changes in behaviour. To test the idea that territorial behaviour can cause population change, Moss *et al.* (1994) increased the aggression of some individual cock red grouse on a study area by implanting them with testosterone (Figure 7), the effects of which lasted for about 6 weeks.

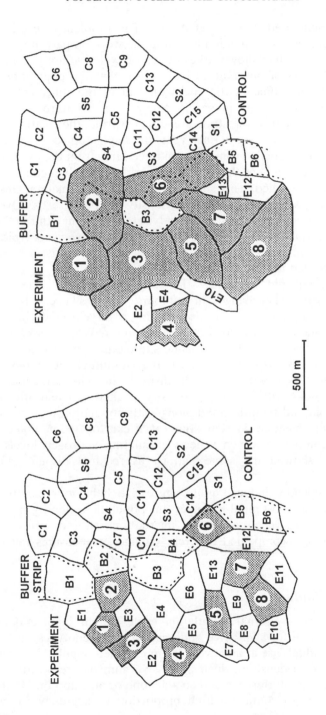

Fig. 7. Effects of testosterone implants on spring territory size and numbers of red grouse in spring 1993. Shaded territories are of implanted birds before (left) and after (right) implants. Similar results occurred in 1992. After Moss *et al.* (1994).

The experiment used a crossover design. The problem of cycle stage affecting the outcome was avoided by doing the work on part of an estate where shooting bags had shown no evidence of cycles with a period ≤ 10 years. After 3 years of observation had shown that the population was effectively constant, some of the cocks on half of the study area were implanted with testosterone in spring. Sham implants were done with cocks on the other half of the study area. Next spring, the treatment and control halves were reversed. In each year, the implanted cocks expanded their territories and expelled some unimplanted birds from the experimental half. The number of hens that left the experimental halves equalled the number of cocks expelled. This showed that changes in male aggression can cause changes in the population density of both sexes. Overall, population density on the experimental halves fell by about a third relative to the controls, which, if repeated for the three successive years typical of natural cyclic declines in that region of Scotland (Watson *et al.*, 1984a), would have resulted in a three-fold decline.

This experiment did not show that natural changes in territorial behaviour caused cyclic changes in numbers. Aggressiveness, however, has changed during red grouse cycles. During a 16-year study involving two cyclic population fluctuations at Kerloch moor, Watson *et al.* (1994) measured aggressiveness as the 'residual dispute rate'. This was the rate at which territorial birds disputed with each other at mutual boundaries, after allowing for the effects of density on the dispute rate. The residual dispute rate increased along with population density, peaked one year after each population peak, and then declined along with population density. Moss *et al.* (1996), during their 11-year study at Rickarton moor, noted that supra-orbital comb size, which reflects circulating androgen levels and aggressiveness, showed the same pattern as residual dispute rate at Kerloch.

In short, artificially induced male aggressive behaviour can be the efficient cause of substantial changes in population density in both sexes, and natural cyclic population fluctuations in red grouse have been found to be accompanied by cyclic changes in measures reflecting aggressiveness.

2. Genetic Changes

Chitty (1967) proposed that population cycles might involve density-dependent selection for aggressive and unaggressive genotypes, such that aggressive individuals are at an advantage in crowded populations and are selected for at high densities. Such aggressive animals are postulated to cause great mutual interference and so a decline occurs, and the declining population comes to contain a high proportion of aggressive animals.

When low density is reached, there is no longer any advantage in being aggressive and so the population increases again.

Moss *et al.* (1984) tested whether a measure of the inherent ability of cocks to dominate others changed during a population cycle in red grouse. They removed eggs from a wild cycling population and hatched and reared the birds in captivity. They then measured the fully grown cocks' 'social dominance rank', which is similar to the pecking order in poultry and has a high heritability (Moss *et al.*, 1985). The results (Figure 8) indicated selection for inherently subordinate types during the increase phase of a cyclic population fluctuation, and for dominant types during the decline. They refuted the specific prediction (Krebs, 1985b), based on Chitty's (1967) hypothesis, that aggressive types should be selected for during cyclic population increases, but left open other interpretations of Chitty's general hypothesis.

The results in Figure 8 led to the idea that the birds were more tolerant of each other during cyclic population increases and less tolerant during declines. The main demographic cause of annual changes in red grouse density was variation in recruitment (Moss and Watson, 1991), and so a higher rate of recruitment seemed to be associated with greater tolerance. Watson *et al.* (1994) observed that disputes at territorial boundaries were less frequent between kin than between non-kin, so indicating that kin were more tolerant of each other. Perhaps selection for tolerant types was due to kin facilitating the recruitment of their joint offspring. This might be more effective if kin were clustered together as neighbours.

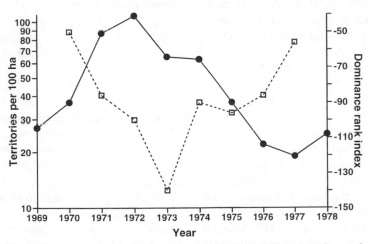

Fig. 8. Changes in an index of inherent dominance (ability of cocks to dominate others, dashed line) during a population cycle (solid line) in red grouse. After Moss *et al.* (1984).

Hence it becomes necessary to consider the spatial organization of individuals.

3. Spatial Organization and Kinship

Increased emigration has been a feature of cyclic population declines in studies of Scottish red grouse and rock ptarmigan (see section V.B). This makes it necessary to think in spatially explicit terms. Another spatial phenomenon is that young territorial cock willow ptarmigan and red grouse tend to settle philopatrically, so forming clusters of related territory owners (Martin and Hannon, 1987; Watson *et al.*, 1994; MacColl *et al.*, 2000; Piertney *et al.*, 1999). This led Mountford *et al.* (1990) to suggest a mechanism for population cycles, wherein population change was related to the size of such kin clusters.

The essential idea is that bigger kin clusters facilitate a higher recruitment rate, and that higher recruitment results in bigger kin clusters and increased population density. During the increase phase of a cycle, this leads to positive feedback between cluster size and recruitment in successive years. At peak densities, crowding halts this positive feedback, and kin clusters decay because they are not being replenished by new recruits. This leads to contrary positive feedback, between smaller kin clusters and lower recruitment, which continues during the decline phase until low densities are reached and kin clusters can grow again. Modelling (Hendry *et al.*, 1997; Matthiopoulos *et al.*, 1998) shows that continued low recruitment during the decline phase could be due entirely to social dynamics involving delayed density dependence in mean cluster size. This might occur because, each year, the development of new clusters and the maintenance of old clusters depend on cluster size and density at the beginning of the year, and these in turn depend on past conditions (Matthiopoulos, 1998; Matthiopoulos *et al.*, 1998).

Two detailed models have confirmed that the Mountford *et al.* (1990) hypothesis is feasible. Hendry *et al.* (1997) showed that a spatially explicit individual-based simulation of territorial behaviour in red grouse, based on realistic parameter values, was destabilized by differential behaviour between kin and non-kin, and could produce realistic population cycles. Matthiopoulos *et al.* (1998) developed an analytical model of the hypothesis, and, using parameters based on field data from two population studies, generated dynamics similar to those of the populations from which the data came.

MacColl *et al.* (2000) studied the effects of kin cluster size on recruitment within years during the late part of a cyclic increase in a wild population of red grouse. They confirmed the risky prediction that a young cock's probability of recruitment was enhanced if he came from a bigger kin cluster. It remains to test this hypothesis during other stages of a cycle, and at the population level.

The kin-facilitation models explain how the proportion of reared young recruited into the breeding population can vary (see section V.B). During declines, kin clusters are smaller and so facilitation of recruitment by kin is weaker. This involves delayed density dependence in kin cluster size (above) and in the proportion of young recruited. In the models, poorer breeding success is not necessary for declines, which can be due entirely to variations in the proportion of young recruited.

As framed above, the kin-facilitation hypothesis seems specific to territorial species and to cocks. There is, however, no reason why kin groups should not take forms other than territorial clusters, or why hen kin groups should not play a role. The prerequisites for this hypothesis are: (1) social behaviour that limits breeding numbers; (2) the occurrence of kin groups that affect recruitment of young birds to the breeding population; and (3) adult mortality and breeding success high enough to allow the size of kin groups to change fast enough to affect recruitment into kin clusters at a rate consistent with the observed cycles in recruitment and density.

In summary, the kin-facilitation hypothesis is consistent with past observations and modelling has shown that it is feasible. Field testing of it has started (MacColl et al., 2000), following the development of new molecular methods for measuring relatedness (Piertney et al., 1999).

VII. SYNTHESIS

Hypotheses about population cycles must explain (1) what drives cycles, (2) intraspecific variations in cycle period, and (3) interspecific synchrony. There is no consensus on (1), and little evidence on what causes (2) and (3). This section is a speculative framework intended to provide a coherent set of ideas for future testing.

A. What Drives Cycles?

No trophic interaction has yet been shown to be necessary for driving any tetraonid cycle, but few rigorous tests of specific hypotheses have been done. The view that trophic interactions drive cycles is still tenable. Alternatively, the spatial organization and interactions of individuals could result in unstable population dynamics (see section VI.B.3).

The main documented demographic cause of cyclic declines in tetraonids (see section V.B) has been lower recruitment associated with (1) fewer young reared to independence, and (2) a smaller proportion of these young surviving the winter and becoming recruited into the breeding population. Given Table 1, a parsimonious demographic hypothesis is that tetraonid population cycles are due primarily to variations in (2).

Two studies (Watson *et al.*, 1984a, 1998) documented more emigration during cyclic declines than during increases. As study areas were quite small ($< 2\,km^2$), emigration need not have been far. This implies the existence of a class of dispersing young, comprising a larger proportion during declines, that is wholly or mostly lost to the local population. Clearly, the suggestion that emigration contributes to declines can be scaled up from the local study area to the landscape scale only if emigrating birds die in population sinks, or if they form a class of 'floaters' that suffers high mortality over the winter, irrespective of the habitat in which they occur.

Population sinks are presumably more capacious in fragmented habitats than in the large tracts of relatively homogeneous habitat where cycles seem to occur (section IV.B.2(g)). By definition, population sinks remove emigrants from areas of better habitat. This is consistent with the density dependence observed in non-cyclic populations in fragmented habitats (Figure 3). In homogeneous tracts, emigrants are presumably less likely to enter sinks and more likely to become floaters, destined seldom or never to enter the breeding population. Behavioural studies and experiments on marked populations of red (Watson and Jenkins, 1968; Watson, 1985) and blue (Zwickel, 1980) grouse have identified such a class. The blue grouse populations studied by Zwickel (1980) were not cyclic and so floaters are not confined to cyclic populations. The suggestion is of a bigger proportion of floaters during cyclic declines (Jenkins *et al.*, 1963, 1967). This is consistent with the lore describing widespread movements of large flocks of grouse and ptarmigan during cyclic declines (Siivonen, 1952; Keith, 1963).

Fragmented habitat is likely to engender more mortality of eggs or chicks from increased numbers of generalist predators, or more emigration of young followed by death in habitat sinks. Because cyclic populations occur in homogeneous tracts, they should produce a higher proportion of young birds than non-cyclic populations in fragmented habitat (Bergerud, 1988). This should facilitate the development of greater population densities (Dymond, 1947). An experiment with red grouse (Moss *et al.*, 1996) prevented a population cycle by removing cocks in the increase phase, so preventing peak density (Figure 9). The control population peaked and then showed the predicted cyclic decline, but the experimental population showed no cyclic decline. Hence peak numbers may be necessary for cyclic declines, and large areas of fairly homogeneous habitat necessary for peak numbers.

A working hypothesis for the effects of fragmentation is that tetraonid population cycles involve stepwise delayed density dependence in recruit-

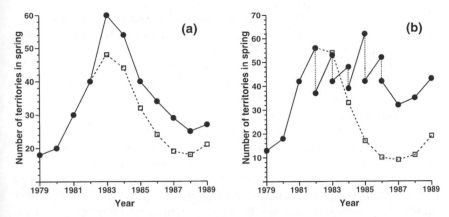

Fig. 9. Numbers of spring territories of red grouse during (a) an unperturbed population cycle (control, 318 ha), and (b) a cycle perturbed by removing cocks (experiment, 203 ha) in the increase phase. The vertical dotted lines in (b) show numbers before and after removals in spring. The dashed lines show predictions assuming no removals, made in spring 1982 from a model developed previously at another study area. After Moss *et al.* (1996).

ment, such that a cyclic population decline occurs only if population density exceeds an upper density threshold. This threshold would not usually be exceeded in fragmented habitats, where there is more predation and more density-dependent dispersal from patches of better habitat into population sinks. Different populations, including different sets of birds on the same ground at different times, may have different thresholds.

B. Variations in Cycle Period

The same species can show several cycle periods, and species with different mean vital rates can show the same period (see section IV.B.2(e) and (f)). These observations refute hypotheses that involve mean vital rates, habitats, and other species-specific aspects as necessary causes of a particular cycle period. Fieldwork that tests hypotheses which explain intraspecific variation in cycle period has not been attempted. This is partly because it would be very difficult, and partly because little attention has been paid to the problem.

It may be coincidence that the three most commonly reported cycle periods, 3–4, 6–7 and 10 years, are approximate multiples of 3–4 years (Siivonen, 1952). However, simple models involving delayed density dependence show increasing instability with increased recruitment rates (May, 1974, 1976). This progression can be through cycles with a given period, to cycles with half the period (cycle doubling). The observation that some trajectories consist of a mixture of 10- and 6-year periods (see section IV.B.2(a)) is consistent with cycle doubling (Watson *et al.*, 1998), but there are other possible explanations.

The Moran effect can account for interspecific synchrony in cyclic species with different vital rates (section IV.B.2(f)), though it is not clear to what extent it can explain variations in cycle period.

Entrainment (see section VI.B.2(d)) of cycle period by cyclic weather patterns, or by cyclic impacts of resources or natural enemies, could account for interspecific synchrony and for variations in cycle period. Entrainment might involve final as well as efficient causation, because the timing of cycles could involve investing more into reproduction in years of predictably good conditions for breeding (Watson *et al.*, 1998), and investing more into survival in years of predictably poor conditions for breeding. In this context, predictability need not be perfect, but just enough to increase the fitness of animals that adjust their investment into reproduction or survival as if they were predicting cycles in resources or enemies.

VIII. CONCLUSION

We have considered factors that drive tetraonid cycles, and those that determine their period, at two hierarchical levels. First, at the demographic level, hypotheses that involve particular mean vital rates and other species-specific aspects as necessary causes of particular cycle periods are refuted by the observation of synchronous fluctuations among species with different vital rates. The main documented demographic cause of changes in the size of tetraonid breeding populations has been variations in the recruitment of young birds to the breeding population. In seven detailed studies, involving two *Lagopus* species, lower recruitment during cyclic declines has been associated with lower breeding success and with a smaller proportion of the reared young surviving over winter and becoming recruited into the breeding population next spring. However, mean breeding success differed among populations within species, such that cyclic increases in some populations occurred while breeding success was lower than during declines in other populations. Numerous anecdotal observations that cycles are associated with large tracts of unfragmented habitat imply that explanations of cycles must be spatially explicit.

Second, we need to unravel the efficient causes of the demographic processes. Weather probably contributes to long-term trends in numbers, to synchrony among fluctuations in different species, and to partial synchrony among fluctuations of spatially separate parts of the same species. Weather may also affect cycle periods. Trophic interactions may be sufficient to drive population cycles, but no hypothesis based on this postulate has so far been substantiated. Developments in modelling and molecular techniques now permit the testing of other hypotheses, based on the premise that population dynamics are the emergent results of individuals' adaptive actions.

At the demographic level, a parsimonious demographic hypothesis for tetraonid population cycles is that they are due primarily to variations in the proportion of independent young that survives the winter and becomes recruited to the breeding population. A working hypothesis that accounts for the effects of habitat fragmentation is that recruitment shows stepwise delayed density dependence and that the upper threshold is exceeded only when predation and dispersal are limited, as in large blocks of continuous habitat. These hypotheses are consistent with hypotheses that cycles are driven by trophic interactions and with those invoking individual behaviour.

ACKNOWLEDGEMENTS

We thank P.J. Bacon, X. Lambin, J. Matthiopoulos, S. Piertney, R.J. Delahay, S. Redpath and P. Turchin for helpful criticisms of the manuscript.

REFERENCES

Anderson, R.M. and May, R.M. (1978). Regulation and stability of host–parasite population interactions. I. Regulatory processes. *J. Anim. Ecol.* **47**, 219–247.

Andersson, M. and Erlinge, S. (1977). Influence of predation on rodent populations. *Oikos* **29**, 591–597.

Andreev, A.A. (1988). The ten year cycle of the willow grouse of Lower Kolyma. *Oecologia* **76**, 261–267.

Andrén, H., Angelstam, P., Lindström, E. and Widén, P. (1985). Differences in predation pressure in relation to habitat fragmentation: an experiment. *Oikos* **45**, 273–277.

Angelstam, P., Lindström, E. and Widén, P. (1985). Synchronous short-term population fluctuations of some birds and mammals in Fennoscandia – occurrence and distribution. *Holarct. Ecol.* **8**, 285–298.

Beaudette, P.D. and Keppie, D.M. (1992). Survival of dispersing spruce grouse. *Can. J. Zool.* **70**, 693–697.

Bendell, J.F. and Elliott, P.W. (1967). Behaviour and the regulation of numbers in blue grouse. *Can. Wildl. Serv. Rep. Ser.* No. 4.

Bergerud, A.T. (1970). Population dynamics of the willow ptarmigan *Lagopus lagopus alleni* L. in Newfoundland 1955–1965. *Oikos* **21**, 299–325.

Bergerud, A.T. (1988). Population ecology of North American grouse. In: *Adaptive Strategies and Population Ecology of Northern Grouse* (Ed. by T. Bergerud and M.W. Gratson), pp. 578–685. University of Minnesota Press, Minneapolis.

Bergerud, A.T. and Gratson, M.W. (Editors) (1988). *Adaptive Strategies and Population Ecology of Northern Grouse*. University of Minnesota Press, Minneapolis.

Berryman, A.A. (1978). Population cycles of the Douglas-fir tussock moth (*Lepidoptera: Lymantriidae*): the time-delay hypothesis. *Can. Entomol.* **110**, 513–518.

Birse, E. (1971). *Assessment of Climatic Conditions in Scotland. 3. The Bioclimatic Subregions*. Macaulay Institute for Soil Research, Aberdeen.

Boonstra, R., Hik, D., Singleton, G.R. and Tinnikov, A. (1998). The impact of predator-induced stress on the snowshoe hare cycle. *Ecol. Monogr.* **79**, 371–394.

Borchtchevski, V.G. (1993). *Populyatsionnaya Biologia Glucharya, Printsipi Structurnoy Organizatsiy*. TSNIL Ochotnichevo Chozyayctva i Zapovednikov, Moskva.

Brinkmann, A. (1922). Lirypens entoparasiter. *Bergens Mus. Årb. 1921–22. Naturv. Rekke nr. 3. Bergen*. (Cited by Gelting, 1937.)

Cattadori, I.M. and Hudson, P.J. (1999). Temporal dynamics of grouse populations at the southern edge of their distribution. *Ecography* **22**, 374–383.

Chitty, D. (1954). Tuberculosis among wild voles: with a discussion of other pathological conditions among certain mammals and birds. *Ecology* **35**, 227–237.

Chitty, D. (1967). The natural selection of self-regulatory behaviour in animal populations. *Proc. Ecol. Soc. Aust.* **2**, 51–78.

Chitty, D. (1969). Regulatory effects of a random variable. *Am. Zool.* **9**, 400.

Chitty, D. (1991). This week's citation classic. *Curr. Cont.* **22**, 8.

Chitty, D. (1996). *Do Lemmings Commit Suicide? Beautiful Hypotheses and Ugly Facts*. Oxford University Press, New York and Oxford.

Clarke, C.H.D. (1936). Fluctuations in numbers of ruffed grouse *Bonasa umbellus* (Linné), with special reference to Ontario. *Univ. Toronto Studies, Biol. Ser.* No. 41. (Cited by Keith, 1963.)

Cole, L.C. (1954). Some features of random population cycles. *J. Wildl. Mgmt* **18**, 2–24.

Darwin, C. (1859). *The Origin of Species by Natural Selection*, 6th. edn. J.M. Dent and Sons Ltd, London, 1928 edn.

Davis, D.E. (1957). The existence of cycles. *Ecology* **38**, 163–164.

Delahay, R.J. (1995). *The epidemiology and pathological effects of* Trichostrongylus tenuis *(Nematoda) in red grouse* (Lagopus lagopus scoticus). Ph.D. thesis, University of Aberdeen.

Delahay, R.J. and Moss, R. (1996). Food intake, weight changes and egg production in captive red grouse before and during laying: effects of the parasitic nematode *Trichostrongylus tenuis. Condor* **98**, 501–511.

Delahay, R.J., Speakman, J.R. and Moss, R. (1995). The energetic consequences of parasitism: effects of a developing infection of *Trichostrongylus tenuis* (Nematoda) on red grouse (*Lagopus lagopus scoticus*) energy balance, body weight and condition. *Parasitology* **110**, 473–482.

Dempster J.P. (1975). *Animal Population Ecology*. Academic Press, London.

Desy, E.A. and Thompson, C.F. (1983). Effects of supplemental food on a *Microtus pennsylvanicus* population in central Illinois. *J. Anim. Ecol.* **52**, 317–376.

Dobson, A.P. and Hudson, P.J. (1992). Regulation and stability of a free-living host–parasite system: *Trichostrongylus tenuis* in red grouse. II. Population models. *J. Anim. Ecol.* **61**, 487–498.

Dobson, A.P. and Hudson, P.J. (1994). Population biology of *Trichostrongylus tenuis* in the red grouse, *Lagopus lagopus scoticus*. In: *Parasitic and Infectious Diseases* (Ed. by M.E. Scott and G. Smith), pp. 301–319. Academic Press, San Diego.

Dolbeer, R.A. and Clark, W.R. (1975). Population ecology of snowshoe hares in the central Rocky Mountains. *J. Wildl. Mgmt* **39**, 535–549.

Dougall, J.D. (1875). *Shooting: its Appliances, Practice and Purpose*. Sampson Low, Marston, Low and Searle, London.

Dymond, J.R. (1947). Fluctuations in animal populations with special reference to those in Canada. *Trans. Roy. Soc. Can.* **41**, 1–34. (Cited by Keith, 1963.)

Elton, C. (1924). Periodic fluctuations in the numbers of animals: their causes and effects. *Br. J. Exp. Biol.* **2**, 119–163.

Elton, C. (1931). The study of epidemic diseases among wild animals. *J. Hygiene Camb.* **31**, 435–456.

Elton, C., Ford, E.B., Baker, J.R. and Gardner, A.D. (1931). The health and parasites of a wild mouse population. *Proc. Zool. Soc. Lond.* **104**, 657–721.

Elton, C., Davis, D.H.S. and Findlay, G.M. (1935). An epidemic among voles *(Microtus agrestis)* on the Scottish border in the spring of 1934. *J. Anim. Ecol.* **4**, 277–288.

Erikstad, K.E. (1985). Growth and survival of Willow Grouse chicks in relation to home range, brood movement and habitat selection. *Ornis Scand.* **16**, 181–190.

Falck, W., Bjørnstad, O.N. and Stenseth, N.C. (1995). Bootstrap estimated uncertainty of the dominant Lyapunov exponent for Holarctic microtine rodents. *Proc. Roy. Soc. Lond. B.* **261**, 159–165.

Findlay, G.M. and Middleton, A.D. (1934). Epidemic disease among voles *(Microtus)* with special refernce to *Toxoplasma. J. Anim. Ecol.* **3**, 150–160.

Gardarsson, A. (1971). *Food Ecology and Spacing Behavior of Rock Ptarmigan* (Lagopus mutus) *in Iceland*. Ph.D. thesis, University of California, Berkeley.

Gardarsson, A. (1988). Cyclic population changes and some related events in rock ptarmigan in Iceland. In: *Adaptive Strategies and Population Ecology of Northern Grouse* (Ed. by T. Bergerud and M.W. Gratson), pp. 300–329. University of Minnesota Press, Minneapolis.

Gelting, P. (1937). Studies on the food of the East Greenland ptarmigan. *Meddr om Grønland* 116.

Gimingham, C.H. (1972). *Ecology of Heathlands*. Chapman & Hall, London.

Ginzburg, L.R. and Inchausti, P. (1997). Asymmetry of population cycles: abundance-growth representation of hidden causes of ecological dynamics. *Oikos* **80**, 435–447.

Giraudoux, P., Delattre, P., Habert, M., Quéré, J.P., Deblay, S., Defaut, R., Duhamel, R., Moissenet, M.F., Salvi, D. and Truchetet, D. (1997). Population dynamics of the fossorial water vole *(Arvicola terrestris scherman)*: a land use perspective. *Agric. Ecosyst. Environ.* **66**, 47–60.

Green, R.G. and Evans, C.A. (1940). Studies on a population cycle of snowshoe hares on the Lake Alexander area. III. Mortality according to age groups and seasons. *J. Wildl. Mgmt* **4**, 347–358.

Gudmundsson, F. (1960). Some reflections on ptarmigan cycles in Iceland. *Proc. Int. Orn. Congr.* **12**, 259–265.

Hannon, S.J. and Zwickel, F.C. (1979). Probable non-breeders among female Blue Grouse. *Condor* **81**, 78–82.

Hanski, I., Hansson, L. and Henttonen, H. (1991). Specialist predators, generalist predators, and the microtine rodent cycle. *J. Anim. Ecol.* **60**, 353–367.

Haukisalmi, V. and Henttonen, H. (1990). The impact of climatic factors and host density on the long-term population dynamics of vole helminths. *Oecologia* **83**, 309–315.

Hendry, R., Bacon, P.J., Moss, R., Palmer, S.C.F. and McGlade, J. (1997) A two-dimensional individual-based model of territorial behaviour: possible population consequences of kinship in red grouse. *Ecol. Model.* **105**, 23–29.

Hik, D. (1995). Does risk of predation influence population dynamics? Evidence from the cyclic decline of snowshoe hares. *Wildl. Res.* **22**, 115–129.

Hines, J.E. (1986). Survival and reproduction of dispersing blue grouse. *Condor* **88**, 43–49.

Hjeljord, O. and Kiær, A. (1991). Jaktjournalen fra 'Rypa'. *Villreinen*, 57–59.

Holstad, Ø., Karbøl, G. and Skorping, A. (1994). *Trichostrongylus tenuis* from willow grouse (*Lagopus lagopus*) and ptarmigan (*Lagopus mutus*) in northern Norway. *Bull. Scand. Soc. Parasitol.* **4**, 9–13.

Hörnfeldt, B. (1978). Synchronous population fluctuations in voles, small game, owls, and tularemia in northern Sweden. *Oecologia* **32**, 141–152.

Hörnfeldt, B. (1994). Delayed density dependence as a determinant of vole cycles. *Ecology* **75**, 791–806.

Hörnfeldt, B., Löfgren, O. and Carlsson, B.-G. (1986). Cycles in voles and small game in relation to variations in plant production indices in Northern Sweden. *Oecologia* **68**, 496–502.

Hudson, P.J. (1986a). The effects of a parasitic nematode on the breeding production of red grouse. *J. Anim. Ecol.* **55**, 85–92.

Hudson P.J. (1986b). *Red Grouse, the Biology and Management of a Wild Gamebird*. The Game Conservancy Trust, Fordingbridge.

Hudson P.J. (1992). *Grouse in Space and Time*. The Game Conservancy Trust, Fordingbridge.

Hudson, P.J. (1993). Red grouse. In: *The New Atlas of Wintering Birds in Britain and Ireland: 1988–1991* (Ed. by D.W. Gibbons, J.B. Reid and R.A. Chapman), pp. 126–127. T. and A.D. Poyser, London.

Hudson, P.J. and Dobson, A.P. (1997). Transmission dynamics and host–parasite interactions of *Trichostrongylus tenuis* in red grouse. *J. Parasitol.* **83**, 194–202.

Hudson, P.J., Dobson, A.P. and Newborn, D. (1985). Cyclic and non-cyclic populations of red grouse: a role for parasitism? In: *Ecology and Genetics of Host–Parasite Interactions* (Ed. by D. Rollinson and R.M. Anderson), pp. 77–89. Linnean Society of London, Academic Press, London.

Hudson, P.J., Dobson, A.P. and Newborn, D. (1992). Regulation and stability of a free-living host–parasite system: *Trichostrongylus tenuis* in red grouse. I. Monitoring and parasite reduction experiments. *J. Anim. Ecol.* **61**, 477–486.

Hudson, P.J., Dobson, A.P. and Newborn, D. (1999). Prevention of population cycles by parasite removal. *Science* **282**, 2256–2258.

Hutchinson, G.E. (1948). Circular causal systems in ecology. *Ann. NY Acad. Sci.* **50**, 221–246.

Irving, L., West, G.C., Peyton, L.J. and Paneak, S. (1967). Migration of willow ptarmigan in Arctic Alaska. *Arctic* **20**, 77–85.

Jenkins, D., Watson, A. and Miller, G.R. (1963). Population studies on red grouse *Lagopus lagopus scoticus* (Lath.). *J. Anim. Ecol.* **40**, 317–376.

Jenkins, D., Watson, A. and Miller, G.R. (1967). Population fluctuations in the red grouse *Lagopus lagopus scoticus*. *J. Anim. Ecol.* **36**, 97–122.

Johnsgard, P.A. (1983). *The Grouse of the World*. Croom Helm, Beckenham.

Jørgensen, E. and Blix, A.S. (1985). Effects of climate and nutrition on growth and survival of willow ptarmigan chicks. *Ornis Scand.* **16**, 99–107.

Kaitala, V., Ranta, E. and Lindström, J. (1996). Cyclic population dynamics and random perturbations. *J. Anim. Ecol.* **65**, 249–251.

Keith, K.B. (1963). *Wildlife's Ten-year Cycle*. University of Wisconsin Press, Madison.

Keith, L.B. and Windberg, L.A. (1978). A demographic analysis of the snowshoe hare cycle. *Wildl. Monogr.* **58**, 1–70.

Keith, L.B., Bloomer, S.E.M. and Willebrand, T. (1993). Dynamics of a snowshoe hare population in fragmented habitat. *Can. J. Zool.* **71**, 1385–1392.

Krebs C.J. (1985a). *Ecology: the Experimental Analysis of Distribution and Abundance*, 3rd edn. Harper & Row, New York.

Krebs, C.J. (1985b). Do changes in spacing behaviour drive population cycles in small mammals? In: *Behavioural Ecology* (Ed. by R.M. Sibly and R.H. Smith), pp. 295–312. Blackwell Scientific Publications, Oxford.

Krebs, C.J. and DeLong, K.T. (1965). A *Microtus* population with supplemental food. *J. Mammal.* **46**, 566–573.

Krebs, C.J., Gilbert, B.S., Boutin, S., Sinclair, A.R.E. and Smith, J.N.M. (1986). Population biology of snowshoe hares. I. Demography of food-supplemented populations in the southern Yukon, 1976–84. *J. Anim. Ecol.* **55**, 963–982.

Krebs, C.J., Boutin, S., Boonstra, R., Sinclair, A.R.E., Smith, J.N.M., Dale, M.R.T., Martin, K. and Turkington, R. (1995). Impact of food and predation on the snowshoe hare cycle. *Science* **269**, 1112–1115.

Lack, D. (1954a). *The Natural Regulation of Animal Numbers*. Oxford University Press, Oxford.

Lack, D. (1954b). Cyclic mortality. *J. Wildl. Mgmt* **18**, 25–37.

Lambin, X., Elston, D.A., Petty, S.J. and MacKinnon, J.L. (1998). Spatial asynchrony and periodic travelling waves in cyclic populations of field voles. *Proc. Roy. Soc. Lond. B.* **265**, 1491–1496.

Lauckhart, J.B. (1957). Animal cycles and food. *J. Wildl. Mgmt* **21**, 230–234.

Lele, S., Taper, M.L. and Gage, S. (1998). Statistical analysis of population dynamics in space and time using estimating functions. *Ecology* **79**, 1489–1502.

Leopold, A. (1933). *Game Management*. Charles Scribner's Sons, New York and London.

Leslie, G. (1959). The properties of a certain lag type of population growth and the influence of an external random factor on a number of such populations. *Physiol. Zoöl.* **32**, 151–159.

Levine, N.D. (1980). Weather and the ecology of bursate nematodes. *Int. J. Biomet.* **24**, 341–346.

Lindén, H. (1981). Hunting and tetraonid populations in Finland. *Finn. Game Res.* **39**, 69–78.

Lindén, H. (1988). Latitudinal gradients in predator–prey interactions, cyclicity and synchronism in voles and small game populations in Finland. *Oikos* **52**, 341–349.

Lindén, H. (1989). Characteristics of tetraonid cycles in Finland. *Finn. Game Res.* **46**, 34–42.

Lindström, E.R., Andrén, H., Angelstam, P., Cederlund, G., Hörnfeldt, B., Jäderberg, L., Lemnell, P.A., Martinsson, B., Sköld, K. and Swenson, J.E. (1994). Disease reveals the predator: sarcoptic mange, red fox predation, and prey populations. *Ecology* **75**, 1042–1049.

Lindström, J. (1994). Tetraonid population studies – state of the art. *Ann. Zool. Fenn.* **31**, 347–364.

Lindström, J., Ranta, E. and Lindén, H. (1996). Large-scale synchrony in the dynamics of capercaillie, black grouse and hazel grouse populations in Finland. *Oikos* **76**, 221–227.

Lovat, Lord (1911). Moor management. In: *The Grouse in Health and in Disease* (Ed. by Lord Lovat), pp. 372–391. Smith, Elder and Co., London.

MacColl, A.D.C., Piertney, S.B., Moss, R. and Lambin, X. (2000). Spatial arrangement of kin affects recruitment success in young male red grouse. *Oikos* **90**, 261–270.

Mackenzie, J.M.D. (1952). Fluctuations in the numbers of British tetraonids. *J. Anim. Ecol.* **21**, 128–153.

Mackin-Rogalska, R. and Nabaglo, L. (1990). Geographical variation in cyclic periodicity and synchrony in the common vole, *Microtus arvalis*. *Oikos* **59**, 343–348.

MacLulich, D.A. (1937). Fluctuations in the numbers of the varying hare (*Lepus americanus*). *Univ. Toronto Studies, Biol. Ser.* No. 43. (Cited by Keith, 1963.)

Marcström, V., Kenward, R.E. and Engren, E. (1988). The impact of predation on boreal tetraonids during vole cycles: an experimental study. *J. Anim. Ecol.* **57**, 859–872.

Martin, K. and Hannon, S.J. (1987). Natal philopatry and recruitment of willow ptarmigan in north central and northwestern Canada. *Oecologia* **71**, 518–524.

Matthiopoulos, J. (1998). *Modelling the kin-selection hypothesis for red grouse population cycles.* Ph.D. Thesis, University of Aberdeen.

Matthiopoulos, J., Moss, R. and Lambin, X. (1998). Models of red grouse cycles. A family affair? *Oikos* **82**, 574–590.

May, R.M. (1974). Biological populations with non-overlapping generations, stable points, stable cycles and chaos. *Science* **186**, 645–647.

May, R.M. (1976). Simple mathematical models with very complicated dynamics. *Nature* **261**, 459–467.

May, R.M. (1999). Crash tests for real. *Nature* **398**, 371–372.

May, R.M. and Anderson, R.M. (1978). Regulation and stability of host–parasite population interactions. II. Destabilizing processes. *J. Anim. Ecol.* **47**, 249–267.

Medawar, P.B. (1967). *The Art of the Soluble.* Penguin Books, Harmondsworth, Middlesex.

Medawar, P.B. (1969). Induction and intuition in scientific thought. *Mem. Am. Philos. Soc.* 75.

Middleton, A. (1934). Periodic fluctuations in British game populations. *J. Anim. Ecol.* **3**, 231–249.

Miller, G.R. and Watson, A. (1978). Territories and the food plant of individual red grouse. I. Territory size, number of mates and brood size compared with the abundance, production and diversity of heather. *J. Anim. Ecol.* **47**, 293–305.

Miller, H.G. and Cooper, J.M. (1976). Tree growth and climatic cycles in the rain shadow of the Grampian mountains. *Nature* **260**, 697–698.

Moran, P.A.P. (1953). Statistical analysis of the Canadian lynx cycle. II. Synchronization and meteorology. *Aust. J. Zool.* **1**, 291–298.

Moss, R. (1968). Food selection and nutrition in ptarmigan (*Lagopus mutus*). *Symp. Zool. Soc. Lond.* **21**, 207–216.

Moss, R. (1997). Grouse and ptarmigan nutrition in the wild and in captivity. *Proc. Nutr. Soc.* **5**, 1137–1145.

Moss, R. and Hanssen, I. (1980). Grouse nutrition. *Nutr. Abstr. Rev. Ser. B.* **50**, 555–567.

Moss, R. and Oswald, J. (1985). Population dynamics of Capercaillie in a Northeast Scottish glen. *Ornis Scand.* **16**, 229–238.

Moss, R. and Watson, A. (1984) Maternal nutrition, egg quality and breeding success of Scottish ptarmigan *Lagopus mutus*. *Ibis* **126**, 212–220.

Moss, R. and Watson, A. (1985). Adaptive value of spacing behaviour in population cycles of red grouse and other animals. In: *Behavioural Ecology* (Ed. by R.M. Sibly and R.H. Smith), pp. 275–294. Blackwell Scientific Publications, Oxford.

Moss, R. and Watson, A. (1990). Breeding success and movement as determinants of breeding density in tetraonid birds. *Trans. Int. Un. Game Biol.* **19**, 85–92.

Moss, R. and Watson, A. (1991). Population cycles and kin selection in red grouse *Lagopus lagopus scoticus*. *Ibis* **133** (suppl. 1), 113–120.

Moss, R., Watson, A. and Parr, R. (1975). Maternal nutrition and breeding success in red grouse *(Lagopus lagopus scoticus)*. *J. Anim. Ecol.* **44**, 233–244.

Moss, R., Watson, A. and Rothery, P. (1984). Inherent changes in the body size, viability and behaviour of a fluctuating red grouse (*Lagopus lagopus scoticus*) population. *J. Anim. Ecol.* **53**, 171–189.

Moss, R., Rothery, P. and Trenholm, I.B. (1985). The inheritance of social dominance rank in red grouse (*Lagopus lagopus scoticus*). *Aggress. Behav.* **11**, 253–259.

Moss, R., Watson, A. and Parr, R. (1988). Mate choice by hen red grouse *Lagopus lagopus* with an excess of cocks – role of territory size and food quality. *Ibis* **130**, 545–552.

Moss, R., Trenholm, I.B., Watson, A. and Parr, R. (1990). Plant growth and nitrogen metabolism of red grouse *Lagopus lagopus scoticus* in spring. *Ornis Scand.* **21**, 115–121.

Moss, R., Watson, A., Trenholm, I. and Parr, R. (1993). Caecal threadworms *Trichostrongylus tenuis* in red grouse *Lagopus lagopus scoticus*: effects of weather and host density upon estimated worm burdens. *Parasitology* **107**, 199–209.

Moss, R., Parr, R.A. and Lambin, X. (1994). Effects of testosterone on breeding density, breeding success and survival of red grouse. *Proc. Roy. Soc. Lond. B.* **255**, 91–97.

Moss, R., Watson, A. and Parr, R. (1996). Experimental prevention of a population cycle in red grouse. *Ecology* **77**, 1512–1530.

Moss, R., Elston, D.A. and Watson. A. (2000). Spatial asynchrony and demographic travelling waves during red grouse population cycles. *Ecology* **81**, 981–989.

Mossop, D.H. (1988). Winter survival and breeding strategies of willow ptarmigan. In: *Adaptive Strategies and Population Ecology of Northern Grouse* (Ed. by A.T. Bergerud and M.W. Gratson), pp. 330–378. University of Minnesota Press, Minneapolis.

Mountford, M.D., Watson, A., Moss, R., Parr, R. and Rothery, P. (1990). Land inheritance and population cycles of red grouse. In: *Red Grouse Population Processes* (Ed. by A.N. Lance and J.H. Lawton), pp. 78–83. Royal Society for the Protection of Birds, Sandy, Bedfordshire.

Murdoch, W.W. (1994). Population regulation in theory and practice. *Ecology* **75**, 271–287.

Murray, J.D. (1993). *Mathematical Biology*. 2nd, corrected edn. Springer, New York.

Myrberget, S. (1984a). Population cycles of Willow Grouse *Lagopus lagopus* on an island in North Norway. *Faun. Norv. Ser. C.* **7**, 46–56.

Myrberget, S. (1984b). Population dynamics of Willow Grouse *Lagopus lagopus* on an island in North Norway. *Faun. Norv. Ser. C.* **7**, 95–105.

Myrberget, S. (1985). Egg predation in an island population of Willow Grouse *Lagopus lagopus*. *Faun. Norv. Ser. C.* **8**, 82–87.

Myrberget, S. (1986). Annual variation in clutch sizes of a population of Willow Grouse *Lagopus lagopus*. *Faun. Norv. Ser. C.* **9**, 74–81.

Myrberget, S. (1988). Demography of an island population of willow ptarmigan in northern Norway. In: *Adaptive Strategies and Population Ecology of Northern Grouse* (Ed. by A.T. Bergerud and M.W. Gratson), pp. 379–422. University of Minnesota Press, Minneapolis.

Myrberget, S. (1989). Norwegian research on willow grouse: implications for management. *Finn. Game Res.* **46**, 17–25.

Myrberget, S., Erikstad, K.E. and Spidsø, T.K. (1977). Variations from year to year in growth rates of Willow Grouse chicks. *Astarte* **10**, 9–14.

Newton, I. (1989). *Lifetime Reproduction in Birds*. Academic Press, London.

Nielsen, Ó.K. and Cade, T.J. (1990). Seasonal changes in food habits of gyrfalcons in NE Iceland. *Ornis Scand.* **21**, 202–211.

Nielsen, Ó.K. and Pétursson, G. (1995). Population fluctuations of gyrfalcon and rock ptarmigan: analysis of export figures from Iceland. *Wildl. Biol.* **1**, 65–71.

Nisbet, R.M. and Gurney, W.S.C. (1982). *Modelling Fluctuating Populations*. John Wiley & Sons, Chichester.

O.E.D. (1971). *The Oxford English Dictionary*, compact edn. Oxford University Press, Oxford.

Oksanen, L. and Lundberg, P. (1995). Optimization of reproductive effort and foraging time in mammals: the influence of resource level and predation risk. *Evolut. Ecol.* **9**, 45–56.

Page, R.E. and Bergerud, A.T. (1988). A genetic explanation for ten-year cycles of grouse. In: *Adaptive Strategies and Population Ecology of Northern Grouse* (Ed. by A.T. Bergerud and M.W. Gratson), pp. 423–438. University of Minnesota Press, Minneapolis.

Piertney, S.B., MacColl, A.D.C., Lambin, X., Moss, R. and Dallas, J.F. (1999). Spatial distribution of genetic relatedness in a moorland population of red grouse (*Lagopus lagopus scoticus*). *Biol. J. Linnean Soc.* **68**, 317–331.

Pollard, E., Lakhani, K.H. and Rothery, P. (1987). The detection of density-dependence from a series of annual censuses. *Ecology* **68**, 2046-2055.

Popper, K.R. (1959). *The Logic of Scientific Discovery*. Hutchinson, London.

Popper, K.R. (1963). *Conjectures and Refutations; the Growth of Scientific Knowledge*. Routledge and Kegan Paul, London.

Popper, K.R. (1981). *Objective Knowledge*. Revised edn. Oxford University Press, Oxford.

Potapov, R.L. and Flint, V.E. (1987). *Ptitsi SSSR. Kuroobrazniye, Zhuravleobrazniye*. Nauka, Leningrad.

Potts, G.R., Tapper, S.C. and Hudson, P.J. (1984). Population fluctuations of red grouse: analysis of bag records and a simulation model. *J. Anim. Ecol.* **53**, 31–36.

Ranta, E., Lindström, J. and Lindén, H. (1995a). Synchrony in tetraonid population dynamics. *J. Anim. Ecol.* **64**, 767–776.

Ranta, E., Kaitala, V., Lindström, J. and Lindén, H. (1995b). Synchrony in population dynamics. *Proc. Roy. Soc. Lond. B.* **262**, 113–118.

Romanov, A.N. (1979). *Obiknovenniy Gluchar*. Nauka, Moskva.

Rothery, P., Moss, R. and Watson, A. (1984). General properties of predictive population models in red grouse (*Lagopus lagopus scoticus*). *Oecologia* **62**, 382–386.

Royama, T. (1981). Fundamental concepts and methodology for the analysis of animal population dynamics, with particular reference to univoltine species. *Ecol. Monog.* **54**, 429–462.

Royama, T. (1992). *Analytical Population Dynamics*. Chapman & Hall, London.

Salomonsen, F. (1939). Moults and sequence of plumages in the rock ptarmigan (*Lagopus mutus* [Montin]). *Vidensk. Meddr Dansk naturh. Foren.* **103**, 1–491.

Saucy, F. (1994). Density dependence in time series of the fossorial form of the water vole, *Arvicola terrestris*. *Oikos* **71**, 381–392.

Savory, J. (1989). The importance of invertebrate food to chicks of gallinaceous species. *Proc. Nutr. Soc.* **48**, 113–133.

Schaffer, W.M. and Tamarin, R.H. (1973). Changing reproductive rates and population cycles in lemmings and voles. *Evolution* **27**, 111–124.

Schieck, J.O. and Hannon, S.J. (1989). Breeding site fidelity in willow ptarmigan: the influence of previous reproductive success and familiarity with partner and territory. *Oecologia* **81**, 465–472.

Schroeder, M.A. (1985). Behavioral differences of female grouse undertaking short and long migrations. *Condor* **87**, 281–286.

Selås, V. (1997). Cyclic population fluctuations of herbivores as an effect of cyclic seed cropping of plants: the mast depression hypothesis. *Oikos* **80**, 257–268.

Semenov-Tian-Shansky, O.I. (1959). *Ecologia Teterevinich Ptits. Trudi Laplandskovo Gosudarstvennovo Zapovednika* V. Glavnoe Upravleniye Ochotnichevo i Zapovednikov pri Sovyete Ministrov RCFR, Moskva.

Seton, E.T. (1929). *Lives of Game Animals*. Doubleday, Doran & Co., New York.

Shaw, J.L. (1988a). Arrested development of *Trichostrongylus tenuis* as third stage larvae in red grouse. *Res. Vet. Sci.* **45**, 256–258.

Shaw, J.L. (1988b). *Epidemiology of the caecal threadworm* Trichostrongylus tenuis *in red grouse* (Lagopus lagopus scoticus). Ph.D. thesis, University of Aberdeen.

Shaw, J.L., Moss, R. and Pike, A.W. (1989). Development and survival of the free-living stages of *Trichostrongylus tenuis*, a caecal parasite of red grouse *Lagopus lagopus scoticus*. *Parasitology* **99**, 105–113.

Siivonen, L. (1948). Decline in numerous mammal and bird populations in North-Western Europe during the 1940s. *Pap. Game Res.* No. 2.

Siivonen, L. (1952). On the reflection of short-term fluctuations in numbers in the reproduction of tetraonids. *Pap. Game Res.* No. 9.

Sinclair, A.R.E. and Gosline, J.M. (1997). Solar activity and mammal cycles in the northern hemisphere. *Am. Nat.* **149**, 776–784.

Sinclair, A.R.E., Gosline, J.M., Holdsworth, G., Krebs, C.J., Boutin, S., Smith, J.N.M., Boonstra., R and Dale, M. (1993). Can the solar climate synchronize the snowshoe hare cycle in Canada? Evidence from tree rings and ice cores. *Am. Nat.* **141**, 173–198.

Small, R.J. and Rusch, D.H. (1989). The natal dispersal of ruffed grouse. *Auk* **106**, 72–79.

Small, R.J., Marcström, V. and Willebrand, T. (1993). Synchronous and nonsynchronous fluctuations of some predators and their prey in central Sweden. *Ecography* **16**, 360–364.

Smith, C.H. (1983). Spatial trends in Canadian Snowshoe Hare, *Lepus americanus*, population cycles. *Can. Field-nat.* **97**, 151–160.

Sonin, M.D. and Barus, V. (1981). A survey of nematodes and acanthocephalans parasitizing the genus *Lagopus* (Galliformes) in the Palearctic region. *Helminthologia* **18**, 145–157.

Steen, H. and Erikstad, K.E. (1996). Sensitivity of willow grouse *Lagopus lagopus* population dynamics to variations in demographic parameters. *Wildl. Biol.* **2**, 27–35.

Turchin, P. (1993). Chaos and stability in rodent population dynamics: evidence from non-linear time-series analysis. *Oikos* **68**, 167–172.

Turchin, P. and Hanski, I. (1997). An empirically based model for latitudinal gradient in vole population dynamics. *Am. Nat.* **149**, 842–874.

Turchin, P. and Taylor, A.D. (1992). Complex dynamics in ecological time series. *Ecology* **73**, 289–305.

Watson, A. (1965). A population study of ptarmigan (*Lagopus mutus*) in Scotland. *J. Anim. Ecol.* **34**, 135–172.

Watson, A. (1985). Social class, socially-induced loss, recruitment and breeding of red grouse. *Oecologia*, **67**, 493–498.

Watson, A. and Hewson, R. (1973). Population densities of mountain hares (*Lepus timidus*) on western Scottish and Irish moors and on Scottish hills. *J. Zool.* **170**, 151–159.

Watson, A. and Jenkins, D. (1968). Experiments on population control by territorial behaviour in red grouse. *J. Anim. Ecol.* **37**, 595–614.

Watson, A. and Moss, R. (1979). Population cycles in the Tetraonidae. *Ornis Fenn.* **56**, 87–109.

Watson, A. and O'Hare, P.J. (1979). Red grouse populations on experimentally treated and untreated Irish bog. *J. Appl. Ecol.* **16**, 433–452.

Watson, A. and Shaw, J.L. (1991). Parasites and Scottish ptarmigan numbers. *Oecologia* **88**, 359–361.

Watson, A., Hewson, R., Jenkins, D. and Parr, R. (1973). Population densities of mountain hares compared with red grouse on Scottish moors. *Oikos* **24**, 225–230.

Watson, A., Moss, R., Phillips, J. and Parr, R. (1977). The effect of fertilizers on red grouse stocks on Scottish moors grazed by sheep, cattle and deer. In: *Écologie du petit gibier et aménagement des chasses* (Ed by P. Pesson), pp. 193–212. Gauthier-Villars, Paris.

Watson, A., Moss R., Rothery, P. and Parr, R. (1984a). Demographic causes and predictive models of population fluctuations in red grouse. *J. Anim. Ecol.* **53**, 639–662.

Watson, A., Moss, R. and Parr, R. (1984b). Effects of food enrichment on numbers and spacing behaviour of red grouse. *J. Anim. Ecol.* **53**, 663–678.

Watson, A., Moss, R., Parr, R., Mountford, M.D. and Rothery, P. (1994). Kin landownership, differential aggression between kin and non-kin, and population fluctuations in red grouse. *J. Anim. Ecol.* **63**, 39–50.

Watson, A., Moss, R. and Rae, S. (1998). Population dynamics of Scottish Rock Ptarmigan cycles. *Ecology* **79**, 1174–1192.

Watson, A., Moss, R. and Rothery, P. (2000). Weather and synchrony in 10-year population cycles of rock ptarmigan and red grouse in Scotland. *Ecology* **81**, 2126–2136.

Weeden, R.B. and Theberge, J.B. (1972). The dynamics of a fluctuating population of Rock Ptarmigan in Alaska. *Proc. Int. Orn. Congr.* **15**, 90–106.

Williams, J. (1985). Statistical analysis of fluctuations in red grouse bag data. *Oecologia* **65**, 269–272.

Wilson, E. and Leslie, A.S. (1911). Grouse disease. In: *The Grouse in Health and in Disease* (Ed. by Lord Lovat), pp. 185–206. Smith, Elder and Co., London.

Wilson, E.O. (1975). *Sociobiology – the New Synthesis.* Harvard University Press, Cambridge, MA.

Wilson, G.R. (1983). The prevalence of caecal threadworms (*Trichostrongylus tenuis*) in red grouse. *Oecologia* **58**, 265–268.

Wissler, K. and Halvorsen, O. (1977). Helminths from willow grouse (*Lagopus lagopus*) in two locations in north Norway. *J. Wildl. Dis.* **13**, 409–413.

Wolff, J.O. (1980). The role of habitat patchiness in the population dynamics of snowshoe hares. *Ecol. Monog.* **50**, 111–130.

Zwickel, F.C. (1980). Surplus yearlings and the regulation of breeding density in blue grouse. *Can. J. Zool.* **58**, 896–905.

Zwickel, F.C., Bendell, J.F. and Ash, A.N. (1983). Population regulation in blue grouse. In: *Natural Regulation of Wildlife Populations* (Ed. by F.L. Bunnell, D.S. Eastman and J.M. Peek), pp. 212–225. University of Idaho, Moscow.

APPENDIX

Density-dependent Terminology

A factor, such as a *per capita* vital rate, is said to be density dependent if its size or strength varies disproportionately with population density. If this variation is linear, we have linear density dependence. 'Non-linear' density dependence means the relationship is non-linear. 'Stepwise' is an extreme form of non-linear density dependence with a step function at an upper or a lower density threshold. 'Delayed' density dependence occurs when the strength of the factor is related to density at some time previously, by a specified 'time difference' or 'lag'. 'Direct' density dependence implies no time lag, and the unqualified term density dependence usually implies direct linear density dependence.

Many simple population models involve reproductive rates decreasing and mortality rates increasing with density. In this case it follows that direct linear density dependence usually involves negative feedback that has a stabilizing effect on model populations. Delayed linear density dependence is often destabilizing and can generate model cycles.

A time series of population counts or indices, typically reported at yearly intervals for tetraonids, is a 'population trajectory'. The annual rate of population change between year $t - 1$ and year t is directly density dependent if it is related to the size or density of the population in year $t - 1$. In this case the time lag is zero and the density dependence is called 'first-order'. 'Second-order' density dependence occurs when the rate of population change is related to population size in year $t - 2$, and so on.

Ecophysiology of Trees of Seasonally Dry Tropics: Comparisons among Phenologies

DEREK EAMUS AND LYNDA PRIOR

I. INTRODUCTION

The subject matter of this review is the seasonally dry tropical and sub-tropical woodlands and forests of the world. We follow Specht (1981) in differentiating woodland (typically <30% canopy cover) from forest (typically >30% cover) on the basis of percentage canopy cover but clearly discrete boundaries do not exist. The definition of a dry season is more problematic. However, we propose that a dry season has two attributes. First, it is a predictable annual event, and second, in the driest 3 months of

ADVANCES IN ECOLOGICAL RESEARCH VOL. 32
ISBN 0-12-013932-4

the year, less than 10% of annual precipitation occurs and typically less than 25 mm per month falls. In few sites does absolutely no rainfall occur in the dry season, if a sufficiently long (a century or more) time average is taken.

Seasonally dry tropical areas are occupied largely by savanna, but also include areas of dry forest in which grasses are mostly absent. Savannas are here defined as:

> tropical or sub-tropical biomes with a tall (>30 cm) continuous grass understorey during the wet season and a discontinuous tree canopy. Grasses are usually dominated by those with the C4 photosynthetic pathway. Rainfall is highly seasonal, with the wettest period occurring during the warmest months.

Dry tropical forests and savanna vegetation types occupy far greater total areas worldwide than does wet tropical rainforest (Olivares and Medina, 1992; Murphy and Lugo, 1995). These seasonally dry tropical areas are distinguished from wet tropical areas by a marked dry period that occurs each year. This means that closed forest canopies do not develop, except in small areas where topographic factors lead to permanently high soil moisture content, and which are thus not truly dry. Conversely, shallow and freely draining soils can also support savannas in the middle of areas otherwise covered in rainforest. This clearly illustrates the importance of soil water availability over the year, rather than rainfall alone, as a determinant of vegetation structure in seasonally dry systems. Seasonally dry tropical areas do, however, have a reliable and pronounced wet season, which distinguishes them from deserts.

Rather than become embroiled in semantic discussion as to the definition of savannas, we must accept that savannas represent a region along a continuum extending from desert at one extreme to tall closed rainforest at the other, with subtle shifts and mergers occurring at boundaries. Vegetation units occur as segments of continua, not as distinct separate units (Murphy and Lugo, 1995).

The co-existence of trees and grasses constitutes perhaps the most striking feature of savannas; this has been reviewed by Scholes and Archer (1997). These authors conclude that traditional simple models based on separation in rooting depth of trees and grasses are inadequate, and that the effects of browsers, grazers and fires on tree recruitment must be considered. In many parts of the world, savanna reverts to woodland in the absence of fire or other disturbance. Thus the distinction between savanna and dry tropical forest or woodland is somewhat arbitrary. In both biomes, trees must contend with seasonal drought and high temperatures, to which conditions they can be expected to share similar physiological responses.

Structurally, seasonally dry woodlands contain a seasonal grass understorey. Typically three layers of vegetation (grass, understorey herbs and forbs, overstorey dispersed tree layer) occur. Epiphytes and vines are absent. In seasonally dry forests, the grass layer and epiphytes are absent, but vines can be present. The upper canopy can vary between <3 m height for shrublands, to <10 m for low woodlands, to >30 m for tall forests.

Savannas are important for several reasons, including their conservation (genetic) and cultural values, their economic value (tourism, pastoral/beef industry, agriculture) and their aesthetic value, among others. They support an increasing number of people globally. They are also major determinants of regional climate and have a significant role to play in regional water balances and global carbon cycles. Any attempt at sustainable resource management within savannas and any attempt at modelling savanna functioning at the landscape scale requires knowledge about the behaviour of savanna trees, particularly in relation to water and carbon fluxes. The aim of this chapter is to provide a review of what is known about the ecophysiology of trees in seasonally dry woody ecosystems. In particular, we shall compare and contrast daily and seasonal patterns of behaviour of different phenological guilds; this approach provides a unifying conceptual framework within which to consider tree ecophysiology. Savannas form an extensive but not exclusive reference ecosystem throughout this chapter. Where relevant and possible, comparative values for temperate or wet tropical ecosystems are presented. We focus on water and carbon dioxide (CO_2) fluxes and related ecophysiology for the following reasons: first, seasonally dry forests are subject to regular and predictable annual drought, which is a major determinant of ecosystem structure and function. Temperature and light are generally not limiting to the functioning of these systems. Second, carbon influx and attendant processes are coupled to water availability and drive all downstream processes.

A. Distribution and Climate of Seasonally Dry Tropics

Native savannas occupy large areas of Africa and Australia, as well as parts of Central and South America. Savannas that have arisen because of human activity can be found in India and other parts of Asia. Savannas often have regional names, including the 'miombo' woodland of Angola and Zambia, the 'cerrado' and 'caatinga' of Brazil and the 'llanos' of Venezuela and Colombia. Bushveld and thornveld of southern Africa are also seasonally dry woodlands. Dry woodlands of the 'chaco' occur in the west of Central America and in the Amazon lowlands. Seasonally dry forests include dipterocarp forest in Thailand, and dry deciduous forests in Mexico and Venezuela.

In most savannas, mean annual temperatures are higher than 20°C, although at higher elevations in Brazil and East Africa mean annual temperatures can be lower than this. The mean temperature of the coldest month is generally higher than 12°C, although occasional values of 4°C have been recorded in eastern Australia (Archibald, 1995). Savannas that are close to the equator and/or close to the coast have small fluctuations in mean temperature between wet and dry seasons, but savannas at the margins of the tropics or at higher elevations experience larger temperature fluctuations and frosts may occur occasionally. Mean temperatures are higher than 20°C for each month in most savannas.

Rainfall is highly seasonal, with distinct wet and dry seasons. Rainfall can be bi-modal (Central and Southern Africa) or uni-modal (Central America, India, Australia) and usually lies in the range 250–2000 mm yr^{-1}. In Africa and Australia, less than 25 mm total rain falls during the dry season, while in Guianan savannas, rainfall in the 'dry season' can exceed 200 mm (Archibald, 1995). Savannas are distinguished from temperate seasonal climates by the reversal of the association between rainfall and temperature.

Soil and atmospheric water content are coupled to seasonality of rainfall. In the wet season water can be supra-abundant and flooding may occur. This contrasts with very dry surface soils (upper 0.5 m) during the dry season. Soil water potential in the upper soil profile can decline from zero (wet season) to −3.5 MPa or lower (Goldstein et al., 1986; Holbrook et al., 1995; Franco et al., 1996) (see section III). In a west African humid savanna gravimetric soil water content varied between 0.18 g g^{-1} at 2 m depth and 0.10 g g^{-1} in the top 10 cm in the wet season and between 0.12 g g^{-1} at 1.6 m and 0.01 g g^{-1} in the top 10 cm in the dry season (Le Roux et al., 1995). There may also be large seasonal fluctuations in depth to groundwater. In northern Australia, depth to groundwater increases over the dry season by up to 12 m in north Australia (Cook et al., 1998). Vapour pressure deficit (VPD) here ranges between 0.4–0.8 kPa in the wet season and 0.5–2.5 kPa in the dry season (Duff et al., 1997), similar to values recorded in a west African humid savanna (Le Roux and Bariac, 1998). VPD peaks between midday and mid-afternoon, declining thereafter.

Because solar radiation loads are high all year, potential evaporation rates are approximately 7 mm day^{-1} in north Australia, and 1600 mm yr^{-1} for miombo of equatorial Africa (Menaut et al., 1995). Similarly, in the caatinga of Brazil, potential evaporation is generally above 2000 mm yr^{-1} (Sampaio, 1995, calculated evaporation to be 1.6–5.3 mm day^{-1} for Brazilian caatinga).

Generally, in savannas, the ratio of annual potential evapotranspiration to annual rainfall is between 1.2 and 1.8 (Murphy and Lugo, 1995;

Sampaio, 1995), but this is highly seasonal. In the wet season, rainfall can exceed potential evapotranspiration, but in the dry season the reverse is true.

II. PHENOLOGY

A. Phenological Guilds

Woody species of savannas may be evergreen, deciduous or semi-deciduous. There is considerable variation, at ecosystem-level, in the relative proportions of these guilds. African and Indian savannas are dominated by deciduous species (Menaut and Cesar, 1979; Shukla and Ramakrishnan, 1982; Chidumayo, 1990; Yadava, 1990). In contrast, the llanos savannas of South America are dominated by evergreen species (Monasterio and Sarmiento, 1976; Sarmiento et al., 1985), although individual patches may be dominated by semi-deciduous or deciduous species (Medina, 1982). Similarly, seasonally dry forests of Costa Rica are dominated by semi-deciduous or deciduous species (Borchert, 1994a). Venezuelan tropical dry forests are dominated by deciduous species, with a few evergreen species also present (Sobrado, 1997).

Australian savannas differ from other savannas in having an approximately equal number of species (but not standing biomass; evergreens dominate in terms of biomass) in each of four phenological guilds (Williams et al., 1997b; Figure 1). Deciduous species lose all of their leaves every year for 1–3 months in north Australian savannas, or longer where the dry season is particularly long (Williams et al., 1997b). Evergreens retain all, or almost all, of their canopy, throughout the year. Semi-deciduous species lose more than 50% of their canopy each year, while brevi-deciduous species lose between 10 and 50% of their canopy each year, but this is very dependent on the length and magnitude of the wet season (Williams et al., 1997b). Although 50% of species are deciduous or semi-deciduous in Australian savannas, the evergreen species account for approximately 90% of the projected canopy cover. Consequently during the dry season total tree canopy cover declines by only approximately 15%.

Within Australia deciduous species have mainly pantropical affinities (Bowman et al., 1988) and are generally broad-leaved. Curiously, the abundance of deciduous species declines along a gradient of declining rainfall from coastal north Australia to inland central Australia (Egan and Williams, 1995; Williams et al., 1996). This is in contrast to tropical forests and savannas on other continents, where the proportion of deciduous species increases as dry season severity increases (Reich, 1995). This is presumably a function of the extremely high degree of

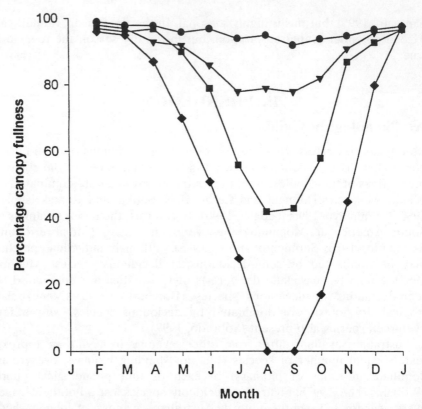

Fig. 1. Four phenological guilds are recognized in Australian savannas (Williams *et al.*, 1997). Evergreen species (●) retain an almost full canopy all year; brevideciduous species (▼) never lose more than 50% of their canopy, the amount lost depending on the duration of the wet season; semi-deciduous species (■) lose more than 50% of their leaves every year; deciduous species (◆) are leafless for at least 2 months every year. Re-drawn from Williams *et al.* (1997).

dominance by Acacias and Eucalypts (which are sclerophyllous and predominantly evergreen; Ashton and Attiwell, 1994; Gill, 1994) throughout Australia, including its savanna areas.

B. Environmental Control of Leaf Flushing

Leaf fall in tropical forests and savannas usually peaks in the dry season (Wright and Cornejo, 1990; van Schaik *et al.*, 1993; Sun *et al.*, 1996). By contrast, there is considerable inter-annual, inter-site and inter-specific variation in the timing of leaf flushing. In Costa Rican dry forest, rehydration of stems always preceded leaf flushing or flowering (Borchert, 1994a).

Many trees rehydrated soon after leaf shedding, which allowed leaf flushing to occur during the dry season. Deciduous lightwood and softwood trees generally fell into this category, while deciduous hardwood trees, which desiccated strongly, remained bare to the end of the dry season. Evergreen trees exchanged most leaves during the dry season (Borchert, 1994c). Medina and Francisco (1994) observed that, in a Venezuelan savanna, leaf exchange in *Curatella americana* (evergreen) occurs in the middle of the dry season, but in *Godmania macrocarpa* (deciduous) leaf flushing occurs at the start of the wet season.

The cause of such variation in timing and intensity of leaf phenophases has been much debated (Reich, 1995; Wright, 1996). Day length (Opler *et al.*, 1976; Bullock and Solis-Magallanes, 1990), temperature (Specht, 1986), vapour pressure deficit (Wright and Cornejo, 1990; Duff *et al.*, 1997) and irradiance (Wright and van Schaik, 1994; Wright, 1996) have all been identified as environmental cues controlling leaf fall and leaf flush. However, Reich and Borchert (1982, 1984), Borchert (1991, 1994a,b) and Reich (1995) strongly argue for endogenous whole-plant control that is subject to environmental perturbation.

Wright and Cornejo (1990) showed little impact on leaf fall of a 2-year irrigation experiment in the field – only four of 29 species showed delayed leaf fall after irrigating in the dry season to extend the wet season. In contrast, in a Costa Rican study, Borchert (1994b) observed that leaf flushing was initiated in *Tabebuia ochracea* within 1 week of irrigation. In the savannas of northern Australia, a dry season irrigation experiment (Myers *et al.*, 1998) showed that leaf flushing of a common deciduous species (*Terminalia ferdinandiana*) occurred significantly earlier (by 4 weeks) in response to increased soil water availability. Flushing was initiated within 10 days of irrigation starting. Furthermore, the decline in canopy cover associated with the onset of the subsequent dry season was delayed by 2 weeks in the irrigated plots. For a second species (*Planchonia careya*), Myers *et al.* (1998) found that the attainment of full canopy was significantly earlier in the irrigated plots, but high inter-tree variation masked any differences in timing of leaf flushing or initial canopy decline. In contrast to these results, there was little impact of irrigation on canopy cover or timing of leaf flushing in evergreen species, although leaf lifespan was increased (Myers *et al.*, 1998). This supports the view that evergreens, postulated as having deeper roots and therefore having access to deeper reserves of water in the dry season, are able to maintain an almost completely full canopy in the dry and avoid drought (Sobrado, 1986; Nepstad *et al.*, 1994; Myers *et al.*, 1997). However, the inverse argument – that deciduous trees are facultatively deciduous and lose leaves in response to soil drying – appears to be poorly supported. Both species studied shed leaves at the start of the dry season despite irrigation maintaining a high soil water availability, and one species – *Planchonia* – showed little response in terms of leaf flushing to dry season irrigation. Therefore, within the same phenological grouping, leaf fall and leaf flush appear to be under the control of different mechanisms.

Leaf fall in deciduous species occurs early in the dry season because of a depletion of water stored in the tree (Reich and Borchert, 1984; Borchert, 1994a; Reich, 1995). When the canopy is reduced or absent for a sufficient time, stems rehydrate and leaf flush can be initiated. This can explain why leaf flush is frequently initiated prior to rains (but generally after VPD starts to decline; Duff *et al.*, 1997). The patterns of change in stem diameter in the Myers *et al.* (1998) study are consistent with this hypothesis.

The interaction between wood density and groundwater availability may also have a role to play in determining phenology and species distribution (Borchert, 1994c). As stemwood density increases, water content, and hence potential for water storage, declines linearly (Borchert, 1994c). In Costa Rica, deciduous hardwoods on sites with little access to groundwater have low stemwood water contents and little potential for storage. Leaf drop occurs early in the dry season and there is minimal stem rehydration during the dry season after leaf drop. Consequently, leaf flush does not occur until after the onset of significant rains and rehydration. In contrast, deciduous lightwoods and deciduous softwoods have a high storage capacity. In both cases, leaf initiation occurs in the dry season after stems rehydrate. However, full stem expansion and leaf growth often only occur after heavy rains (Borchert, 1994c). Thus it is the elimination of water deficits within the tree that initiates leaf flush, and not an environmental cue such as day length or temperature.

III. TREE WATER RELATIONS

A. Foliar Water Potential

Water availability is a key factor in determining savanna structure and function (Scholes and Walker, 1995). As water availability increases, tree height and tree density increase so that standing biomass increases. Trees, being perennial, must survive the 2- to 8-month dry season and must either avoid (deciduous) or tolerate (evergreen) this drought. Given the extent and diversity of savannas/dry tropical forests worldwide, there have been relatively few detailed studies of seasonal patterns of tree water status in these biomes (Le Roux and Bariac, 1998).

Pre-dawn leaf water potential (Ψ_{pd}) has been used extensively as a surrogate measure of soil water availability (Sala *et al.*, 1981; Le Roux and Bariac, 1998). This use is based upon the assumptions that (a) rehydration of leaves occurs rapidly enough for leaf water potential pre-sunrise to equal that of the soil–root interface; and (b) there is some relationship between the proportion of roots at various depths (and hence soil water contents) and the final equilibrium water potential attained by the leaf; and (c) that lateral heterogeneity of soil water content does not prevent the use of bulk soil moisture content as a suitable explanatory variable for plant water status (Ameglio and Archer, 1996).

Pre-dawn leaf water potential is high in the wet season and declines as the dry season progresses. This decline is both a function of declining soil moisture content and declining atmospheric water content (increasing leaf-to-air vapour pressure deficit). In a study of eight species of a north Australian savanna, Ψ_{pd} of mature (10–15 m tall) trees varied between −0.02 MPa in the wet season and −1.5 MPa in the dry season (Duff *et al.*, 1997). For smaller trees, the decline in Ψ_{pd} was larger such that dry season minima were as low as −2.5 MPa (Prior *et al.*, 1997a). Interestingly, in a detailed study of *Eucalyptus tetrodonra* (one of the two canopy domi-nants that account for >80% of standing biomass in these savannas), the impact of the dry season upon tree water status decreased as tree height increased (Prior and Eamus, 1999). Thus, as soil and atmospheric water content declined from the wet to the dry season, Ψ_{pd} declined and the slope of the relationship between tree height and Ψ_{pd} increased (Figure 2). Such a response demonstrates the importance of rooting volume in maintaining favourable plant water status as water content of surface soil decreases.

The decline in Ψ_{pd} through the dry season is also reflected in the decline in midday leaf water potential. As soil water potential declined from close to zero in the wet season to −2.0 MPa in the top 30 cm of soil in the Brazilian cerrado, leaf water potentials declined to −2.5 MPa (Franco, 1998). Similarly midday leaf water potentials declined to −3.0 MPa in smaller trees and −2.5 MPa in tall trees (Myers *et al.*, 1997; Prior *et al.*, 1997a,b;) in a northern Australian savanna. In an upland savanna in Costa Rica, Borchert (1994a,b) observed leaf water potentials as low as −4.0 MPa.

Similar patterns of seasonal leaf water potential have been observed in savannas around the world. Medina and Francisco (1994) showed that, in a Venezuelan savanna, the highest leaf water potential (close to zero; collected at sunrise) declined from −0.1 MPa in the wet season to −0.8 MPa in the dry season in young *Curatella americana* leaves and from −0.3 MPa to −1.2 MPa in *Godmania macrocarpa* leaves. Similarly, midday values declined from −0.5 to 1.2 MPa and from −1.4 to −2.5 MPa for the two species, respectively. Goldstein *et al.* (1986) showed seasonal declines in leaf water potential for four tree species growing in a South American savanna of approximately 1.0 MPa. Seasonal minimum leaf

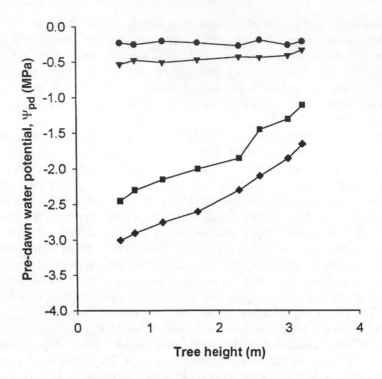

Fig. 2. Tree height influences the extent of the dry-season decline in water status of *Eucalyptus tetrodonta*. Short (young) trees suffer the most. Measurement made in: ●, May (early dry season); ▼, June; ■, August; ◆, October (late dry season). Re-drawn from Prior and Eamus (1999).

water potentials in 38 Costa Rican dry forests ranged from −0.8 MPa to less than −4.0 MPa (Borchert, 1994b).

The oft-stated view that soil water potentials of less than (more negative than) −1.5 MPa represent the 'wilting point' of plants, i.e. represent the limit of plant available water, is clearly untenable within the savanna environment. Even pre-dawn leaf water potential can be as low as this and leaves still have open stomata and photosynthesize as leaf water potential declines through the day (see below).

Seasonal declines in leaf water potential are the result of declines in both soil and atmospheric water content resulting from marked seasonality of rainfall and vapour pressure deficit. However, the documentation of such declines gives no conceptual framework within which to interpret between-species variation. The next section attempts to interpret such differences in the context of contrasting phenologies.

1. Phenological Comparisons of Seasonal Changes in Water Potential

In Venezuelan dry tropical forest, Ψ_{pd} values declined at the end of the wet season in both evergreen and deciduous species (Sobrado, 1986). The decline was more rapid in the deciduous species, which shed their leaves in the mid dry season. The evergreen species attained the same Ψ_{pd} (−2.8 MPa) about 2 months later (Sobrado, 1986). Evergreen trees in the wetter Venezuelan llanos showed only slight seasonality in pre-dawn and midday leaf water potentials (Sarmiento et al., 1985; Goldstein and Sarmiento, 1987).

The lowest Ψ_{pd} recorded for saplings of the deciduous Australian savanna tree, *Terminalia ferdinandiana*, was −1.18 MPa, at the start of leaf shedding in the early dry season (Prior et al., 1997b). At the same time, Ψ_{pd} of co-occurring evergreen *Eucalyptus tetrodonta* saplings was −0.48 MPa, and this continued to decrease to a minimum of −2.45 MPa late in the dry season (Prior et al., 1997a). Thus the evergreen species was both better able to extract water from drying soil (possibly by having deeper roots) and to retain functional leaves at lower Ψ_{pd} than was the deciduous species. In mature trees also, Ψ_{pd} in the early dry season tended to be lower in deciduous and semi-deciduous species than in evergreen species (Myers et al., 1997).

Different patterns of water uptake and water relations can occur within a genus within a phenological guild. In a study of two deciduous shrub species in a West African humid savanna, Le Roux and Bariac (1998) observed that two co-occurring species exhibited marked differences in the magnitude of the dry-season decline in minimum leaf water potential. Furthermore, the relationship between water content of the upper 60 cm of soil and leaf water potential differed significantly. Pre-dawn and midday leaf water potentials of *Cussonia barteri* were not correlated with water content of the 0–60 cm profile and when the water potential of this layer was below −1.5 MPa the Ψ_{pd} was only −0.5 MPa. In contrast, *Crossopteryx febrifuga* showed significant declines in leaf water potential as the upper soil profile dried and pre-dawn and midday leaf water potentials were lower for this species than for *Cuss. barteri*. Clearly *Cuss. barteri* was accessing deeper water than was *Cross. febrifuga*. Similarly, in Costa Rican dry forest, there was a variety of seasonal responses in water relations within deciduous species. Seasonal minimum leaf water potentials were lowest in deciduous hardwood trees (average of −3.7 MPa), highest in deciduous lightwoods (−1.5 MPa) and intermediate in deciduous softwoods (−2.5 MPa), evergreen softwoods (−2.5 MPa) and evergreen lightwoods (−2.0 MPa) (Borchert, 1994c). Pelaez et al. (1994) showed a similar result, which highlights the caution required in characterizing water use on the basis of phenology alone.

B. Solute Potential and Osmotic Adjustment

The ability to maintain turgor as cell water content and leaf water potential decrease can contribute to drought tolerance (Morgan, 1984). High turgor maintenance capacity is associated with low osmotic potentials and a large difference between osmotic potentials at full turgor (π_{100}) and the turgor loss point (π_0) (Jones and Turner, 1978). Solute accumulation in response to water stress is termed 'osmotic adjustment' (often erroneously called 'osmoregulation') and involves an increase in the number of solute molecules per cell rather than a decrease in the amount of water in the cell (Munns, 1988). A decrease in osmotic potential at full turgor is evidence of osmotic adjustment (Morgan, 1984). However, a passive increase in cellular solute concentration resulting from loss of water can also help maintain positive turgor during drought stress (Evans et al., 1992).

Osmotic potentials were lower in woody species from Venezuelan dry forest (annual rainfall 900 mm) (Sobrado, 1986) than those from Venezuelan savanna (annual rainfall 1300 mm) (Goldstein et al., 1987), northern Australian savanna (annual rainfall 1650 mm) (Myers et al., 1997; Prior and Eamus, 1999) or Guinean savanna (annual rainfall 1200 mm) (Le Roux and Bariac, 1998). These low osmotic potentials enable leaves to maintain turgor at the low leaf water potentials prevailing in this dry environment.

The osmotic potential of *Crossopteryx febrifuga* was significantly lower than that of *Cussonia barteri*, a co-occurring shrub of a West African humid savanna (Le Roux and Bariac, 1998). In addition, as the leaves dried during the dry season, a passive increase in solute concentration (resulting from reduced water content rather than active solute accumulation) was observed only in *Crossopteryx febrifuga*. The association of a lower solute potential and osmotic accumulation with water uptake from the upper soil profile are entirely consistent.

Drought-induced osmotic adjustment has been demonstrated in a wide range of species (Morgan, 1984), including saplings of the Australian savanna trees *E. tetrodonta* and *T. ferdinandiana* (Table 1). This osmotic adjustment enabled the saplings to maintain positive turgor overnight throughout the year, although they probably lost turgor during the day at the end of the dry season (Prior and Eamus, 1999). By contrast, osmotic adjustment was not detected in mature trees of these or five other Australian savanna species (Myers et al., 1997). However, Ψ_{pd} was higher throughout the year than the wet season value of π_0, so that osmotic adjustment was not necessary for overnight recovery of turgor during the dry season (Myers et al, 1997; Table 1).

Osmotic adjustment did not occur in Venezuelan evergreen savanna trees during the dry season (Goldstein and Sarmiento, 1987), but there

Table 1

Comparison of some water relations parameters for species from Mediterranean and seasonally dry tropical environments

Species	Ψ_{pd} Wet	Ψ_{pd} Dry	π_0 Wet	π_0 Dry	π_{100} Wet	π_{100} Dry	OA	Comments	Reference
Seasonally dry tropical forest/savanna species									
Allosyncarpia ternata	−0.5	−1.6	−2.46	−2.82	−2.17	−2.48	0.31	Dry hilltop site, Australia	9
Allosyncarpia ternata	−0.3	−0.1	−2.23	−2.29	−2.08	−2.08	0	Wet ravine floor	9
Eucalyptus miniata	−0.2	−0.8	−1.98	−2.08	−1.81	−1.83	0.02	Australian savanna, mature, evergreen	5
Eucalyptus tetrodonta	−0.1	−0.8	−2.06	−2.13	−1.83	−1.93	0.10		
Erythrophleum chlorostachys	−0.2	−1.1	−2.13	−2.37	−1.95	−2.23	0.28	Australian savanna, mature, semi-deciduous	5
Xanthostemon paradoxus	−0.1	−1.2	−1.69	−1.77	−1.39	−1.50	0.11		
Eucalyptus clavigera	−0.2	−0.6	−2.60	−2.70	−2.16	−2.29	0.13	Australian savanna, mature, deciduous	5
Planchonia careya	−0.1	−0.7	−1.73	−1.83	−1.62	−1.58	–		
Terminalia ferdinandiana	−0.1	−0.9	−1.8	−1.72	−1.54	−1.48	–		
Eucalyptus tetrodonta	−0.2	−2.5	−1.75	−2.80	−1.33	−2.25	0.92	Australian savanna, sapling, evergreen	6
Terminalia ferdinandiana	−0.1	−1.2	−1.32	−1.58	−1.18	−1.39	0.21	Australian savanna, sapling, deciduous	6
3 evergreen spp.	−1.2	−3.0			−3.1	−4.4	1.3	Venezuelan dry forest; 1 tree and 2 shrubs pre-dawn π, not π_0, but similar water content so values comparable	8
3 deciduous spp.	−0.6	−2.8			−1.5	−3.1	1.2	Venezuelan dry forest; 2 trees and 1 vine pre-dawn π, not π_0 estimated OA adjusted for change in H_2O content	8
Byrsonima crassifolia	−0.25	−0.6		−1.5				Evergreen tree of Venezuelan savanna	7
Curatella americana	−0.45	−0.7		−2.8					
Bowdichia virilioides	−0.3	−0.8		−1.4					
Caesearia sylvestris	−0.35	−1.2		−2.3					
Cussonia barteri	−0.2	−0.7	−1.37	−1.72	−1.00	−1.15	0.15	Guinean deciduous shrubs	2
Crossopteryx febrifuga	−0.2	−0.7	−1.73	−2.17	−1.44	−1.67	0.23		

Table 1 (*Continued*)

Species	Ψ_{pd} Wet	Ψ_{pd} Dry	π_0 Wet	π_0 Dry	π_{100} Wet	π_{100} Dry	OA	Comments	Reference
Species from Mediterranean environments									
Quercus dumosa	−0.1	−1.1			−2.2	−3.1	0.9	Evergreen, chaparral	1
Ceanothus greggii	−0.1	−2.7			−2.1	−3.1	1.0	Evergreen, chaparral	
Arctostaphylos glandulosa	−0.3	−1.7			−2.3	−2.9	0.6	Evergreen, chaparral	
Eucalyptus behriana		−3.5			−1.63	−1.93	0.30	Evergreen, seedlings	4
Eucalyptus behriana	−2.6	−4.5			−2.8	−3.7	0.9	Mature	3
Eucalyptus microcarpa		−3.6			−1.72	−1.98	0.26	Evergreen, seedlings	4
Eucalyptus microcarpa	−1.8	−4.0			−2.8	−3.5	0.7	Mature	3
Eucalyptus polyanthemos		−3.6			−1.63	−2.14	0.51	Evergreen, seedlings	4

Note: Ψ_{pd} is pre-dawn leaf water potential, π_0 is osmotic potential at turgor loss point, π_{100} is osmotic potential at full turgor, and OA is osmotic adjustment, all in MPa. Deciduous species do not have leaves during the driest time of year, therefore dry season measurements presented here are the minimum values when leaves were present, and were generally not made at the same time as the dry season measurements on evergreen species.

References: 1, Bowman and Roberts (1985); 2, Le Roux and Bariac (1998); 3, Myers and Neales (1984); 4, Myers and Neales (1986); 5, Myers *et al.* (1977); 6, Prior and Eamus (1999); 7, Sarmiento *et al.* (1985); 8, Sobrado (1986); 9, Fordyce *et al.* (1997).

was little seasonality in leaf water potentials and minimum leaf water potential was almost always higher than π_0 (Sarmiento *et al*, 1985). However, in Venezuelan seasonally dry tropical forests, which receive less rainfall than the savanna areas, Ψ_{pd} values fell to about $-3.0\,MPa$ in both evergreen and deciduous species. Pre-dawn turgor was always positive owing to a concomitant decrease in leaf osmotic potential (Sobrado, 1986).

For a range of woody species from seasonal tropical environments on three continents, the extent of osmotic adjustment has been found to be proportional to the decrease in Ψ_{pd} between the wet and dry periods and independent of leaf phenology (Figure 3). In other words, osmotic adjustment is proportional to the degree of stress experienced by the leaf tissue.

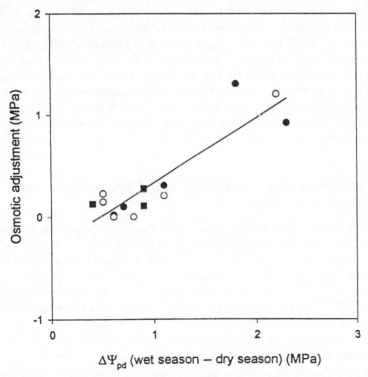

Fig. 3. The degree of osmotic adjustment increases as the difference between wet and dry season pre-dawn water potential ($\Delta\Psi_{pd}$) increases, regardless of phenological guild. Data are from Myers *et al.* (1997), Prior and Eamus (1999), Sobrado (1986), Le Roux and Bariac (1998) and Fordyce *et al.* (1997). Closed circles represent evergreen species, closed squares are semi-deciduous species, and open circles are deciduous species.

C. Hydraulic Properties and Water Transport

Plants balance their root growth, internal water transport capabilities and stomatal behaviour such that they maintain positive carbon assimilation while preventing leaf desiccation. Large xylem vessels are efficient at transporting water but are generally more susceptible to blockage by air (embolism) during water stress, compared to small vessels. There is a trade-off between efficiency and security of the water transport system (Tyree and Sperry, 1989; Tyree et al., 1994; see below).

There are several recent reviews of hydraulic conductivity, hydraulic architecture and xylem embolism (Tyree and Sperry, 1989; Tyree and Ewers, 1991; Tyree et al, 1994), including one on hydraulic architecture of tropical plants (Tyree and Ewers, 1996). Most studies, however, have been conducted on temperate species or tropical rainforest trees. Trees from seasonally dry systems have been relatively neglected.

Xylem conduits consist of tracheids in conifers and vessels in angiosperms. Conduits vary greatly in diameter, and even more in length (Tyree et al., 1994). Typically, tracheids are 1–3 mm in length, while vessels are 0.1–10 m long. In flowing to the leaves of a tree, water passes through many conduits. Movement between conduits requires passage through the pores of pit membranes. (Note that a pit membrane is not a semi-permeable phospholipid bilayer membrane as is found in living cells, but rather a middle lamella with a very thin layer of primary wall on either side. Xylem pit membranes are not metabolically active.)

1. Wood Anatomy of Conifers and Diffuse-Porous and Ring-Porous Trees

Differences in wood anatomy between ring-porous, diffuse-porous and coniferous trees affect their hydraulic characteristics. Most tropical trees are angiosperms, but conifers are found in Southeast Asia, Australia and New Guinea, especially in montane rainforests and seasonally dry areas (Whitmore, 1985). Coniferous xylem, with numerous small tracheids, has a relatively low conductivity and is less vulnerable to embolism than xylem of angiosperm trees (Tyree and Ewers, 1991; Wang et al., 1992). Smaller vessels of diffuse-porous wood are less conductive and less vulnerable than large-diameter vessels of earlywood in ring-porous species.

Ring-porous wood contains growth rings demarcated by much longer, wider vessels in earlywood (formed in spring) than in latewood (formed in summer/autumn) (Carlquist, 1988). Ring-porous trees generally contain between one and four, sometimes as many as 12, rings in the sapwood, compared with 20–100 rings for diffuse-porous and up to 150–200 for conifers (Ewers and Cruiziat, 1991). In ring-porous temperate trees, the wide earlywood vessels that conduct most of the sap embolize during autumn, while the much less conductive (and 'safer') latewood vessels function for several years (Zimmermann, 1983; Cochard and Tyree, 1990; Lo Gullo et al., 1995). Whether some drought-deciduous tropical trees function similarly has not been reported.

Many temperate Northern Hemisphere trees are easily classified as either ring-porous or diffuse-porous, but trees from other areas, such as the tropics and temperate areas of the Southern Hemisphere, often are not. For example, Ingle and Dadswell (1953a) stated that no eucalypts are ring-porous, but in some species vessels are markedly wider in early-wood than in latewood, and Carlquist (1988) considers these to be ring-porous. In addition, maximum vessel length often exceeds 1 m in various Eucalyptus species (Skene and Balodis, 1968; Franks et al., 1995), including E. tetrodonta (L.D. Prior, unpublished data), a dominant tree over large areas of north Australian savanna. Maximum vessel lengths in American diffuse-porous species are generally less than 60 cm, with most vessels being less than 10 cm long (Zimmermann and Jeje, 1981). We therefore need to be cautious in applying generalizations based on Northern Hemisphere diffuse-porous species to tropical and Southern Hemisphere species.

2. Hydraulic Conductance and Conductivity

Hydraulic conductance (L_p) is defined as flow rate per pressure *difference*. The value of L_p is obtained from the relationship between sap flow rate (Q) and the driving force, which is the water potential difference between the root (Ψ_R) and the leaf (Ψ_L) (note that these include a gravitational component):

$$L_p = Q/(\Psi_R - \Psi_L) \tag{1}$$

Leaf water potential is averaged over an adequate sample of transpiring leaves. Root water potential is assumed to stay constant throughout the day, and may be approximated by the value of pre-dawn leaf water potential. This relationship applies under steady-state conditions, when transpiration and uptake are equal. During transient conditions, there is also a capacitance (storage) component, but this is usually small compared with water uptake (Moreshet et al., 1990; Tyree et al., 1991; Goldstein et al., 1998).

Hydraulic conductance (and conductivity, see below) values are usually scaled to sapwood area (or stem cross-sectional area) and/or to leaf area. Generally, hydraulic conductance (leaf area basis) is higher in species with high transpiration rates (Figure 4). Values for woody plants from a range of environments are shown in Table 2. The patchiness of the data

Table 2

Hydraulic conductance of whole trees or shrubs from a range of environments. Values are scaled to sapwood area ($g\,m^{-2}\,s^{-1}\,MPa^{-1}$) and/or leaf area ($mg\,m^{-2}\,s^{-1}\,MPa^{-1}$)

Species	Hydraulic conductance				Comments	Method	Reference
	Sapwood area basis		Leaf area basis				
	Well-watered	Droughted	Well-watered	Droughted			
Conifers							
Abies bornmulleriana	67				Saplings	S	7
Juniperus virginiana		20	21			P	4
Larix sp.			8.1			S	17
Picea abies	61	13	6.5			S	17
Picea abies	56	3				S	7
Picea sitchensis			17	17		S	19
Pinus pinaster	72				Saplings	S	9
Pinus pinaster	100		53			S	7
Pinus pinaster	115					S	11
Pinus sylvestris	31 (average)		50	23		S	10
Pinus sylvestris	34		38			S	8
Pinus sylvestris	66		52			P	18
Pinus sylvestris			137	89		P	18
Pinus sylvestris						S	9
Temperate shrubs							
Distylium lepidotum			126	54	Evergreen	P	14
Dodonea viscosa			72	45		P	14
Hibiscus glaber			171	99	Evergreen, xerophytic	P	14
Larrea tridentata			65	24		P	12
Ligustrum micranthum			117	54		P	14
Wikstroemia pseudoretusa			114	54	Semi-deciduous	P	14

Table 2 (*Continued*)

						Method	Ref
Temperate angiosperm trees							
Juglans nigra			256		Semi-ring-porous	P	4
Quercus alba			117		}	P	4
Quercus marilandica			36	9	}	P	16
Quercus petraea	18–61				Ring-porous	S	1
Quercus petraea	63				}	S	2
Quercus petraea	13–61	4–50			}	S	3
Quercus rubra			31	9	}	P	16
Tropical rainforest trees							
Cecropia insignis			169		}	S	13
Cecropia obtusifolia			49		}	S	13
Coccoloba manzanillensis			59		Evergreen, pioneer	S	13
Miconia argentea			178		}	S	13
Palicourea guianensis			23		}	S	13
Trees of savannas/seasonal tropical forests							
Bursonima crassifolia			101		}	S	5
Curatella americana			106		Evergreen	S	5
Eucalyptus tetrodonta	40	29	18	9	}	S	15
Cecropia longipes				26	Evergreen;	S	6
Ficus insipida				53	abnormally wet	S	6
Luehea seemannii				27	dry season	S	6
Cochlospermum vitifolium			38		}	S	5
Genipa caruto			54		Deciduous	S	5
Terminalia ferdinandiana	125		31		}	S	15
Anacardium excelsum			4		Brevi-deciduous; abnormally wet dry season	S	6
Spondias mombin			29		Facultatively deciduous; abnormally wet dry season	S	6

Note: Method refers to whether transpiration was measured using sap flow sensors (S) or scaled up from porometry measurement (P; these may produce an overestimate of transpiration and therefore conductance).

References: 1, Bréda *et al.* (1993); 2, Bréda *et al.* (1995); 3, Cochard *et al.* (1996); 4, Ginter-Whitehouse *et al.* (1983); 5, Goldstein *et al.* (1989); 6, Goldstein *et al.* (1998); 7, Granier *et al.* (1989); 8, Irvine *et al.* (1998); 9, Jackson *et al.* (1995b); 10, Loustau and Granier (1993); 11, Loustau *et al.* (1996); 12, Meinzer *et al.* (1988); 13, Meinzer *et al.* (1995); 14, Mishio (1992); 15, Prior (1997); 16, Reich and Hinckley (1989); 17, Schulze *et al.* (1985); 18, Whitehead *et al.* (1984); 19, Lu *et al.* (1996).

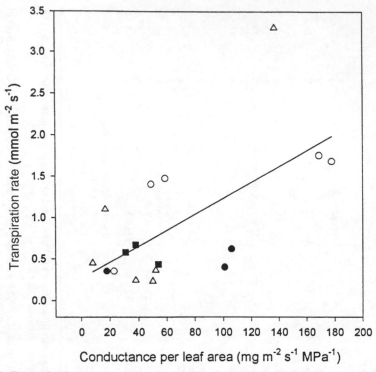

Fig. 4. Transpiration rate increases with increasing hydraulic conductance (expressed per unit leaf area) of stems. Triangles represent conifers; open circles are rainforest species; closed circles are evergreen savanna species; closed squares are deciduous savanna trees; and open squares are temperate trees.

and different methods used to determine transpiration make it difficult to draw generalizations about the different groups of plants. For example, there are few values for temperate trees other than *Quercus* spp., and some of these were derived from scaled-up porometry data. However, conductance does tend to be lower in trees from seasonally dry tropical areas than in tropical rainforest gap species. This is probably a reflection of the larger, year-round, availability of water in rainforests. There are few consistent differences between conductance in evergreen compared with deciduous tropical species. It may not be valid to include deciduous trees measured by Goldstein *et al.* (1998) in the comparison, since measurements were made in the dry season and may be much lower than wet season values.

Hydraulic conductivity (k_h) is defined as the flow rate per pressure *gradient* ($\Delta\Psi_W/l$, where $\Delta\Psi_W$ is the difference in water potential between two points in the plant, and l is path length). This can be written:

$$k_h = Ql/\Delta\Psi_W \tag{2}$$

where Q = flow rate (ml s^{-1}).

In order to scale for size, conductivity measurements may be divided by leaf area (often termed 'leaf specific conductivity'), or by stem or sapwood cross-sectional area ('specific conductivity'). However, in the SI system the term 'specific' is reserved to describe a value per unit mass, so we will refer to conductivity (leaf area basis), (k_l), and conductivity (sapwood area basis), (k_s).

Hydraulic conductivity of a cylinder is proportional to the fourth power of its radius (Poiseuille's law). The k_h of trunks, stems and branches is therefore largely determined by the number and size distribution of xylem conduits, but is also modified by properties of the inter-conduit pit membranes, which add to the resistance of the system (Tyree and Sperry, 1989). Actual conductivities of different species range between 20% and 100% of the theoretical maximum k_h (Tyree and Ewers, 1991).

Hydraulic conductivity values for stem segments from a range of woody species are shown in Table 3. Vines and lianas generally have the highest conductivity values, followed by tropical shrubs and rainforest trees, with conifers and savanna trees having the lowest values (these aspects will be discussed further in section III.C.8). Values of k_l and k_s were lower in savanna than rainforest trees, probably because high soil water availability enables rainforest trees to maintain high rates of transpiration throughout the year, whereas soil water is more limited in savannas during the dry season.

A study of four deciduous and two evergreen trees from Venezuelan dry forest found that the maximum k_h of the drought-deciduous species was 2–6 times that of the evergreen species, but was severely reduced at leaf fall (Sobrado, 1993; Table 3). Another study of 20 tropical vine and tree species also found that, within these two growth forms, deciduous plants generally had higher k_s values than did evergreen plants (Gartner, 1991; Table 3). These findings are consistent with surveys showing that plants of xeric habitats or those active in the dry season tend to have smaller diameter vessels and tracheids than those from more mesic sites and those active in wetter seasons (Carlquist and Hoekman, 1985 – cited by Gartner et al., 1990). By contrast, Goldstein et al. (1987) found that the k_l of stem segments and the conductance of whole trees from Venezuelan savanna was substantially higher in two evergreen than two deciduous species. However, these evergreen species maintain high water potentials throughout the dry season, and it has been suggested that they have extensive root systems that allow them access to subsoil water (Goldstein et al., 1987), as well as effective stomatal control of transpiration (Sobrado, 1996). The large k_l values in the evergreen species were largely due to a high ratio

Table 3

Hydraulic parameters of stem segments from trees, shrubs and lianas from a
range of environments

Species	$HV \times 10^4$	$k_l \times 10^3$	k_s	DBH (mm)	Comments	Ref.
Conifers						
Abies balsamea	2.8	0.34	1.35	15		3
Thuja occidentalis	0.4	0.069	1.7	15		3
Tsuga canadensis	1.1	0.12	1.1	15		3
Temperate angiosperm trees						
Acer saccharum	1.5	0.5	2.5	15	Diffuse-porous	3
Betula papyrifera		0.74			Diffuse-porous	3
Populus angustifolia	2.1	1.04	3.9	15	Diffuse-porous	3
Populus balsamifera	2.5	0.75	3.0	15	Diffuse-porous	3
Populus deltoides	2.9	1.01	4.8	15	Diffuse-porous	3
Populus grandidentata		0.62			Diffuse-porous	3
Eucalyptus grandis	4	2.5	6.5	15–30	Diffuse-porous, evergreen	8
Tropical vines and lianas						
Aristolochia taliscana			41	3–20	Evergreen	1
Adenocalymma inundatum			1.5	3–20	Brevi-deciduous	1
Combretum fruticosum			17	3–20	Deciduous	1
Dieterlea fusiformis			88	3–20	Deciduous	1
Entadopsis polystachya			210	3–20	Deciduous	1
Gaudichaudia mcvaughii			20	3–20	Deciduous	1
Gouania rosei			110	3–20	Deciduous	1
Ipomoea bracteata			32	3–20	Deciduous	1
Paddiflora juliana			40	3–20	Deciduous	1
Serjania brachycarpa			9	3–20	Deciduous	1
Bauhinia fassoglenis	0.14	11	171			3
Bauhinia vahii	0.24	6.8	35			3
Tropical shrubs						
Bauhinia aculeata	1.58	6.2	7			3
Bauhinia galpinii	0.6	5.8	11			3
Tropical rainforest trees						
Bauhinia blakeana	1.2	11	14			3
Bauhinia variegata	0.94	12.3	15			3
Ochroma pyramidale	10	2.0	2.1	45	Evergreen	3
Pseudobombax septenatum	12	1.8	1.6	45	Deciduous	3
Schefflera morotoni	20	4.5	2.2	45		3
Ficus dugandii	6.1	5.2	14	15		3
Ficus glabrata	2.2	2.1	11	15		3
Ficus yoponensis	2.0	2.3	14	15		3
Ficus citrifolia	2.2	1.5	7.9	15	Hemi-epiphyte	3
Ficus colubrinae	1.8	2.3	34	15	Hemi-epiphyte	3
Ficus obtusifilia	1.8	2.2	17	15	Hemi-epiphyte	3
Ficus pertusa	1.0	0.66	7.3	15	Hemi-epiphyte	3
Clusia uvitana	1.4	0.15	1.1	15	CAM-hemi-epiphyte	3

Table 3 (*Continued*)

Species	HV × 10^4	k_l × 10^3	k_s	DBH (mm)	Comments	Ref.
Trees of savannas/seasonal tropical forests						
Eucalyptus miniata	3.2	0.67	2.2	3.2	Evergreen	4
Eucalyptus tetrodonta	1.8	0.59	3.1	3.1	Evergreen	4
Byrsonima crassifolia	4.5	0.41	0.91	11	Evergreen	2
Curatella americana	3.1	0.13	0.43	11	Evergreen	2
Curatella americana	1.55	0.23	1.5	5.0	Evergreen	6
Capparis indica			1.0	3–20	Evergreen	1
Capparis aristiguetae	1.2	0.026	0.23	4.4	Evergreen	5
Capparis aristiguetae	2.1	0.016	0.09	5.7	Evergreen	7
Morisonia americana	1.1	0.025	0.23	4.4	Evergreen	5
Morisonia americana	2.8	0.035	0.14	6.1	Evergreen	7
Beureria cumanensis	1.11	0.066	0.50	4.3	Deciduous	5
Beureria cumanensis	2.94	0.100	0.41	4.3	Deciduous	7
Coursetia arborea	0.77	0.098	1.50	4.4	Deciduous	5
Coursetia arborea	0.81	0.092	1.26	3.0	Deciduous	7
Lonchocarpus dipteroneurus	0.50	0.065	1.31	4.3	Deciduous	5
Lonchocarpus dipteroneurus	0.88	0.096	0.98	3.8	Deciduous	7
Pithecellobium dulce	0.68	0.048	0.59	4.4	Deciduous	5
Pithecellobium dulce	1.53	0.071	0.54	3.5	Deciduous	7
Cochlospermum vitifolium	0.79	0.027	0.35	11	Deciduous	2
Genipa caruto	1.06	0.056	0.52	11	Deciduous	2
Caesalpinia eriostachys			1.8	3–20	Deciduous	1
Cnidoscolus spinosus			2.7	3–20	Deciduous	1
Cordia alliodora			2.6	3–20	Deciduous	1
Guapira sp.			1.7	3–20	Deciduous	1
Heliocarpus pallidus			5	3–20	Deciduous	1
Ipomoea wolcottiana			2.2	3–20	Deciduous	1
Psidium sartorianum			1.2	3–20	Deciduous	1
Ruprechtia fusca			2.4	3–20	Deciduous	1
Spondias purpurea			2.7	3–20	Deciduous	1

Note: HV (Huber value, m^2 xylem cross-sectional area/m^2 leaf area). Units for k_l and k_s are $kg\,s^{-1}\,m^{-1}\,MPa^{-1}$. Stem diameter at breast height (DBH, mm) is presented since hydraulic parameters change according to DBH (Patino *et al.*, 1995). Data for many species have been normalized to a stem diameter of 15 mm or 45 mm (Patino *et al.*, 1995). Where available, Huber values have sometimes been used to convert between k_s and k_l.

References: 1, Gartner (1991); 2, Goldstein *et al.* (1987); 3, Patino *et al.* (1995, and references contained therein); 4, L.D. Prior (unpublished); 5, Sobrado (1993); 6, Sobrado (1996); 7, Sobrado (1997); 8, Van der Willigen and Pammenter (1998).

of cross-sectional area of conducting tissue to total leaf area (Goldstein *et al.*, 1987). Goldstein *et al.* (1987) suggested that an efficient water transport system is required to keep pace with high transpiration rates during the dry season without causing an excessive drop in leaf water potential. However, such a strategy of maintaining high leaf water potential by facilitating large flows of water requires a large and reliable supply of accessible water to avoid extreme soil water deficits. Only the most favoured microsites within savanna landscapes could support such trees.

3. Water Storage Capacitance

Water storage capacitance is defined as the mass of water that can be extracted per MPa change in water potential of the tissue, either per unit volume or per unit dry mass (Tyree and Ewers, 1996). This topic has been reviewed by Holbrook et al. (1995).

Large leaf and stem water capacitances could substantially reduce the maximum rate of water uptake by the roots during the morning, and spread the period of water uptake over more hours in the diurnal cycle. Internally stored water could allow stomata to stay open for longer each day, enhancing carbon uptake. The range in wood density (0.15–1.1 g cm^{-3}) and hence in stem water storage capacity is much greater among tropical trees than among temperate trees (0.4–0.8 g cm^{-3}) (Borchert, 1994c). Calculations of diurnal water storage and release showed that stem and leaf water storage contributed, respectively, 16% and 5% of daily transpiration in *Thuja occidentalis*, 14% and 3% in *Acer saccharum* and only <0.5% and 2% in *Schefflera morotoni*. The contribution was low for *Schefflera* because there was a very narrow diurnal range in stem water potential (Tyree and Ewers, 1991). In five tree species from a seasonally dry tropical forest, diurnal water storage capacity ranged between 9% and 15% of total daily water use (Goldstein et al., 1998). The contribution was proportionally larger in large trees, and could partially compensate for decreases in hydraulic conductivity with tree size (Goldstein et al., 1998). Stem storage of water is likely to have a significant role in phenology (Borchert, 1994a; Holbrook et al., 1995; see above).

4. Xylem Embolism

Xylem conduits are prone to embolism because xylem sap is under tension, typically between −1 and −2 MPa (Tyree and Sperry, 1989), or lower in species adapted to arid conditions. This means that water must remain liquid at pressures considerably below its vapour pressure. Cavitation must be prevented if continuity of the water column is to be maintained.

Emboli may occur as a result of drought or freezing. The mechanisms are different for the two stresses (Sperry and Pockman, 1993). Since most savannas and seasonally dry tropical forests rarely experience freezing temperatures, this review will concentrate on drought-induced embolism.

Drought-induced cavitation in xylem occurs through air-seeding (Sperry and Tyree, 1988, 1990; Cochard et al., 1992; Jarbeau et al., 1995; Pockman et al., 1995; Sperry et al., 1996). Air does not easily penetrate the pores of a wet membrane, but will do so if the pores are large enough and there is a sufficient pressure difference between the two sides of the membrane. The critical pore diameter (d) or pressure difference (ΔP) can be approximated from a simplified version of the capillarity equation (Zimmermann, 1983):

$$d \times \Delta P \approx 0.3 \tag{3}$$

where d is measured in μm and ΔP in MPa. Air-seeding occurs first through the largest pores in the conduit wall, which are located in the inter-conduit membranes. The maximum pressure difference to which an inter-conduit membrane could be exposed occurs if a neighbouring vessel becomes air-filled, for example because of mechanical injury or insect damage. The pressure in the air-filled conduit is then atmospheric (approximately 0.1 MPa), compared with that in the functional vessel (Zimmermann, 1983) of approximately −1 to −3 MPa.

A safe pit membrane (i.e. resistant to propagation of air) has narrow pores, but also needs to be strong enough to resist substantial pressure differences without rupturing. Vulnerability to cavitation depends not only on the diameter of pit membrane pores, but also on conduit length. Long conduits have a larger contact surface between cavitated conduits and those that are still functioning, and the consequences of them failing are worse than for short conduits (Lo Gullo *et al.*, 1995).

5. Vulnerability Curves

The relationship between loss of hydraulic conductivity and the xylem water potential that induced the loss of conductivity is shown in a vulnerability curve (Figure 5 provides examples using two tree species from seasonally dry forests in Venezuela).

Values of xylem water potential corresponding to a 50% loss of conductivity for temperate trees range between −1.2 MPa in *Populus deltoides* (Tyree *et al.*, 1992) and −11 MPa in *Ceanothus megacarpus* (Kolb and Davis, 1994). For Bornean rainforest trees, values were between −0.18 MPa in *Xerospermum laevigatum* and −6.3 MPa in *Homalium moultonii*, but were less than −1.0 MPa for most species (Tyree *et al.*, 1998).

In the evergreen savanna tree *Curatella americana*, 50% of hydraulic conductivity was lost at −1.5 MPa (Figure 5). This species appears able to access subsoil water and maintains high leaf water potentials throughout the year (Sobrado, 1996). Another two evergreen tree species from Venezuelan dry forest lost 50% of conductance at about −2.4 MPa, compared with −1.65, −1.77, −2.42 and −3.82 MPa for four deciduous species (Sobrado, 1997). Thus there is considerable overlap for the two phenological guilds, and we need data from more species, and from more areas (especially trees from African and Australian savannas), before we can

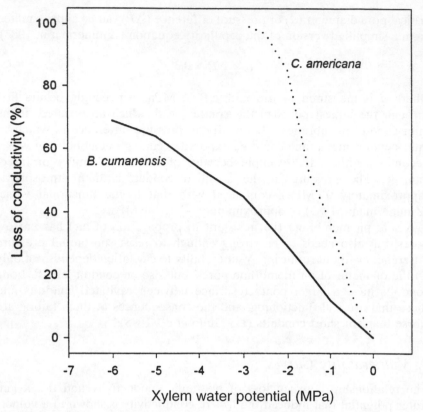

Fig. 5. As xylem water potential declines, the percentage embolism for the tree species *Curatella americana* and *Beureria cumanensis* increases. Re-drawn from Sobrado (1996).

draw conclusions about possible differences in vulnerability between ever-green and deciduous trees. We also do not know whether xylem embolism is involved in the process of leaf shedding by drought-deciduous trees. Dry season leaf water potentials were much lower in four deciduous than in two evergreen tree species (Sobrado, 1993), so that extent of embolism would vary, even when vunerability curves are similar.

In general, the vulnerability of species correlates with the xylem pres-sures they experience in the field (Tyree and Sperry, 1989). For tropical tree species, xylem water potentials that cause 50% loss of conductivity are least negative in dipterocarp forest (high soil water-holding capacity), slightly lower and more variable in heath forest (low soil water-holding capacity, and subject to occasional drought), and most negative in tropical, seasonally dry forest or savannas (Figure 6; Tyree *et al.*, 1998). Tyree *et al.* (1998) suggest that other mechanisms, such as stomatal control to avoid embolism-inducing xylem tensions, are cost-effective adaptations against occasional drought, but that the resulting reduction in productivity places a greater premium on resistance to embolism when drought is annual and predictable.

6. Trade-off between 'Safety' and 'Efficiency' of Xylem

The features that make xylem safe – short vessels (or tracheids), separated by a thick, strong pit membrane with narrow pores – also add to its resistance. Additionally, within an individual tree, conduit size and size of pores in the pit membrane are correlated, so that large vessels are more vulnerable to cavitation than small ones (Tyree and Sperry, 1989; Sperry and Saliendra, 1994; Alder et al., 1996). There is a trade-off between safety and efficiency of xylem.

The relationship between conduit diameter and size of pit membrane pores does not necessarily hold between species. For a range of 57 trees from widely varying environments, Tyree et al. (1994) found there was a weak but statistically significant correlation between conduit diameter and xylem potential at which 50% of hydraulic conductivity is lost. This contrasts with freezing-induced embolism, for which the correlation was very strong. Nonetheless, Tyree et al. (1994) concluded that wet, warm environments tend to favour species with wide conduits, whereas cold or dry environments tend to favour species with narrow conduits.

Studies of wood characteristics of tropical trees give results consistent with these expectations. Wood from 19 species of a very dry Venezuelan

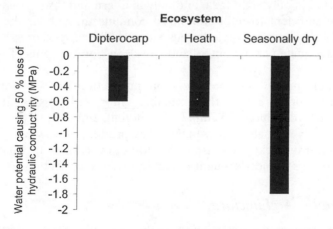

Fig. 6. Xylem water potential causing 50% loss of hydraulic conductivity decreases from dipterocarp, through heathland to seasonally dry forests/savannas. Re-drawn from Tyree et al. (1998).

forest had features that would contribute to hydraulic safety, such as numerous grouped vessels of narrow, short vessel elements (vessel length was not examined), and very small inter-vessel pits (Lindorf, 1994). Wide vessels were found in only one species, *Acacia tortuosa*, which can obtain water from deep within the soil profile. In Mexican deciduous forest, there was more diversity in vessel diameter categories, and a good representation of medium-sized and moderately large vessels was found (Barajas-Morales, 1985, cited in Lindorf, 1994). In trees of a Venezuelan cloud forest, wide vessels predominated, but mean vessel diameter was smaller than in the Mexican deciduous forest (Perez Mogollon, 1989, cited in Lindorf, 1994). This probably reflects the fact that xylem of drought-deciduous trees usually transports water only when water is readily available.

7. Recovery from Embolism

Embolized conduits may become functional again through bubble dissolution. In a few species, refilling of xylem conduits may also occur when gas is expelled from very dry branches, where the ends of conduits are exposed to the air through open vessels or dry pit membranes (Yang and Tyree, 1992). Xylem conductivity can recover from embolism when xylem pressure is positive, or at pressures only slightly below atmospheric (Yang and Tyree, 1992).

Root pressures can be effective in repairing embolism in herbaceous plants, but embolism reversal in tall trees is more problematic (Tyree and Sperry, 1989). Among tropical plants, positive xylem pressures have been detected in only eight taxa, and only in a fern and three grass species were these sufficient to refill embolized conduits throughout the shoots. None of 29 species of dicotyledonous vines exhibited root pressures that would be adequate to refill embolized vessels in canopy stems (Tyree and Ewers, 1996).

Temperate ring-porous trees rely on production of new earlywood vessels each spring, rather than refilling embolized vessels. It is not known whether deciduous savanna trees can refill embolized xylem vessels during the early wet season or whether they produce new xylem that only functions until the next dry season. We do not even know to what extent embolism occurs in most drought-deciduous trees (see section IX).

8. Hydraulic Architecture

'Hydraulic architecture' describes how the hydraulic conductivity of the xylem in various parts of a tree is related to the leaf area it must supply (Zimmermann, 1978). By investigating hydraulic architecture, we can predict how much water can be conducted to various parts of a tree, the resulting water potentials and pressure gradients at varying levels of transpirational flow, how vulnerable the tree will be to embolism, and where embolism is most likely to occur.

About one half of a tree's resistance is located in the root system (Running, 1980; Moreshet et al., 1990; Tyree et al., 1995, 1998), the other half in the shoot. Generally, k_l for minor branches is 10 to 1000 times lower than for major branches (Tyree and Sperry, 1989). Since the pressure gradient ($\Delta\Psi_W/l$) in the stem is equivalent to transpirational flux density divided by k_l, most of the water potential drop in the shoot xylem occurs in small branches, twigs and petioles. Nodal areas also present a distinct hydraulic constriction, with conductivity through junctions often half that of the branch itself (Zimmermann, 1978). In addition, k_h of leaf blades is very low, and there are presumably large gradients in water potential within them (Yang and Tyree, 1994).

Hydraulic resistance was much higher in leaves of evergreen than in deciduous trees of Venezuelan dry tropical forest (Sobrado, 1997/98). Leaves contributed 92–96% of total resistance of shoots (3–5 mm diameter) from evergreen trees, but only 69–76% of total resistance of shoots from deciduous trees. Such resistances were calculated to cause a drop in water potential across a leaf of 1.0–1.7 MPa in deciduous species and 1.8–1.9 MPa in evergreen species (Sobrado, 1997/98). These results are consistent with those of Borchert (1994b), who found greater differences in water potential between leaves and stems in evergreen (c. 1.2 MPa) than deciduous (c. 0.1–1.0 MPa) trees.

Vessel size and k_l decrease from base to apex, where water potentials are always more negative (Zimmermann, 1978; Patino et al., 1995; Tyree and Ewers, 1996). This may also apply to root systems; in the proteaceous shrub Banksia prionotes, k_s, decreased 5- to 20-fold from the base to the top of sinker roots, so that absolute conductance was relatively constant along its length, despite a 10- to 15-fold decrease in cross-sectional area (Pate et al., 1995). The relatively high conductivities of the trunk and main stem means that the absolute conductance per unit leaf area of some woody species is nearly independent of plant size (Yang and Tyree, 1994).

The Huber value is defined as the sapwood cross-sectional area (or sometimes the stem cross-sectional area) divided by the leaf area distal to the segment. It is a measure of the investment of stem tissue per unit leaf area supplied (Tyree and Ewers, 1991). Obviously the Huber value will change seasonally in deciduous species, so it is important to measure it when leaf area is maximal. Conductivity (leaf area basis) is the product of the Huber value and k_s (Tyree and Ewers, 1991). Thus, plants may compensate for a low k_s by having a higher Huber value (Pallardy, 1989). This can happen within a species; for example, Toxicodendron diversilobum grows as a vine when support is present, but as a shrub when support is absent. Narrow stems of supported plants had lower Huber values (xylem transverse area/leaf area), but wider vessels and higher k_s, than those of unsupported plants (Gartner, 1991).

In tropical dry forests of Venezuela, the Huber value was higher in stems of six evergreen and one drought-deciduous tree than in stems of the remaining five deciduous trees (Goldstein et al., 1987; Sobrado, 1997). Lianas have very wide vessels and high k_s but relatively small sapwood areas and low Huber values (Table 3; Tyree and Ewers, 1996). They have very little heartwood and rely on external plants or objects for mechanical support (Tyree and Ewers, 1996).

Zimmermann's (1978) 'segmentation hypothesis' states that during periods of severe drought, water potentials will always be lowest in the most peripheral parts of the tree, and this is where embolism will first occur, provided vulnerability of these parts is similar or greater. Leaves and twigs will be sacrificed first, protecting the vital main stem and major branches. This has been demonstrated in several temperate species (Tyree et al., 1991, 1993), but not in tropical trees.

It can be useful to integrate the factors affecting the balance between water potential gradient and transpiration in plants into an explicit equation. Sap flow rate, Q, can be expressed as

$$Q = E \times A_l \tag{4}$$

where E is the transpiration rate and A_l is the leaf area. From Pearcy et al. (1989),

$$E = G_s D \tag{5}$$

where G_s is stomatal conductance and D is leaf-to-air vapour pressure deficit (expressed as a mole fraction).

The conductivity per unit sapwood area, k_s, is defined by

$$k_s = k_h / A_s$$

where k_h is hydraulic conductivity and A_s is the sapwood cross-sectional area. We can therefore rewrite (2) as

$$k_s A_s = G_s D A_l l / \Delta \Psi_W \tag{6}$$

Whitehead (1998) hypothesized that trees growing in conditions of different evaporative demand will adjust G_s, k_s, A_s or A_l as a result of a homeostatic response to maintain the water potential gradient within narrow limits. Thus, two stands of *Pinus sylvestris* growing under different conditions (Mencuccini and Grace, 1995) exhibited a lower ratio of foliage area to sapwood cross-sectional area at warmer, drier sites than at cooler wetter sites. Trees of northern Australian savannas also appear to maintain fairly constant water potential gradients between roots and leaves throughout the year, despite large seasonal variations in soil and atmospheric water availability. Assuming mean water potential of fine roots is equivalent to pre-dawn leaf water potential, water potential difference between roots and leaves of *Eucalyptus tetrodonta* trees was 1.7 MPa and 1.6 MPa in the late wet season and the late dry season, respectively (Myers *et al.*, 1997). For saplings, these values were 1.3 MPa and 1.6 MPa, respectively (Prior *et al.*, 1997a). Decreased stomatal conductance prevented development of excessive leaf water potential differences.

9. Seasonal Decreases in Hydraulic Conductance

Drought-induced changes in whole-tree hydraulic conductance have been demonstrated in conifers, temperate trees and shrubs and in one study of a savanna evergreen tree (Table 2). In addition, many studies have found seasonal changes in embolism in stems of woody plants (see section III.C.9(d)), but this is only one of many possible reasons for a decrease in hydraulic conductance of whole trees. These reasons include:

(a) Decrease in leaf area. A decrease in leaf area will lead to a decline in flow for a particular pressure difference, and therefore a lower absolute hydraulic conductance, as well as a lower apparent k_s. Hydraulic conductance may also decline on a leaf area basis, since lower leaves on a branch, and lower branches on a tree, are often shed first, giving a longer average pathway for water to travel. This would depend on the hydraulic architecture of the tree, and the location of the major resistances to water flow.

Fully deciduous savanna trees represent an extreme case. These trees shed all their leaves during the dry season, so there is no flow of water and zero conductance. It may be argued that this is simply due to sealing of the xylem vessels during petiole abscission, and that the stem of the tree retains a high conductance. Whether this is so could be tested by measuring flow that occurs after cutting the tips off branches and imposing a pressure gradient on the tree, for example with a high-pressure flowmeter such as described by Tyree *et al.* (1995). Even evergreen savanna trees lose some leaf area during the dry season (Williams *et al.*, 1997b; O'Grady *et al.*, 1999), and a consequent decrease in hydraulic conductance would be expected. This especially applies to saplings and smaller trees (Prior *et al.*, 1997a; Williams *et al.*, 1997b).

(b) Death of roots.   Loss of roots would reduce hydraulic conductance of the whole tree, as well as its apparent k_s and k_l. Species may differ in production and turnover of fine roots, and how active these remain during drought. Many trees produce fine roots in response to rain, and these fine roots may die during periods of drought (D. Bowman, personal communication).

(c) Decrease in sapwood cross-sectional area.   It is theoretically possible that heartwood formation (possibly following embolism) occurs at the inner edge of sapwood during the dry season, and likely that sapwood formation primarily occurs during the early wet season. This would decrease the area of sapwood and thus hydraulic conductance and k_l.

Several trees in Bornean dipterocarp and heath forests had smaller hydroactive areas during the dry period than during the wet period (Becker, 1996), and the probable emboli in this inner part of the sapwood may lead to heartwood development. However, the proportion of sapwood in mature *E. tetrodonta* trees (common in northern Australian savannas, and relatively insensitive to drought) was constant throughout the dry season (A.P. O'Grady, unpublished data). In this species, trunk expansion and leaf flushing occurred through to the end of the dry season (Myers *et al.*, 1998), probably indicating formation of new xylem during most of the dry season.

(d) Decrease in efficiency of sapwood in conducting water (k_s), which may be due to xylem embolism.   Blockage of xylem vessels by air or plugging with tyloses, gums, suberization or lignification (Zimmermann, 1983) reduces hydraulic conductance. For example, in several *Quercus* spp., earlywood vessels are completely blocked by tyloses within a year of their formation (Cochard and Tyree, 1990). Other changes may occur in xylem conduits. For example, conifers may experience irreversible loss of conductivity when dried to very low water potentials, probably as the result of sealing of the inter-tracheid torus (Sperry and Tyree, 1990). Older xylem vessels may also be selectively embolized as a result of increases in permeability of their inter-vessel pits to air; this increased permeability is associated with degradation of the pit membrane, and may be a step in initiating heartwood formation (Sperry *et al.*, 1991).

Seasonal changes do occur in the degree of embolism in woody plants. In several temperate Northern Hemisphere trees xylem embolism of 20–50% has been measured during summer, compared with freezing-induced embolism of 80–90% during winter (Cochard and Tyree, 1990; Tognetti and Borghetti, 1994; Magnani and Borghetti, 1995). In California, xylem embolism was 48% at the beginning of summer and 78% at the end in the facultatively deciduous shrub *Salvia mellifera*, compared with only 12%

and 17% at the beginning and end of summer, respectively, in the ever-green *Ceanothus megacarpus* (Kolb and Davis, 1994).

Sobrado (1997) studied embolism in four drought-deciduous and two evergreen species of a Venezuelan tropical dry forest. In deciduous species, loss of conductivity due to embolism in terminal branches ranged between 8% and 19% during the wet season, increasing to 38–79% during the dry season. By contrast, in the evergreen species it was between 30% and 35% during the wet season, and between 40% and 48% during the dry season. In an earlier study, Sobrado (1993) found that, during the dry season, wood water content in drought-deciduous species declined and the minimum value was recorded when leaf fall was complete. At this time, the volumetric fraction of gas increased, indicating air entry into xylem vessels. In contrast, wood water content and volume of gas did not change significantly through the year in evergreen species (Sobrado, 1993). Differences in extent of embolism between deciduous and ever-green species were attributed to differences in root depth and water availability (Sobrado, 1997).

It is not clear what role, if any, is played by embolism formation in inducing leaf fall in deciduous species. In Venezuelan dry forest, leaf fall in deciduous trees coincided with a decrease in water content of terminal branches, but usually occurred before any marked increase in gas volume (Sobrado, 1993). In these species, Ψ_{pd} values fell to about $-2.8\,\mathrm{MPa}$ (Sobrado, 1986), and dry-season embolism was between 38% and 79%. However, in two deciduous species of northern Australian savannas, water potentials of terminal twigs did not fall below $-1.5\,\mathrm{MPa}$ (Duff *et al.*, 1997) and, from vulnerability curves of other species, there is unlikely to be extensive embolism in these species. It has not been possible to measure directly embolism in these species because the sapwood contains an exudate that partially blocks xylem after a cut is made (Prior, 1997; D. Thomas, personal communication). There was a wide range of seasonal minimum stem water potentials (-1.5 to $< -4\,\mathrm{MPa}$) in deciduous trees in a Costa Rican dry forest, implying there may be varying degrees of embolism in stems of different species (Borchert, 1994b). The three deciduous hardwoods all had minimum stem water potentials around $-4\,\mathrm{MPa}$, so embolism in this group is likely to be substantial unless they are very resistant.

(e) Changes in hydraulic conductance at soil–root interface. Hydraulic conductance may vary with transpiration rate, and the site of variability appears to be the root (Koide, 1985). Passioura and Munns (1984) found that hydraulic conductance of barley and lupin plants may vary diurnally, and independently of transpiration rate. When water flows into an intact root system, to reach the xylem it must cross the root epidermis, the cortex,

and then the endodermis. Direct control of hydraulic conductance is exerted at the living membranes within the root. Root hydraulic conductance is influenced by root age (Lopez and Nobel, 1991), temperature (Radin, 1990; Lopez and Nobel, 1991) and abscisic acid (ABA) (Eamus et al., 1995). It is thus possible the plant can exert some short- to medium-term control of water uptake by changing the hydraulic conductance of the root system via effects of ABA on root membranes.

Since we rarely measure root water potential directly, but rather infer it from soil water potential or Ψ_{pd}, changes in hydraulic conductance at the soil–root interface will cause changes in apparent hydraulic conductance of the whole tree. Increases in soil-to-root conductances in drying soil have often been attributed to poor contact between root and soil. However, there is evidence that solutes accumulate either in the root or just outside it, creating large osmotic pressures, that give the appearance of an interfacial resistance (Stirzaker and Passioura, 1996).

Large seasonal changes in soil water content are characteristic of savannas. Savanna trees are therefore likely to experience seasonal changes in hydraulic conductance between the bulk soil and the root, as well as between the root surface and the xylem. O'Grady et al. (1999), studying savanna trees in north Australia, suggest that hysteresis in the transpiration versus vapour pressure deficit curve may be partially attributed to decreases in soil hydraulic conductance at the soil–root interface. Williams et al. (1998), in a study of seasonal variation of evapotranspiration from a Brazilian rainforest, concluded that soil and root hydraulic resistance increased during the dry season, causing a decline in evapotranspiration.

IV. ROOT DISTRIBUTION

Evergreen trees tolerate periods of six or more months without significant rainfall and maintain a full canopy. In addition, stomatal conductance and photosynthesis, although reduced during the dry season, remain higher than would be expected a priori from consideration of the seasonality of water availability alone (see below). Indeed, transpiration rates per tree can be the same in the dry season as the wet season in some systems (O'Grady et al., 1999). Clearly, uptake of water by roots must occur throughout the dry season, despite the water table falling to depths of 5–20 m.

Direct observation of roots has been made at depths of ≥ 60 m in the Kalahari (Jennings, 1974). Stone and Kalisz (1991) report roots to depths of >20 m in 11 tree species, while in the Sonoran Desert, USA, tree roots to depths of ≥ 50 m have been found (Phillips, 1963). Trees generally have roots to greater depths than shrubs or grasses (Canadell *et al.*, 1996). In a review of 290 observations, covering 253 species in 11 biomes, Canadell *et al.* (1996) show that boreal forest, croplands, temperate deciduous forests and tundra have very shallow rooting depths (<5.0 m). Temperate coniferous forest, temperate grassland and tropical deciduous forest have intermediate root depths (<10 m), and deserts, sclerophyllous shrubland and forest, tropical evergreen forest and tropical grassland and savannas have deep roots (>15 m). As may be expected, plants from arid environments, or from environments with a seasonal rainfall, showed the deepest rooting. Sclerophyllous trees, especially Eucalypts, may have particularly deep roots. Furthermore, tap roots, which are specialized for deep growth, are present in 75% of tropical trees (Canadell *et al.*, 1996). The presence of hardpans, rocky strata and compact clay layers are not impenetrable barriers to root growth (Canadell *et al.*, 1996). Macro-pores and channels, through cracking and dissolution of material, and acid digestion by acids released by roots, allow deep penetration through very hard layers. This is further evidenced by the fact that percolation of water through such hard layers occurs faster than predicted from a knowledge of the hydraulic conductivity of non-fractured layers.

In a second major review of 200 data sets, Vogt *et al.* (1996) show that there were no significant or consistent patterns for above- and below-ground biomass accumulated across different climatic forest types. Soil organic matter varied significantly according to soil chemistry – for example, ultisols and oxisols had high total living and dead organic matter accumulations, especially in cold or tropical regions. Of particular note was the observation that deciduous forests tended to accumulate less aboveground (and total, and thus by difference, less root biomass) biomass than evergreen and semi-deciduous forests growing on the same soil series (Vogt *et al.*, 1996). This supports the view that deciduous species have a smaller rooting volume (and by inference smaller root biomass) than evergreen species (Sobrado, 1986).

Analyses in the 1980s showed that fine root biomass and production in the cold temperate zone could be accounted for by variation in mean annual temperature, the ratio of mean annual temperature to annual precipitation, and soil nitrogen (N) dynamics/pool size. More recent analyses show that different variables are able to account for different amounts of variation in fine root biomass in different climates and forests types (Vogt *et al.*, 1996). Climatic variables could not account for any variation in fine root biomass in deciduous species. However, soil nutrient dynamics did account for much of the variation in deciduous species fine root biomass. In the evergreen species, climatic (e.g. mean annual temperature, mean annual precipitation) and soil nutrient status (e.g. litterfall N/P ratio, soil Ca content) are significant variables accounting for differences in fine root biomass. Precipitation explains a low proportion of variation in fine root biomass in boreal and cold temperate zones but where N, P or K availability limit growth (such as in savannas), root biomass is strongly correlated with N, P or K transfer from litterfall to soil. In tropical broadleaf deciduous forest, the ratio of N/P in litterfall can explain 99% of variation in fine root net primary productivity (Vogt *et al.*, 1996). Precipitation may often not correlate well with root dynamics because this does not take into account soil storage capacity. Factors that determine the amount of fine roots present are poor predictors of the amount of fine roots produced per year (Vogt *et al.*, 1996).

In a West African humid savanna, Mordelet *et al.* (1997) observed that both tree and grass roots were mostly confined to the top 20 cm of soil, with a peak of tree root biomass at 10 cm. Similarly, Castellanos *et al.* (1991) show that approximately 65% of all roots in a dry deciduous tropical forest in Mexico occur in the top 20 cm of soil. Seghieri (1995) showed that in a Cameroon savanna, tree root profiles were mostly confined to the upper 40 cm with only a small number of deeper tap roots penetrating to 1.5 m or more (the limit of the excavation). *Parkia biglobosa*, a tree indigenous to most of the savannas of west Africa, maintains 60% of its root biomass in the top 20 cm of soil (Tomlinson *et al.*, 1998). However, as with the majority of such studies, only shallow (<100 cm) excavations were made. Therefore it is difficult to assess how much root material was deeper. It is pertinent to note that in many studies (Seghieri, 1995; Smit and Rethman, 1998; Tomlinson *et al.*, 1998) there are significant numbers of coarse roots (>1 cm diameter) at 50–150 cm depth. It is likely that these roots proliferate at a depth similar to that observed for jarrah (Kimber, 1974). Furthermore it is clear that for semi-deciduous, brevi-deciduous and evergreen species, which transpire throughout the dry season, there must be substantial root biomass at much greater depths to account for the water transpired in the dry season. Thus Cook *et al.* (1998) have shown that significant amounts of roots in a north Australian savanna must reach depths of 6 m to supply the water requirements of the dominant evergreens in the dry season. Carbon *et al.* (1980) have shown that roots of *Eucalyptus marginata* (jarrah) extend to 20 m in dry sclerophyll forests in Australia. Of particular interest is the observation that roots of jarrah appear to be bimodal – with peaks of root biomass occurring at shallow (less than 1 m depth) and deeper depths (14–15 m; Kimber, 1974). Such a distribution is likely to occur where capillary rise and a permanent groundwater reservoir exist. Seghieri (1995) and D. Eamus, X. Chen, A.P. O'Grady, G. Kelley and L. Hutley (unpublished observations) note that many savanna tree species have a 'double' root system, that is, shallow lateral roots (less than 50 cm depth) and a number of deep tap roots going many metres down. Using a novel lithium chloride tracer, Haase *et al.* (1996) show water uptake in a seasonally dry Mediterranean from depths of 28 m.

Savanna soils are patchy with respect to nutrient availability, both spatially and temporally. This patchiness is reflected in root distribution. Thus Mordelet *et al.* (1997) show root density is far higher in nitrogen-rich areas (close to termite mounds and close to root stumps) than in nitrogen-poor areas. Lateral roots can extend 10–20 m away from the trunk, or three to six times the radius of the crown (Mordelet *et al.*, 1996; Tomlinson *et al.*, 1998). Fine root biomass usually peaks in the wet season and declines in the dry season (Visalakshi, 1994; Sundarapandian and Swamy, 1996), presumably a reflection both of declines in soil water availability and hence nutrient availability. Root distribution is also a function of soil type. Seghieri (1995) has shown that soil depth and drainage characteristics determine the depth and pattern of root distribution in a Cameroon savanna. Fine and coarse root distribution can differ (Smit and Rethman, 1998). Thus 66% of fine roots were found in the first 40 cm of soil but coarse roots were essentially absent in the first 20 cm with a peak distribution between 20 and 60 cm (Smit and Rethman, 1998). In the 80–100 cm depth, coarse roots accounted for 75% of root biomass.

Hydraulic lift, whereby a few deep large roots move water up the soil profile during the night, followed by re-uptake during the day by shallow roots in the upper profile (Caldwell *et al.*, 1998), could theoretically support dry season transpiration. In a study of Kenyan and west Australian seasonally dry ecosystems, Burgess *et al.* (1998) show that hydraulic lift and reverse hydraulic lift occur. Before rains occur, flow of water in lateral roots of *Grevillea robusta* was negative (that is, away from the trunk towards root tips) at night and positive (towards the leaves) when transpiration demand was high (midday). This was taken as evidence of hydraulic lift. Significant water flow at night occurred through lateral roots even when flow through the trunk was negligible, indicating stem recharge and reverse hydraulic lift. These results were confirmed in *Eucalyptus camaldulensis* in Western Australia (Burgess *et al.*, 1998). After rain, lateral roots appeared to supply water from the upper wet profile into the deeper dry profile. Water flow in shallow lateral roots and deep tap roots was strongly and inversely correlated. Therefore roots were redistributing water along gradients of soil water potential and this flow was not simply to recharge root stores (Burgess *et al.*, 1998). Such data do not support the recent controversial interpretations of water transport in plants (Pockman *et al.*, 1995; Milburn, 1996). It remains to be seen whether such redistribution of water both up and down the soil profile is a common phenomenon in seasonally dry ecosystems.

A. Isotopic Signatures and Root Water Uptake

Direct determination of below-ground processes is difficult to achieve. Seasonally dry tropical forests are particularly difficult to study because of high temperatures, the presence of lateritic hardpans in soils and high species diversity. Stable isotope analyses of soil and plant water can be used to investigate partitioning of water resources between different plant functional groups (Ehleringer et al., 1993). However, the majority of such studies have been in temperate zones, partially because of poor differences in isotope signatures of different rainfall events in the wet season. Jackson et al. (1995a) have shown that while lake and stream hydrogen isotope composition (deuterium content, δD ‰) were similar to the weighted mean of annual precipitation, evaporation of soil water from the surface resulted in enrichment of heavy isotopes of hydrogen and oxygen. Most importantly, drought-deciduous species had higher xylem δD values than evergreen species. This was because deciduous species were accessing water from shallower soils than evergreen species. Further support of this conclusion was obtained from the relationship between pre-dawn xylem water potential and xylem water δD. Deciduous species exhibited higher δD values than evergreen species but also more negative pre-dawn potentials, as expected from their shallower roots. In addition, evergreen shrubs and small trees exhibited δD values resembling those of deciduous trees, a result ascribed to their short stature and hence presumably more shallow roots (Jackson et al., 1995a).

Le Roux et al. (1995) also used isotopic analyses of soil and xylem water in a West African humid savanna. In this study there were very few woody roots below 1.2 m and the majority of both grass and shrub roots occurred in the top 60 cm. The isotopic signature of stem water showed that both grasses and shrubs utilized water in the upper 30 cm. Le Roux et al. (1995) conclude that there is very little partitioning of water resources between shrubs and grasses in this system, that is, competition for water occurs. It should be noted that the shrubs in this study were deciduous. In contrast, at the same site, Le Roux and Bariac (1998) showed partitioning of water resources between two deciduous shrubs.

Age and season influence the depth of water uptake in cool savanna in Arizona (Weltzin and McPherson, 1997). Trees and saplings extract water all year from deep soil, and young seedlings extract water from a shallower depth than grasses and older saplings. This pattern may enhance germination and very early establishment of seedlings (Weltzin and McPherson, 1997). As the dry season progresses, extraction of water occurs from deeper and deeper soil.

V. GAS EXCHANGE

A. Stomatal Conductance and Transpiration

1. Stomatal Behaviour and Responses to the Environment

Stomata are the pores through which CO_2 and H_2O diffuse into and out of leaves. Stomatal aperture is affected by both internal controls, which include root and leaf water status, abscisic acid (ABA) levels in xylem and leaf, and leaf internal CO_2 concentration, and external factors, which include light flux density, temperature, and soil and atmospheric water content (Eamus, 1999). Within savannas the major determinants of stomatal aperture (apart from normal diurnal patterns of opening and closing imposed by day/night transitions) are soil and atmospheric water content and temperature (Martin et al, 1994; Pitman, 1996; Eamus and Cole, 1997; Prior et al., 1997a; Franco, 1998). Most studies have found that stomatal conductance (G_s) is larger in the wet season than the dry season, and larger in the morning than the afternoon, especially in the dry season (Martin et al., 1994; Hogan et al., 1995; Pitman, 1996; Eamus and Cole, 1997; Prior et al., 1997a,b; Franco, 1998). Midday depressions of G_s are also evident in a range of species in both wet and dry seasons (Schulze et al., 1980; Meinzer et al., 1993; Fordyce et al., 1997).

It is possible to distinguish two causes for these patterns, one long-term and one short-term. First, there is the seasonal impact of changes in soil water content. As soil water availability declines as the dry season progresses, Ψ_{pd} also declines (Duff et al., 1997; Myers et al., 1997; Franco, 1998). Maximum G_s and Ψ_{pd} are negatively and linearly or curvilinearly correlated (Figure 7; Reich and Hinckley, 1989; Pitman, 1996; Fordyce et al., 1997; Myers et al., 1997; Prior et al., 1997a,b). Second, there is a daily and seasonal response of stomata to the increasing leaf-to-air vapour pressure difference (LAVPD) that occurs diurnally and seasonally (see below).

There are two mechanisms coupling soil water availability and G_s. First, drying soils cause increased synthesis of ABA in roots and subsequent transport in the transpiration stream to leaves, where stomata close in response to increased supply of ABA (Gowing et al., 1993; Loewenstein and Pallardy, 1998; Thomas and Eamus, 1999). Foliar and xylem ABA contents are correlated with G_s (Gowing et al., 1993; Thomas and Eamus, 1999). Second, as soil water availability declines, the water column in the xylem is put under increasing tension and xylem cavitation can occur (see section V.C). Declines in stem hydraulic conductivity as pre-dawn leaf potential declined have been observed in *Eucalyptus tetrodonta*, an evergreen tree of north Australian savannas (Thomas and Eamus, 1999), and in several other tree species (Franks et al., 1995; Williams et al., 1997a).

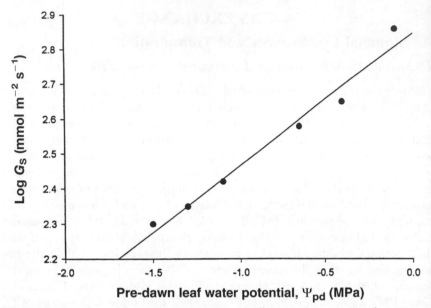

Fig. 7. As the dry season progresses, Ψ_{pd} declines and consequently stomatal conductance (G_s) declines in a range of north Australian savanna species. Redrawn from Eamus and Cole (1997).

Similarly a reduction in stem hydraulic conductivity can reduce G_s (Sperry and Pockman, 1993). It is possible that increased embolism and decreased stem hydraulic conductivity as pre-dawn water potential declines through the dry season is a simple mechanism by which G_s can be simultaneously coupled to a decline in both soil and atmospheric water content (Thomas and Eamus, 1999). However, this is not readily reversible and is unlikely to account for diurnal patterns of stomatal behaviour.

A cause of the decline in G_s observed between morning and afternoon and wet and dry seasons is increased LAVPD. Stomata close as LAVPD increases, and LAVPD increases between morning and afternoon and between wet and dry seasons. Stomatal conductance may decline linearly or log-linearly as LAVPD increases (Olivares and Medina, 1992; Verhoef *et al.*, 1996; Eamus and Cole, 1997; Prior *et al.*, 1997b; Thomas and Eamus, 1999). Meinzer *et al.* (1997) showed there were strong, species-specific correlations between G_s and vapour pressure difference from leaf to boundary layer, but not from leaf-to-bulk air vapour pressure difference. Most importantly, the relationship between canopy conductance and leaf-to-bulk air vapour pressure difference for the four species studied collapsed to one relationship describing all species when canopy conductance was normalized by the ratio of leaf area to sapwood area (approximately equivalent to the inverse of the Huber value; see section III.C.8).

The response function of stomata to increasing LAVPD varies with plant water status (Prior *et al.*, 1997a; Thomas and Eamus, 1999). The slope of the relationship between $\log G_s$ and LAVPD increased between mid-wet season and early dry season in *E. tetrodonta* saplings in a north Australian savanna. During this period pre-dawn water potential declined from > -0.5 MPa to between -0.5 and -1.5 MPa (Prior *et al.*, 1997a). Similarly, Thomas and Eamus (1999) showed that drought increased stomatal sensitivity to LAVPD, possibly through a change in the ratio of leaf area to root biomass.

Declines in G_s as soil or atmospheric water content decline may not always be sufficient to reduce transpiration (Monteith, 1995). In well-watered plants there are three response regions in the relationship between G_s and transpiration rate (E; Figure 8). Note that in Figure 8, the data points in region C were obtained for low values of LAVPD, in region A, moderate values of LAVPD were imposed, and for region C, large values of LAVPD were imposed. As one moves along the line joining the points from region C to B, LAVPD is increasing in steps of approximately 0.5 kPa. In region C, which is obtained for low values of LAVPD, E is not regulated by stomata and, as LAVPD increases, E increases approximately proportionally. This is made possible by the fact that the hydraulic architecture of the plant is sufficient to supply water at rates that support

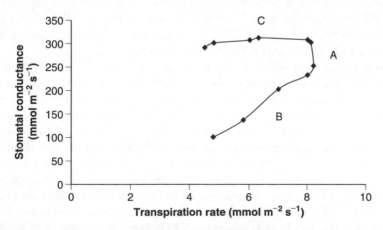

Fig. 8. Stomatal conductance (G_s) shows three response regions to increasing transpiration rate. In region C G_s is unresponsive to increasing transpiration rate; in region A it decreases slightly while E remains constant, and in region B it declines significantly, causing E to decline substantially also. Reproduced from Thomas and Eamus (1999).

this value of E. In region A, at intermediate values of LAVPD, a transition occurs in stomatal responses such that aperture declines in proportion to increasing LAVPD and E is constant. At larger values of LAVPD, stomata respond in a 'feedforward' manner (see Farquhar and Cowan, 1977; Thomas and Eamus, 1999) such that E declines with increasing LAVPD. Thomas and Eamus (1999) have shown that, as drought develops in E. *tetrodonta*, region C is lost first, then region A, so that eventually the entire response of G_s to increasing LAVPD is confined to region B. There is, therefore, an interaction between plant water status and LAVPD in determining stomatal responses to LAVPD.

Pitman (1996) studied stomatal behaviour of *Hopea ferrea*, an evergreen canopy emergent of tropical dry evergreen forests in Thailand. He adopted the empirical approach of Jarvis (1976) to model responses of G_s to changes in light flux density, temperature, soil water potential and LAVPD, and determined the sensitivity of G_s to changes in these variables. Good agreement between the modelled and observed values of G_s were obtained for periods of high and low soil water availability. He concluded that light flux density was the major determinant of G_s, followed by soil water potential. Unlike most other studies, he found little response of G_s to LAVPD. However, there are two reasons for this anomaly. First, the range of LAVPD experienced was very small ($<2.0\,\text{kPa}$). It is likely that, had a larger range of LAVPD been used, a response for G_s would have been observed (Thomas and Eamus, 1999). Second, he pooled all the data that were collected between 06.00 and 18.30 h. During this time there are significant changes in light flux density, LAVPD and temperature. If only data from 10.00 to 15.00 h had been used, when temperature and light flux density are more consistent, a response to LAVPD may have been observed.

Some patterns of differential sensitivity of stomata of evergreen and deciduous species to changes in Ψ_{pd} and LAVPD have been noted. Stomata were more sensitive to declining Ψ_{pd} in deciduous trees than in evergreen trees (Myers *et al.*, 1997). This pattern possibly reflects the fact that leaves of evergreen species must tolerate lower Ψ_{pd} than leaves of deciduous trees during the dry season, and that to gain the benefit of maintaining leaves in the dry season requires the stomata to remain open as Ψ_{pd} declines. By contrast, stomatal sensitivity to increasing LAVPD may be greater in evergreen than in deciduous species (Myers *et al.*, 1997). This may reflect the fact that deciduous trees maintain leaves only during the wet season when LAVPDs are low. In addition, payback time (leaf lifespan) for deciduous leaves to fix carbon is relatively short, and they may compensate by having stomata that can remain open as much as possible in the wet season by being relatively insensitive to LAVPD.

2. Coupling of Transpiration to Atmospheric Conditions

Transpiration can be a major pathway for the discharge of groundwater. Global demand for clean water and hence utilization of groundwater increases annually. The sustainable management of groundwater resources requires knowledge of the role of vegetation in catchment hydrology.

A priori reasoning suggests that water use by trees should decline in the dry season because (a) water availability in the upper soil profile declines in the dry season; (b) G_s is lower in the dry season than in the wet season (see above); and (c) there is a decline in leaf area per tree. This decline can be 100% for deciduous trees and up to 30% for evergreen trees (Williams et al., 1997b). Leaf-scale measurements support this a priori reasoning. Sobrado (1996) observed a decline in transpiration rate, E, of up to 50% in an evergreen tree in Venezuelan savanna while Prior et al. (1997a,b) observed a 40–70% decline in transpiration between wet and dry seasons. However, in these cases, E was calculated from leaf-scale measurements of G_s using portable porometers. Such measurements routinely overestimate E by up to 10-fold (Mulkey et al., 1996) and do not take into account seasonal changes in leaf area per tree, the influence of the boundary layer on E and within-canopy variation in microclimate and hence E from leaves. Partitioning of the control of transpiration into stomatal and boundary layer conductances show the importance of the boundary layer (Meinzer et al., 1997). Leaf-scale estimates of E can be significantly improved if the LAVPD of the boundary layer, rather than the bulk air, is used to calculate E (Meinzer et al., 1997).

There are few estimates of whole-tree water use in savannas or dry tropical forests (but see section D below). For example, a recent review of 52 studies presented data for a range of tropical rainforest species but no savanna species (Wullschleger et al., 1998). Transpiration of several species of tropical tree, measured using sapflow techniques during an unusually wet dry season in Panama, ranged from 0.6 to 2.8 mmol m^{-2} s^{-1} (Meinzer et al., 1997). Unfortunately seasonal patterns were not shown.

In contrast to estimates of E derived from leaf-scale measurements, measurements based on sapflow techniques of whole-tree water use by evergreens showed little variation between seasons (O'Grady et al., 1999). There are several reasons for this unexpected result. First, the proportional decline in leaf area per tree is equal to the proportional increase in LAVPD between the wet and dry season. Second, storage of water in the top 6 m of soil is sufficient to account for the rate of water use in the dry season (Cook et al., 1998) and therefore water availability is not limiting E despite a very dry upper 1 m soil profile. Finally, stomata of many species of tree do not close sufficiently to prevent increased E as LAVPD increased (see above), except when drought stress is experienced or

LAVPD is very large. In aerodynamically rough canopies (such as open forests and woodlands), E should be closely coupled to LAVPD if soil water is not limiting (Jarvis and McNaughton, 1986).

O'Grady et al. (1999) showed there was no difference in rate of transpiration per leaf area between two species of evergreens. This conclusion can be extended to five species in the savannas of north Australia (A.P. O'Grady, personal communication). Similarly, Meinzer et al. (1997) concluded that transpiration rates, when normalized by branch-specific ratio of leaf area to sapwood area (inverse of Huber value), did not differ between four contrasting species in a tropical Panamanian forest. Similarly, Andrade et al. (1998) showed that stomatal conductance in five disparate tree species growing in a seasonally dry forest responded similarly to variation in total soil–tree hydraulic conductance. These results suggest that large-scale modelling of water use by savanna vegetation may not require excessively large numbers of measurements of large numbers of species. It is likely that water use per sapwood area of savanna vegetation, on a large scale, does not differ between species, and only varies with time of day, season, stand density and soil characteristics, all of which can be measured remotely. It is also likely, at the canopy scale, that canopy conductance responses to LAVPD are essentially species independent (Granier et al., 1996; Meinzer et al., 1997).

The relative effects of stomatal conductance and boundary layer conductance can be evaluated from the dimensionless decoupling coefficient, Ω. A high value (close to 1) of Ω indicates that boundary layer conductance is low, and that changes in G_s have little effect on transpiration, so that transpiration is mostly determined by radiation. A low value (close to zero) indicates that transpiration varies almost in direct proportion to G_s. In Panamanian lowland tropical forest, G_s was often equal to or larger than boundary conductance so that E was strongly uncoupled from the bulk atmospheric VPD (Meinzer et al., 1995, 1997). Here Ω ranged from 0.82 to 0.9. In a number of broadleaf tropical forests, estimates of Ω varied between 0.6 and 0.9, while in small individuals of forest gap pioneers in Panama, Ω was about 0.6–0.8 (Meinzer et al., 1995, 1997). These systems have a relatively high LAI (≥ 2). This compares with values of around 0.1 for needle-leaved, aerodynamically rough coniferous trees (Jarvis and McNaughton, 1986). In savannas, with well-spaced trees, relatively low canopy density, and small rather than large leaves, Ω is likely to be low (<0.5) because the ratio of canopy conductance to boundary layer conductance is low. It is also likely that dry-season values of Ω will be lower than wet-season values because of the decline in average stomatal conductance in the dry season.

San Jose et al. (1998) showed that Ω varied between 0.03 and 0.58 over a typical non-rainy wet season day in the Orinoco Llanos of Venezuela, and this variability was because of changes in the ratio of aerodynamic conductance to surface conductance over the day. The low values of Ω show that transpiration is well coupled to atmospheric VPD and that changes in both stomatal conductance and VPD do have a large impact on transpiration rate. Similarly, Miranda et al. (1997) estimate values of Ω of 0.32 and 0.17 in the wet and dry seasons, respectively. They also conclude that there is significant control of transpiration through stomatal aperture.

For a closed canopy of a cultivated grass (*Brachiara decumbens*) in the Orinoco Llanos of Venezuela, evapotranspiration flux density was mainly driven by net radiation, particularly when net radiation exceeded $400 \, W \, m^{-2}$ (San Jose et al., 1998a). Such poor coupling of canopy transpiration to atmospheric VPD is to be expected for short, closed canopies (Jarvis and McNaughton, 1986).

In a number of ecosystems, stomata behave in a manner to ensure that vapour phase conductance and hydraulic (liquid phase) conductance are balanced. Consequently leaf water potential is maintained within narrow limits, despite significant changes in soil and atmospheric water content (Kuppers, 1984; Sperry and Pockman, 1993; Meinzer et al., 1995). It appears likely that these principles also apply to savannas.

B. Hysteresis in G_s and Transpiration

Hysteresis in stomatal behaviour in leaf-scale studies in the lab has been observed for the past 30 years. In temperate zones, hysteresis has been observed in the relationship between sapflux and leaf water potential in *Eucalyptus marginata* trees of Western Australia and in cool-temperate wetland species (Takagi et al., 1998). However, only recently has hysteresis been observed in tropical, seasonally dry vegetation. Pitman (1996) observed hysteresis in the relationship between G_s and three environmental variables, namely, solar irradiance, temperature and VPD. The degree of hysteresis was largest for all three variables when soil moisture content was largest. This is in contrast to the data of O'Grady et al. (1999), who showed that the degree of hysteresis between transpiration rate and LAVPD was largest in the dry season. Hysteresis in transpiration and LAVPD (and hence the behaviour of stomata) is likely to be caused by (a) the decline in the contribution of water stored in the stem with time during the day; (b) the decline in soil–root–leaf hydraulic conductivity with time during the day; or (c) a combination of (a) and (b). The cause of the disparity between Pitman's and O'Grady's data remains unknown, but differences in the contribution of water stored in the stem may contribute. Water stored in stems of trees in a tropical seasonal Panamanian forest accounted for 9–15% of daily water transpired (Goldstein et al., 1998). This stored water regulated the water status of leaves that were exposed to large diurnal variation in evaporative demand (Goldstein *et al.*, 1998). In addition, the rate of change of LAVPD may differ between Pitman's and O'Grady's sites. Such differences were able to account for day-to-day differences in the degree of hysteresis in cool-temperate wetland trees (Takagi *et al.*, 1998).

C. Photosynthesis

An understanding of the carbon cycle of ecosystems is fundamental to the complete understanding of the functioning of any ecosystem. In addition the Kyoto protocol requires governments, as signatories, to quantify the amount of carbon in and moving through major ecosystems. An important step in this quantification is an understanding of the photosynthetic characteristics of an ecosystem, including information on patterns of daily and seasonal change in C assimilation.

1. Daily and Seasonal Patterns of C Assimilation

Assimilation rates of savanna species are larger in the wet season than in the dry season, and in the dry season assimilation rates are usually larger in the morning than in the afternoon (Hogan *et al.*, 1995; Le Roux and Mordelet, 1995; Sobrado, 1996; Eamus and Cole, 1997; Prior *et al*, 1997a; Franco, 1998). Such behaviour is a function of declining soil water content, supra-optimal leaf temperature and increasing LAVPD. (Stomatal responses to humidity should be considered in relation to LAVPD since this, rather than VPD, provides the driving force for water loss from leaves. Leaf temperature is frequently higher than air temperature, especially when stomatal conductance is low and transpirational cooling reduced. At such times, LAVPD can be considerably higher than VPD.)

As soil or atmospheric water content declines, stomatal conductance is reduced (see section V.A, above). This will limit assimilation by reducing the supply of CO_2 to chloroplasts. This was demonstrated in four Australian savanna species by the decline in the ratio of CO_2 concentration inside the leaf (C_i) to the CO_2 concentration of ambient air outside the leaf (C_a) between morning and afternoon in the wet season (Eamus and Cole, 1997). Such changes in C_i/C_a ratio are indicative of non-stomatal limitations to photosynthesis (Lauer and Boyer, 1992). However, additional factors, especially in the dry season, can reduce photosynthetic rate independently of reduced stomatal conductance. Leaf temperature can become supra-optimal for photosynthesis, particularly when soil water availability is low and transpirational cooling is reduced (Prior *et al.*, 1997a). In saplings of the savanna tree *Eucalyptus tetrodonta*, high leaf temperatures at the end of the dry season could account for a 16% decline in assimilation rates in the afternoon compared with the morning, independent of changes in C_i (Prior et al., 1997a). Similarly, Sharkey (1984) has shown that high transpiration rates per se are able to reduce photosynthesis independently of stomatal conductance.

Midday depression of assimilation occurs in many species, especially those subject to any combination of high temperature, high radiation loads and low atmospheric and soil water content, as commonly occurs in seasonally dry ecosystems (Fordyce et al., 1997; Pathre et al., 1998). Causes of such a decline include feedback inhibition of assimilation through carbohydrate accumulation (Foyer, 1988), photoinhibition (Correia et al., 1990; Prior, 1997), decreased carboxylation efficiency (Demming-Adams et al., 1989) and increased LAVPD (Cowan and Farquhar, 1977; Fordyce et al., 1997). However, it is apparent that there is an interaction between temperature, LAVPD and photosynthetic photo flux density (PPFD) such that a high value of any two can significantly reduce assimilation rate. At low LAVPD, temperature appears to be the least significant factor in causing a decline in assimilation, and low LAVPD can significantly reduce the impact of high PPFD (Pathre et al., 1998). Thus LAVPD appears to be the dominant factor in causing midday declines in assimilation. Most, but not all, of this decline can be explained by the influence of reduced G_s on CO_2 supply.

Leaf age influences assimilation rate. Old leaves tend to have a reduced capacity for photosynthetic carbon gain and also have a reduced ability to regulate water loss (Reich, 1984; Reich and Borchert, 1988). In a study of Curatella americana, an evergreen tree of Venezuela, assimilation rates were lowest in young expanding leaves and in old mature or senescing leaves (Sobrado, 1996). Interestingly, foliar nitrogen concentrations declined approximately linearly as leaves aged and specific leaf area (SLA; leaf area/dry weight, $m^2 g^{-1}$) also decreased with leaf age. Consequently there was not a simple clear relationship between assimilation rate and foliar nitrogen content (mass basis). Loss of nitrogen with leaf age is a common response before senescence and is a principal cause of the decrease in photosynthetic capacity observed in older leaves. Increased C_i/C_a ratio with declining assimilation rate provides strong evidence that a decreased biochemical capacity for photosynthesis occurs as leaves age (Martin et al., 1994).

Assimilation rate and stomatal conductance declined more rapidly with leaf age in deciduous species compared to evergreen species in 18 species of Costa Rican tropical deciduous forest (Martin et al., 1994). For deciduous species, the decline in photosynthetic rate of deciduous leaves was attributed both to leaf age (senescence) and the onset of drought. There was little evidence of an age-related decline in photosynthetic rate for evergreen species, especially those growing on moist sites, in the early dry season (Martin et al., 1994). Specific leaf area decreases with leaf age (Sobrado, 1996; Prior, 1997) and Martin et al. (1994) expressed all assimilation data on a leaf area basis. Therefore the differences in photosynthetic rate between old and young leaves observed by Martin et al. (1994) may underestimate differences in photosynthetic rate expressed on a dry weight basis. These results support the conclusions of Reich et al. (1991), who showed that age-related decline in assimilation rate was more pronounced in short-lived (i.e. deciduous) leaves than in long-lived leaves.

The season during which leaves expand may influence their photosynthetic and stomatal performance. Leaves that flush and expand at the end of the wet season experience conditions of high light flux density and large LAVPD, in contrast to leaves that flush and expand in the late dry/ early wet. Long-lived leaves will experience the full range of environmental conditions and therefore leaf-scale adaptations (e.g. differences in SLA; N content) will be small, in contrast to short-lived leaves, where one population may experience predominantly dry season conditions and another population experience wet season conditions. Consequently leaf-scale adaptations are larger in short-lived species (Kitajima et al., 1997). Thus Kitajima et al. (1997) observed that photosynthetic rate (expressed on an area basis) of leaves emerging in the late wet season (measured in the dry season) was larger than that of leaves emerging in the early wet and measured in the wet season. Furthermore, the difference between these two populations of leaves increased as leaf lifespan decreased. Differences in SLA were able to account for these differences. Allocation of N per unit dry mass did not differ between populations of leaves. It is pertinent to note that this is the only study in which the rate of light-saturated assimilation is larger in the dry season than in the wet season and it remains to be seen whether such seasonal differences in leaf characteristics are a common phenomenon.

Stomatal sensitivity to LAVPD, of leaves that developed in the dry season, was significantly larger than for those that developed in the wet season (Thomas and Eamus, 1999). Leaves of two tropical grasses, exposed to different levels of atmospheric water content during development, similarly differed in stomatal sensitivity to LAVPD (Kawamitsu et al., 1993).

2. Phenological Comparisons

In both tropical and temperate environments, deciduous species have a larger photosynthetic rate per unit dry weight than evergreen species (Chabot and Hicks, 1982; Reich et al., 1992; Prado and De Moraes, 1997; Eamus and Prichard, 1998; Table 4). However, because deciduous species

Table 4

A summary of some of the recently published data for light-saturated assimilation rate (A_{max}; expressed on a dry weight or area basis), specific leaf area (SLA) and foliar nitrogen content for a number of deciduous (Decid), semi-deciduous (SD), evergreen (E green) and unknown phenology (?) species of seasonally dry woodlands and forests. Data are for wet season periods

Species	Type	A_{max} (μ mol g^{-1} s^{-1})	SLA (m^2 g^{-1}) $\times 10^{-1}$	A_{max} (μmol m^{-2} s^{-1})	N content (mg g^{-1})	Reference
Calycophyllum candidissimum	Decid			4		Martin *et al.* (1994)
Cordia alliodora	Decid			6		Martin *et al.* (1994)
Guazuma ulmifolia	Decid			5		Martin *et al.* (1994)
Luehea candida	Decid			5		Martin *et al.* (1994)
Myrospermum	Decid			8		Martin *et al.* (1994)
Apeiba tibourbou	Decid			1		Martin *et al.* (1994)
Astronium graveolens	Decid			2		Martin *et al.* (1994)
Tabebuia ochracea	Decid			0.3		Martin *et al.* (1994)
Cassia emarginata	Decid			3		Martin *et al.* (1994)
Tabebuia rosea	Decid			2.7		Martin *et al.* (1994)
Jacquina pungens	Decid			11		Martin *et al.* (1994)
Pseudobombax septenatum	Decid	0.0103	0.1493	8		Hogan *et al.* (1995)
Godmania macrocarpa	Decid	0.0083	0.18		23.6	Medina and Francisco (1994)
Cochlospermum fraseri	Decid	0.0199	0.2676		17.7	Eamus *et al.* (1999b)
Planchonia careya	Decid	0.0101	0.10908		13.5	Eamus *et al.* (1999b)
Terminalia ferdinandiana	Decid	0.0102	0.10914		13.6	Eamus *et al.* (1999b)
Erythrophleum chlorostachis	SD	0.0109	0.14824		22	Eamus *et al.* (1999b)
Eucalyptus clavigera	SD	0.0072	0.0864		10.4	Eamus *et al.* (1999b)
Xanthostemum paradoxus	SD	0.0125	0.14875		11	Eamus *et al.* (1999b)
Humboldtiella arborea	Decid	0.0268	0.185		3.15	Sobrado (1991)
Mansoa verrucifera	Decid	0.0175	0.103		2.71	Sobrado (1991)
Lonchocarpus dipteroneurus	Decid	0.0242	0.227		4.08	Sobrado (1991)
Beureria cumanensis	Decid	0.0116	0.115		2.87	Sobrado (1991)
Pithecellobium dulce	Decid	0.0151	0.134		2.59	Sobrado (1991)
P. ligustrinum	Decid	0.0154	0.142		3.5	Sobrado (1991)
Planchonia careya	Decid	0.00904	0.1264		12	Eamus and Prichard (1998)
Terminalia ferdinandiana	Decid	0.0107	0.1513		15.8	Eamus and Prichard (1998)
Terminalia ferdinandiana	Decid	0.0175	0.1925		12.2	Prior *et al.* (1997b)
Mean for deciduous		**0.014**	**0.15**	**4.7**	**10.67**	
		±0.00136	±0.0107	±0.92	±1.75	

Table 4 (*Continued*)

Roupala montana	E'green	0.0102		13		Franco (1998)
Anacardium excelsum	E'green	0.0098	0.087924	10		Hogan et al. (1995)
Cecropia longipes	E'green	0.0124	0.12152	16		Hogan et al. (1995)
Didymopanax morototoni	E'green	0.011	0.1798	18		Hogan et al. (1995)
Ficus obtusifolia	E'green	0.0136	0.1518	16		Hogan et al. (1995)
Luehea seemannii	E'green	0.0099	0.141848	13		Hogan et al. (1995)
Curatella americana	E'green	0.011	0.1287		15.8	Medina and Francisco (1994)
Eucalyptus tetrodonta	E'green		0.1375		8.5	Prior et al. (1997a)
Andira inermis	E'green			9		Martin et al. (1994)
Cassia grandis	E'green			4.5		Martin et al. (1994)
Licania arborea	E'green			8		Martin et al. (1994)
Pithecollobium saman	E'green			10		Martin et al. (1994)
Psidium guajava	E'green			6		Martin et al. (1994)
Simarouba glauca	E'green			8.5		Martin et al. (1994)
Thouinidium decandrum	E'green			1.5		Martin et al. (1994)
Eucalyptus miniata	E'green	0.0081	0.13446		17	Eamus et al. (1999b)
Eucalyptus tetrodonta	E'green	0.0073	0.11169		9.1	Eamus et al. (1999b)
Curatella americana	E'green	0.011338	0.10771		17.7	Sobrado (1996)
Eucalyptus tetrodonta	E'green	0.00635	0.1045		6.8	Eamus and Prichard (1998)
Eulcayptus miniata	E'green	0.0074	0.1194		8.6	Eamus and Prichard (1998)
Allosyncarpia ternata	E'green	0.00921	0.0524		9.1	Fordyce et al. (1997)
Allosyncarpia ternata	E'green	0.00691	0.054		9.2	Fordyce et al. (1997)
Memora sp.	E'green	0.0078	0.058		2.05	Sobrado (1991)
Capparis verrucosa	E'green	0.0089	0.061		3.15	Sobrado (1991)
C. aristiguetae	E'green	0.0069	0.05		2.21	Sobrado (1991)
Morisonia americana	E'green	0.0068	0.054		2.62	Sobrado (1991)
Eperua obtusata	E'green	0.012658			13.4	Coomes and Grubb (1998)
Carraipa longipedicellata	E'green	0.010417			11.9	Coomes and Grubb (1998)
Iryanthera add. Ellipica	E'green	0.012048			10.3	Coomes and Grubb (1998)
Protium carolense	E'green	0.012048			12.5	Coomes and Grubb (1998)
Hevea pauciflora	E'green	0.016667			17.8	Coomes and Grubb (1998)
Parkia igneiflora	E'green	0.012821			12.7	Coomes and Grubb (1998)
Bombacopsis cf amazonica	E'green	0.009615			11.1	Coomes and Grubb (1998)
Mean for evergreen		**0.010** ±0.00051	**0.103** ±0.0095	**10.27** ±1.34	**10.08** ±1.12	

Table 4 (*Continued*)

Species	Type	A_{max} (μ mol g^{-1} s^{-1})	SLA (m^2 g^{-1}) × 10^{-1}	A_{max} (μmol m^{-2} s^{-1})	N content (mg g^{-1})	Reference
Aegiphyla lhotkhiana	?	0.008333	0.078	9.4		Prado et al. (1997)
Annona coriacea	?	0.006711	0.0624	9.3		Prado et al. (1997)
Aspidosperma tomentosum	?	0.007092	0.0723	10.2		Prado et al. (1997)
Bauhinia holophylla	?	0.006993	0.0727	10.4		Prado et al. (1997)
Bowdichia virgilioides	?	0.005952	0.0548	9.2		Prado et al. (1997)
Campomanesia aromatica	?	0.006711	0.0705	10.65		Prado et al. (1997)
Caryocar brasiliense	?	0.008475	0.0797	9.4		Prado et al. (1997)
Connarus suberosus	?	0.006711	0.0819	12.2		Prado et al. (1997)
Davilla rugosa	?	0.006024	0.0615	10.2		Prado et al. (1997)
Didymopanax vinosum	?	0.006757	0.1189	17.6		Prado et al. (1997)
Duguetia furfuracea	?	0.005988	0.0581	9.7		Prado et al. (1997)
Gochnatia floribunda	?	0.005952	0.0964	16.2		Prado et al. (1997)
Kielmeyera coriacea	?	0.004878	0.0512	10.5		Prado et al. (1997)
Miconia albicana	?	0.006536	0.0843	12.9		Prado et al. (1997)
Miconia ligustroides	?	0.007634	0.1069	14		Prado et al. (1997)
Piptocarpha rotundifolia	?	0.00625	0.1331	12.3		Prado et al. (1997)
Qualea dichotoma	?	0.006993	0.0762	10.9		Prado et al. (1997)
Styrax camporum	?	0.004762	0.0386	8.1		Prado et al. (1997)
Tibouchina stenocarpa	?	0.007353	0.1456	19.8		Prado et al. (1997)
Tocoyena formosa	?	0.006329	0.0411	6.5		Prado et al. (1997)

have thinner leaves than evergreen species, and there is less leaf tissue per unit leaf area (i.e. SLA is larger; Sobrado, 1991; Medina and Francisco, 1994; Reich *et al.*, 1995; Prado and De Moraes, 1997; Eamus and Prichard, 1998), photosynthetic rates per unit leaf area may be similar or lower in deciduous than evergreen species (Medina, 1984; Sarmiento *et al.*, 1985; Goldstein *et al.*, 1989; Prado and De Moraes, 1997; Eamus and Prichard, 1998).

The larger photosynthetic rate per unit dry weight of deciduous species results from a larger total investment in leaf N content in deciduous species (Medina and Francisco, 1994; Kitajima *et al.*, 1997; Prado and De Moraes, 1997; Eamus and Prichard, 1998; Table 4). A linear relationship between leaf N content (area or mass basis) and the rate of light-saturated photo-synthesis, A_{max} (area or mass basis), is generally observed (Evans, 1989; Reich *et al.*, 1992, 1994, 1995). Figure 9 shows that, for a range of tree species from a range of seasonally dry ecosystems, N content (mass basis) increases linearly with A_{max}, with no clear distinction between evergreen and deciduous species. The slope of the relationship for seasonally dry ecosystems (3.6) is within the range observed in a diverse range of natural ecosystems (slope 0.8–20; Reich *et al.*, 1991, 1992, 1994).

Nitrogen content (mass basis) increases with increasing SLA (Poorter and Evans, 1998). Consequently the assimilation rate (A) increases with

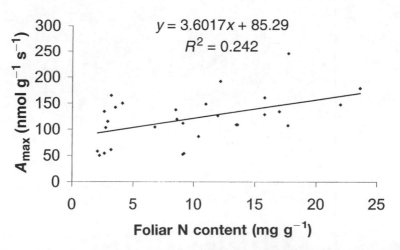

Fig. 9. There is a significant increase in light-saturated assimilation rate (A_{max}) as foliar N content increases. Data from Coomes and Grubb (1998), Hogan *et al.* (1995), Medina and Francisco (1994), Prior *et al.* (1997a,b), Prado and De Moraes (1997), Eamus *et al.* (1999b), Sobrado (1991, 1996), Eamus and Prichard (1998) and Fordyce *et al.* (1997).

increasing SLA. In an analysis of a range of tree species from several seasonally dry ecosystems, deciduous and evergreen trees occur at opposite ends of a single relationship (Figure 10; Table 4) between maximum assimilation rate and SLA. The slope of the relationship describing the log–log plot of assimilation and SLA (0.86) is similar to that observed in a diverse range of ecosystems (Reich et al., 1992, 1994; Reich and Walters, 1994).

The ratio of A_{max} to N content (both on a mass basis, known as photosynthetic nitrogen use efficiency, PNUE; Poorter and Evans, 1998) varies according to soil nutrient availability (Reich et al., 1995), life-form (Field and Mooney, 1986) and phenologies (Sobrado, 1991; Medina and Francisco, 1994). Assimilation rate increases with increasing investment of N in photosynthetic apparatus (Evans, 1989; Medina and Francisco, 1994; Figure 9). Photosynthetic nitrogen use efficiency also increases with SLA (Poorter and Evans, 1998; Figure 11). However, there appears to be no consistent pattern of PNUE for deciduous and evergreen species. In a detailed study of PNUE for deciduous and evergreen species in southern Wisconsin, USA, Reich et al. (1995) observed that the slope of the relationship between photosynthesis and foliar N content (mass or area basis) was larger in broad-leaved deciduous species

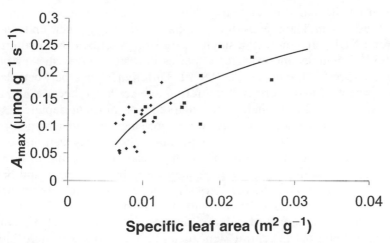

Fig. 10. There is a significant increase in light-saturated assimilation rate (A_{max}) as specific leaf area (SLA) increases. Data from Coomes and Grubb (1998), Hogan et al. (1995), Medina and Francisco (1994), Prior et al. (1997a,b), Prado and De Moraes (1997), Eamus et al. (1999b), Sobrado (1991, 1996), Eamus and Prichard (1998) and Fordyce et al. (1997). Evergreen (diamonds) and deciduous (squares) species tend to occur at opposite ends of the regression.

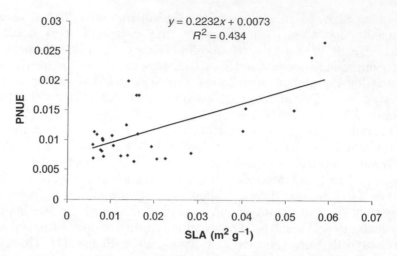

Fig. 11. There is a significant increase in photosynthetic nitrogen use efficiency (PNUE) as specific leaf area (SLA) increases. Data from Coomes and Grubb (1998), Hogan *et al.* (1995), Medina and Francisco (1994), Prior *et al.* (1997a,b), Prado and De Moraes (1997), Eamus *et al.* (1999b), Sobrado (1991, 1996), Eamus and Prichard (1998) and Fordyce *et al.* (1997).

than in needle-leafed evergreens. They concluded that species with long leaf lifespans and low SLA tend to have lower A_{max} per unit leaf N (lower PNUE). In contrast, a single regression described the relationship for both deciduous and evergreen species in a study of north Australian savanna species (Eamus *et al.*, 1999b). Different slopes between deciduous, broadleaf and evergreen coniferous species arose because the conifers were found on, and were adapted to, nutrient-depleted soils, whereas the deciduous species were growing on nutrient-rich soils (Reich *et al.*, 1995). In the north Australian study, evergreen and deciduous species co-occur and do not occupy locations differing in nutrient availability, consequently the same relationship between A_{max} and N was observed (Eamus and Prichard, 1998). Similar variability exists within two Venezuelan studies. Photosynthetic nitrogen use efficiency was higher in the dominant deciduous species on a Venezuelan savanna (Sobrado, 1991) but in central Venezuela, PNUE was lower in deciduous species than in evergreen (Medina and Francisco, 1994). It is likely that local conditions (soil nutrient and water availability, micro-climate) are more important determinants of PNUE than phenology. In a plot of PNUE against SLA, deciduous and evergreen species occur on the same line (Figure 11).

D. Relationships between Carbon Gain and Water Loss

1. Instantaneous Transpiration Efficiency

The ratio of instantaneous assimilation rate to transpiration rate yields the instantaneous transpiration efficiency (ITE; often mistakenly referred to as water-use-efficiency (WUE); Eamus, 1991). A large ITE represents an optimization response in water-limited environments.

Eamus et al. (1999a) found that instantaneous transpiration efficiency in eight evergreen, semi-deciduous and deciduous species in a northern Australian savanna was largest in the dry season, and lower in the wet season or after initial rains at the end of the dry season (Eamus et al., 1999a). Similarly, ITE in the Venezuelan evergreen Curatella americana was higher in the dry than in the wet season, particularly in old leaves (Sobrado, 1996).

In northern Australia, in saplings of both Eucalyptus tetrodonta (evergreen) and Terminalia ferdinandiana (deciduous), ITE was higher in the transitional periods (when Ψ_{pd} values were between −0.5 and −1.5 MPa) than during the wet season (Prior et al., 1997a,b). During the driest period ($\Psi_{pd} < −1.5$ MPa), when only the evergreen species had leaves, ITE was the same as in the transitional period in the morning, but declined markedly in the afternoon. This was due to both very high leaf temperatures (supra-optimal for photosynthesis) and high LAVPDs. Interestingly, stomata were most responsive to LAVPD during the transitional period. During the wet season, LAVPDs were uniformly low, and G_s high, while during the late dry season, G_s was consistently low due to severe soil drought. During the wet season, ITE was similar for both species, but was lower in the deciduous species during the transition periods, when leaves had started to senesce.

Drought stress may also lead to decreases in ITE. For Acacia auriculiformis in northern Australia, ITE decreased markedly between the mid-wet and the dry seasons, mostly due to large increases in LAVPD causing large increases in transpiration (Cole, 1994). Similarly, Franco (1998) showed that the decrease in G_s of an evergreen tree in a Brazilian savanna in the dry season was smaller than the decrease in A, consequently ITE declined. Part of the reason for this was the differential impact of leaf age on G_s and A. As leaves age ITE generally declines because the ability of stomata to regulate water loss is lost to a larger extent than the ability to fix carbon (Reich and Borchert, 1988; Martin et al., 1994; Franco, 1998). In addition, leaf ageing usually coincides with increasing LAVPD, and hence greater transpirational loss for a given G_s.

Some studies have found higher ITE in deciduous than in evergreen species (Sobrado, 1991; Medina and Francisco, 1994; Eamus and Prichard, 1998), but others have found ITE to be similar for both phenological guilds (Goldstein *et al.*, 1989; Martin *et al.*, 1994; Prior *et al.*, 1997a,b; Eamus *et al.*, 1999a). High ITE represents an optimization response of resource use in water-limiting environments. Evergreen woody species may be less limited by water availability (Myers *et al.*, 1997) because of extensive and deep root systems that provide water for plant use during the dry season, whereas deciduous woody species have shallower roots (Canadell *et al.*, 1996). It could also be argued that for most of the time that deciduous trees photosynthesize, conditions are wet and there is little need to optimize water use.

Higher ITE in deciduous trees is not consistent with the predictions of Lloyd and Farquhar (1994), who propose that species with short-lived leaves should have a larger $\delta E/\delta A$ (and hence a lower ITE) than species with longer-lived leaves ($\delta E/\delta A$ is the marginal unit water cost of plant carbon gain (see Thomas *et al.*, 1999a,b), calculated as the ratio of the slopes of E against G_s to A against G_s; see section VIII.D). A central feature of the Lloyd and Farquhar (1994) analyses, apart from the assumption that stomata optimize their behaviour, was the use of $C_i : C_a$ ratio to calculate $\delta E/\delta A$. It has been extensively shown that the $C_i : C_a$ ratio can decrease with increasing LAVPD if the proportional closure of stomata is larger than that of the decline in assimilation, but it can also increase if the opposite occurs (Eamus and Cole, 1997; Prior *et al.*, 1997a). Therefore the use of the $C_i : C_a$ ratio as an indicator of optimal behaviour of stomata may lead to errors in savanna systems.

2. Isotope Discrimination

Instantaneous leaf-scale values may not truly reflect whole-plant leaf lifespan water use efficiency (WUE). In contrast, ^{13}C leaf discrimination values – which show the extent to which leaves discriminate against the heavy (^{13}C) isotope of carbon – may more accurately represent leaf WUE over the lifetime of the leaf (Farquhar *et al.*, 1989). In an early study of ^{13}C leaf discrimination values, Goldstein *et al.* (1989) found no significant differences in $\delta^{13}C$ (the ratio of ^{13}C to ^{12}C compared with an international standard) between five evergreen and three deciduous species of a Venezuelan llanos. Typical $\delta^{13}C$ ranged between -26.74 and $-30.23‰$. Similarly they could find no significant differences in ITE.

Medina and Francisco (1994) showed that, for two species of savanna trees, $\delta^{13}C$ values tended to increase (become less negative) as the dry season progressed. An increase in $\delta^{13}C$ values is indicative of a larger WUE of the leaves. Furthermore, young leaves showed consistently larger WUE than old leaves, a result in agreement with those of Martin *et al.* (1994).

In a recent study across a rainfall gradient (from $1800\,mm\,yr^{-1}$ to $216\,mm\,yr^{-1}$) in northern Australia, Schulze *et al.* (1998) observed no trend in community carbon isotope discrimination (Δ, which is negatively related to WUE; see Farquhar *et al.*, 1989) as annual rainfall decreased from 1800 mm to 450 mm. However, as rainfall declined further, Δ decreased (WUE increased). This contrasts with the results of Stewart *et al.* (1989), who observed linearly declining Δ as rainfall decreased from 1700 mm to 350 mm. Unfortunately Stewart *et al.* (1989) pooled data for trees and shrubs, so this study is not directly comparable with that of Schulze *et al.* (1998).

Deciduous trees have a larger SLA and a larger N concentration than evergreen trees (Sobrado, 1991; Reich *et al*, 1995; Eamus and Prichard, 1998; Schulze *et al.*, 1998). Nitrogen, SLA and assimilation are tightly linked and an expectation that this would be reflected in Δ was partially supported (Schulze *et al.*, 1998). Carbon isotope discrimination increased with increasing N content (mass basis) and increasing SLA. Clearly, deciduous trees have high SLA and high N content (mass basis). These features support a high assimilation rate, which requires a large stomatal conductance to support a large CO_2 influx. Consequently the transpiration rate tends to be large and WUE may potentially be low (and consequently Δ is large).

3. Optimization Theory

Cowan and Farquhar (1977) proposed that stomata behave in a manner such that the sensitivities of the rates of transpiration (E) and C assimilation (A) to changes in conductance (G_s) (i.e. $(\delta E/\delta G)/(\delta A/\delta G)$) remain constant. This occurs if the marginal unit water cost of carbon gain ($\delta E/\delta A$) is a constant (Cowan and Farquhar, 1977). Several tests of this theory have shown $\delta E/\delta A$ to be reasonably constant over a day or two (Mooney and Chu, 1983; Williams, 1983; Lloyd, 1991; Berninger and Hari, 1993). However, several data sets reveal significant variation in $\delta E/\delta A$ (Grieu *et al.*, 1988; Guehl *et al.*, 1991). Savannas represent a highly pertinent environment within which to test optimization theories because of the occurrence of very large annual fluctuations in soil and atmospheric water content.

Lloyd and Farquhar (1994), using a simplified method for calculating $\delta E/\delta A$, observed that biomes with consistently high water availability had a good linear relationship between inferred $\delta E/\delta A$ and mean LAVPD experienced during photosynthesis. Thus, tropical forests, drought-deciduous forests, temperate evergreen forests, mangroves and tundra all fell on the same line (Lloyd and Farquhar, 1994). However, in biomes where evaporative demand is high and water availability is periodic (savannas, seasonal forests), a high $\delta E/\delta A$ (non-conservative water use; $\delta E/\delta A > 1000$) is the most successful strategy to adopt. When evaporative demand is high and water availability is episodic, a low $\delta E/\delta A$ (conservative water use) is the optimal strategy. Plants with a rapid phenological development but short payback interval (i.e. deciduous trees in savannas) are predicted to have a less conservative strategy for water use (larger $\delta E/\delta A$) while plants with a slower phenological development over a longer period (evergreen species) should have a more conservative strategy for water use (smaller $\delta E/\delta A$) (Lloyd and Farquhar, 1994). Givnish (1986) has also proposed that absolute values of $\delta E/\delta A$ are associated with the hydraulic conductivity of the plant.

There has been only one study of stomatal optimization theory of savanna species (Thomas et al., 1999a,b). Several important features were apparent in this study. First, stomata did not behave in a manner that optimized $\delta E/\delta A$ when either LAVPD or soil moisture content was varied. As LAVPD increased, $\delta E/\delta A$ increased in all five species studied. Species occurring in more xeric conditions tended to show larger changes in $\delta E/\delta A$ than species growing in more mesic environments. The most deciduous species tended to have a smaller value of $\delta E/\delta A$ than the most evergreen species, in contradiction to the prediction by Lloyd and Farquhar (1994). However, the analyses of Lloyd and Farquhar (1994) assume that $\delta E/\delta A$ is constant, an assumption shown to be invalid (Thomas and Eamus, 1999).

As drought developed, Ψ_{pd} declined and G_s declined log-linearly (Thomas and Eamus, 1999). In addition, $\delta E/\delta A$ declined substantially. Furthermore, the rate of increase of $\delta E/\delta A$ as LAVPD increased was reduced as drought progressed (Thomas and Eamus, 1999). This decline in the rate of increase of $\delta E/\delta A$ presumably reflects a more conservative use of soil water as this availability declines and evaporative demand (LAVPD) increases.

E. Canopy- and Landscape-Scale CO_2 and H_2O Exchange Rates

1. Canopy Scale

Catchment- and regional-scale predictions of carbon and water fluxes require estimates of canopy-scale exchanges. Three methodologies may provide these estimates. First, canopy-scale fluxes of water can be assessed using sapflow measurements of individual trees followed by scaling up (Cook et al., 1998; O'Grady et al., 1999). Second, eddy covariance or Bowen ratio techniques (Grace et al., 1995; San Jose et al., 1998b; Tenhunen et al., 1998) can be applied to CO_2 and water fluxes. Finally, remotely sensed information using aircraft or satellite-mounted sensors can provide estimates of regional temperature and evapotranspiration (Running et al., 1989; Brunet et al., 1991), woodland and forest tree density and leaf area index, rates of photosynthesis, canopy chlorophyll and N contents, and other parameters (Field et al., 1994). Synthetic aperture radar data have been used for measurements of vegetation classification and for structural attributes of savanna woodlands (Ahmad et al., 1998).

Tropical forests in southwest Amazonia experience a mild, short dry season (Grace et al., 1995). Peak assimilation rates (expressed per unit ground area) measured using eddy covariance techniques were typically 15μmol m^{-2} s^{-1} in light-saturated conditions, a value remarkably close to values obtained from leaf-scale measurements of seasonally dry forests (see section V.C.1). Similarly bulk stomatal conductance of the canopy ranged from 0.4 to 1.0 mol m^{-2} s^{-1}, in agreement with leaf-scale measurements of seasonally dry forests.

Two field studies in the Amazon forest showed minimal variation in assimilation rate between seasons (Grace et al., 1995, 1996), although recent modelling suggests that reductions in dry season gas fluxes can occur in response to changes in soil water content and soil–root hydraulic resistance (Williams et al., 1997b). However, the degree of seasonality is small for their site because the dry season is short and the site receives frequent but low-intensity rainfall. In contrast, Miranda et al. (1997) observed large seasonal changes in gas exchange characteristics in nearby cerrado vegetation, where seasonality is much more pronounced. Thus canopy exchange rates (expressed per unit ground area) were 12 and 4μmol m^{-2} s^{-1} in the wet and dry season, respectively, and LAI decreased from 1 to 0.4. Apparent ecosystem quantum efficiency declined from wet to dry season (from 68 mol photon (mol C)$^{-1}$ to 77 mol photon (mol C)$^{-1}$). These values are considerably higher than comparable values for mixed deciduous hardwood forests in the USA (Wofsy et al., 1994), Brazilian rainforest (Grace et al., 1995) or Nothofagus forest of New Zealand (Hollinger et al., 1994). This is probably a function of the high degree of sclerophylly (Miranda et al., 1997). There was no influence of season upon the relationship between $C_i : C_a$ ratio and VPD (Miranda et al., 1997), in contrast to many leaf-scale studies (see section V.C.1). In the wet season, the cerrado vegetation was a net sink for CO_2 but for a brief period in the dry season it was a net source.

Verhoef et al. (1996) measured fluxes of CO_2 and H_2O over a deciduous savanna in Niger, west Africa, from the end of the wet season through to the middle of the dry season. Leaf stomatal conductance (measured with a porometer) declined after the cessation of rains as soil and atmospheric water content declined (see section V.A.1). Transpirational H_2O and photosynthetic CO_2 flux from/to the canopy showed peak values of about $6 \, \text{mmol m}^{-2} \text{s}^{-1}$ and $10 \, \mu\text{mol m}^{-2} \text{s}^{-1}$, respectively, shortly after the end of the wet season. Over the subsequent 15 days as G_s declined, transpiration and photosynthesis declined by 50%. Photosynthetic CO_2 flux linearly increased with increasing leaf-scale G_s, indicating a low Ω value for this sparsely wooded (LAI = 0.32) and low-lying (<3 m) savanna. This study showed that both VPD and soil moisture determined transpiration and rates of photosynthesis. Canopy quantum yield and maximum rates of photosynthesis declined with decreasing soil and atmospheric water content (Verhoef et al., 1996). Similar results were obtained by Monteny et al. (1997) for a similar site, where peak assimilation rates were approximately $12 \, \mu\text{mol m}^{-2} \text{s}^{-1}$. Declines in soil moisture after the end of the wet season resulted in a rapid decline in quantum yield and light-saturated rates of photosynthesis. Monteny et al. estimated that grasses represented 65% of the total evapotranspiration and that, as soil water content declined, more sensible heat was transferred to the atmosphere so that leaf temperature became supra-optimal for photosynthesis.

Half-hourly estimates of instantaneous transpiration use efficiency (ITE) of the Sahelian savanna declined curvilinearly as VPD increased (Verhoef et al., 1996). The clear relationship between VPD and ITE suggests that CO_2 fluxes can be predicted from a knowledge of VPD and E only (Verhoef et al., 1996). Interestingly, on a daily time frame, ITE was a linear function of VPD (and also soil water content), rather than a curvilinear function of VPD as observed when half-hourly averages were used. This is probably because of hysteresis in the response of G_s to VPD.

A comparison of eddy covariance measurements of CO_2 flux and model outputs for a Sahelian savanna in Niger, west Africa (Hanan et al., 1998), showed coefficients of determination of 0.8 when literature-based values for quantum yield and Rubisco (ribulose bisphosphase carboxylase) capacity were used in the model. However, when seasonal changes in these physiological parameters was accounted for, the coefficient of determination increased to 0.93. Physiological parameters controlling photosynthesis were highly seasonal, in contrast to the Jarvis functions used to describe G_s (Hanan and Prince, 1997). It was observed that, during the short wet season (100 days), peak rates of photosynthesis were as high as in more mesic ecosystems, but annual carbon sequestration was small because LAI was very low and the wet season was short. Thus leaf area duration (LAI × duration) and annual photosynthetic carbon uptake appear to be correlated (Hanan et al., 1998).

The patchy distribution of shrubs and trees of savannas introduces significant heterogeneity into spatial distributions of radiation, momentum and gas fluxes (Tuzet et al., 1997). Such spatial (and temporal, given the seasonality of soil water availability) variability must be accounted for in canopy-scale measures of water and CO_2 fluxes.

Tuzet *et al.* (1997) and D. Eamus, X. Chen, G. Kelley, A.P. O'Grady and L. Hutley (unpublished observations of roots in Northern Territory savannas) have shown that the partitioning of water and CO_2 fluxes between the woody and grass components of the vegetation varies according to soil water content. In the wet season, grasses can dominate total water and CO_2 flux, but trees and shrubs dominate in the dry season. Similarly the partitioning of available energy between sensible heat and evaporation varies between seasons such that in the wet season sensible heat and evaporation are approximately equal but in the dry season sensible heat exceeds evaporation (Miranda *et al.*, 1997).

F. Scaling Up to Landscapes

There is a significant relationship between LAI and canopy CO_2 exchange rate for a number of ecosystems (Figure 12). It is noteworthy that the few savanna sites that have been studied fit the same line as sites with LAI of

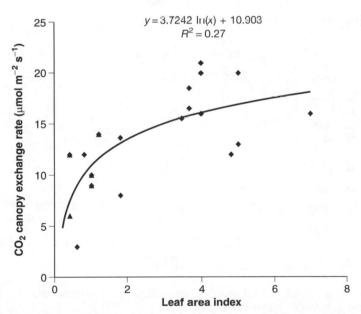

Fig. 12. As leaf area index (LAI) increases, the rate of CO_2 flux to the canopy increases. The diamonds are data from a wide range of ecosystems, and the triangles are savanna sites. The data have been taken from a wide range of sources.

over 6. Given the simple relationship between (foliar N content (mass basis)) $\times P/Et$ and LAI (Figure 13; equation from Baldocchi and Meyers, 1998), it is clear that canopy CO_2 exchange rate can be predicted from a knowledge of foliar N content (mass basis) and the ratio of precipitation to annual equilibrium evaporation, since:

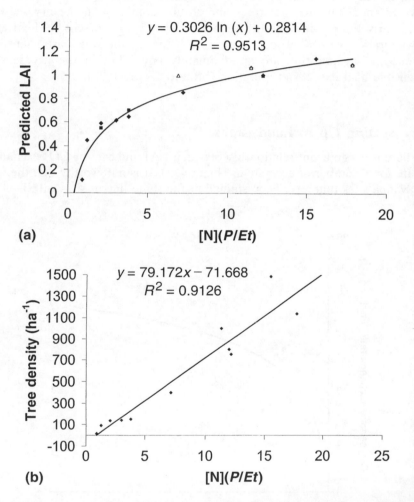

Fig. 13. Along a rainfall gradient of approximately 1600 mm, there is a clear relationship between either (a) leaf area index and [N](P/Et) or (b) tree density and [N](P/Et), where [N] is the foliar N content, P is the precipitation, Et is the potential evaporation. For Figure 13(a) data are recalculated from Schulze *et al.* (1998) (diamonds), Bowman (1996) (squares) and O'Grady *et al.* (1999) (triangles).

$$CO_2 \text{ flux} = 3.72 \times \ln{(LAI)} + 10.9$$

and

$$LAI = 0.3026 \times \ln{([N]P/Et)} + 0.2814$$

Therefore

$$CO_2 \text{ flux} = 3.72 \times \ln{(0.30 \times \ln{([N]P/Et)} + 0.2814)} + 10.9$$

This equation yields a prediction of peak growing season CO_2 flux for canopies over a large range of $[N]P/Et$ values, including those exhibited by seasonally dry woodlands and forests (Figure 13).

Savannas cover a land surface of approximately 15×10^{12} m^2 (Miranda et al., 1997). If we add xerophytic woodlands and other tropical seasonally dry ecosystems, the total land area covered is about 25×10^{12} m^2 (IPCC, 1995). Using eddy covariance data recently obtained during the wet, early dry and late dry seasons (Eamus et al., 2001) and integrated for net 24-hr total carbon fluxes, we obtained total annual C sequestration of $0.75 \, \text{t ha}^{-1} \, \text{yr}^{-1}$ (or $6.2 \, \text{mol C m}^{-2} \, \text{yr}^{-1}$). This compares well with $0.32 \, \text{t ha}^{-1} \, \text{yr}^{-1}$ for a Sahelian fallow savanna (Hanan et al., 1998) and $2-5 \, \text{t ha}^{-1} \, \text{yr}^{-1}$ for temperate deciduous forests (Goulden et al., 1996; Greco and Baldocchi, 1996). Clearly, seasonally dry forests represent globally significant sites of C exchange between the atmosphere and vegetation.

VI. COST–BENEFIT ANALYSES FOR LEAVES OF SAVANNA TREES

A. Theory

Leaves incur a cost in their construction and also in their maintenance. Construction costs are the sum of all the carbon and energy utilized in producing a net gain in dry weight, including carbon incorporated into biomass and carbohydrate consumed to produce ATP and reductant for biosynthetic processes and transport processes (Chiariello et al., 1989). The benefit to the plant of a leaf is clearly the carbon fixed in photosynthesis. A priori reasoning suggests that a leaf should return more investment to the plant than it costs to construct and maintain it.

Construction costs of leaves can be calculated from detailed investigations of biochemical pathways utilized during construction of the principal components of leaves (Penning de Vries, 1975). Alternatively, elemental analyses of the major components of biomass can be undertaken

(McDermitt and Loomis, 1981). Such analyses are very labour and equipment intensive. Merino *et al.* (1982) used growth and CO_2 exchange analyses to calculate construction costs, but this method is also slow and can be difficult in some environments. Measurements of organic nitrogen content, ash-free heat of combustion and ash content are required to determine the construction cost, for which the equation developed by Williams *et al.* (1987) is often used:

$$C = \{(0.06968\,H_c - 0.065)(1 - A) + [(kN/14.0067)(180.15/24)]\}/0.89$$

where C is the construction cost (g glucose equivalents (g dry wt)$^{-1}$); H_c is the ash-free heat of combustion (kJ g^{-1}); A is the ash content (g ash g^{-1}); N is the total Kjeldahl nitrogen (g N (g dry wt)$^{-1}$); and k is a factor that has the value +5 when N is imported as nitrate into the plant, giving the maximum construction costs, or -3 when N is imported as ammonia, giving minimum costs.

Maintenance costs (g glucose equivalents (g dry wt)$^{-1}$ day^{-1}) are calculated following Merino *et al.* (1984), using biochemical pathway analyses. The following maintenance coefficients are used:

Fat   0.0425 g g^{-1}
Protein   0.028 g g^{-1} (minimum), 0.053 g g^{-1} (maximum)
Ash   0.06 g g^{-1} (minimum), 0.01 g g^{-1} (maximum)

Maintenance costs of leaves include all processes requiring energy but not resulting in a net increase in dry matter, such as maintenance of ion gradients across lipid membranes and turnover of organic compounds (Chiariello *et al.*, 1989). Maintenance costs can be calculated from ash, lipid and protein contents of leaves and their maintenance coefficients (Merino *et al.*, 1984).

Williams *et al.* (1987) utilized the concept of glucose as equivalent energy units to modify the calculation of construction costs developed by Penning de Vries (1975). A comparison of the biochemical approach, the elemental analyses approach, the growth and CO_2 gas exchange method and the heat of combustion method showed good agreement (Merino *et al.*, 1982; Williams *et al.*, 1987). The heat of combustion method is faster and less costly than the alternative methodologies.

B. Phenological Comparisons

Heat of combustion is higher in leaves of evergreen than deciduous species (Sobrado, 1991; Eamus and Prichard, 1998). The heat of combustion of leaves is positively related to the glucose equivalent (GE) (McDermitt and

Loomis, 1981), and therefore GE provides a measure of the amount of glucose required to provide the carbon and electrons contained in the leaf (Williams *et al.*, 1987). Since a high heat of combustion means a high energy storage of biomass, leaves of evergreen species must have a higher energy storage of biomass than those of deciduous species. This is a result of the higher degree of sclerophylly and larger investment in secondary defence compounds in evergreen species.

Heat of combustion provides an estimate of construction costs of leaves (McDermitt and Loomis, 1981). A high lipid content of leaves is associated with high construction costs (Merino *et al.*, 1984), and lipid content has been found to be significantly higher in evergreen than in deciduous species. These characteristics explain the higher foliar construction cost of evergreen species. High lipid content may be associated with defensive compounds in evergreen leaves and the smaller cells (and hence proportionally more cell wall material) of sclerophyllous evergreen species.

Poorter (1994) has concluded that there is very little evidence for differences in construction costs between deciduous and evergreen species. Similarly, within tree species, Merino (1987) found no difference in construction costs between evergreen and deciduous species. However, Eamus and Prichard (1998) found construction costs of evergreen species to be larger than those of deciduous or semi-deciduous species. This is in contrast to results obtained in other studies (Merino *et al.*, 1982, 1984; Williams *et al.*, 1987). However, from a theoretical consideration, construction costs of leaves of evergreen species should be higher than those of deciduous species because of the smaller cells, thicker cell walls and hence larger proportion of structural material in long-lived evergreen species (Orians and Solbrig, 1977; Chabot and Hicks, 1982; Williams *et al.*, 1989). Longer-lived leaves are also more likely to be subject to herbivore attack than short-lived leaves (Reich *et al.*, 1992). Consequently, investment in secondary compounds for defence may be higher in leaves of evergreen trees than in those of deciduous trees. This may also contribute to the larger leaf construction costs of evergreen species (Reich *et al.*, 1992). The results presented by Eamus and Prichard (1998) support the hypothesis that leaf construction costs are correlated with lifespan.

In a detailed study of seven co-occurring *Piper* species in a tall evergreen rainforest in Mexico, the ratio of cost to benefit was correlated with leaf lifespan, a result in close agreement with that found in a study conducted in north Australia (Williams *et al.*, 1989). It is clear that deciduous and evergreen species have adopted alternative survival strategies. Deciduous species invest large amounts of nitrogen in leaves to support a very large assimilation rate each day of the wet season when soil water is freely available. Their short-lived leaves fix large amounts of carbon for a short time. Evergreen species do not invest large amounts of nitrogen into their leaves, and assimilation rates are consequently lower, but they fix carbon for 12 months and hence the return to the tree occurs over a longer time.

Maintenance costs of leaves are significantly higher for deciduous compared to evergreen species (Merino *et al.*, 1982, 1984; Sobrado, 1991). Low maintenance costs are associated with long-lived sclerophyllous leaves (Merino *et al.*, 1984). The higher foliar nitrogen content of deciduous species suggests a higher protein content, which is expensive to maintain due to protein turnover. Thus the high A_{max} of leaves of deciduous species is expensive to maintain because of the amount of enzymes involved in photosynthesis. The higher lipid content of leaves of evergreen species was more than offset by the higher nitrogen (hence protein) and ash content of leaves of deciduous species, thereby making the maintenance costs of leaves of deciduous trees higher than that of leaves of evergreen trees.

C. Leaf Lifespan as Determinant of Leaf Characteristics

On average, deciduous trees have shorter leaf lifespans than evergreen trees. It is also clear that, as leaf lifespan increases, several leaf attributes change. Maximum assimilation rate (on a dry weight basis), foliar N content, SLA and maximum stomatal conductance, all decline with increasing leaf lifespan for a large range of environments, including seasonally dry environments (Figures 9–11; Reich *et al.*, 1992, 1994; Eamus and Prichard, 1998). Because assimilation rate is highly dependent on N content, and possibly a single universal relationship exists for this (Reich *et al.*, 1992), the observation that evergreen trees exhibit lower assimilation rates, larger SLA and lower stomatal conductance is attributed to their longer leaf lifespan. It is also likely that deciduous species with relatively long-lived leaves (9–10 months) will have attributes more closely resembling those of evergreen species with relatively short leaf lifespans (12–24 months) than those of deciduous species with very short leaf lifespans (<6 months) (Reich *et al.*, 1992). Given the relationships between leaf lifespan, relative growth rate and leaf-mass ratio (the ratio of leaf mass to whole plant mass) and forest production efficiency (Reich *et al.*, 1992), it is clear that leaf lifespan is an important integrator of plant, canopy and forest function. We must concur with Reich *et al.* (1992) that evergreen and deciduous are two ends of a gradient of leaf lifespan. Furthermore, within seasonally dry forests, evergreen species can have relatively short leaf lifespans (Williams *et al.*, 1997b) and thus have leaf attributes more similar to deciduous species than to evergreens with leaf lifespans of two or more years. We would suggest that it is likely that stand-level canopy production efficiency is a function of weighted average canopy leaf lifespan.

VII. LARGE-SCALE STRUCTURE AND FUNCTION

Composition, structure and dynamics of savannas depend primarily on plant available moisture (PAM) and plant available nutrients (PAN), with fire and herbivory as secondary determinants (Walker and Langridge, 1997). If an adequate model of savanna structure and function can be developed using the PAM/PAN concept, it is likely that predictions will be possible for all savanna sites concerning functional attributes (e.g. productivity, transpiration rates) (Walker and Langridge, 1997).

Walker and Langridge (1997) and Williams *et al.* (1996) showed that variation in structural and compositional attributes of tropical savannas (tree height, percentage tree cover, tree basal area, deciduous tree richness, woody species richness, total leaf biomass) can be well described by knowledge of the PAM/PAN attributes. Plant available moisture is determined by both the amount of water available to a plant and the duration of availability. PAM is thus a function of root depth, soil characteristics and the distribution of rainfall in time. Plant available nutrients can, to a large extent, be estimated from measurements of soil depth, soil texture and available calcium, magnesium, potassium and phosphorus (Walker and Langridge, 1997). However, as Walker and Langridge (1997) acknowledge, the availability of soil data (depth, water-holding characteristics, nutrient exchange properties) is frequently limited. Williams *et al.* (1996) used percentage clay content as a surrogate measure of PAN, which greatly simplified data acquisition.

An alternative approach to estimate the productivity of seasonally dry tropical areas may be to use a simple global empirical scaling index such as that developed by Baldocchi and Meyers (1998) for boreal and temperate systems and tropical evergreen systems. For these systems, LAI could be predicted from knowledge of annual potential evaporation, annual precipitation and foliar N content. Leaf area index determines the maximum potential for carbon and water fluxes to and from canopies. Leaf area index is also highly correlated with a range of ecologically significant variables, including net primary productivity, site water balance and annual temperature (Waring and Schlesinger, 1985; Neilson, 1995). It is apparent that, for a range of seasonally dry forests, there is a significant relationship between (foliar N content $\times$ P/Et) and LAI or tree density (Figure 13). Thus, for the savannas of north Australia, covering a rainfall gradient of almost 1500 mm, and for other sites in Africa, tree density (which is highly correlated with leaf area and stem volume) or LAI can be predicted ($r^2 > 0.9$) from the following equation (Baldocchi and Meyers, 1998):

$$\text{tree density} = [N]\, P/Et$$

where [N] is foliar N content in $mg\,g^{-1}$, P is the annual precipitation and Et is the annual equilibrium evaporation.

Foliar N content provides at least a simple and crude estimate of nutrient availability, while the term P/Et is a surrogate measure of water availability. The $[N]P/Et$ relationship for tree density and LAI may be easier to use than the PAM/PAN model since the data required are far more widely available.

VIII. CONCLUSIONS AND FUTURE DIRECTIONS

Seasonally dry forests represent an important class of vegetation globally. Unlike most temperate systems, temperature and light availability are infrequently limiting for productivity. However, water can be very limiting for a significant part of the year (2–8 months) in the majority, but not all, seasonally dry woodlands and forests (O'Grady et al., 1999).

Deciduous and evergreen species represent two ends of a continuum of leaf lifespan. Useful comparisons can be made between the strategies employed by these two extremes. Thus cost–benefit analyses of maintenance and construction costs reveal significant differences in the trade-off between nitrogen invested, assimilation of carbon, SLA and leaf lifespan. Species with short-lived leaves exhibit a suite of related characteristics (see Table 5), including high N investment, high SLA and a high rate of light-saturated assimilation. However, it is true to say that a deciduous tree with a leaf lifespan of 9 months probably has more in common with an evergreen tree with a leaf lifespan of 12 months than with a deciduous tree with a leaf lifespan of 3 months.

Because of their open canopy and low Ω values, the rates of leaf- and canopy-scale CO_2 assimilation in seasonally dry forests are broadly comparable, this is not the case in rainforests, coniferous forests and other closed-canopy forests, where Ω is much larger. The rate of canopy CO_2 uptake by seasonally dry forests is also comparable to that of many other woodlands and forests where LAI ranged from 2 to 6. This seems surprising, given the low soil nutrient content and low LAI of seasonally dry systems. It also raises the question – why have a closed forest canopy with a high LAI (>3) if canopy CO_2 exchange rates are not proportionally larger?

Leaf area index and tree density, which are major determinants of ecosystem productivity and water use, can be predicted with surprising ease from knowledge of foliar N content and the ratio of rainfall to equilibrium evaporation rate. It remains to be seen whether such relationships continue as more data are published. However, this simple

Table 5

A summary of some of the characteristics associated with deciduous and evergreen phenologies in seasonally dry woodlands and forests

Attribute	Deciduous	Evergreen
Specific leaf area	High	Low
N content per unit dry wt	High	Low
A_{max} (wt basis)	High	Low
Leaf longevity	Low	High
Construction costs	Low	High
Maintenance costs	High	Low
Cost–benefit ratio	Low	High
Decline in leaf water potential between wet and dry season	Larger and faster	Smaller and slower
Resistance to water flow in stem or leaf	Small	Large
Huber value	Small	Large
Embolism during the dry season	Larger or smaller	Smaller or larger
Root depth	Shallower	Deeper

relationship may prove useful when attempting to estimate ecosystem productivity and C balances.

During the 1980s and early 1990s there were many leaf-scale studies of different species in seasonally dry ecosystems. Such studies highlighted the differences between species in assimilation rate, SLA, transpiration rate and other variables. However, more recent studies, at leaf, tree and canopy scale, suggest that similarities are more important than differences. O'Grady et al. (1999) has shown that transpiration rate can be estimated with suitable precision for any tree species from a single relationship between DBH (diameter at breast height), leaf area and transpiration rate. Similarly Meinzer et al. (1997) show that stomatal responses to VPD of a number of species are essentially identical. These data suggest that modelling of the savanna ecosystem function will not require large numbers of leaf- and species-scale measurements.

As in most environments, below-ground processes are not so well understood as above-ground ones. Most statements about rooting depths for savanna evergreen and deciduous trees are based on circumstantial evidence, such as Ψ_{pd} values (e.g. Myers et al., 1997; Prior et al., 1997a) or anecdotal evidence or unspecified sources (e.g. Olivares and Medina,

1992). There are few published studies of rooting depth or distribution, and fewer still of seasonal growth patterns. How does a deep-rooted tree cope with seasonal water-table fluctuations of up to 10 m, as can occur in northern Australian savannas? Do fine roots die as the saturated zone rises to surround them? If not, how do they survive this inundation? How many deep roots are needed to supply the tree's water requirements during the dry season?

Functional wood anatomy of tropical species needs further investigation. Are there generalized differences between the wood of evergreen and deciduous species? Does xylem embolism play a role in leaf abscission in some deciduous species? In those species that are extensively embolized, is xylem refilled, or is new xylem produced?

Comparisons between winter-deciduous, drought-deciduous and evergreen species may allow us to separate characteristics of deciduousness *per se* from what may be responses to a cold, nutrient-rich environment or a tropical environment with a marked dry season. So far, relationships between leaf lifespan and specific assimilation rates, SLA and leaf N content appear to hold for both tropical and temperate environments.

There have been many generalizations about differences between tropical evergreen and deciduous species. Most have been based on a very limited number of species comparisons (2–6) from only one environment. Which of these hold from a global perspective? There is a wide diversity in characteristics of deciduous trees. Some deciduous trees are leafless for a mere week or two, others for 4 months or more. With such a range in leaf phenological characteristics within the deciduous habit, it is not surprising that there is a corresponding diversity in physiological behaviour.

Briefly-deciduous trees are not leafless long enough to avoid drought, and their leaves may have an average lifespan equal to or longer than that of some evergreen leaves. These deciduous trees may share with evergreen trees similar adaptations to seasonal drought, such as deep roots, low solute potentials and capacity for osmotic adjustment, and effective stomatal control of transpiration.

Some deciduous species (e.g. fully deciduous species of northern Australia; Duff *et al.*, 1997; Myers *et al.*, 1997) shed their leaves while water potentials are still high, whereas others (e.g. from Venezuelan dry forest; Sobrado, 1996) are severely dehydrated before leaf loss occurs. In some species, leaf flush occurs during the dry season, whereas leaves of other species do not flush until after rain falls.

It is clear that the future of ecophysiological research, in all large ecosystems, will require input from multidisciplinary teams, including plant physiologists, ecophysiologists, hydrologists, micro-meteorologists, remote sensors and modellers. The challenge for tropical ecosystem research is to conduct long-term, detailed, year-long studies, as opposed to short field campaigns during the most 'apparently active' growth period.

REFERENCES

Ahmad, W., vanZyl, J.J., Menges, C., O'Grady, A. and Hill, G.J.E. (1998). Preliminary results of supervised and unsupervised AIRSAR data classification techniques in the tropical savannas of northern Australia. PACRIM workshop, Sydney, 26–28 July.

Alder, N.N., Sperry, J.S. and Pockman, W.T. (1996). Root and stem xylem embolism, stomatal conductance, and leaf turgor in *Acer grandidentatum* populations along a soil moisture gradient. *Oecologia* **105**, 293–301.

Ameglio, T. and Archer, P. (1996). Significance of pre-dawn water potential in heterogeneous soil water content distribution. *Agronomie* **16**, 493–503.

Andrade, J.L., Meinzer, F.C., Goldstein, G., Holbrook, N.M., Cavelier, J., Jackson, P. and Silvera, K. (1998). Regulation of water flux through trunks, branches, and leaves in trees of a lowland tropical forest. *Oecologia* **115**, 463–471.

Archibald, O.W. (1995). Tropical savannas. In: *Ecology of World Vegetation*, pp. 60–94. Chapman & Hall, London.

Ashton, D.H. and Attiwill, P.M. (1994). *Australian Vegetation*, pp. 157–196. Cambridge University Press, Cambridge, UK.

Baldocchi, D. and Meyers, T. (1998). On using eco-physiological, micrometeorological and biogeochemical theory to evaluate carbon dioxide, water vapor and trace gas fluxes over vegetation: a perspective. *Agric. Forest Meteorol.* **90**, 1–25.

Barajes-Morales, J. (1985). Wood structural differences between trees of two tropical forests in Mexico. *IAWA Bull.* **6**, 355–364.

Becker, P. (1996). Sap flow in Bornean heath and dipterocarp forest trees during wet and dry periods. *Tree Physiol.* **16**, 295–299.

Berninger, F. and Hari, P. (1993). Optimal regulation of gas exchange: evidence from field data. *Ann. Bot.* **71**, 135–149.

Borchert, R. (1991). Growth periodicity and dormancy. In: *Physiology of Trees* (Ed. by A.S. Raghavendra), pp. 219–242. John Wiley, New York.

Borchert, R. (1994a). Induction of rehydration and budbreak by irrigation or rain in deciduous trees of a tropical dry forest in Costa Rica. *Trees* **8**, 198–204.

Borchert, R. (1994b). Water status and development of tropical trees during seasonal drought. *Trees* **8**, 115–125.

Borchert, R. (1994c). Soil and stem water storage determine phenology and distribution of tropical dry forest trees. *Ecology* **75**, 1437–1449.

Bowman, D.M.J.S. (1996). Diversity patterns of woody species on a latitudinal transect from the monsoon tropics to desert in the Northern Territory, Australia. *Aust. J. Bot.* **44**, 571–580.

Bowman, D.M.J.S., Wilson, B.A. and Dunlop, C.R. (1988). Preliminary biogeographic analysis of the Northern Territory flora. *Aust. J. Bot.* **36**, 503–517.

Bowman, W.D. and Roberts, S.W. (1985). Seasonal and diurnal water relations adjustments in three evergreen chaparral shrubs. *Ecology* **66**, 738–742.

Bréda, N., Cochard, H., Dreyer, E. and Granier, A. (1993). Field comparison of transpiration, stomatal conductance and vulnerability to cavitation of *Quercus peraea* and *Quercus robur* under water stress. *Ann. Sci. Forestières* **50**, 571–582.

Bréda, N., Granier, A. and Aussenac, G. (1995). Effects of thinning on soil and tree water relations, transpiration and growth in an oak forest (*Quercus petraea* (Matt.) Liebl.) *Tree Physiol.* **15**, 295–306.

Brunet, Y., Nunez, M. and Lagouarde, J.-P. (1991). A simple method of estimating regional evapo-transpiration from infrared surface temperature data. *ISPRS J. Photogramm. Remote Sensing* **46**, 311–327.

Bullock, S.H. and Solis-Magallanes, J.A. (1990). Phenology of canopy trees of a tropical deciduous forest in Mexico. *Biotropica* **22**, 22–35.

Burgess, S.S.O., Adams, M.A., Turner, N.C. and Ong, C.K. (1998). The redistribution of soil water by tree root systems. *Oecologia* **115**, 306–311.

Caldwell, M.M., Dawson, T.E. and Richards, J.H. (1998). Hydraulic lift – consequences of water efflux from roots of plants. *Oecologia* **113**, 151–161.

Canadell, J., Jackson, R.B., Ehleringer, J.R., Mooney, H.A., Sala, O.E. and Schulze, E.-D. (1996). Maximum rooting depth of vegetation types at the global scale. *Oecologia* **108**, 583–595.

Carbon, B.A., Bartle, G.A., Murray, A.M. and McPherson, D.K. (1980). The distribution of root length and the limits to flow of soil water to roots in a dry sclerophyll forest. *Forest. Sci.* **25**, 656–664.

Carlquist, S. (1988). Comparative wood anatomy: systematic, ecological, and evolutionary aspects of dicotyledon wood. In: *Springer Series in Wood Science* (Ed. by T.E. Timell). Springer-Verlag, Heidelberg.

Castellanos, J., Maass, M. and Kummerow, J. (1991). Root biomass of a dry deciduous tropical forest in Mexico. *Plant and Soil* **131**, 225–228.

Chabot, B.F. and Hicks, D.J. (1982). The ecology of leaf life spans. *Ann. Rev. Ecol. Systematics* **13**, 229–259.

Chiariello, N.R., Mooney, H.A. and Williams, K. (1989). Growth, carbon allocation and cost of plant tissues. In: *Plant Physiological Ecology. Field Methods and Instrumentation.* (Ed. by R.W. Pearcy, J.R. Ehleringer, H.A. Mooney and P.W. Rundell), pp. 327–365. Chapman & Hall, London.

Chidumayo, E.N. (1990). Above-ground woody biomass structure and productivity in a Zambian woodland. *Forest Ecol. Manag.* **36**, 33–46.

Cochard, H. and Tyree, M.T. (1990). Xylem dysfunction in *Quercus*: vessel sizes, tyloses, cavitation and seasonal changes in embolism. *Tree Physiol.* **6**, 393–407.

Cochard, H., Cruiziat, P. and Tyree, M.T. (1992). Use of positive pressures to establish vulnerability curves: further support for the air seeding hypothesis and possible problems for pressure–volume analysis. *Plant Physiol.* **100**, 205–209.

Cochard, H., Breda, N. and Granier, A. (1996). Whole tree hydraulic conductance and water loss regulation in *Quercus* during drought: evidence for stomatal control of embolism? *Ann. Sci. Forestières* **53**, 197–206.

Cole, S.P. (1994). *Field and laboratory studies of growth and photosynthesis of Acacia auriculiformis in the NT of Australia.* Ph.D. thesis, Northern Territory University, Australia.

Cook, P.G., Hatton, T.J., Pidsley, D., Herczeg, A.L., Held, A., O'Grady, A. and Eamus, D. (1998). Water balance of a tropical lowland ecosystem, Northern Australia: a combination of micro-meteorological, soil physical and groundwater chemical approaches. *J. Hydrol.* **210**, 161–177.

Coomes, D.A. and Grubb, P.J. (1998). A comparison of 12 species of Amazonian caatinga using growth rates in gaps and understorey, and allometric relationships. *Funct. Ecol.* **12**, 426–435.

Correia, M.J., Chaves, M.M.C. and Pereira, J.S. (1990). Afternoon depression in photosynthesis of grapevine leaves – evidence for a high light stress effect. *J. Exp. Bot.* **41**, 417–426.

Cowan, I.R. and Farquhar, G.D. (1977). Stomatal function in relation to leaf metabolism and environment. In: *Integration of Activity in the Higher Plant* (Ed. by D.H. Jennings), pp. 205–229. Springer-Verlag, Berlin.

Demming-Adams, B., Adams, W.W., Winter, K., Meyer, A., Schreiber, U., Pereira, J.S., Kruger, A., Czygan, F.C. and Lange, O.L. (1989). Photochemical efficiency of photosystem II, photon yield of O_2 evolution, photosynthetic capacity and carotenoid composition during the mid-day depression of net CO_2 uptake in *Arbutus unedo* growing in Portugal. *Planta* **177**, 377–387.

Duff, G.A., Myers, B.A., Williams, R.J., Eamus, D., O'Grady, A. and Fordyce, I.R. (1997). Seasonal patterns in soil moisture, vapour pressure deficit, tree canopy cover and predawn water potential in a northern Australian savanna. *Aust. J. Bot.* **45**, 211–224.

Eamus, D. (1991). The interaction of rising CO_2 levels and temperature with water-use-efficiency. *Plant Cell Environ.* **14**, 25–40.

Eamus, D. (1999). Stomatal physiology. In: *Plants in Action* (Ed. by B.A. Atwell, P. Kriedmann, C. Turnbull, D. Eamus and R.L. Bieleski), pp. 467–470. Macmillan, Australia.

Eamus, D. and Cole, S.C. (1997). Diurnal and seasonal comparisons of assimilation, phyllode conductance and water potential of three Acacia and one Eucalyptus species in the wet–dry tropics of Australia. *Aust. J. Bot.* **45**, 275–290.

Eamus, D. and Prichard, H. (1998). A cost–benefit analysis of leaves of 4 Australian savanna species. *Tree Physiol.* **18**, 537–546.

Eamus, D., Narayan, A. and Berryman, C.A. (1995). The influence of drought and abscisic acid on root hydraulic conductivity and ion transport properties of *Abelmoschus escalentus*. *S. Pacific J. Nat. Sci.* **14**, 187–209.

Eamus, D., Myers, B., Duff, G. and Williams, R. (1999a). A cost–benefit analysis of eight Australian savanna tree species of differing phenology. *Photosynthetica* **36**, 575–586.

Eamus, D., Myers, B.A., Duff, G.A. and Williams, R.J. (1999b). Seasonal variation in photosynthetic rate of eight savanna tree species of Australia. *Tree Physiol.* **19**, 665–672.

Eamus, D., Hutley, L.B. and O'Grady, A.P. (2001). Daily and seasonal patterns of carbon and water fluxes above a north Australian savanna. *Tree Physiol.* (in press).

Egan, J.L. and Williams, R.J. (1995). Life-form distributions of woodland plant species along a moisture availability gradient in Australia's monsoonal tropics. *Aust. Syst. Bot.* **9**, 205–217.

Ehleringer, J.R., Hall, A.E. and Farquhar, G.D. (1993). *Stable Isotopes and Plant Carbon/Water Relations*. Academic Press, San Diego.

Evans, J.R. (1989). Photosynthesis and nitrogen relationships in leaves of C_3 plants. *Oecologia* **96**, 169–178.

Evans, R.D., Black, R.A., Loescher, W.H. and Fellows, R.J. (1992). Osmotic relations of the drought-tolerant shrub *Artemisia tridentata* in response to water stress. *Plant Cell Environ.* **15**, 49–59.

Ewers, F.W. and Cruiziat, P. (1991). Measuring water transport and storage. In: *Techniques and Approaches in Forest Tree Ecophysiology* (Ed. by J.P. Lassoie and T.M. Hinckley), pp. 91–115. CRC Press, Boca Raton, FL.

Farquhar, G.D., Ehleringer, J.R. and Hubick, K.T. (1989). Carbon isotope discrimination during photosynthesis. *Ann. Rev. Plant Physiol. Mol. Biol.* **40**, 503–537.

Field, C. and Mooney, H. (1986). The photosynthesis–nitrogen relationship in wild plants. In: *On the Economy of Plant Form and Function* (Ed. by T. Givnish), pp. 25–55. Cambridge University Press, Cambridge.

Field, C.B., Gamon, J.A. and Peñuelas, J. (1994). Remote sensing of terrestrial photosynthesis. In: *Ecophysiology of Photosynthesis* (Ed. by E.D. Schulze and M.M. Caldwell). Springer-Verlag, Berlin.

Fordyce, I.R., Duff, G.A. and Eamus, D. (1997). The water relations of *Allosyncarpia ternata* (Myrtaceae) at contrasting sites in the monsoonal tropics of northern Australia. *Aust. J. Bot.* **45**, 259–274.

Foyer, C.H. (1988). Feedback inhibition of photosynthesis through source–sink regulation of leaves. *Plant Physiol. Biochem.* **26**, 483–492.

Franco, A.C. (1998). Seasonal patterns of gas exchange, water relations and growth of *Roupala montana*, an evergreen savanna species. *Plant Ecol.* **136**, 69–76.

Franco, A.C., Nardoto, G.B. and Souza, M.P. (1996). Patterns of soil water potential and seedling survival in the cerrados of Central Brazil. In: *Proceedings of the 1st International Symposium on Tropical Savannas: Biodiversity and Sustainable Production of Food and Fibers in the Tropical Savannas* (Ed. by R.C. Pereira and L.C.B. Nasser), pp. 277–280. EMBRAPA-CPAC Planaltina, Brazil.

Franks, P.J., Gibson, A. and Bachelard, E.P. (1995). Xylem permeability and embolism susceptibility in seedlings of *Eucalyptus camaldulensis* Dehnh. from two different climatic zones. *Aust. J. Plant Physiol.* **22**, 15–21.

Gartner, B.L. (1991). Stem hydraulic properties of vines vs. shrubs of western poison oak, *Toxicodendron diversilobum. Oecologia* **87**, 180–189.

Gartner, B.L., Bullock, S.H., Mooney, J.A., Brown, B. and Whitbeck, J.L. (1990). Water transport properties of vine and tree stems in a tropical deciduous forest. *Amer. J. Bot.* **77**, 742–749.

Gill, A.M. (1994) *Eucalyptus* open-forests. In: *Australian Vegetation*, pp. 197–226. Cambridge University Press, Cambridge.

Ginter-Whitehouse, D.L., Hinckley, T.M. and Pallardy, S.G. (1983). Spatial and temporal aspects of water relations of three tree species with different vascular anatomy. *Forest Sci.* **29**, 317–329.

Givnish, T. (1986). Optimal stomatal conductance, allocation of energy between roots and leaves and the marginal cost of transpiration. In: *On the Economy of Plant Form and Function* (Ed. by T. Givnish), pp. 171–213. Cambridge University Press, Cambridge.

Goldstein, G. and Sarmiento, G. (1987). Water relations of trees and grasses and their consequences for the structure of savanna vegetation. In: *Determinants of Tropical Savannas* (Ed. by B.H. Walker), pp. 13–38. IRL Press, Oxford.

Goldstein, G., Sarmiento, G. and Meinzer, F. (1986). Patrones diarios y estacionales en las relaciones hidricas de arboles siempreverdes de la sabana tropical. *Acta Oecological/Oecologia Plantarum* **7**, 107–119.

Goldstein, G., Rada, F. and Catalan, A. (1987). Water transport efficiency in stems of evergreen and deciduous savanna trees. In: *Proceedings of the International Conference on Measurement of Soil and Plant Water Status*, vol. 2, Plants, pp. 267–274. Utah State University, Utah.

Goldstein, G., Rada, F., Rundell, P., Azocar, A. and Orozco, A. (1989). Gas exchange and water relations of evergreen and deciduous tropical savanna trees. *Ann. Sci. Forestières* **46** (suppl.), 448s–453s.

Goldstein, G., Andrade, J.L., Neinzer, F.C., Holbrook, N.M., Cavelier, J., Jackson, P. and Celis, A. (1998). Stem water storage and diurnal patterns of water use in tropical forest canopy trees. *Plant Cell Environ.* **21**, 397–406.

Goulden, M.L., Munger, J.W., Fan, S.M., Daube, B.C. and Wofsy, S.C. (1996). Exchange of carbon dioxide by a deciduous forest: response to inter-annual climate variability. *Science* **271**, 1576–1579.

Gowing, D.J.G., Jones, H.G. and Davies, W.J. (1993). Xylem-transported abscisic acid: the relative importance of mass and its concentration in the control of stomatal aperture. *Plant Cell Environ.* **16**, 453–459.

Grace, J., Lloyd, J., McIntyre, J., Miranda, A., Meir, P., Miranda, H., Moncrieff, J., Massheder, J., Wright, I. and Gash, J. (1995). Fluxes of carbon dioxide and water vapour over an undisturbed tropical forest in south-west Amazonia. *Global Change Biol.* **1**, 1–12.

Grace, J., Malhi, Y., Lloyd, J., McIntyre, J., Miranda, A.C., Meir, P. and Miranda, H. (1996). The use of eddy covariance to infer the net carbon dioxide uptake of Brazilian rain forest. *Global Change Biol.* **2**, 209–217.

Granier, A., Bréda, N., Claustres, J.P. and Colin, F. (1989). Variation of hydraulic conductance of some adult conifers under natural conditions. *Ann. Sci. Forestières* **46** (suppl.), 357s–360s.

Granier, A., Biron, P., Bréda, N., Pontailler, J.Y. and Saugier, B. (1996). Transpiration of trees and forest stands: short and long-term monitoring using sapflow methods. *Global Change Biol.* **2**, 265–274.

Greco, S. and Baldocchi, D. (1996). Seasonal variations of CO_2 and water vapour exchange rates over a temperate deciduous forest. *Global Change Biol.* **2**, 183–197.

Grieu, P., Guehl, J.M. and Aussenac, G. (1988). The effects of soil and atmospheric drought on photosynthesis and stomatal control of gas exchange in three coniferous species. *Physiol. Plantarum* **73**, 97–104.

Guehl, J.M., Aussenac, G., Bouachrine, J., Zimmermann, R., Pennes, J.M., Ferhi, A. and Grieu, P. (1991). Sensitivity of leaf gas exchange to atmospheric drought, soil drought and water use efficiency in some Mediterranean *Abies* species. *Can. J. Forest. Res.* **21**, 1507–1515.

Haase, P., Pugnaire, F.I., Fernandez, E.M., Puigdefábregas, J., Clark, S.C. and Incoll, L.D. (1996). An investigation of rooting depth of the semiarid shrub *Retama sphaerocarpa* (L.) Boiss. by labelling of ground water with a chemical tracer. *J. Hydrol.* **177**, 23–31.

Haman, N.P. and Prince, S.D. (1997). Stomatal conductance of West Central Supersite vegetation in HAPEX-Sahel: measurements and empirical models. *J. Hydrol.* **188–189**, 536–562.

Haman, N.P., Kabat, P., Johannes Dolman, A. and Elbers, J.A. (1998). Photosynthesis and carbon balance of a Sahelian fallow savanna. *Global Change Biol.* **4**, 523–538.

Hogan, K.P., Smith, A.P. and Samaniego, M. (1995). Gas exchange in six tropical semi-deciduous forest canopy tree species during the wet and dry seasons. *Biotropica* **27**, 324–333.

Holbrook, N.M., Whitbeck, J.L. and Mooney, H.A. (1995). Drought responses of neotropical dry forest trees. In: *Seasonally Dry Tropical Forests* (Ed. by S.H. Bullock, H.A. Mooney and E. Medina), pp 243–276. Cambridge University Press, Cambridge.

Hollinger, D.Y., Kelliher, F.M., Byers, J.N., Hunt, J.E., McSeveny, T.M. and Wier, P.P. (1994). Carbon dioxide exchange between an undisturbed old growth temperate forest and the atmosphere. *Ecology* **75**, 134–150.

Ingle, H.D. and Dadswell, H.E. (1953a). The anatomy of the timbers of the south-west Pacific area. II Apocynaceae and Annonaceae. *Aust. J. Bot.* **1**, 1–26.

Ingle, H.D. and Dadswell, H.E. (1953b). The anatomy of the timbers of the south-west Pacific area. III Myrtaceae. *Aust. J. Bot.* **1**, 353–401.

IPCC (1995). *Climate Change 1995* (Ed. by R.T. Watson, M.C. Zinyowera, R.H. Moss and D.J. Dokken). Cambridge University Press, Cambridge.

Irvine, J., Perks, M.P., Magnani, F. and Grace, J. (1998). The response of *Pinus sylvestris* to drought: stomatal control of transpiration and hydraulic conductance. *Tree Physiol.* **18**, 393–402.

Jackson, C., Cavelier, J., Goldstein, G., Meinzer, C. and Holbrook, N.M. (1995a) Partitioning of water resources among plants of a lowland tropical forest. *Oecologia* **101**,197–203.

Jackson, G.E., Irvine, J. and Grace, J. (1995b). Xylem cavitation in Scots pine and Sitka spruce saplings during water stress. *Tree Physiol.* **15**, 783–790.

Jarbeau, J.A., Ewers, F.W. and Davis, S.D. (1995). The mechanism of water-stress-induced embolism in two species of chaparral shrubs. *Plant Cell Environ.* **18**, 189–196.

Jarvis, P.G. (1976). The interpretation of the variations in leaf water potential and stomatal conductance found in canopies in the field. *Phil. Trans. Roy. Soc. Lond.* B. **273**, 593–610.

Jarvis, P.G. and McNaughton, K.G. (1986). Stomatal control of transpiration: scaling up from leaf to region. *Adv. Ecol. Res.* **15**, 1–49.

Jennings C.M.H. (1974). *The hydrology of Botswana.* Ph.D. thesis, University of Natal, South Africa.

Jones, M. M. and Turner, N. C. (1978). Osmotic adjustments in leaves of sorghum in response to water deficits. *Plant Physiol.* **61**, 122–126.

Kawamitsu, Y., Yoda, S. and Agata, W. (1993). Humidity pretreatment affects the responses of stomata and CO_2 assimilation to vapor pressure difference in C_3 and C_4 plants. *Plant Cell Physiol.* **34**, 113–119.

Kimber, P.C. (1974). *The Root System of Jarrah* (Eucalyptus marginata). Forests Department of Western Australia Research Paper No. 10.

Kitajima K., Mulkey, S.S. and Wright, S.J. (1997). Seasonal leaf phenotypes in the canopy of a tropical dry forest: photosynthetic characteristics and associated traits. *Oecologia* **109**, 490–498.

Koide, R. (1985). The nature and location of variable hydraulic resistance in *Helianthus annuus* L. (Sunflower). *J. Exp. Bot.* **36**, 1430–1440.

Kolb, K.J. and Davis, S.D. (1994). Drought tolerance and xylem embolism in co-occurring species of coastal sage and chaparral. *Ecology* **75**, 648–659.

Kuppers, M. (1984). Carbon relations and competition between woody species in a Central European hedgerow. II. Stomatal responses, water use and hydraulic conductivity in the root/leaf pathway. *Oecologia* **64**, 344–354.

Lauer, M. and Boyer, J.S. (1992). Internal CO_2 measured directly in leaves. Abscisic acid and low water potential cause opposing effects. *Plant Physiol.* **98**, 1310–1316.

Le Roux, X. and Bariac, T. (1998). Seasonal variations in soil, grass and shrub water status in a West African humid savanna. *Oecologia* **113**, 456–466.

Le Roux, X. and Mordelet, P. (1995). Leaf and canopy CO_2 assimilation in a west African humid savanna during the early growing season. *J. Trop. Ecol.* **11**, 529–545.

Le Roux, X., Bariac, T. and Mariotti, A. (1995). Spatial partitioning of the soil water resource between grass and shrub components in a West African humid savanna. *Oecologia* **104**, 147–155.

Lindorf, H. (1994). Eco-anatomical wood features of species from a very dry tropical forest. *IAWA J.* **15**, 361–376.

Lloyd, J. (1991). Modelling stomatal responses to environment in *Macademia integrifolia. Aust. J. Plant Physiol.* **18**, 649–660.

Lloyd, J. and Farquhar, G.D. (1994). ^{13}C discrimination during CO_2 assimilation by the terrestrial biosphere. *Oecologia* **99**, 201–215.

Loewenstein, N.J. and Pallardy, S.G. (1998). Drought tolerance, xylem sap abscisic acid and stomatal conductance during soil drying: a comparison of young plants of four temperate deciduous angiosperms. *Tree Physiol.* **18**, 421–430.

Lo Gullo, M.A., Salleo, S., Piaceri, E.C. and Rosso, R. (1995). Relations between vulnerability to xylem embolism and xylem conduit dimensions in young trees of *Quercus cerris. Plant Cell Environ.* **18**, 661–669.

Lopez, F.B. and Nobel, P.S. (1991). Root hydraulic conductivity of two cactus species in relation to root age, temperature and soil water status. *J. Exp. Bot.* **42**, 143–149.

Loustau, D. and Granier, A. (1993). Environmental control of water flux through Maritime pine (*Pinus pinaster* Ait.). In: *Water Transport in Plants under Climatic Stress* (Ed. by M. Borghetti, J. Grace and A. Raschi), pp. 205–218. Cambridge University Press, Cambridge.

Loustau, D., Berbigier, P., Roumagnac, P., Arruda-Pacheco, C., David, J.S., Ferreira, M.I., Pereira, J.S. and Tavares, R. (1996). Transpiration of a 64-year-old maritime pine stand in Portugal. 1. Seasonal course of water flux through maritime pine. *Oecologia* **107**, 33–42.

Lu, P., Biron, P., Granier, A. and Cochard, H. (1996). Water relations of adult Norway spruce (*Picea abies* (L) Karst) under soil drought in the Vosges mountains: whole-tree hydraulic conductance, xylem embolism and water loss regulation. *Ann. Sci. Forestières* **53**, 113–121.

Magnani, F. and Borghetti, M. (1995). Interpretation of seasonal changes of xylem embolism and plant hydraulic resistance in *Fagus sylvatica. Plant Cell Environ.* **18**, 689–696.

Martin, C.E., Loeschen, V.S. and Borchert, R. (1994). Photosynthesis and leaf longevity in trees of a tropical deciduous forest in Costa Rica. *Photosynthetica* **30**, 341–351.

McDermitt, D.K. and Loomis, R.S. (1981). Elemental composition of biomass and its relation to energy content, growth efficiency, and growth yield. *Ann. Bot.* **48**, 275–290.

Medina, E. (1982). Physiological ecology of neotropical savanna plants. In: *Ecology of Tropical Savannas*, Ecological Studies vol. 42 (Ed. by B.J. Huntley and B.H. Walker), pp. 308–335, Springer-Verlag, Berlin.

Medina, E. (1984). Nutrient balance and physiological processes at the leaf level. In: *Physiological Ecology of Plants of the Wet Tropics* (Ed. by E. Medina, H.A. Mooney and C. Vazquez-Yanes), pp. 139–154. Proceedings of an International Symposium held in Oxatepec and Los Tuxtlas, Mexico. Dr W. Junk, The Hague.

Medina, E. and Francisco, M. (1994). Photosynthesis and water relations of savanna tree species differing in leaf phenology. *Tree Physiol.* **14**, 1367–1381.

Meinzer, F.C., Goldstein, G., Holbrook, N.M., Cavelier, J. and Jackson, P. (1993). Stomatal and environmental control of transpiration in a lowland tropical forest tree. *Plant Cell Environ.* **16**, 429–436.

Meinzer, F.C., Goldstein, N.M., Jackson, G., Holbrook, P., Gutiérrez, M.V. and Cavelier, J. (1995). Environmental and physiological regulation of transpiration in tropical forest gap species: the influence of boundary layer and hydraulic properties. *Oecologia* **101**, 514–522.

Meinzer, F.C., Andrade, J.L., Goldstein, G., Holbrook, N.M., Cavelier, J. and Jackson, P. (1997). Control of transpiration from the upper canopy of a tropical forest: the role of stomatal, boundary layer and hydraulic architecture components. *Plant Cell Environ.* **20**, 1242–1252.

Menaut, J.C. and Cesar, J. (1979). Structure and primary productivity of Lamto savannas, Ivory Coast. *Ecology* **60**, 1197–1210.

Mencuccini, M. and Grace, J. (1995). Climate influences the leaf area/sapwood area ratio in Scots pine. *Tree Physiol.* **15**, 1–10.

Menaut, J.C., Le Page, J.M. and Abbadie, L. (1995). Savanna, woodlands and dry forests in Africa. In: *Seasonally Dry Tropical Forests* (Ed. by S.H. Bullock, H.A. Mooney and E. Medina), pp. 64–92. Cambridge University Press, Cambridge.

Merino, J. (1987). The costs of growing and maintaining leaves of Mediterranean plants. In: *Plant Response to Stress. Functional analysis in Mediterranean ecosystems* (Ed. by J.D. Tenhunen, F.M. Catarina, O.L. Lange and W.C. Oechel), pp. 553–564. Springer-Verlag, Berlin.

Merino, J., Field, C. and Mooney, H.A. (1982). Construction and maintenance cost of Mediterranean-climate evergreen and deciduous leaves I. Growth and CO_2 exchange analysis. *Oecologia* **53**, 208–213.

Merino, J., Field, C. and Mooney, H.A. (1984). Construction and maintenance costs of Mediterranean-climate evergreen and deciduous leaves. II. Biochemical pathway analysis. *Acta Oecologica/Oecologica Plantarum* **5**, 211–229.

Milburn, J.A. (1996). Sap ascent in vascular plants: challengers to the cohesion theory ignore the significance of immature xylem and the recycling of Munch water. *Ann. Bot.* **78**, 399–407.

Miranda, A.C., Miranda, H.S., Lloyd, J., Grace, J., Francey, R.J., McIntyre, J.A., Meir, P., Riggan, P., Lockwood, R. and Brass, J. (1997). Fluxes of carbon, water and energy over Brazilian cerrado: an analysis using eddy covariance and stable isotopes. *Plant Cell Environ.* **20**, 315–328.

Mishio, M. (1992). Adaptations to drought in five woody species co-occurring on shallow-soil ridges. *Aust. J. Plant Physiol.* **19**, 539–553.

Monasterio, M. and Sarmiento, G. (1976). Phenological strategies of plant species in the tropical savanna and the semi-deciduous forest of the Venezuelan Llanos. *J. Biogeog.* **3**, 325–356.

Monteith, J.L. (1995). A reinterpretation of stomatal responses to humidity. *Plant Cell Environ.* **18**, 357–364.

Monteny, B.A., Lhomme, J.P., Cehbouni, A., Troufleau, D., Amado, M., Sicot, M., Verhoef, A., Galle, S., Said, F. and Lloyd, C.R. (1997). The role of the Sahelian biosphere on the water and the C cycle during the HAPEX-Sahel Experiment. *J. Hydrol.* **188–189**, 516–535.

Mooney, H.A. and Chu, C. (1983). Stomatal responses to humidity of coastal and interior populations of a Californian shrub. *Oecologia* **57**, 148–150.

Mordelet, P., Barot, S. and Abbadie, L. (1996). Root foraging strategies and soil patchiness in a humid savanna. *Plant & Soil* **182**, 171–176.

Mordelet, P., Menaut, J. and Mariotti, A. (1997). Tree and grass rooting patterns in an African humid savanna. *J. Veget. Sci.* **8**, 65–70.

Moreshet, S., Cohen, Y., Green, G.C. and Fuchs, M. (1990). The partitioning of hydraulic conductances within mature orange trees. *J. Exp. Bot.* **41**, 833–839.

Morgan, J.M. (1984). Osmoregulation and water stress in higher plants. *Ann. Rev. Plant Physiol.* **35**, 299–319.

Mulkey, S.S., Kitajima, K. and Wright, S.J. (1996). Plant physiological ecology of tropical forest canopies. *TREE* **11**, 408–413.

Munns, R. (1988). Why measure osmotic adjustment? *Aust. J. Plant Physiol.* **15**, 717–726.

Murphy, P.G. and Lugo, A.E. (1995). Dry forests of Central America and the Caribbean. In: *Seasonally Dry Tropical Forests* (Ed. by S.H. Bullock, H.A. Mooney and E. Medina), pp. 64–92. Cambridge University Press, Cambridge.

Myers, B.A., and Neales, T.F. (1984). Seasonal changes in the water relations of *Eucalyptus behriana* F. Muell. and *E. microcarpa* (Maiden) Maiden in the field. *Aust. J. Bot.* **32**, 495–510.

Myers, B.A. and Neales, T.F. (1986). Osmotic adjustment, induced by drought, in seedlings of three *Eucalyptus* species. *Aust. J. Plant Physiol.* **13**, 597–603.

Myers, B.A., Duff, G., Eamus, D., Fordyce, I., O'Grady, A. and Williams, R.J. (1997). Seasonal variation in water relations of trees of differing leaf phenology in a wet–dry tropical savanna near Darwin, northern Australia. *Aust. J. Bot.* **45**, 225–240.

Myers, B.A., Williams, R.J., Fordyce, I., Duff, G.A. and Eamus, D. (1998). Does irrigation affect leaf phenology in deciduous and evergreen trees of the savannas of northern Australia? *Aust. J. Ecol.* **23**, 329–339.

Neilson, R.P. (1995). A model for predicting continental scale vegetation distribution and water balance. *Ecol. Appl.* **7**, 362–385.

Nepstad, D.C., de Carvalho, C.R., Davidson, E.A., Jipp, P.H., Lefebvre, P.A., Negreiros, G.H., da Silva, E.D., Stone, T.A., Trumbore, S.E. and Vieria, S. (1994). Amazonian forests and pastures. *Nature* **372**, 666–669.

O'Grady, A.P., Eamus, D. and Hutley, L.B. (1999). Transpiration increases during the dry season: patterns of tree water use in eucalypt open-forests of northern Australia. *Tree Physiol.* **19**, 591–597.

Olivares, E. and Medina, E. (1992). Water and nutrient relations of woody perennials from tropical dry forest in Mexico. *J. Veget. Sci.* **3**, 383–392.

Opler, P.A., Frankie, G.W. and Baker, H.G. (1976). Rainfall as a factor in release, timing, and synchronization of anthesis by tropical trees and shrubs. *J. Biogeog.* **3**, 231–236.

Orians, G.H. and Solbrig, O.T. (1977). A cost–income model of leaves and roots with special reference to arid and semi-arid areas. *Am. Nat.* **111**, 677–690.

Pallardy, S.G. (1989). Hydraulic architecture and conductivity: an overview. In: *Structural and Functional Responses to Environmental Stresses: Water Shortage* (Ed. by K.H. Kreeb, H. Richter and T.M. Hinckley), pp. 3–19. SPB Academic Publishing, The Hague.

Passioura, J.B. and Munns, R. (1984). Hydraulic resistance of plants. II. Effects of rooting medium, and time of day, in barley and lupin. *Aust. J. Plant Physiol.* **11**, 341–350.

Pate, J.S., Jeschke, W.D. and Aylward, M.J. (1995). Hydraulic architecture and xylem structure of the dimorphic root systems of South-West Australian species of Proteaceae. *J. Exp. Bot.* **46**, 907–915.

Pathre, U., Sinha, A.K., Shirke, P.A. and Sane, P.V. (1998). Factors determining the midday depression of photosynthesis in trees under monsoon climate. *Trees* **12**, 472–481.

Patino, S., Tyree, M.T. and Herre, E.A. (1995). Comparison of hydraulic architecture of woody plants of differing phylogeny and growth form with special reference to free-standing and hemiepiphytic *Ficus* species from Panama. *New Phytol.* **129**, 125–134.

Pearcy, R.W., Schulze, E.-D. and Zimmermann, R. (1989). In: *Plant Physiological Ecology – Field Methods and Instrumentation.* Chapman & Hall, London.

Pelaez, D.V., Distel, R.A., Boo, R.M., Elia, O.R. and Mayor, M.P. (1994). Water relations between shrubs and grasses in semi-arid Argentina. *J. Arid Environ.* **27**, 71–78.

Penning De Vries, F.W.T. (1975). The cost of maintenance processes in plant cells. *Ann. Bot.* **39**, 77–92.

Perez Mogollon, A. (1989). Caracterizacion ecoanatomica del leno de 40 especies del bosque La Mucuy, Estado Merida, Venezuela. *Revista Forestal Venezolana* **34**, 43–51.

Phillips, W.S. (1963). Depth of roots in soil. *Ecology* **44**, 424.

Pitman, J.I. (1996). Ecophysiology of tropical dry evergreen forest, Thailand: measured and modelled stomatal conductance of *Hopea ferrea*, a dominant canopy emergent. *J. Appl. Ecol.* **33**, 1366–1378.

Pockman, W.T., Sperry, J.S. and O'Leary, J.W. (1995). Sustained and significant negative water pressure in xylem. *Nature* **378**, 715–716.

Poorter, H. (1994). Construction costs and payback time of biomass: a whole plant perspective. In: *A Whole Plant Perspective on Carbon–Nitrogen Interactions* (Ed. by J. Roy and E. Garnier), pp. 111–127. SPB Academic Publishing, Netherlands.

Poorter, H. and Evans, J.R. (1998). Photosynthetic nitrogen-use efficiency of species that differ inherently in specific leaf area. *Oecologia* **116**, 26–37.

Prado, C.J.B.A. and De Moraes, J.A.P.V. (1997). Photosynthetic capacity and specific leaf mass in twenty woody species of Cerrado vegetation under field conditions. *Photosynthetica* **33**, 103–112.

Prior, L.D. (1997). *Ecological physiology of* Eucalyptus tetrodonta *F. Muell and* Terminalia ferdinandiana *Excell saplings in the Northern Territory.* Ph.D. thesis, Northern Territory University, Darwin.

Prior, L.D. and Eamus, D. (1999). Seasonal changes in leaf water characteristics of *Eucalyptus tetrodonta* and *Terminalia ferdinandiana* saplings in a northern Australian savanna. *Aust. J. Bot.* **47**, 587–599.

Prior, L.D., Eamus, D. and Duff, G.A. (1997a). Seasonal and diurnal patterns of carbon assimilation, stomatal conductance and leaf water potential in *Eucalyptus tetrodonta* saplings in a wet–dry savanna in northern Australia. *Aust. J. Bot.* **45**, 241–258.

Prior, L.D., Eamus, D. and Duff, G.A. (1997b). Seasonal trends in carbon assimilation, stomatal conductance, pre-dawn leaf water potential and growth in *Terminalia ferdinandiana*, a deciduous tree of northern Australian savannas. *Aust. J. Bot.* **45**, 53–69.

Radin, J.W. (1990). Responses of transpiration and hydraulic conductance to root temperature in nitrogen- and phosphorus-deficient cotton seedlings. *Plant Physiol.* **92**, 855–857.

Reich, P.D. (1984). Loss of stomatal function in ageing hybrid poplar leaves. *Ann. Bot.* **53**, 691–698.

Reich, P.B. (1995). Phenology of tropical forests: patterns, causes, and consequences. *Can. J. Bot.* **73**, 164–174.

Reich, P.B. and Borchert, R. (1982). Phenology and eco-physiology of the tropical tree *Tabebuia neochrysantha* (Bignoniaceae). *Ecology* **63**, 294–299.

Reich, P.B. and Borchert, R. (1984). Water stress and tree phenology in a tropical dry forest in the lowlands of Costa Rica. *J. Ecol.* **72**, 61–74.

Reich, P.B. and Borchert, R. (1988). Changes with leaf age in stomatal function and water status of several tropical tree species. *Biotropica* **20**, 60–69.

Reich, P.B. and Hinckley, T.M. (1989). Influence of pre-dawn water potential and soil-to-leaf hydraulic conductance in two oak species. *Funct. Ecol.* **3**, 719–727.

Reich, P.B. and Walters, M.B. (1994). Photosynthesis-nitrogen relations in Amazonian tree species. *Oceologia* **97**, 73–81.

Reich, P.B., Uhl, C., Walters, M.B. and Ellsworth, D.S. (1991). Leaf lifespan as a determinant of leaf structure and function among 23 Amazonian tree species. *Oecologia* **86**, 16–24.

Reich, P.B., Walters, M.B. and Ellsworth, D.S. (1992). Leaf life-span in relation to leaf, plant, and stand characteristics among diverse ecosystems. *Ecol. Monogr.* **62**(3), 365–392.

Reich, P.B., Walters, M.B., Ellsworth, D.S. and Uhl, C. (1994). Photosynthesis–nitrogen relations in Amazonian tree species. *Oecologia* **97**, 62–72.

Reich, P.B., Kloeppel, B.D., Ellsworth, D.S. and Walters, M.B. (1995). Different photosynthesis-nitrogen relations in deciduous hardwood and evergreen coniferous tree species. *Oecologia* **104**, 24–30.

Running, S.W. (1980). Field estimates of root and xylem resistances in *Pinus contorta* using root excision. *J. Exp. Bot.* **31**, 555–569.

Running, S.W., Ramakrishna, R.N., Peterson, D.J., Band, L.E., Potts, D.F., Pierce, L.L. and Spanner, M.A. (1989). Mapping regional forest evapotranspiration and photosynthesis by coupling satellite data with ecosystem simulation. *Ecology* **70**, 1090–1101.

Sala, D.E., Lauenroth, W.K., Parton, W.J. and Trlica, M.J. (1981). Water status of soil and vegetation in a shortgrass steppe. *Oecologia* **48**, 327–331.

Sampaio, E.V.S.B. (1995). Overview of the Brazilian caatinga. In: *Seasonally Dry Tropical Forests* (Ed. by S.H. Bullock, H.A. Mooney and E. Medina), pp. 35–63. Cambridge University Press, Cambridge.

San Jose, J.J., Bracho, R. and Nikonova, N. (1998a). Comparison of water transfer as a component of the energy balance in a cultivated grass (*Brachiaria decumbens* Stapf.) field and a savanna during the wet season of the Orinoco Llanos. *Agric. Forest Meteorol.* **90**, 65–79.

San Jose, J.J., Montes, R.A., Fariñas, M.R. (1998b). Carbon stocks and fluxes in a temporal scaling from a savanna to a semi-deciduous forest. *Forest Ecol. Manage.* **105**, 251–262.

Sarmiento, G., Goldstein, G. and Meinzer, F. (1985). Adaptive strategies of woody species in neotropical savannas. *Biol. Rev.* **60**, 315–355.

Scholes, R.J. and Archer, S.R. (1997). Tree–grass interactions in savannas. *Ann. Rev. Ecol. Systematics* **28**, 517–544.

Scholes, R.J. and Walker, B.H. (1995). *An African Savanna. Synthesis of the Nylsvey Study.* Cambridge University Press, Cambridge.

Schulze, E.-D., Lange, O.L., Evenari, M., Kappen, L. and Buschbom, U. (1980). Long-term effects of drought on wild and cultivated plants in the Negev desert. II Diurnal patterns of net photosynthesis and daily carbon gain. *Oecologia* **45**, 19–25.

Schulze, E.-D., Cermak, J., Matyssek, R., Penka, M., Zimmermann, R., Vasicek, F., Gries, W. and Kucera, J. (1985). Canopy transpiration and water fluxes in the xylem of the trunk of *Larix* and *Picea* trees – a comparison of xylem flow, porometer and cuvette measurements. *Oecologia* **66**, 475–483.

Schulze, E.-D., Williams, R.J., Farquhar, G.D., Schulze, W., Langridge, J., Miller, J.M. and Walker, B.H. (1998). Carbon and nitrogen isotope discrimination and nitrogen nutrition of trees along a rainfall gradient in northern Australia. *Aust. J. Plant Physiol.* **25**, 413–425.

Seghieri, J. (1995). The rooting patterns of woody and herbaceous plants in a savanna; are they complementary or in competition? *Afr. J. Ecol.* **33**, 358–365.

Sharkey, T.D. (1984). Transpiration-induced changes in the photosynthetic capacity of leaves. *Planta* **160**, 143–150.

Shukla, R.P. and Ramakrishnan, P.S. (1982). Phenology of trees in a sub-tropical forest in North-Eastern India. *Vegetatio* **49**, 103–109.

Skene, D.S. and Balodis, V. (1968). A study of vessel length in *Eucalyptus obliqua* L'Herit. *J. Exp. Bot.* **19**, 825–830.

Smit, G.N. and Rethman, N.F.G. (1998). Root biomass, depth distribution and relations with leaf biomass of *Colophospermum mopane*. *S. Afr. J. Bot.* **64**(1), 38–43.

Sobrado, M.A. (1986). Aspects of tissue water relations and seasonal changes of leaf water potential components of evergreen and deciduous species coexisting in tropical dry forests. *Oecologia* **68**, 413–416.

Sobrado, M.A. (1991). Cost–benefit relationships in deciduous and evergreen leaves of tropical dry forest species. *Funct. Ecol.* **5**, 608–616.

Sobrado, M.A. (1993). Trade-off between water transport efficiency and leaf life-span in a tropical dry forest. *Oecologia* **96**, 19–23.

Sobrado, M.A. (1996). Embolism vulnerability of an evergreen tree. *Biol. Plantarum* **38**, 297–301.

Sobrado, M.A. (1997). Embolism vulnerability in drought-deciduous and evergreen species of a tropical dry forest. *Acta Oecologia* **18**, 383–391.

Sobrado, M.A. (1997/98). Hydraulic conductance and water potential differences inside leaves of tropical evergreen and deciduous species. *Biol. Plantarum* **40**, 633–637.

Specht, R.L. (1981). Foliage projective cover and standing biomass. In: *Vegetation Classification in Australia* (Ed. by A.N. Gillison and D.J. Anderson), pp. 10–21. CSIRO, Canberra.

Specht, R.L. (1986). Phenology. In: *Tropical Plant Communities. Their Resilience, Functioning and Management in Northern Australia* (Ed. by H.T. Clifford and R.L. Specht), pp. 78–90. University of Queensland, Brisbane.

Sperry, J.S. and Pockman, W.T. (1993). Limitation of transpiration by hydraulic conductance and xylem cavitation in *Betula occidentalis*. *Plant Cell Environ.* **16**, 279–287.

Sperry, J.S. and Saliendra, N.Z. (1994). Intra- and inter-plant variation in xylem cavitation in *Betula occidentalis*. *Plant Cell Environ.* **17**, 1233–1241.

Sperry, J.A. and Tyree, M.T. (1988). Mechanism of water stress induced xylem embolism. *Plant Physiol.* **88**, 581–587.

Sperry, J.S. and Tyree, M.T. (1990). Water-stress-induced xylem embolism in three species of conifers. *Plant Cell Environ.* **13**, 427–436.

Sperry, J.S., Perry, A.H. and Sullivan, J.E.M. (1991). Pit membrane degradation and air-embolism formation in ageing xylem vessels of *Populus tremuloides* Michx. *J. Exp. Bot.* **42**, 1399–1406.

Sperry, J.S., Saliendra, N.Z., Pockman, W.T., Cochard, H., Cruiziat, P., Davis, S.D., Ewers, F.S. and Tyree, M.T. (1996). New evidence for large negative xylem pressures and their measurement by the pressure chamber method. *Plant Cell Environ.* **19**, 427–436.

Stewart, G.R., Turnbull, M.H., Schnidt, S. and Erskine, P.D. (1989). [13]C natural abundance in plant communities along a rainfall gradient: a biological integrator of water availability. *Aust. J. Plant Physiol.* **22**, 51–55.

Stirzaker, R.J. and Passioura, J.B. (1996). The water relations of the root–soil interface. *Plant Cell Environ.* **19**, 201–208.

Stone, E.L. and Kalisz, P.J. (1991). On the maximum extent of tree roots. *Forest Ecol. Manag.* **46**, 59–102.

Sun, C., Kaplin, B.A., Kristensen, K.A., Munyaligoga, V., Mvukiyumwami, J., Kajondo, K.K. and Moermond, T.C. (1996). Tree phenology in a tropical montane forest in Rwanda. *Biotropica* **28**(4b), 668–681.

Sundarapandian, S.M. and Swamy, P.S. (1996). Fine root biomass distribution and productivity patterns under open and closed canopies of tropical forest ecosystems at Kodayar in Western Ghats, South India. *Forest Ecol. Manag.* **86**, 181–192.

Takagi, K., Tsuboya, T. and Takahashi, H. (1998). Diurnal hystereses of stomatal and bulk surface conductances in relation to vapour pressure deficit in cool temperate wetland. *Agric. Forest Meteorol.* **91**, 177–191.

Tenhunen, J.D., Valentini, R., Köstner, B., Zimmermann, R. and Granier, A. (1998). Variation in forest gas exchange at landscape to continental scales. *Ann. Sci. Forestières*, **55**, 1–11.

Thomas, D.S. and Eamus, D. (1999). The influence of predawn leaf water potential on stem hydraulic conductivity and foliar ABA concentrations and on stomatal responses to atmospheric water content at constant C_i. *J. Exp. Bot.* **50**, 243–251.

Thomas, D.S., Eamus, D. and Bell, D. (1999a). Optimisation theory of stomatal behaviour. I. A critical evaluation of five methods of calculation. *J. Exp. Bot.* **50**, 385–392.

Thomas, D.S., Eamus, D. and Bell, D. (1999b). Optimisation theory of stomatal behaviour II. Stomatal responses of several tree species of north Australia to changes in light, soil and atmospheric water content and temperature. *J. Exp. Bot.* **50**, 393–400.

Tognetti, R. and Borghetti, M. (1994). Formation and seasonal occurrence of xylem embolism in *Alnus cordata*. *Tree Physiol.* **14**, 241–250.

Tomlinson, H., Traore, A. and Teklehaimanot, Z. (1998). An investigation of the root distribution of *Parkia biglobosa* in Burkina Faso, West Africa, using a logarithmic spiral trench. *Forest Ecol. Manag.* **107**, 173–182.

Tuzet, A., Castell, J-F., Perrier, A. and Zurfluh, O. (1997). Flux heterogeneity and evapotranspiration partitioning in a sparse canopy: the fallow savanna. *J. Hydrol.* **188–189**, 482–493.

Tyree, M.T. and Ewers, F.W. (1991). The hydraulic architecture of trees and other woody plants. *New Phytol.* **119**, 345–360.

Tyree, M.T. and Ewers, F.W. (1996). Hydraulic architecture of woody tropical plants. In: *Tropical Forest Plant Ecophysiology* (Ed. by S.M. Mulkey, R.L. Chazdon and A.P. Smith), pp. 217–243. Chapman & Hall, New York.

Tyree, M.T. and Sperry, J.S. (1989). The vulnerability of xylem cavitation and embolism. *Ann. Rev. Plant Physiol. Mol. Biol.* **40**, 19–38.

Tyree, M.T., Snyderman, D.A., Wilmot, T.R. and Machado, J.-L. (1991). Water relations and hydraulic architecture of a tropical tree (*Schefflerea morotoni*).

Data, models and a comparison with two temperate species (*Acer saccharum* and *Thuja occidentalis*). *Plant Physiology* **96**, 1105–1113.

Tyree, M.T., Alexander, J. and Machado, J.-L. (1992). Loss of hydraulic conductivity due to water stress in intact juveniles of *Quercus rubra* and *Populus deltoides*. *Tree Physiol.* **10**, 411–415.

Tyree, M.T., Cochard, H., Cruiziat, P., Sinclair, B. and Ameglio, T. (1993). Drought-induced leaf shedding in walnut: evidence for vulnerability segmentation. *Plant Cell Environ.* **16**, 879–882.

Tyree, M.T., Davis, S.D. and Cochard, H. (1994). Biophysical perspectives of xylem evolution: is there a tradeoff of hydraulic efficiency for vulnerability to dysfunction? *IAWA J.* **15**, 335–360.

Tyree, M.T., Patino, S., Bennink, J. and Alexander, J. (1995). Dynamic measurements of root hydraulic conductance using a high-pressure flowmeter in the laboratory and field. *J. Exp. Bot.* **46**, 83–94.

Tyree, M.T., Patino, S. and Becker, P. (1998). Vulnerability to drought-induced embolism of Bornean heath and dipterocarp forest trees. *Tree Physiol.* **18**, 583–588.

van Schaik, C.P., Terborgh, J.W. and Wright, S.J. (1993). The phenology of tropical forests: adaptive significance and consequences for primary producers. *Ann. Rev. Ecol. Systematics* **24**, 353–377.

Van der Willigen, C. and Pammenter, N.W. (1998). Relationship between growth and xylem hydraulic characteristics of clones of *Eucalyptus* spp. at contrasting sites. *Tree Physiol.* **18**, 595–600.

Verhoef, A., Allen, S.J., De Bruin, A.R., Jacobs, C.M.J. and Heusinkveld, B.G. (1996). Fluxes of carbon dioxide and water vapour from a Sahelian savanna. *Agric. Forest Meteorol.* **80**, 231–248.

Visalakshi, N. (1994). Fine root dynamics on two tropical dry evergreen forests in Southern India. *J. BioSci.* **19**, 103–116.

Vogt, K.A., Vogt, D.J., Palmiotto, A., Boon, P., O'Hara, J. and Asbjornses, H. (1996). Review of root dynamics in forest ecosystems grouped by climate, climatic forest type and species. *Plant Soil* **187**, 159–219.

Walker, B.H. and Langridge, J.L. (1997). Predicting savanna vegetation structure on the basis of plant available moisture (PAM) and plant available nutrients (PAN): a case study from Australia. *J. Biogeog.* **24**, 813–825.

Wang, J., Ives, N.E. and Lechowicz, M.J. (1992). The relation of foliar phenology to xylem embolism in trees. *Funct. Ecol.* **6**, 469–475.

Waring, R.H. and Schlesinger, W.H. (1985). *Forest Ecosystems: Concepts and Management*. Academic Press, San Diego.

Weltzin, J.F. and McPherson, G.R. (1997). Spatial and temporal soil moisture resource partitioning by trees and grasses in a temperate savanna, Arizona, USA. *Oecologia* **112**, 156–164.

Whitehead, D. (1998). Regulation of stomatal conductance and transpiration in forest canopies. *Tree Physiol.* **18**, 633–644.

Whitehead, D., Edwards, W.R.N. and Jarvis, P.G. (1984). Conducting sapwood area, foliage area, and permeability in mature trees of *Picea sitchensis* and *Pinus contorta*. *Can. J. Forest Res.* **14**, 940–947.

Whitmore, T.C. (1985). *Tropical Rain Forests of the Far East*. Oxford University Press, Oxford.

Williams, J.E., Davis, S.D. and Portwood, K. (1997a). Xylem embolism in seedlings and resprouts of *Adenostoma fasciculatum* after fire. *Aust. J. Bot.* **45**, 291–300.

Williams, K., Percival, F., Merino, J. and Mooney, H.A. (1987). Estimation of tissue construction cost from heat of combustion and organic nitrogen content. *Plant Cell Environ.* **10**, 725–734.

Williams, K., Field, C.B. and Mooney, H.A. (1989). Relationships among leaf construction cost, leaf longevity, and light environment in rain-forest plants of the genus *Piper. Am. Nat.* **133**, 198–211.

Williams, M., Malhi, Y., Nobre, A. D., Rastetter, E.B., Grace, J. and Pereira, M.G.P. (1998). Seasonal variation in net carbon exchange and evapotranspiration in a Brazilian rainforest: a modelling analysis. *Plant Cell Environ.* **21**, 953–968.

Williams, R.J., Duff, G.A., Bowman, D.M.J.S. and Cook, A. (1996). Variation in the composition and structure of tropical savannas as a function of rainfall and soil texture along a large-scale climatic gradient in the Northern Territory. *J. Biogeog.* **23**, 747–756.

Williams, R.J., Myers, B.A., Muller, W.J., Duff, G.A. and Eamus, D. (1997b). Leaf phenology of woody species in a tropical savanna in the Darwin region, northern Australia. *Ecology* **78**, 2542–2558.

Williams, W.E. (1983). Optimal water-use efficiency in a Californian shrub. *Plant Cell Environ.* **6**, 145–151.

Wofsy, S.C., Goulden, M.L., Munger, J.W., Fan, S.M., Bakwin, P.S., Daube, B.C., Bassow, S.L. and Bazzaz, F.A. (1993). Net exchange of CO_2 in a mid-latitude forest. *Science* **260**, 1314–1317.

Wright, S.J. (1996). Phenological responses to seasonality in tropical forest plants. In: *Tropical Forest Plant Ecophysiology* (Ed. by S.S. Mulkey, R.L. Chazdon and A.P. Smith), pp. 440–460. Chapman & Hall, New York.

Wright, S.J. and Cornejo, F.H. (1990). Seasonal drought and leaf fall in a tropical forest. *Ecology* **71**, 1165–1175.

Wright, S.J. and van Schaik, C.P. (1994). Light and the phenology of tropical trees. *Am. Nat.* **143**, 192–199.

Wullschleger, S.D., Meinzer, F.C. and Vertessy, R.A. (1998). A review of whole-plant water use studies in trees. *Tree Physiol.* **18**, 499–512.

Yadava, P.S. (1990). Savannas of north-east India. *J. Biogeog.* **17**, 385–394.

Yang, S. and Tyree, M.T. (1992). A theoretical model of hydraulic conductivity recovery from embolism with comparison to experimental data on *Acer saccharum. Plant Cell Environ.* **15**, 633–643.

Yang, S. and Tyree, M.T. (1994). Hydraulic architecture of *Acer saccharum* and *A. rubrum*: comparison of branches to whole trees and the contribution of leaves to hydraulic resistance. *J. Exp. Bot.* **45**, 179–186.

Zimmermann, M.H. (1978). Hydraulic architecture of some diffuse-porous trees. *Can. J. Bot.* **56**, 2286–2295.

Zimmermann, M.H. (1983). Xylem structure and the ascent of sap. In: *Springer Series in Wood Anatomy* (Ed. by T.E. Timell). Springer-Verlag, Berlin.

Zimmermann, M.H. and Jeje, A.A. (1981). Vessel-length distribution in stems of some American woody plants. *Can. J. Bot.* **59**, 1882–1892.

Meta-analysis in Ecology

JESSICA GUREVITCH, PETER S. CURTIS AND MICHAEL H. JONES

ADVANCES IN ECOLOGICAL RESEARCH VOL. 32
ISBN 0-12-013932-4

I. SUMMARY

Meta-analysis is the statistical synthesis of the results of separate studies. It was adapted from other disciplines for use in ecology and evolutionary biology beginning in the early 1990s, and, at the turn of the century, has begun to have a substantial impact on the way data are summarized in these fields. We identify 119 studies concerned with meta-analysis in ecology and evolution, the earliest published in 1991 and the most recent in 2000. We introduce the statistical methods used in modern meta-analysis with references to the well-developed literature in the field. These formal, statistically defensible methods have been established to determine average treatment effects across studies when a common research question is being investigated, to establish confidence limits around the average effect size, and to test for consistency or lack of agreement in effect size as well as explanations for differences in the magnitude of the effect among studies. Problems with popular but statistically flawed methods for the quantitative summary of research results have been pointed out, and their use is diminishing. We discuss a number of challenges and threats to the validity of meta-analysis in ecology and evolution. In particular, we examine how difficulties resulting from missing data, publication bias, data quality and data exclusion, non-independence among observations, and the combination of dissimilar data sets may affect the perceived utility of meta-analysis in these fields and the soundness of conclusions drawn from its application. We highlight particular applications of meta-analysis in ecology and evolution, discuss several controversies surrounding individual meta-analyses, and outline some of the practical issues involved in carrying out a meta-analysis. Finally, we suggest changes that would improve the quality of data synthesis in ecology and evolutionary biology, and predict future directions for this emerging enterprise.

II. INTRODUCTION

If one browses through ecology journals published before the 1960s, it becomes apparent that statistical tests were not commonly employed in ecological research prior to that time. The integration of formal statistical methods into scientific practice subtly but profoundly changed the perspective of ecologists. While anyone trained in modern ecology is now familiar with at least basic statistical methods for quantifying and comparing responses within a study, many are not yet fully aware of dramatic new developments for the quantitative synthesis of research results across independent studies. Modern statistical techniques for quantitative research synthesis, collectively known as *meta-analysis*, were first introduced to the fields of ecology and evolution in the early 1990s (Table 1 and Figure 1; Arnqvist and Wooster, 1995a). Glass introduced the term meta-analysis, defining it as 'the statistical analysis of a large collection of analysis results from individual studies for the purpose of integrating the findings' (Glass, 1976, p. 3), contrasting it with the primary analysis of individual studies. A more recent definition that emphasizes contemporary approaches is that meta-analysis is a set of 'statistical methods designed to draw rigorous inferences from multiple studies' (H. Caswell, personal communication). Meta-analysis is typically used to synthesize the results of published studies, but it may also serve to combine published or unpublished results by an individual investigator or research group, or by a group of investigators who have agreed, either in advance or after the work is completed, to combine their results. We contrast

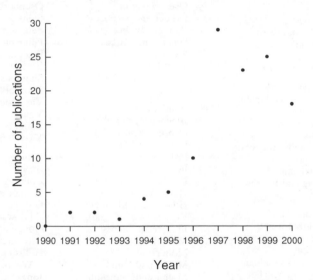

Fig. 1. Number of papers published per year on meta-analysis in the fields of ecology and evolution. The list (references are in Table 1) is inclusive and non-selective, and contains, in addition to strictly defined meta-analyses, papers on meta-analysis methodology, comments, reviews and critiques of meta-analyses in these fields. Several papers claim to be meta-analyses but do not meet the definitions laid out in the text of this review. The purpose of being more inclusive rather than more selective was to gather all of the literature on the topic to date for other researchers interested in various aspects of the application of meta-analytic techniques in these research fields: further sorting and selection is therefore available to the reader. We attempted to gather references to all recent quantitative syntheses and discussions of meta-analysis applications by searching the Web of Science (ISI) using keywords, references to key papers, and papers cited in other references. All papers were then reviewed for their appropriateness for inclusion in this review.

Table 1
Papers on meta-analysis in ecology and evolutionary biology included in Figure 1

Year	Authors	Year	Authors	Year	Authors
1991	Jarvinen	1997	Hugueny and	1999	Arft *et al.*
	Marchant and	(cont.)	Guegan		Byers and Waller
	McGrew		Kraak		Downing *et al.*
1992	Gurevitch *et al.*		Leamy		Englund and
	VanderWerf		Liermann and Hilborn		Evander
			Markow and Clarke		Englund *et al.*
1993	Gurevitch and		McCarthy		Goldberg *et al.*
	Hedges		McGrew and		Gurevitch and Hedges
1994	FernandezDuque		Marchant		Hedges *et al.*
	and Valeggia		Miller and Fair		Medlyn *et al.*
	Poulin		Møller and		Møller
	Tonhasca and Byrne		Thornhill (a, b)		Møller and Alatalo
	Wooster		Myers *et al.*		Møller and Shykoff
1995	Arnqvist and		Osenberg *et al.*		Osenberg *et al.* (a, b)
	Wooster (a,b)		Palmer and Strobeck		Palmer
	Peterman		Pomiankowski		Petersen *et al.*
	Turchin		Schalk and Forbes		Peterson *et al.*
	Vasquez *et al.*		Swaddle		Planque and Fredou
			Thrush *et al.*		Riessen
1996	Arnqvist *et al.*		Whitlock and Fowler		Simmons *et al.*
	Brett and Goldman				Thornhill *et al.*
	Britten	1998	Bender *et al.*		Van Dongen *et al.*
	Csada *et al.*		Blackenhorn *et al.*		Vollestad *et al.*
	Curtis		Cebrian *et al.*		Wand *et al.*
	Dahl and Greenberg		Curtis and Wang		Xiong and Nilsson
	Ellison		Fiske *et al.*	2000	Arnqvist and Nilsson
	Frankham		Folt *et al.*		Brook *et al.*
	Leung and Forbes		Hartley and Hunter		Collie *et al.*
	Poulin		Herrera *et al.*		Connor *et al.*
			Hilborn and Liermann		Gliwicz and
1997	Abouheif and		Koricheva *et al.* (a,b)		Glowacka
	Fairbairn		Lardicci and Rossi		Gough *et al.*
	Adams *et al.*		McCann *et al.*		Gurevitch *et al.*
	Bauchau		Møller		Hollister and
	Brett and Goldman		Møller and Ninni		Webber
	Brett and Mueller-		Møller and Thornhill		Jones
	Navarra		Murray		Lempa *et al.*
	Cote and Sutherland		Myers		Leung *et al.*
	Dodds		Myers and Mertz		Mosquera *et al.*
	Dolman and		Piegorsch *et al.*		Pither and Taylor
	Sutherland		Proulx and Mazumder		Poulin
	FernandezDuque		Van Zandt and		Rosenberg *et al.*
	Hamilton and Poulin		Mopper		Schmitz *et al.*
	Hechtel and Juliano		Vernier and Fahrig		Sokolovska *et al.*
	Houle		Westoby		Windig and Nylin

contemporary meta-analysis with other approaches to reaching conclusions from a body of data obtained from a set of independent studies in Section IV.

Meta-analysis can address many of the inferential issues familiar from classical statistics, albeit at a different level (i.e. across studies), including parameter estimation (point estimates and confidence intervals) and hypothesis testing, using parametric or non-parametric models. In addition, it can provide additional information not offered by classical statistical methods, particularly about the consistency of the results across studies. The synthesis of research results is a universal and venerable occupation in science (see, e.g. Cooper and Hedges, 1994b, for a lucid overview of this topic); indeed, scientific papers almost always begin with putting their results into the context of what else is known about the topic. Meta-analysis provides tools to make this process quantitative and more rigorous, just as classical statistics allowed rigorous quantitative inferences to be made about the results of single experiments.

This review is aimed at a range of ecologists, from those who may have heard the term meta-analysis, but are not sure what exactly it entails, to those who have read a particular meta-analysis paper and wish to put it into a more general context, to those who may be undertaking a meta-analysis themselves. Our goals in writing this chapter are to introduce what meta-analysis is and is not; to review briefly its precedents; to identify all publications concerning meta-analysis in ecology and evolution to date and to highlight the recent history of this topic; to consider some of the controversies concerning its application in this field and consider some of the difficulties that arise in the synthesis of multiple studies; and, finally, to illustrate its application in ecology with several recent meta-analyses in the area of global change biology.

Meta-analysis can be viewed as a tool that enables investigators to see a larger picture, one that is not apparent when looking at some, or even all, of the component studies individually. In this sense, meta-analysis resembles a synthetic, composite photograph in which large numbers of small, individual photos of many different subjects are arranged to create a single, unique larger image that comes into focus only when seen from a greater distance. In this analogy, each of the small individual photos represent the individual studies or data records, and the composite picture is the result of meta-analysis. We suggest that the adoption of these techniques in the discipline of ecology will transform the way research results are understood, much as meta-analysis has in other disciplines, and with an impact potentially as great as that of the introduction of statistical analysis in ecology in the middle of the twentieth century.

Meta-analysis raises philosophical issues regarding the ability to reach a general understanding based upon a body of data from independent studies. The issue of generalizing research results is a particularly ambiguous and troubling one in the field of ecology, where we seek to understand natural systems, and yet work with such a great diversity of organisms, systems and levels of organization. On the one hand, most ecologists, like other scientists, are trained in graduate school to be cautious about over-extrapolating their results. As a consequence, they may confuse scientific rigor with conservatism, hesitating to extend their conclusions to other organisms or conditions. On the other hand, we all begin learning formal ecology from textbooks, which often use the results of particular experiments as examples to illustrate or prove the existence of important phenomena. Perhaps as a result, ecological thinking can demonstrate a curious kind of naivete in accepting individual experimental results as if they constituted the entire truth about nature – the habit of accepting 'textbook examples' (or alternatively, the most recently published study) as if a single experimental result could conclusively prove the reality of a particular ecological phenomenon, or tell us all we might ever want to know about it. Somewhere between the opposite extremes of hesitating to extend the implications of particular results, and over-generalizing from exemplary experiments, ecologists and evolutionary biologists need to consider more deeply the issue of how we use experimental evidence to make generalizations about nature.

Ecological studies, while highly diverse in methodology, subjects and systems, often address questions of broader interest that may be relevant to other species, systems and settings. Skeptics of ecological meta-analysis question the validity of obtaining any quantitative summary of the results of a diverse body of experimental data, owing to the inevitable inadequacies in the primary data as well as to perceived shortcomings in meta-analytic techniques. But there is nothing out of the ordinary in wishing to summarize the findings of a group of studies, as is routinely done in review series such as this one. What is different in meta-analysis is that a formal methodology has been developed to quantify syntheses and test hypotheses about the overall results.

How can the results of different experiments be synthesized quantitatively in a rigorous way? First, we must define what we are attempting to accomplish in a quantitative synthesis. In summarizing the available evidence about an effect (e.g. the effect of predation in field studies) in which we are interested, some of the important questions one might wish to answer are: How large is the overall effect (does predation have a large effect, a small effect, or no detectable effect on prey density across studies)? Can we be confident that this effect is greater or less than zero (is the estimated value of the effect significantly different from zero, when sampling variance is taken into account)? Are the results consistent across studies or, if not, are there systematic differences among categories of studies in the magnitude of the effect (e.g. among trophic levels, or for studies of long versus short duration)? Meta-analysis statistics provide straightforward means by which such questions can be answered. We next turn briefly to the basic statistical methods for meta-analysis, and examine why contemporary meta-analytic methods are superior to the more familiar alternatives for synthesizing the results of multiple studies.

III. STATISTICAL APPROACHES IN ECOLOGICAL META-ANALYSIS

A. Scaling Responses across Studies Using Metrics of Effect Size

Conducting a meta-analysis requires that the results of separate studies are put onto a common scale, so that they can be compared and averaged. Glass' insight into one way in which it could be done signalled the beginning of modern meta-analysis (Cooper and Hedges, 1994b). One of the most common approaches to combining studies in contemporary meta-analysis is to standardize the outcomes using some metric of *effect size*. Various effect size metrics have been proposed, and some that are commonly used in meta-analysis are listed in Table 2. We discuss the issue of the choice of effect size metrics below.

Two commonly used metrics in ecology, the standardized mean difference, Hedges' d, and the log response ratio, lr, are typically used where the outcome expresses the magnitude of the response to an experimental treatment by comparing an experimental to a control group. For example, it might be meaningful to say that the mean mass of organisms in the experimental group was one standard deviation greater than that in the control group (i.e. $d = 1.0$), or that it was 1.25 times the mass in the control group (i.e. $lr = \ln 1.25$; Figure 2). In some research areas the outcomes are reported as correlation coefficients, and these can be used as a metric of effect size in a meta-analysis (because Z has superior statistical properties, correlation coefficients are transformed using Fisher's Z-transform before carrying out the analysis, Table 2).

In experiments in which the results are categorical, a common metric taken from medical meta-analysis is the odds ratio (or other members of the family of measures to which it belongs; see Rosenberg *et al.*, 2000). Imagine that responses are presented in the form of 2×2 contingency tables. For example, we might be interested in whether or not seeds were removed by dispersers (i.e. the outcome is expressed as numbers removed/not removed), when seeds were experimentally colored red or left uncolored (colored/uncolored). The numbers in each cell of the contingency table are expressed as in Table 3. Following the notation in

Table 2
Summary of some common effect metrics and their sampling variances

Metric	Symbol	Equation	Sampling variance
Hedges' d	d	$d = \dfrac{(\bar{X}^E - \bar{X}^C)}{S} J$	$v_d = \dfrac{N^C + N^E}{N^C N^E} + \dfrac{d^2}{2(N^C + N^E)}$
Response ratio	lr	$lr = \ln\left(\dfrac{\bar{X}^E}{\bar{X}^C}\right)$	$v_{lr} = \dfrac{(s^E)^2}{N^E(\bar{X}^E)^2} + \dfrac{(s^C)^2}{N^C(\bar{X}^C)^2}$
Correlation coefficient – Fisher's z-transform of r	z	$z = \dfrac{1}{2}\ln\left(\dfrac{1+r}{1-r}\right)$	$v_z = \dfrac{1}{N-3}$
Odds ratio relative odds	$\ln OR$	$OR = \dfrac{P_t(1 - P_c)}{P_t(1 - P_t)}$	$v_{\ln OR} = \dfrac{1}{T} + \dfrac{1}{C} + \dfrac{1}{t} + \dfrac{1}{c}$

Symbols are as follows: $\bar{X}^E$ and $\bar{X}^C$ are the means of the experimental and control groups, respectively, S is their pooled standard deviation, and N^E and N^C are their respective sample sizes; the term J corrects for small-sample bias (Hedges and Olkin, 1985). Pearson's correlation coefficient, r, is z-transformed, with its associated sample size, N. The odds ratio is explained in the text.

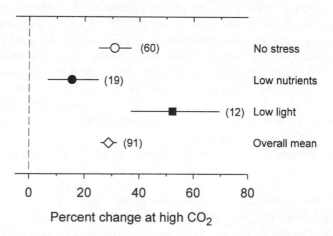

Fig. 2. Results of a meta-analysis of the effects of environmental stress on the biomass responses of trees to elevated CO_2. Experimental treatments were: no stress, low nutrients, or low light levels. Means ±95% confidence intervals (CIs), with number of studies in parentheses. (Data from Curtis and Wang, 1998.)

Table 3, the rate of response for the treatment group, P_t (seeds colored red), is

$$P_t = \frac{T}{n_t}$$

where T is the number of seeds exhibiting a response ('removed') in the treatment group, and n_t is the total number (responders and non-responders) in the treatment group. The rate of response for the control group, P_c (uncolored seeds), is

$$P_c = \frac{C}{n_c}$$

where C is the number of seeds exhibiting a response ('removed') in the control group, and n_c is the total number (responders and nonresponders) in the control group. The odds ratio and its sampling variance is given in Table 2. Similarly, responses in other ecological studies could fit a wide variety of possible categorical outcomes (dead/alive, mated/unmated, metamorphosed/remained larval, etc.), and although this metric has been used more commonly in medical research, it is appropriate in many cases of ecological research as well.

The choice of effect size metric can potentially have a substantial impact on the results of a meta-analysis. Osenberg and colleagues (Osenberg et al., 1997, 1999b; Osenberg and St Mary, 1998) have criticized the use of standard effect size metrics in ecology and evolution. Instead, they suggest that each time a meta-analysis is conducted, the authors should model the biological process being studied as well as the spatial/temporal scales of the experiments, and, based upon the model used, construct appropriate effect size metrics. They criticize the uncritical adoption of standard effect size metrics in meta-analysis, particularly the use of d. A major criticism of d that they raise is based upon the possibility that d may confound the differences between treatment means with what are effectively artifactual

Table 3
2 × 2 contingency table (see text)

	Treatment	Control	Total
Removed	T	C	$T + C$
Not removed	t	c	$t + c$
Total	$n_t = T + t$	$n_c = C + c$	$T + C + t + c$

differences in variance among studies (e.g. due to experimental design or spatial heterogeneity). This echoes the argument made by Hurlbert (1994) criticizing the use of *d* in ecological meta-analysis. In other words, the number of standard deviations by which the experimental and control group means differ is, in such cases, not an accurate reflection of the true magnitude of the effect being studied. It would also be true, in such cases (but not discussed by Osenberg and colleagues) that in the primary analysis of each of such studies, standard statistical analyses such as ANOVA (analysis of variance), regression or *t*-tests would generally be inappropriate as well. They also feel that *d* would not effectively capture the biologically most meaningful measure in combining the results of many ecological studies.

We could not disagree more strongly with the arguments of Osenberg and his colleagues that different effect size metrics should be used each time a meta-analysis is carried out, although we enthusiastically second their recommendation that meta-analysts think carefully about their analysis (including the choice of effect size metric and the interpretation of the results). If a comparison between the experimental and control groups is not effectively expressed in terms of standard deviation units because there are systematic, artifactual differences in the magnitude of the variances among studies, a ratio-based metric such as *lr* (Hedges *et al.*, 1999) should overcome that problem.

There are two major objections to creating new metrics for each meta-analysis: first, lack of standardized measures makes evaluation of the results of the meta-analysis very difficult, and second, for most ecologists, determining the statistical properties of novel statistics is essentially out of reach. The use of standard metrics means that anyone reading a meta-analysis can understand the results, and can compare results among different meta-analyses. This is analogous to why we have uniformly adopted the SI system for biological measurements, rather than creating the biologically most meaningful metric based upon constructing a conceptual or mathematical model each time we measure an organism or field plot. One can run into serious and largely invisible statistical potholes in using novel metrics with unknown sampling distributions and unknown properties, and the use of conventional meta-analysis methods for calculating means, confidence intervals, conducting homogeneity tests, and other analyses of interest on such metrics is likely to result in misinformation. A more minor limitation to the suggestion of Osenberg and co-workers is that for most meta-analyses in ecology there will not be a single way to model all studies one is interested in combining, and it is unlikely that they will all be on the same spatial or temporal scale except for meta-analyses of unusually limited scope. There is an alternative to creating new metrics for each meta-analysis on the one hand, and on the other having a single metric which is sometimes highly unsatisfactory for particular ecological data. That is to have a body of well-understood metrics (perhaps, say, a half-dozen) to choose from that represent a range of biologically meaningful types of comparisons between groups. This may represent a satisfactory compromise between the two positions for most ecological meta-analyses.

B. Combining Results across Studies

Once one has calculated an appropriate effect size for each study, these measures of response can be combined in several ways. There are many advantages to using weighted analyses (see Gurevitch and Hedges, 1999; Hedges and Olkin, 2001), in which effect sizes are weighted by the inverse of their sampling variances. The weights are typically chosen to provide unbiased estimates with minimum variance. One might first determine the weighted grand mean effect size, $\bar{E}$, where

$$\bar{E} = \frac{\sum_{i=1}^{n} w_i E_i}{\sum_{i=1}^{n} w_i}$$

n is the number of studies, and E_i is the effect size for the ith study. The weight for the ith study is the reciprocal of its sampling variance, $w_i = 1/v_i$ (see Table 2). The variance of $\bar{E}$ is:

$$s_{\bar{E}}^2 = \frac{1}{\sum_{i=1}^{n} w_i}$$

Using $s_{\bar{E}}^2$, the confidence interval around $\bar{E}$ is:

$$CI = \bar{E} \pm t_{\alpha/2[n-1]}(s_{\bar{E}})$$

where t is the two-tailed critical value found from the Student's t-distribution at the critical level, α, at $n-1$ degrees of freedom. The grand mean effect size thus presents one with a means for assessing the magnitude of the effect across all studies, and its confidence interval offers a way to evaluate whether the effect overlaps zero or is significantly greater or less than zero.

C. Explaining Differences in Response among Studies

Beyond the bare bones of obtaining a mean effect across studies and the confidence interval around that mean, one might wish to ask, are the results consistent across studies, and if not, can we explain differences in the effect beyond those due to random sampling error? The appropriate analysis will depend, of course, upon the nature of the questions one is posing, and on the nature of the data. Categorical (ANOVA-analog) and continuous (regression-analog) approaches have both been developed for meta-analytic data, although the first has been used more commonly in ecological and evolutionary applications. Both depend upon weighting effect sizes by the inverse of the sampling variances. Categorical approaches rely upon homogeneity tests. The body of results is tested to determine whether they are consistent with one another across studies, after accounting for sampling error, or whether there is genuine heterogeneity in the magnitude of the effect among studies. If studies are heterogeneous, it is often of interest to test whether there are consistent differences among categories of studies that are hypothesized to respond in different ways (carnivores versus herbivores, long-term versus short-term studies, etc.). Continuous models are useful where the effect sizes are hypothesized to depend upon an independent variable (e.g. productivity, Goldberg *et al.*, 1999; Figure 3).

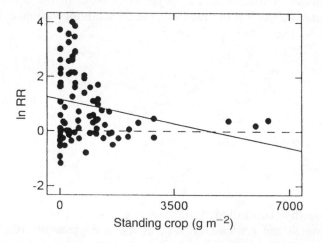

Fig. 3. Effect of competition for plants (expressed as log response ratio, RR, of plant biomass with reduced competition compared to that with competitors present) as a function of standing crop in the community. Reproduced with permission from Goldberg *et al.* (1999), Figure 1D.

One of the most important distinctions in the type of analysis for both categorical and continuous data is between fixed and random effects analyses. In simple fixed effects models it is assumed that all studies share a common 'true' effect size, and differ only by sampling error. In contrast, random effects models assume that there is random variation among studies in the 'true' effect. Mixed models combine random variation among studies within a category with fixed differences among categories (Gurevitch and Hedges, 1993, 2001). Fixed versus random effects models differ in these and other assumptions, and their results have somewhat different interpretations (e.g. Gurevitch and Hedges, 1993, 1999, 2001; Raudenbush, 1994). The methods for data analysis based upon fixed, random and mixed models for categorical and continuous data can be found in textbooks (e.g. Hedges and Olkin, 2001) and are available in some software packages (e.g. Rosenberg et al., 2000).

Other statistical approaches in meta-analysis include the use of resampling tests (randomization and bootstrapping) for both continuous and categorical analyses, where parametric tests may not be appropriate (Adams et al., 1997; Rosenberg et al., 2000). A subtle difference between standard parametric approaches and randomization tests concerns the implications regarding the universe to which one is generalizing. Parametric tests are based upon the perspective that the studies in the meta-analysis represent a population of experimental results that *could* have been done, and therefore the meta-analysis results apply to some broader population of studies beyond the actual ones included in the synthesis. Randomization tests, in contrast, are sometimes seen as viewing the data set in hand as the entire universe, with the conclusions legitimately applying only to those studies. The latter perspective may be easier to justify, at least in meta-analyses in the field of ecology. Another recent development is a technique for factorial meta-analysis, where the studies being synthesized have all manipulated the same two treatment factors at each of two levels (e.g. competition and predation; Gurevitch et al., 2000). This technique allows one to evaluate not only the main factors, but also their interaction across studies. Bayesian methods have also been applied to meta-analysis in ecology and evolutionary biology (Ellison, 1996; Liermann and Hilborn, 1997; Hilborn and Liermann, 1998; Myers and Mertz, 1998; Piegorsch et al., 1998).

IV. LIMITATIONS TO TRADITIONAL METHODS FOR DATA SYNTHESIS

The most traditional method for synthesizing the results of a body of studies is the narrative review, in which an expert in the field provides an overview, evaluation and conclusions based upon the literature on a particular question or topic. While meta-analysis offers an alternative to the traditional narrative review, it will hardly make *Advances in Ecological Research* and other journals that publish narrative reviews obsolete. Narrative reviews serve many valuable functions, and continue to be published in those disciplines in which meta-analysis holds a firmly established role. Some of the things narrative reviews can offer are the authors' perspective on the status of a discipline, evaluation of current techniques and the state of the art, and provocative questions and directions for future research. But narrative reviews also suffer from some inherent flaws. They are almost unavoidably subjective, both in their choice of studies from those available and in their conclusions (e.g. Light and Pillemer, 1984; Cooper and Dorr, 1995; Peipert and Bracken, 1997; Davidoff, 1999; Swales, 1999). Even when reviewers try their best to avoid subjectivity and bias, the selection of studies and the evaluation criteria often are eccentric or haphazard. The impressions of the reviewers are too often based largely upon the Abstract and Discussion sections of papers rather than on detailed examination of the actual data. Most importantly, narrative reviews cannot provide the information that a meta-analysis can. In particular, only a quantitative summary of the results can answer questions such as: What is the magnitude of the response overall? Is it consistent across studies or not? What explanatory variables might account for differences in the magnitude of the response among studies?

A second conventional (if less venerable) approach to research synthesis in ecology can be called 'vote-counting'. In attempting to transcend the limitations of strictly narrative reviews, over the past two decades ecologists unfamiliar with the literature on meta-analysis in other disciplines have devised at least two basic quantitative approaches to synthesize research results. The most common of these approaches is simply to count the number of statistically significant and non-significant outcomes and then weigh these counts against each other (sometimes with the use of statistical tests) to determine the magnitude and importance of the effect of interest. This might entail, for example, attempting to evaluate the existence and magnitude of the effect of competition in field experiments, with the assumption that the importance of the effect will be reflected by having it detected by a large proportion of the studies testing for it. This approach is known as vote-counting, as if each study casts a vote for or against the effect, and it has been used in many other fields as well as in ecology. However, vote-counting has such serious flaws and limitations that it is essentially never advisable to employ it. In other disciplines, these flaws have become well known and are generally widely understood, and vote-counts are no longer published. In addition, there are more subtle limitations to vote-counting that are at least in part ameliorated by using meta-analysis, as explained below. Unfortunately, vote-count reviews continue to be published in ecology (see, e.g. Gurevitch and Hedges, 1999), although the problems with this approach have been pointed out in this discipline for the better part of a decade (e.g. Gurevitch and Hedges, 1993).

The central problem with vote-counting concerns statistical power. The statistical significance of the outcome of an experiment depends both on the magnitude of the observed response, on the variability in the data, and on the sample size, which together determine the likelihood that the experiment will succeed in detecting a real response. This results in a negative bias, because the ability to detect real effects (i.e. to reject the null hypothesis) is limited when sample sizes are small and the magnitude of the effects are modest. (By negative bias, we mean that there is a bias against detecting true effects, because we fail to reject the null hypothesis too often when in fact it should be rejected.) Narrative reviews are subject to the same problem, because the reviewer often relies upon the statistical significance of the results in evaluating the outcome of the studies being reviewed. Because ecological studies typically have small sample sizes and modest effects, they are particularly vulnerable to this negative bias. It is also common to decide whether two studies agree or disagree based upon the statistical significance of their outcomes, but when statistical power is low, even studies with identical underlying effects have a fairly large chance of disagreeing by chance alone (e.g. Gurevitch and Hedges, 1999). In statistical terms, vote-counting is not a very good procedure: it has low power itself to detect results, the conclusions drawn are highly biased, and, counter-intuitively, its statistical power actually declines as the number of studies reviewed increases (the reliability of the test actually becomes worse as one gains more information; Hedges and Olkin, 1980, 1985). Readers should note, however, that there is a statistically robust variant of vote-counting that may be of use when the available data are extremely limited (Hedges and Olkin, 1985). Vote-counting, like narrative reviews, cannot provide reliable information on the magnitude or consistency (homogeneity) of the results of the studies being reviewed. Standard techniques for meta-analysis are not subject to these problems and limitations.

A more subtle limitation with vote-counting that is more likely to be resolved in carrying out a meta-analysis is the lack of specificity in what one is trying to answer in synthesizing results. The 'effect' being evaluated is often only vaguely specified, in contrast to the well-defined 'effect size' used in meta-analysis. In attempting to determine the importance of an effect, vote-count reviews often do not distinguish between statistical significance, biological significance, and biological importance, and confuse the frequency with which effects are detected with their magnitude and importance. In evaluating the statistical significance of each study, since each study used different statistical models and different treatments, it is not so clear what the statistical significance being evaluated is, nor what the effect is whose magnitude is being considered. In conducting a meta-analysis, each of these and many other issues must be carefully weighed, and a decision must be reached and justified. These decisions should be specified in the published meta-analysis.

Another conventional, but flawed, approach to quantitative research synthesis is to calculate standardized effect sizes, but to use more familiar statistical techniques like ANOVA and ordinary least-squares regression to carry out quantitative syntheses of the effect size estimates across studies. This is not advised, and we briefly review the reasons below. Presumably, these reviewers acknowledge the utility of using standard effect size measures (as introduced above) for integrating results across studies, and may even be convinced of the inappropriateness of vote-counting, but are unfamiliar with the statistical techniques used in meta-analysis. The issues involved are spelled out in more detail by Gurevitch and Hedges (1999) and Hedges and Olkin (2001).

Population estimates based on large sample sizes are more precise than those based upon small sample sizes. Because studies in a meta-analysis data set may differ by orders of magnitude in sample size, sampling variances also commonly vary enormously in such data sets. For this reason, concern about violating the usual statistical assumption of homogeneity of variances is often much more serious in meta-analysis than in primary statistical analyses. Data transformation cannot eliminate this problem, and even very high levels of heteroscedasticity may be cryptic, escaping the notice of the analyst who only looks at effect sizes but not at their sampling variances. ANOVA and ordinary least-squares regressions may perform very poorly (i.e. give inaccurate results) in such circumstances. Standard meta-analytic techniques avoid this problem because the analyses explicitly take sampling variance into account.

To illustrate this problem, consider that in a conventional primary analysis, data collected on individuals (organisms, plots, etc.) can be represented by points on a graph. The graph could be a scattergram, for example, where responses of individuals are hypothesized to be dependent upon some other variable. Alternatively, the points might merely illustrate the degree of scatter about the mean. These individual points are known with a fair degree of certainty, because they have been measured directly (there may be a small amount of measurement error associated with them, but we can assume that that will be minor relative to other sources of variation). In a meta-analysis, the data are no longer measurements on individuals known with some certainty, but rather are estimates of population parameters (such as the effect sizes in each study). As in a primary analysis, the researcher might be interested in relating explanatory variables to the outcomes (which here are effect sizes). One might picture these meta-data not as points on a graph, but rather as clouds on a graph. Each cloud (the effect sizes in each study) will be different in size from the others, because these are population estimates, which are known with greater or lesser certainty in each study. The magnitude of each 'cloud' is inversely proportional to its sampling variance (Table 2); studies with large sample sizes approach points (i.e. their effect sizes are known fairly precisely), while those with small sample sizes are large clouds with a lot of uncertainty as to where the actual effect size is located in the cloud. ANOVA, regression and other classical statistical methods are not robust to violations of the assumption that this sampling variance is equal among points (i.e. studies). Again, meta-analysis avoids this problem by explicitly taking sampling variance into account.

V. A BRIEF HISTORY OF META-ANALYSIS IN ECOLOGY AND EVOLUTIONARY BIOLOGY

A. Origins of Contemporary Meta-analysis

While modern methods for meta-analysis have been developed largely in the last quarter century, these techniques have old roots, traceable to methods that include the combined tests of statistical significance developed by such luminaries as Cochran (1937), Fisher (1932), Pearson (1904, 1933) and Tippett (1931). The modern methods, however, are both more powerful and much more useful than those developed earlier.

The development of formal techniques and approaches for modern quantitative data synthesis began in the 1970s in the social sciences, particularly in clinical, educational, social and industrial psychology (see Cooper and Hedges, 1994b; Hunt, 1997). In the following decade, as researchers became aware of these tools and the statistical techniques available were further developed and refined, there was an explosion of interest in meta-analysis in medical research (e.g. Sacks et al., 1987; Chalmers et al., 1989; Mann, 1990, 1994). Cooper and Hedges (1994a, p. 7) state that:

> Research synthesis in the 1960s [in the social sciences] was at best an art, at worst a form of yellow journalism. Today, the summarization and integration of studies is viewed as a research process in its own right; it is held to scientific standards and applies the techniques for data gathering and analysis developed for its unique purpose.

These 'near-revolutionary developments' (Cooper and Hedges, 1994b) in research integration experienced in the behavioral and medical sciences over the past 20 years have only recently begun to have an impact on the field of ecology. As the discipline earlier made the transition from description and classification to modern quantitative approaches, research synthesis in ecology is poised to make the transition from descriptive to formal quantitative techniques. Ecologists in earlier periods generally possessed an intimate knowledge of the biology and natural history of the organisms they studied and about the environments in which they were found. The richness of detail that was once common in describing individual organisms, or the alternative, the imperative to classify and categorize organisms and systems, eventually gave way to an emphasis on representing (statistical) populations by means and variances, and comparing them with other populations using statistical hypothesis testing. The introduction of statistical methods into ecological and evolutionary research was initially strongly resisted in some quarters (see Preface to Simpson *et al.*, 1960), but ultimately changed the very nature of the science. This change coincided with many others in the discipline, and was basic to completing the transition of ecology from natural history to a modern scientific discipline. The fundamental shift in outlook that this entailed may be echoed, in some ways, by that resulting from the gradual acceptance of modern methods for the statistical synthesis of research results in ecology.

B. Publications in Ecological Meta-analysis

We attempted to collect all papers concerned with formal meta-analysis in ecology and evolution. We conducted an exhaustive search, relying primarily on the ISI Web of Science on-line scientific publication database. We searched for papers by keywords and by citations of known key references in the field. We then examined the articles found to determine if they were appropriate. It was our intention to be highly inclusive; papers were not screened for quality, proper use of statistical methods, or other selective criteria. Both actual meta-analyses as well as papers concerned with meta-analysis methodology, application and controversies were included in our comprehensive list. The purpose of using very broad selection criteria was to collect all potentially useful papers for future use by readers interested in this topic, who might choose to screen the papers we found using different criteria of their own.

The first meta-analysis in ecology was published in 1991, and the number of publications concerned with the use of this approach has continued to increase since then (Figure 1). We identified 119 publications concerned with meta-analysis in ecology and evolution through 2000. While it is likely that the slight decline in number of publications in 2000 is due to random variation, the trajectory in the future obviously remains to be seen. Although it is clear that the volume of publications in meta-analysis in ecology and evolutionary biology will never equal the hundreds of meta-analyses published in medicine each year, there are a number of reasons to suggest that meta-analysis is beginning to become firmly established in this field, as we will illustrate. From its introduction, meta-analysis has been applied – and debated – in a wide range of subdisciplines in the field, rather than being restricted to any particular area (as illustrated by the subjects touched upon in the titles of the papers cited in Table 1). Some of these efforts have been inspired by a few influential papers, but the diversity of applications also suggests the independent discovery of these techniques by various authors at the same time that experimental data in a variety of subdisciplines within ecology surpassed a critical mass during the 1990s.

Meta-analysis has been used for the analysis of the results of different experiments by an individual or group (e.g. Hechtel and Juliano, 1997), as well as for sweeping syntheses of the literature on a topic (e.g. Myers and Mertz (1998) included more than 500 fish populations, while Curtis and Wang (1998) evaluated over 500 reports of effects of elevated CO_2 on woody plants). Organisms serving as the focus of ecological or evolutionary meta-analyses have included plants (from trees, e.g. Curtis, 1996; to seagrass, Cebrian et al., 1998), apes (e.g. Marchant and McGrew, 1991), fish (e.g. Myers et al., 1997; Folt et al., 1998) insects (e.g. Tonhasca and Byrne, 1994; Koricheva et al., 1998a) and birds (e.g. Jarvinen, 1991; Cote and Sutherland, 1997), as well as broad arrays of organisms (e.g. aquatic food webs, Brett and Mueller-Navarra, 1997; competing populations, Gurevitch et al., 1992; and lekking species, Fiske et al., 1998). Meta-analysis has been used to address problems ranging from assessing issues of applied importance in conservation ecology (e.g. Bender et al., 1998; Hilborn and Liermann, 1998) to evaluating the strength of evidence for phenomena predicted by evolutionary theory (e.g. Britten, 1996; Møller and Thornhill, 1998). Other papers listed in Table 1 include those that have made suggestions for applications of meta-analysis in ecology, promoted or questioned its usefulness and validity, and developed new methodology for its use.

C. Reviews, Symposia and Other Activities

The first general review of meta-analysis in ecology was published in 1995 (Arnqvist and Wooster, 1995a); this is the second. In addition to publications, various other activities concerning meta-analysis in the field of ecology have occurred in recent years. In 1996, a symposium was held at the Ecological Society of America's annual meeting entitled 'Meta-analysis in Ecology' that sought to introduce meta-analysis more broadly to the ecological community and demonstrate its range of applicability (Brett, 1997). Symposium presentations ranged from overviews of available techniques for meta-analysis to case studies of applications of meta-analysis to ecological problems. Participants identified a range of issues of importance with respect to the wider use of meta-analysis in ecology. A software package (MetaWin 1.0, Rosenberg *et al.*, 1997), specifically targeted at ecological meta-analysis, was introduced at this symposium.

Also in 1996, a working group was convened at the National Center for Ecological Analysis and Synthesis (Santa Barbara, USA) to help evaluate and guide the application of meta-analysis to ecological questions (Osenberg *et al.*, 1999a). Through a series of workshops, participants examined the linkage between effect size metrics and ecological models, evaluated the statistical properties of these metrics, and conducted meta-analyses of published data to address a broad range of ecological problems, including plant community ecology (Goldberg *et al.*, 1999), predator–prey interactions in stream ecosystems (Englund *et al.*, 1999), and marine nutrient cycling (Downing *et al.*, 1999). A common thread in this work was the recognition of the unique features of ecological data as distinct from, say, psychological or medical data. This critical point was further developed by Osenberg *et al.* (1999b) who examined the nature of hypothesis testing in ecological meta-analysis, and by discussions of statistical methods tailored to ecological applications by Gurevitch and Hedges (1999) and Hedges *et al.* (1999).

It is fair to say that currently the awareness and understanding of meta-analysis among ecologists and evolutionary biologists is still highly uneven. Methods used for recent quantitative syntheses in ecology and evolutionary biology have also spanned a gamut of approaches. Some authors have developed and applied sophisticated extensions of meta-analysis statistical techniques, taking into account the peculiarities of the data sets with which they worked, while others continue to use vote-counts, or even more curiously, combine meta-analysis methods with vote-counting. Ecological journals continue to publish inappropriate use of ANOVA, goodness-of-fit tests, and other methods designed for primary data analysis where meta-analysis methodology should be applied, as well as vote-counts that call themselves meta-analyses and others written by authors who are apparently unaware of meta-analysis (e.g. see Gurevitch and Hedges, 1999). Sometimes such papers have even been published back-to-back with sophisticated applications of meta-analysis.

D. Examples of Several Recent Controversies

One of the more controversial applications of meta-analysis in this field has been to evaluate evidence for a hotly debated area in evolutionary theory, fluctuating asymmetry and developmental instability (Møller and Thornhill 1997a,b, 1998; Thornhill *et al.*, 1999). Fluctuating asymmetry refers to deviations from symmetry, typically in animal morphology. Fluctuating asymmetry is thought to represent one form of developmental instability, which is a reflection of the ability (or inability) of individuals to undergo stable development under given environmental conditions. Controversy swirls around many aspects of this topic, including whether it is a genetically based trait (i.e. is heritable), and whether it is under sexual selection (i.e. more asymmetric individuals are at a disadvantage in attracting mates). Møller and Thornhill (1997a,b) integrated heritabilities of individual fluctuating asymmetry from 34 studies of 17 species and found that across all studies, heritability was significantly greater than zero. They concluded that this provided evidence for the existence of an additive genetic component to developmental stability. Seven commentaries on and critiques of Møller and Thornhill's meta-analysis were published (Houle, Leamy, Markow and Clarke, Palmer and Strobeck, Pomiankowski, Swaddle, Whitlock and Fowler, as well as a reply by Møller and Thornhill, in the *Journal of Evolutionary Biology* (Møller and Thornhill, 1997b)). Many of these authors took the opportunity to discuss the general merits of meta-analysis, in addition to commenting on the validity of the specific conclusions drawn. One point of concern among a number of the reviewers was the combination of effect sizes drawn from studies of either differing quality or, more importantly, from different species and on different morphological traits. These concerns reflect the 'garbage-in, garbage-out' and 'apples versus oranges' problems, respectively, that we consider in more detail below (see sections VI.D and VI.F). Others questioned the objectivity of the meta-analysis. The spirited debate clearly demonstrated the emergence, and controversial nature, of meta-analysis as a new tool for testing evolutionary theory. Further papers by Møller, Thornhill and colleagues, and by their critics, have continued the debate on both fluctuating asymmetry and on the use of meta-analysis in evolutionary research (Palmer, 1999, Thornhill *et al.*, 1999).

Another controversial application of meta-analysis involved a test of the trophic cascade hypothesis (Brett and Goldman, 1996, 1997) and led to various papers criticizing, debating and elaborating on that meta-analysis (e.g. Osenberg *et al.*, 1999b). The meta-analyses of Brett and Goldman (1996, 1997) failed to support either of the two current models relating predation rate to prey numbers. Consequently, McCann *et al.* (1998) developed a new type of prey-dependent model, incorporating zooplankton interference and corresponding to a more reticulate food web, that more closely described the meta-analysis results. It is instructive to note the considerable overlap in the conceptual and methodological problems to be surmounted for the successful adoption of meta-analysis by the ecological and evolutionary communities. In evaluating the 'state-of-the-field' in meta-analysis in ecology, it is encouraging to note that we may be moving beyond the integration of results for the purpose of testing existing hypotheses (e.g. Wand *et al.*, 1999), or providing parameter estimates for existing models (e.g. Medlyn *et al.*, 1999), to the development of new approaches or theories as a response to newly emerging perspectives resulting from meta-analytic synthesis.

VI. REAL AND PERCEIVED DIFFICULTIES IN ECOLOGICAL META-ANALYSIS

Although the utility of meta-analysis clearly is becoming more widely appreciated among ecologists, and statistical tools tailored to the needs of these researchers are being developed and disseminated, there remain a number of issues that present various impediments to their use of meta-analysis. While these issues are not unique to ecology and represent general classes of problems that apply in other disciplines as well, there is a distinct ecological aspect to their manifestation that we focus on here. In the following section we discuss difficulties arising from missing data, publication bias, data exclusion, non-independence among observations, and the combination of dissimilar data sets.

A. Missing Data

In our experience, the most serious impediment to the use of standard parametric meta-analysis methods for integrating ecological data is incomplete reporting of measurement statistics in the primary literature. Most common is the failure to unambiguously report sample sizes and/or standard deviations of response measures (i.e. papers commonly fail to report any measure of variation around the means, correlation coefficients, or whatever measure of outcome is being used to report the results of the experiment). We find this situation surprising given the attention paid to the need for statistical rigor in the editorial policies of most ecological journals, to say nothing of the curricula of our graduate education programs in ecology and evolution. Nonetheless, the net result is often a significant reduction in the number of usable studies and consequent loss of information in the analysis.

Several options are available to correct this situation. The long-term solution must be to raise publication standards. Sloppy reporting of results (such as the omission of sample sizes) should simply not be acceptable in mainstream ecological journals, even though it is currently fairly ubiquitous. Publication of data in graphical form is perfectly acceptable, though, and meta-analysts routinely scan and digitize data from figures (e.g. Gurevitch and Hedges, 2001). Standards can be enforced through tightened editorial policies and more attention to this problem in the peer review process. In the short term, or for already published work, the meta-analyst can contact authors directly with a request to supply the missing data. Although this approach can produce unexpected levels of assistance and perhaps even lead to new professional contacts, it is almost always very time consuming, and generally has a low level of return.

B. Possible Options when Most Available Data Are Reported Poorly

One is still left with an enormous quantity of published ecological information in which sample sizes, standard deviations, or even means may be missing. Many reviewers want to know if there is any way to summarize such data, arguing that some information, even if of relatively low quality, is much better than no information. Clearly, if one can calculate a consistent measure of effect size across studies, one can estimate the (unweighted) grand mean. But how can one assess the magnitude of the variation around that mean, or test whether classes of studies differ in their mean effect sizes, since all of the relevant tests rely upon knowing the sampling variances?

One possibility that has been suggested is to use randomization methods (Adams et al., 1997). In this approach, confidence limits are constructed by bootstrapping the (unweighted) effect size data, and homogeneity tests are carried out using randomization, where the significance of the homogeneity statistic on the actual data is tested against a distribution created by randomly reassigning effects among categories many times. Continuous models can also be analyzed using randomization procedures on unweighted data to test for the significance of the slope (Rosenberg et al., 2000). The power and reliability of this approach will depend upon the error structure of the data set, yielding results that may be quite similar or quite different from those that would have been obtained if a parametric, weighted analysis had been possible (Gurevitch and Hedges, 1999).

Alternatively, one could carry out parametric tests such as ANOVA and regression on the unweighted effect sizes, but, as discussed above, the precision, statistical power and Type II error rates will be compromised, and the reliability of the results will likewise be unpredictable. A major dilemma with either of these approaches is not only that the results will not be as good as those from standard weighted procedures, but also that it is impossible to determine just how bad or good they are. Other problems also exist when one is forced into these sorts of compromises, including loss of the ability to separate within-study sampling error from between-study variation in true effects (Gurevitch and Hedges, 1999).

C. Publication Bias and the Validity of Quantitative Synthesis

Publication bias is the selective publication of articles with particular results, rejecting papers that do not conform to these results (Begg, 1994). Publication bias typically refers to the tendency for editors to reject articles that fail to demonstrate statistically significant results (regardless of the particular findings), but it may also include a selective bias in favor of publishing those studies that confirm conventional wisdom. In contrast to the negative bias that can occur when combining the results of different studies using vote-counts (diminishing the frequency or magnitude of the effect being studied), publication bias typically is a systematic positive bias, resulting in a distortion that artifactually magnifies the magnitude of the effect of interest. Thus, if failure to reject the null hypothesis leads to higher publication rejection rates (or even self-selection by authors, leading to lower submission rates), then the combined results of a group of studies will be upwardly biased (Begg and Berlin, 1988).

It is important to recognize that publication bias, if it exists, will not only threaten the validity of a meta-analysis of that group of studies, but will affect *any* attempt to synthesize the literature on a topic, or to generalize from it (L.V. Hedges, personal communication). The conclusions of narrative reviews, then, are as vulnerable to publication bias as is meta-analysis. Evaluating the results of even a single paper potentially subjects one to the effects of publication bias; if a paper demonstrating an effect were put into the context of five more papers that failed to demonstrate that effect, the interpretation of the results of the first paper would no doubt be different. If those papers that fail to demonstrate the effect are rejected for publication, that context is gone and the interpretation of the results of that single published paper could lead to biased conclusions.

While one may suspect that publication bias exists, its extent and the degree to which it influences literature reviews remains conjectural unless it is investigated further. There have been a number of formal studies of publication bias in other disciplines (e.g., see Rosenberg *et al.*, 2000 for a brief review), and three papers that address this issue in ecology and evolution (Csada *et al.*, 1996; Bauchau, 1997; Palmer, 1999). The results of these investigations have been mixed, with some studies showing the likely existence of publication bias, while others suggest that its effects may be small. Meta-analysts have developed a series of approaches for detecting and quantifying possible cases of publication bias, and while they have not yet been applied in ecological meta-analyses, they would be well worth exploring (e.g. Kleijnen and Knipschild, 1992; Begg, 1994). Both graphical and analytical approaches can be used for detecting publication bias and estimating its magnitude.

The most familiar of the graphical methods are the examination of 'funnel plots', which are scatterplots of effect size graphed against sample size (Light and Pillemer, 1984; Figure 4). In the absence of publication bias, a funnel plot is expected to show a great deal of scatter in the magnitude of the measured effect sizes when sample sizes are small, with the scatter diminishing as sample size increases. This is because sampling theory predicts greater variance around the 'true' effect size when sample sizes are small; the measured effect sizes 'funnel down' or converge to the true effect size as sample sizes become larger. Publication bias can result in a dearth of points around zero at small sample sizes, if small studies reporting no significant effects are systematically rejected for publication (i.e. few or no effect sizes close to zero in value are reported for small sample sizes). Publication bias can also result in 'missing' points for larger negative (or positive) effect sizes, particularly at small sample sizes, if studies with unexpected values for the effect are routinely rejected. While funnel plots can be very useful for data exploration, they must be interpreted with some caution, because publication bias is not the only factor that can influence their appearance. For example, publication bias can result in a correlation between sample size and effect size, particularly when the true effect is moderate, because a 'bite' has been taken out of the collection of points for small effect sizes at low sample sizes (Begg, 1994; Figure 5). But other factors can also create such a correlation: for example, if experimentalists use larger sample sizes when hoping to detect small effects, but can 'get away with' smaller sample sizes when expecting larger

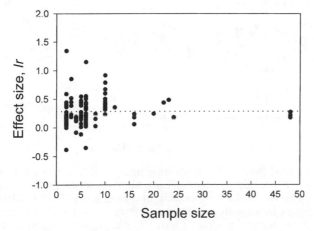

Fig. 4. 'Funnel plot' of effect size (log response ratio, lr) plotted against study sample size; data set as in Figure 2 for responses of trees to elevated CO_2. The dotted line indicates the mean effect size.

effects, the funnel plot will resemble Figure 5 as well. Funnel plots also have a number of other limitations (Wang and Bushman, 1998). A statistical test that evaluates the potential for publication bias in a data set in a similar manner to that of funnel plots is the weighted rank correlation test developed by Begg and Mazumdar (1994). So, although funnel plots are one of the most common tools for detecting publication bias, there are other alternatives that should be evaluated for that purpose.

Other graphical methods for data exploration in meta-analysis that are useful in detecting potential publication bias include weighted histograms and normal quantile plots (Wang and Bushman, 1998; Rosenberg *et al.*, 2000). Weighted histograms differ from ordinary histograms in that the bars are determined by the combined weights of the studies within a 'bin', rather than by frequencies, and they can be used to indicate various anomalies, including publication bias (see Rosenberg *et al.*, 2000). In a normal quantile plot, the data are ordered, and the quantiles are plotted against a standard normal distribution (i.e. with a mean of 0 and a standard deviation of 1.0). Confidence limits can be plotted around the results. Wang and Bushman (1998) detail three uses of such plots in

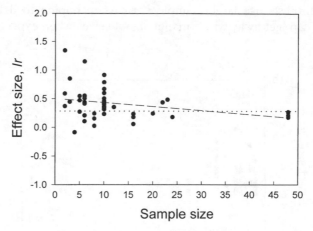

Fig. 5. Hypothetical funnel plot illustrating one possible indication of publication bias. Data set was created by manipulating the data set in Figure 4 by removing 56 of the studies in the lower left part of the graph of 102 total studies (i.e. removing many of those with the smallest effects at the smallest sample sizes) to create 'bias'. A regression line (dashed) indicates a negative relationship between effect size and sample size. Readers might note that it was necessary to remove more than half the published studies before such a negative relationship becomes visually apparent or statistically detectable.

meta-analysis: to check the normality assumption, to investigate whether all studies are likely to come from a single population of studies, and to search for publication bias. If the data fall relatively evenly along a straight line (with slope equal to the standard deviation and the Y coordinate of the center point equal to the mean), and within the confidence bands, the studies probably come from a single population of studies, are normally distributed, and probably do not evidence publication bias (Wang and Bushman, 1998). Publication bias and other causes of non-normal distributions might result in a gap in the points around zero, or in data that have peculiar non-linearities, such as a U-shaped distribution, with the tails (high and low values) extending upward outside of the confidence limits (Wang and Bushman, 1998; Figure 6). Graphical data exploration techniques are useful in meta-analysis for a variety of purposes, not limited to detecting publication bias (e.g. Rosenberg *et al.*, 2000).

There are two general types of non-graphical statistical approaches to detecting and quantifying publication bias. The first is to estimate the magnitude of the problem by calculating a so-called 'fail-safe' number; the second is to model the bias and its impact on the results of the meta-analysis. Rosenthal (1979), imagining that studies that failed to reject the null hypothesis might remain unpublished in a filing cabinet, came up with the following solution to what he called the 'file drawer problem'. He proposed a simple method for estimating the number of unpublished studies with an effect of zero (the 'fail-safe number') that would be needed

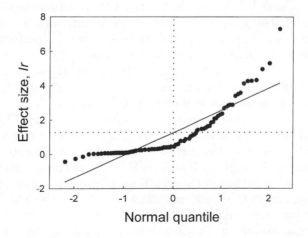

Fig. 6. Normal quantile plot (see text) from data set in Figure 4.

in order to overturn the conclusion that the average effect across studies was significantly greater (or less) than zero (Begg, 1994). If this number is 'sufficiently large', the reviewer might conclude that it is unlikely that so many unpublished studies actually exist, giving more confidence in the conclusion that there was a genuine effect when averaged across studies. 'Sufficiently large' is subjective, but a rule-of-thumb suggested by Rosenthal (1979) is $5k + 10$, where k is the number of studies. An approach for calculating 'fail-safe' number that is more similar to conventional weighted methods for analyzing data in meta-analysis has been suggested, as have other approaches (M.S. Rosenberg, personal communication, and see Rosenberg *et al.*, 2000). The second set of approaches to accounting for publication bias is to adjust the results of the analysis using weighted distribution theory (Begg, 1994). These complex methods are still under development and have not yet been widely applied in any field, including ecology.

D. Data Exclusion

When a meta-analysis is based upon published data, the question arises, how comprehensive does a literature search have to be? There will almost always be a need to restrict one's literature search in some way, if only in acknowledging financial and time constraints on the meta-analysis enterprise. Laird (1990) described attempting an exhaustive search for all published and unpublished literature on a topic to be 'one of life's mistakes that we only make once' (cf. Sharpe, 1997). However, there are two important points to be considered when devising ways to limit the scope of one's search. The first is the need to avoid biasing the search. Englund *et al.* (1999) discussed this issue specifically for ecological meta-analysis, recommending that several meta-analyses be performed using different selection criteria to test for the robustness of the conclusions. The meta-analyst should state explicitly, and *a priori*, the domain of his or her search (e.g. across certain journals, or years, or only using certain databases) and then attempt as thorough an initial search (i.e. to identify potentially useful papers) as possible within that domain. The second point, and arguably the more important one, relates to the conclusions one hopes to draw from the meta-analysis. If the goal is to generalize the meta-analysis findings to all studies that have been conducted in the field, regardless of publication status, time of publication or publication outlet, then a complete search, including unpublished results, would be preferred; if particular areas of the literature are systematically omitted, then one cannot extend one's conclusions to those areas (Sharpe, 1997). If the goal is to produce a quantitative estimate of central tendency across a body of work, and perhaps explore the effect of various moderator variables on the magnitude of a treatment effect, a less intensive search may suffice. Of course, one must take care to select publications in an unbiased manner.

After potentially useful studies have been identified, further decisions must be made regarding which studies will actually be included in the meta-analysis. A persistent concern in meta-analysis is whether to combine high- and low-quality studies (Peipert and Bracken, 1997; Sharpe, 1997). Critics of meta-analysis have sometimes dismissed research syntheses as 'garbage in, garbage out'. Meta-analysts have often favored inclusion of all available studies, coding for quality so that the effects of including lower-quality studies could be tested directly (see below), while others favor screening for quality initially, excluding deficient studies from the database. Publication in peer-reviewed journals may in itself be viewed as adequate quality control, but failure to publish in such journals may be due to a number of factors, perceived quality being only one of them. Moreover, the selectivity or rigor of review varies considerably among journals. Neither approach is entirely satisfactory.

Rather than excluding results based on subjective assessments of quality, coding studies based on one or more measures of internal or statistical validity may be useful (Wortman, 1994). For example, criteria that are used to categorize the quality of each study might be whether treatments were fully replicated (versus pseudo-replicated), whether treatments were randomly assigned to subjects, whether there was confounding of factors, etc. With such 'research quality' moderator variables in place it is possible to test the hypothesis that results from 'poor-quality' studies differ from those of 'high-quality' research, and if so, should be excluded. Sharpe (1997) describes four separate meta-analyses in psychology that used an assortment of composite indexes of research quality that included measures of internal and statistical validity as well as other assessments. In no case, however, were categories defined on the basis of these indexes of research quality related to the magnitude of the treatment effect sizes. In other cases there has been no difference in mean results between high- and low-quality studies, but the latter exhibit more 'noise'. It is clear that there is no simple solution to this problem. However, insofar as 'study quality' is related to sample size or degree of replication, and hence precision, a standard weighted meta-analysis effect size estimate accounts for this source of variation among studies. That is, while we might expect poorly or pseudo-replicated studies to report spuriously high (or low) differences between treatment and control groups, we also expect them to have larger standard errors (i.e. lower precision), which will tend to discount the magnitude of between-group differences.

E. Non-Independence among Observations

One assumption of conventional meta-analysis, in common with most other inferential statistics, is that results of different individual studies, or observations within the database, are independent of one another. It is not known how robust or sensitive meta-analysis results are to different kinds of violations of this assumption, and, as in primary analyses, non-independence is still an unresolved problem. In primary research, control over experimental design can be employed to avoid violating assumptions of independence, and sometimes there are ways of statistically modeling and accounting for autocorrelation if it exists in a data set. In meta-analysis, the investigator has both a lack of control over experimental design and a more limited array of statistical tools at his or her disposal. For example, there is currently no way to accommodate non-independence of measurements through time, as one can in primary research using repeated measures ANOVA. However, if the between-measure correlations are known, multivariate methods have been developed to account for these dependencies (Hedges and Olkin, 1985). The issue of non-independence in ecological meta-analysis also is discussed by Gurevitch and Hedges (1999).

One approach to this issue has been to allow only one effect size estimate from any one published report (e.g. VanderWerf, 1992). Results appearing in separate publications are assumed to come from different experiments (and thus be independent of one another) and, conversely, results appearing in the same publication are considered necessarily statistically non-independent. However, both of these assumptions may be incorrect under some circumstances. Most obviously, those who choose to publish results of large, multi-parted experiments in single, large papers ('lumpers') will be treated differently from those who divide their results into several smaller papers ('splitters'). It also is not uncommon to encounter the same experimental results in more than one publication. Clearly, the 'publication' is not a quantity of sufficiently rigorous definition to be useful as a measure of statistical independence.

Fully crossed, multi-factorial experimental designs are common in ecological research, and present another dilemma. Where main treatment effects are independent in the context of the primary study, should they be considered independent in the context of the meta-analysis? For example, in studies of the effects of elevated CO_2 on plant growth, the CO_2 treatment is often crossed with another factor, such as soil nitrogen availability (e.g. Bazzaz and Miao, 1993). Authors typically report response means for all treatment combinations, such that in this example two CO_2 effect sizes can be calculated and added to the meta-analysis database: one CO_2 effect size for high nitrogen conditions (ambient CO_2, high nitrogen compared to elevated CO_2, high nitrogen) and one CO_2 effect size for low nitrogen conditions (ambient CO_2, low nitrogen compared to elevated CO_2, low nitrogen). Although these results are from the same experiment and would normally be reported in the same publication, they might be argued to represent two independent estimates of the effect of CO_2 on plant growth. Does it make sense to combine them? The answer depends upon the goals of the summary. Information about responses over a range of nitrogen availability may be sufficiently valuable that one would not want to omit either response, because including them both enables one to generalize more broadly. On the other hand, the details of how the experiment was conducted might conceivably cause the responses to elevated CO_2 to be so highly correlated at the two nitrogen levels that they do not provide independent information about those responses, compromising their value for the meta-analysis. The decision to include or omit studies is a scientific as well as a statistical one.

The situation may be made more complicated, however, by the incorporation of multiple species, or genotypes, within a factorial design. In the above example, each experimental unit consisting of a specific CO_2 and soil nitrogen treatment could contain two (or more) different species, resulting in a factorial, split-plot design, with CO_2 and nitrogen as the main plots and species as the sub-plot. In this example, four 'independent' CO_2 effect size estimates could be calculated (response to elevated CO_2 at low N and at high N for each of the two species). Although the species share an experimental unit, and are therefore not strictly independent in their response to the treatments, they could be so different biologically (e.g. wheat versus oak) that we would reasonably expect them to respond very differently to the treatments. Given a lack of strict statistical independence among effect size estimates in such an experiment, one could argue that species differences should be ignored and only the average effect size across species be included in the meta-analysis, or that the results from only one of the species be used. Because this approach can result in a considerable loss of information, an alternative is to consider the responses of different species to a common treatment within a single study as effectively independent of one another. In the latter case, a single study examining many species can contribute a large number of observations to a meta-analysis.

There may be other, less obvious, sources of non-independence among effect size estimates in an ecological meta-analysis database. The magnitude or direction of treatment effect sizes among species could be correlated with their degree of phylogenetic relatedness. The problem of phylogenetic non-independence has been widely discussed in the evolutionary literature (Harvey and Pagel, 1991; Silvertown and Dodd,

1996) and it is likely that some of the same issues apply to meta-analysis. However, while it may be possible for a primary researcher to select species based on known phylogenetic relationships, this is rarely the case when synthesizing research results. It may be impossible in most cases to conduct phylogenetically independent contrasts *sensu stricto* (Felsenstein, 1985) among effect size estimates (P.S. Curtis, unpublished data). A variation of non-independence based on evolutionary phylogeny is that of non-independence based on academic phylogeny. That is, it might be hypothesized that researchers working in the same lab, or simply trained in the same lab, might, by virtue of common techniques or viewpoints, publish results that are more similar in terms of treatment effects sizes than do those from unrelated labs. A preliminary analysis of patterns of results from the elevated CO_2 literature revealed no such relationship (L. Hedges, personal communication) but this issue has certainly not been widely investigated. Research reviewers should understand that when independence of results within the meta-analysis database is not achieved, the standard error of mean effects will be underestimated, leading to increased probability of Type I error (Gleser and Olkin, 1994). A prudent course of action under these circumstances might be to use a more conservative standard for rejecting the null hypothesis in significance tests (i.e. the α level) from 0.05 to 0.01 or even lower.

F. Apples, Oranges and Other Challenges to the Validity of Meta-analysis

Another objection raised by critics of meta-analysis is that these techniques combine unlike studies, producing meaningless results. Glass, an early developer and proponent of meta-analysis in psychology, replied to this contention that it is a good thing to combine apples and oranges if one wishes to understand something about fruit (as cited by Smith *et al.*, 1980). This argument has, however, not satisfied all critics. Clearly, each meta-analysis must provide a justification for the scope of the review. Too broad a focus will risk meaningless results, while too narrow a focus will not only risk being uninteresting, but can also encourage misleading extrapolation if the conclusions are extended to studies outside the domain of the synthesis (Sharpe, 1977). Evaluating results for agreement among studies' outcomes using homogeneity tests, and grouping similar studies together, can also be a way to address this issue. Unfortunately, the number of 'similar' studies (however that is defined) available to partition by study category in a given meta-analysis may not be great enough to provide for meaningful subdivision. For example, if the data base contains three studies on apples, two on oranges, and one each on bananas, pomegranates and mangoes, meaningful partitioning into homogeneous categories based on kinds of fruit may be difficult. If all of the studies agree in their responses, however, this may be neither necessary or desirable. Before combining effect sizes, Hedges *et al.* (1999) recommend comparison of the between-study variance to the average within-study variance. If the between-study variation is many times the average within-study sampling error variation, the studies may be too dissimilar to warrant combination. Ultimately, the question of 'apples and oranges' raises fundamental issues regarding the nature of generalizing from experimental results to truths about nature that cannot be resolved simply.

In addition to discussing the threats to meta-analysis validity addressed above (publication bias, 'garbage in garbage out' and 'apples and oranges'), Sharpe (1997) also considered other possible explanations for continued opposition to the application of meta-analysis among some in the social sciences, despite its general acceptance. Poor first impressions based upon early meta-analyses, condemning meta-analysis on the basis of problematic individual applications of this approach, assuming that the results of meta-analysis will appear to be more definitive than they actually are and cut off future research, and the purportedly descriptive or atheoretical nature of quantitative synthesis are all possible reasons. We would add that meta-analysis is by its very nature a powerful but fairly blunt instrument, and that expecting it to reveal fineness and subtlety of detail risks disappointment. Quantitative research synthesis is in its infancy, and we are still exploring what it can do well, and what tasks it inevitably will do poorly.

VII. CASE STUDIES OF RECENT APPLICATIONS OF META-ANALYSIS IN GLOBAL CHANGE BIOLOGY

Research syntheses can be organized in a number of ways depending on data availability and study objectives. In this section we describe three different approaches to using meta-analysis as a data integration tool as applied by three different research groups examining effects of global change on plants and ecosystems. The first example illustrates the approach of comprehensive literature searching, in which previously published studies are mined for any data relevant to the review objectives. The second example is one where a group of researchers combined data from their independent and otherwise uncoordinated experiments for purposes of hypothesis testing and model development. The final example describes the efforts of a large group of independent investigators who agreed to collect data in a common format with the goal of conducting coordinated integration and synthesis of data from their individual studies.

A. The Elevated CO_2 Meta-analysis Project (CO_2MAP)

Understanding the ecological consequences of rising atmospheric CO_2 has engaged scientists in a variety of disciplines for over 20 years. Strain and Cure (1994) documented an average of 90 elevated CO_2 papers per year published between 1989 and 1992, while a recent search of the Institute for Scientific Information database for a single year, 1998, yielded over 500 elevated CO_2 citations. Synthesis of this body of research resulted in an average of 19 review articles published per year between 1989 and 1992 and (at least) 12 reviews published in 1998. CO_2MAP was initiated in 1995 at the Ohio State University with three primary objectives: (1) the establishment of a comprehensive, digital database of all studies published to date on the response of vegetation to elevated CO_2; (2) integration and synthesis of these results using meta-analytic methods; and (3) distribution of this database via a server at the Carbon Dioxide Information Analysis Center of Oak Ridge National Laboratory. This approach typifies that of many meta-analyses in which a small research group focuses solely on previously published material, but the cumulative, ongoing database is more like the approach taken specifically in some areas of medical meta-analysis.

The CO_2MAP database was originally restricted to woody plant species and covered 83 experiments with 41 different species. The literature search strategies and data extraction methods used are described in more detail below (see section VIII). Curtis (1996), in the first meta-analysis of the elevated CO_2 literature, provided quantitative support for several general conclusions reached by previous reviewers and contributed a number of additional insights into the nature of CO_2 responses in trees. These results were extended by Curtis and Wang (1998), following the addition of 415 studies and 18 species to the database. They also introduced the use of the weighted log ratio as an estimator of CO_2 effect size. This metric was further described by Hedges *et al.* (1999). The CO_2MAP database was expanded to include herbaceous species in 1997. Using this database, Wand *et al.* (1999) examined the responses of C_3 and C_4 species to elevated CO_2 as a test of differences among these plant functional types. The complete meta-database for both woody and herbaceous species is available at: http://cdiac.esd.ornl.gov (Curtis *et al.*, 1999; Jones *et al.*, 1999).

B. CO_2 Model/Experiments Activity for Improved Links (CMEAL)

This multi-investigator project was initiated in 1995 with a broad objective to re-evaluate the way elevated CO_2 responses are handled in ecosystem models (LeFlohic, 1998). In addition to the detailed intercomparison of a number of current ecosystem-level models (e.g. BIOME-BGC, CENTURY, GEM) an important part of this project was a meta-analysis of existing data for the purpose of model parameterization, setting constraints on model structure, and formulating tests of alternative hypotheses regarding ecosystem responses to CO_2 enrichment. The meta-analysis component of this work was also envisioned as a means to search for mechanisms controlling ecosystem carbon storage that could be further explored both experimentally and with models. Thus, the quantitative integration of existing data was seen as a fundamental step in the linkage of empirical data to models and back to the generation of new experimental results.

Unlike CO_2MAP, CMEAL did not draw from the entire elevated CO_2 literature but rather focused on a relatively small number of experiments (~20) conducted under more natural conditions, whose results were regarded *a priori* as being more relevant to ecosystem-scale questions than, for example, results from experiments using potted plants grown inside controlled environment chambers. Scientists representing six of these experiments were co-investigators within CMEAL and agreed to contribute primary data to the meta-analysis. These six experiments were not, however, otherwise coordinating data collection or analysis efforts. That is, while the targeted experiments were similar with regard to certain aspects of scale and methodology, there was no necessary standardization of measurement parameters or techniques.

Peterson *et al.* (1999) conducted a meta-analysis of the responses of 39 plant species grown at ambient CO_2 and 10 species grown at both ambient and elevated CO_2. They used a regression model to evaluate the effects of elevated CO_2 on the photosynthesis : leaf nitrogen relationship, finding that CO_2 enrichment significantly increased photosynthetic nitrogen use efficiency, but that the magnitude of this effect depended on the vegetation type (e.g. evergreen versus deciduous trees). Although this aspect of the meta-analysis was quite successful, the lack of standardization among investigators in data collection and reporting procedures presented considerable difficulties (A. Peterson, personal communication). Efforts to integrate the meta-analysis results into model development are ongoing.

C. The International Tundra Experiment (ITEX)

The International Tundra Experiment (ITEX), established in 1990, is a collaborative research effort examining the response of circumpolar plant species to passive increases in summer warming (Henry and Molau, 1997). There are nearly 40 ITEX sites located in arctic and alpine habitats in 13 countries. ITEX was designed to provide an understanding of how the same taxa located in different geographical areas respond to atmospheric warming and natural climatic variability, and how changes in those species and their environments will affect overall ecosystem structure and function. A manual was developed by ITEX participants defining common experimental protocols, including field chamber design, study species and data collection. However, experimental methods differed slightly among investigators, and experiments were initiated at different times among the many locations. In this sense, ITEX is not a single large experiment, but rather a collection of closely coordinated studies, making meta-analysis the appropriate method for statistical analysis of the entire ITEX dataset.

In 1996 a workshop was held at the National Center for Ecological Analysis and Synthesis to conduct a meta-analysis of ITEX data collected during the first years of the experiment. Prior to and during the workshop, individual participants from around the globe organized their data into a final, standardized format. Several teams then conducted exploratory meta-analyses of different response variables. The results of the ITEX meta-analysis – covering the first four years of this collaborative project – were published recently in *Ecological Monographs* (Arft *et al.*, 1999). The meta-analysis showed that tundra plants in general increased vegetative and reproductive growth in response to warmer summer temperatures. Vegetative biomass increased most in low arctic and alpine species, while reproduction increased most in high arctic plants. Herbaceous species tended to respond more strongly than woody species, particularly in vegetative growth.

Using meta-analysis to synthesize the results of the coordinated ITEX data proved highly successful, but was not without its difficulties. In particular, gathering and collating many disparate data sets into one common data format ready for analysis was a considerable task, requiring substantially more effort than anticipated. The strategy of having multiple investigative teams conduct meta-analyses of different data components was useful for exploratory purposes during the workshop, but was not adequate for the final synthesis (due perhaps to the limited time frame available for the group to work together on the analysis, as well as to a possible case of 'too many cooks' going in too many different directions). In the end, a single analyst working closely with a few investigators was most successful in integrating the results to complete the research synthesis. The resulting manuscript was then circulated to the main group for comments, revised, approved by the group, and finally published.

VIII. PRACTICAL CONSIDERATIONS IN CARRYING OUT META-ANALYSES IN ECOLOGY

In this section we provide an overview of how the CO_2 Meta-Analysis Project operates, as a practical reference for other investigators. As described above, CO_2MAP is fairly typical for a large meta-analysis research program, relying on the published literature for all input data. The project is organized around two separate but integrated activities: (a) identifying and acquiring relevant literature, and (b) using specific hypotheses to frame meta-analyses of that literature. While it may be true that attempting an exhaustive search for all published and unpublished literature on a subject is a once-in-a-lifetime mistake, our experience has shown that meta-analyses involving large numbers of studies are certainly possible, but also clearly benefit from good organization and advanced planning.

A. Data Identification

Data identification at CO_2MAP involves literature searches, manuscript acquisition and archiving, and evaluation of manuscripts for relevance to particular research questions (Figure 7). Identification of elevated CO_2 papers relies primarily on on-line bibliographic services such as those provided by the Institute for Scientific Information. This phase of the search is as comprehensive as possible, although the focus is strictly on studies published in the peer-reviewed literature. That is, the goal is to attempt to maintain a record of all elevated CO_2 studies published. Once identified, a reference is entered into the master electronic bibliography and assigned an accession number. This number identifies not only that specific citation, but also the paper copy of the publication if it is acquired, and any data collected from that publication. Abstracts and keywords are included in the bibliographic database whenever possible, facilitating

Fig. 7. Schematic overview of the CO_2 Meta-Analysis Project procedures.

future searches of the database. Copies of papers are acquired for reference purposes and evaluation.

The actual meta-analyses begin with a search of the master bibliographic database, acquisition of potentially relevant papers, and evaluation of each paper for its usefulness based upon the constraints of the specific hypotheses or analyses being conducted. Two copies of each paper are retained; an archival clean copy, and a second copy for detailed annotations on the specifics of data collection, and for later data checking and quality control.

B. Data Collection

Data collection involves four components; data extraction and recording, data entry, data checking and data storage (Figure 7). Two types of data are extracted from each study: meta-data (methods and experimental conditions) and response data. Meta-data are used to provide background information for subsequent analyses or interpretation and to place studies within specified categorical groups. Since meta-data often include methodological details that will not be used as categorical variables, a separate electronic file is maintained of all meta-data, in which a single record is identified with an individual study's accession number.

Response data are the numerical data quantifying the species or system responses to the experimental treatments. Response data form the core of the data record although, as noted above, each data record also contains the meta-data necessary to partition responses by categorical groups during the actual meta-analysis. Data records are identified by their accession number and by an additional page number. That is, each data record has an accession number relating it to the paper from which it came, and a unique page number identifying it as one of the (perhaps many) records to have been derived from that paper. This dual identification system is critical for accuracy in data entry and ease of data checking.

Response data are reported in the primary literature as text, tables or figures. To extract data from figures, we first scan and digitize the figures and then use image analysis software to determine values (typically means and standard errors) from the digitized information (e.g. see Gurevitch and Hedges, 2001). Meta-data and response data are recorded on standardized data sheets, with one data record per sheet. These data may be recorded entirely by hand, but multiple copies of partially completed data sheets may help expedite data collection. For example, the species name or CO_2 treatment levels may be the same for all records, and can be pre-printed.

Spreadsheet templates are used for data entry into the computer. These look identical to the paper data sheet, helping to minimize transposing errors during data entry. Internal error checking is performed by the spreadsheet software as each cell is completed. Other software specifically designed for expediting data entry and error checking is also available commercially. Post-entry data checking is typically performed by someone other than the person conducing the data entry. Data storage includes electronic backups, as well as the annotated copy of each manuscript from which data are mined.

These methods for searching and mining the literature and for data entry work well for the CO_2 Meta-Analysis Project, and may be useful as a framework for other projects. While the CO_2MAP work is on-going, a similar approach – and identical concerns – would apply for a single literature-based meta-analysis.

IX. CONCLUSIONS: NEW DIRECTIONS

Meta-analysis is poised to begin having a substantial impact on ecological research and on ecological thinking. It will almost certainly eventually be adopted for use in informing policy, as it has been in other disciplines where its use in basic research has become fairly standard. Some ecologists and evolutionists will never accept it, but a great many will surely embrace it because the tools it offers are too powerful to ignore. As with any set of statistical techniques, there is a risk that meta-analysis will be used poorly (as, for example, ANOVA has been extensively misused in ecology). One has to understand the methods one is using, including their limitations, assumptions and pitfalls, whether one is measuring CO_2 uptake, doing a t-test, or carrying out a meta-analysis. Thoughtful implementation of these methods will surely provide a wealth of information that is currently inaccessible to us; inappropriate application of meta-analysis will surely produce misleading results.

Many developments can be made in the usefulness and accuracy of meta-analysis in ecology, as well as in other disciplines. These range from the purely statistical (e.g. extension of GLM (General Linear Models) approaches in meta-analysis; Rosenberg *et al.*, 2000) to those concerned largely with ecological and evolutionary issues, to those somewhere in between. As an example of the latter, a better understanding of how robust meta-analysis results are to various types of non-independence (as discussed above) would be enormously useful (as it would be for primary analyses). Not only do better methods need to be worked out to detect and correct for publication bias, but in a larger context, greater awareness of publication bias may change the criteria for publication. As these issues continue to be discussed, reviewers and editors may begin to realize that results that are 'not significant' are not necessarily 'not informative' or 'not interesting'. Wider acceptance and implementation of meta-analysis may therefore change the way papers are judged for acceptance for publication. As anyone who has been involved in this enterprise would agree, we fervently hope that this will also include higher standards for data reporting (i.e. explaining clearly what was done in an experiment, reporting sample sizes and standard deviations). As meta-analysis becomes more widely known in ecology, people will also be interested in applying these techniques to kinds of data that require new methodology, for example, to non-experimental data.

We end this review as we began it, by predicting that the incorporation of meta-analysis as a routine and familiar approach in ecology and evolution will fundamentally, if subtly, change the nature of these scientific disciplines in both predictable and unpredictable ways. If implemented thoughtfully, the change should be for the better.

ACKNOWLEDGMENTS

This work was supported in part by the Terrestrial Ecosystems and Global Change (TECO) Program, National Science Foundation grant No. IBN-97-27159 to P.S.C. We apologize for any omissions in the papers cited in meta-analysis in ecology and evolutionary biology and for any included inappropriately; no search is ever perfect. The comments and suggestions of Hal Caswell and Dave Raffaelli improved the quality of the paper, and we thank them both. Thanks are also due for stimulating discussion and thoughtful comments to J.G.'s lab group: Kerry Brown, Wei Fang, Tim Howard, Laura Hyatt, Matt Landis, Maria Miriti and Richa Misra. We wish to thank Larry Hedges for his interest and advice on meta-analysis in ecology.

REFERENCES

Abouheif, E. and Fairbairn, D.J. (1997). A comparative analysis of allometry for sexual size dimorphism: assessing Rensch's rule. *Am. Nat.* **149**, 540–562.

Adams, D.C., Gurevitch, J. and Rosenberg, M.S. (1997). Resampling tests for meta-analysis of ecological data. *Ecology* **78**, 1277–1283.

Arft, A.M., Walker, M.D., Gurevitch, J., Alatalo, J.M., Bret-Harte, M.S., Dale, M., Diemer, M., Gugerli, F., Henry, G.H.R., Jones, M.H., Hollister, R.D., Jonsdottir, I.S., Laine, K., Levesque, E., Marion, G.M., Molau, U., Nordenhall, U., Razzhivin, V., Robinson, C.H., Starr, G., Stenstrom, A., Stenstrom, M., Totland, O., Turner, P., Walker, L.J., Webber, P.J., Welker, J.M. and Wookey, P.A. (1999). Responses of tundra plants to experimental warming: meta-analysis of the International Tundra Experiment. *Ecol. Monogr.* **69**, 491–511.

Arnqvist, G. and Nilsson, T. (2000). The evolution of polyandry: multiple mating and female fitness in insects. *Anim. Behav.* **60**, 145–164.

Arnqvist, G. and Wooster, D. (1995a). Meta-analysis – synthesizing research findings in ecology and evolution. *TREE* **10**, 236–240.

Arnqvist, G. and Wooster, D. (1995b). Statistical power of methods of meta-analysis – reply. *TREE* **10**, 460–461.

Arnqvist, G., Rowe, L., Krupa, J.J. and Sih, A. (1996). Assortative mating by size: a meta-analysis of mating patterns in water striders. *Evol. Ecol.* **10**, 265–284.

Bauchau, V. (1997). Is there a 'file drawer problem' in biological research? *Oikos* **79**, 407–409.

Bazzaz, F.A. and Miao, S.L. (1993). Successional status, seed size, and responses of tree seedlings to CO_2, light and nutrients. *Ecology* **74,** 104–112.

Begg, C.B. (1994). Publication bias. In: *The Handbook of Research Synthesis* (Ed. by H. Cooper and L.V. Hedges), pp. 399–410. Russell Sage Foundation, New York.

Begg, C.B. and Berlin, J.A. (1988). Publication bias: A problem in interpreting medical data. *J. Roy. Stat. Soc. Ser. A.* **151,** 419–463.

Begg, C.B. and Mazumdar, M. (1994). Operating characteristics of a rank correlation test for publication bias. *Biometrics* **50,** 1088–1101.

Bender, D.J., Contreras, T.A. and Fahrig, L. (1998). Habitat loss and population decline: a meta-analysis of the patch size effect. *Ecology* **79,** 517–533.

Blanckenhorn, W.U., Reusch, T. and Muhlhauser, C. (1998). Fluctuating asymmetry, body size and sexual selection in the dung fly *Sepsis cynipsea* – testing the good genes – assumptions and predictions. *J. Evol. Biol.* **11,** 735–753.

Brett, M.T. (1997). Meta-analysis in ecology. *Bull. Ecol. Soc. Am.* **78,** 92–94.

Brett, M.T. and Goldman, C.R. (1996). A meta-analysis of the freshwater trophic cascade. *Proc. Natl Acad. Sci. USA* **93,** 7723–7726.

Brett, M.T. and Goldman, C.R. (1997). Consumer versus resource control in freshwater pelagic food webs. *Science* **275,** 384–386.

Brett, M.T. and Muller-Navarra, D.C. (1997). The role of highly unsaturated fatty acids in aquatic food web processes. *Freshw. Biol.* **38,** 483–499.

Britten, H.B. (1996). Meta-analyses of the association between multilocus heterozygosity and fitness. *Evolution* **50,** 2158–2164.

Brook, B.W., O'Grady, J.J., Chapman, A.P., Burgman, M.A., Akcakaya, H.R. and Frankham, R. (2000). Predictive accuracy of population viability analysis in conservation biology. *Nature* **404,** 385–387.

Byers, D.L. and Waller, D.M. (1999). Do plant populations purge their genetic load? Effects of population size and mating history on inbreeding depression. *Ann. Rev. Ecol. Syst.* **30,** 479–513.

Cebrian, J., Duarte, C.M., Agawin, N.S.R. and Merino, M. (1998). Leaf growth response to simulated herbivory: a comparison among seagrass species. *J. Exp. Mar. Biol. Ecol.* **220,** 67–81.

Chalmers, I., Enkin, M. and Keirse, M.J.N.C. (1989). *Effective Care in Pregnancy and Childbirth.* Oxford University Press, Oxford.

Cochran, W.G. (1937). Problems arising in the analysis of a series of similar experiments. *J. Roy. Stat. Soc.* **4** (suppl.), 102–118.

Collie, J.S., Hall, S.J., Kaiser, M.J. and Poiner, I.R. (2000). A quantitative analysis of fishing impacts on shelf-sea benthos. *J. Anim. Ecol.* **69,** 785–798.

Connor, E.F., Courtney, A.C. and Yoder, J.M. (2000). Individuals–area relationships: The relationship between animal population density and area. *Ecology* **81,** 734–748.

Cooper, H. and Dorr, N. (1995). Race comparisons on need for achievement: A meta-analytic alternative to Graham's narrative review. *Rev. Ed. Res.* **65,** 483–508.

Cooper, H. and Hedges, L.V. (Editors) (1994a). *The Handbook of Research Synthesis.* Russell Sage Foundation, New York.

Cooper, H. and Hedges, L.V. (1994b). Research synthesis as a scientific enterprise. In: *The Handbook of Research Synthesis* (Ed. by H. Cooper and L.V. Hedges), pp. 3–14. Russell Sage Foundation, New York.

Cote, I.M. and Sutherland, W.J. (1997). The effectiveness of removing predators to protect bird populations. *Cons. Biol.* **11,** 395–405.

Csada, R.D., James, P.C. and Espie, R.H.M. (1996). The 'file drawer problem' of non-significant results: does it apply to biological research? *Oikos* **76**, 591–593.

Curtis, P.S. (1996). A meta-analysis of leaf gas exchange and nitrogen in trees grown under elevated carbon dioxide. *Plant Cell Envir.* **19**, 127–137.

Curtis, P.S. and Wang, X.Z. (1998). A meta-analysis of elevated CO_2 effects on woody plant mass, form, and physiology. *Oecologia* **113**, 299–313.

Curtis, P.S., Cushman, R.M. and Brenkert, A.L. (1999). *A database of woody vegetation responses to elevated atmospheric CO_2*. ORNL/CDIAC-120, NDP-072. Carbon Dioxide Information Analysis Center, US Department of Energy, Oak Ridge National Laboratory, Oak Ridge, TN.

Dahl, J. and Greenberg, L. (1996). Impact on stream benthic prey by benthic vs. drift feeding predators: a meta-analysis. *Oikos* **77**, 177–181.

Davidoff, F. (1999). In the teeth of the evidence: The curious case of evidence-based medicine. *Mount Sinai J. Med.* **66**, 75–83.

Dodds, W.K. (1997). Interspecific interactions: constructing a general neutral model for interaction type. *Oikos* **78**, 377–383.

Dolman, P.M. and Sutherland, W.J. (1997). Spatial patterns of depletion imposed by foraging vertebrates: theory, review and meta-analysis. *J. Anim. Ecol.* **66**, 481–494.

Downing J.A., Osenberg, C.W. and Sarnelle, O. (1999). Meta-analysis of marine nutrient-enrichment experiments: variation in the magnitude of nutrient limitation. *Ecology* **80**, 1157–1167.

Ellison, A M. (1996). An introduction to Bayesian inference for ecological research and environmental decision-making. *Ecol. Appl.* **6**, 1036–1046.

Englund, G. and Evander, D. (1999). Interactions between sculpins, net-spinning caddis larvae and midge larvae. *Oikos* **85**, 117–126.

Englund, G., Sarnelle, O. and Cooper, S.D. (1999). The importance of data-selection criteria: meta-analyses of stream predation experiments. *Ecology* **80**, 1132–1141.

Felsenstein, J. (1985). Phylogenies and the comparative method. *Am. Nat.* **125**, 1–15.

FernandezDuque, E. (1997). Comparing and combining data across studies: alternatives to significance testing. *Oikos* **79**, 616–618.

FernandezDuque, E. and Valeggia, C. (1994). Meta-analysis – a valuable tool in conservation research. *Cons. Biol.* **8**, 555–561.

Fisher, R.A. (1932). *Statistical Methods for Research Workers*, 4th edn. Oliver and Boyd, London.

Fiske, P., Rintamaki, P.T. and Karvonen, E. (1998). Mating success in lekking males: a meta-analysis. *Behav. Ecol.* **9**, 328–338.

Folt, C.L., Nislow, K.H. and Power, M.E. (1998). Implications of temporal and spatial scale for Atlantic salmon (*Salmo salar*) research. *Can. J. Fisheries Aquat. Sci.* **55**, 9–21.

Frankham, R. (1996). Relationship of genetic variation to population size in wildlife. *Cons. Biol.* **10**, 1500–1508.

Glass, G.V. (1976). Primary, secondary and meta-analysis. *Educational Researcher* **5**, 3–8.

Gleser, L.J. and Olkin, I. (1994). Stochastically dependent effect sizes. In: *The Handbook of Research Synthesis* (Ed. by H. Cooper and L.V. Hedges), pp. 339–356. Russell Sage Foundation, New York.

Gliwicz, J. and Glowacka, B. (2000). Differential responses of *Clethrionomys* species to forest disturbance in Europe and North America. *Can. J. Zool.* **78**, 1340–1348.

Goldberg, D.E., Rajaniemi, T., Gurevitch, J. and Stewart-Oaten, A. (1999). Empirical approaches to quantifying interaction intensity: competition and facilitation along productivity gradients. *Ecology* **80**, 1118–1131.

Gough, L., Osenberg, C.W., Gross, K.L. and Collins, S.L. (2000). Fertilization effects on species density and primary productivity in herbaceous plant communities. *Oikos* **89**, 428–439.

Gurevitch, J. and Hedges, L.V. (1993). Meta-analysis: combining the results of independent experiments. In: *Design and Analysis of Ecological Experiments* (Ed. by S.M. Scheiner and J. Gurevitch), pp. 378–398. Chapman & Hall, New York and London.

Gurevitch, J. and Hedges, L.V. (1999). Statistical issues in ecological meta-analysis. *Ecology* **80**, 1142–1149.

Gurevitch, J. and Hedges, L.V. (2001). Meta-analysis: combining the results of independent experiments. In: *Design and Analysis of Ecological Experiments,* 2nd edn. (Ed. by S.M. Scheiner and J. Gurevitch), pp. 347–369. Oxford University Press, New York and Oxford.

Gurevitch, J., Morrow, L.L., Wallace, A. and Walsh, J.S. (1992). A meta-analysis of competition in field experiments. *Am. Nat.* **140**, 539–572.

Gurevitch, J., Morrison, J.A. and Hedges, L.V. (2000). The interaction of competition and predation: a meta-analysis of field experiments. *Am. Natur.* **155**, 435–453.

Hamilton, W.J. and Poulin, R. (1997). The Hamilton and Zuk hypothesis revisited: a meta-analytical approach. *Behaviour* **134**, 299–320.

Hartley, M.J. and Hunter, M.L. (1998). A meta-analysis of forest cover, edge effects, and artificial nest predation rates. *Cons. Biol.* **12**, 465–469.

Harvey, P.H. and Pagel, M.D. (1991). *The Comparative Method in Evolutionary Biology.* Oxford University Press, Oxford.

Hechtel, L.J. and Juliano, S.A. (1997). Effects of a predator on prey metamorphosis: plastic responses by prey or selective mortality? *Ecology* **78**, 838–851.

Hedges, L.V. and Olkin, I. (1980). Vote counting methods in research synthesis. *Psychol. Bull.* **88**, 359–369.

Hedges, L.V. and Olkin, I. (1985). *Statistical Methods for Meta-Analysis.* Academic Press, New York.

Hedges, L.V. and Olkin, I. (2001). *Statistical Methods for Meta-Analysis in the Medical and Social Sciences.* Academic Press, New York (in press).

Hedges, L.V., Gurevitch, J. and Curtis, P.S. (1999). The meta-analysis of response ratios in experimental ecology. *Ecology* **80**, 1150–1156.

Henry, G.H.R. and Molau, U. (1997). Tundra plants and climate change: the International Tundra Experiment (ITEX). *Global Change Biol.* **3** (Suppl. 1), 1–9.

Herrera, C.M., Jordano, P., Guitian, J. and Traveset, A. (1998). Annual variability in seed production by woody plants and the masting concept: reassessment of principles and relationship to pollination and seed dispersal. *Am. Nat.* **152**, 576–594.

Hilborn, R. and Liermann, M. (1998). Standing on the shoulders of giants: learning from experience in fisheries. *Rev. Fish Biol. Fisheries* **8**, 273–283.

Hollister, R.D. and Webber, P.J. (2000). Biotic validation of small open-top chambers in a tundra ecosystem. *Global Change Biol.* **6**, 835–842.

Houle, D. (1997). A meta-analysis of the heritability of developmental stability – comment. *J. Evol. Biol.* **10**, 17–20.

Hugueny, B. and Guegan, J.F. (1997). Community nestedness and the proper way to assess statistical significance by Monte-Carlo tests: comments. *Oikos* **80**, 572–574.

Hunt, M. (1997). *How Science Takes Stock: The Story of Meta-analysis.* Russell Sage Foundation, New York.

Hurlbert, S.H. (1994). Old shibboleths and new syntheses. *TREE* **9**, 495–496.

Jarvinen, A. (1991). A meta-analytic study of the effects of female age on laying-date and clutch-size in the great tit *Parus-major* and the pied flycatcher *Ficedula hypoleuca. Ibis* **133**, 62–66.

Jones, A. (2000). Effects of cattle grazing on North American arid ecosystems: a quantitative review. *West. N. Am. Nat.* **60**, 155–164.

Jones, M.H., Curtis, P.S., Cushman, R.M. and Brenkert, A.L. (1999). *A comprehensive database of herbaceous vegetation responses to elevated atmospheric CO_2.* ORNL/CDIAC-124, NDP-073. Carbon Dioxide Information Analysis Center, US Department of Energy, Oak Ridge National Laboratory, Oak Ridge, TN.

Kleijnen, J. and Knipschild, P. (1992). Review articles and publication bias. *Arzneimittel-Forschung/Drug Res.* **42**, 587–591.

Koricheva, J., Larsson, S. and Haukioja, E. (1998a). Insect performance on experimentally stressed woody plants: a meta-analysis. *Ann. Rev. Entomol.* **43**, 195–216.

Koricheva, J., Larsson, S., Haukioja, E. and Keinanen, M. (1998b). Regulation of woody plant secondary metabolism by resource availability: hypothesis testing by means of meta-analysis. *Oikos* **83**, 212–226.

Kraak, S.B.M. (1997). Fluctuating around directional asymmetry? *TREE* **12**, 230.

Laird, N.M. (1990). A discussion of the Aphasia Study. In: *The Future of Meta-analysis* (Ed. by K.W. Wachter and M.L. Straf), pp. 47–52. Russell Sage Foundation, New York.

Lardicci, C. and Rossi, F. (1998). Detection of stress on macrozoobenthos: evaluation of some methods in a coastal Mediterranean lagoon. *Mar. Environ. Res.* **45**, 367–386.

Leamy, L. (1997). Is developmental stability heritable? Commentary. *J. Evol. Biol.* **10**, 21–29.

LeFlohic, J. (1998). CMEAL. CO_2 Models/Experiments Activity for Improved Links (Online): *http://www.gcte-focus1.org/activities/Cmeal/cmeal.html* (2001, Jan. 4).

Lempa, K., Martel, J., Koricheva, J., Haukioja, E., Ossipov, V., Ossipova, S. and Pihlaja, K. (2000). Covariation of fluctuating asymmetry, herbivory and chemistry during birch leaf expansion. *Oecologia* **122**, 354–360.

Leung, B. and Forbes, M.R. (1996). Fluctuating asymmetry in relation to stress and fitness: effects of trait type as revealed by meta-analysis. *Ecoscience* **3**, 400–413.

Leung, B., Forbes, M.R. and Houle, D. (2000). Fluctuating asymmetry as a bioindicator of stress: comparing efficacy of analyses involving multiple traits. *Am. Nat.* **155**, 101–115.

Liermann, M. and Hilborn, R. (1997). Depensation in fish stocks: a hierarchic Bayesian meta-analysis. *Can. J. Fisheries Aqua. Sci.* **54**, 1976–1984.

Light, R.J. and Pillemer, D.B. (1984). *Summing Up: The Science of Reviewing Research.* Harvard University Press, Cambridge, MA.

Mann, C. (1990). Meta-analysis in the breech. *Science* **249**, 476–480.

Mann, C. (1994). Can meta-analysis make policy? *Science* **266**, 960–962.

Marchant, L.F. and McGrew, W.C. (1991). Laterality of function in apes – a meta-analysis of methods. *J. Hum. Evol.* **21**, 425–438.

Markow, T.A. and Clarke, G.M. (1997). Meta-analysis of the heritability of developmental stability: a giant step backward – comment. *J. Evol. Biol.* **10**, 31–37.

McCann, K.S., Hastings, A. and Strong, D.R. (1998). Trophic cascades and trophic trickles in pelagic food webs. *Proc. Roy. Soc. Lond. Ser. B.* **265**, 205–209.

McCarthy, M.A. (1997). Competition and dispersal from multiple nests. *Ecology* **78**, 873–883.

McGrew, W.C. and Marchant, L.F. (1997). On the other hand: current issues in and meta-analysis of the behavioral laterality of hand function in nonhuman primates. *Yearbk Phys. Anthropol.* **40**, 201–232.

Medlyn, B.E., Badeck, F.-W., de Pury, D.G.G., Barton, C.V.M., Broadmeadow, M., Ceulemans, R., de Angelis, P., Forstreuter, M., Jach, M.E., Kellomäki, S., Laitat, E., Marek, M., Philippot, S., Rey, A., Strassemeyer, J., Laitinen, K., Liozon, R., Portier, B., Roberntz, P., Wang, K. and Jarvis, P.G. (1999). Effects of elevated [CO_2] on photosynthesis in European forest species: a meta-analysis of model parameters. *Plant Cell Envir.* **22**, 1475–1495.

Miller, C.K. and Fair, J.M. (1997). Effects of blow fly (*Protocalliphora spatulata*: Diptera: Calliphoridae) parasitism on the growth of nestling savannah sparrows in Alaska. *Can. J. Zool.* **75**, 641–644.

Møller, A.P. (1998). Developmental instability as a general measure of stress. *Stress Behav.* **27**, 181–213.

Møller, A.P. (1999). Developmental stability is related to fitness. *Am. Nat.* **153**, 556–560.

Møller, A.P. and Alatalo, R.V. (1999). Good-genes effects in sexual selection. *Proc. Roy. Soc. Lond. Ser. B.* **266**, 85–91.

Møller, A.P. and Ninni, P. (1998). Sperm competition and sexual selection: a meta-analysis of paternity studies of birds. *Behav. Ecol. Sociobiol.* **43**, 345–358.

Møller, A.P. and Shykoff, J.A. (1999). Morphological developmental stability in plants: Patterns and causes. *Int. J. Plant Sci.* **160**, S135–S146.

Møller, A.P. and Thornhill, R. (1997a). A meta-analysis of the heritability of developmental stability. *J. Evol. Biol.* **10**, 1–16.

Møller, A.P. and Thornhill, R. (1997b). Developmental instability is heritable – reply. *J. Evol. Biol.* **10**, 69–76.

Møller, A.P. and Thornhill, R. (1998). Bilateral symmetry and sexual selection: a meta-analysis. *Am. Nat.* **151**, 174–192.

Mosquera, I., Cote, I.M., Jennings, S. and Reynolds J.D. (2000). Conservation benefits of marine reserves for fish populations. *Anim. Cons.* **3**, 321–332.

Murray, B.R. (1998). Density-dependent germination and the role of seed leachate. *Aust. J. Ecol.* **23**, 411–418.

Myers, R.A. (1998). When do environment-recruitment correlations work? *Rev. Fish Biol. Fisheries* **8**, 285–305.

Myers, R.A. and Mertz, G. (1998). Reducing uncertainty in the biological basis of fisheries management by meta-analysis of data from many populations: a synthesis. *Fisheries Res.* **37**, 51–60.

Myers, R.A., Bradford, M.J., Bridson, J.M. and Mertz, G. (1997). Estimating delayed density-dependent mortality in sockeye salmon (*Oncorhynchus nerka*): a meta-analytic approach. *Can. J. Fisheries Aqua. Sci.* **54**, 2449–2462.

Osenberg, C.W. and St Mary, C.M. (1998). Meta-analysis: synthesis or statistical subjugation? *Integrative Biol.: Issues, News Views* **1**, 43–48.

Osenberg, C.W., Sarnelle, O. and Cooper, S.D. (1997). Effect size in ecological experiments: the application of biological models in meta-analysis. *Am. Nat.* **150**, 798–812.

Osenberg, C.W., Sarnelle, O. and Goldberg, D.E. (1999a). Meta-analysis in ecology: concepts, statistics, and applications. *Ecology* **80**, 1103–1104.

Osenberg, C.W., Sarnelle, O., Cooper, S.D. and Holt, R.D. (1999b). Resolving ecological questions through meta-analysis: goals, metrics, and models. *Ecology* **80**, 1105–1117.

Palmer, A.R. (1999). Detecting publication bias in meta-analyses: a case study of fluctuating asymmetry and sexual selection. *Am. Nat.* **154**, 220–233.

Palmer, A.R. and Strobeck, C. (1997). Fluctuating asymmetry and developmental stability: heritability of observable variation vs. heritability of inferred cause. *J. Evol. Biol.* **10**, 39-49.

Pearson, K. (1904). Report on certain enteric fever inoculation statistics. *Br. Med. J.* **3**, 1243–1246.

Pearson, K. (1933). On a method of determining whether a sample of size *n* supposed to have been drawn from a parent population having a known probability integral has probably been drawn at random. *Biometrika* **25**, 379–410.

Peipert, J.G. and Bracken, M.B. (1997). Systematic reviews of medical evidence: The use of meta-analysis in obstetrics and gynecology. *Obst. Gynecol.* **89**, 628–633.

Peterman, R.M. (1995). Statistical power of methods of meta-analysis. *TREE* **10**, 460.

Petersen, J.E., Cornwell, J.C. and Kemp, W.M. (1999). Implicit scaling in the design of experimental aquatic ecosystems. *Oikos* **85**, 3–18.

Peterson, A.G., Ball, J.T., Luo, Y., Field, C.B., Reich, P.B., Curtis, P.S., Griffin, K.L., Gunderson, C.A., Norby, R.J., Tissue, D.T., Forstreuter, M., Rey, A., Vogel, C.S. and CMEAL Participants (1999). The photosynthesis–leaf nitrogen relationship at ambient and elevated atmospheric carbon dioxide: a meta-analysis. *Global Change Biol.* **5**, 331–346.

Piegorsch, W.W., Smith, E.P., Edwards, D. and Smith, R.L. (1998). Statistical advances in environmental science. *Stat. Sci.* **13**, 186–208.

Pither, J. and Taylor, P.D. (2000). Directional and fluctuating asymmetry in the black-winged damselfly *Calopteryx maculata* (Beauvois) (Odonata: Calopterygidae). *Can. J. Zool.* **78**, 1740–1748.

Planque, B. and Fredou, T. (1999). Temperature and the recruitment of Atlantic cod (*Gadus morhua*). *Can. J. Fisheries Aqua. Sci.* **56**, 2069–2077.

Pomiankowski, A. (1997). Genetic variation in fluctuating asymmetry – comment. *J. Evol. Biol.* **10**, 51–55.

Poulin R. (1994). Meta-analysis of parasite-induced behavioral changes. *Anim. Behav.* **48**, 137–146.

Poulin, R. (1996). Helminth growth in vertebrate hosts: does host sex matter? *Int. J. Parasitol.* **26**, 1311–1315.

Poulin, R. (2000). Manipulation of host behaviour by parasites: a weakening paradigm? *Proc. Roy. Soc. Lond. Ser. B.* **267**, 787–792.

Proulx, M. and Mazumder, A. (1998). Reversal of grazing impact on plant species richness in nutrient-poor vs. nutrient-rich ecosystems. *Ecology* **79**, 2581–2592.

Raudenbush, S.W. (1994). Random effects models. In: *The Handbook of Research Synthesis* (Ed. by H. Cooper and L.V. Hedges), pp. 301–321. Russell Sage Foundation, New York.

Riessen, H.P. (1999). Predator-induced life history shifts in *Daphnia*: a synthesis of studies using meta-analysis. *Can. J. Fisheries Aqua. Sci.* **56**, 2487–2494.

Rosenberg, M.S., Adams, D.C. and Gurevitch, J. (1997). *Meta Win: Statistical Software for Meta-Analysis with Resampling Tests.* Ver. 1.0. Sinauer Associates, Sunderland, MA.

Rosenberg, M.S., Adams, D.C. and Gurevitch, J. (2000). *Meta Win: Statistical Software for Meta-Analysis with Resampling Tests.* Ver. 2.0. Sinauer Associates, Sunderland, MA.

Rosenthal, R. (1979). The 'file drawer problem' and tolerance for null results. *Psychol, Bull.* **86**, 638–641.

Sacks, H.S., Berrier, J., Reitman, D., Ancona-Berk, V.A. and Chalmers, T.C. (1987). Meta-analyses of randomized controlled trials. *New Engl. J. Med.* **316**, 450–455.

Schalk, G. and Forbes, M.R. (1997). Male biases in parasitism of mammals: effects of study type, host age, and parasite taxon. *Oikos* **78**, 67–74.

Schmitz, O.J., Hamback, P.A. and Beckerman, A.P. (2000). Trophic cascades in terrestrial systems: A review of the effects of carnivore removals on plants. *Am. Nat.* **155**, 141–153.

Sharp, D. (1997). Of apples and oranges, file drawers and garbage: why validity issues in meta-analysis will not go away. *Clin. Psych. Rev.* **17**, 881–901.

Silvertown, J. and Dodd, M. (1996). Comparing plants and connecting traits. *Phil. Trans. Roy. Soc. Lond.* **351,** 1233–1239.

Simmons, L.W., Tomkins, J.L., Kotiaho, J.S. and Hunt, J. (1999). Fluctuating paradigm. *Proc. Roy. Soc. Lond. Ser. B.* **266**, 593–595.

Simpson, G.G., Roe, A. and Lewontin, R.C. (1960). *Quantitative Zoology,* revised edn. Harcourt, Brace and Co., New York.

Smith, M.L., Glass, G.V. and Miller, T.I. (1980). *The Benefits of Psychotherapy.* Johns Hopkins Press, Baltimore, MD.

Sokolovska, N., Rowe, L. and Johansson, F. (2000). Fitness and body size in mature odonates. *Ecol. Entomol.* **25**, 239–248.

Strain, B.R. and Cure, J.D. (1994). *Direct effects of atmospheric CO_2 enrichment on plants and ecosystems: an updated bibliographic data base.* Oak Ridge National Laboratory/CDIAC-70, Oak Ridge, TN.

Swaddle, J.P. (1997). On the heritability of developmental stability – comment. *J. Evol. Biol.* **10**, 57–61.

Swales, J.D. (1999). Evidence-based medicine and hypertension. *J. Hypertension* **17**, 1511–1516.

Thornhill, R., Møller, A.P. and Gangestad, S.W. (1999). The biological significance of fluctuating asymmetry and sexual selection: a reply to Palmer. *Am. Nat.* **154**, 234–241.

Thrush, S.F., Schneider, D.C., Legendre, P., Whitlatch, R.B., Dayton, P.K., Hewitt, J.E., Hines, A.H., Cummings, V.J., Lawrie, S.M., Grant, J., Pridmore, R.D., Turner, S.J. and Mcardle, B.H. (1997). Scaling-up from experiments to complex ecological systems: where to next? *J. Exp. Mar. Biol. Ecol.* **216**, 243–254.

Tippett, L.H.C. (1931). *The Methods of Statistics.* Williams & Norgate, London.

Tonhasca, A. and Byrne, D.N. (1994). The effects of crop diversification on herbivorous insects – a meta-analysis approach. *Ecol. Entomol.* **19**, 239–244.

Turchin, P. (1995). Chaos in microtine populations. *Proc. Roy. Soc. Lond. Ser. B.* **262**, 357–361.

Van Zandt, P.A. and Mopper, S. (1998). A meta-analysis of adaptive deme formation in phytophagous insect populations. *Am. Nat.* **152**, 595–604.

VanderWerf, E. (1992). Lack's clutch size hypothesis – an examination of the evidence using meta-analysis. *Ecology* **73**, 1699–1705.

Van Dongen, S., Sprengers, E., Lofstedt, C. and Matthysen, E. (1999). Heritability of tibia fluctuating asymmetry and developmental instability in the winter moth (*Operophtera brumata* L.) (Lepidoptera, Geometridae). *Heredity* **82**, 535–542.

Vasquez, R.A., Bustamante, R.O. and Simonetti, J.A. (1995). Granivory in the Chilean matorral: extending the information on arid zones of South America. *Ecography* **18**, 403–409.

Venier, L.A. and Fahrig, L. (1998). Intra-specific abundance–distribution relationships. *Oikos* **82**, 483–490.

Vollestad, L.A., Hindar, K. and Møller, A.P. (1999). A meta-analysis of fluctuating asymmetry in relation to heterozygosity. *Heredity* **83**, 206–218.

Wand, S.J.E., Midgley, G.F., Jones, M.H. and Curtis, P.S. (1999). Responses of wild C_4 and C_3 grass (Poaceae) species to elevated atmospheric CO_2 concentration: a test of current theories and perceptions. *Global Change Biol.* **5**, 723–741.

Wang, M.C. and Bushman, B.J. (1998). Using the normal quantile plot to explore meta-analytic data sets. *Psychol. Meth.* **3**, 46–54.

Westoby, M. (1998). A Leaf–Height–Seed (LHS) plant ecology strategy scheme. *Plant Soil* **199**, 213–227.

Whitlock, M.C. and Fowler, K. (1997). The instability of studies of instability – comment. *J. Evol. Biol.* **10**, 63–67.

Windig, J.J. and Nylin, S. (2000). How to compare fluctuating asymmetry of different traits. *J. Evol. Biol.* **13**, 29–37.

Wooster, D. (1994). Predator impacts on stream benthic prey. *Oecologia* **99**, 7–15.

Wortman, P.M. (1994). Judging research quality. In: *The Handbook of Research Synthesis* (Ed. by H. Cooper and L.V. Hedges), pp. 97–110. Russell Sage Foundation, New York.

Xiong, S.J. and Nilsson, C. (1999). The effects of plant litter on vegetation: a meta-analysis. *J. Ecol.* **87**, 984–994.

Advances in Ecological Research
Volume 1–32

Cumulative List of Titles

Aerial heavy metal pollution and terrestrial ecosystems, **11**, 218

Age determination and growth of Baikal seals (*Phoca sibirica*), **31**, 449

Age-related decline in forest productivity: pattern and process, **27**, 213

Analysis of processes involved in the natural control of insects, **2**, 1

Ancient Lake Pannon and its endemic molluscan fauna (Central Europe; Mio-Pliocene), **31**, 463

Ant-plant-homopteran interactions, **16**, 53

The benthic invertebrates of Lake Khubsugul, Mongolia, **31**, 97

Biogeography and species diversity of diatoms in the northern basin of Lake Tanganyika, **31**, 115

Biological strategies of nutrient cycling in soil systems, **13**, 1

Bray-Curtis ordination: an effective strategy for analysis of multivariate ecological data, **14**, 1

Can a general hypothesis explain population cycles of forest lepidoptera?, **18**, 179

Carbon allocation in trees: a review of concepts for modelling, **25**, 60

Catchment properties and the transport of major elements to estuaries, **29**, 1

Coevolution of mycorrhizal symbionts and their hosts to metal-contaminated environments, **30**, 69

Conservation of the endemic cichlid fishes of Lake Tanganyika: implications from population-level studies based on mitochondrial DNA, **31**, 539

The cost of living: field metabolic rates of small mammals, **30**, 177

A century of evolution in *Spartina anglica*, **21**, 1

The climatic response to greenhouse gases, **22**, 1

Communities of parasitoids associated with leafhoppers and planthoppers in Europe, **17**, 282

Community structure and interaction webs in shallow marine hardbottom communities: tests of an environmental stress model, **19**, 189

The decomposition of emergent macrophytes in fresh water, **14**, 115

Delays, demography and cycles: a forensic study, **28**, 127

Dendroecology: a tool for evaluating variations in past and present forest environments, **19**, 111

The development of regional climate scenarios and the ecological impact of greenhouse gas warming, **22**, 33

Developments in ecophysiological research on soil invertebrates, **16**, 175

The direct effects of increase in the global atmospheric CO_2 concentration on natural and commercial temperate trees and forests, **19**, 2

The distribution and abundance of lakedwelling Triclads—towards a hypothesis, **3**, 1

Index

THE
DAMOCLES SYNDROME

THE
DAMOCLES
SYNDROME

Psychosocial Consequences
of Surviving Childhood Cancer

Gerald P. Koocher and John E. O'Malley

McGRAW-HILL BOOK COMPANY

New York / St. Louis / San Francisco
Auckland / Bogotá / Hamburg / Johannesburg / London
Madrid / Mexico / Montreal / New Delhi / Panama / Paris
São Paulo / Singapore / Sydney / Tokyo / Toronto

This volume is dedicated to
the patients and families who made it possible
in the hope others would benefit.

LIBRARY OF CONGRESS CATALOGING IN PUBLICATION DATA

Koocher, Gerald P.
  The Damocles syndrome.

  Includes bibliographical references and index.
  1. Tumors in children—Psychological aspects.
  2. Tumors in children—Social aspects.
  I. O'Malley, John E., joint author. II. Title.
  [DNLM: 1. Neoplasms—In infancy and childhood
  2. Neoplasms—Psychology. QZ200 K825d]
  RC281.C4K64   362.1'9892994   80-22462

ISBN 0-07-035340-9

123456789   DODO   8987654321

The editors of this book were Lawrence B. Apple, Suzette H. Annin, and Michael Hennelly. The designer was Christopher Simon, and the production supervisor was Teresa F. Leaden. It was set in Baskerville by University Graphics, Inc..

It was printed and bound by R. R. Donnelley & Sons Co.

Contents

Contributors

William R. Beardslee, M.D.

Assistant in Psychiatry, Children's Hospital Medical Center and Judge Baker Guidance Center, Boston, Massachusetts
Instructor in Psychiatry, Harvard Medical School, Boston

Diana J. Foster, M.S.W.

Chief Research Social Worker, Sidney Farber Cancer Institute, Boston, Massachusetts

Janis L. Gogan, Ed.M., M.B.A.

Management Consultant, Arlington, Massachusetts
Formerly: Research Associate, Sidney Farber Cancer Institute, Boston

Norman Jaffe, M.D.

Division Chief, Division of Solid Tumors, Pediatric Department, M.D. Anderson Hospital and Tumor Institute, Houston, Texas Professor of Pediatrics, University of Texas System Cancer Center, Houston, Texas

Beth Kemler, D.S.W.

Senior Psychiatric Social Worker, Children's Hospital Medical Center, Boston, Massachusetts

Gerald P. Koocher, Ph.D.

Associate in Psychology, Sidney Farber Cancer Institute and Unit Chief for Inpatient Psychology, Children's Hospital Medical Center, Boston, Massachusetts, Assistant Professor of Psychology, Harvard Medical School, Boston

John E. O'Malley, M.D.

Associate Psychiatrist, Sidney Farber Cancer Institute and Children's Hospital Medical Center, Boston, Massachusetts, Assistant Professor of Psychiatry, Harvard Medical School, Boston, Massachusetts

Lesley A. Slavin, B.A.

Research Associate, Sidney Farber Cancer Institute, Boston, Massachusetts

Acknowledgment

During the conduct of the study reported here and the preparation of this volume the authors and contributors were supported entirely or in part by National Cancer Institute Grant CA18429 CCG, Psychosocial Sequelae of Childhood Cancer.

Foreword

Out of This Nettle, Danger,
We Pluck This Flower, Safety

If the purpose of a foreword is to provide perspective, let me begin by sharing my own excitement at the very existence of this book, let alone its excellence. For the fact is that the investigation described in this book simply would not have been possible a generation ago. This is not a matter of new methods in behavioral science or in statistics, although there have been major improvements in methodology in recent decades. Nor is it a matter of new funding sources or new patterns of collaboration between behavioral scientists and biomedical specialists, although these, too, have changed for the better. Simply put, there were so few survivors of childhood cancer when I graduated from medical school that the identification of a cohort of suitable size would have been impossible at a single institution; moreover, the study of psychosocial status following survival would have had limited public health importance because of the small size of the population for whom it would have been pertinent. To take but a single example, a generation ago fewer than 20 percent of children with acute lymphocytic leukemia survived two years after the diagnosis and fewer still five years later. Yet, current data demonstrate a 90 percent survival at two years and as many as 70 percent at five years (Smithson et al., 1980). Equally dramatic changes have occurred in the efficacy of treatment for other childhood cancers, though not yet for all. The rate of progress can only be characterized as exhilarating. We have every reason to be confident that the results of today's best treatments are better than the follow-up data reported in this book and that tomorrow's will be even more gratifying.

At a time when death was inevitable and relatively rapid, the role of the physician was limited to making the patient as comfortable as possible and to supporting the family during the grieving process. With the possibilities created by the new developments in molecular biology, the focus of medical intervention necessarily shifted to the preservation of physiological competence during heroic

xi

anticancer treatments, which threaten normal as well as malignant cells. Concern for the psychosocial impact and for quality of life only began to assume importance as survival increased in frequency. But while one could speculate on what the experience must be like for patient and family, it only became possible to do empirical studies on what that experience is like when enough patients had survived to be able to assess their response.

Of course, more has changed than the odds of survival and the types of treatment. It was the received wisdom, when I began my clinical training in the 1950s, that the diagnosis of cancer was to be withheld from the patient except in such special circumstances as that of the businessman who "needed to know" in order to make appropriate financial decisions or the unusual patient thought to be "strong enough" to withstand the shock of the terrible news. Certainly, all were agreed that children should not be told. To do so would be cruel; there were no practical steps they needed to take; the important thing was to preserve hope. Now, it has become the conventional wisdom that all patients are to be told, frankly and fully—and whether they want to hear or not.

From today's standpoint, yesterday's practices may be difficult to understand. For one thing, earlier attitudes were part of a long tradition of paternalism by the physician toward the patient. The doctor was to assume the worry, spare the patient the distress, and make the decisions, usually in concert with the family who, together with the physician, attempted to sustain the patient's morale by preserving hope of cure. It is only in recent years that the earlier ethic has been displaced by such concepts as the autonomy of the patient, full disclosure, truth as a primary value, and a contract basis for the physician-patient relationship (Koocher, 1976). It may be difficult for some to believe that patients did not "know" that they had cancer, whatever euphemisms doctors employed. The fact is that many patients then—and many now—acted as if they did not "know," even when they had been told and told repeatedly. In similar vein, some of those not "told" were quite aware of their situation but accepted the conspiracy of silence which surrounded them; just as the family attempted to "protect" the patient from unpleasantness, the patient "protected" the family (and the doctor) from the need to face openly what they had not the courage to acknowledge. What is at stake is the all-too-human capacity not to see and not to hear, at a conscious level, when information threatens psychological equilibrium.

In addition to the ethical questions that earlier physicians avoided, previous medical practices ignored the behavioral consequences immanent in any attempt to deceive, however well-intentioned. The issue, after all, is not one for the patient alone, but for patient, family, and doctor. Keeping, or attempting to keep, the secret inevitably distorts relationships among members of the group and makes it impossible to share the feelings each may have toward the other. The patient now not only has to face the threat to his life but must do so without being able to call on those from whom help should most be expected.

The findings in this study make it abundantly clear that truth telling is associated with better psychological outcomes than fabrication. I would argue, as the authors do, that the essential element is not the "truth" but the climate of emotional support provided to the patient and family. Lest ethicists object, I hasten to add that I do not minimize the value of honesty. "Honesty," however, is not enough and becomes a shroud for sadism when patient and family have their noses rubbed in the "facts." Patients *should* be told the truth but be allowed to fashion their own version of the truth if they find that necessary as a tactic for survival. Today, the "facts" are far from simple. When survival is possible for many patients and one can not identify in advance who will do well and who not, is it more truthful to believe that one will be a survivor or a victim? Even statements of probability are difficult to translate in meaningful psychological terms except when decisions are to be made; i.e., do I prefer treatment A with probability X of survival over treatment B with probability Y, when A has so and so many more side effects associated with it in the short run or the long run? Wisdom in psychosocial management inheres in truthfulness *and* sensitivity. The most accurate version of current knowledge should be made available so that child and family can make the most informed decisions, when decisions are to be taken. It should not be reiterated ruthlessly if it is translated into a rosier version by patient and family, except when mythopoesis leads to behavior that interferes with the continued treatment necessary for the most favorable outcome.

On the evidence presented by Drs. Koocher and O'Malley, the long-term outcome of survivors of childhood cancer is a tribute to the resiliency of the human spirit as well as to the humane care these patients received. What is remarkable is how many of the survivors are in good psychological health, not the number who have symptoms or the few with serious problems of adjustment. One might well expect that children undergoing treatment today will have a still better psychosocial outcome, even without further improvement in care, because of the assurance they can now receive about the better odds they face. Bear in mind that the follow-up sample includes many children who were treated at a time when doctors could offer hope but little in the way of a favorable prognosis supported by facts, for there were no "facts" on survival. The psychological dilemma has been transformed from one of adapting to the imminence of death to one of coping with uncertain survival: hence the "sword of Damocles," a metaphor for a devoutly desired good obtained at the cost of continuing danger. So long as the sword hangs suspended on a slender thread, albeit one growing ever stronger, how best can we enable the patient to relish the banquet of life medical advance has provided? The patients in this study instruct us.

This study will repay careful reading and rereading because of the wealth of information it contains on the psychosocial adjustment of the largest group of survivors of childhood cancer yet investigated in a systematic way. We need no longer guess, as we had to in the past; we can now know with reasonable confidence

what is likely to be the case. More than that, the authors offer thoughtful recommendations about modes of care for such children from the time of diagnosis
through treatment to continuing follow-up. They correctly emphasize: the crucial
role of *social support* from the time of the first medical encounter; the need for
evaluating *the child in the context of the family;* sensitive respect for *denial;* the
importance of assisting the family to provide the *financial and social resources*
necessitated by a prolonged period of treatment; the challenge of *altering social
attitudes* toward cancer victims and of reinforcing options for *employment and
insurability;* the value of *openness* as a key element in the relationship between
clinician and family; and the fact that cancer treatment is a *long-term and continuing enterprise* because of the as yet unsettled questions of delayed toxic effects
and second tumors.

If I were to single out one point for emphasis, that point would be the crucial
need for enhancing coping capacity in place of the outdated focus on rehabilitation.
In the authors' words: "Rather than working to restore lost functions, we should
be working to prevent or minimize the psychosocial losses patients and their families are likely to experience. Preventive psychotherapeutic intervention aimed at
sustaining the child patient's ability to relate in the community and facilitating a
pattern of open communication in the family is of critical importance." Here, what
is needed is the design of services based on the application of the knowledge this
book epitomizes, followed by the systematic evaluation of the efficacy of such services by controlled clinical trials. It is not enough to "mean well" in dealing with
the child with cancer; it is essential to "know well." To know implies having data
rather than mere opinion. We know enough now to do better than we did a generation ago, but there is much that we still need to find out. Systematic scientific
study alone permits us to reduce ignorance and expand knowledge (Eisenberg,
1977).

Still and all, what I would like to leave with the reader is the realization of the
immensity of change that medical progress has made possible in less than one
medical lifetime. I still recall my despair when I learned not many years ago that
the 8-year-old child of a good friend had developed leukemia. Although trials with
cancer chemotherapy had begun, I mourned with him in the expectation of the
tragic loss of his only child. It is now twenty years later and that child is a healthy
young adult, a miracle neither of us dared to hope for. That outcome is tribute
indeed to the creative imagination and the dedicated work of the biomedical scientists who brought order out of chaos. If we now worry about psychosocial consequences, that very worry is a welcome one, for it is a measure of how far we
have come. It is in that spirit that this book should be read.

LEON EISENBERG

Maude and Lillian Presley Professor of Psychiatry
Harvard Medical School
Boston, Massachusetts

REFERENCES

Smithson, W. A., Gilchrist, G. S. & Burgert, E. O. Childhood acute lymphocytic leukemia. *Cancer,* 1980, *30,* 158–181.

Koocher, G. P. (ed.). *Children's rights and the mental health professions.* New York: Wiley, 1976.

Eisenberg, L. The social imperatives of medical research. *Science,* 1977, *198,* 1105–1110.

Introduction

According to an anecdote related by Cicero, Damocles was a courtier under the rule of Dionysius I, tyrant of Syracuse (ca. 432–367 B.C.). As one is wont to do when in the employ of tyrants, Damocles lavished praise and attention on his king in a rather transparent attempt to ensure his own survival. Dionysius offered to show Damocles the true nature of his happiness, and invited him to be the guest of honor at a magnificent banquet. Delighted not only by his apparent new-found favor with his king, but also by the prospect of a wondrous experience, Damocles readily accepted the invitation. At the banquet he found himself surrounded with every luxury wealth could provide, but when Damocles looked up he discovered that he was seated directly beneath a naked sword suspended above his head by a single horsehair. This clearly and dramatically emphasized the true nature of the tyrant's happiness.

The families of children under treatment for cancer now find themselves in a similar predicament. Thanks to recent progress in the treatment of childhood malignancies, children who certainly would have died fifteen years ago may now have a fifty/fifty chance of surviving for five years and perhaps ultimately being cured of their disease. Yet the nature of cancer is that the disease may recur even after prolonged periods of apparent good health.

Stress and anxiety abound when a diagnosis of cancer is first revealed to the family. For many people the word "cancer" is a synonym for "death." The medical persons who present the diagnosis, however, often provide a substantial measure of hope as they discuss the treatment, which is generally undertaken with curative intent. As the disease responds to the first courses of treatment and symptoms remit, a hopeful sense of security may develop despite a plethora of adverse side effects. At the time of our interviews with long-term survivors of childhood cancer and their families, most were supportive of our project and expressed considerable gratitude to the staff members who had successfully treated them. At the same time there was often a conscious or subliminal awareness that a substantial risk, much like the sword of Damocles, hangs over their futures.

As might be expected, the psychological pressures on cancer patients and their families are intense and do not subside fully even when the disease is "under control." This volume is an attempt to chronicle the psychological events which accompany and follow the diagnosis and treatment of malignancies in childhood. Our goal was to explore the quality of life among survivors and their families, and to seek means of facilitating the coping and adaptation of children currently being treated for cancer.

Chapter 1 is a selective review of the psychosocial literature on issues related to the treatment of the child with cancer. Written by Lesley Slavin, our project research associate, the focus of the chapter is on evolving issues. As the prognosis for these children has changed there have been parallel changes in the needs of their families and the concerns of professionals. This chapter is intended to set the tone and context within which our study of long-term survivors began.

Chapter 2 addresses survival rates and risks of cancer among the long-term survivors as a group. Written by Dr. Koocher with the assistance of William Fine, the project's registrar, this chapter discusses the computerized registry of long-term cancer survivors, demographic information about the survivor population, and some of the long-term risks these former patients face, including the possibility of second tumors and the potential impact of cancer treatments on their progeny.

Chapter 3 describes the methodology of the project in enough scientific detail to permit replication of key aspects by other researchers. Written by Drs. Koocher and O'Malley, this chapter highlights the project's goals and explains the research procedures, including the selection of participants and of measurement instruments and interview procedures. The problem of choosing control groups for the study population is explored, along with a discussion of the rationales used in grouping patients for data analyses.

Chapter 4, written by Dr. Norman Jaffe, original coinvestigator on the project, in consultation with Drs. O'Malley and Koocher, is an elaboration of the long-term medical risks to survivors introduced in Chapter 2. The specific types of late medical consequences of current treatments for childhood cancer are summarized under the headings of chemotherapy, radiation therapy, and surgery. Additional data gleaned from physical examinations of the first 100 participants interviewed in the project are presented as a means of demonstrating the nature and types of long-term medical complications which our survivors confront.

Chapter 5, by Dr. Koocher, explores the psychological adjustment of the patients we interviewed as measured with the psychological tests discussed in Chapter 3. This chapter also summarizes the key psychological variables which appear to relate to either good or poor coping by long-term survivors. Both demographic data and objective test scores are analyzed in this chapter.

Chapter 6, by Dr. O'Malley, presents the findings of extensive psychiatric interviews with our participants. The results of standardized psychiatric interviews and of more open-ended content interviews with the survivors are reported. Findings include the nature and type of psychiatric symptoms noted among the survivors and their fantasies and beliefs regarding the cancer experience.

Chapter 7 offers a detailed discussion of the interviews with parents, conducted in tandem with the survivors' interviews. It was written by Diana Foster with the assistance of Drs. O'Malley and Koocher and includes information on the stresses encountered by parents, the supports which they found useful for coping, the many different issues they had to struggle with, and their recommendations for improving the care system for today's patients. These interviews provide special insights into the less obvious toll serious childhood illness takes on a family, as well as highlighting some surprising sources of help which many families found.

Chapter 8 explores the reactions of siblings to having a cancer survivor as a brother or sister. Janis Gogan and Lesley Slavin, who served consecutively as research associates on our project, conducted the interviews with siblings and wrote this chapter. The material enriches the picture of families' long-term coping processes and brings out some of the special stresses which fall on the siblings of the child with cancer.

Chapter 9 addresses the special problems of living with survivorship which our former patients must face. Written by Dr. Koocher with the assistance of Dr. O'Malley and Ms. Foster, this chapter includes data on the effect of physical impairment, employment discrimination, difficulty in obtaining insurance, and on marital issues. The chapter also addresses the issue of whether the child should be told about a diagnosis of cancer and presents data on the coping of survivors who were deliberately lied to about their diagnosis "for their own good."

Chapter 10 reports on the results of a special subproject of the main study conducted by Dr. Kemler as part of her doctoral dissertation. Dr. Kemler considered the phenomenon of anticipatory grief among the parents of children who have survived cancer. Her chapter addresses the issue of what happens when a parent prepares to suffer the loss of a child, and then is faced with a new situation when the child survives. The potential difficulties in day-to-day parenting and parents' perceptions of the survivor children are the focus of her presentation.

Chapter 11, written by Dr. Beardslee, applies his well-developed life-history interview technique as a means of examining three of our participants in detail. Three quite different men who all survived childhood cancer and were all well-adjusted psychologically at the time of their participation in our study were extensively reinterviewed by Dr. Beardslee. The case histories he develops in this chapter forcefully illustrate how adaptive the use of psychological denial can be in struggles to cope with the stresses of childhood cancer. The case histories also provide a close-up of the more global data reported in Chapters 5 and 6.

Chapter 12, written by Drs. O'Malley and Koocher, reviews the key findings of our project and translates them into specific recommendations for improving current patient care, including practical suggestions for oncologists, mental health professionals, and others who provide services to child cancer patients and their families. The material focuses on the prevention of adverse emotional consequences among those who will be tomorrow's long-term survivors.

Several appendixes are included at the end of the volume, and each is intended to convey specific data or criteria which might be helpful to other researchers who wish to replicate aspects of our study or push on with related work of their own. Special thanks are due to Drs. Michael Rutter and Eugenia Waechter for permission to reprint some research materials developed by them in our appendixes.

Thanks are due to a number of people, not previously mentioned, without whom the conduct of this project and ultimately the production of this volume would not have been possible. William Fine, project registrar, and Diane MacLachlan, registry secretary, managed our tracking of former patients and made it possible for us to locate, contact, and schedule survivors for interviews with ease; they both also provided us with important data from demographic or medical data banks on short notice. Dr. Fred Li of the Division of Epidemiology oversaw the operation of the registry and provided valuable continuing consultation on participant selection and medical risks. Judith Rawlins, our project secretary, is also in large measure responsible for the quality of this volume. Judith is an efficient and tireless worker, a careful manuscript processor, and a sensitive listener who has served both the staff of our project and our participants well.

Special thanks are due to one more group of people: the survivors and their families, who so graciously and willingly participated in this study. They gave of themselves openly, and at times painfully, so that the next generation of childhood cancer survivors might benefit from their experiences.

G. P. K.
J. E. O.

Chapter 1

Evolving Psychosocial Issues in the Treatment of Childhood Cancer: A Review

The prognosis for most childhood malignancies has changed dramatically over the last two decades. Childhood cancer, once seen as an acute, almost invariably fatal disease, is now regarded as a life-threatening, chronic illness. Most patients have long periods of remission and good health after diagnosis and initial treatment for cancer, and for many, long-term survival and "cure" are real possibilities. This shift in the medical outlook for children with cancer is a point of obvious importance in any study of long-term survivors, and we return to it many times in this volume (see especially Chapter 2). What may not be quite so obvious is the profound effect which the lengthening course of the disease and the gradual improvement in prognosis have had on the approach of mental health professionals and researchers working in pediatric oncology. Indeed, recognizing the evolving nature of the prognosis and treatment of childhood cancer is essential to any meaningful discussion of the psychosocial aspects of the disease.

There is a considerable body of literature on the psychological and emotional aspects of childhood cancer. Although rigorous research is lacking and the work is largely descriptive and anecdotal, it nevertheless reveals a fairly clear and detailed picture of the "cancer experience" for the children and their families. However, the picture is not a static one. This chapter presents a selective review of the literature on childhood cancer divided into two sections: patient issues and family issues. Special attention is paid to the way the cancer experience has changed as a result of the evolving medical outlook and to the new issues which are emerging as childhood cancer is increasingly viewed as a chronic disease.

By Leslie A. Slavin.

1

Issues for Patients

The parents of children with cancer have been the major focus of much psychosocial research in childhood tumors. This emphasis is especially marked in the earliest, most seminal studies in this field (Bozeman et al., 1955; Friedman et al., 1963; Chodoff et al., 1964; Hamovitch, 1964; Binger et al., 1969). Certainly, it would be a mistake to assume that the patient's experience with cancer can be understood without consideration of his/her role as part of a family, or that the child can be helped effectively to cope with the illness and attendant anxieties without considering the parents and siblings in the intervention strategy. However, in focusing on the parents and parental coping, issues relating directly to the child's illness experience have sometimes been overlooked or dealt with superficially (Spinetta, 1977a).

This section on patient issues is an attempt to cull from the literature data and ideas relating specifically to the child with cancer. We hope that it will suggest directions for further research on patient issues and provide background for considering the results of the psychological and psychiatric evaluations of cancer survivors presented elsewhere in this volume (Chapters 5 and 6).

The Fatally Ill Child

When the early work on psychosocial aspects of childhood cancer was undertaken, little or no effective treatment was available to most patients, and children almost always died—often very rapidly. As a result, the child with cancer was regarded as "the dying patient," virtually from the point of diagnosis on, and the psychosocial literature focused on death issues. Caregivers and parents were especially anxious to know what to tell the child about the illness and the prognosis. Questions about the child's awareness of impending death were generally seen as most relevant both by investigators seeking to understand the child's experience with cancer and by health care professionals seeking to provide good patient care.

Children and Death

The death of a child is a difficult thing to face or accept in our culture—in an age of medical advancement when childhood mortality is low. It was even more difficult to discuss these issues in the fifties and early sixties before the work of Elisabeth Kübler-Ross (1969) became popular and an acceptance of the need to talk about death became more widespread. More recent popular discussions of death and dying have, we hope, begun to dispel the death taboo once strongly ingrained in American culture.

Health care professionals who care for dying children certainly are not immune either to the feelings of horror and despair engendered by a child's death or to the influence of the cultural death taboo. Death is difficult for most people to talk about, and many feel that children should not be touched by such tragedy. Early writing on the emotional management of the fatally ill child strongly affirmed that "life and not death is the child's business" (Plank, 1964, p. 641). The "protective approach" (Share, 1972)—shielding the child with cancer and any young siblings from information about the seriousness of the illness—was the generally accepted policy for many years among those who cared for these patients (Gogan et al., 1977). Most professional caregivers hoped to help the dying child be a child, and believed they could best do so by protecting the child from knowledge of impending death and by striving to create an atmosphere of cheerful normality (Toch, 1964). This policy was based on several assumptions about the child's awareness of death which drew on the findings of research dealing with the development of the conception of death and the fear of death in children.

The Child's Fear and Conception of Death　　Studies attempting to describe children's conceptions of death (Anthony, 1940; Nagy, 1948; Kübler-Ross, 1969; Koocher, 1973; White et al., 1978) have consistently revealed a developmental maturation in children's understanding. This maturational process has been related to the stages of cognitive development described by Piaget (Koocher, 1973; White et al., 1978). Most of these studies were conducted with healthy children and sought to describe normal development.

In general, research has suggested that young children (under age 5) do not understand either the permanence or the universality of death. They see it as reversible, and akin to separation (Share, 1972). In middle childhood (ages 6–9), death is usually understood as an external process involving physical harm to a person, often coming as punishment for wrongdoing. Nagy (1948) reported that Hungarian children in this age group conceptualized death as a person; however this does not seem to be the case for American children (Koocher, 1973). Older children (aged 10 and over) and adolescents are likely to attain a more complete conception of death as an internal process involving cessation of bodily functions (White et al., 1978) which is permanent and inevitable.

A maturational pattern in the development of the fear of death which parallels the development of the concept of death has been noted (Natterson and Knudson, 1960). Observations of hospitalized, fatally ill children by both researchers and clinicians suggest that for children under age 5 the strongest anxiety is the fear of separation. Children aged 5 to 10 are seen as most fearful of bodily mutilation, and only children over 10 are seen as experiencing a strong fear of death per se (Natterson and Knudson, 1960; Green, 1967; Schowalter, 1970; Adams, 1976).

To Tell or Not to Tell Controversy

The Protective Approach　　A number of clinicians (Plank, 1964; Toch, 1964; Howell, 1966; Evans, 1968) used the research described above to defend and advocate the policy of telling children with cancer less than the whole truth about their diagnosis and prognosis. This argument is based on three rationales (Share, 1972): first, the idea that children under age 10 are not capable of a real understanding of death and do not experience anxiety about death. Those who take this position agree that since death is not a prominent issue developmentally, children will not worry about dying unless knowledge of the true nature of their illness is forced upon them. Second, these clinicians argue that children do not want or need much information about their disease and should not be given more information than they request. This rationale is based on observations that few patients, including adolescents, ask many questions about the nature of the illness or initiate talk about death with the adults who care for them (Richmond and Waisman, 1955). The third rationale is the assumption that the child's immature ego defenses are inadequate to cope with the distress and anxiety which knowledge of a fatal prognosis would entail (Plank, 1964; Evans, 1968).

These arguments were challenged in the late sixties as researchers and clinicians began to question the wisdom and efficacy of the protective approach, giving rise to a "to tell or not to tell" controversy which focused on younger school-age children. Vernick and Karon (1965) used a "life-space" interview technique to study a large group of leukemic patients. Their observations suggested that critically ill children sense the deep concern of their parents and the medical staff, despite the adults' efforts to behave in a cheerful, normal manner. They concluded that the tendency among fatally ill children to remain passive and ask few questions about death reflected the children's perceptions of adult fears of this topic, rather than their own lack of awareness of impending death.

Some investigators (Morrisey, 1965; Waechter, 1971; Spinetta, 1974) have questioned the relevance of research on the development of the concept of death, which used only healthy children, to the issue of managing children who are seriously ill. They suggest that what is true of healthy children may not be generalizable to those with a fatal disease. Results of a number of controlled studies conducted with child cancer patients who had not been told their diagnosis or prognosis support this view (Waechter, 1971; Spinetta et al., 1973; Spinetta and Maloney, 1975). When given storytelling tasks, patients between the ages of 6 and 10 demonstrated an awareness of the seriousness of their illness and of the threat of death which was in striking contrast to their parents' beliefs about what the children "knew." Results of standardized tests showed significantly more anxiety among fatally ill children than among chronically ill or healthy controls.

Although acknowledging that what these children fear may not involve a fully developed adult concept of death, Spinetta (1974) argues that these patients do experience a great deal of grief and anxiety related to the seriousness of their illness. He insists that they deserve help in coping with these feelings from the adults who care for them. A number of clinicians (Vernick, 1973; Lansky, 1974; Drotar, 1977) report that children are responsive to their initiation of discussions about fears and fantasies related to death. They suggest that such openness can help children gain a sense of security and trust in parents and caregivers.

The Open Approach   To summarize, those who are critical of the protective approach and who advocate openness argue as follows. First, research on healthy children's concepts of death is not wholly relevant to fatally ill children; even very young children who are dying experience a great deal of fear about the seriousness of their illness. Second, the observed passivity and lack of questioning about death by these children simply indicates that adults' discomfort and silence make it difficult for children to raise the issue. Finally, since children do experience and cope with a great deal of anxiety about the illness, there is no reason to believe that their coping skills are inadequate, and there is evidence which suggests that discussing fears and fantasies about death can be supportive of good coping.

In recent years, the open approach (Share, 1972) has been adopted by most professionals who treat child cancer patients. This is due, at least in part, to an acknowledgment among caregivers that children often simply cannot be protected from awareness of the serious nature of their illness. However, this shift may also reflect the caregivers' response to the improved prognoses for most of these patients and the fact that most of the children will experience periods of relatively good health—it is now easier for professionals to be hopeful and to offer children and parents a good dose of hope along with the whole truth about the diagnosis and prognosis.

Broader Issues

As caregivers adopted the open approach to communication with the child cancer patient, new questions replaced the "to tell or not to tell" issue. Instead of asking whether the fatally ill child should be told the diagnosis/prognosis, clinicians became concerned with how these children can be helped to cope with the stresses which accompany their illnesses (Vernick and Karon, 1965; Binger et al., 1969; Waechter, 1971). Researchers began trying to broaden the scope of knowledge about the fatally ill child.

Other investigators have been concerned with the personal relationships of the dying child (Spinetta et al., 1974). During the course of their treatment, patients were asked to place dolls representing doctor, nurse, mother, and father in a dollhouse replica of a hospital room which included a bed containing the child patient. As the children's medical conditions worsened, the distance from the bed at which children placed the dolls increased significantly. The authors suggest that this increased distance reflects the dying child's increased feelings of isolation and loneliness (Spinetta et al., 1974).

Coping with the Threat of Death   As discussed above, earlier writings maintained that children are unable to cope with the threat of death because of their immature psychological defenses (Plank, 1964; Evans, 1968). More recently, attempts have been made to explore the strategies through which these children do cope with fatal illness and ways they can be helped to cope more effectively.

One of the fatally ill child's main coping tasks has been described as "maintaining the continuity and integrity of his identity" in the face of the assault which the awareness of fatal illness makes on the child's self-image (Hoffman and Futterman, 1971, p. 75). As do other writers (Richmond and Waisman, 1955), these investigators note that children are prone to withdraw into passivity in the face of this attack on their self-concept. Both play activity and direct communication about illness-related feelings can help children express and thereby master anxieties related to disease and treatment (Hoffman and Futterman, 1971). The dying child's need for a sense of control can be fostered by the primary physician as well, through careful explanations of the diagnosis and treatment and by anticipatory discussions of changes in medication or special procedures (Green, 1967). Such interventions allow the child a more active role in the treatment.

The development of a transitory school phobia among fatally ill children has been seen as directly related to separation anxiety in the child and the parent which is exacerbated by the real threat of death posed by the illness (Futterman and Hoffman, 1970; Lansky et al., 1975). Some researchers suggest that a temporary maladjustment of this kind may represent a way of coping with almost overwhelming stress and may occur as part of an adaptive process (Futterman and Hoffman, 1970). These investigators note the profound effect on the child's adaptation of the parent's ability or inability to cope successfully with illness-related anxiety (Futterman and Hoffman, 1970). Case material has been presented to illustrate the interaction between parent and child coping which is involved in the etiology of the specific symptom of school phobia (Futterman and Hoffman, 1970; Lansky et al., 1975). However, most researchers have focused solely on the parental component of family coping with fatal childhood illness. These topics are explored below in the section on family issues.

The Child with a Life-Threatening Chronic Illness

In spite of advances in treatment and improved prognoses, caring for dying children remains very much a part of the work of those who treat child cancer patients. As a result, a good deal of the literature on the fatally ill child discussed above continues to be relevant and helpful for cancer professionals. However, if the terminal stage of a child's cancer is reached, it now does not occur until after a long course of treatment which often includes several periods of remission and relative health. Although not all children with cancer will survive, each child has rehabilitative potential, if only for a short time (Clapp, 1976). Health care professionals are now being warned against committing "psychological euthanasia" (Van Eys, 1977, p. 165) by assuming that a child with cancer will die and therefore failing to strive for full physical and psychological health for that child. The possibility of a biological cancer cure now forces both parents and caregivers to be concerned about facilitating normal emotional, social, and intellectual development during the child's treatment.

Living with Cancer

Changes in cancer treatment, as well as changes in prognosis, have raised new issues for patients. Any major shift in treatment can be expected to affect the nature of the cancer experience and its coping demands on patients and their families. Some rarer and more experimental modes of treatment, such as those involving bone-marrow transplantation or other procedures involving prolonged sterile isolation, raise very specific emotional problems for patients, parents, and caregivers. These have been described in some detail by clinicians who work with such patients (Kohle et al., 1971; Kellerman et al., 1977; Powazek et al., 1978; Patenaude et al., 1979).

Although efforts are being made to reduce the negative impact of cancer treatment, standard therapies for childhood cancers still involve radical and invasive interventions and an emphasis on outpatient rather than inpatient treatment (Wollnik, 1976). Following hospitalization for initial diagnosis and treatment of a malignancy, present practice often makes it possible for the child with cancer to begin a process of "reentry" (Kagen-Goodheart, 1977) into the home/school environment. At the same time the child is usually starting a long and difficult outpatient treatment program. The reentry process is frequently made more difficult emotionally by changes in physical appearance which are side effects of treatment.

Changes in Body Image   Successes in treatment for many forms of childhood cancer have come at a rather high physical cost to the patients themselves (Jaffe et al., 1979). Present methods of treatment usually cause the child with cancer to experience a good deal of physical discomfort and some striking changes in physical appearance. Frequently, the "cure" seems worse than the disease, which can be extremely difficult for children to understand. Some of the unpleasant physical effects which frequently accompany chemotherapy are temporary changes, such as nausea, vomiting, and hair loss. Other changes may be lasting physical problems, such as the spinal curvatures often associated with radiotherapy, amputations often necessary for treatment of bone tumors, and other forms of mutilating surgery. Cancer treatment also involves the threat of a variety of late physical effects, including the possibility of therapy-induced sterility (Jaffe, 1975) and heightened risk of the development of a new malignancy (Li et al., 1975). Additional risks are discussed in Chapter 2.

Concern about children's potential loss of self-esteem as a result of physical changes caused by cancer treatment has been expressed by a number of writers (Clapp, 1976; F. L. Johnson et al., 1979; Van Eys, 1977; Kagen-Goodheart, 1977). Lack of self-confidence because of physical changes can have a negative effect on children's peer relationships and willingness to attend school, thus affecting their emotional and academic development. The patient's age has been seen as an important factor in this respect. As an example Johnson et al. (1979) point out that hair loss, while potentially quite disturbing for an adolescent patient, probably will not be much of a problem for a 3-year-old.

Special Problems of Adolescents   As survival time has lengthened for children with cancer, new studies have paid special attention to the unique difficulties experienced by adolescent patients. Adolescence is seen by many as an especially stressful period of life, even in the best circumstances (Easson, 1970; Clapp, 1976). Strong peer pressure favors sports and dating, and most teenagers experience some fear of rejection by peers. Probably at no other time in a person's life are physical appearance, athletic performance, and peer acceptance as highly valued in American culture as they are during the teen years. For cancer patients, the normal physical changes which constitute the process of maturing sexually and physically are augmented by the disturbing physical effects of disease and treatment. These effects often involve impairment of athletic ability and lessening of physical attractiveness. To the adolescent, such side effects of treatment may be much more alarming than the threat of death (Plumb and Holland, 1974).

However, as discussed above, the threat of death is understood quite fully by adolescent patients, and is often recognized by their peers as well. This fact may make friendships even more difficult because of mutual discomfort with the issue of death. Fear of rejection may be further aggravated by the influence of social myths about cancer and the fear of contagion on peers (Van Eys, 1977). Fears associated with the cancer diagnosis and changes in physical appearance can cause the adolescent patient to withdraw from most peer contacts if the opportunity to discuss and overcome these feelings is not provided (Kagen-Goodheart, 1977).

One of the major developmental tasks of adolescence is separation from parents and establishment of an independent identity (Erikson, 1959; Easson, 1970). The practical necessity of depending on parents and caregivers during illness often threatens adolescent patients' first attempts to establish independence and a sense of control over their own lives. This necessary regression and dependence may constitute an additional assault on their self-esteem. Already strained communication between parents and their newly diagnosed teenager may make it difficult for the patient to use parents for emotional support (Drotar, 1977). If the patient also withdraws from friends and classmates, the need for psychosocial support from a concerned professional becomes especially evident. Many writers stress the adolescents' need for both honesty and support from professional caregivers (Clapp, 1976; F. L. Johnson et al., 1979).

School Issues   School is the child's occupation and the main focal point of the child's life—at least between the ages of 6 and 16. As caregivers focus attention on quality-of-life issues, problems related to the child patient's school functioning are seen as increasingly important. This has led to an emphasis on facilitating the child's regular school attendance in a normal classroom setting whenever possible (Greene, 1975; Kagen-Goodheart, 1977; Katz et al., 1977; Kaplan et al., 1973). A positive school experience can provide the child with a sense of accomplishment and social acceptance, strengthening faltering self-esteem and lessening maladaptive emotional responses to the illness (Kagen-Goodheart, 1977).

Several authors have described interventions by medical center personnel with educators aimed at easing initial academic reentry and establishing communication between hospital and school which can continue throughout the course of the illness (Greene, 1975; Katz et al., 1977; Clapp, 1976; F. L. Johnson et al., 1979). This communication is especially important since current treatment for the majority of these children involves periodic outpatient visits requiring frequent school absences over a period of two or more years. Specifically, medical staff must periodically provide clear information about appropriate physical limits on the sick child's activities to the school (Greene, 1975; Clapp, 1976). Several authors (Greene, 1975; Katz et al., 1977; Kirten and Liverman, 1977) have suggested that teachers, school nurses, or other authorities should prepare the child's classmates for his or her initial return to school by explaining the child's disease and physical changes. Kaplan et al. (1973) point out that school personnel need to confront their own feelings about illness and their fears about death in order to respond realistically to the needs of the seriously ill child.

Coping with Cancer Treatment   The experience of cancer patients and their families has been described as "living in limbo" (Cohen and Wellisch, 1978). Improved prognoses and lengthened survival for childhood cancer patients means that they and their families must cope with long-term uncertainty, balancing an awareness of the possibility of death with a realistic hope for cure. As discussed in Chapter 2, this uncertainty may be relieved to some extent by passing specific milestones some years after diagnosis, but the threat of recurrence or risk of developing a second malignancy may never entirely fade for these survivors. This raises a fundamental and complex problem suggested by the title of this volume: how can children cope with the stress of such long-term uncertainty?

Existing psychosocial research has failed to address a whole range of important questions about the way children experience and adapt to life-threatening illness (Spinetta, 1977a). These questions include the nature of the coping strategies children employ, whether these vary as a function of the specific type of cancer, age-related coping differences, and how children's coping might be facilitated by parents and caregivers.

In setting forth a framework for future research in this area, Spinetta (1977a) suggests that four coping tasks, originally described by Lazarus (1976), may be helpful in evaluating the adaptational efforts of children with cancer. These coping tasks are (1) tolerating or relieving distress associated with the illness; (2) maintaining a sense of personal worth; (3) maintaining positive personal relationships with parents, peers, and caregivers; and (4) meeting the specific requirements of particular stressful situations, using the resources available.

Several specific coping behaviors observable in children with cancer even at a very young age have been identified, including preparing for anticipated problems (such as hair loss, new medications); distinguishing between that which can be changed and that which must be endured; and seeking information necessary to meet each new stress (Spinetta, 1977a). Several authors have emphasized the importance of providing the child with pertinent information in order to facilitate realistic coping (F. L. Johnson et al., 1979; Clapp, 1976).

Finding an acceptable outlet for feelings of anxiety, anger, and fear, and gaining a sense of mastery over the environment have been identified as important coping tasks among seriously ill children (Adams, 1976). Group play sessions are aimed at enhancing children's coping by helping them express their feelings, increase self-control, induce a feeling of mastery and competence, and resolve frightening treatment experiences. Group sessions also provide continuing peer interaction which is seen as helpful in the adaptation process (Adams, 1976).

Spinetta (1977b) has explored the impact of family communications about the illness on the child's coping and the effectiveness of intense denial as a coping strategy among child cancer patients. He views denial as closely related to silence and closed patterns of family communications. He theorizes that children with cancer can choose to deal with the illness within the family either by means of silence and denial or with open communication, and that the child's choice of coping style is determined both by whether parents have rewarded or discouraged open discussion of feelings in the past and by whether they initiate communication and convey acceptance of such sharing during treatment. Spinetta suggests that each style of coping involves a different form of anxiety. The child who chooses silence will experience tension and feelings of isolation caused by excessive denial. Avoidance of communication about the reality of the illness will put a distance between the child and his sources of support. The child who openly communicates concerns will experience and express anxiety about the illness itself, treatment, and the threat of death. Spinetta argues that the child who chooses openness deals with anxiety stemming from an awareness of the known, rather than with fear of the unknown, and is able to seek support from family members. In Spinetta's view, the open coping style is more effective because it can strengthen bonds among family members, creating support for all of the child's adaptive efforts. This view is supported by Spinetta's research (1977b) comparing children with cancer from families with "open" and with "closed" communication patterns. His results suggest that children from open families have greater self-esteem and are more willing to express anxiety and anger about the illness, more accepting of unpleasant feelings, and more willing to express their desire for closer familial relations.

Long-Term Uncertainty/Late Effects   Work on coping with a life-threatening illness, described above, focuses on patients currently undergoing treatment. Some authors (Kagen-Goodheart, 1977; Lucas, 1977) have noted that the point of voluntary cessation of treatment and the period immediately following it can be extremely stressful for the patient and the family. This point is the beginning of a potentially very long, treatment-free, disease-free period which may stretch, if all goes well, to the survivor's death in old age from causes unrelated to the malignancy (Van Eys, 1977). Presumably, the task of coping with uncertainty continues, on some level, for these persons for an indefinite period of time.

Since the possibility of disease-free survival is relatively new, few studies have attempted to evaluate the quality of life or psychosocial adjustment of those children who have been "cured" of cancer. Two surveys, each involving over 100 long-term cancer survivors, have been conducted (H. A. Holmes and Holmes, 1975; Li and Stone, 1976). In these studies former patients were surveyed by mailed questionnaires or telephone interviews inquiring about their present life with respect to residual physical disability, health, marriage and family, employment, and education. A large majority of former patients in both studies reported reaching or surpassing their premorbid expectations in education, and generally enjoying normal or near-normal lives. These investigators concluded that the survivors had made excellent adjustments and suffered from very few residual problems related to their disease or treatment. The researchers expressed the belief that the potential for a high quality of extended life for most survivors was apparent (H. A. Holmes and Holmes, 1975; Li and Stone, 1976).

Neither of these studies attempted to assess mental health or psychological adjustment in their samples, except through superficial self-report and inference drawn from level of education, employment, and marital status. In addition, studies of adults who have recovered from cancer have shown that employment and insurance discrimination against former cancer patients may constitute a serious problem (McKenna, 1974; Wheatley et al., 1974; Ashenburg, 1975; Stone, 1975; Cunnick and Wright, 1977). These issues may also affect survivors of childhood cancer when they reach adulthood (see Chapter 9).

The question of long-term psychosocial adjustment has been explored in a small preliminary study of 18 cancer survivors treated for malignancies between the ages of 2 and 5 (Fergusson, 1976). On a range of psychological tests half of the children showed no evidence of residual problems; seven (38.9%) showed evidence of mild behavioral adjustment problems and two (11.1%) showed a moderate amount of difficulty. This investigator stresses that intervening family problems may account for some of the children's difficulties, and concludes that psychological damage does not necessarily follow treatment for cancer in early childhood (Fergusson, 1976).

Family Issues

The Family of the Fatally Ill Child

Since the sixties researchers have shown a good deal of interest in the experiences and problems of families of fatally ill children. Until quite recently, the psychosocial literature has been primarily concerned with family reactions to the child's impending death. A number of major studies of these families have explored the nature of their cancer experience, their coping responses, and their emotional adjustment to the crisis of a child's fatal illness (Bozeman et al., 1955; Murstein, 1960; Natterson and Knudson, 1960; Friedman et al., 1963; Chodoff et al., 1964; Hamovitch, 1964; Binger et al., 1969; Lowenberg, 1970; Futterman and Hoffman, 1973; Kaplan et al., 1973; Knapp and Hansen, 1973; Lascari and Stehbens, 1973; Stehbens and Lascari, 1974; Kaplan et al., 1976). Table 1-1 summarizes the samples studied and the main methods of investigation used in each of these projects. The discussion which follows is an attempt to describe the cancer

Table 1-1 Major Studies of Families with Fatally Ill Children

Authors	Date	Subjects	Children's Diagnoses	Method	Timing of Study
Bozeman et al.	1955	18 mothers	Leukemia	Formal and informal interviews; staff observations; Thematic Apperception Test	During treatment
Murstein	1960	Parents of 20 patients	10 leukemia 10 other cancer	Ratings by physician and nurse; projective and objective psychological testing	During treatment
Natterson & Knudson	1960	33 mothers	22 leukemia 11 other fatal illness	Staff observations; social work interviews	During treatment
Friedman et al. and Chodoff et al.	1963 1964	One or both parents of 27 patients: 26 mothers, 20 fathers	20 leukemia 7 other cancer	Weekly interviews; questionnaire; systematic observations	During treatment After death of child: 18 parents (8 couples)

Table 1-1 Major Studies of Families with Fatally Ill Children (*Continued*)

Authors	Date	Subjects	Children's Diagnoses	Method	Timing of Study
Hamovitch	1964	Parents of 82 patients	64 leukemia 18 other cancer	Structured interviews; questionnaires; staff observations; recordings of staff meetings	During treatment and follow-up after death of child
Binger et al.	1969	Parents of 20 patients	Leukemia	One loosely structured interview (2–3 hrs.)	After death of child
Futterman & Hoffman	1973	23 sets of parents	Leukemia	Open-ended interviews; informal staff observation	During treatment; some after-death follow-up
Kaplan et al.	1973	50+ families	Leukemia	Clinical observations to assess coping	During treatment
Knapp & Hansen	1973	5 groups of 8–10 parents; total 45 parents of 26 children	Leukemia	Observations during group meetings; parental evaluation of group experience	During treatment
Lascari & Stehbens *and* Stehbens & Lascari	1973 1974	Parents of 20 patients: 13 fathers, 16 mothers seen, 4 families answered questionnaires	Leukemia	Home interview (2–3 hours) or questionnaire	After death of child
Kaplan et al.	1976	40 families with 173 members (part of Kaplan et al. 1973 sample)	Leukemia	Home interview	Follow-up after death of child

experience of these families, based on the results of this body of research, and drawing as well on the clinical and theoretical observations of other writers concerned with childhood cancer as a fatal illness.

For the most part, research studies have focused on parents, rather than on the family as a whole, and concentrated on mothers rather than on fathers. Control groups have generally not been used and the emphasis has been on getting a broad and in-depth view of the parents' experience rather than on collecting data to prove specific hypotheses.

In addition, most of the research deals specifically with parents of children with leukemia. Acute leukemia is the most common form of childhood cancer, and great strides have been made recently in improving its treatment and prognosis (Simone, 1974). However, for many years, while rapid progress was being made with a number of solid tumors of childhood, the prognosis for leukemia remained "invariably fatal" (Bozeman et al., 1955). Thus, until the mid-1970s leukemia was often used by researchers as a prototype for fatal childhood illness.

For example, in 1960, Murstein compared parents of children with leukemia to parents of children with other malignancies and found that overall emotional adjustment was poorer among parents of leukemics. Murstein attributed this finding to the hope for cure extended to parents of children with solid tumors but necessarily withheld from parents of leukemics. Most of the more recent literature (summarized in a later section of this chapter) studies all child cancer patients as a group and discusses childhood malignancies in general as life-threatening rather than fatal.

The Cancer Diagnosis

Initial Reactions of parents on hearing their child's cancer diagnosis for the first time have been universally described with such terms as shock, disbelief, numbness, feeling stunned. Parents react this way even when they have strongly suspected the true nature of their child's illness before diagnosis (Friedman et al., 1963; Binger et al., 1969). Mothers in the Bozeman et al. (1955) study described the impact of the news as like an actual physical blow: "An iron safe dropped on me" (p. 4). Parents are often unable to really hear anything that is said to them in their initial conference with the physician after the word "cancer" or "leukemia" is used for the first time. Most parents need to be given the same information about the disease and treatment a day or two later in a follow-up session, after they have had a chance to absorb the initial shock of hearing the diagnosis (Peironi, 1967).

Many investigators report that in spite of the parents' emotional shock and disbelief, they are able to mobilize themselves fairly rapidly to act on their child's behalf (Hamovitch, 1964; Binger et al., 1969). Some observations suggest that parents characteristically progress from initial numbness to a split between emotional nonacceptance of the diagnosis and prognosis and an intellectual acceptance of the reality. This acceptance allows parents to accomplish necessary practical tasks (Chodoff et al., 1964). Other observers have described universal denial among the mothers they studied; denial was viewed as manifested whenever a mother screened out the reality of the situation or made a compulsive effort to reverse it (Bozeman et al., 1955). Often, this meant demanding additional consultations and examinations in an attempt to prove that some mistake had been made in diagnosing the child. However, in spite of efforts to disprove the leukemia diagnosis, none of these parents extended their denial to the fact that their child was indeed ill, and so they remained able to fulfill their parental roles in the hospital setting.

Anticipatory Grief   Parents' responses to the devastating news that their child has a fatal illness have been seen by many as analogous to a grief reaction in anticipation of the loss of the beloved child (for a more complete discussion of anticipatory grief, see Chapter 10). In addition to this ultimate loss, the cancer diagnosis also represents enormous immediate losses to parents—for instance, future goals which must be postponed or given up completely (Kaplan et al., 1973). The threat to the child's life has also been described as representing symbolically the threat of death to the mother herself, and as stimulating her own death fears (Natterson and Knudson, 1960). Other observers have stressed the role of the parents' fears of separation in anticipatory grieving (Richmond and Waisman, 1955; Futterman and Hoffman, 1970; Sourkes, 1977). Many have emphasized that the experience of these families cannot be understood without recognizing the effect of their grief on all their choices, actions, and responses (Kaplan et al., 1973; Pearse, 1977; Sourkes, 1977).

A number of investigators have identified parents' initial numbness and denial as the beginning of an anticipatory grief "process" (Friedman et al., 1963; Chodoff et al., 1964; Hamovitch, 1964; Binger et al., 1969). Several writers have suggested that parents go through stages of mourning before the child dies which are similar to the stages of the dying patient outlined by Kübler-Ross (1969) (Heffron et al., 1973; Knapp and Hansen, 1973; Kartha and Ertel, 1976). Natterson and Knudson (1960) observed a similar pattern which they described as triphasic: initial denial, efforts to prolong the child's life, and finally calm acceptance as death approaches. Many of the studies of parents (see Table 1-1) note a number of common responses which tend to affirm this general pattern, including anger, hostility, self-blame, guilt, apathy, weakness, and somatic symptoms.

In this literature, discussions of anticipatory mourning are closely related to discussions of coping. The words "grieving" and "mourning" often denote the behavior and responses used to cope with loss or threatened loss. In fact, parental anticipatory mourning has been identified as one of several coping tasks facing parents of fatally ill children (Futterman and Hoffman, 1973). These investigators delineate five interwoven processes constituting the parents' anticipatory mourning task: (1) acknowledgment—true realization that the child's death is inevitable; (2) grieving—the experience and expression of sadness and pain; (3) reconciliation—development of a perspective about the child's death which preserves a sense of the worth of the child's life and of life in general; (4) detachment—withdrawal of emotional investment from the child as a growing being with a real future; and (5) memorialization—development of a mental representation of the dying child which will endure beyond the child's death (pp. 130–131).

Table 1-2 summarizes five schemes conceptualizing the experiences of parents of fatally ill children over the course of the illness. Because each vocabulary was designed to clarify the underlying meaning of a group of responses and behaviors reported almost universally by researchers and clinicians, many of the phases, stages, and processes described in these five schemes are to some extent equivalent.

Parental Coping during Treatment

The Nature of the Stress It is clear that treatment for childhood cancer involves major emotional stresses for parents. In addition to the grief reactions and emotional pain involved in the threat of the loss of the child, there are substantial practical stresses in day-to-day living which affect the whole family as it mobilizes to respond to the crisis. The sick child needs special parental care and attention; frequent hospitalizations or visits to the doctor are necessary. These circumstances cause changes in family routines and plans which are difficult and disruptive for everyone.

Healthy siblings continue to need parental care and attention, as well as special help understanding the patient's illness and the changes in parents' behavior. Shifts in roles and household tasks and responsibilities of family members are usually required, and financial difficulties often arise. Once the child is hospitalized and begins treatment, parents quickly become aware of a subtle shift in authority from themselves as primary caretakers to the medical staff (Chodoff et al., 1964). This is one important component of the threat to the parents' self-esteem posed by their child's diagnosis and treatment.

Some specific coping problems are implied by the usual course of the disease. Many children with cancer experience a period of relatively good health or remission of the disease during treatment. These remissions have been increasingly frequent as treatment has improved. The pattern of remission and relapse in the course of childhood leukemia can cause special emotional difficulty for parents, who respond to remission either with a great deal of renewed hope or with doubts that the original diagnosis could possibly have been correct. These hopes are smashed, and painful grief is renewed, when relapses occur (Bozeman et al., 1955).

Discussions of parental coping with the anticipated death of their child from cancer have sought to explain how parents meet the difficult emotional and practical demands of their situation. The problem of caring for a child while at the same time grieving for the eventual loss of his or her life is inherently stressful. Parents of fatally ill children face a number of very difficult "adaptive dilemmas" (Futterman and Hoffman, 1973) corresponding to the conflicting nature of the

Table 1-2 Attempts to Conceptualize the Emotional/Psychological Experiences of Parents of Fatally Ill Children

Natterson & Knudson (1960) Triphasic Reaction of Mothers	Chodoff et al. (1964) Natural History of Adjustment	Lowenberg (1970) Approach vs. Avoidance Coping	Futterman & Hoffman (1973) Anticipatory Mourning Processes	Knapp & Hansen (1973) Stages of Anticipatory Grief (after Kübler-Ross)	Reported Reactions or Behaviors
Initial disturbed reaction: deny reality	Experience of shock, unreality Intellectual acceptance/emotional nonacceptance	Avoidance coping	Process of acknowledgment	Denial	Shock, disbelief; isolation of affect; efforts to disprove diagnosis; unrealistic planning for the future; inability to mobilize; avoidance of discussions of death
			Process of reconciliation	Anger	Hostility toward staff; anger at God/fate; anger at child; self-blame
Interim more rational reaction: direct energy toward realistic measures that offer hope of saving child's life		Approach coping		Bargaining	Seeking new medical information to foster hope; use of religion—promises to God; participation in care in effort to prolong life; seeking explanations for child's illness

Table 1-2 Attempts to Conceptualize the Emotional / Psychological Experiences of Parents of Fatally Ill Children (*Continued*)

Natterson & Knudson (1960) Triphasic Reaction of Mothers	Chodoff et al. (1964) Natural History of Adjustment	Lowenberg (1970) Approach vs. Avoidance Coping	Futterman & Hoffman (1973) Anticipatory Mourning Processes	Knapp & Hansen (1973) Stages of Anticipatory Grief (after Kübler-Ross)	Reported Reactions or Behaviors
	Curtailment of hope; anticipatory grieving		Process of grieving	Depression	Crying, sighing; apathy, weakness; somatic symptoms; withdrawal from social contacts; sadness; willingness to talk about feelings and the death of the child; remembering events from the child's life
Integrated terminal reaction: direct energy away from child	Detachment / philosophical resignation		Process of memorialization Process of detachment	Acceptance	Feeling calm; making plans for funeral; anticipating life without child; affirming value of child's life; expressing hope death will come quickly; giving up hope of cure; withdrawing emotional investment in child's future

demands that must be met during treatment. To cope with the child's illness these parents must simultaneously maintain hope and acknowledge the ultimate loss of the child; attend to immediate needs and plan for the future; cherish the child and allow separation; maintain day-to-day functioning and express disturbing feelings; care actively for the child and delegate responsibility to medical specialists; trust the physician and acknowledge his or her limitations; and care for the child and prepare for death through detachment (Futterman and Hoffman, 1973).

The Function of Coping Behavior and Tasks   Chodoff et al. (1963) have delineated two basic functions of coping: internal or defensive, aimed at protecting the self from disruptive anxiety and judged for effectiveness by the degree of comfort that results; and external, aimed at mastering a problem and judged for effectiveness in social terms. Along with other authors (Futterman and Hoffman, 1973; Kaplan et al., 1973) Chodoff et al. stress the positive social aspects of coping rather than the internal defense mechanisms, while continuing to discuss the importance of the defensive function of many coping strategies. Similarly, Lowenberg (1970) has suggested that the behavior of parents of fatally ill children is governed by either an "approach" or an "avoidance" orientation. Approach behavior is aimed at mastery of a problem or threat; avoidance behavior, at escaping the stressful or threatening reality, either through physical avoidance or cognitive distortion.

Other researchers have identified comprehension of the reality of the situation as the essential initial parental coping task (Kaplan et al., 1973; Kaplan et al., 1976). Specifically, these authors suggest that parents of a fatally ill child must understand—if they are to function effectively—that their child is going to be sick for a long time and will eventually die. Attempts to master the threatening reality cannot be successful if psychological protection in the form of strong denial/avoidance keeps parents from comprehending their true situation (Kaplan et al., 1973). Others have discussed the danger of intense denial in terms of the possibility of seriously impaired reality testing. Excessive defensive measures can compromise optimal care of the child or prevent the accomplishment of parental anticipatory grief work, resulting in severe acute grief reactions after the child's death (Friedman et al., 1963; Chodoff et al., 1964; Lowenberg, 1970; Kaplan et al., 1976).

A more complex view of the coping process (Futterman and Hoffman, 1973) suggests that successful coping involves accomplishing a number of specific tasks throughout the treatment period. Each of these tasks involves elements of the two aspects of coping—internal psychological protection of the person, and external mastery of the physical/social/emotional reality. The tasks include maintaining confidence (a sense of their own worth, a sense of mastery or control); maintaining emotional/interpersonal equilibrium; reorganizing their lives (integrating the experience of the child's illness and death into their personalities); and anticipatory mourning.

Coping Behavior   Studies of parents of fatally ill children have reported a number of common behaviors as efforts to accomplish coping tasks. Some of the observed behavior or responses can be seen as directed toward the function of psychological protection from overwhelming anxiety; others can be characterized as attempts to master the threatening situation and maintain a sense of control (Lowenberg, 1970). The observed protective behavior or strategies include isolation of affect, increased motor activity, denying the diagnosis or prognosis, seeking explanations for the development of the disease to avoid guilt, putting trust in the primary physician, avoiding discussions of death, avoiding visits to the child, and hostility toward the medical staff. Coping behavior aimed at mastery or control includes making practical, necessary arrangements for care and transportation; participating in the child's medical care; seeking medical information about the disease in an attempt to master it intellectually; allowing oneself to feel and express sorrow—grieving, giving and using emotional support, and talking openly about the illness.

Several of these responses were identified above as indicators of different stages of parental anticipatory grief (see Table 1-2), underscoring the similarity between parental coping with fatal illness and the anticipatory grief process as it is most often discussed. Neither of these concepts has been well-defined, and discussions in this literature often use them almost interchangeably. Parents' use of a particular coping behavior or strategy can indicate their stage of anticipatory grieving and also the nature of the stress they are facing at a given point in their child's treatment.

Although there will be elements of both the internal/protective and external/mastery aspects of coping in parents' behavior at all times in the course of treatment, protective responses will be stronger during the higher stress points such as diagnosis and relapse. As parents have time to do some of their grief work they will be likely to use protective or avoidance strategies less (Lowenberg, 1970). After the initial turmoil, parental emotional/grief reactions are usually brought under control, and many parents develop "conscious regulation of emotion" (Futterman and Hoffman, 1973). This strategy functions as protection, but it differs from unconscious defenses such as denial. Parents often learn to regulate their feelings intentionally, delaying or limiting some emotional reactions or expressions of feelings in order to maintain their equilibrium and continue to function competently.

Some researchers (Kaplan et al., 1973) have stressed the importance of the coping style which is adopted by the family early on, maintaining that maladaptive coping in the first one to four weeks often persists throughout the illness. Many families studied (Kaplan et al., 1973; Kaplan et al., 1976) adopted largely protective, defensive coping styles at the time of diagnosis and failed to comprehend and face the reality of the child's fatal illness. Because of their failure to accomplish this initial coping task these families were unable to make better adaptations later. Many of these families did not move into behavior aimed at mastering their situation because they persisted in using strongly protective strategies and remained unwilling to deal directly with their real problem. As a result, frequent adjustment problems appeared among family members after the child's death (Kaplan et al., 1976).

Family Communication is an aspect of coping behavior which has been given a great deal of attention in this literature. Good communication and honesty between parents and medical staff has been seen as important for parental adjustment (Lascari and Stehbens, 1973; Stehbens and Lascari, 1974), and several authors have stressed the role of openness and honesty within the family in facilitating effective coping and mutual emotional support. The "to tell or not to tell" issue—the question of whether to inform the child of the cancer diagnosis (discussed above)—relates to the larger question of the effect of open versus closed patterns of family communication on the ability of all family members to cope with the crisis of fatal illness. Many writers have noted the difference between simply "telling" the patient the facts about the diagnosis and prognosis and communicating openly about feelings, fears, and hopes. In the same way, although it is true that a patient's mother and father are usually both told the same facts about the child's illness, they may not choose to talk openly together about feelings or to share their grief. Sometimes, one parent wishes to protect the other from painful feelings or to project an image of strength for the spouse's benefit. Failure to communicate openly can make adjustment very difficult and place greater strain on the marriage (Binger et al., 1969; Kaplan et al., 1973; Pearse, 1977; Sourkes, 1977).

An important function of parents' support group meetings or other psychosocial intervention can be to teach parents to talk out some of their problems, and to help them establish more open communications within their families when such patterns have not existed previously (Heffron et al., 1973; Knapp and Hansen, 1973; Gilder, 1976; Kartha and Ertel, 1976). Parents often need special help communicating with the patient's healthy siblings about the illness. A number of authors have discussed the special problems experienced by the patient's brothers and sisters, including feelings of jealousy because of special attention given to the sick child, guilt that they might somehow have caused the illness, fear of becoming sick themselves, and feelings of grief and loss (Binger et al., 1969; Feinberg, 1970; Binger, 1973; Heffron et al., 1973; Kaplan et al., 1973). Parental communication with the patient's siblings has been identified as important because honest discussion can dispel children's fears and fantasies, help them express stressful emotions, and give them confidence that their parents will continue to love and protect them.

Sources of Emotional Support

The ability to use relationships for emotional support has been singled out as an important component of effective coping among parents of fatally ill children (Bozeman et al., 1955; Lowenberg, 1970; Futterman and Hoffman, 1973; Kaplan et al., 1973). Open communication within the family has been advocated partly because relationships with family members, especially a spouse, are usually the most important source of emotional support.

The term "support" has been used rather loosely in the literature to describe ways of relating which facilitate successful parental coping and which are perceived by parents as warm, affirming, and helpful. According to the mothers in one study (Bozeman et al., 1955), emotional support came from relationships in which the other person offered reassurance about the mother's capacity to function, was sensitive to her need to talk about the illness at times and to avoid talking about it at other times, was able to listen to her expressions of feeling, offered an unqualified willingness to help, accompanied her to the hospital, and expressed concern about her well-being (p. 11).

Grandparents   Bozeman et al. (1955) report that, although siblings—especially sisters—husbands, and some friends generally provided emotional support, the mothers studied did not find their own mothers very helpful in coping with the child's illness. In fact, grandmothers were often seen as a source of additional stress. Other investigators have also reported stressful relationships between parents and grandparents of sick children (Friedman et al., 1963; Binger et al., 1969). Grandparents can find believing the diagnosis even more difficult than the parents do and may push parents to seek second and third medical opinions. Parents sometimes find themselves forced to provide support to mourning grandparents rather than receiving comfort and help in their own grief.

Friendships with peers are often difficult for parents to maintain through the stressful period of treatment, when they have little time or energy for social engagements. Parents' friends may withdraw from them for a number of reasons, such as myths related to cancer and fear of contagion, discomfort and pain in the face of the threat of death, and a feeling that they are unable to be helpful with such an overwhelming problem. As a result, several authors have observed progressive social isolation among parents of fatally ill children (Bozeman et al., 1955; Friedman et al., 1963; Lansky, 1964).

Relationships with Other Parents of Children with Cancer may be formed in formal parents' groups or informally in the inpatient unit or clinic waiting room. Shared problems and mutual understanding often help to form strong bonds between the parents of sick children. These relationships are repeatedly cited as major sources of emotional support (Bozeman et al., 1955; Friedman et al., 1963; Binger et al., 1969; Knapp and Hansen, 1973).

Staff Members   Support from relationships with medical professionals, especially nurses and the primary physician, has been considered important in the process of adjustment (Futterman and Hoffman, 1973; Lascari and Stehbens, 1973). A number of writers have offered advice to physicians on how to develop supportive relationships with parents of fatally ill children, suggesting that when medical treatment is unsuccessful, psychological/emotional support becomes an especially important function of the medical team (Friedman et al., 1963; Green, 1967; Evans et al., 1969).

In general, the research on parents of fatally ill children has been carried out at times and in settings where little routine mental health support was offered to patients aside from the possibly supportive role of the research interviews themselves. Some researchers (Binger et al., 1969; Kaplan et al., 1973) suggest that early psychosocial intervention with parents could greatly promote successful coping. Reports from mental health professionals now working in this area affirm this view (Lansky, 1974; Drotar, 1977; Kagen-Goodheart, 1977; Sourkes, 1977). Sourkes (1977) stresses that in addition to developing supportive relationships with individual members of the family, the therapists' role should be to help family members to support one another. In the same way, those who have worked with groups of these parents aim at the development of support among the group members (Heffron et al., 1973; Knapp and Hansen, 1973).

The Value of Religious Beliefs for parental support has often been investigated (Chodoff et al., 1964; Friedman et al., 1963; Bozeman et al., 1955; Binger et al., 1969; Murstein, 1960; Lascari and Stehbens, 1973). Many studies suggest that whether religious faith is helpful depends on the parents' religious orientation before the child became ill. A few "returns to faith" have been noted among those estranged from their religions (Friedman et al., 1963). Most parents who have been comforted by their religion in the past are able to find emotional support in their beliefs during the crisis, and parents seldom denounce strongly held beliefs as the result of their child's fatal illness (Bozeman et al., 1955; Friedman et al., 1963). Emotional support from religion sometimes includes a relationship with a member of the clergy. Such a relationship is probably most helpful if the cleric was involved with the family before the diagnosis (Binger et al., 1969).

Use of religion as a support may change as parents go through anticipatory grief and try different means of coping with changing demands. Parents often tend to turn to God early on, in the hope of being granted a "cure," later giving up their involvement in religion when hope for cure has waned (Bozeman et al.,

1955). The bargaining strategy, discussed above, implies that parents may "give religion a try" at one stage of the illness.

Several writers have emphasized the role of a "search for meaning" in the coping process (Friedman et al., 1963; Chodoff et al., 1964; Futterman and Hoffman, 1973). This term refers to parents' attempts to deal with existential questions—to integrate the fact of their child's illness into their way of understanding the meaning and nature of life itself. This search is expressed in explicitly religious terms by some parents and in more humanistic, philosophical terms by others.

Akin to the search for meaning is the search for an explanation of the etiology of the disease. For some parents, a conviction that their own failure caused their child's disease can bring a feeling of relief, because any explanation—even one involving self-blame—is preferable to the idea that all events are random, irrational, and meaningless, which is implied by accepting that there is no explanation for the loss of their child (Chodoff et al., 1964). In most cases, however, the search for a cause of the illness is motivated by parents' need to exonerate themselves and overcome guilt feelings (Futterman and Hoffman, 1973).

Hope has often been mentioned in the literature as playing a supportive role in parental coping, and parents themselves universally emphasize the importance of this element (Friedman et al., 1963; Chodoff et al., 1964; Futterman and Hoffman, 1973; Knapp and Hansen, 1973). The persistence of hope for a more favorable outcome does not require intellectual denial of the child's prognosis, and so it is different in an important way from defense patterns that potentially may greatly distort reality (Friedman et al., 1963). The nature of parents' hope often evolves and changes focus through the course of treatment. Their initial hope for the development of a curative drug gives way to hope for just one more remission. As death approaches, hope endures, but the focus is greatly narrowed. Parents hope for one more good day for the patient, and finally for a peaceful and painless death for their child (Friedman et al., 1963).

Marital Support and Stress   Parents frequently report that their spouse has been their primary source of support in coping with the child's illness (Bozeman et al., 1955; Hamovitch, 1964; Binger et al., 1969). On the other hand, marital difficulties and lack of support from the spouse have also been reported; and many authors have expressed concern about the great stress which the child's fatal illness brings to bear on the parents' marriage (Murstein, 1960; Hamovitch, 1964; Binger et al., 1969; Heffron et al., 1973; Kaplan et al., 1973).

The nature of anticipatory grief may aggravate marital stress. The two parents are likely to experience different stages of emotional response (shock, anger, depression) at different times and therefore they can become "out of sync" with one another (Sourkes, 1977). Or parents may choose different coping styles from the start, and their discrepant styles may make it difficult or impossible for them to give needed support to one another (Kaplan et al., 1973). If one partner wants to communicate openly about the child's illness, while the other tries to avoid such discussions, neither of them will receive a satisfying kind of support.

Traditional male and female roles sometimes contribute to feelings of estrangement between husbands and wives. Particularly in the earlier studies, which were conducted at a time when gender roles were quite inflexible, direct care of the child generally fell primarily to the mother, while economic necessity demanded that fathers continue to work. Several investigators (Bozeman et al., 1955; Binger et al., 1969; Stehbens and Lascari, 1974; Kartha and Ertel, 1976) note a tendency for fathers to withdraw into their jobs, using them as an escape from the painful reality of the child's illness.

Most investigators have found that in spite of the very real stress which the crisis of a child's fatal illness exerts on these couples, their marriages generally survive. In some cases, families can be brought closer together by facing the common problem (Stehbens and Lascari, 1974). Heightened marital stress but a low divorce rate has been reported among parents of children with cancer (Lansky et al., 1978). Some have emphasized that the experience of these parents, though extremely painful, is often growth-producing (Futterman and Hoffman, 1973). These writers suggest that just as successful resolution of developmental crises facilitates growth, so can successful resolution of situational crises, such as the loss of a child, have positive developmental consequences (Futterman and Hoffman, 1973).

The quality of the marriage before the diagnosis is an important factor in how well parents will adjust to the crisis together (Hamovitch, 1964). Families with preexisting marital problems are likely to have special difficulties, since a family structure which is already weak at the time of diagnosis may be severely taxed by the stress associated with the child's illness (Hamovitch, 1964). Similarly, single parents of children with cancer face a number of special problems (Kaplan et al., 1973).

The Child's Family: New Issues

The great majority of research investigating the psychosocial effects of childhood cancer on the patient's family has been based on the now out-of-date assumption that childhood cancer is an inevitably fatal disease. In one of the few recent reports, Johnson et al. (1979) discuss childhood malignancies as chronic, life-threatening illnesses and consider a number of issues which interested earlier researchers (e.g., Chodoff et al., 1964; Binger et al., 1969). Like the earlier investigators, Johnson et al. (1979) report that parents react with shock and grief to the initial disclosure of their child's cancer diagnosis; even though cancer treatment has become much more successful for both adult and child patients, most people continue to equate "cancer" with death. As a result, in spite of reassuring information about the probability of long-term survival and even the possibility of cure, the only information that parents may take with them from their initial conference with the diagnosing physician is the certainty that their child has cancer and is therefore going to die.

Thus, parents still need continued education about the illness on a level they can fully grasp, in order to form a realistic understanding of their child's condition and chances for survival (Clapp, 1976; Johnson et al., 1979). Although the medical facts about the prognosis for childhood cancer have changed over the last two decades, the initial emotional meaning of the diagnosis, for many parents, remains much the same. Unfortunately, many children with cancer still die of their disease, and observations on the effect of the impending loss of a child on parents are still relevant.

However, a number of investigators suggest that, after the initial shock, these families are now faced with a number of new, complex emotional and practical problems as a result of the long periods of treatment and the long-term uncertainty about the future which accompany improved prognoses for childhood cancer (Clapp, 1976; Johnson et al., 1979; Kagen-Goodheart, 1977; Lucas, 1977; Koch et al., 1974). Researchers and workers in pediatric oncology are just beginning to explore and discuss the nature of these new adaptational demands on the families of children with cancer.

Practical Demands

Much of the new treatment for childhood cancer is carried out on outpatients in centralized cancer treatment centers. A number of practical difficulties confront parents as they make the transition from their child's initial diagnostic inpatient admission to a lengthy program of rigorous outpatient treatment and as they adjust to caring for the child at home.

The Nature of Current Treatment   Coping with outpatient cancer treatment for a child involves a physical effort which can be exhausting for parents and strain the entire family. Frequently, the treatment center is far from the family's home, making overnight accommodations necessary. Transportation to and from the outpatient clinic and care of children left at home are constant concerns. The "incidental" expenses involved in such arrangements can constitute a serious financial burden for the family (Evans, 1975; Kagen-Goodheart, 1977; Johnson et al., 1979). This financial strain is not relieved by private health insurance, and although limited help from organizations such as the American Cancer Society and the Leukemia Society of America is sometimes available for certain of these expenses, most families find these costs a cause of significant stress (Johnson et al., 1979).

Other aspects of current childhood cancer treatment are potentially stressful for the family. The harsh nature of many cancer therapies necessitates the parents' informed consent to extremely complicated treatment plans. Sometimes they must also consent to their child's random assignment to one of several possible regimens. The implied element of chance in deciding the child's treatment can be most disturbing to parents. Consent forms which detail every possible side effect of each drug the child will receive are a necessary part of informed consent. These statements about side effects can be very frightening to parents, especially when they must make difficult decisions in the midst of the shock which accompanies hearing the cancer diagnosis for the first time (Johnson et al., 1979).

Another salient feature of current treatment for childhood cancer is the elective cessation of treatment following a prolonged period of effective disease control. "Coming off treatment" can be a very stressful time for the whole family (Kagen-Goodheart, 1977; Lucas, 1977; Johnson et al., 1979). Parents and patients usually put a great deal of trust in medical staff and form a healthy dependence on the treatment center both for medical care and for emotional support. Often, they find it difficult to believe that the child can do well without drugs. Even if the family is truly relieved that the ordeal of treatment is possibly over, they may continue to experience anxiety about the real possibility of recurrence for a long time.

Creating a Normal Home Life   The reentry of the newly diagnosed child into the home presents a number of challenges to parents. One area of difficulty is balancing the needs of the sick child with those of healthy siblings. Young children often assume that since their sister or brother is home from the hospital, life can go on as usual (Kagen-Goodheart, 1977). Unfortunately, this is not possible, and the sick child must continue to receive special care and attention from the parents. In addition, outpatient treatment frequently requires that parents leave their healthy children in the care of others. Parental focus on the patient can also cause jealousy and resentment in the child's brothers and sisters (Binger, 1973; Clapp, 1976; Kagen-Goodheart, 1977; Cairns et al., 1979; Johnson et al., 1979).

Mental health professionals' work with siblings to help them with their feelings about the illness has been reported and advocated (Feinberg, 1970; Sourkes, 1980). However, the burden for meeting the emotional needs of healthy siblings usually falls on the parents. Many writers have stressed the importance of open communication between parents and their children in preventing disturbed sibling reactions (Binger et al., 1969; Kaplan et al., 1976). Including sisters and brothers in trips to the clinic or on inpatient visits has also been suggested as a means of helping them understand what is happening to the patient. This can dispel fantasies and fears siblings may develop about the treatment center (Lindsay and MacCarthy, 1974).

Parents often find it difficult to exercise appropriate discipline or set reasonable limits on the sick child's behavior. A common mistake of parents is overindulgence of and overgenerosity toward the patient, which can lead to behavior problems in the sick child and aggravate sibling jealousy (Kagen-Goodheart, 1977; Cairns et al., 1979; Johnson et al., 1979). Overprotecting the sick child may foster regression and undermine the patient's efforts at control and mastery. Several writers (Kagen-Goodheart, 1977; Lucas, 1977; Van Eys, 1977; Johnson et al., 1979) stress the importance of maintaining realistic expectations in the family so that the sick child's social development can continue normally.

Providing as normal a life as possible for children with cancer has become a major focus of the psychosocial literature, as long-term survival has increased. Van Eys (1977) and his colleagues have explored the concept of normality, suggesting that a sense of what is normal for these children involves a realistic appraisal of both the negative effects of the disease and the child's continuing ability to grow, learn, and cope with difficulties. Some authors believe that a focus on living life and striving for growth can help assure the survivor's well-being if treatment is successful and can also give parents a sense that their child lived as fully as possible with their help if death should occur (Kagen-Goodheart, 1977; Lucas, 1977). Recent work on home care during the terminal phase of the illness and letting the child die at home (Martinson, 1976; Fortunato and Komp, 1979) also reflects the philosophy of savoring life as fully and as normally as possible up to its final moments.

Emotional Demands

Setting Priorities   Clearly, parents of children with cancer are burdened with an enormous task. Lucas (1977) writes: "The issue when a ten-year-old is diagnosed is just as much, if not more so, preparing him for adolescence as for a possible death" (p. 3). What parent can face the task of preparing even an absolutely healthy child for adolescence without considerable anxiety? How does one combine that task with the emotional shock of facing the possibility of the child's death, at the same time shouldering the physical and financial burdens of outpatient cancer treatment and attending to the heightened needs of a spouse and other children for emotional support and attention? One of the most difficult emotional tasks of parents is recognizing their own limitations, setting priorities, and conserving their energy for the long haul (Spinetta et al., 1976). One important fact for parents to remember is that a "normal" life for their child with cancer does not mean a perfect life or a completely smooth childhood.

Kagen-Goodheart (1977) has emphasized the stress which cancer treatment brings to bear on parents' marital relationships, noting that parents need help in sorting out what is ultimately most important to them and to their marriage. She suggests that parents should be encouraged to take some time alone with each other regularly, despite the other demands on their time and energy during their child's treatment. Similarly, Spinetta et al. (1976), in a pamphlet for parents about the emotional aspects of leukemia, suggest that when their child begins cancer treatment, parents should ask themselves a number of questions about their goals for themselves, their children, and their marriage.

Uncertainty Now that a fatal outcome for childhood cancer is so much less certain and there are realistic grounds to hope for long-term survival or cure, parental coping tasks have changed. It is no longer necessary for parents to resign themselves to the child's inevitable death and strive to prepare themselves emotionally. Instead they must try to prepare themselves and their child for continuing life, as well as for the possibility of death.

Research and clinical observations suggest that parents' failure to prepare emotionally for their child's survival as well as for death may have serious consequences for future parent-child relationships and for the child survivor's psychosocial adjustment. A variety of disturbed reactions have been observed among children who unexpectedly survived acute, life-threatening, nonmalignant illnesses (Green and Solnit, 1967; Benjamin, 1978). The effect of unresolved anticipatory grief on families of children who have survived cancer is discussed in Chapter 10.

Summary

As the treatment and prognosis for childhood cancer evolve, the emotional, social, and psychological issues confronting patients and their families are changing as well. This chapter has attempted to outline these changes and to summarize, in part historically, the major themes discussed in the psychosocial literature on childhood cancer.

Issues which concerned researchers and clinicians early on, when childhood cancer was almost certainly fatal, include the child's concept of death and fear of it, controversy over what the child should be told about the illness, the nature of the dying child's inner experiences—particularly feelings of isolation and anxiety—and the child's ability to cope with the threat of death.

Similarly, the early literature on the family of the child focused on death, emphasizing parental coping with the child's impending death. Various researchers have been interested in a number of common areas, including parental anticipatory grief, sources of emotional support for parents, marital support and stress, and the role of open family communication in coping.

With recent successes in treatment, childhood cancer is now viewed as a chronic life-threatening illness, and accepting impending death can no longer be considered the family's primary initial coping task. Rather, patient and family must live with a great deal of uncertainty. As a result, more recent literature on the child with cancer has focused on problems of living with cancer rather than on problems of dying. These problems include treatment-induced changes in the child's appearance; adjustment at home and in school after diagnosis; the special social pressures on adolescent patients; and coping with uncertainty.

Literature on the family has emphasized the practical and emotional burdens imposed on parents by their child's cancer treatment. These burdens include the physical effort necessary for frequent outpatient cancer therapy; balancing the needs of the patient in the home with those of healthy siblings; fostering the patient's normal social and emotional development while coping with long-term uncertainty; and dealing with unresolved anticipatory grief if the child survives.

Concern about coping with uncertainty during the treatment period leads naturally to a relatively new set of questions about how patient and family cope with the child's long-term survival and apparent medical cure. Cancer survivors often have some kind of physical impairment as a result of their treatment. That children who survive cancer and members of their families are at risk for psychological/emotional problems and social handicaps is suggested by a variety of research evidence, including studies of families of children who have died of cancer that reveal frequent adjustment problems; observations of maladjustment among children who have survived acute life-threatening illnesses; and studies suggesting increased adjustment problems among children with a variety of chronic disabilities.

Two recent surveys have investigated the quality of life of cancer survivors by asking about their employment and their marital and health status, with encouraging results. However, other research on a small group of cancer survivors revealed evidence of mild to moderate psychosocial difficulties in half of the sample.

The majority of the survivors studied in the research project reported in the rest of this volume were treated for cancer during the time when cancer was viewed as a fatal illness. Some were the subjects of pioneering efforts at cancer treatment. As a result, they were treated in a climate in which, though cure was often hoped for, death was expected. Their families' recollections and the problems they are now experiencing may prove very helpful in understanding the issues confronting patients and families in treatment today, when expectations of long-term survival are much greater.

Chapter 2

Survival Rates and Risks

Cancer in childhood, a relatively rare event, nevertheless ranks second only to accidents as a cause of death in children between the ages of 5 and 14. The mortality rate from malignant neoplasms in this age group is 5 per 100,000, accounting for 14.3 percent of deaths among children in this range (U.S. Department of Health, Education, and Welfare, 1978). As Table 2-1 illustrates, cancer is a leading cause of death through young adulthood. The incidence of all childhood malignancies is less than 5 per 100,000 children in the population per year.

Given the low number of new cases and the comparatively high number of deaths in this small group, a large pool of childhood cancer survivors would seem quite difficult to find—although a prerequisite to the study of any human phenomenon is the ability to define and locate an appropriate group of people to study. We were able to identify a substantial group of former patients for study by using a computerized registry of childhood cancer survivors at Boston's Sidney Farber Cancer Institute (formerly the Children's Cancer Research Foundation). The registry lists all patients who were diagnosed before age 18, were treated at the Institute from January, 1948, and survived at least sixty months following diagnosis. Most lived in New England at the time of diagnosis and treatment. The registry is an unusual research tool, making it possible to categorize, identify, and locate a unique group of people: those for whom the war on cancer has been most successful.

Files on each patient include name, dates of birth and diagnosis, tumor site and histology, treatment administered, and physical, laboratory, or other findings noted at follow-up. Participation in Institute-sponsored research projects is also recorded. A series of medical studies has been conducted and is continuing with

By Gerald P. Koocher.

certain subpopulations of the survivor group (Li et al., 1975; Li and Stone, 1976; Li, 1977a, 1977b; Li et al., 1978). None of these studies, however, have given serious attention to the psychosocial difficulties related to long-term survival of childhood cancer.

Table 2-1   Rates of Leading Causes of Death in Childhood and Young Adulthood

Age Group	Cause of Death by Rank	N	Deaths per 100,000
Birth to 4 years	1. Accidents	3,439	27.9
	2. Congenital abnormalities	1,114	9.0
	3. Malignant neoplasms	656	5.3
	All causes	8,606	78.2
5–14 years	1. Accidents	6,308	17.0
	2. Malignant neoplasms	1,849	5.0
	3. Congenital abnormalities	745	2.0
	All causes	12,901	34.7
15–24 years	1. Accidents	24,316	59.9
	2. Homicide	5,038	12.4
	3. Suicide	4,747	11.7
	4. Malignant neoplasms	2,659	6.5
	All causes	46,081	113.5

Adapted from: *Facts of Life and Death,* U.S. Department of Health, Education, and Welfare Publication No. (PHS) 79-1222, 1978.

Tracking the Patients

To facilitate the locating of patients for study and to assure maintenance of an accurate and representative sample, the registry must be kept up to date. The most critical task is keeping patients' addresses current many years after treatment. Because of the high mobility of Americans and the especially high mobility of late adolescents and young adults, this is no mean feat.

The fact that our survivors were treated for a serious prolonged illness with specialized care does make tracking them a bit easier. Many former patients continue to return for annual physical examinations, despite continuous periods of good health. Nonetheless, some former patients are lost to routine follow-up, and special techniques may be needed to locate them. Practical methodological assistance has been provided by Boice (1978). In a report on women who were treated for tuberculosis in Massachusetts between 1930 and 1954, he describes systematic techniques for locating study subjects many years after treatment.

Who Are the Survivors?

The persons listed in the survivor registry range in age from 5 years (i.e., diagnosed at birth and in remission ever since) to 47. The median age is 23 years. They represent a reasonable cross section of socioeconomic levels, although only 2 to 3 percent are nonwhites. The major reason for this racial imbalance is the referral pattern from local physicians to different hospitals. There are no major differences between whites and nonwhites in overall incidence of childhood malignancies. While access to medical care and early diagnosis are important in cancer survival, data on whether children of different races or socioeconomic groups have differential survival rates are not available. The sex ratio of patients in the registry is 56 percent male to 44 percent female, or 1.3:1. This is not unexpected considering the slight male predominance for many cancers to begin with (for example, in acute lymphoblastic leukemia the male-female ratio is 1.4:1).

The diagnoses of persons listed in the registry also conform to estimated survival statistics for childhood cancer patients at large, except that survivors of childhood brain tumors are underrepresented. Brain tumor patients were traditionally treated on the neurosurgical service of the Children's Hospital Medical Center and were not logged into the Cancer Institute's patient registry. The number of persons listed as five-year survivors (Jan. 1948–Dec. 1976) is presented in Table 2-2 by diagnostic category. Seventy-nine percent of the patients who survived at least five years after diagnosis were known to be alive and locatable in 1976.

Table 2-2   Sidney Farber Cancer Institute Registry of Five-Year Survivors (Jan. 1948–Dec. 1976)

Type of Malignancy	N	Known Dead	Known Alive	Lost to Follow-up
Leukemias	52	22	27	3
Non-Hodgkin's lymphomas	62	2	54	6
Hodgkin's	83	16	64	3
Nerve sheath	14	0	·11	3
Retinoblastoma	8	1	6	1
Neuroblastoma	75	5	66	4
Brain / spinal cord	10	6	3	1
Ewing's	30	6	23	1
Osteosarcoma	19	4	15	0
Blood vessel	10	2	6	2
Teratoma / germ cell	17	0	15	2
Soft tissue sarcoma	53	3	47	3
Wilms's tumor	138	15	112	11
Melanoma	6	0	5	1
Other	24	0	21	3
Total	601	82	475	44

Many patients become "five-year survivors" every year. At the Sidney Farber Cancer Institute this number has recently averaged between sixty and eighty patients per year; in 1977 it was seventy-two. Table 2-3 shows the diagnostic classification of these seventy-two survivors. Although survival figures were not as good in the past, they are expected to show continued improvement in the next several years because of recent therapeutic gains.

What Does Five-Year Survival Mean?

Five-year survival has been taken as a general benchmark in assessing long-term cancer prognosis and the probability of recurrence. Unfortunately this judgment fails to consider the fact that cancer is in fact several different disease entities, each with its own natural history and course. The most realistic prognoses are those based on relapse rates of patients on and off all treatment for the particular illness. Life table probabilities of survival or disease-free survival are studied by plotting actual survival statistics for a group of patients over a period of months or years, as illustrated in Figure 2-1. Figure 2-1 displays the observed survival statistics for 50 patients with non-Hodgkin's lymphoma over a sixty-month span (Weinstein and Link, 1979). For this group of patients twenty-four months of survival is an important benchmark. For other lymphomas one year after diagnosis could be the critical interval. For acute lymphoblastic leukemia in children two years off treatment and an additional four disease-free years following the elective cessation of chemotherapy are required before one can talk about "cure"

Table 2-3 Sidney Farber Cancer Institute
Registry of New Five-Year Survivors in 1977

Type of Malignancy	N
Leukemias	23
Non-Hodgkin's lymphomas	8
Hodgkin's	9
Nerve sheath	0
Retinoblastoma	3
Neuroblastoma	4
Brain / spinal cord	0
Ewing's	1
Osteosarcoma	2
Blood vessel	0
Teratoma / germ cell	2
Soft tissue sarcoma	7
Wilms's tumor	10
Melanoma	0
Other	3
Total	72

with any confidence. New therapies are also frequently changing the probability level at which the survival curve levels off.

Studies which followed five-year survivors over a twenty-year period (five to twenty-four years after initial diagnosis) suggest 79–83 percent projected survival rates (Li et al., 1978). These figures are considerably lower than the 97 percent survival rate among persons of comparable ages in the general population over a comparable span of two decades. Those who die five to nine years after diagnosis generally succumb to a recurrence of the initial cancer, while those who die in the subsequent decade are most likely to experience a second primary neoplasm, fail-

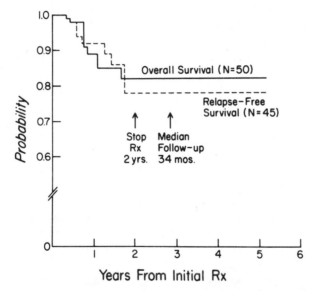

Figure 2-1. Survival Plot for Fifty Children with Non-Hodgkin's Lymphomas *(Reproduced by permission from Weinstein and Link, 1979)*

ure of a vital organ, or infection (Li et al., 1978). Most of the participants in our study were treated before the advent of multimodal intensive therapy (i.e., multiple-agent or high-dose chemotherapy alone or in combination with radiation therapy). Although these treatments substantially improve short-term survival, they have the potential to increase morbidity and mortality after five years.

Risk of Second Tumors

As the above data suggest, long-term remission or control of a single malignancy does not end the risk of mortality for the child with cancer. For a substantial number of these patients, second tumors may present a whole new set of treatment problems. While the "cause" of cancer is unknown, there are a number of significant etiological factors which are known to be related to it, including environmental toxins, viral infections, exposure to radiation, and individual genetic or "host" factors. A person who has developed one form of cancer has clearly been subjected to some etiological factors predisposing him or her to the disease. It follows logically, therefore, that these same factors may create an environment of some continuing potential risk greater than that experienced by a person who has never had cancer. In addition, many cancer patients are treated with ionizing radiation and chemotherapy, which may have their own carcinogenic effects years later. The cumulative risk of these long-term hazards may be greater for children than for adults simply because children have a longer potential life span during which a second tumor might develop.

Retrospective studies of the development of second tumors among childhood cancer survivors suggest that they have a cumulative probability of 12 percent of developing a new cancer during the period from five to twenty-four years after the diagnosis of the first cancer (Li et al., 1975; Li, 1977b). This frequency is approximately twenty times greater than the expected rate for the general population. The risk of a second malignancy varied with the time elapsed since the initial diagnosis. In the first four years after diagnosis the risk has been estimated as 1 new cancer per 1,000 person-years. The rates per 1,000 person-years for subsequent five-year intervals were 2.3, 3.6, 14.0, and 5.1 respectively. It seems that the risk increases over time and peaks at fifteen to nineteen years after initial diagnosis, declining thereafter (Li, 1977b).

Prior research has suggested that radiation per se may induce from one to five cancers per million person-years per rad delivered (Hutchison, 1972). For readers unfamiliar with the term rad, or radiation absorbed dose, it is a measure which takes into account biological and time factors as well as the amount of radiation emitted by a particular machine. It is more an estimate of what is absorbed by a cell than of what leaves the x-ray machine. The second tumors in our participants fall within this predicted range, the incidence being 1.8 neoplasms per million person-years per rad. The occurrence of nearly all lesions within previously irradiated sites on the body strongly implicates ionizing radiation as a substantial etiological factor. Approximately 41 percent of the second tumors discovered in our sample are benign.

Host or genetic susceptibility may have an etiological role, but it is not always possible to evaluate this as thoroughly as one would like. In addition, the oncogenic influences of chemotherapy may also be obscured by the more intense effects of irradiation. More detailed observations over longer periods of time are needed to document the precise risks of these factors in humans. In general, it is clear that the immediate gains from cancer treatments (i.e., radiation and chemotherapy) outweigh the later risks. On the other hand, the long-term risks must be carefully considered as complicating factors when new treatment plans and long-term medical follow-up are developed.

Progeny of Childhood Cancer Survivors

Genetic studies of childhood cancer patients have raised the possibility that some forms of childhood malignancy may be heritable (Knudson, 1971; Knudson et al., 1973). In addition, ionizing radiation and chemotherapy in the relatively intense ranges used to treat cancer may result in sterility, delayed puberty, or other potentially mutagenic effects (see Chapter 4). Until recently, relatively little was known about the long-term fertility and reproductive history of childhood cancer survivors. The existence of our survivor registry has made such investigations possible.

In a sample of long-term childhood cancer survivors drawn from the Sidney Farber Cancer Institute and the Kansas University Medical Center (Li et al., 1979), some interesting and optimistic findings have emerged. In a survey of 146 former patients (84 women and 62 men) covering 286 completed pregnancies, the following data were obtained: 242 live births (including one set of twins), 1 stillbirth, 25 spontaneous abortions, and 19 therapeutic abortions. Seven of the liveborn infants died within the first two years of life, but this frequency is not out of line with expected mortality for children in that age group as a whole. Compared with their cousins and with published figures for the general population, the progeny revealed no excess of cancer, congenital abnormalities, or other diseases.

Two of the offspring did develop cancer. One was a child with retinoblastoma, born to a father who had been successfully treated for bilateral hereditary retinoblastoma. The other child developed acute myelocytic leukemia, following her mother's treatment with radiation for a brain tumor in childhood. This frequency is not significant, but since childhood cancer is so rare to begin with, much more data must be gathered before any conclusive statements can be made. It is probable that most of the childhood cancer survivors in our sample had malignancies without strong hereditary components (Li and Jaffe, 1974; Li et al., 1979). Chromosome and immunological studies of a few offspring did not reveal signs of preconception damage from exposure to radiation or cancer chemotherapy. The outlook for good health among the progeny of childhood cancer survivors whose childbearing potential has not been compromised through sterility seems good.

Summary

1. Improved treatments for childhood malignancies have substantially increased the likelihood of long-term survival. But because these improvements are so recent, information is still scant on many aspects of the survivors' lives and health.

2. Estimates on survival vary by type of malignancy and treatment, but even

after long remission many childhood cancer survivors remain at substantial risk for second tumors.

3. Potential organ failures and infections are also greater hazards for the childhood cancer survivor than for his or her age-mate with no history of cancer.

4. Many of the former patients studied have married and become parents. Happily, there has been no excess of cancer or congenital abnormalities among the progeny.

5. Although the long-term survivor of childhood cancer can look forward to a more stable and healthy future than ever before, some greater-than-average-risks and uncertainties still remain.

Chapter 3

Study Methods

The study described in this book was initiated by Drs. Norman Jaffe and John O'Malley in 1975. The computerized long-term survivor registry described in Chapter 2 is a unique source of information for exploring the quality of life following treatment of childhood malignancies. A grant from the National Cancer Institute (CA18429 CCG), initiated by Drs. Jaffe and O'Malley, led to the formation of the psychosocial research team which undertook this study in October 1975. This chapter summarizes the basic research strategies and methods applied from the inception of the project until its completion in February 1980.

Project Goals

The project was designed to study the psychological and social consequences of childhood cancer with attention to both the former patients and their families. The computerized registry was updated and refined to facilitate the selection of a variety of former patients as possible research participants. An interdisciplinary team encompassing oncology, psychology, psychiatry, and social work was assembled to study the response of the whole family to the childhood cancer experience. The team was also prepared to formulate and carry out psychotherapeutic intervention to correct or ameliorate emotional problems identified among study participants.

Specific goals of the study included the following:

1. To assess the nature and incidence of psychosocial consequences among childhood cancer survivors and their families.

2. To determine the nature of the psychological stresses attending treatment for childhood malignancies and the late effects of these stresses.

By Gerald P. Koocher and John E. O'Malley.

3. To explore the relationships between specific variables and successful long-term adaptation to the childhood cancer experience.

4. To formulate recommendations for the care of future child cancer patients with the goal of reducing long-term psychological problems.

Participants

All participants in the study were selected on the basis of four criteria:

1. They had been treated for a childhood malignancy which began before age 18 and were currently aware of their diagnosis.

2. Diagnosis and initiation of treatment had begun at least sixty months earlier.

3. All treatments for cancer had been over for at least twelve months.

4. All were free of disease at the time of participation in the study.

Ultimately, 121 former patients were interviewed, along with many other family members. The data obtained from 4 former patients were ultimately excluded from statistical analysis, reducing the main data base to 117. One of these persons was discovered to have active disease just before participating in the study. Another had never been informed by her parents that she had been treated for cancer because of their desire to protect her. That situation is unfortunately not as rare as one might think; we did not learn of it until the family arrived for interviews. Two additional former patients had sustained substantial handicaps (i.e., paraplegia and anoxic brain damage) as a result of surgical complications unrelated to cancer. Both had substantial psychosocial problems, but not simply because they were cancer survivors.

Descriptive data on the population studied are summarized in Table 3-1. The mean socioeconomic level of the sample was "middle class," with a fairly typical

Table 3-1 Descriptive Data on Study Sample: 117 Survivors

Variable	Mean Years	S.D.	Range
Age at diagnosis	5.65	5.20	0–18 years
Years since diagnosis	12.49	5.28	5.33–32.67 years
Years since end of treatment	12.22		
Age when seen	18.09	6.66	5.6–37 years
Years of education	10.58	4.02	1st grade–master's degree (18 years)

distribution pattern (Hollingshead, 1957). The sex distribution was 47 percent female and 53 percent male, which is quite reasonable considering the slight male preponderance in incidence of most childhood malignancies.

There was much variability in the course of treatment and recovery for our participants. Some had been treated only with surgery and a few days or weeks of hospitalization. Others had had combinations of surgery, chemotherapy, and radiation for five years and more. Some were diagnosed and treated as early as 1947; others did not develop cancer until as late as 1970. Twenty-two of the participants had one or more relapses (recurrence of original disease) or second tumors (a second form of malignancy) before their follow-up interview, although for all, at least five years had elapsed since their most recent episode at the time they were seen. Most of the survivors in our sample, and most long-term survivors of childhood cancer in general, have experienced a prolonged continuous remission after the initiation of treatment. Some of the implications of these differences in disease/treatment histories are discussed in Chapter 8.

Selection

The selection of participants was coordinated by the supervisor of the registry and guided by the criteria specified above. To ensure a wide age range, participants were initially selected from only three diagnostic categories: neuroblastoma (peak incidence in infancy and early childhood), leukemia (peak incidence in middle childhood), and bone tumors (peak onset in adolescence). Later in the study the registrar was instructed to select such additional former patients as would ultimately bring our study sample into line with the overall representation of each sort of cancer in the survivor population at large; only for brain tumor survivors were we unsuccessful (see Chapter 2).

The registrar provided a list of potential participants to a senior physician at the Cancer Institute who was known to the family in question. The physician telephoned the family to inform them about the study and to request permission to mail them additional information and consent forms. After the mailing, a secretary telephoned the family to ask whether they would be willing to schedule an appointment for participating in the study. The refusal rate was less than 4 percent. Most of the families expressed both great gratitude for the medical care they had received and a high degree of altruism and willingness to participate for the benefit of future patients.

Refusals seemed to be related to individual issues rather than generalizable ones. For example, one former patient, now 19 years old, told the physician who telephoned him, "I've been well ever since I left that place and I'm not coming back." The mother of a 6-year-old former patient declined to participate with her child because she "knew" it would "upset him" to recall his hospitalization five years earlier.

Measures

Overall Adjustment

A *Combined Adjustment Rating* was obtained for each participant using the system devised by Srole (Srole et al., 1962) and clarified by Michael and Kirkpatrick (1962). Independent ordinal ratings from 0 (no significant symptoms) to 6 (seriously incapacitated, unable to function) were assigned by a psychiatrist and a clinical psychologist after individual interviews. These independent ratings were then summed to obtain a combined ordinal rating. This combined score is referred to as the Combined Adjustment Rating; the scale below shows the descriptions suggested by Michael and Kirkpatrick for these combined ratings:

    0– 1 = "well" patient
    2– 3 = mild symptoms
    4– 5 = moderate symptoms
    6– 7 = marked symptoms
    8– 9 = severe symptoms
    10–12 = incapacitating symptoms

Interrater reliability was high, the two independent ratings yielding a Pearson correlation coefficient for all interviewees of .85 ($p = .001$). Because several of the categories contained only small numbers of participants, categories were combined for purposes of data analysis in order to compare well-adjusted participants with those having adjustment problems. All participants with combined ratings of 0 or 1 were considered "well," as suggested by Michael and Kirkpatrick (p. 399). Thus, any participant given a mild pathology rating by only one of the two interviewers was rated "well." Participants with a Combined Adjustment Rating of 2 or higher were combined into an "adjustment problems" group. Thus in our data any significant differences between these two groups are based on a measure arrived at by substantial interrater agreement.

Psychiatric Assessment

The psychiatric assessment of each participant consisted of three basic elements: a standardized psychiatric interview, a mental status examination, and an open-ended content interview.

The Standardized Psychiatric Interview was a modification of the interview schedule devised by Rutter and Graham (1968), originally standardized for children aged 7 to 12 but used for all participants in this study, with minor adaptations for adults. The interview schedule is reproduced in Appendix A.

A Mental Status Examination was also conducted with each participant and consisted of evaluation of the following areas: appearance, including any motor handicap; mood and affect, including a clinical judgment on fluctuation and range of affect; presence of anxiety; depression; euphoria; appropriateness of affect; and flatness of affect. Coping mechanisms were also explored, including intellectualization, rationalization, avoidance, reaction formation, denial, repression, regression, and rejection. The interviewer recorded the presence or absence of these processes or inability to make a judgment. Thought process was noted as either intact or demonstrating thought disorder. Clinical judgments were made on self-concept, object relations, and identification. These judgments involved considering the view each person had of his or her self as a person independent of and apart from all other people, including body image or body identity—a conceptualization of the body structure and function that grows out of the awareness of the self and one's body. Identification is the process by which a person incorporates within the self a mental picture of another person and then thinks, feels, and acts as he or she conceives that other person to think, feel, and act. Each participant's concept of self was then rated as not abnormal, slightly abnormal, or markedly abnormal. A notation was made of each participant's awareness of difficulties, ranging from "no" to "much" awareness.

The Content Interview was a semistructured, open-ended discussion of specific material related to cancer in general and the participant's recollections in particular. Responses were recorded verbatim for subsequent analysis. The specific content areas addressed are presented in Appendix B. The interview generally lasted from 45 to 60 minutes.

Psychological Assessment

The psychological interview included objective measures of intellectual functioning, social maturity, depression, anxiety, death-related anxiety, and self-esteem. A set of projective test cards was also presented, and the session ended with an unstructured discussion of issues raised earlier by the participant.

Intellectual Functioning is an important variable both because of the role it plays in psychosocial adjustment and because some of the study instruments assume a basic level of verbal ability. Estimates of verbal intellectual abilities were obtained by administering the three subtests of the Wechsler scales most closely correlated with overall verbal IQ (i.e., Information, Similarities, and Vocabulary). Subtest scores were prorated to obtain an estimated verbal IQ. The Wechsler Adult Intelligence Scale was used with participants aged 16 years and up, and the Wechsler Intelligence Scale for Children—Revised was used with those under age 16.

Social Maturity was assessed using the Vineland Social Maturity Scale (Doll, 1965), a measure of socialization and self-help skills, to obtain a Social Quotient.

Older participants were not scored on this instrument because the Social Quotient curve becomes asymptotic and hence relatively meaningless for adults in their mid-twenties or older. All of the participants not rated with this instrument were 25 or older.

Depression, Anxiety, and Death Anxiety were measured with paper and pencil self-report checklists. The Depression Scale was a modification of the Zung (1965) Self-Rating Depression Scale prepared by Conte and her colleagues (Conte et al., 1975). A short form of the Taylor Manifest Anxiety Scale (Bendig, 1956) measured anxiety. Death anxiety was explored using the Death Anxiety Questionnaire devised by Conte et al. (1975). All three research instruments have been previously tested with children as young as age 9 (Koocher et al., 1976) and with college students and adults (Conte et al., 1975).

Self-Esteem was assessed using the Index of Adjustment and Values (IAV), which measures self-rating, satisfaction with self, and self-ideal discrepancy. This study used a modified version of the original IAV developed by Bills (Bills et al., 1951; Bills, 1961). It consists of thirty adjectives connoting positive social value arranged in a three-column checklist. In the first column the participants check whether each adjective is self-descriptive "Most of the time," "About half the time," or "Hardly ever." In the second column testees check "Like being as I am," "Neither like or dislike it," or "Dislike being as I am," with regard to their self-ratings, yielding a satisfaction-with-self score. In the third column testees respond for each adjective to the statement "I wish I were like this," checking off "Most of the time," "About half of the time," or "Hardly ever." By assigning weights of 3, 2, or 1 to each check mark, scores for each column ranging from a low of 30 to a high of 90 were obtained. The higher the score, the more positive the self-rating. A self-minus-ideal discrepancy score is obtained by subtracting the self-rating (column one) from the ideal-self rating (column three).

Wylie (1961, 1974) rates this instrument favorably in her critical review of the self-concept literature. The instrument's reliability, validity, and utility have been established with a variety of populations, including children as young as age 6 (Koocher, 1971, 1974; Wylie, 1974).

The Projective Test consisted of five cards selected from the Thematic Apperception Test (TAT) (Murray, 1943) and four drawings of hospital scenes developed by Eugenia Waechter (1971). The TAT cards (1, 3GF, 8BM, 13B, and 14) were selected on the basis of prior use (Waechter, 1968) and their ability to elicit themes related to sadness, loneliness, personal motivation, and individual reflection. The Waechter pictures are reproduced in Appendix C.

The instructions given to each participant were to "tell a story" about each of the nine stimulus cards, including:

"What is happening in this picture?"
"What might have happened just before?"
"What are the people in the picture thinking, feeling, or wanting?"
"How will the story end?"

Vague probes such as "Could you tell me a bit more about that?" were used to facilitate the embellishment of thin stories. All of the projective interviews were tape-recorded for later analysis. The full psychological interview generally lasted from 60 to 90 minutes, depending on the age and verbal spontaneity of the person being interviewed.

Family Interviews

Interviews with family members, including the survivors' parents, siblings, and spouses, were conducted by a social worker and a research assistant. A study of existing family assessment techniques and instruments failed to produce a means of addressing the issues we were most concerned about, so we developed a series of four structured interview schedules designed especially for this study. These interviews were designed to gather a history of the family and of medical status in the interval since active treatment, as well as parents', siblings', and spouses' memories, feelings, and views of events.

The Family and Medical-Interval History was mailed out to each family before its arrival for participation in the study. Parents or participants completed the questionnaire at home and reviewed the contents with a social worker at the time of the interview. The questions were designed to reflect key changes in demography, medical status, and family structure in the interval between the active treatment for cancer and the follow-up interview (the average interval was 12–13 years). Other items covered in this portion of the interview included medication use in the previous two years, contacts with social and rehabilitation agencies, current health care practices, educational progress, and employment data.

The Parent Interview addressed the socioeconomic, educational, and social activities of the parents both at the present time and during the period their child was being treated for cancer. Special attention was paid to areas of emotional stress and support throughout the course of the illness. Other questions explored ways in which the parents' current behavior is a result of the family's cancer experience. Parents were asked to describe their own feelings about and behavior toward the survivor and any other children in the family before, during, and after the period of active treatment. The social worker also inquired about current and future concerns among parents with respect to their child and the cancer experience.

The interview with the social worker, including the completion of consent forms and the two interview schedules noted above, generally lasted from two to two and a half hours. When both parents were able to participate the interview was a joint one, and took place while the participant and other family members were being seen separately.

The Sibling and Spouse Interviews were conducted by a research assistant and usually took 30 to 60 minutes. For siblings, the interview focused on memories of the treatment period, the extent of their knowledge about their sib's illness, their perceptions of changes in their sib's personality as a result of having had cancer, and their own emotional reaction to past and present stresses on the family. The spouses who were available for interview were asked about their knowledge of the participant's medical history, how they learned of it, and what effect it had on their relationship. In particular, we were interested in how the participant's cancer history influenced the decision to date and eventually marry. Communication between husband and wife, especially on illness and handicap-related issues, was a special focus.

Procedures

Participants generally spent a full day at the Cancer Institute, half the day being devoted to a complete medical checkup and half to the psychosocial study. Some participants who had recently completed a medical examination were seen only for psychosocial evaluation.

The participant and the family were greeted by our social worker, who answered any lingering questions about participation in the study, reviewed the nature of the research project, and obtained their informed consent to participate. She then interviewed the participant privately for a few minutes to discuss the confidentiality of the study interviews and complete the drug-use schedule. Then the social worker began the parent interview, the siblings and spouse met with the research assistant, and the participant met with either the psychiatrist or the psychologist. About half of the participants were seen first by each. The individual components of the Combined Adjustment Rating were assigned independently by the psychologist and psychiatrist on the basis of their interviews with the patient. No objective psychological test scores were available to influence the assignment of ratings.

When psychological problems sufficient to warrant counseling were uncovered in the interviews, the findings were discussed with the appropriate family members and followed up with brief counseling by the project staff, referral to community agencies, or both.

Travel expenses and subsidies for pay lost because of study participation were provided as needed. The availability of such funds helped to ensure that geographic dispersion and economic factors did not affect the ability of families to participate in the study. Some participants came from as far away as Florida and Ohio to be interviewed.

Data Analyses

As noted earlier in this chapter, the main data base for the study reported in this book consists of 117 childhood cancer survivors. Variations in total number for a particular measure are noted on the table for that measure; for example, one participant who was totally blind as a result of treatment for her optic nerve tumor was obviously unable to respond to the projective test cards, and her scores on some instruments (e.g., Vineland Social Quotient) were not comparable to norms for the sighted. Another participant was found to have suffered severe anoxia and resulting brain damage as a result of postsurgical difficulties in the recovery room of a rural hospital; his speech was too limited for full participation in the study. However, his parents and siblings were able to provide considerable information. Such exceptional cases account for the fluctuating numbers of participants reported in the data analyses which follow.

Control Group: Theoretical and Administrative Problems

In most scientific research a control group is of critical importance in exploring the impact of a treatment or effect. Typically a control group is composed of persons who are similar to the group under study but who differ with respect to the main independent variable—that factor which is hypothesized to influence later behavior. In this study the independent variable is the fact of having been successfully treated for childhood cancer. Most illness-related research compares a group of persons who have had the specific illness with a group who have not had it or who have had a different illness. This comparison makes it possible to explore differences related to the independent variable under study.

Early in our formulation of this project it became clear that the uncertainty of outcome and chronic life-threatening nature of childhood cancer constitute a critical psychological barrier to adaptation for the patients and their families. The problem was to devise a means of studying the effect of this variable—uncertainty of survival—with reference to a control group.

The problems of choosing a control group are related to the unique nature of surviving childhood cancer. Cancer is actually a number of different diseases varying in symptoms, prognosis, and response to treatment. Given the ongoing difficulties of cancer survivors, it seemed inappropriate to attempt to compare them with a group of healthy persons. Nor would it have been appropriate to compare long-term survivors of childhood cancer with patients currently in active treatment for cancer and hence at greater immediate survival risk. What is the ideal control group for patients successfully treated, at least so far, for a chronic life-threatening illness which began five or more years ago?

We do not know the range or normative values of Combined Adjustment Rating scores for the population of "normal" people corresponding in age range, sex, socioeconomic status, and other ways to our cancer survivor population. The population studied by Srole et al. (1962) using Michael and Kirkpatrick's instrument is not at all comparable. A research effort far beyond the scope of our project would have been needed to accumulate these data. In addition, it is not clear that a group of "normal volunteers" actually representing the adjustment of the community at large could be located without incorporating additional sources of potential bias. As a result, the one question we cannot answer is: How does the survivor of childhood cancer compare with a matched person-on-the-street who is not a survivor of childhood cancer? We decided instead to address parallel questions of adjustment within the cancer survivor group and among survivors of other chronic illnesses.

We decided to seek out a group of persons who had been treated successfully for chronic childhood illnesses five or more years ago. In addition, we hoped to use illnesses with a defined endpoint following which the patient could assume that he or she was permanently cured. This would contrast with the long-term uncertainty of recurrence faced by childhood cancer survivors. We also hoped to find illnesses for which the patient's experience of treatment approximates the experiences of some cancer patients.

Many of the cancer survivors in our sample who had been treated for neuroblastoma, for example, were diagnosed at birth or during the first year of life, were treated in a single hospital surgery stay, and had been well from that point on. Of course, their parents had to deal with feelings about the illness or defect in their infant and live with the fear of recurrence. We planned to compare such survivors to youngsters treated early in life for congenital birthmarks or webbed fingers. These children were also born with noteworthy physical abnormalities, experienced early hospitalization and surgery, and had been well ever since. At the same time, their congenital problems were not life-threatening and not likely to recur.

Bone cancer survivors are generally in late childhood or early adolescence at the time of diagnosis, and the disease is often first manifested in a bruise or athletic injury. Amputation, prolonged chemotherapy, or radiation treatments are often needed. We reasoned that youngsters who experienced amputations as a result of infection (e.g., gangrene) might be suitable controls for these cancer patients. While the gangrene victims did not undergo prolonged chemotherapy or radiation treatments, they did go through a painful, disfiguring illness. Unlike the cancer patients, the gangrene amputees would not need to fear death or recurrence after treatment.

Youngsters who develop nephrotic syndrome were considered potential controls for leukemia survivors. Nephrotic syndrome is not necessarily life-threatening, but it does involve changes in body image as a result of extensive tissue swelling. The syndrome is treated with some of the same metabolism-altering drugs used on cancer patients (i.e., prednisone and chlorambucil), and the physical status of patients must also be monitored frequently. Both leukemics and nephrotic syndrome patients enjoy prolonged remissions. Unlike the leukemias, however, nephrotic syndrome does not pose a danger to life either in the long run or in the possibility of relapse.

The illnesses ultimately represented among the control participants included nevi (birthmarks), syndactyly (webbed fingers), gangrene, nephrotic syndrome, chronic urinary tract infections, thyroid toxicosis, Guillain-Barré syndrome, and congenital cardiac defects. Each of these illnesses has a chronic phase, a specific treatment phase, and a distinct endpoint at which the patient is pronounced cured and free of residual danger of relapse and death.

To locate potential control group participants, we sought people who had been successfully treated for the condition in question five or more years earlier to match the time since treatment of our study group. An initial search through the medical records and surgical logs of Boston's Children's Hospital yielded the names of approximately 250 potential participants. Letters inviting participation and offering to provide additional information about the study were sent to each family's last known address. Nearly 200 were returned marked "Moved: no forwarding address." This was not totally unexpected, since many of the addresses were five or more years old.

To those letters presumed delivered the response rate (the return of an enclosed postcard) was approximately 8 percent. The Human Subject Protection Committee of the hospital did not authorize us to contact nonresponders. Notices seeking appropriate volunteer participants were subsequently placed in the employee newsletters of the Sidney Farber Cancer Institute and the Children's Hospital Medical Center. These notices yielded a few additional candidates, and were followed by renewed postal solicitations over a two-year period. Ultimately, a group of 22 appropriate control group participants were located and interviewed in the same way as the cancer survivors. The data provided by each of these control subjects were compared with the data of a matched cancer survivor for purposes of analysis. When possible, participants were matched for diagnosis (i.e., nephrotic syndrome with leukemia, gangrene with osteogenic sarcoma, congenital nevus with neuroblastoma, etc.). All were successfully matched for sex, age at diagnosis, age when seen, socioeconomic level, and level of intellectual functioning.

Clearly, the control group members differ in many significant ways from their matched cancer survivor counterparts. The rate of positive response to our invitations was much higher (96 percent) among the cancer survivors. Motivations to participate clearly differed qualitatively. Stability of residence in the preceding five years was also greater among the noncancer control participants, with all the implications that may carry (e.g., greater family stability, less life stress, etc.). Still, in the circumstances described and given the uniqueness of childhood cancer survival, this control group is probably the best obtainable. Results obtained in the matched group comparisons are presented in Chapter 5.

Comparison of Survivors by Level of Adjustment

The comparison group concept, rather than the model of an independent control group, is the main basis for data analysis. That is to say, in most of the data interpretations in the chapters that follow, well-adjusted childhood cancer survivors are compared to those whose psychosocial adjustment is less good. In this way it is possible to highlight the factors and tests which seem to differentiate well between these two groups of long-term survivors.

There is no "normal" or healthy control group and only a small control group composed of persons cured of nonneoplastic diseases. While these facts may tend to limit the generalizability of the data presented with regard to other illnesses, the implications for childhood cancer patients are clear enough. There are indeed a number of variables which seem to characterize those survivors who adapt and cope well with the psychological stresses of childhood cancer, as opposed to those who have substantial difficulties. The chapters which follow detail and discuss these factors.

Chapter 4

Late Medical Consequences of Childhood Cancer

A key point of this book is that medical techniques developed to treat childhood cancer over the past decade have yielded large dividends. The optimistic outlook for improved cure rates with combined therapies has been substantiated. This is evident in the increased numbers of long-term survivors being reported (Pinkel, 1971; Simone et al., 1972; Jaffe et al., 1977; Jenkin et al., 1979). However, optimism must be tempered by the realization that serious medical complications may be induced by therapy. The complications may appear as organic and structural changes in the former patient many years after treatment, and there is a potential adverse effect on offspring. This chapter reviews published reports of delayed medical consequences in an effort to foster a realistic attitude toward the risks former patients confront.

We analyze below the long-term medical complications of chemotherapy, radiation therapy, and surgery, and potential effects on progeny. In addition, medical data obtained from careful physical examination of the first 100 participants interviewed are reviewed.

Chemotherapy

Methotrexate, 6-Mercaptopurine, and arabinosyl cytosine (the latter two known to patients as "6-MP" and "ara-C") are major chemotherapeutic agents used in the treatment of childhood cancer. They work by disrupting normal cell metabolism as well as the proliferation of cancer cells. Both methotrexate and 6-MP have been incriminated in the development of liver damage (i.e., hepatic fibrosis). Early reports noted an incidence varying between 10 and 84 percent (McIlvanie and MacCarthy, 1959; Hutter et al., 1960; Einhorn and Davidsohn,

By Norman Jaffe, John E. O'Malley, and Gerald P. Koocher.

51

1964). However, percentages may have been overestimated since such problems have not been prominently mentioned in recent years with increasing reports of long-term cancer survivors.

Long-term methotrexate treatment, used for many types of childhood cancer, may result in skeletal problems, including osteoporosis, growth arrest, and dental abnormalities (Ragab et al., 1970). These findings too, however, have not received prominent mention in recent research reports.

Introduction of methotrexate in the spinal fluid, a frequent prophylactic measure in the treatment of childhood leukemias, may cause neurological problems, including cranial nerve palsy, paraplegia, encephalopathy, loss of motor coordination, and even sudden death (Duttera et al., 1972; Kay et al., 1972; McIntosh et al., 1976; Eiser and Lansdown, 1977). The medication is frequently used with brain irradiation to destroy leukemia cells which may have found their way to the brain or spinal fluids where they could not be reached by other routes of treatment. Computerized axial tomographic studies (i.e., CAT-scan x-rays) of the brains of persons so treated have revealed several types of abnormalities (Peylan-Ramu et al., 1977). Neurological and psychological changes have also been reported in long-term leukemia and lymphoma survivors treated with spinal injections of methotrexate alone (Meadows and Evans, 1976).

The antibiotic most commonly employed as an antitumor drug in the children who are now long-term cancer survivors is actinomycin-D. In addition to its cancericidal properties, actinomycin-D also enhances the effect of radiation therapy and may cause an exaggeration of radiation-induced consequences. It has also been noted to inhibit regeneration of the liver after a partial surgical removal (Filler et al., 1969). The result may be additional liver function problems as the patient grows older.

Adriamycin and daunorubicin, two other powerful antibiotics with antitumor action, may be responsible for heart problems (i.e., cardiomyopathy), particularly if doses of more than 500 mg per meter squared of body surface are administered. The effects of these two drugs may also be exacerbated by radiation therapy to the chest (Greenwood et al., 1974).

Bleomycin, another potent antibiotic, may cause diffuse lung disease. It has not been used extensively to treat children, but an increasing number of patients are currently under treatment with this drug. Long-range complications may be anticipated as a result.

Another family of drugs, the alkylating agents, have contributed substantially to the successful treatment of the child with cancer. These drugs include nitrogen mustard, chlorambucil, and cyclophosphamide (also known to patients as Cytoxan). Sterility is a potential long-term side effect of these drugs. Approximately 60 percent of women patients develop amenorrhea and a high likelihood of permanent infertility following treatment with nitrogen mustard, procarbazine oncovin, and prednisone. This combination of drugs, known by the acronym MOPP, is often used to treat Hodgkin's disease (Sherins et al., 1975). Similar complications have been noted with the use of Cytoxan, which may cause direct damage to the ovaries (Warne et al., 1973). The amenorrhea may reverse after completion of treatment. Some women have become pregnant while receiving Cytoxan therapy, and girls who were exposed to the drug before puberty have developed normal ovarian function (Li and Jaffe, 1974).

Males treated with MOPP for Hodgkin's disease have a high likelihood of sterility (Sherins and DeVita, 1973; Asbjørnsen et al., 1976). Cytoxan and chlorambucil have been known to induce sterility in males, but this effect seems to depend on the dosage. A small percentage of men treated with nitrogen mustard have become fertile again after treatment stops. In general the risk of sterility in males seems to be greatest during early adolescence. Both men and women may experience progressive fertility impairment, associated with hormonal deficiencies, a considerable time after the end of treatment (Chapman et al., 1979a, 1979b).

Cytoxan has also been incriminated as a cause of lung complications (i.e., interstitial pneumonitis and pulmonary fibrosis) and kidney problems (i.e., hemorrhagic cystitis), especially when administered concurrently with radiation therapy (Johnson and Medows, 1971; Alvarado et al., 1978).

Radiation Therapy

The major effects induced by radiation therapy are structural changes of organs, soft tissue, and bone. The effects on growth depend on the anatomic site, the radiation dose, and the patient's age at the time of treatment. Soft tissue and bone deformities as a result of radiation therapy, including reductions in muscle mass and increases in bone fragility, have been well-documented.

Many long-term survivors of Wilms's tumor, treated by removal of a kidney, develop spine deformities after radiation therapy. These include curvature of the spine (i.e., kyphoscoliosis) and a reduction in height. The long-term survivors discussed in most current research literature, including our study, received radiation therapy delivered with 250-kilovolt equipment and doses on the order of 3000 rads (radiation absorbed dose). More recently, megavoltage radiation has been used, with the result that spinal deformities which develop have been less severe (Heaston et al., 1979).

Radiation therapy may also produce deformities in other organs or soft tissue. These include lack of breast development in young women and interference in the functioning of the remaining normal kidney following removal of a cancerous one. Sterility in both males and females following radiation treatment to or in the vicinity of the gonads is well-documented (Lushbaugh and Casarett, 1976). There have also been reports of heart inflammation (i.e., myocarditis and constrictive pericarditis) in the wake of chest irradiation.

The long-term effects of radiation on body sites of endocrine glands may include hormonal disruption years later. In addition to the gonadal effects, growth and thyroid hormones may be affected. Results may include short stature and metabolic disruption.

Second Malignant Neoplasms

Long-term survival may be complicated by the development of new tumors (see Chapter 2). The risk of leukemia following combined radiation and chemotherapy treatments for Hodgkin's disease, for example, increases with time after the end of treatment and is approximately 4 percent after seven years (Desforges, 1979); survival averages only a few months after the secondary leukemia is diagnosed. While the risk of leukemia following ionizing radiation in general has been recognized for many years, the actual incidence is low.

Many anticancer drugs are also potentially carcinogenic over the long term. Specific drugs implicated in human cancers include the alkylating agents, methotrexate, and MOPP. Alkylating agents appear to have a particular potential for inducing leukemia, and the risk of developing a second malignant lymphoma following treatment for Hodgkin's disease is reported to be 4.4 percent after ten years (G. E. Holmes and Holmes, 1978).

Surgery

Among the most frequent postsurgical consequences of successful treatment are the loss of a limb or of limb movement and compromise or loss of function attendant on removal of a cancerous organ. Interruption of nerve pathways during surgery has also resulted in instances of retrograde ejaculation and Horner's syndrome (a depression of the eyeball and drooping of the eyelid). The extent of surgery needed to control the disease, the tumor location, and the skill of the surgeon are the key factors involved in long-term postsurgical consequences.

Progeny

There are few data on the effects of combination therapies on the progeny of survivors of childhood malignancies. One report suggests an increased incidence of abnormal children among women who have been treated with combined chemotherapy and radiation (G. E. Holmes and Holmes, 1978). Another study which considered the problem of inherited traits as well as the effect of preconception exposure to radiation and chemotherapy for cancer found a no higher than normal number of congenital abnormalities or other diseases (Li et al., 1979). Chromosome and immunological studies have not revealed damage either. These findings, also reviewed in Chapter 2, should be considered preliminary but encouraging. Further investigation, preferably through large-scale collaborative studies, is needed for conclusive data.

Risks versus Benefits

Although the risks associated with current cancer therapies may appear high, the result of less aggressive treatment is death for more patients. Late physical consequences are not uncommon, but work aimed at improving treatment and reducing long-term risks continues. Only patients who survive sustain late effects, and with increased patient survival comes increased potential for the effective treatment of the consequences.

The First 100 Participants in Our Sample

The data which follow were collected in physical examinations of the first 100 participants in this study. Table 4-1 shows the percentage treated with radiation and chemotherapeutic agents. None of these 100 participants had been treated

Table 4-1 Percentage of First 100 Interviewees Treated with Chemotherapy or Radiation

Type of Therapy	%
Chemotherapy	
Yes	92
Actinomycin-D	42
Cyclophosphamide	34
Vincristine	24
Chlorambucil	19
Methotrexate	15
Other agents	39
No	8
Radiation	
Yes	86
Females exposed to pelvic or abdominal radiation	67
No	14

Note. Total is over 100% because of wide use of combined drug/radiation therapy.

with adriamycin, bleomycin, or L-asparaginase; about half of those treated with radiation had had associated treatment with actinomycin-D.

Chemotherapy

Physical examinations did not reveal evidence of permanent heart, liver, lung, neurological, or gastrointestinal dysfunction which could be directly attributed to chemotherapy. One man who had been treated with Cytoxan for two years did have aspermia. This type of sterility was suspected in four other participants who were not tested. Another male who had been treated for two years with chlorambucil did have a normal sperm count. Both participants had had chemotherapy before puberty. Another participant reported repeated incidents of blood in the urine following two years of treatment with Cytoxan, but this problem eventually resolved itself and was no longer in evidence five years after treatment ended.

Radiation Therapy

Thirty-two female participants had received radiation therapy to the pelvis or abdomen. For six of them the radiation sites involved both ovaries. Radiation therapy for all thirty-two was administered before puberty, and all had primary amenorrhea and an absence of secondary sexual characteristics. The doses of radiation varied from 2000 to 4000 rads. These women had also been treated with diverse chemotherapeutic agents.

Three other female patients who received radiation therapy to the breasts with orthovoltage equipment had poor breast development. One of these women reported inadequate lactation during her three pregnancies. In contrast, two women who had received lung irradiation with supervoltage equipment for spread of Wilms's tumor to the lungs appeared to have normal breast development when examined years later.

Radiation effects on the skeleton, principally abnormalities of growth and development, were observed in all who had been treated with the older orthovoltage equipment. Approximately 80 percent of those who received radiation to the spine for Wilms's tumor or neuroblastoma had some form of curvature (kyphoscoliosis). Ten required surgical correction (Riseborough et al., 1976; Mayfield et al., 1977). The deformity was more severe in young children whose bones had attained only a small fraction of full growth at the time of irradiation.

Discrepancies in the growth of extremities were noted in six participants who received radiation therapy for Ewing's sarcoma. The irradiated limb was smaller and had less bulk. Four of the six underwent corrective surgery. Radiation-induced necrosis of the clavicles was also noted in three participants who had received radiation therapy to the cervical areas. Other bones exposed to radiation therapy displayed various degrees of radiation effects.

Two persons treated with radiation therapy to the lungs for the spread of Wilms's tumor had restrictive lung disease, not evident clinically but detected by pulmonary function studies in a separate study (Wohl et al., 1975). Three persons treated for Wilms's tumor, including one survivor with bilateral Wilms's tumor, had reduced kidney function in the remaining kidney.

No abnormality in liver function was detected in any of the participants, contrary to expectations suggested by the literature. The integrity of the liver of ten consecutive patients was also examined by repeat radioisotope scanning. All ten had received radiation therapy to all or part of the liver during treatment for Wilms's tumor or neuroblastoma and diminished radioisotope uptake had been detected. On repeat testing some four to five years later, four of the ten had residual defects, one having an enlarged spleen. This participant also had persistent low platelet counts varying between 80,000 and 100,000 (normal range is 150,-000–300,000).

Three participants had undersecretion of the pituitary gland following radiation to the auditory canal or nasopharynx for rhabdomyosarcoma. They were all short, and tests had revealed the absence or a low level of pituitary growth hormone. Two of these three also had hypothyroidism, attributed partially to radiation involving the thyroid gland during treatment of the lymph nodes in the neck; pituitary and thyroid replacement hormones corrected the condition.

Abnormalities in thyroid function were noted in three other participants who had been treated for Hodgkin's disease with irradiation to the neck. Five years later, these patients manifested hyper- or hypothyroidism. Eventually, the conditions stabilized as hypothyroidism in one person, hyperthyroidism in another, and euthyroidism in the third. All three had been diagnosed by lymphangiography before radiation therapy was initiated and had therefore been exposed to additional radiation.

Other abnormalities attributed to radiation included hyperpigmentation or atrophy of the skin, capillary inflammation, and atrophy of subcutaneous tissue and muscle at the radiation sites.

Surgery

Delayed effects as a result of surgery included single eye removal, blindness, amputations, removal of the ovaries, removal of a kidney, and retrograde ejaculation following extensive surgery for cancer of the testis. Two participants had permanent uterosigmoidostomies, and one of the two also had a colostomy following treatment for cancer of the uterus. Most of these survivors appeared to have adjusted well to their deformities or handicaps and participated actively in school and socially. Those who had undergone surgery confined to the abdomen with minimal visible defects generally did not appear to have residual physical or social handicaps.

Progeny

The reproductive and marital status of the first 100 participants is summarized in Table 4-2. Seven female participants were married and had produced fifteen normal, healthy children; three of them had also experienced spontaneous abortions. The drugs administered to these seven had included methotrexate, 6-MP, chlorambucil, nitrogen mustard, and actinomycin-D; three had also received radiation to the hemipelvis or abdomen ranging from 2000 to 4035 rads.

Eight male participants were married and five had fathered normal children. The chemotherapeutic agents administered to them had included chlorambucil, Cytoxan, mitomycin-C, and actinomycin-D.

Table 4-2 Reproductive and Marital Status of First 100 Persons Interviewed

Age at Interview	Single	Married	Divorced and Remarried	Number Who Have Children	Number of Children		Documented Aspermia or Ovarian Failure
					Natural	Adopted	
Males (N = 52)							
11 or less	4						
12–17	19						
18+	20	8	1	5	13	2	1
Females (N = 48)							
11 or less	7						
12–17	16						4
18+	17	7	1	7	15	0	3

Chromosomal analyses were performed on 89 percent of the progeny and failed to reveal any abnormalities. There was also no evidence of tumor development or congenital abnormalities in the progeny.

Conclusions

1. This study reveals that many long-term survivors have had medical complications, particularly the delayed effects of radiation—major abnormalities in skeletal growth and development. In addition, radiation to the ovaries of more than 2000 rads before puberty causes a failure of secondary sexual development. Reproductive abnormalities are also anticipated for these women.

2. Chemotherapy, which has been considered relatively free of side effects, may indeed cause fertility complications. Although not encountered in our participants, adriamycin-induced heart failure and bleomycin-induced lung complications will

probably be encountered more often with the increasing use of these agents (Minow et al., 1975; Samuels et al., 1976).

3. In addition to these specific consequences of radiation therapy and chemotherapy, a recent study reveals potentially lower survival in the first two decades after diagnosis and treatment for cancer victims than for persons of similar age in the general population: 80 percent versus 97 percent. Recurrence of cancer accounts for most deaths during the 5–9-year period, and in subsequent years death may be due to the development of a second malignant neoplasm, organ failure, or infection (Hutter et al., 1960; Li et al., 1975). Rapidly evolving treatment leaves many unknowns to be evaluated; although there is much basis for optimism, it must be well mixed with caution.

Chapter 5

Psychological Adjustment

The global psychological adjustment of our participants was approached in a number of ways. The Combined Adjustment Rating assigned by the psychologist and the psychiatrist was supplemented by a number of personality, socialization, and problem-solving measures described in Chapter 3. These included an estimate of verbal intellectual ability; self-report measures of depression, manifest anxiety, death anxiety, and self-esteem; a measure of socialization and self-help skills; and a series of projective personality assessment cards. Additional variables which were analyzed in relation to the Combined Adjustment Rating included the participant's age at diagnosis, time elapsed since active treatment, duration of treatment, type of cancer, and the incidence of disease recurrence during or after initial treatment. This chapter reports on the findings with respect to these factors.

Combined Adjustment Rating

As noted in Chapter 3, this measure was based on clinical impressions and was obtained by summing ordinal ratings of psychological symptoms assigned independently by the psychologist and the psychiatrist who interviewed each patient. Interrater agreement was perfect in 70 percent of the cases. In another 11 percent of the cases one rater assigned a rating of 1 and the other assigned a rating of 0. In such cases, the combined rating is 1, which counts as "well-adjusted" (Michael and Kirkpatrick, 1962). In the remaining 19 percent of the cases the judges disagreed by more than one rating unit only 4 percent of the time. The Pearson correlation coefficient between ratings assigned by the two raters was .8522 for all cancer survivors and controls interviewed ($N = 139$), which is statistically significant ($p = .001$).

By Gerald P. Koocher.

Fifty-three percent of the participants received a Combined Adjustment Rating of 1 or 0 indicating good adjustment. See Table 5-1 for the distribution of ratings and Table 5-2 for the range, the mean, and the standard deviation.

Summary of Psychological Test Data

Table 5-2 presents a summary of the psychological test data for the full sample of 117 childhood cancer survivors. Estimated Verbal IQ and Vineland Social Quotient scores were slightly above average and narrower in range than in the population at large, but not significantly so. It appears that surviving childhood cancer does not per se impair verbal skills or lower the levels of socialization and self-help skills. Initially, we had hypothesized that these former patients would experience some degree of parental overprotection, with the result that their later social development might be somewhat retarded, as suggested by Green and Solnit (1964). Our data do not support this conclusion for long-range prediction. Although some of our participants may indeed have been overprotected during and immediately after the onset of their illness, they did not show any lasting effects; at least such effects were not detectable with our instrument years later.

The range and variability of scores on the Index of Adjustment and Values are not unusual or striking with regard to the whole population. Our later comparison

Table 5-1 Combined Adjustment Ratings (N = 117)

Descriptions and Ratings	N	%
Well-Adjusted: No evidence of symptoms (0–1)	62	53
Adjustment Problems	55	47
Mild: Mild symptoms, but functioning adequately (2–3)	30	25.6
Moderate: Moderate symptoms; no apparent interference with life adjustment (4–5)	12	10.2
Impaired: (A) *Marked:* Moderate symptoms; impaired functioning (6–7)	10	8.5
(B) *Severe:* Severe symptoms, yet functioning with some difficulty (8–9)	3	2.7
(C) *Incapacitated:* Severe symptoms; unable to function (10–12)	0	0

Note. Categories as defined by Michael and Kirkpatrick (1962). The terms "well-adjusted" and "adjustment problems" are operational definitions adopted by the authors of this volume (see Chapter 3).

between "well-adjusted" and "adjustment problems" subgroups, however, revealed some interesting patterns (see below). As a sample, the group does not seem to differ from the populations of "normals" reported in the literature (Bills et al., 1951; Koocher, 1971, 1974).

The range and variability of scores on the Death Anxiety Questionnaire, the Depression Scale, and the Manifest Anxiety Scale also do not deviate significantly from those expected in the general population (Bendig, 1956; Conte et al., 1975; Koocher et al., 1976). Again, scores on these instruments do not distinguish childhood cancer survivors from other people.

Table 5-2 Summary of Psychological Test Data

Test	N[a]	Mean	S.D.	Range
Combined Adjustment Rating	117	1.91	2.26	0–9
Estimated Verbal IQ	117	107.59	11.97	60–136
Vineland Social Quotient	109	106.62	10.52	75–129
Index of Adjustment and Values				
Self-rating	108	77.93	7.79	55–90
Satisfaction-with-self	108	77.17	10.09	42–90
Ideal-self	108	85.04	4.79	61–90
Self-minus-ideal discrepancy	108	7.38	6.46	0–28
Death Anxiety Questionnaire	108	7.94	4.90	0–25
Depression Scale	108	9.41	6.14	0–34
Manifest Anxiety Scale	108	6.15	4.26	0–20

[a]Sample size varies by instrument as a function of the participants' ages.

Control Group of Chronic Illness Survivors

As discussed in Chapter 3, we were able to assemble a small group of people who had been successfully treated for a chronic childhood illness five or more years earlier. In none of these cases were disease recurrence and possible future death from the illness real concerns for the patient or the family at the conclusion of treatment. In this sense the group constitutes a control for the chronic illness aspect of cancer in childhood, but without the long-term uncertainties faced by cancer patients and their families. We ultimately interviewed twenty-two such survivors and matched them with twenty-two cancer survivors.

The groups were compared on a number of dimensions. The results are summarized in Table 5-3. Careful matching ensured that the two groups did not differ significantly in sex, age at diagnosis, age at interview, socioeconomic status, years of education, Estimated Verbal IQ, time elapsed since diagnosis, or current level of social functioning as measured on the Vineland Social Maturity Scale. The

Table 5-3 Comparison of Chronic Illness Control Group and Matched Cancer Survivor Group (N = 44 in matched groups of 22)

Variable	Mean	S.D.	t (for matched samples)	Significance Level
Age at Diagnosis				
Cancer group	5.70	5.38		
Chronic illness group	7.03	4.29	−1.61	(N.S.)
Age at Interview				
Cancer group	17.37	6.39		
Chronic illness group	17.53	6.99	−0.45	(N.S.)
Years of Education				
Cancer group	9.64	3.62		
Chronic illness group	9.68	4.25	−0.09	(N.S.)
Estimated Verbal IQ				
Cancer group	103.82	12.85		
Chronic illness group	110.46	14.18	−1.57	(N.S.)
Time Elapsed since Diagnosis				
Cancer group	11.67	4.34		
Chronic illness group	10.50	5.87	1.28	(N.S.)
Vineland Social Quotient				
Cancer group	106.58	11.71		
Chronic illness group	111.79	13.16	−1.53	(N.S.)
Combined Adjustment Rating				
Cancer group	3.18	2.50		
Chronic illness group	0.59	0.80	4.63	p = .001, with 21 df
Index of Adjustment and Values: Satisfaction with Self				
Cancer group	70.95	11.08		
Chronic illness group	78.10	6.97	−2.99	p = .007, with 21 df
Manifest Anxiety Scale				
Cancer group	7.61	5.47		
Chronic illness group	4.95	2.78	1.92	p = .063

Note. Values for several of the psychosocial variables which proved not to be statistically significant are omitted.

groups did differ substantially on three of the variables tested: (1) The Combined Adjustment Ratings of the cancer survivors were significantly higher (denoting greater psychopathology) than the ratings of the control group. (2) The former cancer patients reported significantly lower levels of satisfaction with themselves than did the chronic illness survivors. (3) The former cancer patients also reported more manifest anxiety than did the control group, but that difference did not reach statistical significance.

Differentiating among the Survivors

Since the child who survives cancer seems to be at greater risk for psychological maladjustment than children who survive some other chronic but not life-threatening illnesses, it is important to discover additional clues to the contributory factors. Some of the childhood cancer survivors we interviewed were clearly better adjusted than others; 53 percent showed no maladjustment (see Table 5-1). What of the 47 percent who did have some symptoms? To address this question we tested specific hypotheses about factors which could facilitate or inhibit coping among the survivors.

Gender and Family Income

To test whether scores on the psychological tests or the Combined Adjustment Ratings were related to gender, we divided the data pool and conducted a series of statistical comparisons. The sexes did not differ significantly on these variables. Family income, however, was significantly and positively correlated with favorable psychological adjustment. The family economics issues are detailed in Chapter 7.

Type of Cancer

Since the varieties of cancer are treated differently (i.e., with surgery, radiation therapy, chemotherapy, or some combination thereof) and have different consequences depending on tumor site and pathology, we subdivided our sample accordingly. These data are summarized in Table 5-4, in which the numbers of "well-adjusted" and "adjustment problems" participants are listed by diagnosis. Some diagnoses are omitted because our sample had too few representatives to make a subdivision meaningful.

Interestingly, the lowest percentages of psychological symptoms were found among the survivors of neuroblastoma and Wilms's tumor. This finding is striking because of the peak age incidence of these two tumors: both develop predominantly during infancy and early childhood. If detected early, both are among the "most curable" of childhood malignancies. In our sample most of the neuroblastoma and Wilms's tumor patients had undergone surgical excision of the tumor (one kidney in the case of Wilms's tumor) and had been "well" ever since. The mean age at diagnosis was 18 months for our neuroblastoma survivors and 46 months for the Wilms's tumor survivors. These data suggest that extreme youth at the time of diagnosis and a prolonged continuous remission of disease are important factors in long-term psychological adjustment.

The highest incidence of adjustment problems was found among survivors of Hodgkin's disease and acute lymphoblastic leukemia. At the present time active

Table 5-4 Psychological Adjustment Ratings of Survivors by Diagnosis

Diagnosis	Well-Adjusted	Adjustment Problems	% with Some Problems
Neuroblastoma[a]	18	11	37.9
Bone tumors			
Ewing's sarcoma	6	5	45.5
Osteogenic sarcoma	3	4	57.1
Wilms's tumor[a]	12	7	36.8
Acute lymphoblastic leukemia[b]	3	5	62.5
Hodgkin's disease	5	9	64.3
Others including: Non-Hodgkin's lymphomas and soft tissue sarcomas	14	15	51.7

Note. N = 107; 10 participants were excluded from tabulation because they represented diagnostic groups too small to be of statistical interest.

[a]Peak incidence in infancy and early childhood. The mean age at diagnosis in our sample was 18.07 months for neuroblastoma and 45.82 months for Wilms's tumor.

[b]Treatment was longest for these patients. Most were in active treatment for 48 to 60 months, but two were treated for 150 and 171 months respectively. Five also had one or more relapses, which led to additional treatment.

treatment for newly diagnosed leukemia may be electively discontinued after only 18 to 24 months of remission. At the time when most of our survivors were treated, however, some of the newer therapies were not available and treatment tended to average 4 to 5 years. Two patients in our sample had been treated for 12.5 and 14.25 years respectively. Active treatment for Hodgkin's disease has not generally been as prolonged, but the side effects may be. Each patient undergoes a diagnostic procedure known as a staging laparotomy when the disease is discovered, and the spleen is removed in the process. As a result of the splenectomy, and the radiation and chemotherapy which may follow, many of these patients experience prolonged deficiencies in their immune systems. That is to say, they may have difficulty in fighting off infections which would not threaten the healthy person. For this reason, many are instructed to take antibiotics as a prophylaxis for many years.

Given the prolonged course of treatment for these two types of cancer and the related side effects, one might wonder whether patient and family experience greater than usual uncertainty about the outcome. The effect of uncertainty on survivors of childhood cancer will be difficult to explore further because uncertainty is a difficult concept to quantify and measure. In addition, the rapidly evolving nature of cancer treatment necessarily increases the level of uncertainty among patients and families from time to time.

Relapses and Recurrences

The prognostic implications of disease recurrence vary with the type of cancer and the time of the recurrence. In leukemia, for example, the aim is to achieve and maintain a prolonged remission of disease. Relapse may mean a worsening of the long-term prognosis, especially if it occurs during active treatment (i.e., the prime treatment is not working effectively enough). In the case of Wilms's tumor, on the other hand, discovery of metastases in the lungs after excision of the original tumor is not necessarily a sign of doom, since these recurrences can often be successfully treated as well. Regardless of the meaning to the cancer specialist, however, the impact of the relapse or recurrence on the patient and the family can be substantial.

If one has been coping in part by trusting in the treatment and hoping that it will work, new doubts arise. Such thoughts as "What if their next try doesn't work?" and "Will it keep coming back?" are natural reactions. If long-term coping depends on the ability to "forget about" the possibility of recurrence or at least to "stop worrying about it until it happens," coping will clearly be inhibited by a return of the disease. If one becomes preoccupied with worries about possible

Table 5-5 Adjustment as a Function of Disease Recurrence (N = 117)

Combined Adjustment Rating	N with One or More Relapses/ Recurrences	N with Single Continuous Remission
Well-adjusted (0–1)	6	56
Adjustment problems (2–9)	16	39

Note. Fisher's Exact p = .003.

recurrence of the malignancy, extreme psychological debilitation is possible even in the face of continued good physical health.

Twenty-two of our childhood cancer survivors had experienced one or more relapses during the course of their treatment or at some later time. Five were leukemia patients; the other seventeen had been variously diagnosed. In two cases the second cancer was classified as a "second primary tumor" and was essentially a different type of cancer from the one treated earlier. For the other twenty survivors the additional episodes (three for one person, two for two others, and one each for the rest) were either recurrences or metastases related to the original tumor. At the time of our follow-up interviews, all twenty-two had survived at least five years after diagnosis for the most recent recurrence, had been off all treatment for at least three years, and were free of disease.

Sixteen of the twenty-two were given a Combined Adjustment Rating of 2 or higher, indicating problems of adjustment. Table 5-5 shows that among all one hundred seventeen cancer survivors, those who had relapses or recurrences after the initiation of treatment were much more likely to suffer psychological adjustment problems than those who did not have recurrences. Relapsed patients and those with second tumors or recurrences seem to be at substantially greater psychological risk, even when the returned disease is successfully treatable.

Psychological Test Data

We divided our 117 cancer survivors into two groups—those who by the Combined Adjustment Rating were regarded as psychologically well-adjusted and those with psychological adjustment problems—and compared them for differences on three demographic variables and in scores obtained in formal psychological testing. The three demographic variables were (1) age at the time of diagnosis, (2) age at the time of interview, and (3) number of years of education. The two groups did not differ significantly on any of these variables.

Of the psychological tests, only the Vineland Social Quotient failed to differentiate the two groups. Significant differences were found between the groups on all the other psychological test instruments (see Table 5-6). With respect to Estimated Verbal IQ, the Index of Adjustment and Values (i.e., measures of self-esteem, satisfaction-with-self, ideal-self concept, and self-minus-ideal discrepancy), and self-reports of death anxiety, depression, and manifest anxiety, the scores of survivors with adjustment problems differed significantly (in the direction of reduced level of functioning) from the scores of those who had been rated well-adjusted.

Intellectual functioning in the survivors with psychological adjustment problems was somewhat lower and more variable than in their well-adjusted peers. The problem group also reported generally lower self-esteem, lower satisfaction with themselves, less ambitious ideal selves, and a greater gulf between their actual self-concept and their idealized self. This pattern suggests pervasive self-concept problems among those with adjustment difficulties. Ideation related to dying was also more frequent among patients in the problem group. This finding adds support to the notion that an increased preoccupation with death, perhaps resulting from the inability to repress or use adaptive denial, is associated with reduced coping effectiveness over the long term. Self-reports of depression and anxiety lev-

Table 5-6 Comparison of Psychological Test Scores of Well-Adjusted and Adjustment-Problems Subgroups

Psychological Test	N^a	Mean	S.D.	F	(2-tailed p)	t^b	(2-tailed p)
Estimated Verbal IQ							
Well-adjusted	62	110.35	9.50				
Adjustment problems	55	104.47	13.69	2.08	.006	2.72	.007
Self-Esteem (IAV)							
Well-adjusted	57	80.27	6.12				
Adjustment problems	51	75.40	8.62	1.98	.013	3.40	.001
Satisfaction-with-Self (IAV)							
Well-adjusted	57	80.38	8.64				
Adjustment problems	51	73.71	10.47	1.47	.163	3.62	.001
Ideal-Self Concept (IAV)							
Well-adjusted	57	86.16	3.88				
Adjustment problems	51	83.83	5.39	1.93	.018	2.60	1.01
Self-minus-Ideal Discrepancy (IAV)							
Well-adjusted	57	5.96	5.30				
Adjustment problems	51	8.90	7.27	1.88	.023	−2.41	.017
Death Anxiety Questionnaire							
Well-adjusted	57	7.04	4.66				
Adjustment problems	51	8.98	5.00	1.15	.612	−2.08	.040
Depression Scale							
Well-adjusted	57	7.39	4.29				
Adjustment problems	51	11.69	7.10	2.73	.001	−3.75	.001
Manifest Anxiety Scale							
Well-adjusted	57	4.93	3.28				
Adjustment problems	51	7.52	4.82	2.15	.007	−3.21	.002

[a]Sample size varies by instrument as a function of the participant's age.
[b]When F is significant, homogeneity of variance does not exist and the meaning of t may be compromised.

els also yielded higher and more variable scores among those who had been independently rated as having adjustment difficulties.

Correlation and Regression Data

As a pattern of factors seemed to be correlated with the assigned Combined Adjustment Ratings, selective correlations were carried out. The results of these analyses are presented in Table 5-7. Eight variables were found to correlate significantly with the Combined Adjustment Ratings. Five (age at diagnosis, Estimated Verbal IQ, reported level of death anxiety, time elapsed since diagnosis, and the duration of initial active treatment) each account for small portions of the variance (less than 7 percent each). Three (depression, manifest anxiety, and self-

Table 5-7 Correlations of Combined Adjustment Rating with Other Variables

Variable	Pearson r	N	Significance Level	% of Variance Accounted for (Omega)
Age at Diagnosis	0.1772	117	.028	3.13
Estimated Verbal IQ	−0.2626	117	.002	6.89
Death Anxiety Questionnaire	0.2115	108	.014	4.47
Depression Scale	0.4820	108	.001	23.23
Manifest Anxiety Scale	0.4315	108	.001	18.62
Self-minus-Ideal Discrepancy	0.3473	108	.001	12.06
Time since Diagnosis	−0.1545	117	.048	2.39
Duration of Treatment	0.1546	117	.048	2.39

[a]*Omega* is a power test for correlation coefficients and indicates the approximate percentage of the variance accounted for by any given r (*Omega* = r^2).

esteem problems as manifested in self-minus-ideal discrepancy score) each account for substantially greater percentages of the variance (12–23 percent).

Finally, a stepwise multiple regression was conducted using the Combined Adjustment Rating as the dependent variable. Eight variables thought to have the greatest potential for predicting adjustment were tested: age at the time of diagnosis, Estimated Verbal IQ, death anxiety scores, depression scores, manifest anxiety scores, self-minus-ideal discrepancy scores, time elapsed since diagnosis, and the duration of initial treatment. The data are summarized in Table 5-8, and show the substantial significance of age at diagnosis, verbal IQ, current level of depression, self-esteem problems, and time elapsed since diagnosis as predictive of psychological adjustment problems among long-term survivors of childhood cancer.

Projective Test Data

The nine stimulus pictures used to evoke projective responses, and the instructions used when they were administered, are described in Chapter 3. One clinical observation became particularly salient during the first two years of data collection in relation to the themes produced in response to the pictures. It was evident that some interviewees had difficulty in responding to the standard probes used to elicit stories and especially in formulating conclusions to stories. The standard probes were: "What seems to be happening in this picture?"; "What might have hap-

Table 5-8 Multiple Regression with Combined Adjustment Rating as the Dependent Variable

Independent Variable	B	Standard Partial Regression Coefficient (β)	Standard Error of B	F	(B − 0/SE of B)
Age at Diagnosis	0.00918	0.2612	0.00313	8.597	2.934***
Estimated Verbal IQ	−.04426	−.2391	0.01651	7.186	−2.681***
Death Anxiety Questionnaire	0.00199	0.0046	0.04283	0.002	0.047
Depression Scale	0.12392	0.3558	0.04395	7.949	2.820***
Anxiety Scale	0.03329	0.0664	0.06084	0.299	0.547
Self-minus-Ideal Discrepancy (IAV)	0.06816	0.2000	0.03069	4.931	2.2200**
Time since Diagnosis	0.00587	0.1718	0.00320	3.367	1.8344*
Duration of Treatment	.000050	0.0598	0.00013	0.156	0.3854

* $p < .05$ with 9 and 91 df; one-tailed.
** $p < .025$ with 9 and 91 df; one-tailed.
*** $p < .005$ with 9 and 91 df; one-tailed.

pened just before?"; "What are the people thinking, feeling, or wanting?"; and "How will the story end?" The people who were unwilling or unable to "end" their stories often seemed to exhibit psychological symptoms or signs of related adjustment problems. A plausible hypothesis was that the unfinished stories reflected the storyteller's own insecurity or uncertainty about the future and what it holds. To test the validity of the clinical observation, we devised a procedure to explore the relationship between Combined Adjustment Rating and story endings.

Two judges, our research assistant and our secretary, listened to tape-recorded interviews with 116 of the cancer survivors and the 22 chronic illness control subjects. The taped segments contained only the responses to the nine stimulus cards elicited by the standard instructions and probes. The judges did not know any relevant ratings, test scores, or other data about the interviewees, and had never met most of them. The judges were asked to listen to each story and note whether the theme evoked was "resolved," "unresolved," or "left ambiguous."

Stories which had a single specific ending, described spontaneously or in response to the interviewer's probe, no matter how superficial, were regarded as "resolved." For example: "The little girl is sick in bed, and before the doctor was there and gave her medicine. She feels sick and tired. In the end she gets better." Some of the stories ended happily, some with sadness, and some with a neutral emotional tone, but they were considered resolved so long as a specific ending was provided.

Occasionally an interviewee would "not know" or decline to verbalize an ending. For example: "The little girl is sick in bed, and before the doctor was there and gave her medicine. She feels sick and tired. I can't tell how it will end. I don't know . . . I can't guess." These stories were classified as unresolved. In some cases the interviewee gave multiple or ambiguous endings. For example: " . . . it could go either way. Maybe she'll get better, but she could possibly die too? I can't tell which it will be."

The interjudge reliability was very good. The judges listened to 138 people telling nine stories each (a total of 1,242 stories) over a six-month period and disagreed less than 1 percent of the time. When disagreements did occur, they were often about whether a given response was "ambiguous" or "unresolved," rather than "resolved" versus the other two categories. Tables 5-9 and 5-10 present our analyses of these data.

Table 5-9 shows the frequency of ambiguous or unresolved responses on one

Table 5-9 Comparison of Chronic Illness Control Group and Cancer Survivor Sample: Ambiguous/Unresolved Themes

	Chronic Illness Control *(N = 22)*	*Cancer Survivors* *(N = 116)*[a]
No ambiguous or unresolved themes	17	65
One or more ambiguous or unresolved themes	5	51

Note. Fisher's Exact p = .0496.
[a]One survivor was totally blind from optic nerve cancer and could not be tested.

or more of the nine stimulus cards for the chronic illness control group subjects and the childhood cancer survivors. The cancer survivors were significantly more likely to produce an ambiguous or unresolved theme at least once than were the control subjects. In Table 5-10 the data are analyzed a step further: the frequency of ambiguous or unresolved responses is shown as a function of the Combined Adjustment Ratings assigned to the cancer survivors. This time the results were highly significant: the survivors with adjustment problems produced unresolved and ambiguous themes with far greater frequency than did their better-adjusted peers.

Table 5-10 Comparison of Well-Adjusted and Adjustment-Problems Subgroups: Ambiguous/Unresolved Themes ($N = 116$)[a]

	Well-Adjusted (0–1)	Adjustment Problems (2–9)
No ambiguous or unresolved themes	44	21
One or more ambiguous or unresolved themes	17	34

Note. Fisher's Exact $p = .0002$.
[a]One survivor was totally blind from optic nerve cancer and could not be tested.

Summary

It seems evident from the data presented in this chapter that survivors of childhood cancer are at substantially greater psychological risk than are the survivors of other chronic, but not life-threatening, childhood illnesses. This tendency is reflected both in our own observations of their adjustment during personal interviews and in their self-descriptive responses to objective measures of anxiety and self-satisfaction.

1. A number of other variables tends to distinguish well-adjusted survivors from those whose adjustment is compromised in some respect. Factors which seem related to optimal long-term psychological adjustment include:

(a) having a type of cancer with a relatively short treatment course and a minimum of permanent side effects,

(b) having a relapse- or recurrence-free recovery period, and

(c) having disease onset during infancy or early childhood. It also seems that the further away in time one gets from the diagnosis of cancer in a period of relatively good health, the less likely one is to suffer prolonged psychological problems.

2. Those long-term survivors who do have adjustment problems differ from their better-adjusted peers on a variety of self-report personality and mood measures.

3. Their verbal skills may also be slightly lower, or at least more variable, than those of well-adjusted survivors.

4. There is also substantial evidence to suggest that those survivors who have persistent unresolved concerns about the outcome of their disease are at risk for long-term psychological adjustment problems. In this sense the adaptive use of defense mechanisms such as denial to avoid preoccupation with an uncertain long-range outcome seems to be of critical importance. The application of this principle is illustrated by the case material presented in Chapter 11. Patients who lack confidence in a favorable outcome of their cancer treatment, who experience a recurrence of disease, or who are frequently reminded of the threat to their health posed by having had cancer are at the greatest risk of all.

5. Certainly the prediction of psychosocial adjustment among survivors of childhood cancer is a complex problem which will not be fully resolved by a single cross-sectional retrospective study such as this project. Still, it is clear that we have a number of strong clues on which to base new modes of care for current patients as well as long-term survivors.

Chapter 6

The Psychiatric Interview

The purposes of conducting a comprehensive psychiatric evaluation in this population were (1) to determine whether there were symptoms; (2) to identify what coping mechanisms were used; (3) to evaluate the survivors' current psychosocial functioning; and (4) to "hear" what survivors had to say about their experience. We hoped to learn how they handled stress in general and cancer in particular. The psychiatric interview was divided into two parts: (1) a standardized psychiatric interview and mental status examination; and (2) a semistructured, open-ended interview.

Because this was a retrospective study, we expected to encounter some distortions, memory lapses, and confusion about past events. However, we believed that these memories, distorted or not, represent what the survivors believe about events they experienced, and are thus quite important. The interviews also provided the opportunity to compare and contrast the survivor's memories and beliefs with those of the parents, which sometimes differed substantially. The topics covered in the semistructured interview are listed in Appendix B.

Results

Discussion of the results is divided into two sections: (1) the standardized psychiatric interview and mental status examination, and (2) the semistructured, open-ended interview.

Psychiatric Interview and Mental Status Examination

Rutter and Graham Interview Schedule   Each item on the Interview Schedule was correlated with the Combined Adjustment Rating for the long-term survivor population as a whole, for those survivors under 12 years of age, and for those over 12 years of age. The results are presented in Table 6-1.

By John E. O'Malley.

74

Some of the correlations that were significant for the population as a whole were not significant for survivors under 12: apprehension entering the interview, distractibility, depressed or sad mood, adequacy of peer relations. Two items, mannerisms and lack of spontaneous talk, were significantly correlated with the adjustment ratings for the group under age 12 but not for the group over age 12.

The Mental Status Examination consisted of an evaluation of the following areas: appearance, including the presence or absence of any visible motor handi-

Table 6-1   Correlation of Items on Rutter and Graham Interview Schedule and Survivors' Combined Adjustment Ratings

	Correlation Coefficients		
Items	Survivors Aged under 12 (N = 18)	Survivors Aged over 12 (N = 99)	All Survivors (N = 117)
1. Apprehension entering interview	(N.S.)	.46***	.38***
2. Apprehension with other things	.49*	.67***	.63***
3. Preoccupation with anxiety topics	.51*	.70***	.68***
4. Preoccupation with depressive topics	.51*	.63***	.60***
5. Anxious expression	.66**	.60***	.60***
6. Sad expression	.57**	.55***	.55***
7. Adequacy of peer relations	(N.S.)	.49***	.46***
8. Tearfulness	(N.S.)	(N.S.)	(N.S.)
9. Tremulousness	(N.S.)	(N.S.)	(N.S.)
10. Startle	(N.S.)	(N.S.)	(N.S.)
11. Muscular tension	.47*	.21*	.24**
12. Mannerisms	.51*	(N.S.)	(N.S.)
13. Overactivity	(N.S.)	(N.S.)	(N.S.)
14. Fidgetiness	(N.S.)	(N.S.)	(N.S.)
15. Attention span	(N.S.)	(N.S.)	(N.S.)
16. Distractibility	(N.S.)	.32***	.29***
17. Anxiety	.53*	.65***	.61***
18. Emotional responsiveness	.53*	.46***	.46***
19. Relationship with examiner	.73***	.32***	.38***
20. Depressed or sad mood	(N.S.)	.57***	.53***
21. Disinhibition	(N.S.)	(N.S.)	(N.S.)
22. Lack of spontaneous talk	.73***	(N.S.)	.22**
23. Lack of smiling	.53*	.33***	.35***
24. Overall psychiatric state	.68***	.73***	.72***
Total Interview Score	.64**	.76***	.72***

*p = < .05.
**p = < .01.
***p = < .00l.

cap; mood and affect, which included a clinical judgment on fluctuation and range of affect; presence of anxiety; depression; euphoria; appropriateness of affect; and flatness of affect. Coping mechanisms were also explored. These coping mechanisms are unconscious ego defense mechanisms and include:

intellectualization: reasoning or logic is used in an attempt to avoid confrontation with an objectionable impulse or emotion;

rationalization: irrational behavior, motives, or feelings are made to appear reasonable;

avoidance: an aspect of external reality which has caused unpleasant emotions is ignored;

reaction formation: person develops a socialized attitude or interest that is the antithesis of a basic wish or impulse;

denial: an aspect of external reality is rejected;

repression: person removes from consciousness ideas, impulses, or feelings that are unacceptable;

regression: person undergoes a partial or total return to earlier patterns of adaptation;

projection: person attributes to another the ideas, thoughts, feelings, and impulses that are part of his or her inner perceptions but are emotionally unacceptable.

Judgments were made by evaluating the interview in relation to medical data, current physical examination, and the interviewee's degree of awareness of his or her problems. Thought processes were described as either intact or demonstrating the presence of a thought disorder. Clinical judgments were made on the interviewee's self-concept, object relations, and identifications. Judgments of self-concept and of object relations involve considering the view each person has of his or

Table 6-2 Mental Status Examination Items: Discrimination of Well-Adjusted and Adjustment Problems Survivors

Examination Item	Chi Square	d.f.	Significance Level
Mood fluctuation	9.44	2	.009
Range of affect	9.45	2	.009
Anxiety	30.71	2	.0001
Depression	20.60	2	.0001
Euphoria	0.03	1	(N.S.)
Appropriateness	9.22	1	(N.S.)
Flatness	4.37	1	.04

Note. $N = 113$; valid data unavailable on four survivors.

her own body as a person or object in space independently and apart from all other objects; that is, body image, or body identity, as a conceptualization of the body structure and function that grows out of the awareness of the self and one's body and intended action. Identification is the process by which the person incorporates within him or herself a mental picture of a person and then thinks, feels, and acts as he or she conceives that person to think, feel, and act. Each interviewee's concept of self was then rated as having no abnormalities, slight abnormality, or marked abnormality, again using clinical judgment.

Mood and Affect Specific mood and affect items were used to compare the presence or absence of mood problems in the interview with the two combined Adjustment Rating groups, "well adjusted" (rated 0–1) and "adjustment problems" (rated 2 or more). These data are summarized in Table 6-2, and related correlation coefficients are summarized in Table 6-3. Fluctuation of mood, range of affect, anxiety, depression, and flatness of affect all significantly differentiated

Table 6-3 Correlation of Combined Adjustment Rating and Clinical Interview Judgments

Problem	Correlation Coefficient	Significance Level
Self-concept	.58	.001
Object relations	.46	.001
Identification	.07	(N.S.)
Lack of awareness	.42	.001

Note: N = 113; valid data unavailable on four survivors.

the two groups. The adjustment-problems group was significantly more likely to have difficulties with self-concept and poorer object relationships. Problems with identification as a function of the Combined Adjustment Rating were not statistically significant.

Coping Mechanisms were evaluated in the interview, and the results are presented in Table 6-4. It was clear that most of the coping mechanisms were universally used by the interviewees and that these mechanisms were not used differently by adjusted versus maladjusted participants. Since most participants used these mechanisms, it is important to consider the quality of use and the benefits provided. Lazarus (1976), for example, clearly differentiates between adaptive and maladaptive denial. Since almost all of the participants used denial, differentiation of the adjusted from the maladjusted group must depend on the quality of denial rather than its presence or absence. It seemed that those participants who were having difficulty in their social and emotional adjustment also had difficulty using denial effectively. There tended to be gaps in the denial or a great deal of anxiety associated with attempts to make the denial work.

Psychological Adjustment Rating   Table 5-1 presents the percentage of study participants falling in each of the mental health categories established by our Combined Adjustment Rating; 47 percent had mild to severe symptoms with varying degrees of difficulty functioning. Most were judged to have no symptoms or to have mild symptoms with no difficulty functioning. Several case composites follow which illustrate the scoring procedure in the psychiatric interview.

(1) Overall Psychiatric Rating of 0 (no symptoms)

David is a 12-year-old boy who was treated for a neuroblastoma of the kidney at age 2. He is in excellent health currently and doing well in junior high school. He appeared comfortable and related easily to the examiner. He had no recall of his surgery or hospital stay, but indicated that his mother told him at 5 years 6 months that he had a "kidney tumor removed." This information was provided in response to his concern about why he had such a big scar. He remembered that he heard the word "cancer" at school in third grade and asked if he had had cancer. David was relieved to learn that the cancer was gone and believed that he could not get it again. He had told all his friends about his cancer without any negative responses. The family apparently discussed his cancer openly when questions arose. David thought that he might somehow be "special" to be spared from

Table 6-4   Frequency of Coping Mechanisms As Determined by Clinical Judgment

Coping Mechanism	Frequency	%
Denial	113	97
Intellectualization	109	93
Rationalization	110	94
Avoidance	108	92
Repression	81	69
Reaction formation	50	43
Projection	2	2
Regression	1	1

Note. N = 114; valid data unavailable on three survivors.

death and feels his life is more meaningful (e.g., he "pays more attention to other people," "tries to enjoy every day").

David would like to be a doctor and care for "sick people." He plans to marry and have children of his own when he is older. He believes that the diagnosis should be told to children old enough to understand about it (he believed age 5 was old enough), although one didn't have to "scare them about death."

(2) Overall Psychiatric Rating of 2 (mild symptoms)

Alice is a 22-year-old single woman who was ten years beyond the diagnosis and treatment of a lymphoma. She had no obvious physical impairment and seemed poised and confident. Nonetheless she was anxious throughout the interview. She had some difficulty remembering events before and during treatment of her cancer. She remembered being scared and sometimes angry at herself for being such a "baby" about things. Alice currently worries when she gets sick or when she has her annual checkup that the cancer might be returning. At other times she rarely thinks about it. However, she believed that there was little likelihood of recurrence but "couldn't be absolutely certain."

She was vaguely dissatisfied with her life and current career choice. She wasn't sure whether marriage would happen for her although she does want children.

Alice related that she rarely tells friends about her cancer and tried to hide it when she was younger. She refuses to wear a two-piece bathing suit since kids teased her about a scar when she was younger. She has not been involved in psychotherapy, but has been "thinking about it." She has lived her life "more cautiously" since learning that she had cancer.

(3) Overall Psychiatric Rating of 6 (moderate symptoms, some impairment of functioning)

Mark is a 34-year-old man who had his left arm amputated at age 16 for osteogenic sarcoma. In the eighteen years since his cancer was found, Mark has had increasing difficulties in school, work, and his social environment. He withdrew from high school and his friends. He described himself as being very depressed and anxious much of the time. He continues to be unable to maintain any successful interpersonal relationships or find gainful employment.

Mark felt that his cancer has "ruined" his life. He is angry and bitter about his situation. He felt that children should not be told that they have cancer. Psychiatric help was recommended and accepted by Mark, but was discontinued abruptly after the third session when he acted on an impulse to go on a trip to another state.

Content Interview Responses

The frequencies of replies to questions asked about the cancer experience are listed in Table 6-5. (Interview items are listed in Appendix B.) Each response

Table 6-5 Responses in Content Interview (N = 112, except where noted)

Topic	N	%
How learned diagnosis		
Parent	69	61.6
Doctor	17	15.2
Friend	4	3.6
Self	14	12.5
Other	8	7.1
Reaction to diagnosis		
Shock	36	32.1
Relief	34	30.4
Other	42	37.5
Cause of cancer		
Unknown	75	67.0
Injury	11	9.8
Agent	15	13.4
Other	11	9.8
Chance of getting same cancer		
No chance	59	52.7
Same	19	17.0
More	24	21.4
Don't know	10	8.9
Chance of getting different cancer		
No chance	21	18.8
Same	65	58.0
More	17	15.2
Don't know	9	8.0
Change in religious beliefs[a]		
None	88	79.3
More	18	16.2
Less	5	4.5
Change in how conduct life[a]		
Debt to pay	12	10.8
More cautious	15	13.5
More meaningful	26	23.4
No change	38	34.2
Other	20	18.1

[a] N = 111.

Table 6-5   Responses in Content Interview (N = 112, except where noted) (*Continued*)

Topic	N	%
Change in thoughts about death[a]		
No change	86	77.5
Little change	1	0.9
Think about it more	21	18.9
Not asked	3	2.7
Change in social relationships		
More friends	4	3.5
Fewer friends	27	24.1
No change	76	67.9
Other	5	4.5
Change in family relationships[a]		
Closer	26	23.4
Farther apart	9	8.1
No change	51	46.0
Overprotected	25	22.5
Current preoccupation		
Future	33	29.4
Cancer recurrence	12	10.7
Current life events	48	42.9
Other	19	17.0
Effect on occupational choice[a]		
None	65	58.6
Some	16	14.4
Much	25	22.5
Other	5	4.5
Plans for future[a]		
Work/School	52	46.8
Marriage	2	1.8
Children	2	1.8
All	50	45.1
Other	5	4.5
Family[a]		
Supportive	87	78.4
Not supportive	21	18.9
Other	3	2.7

[a]$N = 111.$

Table 6-5 Responses in Content Interview (N = 112, except where noted) (*Continued*)

Topic	N	%
Peers		
(1) All know	3	2.6
(2) Few know	29	25.9
(3) Made little difference	2	1.8
(4) Made much difference	1	0.9
(1) and (3)	68	60.7
(2) and (4)	5	4.5
Other	4	3.6
Spouse		
Supportive	19	16.9
Not supportive	2	1.8
Doesn't know at all	1	0.9
Not relevant	88	78.6
Other	2	1.8
Should child be told diagnosis[a]		
Yes	77	69.4
No	9	8.1
Qualified	23	20.7
Other	2	1.8
Should psychosocial aid be available[a]		
Yes	75	67.6
Mandatory	6	5.4
Never	19	17.1
Other	11	9.9
Overall impact of cancer[b]		
None	30	27.3
Some	41	37.3
Great	33	30.0
Other	6	5.4

[a]N = 111.
[b]N = 110.

was compared with the Combined Adjustment Rating using chi square. No one item was found to discriminate significantly between the "good adjustment" and "adjustment problems" groups, although three items approached significance.

Interviewee reaction to the diagnosis approached statistical significance ($p = .073$), indicating that those interviewees judged to be maladjusted also reported having reacted to the diagnosis of cancer with "shock and distress" more often than those without adjustment problems. Those found to be well-adjusted reported reacting on initial diagnosis with some relief upon learning that the cancer was treatable, thus emphasizing hope in their ability to cope.

Interviewees who thought they might have a recurrence of cancer were compared with those who did not express such concerns, as a function of Combined Adjustment Rating, and the resulting chi square approached significance ($p = .071$). Those patients who reported a decrease in social contacts at the time of the initial diagnosis and treatment also tended to be less adjusted at the time of the interview than those who did not report such changes in social relationships (approached significance; $p = .062$).

No other items in the content interview tended to distinguish between the adjusted and the maladjusted group. These statistical results suggest that if patients react with shock and horror to their diagnoses; are at the same time shunned by their friends, schoolmates, and family members; and believe that recurrence is a possibility, they are likely to fare less well than those who do not have these experiences or attitudes. The data suggest that the internal emotional life of the patient and the social context in which it occurs are equally important for determining the ultimate adjustment outcome.

Specification of Responses   Most interviewees said that they learned of their diagnosis from a parent. Only 15 percent reported learning the diagnosis from a physician. In addition to the two predominant emotional responses to the diagnosis, shock or relief, some former patients reported responding to the diagnosis with anger or sadness, and some with feelings of pride or invincibility at having somehow managed to conquer the illness. Although most had no notion of the etiology of their disease, some believed that a previous injury might have caused their cancer or that it was congenital.

When the interviewees were asked their thoughts about the possibility that cancer might recur, over half expressed the belief that they had little or no chance of getting the same type of cancer again. Another substantial group believed that they had about the same chance of getting a different type of cancer as the rest of the general population. Interviewees who believed that there was no chance of recurrence of their original cancer or any other cancer expressed the belief that they were somehow immune as a result of their successful cancer treatment.

A series of questions was asked about changes in various aspects of their lives due to the cancer experience. Very few reported any change in religious beliefs as a result of the experience of cancer. We had expected that religion might play a significant role in coping with such a severe stress, but we did not find that to be the case. Many felt that because of the successful cancer treatment they had "some debt to pay back to society" or that life had become "more meaningful" or that they were somehow "special" to have been spared from death.

Others indicated that they tend to lead their lives more cautiously, attempting to avoid risks and giving more attention to their health. Many interviewees believed strongly that the illness had brought about a change in their conduct of living and reported feeling driven to repay that "debt." Those who believe that they are "special" as a result of surviving seem to do so to find a personal explanation of why they were spared while other cancer patients they knew were not. Their feeling of specialness did not correlate with increased risk-taking activities, as one might predict. Nor did they define their specialness in specific religious terms. Rather, they felt that whatever "life force" was controlling life and death, they were spared.

Few reported changes in their thoughts or reflections about death as a result of their experience. Interestingly, every interviewee reported some thoughts or personal reflections about death, including our very young patients. None felt particularly invulnerable to death because of the experience or believed that they were currently closer to death than their peers.

Some interviewees believed they had lost friends because of a public fear that cancer is contagious or because of peers' feelings of revulsion at the loss of a limb or hair. It was this subgroup which tended to be more poorly adjusted. It is not clear whether the perception of loss of friends was accurate or whether the patients' own withdrawn and depressed behavior contributed to losing friends. However, many reported that friends, family, extended family, and neighbors believed that the cancer might be contagious.

Some former patients believed that they had been overprotected by their families. They compared the freedom and privileges they enjoyed with those permitted to their siblings, and found they were granted privileges more slowly. Some reported that their family drew emotionally closer together because of the experience, although, surprisingly, a fifth of the former patients felt that the family was not helpful in any way. Most of these people reported that no one in the family was willing to listen to feelings, fears, and anger about the illness.

Many patients believe that having had cancer affected their occupational choice, particularly those interested in health-related fields. Those who picked nursing, occupational therapy, or medicine could articulate directly that their choice was due to their experience with their illness. An important finding was that most of the patients were future-oriented, as shown by their plans for marriage, employment, schooling, and so forth. Approximately 60 percent of those over 18 had shared the fact of having had cancer with their friends in adulthood. This generally resulted in no particular difficulties or stresses, in contrast to reports of childhood or adolescent sharing, when many reported losing friends, becoming scapegoats, or somehow being ostracized because of their cancer. Former patients who were married reported that their spouses were informed of the illness before marriage and were generally supportive.

Summary

A standardized and semistructured psychiatric interview with 117 childhood cancer survivors revealed:

1. Approximately half had some psychiatric symptoms, with a range of mild to severely impaired functioning.

2. The majority of those with symptoms were only mildly affected and had no difficulty in overall functioning.

3. The Rutter and Graham Interview Schedule was useful in distinguishing between well-adjusted interviewees and those with adjustment problems.

4. Certain mental status examination items, including those on mood, range of affect, anxiety, and depression, also distinguished well-adjusted from poorly adjusted former patients.

5. Virtually all of the interviewees used some degree of denial as a coping mechanism, although the population varied widely with respect to adaptive and maladaptive applications of denial.

6. Detailed content-oriented interviews revealed the uniqueness of the cancer experience and its impact on these former patients.

Chapter 7

The Parent Interviews

Although each parent had a unique style of living and self-expression, the parents as a group were surprisingly consistent in many responses. At the beginning of the interview the majority reported that they were participating in the study both because of their desire to help other families who are and will be forced to cope with the experience of having a child with cancer and because they were very grateful that their children had survived. The parents faced enormous tasks from the time they first became aware of their child's symptoms. The usual practical and emotional responsibilities of parenting, to some extent routine and predictable, were suddenly multiplied as a result of the cancer diagnosis. Although logistical problems such as arranging transportation for clinic visits and coping with hospital costs did require substantial attention, parents reported that emotional issues were by far the most difficult matters to cope with for all family members.

As noted in Chapter 3, the parent interviews were designed to address a wide range of topics. The general purpose of the sessions was to gain an understanding of those matters which most directly affected the family during the course of the illness. We hoped to discover which aspects of the experience were consciously considered most important in retrospect.

Demographic Data

General Background

A total of 103 former patients were represented by at least one parent in an office interview. Office interviews were held with 98 mothers, 75 fathers, and 1 uncle who had acted as a surrogate father during the treatment period. In addition

By Diana J. Foster, John E. O'Malley, and Gerald P. Koocher.

86

3 parents were interviewed by telephone, and information was obtained from questionnaires returned by the cancer survivors for another 13 parents who were not seen in person. Thus data on parents were obtained for 119 survivors. Except where otherwise noted, the responses of mother and father are treated as a unit. Sections of Chapter 3 explain why the number of survivors varies from analysis to analysis. Although the data on some may have been excluded from analysis, relevant data from their parents were not, and are reported here.

The mothers ranged in age from 29 to 71 at the time of interview; the range for fathers was 30–75 years. Three couples were adoptive parents. The number of children in the family ranged from 1 to 11, with an average of 3 to 4 per family. At least 39 of the families included children conceived after the cancer diagnosis had been made in their siblings. Two families were Afro-American, and at least 12 additional ethnic heritages were described by the remaining parents. All of the parents spoke English well, although for 12 families it was a second language. In order of decreasing frequency, the non-English primary languages mentioned were Canadian French, Italian, Spanish, German, and Portuguese.

Marital Status

In any discussion among clinicians, the question of what happens to the parents' marriage when a child has cancer often arises. For our sample of 119 survivors, at the time the diagnosis was made 112 of the parents were married, 2 were separated, 4 were divorced, and the status of one couple was unknown. By the time our research interview took place, from five to twenty years later, 99 were still married, 2 were separated, 10 were divorced, and three families had experienced at least one parent death. Two sets of parents, although divorced, were currently living together as a couple, and the status of three couples was unknown. Nineteen parents had at least one change in marital status between diagnosis and our interview with them, and a few had experienced up to three changes. Only 6 parents who were married at diagnosis subsequently divorced, and none of these parents thought the cancer experience was a causal factor in the decision to divorce. Four sets of divorced parents chose to come together for the research interview.

Socioeconomic Status

Social class estimates were assigned using the current educational level and occupation of the primary breadwinner (Hollingshead, 1957). These data are summarized in Table 7-1. The parents fell predominantly in the middle-class categories. Only three parents described themselves as unemployed, but as Table 7-1 shows information on some parents was unavailable. Most of these "no information" parents could not be interviewed personally and were parents of former patients who are now adults. The social-class ratings of adult survivors who were living independently are summarized in Table 7-2.

The income level at the time of our research contact fell primarily in the $15–20,000 per year range. Almost all parents remarked that their incomes had been considerably less at the time the cancer was diagnosed. Parents reported that both were working at interview more often than at diagnosis, which they generally attributed to factors other than the cancer experience. At diagnosis 23 mothers and 113 fathers were employed. At interview the figures were 60 mothers and 110 fathers. Some were retired by the time of the interview.

Table 7-1   Social-Class Distribution of Parents at Interview by Position of Primary Breadwinner

Index of Social Position[a]	Primary Breadwinner		Total Breadwinners	%
	Mother	Father		
I (highest)	0	11	11	9
II	1	18	19	16
III	4	31	35	29
IV	5	28	33	28
V (lowest)	3	4	7	6
Incomplete information	–	–	14	12
Total	13	92	119	100%

[a]Two-Factor Index (Hollingshead, 1957).

Table 7-2   Social-Class Distribution of Adult Survivors Living Independently ($N = 32$)

Index of Social Position[a]	N	%
I (highest)	0	0
II	8	25
III	11	34.4
IV	8	25
V (lowest)	5	15.6

[a]Two-Factor Index (Hollingshead, 1957).

Religious Affiliation

The religious affiliations reported by parents were Roman Catholic, Protestant, Judaic, or none. Some parents said they turned to religion when their child was diagnosed and found it helpful. Others did not find their religion helpful, and indeed a few expressed some anger that religion did not seem to offer more solace. Only a few parents felt that their individual religious beliefs changed as a result of their experience during the cancer period.

Results

Correlation with Combined Adjustment Rating

We conducted a series of analyses to explore the relationship between key facts gleaned from the parents' interviews and the Combined Adjustment Rating assigned to each patient. Few of the variables were significantly correlated with the adjustment rating, and those facts which were related do not seem surprising. The significant correlations are summarized in Table 7-3. Parental income and family socioeconomic status were weakly, but significantly related to overall adjustment, accounting for less than 10 percent of the sample variability. It does not seem unreasonable that financially secure families are better copers, although this relationship does underscore the need to ensure adequate financial stability for the families of catastrophic-disease patients.

The age at which the child reportedly learned about the cancer diagnosis was also correlated with psychological adjustment. The earlier the child learned of it, the better was his or her psychological adjustment at the time of our study. While this correlation accounts for approximately 4 percent of the variability, the meaning is not totally clear. This issue is discussed in detail in Chapter 9.

Parents were asked to list any current problems or concerns about the survivor in the family or in the world at large. The specific concerns parents express are listed in order of frequency in Table 7-4. These concerns were summed to form a score of total number of "concerns" reported, and we found that this summary score correlated significantly with the Combined Adjustment Rating. This finding enhances the validity of the ratings and suggests that there was some independent agreement among the parents, the psychologist, and the psychiatrist on the need for worry about the child's adjustment.

Changes in the parents' marital status, other family changes, recent stress (other than the patient's illness) facing the family, and reports of emotional or financial support available at the time of the illness all proved to be statistically unrelated to the Combined Adjustment Rating.

Content Interview: The Natural History of Treatment

The Beginning

The first professional person involved with the child was most often a local pediatrician or family doctor. A few families used the emergency room of a local hospital or a community pediatric clinic when the symptoms first emerged. It should be remembered that the accurate diagnosis of cancer, especially in a child, is often difficult to make under the best conditions, and the average community pediatrician probably sees less than half a dozen children with cancer in a lifetime of practice.

All the parents talked about the importance to them of the attitude conveyed by their local physician. Whether their experience was recalled positively and supportively (60 percent) or negatively (40 percent), it was important that the physician take their report of their child's symptoms seriously, investigate it reasonably, and be honest about what he or she knows and does not know. An honest, hopeful, and considerate attitude was the most appreciated. The negative experiences many families reported generally reflected their feeling that the physician withheld information, was unsupportive, or was tactless.

The physicians who were most helpful had told parents what tests were to be

Table 7-3   Correlation of Family Data and Survivors' Combined Adjustment Rating ($N =$ 117)

Variable	Pearson r^a	Significance Level	% of Variance Accounted for (Omega)
Parent income	.2763	.002	.078
Socioeconomic status	.3044	.001	.093
Age child learned diagnosis (parental report)	.1915	.032	.037
Sum of parental "concerns"	.3108	.001	.097

[a]Signs removed for clarification: direct positive relationship holds for parental income, socioeconomic status, and good adjustment; inverse relationship holds between the age at which parents believe their child learned of the diagnosis, the sum of their current concerns, and good adjustment.

done and then called both parents to the office in order to let them know about the findings, had consulted with the Medical Center, and had made arrangements for an appointment for the child by the time the parents arrived. They gave the parents time to react and ask questions, and conveyed hope that treatment could be successful if the cancer diagnosis was confirmed. These physicians usually remained in touch with the family and were seen as continuing to be supportive.

Conversely, the parents who remembered this initial phase in a negative way referred primarily to perceptions of the physician's attitude or behavior rather than poor medical care per se. These parents experienced what they felt was condescension (e.g., "You're only an anxious mother"), arrogance (e.g., "What do you mean 'take your child to the city specialist,' I know as much as they do"), premature pessimism (e.g., "You might as well prepare your child for death, there's nothing else to do"), and just plain bad sense (conveying the news over the telephone without any preparation) or avoidance (getting another family member to tell the parents the news). These parents were often still angry and bitter. The parents may not have been perfectly accurate in their accounts. This anger may in part reflect the painfulness of the whole experience, focused or projected onto the physician in order to make it tolerable. In general, however, their recollections were recounted with believable poignancy.

The important practical problem of transporting themselves to the Medical Center, initially and throughout treatment, was of some concern. It was a hidden expense and the most frequently mentioned nonmedical financial burden.

When the parents arrived at the Medical Center with their child they were often frightened, anxious, and confused. The diagnosis of type of cancer was generally made or confirmed within twelve hours of their arrival. Most often the patient was admitted to the hospital and treatment was begun almost immediately. Treatment consisted of surgery, radiation, chemotherapy, or some combination of these. During our interviews the parents consistently stressed their memories of the importance of *how* things were done rather than *what* specifically was done. The attitudes conveyed were especially significant.

Table 7-4   Parents' Concerns about the Former Patient at Interview (N = 119)

		N		
Order of Frequency	Issue	Mentioned as an Issue	Mentioned as Nonissue	Not Mentioned
1	Long-term effects of treatment	90	9	20
2	Recurrence	85	11	23
3	Ability to produce children	66	26	27
4	General physical condition	56	35	28
5	Ability to obtain health or life insurance	49	34	36
6	Emotional stability	40	42	37
7	Whether life will be less full	38	46	35
8	Life expectancy	36	39	44
9	Whether able to get job and be self-supporting	18	58	43
10	Other	14	9	96

Parents felt that courtesy and consideration by all staff involved were most helpful in reducing their anxiety. Having someone spell out what was to happen during this initial period was important. Who that someone was, was less significant.

Confirming the Diagnosis

When all the test results were in, a staff pediatric oncologist generally met with
the parents privately. At this session, the particular diagnosis of cancer was confirmed, described simply, and explained. Visual aids, such as x-rays or a drawing,
were described as helpful by parents. Next, a plan of treatment was presented for
the parents' consideration. This was quite important since it offered hope for successful treatment, conveyed either overtly or implicitly, although no promises were
made.

This was by far the most difficult and stressful time for parents. Regardless of
the number of years that had passed by the time of our interview, they related
these events with much evident emotion. The persistence of a given symptom
rather than the type of symptom per se was what alerted parents to the likelihood
that something was quite wrong with their child and led them to take the child to
the physician. The emotional tension for the parents increased, reaching its zenith
when the diagnosis of the child's disease as cancer was confirmed at a pediatric
medical center. The parents' anxiety level remained high for a minimum of three
months to a year or more. The tension at its peak was often described spontaneously by parents as a state of "emotional shock."

The emotional shock gradually dissipated, but stress peaks of lesser intensity
were precipitated by new or disturbing events during the course of treatment (e.g.,
new medication, side effects of treatment, and surgery). For parents whose child
had a relapse or recurrence, a new high of tension and stress was experienced, but
the "shock" did not last as long as when the initial diagnosis had been made.
Another small peak occurred, unexpectedly for many parents, at the end of active
treatment, which was most often three years after the diagnosis. The stress was
as brief as 10 days for an infant with Wilms's tumor, ranging to 171 months for
at least one leukemia patient. At 5 years after diagnosis, some parents felt that the
"magic cure time" had been reached and often celebrated the event.

Nevertheless, most families at the time of interview still noted that their fear of
recurrence was not far below the level of awareness, no matter how many years
had passed uneventfully. They sometimes described themselves as "lump conscious" or otherwise attuned to any symptoms reminiscent of those which first
appeared in their child's case. Individual families represented the spectrum of this
fear; members of one family stated flatly that they believed the cancer was over
and done with and could not recur, whereas members of another family continued
to be globally fearful about recurrence at the time of our study.

Impact on Parents' Marriage

Since the study was a cross-sectional retrospective one, we had no data on the nature of the parents' marriage before their child's illness except their own reports and memories. The parents were asked whether their experiences of caring for a child with cancer influenced their closeness as a couple and as parents. Their responses are summarized in Table 7-5.

The stress of cancer had at least some effect on every marriage. Although a few families reported a negative effect, most said that the impact was generally positive over the long run. Most became sensitized to what aspects of their relationship

Table 7-5   Reported Impact of Cancer on Marital Closeness (*N* = 176)

	N Mothers	%	N Fathers	%
Closeness as a Couple				
Grew closer	69	70.4	58	74.3
No change	17	17.3	16	20.5
Grew less close	12	12.2	4	5.1
Total	98	99.9	78	99.9
Closeness as Parents				
Grew closer	85	86.7	72	92.3
No change	10	10.2	6	7.7
Grew less close	3	3.1	0	0
Total	98	100	78	100

were good or not so good. For many couples, this was the most severe stress either partner had ever confronted. The emotional shock described by many parents brought their individual styles of expressing feelings and coping into sharp focus.

It was the difference in coping styles rather than one spouse's seeming to care more or less that caused difficulty for many. It sometimes took months or years for each to understand the other's coping style. For example, it was not unusual for one spouse, often the father, to appear very contained and controlled, concentrating on going to work, paying the bills, and seeming unsympathetic to the other's tears and overt expressions of distress. Occassionally the apparently well contained spouse would report during the interview that he had cried every day on the drive home from work, had cried privately, or had gone to pray at church every day.

Typically this spouse had not told the other, believing it to be important to appear "strong." Our interview often provided the first opportunity that seemed acceptable to mention how he had really felt.

Many couples were able to share their feelings with each other from the beginning. They believed that their marriages became stronger through reliance on each other's strengths, and they grew to respect each other more. Family relationships became a conscious priority to the parents and they no longer took them for granted. They reported developing a much deeper sense of unity than they had been aware of before this experience with cancer.

A few couples had been in the process of separating or divorcing at the time of diagnosis. The diagnosis did nothing to alter the decision. The diagnosis did, however, highlight the issues for these couples. They found that they could and did work together on behalf of their child. They also found, occasionally, to their own surprise, that they were not arguing about treatment decisions, visitation rights, or other child-related issues, and the child was not really a source of contention. As they became aware of this process they found it emotionally supportive and began to trust one another more concerning their children, even if they could not resolve or change their personal differences on other issues.

Mental Health

Explicitly or implicitly, all the parents discussed how emotionally overwhelming the cancer experience had been. They were all asked, "With whom did you discuss your worries?" and "Would you have liked to discuss emotional issues with a staff person at the hospital while your child was in treatment?"

In answer to the first question, most responded that they discussed their worries with a spouse, another relative, a friend, or a coworker; a few said they shared worries with no one and kept worries to themselves. Only a few mentioned professional mental health workers with whom they already had some form of relationship. A few had met a social worker at the hospital but remembered the contact as helpful primarily for practical matters such as dealing with insurance problems, transportation, overnight stays, and the like.

In answer to the second question, most answered emphatically that they would indeed have liked to talk with a staff person at the hospital about the emotional issues while their child was in treatment. Parents were quite clear about what they would have sought from such a person. They would have liked the meeting to take place within the first week or so after diagnosis and treatment had begun. The idea of such a meeting, they explained, should be presented by the primary physician as a routine part of the system of care. That way, they would not feel stigmatized by referral to a mental health professional. Initially, they would expect such a meeting to be informative about common issues other parents have experienced, thus giving them some idea of what to expect themselves. They wanted to know that the feeling of being in emotional shock would probably wear off as they became more familiar with place, people, jargon, care system, and routine. Some parents thought that initially one to three meetings, would probably be enough, so long as they had the option to meet again when necessary.

Most parents said that they would have liked to meet either individually or as a couple with a mental health professional. Even those who were generally reluctant to talk about feelings saw this circumstance as an exception. As treatment of their child progressed, individual preferences were more apparent. Some expressed a preference for individual or for couple meetings, others expressed a preference for meeting with other parents in a group. For some, just knowing that a mental health person was available at the Medical Center would be adequate. Parents also reported that referral to a community mental health facility would not be helpful because of anticipated difficulties with care and information coordination.

Interpretation of the reported desire for professional mental health services at the time of treatment must be tempered by recognition of the fact that the parents may very well have wanted to please the interviewers. It is difficult to know whether these reports actually reflect the way they felt during the course of their child's illness.

Most parents in our study felt that the regular staff (physicians, nurses, lab technicians, radiology staff, etc.) was helpful and supportive. Nevertheless, the parents often did not really feel free to discuss their own feelings with staff because the staff's primary concern was—appropriately—for their child. The parents did not want to "take up their time." Therefore, to have had a mental health person available at the Medical Center for the primary purpose of listening to them would have been very helpful.

Many parents feel some degree of guilt when something happens to their child, and these parents were no exception. Many spontaneously spoke of how they had asked themselves, and often the doctors, what they might have done to cause the cancer. Most parents had come to terms with this uncomfortable feeling by the time of the interview, and said that there were no clear answers and in any case, no way they could have done anything differently. A few parents talked of finally recognizing the irrational nature of their magical thinking (i.e., one mother thought perhaps her child developed cancer because she was too greedy in wanting to have as many children as her own mother had had. She had had six, and her own mother had had nine. On the other hand, another mother had worried that it was because she had wanted only two children that her child had developed cancer).

Many parents had also asked themselves the related question of those feeling overwhelmed, "Why me?" or "Why my child?" By the time of the interview most had resolved this question to their satisfaction by accepting that there was no answer. Most parents continued to be interested in the progress of research into the causes of cancer and say they are more alert to related medical reports than they were before the diagnosis. These parents also believe they are much more knowledgeable and assertive consumers of medical care as a result of their experience.

Coping Strategies

The parents were all asked what they thought made it possible for them to endure the experience. They reported that hope and honest communication were most important. Many mentioned faith, although they were not necessarily referring to their formal religious affiliation. Individual parents said that the support of other family members was very important, especially their spouse. Those parents without spouses felt the absence of their partner acutely and talked of friends or other relatives as being significant. Many parents mentioned that their other children helped them to keep things in some perspective, and others noted that the courage of the patient was what kept them going. Parents also reported that a sense of humor helped them endure some stressful events. Trust that their child was getting the best and most up-to-date medical care possible was essential.

The parents generally reported that their child's confrontation with death made them more mindful of their own mortality. The Death Anxiety Questionnaire (Conte et al., 1975) that was administered to the patients (discussed in Chapter 3) was also administered independently to each parent. The scores for each parent were correlated with their own child's score; the results were not statistically significant. On the other hand, when the scores for one parent were matched with the spouse's score, the Pearson correlation coefficient was 0.32, which is significant at $p = .008$ and accounts for 10.2 percent of the sample variance. At the same time, parental scores did not differ significantly from the scores reported for other adults (Koocher et al., 1976).

The majority of parents, when asked their plans for the future as a couple, stated that they would be glad when their children, especially the former patient, reached adulthood. They looked forward to the major responsibility of parenthood being over despite the attachment they feel for their children. They often explained they would continue to care and feel close, and thought that they would still worry, but major decision making on behalf of the child would no longer be theirs.

Lingering Concerns

A few parents claimed to have no residual concern about their child's well-being with respect to the cancer experience, but most parents did have lingering worries. Many expressed concern about the risk of recurrence or increased vulnerability to other cancers, regardless of the number of years their child had been well. Most were concerned about the long-term effects of treatment from surgery, radiation, or chemotherapy. They wondered whether life expectancy would be shorter, or whether some late effects would occur when their child was an adult. These are realistic concerns, but unfortunately ones to which there are no reassuring answers. The former patients were advised to have regular follow-up medical examinations and not to ignore any persistent physical symptoms.

For some parents, the concerns were less with physical problems than with the emotional effects of the experience. Some believed their child was functioning well in general, but noted that the child appeared to have some difficulty forming lasting relationships with members of the opposite sex. A few thought the difficulty related to other people's views of a former patient's residual physical impairment or life expectancy.

A few parents expressed concern about the ability of their child to get a job, enter military service, or obtain health and life insurance. These realistic concerns are discussed in more detail in Chapter 9.

The parents were consistent in expressing regret about having given less attention to the child's siblings, although most felt they could have done little else in the circumstances. They gave many examples of siblings' expressions of jealousy, withdrawal, and anger, as well as reports of some who became overconcerned with their own health. Some families felt that patient and siblings drew closer, especially when siblings could contribute to caring for the patient. Some families found it helpful to have the siblings accompany the patient to the clinic, where they could see the treatment for themselves.

The parents welcomed the aid of grandparents, aunts, and uncles, who often helped in practical ways such as with baby-sitting, transportation, housekeeping, and shopping, and sometimes financially. Only a few parents, however, found that individual relatives were helpful in an emotional sense. Most relatives were described by parents as being so distressed themselves by the child's diagnosis of cancer that it was difficult to share feelings in a way that was useful.

Parental Employment Issues

In most families, at least one parent was working at the time of diagnosis. Most working parents reported that their employers were often supportive, allowing the parents time off to be with their child, often without loss of pay. Other employers were willing to be flexible about time off and allowed it to be made up at the parent's convenience. A few parents reported that they were given preference for keeping a job during layoffs in their companies. Some thirteen parents had to quit work or change jobs to provide for their child's care adequately.

A large number of parents believed they had continued to do their jobs and put the worries about their child aside while working. Some indeed found it a relief to go to work. Other parents reported that they wish they had been able to spend more time with their child. When interviewed, a number of parents said there were times when they wished they could have exchanged roles with their spouse (i.e., the one working to be at home, and vice versa).

Eighty-eight individual mothers and fathers reported that they knew their job performance was adversely affected by worries about their child. Although many found coworkers to be responsive and supportive, these parents were unable to concentrate as well, were distracted easily, and made more mistakes than usual; they expressed much gratitude toward their employers for their understanding.

Financial Issues

A large number of families (88 percent) had at least some form of health insurance coverage for the medical costs incurred. Also, during the years that our sample was in active treatment, outpatient care at our facility (The Jimmy Fund Clinic) was free to all children, regardless of income. This is no longer the case, although no one is denied treatment for financial reasons. Nevertheless, most children had had one or more inpatient hospitalizations, required medicines, and often needed specialized equipment (e.g., wheelchairs, prostheses). Nine percent found these to be burdensome expenses.

Eight families, 7 percent, still had leftover medical debts by the time of our interviews, and a comparison of the 8 former patients in these families with the other 109 former patients showed a striking difference in Combined Adjustment Rating, the 8 in question tending to be less well adjusted than the other 109 ($t = 1.84$, with 115 df, $p = .05$, one-tailed test). We were aware that patients from poorer families tended to fare less well, and this finding provides additional data on that point.

Most of the parents found the cumulative nonmedical expenses a financial burden. Chief among these was transportation, since few families lived very near the Medical Center; this problem was mentioned by 87 percent of the families. These costs consisted primarily of automobile expenses plus parking. Other expenses high on the list were eating away from home (54 percent); overnight expenses when necessary (28 percent); and baby-sitting costs for the other children (27 percent). All told, 4.3 percent took out personal loans or second mortgages on their homes in order to meet expenses, and many others reported that plans for family savings were erased or revised downward. Some families (14 percent) did get additional assistance from governmental or social agencies, but a few never knew that such help was available. A few who did refused such support, preferring to meet the expenses themselves in spite of clear eligibility. A full 76 percent of the families paid at least some of the direct medical expenses themselves.

Other Issues

Many parents expressed the feeling that the child had lost something in school. Although most of the children had not repeated grades, a few parents thought some teachers had been too demanding or too lenient, and that it might have been better for the child to have repeated a grade. Conversely, a few other parents reported particularly thoughtful and appropriate responses by teachers who encouraged a child's strengths. Some parents thought peer relationships had changed and described their child as being either more or less outgoing than before treatment. Many parents observed that their child had been most bothered by visible impairments, including scars, during the period of early adolescence. They frequently described a summer when their son or daughter would not wear a bathing suit, or a year in which they were unhappy about participating in gym.

More positive observations included parents' descriptions of their children as being more self-assured with adults and new situations than could be expected at the child's age. Many parents described their child as being more understanding, sympathetic, and helpful to others with problems than expected, an observation that seemed related to the fact that many of the former patients expressed an interest in human service occupations.

Postresearch Follow-Up

All of the former patients and parents who participated in this study were asked if they had any questions of the research team. Many had questions about current and future functioning, as well as past treatment. Families with medical questions were referred to a pediatric oncologist and related specialists.

As noted in Table 5-1, 47 percent of the former patients had at least mild adjustment problems. Those who had moderate to severe emotional problems were offered assistance with them in the form of an extended evaluation by the psychosocial team, and when appropriate and desired, referrals were made to therapeutic resources nearer their home. These resources were primarily Vocational Rehabilitation Commission offices or mental health professionals or facilities.

All families were contacted by telephone or letter from one to three months after the research interviews in order to address any additional questions they might have and to inquire about any problems evoked by participation in the study. No family expressed a negative response to the experience. Indeed, most parents said that the interview was the first time they felt they had ever talked meaningfully about the experience. It gave them the opportunity to discuss many personal feelings that they had not shared before. They said participation had helped to clarify their own feelings, articulate leftover questions in order to get some answers, and put the experience in better perspective. They were glad to be part of the study and expressed the hope that it would help others facing the same experience.

Summary

Extensive interviews with 190 parents, including 16 interviewed by telephone or mailed questionnaire, representing 119 children who survived cancer revealed:

1. Marriages tended to be stable over time; no parents reported that their child's cancer played a major role in inducing marital discord.

2. Parental income and family socioeconomic status were correlated with the overall psychological adjustment of the child. The lower the economic status, the higher was the likelihood of adjustment problems.

3. The parents' continuing concerns about their child included worries about the long-term effects of treatment, recurrence of cancer, the child's reproductive capacity, and the child's overall physical condition. The frequency of parental concerns was correlated with our independently obtained Combined Adjustment Rating of the child. The more concerned the parents were, the more likely the child was to be rated as having problems.

4. Points in the natural history of cancer treatment which were most stressful included being told the initial diagnosis, which was accompanied by an emotional shock lasting three to twelve months; changes in treatment; disease recurrences; hospitalizations; and the elective cessation of treatment.

5. Parents tended to use their usual coping mechanisms for dealing with the stresses of childhood cancer, although hope and open communication seemed to be the most important.

6. Parents' recommendations to caregivers included the following:
   a. Factual, direct communication about the patient's condition and information about cancer should routinely be provided, with special information on financial resources and assessment of the family's emotional support system.
   b. The diagnosis should first be told to the parents, then the parents and physician together should tell the diagnosis to the child at the beginning of treatment.

7. Parents' recommendations for other parents included:
   a. Parents should seek the best medical care available, meaning that they should take the child to a medical center specializing in the treatment of childhood cancer, rather than simply relying on local physicians whose experience with childhood cancer is likely to be limited.
   b. Parents should ask questions and realize that no question is foolish.
   c. Parents should tell their child about the diagnosis and what is happening as soon as possible.
   d. Parents should have hope; children do survive cancer.
   e. Parents should treat their child as if he or she is going to live, that is to say, try not to overindulge or overprotect the child.
   f. Parents should actively seek someone to talk with about their feelings.

Chapter 8

Interviews with Brothers and Sisters

When a child is seriously ill with cancer, all members of the family are affected. The psychosocial literature on childhood cancer suggests that the healthy sisters and brothers of a sick child may be especially vulnerable to the stress created by life-threatening illness in the family (see Chapter 1, especially Binger et al., 1969; Binger, 1973; Kaplan et al., 1976; Cairns et al., 1979). For the most part, researchers have relied on some form of parental report for data on which to base both descriptions of the nature of the cancer experience for the patients' healthy siblings and assessment of the effect of that experience on siblings' psychosocial adjustment.

Frequent behavior problems among siblings after the child's death have been reported, based on data from interviews with parents (Binger et al., 1969; Kaplan et al., 1976). Many investigators have described a variety of problems among siblings of children undergoing active treatment: heightened jealousy, anger, feelings of abandonment, and guilt. These problems were reported by parents in research interviews (Friedman et al., 1963; Chodoff et al., 1964; Kaplan et al., 1973; F. L. Johnson et al., 1979).

Lavigne and Ryan (1979) recently assessed psychological adjustment among well siblings of children with a variety of chronic illnesses, including a group of sixty children with leukemia. The assessments were based on scores from a paper-and-pencil behavior checklist used by parents to describe their children. These investigators conclude that siblings of chronically ill children are at risk for adjustment and behavior problems. They also note that various illnesses differ in the extent of negative effect on well siblings.

We are aware of only one study which has collected data from the siblings

By Janis L. Gogan and Leslie A. Slavin.

themselves. Cairns et al. (1979) administered a variety of projective and objective psychological tests to schoolaged cancer patients and their healthy brothers and sisters. The results suggest that siblings experience significant distress in a number of areas, including perceived vulnerability to illness and injury, perceived social isolation, general anxiety, and fear of confronting family members with negative feelings.

Our study of survivors of childhood cancer provided an opportunity to investigate the cancer experience of survivors' sisters and brothers through direct interviews with the siblings themselves. This research differs from previous investigations in that we asked siblings to describe their current and past experiences and feelings about the patient and the illness (see also Gogan et al., 1977). Although the results of these interviews have the limitations inherent in self-report and retrospective data, the reports of the siblings may be helpful in forming an understanding of the present, personal reality for siblings of cancer survivors as a group. The data may also suggest new directions for future research and intervention with cancer patients' healthy sisters and brothers.

Participants

Fifty-one brothers and 50 sisters of former cancer patients participated in our study. The 101 siblings represented 55 of the 117 survivors included in the research project. All of the siblings interviewed met the following criteria:

1. Permission to interview was given to us by the survivor and the parents;

2. All were at least 7 years of age at the time of interview and were willing to be interviewed;

3. All were geographically available for interviewing (i.e., within a day's travel);

4. All were born before cancer was diagnosed in the survivor and were thus part of the family during the treatment period, except that because the leukemia patients in our sample were treated for up to 150 months—over 12 years—all their available siblings were interviewed, regardless of birthdate.

Table 8–1 summarizes the data on the siblings' ages at the time of diagnosis and research interview, sibling–survivor age differences, and sibling birth order. It should be noted that many older siblings who were no longer living at home were unavailable for study. As a result, the sample interviewed is younger than the larger potential sample of all living siblings of the 117 survivors seen.

Method

The siblings were interviewed by a research associate (J. L. G.) using a semistructured format including both forced-choice and open-ended questions. Participants were asked about their memories of the diagnosis and treatment period and their thoughts and feelings about the effect of the cancer experience on themselves and on the survivor. In addition, most of the siblings (83) completed the Death Anxiety Questionnaire (Conte et al., 1975). Some of the participants were interviewed at the Sidney Farber Cancer Institute; others preferred to be interviewed at home.

Results

Understanding the Diagnosis

In order to assess their current understanding of the survivor's diagnosis, the siblings were asked to explain what had been the matter with the patient, and why he or she had had to come to the treatment center. Thirty-six percent of those interviewed used the word "tumor" to describe the patient's disease. Many of these

Table 8-1 Characteristics of Siblings

	N	Mean	S.D.	Range
Age of Siblings (Years)				
At survivor's diagnosis	101	6.5	5.4	0–21
At interview	101	17.8	6.2	7–34
Sibling-Survivor Age Difference[a] (Years)				
Older than survivor	43	4.1	2.9	1–11
Younger than survivor	53	4.5	3	1–14

	N		% of Sample
Birth Position of Siblings			
Oldest	33		32.7
Middle	54		53.5
Youngest	14		13.9

[a]Four siblings were twins of survivors; one stepsibling was the same age as the survivor.

were among the 76 percent of siblings who identified the survivor's illness as a form of "cancer." The other 24 percent did not appear to know that the survivor had had cancer. Siblings were probed for specific details about the nature of the illness, and their level of understanding was rated as "good," "fair," or "poor." The majority (58 percent) were rated as having a "fair" understanding of the disease. These siblings were aware both that the survivor had had cancer or a "tumor" and that this illness was life-threatening. Twenty-two percent of the siblings did not demonstrate such awareness and were rated as having a "poor" understanding of the diagnosis. The 20 percent of the siblings rated as having a "good" understanding of the diagnosis met the criteria for a "fair" understanding and in addition were able to explain that cancer is a systemic disease which can spread to different parts of the body. These siblings often exhibited detailed knowledge of the survivor's specific form of cancer as well and used relatively sophisticated terminology in describing it. Although ratings of the siblings' understanding took account of the participants' age by assessing explanations in terms of age-appropriate vocabulary, understanding of the diagnosis is significantly related to siblings age both at diagnosis and at interview, as shown in Table 8-2.

The level of understanding of the illness among the siblings can be taken as a rather crude indication of the amount of open communication within the family about the illness. Most of the survivors seen in our study were treated at a time when parents were advised to protect both the patient and the young siblings from knowledge of the illness and prognosis. The high percentage of siblings who knew

Table 8-2 Relationship of Sibling Age to Reported Understanding of the Diagnosis and Memories of the Cancer Experience

	Age at Diagnosis				Age at Interview			
	0–5	6–10	11–15	16–21	6–12	13–17	18–22	23–34
Understanding of the Diagnosis								
Good	7	4	3	6	0	7	3	10
Fair	28	17	9	3	13	17	15	12
Poor	16	5	1	0	11	9	2	0
chi square = 17.8,* 6 df					26,** 6 df			
Memories of the Diagnosis								
Many	2	7	9	9	0	4	5	18
Some	6	12	4	0	3	8	7	4
None	40	6	0	0	19	18	9	0
chi square = 71,** 6 df					51.2,** 6 df			
Memories of the Treatment								
Many	4	2	9	7	1	7	8	15
Some	34	13	4	2	16	18	12	7
None	14	11	0	0	7	8	1	0
chi square = 35.5,** 6 df					28.7,** 6 df			

Note. Some responses could not be coded.
* p = .01.
** p = .001.

the survivor had been treated for "cancer" and who demonstrated a fair-to-good understanding of the diagnosis at interview may suggest either that parents had abandoned attempts to shield the siblings from this information or that such attempts were unsuccessful. Because of our informed-consent requirement that the survivor know the diagnosis in order to participate in our study, some of the siblings, along with the patient, were informed of the nature of the illness a few days or weeks before the research interviews. However, we did not require that siblings know the diagnosis in order to participate in the project.

The higher level of understanding demonstrated by the older siblings may reflect the parents' tendency to give more information to older children who they feel need less protection. Some of the older siblings reported that their parents told them the nature of the patient's condition early on and asked for their help in shielding the patient from the truth about the diagnosis. A protective attitude endures in some of the siblings' relationships with the survivors.

Siblings who were not given very much information at the time of diagnosis and treatment recalled feeling uncomfortable when they asked questions about the sick brother or sister. A brother, aged 17 at the time of interview, recounted: "I was afraid they would say they didn't want to talk about it." This sense of contraint within the family about the subject of the patient's illness seems often to endure long after active treatment has stopped. A 17-year-old sister who admits she still has unanswered questions about her sibling's illness reported, "We just don't bother talking about it in the family, since it's all over with."

Opinions on Telling versus Not Telling   Because the issue of whether to tell the patient and siblings the cancer diagnosis has generated considerable controversy, siblings were directly asked their opinion about this question. Sixty-seven percent said they believe even young cancer patients should be accurately informed about their diagnosis, treatment, and prognosis. Twelve percent believe that patients should not be told, and 14 percent said "Maybe they should be told," often suggesting specific criteria, such as telling patients "only if they ask" or "only if they are over 10 years old." Six percent of the siblings said they did not know how this should be handled. Similarly, when asked about telling patients' young sisters and brothers, 65.5 percent of the participants responded that siblings should also be informed about the patient's diagnosis, details of the treatment, and prognosis. "Maybe they should be told" was the response of 14.5 percent, and 11 percent said siblings should not be given such information. Nine percent of the siblings asked did not offer an opinion on the subject.

Siblings' Memories of the Cancer Experience

The siblings were asked to relate what they remember about the time the survivor first became sick and to recall details about the illness. They tended to remember more about the period of the survivor's treatment than about the time of diagnosis. Whereas nearly half (48.4 percent) had no memories of the time of diagnosis, only 16 percent had no memories of the treatment period. Thirty-one percent of the siblings were able to relate two or more specific incidents from this period. A majority (53 percent) related at least some recollection (one or two incidents) of the patient's illness. Clear and detailed memories (more than two specific details) of the time of diagnosis were recounted by 28.4 percent of the siblings, and an additional 23.2 percent were able to recall something (one or two details) about the time of the diagnosis.

Because patients' young sisters and brothers often were not told about the seriousness of the illness at the outset, it is not surprising that the time of diagnosis, which parents often remember so vividly, was not as salient for many siblings. Moreover, many of the siblings were infants and a few had not yet been born when the patient was diagnosed. The lengthy treatment period was far more likely to disrupt the entire household both practically and emotionally, and thus leave a lasting impression, even on very young children.

The problem of the reliability of retrospective data plays a role in assessing all of the siblings' memories of the cancer experience. The average interval between the end of the survivor's treatment and the sibling interviews was twelve years. Clearly, siblings' memories of the diagnosis and treatment period cannot be expected to be either complete or strictly accurate, although the reported memories can be seen as representing the personal reality of the siblings themselves. Interestingly, we noted that siblings who were very young during diagnosis and treatment and who come from families that discuss the cancer experience openly tended to recount as "memories" events which they would have been too young to recall as first-hand experience. These incidents have probably become family stories and now seem like actual memories to the participants.

Despite this tendency, age is a significant factor in how much the siblings were able to remember about the cancer experience. As shown in Table 8-2, siblings who were older at the time of the interview had significantly more memories from both the time of diagnosis and the treatment period. Similarly, those who were older when the cancer was discovered also remembered more about the time of diagnosis.

Older siblings' more vivid memories can be attributed to a variety of factors. One practical consideration is the longer attention span of older participants and their willingness to relate more material in the interview. In general, older children tended to be more aware of the effect of the illness on family life at the time of diagnosis and treatment. As noted above, parents are more likely to share distressing information with older children early on, and to give them extra responsibility for child care and household chores during the patient's illness. Whereas a number of older siblings recall taking on adult responsibilities when their parents left them in charge of the other healthy children in the family, many of those who were younger at diagnosis remember the disruption of family routine caused by the illness as only a temporary upset.

Sometimes the disruption of the sibling's life caused by the patient's illness was much more profound than simply taking on extra responsibilities or adjusting to a new household routine. For example, one brother in this sample interrupted his college education and then found himself isolated from his friends when he returned home to help his family during the sibling's treatment for leukemia.

A number of problems seemed to be fairly common experiences during cancer treatment and were recounted by many of the siblings. They often recalled with disappointment that they were not allowed to visit the patient in the hospital because of age restrictions. Some siblings had problems with other children at school. Occasionally they found themselves having to defend their brother or sister from ridicule for baldness or physical impairment or some other side effect of treatment. In a few other cases, misinformed neighborhood parents instructed their children to stay away from the cancer patient's siblings, feeling they were "contaminated." A few siblings felt that they had been called upon to act as a major source of emotional support for one of their parents through the cancer experience.

Jealousy and Guilt

Siblings were questioned about feelings of jealousy and guilt they might have experienced. They were also asked about their current feelings toward the survivor. Almost a fourth of the siblings interviewed (24.5 percent) said they had felt jealous of the patient during the time of active treatment, and 19 percent admitted some residual feelings of jealousy. There were very few reports of past or current guilt feelings. Only 5 percent remembered feeling guilty at the time of treatment.

The incidence of jealousy among siblings during the treatment period is related to their age at the diagnosis, as shown in Table 8-3. Siblings who were aged 6 to 10 at the time of diagnosis reported feeling jealous while the patient was sick significantly more often than any other age group. However, neither age at diagnosis nor age at interview is significantly related to the incidence of reported current jealousy or to the frequency of reported past or current guilt feelings among these siblings.

For the most part, siblings reported that some of their jealousy evolved in response to special privileges and extra attention given to the patient. Some siblings believe that the survivor has been overprotected or that parents have demanded less from the survivor than from the siblings. One sister complained: "I always think I do more than she does." Jealousy arising from the central role the survivor often plays in the family is related to feelings, among a few of the siblings, that they were abandoned or "left out" during the illness.

In many cases, participants reported that they felt jealous during the treatment period when they did not understand the seriousness of the patient's situation. They often said that since learning more about the illness and returning to normality in their family life they no longer feel especially jealous of the former patient. Some jealousy and rivalry among siblings is normal in all families. Our findings suggest that normal jealousy can be heightened when one child in the family is seriously ill. In addition, the experiences of the siblings in our study support the notion that brothers and sisters of sick children can resolve their more intense feelings of jealousy if they are helped to understand the special needs of the patient and if they are reassured that they, too, are important and loved.

Table 8-3 Relationship of Sibling Age to Reports of Remembered and Residual Jealousy

	Age at Diagnosis				Age at Interview			
	0–5	6–10	11–15	16–21	6–12	13–17	18–22	23–34
Jealousy during Treatment								
Some	7	12	3	2	1	9	1	3
None	44	13	10	7	18	25	19	19
Chi Square = 10.7,* 3df					4.75, 3df, N.S.			
Jealousy at Interview								
Some	11	5	2	1	4	6	8	6
None	41	21	11	8	20	27	12	15
Chi Square = 0.63, 3 df, N.S.					4.29, 3 df, N.S.			

Note. Some responses could not be coded.
*p = .01.

Similarly, guilt feelings among siblings seem to be directly related to lack of information and a consequently poor understanding of the patient's illness. Guilt feelings may be harbored by siblings too young to understand fully how illness is caused, who believe they are somehow responsible for their sister's or brother's disease. Each of the five siblings in our study who recalled feelings of guilt during the treatment period also indicated that neither the subject of cancer nor feelings in general were open topics of conversation in their families. Since there were far more families with communication problems in our study than there were siblings who reported feeling guilty, a lack of open family communication may not be a sufficient condition to produce feelings of guilt. However, we hypothesize that it is probably a necessary condition. Our findings support the idea that a family which openly and actively seeks and discusses information and which shares feelings about the illness is less likely to produce such side effects as guilt-ridden siblings.

Most of those participants who remember feeling guilty had learned they were not to blame for causing or exacerbating their sibling's cancer by the time of our interview. However, the guilt-producing effect which misunderstanding and lack of communication can sometimes have on siblings is illustrated rather poignantly by the one participant who still felt guilty about the illness when interviewed as part of our project. When his sister, aged 17 at interview, was 4 years old, her mother instructed her to watch over her infant brother. The baby managed to fall downstairs and when taken to the hospital for x-rays was diagnosed as having Wilms's tumor. The sister was "protected" from the fact that her brother had cancer. She was told by her parents that because of his fall, one of his kidneys had to be removed. Since that time she has felt guilty for having "caused" her brother's condition. Thirteen years later this sister learned that he had been treated for cancer. Since no one told her at that time that cancer is not caused by a fall, she naturally assumed that she had been responsible for causing his malignancy. The brother also had assumed that she was responsible for the physical restrictions placed on him because of his missing kidney, such as his inability to play high school contact sports.

Anxiety

The difficulty of coping with long-term uncertainty and anxiety about recurrence inherent in the experience of cancer survival is an issue of much concern. Such anxiety in the family might be expected to affect patients' siblings in a variety of ways. This topic was addressed indirectly in two parts of the sibling interview. Siblings were asked if they ever worry about getting cancer themselves. They were also questioned about their lingering concerns for the survivor and asked how they think their sister or brother may have changed as a result of having had cancer. In addition, 83 of the study participants completed a Death Anxiety Questionnaire as discussed in Chapter 3.

Approximately one-third of the 101 siblings seen stated that they had worried about getting cancer themselves during the patient's cancer treatment. Only 13 percent reported that this remained a worry for them at the time of our interview. Siblings offered a variety of reasons why they do not continue to worry about getting cancer, such as: "I try not to think negatively," "I've thought about it occasionally, but there are too many other things to be worried about." Often, a sibling's worry about getting cancer is related to an idea about the etiology of the disease. One brother attributes his brother's cancer to pure chance: "His number came up, he's a statistic." This young man sees no good reason to worry about whether he might be unlucky as well, since the matter is beyond his control. One little girl thinks her sister got cancer because she was born prematurely. The girl does not worry for herself because she is not the product of a premature birth.

Siblings' mean score on the Death Anxiety Questionnaire is within the normal range (Conte et al., 1975; Koocher et al., 1976). Interestingly, it is somewhat higher than the overall score of the sample of long-term survivors, suggesting slightly greater anxiety among the siblings than among the former patients themselves.

When asked to describe their perceptions of the extent to which cancer has affected the survivor's life, personality, goals, and activities, a majority of the siblings (58 percent) said that the survivor had changed in some way as a result of the disease, an additional 13 percent stating that the cancer experiences had had a marked effect on their sister or brother. Many of those interviewed discussed the survivor's self-consciousness about scars or more serious impairments, such as the loss of a limb or scoliosis secondary to treatment. Others described the survivor as being more shy, more nervous, more tearful, more "emotional," more dependent on parents, or "spoiled." One sibling said that his brother "probably felt doomed to die" and therefore "tried to get in all the experiences he could" while he was still alive. These "experiences" included running away from home and a variety of irresponsible and delinquent activities.

Many of the siblings noted some positive effects of the cancer experience on the former patient. One young child felt that her sister's treatment-related blindness had improved her memory and her hearing. Others said the survivor now is more courageous, more self-confident, or more conscious of taking care of his or her health. A few noted that their siblings are "repaying society"—for having their lives saved—by choosing careers in medicine or related fields. Two sisters believe their brother has a "special purpose in life" because he was cured of cancer. At home he is regarded as a hero who courageously fought and won the battle against cancer.

Summary

In addition to the unique stories told by each of the 101 siblings interviewed, a number of common threads emerged:

1. Having a brother or sister with cancer had a sustained and profound impact on their lives.
2. Emotional concerns such as feeling left out, jealousy, resentment, and fears for their own health were relatively common in the siblings.
3. It may be that siblings aged 6–10 at the time of cancer treatment are particularly vulnerable to feelings of rivalry and the attendant difficulties.
4. Closed communication systems in families may contribute to the development of behavioral and emotional problems among the cancer patient's siblings.

5. Many of the siblings' problems could apparently have been prevented or ameliorated by providing direct factual information at the time of diagnosis and during treatment.

6. Some siblings reported positive aspects of the cancer experience, including feelings of enhanced closeness to the former patient or other family members. Other reported positive aspects included enhancement of their own emotional growth and development of personal coping skills.

7. Most siblings appear to have resolved any anger toward the patient over time, once the treatment ended. Normal sibling relationships seem to have been restored in most cases.

8. Siblings should clearly not be neglected by the treatment team during the course of a child's illness. They should be seen as an integral part of a whole-family approach to treatment, and acknowledged as important participants in the family's life throughout the illness.

Chapter 9

The Special Problems of Survivors

Thus far, this book has dealt with some of the more obvious psychological consequences of surviving childhood cancer. There are also a number of less obvious but no less stressful issues which the maturing survivor must confront as she or he enters the mainstream of adult society. These include (1) the meaning of residual physical impairments resulting from the cancer treatments, (2) the prospects for social acceptance and marriage, (3) the ease of entry into the work place, (4) the ability to obtain health and life insurance and (5) the matter of family communications and the long-range impact that patterns of openness or secrecy may have on the survivor's psychological adjustment.

This chapter explores these issues in some detail.

Physical and Visible Impairment

Background

As a result of the invasive nature of current treatments for childhood malignancies, some survivors may be left with residual physical disabilities (H. A. Holmes and Holmes, 1975; Jaffe, 1975; Li and Stone, 1976). These could include scoliosis, amputations, scars, sterility, and chronic suppression of the immune system. A number of other investigators have suggested possible relationships between psychological adjustment and a wide range of physical disabilities in childhood (Mattsson, 1972; Pless, et al., 1972; Sandberg, 1976; Steinhausen, 1976).

Pless and Roghmann (1971) compared results from three epidemiological studies of large populations of children. The rate of psychological maladjustment was significantly higher among children with physical disorders than among healthy

By Gerald P. Koocher, John E. O'Malley, and Diana J. Foster.

children in each of the surveys. They also reported that the degree of functional disability experienced by the child, assessed by limitation of normal activities, had a small but direct effect on the formation of behavioral symptoms. Some other studies investigating the relationship between the degree of physical impairment and the level of psychological adjustment have not supported this finding (McAnarney et al., 1974; Seidel et al., 1975). A report by Goldberg (1974) suggests that the visibility of an impairment affects psychological adjustment more than the degree of physical limitation does.

Physical/Visible Impairment Rating

In order to explore the meaning and effect of residual physical impairment on the survivors in our study, we developed a special scale. It was designed to rate both physical and visible impairment to give an objective assessment of the degree to which each person studied is functionally, physically, and visibly impaired at a particular time. Key elements incorporated in the scale are organ integrity, risk of physical dysfunction, independence in performing activities of daily living, and the degree to which the visibility of the impairment might be expected to present a barrier to socialization and vocational choice. The scale is best applied by a health care professional using an accurate and current medical history obtained by direct interview with the patient (and the parents, if the patient is a child).

The scale requires assignment of a score from 0 to 3, increasing with the level of severity, in four separate categories: obviousness of impairment, interference with activities of daily living, need for medical attention or prosthetics, and employability/ability to attend school. The operational definitions and scoring for each category are presented in Appendix D. The scores obtained in each category are summed to obtain an overall rating.

In our study the scale was applied to each of 116 survivors by a biostatistician and a social worker who is also a registered nurse. The biostatistician used data from the medical records, but did not see the participant or talk with the family. The social worker/nurse interviewed the patient or the family or both, but had only minimal medical data available to her. Their independent ratings of the patients were highly correlated (coefficient = .84) but when medical record data and interview material were pooled the two raters agreed perfectly. The distribution of scores is summarized in Table 9-1.

Results

A 2 × 5 contingency table was constructed displaying the distribution of participants in each of the five categories as a function of their psychological adjustment (either "good adjustment" or "adjustment problems," as discussed in Chapter 3). This relationship was found not to be statistically significant (chi square = 3.792; p = .435, with 4 df). The data table was then reorganized into a 2

× 2 format, comparing the two psychological groupings with two physical impairment classes ("none or mild" and "moderate to severe physical/visible impairment); this relationship was also not statistically significant (Fisher's Exact $p = .452$).

Discussion

Contrary to reports in the published literature, among the survivors in our sample the degree of physical impairment resulting from treatment for childhood cancer did not prove to be significantly related to long-term psychological adjustment. Our data suggest that those survivors who do well psychologically do so regardless of the degree of residual impairment or insult. Physical/visible impairment was not a variable which significantly distinguished good copers from the poorer copers. The Combined Adjustment Rating as a function of degree of impairment (arrayed in a 2 × 2 table) was not statistically significant (Fisher's Exact $p =$

Table 9-1 Distribution of Physical/Visible Impairment Rating Scores ($N = 116$)

Score Range	Impairment Rating	N	%
0	None	10	8.6
1	Mild	41	35.4
2–6	Moderate	55	47.4
7–9	Moderately severe	9	7.8
10–12	Severe	1	0.8

.420). Perhaps the most optimisitic interpretation of our data is that invasive treatment per se, including the loss of a limb, an organ, or reproductive function, or some other disfigurement, does not preclude adequate psychological adjustment and is not necessarily a hindrance in the survivor's overall quality of life.

Marriage

Background

Because a number of the survivors in our study were at the age of majority and had married, we decided to explore some of the issues in being a cancer survivor which could be related to the decision to marry. In particular, we wondered about factors which might discriminate between those survivors who chose to marry and those who did not. Special open-ended interviews were held with the spouses of a number of survivors; these interviews focused on a variety of topics, some directly related to marriage and others aimed at broad issues of psychological adaptation.

Particular areas of concern included the future orientation of both survivor and spouse with regard to commitments and planning; the potential for self-concept or body-image problems to inhibit intimacy; worries about infertility and the health of progeny; and factors potentially predictive for the decision to marry.

Marital Statistics

Of the 117 patients in the study sample, 36 were aged 21 or over. We selected 21 as the cutoff point for this analysis because it was the age of the youngest married or engaged survivor in our sample. The mean age of the 36 participants over 21 was 26 years, and the oldest was 37. Sixteen of the 36 had married by the time of our interviews and an additional 4 were engaged or planned to marry within a year. Three had been married and divorced; 2 of these had remarried. The mean age of the married participants was somewhat older than the mean age of the unmarried ones, as might be expected: 28 and 24 years respectively.

For the purpose of analysis the engaged participants are included with the married ones, and their partners are referred to as spouses. We assumed that the engaged participants had made an emotional commitment which made them more comparable to the married survivors than to the single ones, and little would be gained by creation of a subgroup numbering only four. The age of the spouse was generally equivalent to the age of the survivor.

Procedure

Thirteen of the twenty spouses were interviewed. There are no reasons to believe that they are not also representative of the seven who were unavailable for interview. Most of the spouses accompanied the participant to our offices on the day of the interview and were interviewed privately by a research assistant while the participant and family were interviewed in adjoining offices. The interview was semistructured and open-ended, designed to elicit specific responses to questions about how the spouse learned of the cancer diagnosis, how this knowledge influenced the decision to marry the survivor, the nature of the current marital relationship, and cancer-related concerns. The interviews, which lasted from one to two hours, were recorded verbatim.

Results of Content Interview

Information about the Diagnosis came from the survivor for ten of the thirteen spouses during the dating period, usually before they became engaged. If the survivor had a visible handicap, he or she was likely to discuss the cancer history relatively early in dating. A few spouses reported that they learned the diagnosis from other sources, such as mutual acquaintances. In three cases, the spouse-to-be was actually told the details of the diagnosis before the patient was (see section below, "Communicating the Cancer Diagnosis").

The Decision to Marry was not affected by the cancer diagnosis for nine of the thirteen spouses. The remaining four reported that they had hesitated initially because they did not know whether the survivor could have healthy children. Two had also felt that sexual relations would be difficult because of the survivor's physical limitation; both survivors were amputees (one had lost a leg, the other an arm). Some spouses noted that their friends or relatives had discouraged growing intimacy.

Effects of Cancer on the Survivor and the Marriage were perceived variously by the spouses. Five spouses felt that having cancer had no particular effect on the survivor. Four spouses felt that having had cancer was "good" for the survivor, because he or she became more persistent, considerate, or understanding. The remaining four spouses reported a variety of negative effects which they believed were directly related to the survivor's cancer experience. These ranged from a spouse's report of serious psychological problems (two survivors) to milder difficulties, including occasional tension, emotional withdrawal, short temper, decreased appetite, insomnia, and anxiety about disease recurrence.

Six of the thirteen spouses felt the survivor's cancer experience did not affect their relationship. One spouse felt that cancer "has brought us closer together." Five reported mildly negative effects on their marriage. For example, one woman reported that during her first pregnancy she feared that the baby would also get cancer. Another reported that the sexual relationship suffered initially, until she and her husband shared their feelings about his amputation. Two others reported a markedly negative impact on their marriage, because the survivor periodically became depressed and withdrew from daily activities.

Children and Health Issues were also prominent concerns of the spouses. Of the sixteen married survivors, twelve had had children (a total of twenty-six children), and an additional survivor was pregnant at the time of the interview. Of the remaining three, one had divorced after a marriage of less than a year. Thus only two of the currently married couples are classified as child-free.

All spouses with children (ten of the spouses interviewed) reported that their children have developed normally, without any serious health problems. Many spouses reported that they had worried about the survivor's potential sterility, but all had been encouraged to try to have children by the doctors at the cancer center. Three of the spouses reported being more "lump-conscious" and taking their children to the doctor more often than others because they fear the possibility of cancer.

Nine of the spouses reported that they urge the survivor to see a doctor more often than they would others. A few expressed the belief that "Lightning doesn't strike twice in the same place" and claim not to worry about the former patient's health. None of the spouses appeared to realize that cancer survivors have an increased risk of a recurrence or a second cancer, as discussed in Chapter 2. Ten of the spouses reported that while they are concerned about the patient's health, their own health habits have not changed.

Results of Comparisons

Almost half of the group of former patients over age 21 have not married or become engaged. By way of comparison, national statistics reveal that 77.5 percent of American males and 76.1 percent of American females aged 17 to 64 marry. Although it is not unusual for young adults to remain single, the choice might provide clues to the survivors' coping styles. If certain consequences of cancer are associated with a deviation from typical adult development, then well-timed psychotherapeutic intervention in the course of routine medical follow-up care of these persons might be indicated. To determine what, if any, differences exist between childhood cancer survivors who have married or become engaged and those who have not, three hypotheses were formulated:

Hypothesis 1: The greater the severity of a former patient's physical limitations due to cancer, the less likely he or she is to marry.

Hypothesis 2: The more obvious the visible impairment (whether or not the impairment is physically limiting), the less likely the former patient is to marry. Because of social stereotypes, women are more affected by visible impairment than men.

Hypothesis 3: Married survivors are better adjusted than never married survivors.

Physical limitation scores were assigned using data obtained from sections B, C, and D of the Physical/Visible Impairment Rating Scale (Appendix D). Visible impairment scores were assigned using the data obtained from section A of the same instrument. The Mann-Whitney U statistic was applied to determine statistical significance. As predicted, never married females had significantly higher physical limitation scores than married females ($U = 5$; significant at $p = .01$). Males, however, showed the opposite tendency: married males had significantly higher physical limitation scores than never-married males ($U = 25.5$; significant at $p = .05$).

With respect to the visible impairment scores, the results were also as predicted. Never married females had higher scores than married females ($U = 11$; significant at $p = .05$). Married males had higher scores than never married males, and this relationship approached, but did not attain significance ($U = 28.5$).

Similar statistical analyses do not reveal significant differences between the married and the never married in average Combined Adjustment Ratings. However, when the ratings were combined into two categories ($0–1$ = well; and $2–9$

= some evidence of symptoms), analysis did reveal a significant difference between married and never married former patients, the never married having more symptoms (Fisher's Exact p = .0544). Scores of males and females did significantly differ. These data are summarized in Table 9-2.

Table 9-2   Survivors over 21: Combined Adjustment Rating as a Function of Martial Status (N = 36)

Marital Status[a]	Sex	Combined Rating Frequencies		Mean[b]	S.D.	N
		0–1	2–9			
Married or engaged	M	5	5	1.9	2.8	10
	F	5	5	2.1	2.9	10
	Both	10	10	2.0	2.8	20
Never married	M	2	8	2.5	2.0	10
	F	1	5	2.5	2.3	6
	Both	3	13	2.5	2.1	16

[a]Married and Never Married categories arrayed in a 2 × 2 table with Combined Adjustment Ratings of 0–1 and 2–9 yield Fisher's Exact p = .0544.
[b]The mean Combined Adjustment Ratings do not differ significantly by sex.

Discussion

Interviews with the husbands, wives, and engaged partners of former cancer patients have provided us with some interesting data about the quality of the survivors' adult lives. Although many of the married survivors appear to have happy and secure lives, less than half of the spouses reported that the cancer experience had no effect on their marriage. Clearly, a life-threatening illness affects the survivor and those around him or her, even many years after treatment.

The difficulties mentioned by some spouses may or may not have resulted from the patients' cancer experience. The cross-sectional interviews we have reported were not designed to seek causal relationships. We can note with enthusiasm that many former patients appear to have emerged from a trying childhood experience into an adulthood which on the surface is indistinguishable from that of other Americans.

The two problems most often discussed by the spouses were the survivor's ability to conceive children and the sexual relationship. The former issue ought to be thoroughly addressed by the patient's physician as soon as it is possible to assess the patient's fertility or childbearing capacity.

Comments about sexuality were related to cultural norms of attractiveness. Wives' concern about their husbands' impairment seemed to stem from their uncertainty about the more aggressive role they felt they might have to take in lovemaking. Survivor's husbands were generally less concerned about sexual issues than were survivors' wives, perhaps because most of the married survivor females had relatively minor physical impairments. Open communcation alleviated most sexual problems.

The comparison of married with never married survivors raises difficult issues. Why do women with physical limitations and visible impairments tend not to marry, while men with similar handicaps marry more often than men without physical residuals? In the case of the men, the difference may be a function of age, since the never married men average more than five years younger than the married men. The never married women, who did not differ significantly from the married women in age, were probably unable to attain cultural standards of feminine attractiveness. This may result in lowered self-esteem and become a handicap if the women do not take an assertive role in establishing relationships with men. Men with impairments, however, may overcome their limitations by pursuing the culturally accepted masculine norm of assertiveness in developing relationships with women. Social stereotypes may result in males with obvious impairments being seen as "stronger" by virtue of having survived a trauma, whereas females may be regarded as "damaged" victims.

Carter and Glick (1976) have focused on all serious chronic physical limitations and have generally found that persons with such handicaps have substantially reduced chances of marriage. The women with chronic impairments who do marry tend to be those with the least severe types. For men with chronic impairments, the same researchers suggest that the ability to work (and earn a living), not the visibility of the impairment, is the critical variable bearing on marriage.

The lack of a statistically significant relationship between marital status and the Combined Adjustment Rating indicated that never married survivors are not coping demonstrably worse than their married counterparts, even though a greater proportion exhibited mild symptoms. However, we must note that twenty-three out of thirty-six patients aged 21 or older had some psychological symptoms, even though many are able to function well in spite of these mild difficulties.

Employment

Background

The majority of the former patients interviewed for this project have no residual physical impairments visible to others. Most have no substantial physical or medical limitations on their activities. Some, however, encountered employment discrimination solely on the basis of their cancer history when they began to enter the adult world of work. Most of the existing literature on the subject of employment discrimination against the recovered cancer patient has focused on adults, rather than former child cancer patients.

Reports of the extent to which adult cancer patients experience employment discrimination vary widely. Dietz (1978) quotes the American Cancer Society as reporting that of cancer patients who subsequently seek work, 90 percent experience employment discrimination; a National Cancer Institute report (Counts et al., 1976) gives an employment discrimination incidence of 23 percent among adult cancer survivors. Part of the variability is a definitional problem. Discrimination may take many forms. A person may be told that he or she is the chosen candidate to fill a position, for example, only to be rejected after a preemployment physical examination turns up a cancer history. Some companies have established an arbitrary five-year waiting period before hiring a former cancer patient (McKenna, 1974).

Employers who have responded in studies exploring their attitudes about cancer survivors reflect deeper fears of cancer. In one study, 61 percent cited fear of increases in insurance premiums as a justification for not hiring cancer survivors (Counts et al., 1976), in spite of evidence that neither insurance nor Workman's Compensation rates for the employer would increase (McKenna, 1974). Other reasons for not hiring cancer survivors mentioned by employers included fears about decreased productivity, excessive sick leave, increased absenteeism, longterm disability payments, and the possibility of the employee's sudden death.

Once the survivor has a job, he or she may encounter other difficulties, such as the feeling that perhaps a promotion or opportunity for advanced training was denied because of the cancer history. Cancer survivors may have to settle for lower salaries and restricted fringe benefits because of their illness history (Counts et al., 1976). They may also suffer less tangible problems, including stressful or inappropriate responses or avoidance by coworkers and supervisors stemming from fear of contagion.

Studies of 101 cancer patients and 264 employers conducted by the National Cancer Institute (Counts et al., 1976), of 1417 employees who developed cancer at the American Telephone and Telegraph Company (Stone, 1975), and of 148 job applicants who had a cancer history at the Metropolitan Life Insurance Company (Wheatley et al., 1974) all indicate that the reasons employers cite for discriminating against cancer patients and survivors are unfounded. All measures of employee absenteeism, turnover, and job performance were within normal limits for cancer survivors, and there were no increased insurance costs. As one report noted, "The selective hiring of persons who have been treated for cancer, in positions for which they are physically qualified, is a sound industrial practice" (Wheatley et al., 1974).

The United States military policy on applicants with a history of cancer could not be clearer: automatic disqualification. The basic premise for this policy is to have as fit a military force as possible for the nation's defense. There is a subsidiary concern not to encourage anyone to embark on a career when there is a possibility that he or she will not be able to complete it, as well as a fear that the person may become disabled and thereby dependent on the government for care.

Findings

Sixty of the 117 patients in our sample were over 18 years old at the time of the interview; we focused on this group to explore the employment discrimination problem. Only 8 of the 60 were over 30 years old at the time of the interview. Twenty-nine were women, and except for one black man the sample was white. The group was essentially middle class, measured by Hollingshead's (1957) index, and 15 were married. Thirty-seven had completed some education beyond high school, and 3 were not high school graduates. With respect to types of cancer, levels of adjustment, and related variables, the group does not differ substantially from the full sample of 117 survivors.

Interviewees were asked about their current employment status, employment history, and absenteeism. If problems were reported, a distinction was made between those related solely to the cancer history and those linked to physical limitations. There is an obvious potential for bias in this report, since we made no effort to confirm the events reported. On the other hand, if patients sincerely believe that they have been victims of discrimination the cost to their self-esteem is real, whether or not the episodes reported can be validated.

Forty-six of our 60 survivors were working at the time of the interview. One person was still a full-time high school student and had never applied for a job. Twenty-four reported that they had experienced some form of employment discrimination because of their history of cancer, including 11 who had attempted enlistment and were rejected for military service; 3 had also been denied other jobs because of their cancer history. None believed that the rejection was related to a residual physical impairment.

Table 9-3 tabulates employment status and Combined Adjustment Rating for the 60 participants over 18. Those with good psychosocial adjustment (ratings of 0 or 1) were significantly more likely to be employed than those with psychological problems. It is not possible to say whether the psychological difficulties led to prob-

Table 9-3 Survivors over 18: Combined Adjustment Ratings and Employment ($N = 60$)

Combined Adjustment Rating	Employed	Not Employed	Total
Good adjustment (0–1)	28	4	32
Adjustment problems (2–9)	18	10	28

Note. Fisher Exact $p = 0.0342$.

lems in employment or vice versa; however, it is evident that injury to self-esteem follows in the wake of an employment rejection regarded as cancer-related.

Absenteeism on the job was low in our sample. Of the 46 former patients who were working, 43 were absent fewer than five days during the year preceding the interview, 2 missed from six to fifteen days, and only 1 was absent for sixteen days or more. No one claimed to have been denied promotion or given a lower salary than comparable coworkers or reported any problems with the attitudes of coworkers about cancer. It must be remembered that the adult with cancer and the childhood cancer survivor are in quite different situations: our survivors are many more years beyond diagnosis, are in better general health, are on the whole younger, and have had fewer years of work experience than the adult cancer patients surveyed.

Some of the survivors had chosen not to inform their employer, the medical division at work, or coworkers about their cancer history. They gave various reasons for not telling, such as fear of adverse reactions, feeling that it was a private matter, or simply because they "rarely even think of having had cancer anyway."

Discussion

Although our survivors were younger and in better health than adult cancer patients, they were still subject to society's prejudices and stereotypes about cancer. The blows to self-esteem they experienced are obvious and often parallel those experienced by the adult cancer survivor. Unfortunately, few of those who must confront such problems are aware of the potential resources available to help them.

The employment rights of people with a history of cancer are protected by affirmative action rules and regulations, and free legal assistance is available through the U.S. Department of Labor. Some states have passed similar legislation that forbids employers not covered by federal rules and regulations to discriminate against people with a history of cancer. The armed forces offer the option of requesting a waiver from the office of the Surgeon General, entitling the person to enlist.

Insurance

Background

Life insurance plays an important role in providing for a family's financial security, and health insurance is critical to financial survival in today's world of escalating health care costs. The 60 survivors who were over 18 years old at interview were surveyed on their experiences in applying for life and health insurance. They were asked about current insurance holdings, prior applications for policies, and any problems in getting insurance related to their cancer history.

What literature exists on this topic suggests that employed cancer survivors and their spouses fare reasonably well if covered by group health or life insurance.

Approximately 80 percent hold health insurance in group policies (Ashenburg, 1975). Underwriters of individual health insurance may require a waiting period of up to ten years after diagnosis, may exclude coverage for cancer-related treatment, or may require the cancer survivor to pay a higher premium.

Until 1920, life insurance was flatly denied to the cancer survivor (Ashenburg, 1975). Since then, life insurance companies have increasingly tried to accommodate higher-risk applicants by applying higher premiums, five-year waiting periods, or surcharges based on cancer mortality rates (Entmacher, 1975). Although the surcharges are now set specifically by type and site of cancer and policies are more readily available, the actuarial tables used to determine degree of risk may be somewhat behind more favorable current prognoses (Ashenburg, 1975).

Results

Health Insurance was seen as critically important to the survivors in our study. At interview, 52 of the 60 former patients were covered by some form of health insurance, 7 had no health insurance, and 1 person did not know whether he had insurance coverage.

Problems with health insurance coverage because of their cancer history were reported by 7 of the 60 survivors. Most of our sample were covered by group health insurance policies through an employer. All reported difficulties were with nongroup policies. Five participants had been denied health insurance, and 2 had policies which excluded coverage for any medical care to sites where they had received radiation therapy.

Life Insurance coverage was especially important to the married participants, who were concerned about ensuring their family's financial security. Thirty-eight (63.3 percent) of the 60 had some form of life insurance at the time of interview, 11 did not, and 11 were uncertain. Of those who did have life insurance, 9 had a policy that was obtained on their behalf before the cancer was diagnosed.

Twenty-five former patients had been denied a life insurance policy at least once, 8 had been asked to pay a higher premium than usual, and 6 reported they had been told they must wait anywhere from three to twelve years after diagnosis before they would be granted a life insurance policy. No particular pattern of acceptance or rejection for life insurance coverage emerged from the reports given by this sample. However, many of those who had experienced problems described emotional distress at being rejected. These feelings ranged from mild annoyance to a sense that they had been told they were worthless and were not going to live long anyway. Other survivors reported that they had been able to obtain life insurance after their oncologist wrote a letter to the company involved explaining the particular disease, current physical status, and improved prognosis relative to outdated actuarial data.

Discussion

Forty of the 60 recovered childhood cancer patients in our study believe they have experienced discrimination solely because of their history of cancer at least once in their quest for employment, health insurance, or life insurance. Clearly the socioeconomic problems of the childhood cancer patient are not over when the disease has been controlled. Most were unprepared for such discrimination and talked poignantly of how they were made to feel worthless or at immediate risk. Some believed this meant that their prognosis was poor even when they had survived up to seventeen years with no cancer-related health problems. In addition, most of the survivors and the families interviewed were unaware of their rights and of the remedies available to them. A key aspect of social rehabilitation for these patients and families must be information on how to be an effective consumer and an advocate for oneself with regard to these issues.

Communicating the Cancer Diagnosis

Background

Clinicians and researchers caring for child cancer patients and their families have often discussed the question of open communication with patients. There are those who hold that seriously ill children and their young siblings should be protected from the knowledge that they are confronted with a life-threatening illness; other advocate open discussion of the diagnosis and prognosis with all family members. The historical evolution of views on this topic has been described in Chapter 1.

Although the protective approach to communication with child cancer patients was widely advocated in the fifties and sixties, a more open approach has been adopted in recent years by most of those who care for these children (Gogan et al., 1977). Results of extensive surveys conducted in 1961 (Oken) and 1979 (Novack et al.) demonstrate a dramatic shift in physicians' attitudes toward disclosing the cancer diagnosis to both adult and child patients.

Our study provided an opportunity to approach the "to tell or not to tell" issue in a new way. Implicit in the arguments of those who advocate open communication with the family is the assumption that an honest discussion of the diagnosis and prognosis will ultimately result in better psychosocial adjustment for family members and the patient. We therefore decided to examine the effect of the patient's knowledge of the diagnosis on his or her later psychological adaptation, as reflected in the Combined Adjustment Rating.

The "protective" approach to communicating with patients was the prevailing philosophy of the treatment center during the years when most of the survivors in this investigation were in active treatment (Evans, 1968). Nonetheless, many parents did choose to tell their children the diagnosis; others accepted the advice of the professional caregivers not to do so. As a result, the survivors in this sample had learned of their diagnosis in a variety of circumstances. We hypothesized that survivors who had learned their diagnosis early in their cancer experience would tend to be better adjusted than those who had been intentionally misled and learned they had cancer long after the diagnosis was made.

Calculation of a "When Told" Variable

Many of the survivors' reports of when and how they had learned of the diagnosis varied widely from the reports given by their parents. Both the retrospective nature of the study and selective memories may have contributed to this fact. We assumed, however, that the critical factor would be the child's perception of the event and circumstances, since this perception would form the chief basis for the person's later beliefs. Survivors were divided into three groups on the basis of their responses to questions about how and when they learned their diagnosis and their age at diagnosis. The following criteria were used to assign participants to one of the three groups:

Informed Early: Patient was told the diagnosis by parent or physician within one year; or patient was diagnosed in infancy and was told the diagnosis before age 6.

Informed Late: Patient was not told the diagnosis by parent or physician within one year; or patient was diagnosed in infancy and was not told the diagnosis before age 6.

Self-Informed: Patient was not told the diagnosis by parent or physician before learning it another way (told by peers, read their own hospital charts, figured it out by reading about their disease or from radio or television information).

Table 9-4 shows the number of participants in each of the "when told" groups

Table 9-4   "When Told" Group and Age at Diagnosis (*N* = 114)

When Told	Age at Diagnosis 5 and Under	Mean Interval Between Diagnosis and When Told (years)	Age at Diagnosis 6 and Over	Mean Interval Between Diagnosis and When Told (years)	Total
Informed early	30	1.7	18	.3	48
Informed late	19	9.1	24	5.8	43
Self-informed	10		13		23
Total	59		55		

and the mean interval between the age at diagnosis and the age the child learned the diagnosis for the "early" and "late" categories.

Results

The "When Told" Variable and Combined Adjustment Rating findings, summarized in Table 9-5, are statistically significant but must be interpreted cautiously because of small numbers in several categories. Because of these small numbers, some categories were combined and reanalyzed.

Two Combined Adjustment Rating groups—"good adjustment" (rated 0 or 1) and "adjustment problems" (2 or higher)—were used, as detailed in Chapter 3. Two "when told" groups ("informed early" and "informed late") where then compared for psychosocial adjustment, yielding highly significant results (Fisher's Exact $p = .008$). Because our study showed that survivors who were very young at the time of diagnosis tended to be better adjusted at interview (see Chapter 5),

Table 9-5   Combined Adjustment Rating and "When Told" Group ($N = 114$)

Combined Adjustment Rating	Informed Early	Informed Late	Self-Informed	Total
Well (0–1)	32	18	10	60
Mild (2–3)	6	16	7	29
Moderate (4–5)	6	5	1	12
Impaired (6–9)	4	4	5	13
Total	48	43	23	

Note. Chi square = 12.062, significant at $p = .05$, with 6 df.

this test was repeated for those participants who were diagnosed after age 6 ($N = 42$). These results approached significance ($p = .0589$).

A comparison of the self-informed group and the group told by parents or physicians (early or late) for adjustment was not statistically significant ($p = .416$). However, combining all survivors who were not told the diagnosis early (informed late and self-informed) for comparison on adjustment with those informed early did show high statistical significance ($p = .009$).

Open-Ended Questions dealing with the issue of telling the child the cancer diagnosis were asked in interviews with survivors, their parents, and their siblings. All three groups were asked the question: "Should a child with cancer be told the diagnosis?" The majority of participants stated that the child should be told, including 90.3 percent of parents ($N = 104$), 70.1 percent of survivors ($N = 114$), and 71.1 percent of siblings ($N = 101$). Very few parents (4.85 percent) said the child should not be told; 22.5 percent of survivors and 13.1 percent of their siblings agreed with this view. In addition to believing that children with cancer should be told the diagnosis, most parents said that in ideal circumstances, children should be told as soon as possible (84 percent), a smaller proportion stating that children should be told when they ask (9.9 percent). Parents often added that whatever the circumstances, the child should be told at least by age 10. A majority of the 101 siblings interviewed (65.5 percent) thought that brothers and sisters should be told about the diagnosis as well as the patients; 14.5 percent said "Maybe they should be told"; 10.9 percent said that siblings should not be told; and 9.1 percent said they didn't know.

Discussion

The results of these analyses support the hypothesis that early knowledge of the cancer diagnosis is related to good psychosocial adjustment among long-term survivors of childhood cancer. In addition, the majority of the family members interviewed—survivors, parents, and siblings—believe the child with cancer should be told the diagnosis early, despite the fact that such open communication had been discouraged at the time of the diagnosis years earlier. Many of the parents who did not initially share the diagnosis with their child identify this lack of candor as a source of stress or difficulty both during and after treatment.

Several authors have pointed out that "telling" the child per se is not really the most important issue, and that what should be emphasized is providing a climate of openness and support for the child in dealing with his or her serious concerns (Vernick and Karon, 1965; Waechter, 1971; Spinetta and Maloney, 1975). A primary assumption of our study is that how soon the child was told can be seen as a general indication of family openness both to discussing the disease and its implications and to helping the child cope with fears and anxieties. Of course, it is not possible to show conclusively that such open communication of the diagnosis leads to better long-term psychosocial adjustment in this population, since no data are available about either the children's mental health or family communication patterns before the onset of cancer. In addition, a variety of other factors may affect long-term adjustment in this population. But it appears that by using an open approach with patients professional caregivers can provide models of adaptive behavior for parents. Such modeling could help families with children in active treatment learn healthy, open styles of communicating and coping together.

Summary

The special problems inherent in living with survival as a former childhood cancer patient discussed in this chapter include the following:

Physical and Visible Impairment

1. A practical, easily administered test, the Visible/Physical Impairment Rating Scale was devised and applied to measure impairment in our sample.

2. Neither the degree of physical impairment nor the degree of visible impairment related to long-term psychological adjustment among the childhood cancer survivors in our study.

Marriage

1. Almost half of the former patients interviewed who were aged 21 or over had not married, compared to 77.5 percent of males and 76.1 percent of females aged 17-64 in the national population. The low marriage rate among childhood cancer survivors in our sample may be related to their relative youth (aged 21-37) in comparison with the national population.

2. The more marked the physical impairment of the women survivors, the less likely they were to be married. For the men survivors, however, the more marked the impairment, the more likely they were to be married.

3. The greater the visibility of impairment, the less likely the women survivors were to be married. This relationship was not found in the men studied.

4. The never married survivors tended to show more psychological symptoms than the married ones, but the two groups did not differ significantly in overall psychological adjustment.

5. The major concerns of survivors' spouses with respect to the cancer history were the potential health of progeny and sexual functioning. These issues were generally explored before or soon after marriage and were resolved by the time of our interviews with spouses.

Employment

1. Forty percent of the 60 survivors in our sample who were over 18 at the time of interview had experienced some form of employment discrimination based solely on their cancer history, according to their own reports.

2. The better the level of psychological adjustment, the more likely the survivor was to be employed at the time of the study.

3. None of the concerns sometimes cited by employers as reasons for not hiring cancer survivors (e.g., fears of absenteeism or increases in insurance premiums) were found to be justified on the basis of childhood cancer survivors' adult employment records.

Insurance

1. Most adult survivors of childhood cancer were covered by some form of health insurance, usually provided as a group policy through an employer. Few were able to obtain individual health insurance policies; most of the individual policies which had been issued contained clauses excluding a wide range of coverage related to the cancer histories.

2. Almost 64 percent had life insurance coverage of some sort by the time of

interview, but many had been denied a policy at least once, were required to pay a higher than normal premium, or were made to observe a waiting period of some sort.

3. Discrimination or rejection associated with employment and insurance often led to increased anxiety about the disease prognosis and to lowered self-esteem.

Communicating the Cancer Diagnosis

1. The earlier a child was told the diagnosis, the more likely he or she was to be well-adjusted at the time of interview.

2. Directness and openness in all matters associated with the illness seem to foster better adjustment among childhood cancer survivors. It is difficult to know, however, how much family patterns of open communication which predate the onset of cancer contribute to this phenomenon.

Chapter 10

Anticipatory Grief and Survival

Preceding chapters have documented the family crisis ushered in by the diagnosis of cancer; until very recently, this diagnosis was tantamount to a death sentence. Once parents' initial efforts at denial fade, they are faced with complex and often contradictory tasks: to meet the ill child's current physical and emotional needs while preparing for the possibility of eventual death. Since the child is still alive, parents waver between hope and despair, between denial and realistic appraisal, and between experiencing and repressing grief. Feelings and behavior normally associated with grief, such as anger, sadness, guilt, and restlessness, are present in varying degrees. This process, known as anticipatory grief, is an adaptive one, preparing the parent for a traumatic eventuality: the loss of a child. Its function is to prevent the parent from being overwhelmed by the anxiety and depression which attends the threat of such a loss.

Literature

The onset of anticipatory grief at the time of diagnosis has been well-documented by the number of prospective studies of families with a fatally ill child (Richmond and Waisman, 1955; Futterman and Hoffman, 1973; Knapp and Hansen, 1973). The process of anticipatory grief has been most comprehensively studied by Futterman and Hoffman. Over a period of six years, they interviewed twenty-three sets of parents of leukemic children, at various times in the course of the child's illness as well as after the child's death. They defined anticipatory grief as "a set of processes that are directly related to the awareness of the impending loss, to its emotional impact and to the adaptive mechanisms whereby emotional attachment to the dying child is relinquished over time" (1973, p. 130). The processes evolve through the different stages of the illness and according to the parents' changing understanding of the child's life expectancy. The authors contend

By Beth Kemler.

130

that anticipatory grief is an adaptive and necessary process which most parents were able to master. Friedman, Chodoff, Mason, and Hamburg (1963), in another prospective study of the coping behavior of parents of leukemic children, also point to the adaptive quality of anticipatory grief. They note that the few parents who did not experience any anticipatory grief later suffered intense, difficult grief when the child actually died.

The adaptive function of anticipatory grief in preparing parents for the loss of a child is evident. But what happens when the child does not die? How do parents adjust, after years of some internal preparation for a child's death, to the likelihood that their child will live? Lindemann (1944), who coined the phrase "anticipatory grief," raised the possibility that this initially adaptive process may turn out to be a disadvantage if death does not occur as anticipated. Hansen (1973) also raises the question of what happens when the task of mourning has been partially accomplished and then the mourned one survives. His answer is that ambivalence is likely to result.

This view is reflected in Green and Solnit's (1964) study of disturbances of the mother-child relationship which result from an acute or chronic life-threatening illness in the child. The authors believe that such children, though recovered, are still viewed by their mothers as vulnerable to illness and destined to die young. Some of the mothers seem to have experienced a modified grief reaction when informed that their child would probably die. This reaction partially stopped when recovery became likely, but was not completely dispelled. Some of the mothers reported recurring nightmares about losing the child. Clinically, the children often revealed separation difficulties, infantilization, and hypochondriacal complaints. The authors' explanation for this "vulnerable child syndrome" is that the past life-threatening experience persists as an active force which attaches itself to the current experiences of growing up, and that the major reason for its persistence is the mother's unresolved feelings of resentment, guilt, and fear continuing from the time of the illness. The Green and Solnit study highlights the risks for a child who survives a life-threatening illness when the mother has difficulty in resolving her anticipatory grief. Unfortunately, the authors do not clarify what percentage of such children and their mothers are at risk, nor how the findings compare to the general population.

Method

This study, a subproject of the research program described in this volume, was designed to explore the current adaptation of families in which a child has survived cancer. More specifically, its purpose was to assess the current state of resolution of anticipatory grief in both mothers and fathers, in terms of the parent's relationship with the child, the degree of worry about the child's present and future health, and the parent's reinvestment in marriage, work, friendships, and activities.

Fifteen families were selected from the long-term survivor registry, none of whom had been interviewed for the larger study described in Chapter 3. These families were selected from a subset of fifty families in which the child had been diagnosed during the "latency stage" of psychosocial development (aged 5–10) and was currently in adolescence (aged 12–21). These criteria were chosen to hold constant the age and developmental conflicts and tasks of the child for the families studied. No attempt was made to control for the specific type of cancer nor for the number of years elapsed since diagnosis. The forms of cancer represented in the sample were lymphoma (7), sarcoma (5), and leukemia (3). The time elapsed since diagnosis ranged from seven to twelve years.

The families were randomly selected from those living within an hour's traveling time of Boston. This criterion may partly account for the composition of the sample: white, lower-middle-class to middle-class Catholics, most with a high school education. The homogeneity of the sample in social class and religious background is discussed later with respect to generalizability of the results. The refusal rate for participating in this substudy was relatively low (28 percent): those who participated (72 percent) viewed their cooperation as a way of helping other parents and repaying a debt of gratitude to the hospital that took such good care of their children.

A semistructured interview, lasting two to two and one half hours, was conducted individually with fifteen mothers and fifteen fathers. The parent was first asked some open-ended questions about the child's preillness functioning and general family interactional patterns. Next he or she was asked about the period when the diagnosis was learned, focusing on any evidence of anticipatory grief. The interview then proceeded to the time of remission and then to the current situation, focusing on the adaptation of the child and the parent. All the interviews were audiotaped, and ratings based on clinical judgments were then made by the interviewer. An independent judge rated 30 percent of the interviews from the tapes; interrater reliability ranged from 85 percent to 100 percent. Both the interviewer and the independent judge had had ten years of clinical experience in child guidance agencies, working intensively with both children and parents. They were also both doctoral candidates in a clinical social work program. The detailed bases of the ratings are presented in Appendix E.

Presence of Anticipatory Grief

Although the questions pertaining to the time of diagnosis were answered retrospectively, the impressionistic recall of all the parents was very strong. As they spoke of that period, it was as if it had occurred only yesterday. Talking about the diagnosis evoked much emotion; a number of parents stated that it still makes them sad to think about it. Despite the passage of from seven to twelve years, the reporting of events seemed quite reliable, for mothers' and fathers' reports were strongly corroborative.

Of thirty parents, twenty were rated as having experienced strong anticipatory grief around the time of diagnosis. Another eight evidenced a moderate degree of grief, one experienced mild grief, and only one apparently experienced no anticipatory grief. This was a father who confided to the interviewer that he had never believed that his child had cancer and that he thought the child was ill only as a result of the chemotherapy. Since he denied the reality of the illness, he had no reason to begin mourning the loss of his child. For the great majority of parents, the first several months following the diagnosis were fraught with strong emotions, primarily sadness and anger, and less frequently guilt. Twenty-six parents described at least a moderate amount of sadness; twenty-three experienced some anger, commonly expressed as general irritability; nine parents reported feeling guilty at that time.

As Futterman and Hoffman (1973) note, anticipatory grief is initially intense and undifferentiated but gradually subsides to a more stable, chronic condition. This course was reflected in the parents' descriptions of the period of remission. The child appeared fairly healthy and was able to resume most normal activities. However, there were constant reminders that the child had a disease: regular medical checkups; watchfulness for signs of relapse; continuation of chemotherapy, with its attendant side effects, such as nausea and hair loss. Parents reported that despite professional advice to treat the child "normally," it was very difficult to do so. They found themselves being more lenient and indulgent and generally treating the child somewhat differently from the other children in the family. There continued to be some disruption in the parents' life; much energy was still directed toward the child and less was available for outside friendships and activities. As remission continued with no relapses, anticipatory grief diminished in proportion to the rise in hope as the reality of the situation improved. Several parents when asked what was most helpful to them during remission, responded that the child's continued good health provided them with hope.

Current Functioning

Parent-Child Relationship Of major importance is the parent-child relationship, especially in view of Green and Solnit's findings, which alert us to the possible risk for these children. How are they viewed by their parents? One might expect either idealization or negative attitudes about the child, as is reported in accounts of unresolved grief reactions (Parkes, 1972; Wilbur, 1976). Clinicians have long noted a tendency of parents to describe a chronically ill child as "special" or "chosen," a meaning which goes far beyond the actual physical condition. This quality could be attributed to a child who has survived a life-threatening illness, yet these parents do not use such a description. They appear to perceive their child realistically, being able to describe negative as well as positive aspects of the child's personality. The great majority of parents had a positive, realistic view of their child; only one parent seemed to idealize the child, and several had a mildly negative perception of the child. Almost all had reasonable expectations about their child's future in terms of work. None of the parents described the child as "special" or out of the ordinary. On the contrary, they emphasized the child's normality. When asked to describe their child before the illness, many parents began with "He was a normal child." This attitude carried over into their discussion of the child at present: "She's a typical teenager," etc. There seemed to be an investment in portraying the child as well-adjusted now, with a concurrent tendency to downplay problems.

From the parents' reports, it appears that the majority of the children are managing all right. The aspects of the adolescents' lives explored were school attendance and performance, work, peer relationships, and outside activities, and on the whole they are behaving in an age-appropriate way. Of special interest is the fact that school or work attendance was reported to be very high, with very few absences because of poor health. Many of these children excelled academically, but several parents reported a reluctance to push their child in school work. This was related to the illness in that academic success seemed less significant after what the child had been through. Almost all the children had a range of friendships and outside interests appropriate, and important, for their stage of development.

The high percentage of adequate adjustment was based solely on the parents' report, since none of these children were interviewed. But the parent interviews were intensive, and it is likely that these findings are a valid indication of good outward adjustment made by the adolescents. What we do not know from these data are the survivors' internal adjustment and reactions to being cancer survivors. As noted, the parents had a strong investment in seeing their child as normal and well-adjusted. There also appeared to be a hesitancy about discussing the illness and its implications with the adolescent currently. The majority of parents either discuss the illness only with reluctance or actively avoid discussion of it in the family. Understandably, they want to leave this most unpleasant topic in the past and be done with it. As a result, there are indications that the adolescent may be left to deal alone with any continuing worries or questions about the illness and its implications. Children in this position may be inclined to keep their concerns to themselves, which is typical adolescent behavior, but in these children it becomes interwoven with the parents' reluctance to communicate more openly.

A poignant example of this situation is the S family. Fifteen-year-old Ann is doing well: she is a good student, is popular and seen as a leader by her peers, and is active in sports. Moreover, she has a close and seemingly good relationship with her parents. The night before the interview, all three had filled out a mailed questionnaire about the cancer experience, which they had coincidentally received from the long-term follow-up study. Ann retired to bed and her parents later discovered her sobbing inconsolably. She had apparently long believed that she was a freak because of her illness and that therefore no one could really love her. This came as a great shock to her parents, who had assumed that Ann was a happy young girl who no longer thought about the cancer experience. Of course, many teenagers feel they are somehow different and unlovable, which causes them great anguish. For the adolescent who has survived cancer, this feeling may be attached to the illness. Some of this pain will be resolved with time, but some could be alleviated by discussion with an open and caring adult. The example of Ann alerts us to the possibility that the outwardly well-adjusted adolescent survivor may still be internally troubled by the cancer experience.

Other aspects of the parent-child relationship were examined in detail. The majority of the parents (twenty-two) appear to be granting age-appropriate autonomy to their adolescents. Four were judged as "clinging" and another four as inconsistent in dealing with separation. These findings are reflected in the fact that the majority of the adolescents regularly attend school or work, are involved in friendships and activities outside the home, and generally exhibit a degree of independence commensurate with their age. Thus, these results do not support Green and Solnit's (1964) finding of frequent pathological separation difficulties. Unfortunately, a limitation of both studies is the lack of comparison with a disease-free population. Obtaining a control group for this population was not possible. We are therefore unable to say whether these parents have approximately the same or more difficulty in dealing with separation-individuation issues with their adolescent than do parents of children who did not have a life-threatening illness.

In terms of protectiveness, the majority (nineteen parents) seem to be reasonably protective of their adolescents. Seven were rated as overprotective, three as inconsistent, and one as underprotective. The latter is a father who exposes his 15-year-old son to dangerous situations, one of which resulted in a serious accident for the boy. The seven parents who were rated overprotective (all mildly so) connected their attitude to the child's illness. For example, several parents said that although their adolescent occasionally sleeps over night at a friend's house, they prefer to have friends sleep in their house so that they can keep an eye on their child.

A more significant finding concerns discipline and the parents' ability to express anger toward the child. Nine parents said that they rarely, if ever, get angry at the adolescent; three reported feeling angry but not expressing it; one parent reported frequently getting very angry. Most of these reactions contrast with the expression of anger toward the other children in the family. The remaining seventeen parents appeared to be able to express anger appropriately to the adolescent. On the question of discipline, nine parents were judged to be mildly permissive and nine were considered very permissive. Since adolescence is known to be a stormy time marked by rebellion, which typically arouses frustration and anger in parents, these findings of relatively low parental anger level are striking.

Several explanations are possible. First, these adolescents may be, as their parents state, less difficult to manage. Perhaps they are more compliant in their outward behavior or have matured because of the experience of being ill. Another possibility is that many parents have difficulty acknowledging anger toward a sick child or a child who has survived but may still be considered vulnerable. Several parents stated explicitly that they discipline this child differently from the others because of the illness; perhaps they view their anger as potentially harmful to the child. Anger is considered to be a normal reaction to the death of a loved person (Bowlby, 1961); it also occurs when a loved person becomes ill. If this anger is personally unacceptable it may be totally denied. The denial then interferes with the parent's capacity to set limits and controls for the child. Or perhaps the high incidence of denied anger is an outcome of a bargaining process. Kübler-Ross (1969) identifies one phase of anticipatory grief as bargaining, in which the person promises "good behavior" in exchange for the survival or prolongation of life of the dying loved person. She claims that most of these bargains are made with God and are kept a secret. It is conceivable that some of these parents "bargained" for the lives of their children with a promise to treat them better or to not get angry with them in the future. Data were not elicited to support this conjecture, and it is a subject for additional investigation.

When all aspects of the parent-child relationship were considered, two-thirds of the relationships were judged to be appropriate to the child's age and growth-promoting. We do not know how this figure compares with the general population, but it does show that a majority of the parents have been able to reinvest themselves in a relationship with a child who is viewed as having a real future.

Concerns for the Future   Even if the adolescent is viewed as a growing person with a real future, the fact remains that he or she has survived a life-threatening illness and the future has been affected in some way. Some concern for the future health of the child is thus to be expected, based on a realistic acknowledgment of the (small) possibility of future loss or limitation. When asked if they have any concerns about their child's health, fifteen parents mentioned recurrence of the cancer, six spoke of the long-term effects of radiation treatment, and six voiced concern about ability to procreate. It is of interest that a number of parents had questions about their child's future medical condition which they asked the oncologist who called them about participating in the study. This raises the question whether many parental concerns remain unspoken and are not voiced to the physician who sees the child for the annual checkup. Parents commonly express anxiety about the checkup and may not feel comfortable bringing up additional questions at that time. Or perhaps they feel the physician is too busy to take the time, since their child is healthy now and there are others with more pressing problems. Whatever the reason, it is important for the medical staff to be aware that although the child is healthy and the parents have been living with the situation for years, questions and worries may still exist and need to be addressed, especially as the child approaches adulthood.

In the interview, parents were asked if and how often they found themselves worrying about their child's health. The response to this question, as well as other impressions, figured in the formulation of a clinical judgment about whether the parent (1) had a reasonable concern about the child's health, (2) denied any concern, or (3) was overconcerned or preoccupied with the child's health. Only nine parents were judged to have a reasonable degree of concern; seven parents totally denied worrying, and fourteen parents seemed preoccupied. Parents in the latter group made such statements as: "It is always in the back of my mind"; "Cancer is like a dark shadow—it is always there." Several mothers spoke of closely watching their child for signs of recurrence. Thus, despite the passage of many years and the high probability of survival for these children, these parents are still very much worried and anticipate a possible loss in the future. Interestingly, however, not one parent reported a recurring dream about losing the child, as was reported by the parents in the Green and Solnit study. This may indicate a greater degree of resolution of anticipatory grief, since dreams of lost persons have been associated with lack of resolution of grief (Parkes, 1972).

Parents' Adjustment   Freud (1917) described mourning as a slow, gradual, painful process in which there is a preoccupation with the lost person. The process requires much energy, and while it is going on it leaves the bereaved depleted of energy for other things. Investment in other relationships, in life's tasks, and in life's pleasures are evidence of the successful termination of the work of mourning. The same can be said of the process of anticipatory grieving. To assess the present state of anticipatory grief of these parents, we must also consider aspects of their lives separate from their relationship to the child. First, have they reinvested in themselves, as reflected in their own health and their ability to take care of themselves? In the interview, parents were asked about their health at different stages. The majority said that during the period of diagnosis their health had been fine, but three complained of ulcers and one developed a back problem. The number of physical complaints increased only slightly during the period of remission. Many parents mentioned that they "had to" remain healthy so as to be able to care for their sick child. As in most studies of health, these reports by parents on their health are retrospective and susceptible to distortions of time. Nineteen parents described themselves as being in good health at the time of the interview. Of the remaining eleven, four had high blood pressure (on medication), two had acknowledged drinking problems for which they were attending Alcoholics Anonymous, five complained of being overweight, one still suffered from ulcers, and one had a back problem. It should be noted that the age range of these parents is

32 to 57 years, with a mean age of 47. The great majority of these parents appeared to take reasonable care of themselves, as evidenced by their scheduling annual physical checkups, following medical orders, etc. Only four parents seemed to be preoccupied with their health, and none flagrantly ignored their health.

As for their marriages, twenty-two parents expressed current satisfaction. Of these, fully half stated that they were even closer to their spouse now, as a result of having gone through the crisis of caring for a seriously ill child. Of the eight parents voicing dissatisfaction with their marriages, six claimed that they were more distant from their spouse as a result of the cancer experience. These findings support a long-accepted impression: a crisis tests the strength of a relationship. A marriage based on strong mutual bonds will survive the stress, perhaps even being enriched by the sharing and overcoming of a crisis. In contrast, a weak marriage is less likely to weather the storm intact. The disappointment of not being able to count on the partner for support leaves the marriage further depleted. Interestingly, of the fifteen couples in this portion of the study, not one had experienced a marital separation, let alone divorce. One of the dissatisfied wives said she was considering a separation, but had taken no active steps toward it. For several reasons (small sample size; religious homogeneity, most of the parents being Catholic), this finding cannot be accurately compared to the national rate of divorce. Yet it does tend to dispel the notion that the experience of having a child with cancer produces a higher incidence of marital disruption. This is of course a survivor population; perhaps the rate would be higher among families in which the child died.

The great majority of parents said that they enjoyed their work, whether it was employment outside the home or in the home (seven of the women were not employed outside). Nine parents claimed to be deriving greater satisfaction from their work now than they did in the past; none related this directly to their child's having been ill. Only three parents reported finding work less rewarding now, and again this seemed to be independent of the child's illness. Almost all the parents were able to take pleasure in the work they do, either outside or in the home. Those who were finding greater satisfaction now had the energy to try to improve their working situation in whatever way was necessary. Several fathers stated that they were somewhat distracted or that their work was disrupted during the time of diagnosis of the child's illness. Yet work was also clearly a place to escape for them. Mothers reported less opportunity to turn to work for release, since the major responsibility for caring for the ill child generally fell on their shoulders. But several mothers reported finding jobs soon after the child was well enough not to require special care. These mothers found work beneficial in that it provided them with an escape from worries about the child. Although work serves as an important outlet for these parents, the amount of time spent at work did not change significantly. Those fathers who were spending long hours at work had a history of such working hours long before the child ever got sick. A few fathers even commented that as a result of the illness family life had become more important to them than work.

The two areas in which there appeared to be some deterioration of satisfaction were friendships and outside activities. This was rarely stated explicitly but was inferred from the parents' reports. Although the majority derived approximately the same pleasure from friends, nine parents reported feeling less close or spending less time with friends now as compared to before the child's illness. In activities outside the home, twelve parents were judged to be less active now. Why this change? Several explanations are possible, including the effects of the passage of time—as people grow older they may become less involved socially. Perhaps the crisis of cancer in a family causes a reevaluation of priorities, resulting in more free time spent with the family and less time outside. Or is this finding an indication of unresolved anticipatory grief, which leaves the parent with less energy to invest in friendships and activities? One mother, for whom such was clearly the case, stated that she could not afford to be happy because it might upset the balance, as if to say she did not want to tempt fate. It is as though she feels she must pay for her child's survival with her own happiness.

In summary, two-thirds of the parents currently have age-appropriate relationships with their children. A higher proportion report satisfaction in their marriages and most appear to derive satisfaction from their work, whether outside or in the home. Yet fourteen parents (one-half) were judged to be preoccupied with or overconcerned about the child's health. Apparently this worry is somehow kept separate from the emotional investment in their child and themselves.

Differences between Mothers and Fathers

Nearly all the studies of families coping with a fatally ill child focus exclusively on the mothers' reactions; the fathers' responses have received little attention. Knapp and Hansen (1973), who led groups for parents of leukemic children, found that denial was used as a defense more frequently for a longer time by fathers than by mothers in anticipatory grief. The fathers appeared to find it more difficult to accept the diagnosis and the possibility of losing the child. Wilbur (1976) studied five sets of parents of leukemic children in detail. She noted that the fathers used more distancing techniques for coping with the illness than did the mothers: the fathers spoke of their leukemic child in more idealized terms than the mothers, and also expressed a present orientation to the child rather than conceiving of the child as part of future plans. The fathers saw themselves as more isolated and less helpful to the ill child than did the mothers. Wilbur's explanation of her results is that the fathers' coping efforts are restricted by cultural expectations. Fathers spend more time away from the family, have fewer opportunities for direct expression of feelings, and are expected to maintain the appearance of control and strength at times of crisis.

Since previous studies indicate that fathers, for a variety of reasons, seem to deal with anticipatory grief in a different way than do mothers, this study was designed to explore these differences in the present. First, it should be pointed out that the willingness of the fathers to participate in this study represents a potential source of bias. These are fathers who played a fairly active and continuing role throughout the child's illness. Several mothers commented that their husbands were available to them and the child during treatment, in contrast to many other families in which the fathers never appeared at the hospital or clinic. Nevertheless, some generalizable statements can be made. A number of fathers stated that despite their helping to care for the child during the first years of illness, the major burden still fell on the mothers. Fathers had their work, to which they could escape; when the child was hospitalized fathers usually visited in the evenings, and later they only occasionally brought the child for clinic appointments. A few fathers expressed some current guilt about their past behavior, but others were clearly relieved. One result of this often-noted pattern is that fathers typically have less direct contact with the medical staff and receive information indirectly via the mothers. Fathers have less time and fewer opportunities to express their feelings, concerns, and questions to the medical team and to other parents. This fact seemed relevant to the fathers' current willingness to participate in the study. In three families, the mothers were reluctant to participate and it was the fathers who strongly wanted to do so. Fathers made great efforts to come in for the interviews, frequently taking half a day off from work. In two cases, the interviewer had been forewarned by the mothers that their husbands were quiet and probably would not say much. It turned out that these two fathers had a great deal to say and provided two of the longest interviews. Here, again, we noted that years after the illness there is still a need to talk about it, especially if the opportunities to do so in the past have been limited, as is the case for most fathers. The implication is that fathers should be strongly encouraged to come with mothers to the clinic for the child's annual checkup. Time needs to be provided for both parents to allow them the opportunity to express their feelings and questions to the medical staff.

When asked what they thought their role was during the acute phase of the child's illness, the majority of fathers replied in terms of caring for the child. But a number of fathers saw their major role as supporting their wives and families by being strong, keeping a calm exterior, and using humor. This is in line with Wilbur's findings. Yet fathers clearly do experience anticipatory grief. Only two fathers showed either mild grief or none at all. The remaining were judged to have experienced either strong (seven fathers) or moderate (six fathers) grief. Of the mothers, thirteen expressed strong grief and two moderate grief. The difference between mothers and fathers seemed to be in the intensity and duration of feelings expressed, the mothers experiencing stronger grief for a longer time. When the specific affects are considered, there is no significant difference between the number of mothers and fathers who experienced some sadness and anger. There is a difference, however, in the expressed guilt; only three fathers recalled feeling guilty about the illness, whereas six mothers did. Apparently mothers are more likely to feel responsible for their child's illness, to view it as a failure in their maternal performance.

Another difference between mothers and fathers at the time of diagnosis involved their reactions to the child. Three of the fathers commented on resenting the child for getting sick. One of these fathers said that he "pulled back" from his child after the diagnosis, for fear that the hurt would be too great when the child died. This withdrawal from the child continued for several years and eventually was resolved with the help of short-term counseling. None of the mothers retrospectively expressed such anger at the child. In an interesting contrast, several fathers, but no mothers, blamed the child for the illness, whereas more mothers than fathers blamed themselves. Does this reflect a tendency for women to internalize or take upon themselves responsibility for events, whereas men are more likely to externalize the blame?

When the state of anticipatory grief at interview is considered, we find several trends in differences between mothers and fathers. There was no significant difference between mothers and fathers in the age appropriateness of the relationship with the child. In only one aspect of the relationship was there a difference: the ability to acknowledge anger toward the child currently. Fathers seemed to have greater difficulty in acknowledging anger toward the surviving child. It is not that these fathers generally acknowledge less anger toward their children, but rather less anger toward the child who has survived. Seven fathers were unable to acknowledge anger toward the surviving child, but only two mothers did not get angry at the child. This is interesting in light of the higher incidence of fathers' initial blame of the child at the time of diagnosis. Perhaps unconscious guilt for the blame resulted in the denial of any anger toward the child at the time of our interview.

In other aspects of their lives, no significant differences were found between mothers' and fathers' current satisfaction from marriage and work. There was a difference in degree of worry about the child's future health. Six fathers were judged to do a reasonable amount of worrying, but only three mothers were so judged. Four mothers and three fathers denied any worry. Eight mothers seemed preoccupied or overworried, as did six fathers. These figures are too small to be significant, but do indicate a trend. Several fathers commented that they thought their wives still worried about the child, but no wife said this of her husband.

Summary

Theoreticians (Lindeman, 1944; Hansen, 1973) have suggested that anticipatory grief which is aborted because its object survives may lead to difficulties in the ensuing relationship. This concern was borne out in the Green and Solnit study (1964).

1. Childhood cancer survivors and their families are conceivably at risk but in our study were not shown to be. Although the social, religious, and racial homogeneity as well as the small size of the sample limits generalizability, certain trends are evident.

2. The majority of parents (66 percent) appeared currently to have age-appropriate relationships with their adolescents, reflected in the latter's overall adequate social adjustment. Unfortunately, as discussed in Chapter 3, there are no normative studies with which to compare the results, but it is possible that the proportion is not very different for the population at large. However, one striking characteristic of this sample was the relatively low incidence of acknowledged anger toward the adolescent. Several possible explanations were considered, the most likely being that anger is a normal reaction to having an ill child but may be unacceptable to the parent, who denies all anger toward the child. One consequence of the inability to acknowledge anger is a laxity in setting consistent limits for the child.

3. These parents expressed generally positive feelings toward the child, neither idealizing nor being overnegative. Their reported expectations and preparations for the child's future seemed realistic, and they were able to talk about the adolescent in a future tense. Nevertheless, one-third expressed some worry about the child's future health and almost one-half were judged to be overconcerned. How can we reconcile these seemingly disparate results? One explanation is that the worry about the future is encapsulated, so that it remains separate from the ongoing relationship with the child. It seems that the concern about the cancer experience is present, but its implication for the child's future is denied. This could be viewed as denial in the service of the need to survive (Geleerd, 1965). It enables the parent to meet the child's current needs, including helping the adolescent to plan and prepare for the future in spite of concerns about that future. The denial of concern which seven parents expressed did not interfere with their meeting the children's medical needs, such as maintaining annual checkups at the hospital. Even in the extreme instance of the father who never believed his child had had cancer, the denial did not interfere with providing for the child's needs.

4. The findings also corroborate prior speculation that fathers may not experience anticipatory grief as actively as mothers. Retrospectively, the fathers reported experiencing less intense grief for a shorter period at the time of diagnosis. There is, however, no indication that the fathers' anticipatory grief is currently less adequately resolved than the mothers'.

5. Although both the mothers and the fathers are currently able to derive satisfaction from important aspects of their lives, there are differences in their relationships with the child who survived cancer. Many of the fathers continued to have difficulty acknowledging anger toward the child, which was not generally a problem for the mothers. At the same time, more fathers were able to acknowledge a reasonable concern for their child's future health, whereas mothers were often preoccupied by worry about it.

6. The majority of the parents reported currently deriving pleasure from their marriages and work. Having energy available to invest in relationships and in life's tasks and pleasures is an important indicator of resolution of anticipatory grief. What is remarkable is these parents' ability to invest appropriately in their children, their families, and themselves, despite the continuing great concern which 50 percent experienced in connection with the cancer experience. It is as though the majority have not completely resolved the anticipatory grief, but rather have placed it in abeyance so that life can continue satisfactorily despite uncertainty about the future.

Chapter 11

Self-Understanding and Coping with Cancer

This chapter presents three firsthand reports of the experience of having cancer in childhood from people who were part of the larger sample discussed in this volume. Its aim is to provide an exploration of the way people who have had cancer and coped well with it perceive themselves and how they remember their experience.

A small group of survivors who had coped well were selected and interviewed in depth about their experiences. Those selected all had a Combined Adjustment Rating of 0 or 1 (see Chapter 3 for criteria). Each survivor (all three were men) was interviewed a number of times over a period of weeks. The central questions asked the survivor were: How would you tell the story of your own life? How would you characterize yourself and how does having cancer fit into that? What do you remember about the time you were ill? What factors helped you cope then and help you cope now? What factors did not help? What effects do you think the illness had on you? The survivor was asked about his current functioning in work, in the family, and in other relationships, and above all, about how he felt these things had been affected by the illness experience. The questions were open-ended, and each person was allowed to develop the answers as he saw fit. The aim of the interview was to put the person at ease and let him reflect and tell his own story, in his own words. Every effort was made to achieve rapport and not to direct the interviewees' understanding, but to allow it to be presented as fully as possible. The interviewer did not consult the records of the larger study and thus was blind to the findings, except for the Combined Adjustment Rating.

The choice of this method was based on several considerations. First, standardized quantitative data had already been obtained on these survivors. This investigation was seen as a way of enriching the data, not as a substutute for the mea-

By William R. Beardslee.

sures already obtained. Second, our review of the literature showed that there were very few in-depth, open-ended interview studies of survivors of cancer and none of those who had survived cancer as children. It was thought that an open-ended interview offered an important way of trying to characterize just what, if anything, was remembered from the experience, and what, if any, bearing this memory had on the survivor's overall coping. Obviously, some questions overlap questions in the psychiatric interview (see Appendix B and Chapter 6). What was different was the emphasis in this investigation on the survivor's own story and self-understanding. It was also possible to devote considerably more time to each question during the interviews reported here. An earlier study (Beardslee, 1977) investigated the relationship between self-understanding and ways of handling a particularly difficult stress, that of self-chosen political involvement. Clearly, one cannot demonstrate cause in a study based on retrospective accounts; nonetheless, that study raised important questions and drew attention to the importance of self-understanding in dealing with difficult situations. To our knowledge, this has not been well-investigated in the area of the stress of medical illness in general and with respect to cancer in particular. Moreover, the literature on coping with cancer emphasizes the role of denial, so that it was not at all clear at the outset whether self-awareness, reflecting on the past, and self-understanding play any part in improving coping with this difficult illness. An investigation of this sort therefore seemed justified.

The reflections of three different men are presented here. Their anonymity is preserved at their request by nonsubstantive changes in the identifying data. They are at three different life stages: one is in his thirites, is married, has a family, and has a stable job; the second has finished college and is casting about for what he will do; the third is in his third year of high school. They are atypical of the overall sample of good copers in that they were subjected to somewhat more stress than the average cancer survivor discussed in this volume. For two of them the cancer occurred at a later age in childhood than most, for two of the three treatment lasted longer than most (i.e., five years), and all three underwent surgery. Two of the three had surgery more than once, and the third had an amputation. Put another way, judged by external criteria of age at diagnosis, severity of cancer, and duration of treatment, the three fall into the group of those statistically more likely to have had difficulties than the other survivors (see Chapter 5). Thus their coping is all the more remarkable and of all the more interest.

In presenting the three accounts, some editing, condensation and organization of the interview material has taken place, but the general sense of what the survivors said has been maintained as faithfully as possible. Only topics presented by the survivors consistently over a period of time, that is, in several weeks of interviewing, and that seemed to be of major importance, are dealt with in the accounts that follow.

Case One

The subject of the first history is in his early thirties. He grew up in a large family in a small town in Rhode Island. He was the youngest in the family. When asked about his early years he recalled much love and closeness in his family. He does not recall any major conflicts or difficulties in those years. He does remember some financial strain. The family had lived in the town where he grew up for many years and although he does not, some of his siblings live there still. The man himself was tall, friendly, and warm in his manner. He talked easily about himself and seemed very comfortable in going over the events of the past. He clearly had reflected a great deal about what had happened to him. During the course of the interviews, he sometimes cried and at other times laughed as he recalled events.

Before his illness began he remembered himself as a hard-working youngster, conscientious and a "perfectionist." His illness, osteogenic sarcoma, began as a severe pain in his leg when he was 14 years old. He said of the pain:

I can remember the pain in school, it was so bad that I couldn't function. I would just sit there with my head on my desk. The first thing I remember about my illness is something that happened with my cousin. We were at recess one day and he came over and lightly bumped my leg, and I just fell down in pain. It was just something awful . . . it was two or three weeks till I went to the doctor. As soon as I got here he started giving me pain medication and I didn't have pain after that, but before then, it was pain like I had never had before. He referred me to the hospital.

When I first came down to the hospital it was frightening. It's probably improved a lot since then, but back then a person couldn't just come in and be admitted. A person had to go to the clinic down the street. We had thirteen hours of sort of being shuffled around down there. I was sitting down there, in those cold, drab waiting rooms with my parents all the time.

After I was admitted, I think the hardest thing was being away from home. I'd never been away from home before. I'd never been a person who went to camp or anything like that, I'd always been at home. I will never forget that first night up on the sixth floor, looking out . . . it was a rough experience. I was only in the hospital for a week or two at that time, then I came back on an outpatient basis to get chemotherapy.

My family just really pulled together and stayed with me all through the experience. They really helped. My mother had the most trouble adjusting to the experience, she never liked hospitals, and she really had trouble coming here. It was mostly my brothers and my father who brought me back for chemotherapy; that was the way my mother was and I accepted that. My brothers and my father drove me in here for chemotherapy three times a week.

I had a biopsy when I came in. Later I had my amputation. I don't remember worrying about what was going to happen to my leg. One week when I came in for treatment, the doctor told me that they would have to operate. He said, "We are going to try to save your leg, we will probably have to take it off." I cried and my mother cried, but then I felt almost relieved. I remember thinking I would be glad to get rid of the damn thing. I guess that was because I hadn't been able to use it much and it was giving me a lot of trouble.

I remember going into the surgery, and then I remember waking up. I was bandaged all over. I remember looking down and saying, "It's gone." That was it. My mother came in. She has said since that it was the most difficult thing for her to come in. She said that she would never forget what had happened. I said to her, "You know, Mom, I had a wart on my big toe that has always bothered me and I'm glad it's gone." The only time I remember crying was that night before the surgery. I just don't remember going into questioning what would happen that much. I think I was unconsciously aware of what might happen. I remember on the ward, we had a little group of people who all had the same diagnosis. One of them died a little after that. For me it was never an intense "Am I going to die?" and dwelling on that. I guess in my mind that just wasn't going to happen to me.

My family was there with me all the way and the community was too. When I got home from the hospital, my brother Charles, he's the one who doesn't say much, had gotten a car for me. It was an old car which he had shined up. He purchased it for me to run around the fields. I made a race track out in the big fields. I had my jollies smashing that thing up. I had learned to drive when I was ten, so I already knew how to drive. I guess I was a little reckless. Once during the spring of the year, I drove up on the muddy lawn in front of our house, and skidded into the porch, knocking out a support post. Those things might have been a little traumatic for my parents, but they didn't say anything.

The community was tremendously important to us. My family has been in that town for generations. The word was out that the prognosis for me was pretty grave. An example of the support is that some leaders in the community got together and organized a basketball game in the gymnasium of the school. It was a fund-raiser. They raised three or four hundred dollars and presented it to me that night. As another example at the time of the trouble that I had, there was an orthopedic surgeon, a friend of the family, who was retired. He had worked at a hospital in New York for many years, and had written a book about pain in medicine and the spiritual laws. He had given case studies in the book of his experience helping patients spiritually. During the time after my surgery, he arranged to have prayer meetings at my home, where essentially we would get together with some other friends to pray for people in need, which would include me. It was a group with my mother, father, the doctor and his wife, and another couple, friends of the family. I don't remember how long it lasted, but it was a weekly thing, and went on for quite some time. I have always felt that it was quite significant.

The man also reported that while he was in the hospital, one of the nurses had written to the newspaper and described him in a letter that was printed in a national column. He said that he received hundreds of cards and letters of support because of that. In talking about how he coped at that time, and also since then, he said:

I was always very active and I continue to be. I think it was very hard for my parents because I know at the time the doctor told them to let me do whatever I wanted to do, not to prevent me from doing things, and they did let me. They let me experiment and they allowed me flexibility. In my mind I developed the attitude, and I have it today, that I have two legs.

There really haven't been that many obstacles in my functioning, physically and emotionally. Just like with the car, I kept driving and my parents kept letting me drive. I used to drive a lot right on through high school. I had a little accident right after I got my license. I skidded into another car. It was winter. It caused my parents a lot of anxiety, but they didn't prohibit me from driving. I wasn't reckless, taking crazy chances, but I did drive fast. In high school, the kids used to call me the "fender bender," but they rode with me.

The patient continued in school after the surgery. He reported that he had not been particularly involved in extracurricular activities before the surgery or afterward. He continued to be active in the church and was influenced by a minister there. After graduating from high school, he enrolled in a local college, but after a few months he quit and returned home. In looking back, he said he was just not ready for the experience. The following fall, he felt more ready and enrolled in a college recommended by his minister, a thousand miles from home. He went there and completed four years of excellent work. He was active in a fraternity and in various school functions. He also met the woman who was to become his wife, although they did not marry until some time after that. He said of those early years, after finishing high school:

I know one of my biggest concerns when I was eighteen or nineteen was for my future. I always had an ideal as a child of being married and having a family and my own children. I had concerns through the early years of the disability about whether I would be able to find anyone, whether I would be potent, all kinds of things like that. I didn't dwell on it. I wasn't depressed about it or anything, but it was a concern. I remember asking one of the doctors at the clinic if I would be able to function sexually, if I should have any concerns after all the radiation and all of the drugs. He said that there was no reason to be concerned and that I should be normal. After that I just didn't let it worry me. I always got a lot of help from the doctors. I felt that any concern that I had, I could discuss it with them, and I would get a very good answer.

Five years after the surgery, he was without any sign of cancer and was told that he was "cured." He recalled being "choked up" at the time, and in talking about it, tears came to his eyes. He said:

The doctor called me in and said that I could do anything that I wanted to do. It was the first time anyone had told me I was cured. It had a tremendous impact. I had a little camera with me and the doctor called his hospital photographer and had him take a picture of the two of us with it. I have that picture, even now.

He recalled the physician who treated him throughout the course of his illness as another of those people who had influenced him and helped him a lot.

After college, he went to work in a laboratory which specialized in cancer research. He felt this was directly related to his having had cancer. During that time he married. After several years he left that field, as he wanted to work more directly with people. He returned to graduate school and earned a degree in industrial psychology. During that time, and once subsequently, he sought personal psychotherapy. He had had several jobs in industrial psychology over the years, with steady advancement. He is the father of three children, lives in a community where he is active, with his wife, in the church and community affairs. He has recently faced a number of severe life stresses, including the death of one of his parents, some surgery himself, and the serious illness of one of his children and of his wife. There was also some worry about a cancer recurrence at one point, but that proved to be a false alarm.

When asked about what effect his illness has had on his children, he said that he didn't think it had had much effect. He did talk about how they had become aware of his disability. He said:

I guess there is a certain age where they're aware, I think about three years old. Growing up with it is different for my children than if a child saw an amputee on the street for the first time. I say to my wife sometimes that probably our kids will think that daddies with two legs are strange. They have accepted it. I think that my children have just seen me doing things. I answer their questions when they have questions. I tell them I got sick and had to have my leg cut off in order to live. They handle it pretty well. It's really amazing, the capacity of kids. Just like how they handled it when my father died. He was particularly close to them. A few weeks ago out of the clear blue, when my wife was away working, my little girl gave the grace. She said in the grace, "I hope that you have taken care of Grampa." We had had no recent discussions about that, and it had been a year since he had passed away. After dinner we had a little discussion about Grampa, and how much we miss him and so on. It is really amazing, her bringing it up. Kids can really pull things together better than adults. We can learn something from them.

In summing up, he said that he felt that although the experience of having cancer had been a major influence in his life, it had not overwhelmed him or dominated him. He commented several times, in several ways, about his being willing to try difficult tasks because of the experience. He said:

I've always taken the attitude that it wasn't going to stop me. I've always taken risks, probably more risks because of having had cancer. I have always felt and acted as if I had two legs. I do think I am stronger because of the experience. It's hard to verbalize, it's just sort of a gutsy feeling. I have the feeling that if it hadn't happened, I would not be taking action in the things that I am now. I think in a way it solidifies my experience.

In summing up what had helped him he repeatedly talked about the warm, strong, close relationships with others, within the family, with his minister, with people in the community, and with his doctors. He continues to have strong, warm relationships in his own family and in the community. When asked about who he modeled himself on or admired, he said:

I guess I remember modeling myself after people much more as a child. I think my father was probably the prime person because I spent a lot of time with him. I am on my own now.

He described himself as basically having a very positive attitude toward life. He said that he tries to give that attitude to the people he supervises at work. He said he felt reflecting on things had helped him deal with difficult situations in his life and he found the process of talking things over with me and reflecting on them helpful. In terms of the future he hoped for some advancement for himself and a good life for his wife and children. He said:

I don't want to be too caught up in things, in worries. I feel I am a mature person yet I want to be able to see the light side of things too, like a child who doesn't worry about hard situations, you know.

Case Two

The second man was younger and had recently finished college. He was almost the same age as the first survivor at the time his disease was discovered. He also had had surgery, chemotherapy, and radiation, although he had not lost a limb. He is a tall, handsome black man who spoke slowly and carefully. He described himself as independent and fully formed as an individual before the cancer was diagnosed. He emphasized that he had dealt with the experience rationally with his mind. This seemed to be a common thread through much of what he said— the rational, controlled approach to what was happening.

Of his growing up he said:

My parents had two separate, distinct personalities. They were both very strong and very sharp. When one of them sort of slipped up the other stepped right in and let him know he slipped. That environment never gave me room to be slack, to look back and feel sorry for myself or whatever. I think I really had to stay on my toes.

I was always very curious, and my curiosity was never put down by my parents. For example, about being black, they never said, "Don't go play with white kids, be careful about going into an Italian home because Italians supposedly don't like blacks," or anything like that. I had gone to school with white kids from the time I was five. I am curious about a lot of things and if something interests me then I will pretty much not heed what other people think, and just go ahead and find out about it.

I think I go into situations with the attitude of saying, "Listen now. I think I am being honest with you and I want to get to know you because I think you are an interesting person. If you are any kind of good person you will feel the same way about me."

My parents aren't very doting people. They expressed love in more concrete terms. My mother didn't say, "Oh my poor little baby," when the illness happened, or at any other time. She just didn't do it. I was having independent experience for a long time before I had the illness. For example, both my parents worked, and I had to go to school on the bus by myself. It was in a school in a district in a different town from the one where I lived. This was when I was nine. I did that by myself for a year. What I am trying to say is that I was always on my own. I was comfortable being on my own.

In speaking of his illness he said:

It started the summer between seventh and eighth grade. I was twelve. I just remember having a cyst. It started growing and I went away to summer camp. I was supposed to go for a long time, but then my parents told me I had to come back and have an operation before the end of camp. I just remember flashes like I was really having a great time in camp. I wrote to my parents and said I wanted to stay an extra four weeks. They said, "Sorry, you have to come home and have this operation." I was really sad about that.

The next thing I remember was the hospital, and not that much about it. I remember the nurses; a couple of good-looking nurses. I remember being able to go to the ward kitchen and make whatever food I wanted. I think I was in the hospital for about three weeks. I was sort of outgoing so I had the run of the floor. I knew all the other patients. I was only in the hospital a short time. One night a week after the hospitalization for the cyst removal, my father was not home, and my mother called me upstairs. She asked me if I knew what the word malignant meant. I said yes. She said they had run some tests on the matter they removed from the cyst and they found it was malignant and that I would have to start going in for chemotherapy and radiation.

So I started going into the clinic and I had x-ray treatments. Then the doctors did a couple of other tests. I think they were testing the lymph system all over my body. They did not find any other cancerous cells in my lymph nodes but they decided—just to be sure—that they would remove all of the lymph nodes that surrounded the cyst. They cut me down here as well. (He pointed to an area on his chest and abdomen.) I guess originally I had a scar down to here and then they went further down here. That was kind of rough. I was in good spirits except for the night of the surgery. I remember that. It was the second surgery. I was throwing up all over the place and it was really ... I just didn't want to be there. I was in a very bad frame of mind. Then after the surgery things started going up. I was treated like a king. Whatever I wanted my parents would bring me, things like that. I remember all the people I roomed with pretty well.

I can just remember a woman who came in all the time. She must have been in her fifties. I found out later she had had a son who died of cancer, and she was doing volunteer work on her own time. She just came around and talked to kids who were sick. I spent a lot of time just talking to her.

She was very interesting. She showed me like three or four card tricks. I remember those card tricks to this day.

The doctors were definitely very good people. They just had outrageous patience. I guess they have a really good sense of reality too, just a sense of here and now. They all had the attitude that one had to live for the day. I remember them whizzing into the room, just opening the curtains and saying, "This is what we are going to do today." Before you had a chance to bitch or moan they were right on top of everything, energetic.

What I remember about the chemotherapy is that it was fun. There were lots of kids my own age. I was never really nauseous or sick with it. I had a little hair loss but not too much. I was an outpatient. That was sort of a big deal for me because I had to come in every day for it. It was in the winter of my eighth grade—January and February. I came in by myself, all the way, on the bus and my mother would pick me up afterward. I really did it by myself.

It was never like I felt, why did this happen to me? I never really thought of it that way. I just decided that it had happened. I was going to go on from there.

He remembered his friends as being very helpful in getting him back involved in things after his treatment. He said:

I can remember coming home from the hospital and being two or three weeks into chemotherapy, part of my hair had fallen out and the x-ray treatments had discolored my skin. I was a pretty vain person. I had always thought I was not too bad looking and all of a sudden there was this big scar. That was something that really kind of worried me. I had a real good friend of mine who used to be my sister's boyfriend. He, two other friends, and I were standing around. They were going swimming, and he said, "Well, aren't you coming along?" I sort of hemmed and hawed and said, "No, I don't think so." He said, "Well, what do you mean you don't think so," and then he said, "You're either coming or you're not coming." I said, "I don't know, I don't think I'm going." He said, "What's the matter, why don't you want to go swimming?" and I said, "Well, you know, I really don't want people to see my scar, when I swim with no shirt on." He had an incredulous look on his face and just said, "Are you going crazy? Is that the reason you're not going swimming?" He was just so totally put off by it. I thought, well, if he thinks this way about it then maybe I am a little crazy about it. I went swimming and had a good time.

I changed schools between seventh and eighth grades so that I was in a new school system when I came back from having the surgery and the treatments. In eighth grade I just didn't compete in sports at all. I just assumed I couldn't do any sports. In fact, in that year I was exempted from gym. In ninth grade I got back into sports. The same friend who got me to go swimming came to me and said, "Well, are you going out for soccer?" and I said, "Well, I don't know," and he said, "Well, didn't you play in seventh grade?" I said yes. He said, "Well, weren't you pretty good?" and I said yes, and he talked me into it. I went out for it, and it was like the best thing I ever did. It got me back into sort of manly things and doing things for other people. I went on from there and played all through high school and I played in college.

He finished high school and then went on to college. He chose an excellent college on the West Coast. In college he reported getting involved in political theory, believing in it for a time and then giving it up. He maintained an independent, somewhat removed perspective during college, although he had a number of good and close friends.

I was sort of involved in a quasi-radical socialist trip for a while. The stuff I was doing just wasn't being read in my department. The department was very conservative. They would tolerate it but there was no genuine respect or anything. There was nothing really that could be done about it. So I just decided I was there for the status the university would give me and the few friends I could ferret out. There were a lot of good people, a lot of good people. It was stimulating.

When asked about his ideology, he said:

I can't really say that I live by any ideology except my own. Let's say I think Marxism is the most fair system that I can think of in terms of humanity. But in terms of its application I am not a strong enough person to try to bring it about. When I was in college I was less futile about it, and I had some hopes change could take place. I liked it. My thinking was that it was a good system for people and somehow magically it would come about. Now I am a little more conservative. I don't think there is any such thing as radical change. I have never experienced it.

The survivor was interviewed a few months after finishing college. His own independence and his will to do things by himself were shown by the fact that he had chosen not to go directly to graduate school or professional school, although he certainly was capable and had the opportunity. Rather he had chosen to take time off to think and to travel. He felt somewhat disillusioned by the college experience. He reported that it was hard not going on to professional school as many of his friends had, but that he felt he had made the right decision. He reported that his parents had also adjusted to the decision, although they were not particularly happy with it. At the time of the interview, he was actively involved with relationships with others and interested in sports and music. He had searched for and found a job which would enable him to save money and then travel around the world. He had a particular interest in visiting Eastern Europe and the Far East.

In talking about these decisions he said:

I just don't know what I am going to settle on. I just say, listen, if I settle on just this one thing then I am going to put blinders on. I'll just see down that one alley, and I won't see over here and I won't see over there. Whereas now I can go and talk to people of all different sorts; to a doctor, or bartender, to someone who is mature and intelligent or someone who is not. I want to stay objective, young, and open-minded. Before taking this time off I was thinking of going to law school and I still am. I just don't think it is right for me right now. I sort of look at life as a rope. The further along you get the closer you get to the end and the harder it is to do the things you want to do for a long time. So I figure I can put off a lot of serious things right now, such as what I am going to be fifteen or twenty years from now, and concentrate more on sowing my wild oats.

In summing up his experiences with cancer, he said he had just concentrated on getting well. He said religion had not been particularly important to him in dealing with it, although he does remember saying, "God, please help me out of this" after the second operation. He had stopped going to church sometime in his late teens. He reported wondering about what had caused the cancer. He said:

I get this sort of feeling sometimes, that something ridiculous could have been the cause for cancer, like maybe on a certain day I was exposed to a certain train that passed by carrying some unusual chemical. I think my ability to deal with the cancer has a lot to do with my personality. I think my whole personality was formed already. It could have been a setback, but it wasn't. I just turned twelve when it happened. I think a lot had to do with my real sense of independence. I've always had a real sense of independence, and I'm pretty stubborn. I'm the hardest person to convince that I am a stubborn person, because it seems to me that I'll do anything for anybody, but if I don't want to do it, then I genuinely don't do it. Before the thing came up, and now since then, I'm really comfortable being by myself. I think that helped me deal with the reality of the illness, and since then.

Once I found out about the cancer I just fit it in. I didn't do it consciously, but I just tried to fit it into the normal pattern. It's perhaps a very cold and calculating way to think. I wouldn't characterize myself that way, but I would say I'm very calculating. I'm very wary of things, I like to check a lot of things out before I do something, to explore all the options. I just remember being very rational about the experience. For example, when friends asked me about what had happened, I answered them and that was that. I don't think that there was any kind of stigma involved. I think that I was treated pretty equally from the beginning after surgery.

The survivor reported that he was close to his family, and to his friends, and that he particularly appreciated the way his parents encouraged his independence. They had encouraged it in his decision on what college to go to; his parents had wanted him to go to a different school from the one he went to, but supported his choice. Of them, he said:

They never took away decisions that a lot of parents take away from their children, even at a young age. College was one example. Earlier they let me decide when I wanted to drop out of going to one fancy private school and go to another public school. They left that up to me.

In terms of the experience itself, he said that it had really helped him grow.

I think it forced me to toughen up. I think that before I was sick, I was kind of the sissyish type. I was just pretty spoiled. After the illness I got into sports and I got help from that friend of mine, so I think that sort of opened up another side of me that I didn't know was there. I look back and I don't have any bad memories about it or see it as a dark period of my life. I sort of remember it as a fun time, but one that forced me to toughen up.

Case Three

The third survivor interviewed was 16, the youngest of the three described in this chapter. When he was 7, he had a tumor removed and then had been treated with chemotherapy. Several years later he had a relapse, a second surgical procedure, and additional chemotherapy and radiation therapy. It was several years after the end of the most recent treatment when he was interviewed. He was a short, muscular youngster who spoke directly and clearly, but did not elaborate much on his answers. He denied consciously thinking over or considering much of what had happened to him, but he had worked out a way of dealing with things which helped him and which he could describe. He began by talking about his current life, emphasizing his activity and involvement.

I am leading a normal life. I do everything like everybody else. I'm on the ski team and the season is about to start. Right now I'm getting psyched up for skiing. That is really what I love to do, skiing. I play sports all year round. I play soccer in the fall, ski in the winter, baseball in the spring, and baseball and soccer in the summer. What I like about sports is the action. Soccer, for example: I play it rough because that is the way I've been taught. We play a hard game, rough but close. I went out for football as a freshman, but I really didn't like it. It was boring, there was no action. You go in, you come out, and you stand around between plays. In soccer you're on the go all the time.

In skiing, I just like going down and trying to get the best time I can, attacking the hill, pushing really hard. I think over in my mind how I am going to take the turns, how I am going to use my edges if there is ice. I like the action in sports.

He is the youngest of four children, and the only one still living at home. Both parents work. The other children all live in the same general area as the parents, and family gatherings are frequent. The survivor attends high school and reports many friends. He did not remember much of his childhood before surgery, except that the family was a close, caring family and that he had been interested in sports even then. He remembered pain before being hospitalized, and his first hospitalization for surgery on Thanksgiving day, followed by another surgical procedure a few months later.What he remembered most about all this was the help the doctors gave him, the closeness he felt with his family, and the pain of it.

Of his family he said:

We stuck together when I was sick. We never separated and we never laid down, so everybody was just one. They took care of me and spoiled me I guess, when I was sick.

I remember pains, strong pains right in my gut. They would come off and on, and at first my mom wasn't sure what was causing them. I remember they kept coming on in school. They went on for about a week and then we went to the doctor and he said something about how he had to take something out. This is when I had the operation. I had my operation the day before Thanksgiving. I missed the rival-school football game. We were supposed to go, but I ended up in the hospital and missed Thanksgiving at home. My family snuck in a turkey plate for me. I always eat the turkey leg, every year.

Then I knew I just had to get some kind of operation. I didn't know what kind, they didn't tell me, but I had it. A few months later, I had to come back and see my doctor, the one who still sees me. He said I would have to come in for bone marrow and all kinds of tests, like having blue dye put in my feet. I was back on the ward. I remember I was there and I missed New Year's at home. Then I had to come back every two weeks for treatments. After I stopped treatments something recurred on the left side of my neck. I had more treatments for that; about three years of radiation. With the radiation, I used to come in to the hospital and spend about six weeks. We would just go home on weekends. I also had some medication, methotrexate. I remember the methotrexate because I got sick and lost my hair. I started losing it in the fourth grade, and in the fifth I didn't have any, and then later it grew back. Then I lost it again in the sixth and seventh and then it came back again, and came in really thick. I haven't lost it since I've been off treatment for about two years.

When I was on the pills I would really be nauseous and get very sick easily. I didn't want to eat. I lost my taste buds for some things like milk. I still hate milk. I drink it, but I don't really like it. My stomach was always screwed up. We would go out to eat in a restaurant, I would feel sick, and we would come back home again. Then I would feel better and we would go back out again, then I'd get sick again.

When he was asked how he explained the experience to himself or any thoughts about what caused it, he said:

I dealt with it just by thinking about when it was going to be over and when I was going to stop taking the medicine, things like that. Many times I used to get so sick that in ways I just didn't want answers. All of the nurses and doctors were very good. There was one doctor in particular, I still see him. He worked at the hospital, but he lives not far from us now and he runs a Scout troop. I've gone with him on trips with his troop several times.

You're in good hands, especially in the hospital I was in. They treat you like a king. The nurses are really nice and the doctors explain everything. I just didn't really ask many questions. It was more or less my mother or father that asked them. I didn't really want to know what was going on because I didn't feel that good. Mostly, what they told me was what they were going to do when they cut on me. They would explain the basic procedures. They would tell me anything else when I asked.

The duration of his illness was much longer than the other two interviewees', more than five years. It has only been a few years since the end of his treatment. In reflecting on it, he emphasized the closeness and warmth with his family. He said particularly that his mother dealt with it very well.

She drove me in for the chemotherapy. We got much closer, and we can talk much more easily about mostly everything.

Of his own philosophy he said:

I think in my own life, the worst has already happened. My health is much better now. I try to recognize what has to be, accept it and go on from there. In terms of what I've learned, I don't know how I have changed. I missed a lot of school because of all the treatments and could have changed because of that. Being sick certainly affected my sports.

I do think that I have matured more than most kids in the way I look at things. I find I can talk to older people more easily. I am not quiet. I say what I mean and what I feel. I come right out and say it. I'm not scared to ask what is wrong and things like that. I'm not scared to get hurt either. I will take a lot of risks. If you don't take risks, it is going to be a boring life. For example, my friends and I go mountain climbing. We usually go free-climbing and we don't use ropes, we just scale the mountain. We play football and things like that without equipment. Skiing is a lot of fun too. I do a little bit of jumping. There is always the possibility of coming down wrong and breaking your neck or something. I like the challenge. In terms of meeting people I'm willing to take the risks too. I try to be friendly to everybody. If they don't like me it doesn't bother me.

At present he is working hard in school, playing sports, and has a wide variety of friends. He had a brief episode of surgery last spring for an undescended testis and has had to deal with the fact that his father recently had a tumor removed and was treated with radiation. He reported one episode of depression, not severe enough to cause him to seek any kind of psychiatric help, but of concern to him. It was resolved spontaneously after a couple of months. It is noteworthy that the way he dealt with the recent surgery was somewhat similar to the way he deals with feelings about what has happened to him in having cancer, that is, he was extremely active. Right after getting out of the hospital, in fact the next day, he went to baseball practice, although he was supposed to be inactive for two weeks. He also began to play soccer immediately after the operation.

When asked what kind of advice he would give someone who had to go through what he had been through, he said:

Just face the facts, don't worry about it. That's the worst thing you could do—worrying about it. Try to keep your mind occupied by doing other things.

In talking about how his relationships changed after surgery and chemotherapy, he said:

Having the surgery made me a little tougher. I made a lot of good friends and they helped me. People used to call me names when I didn't have any hair and I had a lot of kids stick up for me. I found my friends that way. I got my reputation that way too—that I would stick up for myself. Overall, in terms of what helped me, it was my family and my friends. The overall effect of the experience on me was just getting closer to people, closer to friends, and things like that.

Our conversation ended with a talk about the future. He has plans and a number of hopes for the future. He is not sure what he wants to do, but is sure that it will be something active. He would like to go to Colorado and do some skiing. He has considered working in law enforcement and he has considered college. He is planning a major hiking trip on the Appalachian Trail, and we talked at length about the planning and details of that trip as the interviews ended.

Discussion

Each personal story is unique, and the way each survivor has coped with the stress of cancer in childhood is distinctive. Nonetheless, there are certain common themes in the three accounts presented here which reinforce the more general quantitative findings of the larger study, as well as suggesting additional important ideas for further study.

The first major common theme is the importance of relationships with others in facilitating coping with cancer. Each man called attention to this fact, although each has a different lifestyle. The first survivor's account is very clear on this point: he emphasized the closeness and support of his parents and his siblings, as well as the way the whole town rallied around him and the value of the prayer group in helping him. The second survivor appreciated the clearness and definiteness in his parents' support of him and the fact that they did not baby him or change their expectations of him. He described how friends were particularly valuable in helping him overcome inhibitions and get back into the mainstream of adolescent activities. The third man, younger than the other two, and having had cancer at a younger age, also emphasized the family. Much has been written about the importance of a network of social support in coping with illness (Eisenberg, 1977). The inner perceptions of these three survivors support this general idea, while their differences reflect the wide range of family styles and social networks that can be supportive.

The second important central theme is the role of action following the cancer.

Each of the three was very active physically after recovery; the first survivor through his car, the second and third through competitive athletics. All had been active before the cancer. The illness experience itself involved an enforced passivity, a sense of not being in control. The actions, the activities in sports and driving, served as a helpful counterbalance or compensation for this passivity, at the same time serving as a clear behavioral demonstration of being intact, not ill, and not handicapped.

The third major theme is the use of denial. Clearly, certain aspects of the experience are not as well-remembered as others. The first survivor covered over all the trauma of losing his leg rather quickly. The second, emphasizing rationality, did not remember fears and frightening feelings during his hospitalizations. None of the three wanted to dwell on the negative aspects of his hospitalizations, a central point in all their cancer experiences, each dwelling rather on the positive experiences of knowing the doctors, meeting people, and—above all—on doing well after the experience of hospitalization. On the other hand, there is none of what in psychoanalytic terminology is called pathological denial; that is, in none of these men is there a refusal to see certain aspects of the experience which then limits or obliterates the capacity to test or deal with reality and to function well in the real world. Indeed, in some ways the major handling of the experience— not dwelling on certain painful, frightening things that happened to them, being active in a wide variety of endeavors, and looking to the future—is really more like a conscious decision to behave that way than an unconscious refusal to face or see certain things. In this connection, the recent work of George Vaillant (1977) on adaptive ego defenses and the development of mature defenses over time is relevant. Using a thirty-year longitudinal study of healthy men, Vaillant has described a hierarchy of ego defenses and has persuasively argued that defenses change over time.

Within the group of defenses he describes, denial and suppression are particularly relevant to the stories of these men. Vaillant uses a traditional psychoanalytic definition of denial, as explained above, and describes it as a primitive defense, which might be used in a major way by a child, someone with a serious mental illness, or someone in crisis. The mature equivalent, which develops over time from denial, is suppression, the conscious choosing to put aside, to not consider certain disturbing or painful events. Starting perhaps at the time they were hospitalized or shortly thereafter, these survivors used suppression, that is, dealing with cancer by deliberately not thinking about it and not dwelling on certain painful aspects of treatment. They did not deny the events or memories of them. Use of the term suppression draws attention to the adaptive qualities of what they did, as well as pointing out that they had some control over what they thought about.

Whether denial or suppression is the more appropriate way to describe the ways the men dealt with some of the negative or painful aspects of their treatment, it is striking how much they all do remember and how clearly they remember what happened to them. In the interviews, they seemed to be expressing their ongoing processes of self-understanding. The men had clearly wrestled with many of the questions on their own, long before the interviews. Having cancer was a major life event and, for them at least, it required working through in a major psychological way. The form of this working through is evident in the accounts. All three men, particularly the older two, accepted fully what had happened to them, rather than refusing to believe it had happened or feeling controlled or victimized by it. Thus, the first survivor, rather than becoming overwhelmed by the amputation and complaining about it, concentrated on what he could do. At the same time, through his work in industrial psychology, he used his experience in coping with the illness to help others.

For all three, the psychological work of coming to grips with the experience involved making sense of it: being aware of what was helpful or useful in dealing with it—for example, the support of others—and seeing it in perspective in relation to other events and feelings about their own lives. The two older men were able to reflect considerably about what they had been like before the illness and to see it in the context of their other experiences. Each man had a strong sense of self, was conscious of how he felt about things, and was aware of how he affected others. This too is a kind of self-understanding. All three noted changes in themselves because of the experience. The third survivor commented that he was now more direct, open, and clear in meeting people. The first said he felt he had become more venturesome, risked more, and perhaps even gained more. Thus, the cancer was integrated into the whole of their experience, not seen as an isolated event never to be felt or talked about. In this sense it was accepted and learned from, not denied.

Clearly, one cannot make a causal inference about the relationship between such self-understanding and coping based on retrospective accounts, but it is striking that self-understanding was important to these good copers. That is, they believed it to be important and worked at it.

These histories support the idea that a psychological working through of the event, coming to grips with it emotionally, is indeed a part of a healthy, adaptive response to the stress of cancer. Although the role of denial/suppression is important, what these accounts emphasize is that a much broader perspective is needed in understanding how people deal adaptively with the stress of a major illness such as cancer. Certainly, some aspects of the experience are put away from consideration and not dwelt on. But just as certainly, major aspects of the experience are consciously thought about and dealt with in those who cope adequately. Self-understanding, that is, making sense of their experience and working out an understanding for themselves, was an essential part of successful coping for these three survivors. Much more work is needed to substantiate these preliminary findings, but their implication is that researchers need to pay attention to the process and nature of psychological working through and self-understanding in studying the survivors of serious illnesses. More broadly, these findings suggest that clinicians should be aware of self-understanding and psychological working through in patients as they deal with their illnesses.

Chapter 12

Implications for Patient Care

The dramatic growth in the population of childhood cancer survivors and survivor families in the 1970s has been documented in the preceding chapters. We have discussed in some depth the medical and psychological hazards which survivors and their families face. The real value of this study, however, lies not so much in past events and experience as in the meaning the accumulated information holds for medical and mental health professionals. The purpose of this chapter is to review the key findings of our project for guidance on how to improve the care of those who are now in treatment by learning from the families we studied. Suggestions for improving the psychological care of survivors are also offered, both because the number of survivors is increasing and because the level of adjustment of survivors is so variable.

Summary of Key Findings

Medical Risks

The medical and epidemiological data reviewed in Chapters 2 and 4 suggest that the survivors of childhood cancer remain at risk for recurrence or development of second tumors at a rate that is twenty times greater than that of the general population. Because of a relatively rapid evolution in treatment, it is likely that improvements in survival statistics will continue. At the same time, however, the long-range effects of many new techniques and therapies are necessarily still largely unknown.

Growth arrest, dental abnormalities, neurological impairment, reduced intellectual functioning, and skeletal deformities are all potential late effects of treat-

By Gerald P. Koocher and John E. O'Malley.

ment for childhood cancer. Weaknesses in organ systems and resulting organ failures or impairment, including the liver, kidneys, heart, lungs, and immune system, are all possible. Delayed puberty or sterility has been frequently reported. The long-term risk of second tumors as a result of radiation or chemotherapy, and the enduring side effects of surgery, including amputations, scars, and other mechanical or cosmetic injuries, are also potential problems. Few survivors experience all such complications, and many survivors will not experience any of them, but there are undoubtedly special medical risks attendant on survival.

It is clear that the quality of life for survivors can be quite good. Many go on to lead productive and healthy adult lives, marry, have children, and maintain a quality of life consistent with others in the general population. A healthy adult psychosocial adjustment, however, is not assured.

Emotional Risks

Impairment of mental health may be another major consequence of survival. Although less than half (47 percent) of the survivors we studied had any symptoms, and a quarter had only mild symptoms, 10 percent had moderate symptoms and 11 percent had severe psychological symptoms which impaired their functioning. No specific data exist on the incidence of psychological symptoms among noncancer "normals" in the general population; however, our small-sample control study of children who survive other chronic but not life-threatening childhood illnesses suggests that cancer survivors are at much greater risk for emotional disturbance as a late side effect. The causal role of cancer per se is not entirely clear and caution must be used in making generalizations, but the very real risk has been documented.

In our population of survivors, some seemed to be at greater psychological risk than others. When we compared well-adjusted cancer survivors with those who showed some evidence of adjustment difficulty, a number of variables contributed to differentiating the two groups. Children whose cancer is discovered in infancy or early childhood, whose treatment is short, who do not have relapses and whose families are supportive and communicate openly have the best psychological prognosis.

Survivors who were judged to be poor copers at the time of interview reported more depression, more anxiety, and more self-esteem problems on standardized personality measures than did their cohorts. The poor copers were also more likely than their better-adjusted peers to be unable to complete or resolve projective storytelling tasks. These data seem to reflect the chronic continuing uncertainty faced by all cancer survivors, which is especially salient to those who are not able to cope effectively.

Psychiatric interviews revealed that the poor copers tended to experience greater fluctuation in mood, more obvious anxiety, more depression, and poorer self-esteem than their well-adjusted peers. Denial and suppression of stressful feelings, which are nearly universal psychological defense mechanisms, served many of the survivors quite well, as is also illustrated by the cases described in Chapter 11. While denial is sometimes regarded an an inappropriate coping style in psychiatric patients, it seems to be quite adaptive and even necessary, in varying degrees, for cancer patients and survivors.

In contrast to the medical risks, the emotional hazards which childhood cancer survivors face should be quite amenable to preventive intervention. Laboratory research will ultimately develop more effective and less devastating treatment for cancer, but in mental health, current techniques have great promise. Mental health intervention designed to reduce social isolation, provide family support, and concentrate on the most vulnerable cancer patients at the appropriate time are possible now.

Family Relationships

Interviews with parents revealed the profound effect that their child's cancer had exerted on the entire family. Contrary to popular myth, marital stability seemed unaffected by the cancer experience and, in fact, divorce rates among the survivors' families were lower than in the general population. Whether these statistics would be different if the child patient had died is unknown.

Parental income and socioeconomic status did seem related to the quality of long-term psychosocial adjustment. This relationship clearly points to the need for providing adequate financial support to families faced with this catastrophic chronic illness. Some parents still had residual financial obligations for their child's cancer treatment many years after the end of treatment.

The tone set by physicians and clinics in their own community was of major importance throughout the family's cancer experience. How procedures were carried out and the way in which news was communicated seemed far more important to the parents than the specifics of actual treatment. The attitude of physicians was critical to the parents, who needed warmth, honesty, courtesy, and consideration at the time of diagnosis and treatment. It was important that the caretakers gave families a measure of realistic encouragement and hope, along with a sense that they were cared about and that the best possible care would be provided or found for their child.

Many parents described the cancer experience as having had a positive effect on their marriages. They tended to draw closer and rely on each other for support more than in the past, while becoming more sensitive to each other's needs, coping styles, and parenting skills. Most parents also described the importance of feeling able or permitted to express their own emotions. They believed it was important to have someone at the treatment facility available for this purpose, particularly to discuss what they could expect emotionally from their child and themselves.

They believed that such psychological support could help to deal with guilt feelings and anxiety and expand their repertoire for coping. While this clearly implied that a mental health professional who is a member of the oncology treatment team would be ideal, the parents felt they would be selfish to share their burdens with the child's medical caretakers and did not wish to be singled out as parents with emotional problems. The clear implications for practice with such families are discussed below.

Parents often had lingering concerns about their child's future, both medically and psychosocially. These included worry about disease recurrence, late effects of treatment, and the child's reproductive capacity, and such psychosocial concerns as the child's peer relationships, school functioning, and self-esteem. It is interesting that the parents' reported levels of concern correlated highly with the independent ratings assigned in psychological and psychiatric interviews.

The cancer experience also had a profound effect on siblings, who frequently experienced feelings of being left out, jealousy, resentment, or guilt. Siblings frequently worried about their own health, and they seemed particularly vulnerable to psychological stress in families where closed communication patterns blocked access to factual information about the sick child and the illness. Fortunately, most of the siblings we interviewed appeared to have resolved unpleasant feelings and developed normal sibling relationships with the former patient by the time of our interview. One must wonder about the inability of some siblings to resolve such issues when the cancer patient does not survive. Clearly, the whole family must be included when addressing the mental health needs of childhood cancer patients.

Social Issues

We discovered several special problems or concerns for childhood cancer survivors as they related to aspects of life away from home and hospital. These include the effect of visible physical impairment, marriage for survivors, employment discrimination, insurance problems, and the effects of how and when the survivors learned their illness was a particular form of cancer.

We found that visible physical impairment did not seem to be related to long-term psychosocial adjustment. However, half of the survivors in our sample were over 21 and half of this group were not married. We discovered that the never married females were more likely than the married females to have severer visible impairments, whereas among the males the married had more severe visible impairments than the never married. Although not statistically significant there was a tendency for the never married survivors to have more psychiatric symptoms than did their married peers; there were no significant sex differences. Given the apparent relative stigma of visible handicaps in women and the risks to self-esteem which may accompany delayed puberty, it seems likely that women survivors could benefit from special psychological intervention, which is discussed below.

Once married, the fact of having survived cancer seemed to have little negative effect on the marriage, according to interviews with the spouses of survivors. The risk of recurrence was a negative factor, but sharing discussions of the cancer experience before the marriage was reported by many to have enhanced closeness. Many of the survivors had become parents and all of the progeny were in good health.

Despite industry studies showing that cancer survivors in general are not absent more than other employees, are not poorer job performers, and do not increase business insurance costs, 40 percent of our now adult survivors (those over 18) reported some form of employment or insurance problem linked directly to their cancer history. Survivors who attempted to enlist in the armed services were routinely rejected solely on the basis of their cancer history, despite excellent physical health and an interval of fifteen or more years since treatment for cancer ended. Many of the survivors who did experience some form of discrimination experienced heightened anxiety and lowered self-esteem. Our survivors could generally get health insurance through group plans at work; but those whose circumstances dictated individual rather than group policies often experienced denial or specific exclusions in coverage. Almost half had been denied life insurance, were required to pay higher than normal premiums, or were told of a prolonged waiting period ranging from three to twelve years.

Many of our survivors were treated at a time when the philosophy of care for children with cancer was that the patients should not be told of their diagnosis or prognosis. We found a higher frequency of adjustment problems among those who were not told their diagnosis until late in treatment, or who "found out" independently rather than from their parents or physician. Early information on diagnosis and prognosis, on the other hand, was related to a greater likelihood of good adjustment. We do not conclude that telling, or not telling is per se the critical factor, but rather that the choice made reflects the general attitude and tone of communication in a family. The potential for supplying needed emotional support seems considerably greater in families that communicate more openly.

Survivor-Investigator Relationship

Our relationship with the survivors and family members we studied was unusual, by virtue of the drama inherent in the topics we discussed; the very low refusal rate among those invited to participate is an evident consequence of the overriding importance of the subject to the participants. The survivors and their families almost universally expressed a debt of gratitude to the medical profession in general and to the institution we represented in particular. It is quite possible that they wished to present as good a picture of themselves and their experiences as possible. This is most evident in the occasional comments by parents that their marriage "was strengthened" by the experience of their child's cancer treatment.

Some siblings, and some survivors, expressed the belief that they had been improved as people by virtue of the adversity they experienced. Few objective observers would recommend cancer treatment as a character-building experience, but just this sort of rationalization was quite common among those we interviewed.

Even survivors who remained angry about some aspects of their cancer experiences after many years found individual memories, people, and experiences to praise. The tendency toward rationalization is perhaps representative of hope in the human spirit. The phenomenon of finding some praiseworthy experiences to recount does not invalidate our study by any means; it is a rather special and noteworthy aspect of the investigator-survivor relationship.

The Natural History of Surviving

Change in the treatment of a disease often alters both normal progress or course of the illness and the course of psychological events wtih which patients and their families must cope. We have learned that there seems to be a predictable natural history of surviving, and we can identify with some assurance a series of stressful events and a pattern of coping which emerges over an extended period of survival. For purposes of discussion, we have divided this part of our report into two sections: onset and extended adaptation.

Onset

The onset of childhood cancer is depicted in Figure 12-1 as a function of stress over time. The level of stress experienced has been defined in terms of the amount of adaptive change or energy a person must exert to cope with ecological shifts, whether temperature, population, or psychological changes. In Figure 12-1 time is expressed in days along the horizontal axis; the person's or family's hypothetical stress level is expressed on the vertical axis. The dotted line across the center of the figure represents the normal stress baseline of the given person or family. The day-to-day level of stress generally fluctuates to some degree on either side of the baseline, but there is a considerable rise in both stress and anxiety with the diagnosis of cancer.

Most parents and survivors report that anxiety and stress were highest at the time of diagnosis. Discovery of a life-threatening illness and uncertainty about what is to follow have a profound effect. Many parents described the emotional stress as dropping off a bit as treatment began and "something was being done," but the emotional shock often seemed to last for an extended period that ranged from three to twelve months. During this period the stress level never seemed to drop back to the pre-illness level, and an assortment of events associated with the course of the disease in treatment evoked new stress peaks.

A hypothetical pattern based on these reports is in Figure 12-1. The figure shows a stress peak at diagnosis which trails off in the subsequent days as treatment begins. A week to ten days later our hypothetical patient develops an infection in response to falling blood counts induced by chemotherapy. Perhaps a hospital admission for antibiotics is needed, and inevitably the stress level rises. Three to four weeks after the diagnosis and beginning of treatment, hair loss begins; increased stress accompanies this bodily change. And so it goes, with intermittent hospitalizations, drug reactions, relapses, and other stressful events punctuating an already elevated stress level for both patient and family.

The course illustrated in Figure 12-1 eventually fades and the stress level may approach baseline, but the process is a very gradual one. Some families report a

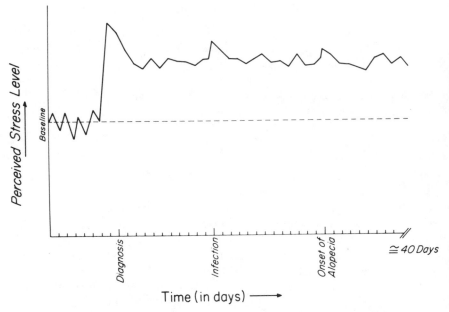

Figure 12-1. Hypothetical Stress/Time Graph: Onset Phase of Cancer

continuing high level of stress until the magical five-year point is reached, although this time limit may have little justification in terms of objective scientific data, as discussed in Chapter 2.

Extended Adaptation

The pattern of coping with stress among long-term survivors is represented in Figure 12-2 by two hypothetical survivors, a good coper and a poor coper. The chart begins at the five-year point, sixty months after diagnosis, and extends over an additional forty months. We have imagined two patients with identical baseline stress levels. Even sixty or more months after diagnosis neither patient has totally returned to the old pattern. The good coper often returns to the baseline, but still deviates from it more than before, especially with respect to certain stressful events. The poor coper is seldom able to reach the baseline, and tends to overreact to stressful events compared to the good coper.

Stress 1 could be the emergence of a symptom similar to the ones which first warned of the original cancer. Stress 2 could be an infection or a similarly "normal" short-term illness. Stress 3 might be the death of a friend or relative from

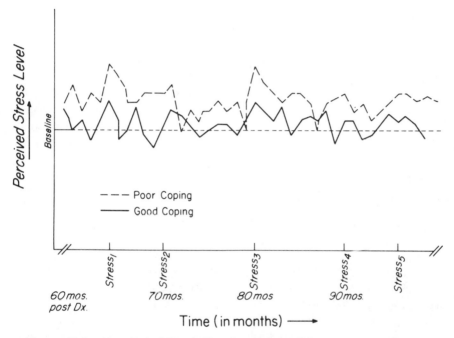

Figure 12-2.   Hypothetical Stress/Time Graph: Good Copers versus Poor Copers

cancer; and so forth. For all survivors, worries seem to lurk just below the surface of consciousness, ready to emerge and cause renewed anxiety in response to memory-jogging events or feelings. The people who cope well seem, for whatever, reason, better able to keep the stresses under control by the use of adaptive denial or other means.

Although the nature of the stressful events and their effect is to some degree predictable, the timing of the events is generally an unknown. Still, advance knowledge of potential stresses can be helpful in itself (Seligman, 1975), both to

the patient and to caregivers. An intervention model based on preventive anticipation of stresses would be expected to provide some potential measure of anxiety
reduction.

Recommendations for Care of Patients

On the basis of the data obtained in this study and the summary of findings
presented above, it is possible to make a series of recommendations for the care of
both newly diagnosed patients and those who are rapidly joining the ranks of the
long-term survivors. These include recommendations for general care as well as
suggestions for medical personnel, mental health professionals, public policy makers, and researchers.

General Care

The needs of childhood cancer patients today are quite different from those of
a decade ago, when long-term survival was relatively rare. A need for support and
sympathy has given way to a need for support, hope, and active treatment by
medical and psychological professionals who approach the patient with curative
intent. The focus has shifted from helping parents to cope with death to helping
the patient and family to deal with life and uncertainty. It is no longer sufficient
to consider only the medical issues facing the patient. Even after medical rehabilitation is well under way and psychological stresses are being effectively managed,
the patient and the family must confront a host of other adjustment issues, not the
least of which are staggering costs of medical care, educational choices, and the
whole matter of a future orientation in the face of uncertainty.

It is evident that rehabilitation is an outdated concept if we are to maximize the
adjustment of these patients. Rather than working to restore lost functions, we
should be working to prevent or minimize the psychosocial losses patients and
their families are likely to experience. Preventive psychotherapy aimed at sustaining the child patient's ability to relate in the community and facilitating open
communication in the family is critical.

Long-term survival of the physical ravages of cancer does not assure uniformly
good adjustment in psychosocial spheres. Systematic long-term follow-up care for
both the medical and the psychological needs of childhood cancer survivors and
their families is needed. Only by routinely attending to psychological needs in the
same way that medical needs are addressed can we hope to minimize the late
psychosocial consequences of childhood cancer.

Primary Medical Care

At Diagnosis the attitude of the family practitioner or local pediatrician seems
to be of paramount importance. Since childhood cancer is a relatively rare event
in most pediatric practices, it is important that professionals be educated on the

changing morbidity and mortality for childhood cancers. Only by being acquainted with recent advances can the local family physician sincerely provide the initial climate of realistic hope and support so necessary to families during the stressful period surrounding the time of diagnosis. Continuing education courses on the newest developments in cancer treatment should also routinely include discussions of a psychological nature on how to communicate with families. So many families reported first encounters made more frightening than necessary by the local physician's lack of current information or seeming lack of appropriate concern that the latter problem seems to be as significant as the former. Specifically, parents expressed the desire to sit down with the physician in private to discuss the possible diagnosis, realities of treatment, prognosis, and possible referral to a major cancer treatment center. Most primary care physicians in the community completed their medical training before the recent advances in care of the child with cancer; these physicians need to be made aware that increasingly successful therapies are indeed available. Only in this way will they be able to confront their own suspicion of a cancer diagnosis honestly and without the fear which could impair comfortable communication with the family.

At the Oncology Treatment Center the watchwords for the best patient care are stability and teamwork. Family members need to gain a feeling of stability, support, and consistency of care during the difficult early days of treatment. They need to feel that staff members are available to provide them with both information and the time to formulate questions. And much time is often needed: even the brightest of family members may have to ask the same questions several times before "hearing" the answers fully. Only by establishing a supportive, trusting relationship from the outset can the medical staff ensure maximum supportive cooperation from the whole family.

Ideally, one senior physician should be the patient's key "doctor" throughout the course of treatment. This arrangement may be difficult when the patient travels to surgeon, to radiologist, to oncologist, and it may be difficult in teaching hospitals, where rotation of interns and residents necessarily leads to service changes and breaks in the continuity of care. The pattern of multiple caretakers on the treatment team is clearly stressful for both the patient and other family members. Perhaps one solution is a model based on private practice, one physician being designated to supervise the patient's care for the duration of treatment regardless of service rotations. Designating such a team captain for the treatment of each patient may make it possible to bridge potential gaps or lapses in communication by channeling and coordinating efforts through a single caretaker.

Given the complex nature of current cancer treatments, including costly diagnostic and therapeutic instruments and diverse staff specialists, most patient care should be coordinated through a comprehensive cancer center. For patients who live at some distance from such centers, much care may ultimately be transferred to competent local hospitals or physicians. It has consistently become evident, however, that basic coordination of care ought to originate in a highly specialized cancer care hospital.

It is also evident that the oncology treatment team should include mental health professionals. Whether these team members are drawn from psychology, psychiatry, or social work does not seem to matter. The critical factor is that the mental health professional must be willing to join fully in the team treatment approach, both to understand fully what the patient and family face and to be accepted as a valued consultant by the treatment team (Koocher et al., 1979). Participation of mental health professionals in the treatment team also implies a recognition of a need for emotional support for those who work in the high-stress medical environment of oncology in general, and pediatric cancer in particular.

Long-Term Medical Follow-up is a relatively new realm in the treatment of childhood cancer, but—as Chapters 2 and 4 indicate—one which cannot be ignored. Such follow-ups pose an interesting dilemma in the light of our discovery of the importance of adaptive denial to adequate psychosocial coping. How ought the physician to deal with the childhood cancer survivor who "does not worry about recurrence" and therefore does not seek regular checkups, or the long-term survivor who had extensive lung irradiation as part of her therapy for cancer and does not see any increased risk associated with her cigarette smoking? Does one bluntly cite statistics and risk precipitating a flood of unnecessary anxiety, or simply permit survivors to continue as they wish, in ignorance of their increased risk levels? One answer is to tell each survivor that we do not know what the future holds for him or her as an individual, but to stress the seriousness of the illness for which they were successfully treated and urge appropriate follow-up and routine health precautions.

It is also important for the caretakers of long-term survivors to be aware of both subtle and obvious late consequences of cancer treatments. The survivor whose growth is retarded or whose puberty is delayed, for example, may experience some significant self-esteem problems which could go unnoticed in a routine medical follow-up. Delayed puberty can be a specially sensitive issue for adolescent females, more so than for males, since delay of menarche or interruption of menstruation as a result of chemotherapy signals reproductive problems with an explicitness that the male does not experience. By recognizing that any symptom of reproductive malfunction can be an issue, the sensitive practitioner can inquire and make referrals as indicated.

Mental Health Care

Scheduled Attention to Every Family is the key principle of good preventive emotional care during the course of treatment for childhood cancer. As noted earlier, parents wanted mental health services, but they did not wish to be singled out as being in need of help. Routine family mental health assessments as part of the clinic admission procedure can help to address this issue. Since parents, patients, and siblings are all at risk for emotional problems, they can be assured that some reactions to stress are normal and inevitable in the circumstances. They can then be told what programs or modes of emotional support and treatment are available, with the message that these can and will be modified to meet their unique needs. By presenting this message at the outset, the treatment team gives notice that the discussion of emotional issues is not only permissible but actively encouraged.

Some families will seek individual psychotherapy for one or more members with problems; other families will seek participation in group discussions or family meetings. Having a variety of modes available maximizes use. Some families or family members may choose never to avail themselves of these services, but will simply draw support from the knowledge that they are available.

The nature of psychotherapeutic services to child cancer patients and their families is quite different from the classical role of the mental health practitioner. In traditional circumstances the therapist attempts to uncover and interpret motives and sources of emotional stress. In the cancer hospital the patients and family members—whatever their psychological adjustment before diagnosis—face inordinate stress and uncertainty. Giving patients and families the opportunity to talk about their concerns and receive information about their experiences is critically important. Being able to anticipate stressful events—such as hair loss, drops in blood counts associated with chemotherapy, and elective cessation of chemotherapy—can lessen the emotional drain even though the actual experience has not been altered (Seligman, 1975). Supportive information-giving, facilitation of communication among family members, and encouraging discussion of emotional issues was strongly endorsed by virtually all of the survivors and family members interviewed.

Special Consideration of Defense Mechanisms is another aspect of the psychotherapeutic care of children with cancer which is quite different from the usual work of the mental health professional. As noted above, there are times when it seems better to avoid confronting patients with stark realities, better not to challenge their use of adaptive denial or other psychological means of coping more effectively. This is not a statement in support of lies or deception, but simply a statement that the emotional climate of the hospital is more important than the factual knowledge the patient has (or believes) per se. That is to say, the patient and family members must feel cared about and must know that all of their questions will be answered directly and honestly. Those who choose to stop asking questions about their condition in the face of failing health need not be reminded of their worsening condition, but they should feel able to ask about and discuss their concerns according to their own timetables.

Community and Reentry Issues are also very important in the mental health care of the child with cancer. The "community" includes the extended family, teachers, neighbors, and—especially—the child's peers. The mental health team must be willing and able to reach out to members of the patient's social milieu and provide information and guidance to those with whom the patient will be interacting. The loss of family and peer contact which sometimes occurs as a result of hospitalization should be minimized upon the patient's return home. Many of the survivors we interviewed, for example, expressed great sadness that they "lost friends" because the friends' parents objected to their playing with the patient out of fear that the cancer was contagious or because of other unnamed anxieties.

A common theme in discussion of aids to rehabilitation of the child with cancer is prevention of interpersonal losses and maintenance of as much normality as possible. Patients should be encouraged, for example, to return to school as soon as possible and to participate in their normal activities to the extent that their physical condition permits. This return to activities requires active discussions with fearful teachers and potentially overprotective parents, but the normalized climate will be supportive for most patients.

Mental health professionals must also recognize the importance of a family systems approach in the equation of family coping. The cancer patient may need prime attention on some occasions: at other times a sibling, a grandparent, or the whole family may be in need. The mental health professional is in a good position to address a concern of many of the parents interviewed in our study: they felt they could not get enough of the physician's time or could not share their personal worries with the "child's doctor." Mental health professionals can, by presenting their availability and orientation properly, increase the efficiency of and family satisfaction with the whole treatment process. Families which would not otherwise be able to support individual members well over the stressful period could be helped to respond much more effectively.

Implications for Public Policy

Availability of and access to effective up-to-date treatment for childhood cancer is a critical issue both for actual survival and for long-term psychological adjustment. No one should be denied such care for any reason. It is therefore imperative that physicians responsible for primary care become knowledgeable both about treatments for childhood cancer and about related support services in their geographic area. Public information programs are much needed to facilitate patient care and to dispel the outdated prejudice that the prognosis for childhood cancer is uniformly poor. Financial support should be available both for the direct medical costs of the child's illness and for the hidden costs (i.e., travel to treatment centers, child care for siblings, and lost parental pay) either through special catastrophic illness insurance or direct government subsidy. Parents should be made aware of available financial support at the outset of the child's treatment to alleviate the additional stress that financial burdens produce.

Public agencies should be prepared to fulfill their role in the rehabilitation and reintegration of the child with cancer in the community. Such services as tuition support, tutoring, special education, psychological counseling, and other facilitative programs should be readily available. As mandated by Public Law 94-142, school buildings and programs should be accessible to all patients ready and able to return to school.

Hospitals and clinics that care for children with cancer must also be willing to provide appropriate numbers of mental health professionals to meet the needs of these patients and their families. It is no longer reasonable to focus solely on physical care to the exclusion of a family's emotional needs, especially where chronic life-threatening illness is concerned.

Because discrimination in employment and insurance coverage seemed to present significant problems for many of the childhood cancer survivors in our study who are now adults, need exists to educate the business community, specifically to dispel unfounded myths about cancer. Some federal laws do protect the person with a history of cancer from discrimination, and many states have also enacted such laws. Unfortunately, many cancer survivors are unaware of these laws or feel too psychologically vulnerable to assert their rights when they encounter such discrimination. Existing laws need to be widely advertised and vigorously enforced. It is worth noting that none of the survivors we interviewed who were adults had encountered employment problems because of residual physical incapacities.

Insurance underwriters should be required to adjust policy rates and coverage to conform more accurately with *current* survival expectations. Studies which have documented the substantial similarity in productivity of former cancer patients and the noncancer worker provide additional evidence that continuing discrimination is unjustified.

As childhood cancer survivors enter the independent adult world, some clear-cut rehabilitative consultation is needed. They should be informed of problems which may confront them because of their cancer history. They should also be advised of potential solutions or remedies to these problems and of resources for assistance.

Implications for Research

Three avenues of research would be worth pursuing as an outgrowth of the study which this volume reports. The first is an examination of the continuing rehabilitation needs of the long-term survivor population, with a longitudinal rather than cross-sectional analysis of needs and the effectiveness of different interventions on overall adjustment. Ideally, such studies would begin with some newly diagnosed patients and follow their progress through treatment and into posttreatment period. The fact that 50 percent of current child patients will indeed survive for at least five years makes such studies feasible. Such research should of necessity also include the whole family, especially siblings and their needs during the periods of family stress.

A second area ripe for study is a series of similar in-depth studies of reactions to other chronic illnesses in order to assess the subtle differences or generalizable similarities in response. Children with cystic fibrosis, for example, may survive for periods of ten, twenty, or more years with their chronic illness, but the outcome is invariably fatal and has known genetic components. These latter two factors may cast a considerably different light on key issues in patient and family adjustment.

A third potential direction for research is the identification, testing, and evaluation of psychotherapeutic approaches. There is every reason to believe that the preventive practices discussed above, along with improved availability of mental health services, have a high potential for reducing both the physical and the long-term psychological morbidity among patients and their families.

Precisely controlled studies will continue to be a difficult matter, for all of the reasons discussed in Chapter 3, but the expansion of comparison group populations and the longitudinal research model could both prove to be helpful methodological improvements. It is clear that continued refinement of our care methods, both medical and psychosocial, is owed to the children who are treated for cancer and their families.

Appendix A

Rutter and Graham Interview Schedule

SCORING CATEGORIES

0 = No Abnormality
1 = Slight Abnormality
2 = Marked Abnormality

1. Apprehension on entering interview
2. Apprehension with other things [size of room, fear of examiner]
3. Preoccupation with anxiety topics [how far the interviewee spontaneously extends answers about these topics]
4. Preoccupation with depressive topics [how far the interviewee spontaneously extends answers about these topics]
5. Anxious expression
6. Sad expression
7. Adequacy of peer relations
8. Tearfulness
9. Tremulousness
10. Startle [extent of startling to sudden extraneous noises or movements]
11. Muscular tension [at rest: clenching of jaw, sitting stiffly, gripping side of chair]
12. Mannerisms or habits [movements which are both repetitive and stereotyped]
13. Overactivity
14. Fidgetiness [other extraneous movements: twisting in chair, fiddling with things]
15. Attention span or persistence [in completing a specific task]
16. Distractibility [response to all visual, tactile, auditory, and other stimuli]
17. Anxiety
18. Emotional responsiveness [to examiner]
19. Relationship with examiner

Reproduced by permission.

20. Depressed or sad mood
21. Disinhibition [apparent lack of social skills]
22. Lack of spontaneous talk
23. Lack of smiling
24. Overall psychiatric state

Schedule for Psychiatric Content Interview

Reflections

Events prior to illness: What was going on in your life before the illness?
How learned of diagnosis; by whom; when?
Reaction at time of diagnosis?
Hospital (treatments): What were the hospital experiences like?
Staff: How did the staff treat you? Do you remember anyone in particular?

Etiology

Thoughts about etiology?
Any treatments attempted other than standard medical treatments?
Immunity: How likely is it that you might have a recurrence? Do you feel your chances of getting a different cancer are any different from the general population?

Life Changes

Religiosity: Were there any changes in your belief because of your experience with cancer?
Concept of life (purpose): How do you conduct your life: Are more cautious?, carefree?, etc.
Concept of death: Has illness interfered with or changed your notion about death?
Social: Was there any change in your social environment?
Family: Was there any change in the family structure, interaction, or relationships?

Current Feelings

Preoccupation: What do you worry about now?
Effect on life, occupation, etc.: Do you think that your illness had any impact on your career choice?
Thoughts of future (goals, planning, etc.): What plans are you making for the future?

Perceptions of the Family

Support: Were your parents available to you to share feelings?
Turmoil: Do you think that your illness caused any family turmoil?
Effect on family: How did the illness affect your family?

Peer Perceptions

Support: Were your friends available to you for support?
Turmoil: Did any of your relationships change after having cancer?
Effect on peers: What reaction did you get from your friends? Did you tell your friends?

Spouse's Perceptions

Support: Did you tell your spouse before marriage that you had cancer?
Turmoil: What reaction did you get?
Effect on spouse: Has your spouse been available to offer support?

Recommendations to Professionals

Diagnosis: Should children be told diagnosis? By what age?
Hospitalizations: Anything that would make the hospital experience more comfortable?
Psychosocial support (what kind, who, etc.): Did you feel it would be helpful to have someone else to talk to other than the family? Who?

Interviewee's Perception of Overall Impact of Disease on Life

Appendix C

Waechter Stimulus Cards

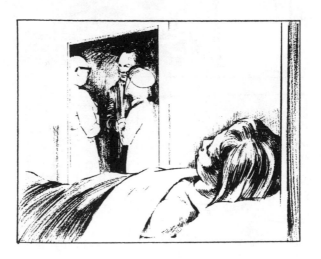

Appendix D

Physical/Visible Impairment Rating Scale

A. Obviousness of Physical Residua

SCORE ASSIGNED:

0 = Physical residua not at all obvious to casual observer; but the individual might have biopsy or I.V. scars

1 = Physical residua would be obvious to a physician during a physical exam, or to an untrained observer when patient is clothed in a bathing suit; or some facial disfigurement is present, but can be covered by cosmetics

2 = Physical residua could be noticed by alert others who observe the patient wearing street clothes; or facial disfigurement remains obvious despite use of cosmetics

3 = physical residua constitute an obvious deformity, even to untrained eye

B. Interference with Activities of Daily Living

SCORE ASSIGNED:

0 = Physical residua do not interfere at all with normal activities

1 = Individual has physical residua which require daily attention, but cares for self independently

2 = Individual requires help with activities of daily living once or twice daily; or cannot live independently

3 = Individual requires more frequent help, and might require institutionalization

C. Medical Attention or Equipment

SCORE ASSIGNED:

0 = Individual requires no special medical attention or equipment; and has no missing organs

1 = Regular checkups advisable; may require prosthesis with no adjust-ment problems; may have missing organ or other dysfunction such as iatrongenic sterility, but careful monitoring is not required

2 = Individual requires more frequent medical attention; may have miss-ing organ or dysfunction, with related problems that need medical attention more than once a year

3 = Individual needs frequent, special medical attention; and intermittent hospitalization for treatment of residual problem

D. *Employability or Ability to Attend School*

SCORE ASSIGNED:

0 = Physical residua do not hinder employment or school attendance at all

1 = Individual has minor limitations in job choice or school activities (e.g., no contact sports or heavy lifting are permitted)

2 = Individual has significant limitation in job choice, but may be able to work or attend school full time

3 = Individual has major limitations in job choice, and is unable to rou-tinely work a full day or attend school full time

The sum of scores for A, B, C, and D is the overall rating.

Rating Criteria: Anticipatory Grief Study

I. *Ratings for Degree of Anticipatory Grief*

First Criterion: Parent's Affective Acknowledgment

1. Acknowledgment of anger, sadness, and guilt
2. Acknowledgment of any two affects listed above
3. Acknowledgment of any one affect listed above
4. No acknowledgment of any emotions associated with grief

Second Criterion: Parental Reports of Affective Intensity

1. Great intensity
2. Moderate intensity
3. Mild intensity
4. Absence of feelings reported

Third Criterion: Parent's Reports of Duration of Feelings of Grief Associated with Child's Illness

1. Years
2. Months
3. Weeks
4. Very brief duration
5. None at all

Fourth Criterion: Parental Reports of Behavior toward the Child during the Illness

1. Appropriately meeting child needs during the illness period
2. Inappropriate dependence (e.g., clinging)

The criteria presented here were used by raters to form the clinical judgments discussed in Chapter 10. The "age-appropriate" criteria used by the raters refer to guidelines as specified by Doll (1965).

3. Resentment or mild pulling back of emotional investment
4. Emotional abandonment

Overall Clinical Rating of Anticipatory Grief

1. Strong
2. Moderate
3. Mild
4. Absent

II. Ratings for Appropriateness of Parent-Child Relationship

First Criterion: Parent's View of Child

1. *Idealized:* Unrealistically favorable view of child with inability to mention negative characteristics
2. *Positive:* Predominantly favorable view of child with balanced ability to recognize some shortcomings
3. *Neutral:* Nonevaluative statements only
4. *Mildly Negative:* Predominantly negative view with some favorable attributes reported
5. *Very Negative:* Unable to see any positive attributes

Second Criterion: Parent's Future Expectations for Child

1. *Grandiose:* Unrealistically imposing expectations given child's actual ability
2. *Reasonable:* Appropriate level of expectations given child's ability level
3. *Limited:* Few expectations for child despite current talents or abilities

Third Criterion: Parent's Reported Handling of Separation-Individuation Issues

1. *Clinging:* Overly close and dependent relationship with child; little or no separation tolerated
2. *Age-Appropriate Separation:* Age-appropriate autonomy permitted with realistic degree of parental concern
3. *Inconsistent:* Fluctuating pattern
4. *Abandonment:* Characterized by essential lack of interest in closeness of relationship with child

Fourth Criterion: Protectiveness Based on Report of Parental Activity

1. *Severe Overprotection:* Parent curtails child's activities which would otherwise be age-appropriate
2. *Mild Overprotection:* Some minimal parental interference without curtailing age-appropriate activities

3. *Reasonable Protectiveness:* Parent permits age-appropriate activity
4. *Inconsistent Protectiveness:* Parent's protectiveness is inconsistent
5. *Underprotective:* Parent knowingly permits exposure of child to dangerous situation(s)

Fifth Criterion: Parent's Reported Use of Discipline

1. *Very Permissive:* No limits set by parents
2. *Mildly Permissive:* Some limits set with wide latitude permitted
3. *Flexible:* Age-appropriate latitude permitted
4. *Very Strict:* Clearly defined, inflexible limits set
5. *Punitive:* Inflexible limits set in conjunction with harsh punishment for infractions

Sixth Criterion: Parent's Reported Ability to Express Anger toward Child

1. Able to express anger toward child appropriately
2. Parent reports getting angry at child, but being unable to express the anger
3. Parent reports rarely, if ever, getting angry with child

Seventh Criterion: Amount of Time Spent with Child

1. Parent reports spending a great deal of time with the child, given the child's age
2. Parent reports spending a reasonable amount of time with the child, given the child's age
3. Parent reports spending very little time with the child, given the child's age

Eighth Criterion: Worry about Child's Health

Parents were asked to rate their concern for their child's health on a 6-point continuum as a function of frequency of worrying:

1———2———3———4———5———6			
Never worry	Worry a little	Worry somewhat	Constant worry

Ninth Criterion: Ability to Discuss Disease and Current Implications with Child

1. Able to discuss issues openly
2. Reluctantly willing to discuss issues, when child wishes to
3. Actively avoid discussing issues
4. Not known

Tenth Criterion: Child's Inclusion in the Family

1. Child is actively included in all family activities
2. Child may be passively omitted from some family activities
3. Child is actively excluded from most family activities

Eleventh Criterion: Parent's Reported Treatment of Survivor Relative to Siblings

1. Survivor treated about the same as siblings
2. Survivor treated more leniently than siblings
3. Survivor treated more harshly than siblings
4. No siblings; does not apply
5. Not known

Overall Clinical Ratings

Relationship with Child:
1. Appropriate
2. Inappropriate

Worry regarding Child's Future:
1. Reasonable degree of concern
2. Denial of any concern
3. Overly concerned

References

Adams, M.A. A hospital play program: Helping children with serious illness. *American Journal of Orthopsychiatry,* 1976, *46,* 416–424.

Alvarado, C. S., Boat, T. F., & Newman, A. J. Late-onset pulmonary fibrosis and chest deformity in two children treated with cyclophosphamide. *Journal of Pediatrics,* 1978, *92,* 443–446.

Anthony, S. *The child's discovery of death.* New York: Harcourt, Brace, 1940.

Asbjørnsen, G., Molne, K., Klepp, O., & Aavaag, A. Testicular function after combination chemotherapy for Hodgkin's disease. *Scandinavian Journal of Haematology,* 1976, *16,* 66–69.

Ashenburg, N. J. *Employability and insurability of the cancer patient.* Paper presented at the New York State Cancer Programs Association, Inc., Rochester, N.Y., November 8, 1975.

Beardslee, W. R. *The way out must lead in: Life histories in the civil rights movement.* Atlanta: Emory University, Center for Research in Social Change, 1977.

Bendig, A. W. The development of a short form of the manifest anxiety scale. *Journal of Consulting Psychology,* 1956, *20,* 384.

Benjamin, P. Y. Psychological problems following recovery from acute life-threatening illness. *American Journal of Orthopsychiatry,* 1978, *48,* 284–290.

Bills, R. E. *Manual for the index of adjustment and values.* University, Ala.: University of Alabama College of Education, 1961.

Bills, R. E., Vance, E. L., & McLean, O. S. An index of adjustment and values. *Journal of Consulting Psychology,* 1951, *15,* 257–261.

Binger, C. M. Jimmy: A clinical case presentation of a child with a fatal illness. In E. J. Anthony & C. Koupernik (Eds.), *The child in his family: The impact of disease and death.* (Yearbook of the International Association for Child Psychiatry and Allied Professions, Vol. 2.) New York: Wiley, 1973.

Binger, C. M., Ablin, A. R., Feuerstein, R. C., Kushner, J. H., Zoger, S., & Mikkelsen, C. Childhood leukemia: Emotional impact on patient and family. *New England Journal of Medicine,* 1969, *280,* 414–418.

Boice, J. D. Follow-up methods to trace women treated for pulmonary tuberculosis, 1930–1954. *American Journal of Epidemiology,* 1978, *107,* 127–139.

Bowlby, J. Processes of mourning. *International Journal of Psycho-Analysis,* 1961, *42,* 317–339.

Bozeman, M. F., Orbach, C. E., & Sutherland, A. M. Psychological impact of cancer and its treatment: The adaptation of mothers to the threatened loss of their children through leukemia. *Cancer,* 1955, *8,* 1–33.

Cairns, N. U., Clark, G. M., Smith, S. D., & Lansky, S. B. Adaptation of siblings to childhood malignancy. *Journal of Pediatrics,* 1979, *95,* 484–487.

Carter, H., & Glick, P. *Marriage and divorce: A social and economic study.* Cambridge, Mass.: Harvard University Press, 1976.

Chapman, R. M., Sutcliffe, S. B., & Malpas, J. S. Cytotoxic-induced ovarian failure in Hodgkin's disease. *Journal of the American Medical Association,* 1979a, *242,* 1882–1884.

Chapman, R. M., Sutcliffe, S. B., Rees, L. H., Edwards, C. R. W., & Malpas, J. S. Cyclical combination chemotherapy and gonadal function: Retrospective study in males. *Lancet,* 1979b, *1*(8111), 285–289.

Chodoff, P., Friedman, S., & Hamburg, D. A. Stresses, defenses and coping behavior: Observations in parents of children with malignant disease. *American Journal of Psychiatry,* 1964, *120,* 743–749.

Clapp, M. J. Psychosocial reactions of children with cancer. *Nursing Clinics of North America,* 1976, *11,* 73–82.

Cohen, M., & Wellisch, D. Living in limbo: Psychosocial intervention in families with a cancer patient. *American Journal of Psychotherapy,* 1978, *32,* 561–571.

Conte, H. R., Bakur-Weiner, M., Plutchnik, R., & Bennett, R. *Development and evaluation of a death anxiety questionnaire.* Paper presented at the 83rd annual meeting of the American Psychological Association, Chicago, September, 1975.

Counts, S., Rodov, M. H., & Wilson, M. T. *Attitudes of employers and cancer patients towards patients' work ability: Two surveys and an action plan.* (Rehabilitation Program, National Cancer Institute Contract No. NO1-CN-55070.) Center for Health Systems Studies, The Fairfax, 4614 Fifth Avenue, Pittsburgh, Pa. 15213, November, 1976.

Cunnick, W., & Wright, B. If your cancer patient asks for a job reference. *Medical Times,* 1977, *105*(3), 29d(80)–32d(80).

Desforges, J. F., Rutherford, C. J., & Piro, A. Hodgkin's disease. *New England Journal of Medicine,* 1979, *301,* 1212–1222.

Dietz, J. H. How doctors can help solve cancer patients' employment problems. *Legal Aspects of Medical Practice,* April, 1978, pp. 25–29.

Doll, E. A. *Vineland Social Maturity Scale.* Circle Pines, Minn.: American Guidance Service, 1965.

Drotar, D. Family oriented intervention with the dying adolescent. *Journal of Pediatric Psychology,* 1977, *2,* 68–71.

Duttera, M. J., Gaelelli, J. F., Kleinman, L. M., Tangera, J. A., & Wittgrove, A. C. Intrathecal methotrexate. *Lancet,* 1972, *1*(7749), 540.

Easson, W. M. *The dying child.* Springfield, Ill.: Charles C Thomas, 1970.

Einhorn, M., & Davidsohn, I. Hepatotoxicity of mercaptopurine. *Journal of the American Medical Association,* 1964, *188,* 802–806.

Eisenberg, L. A friend, not an apple, a day will help keep the doctor away. *American Journal of Medicine,* 1979, *66,* 551–553.

Eiser, C., & Lansdown, R. Retrospective study of intellectual development in children treated for acute lymphoblastic leukemia. *Archives of Diseases of Children,* 1977, *52,* 525–529.

Entmacher, P. S. Insurance for the cancer patient. *Cancer,* 1975, *26,* 287–289.

Erikson, E. Identity and the life cycle. *Psychological Issues,* Monograph 1. New York: International Universities Press, 1959.

Evans, A. E. If a child must die. . . . *New England Journal of Medicine,* 1968, *278,* 138–142.

Evans, A. E. Practical care for the family of a child with cancer. *Cancer,* 1975, *35*(3 Suppl.), 871–875.

Evans, P. R., Saunders, C., & MacCarthy, D. The management of fatal illness in childhood. *Proceedings of the Royal Society of Medicine,* 1969, *62,* 549–554.

Feinberg, D. Preventive therapy with siblings of a dying child. *Journal of the American Academy of Child Psychiatry,* 1970, *4,* 644–668.

Fergusson, J. H. Late psychological effects of a serious illness in childhood. *Nursing Clinics of North America*, 1976, *11*, 83–93.

Filler, R. M., Tefft, M., Vawter, G., Maddock, C., & Mitus, A. Hepatic lobectomy in childhood: Effects of x-ray and chemotherapy. *Journal of Pediatric Surgery*, 1969, *4*, 31–41.

Fortunato, R. P., & Komp, D. M. Death at home for children with acute lymphoblastic leukemia. *Virginia Medical*, 1979, *106*, 124–126.

Freud, S. (1917). Mourning and melancholia. *Standard Edition, 14*, 239–258. London: Hogarth Press, 1957.

Friedman, S., Chodoff, P., Mason, J., & Hamburg, D. Behavioral observations of parents anticipating the death of a child. *Pediatrics*, 1963, *32*, 610–625.

Futterman, E. H., & Hoffman, I. Transient school phobia in a leukemic child. *Journal of the American Academy of Child Psychiatry*, 1970, *9*, 477–493.

Futterman, E., & Hoffman, I. Crisis and adaptation in the families of fatally ill children. In E. J. Anthony & C. Koupernik (Eds.), *The child in his family: The impact of disease and death.* (Yearbook of the International Association for Child Psychiatry and Allied Professions, Vol. 2.) New York: Wiley, 1973.

Geleerd, E. Two kinds of denial. In M. Schur (Ed.), *Drives, affects, behavior* (Vol. 2). New York: International Universities Press, 1965.

Gilder, R., Bushman, P. R., Starz, A. L., & Wolff, J. A. *Group therapy with parents of children with leukemia.* Paper presented at the 53rd annual meeting of the American Orthopsychiatric Association, Atlanta, Ga., March 4, 1976.

Gogan, J. L., O'Malley, J. E., & Foster, D. J. Treating the pediatric cancer patient: A review. *Journal of Pediatric Psychology*, 1977, *2*, 42–48.

Gogan, J. L., Koocher, G. P., Fine, W. E., Foster, D. J., & O'Malley, J. E. Pediatric cancer survival and marriage: Issues affecting adult adjustment. *American Journal of Orthopsychiatry*, 1979, *49*, 423–430.

Goggin, E. L., Lansky, S. B., & Hassanein, K. Psychological reactions of children with malignancies. *Journal of Child Psychiatry*, 1976, *15*, 314–325.

Goldberg, R. T. Adjustment of children with invisible and visible handicaps: Congenital heart disease and facial burns. *Journal of Counseling Psychology*, 1974, *21*, 428–432.

Green, M. Care of the dying child. *Pediatrics*, 1967, *40*,(3, Pt. 2), 492–497.

Green, M., & Solnit, A. J. Reactions to the threatened loss of a child: A vulnerable child syndrome. *Pediatrics*, 1964, *34*, 58–66.

Greene, P. The child with leukemia in the classroom. *American Journal of Nursing*, 1975, *75*, 86–87.

Greenwood, R. D., Rosenthal, A., Cassady, R., Jaffe, N., & Nadas, A. S. Constrictive pericarditis in childhood due to mediastinal irradiation. *Circulation*, 1974, *50*, 1033–1039.

Gullo, S. V., Cherico, D. J., & Shadick, R. Suggested stages and response styles in life-threatening illness: A focus on the cancer patient. In B. Schoenberg, A. C. Carr, A. H. Kutscher, D. Peretz, & I. Goldberg (Eds.), *Anticipatory grief.* New York: Columbia University Press, 1974.

Hamovitch, M. B. *The parent and the fatally ill child.* Los Angeles, Calif.: Delmar, 1964.

Hansen, H. Discussion on Jimmy. In E. J. Anthony & C. Koupernik (Eds.), *The child in his family: The impact of disease and death.* (Yearbook of the International Association for Child Psychiatry and Allied Professions, Vol. 2.) New York: Wiley, 1973.

Heaston, D. K., Libshitz, H. I., & Chan, R. C. Skeletal effects of megavoltage irradiation in survivors of Wilms' tumor. *American Journal of Roentgenology*, 1979, *133*, 389–395.

Heffron, W. A., Bommelaere, K., & Masters, R. Group discussions with the parents of leukemic children. *Pediatrics*, 1973, *52*, 831–840.

Hoffman, I., & Futterman, E. H. Coping with waiting: Psychiatric intervention and study in the waiting room of a pediatric oncology clinic. *Comprehensive Psychiatry*, 1971, *12*, 67–81.

Hollingshead, A. B. *Two-factor index of social position.* Unpublished manuscript, 1957. Available from A. B. Hollingshead, 1965 Yale Station, New Haven, Conn.

Holmes, G. E., & Holmes, F. F. Pregnancy outcome of patients treated for Hodgkin's disease: A controlled study. *Cancer,* 1978, *41,* 1317–1322.

Holmes, H. A., & Holmes, F. F. After ten years, what are the handicaps and life styles of children treated for cancer? *Clinical Pediatrics,* 1975, *14,* 819–823.

Howell, D. A. A child dies. *Journal of Pediatric Surgery,* 1966, *1,* 2–7.

Hutchison, G. B. Late neoplastic changes following medical irradiation. *Radiology,* 1972, *105,* 645–652.

Hutter, R. V., Shipkey, F. H., Tan, C. T., Murphy, M. L., & Chowdhury, M. Hepatic fibrosis in children with acute leukemia: A complication of therapy. *Cancer,* 1960, *13,* 288–307.

Jaffe, N. Non-oncogenic sequelae of cancer chemotherapy. *Radiology,* 1975, *114,* 167–173.

Jaffe, N. The cost of therapy. in J. Van Eys (Ed.), *The normally sick child.* Baltimore: University Park Press, 1979.

Jaffe, N., Murray, J., Traggis, D., Cassady, J. R., Filler, R. M., Watts, H., Weishselbaum, R., & Weinstein, H. Multidisciplinary treatment for childhood sarcoma. *American Journal of Surgery,* 1977, *133,* 405–412.

Jenkin, D., Freedman, M., McClure, P., Peters, V., Saunders, F., & Sonley, M. Hodgkin's disease in children: Treatment with low dose radiation and MOPP without staging laparotomy; A preliminary report. *Cancer,* 1979, *44,* 80–86.

Johnson, F. L., Rudolph, L., & Hartman, J. Helping the family cope with childhood cancer. *Psychosomatics,* 1979, *20,* 241–251.

Johnson, W. W., & Medows, D. C. Urinary-bladder fibrosis and telangiectasia associated with long-term cyclophosphamide therapy. *New England Journal of Medicine,* 1971, *284,* 290–294.

Kagen-Goodheart, L. Re-entry: Living with childhood cancer. *American Journal of Orthopsychiatry,* 1977, *47,* 651–658.

Kaplan, D., Grobstein, R., & Smith, A. Severe illness in families. *Health and Social Work,* 1976, *1,* 72–81.

Kaplan, D. M., Smith, A., Grobstein, R., & Fishman, S. Family mediation of stress. *Social Work,* 1973, *18,* 60–69.

Kartha, M., & Ertel, I. J. Short-term group therapy for mothers of leukemic children. *Clinical Pediatrics,* 1976, *15,* 803–806.

Katz, E. R., Kellerman, J., Rigler, D., Williams, K. O., & Siegel, S. E. School intervention with pediatric cancer patients. *Journal of Pediatric Psychology,* 1977, *2,* 72–76.

Kay, H. E. M., Knapton, P. J., O'Sullivan, J. P., Wells, D. G., Harris, R. F., Innes, E. M., Stuart, J., Schwartz, F. C. M., & Thompson, E. N. Encephalopathy in acute leukemia associated with methotrexate therapy. *Archives of Diseases of Children,* 1972, *47,* 344–354.

Kellerman, J., Rigler, D., & Siegel, S. E. Psychological effects of isolation in protected environments. *American Journal of Psychiatry,* 1977, *134,* 563–565.

Kennedy, B. J., Telegen, A., Kennedy, S., & Havernick, N. Psychological response of patients cured of advanced cancer. *Cancer,* 1976, *38,* 2184.

Kirten, C., & Liverman, M. Special educational needs of the child with cancer. *Journal of School Health,* March, 1977, pp. 170–173.

Knapp, V., & Hansen, H. Helping the parents of children with leukemia. *Social Work,* 1973, *18,* 70–75.

Knudson, A. G. Mutation and cancer: Statistical study of retinoblastoma. *Proceedings of the National Academy of Sciences,* 1971, *68,* 820–823.

Knudson, A. G., Strong, L. C., & Anderson, D. E. Heredity and cancer in man. *Progress in Medical Genetics,* 1973, *9,* 113–158.

Koch, C. R., Hermann, J., & Donaldson, M. H. Supportive care of the child with cancer and his family. *Seminars in Oncology,* 1974, *1,* 81–86.

Kohle, K., Simons, C., Weidlich, S., Dietrich, M., & Durner, A. Psychological aspects in the treatment of leukemia patients in the isolated bed system, "Life Island." *Psychotherapy and Psychosomatics,* 1971, *19,* 85–91.

Koocher, G. P. Swimming, competence, and personality change. *Journal of Personality and Social Psychology,* 1971, *18,* 275–278.

Koocher, G. P. Childhood, death, and cognitive development. *Developmental Psychology,* 1973, *9,* 369–375.

Koocher, G. P. Talking with children about death. *American Journal of Orthopsychiatry,* 1974, *44,* 404–411.

Koocher, G. P., O'Malley, J. E., Foster, D. J., & Gogan, J. L. Death anxiety in normal children and adolescents. *Psychiatria Clinica,* 1976, *9,* 220–229.

Koocher, G. P., Sourkes, B. M., & Keane, W. M. Pediatric oncology consultations: A generalizable model for medical settings. *Professional Psychology,* 1979, *10,* 467–474.

Kübler-Ross, E. *On death and dying.* New York: Macmillan, 1969.

Lansky, S. B. Childhood leukemia: The child psychiatrist as a member of the oncology team. *Journal of the American Academy of Child Psychiatry,* 1974, *13,* 499–508.

Lansky, S. B., Cairns, N. U., Hassanein, R., Wehr, J., & Lowman, J. T. Childhood cancer: Parental discord and divorce. *Pediatrics,* 1978, *62,* 184–188.

Lansky, S., Lowman, J. T., Vats, T., & Gyulay, J. School phobia in children with malignant neoplasms. *American Journal of Diseases in Children,* 1975, *129,* 42–46.

Lascari, A. D., & Stehbens, J. A. The reactions of families to childhood leukemia. *Clinical Pediatrics,* 1973, *12,* 210–214.

Lavigne, J. V., & Ryan, M. Psychological adjustment of siblings of children with chronic illness. *Pediatrics,* 1979, *63,* 616–627.

Lazarus, R. S. *Patterns of adjustment.* New York: McGraw-Hill, 1976.

Li, F. P. Follow-up of survivors of childhood cancer. *Cancer,* 1977a, *39,* 1776–1778.

Li, F. P. Second malignant tumors after cancer in childhood. *Cancer,* 1977b, *40,* 1899–1902.

Li, F. P., Cassady, J. R., & Jaffe, N. Risk of second tumors in survivors of childhood cancer. *Cancer,* 1975, *35,* 1230–1235.

Li, F. P., Fine, W., Jaffe, N., Holmes, G. E., & Holmes, F. F. Offspring of patients treated for cancer in childhood. *Journal of the National Cancer Institute,* 1979, *62,* 1193–1197.

Li, F. P., & Jaffe, N. Progeny of childhood cancer survivors. *Lancet,* 1974, *2* (7882), 707–709.

Li, F. P., Myers, M. H., Heise, H. W., & Jaffe, N. The course of five-year survivors of cancer in childhood. *Journal of Pediatrics,* 1978, *93,* 185–187.

Li, F. P., & Stone, R. Survivors of cancer in childhood. *Annals of Internal Medicine,* 1976, *84,* 551–553.

Lindemann, E. Symptomatology and management of acute grief. *American Journal of Psychiatry,* 1944, *101,* 141–148.

Lindsay, M., & MacCarthy, D. Caring for the brothers and sisters of a dying child. In L. Burton (Ed.), *Care of the child facing death.* London: Routledge and Kegan Paul, 1974.

Lowenberg, J. S. The coping behaviors of fatally ill adolescents and their parents. *Nursing Forum,* 1970, *9,* 269–287.

Lucas, R. H. *Children with cancer: Denying death or denying life?* Paper presented at the meeting of the American Psychological Association, San Francisco, Calif., August, 1977.

Lushbaugh, C. C., & Casarett, G. W. The effects of gonadal irradiation in clinical radiation therapy: A review. *Cancer,* 1976, *37,* 1111–1120.

McAnarney, E. R., Pless, I. B., Satterwhite, B., & Friedman, S. B. Psychological problems of children with chronic juvenile arthritis. *Pediatrics,* 1974, *53,* 523–528.

McIlvanie, S. K., & MacCarthy, J. D. Hepatitis in association with prolonged g-mercaptopurine therapy. *Blood,* 1959, *14,* 80–90.

McIntosh, S., Klatskin, E. H., O'Brien, R. T., Aspres, G. T., Kamerer, B. L., Snead, C., Kalavasky, S. M., & Pearson, H. A. Chronic neurologic disturbance in childhood leukemia. *Cancer,* 1976, *37,* 853–857.

McKenna, R. J. *Employability and insurability of the cancer patient.* Paper presented at National Rehabilitation Conference, New York, 1974.

Martinson, I. The child with leukemia: Parents help each other. *American Journal of Nursing,* 1976, *76,* 1120–1122.

Mattsson, A. Long-term physical illness in childhood: A challenge to psychosocial adaptation. *Pediatrics,* 1972, *50,* 801–811.

Mayfield, J. K., Riseborough, E. J., & Jaffe, N. Irradiation effect on the axial skeleton following treatment for neuroblastoma. *Proceedings: American Society of Clinical Oncology/American Academy of Cancer Research,* 1977, *18,* 279.

Meadows, A. T., & Evans, A. E. Effects of chemotherapy on the central nervous system. *Cancer,* 1976, *37,* 1079–1085.

Michael, S. T., & Kirkpatrick, P. Additional information on the mental health ratings. In L. S. Srole, T. S. Langner, S. T. Michael, M. K. Opler, & T. A. C. Rennie (Eds.), *Mental health in the metropolis.* New York: McGraw-Hill, 1962.

Minow, R. A., Benjamin, R. S., & Gottlieb, J. A. Adriamycin (NSC-123127) cardiomyopathy—an overview with determination of risk factors. *Cancer Chemotherapy Reports,* 1975, *6,* 195–201.

Morrissey, J. R. Death anxiety in children with a fatal illness. In H. J. Parad (Ed.), *Crisis intervention: Selected readings.* New York: Family Service Association of America, 1965.

Murray, H. A. *Thematic Apperception Test.* Cambridge, Mass.: Harvard University Press, 1943.

Murstein, B. I. The effect of long term illness of children on the emotional adjustment of parents. *Child Development,* 1960, *31,* 157–171.

Nagy, M. The child's theories concerning death. *Journal of Genetic Psychology,* 1948, *73,* 3–27.

Natterson, J. M., & Knudson, A. G. Observations concerning fear of death in fatally ill children and their mothers. *Psychosomatic Medicine,* 1960, *22,* 456–465.

Novack, D. H., Plumer, R., Smith, R. L., Ochitill, H., Morrow, G. R., & Bennett, J. M. Changes in physicians' attitudes toward telling the cancer patient. *Journal of the American Medical Association,* 1979, *241,* 897–900.

Oken, D. What to tell cancer patients: A study of medical attitudes. *Journal of the American Medical Association,* 1961, *175,* 1120–1128.

O'Malley, J. E., Koocher, G. P., Foster, D. J., & Slavin, L. S. Psychiatric sequelae of surviving childhood cancer. *American Journal of Orthopsychiatry,* 1979, *49,* 608–616.

Parkes, C. *Bereavement: Studies of grief in adult life.* New York: International Universities Press, 1972.

Patenaude, A. F., Szymanski, L., & Rappeport, J. Psychological costs of bone marrow transplantation in children. *American Journal of Orthopsychiatry,* 1979, *49,* 409–422.

Pearse, M. The child with cancer: Impact on the family. *Journal of School Health,* March, 1977, pp. 174–179.

Peironi, A. Role of the social worker in a children's cancer clinic. *Pediatrics,* 1967, *40*(3, Pt. 2), 534–536.

Peylan-Ramu, N., Poplack, D. G., Blei, C. L., Herdt, J. R., Verness, M., & DiChiro, G. Computer assisted tomography in methotrexate encephalopathy. *Journal of Computer Assisted Tomography,* 1977, *1*, 216–221.

Pinkel, D. Five year follow-up of "total therapy" of childhood lymphocytic leukemia. *Journal of the American Medical Association,* 1971, *216*, 648–652.

Plank, E. Death on a children's ward. *Medical Times,* 1964, *92*, 638–644.

Pless, I. B., & Roghmann, K. J. Chronic illness and its consequences: Observations based on three epidemiologic surveys. *Journal of Pediatrics,* 1971, *79*, 351–359.

Pless, I. B, Roghmann, K., & Haggerty, R. J. Chronic illness, family functioning, and psychological adjustment: A model for the allocation of preventive mental health services. *International Journal of Epidemiology,* 1972, *1*, 271–277.

Plumb, M. M., & Holland, J. Cancer in adolescents: The symptom is the thing. In B. Schoenberg, A. C. Carr, A. H. Kutscher, D. Peretz, & I. Goldberg (Eds.), *Anticipatory grief.* New York: Columbia University Press, 1974.

Powazek, M., Goff, J., Schyving, J., & Paulson, M. A. Emotional reactions of children to isolation in a cancer hospital. *Journal of Pediatrics,* 1978, *92*, 834–837.

Ragab, A. H., Freich, R. S., & Vietti, T. J. Osteoporotic fractures secondary to methotrexate therapy of acute leukemia in remission. *Cancer,* 1970, *25*, 580–585.

Richmond, J., & Waisman, H. A. Psychological aspects of management of children with malignant diseases. *American Journal of Diseases in Children,* 1955, *89*, 42–45.

Riseborough, E. J., Grabias, S. L., Burton, R. I., & Jaffe, N. Alterations occurring in the axial skeleton following irradiation for Wilms' tumor. *Journal of Bone and Joint Surgery,* 1976, *58-A*, 526–536.

Rutter, M., & Graham, P. The reliability and validity of the psychiatric assessment of the child: I. Interview with the child. *British Journal of Psychiatry,* 1968, *114*, 563–579.

Samuels, M. L., Johnson, D. E., Holoye, V. J., & Lanzotti, V. J. Large-dose bleomycin therapy and pulmonary toxicity: A possible role prior to radiotherapy. *Journal of the American Medical Association,* 1976, *235*, 1117–1120.

Sandberg, S. Psychiatric disorder in children with birth anomalies. *Acta Psychiatrica Scandinavia,* 1976, *54*, 1–16.

Schowalter, J. E. The child's reaction to his own terminal illness. In B. Schoenberg, A. C. Carr, D. Peretz, et al. (Eds.), *Loss and grief: Psychological management in medical practice.* New York: Columbia University Press, 1970.

Seidel, U. P., Chadwick, O. F. D., & Rutter, M. Psychological disorders in crippled children. A comparative study of children with and without brain damage. *Developmental Medicine and Child Neurology,* 1975, *17*, 563–573.

Seligman, M. E. P. *Helplessness: On depression development and death.* San Francisco: W. H. Freeman, 1975.

Share, L. Family communication in the crisis of a child's fatal illness: A literature review and analysis. *Omega,* 1972, *3*, 187–201.

Sherins, R. J., & DeVita, V. T. Effect of drug treatment for lymphoma on male reproductive capacity: Studies of men in remission after therapy. *Annals of Internal Medicine,* 1973, *79*, 216–220.

Sherins, R., Winokur, S., DeVita, V. T., Jr., & Vaitukaitis, J. Surprisingly high risk of functional castration in women receiving chemotherapy for lymphoma. *Clinical Research,* 1975, *23*, 343A.

Simone, J. V. Childhood leukemia: The changing prognosis. *Hospital Practice,* 1974, *9*, 59–68.

Simone, J., Aur, R. J. A., Hustu, H. O., & Pinkel, D. "Total therapy" studies of acute lymphocytic leukemia in children: Current results and prospects for cure. *Cancer,* 1972, *30*, 1488–1494.

Sourkes, B. Facilitating family coping with childhood cancer. *Journal of Pediatric Psychology*, 1977, *2*, 65–67.

Sourkes, B. Siblings of the pediatric cancer patient. In J. Kellerman (Ed.), *Psychological aspects of childhood cancer*. Springfield, Ill.: Charles C Thomas, 1980.

Spinetta, J. J. The dying child's awareness of death: A review. *Psychological Bulletin*, 1974, *81*, 256–260.

Spinetta, J. J. Adjustment in children with cancer. *Journal of Pediatric Psychology*, 1977a, *2*, 49–51.

Spinetta, J. J. *The child with cancer: Patterns of communication*. Paper presented at the 57th annual meeting of the Western Psychological Association, Seattle, April 22, 1977b.

Spinetta, J. J., & Maloney, L. J. Death anxiety in the outpatient leukemic child. *Pediatrics*, 1975, *65*, 1034–1037.

Spinetta, J. J., Rigler, D., & Karon, M. Anxiety in the dying child. *Pediatrics*, 1973, *52*, 841–845.

Spinetta, J. J., Rigler, D., & Karon, M. Personal space as measure of a dying child's sense of isolation. *Journal of Consulting and Clinical Psychology*, 1974, *42*, 751–756.

Spinetta, J. J., Spinetta, P. D., Kung, F., & Schwartz, D. B. *Emotional aspects of childhood cancer and leukemia: A handbook for parents*. San Diego: Leukemia Society of America, 1976.

Srole, L. S., Langner, T. S., Michael, S. T., Opler, M. K., & Rennie, T. A. C. (Eds.). *Mental health in the metropolis*. New York: McGraw-Hill, 1962.

Stehbens, J. A., & Lascari, A. D. Psychological follow-up of families with childhood leukemia. *Journal of Clinical Psychology*, 1974, *30*, 394–397.

Steinhausen, H. C. Hemophilia: A psychological study in chronic disease in juveniles. *Journal of Psychosomatic Research*, 1976, *20*, 461–467.

Stone, R. W. Employing the recovered cancer patient. *Cancer*, 1975, *36*, 285–286.

Toch, R. Management of the child with a fatal disease. *Clinical Pediatrics*, 1974, *3*, 418–427.

U.S. Department of Health, Education, and Welfare, Public Health Service, National Center for Health Statistics. *Facts of life and death*. (D.H.E.W. Publication No. (PHS) 79-1222.) Washington, D.C.: U.S. Government Printing Office, November, 1978.

Vaillant, G. *Adaptation to life*. Boston: Little, Brown, 1977.

Van Eys, J. The outlook for the child with cancer. *Journal of School Health*, March, 1977, pp. 165–169.

Vernick, J. Meaningful communication with the fatally ill child. In E. J. Anthony & C. Koupernik (Eds.), *The child in his family: The impact of disease and death*. (Yearbook of the International Association for Child Psychiatry and Allied Professions, Vol. 2.) New York: Wiley, 1973.

Vernick, J., & Karon, M. Who's afraid of death on a leukemia ward? *American Journal of Diseases of Children*, 1965, *109*, 393–397.

Waechter, E. H. *Death anxiety in children with fatal illness*. (Doctoral dissertation, Stanford University, 1968.) Ann Arbor, Mich., University Microfilms No. 69-310.

Waechter, E. H. Children's awareness of fatal illness. *American Journal of Nursing*, 1971, *7*, 1168–1172.

Warne, G. L., Fairley, K. F., Hobbs, J. B., & Martin, F. I. R. Cyclophosphamide-induced ovarian failure. *New England Journal of Medicine*, 1973, *289*, 1159–1162.

Weinstein, H. J., & Link, M. P. Non-Hodgkin's lymphoma in childhood. *Clinics in Haematology*, 1979, *8*, 699–716.

Wheatley, G. M., Cunnick, W. R., Wright, B. P., & Van Keuren, D. The employment of persons with a history of treatment for cancer. *Cancer*, 1974, *32*, 441–445.

White, E., Elsom, B., & Prawat, R. Children's conceptions of death. *Child Development*, 1978, *49*, 307–310.

Wilbur, S. *Coping with cancer: Self-help to parents of leukemic children.* Unpublished Master's thesis, Smith College School of Social Work, Northampton, Mass., 1976.

Wohl, M. E. B., Griscom, N. T., Traggis, D. G., & Jaffe, N. Effects of therapeutic irradiation delivered in early childhood upon subsequent lung function. *Pediatrics,* 1975, *55,* 507–516.

Wollnik, L. Management of the child with cancer on an outpatient basis. *Nursing Clinics of North America,* 1976, *2,* 35–48.

Wylie, R. C. *The self-concept.* Lincoln: University of Nebraska Press, 1961.

Wylie, R. C. *The self-concept* (Vol. 1, rev. ed.). Lincoln: University of Nebraska Press, 1974.

Zung, W. W. K. A self-rating depression scale. *Archives of General Psychiatry,* 1965, *12,* 63–70.

Name Index

Subject Index

About the Authors

GERALD P. KOOCHER, Ph.D., joined the staff of the Sidney Farber Cancer Institute, Children's Hospital, Boston in 1975 as Chief Psychologist. He is an Assistant Professor at Harvard Medical School and Associate Chief Psychologist at Children's Hospital Medical Center. Dr. Koocher has published more than 35 articles and papers.

JOHN E. O'MALLEY, M.D., is Assistant Professor of Child Psychiatry at the Harvard Medical School, an Associate in Psychiatry at the Children's Hospital Medical Center, and an Associate at the Sidney Farber Cancer Institute where he has been the principal investigator for the long-term follow-up of children who have had cancer.

TALK TO ME

RANDOM HOUSE NEW YORK

Anna Deavere Smith

TALK
TO
ME

Listening

Between

the Lines

Library of Congress Cataloging-in-Publication Data
Smith, Anna Deavere.
    Talk to me: listening between the lines / Anna Deavere
Smith.
        p.   cm.
    ISBN 0-375-50150-9 (acid-free paper)
    1. United States—Politics and government—1993–
2. Political culture—United States.   3. Political culture—
Washington (D.C.)   4. National characteristics, American.
5. Presidents—United States.   6. Press and politics—United
States.   7. Politicians—United States—Interviews.
8. Interviews—United States.   I. Title.
E885.S63   2000
306.2'0973'09049—dc21   00-055306

Random House website address: www.atrandom.com
Printed in the United States of America on acid-free paper
98765432
First Edition
Book design by Barbara M. Bachman

THIS BOOK IS DEDICATED TO MY MOTHER, ANNA Y. SMITH,

A TEACHER IN THE BALTIMORE PUBLIC SCHOOLS, WHO WAS ALSO AMONG

THE FIRST PEOPLE TO TALK TO ME.

ACKNOWLEDGMENTS

To my hosts in Washington, the Honorable Amory Houghton and Priscilla Dewey Houghton, for welcoming me into their home and for giving me a base from which to work. For their spirit, humor, friendship, and generosity.

My editor, Ann Godoff, for introducing me to another kind of writing, another way of looking at character, another way of creating voice, another way of inhabiting words and talk.

My agent, Gloria Loomis, for being there, always, with her particular, unique combination of savvy and grace.

Kate Niedzwiecki, for her constancy and her editorial assistance.

Sarah D'Imperio, Ann's assistant.

Jessye Norman, for conversations that influenced the formation of some of the ideas in this book. For her performances, which have taught me many lessons about the relationship of a single voice to an audience. For her passionate interest in this country. For how she speaks to us, all over the world, in our souls, through songs—songs in different languages, songs from all over the world—songs written now, songs written in the past. Some of those songs come from the United States: spirituals about hope in the presence of suffering and unfairness, and then patriotic songs about glory and promise. Songs that she sings and has sung in the acoustic perfection of concert halls, in churches, in opera houses, in schools, against the granite background of monuments, in the huge coldness of convention halls. Songs that manage to bind us, even through our differences. For the magic of her communication to our hearts, beyond words, beyond cultures, across boundaries.

The presidents who were willing to meet with me, and their staffs who made it possible: President Jimmy Carter, President George Bush, President Bill Clinton.

Stephen Rivers, for his diligence in helping me move around the beltway world. Peter Osnos, for early conversations about this book, and his encouragement. Diana Walker, for her humor, inspiration, and generosity, and for her perceptive, sometimes theatrical, photographs of presidents since Carter. Catharine Stimpson, for her common sense. Stephen Hess, at the Brookings Institute, for being the first to translate Washington for me. Riley Temple, for giving me confidence from time to time, right on time.

With gratitude to, and in memory of, Maynard Parker, former editor of *Newsweek,* and Charles Lyons, former chair, Department of Drama, Stanford University.

Alison Bernstein, Andrea Taylor, Christine Vincent, Barron Tenny, and all of the people at the Ford Foundation, for conversations and experiments about how to enliven democracy and the ways in which we talk to one another across the lines of power, race, class, and difference; in institutions, cities, and countries; and between individuals.

Suzanne Sato, a patron saint and wise woman, for helping so many of us take risks—intellectually and artistically—in our disciplines, forms, and communities. For being forward-looking.

The Rockefeller Foundation, Bellagio Study and Conference Center on Lake Como, Bellagio, Italy. Special thanks to Gianna Celli and Susan Garfield for my residency there.

Adria Popkin, for her clerical assistance on the first draft of this book.

David Chalian, Stacey Shorter, Roberta Goodman, Kimber Riddle, Diana Alvarez, Sandra Smith, Jane Kennedy, Irene Mecchi, and Shana Waterman, for their intelligence, friendship, and support.

The artists, core audience, and staff of the Institute on the Arts and Civic Dialogue, who have been experimenting for three summers with the art of conversation in public.

Colleagues and deans at Stanford University, for being flexible and making it possible for me to take the time needed to research, prepare for, and follow the '96 campaign.

The students in my Arts and Civic Dialogue class, Fall 1999, for their energy, inventiveness, openness, appetite for civic responsibility, and, most of all, idealism.

Stephen Richard, Kitty Eisele, Nora Connell, Marcos Najera, Lynette Turner, Matthew Francis, Andrew Goodman, Cori Nelson, Stacey Schwandt, and Eryn Rosenthal, for the research and creativity needed to develop an understanding of the presidency and the press in history and now. For all the logistics and long hours provided to move me through the presidential campaign trail in '96, and to the South, where churches had burned that summer.

This book was inspired, in part, by a project I developed called the "Press and Presidency Project." One of its dimensions was as a project for the theater. It was originally commissioned by the Arena Stage Theater: Doug Wager, artistic director; Stephen Richard, managing director. It was subsequently produced at the Arena Stage Theater, the Mark Taper Forum, and the New York Shakespeare Festival. Its development was also supported by the Intimann Theater and the Goodman Theater. Many thanks to all of the theaters, artistic directors, managing directors, boards of directors, the "Friends of the Press and Presidency Project," and the actors, designers, dramaturgs, historians, stage managers, production assistants, staff, and audiences that dedicated their time, commitment, and talent to giving that project a life—financially, logistically, intellectually, and artistically. Its life in the theater (a play called *House Arrest*) provided the opportunity to represent ideas in the form of character, spoken words, and metaphor in front of live audiences. It also provided the opportunity to talk to actors and other theater artists about language and character in new and different ways. Finally, it provided the opportunity to talk to audiences after shows and to invite them to talk to me, and to one another.

Stanley and Betty Sheinbaum.

Stephen and Daryl Roth.

Gordon Davidson.

Cinder Stanton, Monticello.

The White House.

The Maryland Correctional Institute for Women.

Maggie Williams, Judy Woodruff and Al Hunt, Mike McCurry, Sheila Tate, Jody Powell, Peter Mirijanian, John Sullivan, Susan Mercandetti, Tina Brown, Rhonda Sherman, Wendy Smith, Robert Kaiser, Ben Bradlee and Sally Quinn, and Don Graham.

To all of the people who invited me to their homes, their favorite restaurants, their parties, their offices, and their prison visiting rooms in and around Washington. For your fellowship and your generosity in opening doors that otherwise would have been impossible to open.

I interviewed more than four hundred people in the course of working on this project. To all of the people who provided interviews—most of which do not appear in this book—those hours of interviews, your words, are the heart of the project and the foundation for my work in general. Thank you for talking to me.

CONTENTS

TALK TO ME

WILD WAVES AND BONFIRES

1971

BALTIMORE, MARYLAND

A HOWARD JOHNSON'S PARKING LOT NEAR I-95

I PACKED AN OVERNIGHT BAG AND COUNTED OUT EIGHTY DOLLARS, all the money I had in the world. My mother drove me to a Howard Johnson's near I-95. A car pulled up with four friends, each of whom had come from a different point north of Maryland. At age twenty-one I left my family, my hometown, and, with my four friends, took off for California. We wanted to see America and to make sense, each in our own way, of what to do with all the breakage and promise that had been released through the antiwar movement, the assassinations of Martin Luther King and Bobby Kennedy, the beginning of the environmental movement, and the bra-burning, brief as it was, of the women's movement. And there was the masculine glamour and fashion of the black liberation movement. Years later I would talk to some of those Black Panthers. One of them mused openly, "I think we got caught up in the theater of it. We began to believe we were in a movie." One of the Chicago Eight would similarly say, "It was theater, until the cops showed us the difference between reality and theater, and hauled some of us off to jail."

Was it theater or not? I took off to see for myself. Quite apart from the theater, the sexiness of the antiestablishment voice was another promise, a serious promise that was eking out from under all the chants, all the music, all the pageantry. What was promised, after all was said and done, was a larger idea of "we the people." What was promised was that more voices would matter, that the patrician white male would not be the only one to hold the chair. This promise was made by none other than ourselves, so if we were to ever be disillusioned again, we would have to be the cause of that disillusionment.

My mother tells me she sat in the car and cried for a long time after I left. Her life's work had been to educate me, my four siblings, and hundreds of others who had passed through her classrooms all over Baltimore. Her goal had been to position us firmly in the black middle class.

Her trajectory was one that had been formed in the depression—a colored girl growing up poor in a family of eight in a tough, segregated Baltimore. My father, more fortunate, had been the son of a businessman who had an eighth-grade education and had started a business with a pushcart. His shop had eventually held its own on Pennsylvania Avenue, the street for black businesses during the day and good jazz at night. My grandfather had managed to send all six of his kids to college. My mother and her siblings, too, all went to college.

I suspect that some of those kids my mother taught in the Baltimore public schools, she only wanted to keep out of trouble, heartbreak, and illiteracy. (She never believed there was such a thing as a nonreader.) As for me, she had spent many nights helping me read and write, and I could tell she had faith in me. But life is more than reading, writing, and putting the correct answer on a test. Especially when the tests and the books themselves become suspect, as they did in Wagnerian proportions round about 1968.

It was a rocky road, and I, as the first child, was to make the first solid step. It wasn't to be the step my mother expected. My college education answered few questions. It created many. I came out of college with debts, and, rather than a five-year plan, or even a foothold in the next generation of black success, I had about fifty years' worth of questions about the world I came from and the world I live in. I am still in the process of answering those questions.

WHAT I REMEMBER MOST ABOUT AMERICA ON THAT TRIP WAS THE gorgeous tapestry of autumn in the West Virginia hills, the hamburgers in Texas, and the poverty in Oklahoma, which was beyond anything I could have imagined. We landed finally on Coronado, an island off San Diego, and stayed in the home of a friend whose husband was in the

Navy and out on duty somewhere dangerously close to Vietnam. The place was in stark contrast to what I thought California would offer. Everyone seemed to ride bikes, play tennis, and have blond hair. It was as if nothing of the sixties push to color American culture had happened there. We did boring "survival" jobs during the day and watched the sunset over the Pacific every night, until each one of us figured out, singly, which route we should take next.

One by one we left one another. It was sad. As each person parted, I knew that I may have been watching a series of dreams deferred. I had watched my friends speak their dreams each night. They started out with bluster, and, as the days rolled on, rather than constructing the dreams into plans and realities, they began to leave their sentences unfinished, taking drags on a cigarette where words used to follow, sipping water or wine where a fist used to be pounded, or sighing where a guffaw used to come. The conversation was melting.

One night, in a van that we had driven to a beach in Baja California, just south of the Mexican border, I could feel the palpable pull of the known. It weighed on all my friends. I could feel the weight of it in my own heart. It was an ache. It was time, for them, one by one, to get back to the boyfriend, father, or mother who had caused them to have questions in the first place. They would return with the questions unanswered. This was very different from my project, which was to take, at its word, and with both eyes open, and at the same time one eye piercing suspiciously, the movement's promise to give more voice to more people. I left the van and sat on the beach, with its wild waves and bonfires. The roar of each was wilder than anything I had experienced on the East Coast. I began to fear that my own dreams would meet the air undone. I decided not to speak them to my friends, although that had been the purpose of my trip. The trip with eighty dollars and an overnight bag had been meant to speak my dreams out loud until I had a plan. But dreams don't have to be spoken, they only have to be seen.

Soon after we got back to Coronado, I said good-bye, and went north.

1973

GEARY STREET

SAN FRANCISCO, CALIFORNIA

I arrived, in June 1973, at a five-story building that sat above several store-fronts on Geary Street in downtown San Francisco. Among the store-fronts were a glitzy deli with mounds of chopped liver in the window, called David's Delicatessen, an art gallery, a soup place called Salma-gundi's, and a bar just to the right of that called The Curtain Call. I couldn't afford to buy anything in any of those places. Even for a cup of coffee or an apple, I had to go up the block, where it was fifteen cents cheaper. There were two theaters across the street. One was the theater operated by my school, the American Conservatory Theatre. The other brought the big road shows from New York. Our theater did all the "authentic" stuff, the "real" theater, with "real" acting, "real" intellect, "real" art, and it evoked and used "real" feelings. The other stuff was thought to be mere "spectacle."

You could hear the cable cars and the brassy whistle of the hotel doorman across the street, sharply signaling for cabs as the guests stood waiting in their polished shoes, manicured nails, and perfectly clipped hair. We were a motley bunch, to say the least, in the midst of that down-town finery. But we were just blocks from the Tenderloin, with its myriad tragic stories—drug addicts, prostitutes, pimps, the downs of the down-and-outers—on every corner. Not so destroyed as they would be in the eighties, with the invasion of crack cocaine, but nonetheless in a vari-ety of states of despair, loss beyond repair, and physical and psychological danger. There was the dramatic reminder of hope in the form of the glo-rious choir that belted out from the Glide Memorial Church. Glide wel-comed the richest and the poorest, the luckiest and the most challenged. Some of us went there on Sundays to get a burst of inspiration and to hear good speaking—who knew, you might find Maya Angelou in the pulpit. We could also hear great singing.

SUMMER 1996

THE CAMPAIGN TRAIL

Twenty-three years later I would travel back to San Francisco on a press swing with President Clinton, and I would leave the trip as Clinton went in to visit the Glide church. America seems to me to be addicted to hope. Presidents from time to time visit places like Glide, where hope lives and where someone seems to be tending to those who missed out on the American dream. I wonder how often they visit the places where there is no hope, no hope whatsoever. Has a president in office ever gone without a chaperone to press the hand of a person in profound need?

And then I think about those who have "everything." What are they yearning for, another dollar, a sunnier day? happier progeny? Are they still in the hopeful state, or are they prisoners of their ambition? Is ambition, drive, the same as hope? Does hope exist only for those who are "lost," "lost causes"? Those who have hope are perhaps the motor, the air, the breeze under the soul of the nation.

1973

BEETHOVEN'S NINTH

SAN FRANCISCO

In that summer of '73, we carried sweaters on our piles of scripts and dance clothes because the breeze from the bay was very cold at night, almost like in winter. We had so much to talk about, so many people to talk to—the shoe shine man across the street with the incomprehensible European accent (last time I walked by, in early 2000, he was still there), Tennessee Williams, who was visiting (I actually saw him for real in the elevator), or perhaps one of those people sitting on a corner in the Tenderloin. In this pre-AIDS-consciousness time, it was romantic in all ways, physically, spiritually, intellectually, aesthetically. The twenty-four-hour murmur of electricity under the ground of the cable car was the perfect metaphor. And the foghorns spoke to the darker, lonelier side that could visit you too.

We were 210 students, all there to study identity, change identities, to learn to "be." There are a variety of ways to describe what acting is. "Being," "Seeming," "Becoming," "Lying," "Truth Telling," "Magic," "Transforming." We were new. Some among us had known the building for an hour longer than the others of us. No one ever arrives at the same time as everybody else. We were going to learn how to talk to each other onstage, and through all of this how to take our own special message to the *world*.

On one of the first days I was coming into the building, a tall, thin, aristocratic-looking white woman who appeared to be about my age, and whom we ultimately referred to as the Katharine Hepburn among us, came breathlessly down a narrow hallway, saying to me (whom she had never seen except in that one instant), "Do you know where I can get a drink of water?"

She said this as if she had known me all my life, as if I were a sister, a brother, a friend. She may even have grabbed my hand. I wasn't put off by the fact that she was a stranger. Her presence in that question made me feel in an instant as if I had known her all my life. Having grown up in segregation, I found it odd that a white person would approach me without her own barriers up, and without the expectation that I would have barriers. I was so stunned by her presence that I didn't speak. Besides, I didn't know where to get a drink of water. Just as rapidly and as urgently, she vanished down the hallway and out into the street. I thought that perhaps this was what acting was. Because, as real as it was, realer than real, it also seemed like a moment out of a scene from Chekhov's *Uncle Vanya*, or as if one of Tchaikovsky's symphonies had burst into speech. *Urgency* is the word. And it's one of the top ten in the vocabulary of acting.

Acting is the furthest thing from lying that I have encountered. It is the furthest thing from make-believe. It is the furthest thing from pretending. It is the most unfake thing there is. Acting is a search for the authentic. It is a search for the authentic by using the fictional as a frame, a house in which the authentic can live. For a moment. Because, yes indeed, real life inhibits the authentic.

I knew intuitively that this was metaphorically what it was all about. Later I would learn fancy words for it. I would learn, in all the reading I did about acting, what Joseph Chaikin, a great director, had to say—that presence is the gift of the actor. Presence is a "kind of deep libidinal surrender which the performer reserves for his anonymous audience."

Presence is that quality that makes you feel as though you're standing right next to the actor, no matter where you're sitting in the theater. It's the feeling you have that the performer is right in front of you, speaking to you and only you. It's that wonderful moment when Jessye Norman sings in a quiet, so quiet you can hear a pin drop concert hall to an audience that is attentive like no other. It's a moment when she seems to be singing as she's never sung, and the audience seem to be listening as they've never listened. It's the moment when it's clear that everyone is there for the same reason. It's not that frenzied desire for the diva, but a sudden calm that hits the hall, like it did in one performance I saw in Paris, where they love her so much they named an orchid after her. These moments have a kind of authenticity, because they reach the heart. They speak to us. They speak to us not because they are natural in the sense of normal. They speak to us because they are real in their effort to be together with a very large *you*, the *you* being all men and women.

Politicians have tried to borrow those skills, and they have misused them and ended up speaking to very few.

That genuine moment, that "real" connection, is no small thing. It is not something that happens every day. Is it rare because it calls for a special talent? Is it a moment that can happen only when we don't know each other, when we have so much to learn about each other that we hang on every breath together? It is hard to find those moments in our culture because we think we know so much about each other. Perhaps it is a moment that is dependent not only on the performer or the leader, but on the audience as well. Does this era of focus groups and polls, this desire to get at and quantify the mysteriousness of that "deep libidinal surrender," make it nearly impossible to find those moments of true engagement? Does the overdetermined nature of our time, and the inherent desire to control the public, to control their thoughts, particularly how they work those thoughts into actions that are favorable to the marketplace, create an atmosphere where only the predictable can occur? Those moments of deep libidinal surrender are in fact all about that which is not predictable. And there *is* no anonymous audience. At least that's what the pollsters would like, what commerce would like. They would like to make the anonymous audience *fully* identifiable. With no anonymous audience, there can be no deep libidinal surrender.

Politicians have tried to get the benefit of lessons that performers have learned, presumably because they would like to create the feeling with their audiences that great actors and singers create. They would like to make us feel as though they are speaking to us and only us. But they fail at it. I was surprised to learn that one of Clinton's coaches in 1996 was a graduate of the Yale School of Drama. I wonder if the audience also has that libidinal surrender that they reserve for that one special performance that they so long to adore, to be with, to be enchanted with. If the possibility for surrender is deep, and libidinal, and therefore natural, why is it so hard to find in political life these days? Is it all used up for movie stars? Or money? Or is it simply profoundly in reserve? We're having a hard time connecting in public.

I never knew a group of people like the people I met in the summer of 1973—those 210 actors and all of our trainers. One night I went to hear Beethoven's Ninth performed. I had never heard it live. It was in Grace Cathedral, which sits like a great princess atop Nob Hill in San Francisco. It was so exciting. At one point, as you know, that single human voice comes out after all that music. A tenor exclaims, from the orchestral beauty that has preceded, *"Freunnnnnnden!"* Which means "friends." And then the choral part of the symphony begins—after his call.

When I went to yoga class the next day, I complained of a hot feeling on my forehead. I hadn't been able to sleep. I thought I was feverish and was getting the flu. My yoga teacher listened attentively, looked me square in the eye, and calmly said, "It sounds to me like one of your chakras is opening."

Who ever heard of a piece of music making you feverish? I liked her explanation. Not that I had ever had a chakra open. Many fevers and chakras later, I know, whether it was a fever or my chakras, Beethoven caused it, and that's thrilling. Not only is communication possible across cultures, it is possible across centuries. No great desire to communicate ever dies.

Perhaps it was the sound of the tenor singing *"Freunnnnnnden"* that first opened my heart to the idea that we should all be in a conversation together. By "we" I refer to the potential America, the America that has expanded significantly since the late eighteenth century away from that small group of white men who were the original "we" in "we the people."

When I first went to California to study performance and look for whatever carcasses were left of the "revolution," I thought I was actually in search of the authentic. It came as no surprise to me that the study of acting in the 1970s was about getting "real."

This went hand in hand with what the short-lived "revolution" had in mind. Here we were, in that odd time in the seventies before Nixon was threatened with impeachment—standing in the sawdust of something being constructed. In my college years I thought we were taking apart the throne upon which the white male patriarch had comfortably been perched. The drama of burning bras, the Panthers' guns, Woodstock, et cetera, may have been short-lived. However, a conversation reverberated for three decades in schools and universities and popular culture about who could speak for whom. Women wanted to speak for themselves, people of color wanted to speak for themselves, et cetera.

In this cacophony of sound, where does "we" come from? That's what we're still working on in 2000.

2000

We are in a communications revolution. Yet, as the great Americanist Studs Terkel tells us, "We're more and more into communications and less and less into communication." In this time of a global economy and business mergers happening as often as sunrise and sunset, where is the human merger? Where is real human engagement?

The theater was where I started my quest for the "we" of the new "we the people" the sixties had promised. I soon saw that the theater would be a resource for my quest but that it had serious limitations. It's a business. It's the business of representation, and the people who make all productions "possible" are the same white men in bow ties and women with Chanel bags who have always run "the arts." In thirty years the theater itself has not made very many strides toward creating a bigger "we." It struggles with how to engage younger, diverse audiences, and it has very little to show in terms of a diverse working community. This is how the theater in the year 2000 defines its dilemma: It is worried about its relevance. Yet, in 1973, while I was in school, I had that very question. The theater had been a door into "getting real." Yet it was only that, a door, and only one door, and luckily a kind of revolving door. I would move in the theater and out. I would move in academia and out.

Academia has been a wonderful storehouse of information during the culture wars of the last thirty years. It has pushed itself to be more porous, more absorbent of the world around it. To some extent it was successful, and to some extent it was not. The very schools that had begun to collect and teach information about "us," a bigger "us," struggle with the problem of tenuring sufficient numbers of women and people of color, and of treating them respectfully once they are appointed. Academia too was a revolving door. I would need to find many doors if my goal was to absorb my culture in its moment of promising to find a bigger "we."

To me, the most important doorway into the soul of a person is her or his words, or any other external communication device. I am a student of words. The theater gave me Shakespeare, Molière, Adrienne Kennedy, Sam Shepard. Life would give me other kinds of characters, nestled in the speakings and misspeakings of the people I met in all walks of life. I supposed that words could also be the doorway into the soul of a culture.

I set out across America, on a search for American character. My search was specifically to find America in its language. I interview people and communities about the events of our time, in the hope that I will be able to absorb America. I use the interviews as texts in one-person shows, in which I perform the people I have interviewed. This is a country of many tongues, even if we stick to English. Placing myself in other people's words, as in placing myself in other people's shoes, has given me the opportunity to get below the surface—to get "real."

After almost twenty-five years of my journey, I went to Washington, D.C., with my tape recorder. It was my objective to capture the American presidency in its words. The words of the American presidency are now, more than ever, mediated by the press. For this reason, I determined to look at the relationship of the press to the presidency. I knew that I knew nothing about the president, or any public figure for that matter, that the press didn't tell me. I would have to look at the press too.

WASHINGTON, D.C.

ARRIVED IN WASHINGTON, D.C., ON THE DAY OF THE OJ VERDICT, in the fall of 1995. I was to live in a town house in Georgetown that was a part of a two-house complex. My hosts were Congressman Amory Houghton from Corning, New York, and his wife, Priscilla Dewey Houghton. Priscilla is a lover of the theater, and when they heard that I, a theater artist, needed someplace to sleep and pile my books, she and Amo generously offered an entire empty town house in Georgetown for my use for the five years I would be in and out of Washington. The house itself was the Theresa Fenwick House, a historic monument built in 1826.

When I arrived, workmen were cutting down a two-hundred-year-old cherry tree in the backyard. (Because it was dead, dead on the inside.) My hosts, whom I had yet to meet, were in Corning, the district of the congressman. They were doing exactly what I was doing when I arrived, except miles away—watching the OJ verdict.

The garden and backyard were between the two houses. The kitchen, which served both houses, was on the ground floor of the house I lived in. There was a bumper sticker in the kitchen that said, "The road to hell is lined with Republicans." In Priscilla's handwriting was added, "Except for Amo." Amo is a Republican. Priscilla is a liberal Democrat. She was a Bostonian, and a descendant of abolitionists. Amo's great-grandfather was a glassblower who made Thomas Edison's lightbulbs. The place was grounded in history and current events. In the living room was a photograph, prominently placed, of Amo and George Bush. Not fully nonpartisan upon arrival, I was made instantly nervous by that picture—nervous about meeting Amo, who, at the time, was still only a name to me. But so much for looking at pictures of the past. Current events awaited upstairs, within moments. I went to look for my assistant.

Marcos Najera had gotten to town a day or so before me, from Arizona, where he lived. He was at the top of the house, on the third floor, unpacking my books and converting the space into an office. The doorbell rang. Segrario, the housekeeper, went to answer it. A thin woman with a face lined with character, she was from Spain and had a very thick accent. She came upstairs with a man from the phone company in tow. He was a tall, very well built black man with a West Indian accent. What would Theresa Fenwick think of us all?

"What time is it?"

"The verdict!" somebody said.

We all ran down a flight of stairs to the "red room," a sitting room with a rather large television. We turned on the television. The man from the phone company, who had arrived just seconds before, joined us.

I sat next to Marcos on the couch. The man from the telephone company stood in the doorway. My heart started beating really fast, and it was hard to catch my breath. I surveyed the room through squinted eyes, as if squinting my eyes would protect me from seeing something I didn't really want to see. It was like waiting for something nearly violent to happen.

FALL 1991
CAMBRIDGE, MASSACHUSETTS

I was at Harvard on a fellowship.

Who could possibly forget Anita Hill weekend? We sat in front of our televisions watching an amazing parade. It's difficult to believe that it was only one weekend, the event stayed so imprinted on many of our minds. I did not have a television and had to watch what I could in hallways and lobbies.

On the night of Clarence Thomas's testimony, I was to have dinner with the preeminent teacher of voice for American actors. Her name is Kristin Linklater. She wrote a very important book called *The Thinking Voice.* She has trained many people in her technique and has disciples well placed in schools all over the country. Even as people teach a variety of techniques, it's rare to find someone who did not cross the path of Kristin Linklater, her disciples, or the influence of the notion of a "thinking voice."

At this time, I didn't know her. I knew only of her eminence. I was prepared, and rather nervous about meeting "the master." The plan had been to meet in a restaurant in Boston.

When I called to make last-minute arrangements, she was watching the Hill-Thomas hearings, and she said, "I can't pull myself away from this. Let's meet at my place, watch this, and then decide what to do for dinner." My guess was that people were changing plans all over the country.

We watched the testimony. She was, of course, appalled by the entire display. Her ears were attuned to lies and truths. We were both screaming at the television, using all we had gathered over the years about authentic voice, true-seeming feelings, and grounded speaking.

We sat with our brows furrowed, and with our mouths hanging open. To some extent we were both like impatient teachers. She was the master, I was still in development. We were both appalled at the complete and total lack of authenticity.

All that I had learned about acting from my own work, and from watching my students since the seventies, came to bear as I watched for these intense hours. She, who was the eminence of voice, had a lot to say. What an amazing tutorial I had as we watched this political drama unfold.

"Oh—my—God!" became our descant. Often we would get as far as "Oh, my . . ." and something else would happen that would make us lose words completely. Perhaps we would simply slap our thighs or shake our heads.

Before our very eyes there was a wide display of patriarchal Washington, many of its members speaking to Anita Hill in condescending tones. One among them even inquired, with accusatory tones, why she was not eager to go out with Clarence Thomas. The presumed entitlement took our breath away—but not completely away. We certainly had enough breath to roar at the TV in unison, "Because she didn't *like* him!"

"Oh—my—God!"

It was one of those moments when the truth of the matter comes pouring down from heaven. Men and women live in different universes. Washington and the rest of us live in different universes.

I was so amazed by what I had watched that the next morning I took the T across Boston to a discount center and bought a television, so as not to miss a moment. Friends of mine were visiting from out of town. We huddled around my small color TV and hung on every word. No one could decide what was true or not. It didn't matter.

When the decision came down, many of us were stunned that Thomas was to be appointed after all. How could this *be*? I felt completely disconnected. Where does one go in such a civic moment? You would think there would be halls we could go to, even coffeehouses, someplace for *us* to talk. The pundits talked, and I suppose one could have called in to a talk show. But where could *we* go? Those of *us* who were not linked to any community organization or club? And how many of those clubs and organizations exist? Wouldn't it be wonderful if we had civic organizations where *we* could go and talk about any manner of things in any town? Perhaps these could be as available as, say, AA meetings. I knew of a poetry reading being given in Cambridge by Adrienne Rich. Perhaps this could be the antidote to such an intense feeling of disconnectedness. That is where I went. There was no conversation. I just thought that the safest place to be was in the presence of a poet.

FALL 1995
THERESA FENWICK HOUSE
WASHINGTON, D.C.

As the moments ticked away in the red room, I grabbed on to Marcos as if I were in a horror movie. Lance Ito had forbidden noises of any kind in the courtroom. We watched every gesture. Of OJ, of Cochran, whom I had once interviewed—every blink of every eye. The public spectacle.

As the nation waited, what was it that they wanted? OJ to hang? To hear him confess? To have him repent? As on the scaffold? Most people would say they wanted justice done, but justice being done has become such a spectacle. Democracy and the justice system are owned by television ratings.

I flashed back to a dinner I had in Beverly Hills with a woman who had helped OJ select his "spring palette." Here was a man who may have been on his way to the gallows, selecting the color of his suits. Everything was so overdetermined, everything was based on a guess about "our gaze"—what we would be watching, and how we would feel about what we watched. The jury vote was really supposed to be a sequestered affair, but no one believed it was. There's no privacy in our culture.

I had gone to Los Angeles several months before the trial started. I was given a tour of the media villages being created in and around the courthouse. My guide walked me around a parking lot that was showing the earliest signs of what it was going to become. A few trailers were already there, and equipment from the networks was being piled into them. Then she took me across to the courthouse, and upstairs to a floor that had once had offices. I had visited it when I attended the so-called Rodney King trial—the federal trial that President Bush had ordered after the first trial had brought back all not-guilty verdicts on the cops, and a subsequent riot. The entire floor was in the process of being turned into media central. There were wires and boxes everywhere.

"There's no going back now," she said. And this was months before the coverage started. I did not want it to be true. This structure of exposition is now ready for any event—whether the event warrants it or not—and it's so huge that it kills the character of the event. It promises to bring us closer, but, like overbearing parents, it alienates us from the event. It's like a huge scaffold.

In 1996, when I went to the Republican convention, pundit Jeff Greenfield took me for a walk along a row of trailers that were all electrical wires, machines, and manners of connection. There looked to be enough wiring and enough whirring of electricity to hook the convention to the moon. Yet the Republican convention was so overhooked, it unhooked itself from the public's interest. All the wattage in the world doesn't make us watch if we're not already connected.

And to think that Thomas Edison had gone to my host's great-grandfather to ask him to make lightbulbs.

The verdict was announced. Johnnie Cochran wimpered, just for a split second. He covered his mouth like a Cub Scout and had to stop himself from cheering, it seemed. And then the sobbing started. It was Kim Goldman, Ron Goldman's sister.

No one among us screamed out for joy, even though our group, with two blacks, one Latino, statistically would have been expected to do so.

The verdict was like the Winslow Homer painting of soldiers coming home after the Civil War. All three of us likely had less than cozy relationships with police. Nonetheless, there was something like a deflated balloon about the atmosphere in the room. The press had built a huge scaffold. I don't think they'd built a scaffold like that in a long time, if ever. The scaffold, in the middle of the square. All around America, instant community was created around those few moments.

"Well, we'll never know," one among us said.

How could that be? That we would never know? Wasn't all that exposure, all that talk, all that information, all those testimonies, all of the articles, all of the money, all of the commentators, every kind of expert, the birth of the expert on the air from USC, UCLA, everywhere else, all of this expertise, wasn't it about knowing? How could we not know? "We'll never know." My colleague at Stanford, a biologist named Marcus Felman, warned me several years ago that there is no proof that knowledge would make us a better species, that is to say, no proof that knowledge in and of itself will save us from extinction. There's a lot of money spent, a lot of time spent, a lot of smart and talented people giving over their talents to this enterprise of all news all the time, of telling us all . . . and . . . we'll never know? Evidence wasn't enough? There wasn't enough evidence? Well then, why were so many hours spent?

The man from the phone company stood at the door, shaking his head.

"What do you think of this?" I asked him.

"Look like if you got the money you get away wid anyting. If he didn't have dat money he wouldn't have gotten away wid it."

He looked as if he were at a loss. Segrario wasn't happy with the verdict either. What was it that we wanted? Did we want blood drawn? I wonder. Is there something deep inside of human beings that longs for the scaffold in the middle of the square, where the body is displayed and tortured? Was this what the media were banking on when they built their structures of display? They could never really follow through. Supposedly, we were anticipating truth. On the other hand, we didn't think it was possible.

The two-hundred-year-old cherry tree was being buzz-sawed outside as the four of us talked about the fairs and unfairs of the OJ verdict. We all felt disconnected from the justice system. I was grateful that this time,

ill–Thomas hearing came to a close with news of
was in the company of others. At the time the
I arrived in Washington—did I think that the
to do with the president of the United States? No.
at the time that a scaffold would also be built for the

When the president was finally acquitted, two days before Valentine's Day 1999, the nation did not hold its breath. When I had gone to see the House take their impeachment vote, near Christmas 1998, it was anti-climactic. People roamed around the gallery, chatting as though it were just another day. "Order" was called constantly, to no avail. And as for the rest of the nation, it was Christmas shopping, disconnected from it all.

The phone man asked: "You want how many lines?"

"She needs four," Marcos called out.

"Four?"

"Two phone lines, one for fax, one for e-mail."

He headed into the bedroom. The phone man's job was to connect me, and everybody else, up to the world. All communication is possible.

Television, the Internet, all of the descendants of the lightbulb, and the telephone promise to connect us up like we've never been connected before. Yet connection is much more than spectatorship.

It seems that, since the OJ trial, the courtroom has become ever more present in our lives. The courtroom and the media stand as the places where we resolve our differences—in public. Are the courts, together with the media, a collaborative scaffold building? Isn't there some way other than to immediately head to court that we can work out differences? It gets more and more difficult to negotiate fairness without the aid of the legal system.

"Do you want two lines in the bedroom, or one?"

"Uh . . ." I headed down the steps. On the way down, I heard a crash.

"Oh no." (Marcos.)

There was a long pause, in which I could hear the saw outside, still hacking away at the two-hundred-year-old cherry tree. I stopped dead in my tracks on the steps. Marcos came out.

"We broke a mirror," he said. "We" was kind, because it was actually the man from the phone company who, while moving a dresser to look for a phone jack, caused a mirror to fall.

"Has this mirror been here since 1826 too?" Marcos continued.

"If it's an antique, we're dead," I mumbled. I hadn't even met hosts yet, and I had bad news to report.

"Seven years bad luck," Marcos called.

By now the phone man was ready with an energetically stated alibi: the mirror was shaky in the first place—it wasn't his fault, it was the mirror's. The truth is always mitigated.

What a way to start a journey into the jungle of Washington. The OJ verdict, a saw whirring outside as the two-hundred-year-old cherry tree, dead, dead on the inside, hit the ground, and "we" broke a mirror.

HELEN THOMAS

WHITE HOUSE PRESS CORPS

"Little Match Girl"

My interest in secrets?
You mean why I have been uh
so nosy?
All I know
is
when I was five years old
a lovely woman came to visit our home.
She was a sort of distant relative
very beautiful clothes on and I kept asking her all these questions
and she
turned to me and she said "You're so inquisitive"
and I ran to my sister and said
"What does *inquisitive* mean?"
And I was just, ya know.
So my nosiness has always been—
I have a curiosity
and uh

it could be called nosiness.
I like to think, I like to know a lot of things.
I like to know everything I could possibly know.
I don't like secrecy.
I think it could be detrimental to democracy
and I don't think we should have secrecies
except for maybe the extreme
national security propositions
but otherwise I think we should have an open society and I don't
    believe in secrecy at all.
I think secrecy is uh
I think it's very hurtful to the American people.
I don't think it's necessary.
I think it's fantastic to have the privilege of covering the White
    House because this is where it all happens in terms of our
    country, in terms of the world.
We're the only superpower in the world.
We are the leaders of the world, and so I
I am able to see someone operating
And this office is the center.
You know, so when you're watching them, you feel very lucky.
Watching history every day in the making.
I mean I don't, I'm not personally affected by it because I always
    consider myself the match girl with her nose against the
    windowpane.
And, and I'm an outsider and I want to be that way.
And I'm an observer.
I'm not part of the inside.

CULTURE SHOCK

GETTING READY FOR
THE JOURNEY

ANY ANTHROPOLOGIST HAS RULES, LESSONS, SURVIVAL TECHNIQUES for moving where you don't normally move, in fact, moving where you don't belong. The need for a sense of smell, the need for a sense of humor—whether in a "rough" neighborhood or in finer circles. These are the kinds of things I have been told in the past. I try to take lessons and apply them wherever I am going. I try to pinpoint what sorts of transformations I need in order to "cross the lines." I normally take advice wherever I can, and try to follow it. I had to take information from all sources to get ready for Washington.

As I sat forward at a visiting-room table inside a prison near Washington, a compulsive thief taught me how to dress and fit into a "street environment": "To be honest, in an all-black neighborhood, a lot of people may not know that you're [black]. Maybe you need to change your lipstick to a darker color, like plum."

Later, in a tony restaurant, an anonymous Washington insider advised me, "It's a very tight, Wasp environment, it is a very tubular, closed environment. Your costume designer is going to have to go really to Pappagallo! It's as if they got their stuff at um, at um *Loehmann's.*"

I figured what the prisoner had to say would be helpful in establishment Washington too. A little plum lipstick, a little Loehmann's. I wore the same outfits to visit the prison outside Washington as I wore to visit the White House.

COMPOSING LESSONS LEARNED FROM PAST

INCIDENTS OF CROSSING LINES AND

WEATHERING CULTURE SHOCK, 1959–2000

I am constantly in a state of being, to borrow a phrase from the cultural theorist Homi Bhabha, "almost, but not quite." It's actually not a bad state to be in. It might just be the best state in which to find oneself during the twenty-first century, as our culture wars continue and identity politics moves into its next phase. At such a time as this, it would be useful, I think, to have at least a cadre of people who were willing to move between cultural lines and across social strata. Globalism will require it, so we may as well practice our moves.

I am prepared for difference, live in difference. My pursuit of American character is, basically, a pursuit of difference. Character lives in that which is unique. What is unique about America is the extent to which it does, from time to time, pull off being a merged culture. Finding American character is a process of looking at fragments, of looking at the *un*merged. One has to do the footwork, one has to move from place to place, one has to stand outside. It's not easy, and the danger is that, when you stand outside, you could end up undocumented.

When I visited Thomas Jefferson's home and farm, Monticello, I went on a tour of the site of the slave quarters, which is currently part of an archaeological dig. The archaeologist was named John Meeks. I asked him what the difference would be if an archaeologist, five centuries from now, did a further dig of Jefferson's house and the slave site. He said, "There's going to be no guesswork when you run into the walls of [Jefferson's house]. It's a very substantial house type. Here [at the slave site] we have to really coax the evidence. We have nothing that marks the outside of the house. Just nails, and all outside. Which goes to what we know about slave housing. The activity took place outside the house, not inside."

The most comfortable place to live is inside of what I call one's safe house of identity. I have observed that this is where most people live. Even if they leave a previous identity to enter another identity of choice, they often end up in another safe house, and leave behind any ambiguity that met them as they went from one house to the other. I tend to be more interested in the unsettled part of us.

I am continually leaving safe houses of identity. When you leave the house of what is familiar to you—your family, your race, your social class, your nation, your professional area of expertise—it is not likely that you will find another house that will welcome you with open arms. When you leave your safe house, you will end up standing someplace in the road. I would call these places that are without houses crossroads of ambiguity. On the one hand, they are not comfortable places. On the other hand, in them one acquires the freedom to move. In my work I have moved across many cultural boundaries. For this reason I do not suffer culture shock often. I've developed a lot of stamina for being where I don't "belong."

My journey to Washington showed me that I had less stamina than I thought.

I come from a matriarchy. Pearl Banks Young, my maternal grandmother, told me many stories about her mother, and also about the woman who raised her after her mother died. The woman who raised her was called Sister Annie. She was the Grand Matron of the Eastern Star, the female counterpart to the Masons.

Grandma's subtle power was all too obvious. She was a very small woman, with a high forehead and a warm smile. She automatically engendered trust, not fear. Until the day she died, this rather short woman with a very sweet face had moral authority over all of her eight children and their children. She walked the streets of Baltimore and took buses to take care of her grandchildren. Never one to waste, she would collect pennies dropped on the floors of the homes of her grandchildren. At the end of the year, she would present us each with our pennies rolled in bank paper so that we could turn them in for dollars that we otherwise would not have had. She was a major source of nourishment in all ways. She cooked. She told me stories.

I often accompanied her around the city. We walked and took buses around Baltimore together. Since we had the same type of hair, we would regularly meet to get our hair done in an all-white salon. This in itself felt like a move into a house where I didn't belong. The salon was very different from the black salon I was used to: the smells, the colors, the clientele. Wherever we went, either to a fancy salon such as that one, or to

East Baltimore, where the poverty seemed to me to have its own smell, she would take Kleenex in her pocket in case there was a child with a runny nose.

She was a member of the Harriet Tubman Club. The Harriet Tubman Club was a club of black women, all about Grandma's age. She went on a regular basis, by foot, to pay her dues to the treasurer of the club. I often accompanied her on these occasions. As the treasurer was a short, stocky, brown-skinned woman with a wonderful smile, and as her hallway was cool and dark, and as we never ventured past the hallway, I always thought that Harriet Tubman was being kept alive in some mystical tribal way. I always thought that the club was about action, and not much talk. Grandma never told me about the club meetings or what went on there, she just paid her dues.

In my formative years I experienced a long line of matriarchs, a long line of women, tough and with their feet firmly on the ground, in power. Nothing that I learned from being in a matriarchy prepared me for Washington. Nothing that I learned from walking the varied areas of Baltimore with my grandmother, even as I can remember the determined fearlessness of her stride, or the charm of her warm smile, prepared me for Washington.

I also had a patriarchal side to my worldview. I am coming to believe that the black patriarch is significantly different from the white patriarch. There's a difference in reach. On my father's side, there was a patriarchal culture. The paternal side of my family was drenched in American history. I don't know my "roots," so to speak, but my father's aunts and uncles represented to me, as a child, American history. They looked like they had been here a long time, and many Sundays and holidays were spent visiting my Aunt Hannah in Gettysburg, and playing in the battlefield.

My paternal grandfather was a patriarch. He was called "Pop." He was tall, thin, and aristocratic looking, and had ruled, I am told, with an iron rod. He had an eighth-grade education, started a coffee and tea business with a pushcart in the early part of the twentieth century, and put all six of his children through college. He and I were good friends, because he liked to talk, and I liked to listen. He is the one who taught me the kernel of all that I understand about acting. "If you say a word often enough it becomes you" is what he said.

If Grandma showed me the world on my feet, with few words, and lots of action, Grandpop showed me the world in conversation. When he came to dinner he dominated the conversation. But even after my having grown up with our version of the patriarchy, my education in that matter was completely insufficient for the patriarchy that I met in Washington.

In my adult life I moved in the culture of the arts, which has all manner of behaviors, gracious and supremely ungracious, humanitarian, yet sometimes racist and elitist enough to take your breath away. We are in the business of representation. We are humanitarians, those who study mankind. Yet our world in art is not a diverse world. The hallways of theaters, museums, and other arts institutions are surprisingly empty of people of color (unless those people are sweeping the floors, guarding the doorways, or serving food).

When I got out of acting school, I went to my first meeting with an agent. She had a British accent. All of my classmates came back with tales from similar meetings. My meeting was one of the briefer ones. She quickly, and with no expression on her face, looked at my résumé. She turned it over and glanced at my black-and-white glossy. "I can't possibly send you out to auditions," she said. "I wouldn't want to antagonize my clients."

"Antagonize them?" I asked politely.

"Yes. You don't look like anything. You don't look black. You don't look white."

That was the end of the meeting.

My career was a long series of such meetings, and rejections. Still, none of those interactions prepared me for Washington.

An artist brings to the table, by necessity, a personal voice, a cultural voice, which is organic to where he or she once was. But once these wares are brought to market, the shock, the culture shock, is sharp, and stark. The upside of this rather downbeat tale is that in the arts one develops techniques for developing intimacies with strangers quickly. The most obvious intimacy is that with the audience. You might find yourself baring your soul or your body to complete strangers, either live or on film, an anonymous crowd who sit in the dark.

Being vulnerable in public is a way of life for artists. Yet in Washington I saw public figures being shamed publicly, and wondered at how they would ever recover. At least a movie star has the cover of persona. Politicians pretend not to have a persona. Yet both politicians and movie stars have to deal with a myriad of projections that are cast upon them, and, when they are hit hard in public, they have to survive. It was Raquel Welch who I remember hitting the first warning bell, in a droning voice, seated like a queen, on the Dick Cavett show: "They're treating politicians the way they used to treat movie stars." (She meant poorly, and with scandal lurking.)

That was in 1980. Now, I would imagine, she would say they treat them worse. I am reminded of a story about Marilyn Monroe. The studio didn't want to give her a proper dressing room when she was shooting *Gentlemen Prefer Blondes*. They said this was because she was not the star. Since the star was a brunette, Monroe's response was "I may not be a star, but I am the blonde, and this movie is called *Gentlemen Prefer Blondes*." Dignity does not come without a fight in public life.

The stakes are higher, and there is the added factor of morality in Washington. People in Washington are expected to behave in a "moral" way. Whereas artists have always been thought, if unfairly, to be degenerates. In the arts, there is a rejection process, which is humiliating. In Washington, there is a public shaming process.

NEW YORK–LOS ANGELES
1991–1992

I visited two race riots. One was in Brooklyn between blacks and Jews. The other was the Los Angeles riot in 1992. In Brooklyn I went through the war-torn streets alone, afraid only that my tape recorder, which was my most valuable possession, would be stolen. As for Los Angeles, I went to Watts, to Beverly Hills, to Simi Valley, where an all-white jury had come back with a verdict of not guilty on the videotaped beating of Rodney King, a black man, by four police officers. I went to Koreatown, where so many businesses had burned. I was more afraid in Washington than I was in the embered streets of race riots.

I am an academic and academia has all manners of behavior. Collegiality can be rewarding. Yet all the adages about the atmosphere of backstabbing and petty politics for low wages are true. We're in an era when students come to us to prepare themselves by and large for the marketplace. In the nineties, they were much more likely to gobble up answers than to see education as a process for finding the right questions. I worried that we were allowing them to be so smart, they were not wise. Academia, with all its provosts, deans, presidents, and white-haired emeriti, its colors and processions, offered a smattering of experiences, but they were not the patriarchy in its pure form.

Yet the promise and the disillusion in academia, the complex loyalties, and the quiet brutalities that sometimes appeared, did not prepare me for what I saw in Washington.

WASHINGTON
1995

Washington once sat on a swamp. Now it sits, I think, upon the patriarchy. It is the grandest of patriarchal structures. I learned that popular culture and its few stabs at making the illusion of a multicultural society could not fool me, where gender and race politics are moving, slowly, but are nonetheless moving. We're not so far along as I thought.

Ideally, Washington would be the place from which our national dialogue would emerge. I am told that in FDR's time, you could walk down a street and hear radios sending out his fireside chats. People would gather around radios of neighbors if they did not own radios themselves. Now, most of us have our own home entertainment centers. Even in a South African township, I entered a very small two-room home dominated by an enormous television from which blasted an American soap opera. Hollywood seems to hold the voices and bodies that want to talk to us, not Washington. In Washington they are talking to each other.

Is this because they can't figure out how to talk to a diverse society? What has happened that keeps us from talking to one another, even as we have so much equipment, so much technology to help us do that? Some say that the spirit of Washington is not quite right. That cynicism has overtaken the streets there. People cite Watergate as the beginning of that cynicism. They credit Woodward and Bernstein. Younger journalists seem on the prowl for that story that will land them a town house like the one Woodward has, or a movie deal. On the prowl for a story at any cost. More than a story, they want a coup. If they smell the blood, any blood, of a president, they circle. Others cite Vietnam as a turning point.

THE MADISON HOTEL
WASHINGTON, D.C.
DECEMBER 1995

Early on during my stay in Washington, I met with David Broder for breakfast:

"Vietnam."

"Oh, right."

"I mean you can go back to the battle over the United Nations, after World War I, when the Senate defied the president. But in the time I've worked here, it really turned around with Vietnam. That's when Congress stood up on its hind legs and said, No we don't support what the president's doing."

"I had thought that Watergate was sort of a point for the beginning of what people call the cynicism of our time."

"I think that a man named Murray Marder was the first to use the term *credibility gap*. And he was talking about Johnson and Vietnam."

It was the point when mistrust was bred, when many thought that the patriarchy could not be trusted after all. Perhaps, in terms of credibility, Washington is still on a swamp. Yet for all the mistrust, people still cling to and long for that patriarchal model.

We have from all fronts, for the last thirty years, questioned the moral authority and the intellectual authority of the white male as great explainer. Even as we suspect that the soul of America lives in our diversity, and even as different intellectual and cultural factions have voice, the persona of the white patriarch still thrives. We have challenged it, but it holds on to its chair with ease. We know there is no great explainer—his explanations were shown as false. And we have witnessed the power of divisive forces. David Broder continued:

"It's much, much harder for this generation to build trust for themselves, because the forces that shaped them were divisive forces within the country, not unifying forces. I mean the people who are part of that generation, the biggest things that have occurred in their lives were the civil rights struggle, the women's rights struggle, the battle over abortion, both pro and anti. And most important of all, of course, Vietnam."

It was beginning to make sense to me that the other explanation that I had been given, that is, the Watergate explanation, was too simple.

"We have yet to find among all of these enormously gifted and well-educated men and women anybody who, for very long, has been able to build a real bond of trust with the American people. And somewhere they have to find that in themselves, or it's going to be a really rough passage for the country."

No wonder Washington felt more dangerous than a race riot. It's a bigger, more complicated powder keg that holds among other things the potential for race riots . . . and wars and more. On the other hand, it holds the potential for something remarkable as well.

The language of Washington is in disrepair. Americans don't believe the language that comes out of there. Is it because that credibility gap born nearly forty years ago has never been repaired? To repair it would take more than the patriarchal voice. Perhaps the repair could be helped along by the diversity that we have, by the new canons that have been built, by the stronger, more literate, more articulate populace that we have.

MARK FABIANI

FORMER CLINTON STAFFER

"What Do They Want You For?"

We moved to Washington.
In the first year it was great because it was different from L.A.,
and the seasons
and we were about to go see all of the museums
and the sights and everything.
But after that it became appalling
appalling in its
insularity
appalling in its

strict hierarchy
appalling in its
oneness.
It is a one,
and this is not an original thought,
but it sure is true,
it's a one-company town.
Everybody works for the company,
lives off the company,
attacks the company,
lobbies the company.
You go to a party and,
if you're somebody who works at the White House,
people want to talk to you.
If you're someone who has a business—a really interesting
        business—
Yeah—
unless you're Kevin Costner or somebody
you know
it's like
well, who do you work for?
You don't work on the hill?
You don't work in the White House?
You start.
People look over your shoulder.
I think if people were exposed to it,
they would think even less of Washington than they do already.
I think that if the common person were really exposed to what—
I mean they've heard about it,
and they've read about it,
and they've seen spoofs of it on TV.
But I mean if they really saw it
they would be appalled,
I think.
Appalled!
The pomposity of the
of the whole thing.

Oh yeah.

It's unbelievable.

I mean a relatively mediocre level of talent taking itself seriously.

This is a surreal experience.

The day Hillary was in the grand jury, which was a horrendous
week.

It was a Friday.

Late that Friday night when I was going home, I took the metro.

I got mugged.

It's like dealing with reporters!

You try to develop a rapport.

I mean you try to treat people with some respect.

I had spent a lot of time in L.A. with young black kids and you
know

kids with problems,

and he was looking to be treated with respect.

He was looking for someone to take his threats seriously,

but also to treat him honorably in that,

if you did what he wanted you to do, he would do

what you wanted done.

So if I did everything, you know, he would live up to his part of the
bargain.

He would let me go.

We lived up near the top of King Street in Alexandria.

So I was just walking up to my house.

It was late.

It was like 11:30 on a Friday

or 10:30 on a Friday night.

He turned me around, walked me over to his car with his friend.

Drove around for a couple of hours in Southeast.

Visited ATM machines.

You know I mean he could have

Well he got like sixteen hundred dollars, which I think was more
than he expected to get.

Because one of my credit cards had cash access in addition to the
ATM card.

I don't know what would have happened if he had only gotten the
    four hundred dollars that you get from an ATM card, but he
those things usually don't end that way.
So whatever you can say about the guy, he didn't do what he could
    have done, or what most people would.
I mean when they found who this guy was, I punched him up on
    Lexis-Nexis [when] they arrested him.
It was a really sad story.
He was a former first-round draft pick in the NBA, a big college
star in North Carolina State, and a high school star at DeMatha in
    Washington.
he pled guilty—
Oh he blew out his knee when he was first-year pro from Kansas
    City
and actually had quite a life.
He adopted kids in their teenage years and tried
to help them out, even after he had blown out his knee, and his
    career was over.
But then he fell on hard times and ran out of money
and started using crack, and it was a terrible story.
It was a very sad story.
So later it was a couple—it was a month or two later
and the FBI, early Saturday morning,
had asked me to go out and walk the scene for them.
And it was like freezing cold,
and I'm going out there.
I'm trying to walk up this hill, in this slush and rain
and my beeper goes off.
And I look at it, and it's the first lady calling me.
So I rush to the phone and I say I'm sorry there
was a delay in getting back to you,
I was with the FBI.
She said as cool, as calm as could be
"What do they want you for?"
That put it in perspective for me.
And I waited for her to laugh

or something.
And then she—she—"What do they want you for?"
[He explodes into laughter]
I said "Well Mrs. Clinton, they didn't want me for anything, I'm just
    helping them with the investigation of this thing."
She goes "Oh, oh oh, oh, okay."
I'm thinking this has become such a commonplace part of their lives
that someone who has, you know,
no connection to much of this at all . . .
It was a great moment.
I'll never forget the tone of her voice.
"Oh, what do they want you for?"
I'll never forget when Hillary said "What do they want you for?"
[He keeps laughing]

A TROCHEE IN THE SECOND BEAT

1973

SAN FRANCISCO

MY PURSUIT OF THE AUTHENTIC WITH THE USE OF ACTING AS A frame was not entirely fearless. I was afraid of many things. I was afraid of heights. Circus class was a terrifying prospect once we moved from juggling socks to juggling balls and then clubs. The next step was the trapeze. Then came the day that we all had to hang upside down on the trapeze. I had no choice but to confess my fear. My circus teacher, much to my surprise, looked me straight in the eye, and said, "I understand fear." She still made me hang upside down on the trapeze, but at least I knew that she had heard me, and I heard her. We had communicated; this alone made the task seem doable.

But nothing matched my fear of Shakespeare. This seemed to be an overwhelming task—to speak in Shakespeare, that thick, antiquated language that seemed totally irrelevant to the world around me. Yet it was learning to speak Shakespeare that would catapult me into the quest, into the search, that I am now pursuing with the same vigor that I had all those years ago.

Our Shakespeare teacher was like a racehorse waiting at the gate. Whenever we entered class, she was waiting for us, impatiently drumming her fingers on her leg, or on a table. She was originally from Appalachia. I suspect that she came, like I did, from an oral tradition, only a white one.

She told us on the first day about trochees. Most of us had heard of iambic pentameter: BuhDUH buh DUHbuh DUHbuhDUHbuhDUH.

"Okay?"

"Yes," we mumbled in unison.

"Now, a trochee," she explained, "happens when the iamb goes up-side down. So that instead of Buh DUH, you get BUH duh."

She maintained that if you got a trochee in the second beat, a character was really "losing it" psychologically, and this "loss" made it possible for you to really know something about that character, if you wore his or her words.

Losing it is a good thing in that it is a defeat of an imposed rhythmic structure.

The classic example of everything falling to pieces rhythmically as an indicator of a character's psychological state is King Lear, who says at one point, "Never, never, never, never, never!"

Which is all trochees.

From this idea, I began to see Shakespeare in general as not so frightening at all. I began to perceive him as a jazz musician, who was doing jazz with the given rhythms of his time.

Character, then, seemed to me to be an improvisation on given rhythms. The more successful you were at improvising on language, the more jazz you have, the more likely you could be found in your language, that is, if you wanted to be found in your language. Some people use language as a mask. And some want to create designed language that appears to reveal them but does not. Yet from time to time we are betrayed by language, if not in the words themselves, in the rhythm with which we deliver our words. Over time, I would learn to listen for those wonderful moments when people spoke a kind of personal music, which left a rhythmic architecture of who they were. I would be much more interested in those rhythmic architectures than in the information they might or might not reveal.

Our Shakespeare teacher then gave us an assignment: "Go home, take fourteen lines of Shakespeare, and say them over and over again, until something happens."

That's all she said. Now, in 2000, when my students pay as much as thirty thousand dollars a year for an education, I find that they have little tolerance for metaphor and usually want more from me than those kinds of instructions. Even in the openness of the seventies, some among us did grumble. I was intrigued by the instruction, and was determined to do exactly as she asked.

I went to the Tenderloin, where the down-and-outers were. There were a number of used-book stores there. As Shakespeare was not a hot ticket in that neighborhood, I had my pick of volumes. I found one that was wonderfully well worn. It was red, beat-up, and looked a bit like a Bible. I paid five dollars for it, which at the time seemed like a fortune.

I chose a speech from *Richard III*. I had no scientific way of choosing a speech, I simply turned pages until I found fourteen lines. I chose Queen Margaret. She was speaking of Richard III to his mother in this way:

> *That dog, that had his teeth before his eyes,*
> *To worry lambs, and lap their gentle blood . . .*
> *Thy womb let loose, to chase us to our graves.*

I said these words, as instructed, over and over again "until something happened." Everything happened. Not only did I feel as though I had "become" Queen Margaret, but I had what in the seventies we would have called a "transcendental experience," fully unaided by chemical substances of any kind. I, in fact, "saw" Queen Margaret—she was a small vision, standing in my apartment. She came from the same place that the tooth fairy came from when I was a child. She came from my imagination. She was concocted somehow from the words. Words, it seemed to me, from then on were truly magical, not only by their meaning but by the way we say them, how we manipulate them.

My paternal grandfather had told me when I was a child, "If you say a word often enough, it *becomes* you."

What has happened to the manipulation of words in public speech? Imagine the potential of the magic of words—to communicate, to intoxicate, to *sway* a crowd. To concoct a vision? Without language there is no vision.

We sit and watch our politicians speak, and we change the channel. There seems to be no place for swaying with words.

I was teaching freshmen. These were people who were born in 1981. Nonetheless, I decided to try some old-fashioned oratory on them. I had a videotape of Bobby Kennedy on the occasion of the death of Martin Luther King, in Indiana, and I had a tape of Barbara Jordan, the congresswoman from Texas, during the Nixon impeachment hearings. I played for them Kennedy's speech.

"Could you lower those signs please?" RFK began. "I have some very sad news for all of you and that is that Martin Luther King was shot and killed tonight in Memphis, Tennessee." He quoted Aeschylus. He said that he could understand that people may want to give up on race relations because Martin Luther King had been killed "by a white man." And from the looks of things, it really didn't look very good for race relations. Then he paused. And he said that a member of his family . . . And he paused again and said that a member of his family had been killed (pause) by a "white man."

I sat in the back of the room; the students huddled around the video. I was worried that they would find no connection with the speech. Not so. There was something riveting about this speech, which Kennedy made without notes—and what was riveting, according to the students, was his vulnerability.

Acting, the study of the authentic, puts a high premium on vulnerability. When there is vulnerability there is a greater possibility that something will actually happen. Seated in the back of the darkened room as I was, even having watched this speech a number of times before, I was arrested by Bobby Kennedy's openness about race. Few politicians since have spoken as openly as he did. Race is a particular issue that calls for covered, coded, euphemistic language. Even my students in 1999 found his references to race to be surprisingly "honest." "You don't hear that type of talk now," one of them said. Then what have we been doing all these years? I thought. Yet Kennedy's job was in part to plead for nonviolence. Apparently the city from which he spoke was one of the few that did not burst into riot.

Later in that same session, I ran the tape of Barbara Jordan for them. She held forth with planned cadences—all iambic pentameters, really, but with such clarity, and such courage, and then, quite unexpectedly, as she spoke about the Constitution, in one alarming moment, a trochee appeared; she said, almost in another register, that if the Constitution were to mean nothing, then it might as well be relegated to a "twentieth-century paper shredder." She had been speaking so carefully, so deliberately, naming herself as a person who had not been adequately protected by the Constitution, moving inch by inch over slavery and right up to the present moment, when Nixon had not honored the honorable document, which she herself honored. She reminded me of Queen Margaret. In iambic beat, she spoke to a hushed and attentive audience. She spoke of "ob-fus-cations." She enunciated every consonant, every vowel. And yet it was not stiff, it was music. Why was it music? Because, underneath, one could hear all that was *not said*.

The not-said is as important as the said. Yet not saying is not the same as lying, it is not the same as covering. In authentic speech, it is what is felt that is transmitted. We live in a time when what is felt personally is at a premium, but when what is felt civically is not. We live in a time of coined phrases (phrases that are designed to move like currency) and studied nonchalance.

I asked the freshmen for the most memorable moment in the speech. Knowing nothing about trochees, and very little about Nixon and Watergate, and having been born nearly a decade after, they selected the "twentieth-century paper shredder."

Speaking calls for risk, speaking calls for a sense of what one has to lose. Not just what one has to gain. Clearly for Barbara Jordan, the Constitution in the paper shredder would be a significant, if not earth-shattering loss. Speaking calls for heart.

It seems very hard to find this kind of speaking in public life now. It's not only because of the speakers, the leaders. It's also because the audience doesn't want this type of passionate earnestness, or at least that's what we are told. The public does not trust words. People seem to be looking beyond the spoken word. The word is not enough. When was the last time any of us accepted a person's "word"? We need contracts, we need laws, we need evidence. We need much more than verbal promises.

Perhaps this is why political life is now cluttered with pictures rather than words—photo ops, which make things seem more "real" perhaps. Our "word" is not enough. We need evidence.

Why is it so difficult to find public speech that has trochees in the second beat—or trochees at all? I would have to look for the answer to this as I went on my search to "find" American character in the presidency.

Character depends a great deal on trochees. We must wear our language, the language must not wear us. Language is a dance between you and the other, it is not meant to be camouflage, or cover. The dance of language is not the same as the confessional, which has also permeated our culture.

There is so much talk after all—talk shows, talk therapies—to some extent we are talking ourselves to death. But it's just like food—we can eat junk food, or we can be nourished. And it's not necessary to have volume; birds, after all, fly with only seeds and water. The question is, does the talk make anything happen—or is all our public talk only connected somehow to the marketplace? Is it just one more thing that we consume?

I believe that talk comes from a rather divine place, and that the real conversations are the ones that cause change. I am fully aware that this is not a modern way to think. Yet language is part of what makes us human. We humans are linguistic animals.

1996

SAN FRANCISCO

I was speaking with a scholar of rhetoric, Hayden White, from the University of California at Santa Cruz.

He is more jaded than I about that possibility of an authentic voice. He thought that the power of rhetoric in modern life is that it makes connections that aren't even true.

He is midspeech in a restaurant at the Fairmont Hotel: "So that when I teach ideology . . . you have to ask the question of why it is that so many people who are otherwise quite—may be quite nice people, like people of goodwill . . ."

"Wow."

"Christians and so forth and yet they're still racists—right?"

"Right."

"They seem to think that that's justified."

"Right."

"Or if people who identify democracy with the free market."

"Uh-huh."

"The assumption is that the free market and democracy go hand in hand. If you buy into the free market, you have to take a certain amount of unemployment, a certain amount of exploitation, a certain amount of corruption, and so forth. It has nothing to do with democracy."

"Oh? Yeah."

"So, I mean, that's been the greatest triumph of Western capitalism— it's been to identify democracy . . ."

"Uh-huh."

". . . with the free market."

Our modern American problem is not a lack of communication. The problem is a disconnect between the heart of a voice and the purpose that the voice is meant to serve. The public voice repeats the status quo. And most voices that we hear have been adjusted by the time they get to us. We rely so much on mass communication, and mass communication controls so much of what gets to us. It's very hard to hear an original voice. We are very far from the personal, the one-to-one, the human touch.

Shakespeare's technology was very simple. A printing press, and accepted poetic rhythms of the time. It broke through accepted rhythms. He proved that accepted rhythms were too restrictive to hold humanity. He brought us human character that has lasted centuries. What would it take now to bring across some trochees in the second beat? We have studied nonchalance—the rhythms of distance and coolness—as our iambic pentameter. And, as we are in an age of incredible discovery in the communications field, I wouldn't dare to define what is as prolific as the printing press. Who knows, it's possible that by next year even the e-mail by which I send this to my editor will be replaced by something else.

When I told Hayden White that I believed in authentic voice, it was as if I told him I still believed in Santa Claus. He laughed, and looked at me with both a sparkle, and pity, in his eyes.

STUDS TERKEL

AMERICANIST

"Defining Moment in American History"

Defining moment in American history
I don't think there's one
you can't say Hiroshima.
That's a big moment.
I don't think there's any one.
I can't pick out any one.
It's a combination of many.
I can't think of any one moment I'd say is the defining moment.
But the gradual slippage—
slippage is the word used by Jeb Magruder
one of Nixon's boys that went to jail—during Watergate—
moral slippage.
We accept it daily now more and more.
It happens bit by bit and drop by drop.
It's a gradual kind of thing.
A combination of things.
The funny thing is you see we also have
the technology.
I say less and less the human touch
so I can tell you of another funny
playlet.
The Atlanta airport is a modern airport
and as you leave the gate
there are these trains
that take you to the
uh
concourse
and out to a destination.

You go on these trains
and they're smooth and
quiet and efficient and there's a voice you hear on the train
the voice you know was a human voice—
See in the old days you had robots
the robots imitated humans.
Now you have humans, imitating robots!
So you got this voice
on this train
"Concourse One
Dallas
Fort Worth
Concourse Two
Omaha
Lincoln"
Same voice.
Just!
as the train is about to go
a young couple
rush in
and they're just about to close the pneumatic doors?
And-that-voice
without-losing-a-beat-says
"Because-of-late-entry-we're-delayed-thirty-seconds."
Just then
everybody is looking at this couple
with hateful eyes
the couple is going like this shrinkin'
and [I]
said "Oh my God."
I'd happened to have had a few drinks
before boarding
I do that
to steel my nerves.
And so
I
imitate a train call

holding my hand
over my heart
"George Orwell,
your time has come."
Everybody laughs when I say that
but not on that train!
Silence!
And they're lookin' at me
And so suddenly I'm shrinkin'!
So there I am with the couple
the three of us
at the foot of Calvary
about to be upped you know.
Just then I see a baby
a little baby in the lap of a mother—
I know it's Hispanic cause she's speakin'
Spanish
to her companion—
about a year old
a little baby with a round little face ya know
and so I'm going to talk to the baby
so I say to the baby—
holding my hand over my mouth cause
my breath may be a hundred proof!—
So I say to the baby
"Sir or madam
What is your considered opinion
of the human species?"
And the baby looks
you know the way babies look at ya
clearly
and starts laughing
busting out with a crazy little laugh
and I say
"Thank God
for a human reaction!
We haven't lost yet!"

And so there we have it!
But the human touch
that's disappearing you see.
So we talk about defin—
There ain't no defining moment
for me.
All moments are defining and add up.
There's an accretion of movement that leads to where we are now
when trivia becomes news.
When more and more less and less awareness
of pain of the other.
So this is an interesting dilemma with which we are faced.
I don't know if a used this or not
I was quoting Wright Morris
this writer from Nebraska, who says
"We're more and more into communications and less and less
into communication!"

THE THREE QUESTIONS

1981

MANHATTAN

Jimmy Carter was president at the time. I had left my tenure-track job at Carnegie Mellon University, much to the surprise of my parents and others. Thinking I was simply not cut out for university life, I decided to go to New York, and walk dogs if I had to. Which is what I did. Interestingly enough, I walked the dog of a woman who coached newscasters, some highly public figures—including presidential candidates. She was teaching them to be "natural." I typed her notes to them. The notes, without divulging anything specific, were often about what tie they should wear, or how they could improve their enunciation, or reminders to keep breathing. It was really good old-fashioned common sense. It was easy to observe, at the time, that people were still so enamored of the camera—as if the camera was going to catch something mysterious about them that they themselves weren't fully conscious of. Her work was to firmly plant them in the moment. The moment of who they really "were." The idea being, of course, that the camera sees all, and that what it really wants is who you "are"—who you *really* are. She was kind enough to give me a free lesson one day. It's hard. To be "yourself" in front of the camera. Really hard.

Two of her clients at the time were George and Barbara Bush. I became fascinated with what it meant to groom public figures. It seemed to me that public figures were as interested in authenticity as actors were. Or at least they wanted the *benefits* of authenticity. Yet none of them would have given over three years of their lives, as most actors in training do. It takes at least three intense years in a conservatory to become a transformative being. It was clear that her clients wanted the instant "result" of that training. That result being "presence." In fact, presence can most likely not be taught.

My boss had herself been a student of one of the most important teachers of acting—when everyone was teaching "the method." If you would like a crash course on the method, take a look at Marlon Brando in *On the Waterfront,* particularly that scene in the back of the car, when he says, "I coulda been a contender." It's a cliché now, but it is also startling in its "realness." This idea of performing "realness" is what seems to permeate political and public life now.

The dog walking lasted until I got cast in a couple of plays. Such a windfall of work for an actor is enough to make you believe you *are,* after all, an actor. When that windfall of luck fizzled out, I found myself, once again, at the mercy of the winds of chance.

I worked doing very low-level secretarial jobs out of a temp agency and going to auditions whenever I could. I also had, by now, collected some students here and there, and did private coaching.

Then came the whiff of a turning point, but it was not the type of turning point a careerist would imagine. One of the numerous low-level secretarial jobs I had was in the dimly lit offices of J. P. Stevens. I sat next to a woman called Julia, who had been a secretary there for quite some time. She was, for all intents and purposes, my "boss." I did photocopying and such, she did the heavy lifting. Julia was a very dark-skinned black woman with flawless skin and life pouring out of every pore in her body despite the horrifying lighting and low ceilings of the office. There was more light coming out of Julia's eyes, and her occasional smile, than on the whole floor. Thank God they could afford Julia, because clearly they couldn't afford Con Ed.

At first Julia was rather lukewarm toward me. But I was determined to get her to talk. I would catch her eye and smile whenever I could. I knew that under that layer of professionalism was someone who was full of stories, stories with wonderful rhythms, stories with wonderful performances. I was right. She could barely get through a story without a giggle.

Dismal as the place was, I preferred working there to working in some of the tonier law firms I'd been to, with their sleek wood, fine furniture, and the occasional salacious comment from one man or another who was not the stereotypical geezer you would imagine but rather someone who looked like he was still in junior high, with no hair on his face, a crisp white shirt, and a tie that was too big for his neck. You were also apt to land a boss who was (Gloria Steinem, forgive me for saying this) one of those humorless women in a headband, obsessed with exactly how sharp you had managed to get her pencils. Undoubtedly these women saw through my obedient secretarial manner, to see that I (or any other artist who might cross their path) was likely nearly as educated as they were. And these were always the most disturbing moments. I kept thinking that the women's movement would have not only succeeded at placing women, like this one, in positions that were formerly meant only for men, but also made headway in ensuring that women would be comrades—comrades across race and hierarchies. Not so.

Not to put the women all in one category.

This cast of characters, the women with bluntly clipped hair and the men with ties too big for their necks, would be a descant throughout my working life, and they would show up again in Washington. It's not the ties or the haircuts, it's the lack of light in their eyes that characterizes them.

One advantage to acting is that you move up and down and all across the social circles of our country. You never know what your status will be, and so you understand that status is man-made. It's not written in stone. I've now met with presidents and prisoners. I've been on death row, I've spoken to the nation's best chefs, I've been behind closed doors at Monticello after the place was closed down for the day. I'm a visitor, and from this vantage point I have ever more difficulty understanding the lines that mark us one human—away—from the other.

Jean-Paul Sartre, in an essay on actors, gives the following picture: An actor is on the bus reading the financial pages. If you look closely, you see that the pages are upside down. We should see that the pages could work just as well for the study of humanity if they were upside down. But actors today are more likely to have the financial pages right side up. And perhaps, in this activity, we give over part of what is most useful about us. We're all taking ourselves awfully seriously in America right now. Even the clowns have mortgages.

I certainly preferred working for Julia to working for the associates with whom I was often placed in law firms. Slowly but surely I got her to talk to me. I learned about her circle of friends—I learned about the zany events that had happened to her on her bus rides from her home in New Jersey to work. I saw how easy it was to get people to talk. It could start out as a nearly subversive act, whisperings over workstations—and it could land finally in a full interview over dinner after work.

In the midst of my temp jobs, an unexpected thing happened. I came down with a terrible case of mononucleosis. I had no health insurance and no money.

Then came my big break. I landed a low-level secretarial job at KLM Airlines. I was working for the complaint department. All day long I read complaint letters. These were wide-ranging. There was the man who was outraged about a flight with a drunken soccer team that ended with lost luggage—luggage that had his glaucoma medicine in it. Then there was the woman whose eighty-five-year-old mother had flown in from Egypt to Dulles Airport. KLM was to have provided an escort, as the mother knew nothing about Washington, had never been to the United States, and spoke no English. They failed to send the escort, and so the mother, somehow, ended up in a cab in Washington, D.C., driving around all night, with no idea of where she was and no ability to tell anyone where she needed to be. I loved my job—I laughed out loud from time to time.

I could not have been given a clearer counterpoint to the job I had done previously. Then I had spent a year typing up letters to newscasters and presidential candidates about how to get it "right," how to sound "perfect" for the audience. Now I was reading letters about how very wrong a large airline had been. These letters were *from* the people. The notes to the newscasters were about how to *approach* the people. The letters of complaint were much less inhibited than the notes to newscasters.

I began to see that there was a theater project in this. What exactly it was I didn't know. I wanted to know the relationship of character to language—and, to be even more scientific about it, I wanted to know, What is the relationship of language to *identity*? What does language, the way we render language, tell us about who we are? What does it tell us on an individual level? What does it tell us on a societal level?

So, basically, in the offices of KLM Airlines my project "On the Road: A Search for American Character," which had many sources, began to gel. Everything I read seemed to offer a clue. I had come across something that the writer Eudora Welty had said about her childhood. She would sit in the hallway outside the room where all the adults were talking, and her ears would "open up like morning glories."

My colleagues from KLM were from all over the world. Perched as I was in my little corner, behind a divider, in the complaint department, I read complaints, and listened listened listened to a wide variety of vocal tones that spanned from Holland to the Caribbean, Brooklyn, and onward.

I loved what I was hearing and wanted to hear more of it. How could I hear people authoring their speech, putting themselves in their speech? How could I study speech as a design around identity? How could I study speech as *betrayal*? When does it betray, when does it cooperate? When is it powerful enough to cause action? The wonderful thing about dramatic speech is that it is built to *cause action*.

If I were to go around and listen listen listen to Americans, would I end up with some kind of a composite that would tell me more about America than what is *evidently* there? How could I get underneath the surfaces? I could tell that speech would *have* to be a resource. Look at the way people can dive and dip and breathe and exclaim and come up with all manner of sounds in the course of saying a word. No one among us talks like anyone else.

How could I learn more about those powerful moments when people speak their speech, speak a moment in their lives until the music of the moment overpowers the information they are trying to communicate? I found a key, by sheer luck. I was at a party, in New York, I cannot remember who gave the party or why I was there. But I do remember meeting a linguist. She was not an invited guest, as I recall. She was the date of somebody. Most likely I was the date of somebody myself. It was not an actors' party, it was fancier, which is what leads me to believe this was sort of outside my normal circle.

I don't remember her name. We struck up a conversation. I told her some of the things I was learning in the complaint department and a few of my theories on acting. I told her about my dismay with the "self" technique of most acting teachers. I was on my own for all intents and purposes—for finding even a way to continue the study of acting for myself, let alone my students. At the time it was getting harder and harder to find the difference between psychotherapy and acting in New York. I just couldn't sit in another class and see someone brought to tears by a coach. I had sworn not to go to another one of those kinds of teachers who did psychoanalysis as acting teaching. She understood what I was stumbling around to find—or at least part of it. I told her, in essence, that I wanted to get people to talk to me, in a true way. Not true in the sense of spilling their guts. Not true in the sense of the difference between truth and lies. I wanted to hear—well—authentic speech, speech that you could dance to, speech that had the possibility of breaking through the walls of the listener, speech that could get to your heart, and beyond that to someplace else in your consciousness.

I knew enough to know that this quest was not only about the development of my voice as an artist. To develop a voice, I told her, "I need to develop an ear." She told me she could describe to me how to get people to talk, to really talk to me. She gave me her phone number and told me to call.

It was a Saturday when I called her. I told her more about what I understood. I told her that this "thing" I was after had another tangible sign. I didn't tape-record the conversation, but I can remember and imagine that it sounded something like this, although possibly less coherent or more coherent. It went something like this:

"When they're talking that way, their syntax starts to fall apart, their grammar starts to tumble, they lose words, sometimes they go off words, sometimes they make sounds that have nothing to do with words."

She agreed with me enthusiastically.

"See the thing is," I continued, "it's like jazz. They start out singing a familiar song, with a predictable pattern. If I listen for, say, five minutes, I can tell what that pattern is. They might talk for an entire hour in that pattern. It might be a pattern that they learned from their mother or father or friends or on television. . . ."

We agreed.

"It's usually a composite pattern of, say, their years of hearing and talking."

This was obvious.

"But what I want to do is get them to break that pattern while they're talking to me, because when they break it, they do things that are so specific to them and only them. And if I can take those few moments—it might be only three seconds, it might be a full minute—if I can get a hold of those moments, and reproduce them—then I will seem to be just *like* them."

She thought that was interesting.

"I was a mimic when I was a kid."

She thought that was interesting.

"I'm not interested in mimicry the way an impressionist is on a talk show. You see, I want to use my ability to mimic to sort of get at those moments when people are themselves, becoming themselves in language. I believe identity is a process and that we are every moment making an adjustment, and sometimes those moments happen while we're talking—I mean, people use language to get married, to come to the realization that they're dying. I mean it happens—right—in the words."

I could tell I was making a good impression.

"And, look, this neighborhood where I'm living in Manhattan—it's changing overnight. Every bit of individuality is disappearing. Amsterdam Avenue, where I live, and Columbus Avenue, which is a block away, used to be the service streets for Broadway and Central Park West. But look what's happening. There's no more baker, no more candlestick maker; the shoemaker is closing down, and these huge franchises are moving in. I want to chronicle this disappearance of individual effort, and its replacement with franchised life, in language. We're all going to talk like each other before we know it. In the end, I believe it can be seen, like fossils, in what we say and how we say it to one another."

The vibes were good. She seemed to be with me.

"If I can do this, I can avoid a lot of the so-called psycho technique. I'm talking about an acting technique that was developed by a man named Konstantin Stanislavsky in the last century in Russia. The goal was to have stage behavior look real. This entire century has been smitten with the same idea. That we should look real on stage. It's become almost a religion. The thought was that realness on the outside would flow naturally from realness on the inside. In other words, if, as an actor, you took the time to think and feel like a real person, the result would be that the actor would seem to be acting, externally, like a real person. Think of it, we like performances in movies that seem 'real.' So this was a powerful technique that he had. It has many heirs and has lasted a long time."

She thought this was interesting.

"He did this work during the same era in which Freud was writing. I think that we have other ways of studying and replicating human behavior now. He wanted to rid the stage of stiff, histrionic acting. But we are getting to the point now where we think people act the way they seem to act in television and movies, but the problem is, we often act like what we see in television and movies in real life! I want to find other ways of getting to the inside of a person. I don't think I should base my idea of another person all on my own feelings, which is what Stanislavsky was after." Ultimately I was to believe that the Stanislavsky technique, for all its undeniable success, was a spiritual dead end.

"I'm not the other and can never be the other," I continued. "I can only try to bridge the gap, and I'm looking for ways to bridge the gap."

I hunkered down, and drove on to my ultimate goal—my experiment. "I think we can learn a lot about a person in the very moment that language fails them. In the very moment that they have to be more creative than they would have imagined in order to communicate. It's the very moment that they have to dig deeper than the surface to find words, and at the same time, it's a moment when they want to communicate very badly. They're digging deep and projecting out at the same time."

She was following me.

"The traditional acting technique wants to know who I am in the character. Perhaps it's based on a very humanitarian assumption that we are all the same underneath. I don't believe that. I'm interested in difference. I want to know who the character is, not who I am. Somewhere in all of it, I may learn who I am, too, but that's not the goal. It's in language that I think I can find the other. If I can get people to that moment that they're digging deep, and then I repeat what they have done, I should actually end up seeming quite like them."

She was intrigued.

"And we're in a moment when technology can support what I am doing. Stanislavsky did not have the tape recorder. I do. I am able to study a person's language and breaths very carefully, because I can record it, and listen to it over and over again. I think it's about finding that moment when syntax changes, when grammar breaks down. Those are the moments I should study, if I want to know who a person is."

She thought this was interesting.

"So the idea is that the psychology of people is going to live right inside those moments when their grammar falls apart and, like being in a shipwreck, they are on their own to make it all work out. I mean, I'm talking about something that lasts a few seconds, it's not a catastrophe, and it is seldom frightening or anything like that. Although I suspect there would be circumstances where it *could* be frightening. It could also be joyous, like when you tell someone you love them."

I went on to ask about the variety of situations that leave us putting our words together on our own.

If I simply say those moments as specifically as I possibly can, I am going to know a heck of a lot about who *they* are. If I could wear them in those kinds of moments, I could seem to *be* them. But it's all about finding that moment when syntax changes."

She agreed.

"How much time do you have?" she said.

"You mean now?"

"When you do an interview, how much time do you have?"

I thought about the reality of my life at the time, which was if I could get an interview it was usually over lunchtime.

"Oh, I don't know, about an hour, or forty-five minutes. Seldom more than an hour."

"I can give you three questions that will ensure that their syntax will change in the course of an hour." She had one of those wonderfully efficient and confident vocal tones that people like linguists and anthropologists have. Sometimes they are as direct as accountants are.

I, of course, will never forget this part of the conversation. She stated the questions, quickly. I was writing as fast as I could.

"One is, Have you ever come close to death?"

"Okay."

"Another is, Do you know the circumstances of your birth?"

"Interesting."

"The third is, Have you ever been accused of something that you did not do?"

She went on to say that sometimes asking people about their first day of school is a good one too.

These three questions became the spine of all of my work for the next several years. I had a Panasonic tape recorder that was about eight inches long and five inches wide. I took it to talk to anyone who would talk to me—the lady in the clothing store up the street, the lifeguard at the YMCA pool where I swam, people I met at parties. At the time I had a small group of actors who were working with me, people I had met in different schools and studios.

I would simply walk up to a person and say, "I know an actor who looks like you. If you give me an hour of your time, I will invite you to see yourself performed."

Somewhere in that hour, I would ask those three questions. The result was a performance that I produced myself in a loft in Lower Manhattan, with twenty actors and twenty real people who came with their friends. I played Julia.

I don't ask those questions anymore, but they taught me how to listen—because after I asked the questions, I would listen like I had never listened before for people to begin to sing to me. That singing was the moment when they were really talking.

I've taken that tape recorder, which has now become a Sony professional, and sometimes a DAT recorder, from place to place all over America since the early eighties. I took it finally to Washington, D.C., and listened as hard as I could for the talk, the talk of the big talkers, to turn, if only for a moment, into a song that they and only they can sing.

ALEXIS HERMAN

U.S. SECRETARY OF LABOR

You know, my daddy was very active during his life.
You know
he was the first black to sue the Democratic Party because they
    wouldn't give him an absentee ballot.
He just didn't take no for answers, you know.
He wasn't a fiery man; he was just steady and persistent, you
    know?
But he had this quiet way
of getting people out of trouble, you know,
in the South when they would get arrested or folk would end up in
    jail in the middle of the night or these—we call it police
    brutality now; I don't know what the name was for it then.

So

and on Christmas Eve, we always took these rides out, you know,
and that's how he would put me to sleep and bring me back
home.

So that's kind of what I did with him.

And this one Christmas Eve night we were going over the bay

to Father Warren, he's a priest, and—

And we went for our ride

and he went to one of his meetings over the bay.

My daddy had a silver pistol with a pearl handle,

and he was a peaceful man. I never heard my daddy curse or raise
his voice a day in his life.

He kept his gun right here in the front of his old DeSoto.

Green and white.

We had lots of DeSotos [but] ours was green and white. But
whenever there was trouble,

you know,

something was going on,

the gun came out from under here,

and he would always put it by his side.

Now, I used to like to sit up under my daddy when we would be
riding

and sometimes, you know how daddies put you in their laps and let
you steer the wheel.

But if the gun was on the seat, then I knew that there was a
problem.

I was scared of that gun.

I was scared of that gun

you know. I didn't like that gun because it just was a symbol of
tension and something was wrong, and my daddy could be
hurt.

I didn't want anybody messing with my daddy.

So this particular night the gun is out

we go over the bay

we go over to Father Warren's,

and they were all in their meeting.

And we get back in the car.
In those days, over the bay, dark roads, dirt roads, no lights, the
     church is way back off the road.
And we're coming back from the meeting that night
and
you know
the cars and the lights had come behind us
and my daddy starts driving fast
and we're trying to get around these cars
and they're, you know, pushing us off the side of the road with the
     cars, and he's having—
It's the Klan, yeah.
He pulled over
just stopped
and he said, you know, he said, Poppy's got to get out of this car
and he says, I'm going to put this gun in your hand, and I want you
     to get right down there
and he pointed, like, under the dashboard. And he said
You get down there
and Poppy's going to put this gun in your hand.
And he says, I'm going to have to get out of this car, and I'm going
     to lock this door.
He said, If anybody opens that door
I want you to pull that trigger.
And he took my finger and he put it right on that trigger and he put
     that gun in my hand and I had it just like this and I was down
     under the dashboard.
Oh, yeah. I was tiny.
I was always a small child.
And that's where I got.
I got down on the floor underneath the dashboard by the seat with
     the gun in my hand, and he got out and locked the door, and
     he just started walking to face the Klan.
And he told me don't raise my head
don't look up
don't look out.

You know, I could hear them, you know.
I could hear them.
You know
you could see the car lights and stuff
but mostly I could hear them.
What I remember more than anything were these sounds, you
    know. Yelling, names, and shouting.
I remember that more than anything.
That's why for years I didn't talk about this because I could hear
    those sounds.
"Nigger"
you know
"Get him"
"Kill him"
"Beat him"
you know
just, just sounds.
I just remember—I remember "nigger" more than anything.
What I remember more than anything was just the word "nigger."
    "Get that nigger."
"Here comes that nigger," you know.
So, anyway, I just remember "nigger" more than anything.
So it seemed like forever.
I really don't know how long it was, but it felt like forever that I was
    down there with this gun, and eventually I heard Father
    Warren's voice saying
Alexis, it's all right.
It's all right.
I'm coming to the car.
Don't do anything.
Don't do anything.
It's Father Warren.
It's Father Warren.
I'm coming to the car. I'm coming to the car.
This night they had made a decision to follow Poppy
so they followed,
and luckily they did.

His shirt was torn off.
I remember—because my daddy was a neat man, too.
That was the other thing
and I think, for a child's impression
to see my daddy's white shirt torn off of him
and he had straight black hair that he wore back, and it was, like,
      hanging all down around
you know.
[Pause]
Unfortunately, I think what we've evolved to is not having
quite frankly
almost the absence of the visible and the tangible leaves the
      impression that the problem isn't there
that the issues are not there
you know.
And so I think what you have is this false sense
really
now
that everything is okay
you know
because you don't have the Klan.
So the flip side of that is this immediate conclusion that it's no
      longer a problem
when it still is.
And so I'm trying to figure how to say my feelings of it.
[Pause]
Oh, I can't say this on tape.

TALKING TO JESUS

IN THE BEGINNING WAS THE WORD, AND THE
WORD WAS WITH GOD, AND THE WORD WAS GOD.
THE SAME WAS IN THE BEGINNING WITH GOD.

—*The Gospel According to St. John 1:1–2*

AND THE WORD WAS MADE FLESH, AND DWELT
AMONG US . . . FULL OF GRACE AND TRUTH.

—*The Gospel According to St. John 1:14*

THE WORD WAS MADE FLESH AND DWELT AMONG US. A PERSON? WAS the word? That huge big Bible that loomed out over the pulpit at Union Memorial Methodist Church was said to carry the *word* of the Lord.

There were the black poets, and we knew them because one good thing about segregation was black pride, such pride for all the people of letters—James Weldon Johnson, Paul Laurence Dunbar. And I learned from those poems not to be timid about big sounds—such an extroverted idea of language they had, such a love of sound:

> *'Lias! 'Lias! Bless de Lawd!*
> *Don' you know de day's erbroad?*
> —"In the Morning," Paul Laurence Dunbar

I listened with rapture whenever my paternal grandfather opened his mouth. I asked him to tell the same stories over and over. I would listen to story after story on the porch of Miss Johnson (always Miss although she was married, widowed, a mother and a grandmother). Miss Johnson weighed at the very least four hundred pounds. She couldn't move much further than to a house or two up or down from hers for that reason. She'd call me over, and I would listen, or go down to the store to buy her fatback. She also baby-sat for us from time to time, and would iron. I would sit by the ironing board and listen. I would request her stories as if they were songs or concerts.

The other place for oratory, of course, was the pulpit. Reverend Carrington was the pastor of my church and had been since I was a little girl. His father had been white and British, his mother black. I didn't always pay attention to what was said from the pulpit when Reverend Carrington spoke, even though I was afraid I would go to hell if I didn't. The drone of the ladies in the choir at Union Memorial Methodist Church sounded like a wail:

What a friend we have in
Jeeeee-uh-suuus
All our griefs [quick stop hard on the *f*s]
and sins to bear
What a priv-e-lage to caaauh-ry
every-
thing
to God in prayer!

And the piano and the organ, and the preacher, Reverend Carrington, a slender, shortish man with a neat mustache, light skin, and glasses, sitting in profile, so that we couldn't really see how he might respond to the music.

Oh
what peace we often for-
feit
Oh what needless pain
we bear
All because we do not caaaaa-uh-ry
every-
thing to God in prayer.

This was a pulpit that became political in the nineteen sixties. Black men running for city offices came to talk. We were urged to vote for certain white candidates and not others.

Mrs. Green, somehow Mrs. not Miss, rarely dressed up as the others did. She didn't always wear a hat. Sometimes she wore a scarf. I have a dim memory of her in bedroom slippers. She looked as though she came to church exactly as she was, the way we were told that God was prepared to receive us. She was the only member in the entire church who "got the Holy Spirit." Being of a moderately logical mind, I tried for years to figure out what triggered it. I had to accept the fact that it might happen at any time, that it was unpredictable.

"Yes, Jesus. Thank you, Jesus."

Sometimes she would outcry the wail of the choir. And sometimes these two sounds would go together.

Have we tria-als and tempta-aaay-tions
Is there trouble anywhere
We should never be discouraged
Take it to the Lord in prayer.

Can we find a friend so faithful

"Thankyou Jesus yes Jesus, thank you Jesus yes yes yes thank you Jesus"

And sometimes she would sit and weep while they sang on.

Who will all our sorrows share
Jesus knows our every weakness
Take it to the Lord in prayer.

It seemed that Mrs. Green was the only person with a telephone line to the Lord, because she was the only one who dared call out his name and, in fact, would stop the service to have a conversation in our presence. Well why shouldn't she, if she had that line, why shouldn't she?

We thought this was very funny.

"Don't laugh," my mother said.

"But why does Mrs. Green do that?"

"She believes in Jesus and sometimes that happens. It's called the Holy Spirit."

"Do you get the Holy Spirit?"

Silence.

"Well don't you believe in Jesus?"

"Yes I do."

"Well why don't you do that?"

"Different people believe in Jesus different ways. Different people get the Holy Spirit in different ways."

Are we weak and heavy laden
cumbered with a load of care
Precious Savior still our re-eh-fuge
Take it to the Lord in prayer.

"Well what about Grandma? Doesn't Grandma believe in Jesus?" (Our maternal grandmother, my mother's mother, would by contemporary standards be considered "born again.")

"If you sit next to Grandma in church sometimes you'll see a tear come out of her eye. That means Grandma is getting the Holy Spirit."

"The Holy Spirit is—"

"Yes Jesus Thank you Jesus yes Lord thank you Lord"

"Well how come Grandma doesn't—"

"I said Grandma cries when she—"

"Well then what about you? How come you don't—"

"Ssssh."

She probably thrust a hymnal in our hands by this point.

Do thy friends despise, forsaaakke theee?

The words were sometimes disturbing, but the music was soothing.

Take it to the Lord in prayer
In his arms he'll take and shield thee
Thou—wilt—find—a—solace—there.

Ahhhhhmen.

So there was Mrs. Green, who seemed to have a faster train to Jesus than the preacher himself, because the preacher in our church did not talk to Jesus, he talked to us. When he talked to the Lord, he did so silently, with his hand on his forehead and his face tilted down. Mrs. Green subsided in her experience, talking to Jesus, by walking sometimes up and down the aisle, sometimes sitting with her head bowed in an intense prayer, sometimes crying or moaning. I always wished she'd talk to us. She wasn't interested in talking to us. She had bigger fish to fry.

Since that time, in my travels, I've visited churches where the Mrs. Greens of the world are not so rare. Reverend Carrington wasn't the only one with a through line to God. But the only person in that whole church who seemed to work as hard as Reverend Carrington, or who came prepared to work as hard, was Mrs. Green. She didn't need a uniform, she wore no robes, she wore no ribbons, she came and sat on the outskirts. She didn't come to socialize. She didn't come to join the auxiliary, but she came to work in our community in another way. She came to work in a spiritual way.

Maybe our leaders aren't the only ones who hold the Gospel of America inside of them. Maybe they need some help to release that gospel. They need another kind of partner. I see this in many ways. Reverend Carrington was very educated, and he had been educated to have command of the word. Mrs. Green was not in words at all. She was the perfect partner for Reverend Carrington. She was not a part of the political structure of his church, but her presence was critical. We are a very material culture, with little room for those things that do not add up in numbers. Many participating elements in democracy are managed. Mrs. Green was anything but managed, yet she had something important to offer.

Maybe the very help that politics needs can come from someplace other than the halls of Congress or the desktops of punditry. Maybe our leaders need more voices from the outside. Maybe the voice of a nation lives in the fragmented voices of its people, even the less articulate ones. Maybe the voice of the nation is not so much the leader's plea to the people but the people's plea to the leader, and to something beyond the leader. Maybe the voice of a nation is the plea of the people to the idea of the nation, the plea to make the idea come alive. Perhaps the voice of a nation should be an incantation to the spirit of the nation rather than to a single man.

PEGGY NOONAN

"And Make the Crazy People Cry"

You know what [the press]
is the opposite of, in a way?
You remember in the eighteenth century in
the
in the eighteenth and nineteenth centuries
in the finer and more refined circles in England
It became the habit to go to um
homes for the mentally ill and go see the people there
and be very *moved* by their predicament?
It was a weird
sort of thing.
You wanted to go see the mad people
and then feel.
And almost show all your friends
see how compassionate I am.
I'm deeply moved by
the misery
I'm deeply moved by the misery around me.
But then again I've always been very sensitive.
The *press* is the exact opposite of that
They
they don't
They wanna go to the insane asylum
and make the crazy people cry
[she laughs, fully delighted]
They wanna go to the insane asylum with a fork
and say, "Hey, how'd ya like that Dole?"
"Hey Clinton, what did you mean about Susan MacDougal and her
    legal bills?"
Nyerrrn!

I mean I love to see old 1930s films the 1930s old
tape of the great
ocean liner
landing in New York
and Greta Garbo gets off and you know
says hello to her fans
you know
you know those old
arrival shipping news videos from Movietone?
Do you remember the one with the queen and king of England
coming down the plank?
And some of the photographers start yelling
"Hey, Queen, this way!"
That's what journalism is
at its worst and still at its best
"Hey-Queen-look-this-way"
"Hey King over here"
Click click.

SEGREGATION

1998

WASHINGTON, D.C.

IT WAS THE GRIDIRON DINNER IN 1998. THE GRIDIRON DINNER IS A time when the press spoofs the president. There was mild questioning about whether or not the president would come. Yet it was determined that it would be a mistake for him not to come. Monica Lewinsky was on the tip of everyone's tongue. The room of people dressed in white-tie attire was all abuzz with how the president would get through the evening.

Newt Gingrich stood up to make remarks. He was notably somber. He said that even as it was hard sometimes to read the paper in the morning, he was moved to look around the room and be grateful that he was in "the center of intellectual and political life in America."

I was stunned.

The Gridiron Dinner is not a huge affair. True, there are a lot of people, but they all fit into a fairly normal-sized hotel ballroom. It is not as extensive as, for example, the White House Correspondents' dinner. The room is large, but you could probably see someone at the opposite end of the room without binoculars. And when the president speaks, or the "skit" is done, there's no need for video projection. It was a room, not a football field. Yet Gingrich felt secure to say that the "center of intellectual and political life of America" was represented inside those four walls.

BROWN V. BOARD OF EDUCATION

I grew up in segregation. Although *Brown v. Board of Education* came down when I was four years old, it took until I was a teenager before I actually sat in a classroom with white students or had a white teacher. My world as a young person was a world of almost all black people, except for when we had to go downtown to "take care of business," as my mother would say. There was something intimidating about the big buildings where business was "taken care of." The stores were segregated, so even if we got into a store, we couldn't take the escalator or try on clothes. We only went to black doctors and dentists, unless something was very wrong with us, something Dr. Wooldridge couldn't take care of. Going into white territory gave me butterflies in my stomach.

1998
WASHINGTON, D.C.

By the time I went to Washington, I had traveled to many places in the world. I had met, dined with, even lived among the rich and the poor, the famous and the most unfamous. I had faced large and small audiences, baring my soul to strangers in the dark, never knowing who was there or what they thought. I had survived the ego-battering process of pounding the pavements as an actress, hearing all manner of things, swallowing rejection like the one cup of deli coffee per day that my budget allowed. I had survived the tenure process, with its scary balding white men in suits or in cotton short-sleeved shirts and pen guards, women in Hush Puppies and no-nonsense plaid wool suits, or later hip-looking, sighing, never-to-be-impressed, seen-it-all-heard-it-all men and women with expensive haircuts, designer eyeglasses, and multiracial backgrounds, its football teams and covertible cars, its floats and entourages of deans and provosts and chairmen. I had gasped out loud on several occasions, in my case and the cases of friends, at how closely and blatantly, elusively and subtly, but how oh so real-ly racism and sexism lurked in the halls of ivy, threatening at every turn to force you to sue, make a case, or run. This racism and sexism lurked *even* as these universities were in the process of questioning the canon, and stocking their curricula and libraries with information that would be, we were all told, the antidote to racism in the late twentieth and early twenty-first centuries. And anyone could be the culprit, a secretary (or even a student!), perhaps, who just didn't get "diversity," or a chairman who was outright capricious and nasty, causing you to remember everything you ever learned about the unfair practices of segregation in the old days. After nearly dying on my sword as a young professor at one university, whose name will go unmentioned, I landed somehow on my feet, at a nice and rather fancy place: Stanford, and almost uneventfully made my way into the ranks, but still. It had been rough.

Given that I had been through many culture-inspired wars, I was surprised to feel the return of those same butterflies from the segregation of my youth when I was in Washington, D.C. It is a feeling that something could go wrong, something could go wrong, and you wouldn't have the power to make it right. Why should you have that feeling when you're merely trying to find out something about the place that is said to be a bedrock of where you live? Perhaps I was, as an actress, empathizing at large with those around me.

I think the butterflies came back because of the way people in Washington tend to look at a newcomer. Suspicion, mostly. This is truer of the media's gaze than of the gaze of those in the White House. Perhaps the media has no guards but itself. The White House, after all, has armed services, Secret Service, metal detectors, and an intricate process for finding out who you are before they admit you to the gate. The media, I suppose, has to be its own guard, reporter by reporter, editor by editor, producer by producer, columnist by columnist. Perhaps this is what gives them that scrutinous gaze, that quick look up and down, with their arms across the chest, the head tilted back, and perhaps even a look away, or an actual wander away, when you are introduced. Or perhaps those in the White House are simply better at charm, at least if you are of the same party as the man who captured the place.

1958

BALTIMORE

In segregation, it was not as if we were totally cut off from the white world. Many of our parents and relatives worked for white people, in their homes, in their clubs, in their businesses. We had the opportunity to learn many things about them, because we watched them. They did not work in our houses, or for our businesses, so they never had the opportunity to learn about us the way we learned about them. It would seem, on the face of things, that this would make them less culturally literate. Yet in the year 2000, in our society, cultural literacy is only an idea, and not valued enough to really become an issue. And yet these people, who don't know us or anything about us, although we are constantly learning about them, affect every aspect of our lives. They make decisions about our education, they are our surgeons, they are often our lawyers, our teachers, they edit the major papers (and there's not much of a black press to speak of now, or at least it isn't what it used to be), they hire us (or not) in major corporations. In short, they create our realities in body and mind. The end of segregation helped position people in places they hadn't been before, but it didn't make things go both ways. And they still don't know so much about us. Not that knowing is enough of a solution, as we would see in the nineties.

We believe we know about public figures. They broadcast what they think, and sometimes they broadcast what they feel. Sometimes public figures, and not so public figures, seem to be speaking to us very personally about intimate details of their love lives, their sexual lives, their financial lives, their family lives. Indeed, the president was caused to speak in a taped grand jury testimony that we can all watch about very intimate details of his relationship with his lover. When I watched the grand jury testimony, I was very surprised at the questions the interviewer asked, and the tone with which he asked them. "Did you tell Monica Lewinsky that you were going to leave Mrs. Clinton after you left the White House . . . ?" It was as if Jack Nicholson in *Carnal Knowledge* suddenly turned into a prosecutor as he asked Art Garfunkel about his first sexual experience with Candice Bergen. Those of us who were black in segregation learned some very profound things about the dangers of believing in the false intimacies that television can create. Psychiatrists believed that these types of false intimacies that we made with television were very bad for the health of our identities.

Television was a way that we, as black people, learned about white people. In my generation, it was less likely that we would have the kinds of intimacies that our parents and grandparents had had with whites. It was becoming less likely that we would wash their floors, or wash their clothes, or serve them their food, or take care of their children. Less likely that we would be "living in" with them. Less likely that we would be in their homes. This was in part because of education. We would go "beyond" those jobs. At the time, most of us did not have the foresight to see that the people who did not go beyond those jobs would be replaced in those jobs by members of immigrant groups of other colors. And we certainly couldn't have projected that many of us, men and, more shockingly, women, would not be having those jobs because we would be incarcerated.

Television was not a communicator about everybody. It was peopled with white people. When I turned on the television, except for Amos and Andy, everything I saw was white. I *identified* with white people, but I didn't know very many. In other words, I was brought up identifying with something that was really strange. I was brought up with a false intimacy with people who had nothing to do with me. I was brought up identifying with their world, the problems and joys they had, and the products that they were selling. The downside of this is that white people were not brought up to identify with us. It took us black folk until the nineteen sixties, and the late sixties at that, to publicly question that, and to publicly rally around an idea that we needed to see on television, in jobs, in positions of authority, people who we could *identify* with. Psychiatrists said that black children had a problem because they had no one to identify with, and in particular we had no role models. The fact is, we didn't have any trouble identifying with the other in the first place. My grandmother, a devout Christian woman, had no trouble identifying with the people on her "story" as she called it, her "soap opera."

I don't think the problem was that we had no one to identify with. There were plenty of white people that we did identify with. We cried about *Old Yeller, Bambi, West Side Story, Love Story,* all the sad stories, just like everybody else did. Our overidentification with white people was ultimately analyzed as a problem. But was that the problem? An ability to identify with the other is called empathy. That empathy is a proof of humanity, it is a proof that we don't all stop at the front and back doors, the floors and the ceilings of our physical selves. Empathy and the ability to identify with the other is proof that our color, our gender, our height, our weight is only a frame of something else called the soul. And politically, of course, that proof is the very ingredient we need to get to "we," to get to move from "me" to "us."

So I don't think, in retrospect, that the problem was so simple as we had no one to identify with. I would say, rather, the problem was that white people only had *themselves* to identify with. If it had gone both ways, we would have a different situation. This is what I see in Washington in 2000. The people there have themselves to identify with. Their daily lives do not give them the opportunity to identify with us. We learn about them. We are beginning to know a lot about the pundits and newscasters who tell us the story of our world. Our "hosts" are themselves becoming the subject. But they are not learning about us. The vestiges of segregation are all around us. We do not have our own talk shows in which we simply blast off our ideas to them. The technology is here, or nearly here, for us to do that. The question is, once the technology is here for us, "we the people," to let them know what we're doing—will they be interested to watch? I wonder if, five years from now, I might find "the people" talking—"community people" talking on shows that are not orchestrated by major network programming. That is, community punditry. But pundits are the dominant culture, and the dominant culture is, still, very self-interested.

The desegregation of schools was really the gateway, in my life, for a beginning of an understanding that the world should be larger than those black kids I sat next to during reading, and played with on the playground. People were being shot and jailed in order to get the right to vote or to sit at a lunch counter. Although I was too young for that, I was aware, in my "experimental school," that something was afoot about where I was going to go to school, and who I was going to go to school with. My school was given many of the same privileges as a white school across town. This must have been a part of trying to bring people around to seeing that we weren't simply of inferior intelligence, and I'm sure there were other more complicated political agendas. It played out in a very strange way, because my class was the actual subject population for that experiment.

At various times a year from third grade on, my mother would dress me up, straighten my hair, and send me off for what was a special day. The people from Twenty-fifth Street were coming. Twenty-fifth Street was the Board of Education. We would go to school, seeming to have a perfectly normal lesson. It of course had been rehearsed. There was a crowd of white people sitting in the back watching us learn. We were literally asked to perform the fact that we were learning, as if our tests weren't performance enough. I don't know if those presentations encouraged the white administrators to identify with us. The sum total of all those presentations, in my child's mind, was that I ended up in an integrated junior high.

2000

We like to think that education is the route to learning how to be together. We know that education alone is not the answer because, in part, once we got to the schools we still stayed among ourselves. We stayed well nestled in safe houses of identity. The assumption was that knowledge was the key to getting rid of racism, and knowledge was the key to encouraging us all to live together in that way that Martin Luther King suggested we live together. Many schools, or societies, are still segregated, not by law, but by choice.

I have met many people who know a lot. They aren't necessarily the same as people who move across cultural lines at all, they don't move at all toward that Martin Luther King image of the little black kids and little white kids being together. Not at all. And Washington is full of people whose business it is to know everything. What they lack is the ability to identify with anyone, other than those just like themselves.

Whatever happened to the idea that the media, for example, would "afflict the comfortable, and comfort the afflicted"? They themselves are comfortable. They are living in a highly wired, every day more wired cocoon.

I was looking at *Brown v. Board of Education:*

We come then to the question presented: Does segregation of children in public schools solely on the basis of race, even though the physical facilities and other "tangible factors" may be equal, deprive the children of the minority group of equal educational opportunities? We believe it does. In finding that a segregated law school for Negroes could not provide them equal educational opportunities, this Court relied in large part on those qualities which are incapable of objective measurement but which make for greatness in a law school. In requiring that a Negro admitted to a white graduate school be treated like all other students, we again resorted to intangible considerations, his ability to study, to engage in discussions, and exchange views with other students, in general to learn his profession. Such considerations apply with added force to children in grade and high schools. To separate them from others of a similar age and qualifications solely because of their race generates a feeling of inferiority as to their status in the community that may affect their hearts and minds in a way unlikely ever to be undone.

I would think that segregation would keep *any* of us from learning our profession, particularly if that profession has to do with society, and society's idea of itself, and society's idea of the other. How can the people who serve us, and the people who write about us, put us on the air, be so distant, so self-contained, so segregated from us, and do a responsible job? And if they are relying on communications technology to bring them closer to us, or us to them, that may be shortsighted. Again, I ask, in an age of global mergers, where are our human mergers?

I was speaking with someone working in a corporation, struggling with how to be a whole person in an environment that causes him and his colleagues every day to make "small compromises." He said, "People want to do good, but they don't believe they can. They believe they will be punished for being good, so they repress all that and get on with the job." In every area of American work life we will find this conflict. The desire to "do good" gets more and more repressed, less and less visible, and takes the form of cynicism.

The world of inside Washington, with its politicians and pundits, and the chorus of media, is a place where people do not look for the good very much anymore, they assume they are only looking at the bad. They honor truth, yet they are not looking for truth, they are looking for lies. There is a difference.

Washington has made it clear in the last several years that, even when people go there to try to contribute something good, they may very well be punished, exposed, humiliated. It looks like a very inhospitable place.

Fewer and fewer people want to go there to make contributions to our society. As a black woman, I am particularly sensitive to how it has chewed up and roughed up and sometimes spat out, in a very public way, other black women—Anita Hill, Lani Guinier, Maggie Williams, Alexis Herman.

"We" the people. In the beginning, "we" was a small "we," that "we" was a small community of white men. During the last two centuries, people have slowly, and sometimes in fits and starts, tried to make that "we" seem bigger. We have been trying to make that "we" a "we" that allows more people to have a voice in saying who "we" are. And then we had that one particular forefather who put in our minds an idea—and it's probably a good thing that he did—one particular forefather put on the record the idea that "all men are created equal." As Americans, deep down we have tried, at least, to absorb and to behave as if we believe that. And yet we're still confused. I believe we're confused because that very forefather was confused. Thomas Jefferson wrote "all Men are created equal [and] they are endowed by their Creator with certain unalienable Rights, that among these are Life, Liberty, and the Pursuit of Happiness." It is significant, I am told, that he chose to write the word *happiness* rather than the word *property*. But this same man had slaves. Around 130 of them.

Something I heard from a tour guide at Monticello always rings in my head: "And another thing Thomas Jefferson said about slavery, he said 'Justice is in one scale, self-preservation in the other.' "

America was not a very hospitable place for many people in the beginning. Presumably we are more civilized now. We keep trying, on paper, to make the place healthier for more people. And yet the bloodless assassinations of character that take place every day in the name of keeping the place clean create an atmosphere that is not clean, or healthy, or nurturing to "we the people" at all. People are speaking to us in such planned, designed language that a free flow of ideas is harder and harder to find. We are being given packaged discourse. Even the mainstream seems frozen; there's not enough movement.

But this move toward segregated circles of decision makers, segregated circles of expertise, is not limited to Washington. People stick with their own kind.

The assumption in *Brown v. Board of Education* is that the black kids lose out, and come away from all of this with a feeling of inferiority. What about the white kids? Don't they lose something too? Why do we not all feel inferior, when in fact what we are all losing out on is the opportunity to identify, to know, to be with the other? We are losing out on the wealth of exchange, the wealth inherent in that *human* merger. Separation is how things work, as I saw dramatically in our nation's capital.

The state of separation is what is expected. To move out of your separate place, your safe house of identity, is hard work. You have to be prepared. Because remember the lesson from segregation. The side of power will not be as invested in learning about you as you are in learning about them. It will be hard to find dialogue. You have to simply get inside the circle, be as inconspicuous as possible, get what you need, and get out. But as for really engaging? It rarely happens. And people think the answer to racial strife is demographics? I refer you to Newt Gingrich's comment. In that one ballroom, he said, was "the center of intellectual and political life." It'll be a long time before demographics change that center.

A NONREADER

1997

THE BRONX

My mother had dedicated most of her early teaching career to proving there was no such thing as a nonreader. This was before the days of dyslexia and defined learning disabilities. There would often be a very large boy at our house after school whom she was teaching to read.

During one of the summers that I was doing this project, I met with a boy who lived in the Bronx named Dennis. I spent an afternoon talking to him and to his father. Dennis was not able to read and had been simply graduated to push him on. He had five or six siblings. His father, Dennis Sr., was a single father. Dennis's mother was a drug addict who was suffering from AIDS and who lived under the 125th Street Bridge. When I tried to get Dennis to talk to me about his mother, he said to me very directly, "I don't want to talk about her."

I didn't ask him again.

After having spent quite a while with them, I was most disturbed by the casualness with which the schools dealt with the problem, and the fact that the father had nearly had to sue the school system to get his child tested. He took out a very neat box of all the letters he had written, and all the documents he had collected, while simply trying to get a test. He had even written a letter to the president.

His father told me that one of the teachers at his son's school had simply said to him, "You may as well get used to it, your boy is either going to end up in jail or end up in the graveyard."

Why can't we do anything about these stories? The fact is we can. Why aren't we doing more? What's inhibiting us from looking further than our own immediate circle?

PENNY KISER

MONTICELLO TOUR GUIDE

"Jefferson's Nailery Boys"

Now the boys' incentive in the nailery
was if you
and boy those records were strict but if you were the best producer
    then you would get a
new suit of clothes a red suit or a blue suit
and remember great George?
His son Isaac often won that prize in fact at the age of sixteen if
    you'd done a good job Thomas Jefferson allowed you to learn
    a trade and he took Isaac to Philadelphia where he learned to
    be a tinsmith.
If you didn't do a good job where do you think you'd end up?
Yeah, in the fields
it's called going into the ground
and that would be your job you would go into the ground.
Same with the girls

who worked in the textile industry
and we know that
there was a young boy who worked here and his name was Carey
and we don't know the circumstances
but we know that one day Carey comes to work it's probably hot
and sticky and they're
working over these fires.
He takes his hammer and he hits the boy next to him, Brown,
on the head, he cracks his head wide open
and the overseer
who I think might have been Mr. Bacon at that
time thought that
Brown might die
so
he's in a total panic 'cause he thinks all these young boys might
take their hammers and
we're gonna have a riot here.
So he takes Carey and he puts him in jail.
Now Thomas Jefferson is in Washington.
And he has to write Thomas Jefferson to find out what the
punishment might be.
Now Thomas Jefferson always said that
he loved industry
industry or hard work.
He abhorred or hated severity.
And the overseer said when Thomas Jefferson was here on the
plantation that that whip
was put away as much as possible.
So when he writes Thomas Jefferson
Jefferson writes back and he says we must give Carey the worst
punishment
he has to be an example to these
boys.
What do you think the worst thing could happen to you if you were
a slave?
Death would be pretty bad wouldn't it?
That would kind of be the end of you.

But you know what?
If Thomas Jefferson had you killed, every slave is worth money so
    he's kind of losing
money if he does that
he's got to think of something else where he doesn't lose money.
Sell him to the worst . . .
Yeah,
okay what did he do?
He writes back and he says take Carey and sell him
so far away that his parents will think he's dead,
all the boys around him will think he's dead.
You can imagine
if you don't own anything
think how important your family is
so that's what happens to Carey we think he probably ended up in
    Georgia
say in the cotton fields
we do know—
I have read that if you ever ended up down in the sugarcane
    plantations
on one of those plantations say in the West Indies?
Your life expectancy was only five years.

GARRISON JUNIOR HIGH SCHOOL BALTIMORE, MARYLAND, 1961

I TRAVEL IN PURSUIT OF LANGUAGE. MY TAPE RECORDER IS MY CAMERA. Here I am, two decades into my journey, and I find myself worrying about the future of language, or at least language in America. I have heard about a culture in Cameroon where they have a language with only five hundred words:

> My grandmother she still lives in Central Africa
> And she speaks a language called Sango
> Which has only five hundred words.
> I mean, five hundred? Five hundred?
> It's "I'm hungry." "I'm hot." "How are you?"
> That's it!
> That's it!
> But every time I go back to Africa
> It brings me down on earth.

Imagine. There are people who live in minimal language. We have so many words. Does it change what a human being is, as a species? That woman and I are of the same species, even as we stand thousands and thousands and thousands of words apart.

★　★　★

I T MAY BE THAT CULTURES WITH FEWER WORDS ARE IN LESS DANGER than we are. So many of our words are being contorted, mangled, stretched, distorted in public life. I'm surprised they survive. I'm surprised they mean anything.

So suspicious is the ear. Its structure has changed. We sit with only one ear toward the speaker, and the other is tuned to the nonexistent next beat. In Washington, I found many people who were watching the world from over their shoulders, like smokers, who stand with their heads away to keep from blowing smoke in your face; we are addicted to another direction, to any direction other than straightforward contact.

B EING A NEGRO GIRL FROM BALTIMORE RAISED IN SEGREGATION, INtegrated into "it all" when I was eleven, and newly in junior high school, I was terrified of white kids. We outgrow these things, of course, as Jacob Lawrence, the great painter, told me when I went to visit him in Seattle. "Well it's scary, talking about how brutal it was, the brutality of people being burned and hung by trees. It was scary, frightening. So much so that if you'd walk down the street or you'd see a person, a Caucasian, you would immediately think, Oh this man was a lyncher. I guess as a young person your imagination is very fertile. It's very—you know, it's like seeing goblins. It's like it doesn't take much, but as you develop your experience broadens. So you don't have the same kind of apprehension." History always lurks, changing reality into shadowed moments that are haunted by a past.

And the gorgeous reality of American culture is that our diversity breeds for us a smorgasbord of nightmares, fantasies, justified fears, and unjustified fears. It might seem strange that as a child Jacob Lawrence thought every white person was a lyncher, but think of how many adults think that any black man on a dark street is a thief, a mugger, or a rapist. And so for me, somehow, my fear started with a girl with red hair. Her name was Nancy, and she was in my homeroom class in seventh grade.

She was very mean in the classroom. I don't know much about how she was on the playground, because I didn't have the opportunity to watch her there. We didn't play together on the playground, whites and blacks, Jews and gentiles. We had to go to school together, but no one could tell us how to play at lunchtime. I have been surprised to learn that, more than thirty years later, in many junior and senior highs in this integrated country, students still prefer to sit with their own kind.

Whites didn't play with blacks, or Jews, for that matter, and Reform Jews didn't play with Orthodox Jews, and Orthodox Jews didn't play with Jews fresh from Europe who didn't speak English. Even Jews made fun of a Jewish girl with a Russian accent who brought sandwiches made of meat with a strong smell and purple horseradish, despised her for being so not "of it."

Nancy was quite popular in seventh grade. She had a thick head of hair and freckles, and she sat somewhere near the front of the room in class 7-7. There had been no girl quite as mean as Nancy in James Mosher Elementary School—an all-black school. We had boys who were bullies, and girls who were goody-goodies, but the room was dominated by either a bully on the playground or a teacher's pet in the classroom. So a white girl bully in the classroom was a novel idea.

Nancy sat second from the front in French class, and always seemed to be the first one there. She was not attractive by any stretch of the imagination. Perhaps her brutishness was a compensation for that. She didn't suck up to the teachers enough to be considered a "good student," but she ran the room, with the threat that at any moment her mean spirit would lash out in the form of ridicule. She never said anything racist, as far as I can remember, but there seemed to be the possibility or the threat that she would, since we were on borrowed territory and for some reason the territory seemed to be hers.

Nancy. This is where I began to learn that bullies weren't just the big guys who hid behind buildings and sprang out to steal your lunch money or beat you up. Nancy was never hidden; she was always quite apparent. She sat very tall, very proudly, with her not yet breasts supported by a straight back. In fact, she seemed to like people to see her. She made us all very uneasy, very uncomfortable, because we never quite knew what she'd do, what she'd say.

Stranger still was what happened to Lila. It was the one occasion that we did not need Nancy to exploit our unspoken hostility for us. The entire class came forward with their own individual meannesses. I'll never forget when the whole homeroom class took it upon themselves to beat up Lila. Not physically. There were surely fights, but at least among the girls those fights tended to stay within racial lines. Perhaps we were a little too civilized.

Perhaps beatings are subverted when "shoulds" appear in a group. Those subverted headings transform into another type of hostility. Baltimore, like Washington, is neither North nor South. It wouldn't have been right to behave like southerners. Our situation was not overt. I didn't hear much "nigger" calling. Most of the integration in housing and education happened with the Jews. Perhaps their own situation caused them to be silent about their thoughts. But underneath the silence was contorted aggression.

Lila was beat up with humiliation. The class was predominantly Jewish, at a time when many Jews in Baltimore were not entirely assimilated. My father would drive us across town to the Jewish neighborhoods on Sunday to buy things, since they had celebrated the Sabbath already. Our neighborhoods were quiet; most of the businesses were closed on Sundays, and theirs were wide awake. There were no boyfriends and girlfriends across racial lines, or religious lines. All Jewish holidays were observed. I didn't know why they made us come to school on the High Holy Days, because there was no one there. Our teachers never taught on those days; the eight, or ten, or sometimes as few as three or four of us would simply sit in empty classroom after empty classroom until the end of the day.

Our homeroom teacher was a black woman who was not particularly popular. She was also our science teacher. She had to fight to get control of the room. I can only imagine what it was for her, too, to be in integration for the first time, probably having been educated in segregation (I know, for example, that she had gone to a black college) and now having to teach in this "loaded" integrated school. By Christmastime, we calmed down. She "proved" herself to us and we actually felt warmly toward her. The class decided to buy her a Christmas present. A rumor started that Lila, who was the quietest person in the room, Lila, who never ever had to be told to sit down, to be quiet, to do anything, Lila, who simply came to school and went home, who never seemed to socialize with anyone . . . Lila was not going to chip in for the Christmas present. Her parents wouldn't allow it. This became our headline for two weeks or so: what we were going to do about it, how we were going to vote in terms of ostracizing Lila.

A tall, beautiful black girl (who was pregnant and would soon be forced to leave school) began some of the mockery toward Lila. I remember that it pained me. I also remember how surprised I was that the Jewish kids (again, the predominant population) began to turn against Lila too. What had started as a sort of 50–50 vote about whether to buy a Christmas present at all, now turned into 99 percent for the present, and Lila on her own. No one took her to the schoolyard and threatened to beat her up, no one stuck her head down the toilet, but the daily vote would be taken, the vote toward unanimous for buying the present or not, and as the days went on Lila became stronger and stronger in her position. The teacher would be out of the room. The tall, beautiful black girl would take the vote.

Every day Lila would sit with no expression on her face as we lifted our hands. Her hands stayed firmly planted on the desk. Her parents did not celebrate Christmas, and they would not allow her to buy a present for the teacher. I did not know if the fact of the teacher being black complicated it on another level. Lila never cried, she simply sat quietly as all kinds of things were said, and she never explained anything further. In fact, I don't remember her ever saying anything—it was simply known she would not be chipping in for the gift.

Finally, the teacher got wind of the whole thing and shamed us all by saying, as she should have, that in this spirit she didn't really want a Christmas present, and that Lila should not be forced to participate if her religion wouldn't allow it. I remember this story because it was the first time I saw that a beating—even a public beating—could happen without anyone so much as striking a blow.

WALTER SHAPIRO

COLUMNIST

"Loaded for Bear"

Also the Bush campaign reporters came in,
some of whom
worshiped at the shrine of Marlin Fitzwater,
some of whom
thought that
Bush had gotten an unfair deal in the '92 campaign.
And Bush did.
The press was unbelievably sycophantic on the way up
and too cruel on the way down,
and while I've only read excerpts from Fitzwater's
memoirs
he probably captures
correctly
the unfairness on the way down
and probably glosses over
the gushy excesses on the way up.
Most of the Bush reporters
and these are the Brit Humes of the world—
the Andrea Mitchells have now gone on to the State Department—
the Tom Friedmans, the Ann Devroys felt that their counterparts had
     been too soft on Clinton
so they showed up in Little Rock
loaded for bear.
They were going to show him
what a real press corps was like
not like those sycophants on the plane.
What happened is
Clinton,

who had
loved the press
learned to hate the press during Gennifer Flowers and the draft
    letter
for some cause,
was getting back
to his comfort level with the press in the last three weeks of the
    campaign—
revealing himself in useful ways—
without feeling like that anybody's gonna do a gotcha on him?
You know
coming back and sort of schmoozing in the corridors at two in the
    morning on a campaign plane on a Wednesday night sort of
    half off the record half on the record
not talking about anything newsy?
Reminiscing about odd things
you know but these are little moments where you can get a sense of
    who Bill Clinton is.
Yeah, yeah.
He was beginning to do this again.
Ya know it's like that old
poster for *Jaws*—
Just when you were
Just when you were willing to go back into the water
you know, for *Jaws Four*.
For Clinton—
Just when you thought that you can be seminatural with the press
the guard changed.
Everybody thought Bush was the winner
so their best—both their White House reporters
and the reporters who had been promised the White House in the
    future—had been given
the Bush campaign to cover.
Clinton was seen as the likely loser.
For a lot of news organizations
their wrong reporters had covered the victorious president.
So what happened is

after the election
two-thirds of the people who covered the Clinton campaign
were ordered back to Washington and in their place were the
    people who covered the Bush campaign.
And this had nothing to do with Clinton.
This had to do with lots of assignment editors
and vice presidents for news
had gambled on a Bush victory, and staffed the campaigns
    accordingly.
For lots of the White House reporters
who'd been covering the White House for ten years
fifteen years.
Major temper tantrum if you're pulled off the White House
even if it looks like your guy's gonna lose.
It *is* the White House.

THE EAST COAST
CORRIDOR

I HAVE BEEN TRAVELING UP AND DOWN THE EAST COAST CORRIDOR all my life. First in a car, and when I went to college, in a train. In the five years that I was trying to understand Washington, I traveled the corridor all the time, by Delta or USAir shuttle.

The "corridor" was fun when we took the train. When I was younger, it was significant that the train station was a place where people gathered across class lines and racial lines. I often wish that the theater, onstage and in the audience, would look like Pennsylvania Train Station in Baltimore looked in the nineteen fifties and sixties. But the theater still does not look like that. Neither does the academy, and neither does Congress or most institutions. The message was clear: If people want to move, they have to at least all meet at the train station. (Even in the case of Jim Crow, which I never experienced, you'd have to sit in a special car, but you'd have to gather at the station.) So a train station, for me, was always a good metaphor for a place that was big enough, structurally, for all of us. This kind of a place required a big booming voice, and very clear speech. I loved those voices.

As a ritual, we would go to the train station following the Thanksgiving Day Parade. Every year, my mother said the exact same thing about the drum majorettes: "I feel so sorry for those drum majorettes. Their little legs were so cold, they didn't even have on stockings. Now you know their legs were cold. Those white legs. They were completely red." At the time there were no black drum majorettes. After the parade my brothers liked to watch the trains. I liked to hear the announcements and watch the arrivals and departures of the people. I loved the stories that were told in those arrivals and departures, although I couldn't hear the words. I would stare at the groupings of people in conversation.

"Don't stare," my mother would say.

The voice that announced the trains was usually male in those days, deep and authoritative.

"Announcing
on track num-ber
two
the arrival
of the Silver Constitu*tion*
from Washing-*ton,*
going to
Phila-del-phia
Wil-ming-ton
Delaware
Tren-ton
Newark
New York City
New Haven, Con-nec-ticut
And
Bos-ton
Massachusetts!
Allllllllllllll Aboaaarrrrrrrruhhdd!!!!!!!"

During my college years, the sounds caused quite a bit of adrenaline and hurry when all four of my siblings, my parents, and sometimes my grandfather would come to the train station to say good-bye. They would run, even if we had plenty of time, as if I were going to miss the train. My little sisters, who were only seven and eight years old at the time, would be, of course, nearly beside themselves with the excitement of the flurry of motion and the echoes all over the very tall, stone train station. People even dressed to travel then. The sound of the announcement signaled a flurry of activity: luggage moving, porters moving, high heels clicking on the stone floor, whisks of perfume flashing by; in the winter, it was still politically all right to wear fur. All social classes convened at the train station, and across these lines you saw kisses, hugs, last-minute mementos and gifts, dollars, being handed off. As you ran to your train, out of the corner of your eye you might even catch a sob here and there, or the last moments of an argument. My brother Deaver and I *always* fought before I left, so my brother Maurice, the younger of the two of them, was inevitably left to pull the bags along, while Deaver sulked. You were leaving. And each time you left there was less and less certainty that you would be the same when you came back again, or that *they* would be the same.

The conductor's and the announcer's voices had a mild kind of grandeur that was a cousin to the vocal tones I had heard at funerals—"Ashes—to—ashes"—and at christenings and weddings. These are words that have been said many times, but the person who speaks them understands that each time it must be said as if it matters because it does matter, and we never know what lies ahead, and we never know what just happened, and all words must house respect of those two unknowns.

We are relatively calm about arrivals and departures now. And the way we deal with it is very low-key. We've seen it all before, heard it all before. Airports are the major gateways. You often have to travel very long distances across the airport, taking trains and shuttles and long walkways. It's less about your departure, and more about "getting there," wherever "there" is. There are a series of "theres"—the ticket counter, the gate, and the variety of lounges.

Recently I was in San Francisco, and went to the so-called Red Carpet lounge to speed up my check-in process. The line was all the way out the door. Businessmen and some women with suitcases on wheels were everywhere, it seemed. I remembered that I am a so-called 1K Traveler, which means I can go to an even more exclusive lounge. I went to the 1K lounge and there was a line there too. Then a concierge came over and told me about yet another lounge, across from the 1K lounge, that I might like to know about. I realized that the most efficient place for me to be may be back at the ticket counter in the front, given the fact that everyone is fleeing to the other "special lounges." Maybe the least average thing to be now is "average." If everyone is "special," then what's the point? I was sitting next to a man on a plane who told me that he and his colleagues were so fed up with the airlines they were going to chip in and get their own plane. "I guess somebody will make something like FedEx for air travel," I said.

Sometimes, those who accompany you to major airports cannot go with you past security. The only place I see a mass of human emotion in an airport comparable to what I used to see in the train station is in the arrivals area after an international flight. There, after all the business has been done, all security, all customs, all government affairs are finally over, as you exit, behind a rope you will see clusters of people of all nationalities holding signs, placards, balloons. And speckled between the relatives and lovers, daughters, sons, mothers, fathers are members of that club of mostly colored men from Africa, the Middle East, Latin America waiting with their car service signs to pick up people that they do not know.

Years later, in my time trying to "capture American character in Washington, D.C.," I would fly up and down the eastern corridor to New York and Boston. I became a regular customer on USAir and Delta. Sometimes it was so frequent I felt as if they were tantamount to a subway. In contrast to those old conductors, the flight attendants never enunciate ending consonants, and they have the most peculiar rhythm pattern. We were told in acting school that if we want to take full advantage of getting a message across, we must stress operative words, usually verbs, and never stress prepositions. I marvel each time I hear a flight attendant announcement at their affinity for stressing prepositions, their resistance to elongating vowels, and their tendency to simply let the breath run out at the end of a phrase so that the last word sounds like a motor winding down. Their speaking and breathing patterns have absolutely nothing to do with the thought they are transmitting. So, given that big companies like airlines are sure to instruct people down to the last detail about how to behave on the job, one can only imagine that there is some corporate reason that they do not want us to pay full attention to these messages, or to really listen to them each time they are said.

"WELcomdoDeldairlinesairflightnummertwoeighdynineWITHzerviztoWashingdnNatshnulairporrrrd.KINDLYreadtheinstructshunsINtheseatpoggetinFRONTufyooooou.ForTHOSEpassengersittinginandemergenzyexitrows(BREΛTI I)bewarethatfederalregulationsDOrequirethatyoubeabletoassistothersINtheeventofanemergencylandinnnnng."

On a graph this would look like the flat line in the intensive-care unit. The speech, unlike the conductor's speech, is often associated with women, because although there are male flight attendants, one normally thinks of that job as a woman's job, and if anything it is a job that men have entered into later than women. What I don't understand is why the flight attendants aren't able to give that speech as if they are thinking about what they are saying. When the pilots speak to us, their manner is, by contrast, quite "normal," and lifelike. Especially if they have to bring disappointing news. That news, if anything, is told with a certain amount of charm, and the sound that "we're all in this together." It often starts with the word *Folks,* and if the pilot is particularly good at this, he will sigh after he says "Folks," to lead you to believe that he's peeved a little bit, too. He *wants* to identify with you.

"Folks, this is your captain again. I'm sorry to have to tell you this, but we're going to have to go back to the gate. We're gonna let you off the plane, then we're gonna let you back on the plane, and we'll sit on the runway. We don't know how long that will be. But there's weather at La Guardia and . . ."

The moans of the passengers usually overwhelm the rest of the speech, and the flurry to get on cell phones to call offices and find alternate modes of travel or, in the worst-case scenario, find places other than the lobby of the airport to spend the night.

Notice the safety announcements never start with the word *Folks.* The safety announcer does not want to identify with you. If there is ever a moment when we're all "folks," it would be the moment when we all need those safety instructions.

I was on one commuter plane from Pittsburgh to New York. It was the first time I had ever (and I have sometimes had to travel as much as three times a week) heard the safety announcement make sense. I was so shocked, at how serious the announcement really is, that I struck up a conversation with the flight attendant. She told me that she used to be a police officer, in an urban area. "I'm not foolin' around," she said. I asked her if she had practiced the speech. "Absolutely," she said. "I practice it all the time. It's important. Your safety is important."

She told me that there was a man who wouldn't fasten his seat belt. She went over to him to instruct him to do so. "I take this flight all the time," he mumbled and put his head back into *The New York Times, The Wall Street Journal,* or whatever he was reading. She leaned over, put her finger right in front of his face, and said, "I don't care if you are president of the airline, you're fastening your seat belt."

He fastened it.

Who's listening anymore? What does it take to get people to listen? When do people feel they need to listen? When do they feel they *have* to listen? Only for the banker, the lawyer, the doctor, or the police?

We get so used to hearing things that they have no meaning. And there is, of course, the chance that one day those safety instructions will have meaning. Then it will be stark raving clear. Until that time we live in the expectation of a verbal flat line, a verbal minimum. We live with the expectation that words mean very little, because we have seen it all before, heard it all before. And that is why I find myself going on a quest down memory lane for a time when words meant something in my family, in my church, in my city, in my world.

MIKE McCURRY

FORMER PRESS SECRETARY TO PRESIDENT CLINTON

"A Troubling Time"

We're coming into a domain in which there may be questions that
    in the past never even would have been contemplated here uh
    that are now
you know
asked all the time.
We had [a nominee for a cabinet department post]
withdraw his nomination uh, today
because he is accused of sexual impropriety, and as near as I can
    figure it, it amounts to he had, he made an improp——
    improper, is alleged to have made an improper advance on a
    woman, she complained, it was looked into, the process by
    which it was looked into within the department was irregular,
    the irregularity of that was going to become a big controversy,

the Senate was going to haul everyone up and have open
testimony next week, embarrass this man and his wife, make
his life miserable, and he said screw it I'm just not going to take
the job.
And so the the the boundary of questions that never were asked in
the past
the bar, the threshold
has been lowered and lowered and lowered.
And we, we came very close in the last week for, to a point where I
thought I was going to get asked about what kind of erections
the president has.
I mean quite seriously.
There was and, and that was, and this actually happened on the
trip to Latin America which was great so that we didn't get too
deeply into the subject but there was sort of a collective
judgment made that that was off-limits.
So it's a, it's weird.
It's kind of this merging of our popular culture and tabloid mentality
and the evening shows,
that sort of the tabloid television shows at night
and it's kind of this morphing of what we consider, you know,
civil discourse
and ah so it's it's it's a troubling time.

THEATER AND POLITICS

I. THE PRESIDENT

WINTER 1992
CAMBRIDGE, MASSACHUSETTS

WAS AT HARVARD ON A FELLOWSHIP. ANOTHER FELLOW IN THE SAME program was the former governor of Vermont Madeleine Kunin. We were living in the same apartment building. One day I was coming in as she was rushing out.

"Have to go to New Hampshire and help Bill Clinton! We've got to do everything we can!" she hollered as she took off down the street. She said "we" in a way that made "we" seem like it included me too, and like I and everybody else should follow her wherever she was going. From the freedom in her wave, and the glee in her voice, it certainly seemed that wherever she was going was the right way to go. Political people do seem to have that talent.

SPRING 1992
NEW YORK CITY

Clinton was in the midst of his first campaign for president when my career, or rather my language work, "took off." I was in New York preparing my play *Fires in the Mirror,* about riots between Jews and blacks in Crown Heights, Brooklyn. The riots began when a young black boy was killed by a car in the entourage of the leader (the Grand Rebbe) of the sect of Lubavitcher Jews. In retaliation some young black men killed a Hasidic scholar from Australia. Riots broke out, and police occupied the neighborhood for several days. I created a one-woman performance piece out of the stories I gathered from the people who had witnessed the events.

When I took the Crown Heights text to begin working on it in a theater in New York, one of the designers told me that "no one would care about this. People don't care about these things," she said. Everyone at the table, except for one other designer, agreed. "People in New York just don't care about this stuff." "This stuff " meaning race relations. Race as a concern, as "matter," is like fog in our country, or like floating anxiety. One moment we rest on our laurels—that things are better—after all, people aren't still being chased by dogs as they try to go to school. The next moment it's the most "serious problem our nation has to face."

Given that the eighties had not yielded much conversation on race, I assumed the design team was right. The theater has perhaps not been very hospitable to race issues. Unlike academia, where people can "study" blacks or other ethnicities, and never actually talk about race, in the theater we must embody the material. In academia, professors can glide right over the students' complicated feelings or their own complicated feelings about the subject with the excuse that they have to "cover the material." In the theater we can't simply "cover the material"; we "become the material." In fact our job is to *un*cover the material. So perhaps it makes sense that the theater is about a decade, or perhaps two decades, behind academia (which is not necessarily a bastion of progressive attitudes) in terms of its ability to articulate difference and its ability to think through issues that have to do with representation and identity in an ever more complex society.

April 30, 1992, was the scheduled first performance of my play. On April 29, a jury of all whites in Simi Valley, California, came back with a verdict of not guilty on four police officers who had beaten a black man. The videotape had been seen by most Americans. Few people could believe the verdict. Least of all the young blacks who lived in South-Central L.A. By now, everyone knows the story of what happened.

I knew nothing of what was going on in Los Angeles until I got home that night from dress rehearsal and "tech." Tech is the most insular time in the theater. You live in a world away from everything. When I got home there were a number of messages on my answering machine. All the voices were worried. One was in tears. "Anna, I know you don't usually watch TV—you need to turn it on tonight. You won't believe what is happening." Flames exploded across the screen.

I returned to the theater the next day for what should have been the continuation of "tech" time. It's the time when everyone is pushing ahead in the tunnel to bring the show to its opening. Designers, director, in my case, since there's only one actress (me), the crew, the stage manager. It's a very focused time, which has to last through many adjustments until another crew of people—the critics—come and take their turn at what you've done. Then everyone leaves, and you are left, each night, to your own devices with a crowd of interesting people—most of whom you do not know—who are sitting in the dark. But on good nights you find times in the course of the evening when all of you are apparently there for the same reason—to wonder, to laugh, to cry, to ache about something in the human condition.

This was my New York debut, I was nervous, in fact beyond nervous. The audience, the critics, were all a sea of strangers, scary strangers, and judging from what the designers had said to me on the first day, there was a chance that they "would not care" about the material. There did seem to be something just a little out of kilter about our huffing and puffing to put final touches on a play about a riot when a real riot was going on full force in another city.

This particular day, the day after the riot, was the first preview. The general manager was a woman. She came in with a scowl. "This theater," she said, "is closed." A lot of buildings in New York had closed because New Yorkers were frightened that their city would also burst into flames—a memory I suppose of the multiple riots that rocked the country when Martin Luther King was murdered.

"This theater is closed." She looked braced for an argument.

No one argued.

I decided to go to Times Square to the demonstration that was taking place. The director and costume designer joined me.

The riot was one of those events that cause the public to think, as they do from time to time, that race is one of the most important issues our country has to face. As it turned out, given these circumstances, people not only cared about the subject of the play, they came in droves. In that period, I felt each night as if there were a force pulling me downtown to the theater. There was a real urgency, a real purpose. For the first time in my career, I needed vocal coaching every day. It was because it was the first time I had something to say, and the first time I had a public that consciously knew they needed to hear it.

I finished my run in New York and went immediately to Los Angeles to study that riot. Again, the text was rich. I spoke with 280 people, all of whom would have, like those I spoke with in Crown Heights, gone to the highest mountain to tell their stories to anyone in the world who would listen. The two hardest people to perform were actually those who were in charge, the chief of police, Daryl Gates, and the mayor, Tom Bradley. Strangely enough they were also in better physical shape than anyone else I talked to (other than Anjelica Huston and Charlton Heston).

I then wrote and performed a play about the Los Angeles riots called *Twilight: Los Angeles, 1992.*

For all the entertainment quality to politics, it doesn't seem like too much fun these days. The challenge is you have to run to keep up with those who control the dialogue. So many people have given up on that chase. Perhaps it's because there are so many other things to chase. Or is there something about the barrage of media that feels like an assault? I am reminded of a friend who told me about training to be a tennis star with his father. He had to train even on Christmas Day, in the rain. His father was barraging him with tennis balls. My friend threw down his racquet and walked off the court, but his father kept hitting balls at his back until he was out of view. His father's aim and stroke were so good, he managed to get him squarely in the back each time.

We are running in different directions. We pay taxes, but we don't vote, and they say we don't watch political television unless there's a scandal.

1993
LOS ANGELES

I had created fifteen theater pieces with my method of looking for trochees in everyday speech. Two of them got national recognition. Both of the two recognized ones were about race riots.

I was performing my show about the Los Angeles riots when Lani Guinier was being tossed around by the process.

I met with Lani about what happened. I was surprised at how little help she had been given to move in that enormous Washington machine. When I asked Kweisi Mfume, then the head of the Congressional Black Caucus, why no one had helped Lani, but many people had clearly helped Clarence Thomas, he paused and chuckled as he said good-naturedly, "I think everybody thought she'd be fine. Nobody thought she needed help. It was clear he did."

I then spoke with the person in the Bush administration who was "in charge" of "Anita Hill Weekend." At the time this person, like many people who leave politics, was working in the entertainment industry. In our reflecting back on that period with Clarence Thomas and why it was possible to push that nomination through, I was told, "It just shows you what the power of the presidency can do, okay?"

Both Lani's story and Anita Hill's story smoke-signaled to me that you cannot be in Washington, D.C., without a patron, without a chaperone. You must have someone there who can walk you through what is now an incredibly complicated process. Although we have free speech, and are supposedly expected as citizens to come forward and "do our part," only a few get to do "parts."

Lani developed quite an audience as a result of what had happened to her. I asked her in a public interview, "When you go out and you speak about what happened to you in Washington, who do you think you are talking to?" Her answer took my breath away: "I think I'm talking to the president. I half-expect to come home and find a message on my answering machine saying, 'That was interesting what you said tonight.'"

Politics also seemed to be a place where losing your friends could be par for the course.

FEBRUARY 1994
WASHINGTON, D.C.

I met Clinton for the first time at a dinner at the White House during Black History Month. I was seated at Hillary Clinton's table. I understand that it means a lot to people to be invited to these events, but it felt less like a dinner party and more like an awards ceremony at high school. You were there because you were being recognized for having done well at something—or, as was my case, you were the guest of someone who had done well at something. At the conclusion of the meal, Mrs. Clinton said to all of us at her table, "Would anyone like to dance?" We rose. Only one couple danced.

At the end of the evening Clinton shook hands with each one of us as we left. If you had something to say to the president, it was best to have thought of it in advance. Economy was necessary. I didn't say anything other than "Hello." It was something to call home about.

II. THE PRESS

....

FALL 1993

WASHINGTON, D.C.

The following fall, while performing *Fires in the Mirror,* my play about the Crown Heights riots, in Washington, I was asked by the artistic director of the theater that presented me—the Arena Theater—if I might like to do a play about Washington. I was asked this question as we were driving. I remember looking at a view of monuments as I said, "How about if I do something on the president?"

"What about him?" he said.

"He has to be in the press so much. I wonder how he has time to do his work."

As I looked at the city around me, I was sure there were a million stories. And many of those stories were totally disconnected from this inner circle of monuments and government buildings.

I said, "If I'm really doing a 'Search for American Character,' sooner or later I should look at the president.

"But you know what?" I said. "I know nothing about the president that the press doesn't tell me. I can't really look at the president without looking at the press."

The press are as present with the president as we know him as the Secret Service are. Even more present. The Secret Service are only really visible if you see the president live. Most of us view the president as a product of a camera lens.

FALL 1995
WASHINGTON, D.C.

One of my first meetings in Washington was with Bob Kaiser, managing editor of *The Washington Post*. He had responded immediately to my call for a meeting. Everything about Kaiser is done with great dispatch. His secretary signed a variety of notes he sent me from time to time with her name "to avoid delay." He has a pocket watch, which he carries in the breast pocket of his jacket. As he pulls it out, he explains it away as his "one affectation. Everyone deserves one affectation."

I think one reason for Kaiser's immediate response had to do with a rendition I had done of his colleague Shelby Coffey of the *Los Angeles Times*—Shelby having been a character in my play *Twilight*, about the Los Angeles riots.

We sat in Kaiser's office at the *Post*. "The first thing you have to understand about this town," he said, "is that there are different ways to talk to the press. There's on the record, off the record, background, and deep background."

He looked to see if I was following him. "This conversation is on deep background."

He paused again. "My wife tells me I needed to get that clear with you, because I didn't want to end up like my friend Shelby Coffey."

He made it exceedingly clear that under no circumstances did he want to see himself being performed onstage, by me.

And so that first conversation remains in deep background. It was deep background, although I wasn't talking to the press, the press was talking to me. Nonetheless, I abided by their rules.

The delineation of on the record, off the record, background, deep background would be one of many delineations that would be made from time to time as I tried to understand the world of "the press." If you say the word *press*, members of the press will immediately ask for attention to diversity. *The New York Times* is not going to want to be categorized in the same breath as a tabloid. And, who knows? Perhaps a tabloid doesn't want to be mentioned in the same breath as *The New York Times*. *The Washington Post* is not even going to want to be considered in the same breath as ABC News.

People speak with great concern about the degree to which political journalism is a part of the entertainment media. Yet I learned in my journey that this is not new.

1997

MONTICELLO

It was through my researchers, and their dealings with Monticello, the home of Thomas Jefferson, that I began to become more and more interested in a journalist in Jefferson's day. His name was James Callender.

Callender had written volumes of letters to Jefferson. First, he was looking to Jefferson for patronage and sent him his writings. Jefferson frequently wrote back to him, commending him on the ideas put forth. Callender was from Scotland, well-read, and had the gift of being able to turn a phrase with wit. To make a long story short, Callender went to jail for his writings against John Adams, who was Jefferson's opponent in a presidential election. From jail, he wrote time and time again, asking Jefferson for money and, finally, when Jefferson became president, for a job as postmaster. Jefferson clearly wanted to distance himself from this man, and he wrote as much in a letter to a friend. When Callender got out of jail he went, enraged, to one of Jefferson's associates, demanding his "hush money."

Callender was also a racist. It happened that he was in jail at the same time as a number of slaves who had taken part in a well-known outbreak called Gabriel's Rebellion. His distaste for black people was palpable.

Failing to get the post or the money he wanted, Callender spent a great deal of time exposing his claim that Sally Hemings and Thomas Jefferson had been sexually involved. In fact, Callender is known better now because he is said to have "broken the Sally Hemings story," that is, the now well-known story of Jefferson's supposed fathering of the children of a slave woman, who was a quadroon. She was one-quarter black and was in fact the sister of Jefferson's late wife. So if slaves were "in law," they would have been in-laws.

What amazes me is the time and imagination Callender spent turning this story into entertainment. I am also amazed at how much he did to make an image of Sally that could only be distorted. She was very vulnerable to his pen's distortion; Jefferson was not nearly as vulnerable in that way.

Callender wrote, for example, a very racist takeoff on Hogarth's *Rake's Progress* that was about Jefferson and Sally. He wrote numerous articles and ditties. This one, about Sally Hemings, was sung to the tune of "Yankee Doodle":

Of all the damsels in the green
on mountain or in valley
A lass so luscious ne'er was seen
As Monticellan Sally.

Thick pouting lips! How sweet their grace!
When passion fires to kiss them!
Wide spreading over half the face,
Impossible to miss them.

In glaring red and chalky white
Let others beauty see
Me no such tawdry tints delight
No Black's the hue for me!!!!!

What though my Sally's nose be flat
'Tis harder then to break it
Her skin is sable what of that
'Tis smooth as oil can make it.

If down her neck no ringlets flow
A fleece adorns her head
If on her lips no rubies glow
Their thickness serves instead.

This reminds me of the way Monica Lewinsky and all of the women revolving around that story, Linda Tripp included, got "beaten up" in the media. They were categorized, across the "media"—from tabloids through Jay Leno to the op-ed pages of *The New York Times*—in ways that were disrespectful in terms of physical appearance. I wonder when people look back on those writings generations from now if they will be as horrified as I was when I read some of Callender's writings.

Callender never got what he wanted from Jefferson. He was an alcoholic and died by drowning in the Potomac River. There will be no monument built to James Callender; however, he probably caused quite a headache for Jefferson in his time. Then, and now, his diversions could also divert the public from other matters at hand.

I am not the first to marvel at how much of the public's imagination was taken up by the Monica Lewinsky scandal.

The press are thinking people, many of whom have Ivy League educations, some of whom might be found quoting T. S. Eliot, or waxing poetic about having the opportunity to reread Plato, or any of those "men" from the "canon." But when does being a thinking person become merely being a clever person? Sometimes, tucked into that "cleverness," are troublesome thoughts that we'd best not glide past too quickly. Callender's cleverness could allow his audience to glide over their racist feelings.

After having been in Washington for a while, and having interviewed a few hundred people, I began to long for an interviewee who lacked reverence. Even as most of the press people I interviewed had enormous disdain for Bill Clinton, they still had quite a bit of reverence for the process they themselves were in. It was hard to find anyone who had not bought into the process lock, stock, and barrel. I was looking for a modern-day James Callender. It would be too obvious to go for the stand-up comics— this needed to be someone who was playing even harder than they were.

The press for all their war with those in power, and their charge to reveal any misuse of power, are very much the status quo. They are very middle-class. I found my modern-day Callender in Christopher Hitchens. I was amazed at his likeness with James Callender. Callender was Scottish; Hitchens, English. Both were irreverent. Both felt they had nothing to lose in terms of moving against the grain of the status quo.

We met in Washington on a sunny day at the height of the impeachment proceedings.

FEBRUARY 1999
WASHINGTON, D.C.

Hitchens at the time that I met him had just stepped "out of bounds" by raising questions about Sidney Blumenthal, a Clinton staffer, and doing so in a way that disturbed even Hitchens's closest colleagues. At lunch, amidst a passionate telling of his drama with Sidney Blumenthal, he broke into an account about Clinton's response to Gennifer Flowers's having come forward during the '92 campaign: "Because from the love nest with [the] blonde—who, by the way, you're content to libel and slander— someone who loved you—and say she's a lying minx; she's done it for money—later, and only under oath say, 'Yeah, well, maybe once I did fuck her,' but everyone knows incidentally, should know, it's quite bad manners to screw someone only once. The rudest thing you can do, I would think—one of the rudest things you could do. . . . I think it's very nasty to say, 'Well, I'll fuck you once and not call you again.' I have a good reason to think that was also a lie and why he thinks it would make it better. Yeah, once. What a vulgar thing to say. What a revolting thing to say."

The press gather the information. But they do a lot more than gather and disseminate information. At their best moments, they use their wit to make us question power in a way that we may not have. And they must get our attention in the first place. They have to creep into the brains of the readers, or listeners, and alter the flow of our ideas.

So if I'm listening along, as I was to Hitchens, about an issue that most of us have heard quite a bit about—Gennifer Flowers—I might think I've heard it all before, until he offers up: " 'Well, maybe once I did fuck her,' but everyone knows incidentally, should know, it's quite bad manners to screw someone only once. The rudest thing you can do."

That's a trochee in the second beat. It's not where he seemed to be going. The last thing I expected from him was his way of looking at the situation from a woman's point of view. Normally the women in these accounts become, by association, sluts.

The problem is, politicians are not *allowed* trochees in the second beat. They're scared stiff into iambs. It's the columnists like Hitchens and others, and talk-show hosts, and radio hosts, and comics in this mélange of press/media/entertainment et cetera, who have the trochees.

What would we as a public have to do to give our leaders the courage to take back the trochees—to speak originally—to stop our trains of thought, just when we think we've heard it all before, seen it all before? To get our attention again, they must.

When I met the president the first time, I called home to tell my mother and father. I suppose I called because the president is a powerful man. I didn't call them as I met members of the press. Yet the press represent another kind of power. They have power as a team—they accumulate power with all the words they put forward day after day. It's like a constant drip that affects the way we think, and the way we see the world. They can change us without our full awareness. It happens slowly, bit by bit, that we take on attitudes that are perpetuated in the media. How can we as a public regain control of words?

TODD PURDUM

THE NEW YORK TIMES

"Surf and Turf"

You see, the big thing
this is the other thing—
it's better to be on the press charter,
because the press charter is all first-class seats.
Air Force One has first class seats, too
but it's much roomier,
and it's all designed to compensate the press.
But, um, you know, they try, they do the best they can.
But the network people are particularly—
cushy.
And they have minions to carry their things around,
and we're just all there
but they have burdens we don't have, too.
They have to look great on the tarmac or whatever.
They have to stand up and talk sense off the top of their heads,
whereas we have,
basically always, hours to futz around.
And the two sort of cardinal rules are
if you have an opportunity to eat or go to the
bathroom, you should do either one,
because you do them when you have the chance because
you never know when you'll next have the chance.
But what happens is you keep having food put in front of you,

and I've been on trips where you eat five meals a day.
Literally,
once,
we were coming back from someplace—
Wyoming—Montana, Montana
at two in the morning,
and they served us sort of surf and turf on the plane
—steak and shrimp or lobster.
And we all ate it.
We all ate it all.

ORIENTATION: DINNERS AND LUNCHES

I HAD A LOT OF MEALS IN WASHINGTON. PEOPLE GAVE ME QUITE A bit of orientation and advice for the price of lunch, dinner, or breakfast, as their schedules would have it.

FALL 1993
BREAKFAST WITH HELEN THOMAS
ANA HOTEL
WASHINGTON, D.C.

Any sitting president is only visiting. Early on I had breakfast with Helen Thomas from UPI, the woman who is the first to stand in a press conference and ask a question of "Mr. President." She told me that there was nothing like seeing a president the moment he leaves office. The power is so great that, as he passes the mantle, you can actually see him decrease in size. Obviously this mantle, or this cloak as I have heard it called, is borrowed property. Supposedly, we the public lend that mantle. It is in part a mantle of our trust.

FEBRUARY 1995

DINNER

MORTONS, BEVERLY HILLS, CALIFORNIA

I was filming the movie *The American President*, with Michael Douglas and Annette Bening, directed by Rob Reiner. I was playing the press secretary to the president. By an inexplicable confluence of events, the first major grant for the project on the press and the presidency came through just weeks before I met with Rob and he cast me in the movie. I had done quite a bit of research on the role, and it fed right into what I would be spending the next five years on.

One night I was invited to have dinner with Robert Sheer and Narda Zacchino of the *Los Angeles Times,* along with George Stephanopoulos and his brother. I sat next to George. He gave me one of my first lessons in how stories are created about our times and about the people who lead us:

"Clinton's gonna win in '96 because that's the best narrative."

To me, it seemed early to predict such a thing, but I was all ears.

"A narrative about a guy who is falling and pulls himself up is a good narrative. What the press wants is the most interesting narrative."

I had never thought that our reality was so dependent on narratives. I was hoping that who won had to do with voters. But given that there aren't so many voters, it may be that we need narratives to create a certain fiction.

SPRING 1995

DINNER AT RITA BEAMISH AND PAUL COSTELLO'S HOUSE

WASHINGTON, D.C.

I was going to Washington as a guest of *Newsweek* to attend my first White House Correspondents' dinner. It would be the first of a few.

Rita Beamish, who was an AP correspondent at the time, and her husband, Paul Costello, hosted a small dinner party for me. Among the guests were Andy Rosenthal, from the Washington Bureau of *The New York Times,* his wife, and other journalists. Paul Costello had worked in the Carter administration.

As the evening progressed, there was an enthusiastic and generous in-doctrination into this place I was about to study. It was stranger than other places I had been, and I could tell the preparation was going to have to be significant. I was faced with an absolute tumble of words at that dinner party, unlike anywhere else I had been. It was a cacophony of voices—long tones, short clipped tones, but all relatively loud and ex-cited. The one with longer tones in his voice took on the role of translat-ing, or filling out the shorthand. The conversation went something like this.

"He's the one who wrote such-and-such about so-and-so."

"Oh, no no, tell her about ————"

There would be a guffaw and then an explanation.

And there were moments that were not so funny. I didn't know the difference, so I could only watch the room as though everyone were speaking Turkish. If they smiled I smiled, if they looked serious, I looked serious. At best I was a mirror of their roller coaster of enthusiasms and feelings.

"Well, that was the grocery store scanner scandal."

"Marlin—Fitzwater . . . ," the one with longer tones started out. He was cut off.

"You know Marlin?"

"I don't know anybody," I said.

"He's great. . . ."

"Well . . . ," someone droned.

"No, he's a sweet man. . . ."

"George Bush and I used to jog together."

Bush jogged with members of the press? I thought.

And there was some pontificating:

"Now you have to understand this. Watergate—changed—everything. You see before that tiiiiiime . . . ," the one with longer tones expounded.

"You need to meet Bob Woodward."

"You think he would talk to me?" I said in partial disbelief.

"Oh surrrre."

"Have you met Jane Mayer?"

"Uh, did she write the book about Anita H———"

"Oh, tell her 'bout Naomi. . . ."

And everyone sort of howled in unison.

"Naomi."

"Naomi Novis . . . a woman who . . . ," one of the ones with longer tones explained.

"Who does she work for?"

"I don't think anybody knows."

"Oh come on, don't say that, she's looking for real information."

"Anyway, one time we were leaving a hotel, and she—"

Someone howled.

"She had *emptied* the minibar!"

"Into her suitcase, see."

"She thought it was *free!*"

And they howled about how someone came after her from the hotel with a huge bill, and she opened up her suitcase and gave all the booze back. Right then and there, maybe even on the bus or on the sidewalk just outside the hotel. . . .

These people live with each other on the road, I thought to myself.

"Oh! Judy Woodruff and Al Hunt. . . ."

"They are the classic, inside-the-beltway couple."

"You know who you should contact," the one with longer tones said thoughtfully, "Jody Powell, who was press secretary to Carter. . . ."

"Well, he's with Powell Tate now . . ."

"That's what I was going to say. . . . He has a consultancy. . . ."

Everybody, it seemed, left Washington and had a consultancy, or went to Hollywood. In the course of being in Hollywood to do *The American President,* I had already come across former politicos.

There was some ground being covered by nods. Sentences being finished with laughs or gestures. Oh, this is going to be one tough study. It'll take me a year just to bone up, I thought.

"You're definitely going to travel on the campaign trail, right?"

"That's the plan."

"I can jot all this down for you later if you like. . . ."

The one with longer tones was the most helpful in the bunch.

Then someone suggested emphatically, "You *have* to get on Air Force One."

"I heard it's really expensive."

"You *have* to . . ."

"I heard it was first class and a half."

"Well the *press* plane is first class and a half, that's what you pay."

"But the press plane is not the same as Air Force One."

"Oh no?"

"No."

"It's not the same as Air Force One."

"And by the way, the press plane is not first-class, that's what you pay, or rather what the news organization pays, but it's not first-class."

"Well, for some of the major networks . . ."

"*New York Times, Washington Post,* ABC, NBC, CBS, they all go first-class."

"But Air Force One is a different story."

"You have to be in a news organization. The pool travels on Air Force One. You know what the pool is?"

"Unless you have friends in high places . . ."

"You must know someone who could get you on Air Force One."

"See, the pool is . . ." the one with longer tones began to explain.

They started to brainstorm about how I might do that. No one came up with any solution, just the suggestion.

"Anybody know where I can find a good gym?" I asked.

A good gym turned out to be *the* hardest thing to find. It was easier in the long run getting in to see Clinton than it was finding a good gym.

Washington is, in every way, an *un*body experience.

I wouldn't know for quite some time just how much conflict there is in that town about the body.

For all the talk of Evian and jogging having replaced booze and smoke-filled rooms, the inside-the-beltway crowd seemed to like to down a healthy amount of booze, eat hearty, and talk up a storm. The first thing I would need is a grant to take care of the lunches, breakfasts, and dinners of my subjects. They liked to meet in fancy places.

FALL 1995
LUNCH WITH GEORGE STEPHANOPOULOS
THE OVAL ROOM
WASHINGTON, D.C.

One of the many people I took to lunch that first fall in Washington was George Stephanopoulos. He told me stories of glory and horror. Of talking to the president about his draft scandal in a men's room on the road, during the campaign. Of how the president in his big health care speech went out to face the nation on television only to find the wrong speech on the TelePrompTer, and of how he, George, had to leave his seat and run to the back to where the technical guy was trying to fix it.

"So he had to give the speech with no text?" I said.

"It's worse than no text. A hundred sixty million people . . . okay, let's not exaggerate, are watching you, and what you're seeing on your Tele-PrompTer is another speech text scrolling by at quadruple speed because the way the guy got through it was to go through the state of the union to get to the health care speech. So he's got two TelePrompTers, one with the state of the union at quadruple speed, while he is extemporaneously giving the health care speech."

I gathered that the first term was full of such escapades.

George is a very personable, charismatic guy. It struck me as we talked that he might know something about Air Force One, if it was really some sort of major sign of the culture, and if so how I should go about getting on it.

"People tell me I should try to get on Air Force One as a part of my research."

"That's true, you should," he said, as we were moving from lunch to espressos.

"Any advice on how to do that?"

"How many big donors do you know?"

BEN BRADLEE

FORMER EDITOR, *THE WASHINGTON POST*

"Off the Stage"

Well, it started with television, right?
It started with television.
These guys, uh—they were really performers long before the,

uh, the press was of the, the scribes.
The scriveners were—uh, uh,
Brinkley—uh,
Cronkite,
Sevareid.
These were performers
and uh, uh, it, it got so that what they said was less important than
how they said it and
the authority that they could, uh, force the public to believe they
had.
And then as we got used to this, as this became part of our culture,
they ceased to be reporters of any kind.
They're not.
I mean, they love to think of themselves as reporters and
occasionally they still can report, but in this wonderful time
when we were downstairs in the city room when Hoffman was
here, Dustin.
And he was absorbing and trying to learn how we all talked and
what the culture of—and, you know, not unlike what, I guess,
what you're doing
and we got the word that there was a jumper.
A jumper means that somebody has gone out a window and is
threatening to jump into the street and off himself.
I said to Dustin,
Would you—yeah, you want to see this?
This is a, uh, a kind of a, uh, ritual story.
Happens twice a year and happens to almost all reporters.
They get to cover it.
So, we went down and walked and it was right around the corner.
We walked a block and a half.
And, you know, everybody's looking up this way and a few people
say, Jump, jump. But mostly just looking.
Then they spotted Hoffman
and the whole audience turned around and looked at us.
Just they all looked at *Hoffman!*
Now, if, if, uh, Dan *Rather* did that, he went to cover a jump,
they'd do the same thing.

They *intrude*—upon the event—and this is why the smart editors
      who taught us wanted us off the stage
because,
uh, uh, you *changed* the event by your presence if you're really a
      performer.
It's a cheap thrill for uh—
I mean, I don't suppose that was such a cheap thrill for Hoffman.
He's been seen a thousand times and oohed and aahed over,
but it sure changed it for the poor bastard who was jumping and—
      he didn't jump.
But—uh, they very seldom jump.
But—and, you know, there's a principle in physics—I have the
      book.
I bought this huge physics book, which is so unusual for me—
called the Heisenberg principle, and—
and that is, if you, if you, uh, split an atom,
you don't end up with two half atoms; you end up with two
      different things.
Observing the phenomenon changes the phenomenon.

A BRIEFING

THE BRIEFING ROOM COULD REMIND YOU OF A CLASSROOM OF VERY smart, very aggressive kids—waving their hands, having the right answer. In this case, they are raising their hands to ask the right question, which in Washington is tantamount to the right answer, because the question inscribes an idea in the public's mind regardless of the response. "Mr. President, isn't it true that . . . ?"

It's a little like the day that a substitute is there, or a new teacher, or a student teacher. It isn't like a scene with a substitute in the ghetto. It's like a substitute teacher in Scarsdale or a community like that. The aggression on the part of the kids would never be physical. No one would turn over a desk, or moon the teacher, or throw chalk, or write graffiti, or spit, or do something sexual, or any of those kinds of things. The aggression would be in the form of the fifth-graders proving, and some of them can pull this off, that they are in fact smarter than whoever is in authority in their normal teacher's absence. And if it's a dynamic with the normal teacher, then they're smarter than the normal teacher is, because the kids are actually spokespeople for their *parents*. The normal teacher is the president, the substitute is the press secretary.

In actuality, the press see a lot more of the press secretary than they do of the president. The press secretary briefs daily, sometimes more than once a day. This is even the case on the road, where they make a makeshift briefing situation by putting together a makeshift podium with appropriate signage. I suppose Christianity was like this in the days of colonialism. Missionaries could do their work anywhere. So this religion of getting and delivering information happens under all conditions. The same is true of "filing." The press get the story in the way the postal service gets the mail through all conditions. I was told that in the old days they had to file over the phone, word by word. Now, computers make this quite simple, but also, they make it dangerously fast. We can get information transmitted faster than we can digest what we've just heard.

Mike McCurry was press secretary when I saw my first briefing. A briefing is not a conversation. It's almost athletic. It's a kind of badminton or tennis. There's a team of thirty against one. They are serving—Mike McCurry, who doesn't have a racquet, either ducks or easily hits the birdie or the ball back with his hand. Six to ten serves come on the same subject matter. At my first briefing, Mike had done ten ducks and hits, and suddenly, from another room entirely, came a voice; it was Brit Hume.

"Oh—come—on—Mike!" he yelled, in a rhythm that sounded like a windup for a Sousa march. He yelled this and came storming in. The briefing room of the White House is a little like a den in a basement. It doesn't have a very firm feel, so when Brit Hume stormed in, the floor and the windows shook.

DEE DEE MYERS

FORMER PRESS SECRETARY TO PRESIDENT CLINTON

"The President's Haircut"

Uhm,
we were in L.A.
and the president uh was previously scheduled to get a
haircut
and rather than go
to

uhm a hotel
or
he couldn't go to a salon
but we decided that we would do it on Air Force One save some
time.
So we got to the airport and he got on the plane
he got his haircut.
We were on the tarmac for quite a while but
when the president
you know then everybody,
Christophe got off
buttoned up the plane
and Clinton did something that he almost never does
which is he walked back
to the press section of the plane.
He almost never does it.
And of course one of the women
because
men would never notice this kind of thing
said
"He got his hair cut!
when did he get his hair cut?"
and um you know I, I, I uh think I, I, I, I can remember just
thinking Oh God I—he got his hair cut yes it was obvious—I
didn't deny that yes he did but I didn't want to get into the
details of who had cut it
but somebody else had seen
him and somebody goes, "Oh yeah I saw that guy. Who's that guy
with the long hair, getting off the plane?" At that point I was
running to the front of the airplane.
Well what really there was a little chirping about it and I
think there was a little item on
one of the reporters there put a little item on the wire,
President Clinton got his hair cut onboard Air Force One blah
blah blah
well then somebody from the FAA told
somebody that

while the president sat there and got his hair cut by this
guy Christophe
that it had delayed air traffic.
So we went back and checked with
they checked with the FAA.
It was a blind quote.
Um
one woman had said that delayed air traffic
we checked with the Secret Service
they said no
um and Christophe is um a Beverly Hills coiffeur, he charges
two hundred dollars for a haircut normally of course
the president
wasn't paying two hundred dollars
but that for some the story got out that all these commuter
planes around the country were you know backed up while the
        president was leisurely getting his hair cut.
So
uh
the next day when I went out to brief
you know you can sometimes sense the uh building momentum of
a bad story.
Um
so I walked out there
and I remember I have to look at the transcript
but I can remember Brit Hume
from
ABC News being very obnoxious and saying
"What is this about Clinton getting his hair cut?"
it may have even been the first question I don't really
remember
and then he started this
with "Monsieur *Christophe*!"

c

LOCKED UP

FROM TIME TO TIME WHILE I WAS IN WASHINGTON, I WENT TO VISIT women at the Maryland Correctional Institute for Women. I had first learned about MCIW when I went there to research an article for *The New Yorker* in their special "women's issue." Frankly, it was a verbal vacation. The language of the inmates was so much more energized and varied than the language of the status quo in Washington. The prison was also a strange relief from the intense masculinity of Washington.

But the prison was a very sad place. The number of incarcerated women has increased exponentially over the last fifteen years. The majority of the women in the prison were black. Many of them were from Baltimore, where I grew up. As they told me about the crimes they had committed, the streets of Baltimore came alive in a new way.

I met a woman who was eighteen who had been imprisoned a year before for murder. She had shot someone nine times, as she told me, "once in the head, and the rest in the chest." Most of the women were there for violent crimes, and most of them had been abused or had violence committed against them. One woman had raped another woman. I was stunned by her logic: "What I wanna rape a old woman for, that woman 'bout fifty years old. What I wanna rape a old woman for? When I got my own girl?" I met a very tight-lipped woman who was in for life. She wouldn't tell me why, but she spoke poetically of how she stopped taking the drugs they gave her and woke up to hear the birds every morning and how she was committed to making this her life. She knew it was her life, such as it is. And I was mindful of the extent to which they had no controls, none at all. Their mail, their gifts would be returned if they weren't sent in the exact regulated way. The warden explained to me how frequently people tried to take advantage of things. I learned the multitudes of ways that drugs made it into the jail, cocaine being "passed," for example, in a balloon, through a kiss. A balloon of cocaine swallowed and eventually defecated out of the body.

What strikes me most about the prison mentality is the degree to which both the jailed and the jailers are incarcerated. The warden and I talked at length. He kept emphasizing how strong the guards had to be. It seems that some of them ended up committing crimes while on the job. They were caught bringing drugs into the jail, having sexual interactions with inmates, doing illegal things in collaboration with people "on the outside" for inmates.

I had been told that the relationship of the president to the press was one of captives. They are captives of each other. I know now that that is probably not an appropriate metaphor. The fact of the situation for those who are incarcerated is that there's almost no way out.

I met eighteen-year-old girls who will spend most of their lives in jail. Lives ruined. I saw the dramatic role play that was going on—of girls who really looked like boys or men. One guard in a San Francisco jail explained to me that, for incarcerated men, sex and sexuality was really about "getting off," and that most of these men on the outside were straight. The women, by contrast, were more interested in creating families, staged families, in which someone was the father, someone was the mother, and someone was the child.

What does this darker side of our society tell us about ourselves? It tells me that, as much as we seem to be addicted to hope, we also give up on people if they are truly on the margins. I once asked a psychiatrist if he knew of anyone doing psychoanalysis in the jails. He explained to me that it was problematic. "Who's the client?" "Who's the client?" comes down to "Who's paying?"

I often thought about the prison when the Clintons became more and more criminalized. I thought about the prison when the Monica Lewinsky story broke. For all the talk of this being a "relationship" or an "affair," it seemed to me to live in the same sort of distorted shadows that housed these "relationships" in prisons. Everything fast, furtive, with the possibility of captivity, entrapment, being caught right there. Sexual encounters in a gym, in the laundry room, the kitchen, or sometimes a female guard backing up to the bars and having sex with a male prisoner. Our president was spoken about in the same way. His every move dissected. The press, like the prison warden, gleeful about the captive. Ken Starr gleeful about the captive. Caught in the act. The graphic act. What did it mean that our president was seen in such a shadow—and seen there in a way that could only be interpreted as pathology?

What was the difference between the guard who made me empty my purse at the prison and the guards who made me empty my purse at the White House? What was the difference between clearance at the prison and clearance at the White House? In the case of the prison, it once took the lieutenant governor of Maryland. In the case of the White House, it always took someone on the inside, who cleared the way. Access on the "bottom" was as tough as access at the "top."

HOMI BHABHA

CULTURAL THEORIST

"Sucking the Toe"

The way in which the clothes of leaders
of public leaders in democratic societies
now
, you know let's think of all the stuff you hear
even today about Clinton's hairdress——
you know hairdresser in Los Angeles airport
yeah
I think it's part of this general system
and I want, I want to just give a range of examples that are
absolutely crucially important in the public view of
leadership.

Jacqueline Kennedy
um um uh of course Princess Diana's
uh vestments
(1997)
so what I'm saying this is not some little airy-fairy idea
but, but in a way
now that we do not mark authority so obviously by clothes and
clothes were the way, the way in which the king's body or the
          despot's body was, was
marked out
we mark it
you know
we, we mark it in terms of fashion
and then the other big thing at the moment
is the enormous interest in the unclothed body
sex
lust
I mean I sincerely believe
that the day well
I half-sincerely believe
that the day in which uh Fer——
Princess D——
Whatever her name is Ferg——
Fergie
you know
the day in which her nipples were actually shown in the press
you know photographs of herself naked
sucking the toe of this American boyfriend of hers
uh that was a major major day there was almost nothing then
in royal authority that was enigmatic or charismatic
but on the other—
so things like a haircut are completely quotidian
every day
it allows for this identification, this immediate
identification
and you know the haircut—
Why has the interest in the body of authority and those who

embody authority lasted so long?
You know the thing about the common person, is uh everyday
life, the details they're just next to you
they could be you?
It could've been you instead of Clinton—
It's, it's your, it's your neighbor
it's the boy or the girl next door
uhm uh and so forth right?
that's the everyday
that's the kind of why
President Clinton's hair or Princess Diana's tampon becomes
so interesting.

THE POWER OF

MUTENESS

DECEMBER 1995
A HOTEL
NEW YORK CITY

I HAD BEEN IN WASHINGTON FOR FOUR MONTHS. I WAS IN NEW YORK for a weekend, and I was having my hair and makeup done for an event I had to attend. The person helping me was in the world of fashion but had gotten some Washington insiders ready for photo shoots. She had also coiffed many a newscaster. (I wonder if Huntley and Brinkley had stylists?) Glamour hits Washington too.

I told her about my project—

"Well, you have to talk to [she named a prominent woman newscaster]."

"She refused to give me an interview."

She continued blow-drying my hair. Then she turned off the dryer.

"Oh, what about [she named another one]?"

"She refused to give me an interview."

"You're kidding."

She turned the dryer back on. Then she shut it off.

"Well, of course you've talked to ———"

"She doesn't want to do an interview."

I looked at my stylist. Suddenly I said, "Oh my God. . . . I just realized something. You're naming all white women."

I thought for a minute. A number of the white women I had approached for interviews either would not talk to me or, after they had talked to me, decided they wanted to be off the record, or at least that I could not perform them in a "show."

"I don't even want to think about this," I said.

"No," the stylist said. "Don't go there."

She proceeded with drying my hair. I lifted my hand. She stopped.

I had an awful memory, and thought twice about sharing it, but decided I would.

The person who scheduled my interviews had gotten into a tangle with one well-known radio correspondent. She said she was not interested in meeting with me and wanted to know who had agreed to meet with me. He named the names of a few people. Two of them were women, and both friends of hers. She said she couldn't believe they had agreed and was going to call them up herself, because she couldn't imagine they would have consented to do this.

We were alarmed when this happened. Even given the task of calling movie stars as well as people who toted guns in Los Angeles during the riots, I hadn't had this particular type of problem. I had always had challenges when it came to gaining access, but I hadn't yet had the problem of women calling their friends and saying, "Don't talk to her." Apparently the decision of this correspondent and her colleague was based on something they had *heard* I said when I gave a (free) brown-bag-lunch talk at National Public Radio a year or so before. Very frightening. I had happily spoken at the brown bag for no fee—it was an honor to have been invited—and I was paying a price.

For my work in the theater, I often use release forms. We had to get a special release form created just for Washington. I still wince about the legal fees.

It's expensive to get people to talk to you in Washington.

The guy in our office who did all the calls felt pretty bad about this and other snafus. We decided that this was not as simple as calling up people as we had in Los Angeles and other places to get interviews.

We ended up having to hire a consulting firm to schedule the interviews! It was clear that we did not know what we were doing, in this very peculiar world. We winced about the consultancy fees. Luckily a firm called Powell-Tate was kind enough and generous enough to take us on for just a nominal amount of money. Sheila Tate and her colleagues generously opened doors that would have otherwise remained shut.

Theaters, which often do plays by dead white men, are not prepared for these kinds of expenses, or this type of risk. This is what happens when you dare to move out of the margins and into another place. I was stunned at my sudden realization that women had been the instigators of this falling apart.

Having been educated at a women's college and an all-girls high school, and being a product of feminism, I was confused by this. I was disappointed.

On the face of it, one might expect that the white women in Washington, and white women in general, would be good collaborators. This is not so, unless they themselves have had a reason to have a variety of cross-cultural experiences.

I was saddened by this. I called the two smartest people I could think of to talk about it. One was Gloria Steinem; the other was Barbara Johnson in women's studies at Harvard.

I talked with Barbara Johnson in January 1998, interestingly enough, just before the Monica Lewinsky story "broke."

We were on the phone, and she started off with: "I think that white women have benefited from the power of muteness."

In fact I had called her in part because I had read an article that she had written in which she gave many examples of the power of muteness for white women called "muteness envy." Perhaps the most riveting idea in the article was that every white woman who was nominated for an Academy Award for playing a mute woman had won. So that something about our cultures likes the "mute" white woman.

"Being *next* to power is more power than any of the other positions that they could envisage for themselves. The fear of being estranged or alienated, standing alone, standing up for themselves, standing out. So if the calculation of white women has been that not being alone maximizes your chances of being successful, not being exposed, not being out there, then it's almost second nature not to want someone to perform your identity."

This didn't entirely make sense to me because, after all, I had seen Cokie Roberts and many others on the David Letterman show. If they were afraid of being exposed, why on earth would they go on a show like that? She explained that on those shows they are speaking for themselves.

"Whiteness in women has always been fragile. That is, whiteness is something a woman can lose. In fact, femininity is something a woman can lose. In fact, femininity is something a white woman can lose."

I didn't understand that. "How can you lose whiteness? It's right there on your skin," I said. "How is talking to me a threat to that?"

She explained that the problem was they had no idea what I was going to do with their identity, with their material. "They wouldn't know what your story *is*," she continued.

"Oh, wow!" I said. "Wow!"

"Being a character in your play means being in a different position in the story than I'm in now. I'm trying to maximize my position, and you want me to be in a different position in a different story? No thanks."

I laughed from relief, not because any of this was funny.

It was quiet on the line for a moment. I thought for a moment before asking the dangerously obvious question. "How significant is my race in this?" I said, and then added, "If at all."

"We're in a weird political moment," she said. "In feminism, to the extent that it still exists, there's a huge prestige factor being in your play or in an anthology that's run by black women. The people who are maybe tied to the story of the presidency or the press may not be in the same moment," she said.

Then she added, "I think it's a moment where your race would play an unpredictable role."

CLAUDIA McCLAIN

CONVICTED FOR MURDER
MARYLAND CORRECTIONAL INSTITUTE FOR WOMEN

"Pretty Teeth"

The warden was basically telling us to watch what we say to you and
I said Well if you ask me I'm gonna tell it like it is.
He called me and Tyboria

um
he said
"It'll be a privilege for the segregation inmates
and I don't feel it's in their best interest."
You could look at 'em and just tell how they're livin'
and how they're bein' treated.
And people said
um you know
well
you know
and I told people
it was like
"Just go tell her the truth"
and it was like you know
whether it's gonna hurt me or don't hurt me
I just had to deal with it.
So yesterday I was telling a couple people I'm goin' up here [to talk
        to you]
because
you know they kept
trying to scare me
talking
"Are you gonna do it are you gonna do it?"
You know
kept axing and axing and axing,
and I said "If I said it once I mean yes"
and they kept
you know axing axing axing like they wanted to change our minds.
The officers
the warden called me back
and asked me that.
So
people said "Well Claudia
we know you're gonna go tell it all
everything you know"
and I said "You're right
because I said we're not dogs

we're still human beings regardless of what we might have done."
[She sits closer to the microphone and increases her volume.]
This is on the record!
We had one girl
her name is Zelda Mitchell [a pseudonym]
she has abscesses
an infection in her mouth.
And this other girl
she just caught hepatitis from the dentist using a dirty needle.
[She bares her teeth.]
But see I have pretty teeth
so I don't have to worry.

GRANDPOP'S NIGGER

THE PROBLEM OF GETTING TO "WE" WITH A DIVERSE CULTURE ON THE one hand and a profoundly patriarchal culture on the other has historical veins that are difficult to uproot. To find America in the presidency, I spent a lot of time getting to know Thomas Jefferson. I tripped over those historical veins. Those veins reach all of us. They are powerful veins. A friend of mine has a huge copper beech tree. It is gorgeous and shimmering and expansive. It changes color as the sun changes its position. Wild turkeys congregate under its expanse. I wonder, whenever I gaze at it, how it manages to pull the amount of water it needs from its roots. American history manages to weave its way into our daily lives in such a way. Sometimes the resulting tree shimmers like that copper beech. Sometimes the tree is not so pretty. In such a way American history has even marked my family.

1979
UPPER WEST SIDE RESTAURANT
NEW YORK CITY

My brother is eighteen months younger than I. He was born with platinum blond hair and blue eyes. People would stop my mother on the street and ask her where she got such a pretty little boy. I think they thought she had borrowed him. We have many colors in my family.

When I was a starving actress in New York, my brother would drive up from Baltimore after he got out of work on Fridays. He would spend the weekend and take me to restaurants to which I could otherwise not afford to go. One night at dinner, we started talking, as we often did, about our family. All of my grandfather's kids, that is, my aunts and uncles, left home as soon as they got through college. My father did not. He stayed in Baltimore and worked for my grandfather. Parenthetically, let me say that my father was the only dark-skinned member of his family. I asked my brother, who was very close to my grandfather, why it was that my father had stayed when everyone else had left. His explanation sent chills up my spine: "Don't you know that Daddy was Grandpop's nigger?"

SPRING 1996
MY WORK LOFT
SAN FRANCISCO

I was waiting for my research assistant, Nora, to drop off some Jefferson materials. I looked out the window, and Nora, who is a very petite white woman with a Louise Brooks type of hairstyle, was striding across the street with one of her classmates—a black woman wearing sunglasses. She had a very full head of hair that extended like a pyramid from her head. They had that "it's finally spring" sort of glee in their stride. Even San Francisco has to recover from cold, rainy winters. The confidence that they had, and the ease they had with each other, across cultures, was something that was nonexistent in my generation of women. They wore their intelligence with pride. Things have changed, I thought, as I leaned out the window to greet them.

As they entered, Nora's friend made herself comfortable without removing her sunglasses. She sat quietly as Nora and I went over a few things about Thomas Jefferson and some new material she had found. I said that I was fascinated by Jefferson.

Nora's friend suddenly broke in, with a kind of drone in her voice. "You've read the *Notes* of course?"

"The *Notes*?"

"*Notes on the State of Virginia.*"

I bristled just slightly at what seemed like the slightest bit of condescension, but quickly let it pass. She was a grad student, like Nora, at UC Berkeley. The conversation proceeded something like this.

"No. I haven't read them," I said.

"They're a must."

"What are they like?"

"I'm mixed about them," she said, as she lounged. "It's required, like reading Shakespeare."

"Oh."

"You can pick them up anywhere."

"But what are they like?" I asked again.

I think she may have said that it was very good prose.

I thanked Nora for her work, thanked her friend for her advice, and they left. For some reason I felt like I was Alice in Wonderland.

I was headed out of town to perform in New Haven. I picked up the *Notes* in a bookstore before I left. One night after a performance, I took them out. My heart sank. Thomas Jefferson was a racist, a *real* racist, and there was no way around that fact. I had known this, but now it was palpable. He wrote about blacks as if they were scientific specimens.

> The first difference which strikes us, is that of color. Whether the black of the Negro resides in the reticular membrane between the skin and the scarf skin, or in the scarf skin itself, the difference is fixed in nature. Are not the fine mixtures of red and white, preferable to that eternal monotony, that immovable veil of black, which covers all the motions of the other race? They have less hair on their face and body. They secrete less by the kidneys and more by the glands of the skin, which gives them a very strong and disagreeable odor. They are more ardent after their female. But love for them is more an eager desire than a tender delicate mixture of sentiment and sensation.

Here I was, after a performance, in a dark, pinkish hotel room in New Haven, where the streets roll up at 10:30 at night, and I couldn't believe what I was reading. I was already down a path that had committed to Thomas Jefferson. We had done an enormous amount of research. I had known, of course, of his contradictions: that on the one hand he wrote the Declaration and on the other hand he had slaves. But this? He had not only a political dilemma with blacks but a "scientific" one. And he went further, to speak of "odor": "They secrete less by the kidneys and more by the glands of the skin, which gives them a very strong and disagreeable odor." All the ideas that we fought so hard from 1950 onward especially to dispel, were right there, deeply rooted.

He went on:

> In general, their existence appears to participate more of sensation than reflection. . . . Comparing them with their faculties of memory, they are equal to whites.

I tried to imagine how he did his testing. Did he do it himself, or did he have others do it? What kinds of tests did he use?

> . . . in reason much inferior. In imagination they are dull, tasteless and anomalous. They astonish you with strokes of the most sublime oratory; such as prove their reason and sentient strong, their imagination glowing and elevated. But never could I find that a black had uttered a thought above the level of plain narration.

Suddenly, the experimental elementary school I went to had another context. When our teachers and our parents fought to show that we could learn as well as any others, they were fighting a battle that Thomas Jefferson himself had helped create. When the white administrators sat in the back of our all-black classroom, they were watching the other side of a boxing ring that had been mounted as long ago as the mounting of the country. We may have been showing that we could do the New Math, but math was, of course, the very least of it. I had known all of this, but to see the *Notes* made it almost too palpable to bear. I was deluged with memories and feelings that I didn't even know I had.

He talked about the talent that blacks had for music but wouldn't concede that they could write compositions.

> In music they are more generally gifted than the whites with accurate ears for tune and time, and they have been found capable

of imagining a small catch. Whether they will be equal to the composition of a more extensive run of melody, or of complicated harmony, is yet to be proved.

The entire twentieth century, with the birth of jazz, would prove him wrong.

He even went further and into poetry—to take from us the possibility of making music of language!

Misery is often the parent of the most affecting touches of poetry. Among the blacks is misery enough, God knows, but no poetry. Love is the particular oestrum of the poet. Their love is ardent but it kindles the senses only, not the imagination.

Then, just as I really thought I could read no further, I read the lowest blow of all, which created for me a sudden suspicion about his motives.

Religion indeed has produced a Phillis Wheatley, but it could not produce a poet.

Why did he go after Phillis Wheatley? Why name names? And a woman who is the pride of so many blacks? I felt nauseated.

His imagination is wild and extravagant, [it] escapes incessantly from every restraint of reason and good taste, and in the course of its vagaries, leaves a track of thought as incoherent and eccentric as is the course of a meteor through the sky. Upon the whole, though we admit him to the first place among those of his own colour who have presented themselves to the public judgement, yet when we compare him with the writers of the race among whom he lived, and particularly with the epistolary class, in which he has taken his own stand, we are compelled to enroll him at the bottom of the column.

I felt nauseated because of that flood of memories. Memories that had been readjusted in a thirty-year public and personal therapy of

blacks, whites, all of us, through study, culture, conversation, and sometimes psychoanalysis. The public therapy, at least, was fairly successful. I
was working on this very chapter in an office at Harvard University, the
W.E.B. Du Bois Institute, where I convene the Institute on the Arts and
Civic Dialogue. When W.E.B. Du Bois went to Harvard, he could not live
with the other students. Now there is a plaque on the site where he lived.
In the year 2000, the study of African-American culture is a solid study in
the halls of the major universities in this country. It was a public therapy
that was going on for most of this century but one that came full blast in
the last thirty years: Martin Luther King to Colin Powell.

Jefferson's *Notes* were an unexpected shock. Not only were they a
shock to my intellect, they were a shock to my entire physical system. I
was just getting to know him, was intrigued by his vast array of interests.
I had gone to the music store to buy a pile of CDs of violin compositions,
because he had played the violin. I was planning my own trip to Monticello. I was treating him like any character I would play. Learning as
much as I can, trying to fall in love with him. And all characters require
that love, whether they are presidents, high priests, or child murderers, or
racists.

But the *Notes*. It was like a fast-moving kaleidoscope that forced the
return of terrible pictures, those "self-images" that many of us had before
the term *self-image* emerged. I realized, in that dark, pinkish room in New
Haven, a city with one of the best hospitals in the world on the one hand
and one of the highest infant mortality rates in the country on the other,
that there are so many people who still believe exactly what Jefferson proposed. Some in the human genome project even worry, politically, about
what further discoveries could unleash in this area. Look at the affirmative action debate, be a fly on the wall in a tenure committee, a hiring
committee, read criticism and even straight news carefully in our finest
newspapers and journals, you will see the descendants of these attitudes.

White feelings of superiority are written in stone, as in our monuments. They are deeply encrusted in our presidency, and our Congress.
They are deeply encrusted in our media. And if these attitudes in the
presidency go back to Jefferson and his colleagues, these attitudes in our
media go back to those times too. While Jefferson was writing his *Notes*,
James Callender was concocting his images of Sally Hemings, singing
them, publishing them in the newspapers of the day.

If down her neck no ringlets flow
A fleece adorns her head
If on her lips no rubies glow
Their thickness serves instead.

It's always hard to see what we're doing while we're doing it. I wonder if journalists today worry at all that a writer or student or scholar two hundred years from now will pull out an archive and read what they have written or what they have said on the air and hold it up as both shocking and rooted in the very problems that cripple us.

What though she by the glands secretes
Must I stand shilly shally
Tucked up between a pair of sheets
There's no perfume like Sally.

"We" is still a long way away. We could ignore history and say that things are better now, or even that mixed-race children are the promise of a better future. But that would be naïve. Sally Hemings was a mixed-race child, in fact she was only one-fourth black. An institution called slavery kept her in her place. We have institutions, subtle though they are, that keep many of us "in our place" and relatively silenced in public discourse.

I was dreading my work. It was going to be very hard to love this man. For actors the real test is the degree to which we can love the characters in spite of personal feelings, in spite of politics.

My disappointment almost immobilized me.

I thought back on the lounging graduate student. "You've read the *Notes* of course?"

Having read them, I decided to proceed. What choice do you have? As Anita Hill told me when I interviewed her, "To the extent that I am at peace here now, it's not because this place has fulfilled the promises that we thought it would. It's because I have fulfilled the promises and faced up to its limitations."

KEN BURNS

HISTORIAN

"Teacup: Regarding Sally Hemings"

It doesn't matter.
He owned her
get the story straight.
I mean he could have killed her if he wanted
he owned her
he could have done anything with her
he could have murdered her
they could have said, "Mr. President, where's Sally?"
and he could have said, "Oh I killed her last night, she displeased
    me," and there wasn't a law in the land that
could have touched him
the fact of whether he did or he didn't
this late-twentieth-century obsession with all things
sexual, titillating, and celebrity driven is an anathema to historical
    truth
he owned her and we forget the fact but the fact that
the man who authored the world's words which we consider our
    creed
held in chattel slavery more than two hundred human beings
one of whom
was a young and we are told attractive and potentially lover for
    him but it doesn't matter
the sexual politics are overwhelmed
by the fact that he owned her.
I like the frisson that comes from
both sides
"Yes of course he could have" "but no he absolutely didn't"
But he owned her goddamn it

that's the point he owned her.
And that's what we forget.
And we go "yes yes yes"
I say "Okay."
"So can I tell you about slavery?"
I said
"How would you like to live
in a one-room dirt-floored shack, fourteen by fourteen, in which you
    work fourteen hours a day?
Unless there is a full moon and then you work more,
you are not paid
you can be beaten
you can be separated from your family.
In fact they changed the wedding vows
for slaves
to read "Till death or distance do you part."
You are susceptible to every known disease of which there is no
    cure—
You are denied the possibility of an education, and in fact
in many instances you would be punished for learning a language
    or having a literature or having a culture.
Now tell me how long you would like to live under this.
I would say a generation's too long
a decade's too long, a year is too long,
a month is too long, a week's too long.
I submit if you were asked to do that
you might try it on for twenty minutes."
That's—
he owned her
you know if I own you
when I say he could have killed her
you say
"Hell yes but he wouldn't have."
His nephews murdered one of his slaves
and that slave's crime had been to break a teacup that had
    belonged to their mother
and there-was-no-recourse-in-the-United-States-of-America.

He's both the blessing and the curse
as John Hope Franklin said—
He ensured that we would inherit the poison of indecision on race
and yet he also wrote us the prescription for the antidote
for the serum that would cure us.
Jefferson said that slavery was "like holding a wolf by the ears—
    you didn't like it but you didn't dare let go."

SLAVES ON P STREET

SPRING 1998
WASHINGTON, D.C.

ONE SUNDAY I WENT TO P STREET, AFTER HAVING BEEN IN TOWN
for the Gridiron Dinner, to say hello to Priscilla and Amo Houghton. I
brought along my mother, sister, and niece. We had a terrific time. My
sister and Amo were chatting away, and Priscilla pulled me to the side.
She had a slightly alarmed look in her eyes.

"Oh, Anna, I went to the library to look at the history of the
house. . . ."

She took me by the arm.

"And, Anna . . ."

"I know, Priscilla," I said. "Slaves."

"Yes!"

I wasn't surprised at all. The house had been there since 1826; it made
perfect sense. Priscilla had now versed herself completely in the facts.

"And the really shocking thing about it was in her will, she left slaves.
She left one male slave, aged thirty-six to fifty-five. I mean, that's quite a
range!"

I felt oddly more at home with this news.

"And she left one female slave, thirty-six to fifty-five, and three—
young—boys. Michael, Henry, and James. She left two to one—"

"She split them up?"

"Well, it sounds as if she broke up this couple. She left this one servant woman, Mary, to her nephew, and then a servant man, Sam, to her niece."

I remembered when I first entered this house, and saw photographs of Amo and his family, and how I ultimately learned that Amo's great-grandfather had owned a big glass company, and they had made the light-bulbs for Thomas Edison. His history went way back—and so did Priscilla's. The documentation about Michael, Henry, and James—I felt like this connected me, in another way, to the house. We are all con-nected, in our ways, to a past.

"So this was really horrifying to me to find that out. Isn't it to you?" Priscilla asked.

My sister was putting her daughter into the car seat. Amo, the Repub-lican congressman, was concentrating on my mother, patiently helping her with her now stiff legs, into the car, telling jokes, filling P Street with his laugh. The slave Mary would never have thought she'd see such a sight, right outside the house. History takes a long time. But it gets there.

DENNIS GREEN, SR.

A DAD, A NONREADER

"Sweepin' the Hallways"

I had one over at 126
who said
"Oh he'll just be another statistic."
And I said What do you mean?
"Oh if he's not gonna read or write, Mr. Green,
you might as well look for him in the cemetery
or in jail."
That's it.
Bottom line
I been up in—
one they tell me at the end of the year

or during parent night
"Your son hasn't been doin nothin."
Yet instead
when I start comin to the school
I see my son
out of the classroom
walking the hallways,
and during lunchtime
he's eating pizza
with
the teachers,
having lunch with some of the teachers.
And this is how he's gotten by elementary school,
not being able to read.
They say, he's
the teachers are saying
Okay, since you can't stay in the classroom come um
come clean the book room.
He cleaned the book room
for three years
three whole years
he went inside of a book room
and just cleaned
and during that time
they said
when parent night
comes they say
Oh
I say "Well how come I wasn't contacted?"
"Oh Mr. Green you don't know what your child is doin?"
I said "No, not if I'm not here."
"Oh your child runs the hallway all the time" and
then some of them would tell me
"Oh you know the assistant principal said
your child is nothing but trouble
and if you watch, if you come up here during the day
you'll see your son cleaning up rooms

or sweeping the hallways.
And he eats pizza with the
dean
just to keep him
quiet
or keep things on the down low."
So I told her I don't believe that.
I did go inside the school
and I seen it with my own eyes—
That's the biggest shocking thing I seen in my whole life.

CREATING FICTIONS

A TWO-YEAR-OLD PROFESSOR

FALL 1998
STANFORD UNIVERSITY

MY NIECE HAD COME TO VISIT ME. HER NAME IS ELIZABETH, AND at the time she was two and a half years old. She and her mother (my sister) were driving down to Stanford with me on a day when I was teaching. They wanted to see the campus. I thought of an exercise for my students, all young actors, that would involve Elizabeth.

"Do you have any Legos or crayons or things like that for Elizabeth?" I asked my sister.

Of course she did, she had a purse full.

"I'd like to use Elizabeth today in an experiment in class."

Her mother was all for it.

I entered the class—Freshman Acting. Their optimism and idealism was in stark contrast to the weary cynicism that hung over the more advanced students.

"Today we have a visitor. Her name is Elizabeth Allen. I would like you to observe her and take notes. Then I'll ask some of you to mimic her behavior. The great British director Peter Brook tells us in his book *The Empty Space* that the hardest thing for an actor to portray is a child."

They all eagerly got out their notebooks and pads and took places around the edges of the playing area. I walked Elizabeth to the center of the playing area and sat her down. Her mother carefully put down some crayons and some Legos.

Elizabeth began to draw, and she did so with an amazing amount of concentration. It will be much less relevant twenty years from now when she looks back on this, that she sat in a room alone at two years old being observed by nearly all white grown-ups, or people who in her eyes would have looked like grown-ups.

Was I repeating the scenario at James Mosher Elementary School, when the white throng of educators came to watch us learn?

No. With Elizabeth the situation was different. It was I who was watching, and I was actually watching my students as much as I was watching her.

Suddenly she dropped her crayons and covered her eyes.

My students looked up from their notebooks. Until that point, they had been steadfastly taking notes on every single breath she took. Everything was still, including Elizabeth. I looked to her mother for a clue. She merely shrugged.

Then Elizabeth began to move her hands away from her eyes and back, in peekaboo style. She repeated this several times. My students returned to their note-taking. No one laughed. They took it quite seriously.

Then Elizabeth stopped everything and looked at all of them carefully. Finally she did a very surprising thing. She roared at them. When she got no response, except one laugh, she roared again, longer and more ferociously, like a tiger.

I thanked Elizabeth for coming to our class, and she and her mother left to tour the campus.

I didn't ask my students to mimic Elizabeth. "Originally I wanted you to use this as a life study—but Elizabeth has been an even more valuable model for us than I thought. She has taught us something today about the position of any people who find themselves having to deal with the pressure of the gaze. It is totally abnormal for any of us to stand in front of many, alone, and to be observed. Yet performance and leadership require that. I think you figure out your relationship to being observed when you are very young. Elizabeth is only two, yet she already had a strategy to deal with the anxiety that your silent gaze could have caused. In your presence she became a tiger, which is her favorite animal, and to her it is a ferocious animal. In order to gain power over the moment, she roared at you, not as herself, but as a tiger. This allowed her to stay with you on her terms."

Elizabeth had created a fiction. Her fiction was not a lie. It was a persona. It was a tool that gave her power over us, and allowed her to speak to us, in fact it allowed her to roar, and thus to rule the room, for a moment. She caused the students to stop what they were doing. It was the single moment when they looked up from their pads, in a quandary. Was Elizabeth a tiger? No. Was she lying? No. She was presenting herself "as if" she were a tiger.

What we keep forgetting is that when a public person presents a persona, he or she is simply offering "It's as if I were." That "It's as if I were" is an invitation for us to begin to behave "as if we were" a group. That "as if" is very important for civic action. We are living with the death of metaphor. The media with their high-powered microscope and their incredible capacity to create metaphor behave as though they both love and hate metaphor. They build metaphor, but they insist on the literal, the mundane, the everyday. They take heroic events and try to make us feel as though these events can fit neatly in our living rooms.

Most humans adopt a persona in order to interface with the society around them, no matter how large or small. A person who is caused to move in a large and diverse society must develop a persona that is resilient, and perhaps more complex than, for example, that of a person who has developed a persona to operate in a small town where everyone is the same, and everyone knows everyone. These fictions, these personae are necessary for public life.

Perhaps these fictions are the clothing for greater truths, truths that such an individual accumulates by moving in and out of safe houses of identity in order to be effective in a larger, more complex society. That fiction is a kind of a bargain between the public figure and his or her public. The media seem to be particularly ambivalent about these fictions. On the one hand, they help create them. On the other hand, they are always trying to get under them to "find out exactly who this guy, or this woman, is." The danger of this was revealed most dramatically in the story of Mayor Rudolph Giuliani. Do we really want a society where personal confession goes that far in public? When we dig under a persona to find the "real person," we may not find the real person at all. There are also fictions that are useful to all of "us." These fictions should be allowed to blossom. The most effective fictions are those that allow many people to convene around them for good cause. The most destructive fictions are those that allow many people to convene around them for bad cause.

PLATO: A SUSPICION OF THOSE WHO CREATE FICTIONS IN THE NAME OF ART

....

FALL 1996
WASHINGTON, D.C.

NOW YOU'RE INVITED TO THE TABLE IN
WASHINGTON AND EVERYBODY LOVES . . .
AREN'T WE GLAD TO HAVE THEM AT THE TABLE
AND THEY SENT OUT A LIST AND EVERYBODY
KNEW AND THE NEXT DAY THEY SAY, CAN YOU
BELIEVE THAT STUPID FUCKING STREISAND?
WHO THE FUCK DOES SHE THINK SHE IS
TALKING TO COLIN POWELL ABOUT BOSNIA, YOU
KNOW? WHAT IS SHE, THE SECRETARY OF THE
FRICKIN DEFENSE, YOU KNOW. WHO IS SHE?

—*An Anonymous Man*

I wondered why there was such disrespect for actors in Washington and thought it might be a symptom of something else. The scholar Judith Butler told me that, in order to understand this, I had to go all the way back to Plato. So I called a woman named Shadi Bartsch, who, I was told, was an expert on this kind of thing.

Knowing in advance what my problem was, she had marked out the relevant passages in Plato's *Republic*, Book 10, Section 604: "Here he talks about theater and poetry as all being tainted by the fact that they're at this third remove from reality. Then where theater is concerned, he goes one step further and he says it corrupts people. It corrupts the human soul."

It *corrupts* the human soul. I had always thought that theater was *good* for the human soul.

"Why does it do that? Because it appeals to the baser instincts like pity and anger and grief and all these things, but it does so in a context where these emotions are not justified. We're weeping or we're rejoicing as we're watching something that's not truth."

This was giving me a horrible feeling, and I had that same feeling in Washington. It's that hopeless feeling you get when you know that people are really closed-minded. What a sweeping thing to say about art, but who in the world was I, who am not a philosopher, to question Plato.

"In other words we're warping our souls," she concluded. "In Plato's view."

We are *warping* our souls with theater and poetry?

LOGIC, ETHOS, PATHOS

FEBRUARY 1997

BELLAGIO, ITALY

I packed up everything I had gathered to date on the '96 campaign and in the two years leading up to it. I had a monthlong fellowship at a center that the Rockefeller Foundation runs to provide a workplace for artists and scholars. The setting is an extraordinary villa and grounds that sit on the shore of Lake Como. I was there working on the first stage version of this project.

I was told tales at breakfast of how John F. Kennedy had been to the villa. Apparently he had come to Italy to see the pope and for some reason was diverted and had to spend the night. The point of the story, however, was that (supposedly) an Italian movie star had spent the night with him.

One night at dinner, I found myself sitting next to a very warm woman named Ann Vasaly, from Boston. She was a scholar of antiquity. One of her specialties was the rhetoric of Cicero. Given my desire to understand what I had heard and not heard on the campaign trail, I pumped her for every bit of information I could get.

"There's a way of analyzing rhetoric that comes from Aristotle. He divides rhetoric into sources of persuasion: One is *logos,* which is $2 \times 2 = 4$, you know, the rational form of persuasion.

"And then there is *ethos,* which is extremely important. It's how you present yourself within the speech, what kind of person you become within the speech as it's given."

I asked her to watch some Clinton speeches I had on video and to define for me his rhetoric. I had videos of the two speeches that, by 1997, were considered to be among his best. One was the speech he gave after the bombing in Oklahoma City, and the other was the speech he gave at Ron Brown's funeral. She said she would.

"The third source of persuasion is *pathos,* which, of course, Plato said is the heart of the corruption of rhetoric, because when you move people emotionally, they cease to analyze and instead go along with all sorts of things simply because of that emotional involvement."

Later that week we watched the videos. Ann explained to me that Clinton is all *ethos* because his effectiveness is so dependent on how we feel about him at the moment. I was surprised that he was not *pathos.*

So it's not so much that Clinton made us "feel." It's that he made us feel *about him.*

I have come to the realization that the most powerful fictions are the ones that cause people to convene around them. The fiction then becomes more potent than the author. So it is with the president. We don't have a thoughtful, vital citizenry, and that's not only because the man may not be up to the task. The fiction is not up to the task. The president is only a man who inhabits the fiction. We as a nation can be a part, and we are a part, of creating a better fiction. We just need the space and tools to build it. The pundits, the governors, the media owners, the politicians, the lawyers need to give us the space. Or perhaps we have to show them how much we really want it.

Recently in performances, I was learning to be there *with* the audience rather than to be there *for* them.

1994 (JUST AFTER NELSON MANDELA WAS ELECTED
PRESIDENT IN NEIGHBORING SOUTH AFRICA)
ZIMBABWE
A PHOTOGRAPHIC SAFARI

The most gorgeous part of the safari was when we sat near the watering hole about midday, to see the many species that would gather. But during the rest of the day, we would sit in our Jeeps and watch all the animals, from many species, come to drink the water. The grace of the animals was unlike any piece of art I had ever seen. The giraffes bending, the birds, and finally the flock of elephants who seemed to glide from a long distance. There was room for all. The lion was not there. The lion eats at night, and, with very little work, maintains its place as king. Because nobody preys on the lion.

It would be wonderful if modern civilization could make a watering hole. If we could find some way to create even a fictive one that would allow us to convene and partake of the same thing, each one of us, regardless of our type. The president would ideally be that fiction. A man or woman would play the part of convener—and we could dress that man or woman any way we chose. The most important qualification would be that this fiction must have room for all.

As for going to watch the lions eat, well, it's a whole different feeling. Some of the people on the safari were most excited about that. The guides would tell us stories of kills they had seen just days before. The feeling was—how lucky we would be if we got to see one too.

During the day we sat quietly on a hilltop not far away. At night, while going to find the lions, we would ride slowly for a few moments with the headlights off. And stop. And wait. And move. It was furtive. Our observance. We were hushed, and the guide was hunched forward over the steering wheel. After all, we were in pursuit of the *king* of the jungle. We are waiting to catch him in the act, any act.

Many people assume that political life is theater. The theater is created to illuminate a truth. What truth is our political "theater" illuminating? True theater is not only text and subtext—it is a vast mélange of contradictions and paradoxes, associations and disassociations.

Is it indeed true that the press is the audience for our "political theater"? Is this informing what our theater is? Would the theater be different if it had a larger, more diverse audience? Would our theater look more like the watering hole and less like the guide crouched over the steering wheel of a Jeep furtively moving through the jungle at 2:00 A.M., stalking the lion, who stalks his prey?

MICHAEL DEAVER

Everyone talks about how Reagan was an actor. And they usually do not mean it as a compliment. They may be suggesting that he was a "fake," an "imitation," but an imitation of what? Would Plato have had a problem with Reagan, the actor president? Yet something about our culture embraces that which is "imitation." So much of how we run our lives in a society of mass production is in "imitation" of something. How far are we from truth as Plato would have thought truth to be?

Michael Deaver is the man who is credited with creating the image of Ronald Reagan, and with bringing "visuals" into the White House. He added a lot to "photo ops" as we know them. He now works in a consulting firm.

"I never worried about what Ronald Reagan said. Other people worried about that. And I really never had to worry about what he did, because he was a pro. And I really never changed any belief he ever had, because I couldn't."

What *did* Deaver worry about? He worried about how Ronald Reagan looked. Reagan had taught him that "the camera doesn't lie," so he believed that. It was all for the camera. He talked about the "tape" Reagan walked onto. By tape, he meant the mark on the floor upon which Reagan would stand while talking.

"And one of the things that I always strived to do with Reagan was that when he walked out to the tape, Ronald Reagan knew that that was going to be the best-dressed set he'd ever been on."

"How did you dress the set?"

"First of all, sound and lighting. I mean, lighting is the most important part of it. Ronald Reagan was a guy who was seventy-five years old, so you wanted to light him from the top of his head down, because what you'd do is you'd get the light to bounce off that wonderful head of chestnut hair, and you'd wash his face of wrinkles."

I was amazed at how open he was with all this information.

"If you lighted him either straight on or from down below, he'd have looked eighty-five or ninety years old. I used to kick the press photographers when they'd get down on their knees in front of Reagan and tell them to get up. If you want to take a picture of Ronald Reagan, you do it straight on; you don't do it from down below."

I was curious about how he knew to do this, and why he knew it would matter to the public.

Michael Deaver had grown up in a small town. His father, who worked for Shell Oil Company, had the nicest piano in town. He made a deal with the piano teacher—that the teacher could use their piano to give lessons if he gave lessons to the Deaver boys for free. It was a deal. Although Michael's brother was the one the lessons were meant for, it was clear to the teacher that the real student was "this little guy who stands around and watches during the lessons." Ultimately Deaver can play whatever you could hum. He knows what something needs to sound like. He said that his knack for knowing what something needed to look like came from the same source.

Deaver was onto something very important in our time. We live in a visual, not an oral rhetoric. He could compose ideas about the president by making a series of pictures of him.

1998

GRIDIRON DINNER

I was sitting in the midst of many journalists. Their motto is, "The Grid-iron singes but it never burns." The journalists do skits about the events of the year where they dress in drag and sing lyrics to the tunes of songs in Broadway hits. The president tells jokes too. When Clinton came to the podium, a hush fell over the room. Then I looked at the faces around me. There were three hundred and sixty degrees of intense gazes. These gazes were like laser beams. They were killer gazes.

All the examples that I have given are about watching. When the journalists were watching, it was as if they were trying to see *through* Clinton. The relationship of the eye to the subject is off balance. They were looking for something in his physical being, a tic perhaps, a slipup of some sort, perhaps he would drop something, do anything out of the or-dinary that would show him *up*.

They wanted a slip that would reveal more about Clinton and Monica Lewinsky. After having studied language and body language intensely for the last two decades, I have come to the conclusion that it doesn't always tell us as much as we think it does—particularly if the subject is used to being scrutinized.

The president is assumed to be in a planned physical state. That planned physical state is called, in the minds of those who observe it, an act. They think that the president is always acting, that he is in a constructed reality.

SUMMER 1996
RHETORIC LESSON
FAIRMONT HOTEL
SAN FRANCISCO

I am at breakfast with Hayden White, professor of rhetoric at the University of California at Santa Cruz.

"So, you see, association of images is the rhetoric to me, what image you put together with what other image."

"Okay."

"So, I think that's what rhetoric has to do with now, the association of a politician, not with a particular cause—but with another image."

"Yes, sure."

"Or several images."

So it's not about words, it's not about facts. It's about something else. It's about associations.

The age of the image as rhetoric would seem to follow right out of a time when commercials are more a part of our culture as artistic expression. And advertising is all about associations. But what happens when that technique of creating associations is used not only to get us to consume, to buy? What happens when that technique is the very lifeblood of how we learn to think about our process, how we learn to think about our American identity, our civic identity?

White said to me, "People identify democracy with the free market. This is what all the commentary on the elections in Russia has been—a triumph of democracy. It isn't; it's the triumph of capitalism."

"I see."

"The assumption is that the free market and democracy go hand in hand. If you buy into the free market, you have to take a certain amount of unemployment, a certain amount of exploitation, a certain amount of corruption, and so forth."

"Interesting."

"It has nothing to do with democracy."

"Oh?"

"I mean, that's been the greatest triumph of Western capitalism—it's been to identify democracy with the free market."

FALL 1995

MICHAEL DEAVER

There was one time when this idea of picture making backfired.

While he was president, Ronald Reagan made a trip to Germany for the fortieth anniversary of the end of World War II. Michael Deaver was responsible for organizing the logistics of the visit. The plan was that Reagan and West German Chancellor Helmut Kohl would have a photo op at a cemetery where soldiers were buried. This was to be on the theme of reconciliation.

Deaver went in advance, did some location scouting, and found what he thought was a wonderfully picturesque cemetery. He asked the chief of West German protocol and someone from the American embassy to check out the graves. As it turned out, there was no cemetery free of SS soldiers. They were buried all over Germany. Reagan was advised not to go to the cemetery for the reconciliation "scene." But he was adamant in spite of many vocal people, among them Elie Wiesel, expressing their dismay.

So, they went ahead with the plan. The plane ride itself seemed more somber than the graveyard.

"We were flying from Bonn to Bergen-Belsen that morning, and I mean to tell you it was somber on that airplane. Nancy was all dressed in black. She had said to me, 'You've ruined my husband.' So it was a terrible, terrible time." He concluded with, "*Newsweek,* of course, you know put Waffen-SS flags on the graves for their cover story."

Mixing images can be chemical. It's hardly that images are not strong. The adages all tell us that a picture says a thousand words. The only problem with reliance on the picture, particularly the photograph, is that there is no command really. There is not the opportunity to add breath into the mix. There's not the opportunity to stand in the moment and change the moment with the power of your own diaphragm, your own voice, your own power.

Michael Deaver, who brought movie lights into the White House, told me that at the end of the day, he would go into the East Room and play the piano because it allowed his soul to come forward.

MARLIN FITZWATER

PRESS SECRETARY TO RONALD REAGAN

"Ronald Reagan"

It sounds like that's description of a lack of intellect, or a lack of
    knowledge or whatever.
But having been there, I never saw it that way with Ronald Reagan.
If he got into an argument with Gorbachev, for example, and
    Gorbachev would talk about a 1925 chemical weapons treaty
President Reagan was a little chagrined with himself that he didn't
    know about that
and he knew
it didn't matter.
He didn't really want to know about that.
He didn't want to know about
how many bombs
we're going to allow on B-52s under this new treaty.
Is it ten bombs versus fifteen bombs?
Is it five nuclear warheads per bomb? Is it three nuclear warheads
    per bomb?
He says, You guys solve that problem.
My job is to see that it's done.

Reagan had this kind of instinct for knowing how to push big issues
    and big ideas.
And the mystery
that everyone is still wrestling with—
Did he know
that he knew how to do it?

METAPHOR'S FUNERAL

CIRCA 1959
1312 NORTH BENTALOU STREET
BALTIMORE

FOR MOST OF MY CHILDHOOD, I LOOKED OUT ON A GRAVEYARD. MY desk was by the window, and across the alley behind our backyard was a cemetery.

There was the sight of the graveyard, and the sound of the train. The train went under a bridge that was a half a block away. The graveyard looked like the end of the universe, but the train sounded like eternity.

I didn't find out until I was an adult that my parents were the first blacks to move in on our side of the street. I always remember it being an all-black neighborhood, so the whites must have moved out very fast. By the time I was able to understand such things, most blacks were trying to move out of the neighborhood I grew up in, and to find housing in a pre-dominantly Jewish area in another part of town. We did eventually move from our first house on Bentalou Street to one of those predominantly Jewish areas, and my mother still lives in that house. That neighborhood is now an all-black neighborhood.

Behind Bentalou Street stood a graveyard. We would ride our sleds down its hill during the winter, but other than that we didn't really venture in. There was a No Trespassing sign. The lady who lived next door, Mrs. Johnson, was a friend of the caretaker, and once a year, we would walk with her into the graveyard and to the caretaker's house, which was in the middle. He and his wife were white. They had a grape arbor, and when it was time to pick the grapes, they would prepare several bags full for Mrs. Johnson. She would make grape jelly and pass it out up and down the block.

These trips with Mrs. Johnson into the graveyard were memorable. First of all, because as far as I could tell we were "trespassing," and nothing bad happened. They were also notable since Mrs. Johnson, weighing in at over four hundred pounds, never walked anywhere. Very occasionally she would be driven to church, but most of the time she stayed placed on her porch, or in her kitchen, and we would go to see her. On these occasions, we were quite a parade. The caretakers of the cemetery were likely the first white people I ever visited in their home.

One afternoon, something happened in the graveyard that brought all of us on the even-numbered side of the 1300 block of Bentalou Street to our back porches. It was stunning enough that we all stopped what we were doing.

Whenever there was a funeral, most of us, especially the kids among us, would take note. It was as if whites suddenly invaded the neighborhood. In addition to this being a white graveyard, it was a Catholic graveyard. This was before the sixties, so nothing about the pomp and circumstance of the Catholic Church was yet watered down—the priests wore elaborate hats, burned incense, and spoke Latin. True, there were surely black Catholics somewhere on our street, but most of us were Baptist, Methodist, or some other kind of Protestant.

So across the way, one would see an almost Felliniesque grouping of whites, some in robes, standing outside the dramatic entourage of cars, which had slowly pulled down Bentalou Street, turned the corner, and driven up the very slight hill of the cemetery. This particular funeral was nearly over, a lone car pulled up the hill, and the alley and our backyards burst open with the sound of a woman wailing. I can remember watching this and having chills go up my spine. Everyone from my family except my father, who was working, gathered, from whatever disparate parts of the house or surrounding play areas they had been in.

We watched a funeral of someone we knew nothing about, and yet we were saddened. We didn't know what exactly was going on. But somehow, through the grapevine, we were told that the wailing woman had come from out of town, and had missed the funeral of her father. She had to be held back from the grave. We watched as she was taken, by each arm, back to her car.

It was also an important moment because, in spite of what I was learning about "white people" and how different we were, I could imagine the circumstances, and I felt for that woman.

I came back to that sixties expectation that education is the answer to racial strife and inequality. The idea was that, if we were all educated, if we all learned our ABCs, we could all have the advantages of the American dream. My education was a product of that idea. *Along with that,* as a bonus, an important bonus, was the notion that, having gotten *to know* one another, we would make a better, more equalized society. But as we watch affirmative action burn at the stake, as we watch the numbers of incarcerated people of color climb, we have to ask, what happened?

Education gives us more facts, more evidence, but it does not give us empathy. The proof is staring us right in the face. What profession of people are thought of as the *least* empathetic of all? The media. And they have the resources to *know* everything. In fact, perhaps they know too much to be empathetic.

I suggest here that knowledge will *not* save the world. We have shrunken hearts.

In those days when I stood on the porch, I had perhaps more empathy than I have on this day, with a terrific education. In those days, when I was standing on the back porch, and watching those few white people who came to the graves of their loved ones, my curiosity was enormous. My *desire* to know them, to be among them, was enormous. And when I stood on the front porch, and looked up and down the even side of the street, at all those black folks—or looked across to the odd side of the street at all those white folks, my heart was an open heart. Education did not make me a more empathetic person. It made me a tougher person. It helped me develop a persona, it taught me how to fight, but it did not "open" me to the world. I was born with a certain openness. Life has caused me to resist those things that through the process of education would shut me down.

And, from the looks of it, many of my colleagues, educated as they are, do not have healthy hearts. They may have healthy hearts for those closest to them, but it is difficult for them to imagine the pain of the other.

These very people, who can pay big bucks to go to the theater, or to see other works of art, talk in a vocabulary of "what they identified with," what they "personally connected with." It's rare that they can reach beyond what they can identify with to *feel* for the other side. America needs heart surgery.

1996

LOBBY OF THE ESSEX HOUSE HOTEL

NEW YORK CITY

I have just returned from a magnificent dinner with Studs Terkel, at a "joint," as he called it, named The Crocodile. We have been out all night. Studs has had much more to drink than I could ever handle, and yet, in his eighties, he is wide awake and telling me stories as we sit on a huge sofa in the lobby. And this particular story, of all the stories Studs has told me, stands out as one of the most important. If there is ever a genuine, real funeral for metaphor, Studs should give the eulogy.

He told me the story of his friend Bill, a blues singer, a black man who sang the blues and who laughed when he was angry. And one time Studs was the emcee when Bill was singing the blues.

It was a story about a mule that had died, it was a song called "Plow-hand Blues," and Studs said that it was "a long wail of a blues, like a Spanish flamenco, a *canto hondo,* a deep song," and "Bill's guitar cries out like a human voice"—"this incredible moment" and "just at that moment, these two kids, one black and one white, in the audience, got up and scraped their chairs and walked out, disdainfully." And Studs was furious— he was furious that they ruined Bill's song.

And Studs says that he said to Bill, "They ruined your song those bas—— they ruined your song." And Bill of course laughed at Studs's anger, and Bill said, "What do they know about the blues? What do they know about a mule? It's a horse-and-buggy song to them. What the hell do they know about a mule dying on 'em? This mule died and it was a tragedy for me or my father, but they don't know anything about mules."

Bill said, "It's like me and the bomb." He said, "What do I know about a bomb? They had it in Europe, Italy, Germany, and I saw the rubble, and I saw people crying when their houses fell down, but what do I know?"

And then Studs said to me, "Bill raises the big question, that may answer everything you're searching for!" And he said, "And Bill said, In order to *sing* the blues you have to *experience* it." And so Studs says, "If that's the case, if you have to *experience* the bomb, if you have to *experience* it to understand it, then we're in for it! Do we have to have a bomb fall on us?" he said. "Must our mule die on us in order for us to experience the horror of it?"

Knowing, experiencing, witnessing, is limited in its reach. Just because you "know" doesn't mean you are "of." In fact, there are ways to be "a part of" without direct experience. With all our potential to be brought "up to the minute," many of us are not "a part of."

RICK BERKE

THE NEW YORK TIMES

"Fondling Breasts"

I think, we've always hated sex, these kinds of stories. We've
    always been last. From the beginning, there's a host . . .
It was like a hundred years ago, we just had to . . .
We've always stayed away, the Gennifer Flowers stuff,
the Gary Hart, we've always been the last,
and we've always been very uncomfortable about it, in not
    knowing how to deal with these stories or what to do with
    them.
Sometimes we've been, waited too long, when they've become
    stories that were unavoidable.
But I'd rather be last than stoking the whole thing.
So we've seen a lot of changes in what the *Times*,
because of this scandal,
of what the *Times* would write about, would cover.
I remember covering, I covered, the Thomas-Hill hearings.
And I remember thinking,
Do they put pubic hair on Page One? and, you know, penis, and
    all this?

Because we'd never, like, gone there before.
And I thought that was, like, new ground,
you know, however many years ago that was.
And then I find myself last year writing about oral sex in the *Times*,
on the front page, fondling breasts, and things that I never thought,
you know, my God,
the *Times* would never have touched. So we're very uncomfortable
    with these kinds of stories.

POLICING

W<small>E HAVE BOTH VISIBLE AND INVISIBLE VIOLENCE NOW. THE IN-</small>visible violence is the mean-spiritedness, the lack of forgiveness, the lack of interest in rehabilitation, the numbers of black men and now women incarcerated all across the country. At the *Vanity Fair* Oscar party in 1999, Tom Hayden told me that the biggest supporter of political campaigns in the state of California is the union of prison guards. He told me this just as they were announcing best picture. I was so shocked I missed the announcement.

Cynicism, wit over wisdom, and the prevailing mean spirit entertain us, but at what price?

FALL 1998
SAN FRANCISCO

I began to think that there were reasons for us to fear the media. I was having coffee in a Noe Valley café with Jim Risser one morning. Jim is a Pulitzer Prize winner who runs a journalism program at Stanford called the Knight Fellows. I asked him what he thought about our fear of the media.

"It used to be said that you have no reason to fear the media unless you've done something wrong," he said calmly.

I said, "Well gee, that reminds me of when I was a girl, growing up in segregated Baltimore. When I told my mother I was afraid of the police, she said, The police are here to protect you, you shouldn't be afraid of the police unless you've done something wrong."

He suggested that I ask the Knight Fellows myself.

I met with the group. The Knight Fellows are professional journalists, representing news organizations from all over the world, who take a year off to study whatever they like at Stanford. I asked them, "Should we be afraid of the media?"

The general consensus was "You should be afraid of the media. And if you're not afraid of the reporter him- or herself, you should be afraid of the conglomerates who run the media."

Where are we if the media themselves think we should be afraid of them?

Sometimes when I see how the press treat people, I find myself thinking about the police and the press in a similar light. Neither is a uniformly bad institution. But they do not always use their power responsibly, and there's not a lot we can do about it. Nobody monitors the media. When asked about that, some of them bristle and say, "We monitor each other." People have been fighting police brutality vigorously for forty years. How many citizens' review boards are there, and how effective are they? What can we do to get better media? Just don't buy the papers, people say. Just don't turn on the news. I think that's not a good enough answer.

Both the police and the media represent fairness and unfairness, justice and injustice, and both have the power to practice brutality should they choose to.

SATURDAY NIGHT, NOVEMBER 1995
THERESA FENWICK HOUSE
WASHINGTON, D.C.

I came back to the Houghtons' house on P Street in Georgetown one Saturday after having been out at the Maryland Correctional Institute for Women. I'd stopped off to have a swim on the way. It was fall, and at 6:30 or 7:00 it was dark out. I tried to open the front door. The inside chain was on. This was strange for a Saturday. I thought that perhaps my assistant, Marcos, was upstairs in the office working, but I couldn't remember having asked him to do anything that would keep him working this late on a Saturday. I took a few steps backward to see if lights were on. There were no lights on on the third floor. On the other hand, there *were* lights on in a section of the house across the garden. I knew for certain that the Houghtons were away for the weekend, so this bothered me. I took out my cell phone and called Marcos to see if he was, in fact, upstairs in some way that I could not see from the street. He was not.

I went in through the garden gate, entered the house from the ground level, into the kitchen, and called the police. I explained that I was a guest in the house, that I had returned home and found doors locked in an unusual way, and lights on that shouldn't be on. I worked through the monotoned responses of the 911 operator, who did not seem to be listening at all.

"No, I'm saying that this is *not* my house, that the people who live here are *away*, and there are *lights* on in their house. . . . I'm a *guest*. . . . Well, I'm afraid to go upstairs. . . . Look, this is a congressman's house, it would seem that you would at least . . ."

Finally she droned that she'd send someone by to take a look.

"How long do you think this will take?" I asked.

"There's a lot going on tonight. They'll be there as soon as they can, ma'am." She sighed.

I had visions of sitting in the garden till dawn. I was very tired, and contemplated going to a hotel. But if I did that, and they were destroying the Houghtons' property—or stealing something . . . No, it was clear. I couldn't leave.

It seemed like I had barely hung up the phone and the police were there. Relieved, I went to the garden gate and opened it. Much to my shock, I found myself looking into a semicircle of about a dozen police officers with guns extended toward my face. I had never looked into the barrel of a gun before. The barrel was bigger than I would have thought.

But no sooner did the guns register than they started a very loud chorus: GET BACK!!!! GET BACK!!!! GET BACK!!!!!

My heart started racing. But this was a misunderstanding.

Somewhere, I found the wherewithal to strive for clarity. I thought if I was reasonable, they would be reasonable.

"Actually, I'm the person who called you."

They didn't seem to hear me, or listen.

The officers were all of different races, women and men. As I stepped

forward, they shouted again: GET BACK! GET BACK! GET BACK! GET
BACK!

I tried to explain: "I'm a guest in this house. This is Congressman
Houghton's house. He's away and there are lights on that . . ."

I looked around for a neighbor. The streets were vacant. Not that I
knew anyone on the block anyway.

They lunged closer, bringing their guns even closer to me. GET
BACK! GET BACK!! GET BACK!! GET BACK!!!

I moved forward a little and tried to talk to them, one human being to
another: "I'm just trying to protect their property I'm afraid there's
someone in the—"

GET BACK! GET BACK! GET BACK! GET BACK!

I decided to give them all I had—I put my hands up, began to back
up, and said in the vocal intonations of a confession, "Okay. Okay. Look,
I'm afraid of you. I'm afraid of you! No really. I wrote a play about the
police. You remember Rodney King? I'm afraid of you. I'm afraid. Okay?
So I'm terrified. You've really frightened me."

This time they didn't shout. They were still for a moment. There was
a Latino woman who kind of glanced at the black man in the middle. He
glanced at her but looked quickly back at me. I continued: "You know,
Congressman and Mrs. Houghton are humanitarians. I'm their guest. I
can only *imagine* how they will feel about this."

One of them, the tallest one, who was in the middle, a black man,
stepped forward. They put their guns down. He said, "All right, miss, just
calm—down."

I continued, with more things that I had on my mind, now that I had
their attention: "Here I am trying to be responsible to this property, and
you pull out your guns before finding out a *thing* . . ."

The tall black man was about to lead me into the house as the Latino
woman and an Asian man went to the front door.

"Hey!" I shouted. *"Don't break the door down!"*

They ignored me.

"Look, miss, just—relax," the tall black cop continued. He reminded
me of a physical trainer I had had years ago in San Francisco.

"They can't break the door down! This house is a historic *landmark*." I
moved about, up and down the street, frantically looking for the plaque
that said THERESA FENWICK HOUSE.

"They have to get into the house if they're going to help you, miss," he said, as if he were talking to a child.

"Well, why can't they go in through this way?" I pointed to the kitchen door.

They immediately scurried down the path and into the kitchen. Another crew of them scurried over to the side that the Houghtons lived in. They all seemed like animals, or let's say the animal side of their nature was what I saw. I stood in the street and looked up at the house as their flashlights reflected through the windows. More police cars pulled up.

"My God," I said, "did they send out the entire precinct?"

Then it dawned on me. Well it *is* a congressman's house.

The Asian man officer and the Latino woman officer came out through the front door. "It's all clear."

"How did the inside get locked?"

"I couldn't tell you," the tall black policeman said.

We went into the kitchen, because he wanted to ask me a few questions. As he finished he said, "Now, miss, I want you to understand why we did what we did."

"I know why you did what you did. I was moving forward, and when you screamed, 'Get back,' you wanted me to get back. I wasn't hearing that. All I heard was that you were treating me like a criminal, and I wanted you to know that I was the one who had called you."

"Look, miss . . ."

"So once I stepped back, you put your guns down, but if I hadn't stepped back you probably would have shot me."

"Now, miss."

"That's how people get killed innocently by the police," I continued. "You know we don't know what you know. We didn't go to your school. The only reason I knew to step back was that I had done some research with the Oakland cops, and I know that first you make noise, and then you shoot."

"I just wanted you to understand . . ." and he continued to do "public relations," I suppose because it was, after all, a congressman's house.

The fact is, they did tell me to "get back" and I didn't understand it. They were very literal. I was on the metalevel of right and wrong. And I didn't trust them enough to do anything they were telling me to do. I was so shocked by the guns. I immediately went into a mode of trying to convince them of my innocence. I had an increased understanding of what black men had been telling me all my life.

It took me weeks to get the feel of those gun barrels out of my system. And I thought, If they had shot me, the real story would never be out. All kinds of people would have been brought forward to paint a picture of me as someone who deserved being shot, and another side would have painted a picture of a tragic loss.

Having observed people dealing with the media, and using "confessional" behavior to get them around to their side, I used the vocal tones of a "confession" to bring the police to put their guns down. "Okay. Okay. Look, I'm *afraid* of you," I had conceded. "I'm *afraid*." It had worked, but for days, weeks, I would still see those guns, smell those guns, and feel as I did then, that I was close, very close to something that could have gone another way. Thinking about fair and unfair, right and wrong when they're standing there with all their might and power won't help.

Although we live in a society permeated by media, most people do not, actually, know how to deal with it. And when it happens to them, it's very surprising. I suppose it's like sex. You see it in movies, you see it on television, it's in music and in magazines, but until your first time, you really do not know. And when it's your first time, you're on your own to put the pieces together. It helps to have a decent partner.

I went inside after the police left. The phone rang. It was Priscilla. "I got your message. *Anna,* what's going on?"

I decided not to tell her about the cops and their guns. I knew she would worry.

I told her about the door being mysteriously locked. I had been so caught up with the cops, I had almost forgotten that the door being mysteriously locked was what had started the escapade.

"Oh!" She laughed. She explained that the handyman always chain-locks that door no matter how many times they tell him not to.

Thanks, Mr. Handyman, I said to myself, for causing me a traumatic experience.

There are a variety of ways to keep us back. For folks who are really stuck, in the bottom of the system, those means permeate their lives. We like to believe that America is about fighting your way up and that you can make it with tenacity and brains and guts. That is not true. There are actually many, many ways to keep people back. Not all of us will have to deal with policemen, drugs, abusive mates, and much more. But in the finer and more refined circles of our society, infrastructures do keep many people locked in. Some people don't even know they are locked in until they try to move. Often we are happy to stay exactly where we are. But when you move, you are vulnerable.

GET BACK!!!! GET BACK!!!!! GET BACK!!!!!!

I was also chilled by the realization of how dangerous it is that we actually learn very little about what citizenship requires. If the police have certain techniques, and we don't know what they are, we could literally be dead. The police, like many professions, exist in their small circle. For those of us who have little reason to interact with the police, we end up as strangers in their land; that is, when they make our land their land.

The media are one of those instruments that can, from time to time, keep people back, inasmuch as they perpetuate some aspects of American identity and obliterate others. It's like we are in a state of house arrest. Stay exactly where you are.

SUMMER 1997
NEW YORK UNIVERSITY LAW SCHOOL

I am talking about freedom of the press to a legal scholar at NYU, Bill Nelson. The conversation drifts to policing. I had asked him what the first police force was in America.

"I think the New York City police force is the first police force in the United States, and it's the early eighteen thirties. The London police force is a couple of years earlier than that," he answered.

Nelson had several books out to help me understand a very peculiar time in the earliest days, during Thomas Jefferson's time, when James Callender, a journalist, had gone to jail for things he had written about then President Adams.

"Now, is it true that the London police force was created . . . Apparently they weren't there to fight crime," I offered.

He finished my sentence: "But to keep the lower classes in their place."

"Right," I said.

"That's a big, that's a big job of police at all times. I mean, I think to be realistic about what police do, that's a big job of police forces at all times. That's what the New York City police force mostly does now, right."

"Are you speaking as a lawyer or a historian?"

"As a historian. Friday night. We had dinner with some friends. And, uh, I had in fact gotten a parking space right here, and we walked to the car, we got in and we drove, and shortly before we got there, the police decided to set up a barricade to check out drunk drivers. This was about ten-thirty Friday night. Uh—so I finally got up to the front and he asks me, had I been drinking? I said, Yes, I had two glasses of wine with dinner over the last couple of hours. Uh, and, uh he asked to see my li—— do you have a license? Yes. He asked to see it, and I, by mistake, uh, pull out an NYU ID card, and he says to me, Oh that's not a license, it's an NY—— an NYU ID card. Go ahead. I can't help but think that the police, you know, it was a very polite, nice policeman, but he's dealing with an older white guy who clearly is on the NYU faculty, fine, we'll let him go. He's certainly not gonna treat a nonwhite person that way."

There are current brutalities of the police force against brown and black men. They don't seem to go away. Even when we see the images of them. Even when they are obvious.

Billy clubs and guns are not the only instruments we have in our society to keep people in their places. There are more subtle ways that this is done. The neglect of the educational system, of public schools, in a culture that professes to believe in knowledge as a cure, is the most obvious way.

In Washington people are kept in place in a subtle way. But seemingly small things could have been warnings for what was going to happen to the president.

Washington is a place of organized seating. It is very important to keep your place. If you are not in the club, then you must accept your fate. If you are in the club, you must behave a certain way. In the course of my time there, I saw people misbehave and get their hands slapped. Small slappings in a generation that was hungry for another Watergate.

I didn't know enough to take sides in Washington. I couldn't read the "text" of the place well enough. I only knew broad strokes. My intuition, however, did cause me to pause when something seemed out of balance.

JOE KLEIN

I questioned what happened to Joe Klein when it was discovered that he was the "Anonymous" who wrote *Primary Colors*. Why—is—this—such—a—big—deal? How does it really affect the quality of our lives?

It was before daylight, and I was down in the Theresa Fenwick kitchen making coffee when I opened the papers and saw that Klein's confession was on the front page. It happened just as the '96 campaigns were taking off, and people were in full sweat about the matter. I heard very passionate explanations: "He *lied*. I mean, my *God*, if you're in the press you're not supposed to lie, it gets to the very base of what we *are*."

The fact is, most of us don't believe the press tell the truth. Nevertheless, we believe, and quote what we read as truth. It's nonsensical. It can only mean that we have given up on truth, and only pass information. We're in the "know," but we know that we are not in the "truth."

I called Judith Butler, scholar of rhetoric, to get her take. "Well, I think it has got to be the media's infatuation with itself, in part. You know, they do think they are the center of the world, I think it is maybe the media feels that it was—that it had a hoax played on it, so what it can do now is turn on this guy who clearly has broken ranks with them."

I thought the Joe Klein event was a warning, a warning of what was going to come like the day of the locusts with Clinton and Monica. And for those readers who don't care about Clinton and Monica, it's possible that Clinton and Monica warn us of things to come that we will care about. We will need the media, and they will be off in a language of their own, making their own sets of small slaps, unable to understand us.

ELLEN DeGENERES

Then there was the story of Ellen DeGeneres.

Every year there is a big dinner, called the White House Correspondents' Dinner. It is black tie. News organizations invite celebrities to be among them. The president attends. It's in a huge ballroom at the Hilton. There are small cocktail parties before, and parties after. There is a parade of celebrities with the usual suspects, Annette Bening, and Warren

Beatty. Sharon Stone, George Clooney. *Vanity Fair* usually gives a party. The party that *Vanity Fair* gives after the White House Correspondents' Dinner is a lot like the party they give in Beverly Hills, at Mortons, after the Academy Awards. Sometimes it gets very confusing. For example, just after Clinton brushed by conviction by the skin of his teeth, I went to the *Vanity Fair* Oscar party. Monica Lewinsky was the star guest. She seemed to get at least as much attention as, if not more attention than, that year's best actress, Gwyneth Paltrow. She was surrounded by people I had met in Washington—correspondents from major news organizations and former White House staffers.

Graydon Carter invited Ellen DeGeneres to the White House Correspondents' Dinner in 1997. She came to the dinner with her girlfriend, Anne Heche. This was just before she was to "come out" on her sitcom. Her attendance at the White House Correspondents' Dinner was regarded by many as a publicity ploy.

In the course of the dinner a comic performs, and Clinton makes a speech. It is expected that the president will be funnier than the entertainment, and sometimes he pulls it off.

At a certain point in the evening I noticed that the people in front of me were not looking at the stage— they were looking at something else, and their mouths were hanging open. I turned to see what they were looking at, and I saw two women with their arms around each other. Apparently they displayed more affection than many thought was appropriate. Before the dinner, Graydon Carter was looking straight ahead at the stage, while his guests, Anne Heche and Ellen DeGeneres, were causing quite a stir.

This went further when Graydon Carter took them upstairs to a room in the Hilton to meet the president, and they approached the president with their arms around each other. People from both camps—those who want the sexual status quo to remain soundly heterosexual, and those who fight for gay rights—expressed displeasure. After all, it was a "photo op."

Their behavior, and the general response, did not surprise me. What did surprise me was the following editorial in *The New York Times:*

> After all the hype and exploitation surrounding the actress Ellen
> DeGeneres and Ellen Morgan, the woman she plays on tele-

vision, it was easy to lose sight of what actually was taking place on ABC last night. The "coming out" of the title character on *Ellen* was accomplished with wit and poignancy, which should help defuse the antagonism toward homosexuals still prevalent in society. . . . Unfortunately, Ms. DeGeneres was not immune to exploiting the situation, most notably by her ostentatious display of affection with her lover in front of President Clinton at the White House Correspondents Dinner last weekend.

I understood the text of the editorial, I just didn't understand why an editorial in *The New York Times* would take a moment to refer to her behavior at a dinner that most Americans know very little about.

I did the rounds of asking people to explain to me why this was such a "big deal." One of the people was Paul Costello, who had worked in press relations for quite some time in Washington. He put it this way: "Talking about something Washington can't handle at all. Sex. Any kind of sex. But gay sex? It's just not part of the game, it's just not part of what you do. Washington is a town where you don't talk about foibles, you don't talk about depression. . . . You only talk about strength and manipulation and Machiavellian points of view, you don't let on weakness. It's the most unsexy place, it's the most sexless place in the world."

Okay, so the trespass was a trespass into sex, and sexuality. Still, this is the nineties, we're liberated. I called Judith Butler. She put it this way:

"I mean, it doesn't strike me as gay pride in its finest hour if that's what you're asking me. I mean, I think it's a scream! And the fact that people got so worked up about it is the most interesting part of this. I suppose that people who consider themselves liberal and tolerant in their everyday lives, who nonetheless, people who think [laughing] that you're not supposed to do it in front of the president, think you shouldn't be doing it in public.

"It's okay if that's what you do if you do it in private and they love feeling liberal and tolerant about that. But to do it in that public a setting and in front of the, the symbolic authority of the nation—is really to not have any shame at all."

Counting on a sense of shame is a kind of policing too. But this gets tougher in a diverse society, where that sense of shame begins to disappear in some lifestyles. It may be that the "freer" we get culturally, the more other kinds of restraints begin to appear.

I then went to the Condé Nast building on Madison Avenue, and went into the offices of *Vanity Fair* to talk to the host himself, the editor, who had invited Ellen and Anne to the party. For him it was all fun. When I asked him about the *New York Times* editorial, I felt like some kind of a fuddy-duddy.

"Oh fuck them," he said dismissively as he took a drag of his imported cigarette.

Although he gave the best party in Washington, he himself had never been invited to the White House.

"I've never been invited to the White House, and if I was I wouldn't wanna insult them but I probably wouldn't go."

"Really."

"Well, you know, it's the most uptight place in the world. I'm sure it's a perfectly nice place to live, but I'd be too terrified, it's too built on power."

As I left his very elegant office at Condé Nast, I questioned why he dismissed power, as if he was not himself a prince on a mountain of power, power in the fashion world—a world that affects many more people than Washington affects them. Psychologically, at least, the world of fashion has a greater presence in our everyday lives. Yet in reality, decisions made in Washington have a tremendous effect on how we live our lives. Many of us know more about hemlines and hair color than we do about candidates for office. Graydon Carter is powerful, and his power looked like a heck of a lot more fun than the power I saw in Washington.

There was also the issue of simply how artists are regarded in Washington—which of course has ramifications with regard to how the arts are thought of in this country. We are the only superpower in the world, and we do not support the arts. We do not have financial support and we do not have intellectual support. There is a lot of media about controversy, and there is media about art with celebrity participation. That media goes hand in hand with advertising. There is little or no attention paid to the people who work very hard in the arts because of a series of beliefs, either in the health of their art form or in the health of a community that benefits from the arts. There is ambivalence about artists in Washington. We are still seen, as Rousseau and others saw us, as derelict.

The media are a part of bringing us into the public eye. And when they bring us in they put us in a "place." To move from one place, that is, to move from what is assumed about you, to another place is very hard to do. People who don't seem to be in any one place are very hard to police. Clinton was said to have had a hard time because it wasn't clear "where he stood." Our culture is in transition, even as we know change is inevitable, those who communicate and define culture put up a series of dams. But Congress and the media lately, and in the Lewinsky-Clinton scandal, showed how ineffectual their dams are.

Policing is the protection of property. The status quo is a kind of nonphysical property, which is policed by nonphysical means.

JAMES CARVILLE

"Herd Mentality"

So what!
I mean sure.
But, but see
again
I wasn't put here
to
agree with these people.
I'm not put here to dislike 'em.
I like 'em.
I love
they wonderful
they nice parents
they're very bright people
terrific table manners
they're charming
they witty
they just wrong
that's all!

See the problem is if you think differently than they think they attack
    you
it's only one way to think
and that is the way that they think
and I think it's a shame.
This is my question.
As I understand
that, that
in, on rough terms is that the national media, the media here in
    Washington
they are people who are supposed to be more knowledgeable
in
and closer to the situation than the rest of the people in America
and as such it's their job to inform people what's going on.
I mean
I think that's a reasonable hypothesis
we have a free press in this country.
If so many of them were so wrong
it's my job to tell the American people about that.
It's part of their mission
here is to be right about these things.
They all
make
and they should, they make
make nice salaries
they got nice offices
they have access they go to the right parties
they talk to the right people
they have access and everything
and if they're consistently wrong
then
somebody gotta sort of say
it.
See.
In any other endeavor in life
you will suffer
public humiliation

for you being wrong
any other endeavor
you make the stock market
you make the right investment
you get to add a room to your house
take a trip to Hawaii.
I'm going to Bob Woodward's house tonight
who is a lovely man
as is his wife
Elsa
and they have a
wonderful home in Georgetown
and I'm sure that he sells
millions of books
and you know what?
He should
He was right about a big thing
he has reaped the rewards of that
what about all of these reporters
who were all dead wrong about Whitewater?
The media is the only business that I know,
okay?
That suffers
no penalty for being wrong.
It's, the herd judges itself,
and the herd exonerates itself all the time.
And anybody who criticizes the herd
the herd turns on.
Ask me I know.
They called me a buffoon and this and that.
I criticize the sort of mentality.
I think that what Washington needs more than anything is people
that think different than they think.
I guarantee you
that there are fraternities that have more diversity of thought.

SWINGING

I. THE PRESS AND PRESIDENCY
PROJECT HEADQUARTERS

We WERE IN FULL GEAR. THE ARENA STAGE THEATER, WHERE I WAS in residence, didn't have enough space for our headquarters. We'd outgrown our office there. They rented us a two-bedroom apartment across the street, and we turned it into command central. The empty apartment I walked into in June, with its smell of freshly laid carpeting, eventually housed an enormous amount of activity. These headquarters would end up housing all of the activities that put me on the campaign trail, and all of the activities that would lead to the productions of the play *House Arrest*. Production would follow my journey on the campaigns. It would start as a place that was centered on phones and faxes, and end as a place that was centered on turning four hundred audiotapes into what actors needed to "become" the people I had interviewed. By the end we would create, out of those four hundred audiotapes, ten thousand audio tapes as part of our editing process.

The first team was diverse. Nora, a graduate student in history at Berkeley, was already onboard, and by now had read a library's worth of books. Marcos had been with me in Washington since the first day; Andrew came to us with an interest in history and theater from Amherst; Erin was from Yale. Matthew, a former student of mine at Stanford, who I'd talked into coming to work for me on this project, was born again. He did advance work. Cori was a sensitive poet, who had been a student of mine. She did research. The office was run by Kitty, who was the daughter of Washington politicos. With a background in radio research for Ken Burns's films, her job was to organize and think up the vast range of activities that would entrench me in the campaign of '96. Lynette ran my life from D.C. Others came in and out during the summer and fall. Shawn, a law student at Yale, created dossiers on people alive and dead.

They managed together to make for me an impressive but grueling schedule. It involved going on the Clinton and Bush campaigns, preparing for and attending both conventions, writing for *Newsweek* at the conventions (I had never done political journalism before), going to the presidential and vice presidential debates on both coasts, traveling with Jesse Jackson, going to the "border" in El Paso, Texas, continuing to do interviews of Washington media and White House figures, going to the South to visit churches that had burned that summer, helping with fund-raising for the project, and doing other, tangential things—like visiting Willie Horton in prison.

There were no "down" days between June and election day in November. They had to cut through an enormous amount of red tape to pull this off. They also had to prepare me intellectually for everything that was about to happen. They read books, dug into the Internet, and created a mountain of dossiers. They also chased potential interviewees with the vigor of terriers. They got me "in." None of them was an "insider." Powell-Tate, a consulting agency, generously helped us knock on doors in the fall of '95. We couldn't have done it without them. But basically this motley crew of people freshly out of college in theater, and in history, with no campaign experience, created a schedule for me that was as if I myself was campaigning. It was the hardest work I had ever done, going on that trail and writing about it.

Watching without being soundly in an organization whose business it is to "watch" is hard work. Theaters are not in the business of "watching." They are in the business of "presenting," and usually that presenting is done inside a fairly safe place. It is safe because the risks that theater artists take are usually aesthetic ones. We don't normally face the public until we are "ready." The Arena had to turn itself around in order to do this, and it did. I did too. I was basically doing my work in a setting that was not safe at all.

My schedule—some of it being with the press corps, some of it on my own—looked something like this:

July 19 Atlanta—opening ceremonies of the Olympics

July 21–23 West Coast trip with president—flew with press corps

Denver,

Los Angeles,

Sacramento

San Francisco

July 25 Greensboro and Tuscaloosa, Alabama, attended revival meeting
     for a church that burned in June; Birmingham, Alabama

July 26 Atlanta—Return Olympics

July 27 Columbia, South Carolina, St. John Baptist Church, visited small,
     two-hundred-year-old black church that had burned

July 28 Greeleyville, South Carolina, visited Mt. Zion AME, which had
     burned

July 29 Library of Congress, Washington, D.C., research on past
     conventions

July 30 Fund-raising, Washington; Preparation, Schlesinger interview,
     Library of Congress

July 31 Meeting with Michael Deaver; Preparation, Schlesinger interview

Aug. 1–3 Research, listening to recordings of radio coverage of past
     conventions, Library of Congress

Aug. 4 Interviewed Osborn Elliott, former editor, *Newsweek,* Century
     Club, New York City

Aug. 5 Interviewed Arthur Schlesinger, Cote Basque, New York City

Aug. 5–9 Screened television coverage of past conventions, NBC. Other
     convention prep

Aug. 9 Joined Young Republicans train to San Diego in L.A.

Aug. 9–16 Republican convention, San Diego

It was an adventure. When you're on your own, you have to create
your own advance team.

II. SWINGING WITH CLINTON

I went to visit Ann Lewis, the deputy campaign manager for Clinton in
the '96 campaign. In the midst of the flurry that accompanies a campaign, I was surprised to find her with pearls around her neck, seated
calmly at her desk, with an elegant porcelain dish of fruit on the guest

side of the desk. There was a knife on the plate, and one piece of fruit had been cut. It looked like a still life. I imagined that the pearls, the containment, the fruit were all a kind of centering device. She told me that her strategy for press conferences was to be like a fifth-grade teacher.

"I concluded what I wanted to remind people of was sort of the best fifth-grade teacher in school, the one that all the parents wanted their kids to go to, because that was somebody that—because that was somebody whose word you could depend on or you could believe. She had authority, but she wasn't threatening, and that's who I try to be."

Lewis told me about a trip to California in late July that the president was making and suggested that I try to get on it. I had *Newsweek* credentials, because I was going to be writing for the conventions.

So Kitty went about getting permission—sending letters and making phone calls, until we finally secured authorization, from another very pleasant woman, named Ann Edwards. Kitty took care of the security clearances, and of course billing. The trip would cost us $3,300 for airfare and about $400 for hotels. Kind of an expensive trip to California, considering the fact that the press plane is coach class (except for the bigwigs— *The New York Times, The Washington Post,* et cetera, who fly first class). There's a lot of hierarchy in press travel, and in the briefing room, with the major networks and the *Times* and *Post* getting first dibs.

I went over to *Newsweek* to get briefed by their White House correspondent Bill Turque and by Tom Rosenteil. We also spoke to David Broder, a friend at *The Washington Post,* to find out who was flying for the *Post.* He told us about Kevin Merida, who was "a great guy."

So the day that I was headed out on this "swing," Nora and Kitty came over to the Theresa Fenwick House on P Street to give me my final marching orders before I set off for Andrews Air Force Base. They were very excited. I was very nervous. We sat down at the kitchen table. Nora had in hand a couple of huge dossiers, just in case I was able to do an interview or two. "Like the president," for example? she suggested.

"There's no way that's going to happen," I said.

The idea was that I could use all that time I had on the plane to bone up, just in case an interview with the president came up. We knew that whenever that interview happened I'd have to grab it, and be ready.

Kitty planted an itinerary on the table, right next to Priscilla's bowl of angel cards.

12:30 P.M. Depart P Street for Andrews AFB
1:30–2:30 Check-in, Andrews AFB
3:15 Wheels Up, Press Plane Departs for Denver
4:45 Press Plane Arrives, Denver AFB
Remain Overnight, Brown Palace Hotel

The idea was, I would travel with the press and the president from Denver to Los Angeles to Sacramento and San Francisco. I would leave the press and the president in San Francisco, and have one day at home to prepare for my trip to the South. I would then leave early in the morning (like 4:00 A.M.) to go to Birmingham, where I would visit one of the churches that had burned, and head from there to the Olympics, and onward to South Carolina, where two other churches had burned.

Kitty had lists of people's names, and all sorts of backup plans.

I felt like I used to feel on the morning of an exam, without the adrenaline. Midsentence Kitty looked down at her pager. "It's the White House!"

Nora seemed thrilled by the news. "The *White* House!"

I was starting to have a feeling I knew all too well. It wasn't a good feeling. It was a feeling I associated with a kind of pressure to perform. Even though I was going on the press plane as a "mere" observer, there was something about it that was not just like your normal plane ride. Your normal plane ride, by the way, is not without stress—you have to make sure that you have your ticket, your driver's license, and that you are ready and alert at every turn: at security, that you check all signs to make sure everyone's given you the correct information, et cetera.

But this, with all its details, was more complicated. It wasn't the pressure to perform, say, on opening night on Broadway. Perhaps because it was about being with a group of strangers for several days. Also, opening night on Broadway, or performance at any time, gives you the anticipated release of "it's over." This would be three days of hoping nothing went wrong, and moving in a territory I did not know. I had signs already, from my previous months in Washington, that this was not a summer camp atmosphere, to say the least. I was having a flashback, for some reason, to those days at Elementary School No. 144 when the white people came to watch us learn. But *I* was doing the watching this time, so what was the problem? Well! Maybe the problem was that I was with a planeful of journalists. I was reminded of being on the safari in Zimbabwe. Sleeping in a tent, with the danger of lions lurking.

Kitty was jotting down notes as she talked, presumably to a Clinton staffer. She wrote on a piece of paper, so that Nora and I would know what was happening:

"Ann Matthews"

She moved the paper toward us.

Maybe the trip was being called off. No. It didn't sound like that.

The Sunday papers were on the table. I glanced at them. The previous week a TWA jet had crashed. They still didn't have very much information.

Kitty was getting more and more specific. Her conversation went something like this. "And what will she be able to observe?" She was writing notes. "Uh-huh, uh-huh."

Kitty put down the phone and gave us a long, intense look. There was a pause. "You can get on Air Force One."

I seem to recall that Nora screamed out, or gasped, in a way that you would think of as an eighteenth-century way. She was in her early twenties, but she used expressions like "Heavens," always with the slightest sense of irony. Nora was laughing.

I did not laugh.

"Woah, woah, woah," I said. "Air Force One?"

Kitty nodded.

"I am not prepared to go on Air Force One," I said.

Prepared or not, it seemed to be in the works. "How did that happen?"

"Ann Edwards volunteered it."

"Just like that?"

"Our office did not broach this at all at this point."

"Because I thought the idea was we were going to wait to get some 'big donor' that we might know through the grapevine to get me on Air Force One. That's what George Stephanopoulos said I should do."

It seemed to me that both Nora and Kitty had kind of now-or-never looks on their faces. This was more than I'd bargained for. I was having enough trouble with the press plane part of it, and now Air Force One. I felt very in the dark.

It's interesting, when you work with people you begin to absorb their desires too. Since the day I arrived in Washington, press people had been saying to me, "Oh, you have to go on Air Force One." I didn't know how I felt about it. It was beginning to feel "mandatory."

Kitty simply continued giving me instructions. The official pool reporter on this trip for the newsweeklies is from *Time*. Pool reporters travel in the press "pool" to events that are not open for the entire press. They then report to the rest of the press through something called a pool report about what happened.

"The *Time* reporter is named Jeff McAllister. All you have to do is check with him and see if he'll let you take his seat on Air Force One for a short leg of the trip."

"But why would he do that?"

The doorbell rang. "I'll get it," Nora said.

"It's no big deal. They do it all the time." Kitty was speaking quickly.

It's in moments like these that I tend to speak very slowly. "I don't get it."

"That's what Ann Edwards said. Just let her know if you decide to switch with Jeff. For security reasons, she will need to know if you are going to switch with Jeff."

Nora came back downstairs. "The car is here."

"What else did she say?"

"Most of the events are private fund-raisers, which won't even be open for the pool to observe."

I didn't like the way I was being given this information at the last minute. The call had come from the White House literally as I was leaving. To be perfectly frank, at that point I would much rather have spent the night at the Maryland Correctional Institute for Women, in the cell of a child murderer, than sit on Air Force One. I knew a woman who had allowed her boyfriend to murder her daughter, actually, and from time to time I would talk to her, either in her prison or on the phone. Given what she'd been through, she had a very philosophical view of life that I rather appreciated.

That's a bit of an exaggeration, but I think it is accurate to say that if I had been able to get clearance to spend the night in jail with a child murderer, I would have felt a lot like I did before leaving for the press plane. It's a feeling of dread and fear that one might have before crossing boundaries. I say all of this to admit that, for all my talk about coming out of safe houses of identity, it is not easy. It is not comfortable. How much nicer it would have been to spend the afternoon in the garden, and go out to dinner that night, or even take the shuttle to New York, than to go on this campaign "swing."

"So, that's what the White House said I should do? Ask this guy Jeff McAllister?"

"Yes."

Apparently this was something that was done all the time. Even news organization interns did it, I was told.

Kitty and Nora walked me upstairs. I went over all my gear. Cameras, computer, clothes, itineraries, dossiers, David Maraniss's book. I locked up the house, got in the car that was going to drive me to Andrews Air Force Base, and waved good-bye to them. They looked awfully cheery as I pulled off down P Street.

I was the first to arrive at Andrews. Very military. I was about an hour and a half early. Kitty had given me enough time to get lost twice. The room that I waited in was rather nondescript—large tables, chairs. From being in the briefing room, I had developed a caution about sitting down. Even though I was the first one there, and all the seats were empty, I was worried that I might sit down, unknowingly, in somebody else's seat.

One by one the photographers, cameramen, and writers began to show up in the waiting room. I noticed that all of the photographers and cameramen were carrying or wearing rainproof outerwear. As people arrived, they sat alone, usually, read the paper. It was a fairly quiet place. I noticed here and elsewhere that no one read the paper "idly." They all seemed to read it with a sense of purpose, as though they were looking for something specific, the way we in the theater read reviews.

Air Force One was on the ground, as was the press plane. I tried to get a photograph of Air Force One, but I couldn't fit it in my frame. I noticed a very outgoing, rather upper-class-looking woman with short hair and a red jacket and a baseball cap that said TIME. I had noticed her before in the briefing room. She was a photographer.

III. THE PRESS PLANE

I boarded the press plane. All of the seats have white pieces of paper on them, with the names of publications. Nothing is random. I looked for the seats marked *"Newsweek."*

"But which *Newsweek* seat shall I take?" I asked someone who was in charge. "Any one." This made me nervous. I knew from a ballet I worked on with the Alvin Ailey Dance Company that seating—where a dancer sat on a bus, for example, or where she stood in class—was not to be tampered with. I figured the press would be the same.

I sat in a *Newsweek* seat. A very tall, rather good-looking man got on the plane. He was one of the *Newsweek* photographers. He was looking around for where to sit.

"Is this your seat?" I shouted out, already rising.

"You're fine. You're fine," he said.

After a while Joe Klein got on. I wondered how it must feel for him to be among these folks, many of whom were hostile to him. After the plane took off, I saw that there were more seats in the back, and I left my seat to find a place to stretch out.

This was just like any other plane, except they brought us more food. I had already decided that the safest strategy was the Audrey Hepburn Seafood Diet: "See food. Don't eat it." I wasn't going to eat anything on the plane, except coffee and whatever wilted lettuce and shredded carrots they brought by from time to time. But as for the Chicken McNuggets, the sirloin tips, I was glad to be a vegetarian.

I was sort of napping, and the woman photographer I had noticed before came over. She introduced herself. She was literally the only person on the plane who seemed outgoing in that way. "Diana Walker," she said, extending her hand. She began to talk to me while standing by my seat. She had apparently covered presidents since Carter for *Time.* I wondered if she were the sort of unofficial welcome wagon. She was very elegant, and very nice. And very funny. In the course of the trip, a moment on the bus here, another moment standing at security there, I would get a picture of a very interesting person. I gathered that she lived in Washington, grew up there, was married to someone named Mallory. She seemed "established." Had gone to Foxcroft. Fancy boarding school. For the greater part of the first conversation, she stood in the seat behind me and talked to me over the back of my seat.

I mentioned to her that I was to talk with the reporter from *Time* about taking his place on Air Force One. In a way I was floating the idea.

"Oh, Jeff! He's a great guy," she said. "He'll let you do it."

"But why would he give up his place on Air Force One?"

"It's no big deal."

The plane landed in Denver. We got off the plane and had to get on a bus on the tarmac that would take us to our hotel.

I spotted Todd Purdum, with whom I had dined and spoken several times. He was very well educated, was given to quoting Yeats in the middle of, say, an otherwise uneventful explanation of the day-to-day work of a journalist. I congratulated him on a huge piece he had done on Clinton in *The New York Times Magazine.*

"A group of us are having dinner tonight, want to join us?"

"Sure," I said.

There was a very friendly looking aide—named Kris Engskov. He sounded like he was from the South, or the Midwest. Our conversation went something like this. "Miss Smith?"

"Yes?"

"I was told you wanted to go on Air Force One?"

I wondered who told him. I reiterated what I already knew.

"Jeff's a good guy. He'll let you do it."

Everybody kept saying that Jeff's "a good guy."

We got to the hotel and went to our rooms. Our luggage was delivered. On the one hand, this is simpler than other kinds of travel because they do everything for you; on the other hand, it's odd because you have no control. I imagine the army would be like this.

I met Todd and his friends for dinner. The anxieties, the ennui, the general air of the work to do, the work to be done, permeated things. These were people who wanted to get it "right." This felt nothing like "Boys on the Bus." It seemed uptight.

IV.

The next morning we all went to a speech about "deadbeat dads" and then traveled on to Los Angeles for a speech on juvenile crime.

We were given rooms at the Loews Hotel by the beach in Santa Monica. That night I had dinner with Kevin Merida, a black journalist I had met the day before, and his brother-in-law.

I was, at this point, scheduled to go on Air Force One in the morning, for the ride from Los Angeles to Sacramento. It seemed that I was on for about thirty-five minutes, at the most. Kevin was giving me the lowdown. He kept referring to something called the pool report. "What's a pool report?" I said.

"You'll have to help write it."

I thought he was kidding. But I wasn't sure. I got my hands on a pool report, took it back to my room, and read it.

It was lighthearted in manner—"The president was not feeling our pain tonight." It started with a complaint about how long they had had to wait for the event to begin. At any rate, I concluded that Kevin was joking about the fact that I would have to help write it. He had a laid-back, warm manner.

The next morning we all arose and went downstairs, where we had to wait in a holding area before taking off. Each time we left a hotel, we would have to go through security. We'd bring our bags down early in the morning. Dogs would sniff them, et cetera. The fear, or expectation, that something could endanger the president is palpable always.

We were then whisked away in the entourage of the president. This was much different than traveling on the press plane. The first thing that is unusual is that, when you travel in the entourage of the president, there is no traffic. They shut down the Los Angeles freeways. I had never in my life traveled the 10, the 405, or any Los Angeles freeway without traffic. It is an amazing experience. I can only imagine that this would be very empowering for the boy next door who becomes president. And this would be the least of it.

Then we took a helicopter—a military helicopter. Very dramatic. And then the flight on Air Force One. Air Force One in and of itself is not remarkable, so I don't know what the people who told me I must get on

Air Force One meant. Did they mean I should try to get access to the president on Air Force One? I was not with the president. I was with the press.

The press area on Air Force One is more comfortable than the press area on the press plane, but it feels more like business class than first class on a normal flight. The flight attendants give out souvenirs—Air Force One M&M's, napkins, and so forth. The food's better than it is on the press plane, and it's served on Air Force One china. I was seated next to Kevin Merida. We spent the thirty-five minutes as black folks often do, talking about a black folk. In this case, Jesse Jackson.

Leon Panetta came to the back of the plane, which is where the press were. He spoke very quietly. It was nearly impossible to hear him, and, although he had a huge smile on his face, he did not seem to be making any kind of great effort to be heard. His ease, his smile, was in direct conflict with the urgency of the press. They wanted information on TWA. As he walked off, and some of them tried to get further access, one reporter asked me exactly what he said. I told her what I heard. "That's all I could hear," I said. "You should probably talk to someone else."

I had a sudden pang of fear. I'm not official. She was asking me a question as if I would know the answer. Suddenly I felt as though I were watching surgery and a nurse turned and asked me to pass an instrument. Here is the danger of being an observer. Yet the press observe all the time, and their work requires that they get as close to the subject as possible. How do they do that without getting confused *as* the subject?

The ride on Air Force One was over. I was still in the "pool" and was shuttled to a series of events. Everything the president did was staged within an inch of its life.

When we got to Sacramento, we were taken to the home of a wealthy person where the president was having lunch. We were "held" in the backyard of a neighbor. Lunch was served. The food, the folding tables, the sitting and waiting reminded me of the days when I had done work as an extra in movies. Kevin, and a few others of the pool, were writing the "pool report." In this case, the "pool" was not even inside the house where the fund-raiser was taking place. All they had to go on was what they'd seen of the president as he went into the house.

At one point Kevin asked me a question. It was something like (although I can't remember exactly what it was), "What color were the umbrellas outside the house?" or, "Was that a canopy or an awning?" He wrote down what I said. I had an eerie feeling, and soon moved away from his table.

There is a combination of idleness and sense of importance to the behavior of the press. They are literally trapped or, as Ed Bradley said, held "captive" by the president—hanging on his every word, in spite of their suspicion that his words are not truthful or meaningful. The more cynical ones among them say that they are held captive by the deathwatch—the possibility that he might get killed on their watch, and how important it would be not to miss that. But how they move from idleness to seriousness is what perplexed me. It's a little like veteran movie stars, who can tell jokes before a scene is shot. I have to hide in my trailer and meditate, even before the simplest of scenes.

Diana Walker distracted me—she was taking pictures of me. I saw her out of the corner of my eye. I asked her to stop. She thought it was amusing and kept snapping away. What was worth her film, it seemed, was that I had been in the movie *The American President,* and now I was actually traveling with the real president. I wasn't amused by that, but I was amused by her, and her mock gotcha-ness.

We soon gathered up our gear and took off for the next stop.

Each stop had on the dais, with the president, civic leaders dressed in their finest. There were very long introductions in each case. These people would often give speeches. It seemed that their presence had less to do with what they were saying, and more to do with the fact that they were in proximity to the president, at least for those few moments. This, I suppose, legitimized them—they had been with the president of the United States.

There was one event outside under a cluster of trees. The president was talking again, about "deadbeat dads" and how these deadbeat dads would not be able to get away with deserting their families. I noticed, for the first time, the men in black.

They were dressed in black jumpsuits and carried automatic weapons. They traveled in black vans, whose windows you could not see through. They traveled with black dogs. They lined the roofs of buildings around the event. It's as if the president were the nation's most precious possession.

Again Leon Panetta emerged, and a group of press huddled around him trying to get the latest on TWA. Again, he spoke so softly that he was nearly impossible to hear. Again, he had a huge smile on his face, in direct contrast to their furrowed brows. Again, he walked off before they had seemed to get enough of him. Again he deflected their questions. The onstage presentation continued. What was clear was a subplot, always to the president's staged performances. Life went on behind the scenes.

Someone came out with the "pool report." I read it, and suddenly my heart began to race. The authors had signed my name to the report. Were they joking?

My beeper went off. I called in. Richard Ben Cramer had called. He was in San Francisco working on his book about Joe DiMaggio. He congratulated me on winning the MacArthur award, would I like to meet for dinner? I determined that I would actually be in San Francisco for one night, and that it would be great to have dinner with him.

I went outside and stood on a stairway, watching Clinton work the rope. A sight to behold. He throws himself right into the crowd. Why does it mean so much to the crowd to shake the hand of the president? And while the crowd is grabbing at his hands, the men in black, the Secret Service, the dogs, patrol the crowd. We are all suspects. Any one of us might plunder the crown jewels.

V.

This trip was winding down. Clinton had one more event, inside an air-port, in a rather plain-looking room, almost like a classroom. I was stand-ing in the back. I thought I caught his eye. It was as if he was standing right next to me. Clinton has presence. That "deep surrender."

I picked up my gear and took off. I was approached by J. F. O. McAl-lister, the reporter from *Time*. "I'll take over now," he said. He was going to come back to the pool. It reminded me of getting off a ride at the amusement park. Not quite a roller coaster, but more at stake than a merry-go-round. "Thanks," I said, heading off for the last leg of the trip. A woman journalist from *USA Today* approached me. "Are you okay?" I didn't know what she was referring to. "Was there a problem about your name on the manifest?" I didn't know what she meant. "Not as far as I know." She looked concerned. I looked over my shoulder as I headed to the regular press plane.

The press plane landed in San Francisco, and I headed to our new holding pen, the Hilton, downtown, across from Glide Memorial Church. I waited to have my bags released and took off, with an amazing sense of freedom. What was I free from? I got a cab and went home. That night I had a terrific dinner with Richard Ben Cramer. Newly awarded the MacArthur, I picked up the tab. In a day or two I'd get a call of congratulations from Susan Sontag, who would say, "And don't take your friends out for dinner, it's not a lot of money. It's no more than a modest academic salary." Well, modest or not, it's the only money I've ever gotten in my life that I didn't have to work for or, better said, the only money I ever got that I got by surprise, out of the blue. I ultimately took her advice, but at least that night, I still thought I was rich, and so Richard and I ate well, and drank well. He and I had something in common. As far as presidents are concerned, Richard commented, "We both know these guys are special."

VI.

The next day I went to my loft to do some work. I had just gotten in from the gym, and purposely didn't check the answering machine, because I had a lot of reading to get through. Dossiers of potential interviewees. At this point, I was still learning the language of the culture, and the conventions were in front of me.

I began poring over what my team had gathered about the church burnings. Nora had gone to a gathering of preachers in Washington to take notes while I was on the road, and Kitty had been on the phone all week trying to put together an itinerary. People had been hard to get ahold of. Even as I was reading the material, Matthew was on country roads outside Tuscaloosa predriving all the routes I'd be taking, so that we wouldn't get lost on the way to the interviews we'd scheduled.

Churches had been burned throughout the South since December of the previous year. It was unclear if they were random or connected in some way. My first destination was Greensboro, Alabama, the location of

Rising Star Baptist Church. It was a church that had literally been built by its members. One of them had put up his milk cow as collateral for the land. It was sixty-five years old when it burned, at 3:00 A.M. I would also go to the site of an old slave church, called St. John, which had burned near Columbia, South Carolina, and finally to the church Clinton had chosen to visit during the rash of burnings, Mt. Zion AME in Greeleyville, South Carolina.

I was anxious about going to Birmingham. All that footage of the South in the sixties, the dogs, the fire hoses, the men, the women, being kept away from lunch counters, and schools, those big fat white men with crew cuts.

From the press plane to the country roads of Alabama—what a mix. The press plane is remarkably clear of "race." Kevin Merida and one other woman were the only blacks I saw on the trip with the president. I had thought it was so odd that, in 1996, the U.S. media was not more diverse. I wondered how hospitable or inhospitable it was for reporters of color. The nineties were an odd time. At the very moment when you were inclined to agree that things *are* better, black churches would be burned, and at that same moment as your gaze peruses newsrooms and press planes, the place where "news is made," where the "rough draft of history" is written, you marvel at the lack of writers of color. White women, yes—colored people, no. Left in the dust. Still not a part of making the story.

The phone rang. My assistant was frantic. *"The New York Times* is trying to get ahold of you."

One of the first things an assistant of mine learns is to refer all calls from the press to my press representative. I don't talk directly to the press until it's organized by my rep. (That's odd in and of itself—except that talking to the press requires a specific language, a guarded language. You can even get a "media education." I haven't gone that far yet.)

"Didn't you tell them to call Stephen [my press rep]?"

"I did, but she was very aggressive."

"They have to talk to Stephen."

"He called too. You need to call him back right away. It's urgent."

I called him.

He had just gotten a call from the *Times*. They had assigned someone to find out why I was on Air Force One.

I gave Stephen the whole story. About how Kitty and Nora and I were sitting in the kitchen, and we got this call from the White House, et cetera. He's been around the block several times, is very versed in the worlds of Hollywood, Washington, and *The New York Times*. Normally he allows me to finish my sentences. Suddenly he cut me off.

"It's Maureen," he said emphatically, as though he had the winning answer on a game show. He meant Maureen Dowd. He sensed that she was somehow involved with this, although she herself had not called. When I had arrived in Washington in 1995, I had been told that Dowd had advised her colleagues at *The New York Times* not to talk to me.

I flashed on a moment that had seemed odd to me during the trip. I was walking down a hallway of a high school, just after Clinton had saluted a number of policemen, and I saw Todd Purdum talking to Maureen Dowd. She grabbed Todd and pulled him into a classroom. The door slammed. They had the look of two junior high school kids up to mischief. I had not liked the feeling I had when I saw that, but it felt too much like junior high for me to think this was really serious. Besides, Todd had always been such a gentleman.

Whatever Maureen Dowd was doing, the *Times* was writing a *second* story to back her up.

Stephen interrupted whatever I was saying. "Let's get Kevin Merida on the line."

The *Times* had called Kevin Merida too. My trip on Air Force One was being made to look nearly criminal. They had also called J. F. O. McAllister of *Time* and Ann McDaniel of *Newsweek*, since I had *Newsweek* credentials. The issue seemed to be that I had written the pool report.

I was shocked. "Well, I didn't write it!"

Kevin consented that that was true.

"Well, what's the problem?"

Stephen chimed in that interns write pool reports—they're very informal documents.

Kevin then cautiously added, "Well, remember you did help describe . . ." He was referring to the umbrella, or canopy. I believe I had said no more than "It's yellow," or "it was an umbrella."

"Yeah, but, I didn't *write* it."

He agreed.

I never know if people mean it when they say you're right, or if they just want to get you to stop talking. "Kevin," I said. "Why *did* you put my name on the pool report?"

"It was a kind of salute to you," he said after a pause.

A salute? He had thought it was interesting that I had been in *The American President,* playing a press secretary, and here I was on a press plane. It may have been well-intentioned on his part, but *The New York Times* was certainly not looking at it as a "salute," they were looking at it as serious trespassing. I couldn't help feeling a bit of an edge—a bit of racial edge—about it all. I wondered what would have happened if a white colleague of mine had traveled on Air Force One. I doubt that it would have provoked the same type of response.

"Why don't we tell them that the White House put me on, or told me how to get on? That's really what happened."

"I don't think you need to do that," Stephen said.

"I'm really sorry about this," Kevin said.

This was sounding worse and worse. The guess was that Maureen Dowd was going to write something about it. She had, I was told, "hit the roof" about me being on Air Force One, and perhaps Andy Rosenthal had too.

"Andy Rosenthal?" I said. Andy had been at the first party given for me in D.C. It was at that party that I had heard so much about Air Force One, and about how important it would be to go on Air Force One.

We finally got off the phone. I had plans to go out to dinner. The Slanted Door, a wonderful Vietnamese restaurant. All night I felt lousy. Stephen told me to expect something in the paper the next day. I was going to be leaving for the airport at 4:00 A.M., headed to the sites of the church burnings.

"I GOT THE *NEW YORK TIMES,* IT AIN'T NOTHIN' NEW NEWS BLUES"

....

UNITED AIRLINES RED CARPET LOUNGE

The New York Times wasn't being delivered because I had been out of town so much. The next morning, after I got to the airport and checked in, I bought a copy of *The New York Times.* I didn't want to read it to my-self. I knew already the likelihood was whatever was written was going to be disturbing, I had that same feeling you have when you read a review. On the occasions when I had to read reviews because they would dra-matically affect my immediate future, I had them read to me—I didn't read them alone. So—I called a friend, at 5:00 A.M., and read the articles aloud over the phone in the United Red Carpet Lounge. It was a one-time performance.

> The big story on President Clinton's Western swing this week was that *Newsweek* sent Anna Deavere Smith as its White House correspondent. Let's put aside the absurdity of *Newsweek* assign-ing the writer and actress, who played a White House press secre-tary in the movie *The American President* and is now working on a book and a play about political reporters, to cover a news story.
>
> The White House was philosophical. "She writes plays and Joe Klein writes novels," said a top Clinton aide, slyly. *Newsweek* has a precedent.
>
> And certainly if Ms. Smith is looking to document the feck-lessness of the press, what better evidence than her own instant and bizarre accreditation? The real issue in sending the talented Ms. Smith on the campaign trip is whether it was unfair to give the President such tough competition in performance art.

Robin Pogrebin's article, printed on page 20 of Section A in the *Times,* started, "*Newsweek* yesterday found itself explaining how it was that a performance artist, Anna Deavere Smith, wound up representing the news weekly on Air Force One."

Several things seemed odd in this new land I was visiting. I was iden-tified in each case as a "performance artist." I could be called actress, play-wright. I could also have been called professor, or Stanford professor, or even Ann O'Day Maples Professor of the Arts. In actuality I have been an academic much longer than I have been called a "performance artist." I have been teaching since 1976, have held academic rank in a variety of universities since 1978, and have tenure.

Stranger still is the ease with which these two journalists refer to "performance art." And perhaps what troubled me most about the articles was the use of that term. I'm more worried about the way the identity of that term was misused than about how my identity was being handled. I don't know what a performance artist is. Do the journalists know? From what I can decipher, *performance art* is a catchall phrase meant to serve a variety of people in a variety of art forms, not just theater, who cannot be easily categorized. When my work hit the scene, many people said they had never seen anything like it before. I was soon placed in the category of "performance artist" by the media. There have been some debates about whether or not I am a playwright. I like to think of a playwright in the old way. The word, as you see, is spelled play-w-r-i-g-h-t. It's not w-r-i-t-e. That's not a typo. *Playwright* is like *wheelwright*. A wheelwright makes wheels. A playwright makes plays.

Around about the time that the theater made some efforts to get to a bigger "we," that is, around about the time it was clear that it could no longer mirror society if it made room for only Williams, Simon, O'Neill, Miller, and Shakespeare, a variety of people emerged. They worked outside the limited box of art as mirroring only the lives, dilemmas, and stories of white families, white people, and particularly white heterosexual men. They were of color, they were women, they came to art with questions about society and about art that were not answered by the status quo. This group of people, adventuring to make a bigger expression of who "we" are, often worked in unusual ways, mixing forms, working outside forms. Many of them were called performance artists.

Because of controversies around the National Endowment for the Arts, the term *performance artist* connotes controversy, and even that which is outlandish. I believe that performance art may contribute to a significant change in culture. A change that allows a bigger "we." Here *performance artist* sounds a little sleazy: "whether it was unfair to give the President such tough competition in performance art."

Clinton was being called a performance artist too. Dowd had continued, "Bill Clinton, after all, is a metamorphosis artist, performing roles of New Democrat, Old Democrat, radical liberal and conservative all in his first term." Under this light, the idea of metamorphosis, or art, or performance art did not sound very positive. Moving, changing, evolving is not respected in politics; it is honored in art. I wonder if some scholars of performance would see Maureen Dowd as a performance artist. Would that be an honor or an insult?

Far from the facts is the notion that I was traveling only for *Newsweek*. In fact the Arena Stage paid for my trip, and we had gone to great lengths to get access—a staff of six working day and night.

And then the question of whether I was worthy of credentials in general. Who can be credentialed? "Who is credible?" has been a part of the blood on the floor in the battle to make a bigger "we." The easiest way to silence a voice is to question its credibility. All sorts of people have gotten credentialed in the past. I see colleagues of mine, from the arts, with bylines in *Newsweek* and *Time* and other magazines. No one lifts an eyebrow. Jean Genet, the French writer (and a thief), covered the Democratic convention in '68.

Who is credible? The person who has the most ink, the most airtime? The idea of who is credible and who is not changes with time. Slave narratives were not credible. The story of Sally Hemings was not a credible story for years, although there were slave narratives to support it. Finally there was a debate, and finally there was DNA. Neither history nor science could have stood on its own. Supposedly we have expanded our idea of credibility, we have gained enough evidence that we shouldn't be so quick to judge who is credible and who is not. In Washington they have not expanded that idea.

"Oh they love when Streisand comes to town, yet these same people are the ones who at a dinner party would say, 'What the fuck does she know about Bosnia? Who is she?' " an anonymous insider explained to me.

Misinterpretation is a way of life in Washington and in the press generally. My brush with it was extremely mild, compared with how it works in a real way in the everyday lives of the people whose careers are politics and image building. I have a lot of tape to attest to this. Perhaps one of the clearer statements came from Alexis Herman, secretary of labor: "They want to misinterpret, you know, the feeding frenzy. And unfortunately there is an element today that can paint you to be a very different person, that you may not even recognize. . . . And then the funniest thing to me was that somehow I was labeled a 'Washington insider.' That was really, you know, you're on the outside looking in, trying to bring down the walls, bring down the barriers, to be in the room, to get to the table, you know? And somehow to wear the mantle of a Washington political insider was just funny to me, you know. It was just funny to me."

Probably the biggest fiction being created here was the idea that my being on Air Force One was in the lead of Dowd's column. The idea that I was the "big story" on the president's western swing. Actually, the big story on the swing was the TWA crash. The reporters seemed eager to get details of what had happened, and those details were hard to come by.

So those were some of the subtle fictions and not so subtle fictions being created around my name, around the term *performance artist,* around my trip to follow the president, around my desire to know more about the circle of people who create America and those who tell us about their work. This was a subtle and not so subtle fiction that put a public frame around my search for American character on the campaign trail. What truth was that fiction trying to tell?

Even as Dowd's writing could be enjoyed by some as a kind of performance art itself, a kind of dark insightful clowning, Robin Pogrebin, who had written the second article, seemed to have the task of making this very serious. Why had the *Times* printed *two* stories in section one about thirty-five minutes on Air Force One by a little-known (in the big scheme of things) African American playwright-actress?

Sitting in the little phone cubicle of United Airlines, with my morning coffee, I waited for my flight to Birmingham to board. I thought about how afraid I had always been to go to Birmingham. When I was a girl in Baltimore, we were afraid to go any farther south than Washington, D.C. It was the first place I was called "nigger." My father had a saying, which was that he hadn't been to Mississippi in so many years she could be married by now for all he knew. And then there was the awful news of the four little girls who were killed in the bombing of the Sixteenth Street Baptist Church. I can still remember learning that news from my mother, in our kitchen on Bentalou Street, before we were in integration. That morning I was more afraid of what would be written about me in *The New York Times* than I was of going to Birmingham. I realized how out of balance my reaction was.

VII. O'HARE AIRPORT, CHICAGO, ILLINOIS

I had to change planes in Chicago, and when my plane landed at O'Hare, I called my office to check in. My assistant said that I should call my press representative.

I started looking for a pay phone that wouldn't be too noisy. I decided I better first get to the gate, so that I would be ready to board even if the phone conversations got complicated. I had several calls I knew I had to make. I called my press representative. He was already getting calls, and he needed a response.

"A response? What for?"

"We have to come up with a response right away."

"You mean a response that will be printed?"

"Yes."

I was suddenly worried that we should bring my agent in on this, since she had been a part of the *Newsweek* deal, and a book deal. We decided to conference her in.

"Hello. Hello. Are you there?" They were both on the line.

"Okay, everybody's here."

My agent was curious about what Maynard Parker, the editor of *Newsweek,* would be thinking, since I had been flying with *Newsweek* credentials. Some people thought that when *The New York Times* asked *Newsweek* to comment, their response had sort of left me hung out to dry.

"I haven't talked to him."

To tell the truth, I have never understood this part of the "game." Something goes out, it's not entirely true, and we have to find a way of responding. The whole thing was a disruption in my already overly ambitious schedule, but it was coming clear to me that it was not to be ignored.

"I think we should just tell the truth," I said. "Tell them what really happened. Tell them the White House put me on the plane."

For some reason, neither one of them thought I should say that.

"Why shouldn't we just tell the truth, just say what happened—"

My press rep cut me off. "That's too Talmudic," he said.

"Excuse me?" I said.

Too *Talmudic,* I thought to myself. What did that mean? Did that mean the truth is too studied? It did have a ring to it—"too *Talmudic.*"

My agent agreed with my press rep that I ought to come up with something short and to the point. They waited—I was under the gun. It was a little like a game show, with a loud clock ticking.

"Say that I came to Washington to learn how things work and now I know."

They both laughed. I wasn't laughing at *all*.

"That's good!" one of them said, very animated and relieved.

"See, that's the kind of thing that will work!"

"It's quick, to the point, and it's light," my agent said.

"I like it because it has a couple of layers of meaning. And it has a little bit of an edge," my press rep said.

"What do you mean?" I asked.

"It's sort of like, this is how you play the game. Now I know you guys don't play fair," he said.

"Hmm . . ." I said.

My agent still wanted me to make sure to call Maynard. "Just to check in."

"Okay," I said and hung up.

Just to check in. I looked down at my beeper, the first beeper I ever had; I had gotten it for this project. I was surprised that I hadn't heard anything from the office in Washington, or the theater for that matter. I couldn't imagine that they hadn't read *The New York Times*. They were probably scared to death. All they had done was follow procedures given to them from others.

I quickly dialed the office in Washington. One of the interns brought Kitty to the phone.

"Did you see *The New York Times* this morning?" I asked.

The phone was silent on her end for a few moments. "I was just *sick* when I read it," she responded. She let out a long sigh.

"Maybe you should write a narrative about what exactly happened, I mean with the White House and all, you know, for our own record."

She said she would, and she did.

I hung up.

I still had a few moments left before boarding. I called Richard Ben Cramer. "What do you make of this?" I asked him.

"Don't worry about it, Anna," he droned, in a kind of weary, Jack Nicholson–esque, high pitch. He then said something like "These things last two minutes."

They last two minutes. And Andy Warhol said we have only fifteen. There were a million things I had planned to do with my fifteen—and they didn't include this. My trip to Birmingham was a part of what I would like to do with my fifteen minutes. And somehow it was being sidetracked.

What if I had gotten as many calls about the church burnings as I did about the *New York Times* articles? In retrospect, I decided it would have been nice if just as many people had called when the church burnings started to say, "Anna, why don't you go South and check that out?" I even got a call from one of my funders when the Dowd article appeared. Even my *accountant* wanted to know what was up. Shortly before this happened, perhaps no more than two weeks before, when I had been awarded the prestigious MacArthur award, my mother and my agent could not find the announcement in *The New York Times*. Yet funders, accountants, my deans, friends I hadn't heard from in a long time, knew that I had spent thirty-five minutes on Air Force One.

VIII. THE AIRPORT IN BIRMINGHAM, ALABAMA

The plane landed in Birmingham. It had been a very long day, and I was still due to go to a revival meeting and do a couple of interviews. The airport was spanking new. I didn't expect it to be so modern.

Matthew met me at the gate. He was in a very good mood. I'd asked him to come to the South because he was completely dependable; I knew I could count on him to be meticulous, even anal, in setting things up. He had been in Birmingham and Tuscaloosa for a couple of days. He had driven all the routes we had to drive, had found places where we could eat fresh fish and vegetables, had even found a good swimming pool.

He knew about the *New York Times* pieces. As we walked from the gate to baggage claim, our conversation went something like this.

"They used that picture with your hat," Matthew said.

"You're right."

"Yeah, you had on a sort of weird hat. It's like they picked a picture that made you look kind of weird, like a performance artist, instead of more serious, like a professor."

"Yeah."

"Why'd they put in two pieces about it?"

"One is the straight man, one is the burlesque. They had to put the first one in to let people know who I am, and what I was doing there; otherwise Dowd's column wouldn't have made sense."

"You know," he said, "there comes a—there comes a time when we have to just be delivered from what other people think of us if we're going to be able to go forward and live our lives in the way that God would want us to."

The other reason I took Matthew with me to the churches in the South was that he was born again.

At baggage claim an old, thin, but very fit black man came up to us with a luggage cart. He looked like he had been carrying people's bags all his life. This was not a part-time job while he was waiting to make a million dollars. This was his job, his profession. I asked him about the church in Birmingham, the history of the four little girls being killed. He said he couldn't talk about it.

"You can't talk about it?"

"No, ma'am."

"Why is that?"

"Spike Lee been down here making a movie about it, and we not supposed to talk about it, till he done making his movie."

We waited patiently for my luggage, and it did not turn up. This was not good.

What would I do without proper clothes? I couldn't go to church that night the way I was dressed. In jeans. The old black man waited patiently with us while we tried to sort this through. I tipped him although no bags came. Or maybe he should have tipped me. I had done a remarkably restrained performance. Matthew doesn't like profanity, so, through the entire lost bags ordeal, I was very subdued. Without access to profanity, I had to be imaginative. My imagination left me silent.

IX. SHONEY'S RESTAURANT, TUSCALOOSA, ALABAMA

We drove past a huge Mercedes-Benz plant as we left the airport, on our way to meet Reverend Coleman, pastor of Rising Star Baptist Church. We were set to meet him at a Shoney's restaurant off the main highway.

Matthew had a gift waiting for me in the car. A Bible. He was very excited and gave me a detailed, and animated, description of a huge Christian bookstore in a strip mall. ". . . with these tacky handwritten signs. You know, the kind of signs that tell you what section you are in? Well, they were handwritten!"

We pulled into the Shoney's parking lot. Matthew sat in the car, staking out the parking lot for Reverend Coleman. We didn't know what he looked like. I went inside to buy an orange juice, and to get the benefit of air-conditioning. I remembered suddenly that I was supposed to call Maynard at *Newsweek* to "check in," so I did.

Maynard's vocal tones were melodic—the kinds of tones meant to make you think everything is fine. He said that he thought this thing with me on Air Force One and the *Times*'s response to it would not have blown up if it hadn't been for the Joe Klein story. "It was the two things together, you see," Maynard said.

Having "checked in," I hung up and saw a black gentleman with a huge smile. He came up and looked at me as if he had known me all my life. "Reverend Coleman?" I asked. He nodded and clasped my hand in a firm handshake.

He did not look at all like he was in the middle of a drama, that is, the drama of his church having been burned down. He looked strong and steady. His smile was familiar.

Suddenly I remembered my appearance. "I'm so sorry, you have to excuse the way I look. They lost my luggage."

"You don't need to worry about that." He, by contrast, was pressed and suited for the evening revival meeting.

We went outside to Matthew. We determined that I would drive with Reverend Coleman, and Matthew would follow us. I took out my tape recorder right away. "Okay. The church was sixty-five years old, and it was a brick building that had bricked over siding, and the siding that they had was that asbestos-type siding. Now I don't know exactly what year they rebricked it, but they rebricked it and they remodeled it. There is no elected official in the church. There's professional peoples as relate to education in the church. There's insurance peoples, and just your common everyday peoples that really love that church."

Coleman was not a full-time preacher. He had a "day" job.

"Personally, I did not recognize how many fond memories I had of the church until the building got gone. Then I reflected in my mind the many of times that I have had the visitation of the Holy Spirit in that building."

The church had burned around three or four o'clock in the morning. Reverend Coleman was clearly perplexed that Clinton and others suggested that the burnings were racially motivated. Perplexed because when the cases went to court, no one was tried as if there were racial motivation. To my mind, that didn't mean they weren't racially motivated, it just meant the courts didn't go there. But Coleman had his own ideas about the vandals.

"There is something wrong in their relationship with God," Reverend Coleman told me. "There are several times in the Bible that you see how Satan just motivate an individual."

"Oh?" I said.

"It's not all that black or white, just Satan motivate that person."

We pulled up as people were arriving. We got out of the car and went into the small country church. Matthew was in a suit and tie, I was in slacks. I felt so out of place.

Matthew and I were in a world entirely different from the one of the campaign trail. What went on inside there was the flip side of everything I was seeing in Washington. The droning voices, the sounds, the community. People were talking to Jesus, and they were talking to each other. The preacher, the Reverend Elijah C. Weaver, weighed about 350 pounds. A very dark-skinned man in a purple suit under his white robe. His preaching was more sounds than words.

"And they put Jesus in the lion den . . ."

"*Welll.*"

"Can I get a witness?"

"*Yes.*"

"And when dey put im *in* deah, Jesus wen in dere wif him and made du lion to lay down so they could be a pilla ta Daniel head."

"*Amen. Amen.*"

"And he made du lion da lay down ta be a pilla ta Daniel head!"

"*Welllllll.*"

"An only Jesus could a don it cause dose lion in the lion den
They wan tame like da lion in the circus
See we see a lion in the circus and they be trained

But these lion wan tame
These was *wiilllld* lions in the lions' den.
Am I right about it?" he sang.
    "*Weeeellllll.*"
    "Can I get a witness? Amen. . . . Amen."
    The drone of the music, the sweat of all of us.
"Aaaaaammmaaazzzzing grace!!!!!!!!!!
Howwwwwwwwwwww
Sweet!
The
Souuuuuunnnnnddddddd.
Thaaaaaat saavvveeeuuuuuuvvved aaaaaaah wretch liiiiiike me!"
    Matthew was beside himself. He was crying, I was crying, and laughing. We were both clapping, and singing. We were a mess. We had heard the song many times, but not like this.
    He leaned over, thrilled. "I *knew* we would have an experience with the Holy Spirit, I just *knew* it!"
    What if democracy felt like that? Why is it so entirely rational, even in a time when we know the limits of our reason, even in a time when we know we're so smart that we're not wise. Even in a time when we know we have no proof that knowledge, knowledge alone, and material gain alone, will not make us a better species. And it's dangerous, too, that the right wing has grabbed ahold of the evangelical movement, and wants to hold on to the truth of it. I'm not suggesting that we confuse church and state—I'm just suggesting that we find other ways to talk to each other than through reasoned discussion. Maybe even (God forbid) the arts, which house empathy, if not spirituality, can be useful to us.
    I was enthralled with Reverend Elijah C. Weaver. When I went up to meet him, I felt like a fan of a rock star. He had a white dot in one eye. We begged him to meet us for breakfast the next morning. He was amused by our enthusiasm, I think, and gave us intricate directions to a gas station where we'd rendezvous early the next morning.
    "All right now," he said, as we went off into the night with our chorus of thank-yous. That night we visited the oldest member of the church, and turned in rather late.
    The next morning, I swam with great energy in an Olympic-size pool Matthew miraculously found. We then drove to meet Reverend Weaver

at the gas station. From there we followed him in his long, old Cadillac to a diner, with only black customers. Over grits, biscuits, and bacon and eggs, we talked to him about talking, about how he talks to his congregation. He explained to us that he was talking for the Holy Spirit.

I would visit Reverend Weaver several times, and travel with him each time to another church, to watch him preach, and to hear the music of his congregations. The music of hope:

> *Oh it's another day's journey and I'm glad*
> *About it*
> *So glad*
> *So glad*
> *So glaaaaaaad!*

And the music of warning:

> *Iss gon rain*
> *Iss gon rain*
> *God tol Noah iss gon rain*
> *And when da watuh begin to pour*
> *Knock on da winda and knock on da dooor!*

I would call him on the phone, the way I spoke from time to time with Judith Butler, scholar of rhetoric. I would call him, as I had called her, to talk me through things that I didn't understand by looking at the surface. I realized I needed not only intellectual explanations but spiritual explanations. In neither case could I accept pure doctrine. Judith Butler's insights weren't the be-all and end-all, and neither was the Reverend's Christianity. But to understand "the words" I was hearing in Washington, I needed to look at words for their political potential and their spiritual potential. Most of the words I was hearing were flat compared with what they could be. I needed to understand what was, or was not, beneath the words.

And the swing kept on, all throughout the summer. I went to both conventions, wrote for *Newsweek*—and just kept moving throughout America, with a few more stops in Tuscaloosa to get my battery charged.

Onward to see the end of the tale: Who would be the next president of the United States? No one seemed very excited. There wasn't much suspense. Few people thought it would be Dole.

MIKE WALLACE

60 MINUTES

"Proud"

You're going to believe Richard Nixon?
I wasn't sure what I believed about Jack Kennedy.
I remember that he was going to change the housing situation in
    this country, with a stroke of the pen
which stroke of the pen never
somehow never hit the paper.
Uh uh, Jimmy Carter couldn't persuade anybody to do anything.
He was well-meaning
But he didn't
he didn't make the country
he didn't capture the heart or the attention or the focus of the
    country
the way
certainly the way Roosevelt did and
to a certain degree
that way that
that Truman did
over great
the great skepticism
and people who were looking down their nose at
this haberdasher.
But eventually

but eventually
as far as
as far as Korea was concerned
I'm wandering all over the place
but
Yeah
Well, yeah
It
it's not quite awe.
I want to
I really want to admire him.
I want to say
"Boy am I proud to have that man sitting in the White House."
I, I want to be proud.
He's
he's the top
he's the president.
I want to be proud of my president.
It's as simple and straightforward as that.
And it's—
I can't be proud of Bill Clinton.
I can't be proud of George Bush.
I can't be proud of Jerry Ford.
Can't be proud of,
uh,
Jimmy Carter,
can't be proud of Richard Nixon.
That's a long time.

THEATER HISTORY

SUMMER 1996
LIBRARY OF CONGRESS
WASHINGTON, D.C.

I AM SITTING IN A SMALL ROOM AT THE LIBRARY OF CONGRESS LISTEN-
ing to tapes of the conventions dating back to the first recordings. They
were raucous events. Someone with a gavel was banging away, asking for
order, and the conventioneers did not heed. It sounded like an all-male affair. "Happy Days are here again, here again," et cetera.

NBC TELEVISION ARCHIVES
NEW YORK CITY

I am sitting in a small room at NBC in New York, watching the earliest
television we can find of conventions. It's black-and-white. Huntley and
Brinkley are anchoring. They are smoking on television as they speak.

Everett Dirksen is banging the gavel, trying to speak. He gets a few
sentences into the speech, and the crowd begins to scream.

"Will you let me go on?" he wails. To no avail. The crowd has a mind
of its own. They are clearly not there just to hear the speakers.

SUMMER 1996

REPUBLICAN CONVENTION, ARRIVAL

SAN DIEGO, CALIFORNIA

San Diego was a welcome sight after so many months in Washington. Everything looked so clean and new. *Newsweek* hires firemen to take attendees around the city. When I arrived, a fireman picked me up and took me to my hotel. He was a terrific-looking black guy, jovial and talkative. For a moment, I thought the convention would be fun.

I went to my room, got settled, and hooked up with Rob Maas, the photographer who was assigned to me. I did thirty-five interviews in three days. I never worked so hard in my life.

ON THE FLOOR

I was on the floor of the convention, in the middle of an interview. These kinds of interviews, standing up holding a mike in front of someone's face, can only yield sound bites. There was loads of noise in the background.

Mary Summers is screaming over the noise into my microphone. "I began working in the pro-life movement when I worked for Jesse Helms, and I began working for him after I graduated from law school in 1984. He is one of the most honest men I have ever met. He is one of the most courageous men I've ever met. And he's a very compassionate man. People don't know this, but, contrary to what the popular belief is about him, he is a great promoter of women.

"I think abortion is the greatest social evil in our society, because if we abandon the inalienable right to live, then we're going to lose the rest of our freedom, and if we abandon the right to life of the innocent unborn, then we are going to eventually lose the rest of our freedom and the inalienable rights that our forefathers fought so hard to keep."

Although I had to yell over the noise to continue our conversation, I was still able to do it. If I had been trying to have this conversation in 1932, not only would it have been politically impossible but it would have been technically impossible.

There was much discussion about the Republican convention as "too scripted" because the organizers of the convention were determined to bring the thing in under time. Much of the media complained, and Ted Koppel even left because of this. Television ratings were quite low. What was scripted was the speaking on the part of the stars. I wondered how a huge convention could be controlled. How could they control the crowd? Having listened to and watched several recordings and videos, I knew that audience response could add time to the event.

I asked one of the producers how he could have counted on the audience responses lasting only a specific period of time.

"It all has to do with the music. We told the bandleader not to play music that would get people riled up."

This was the antithesis of what I had been listening to at the Library of Congress. Who demands this control?

It was outside the hall that I found passionate discourse. There were Flip Benham and Rusty Thomas of Operation Rescue, who were holding funerals for fetuses outside the convention hall. There were the Mexicans who set off on a march on the first day of the convention down to the border and back to protest all the anti-immigration propositions. And there were all the born agains, Phyllis Schlafly, the evangelicals, camping out in the peripheries. People on the margins, trying to inch into the center.

The happiest people seemed to be the youngest ones. The Young Republicans became more and more sure of themselves as the week went on. I had traveled into San Diego with them on a train that had come from Chicago. I got on in Los Angeles. By that time they had been up all night for several nights singing "Proud to Be an American" and talking through their ideas about policy. They were carrying the future in their hands, and they knew it. There was no studied nonchalance here. All passion. Just free, wild optimism. As I ran into them in the course of the week, they became hoarser and hoarser. They, it turned out, were responsible for most of the cheering and passion that was felt on the floor.

A scholar at Stanford had told me, "There is a slow glacial move in this country to the right." If I were to go by the health and spirit of the Young Republicans, I would have to believe that was true. It was the older folk who were dissatisfied.

One day I was walking through a parking lot, and I saw a very disgruntled Jack Germond sitting on a crate of some sort.

"How about breakfast?" I asked. "I eat a real breakfast," he said. We'd have to go someplace where they were able to roll out the bacon and eggs and biscuits. I had melon, he had a real breakfast. He was mourning the death of politics as he had known it.

"This is—this is all—this is all showbiz now. There—there's—there's nothin' for them to tell ya. I mean, 'cause it's—the decisions are made in a different way."

It was all very clean in San Diego, all very neat. The only unbridled emotion I saw was inside the hall when the tribute was played to Ronald Reagan. I was right in the middle of the Minnesota delegation. There wasn't a dry eye in the place. Men and women both, weeping.

SUMMER 1996
DEMOCRATIC CONVENTION
CHICAGO

The ambience in Chicago was remarkably different. There was a lot of music. And it wasn't the kind of music to calm a crowd down. Bonnie Raitt was in town. Jessye Norman and Aretha Franklin both sang inside the hall. When Aretha sang "America the Beautiful," people were dancing in the aisles. The convention room floor smelled of french fries and hamburgers. There had been no food on the floor of the Republican convention.

The fringe events at the Republican convention seemed to be about passion held back. The fringe events at the Democratic convention seemed to be about a dying left. Many of them were half empty. What was more remarkable was that there were very few young people at the fringe, progressive events. I got the feeling that it was hard here to figure out where passion should come from, other than the music.

The 1996 Democratic convention didn't really need anybody to monitor the music, because even if they had gotten riled up, it would not have been about an issue.

Something else was lurking underneath the Democratic convention, though. It was a vivid memory of another time. It was the memory of the convention in Chicago, 1968.

There is a kind of political theater that happened in '68, that burst up like flames, but was put out just as quickly. It was so "hot" that even the Beat poet Allen Ginsberg and the French writer Jean Genet had gone to it.

Passion is dangerous. Passion leads to theater, or to a make-believe world. You can begin to believe what you are fighting for is possible. And if you get too wrapped up in that reality, somebody is sure to come along and let you know what reality actually is.

Nobody today needs to worry about getting carried away. In fact, I'd bet we're actually still smarting from some kind of a death blow that was struck in the seventies. That's what it looked like, at the Democratic convention, on the fringes. The tried and true were gray-haired and tired, and I didn't see any descendants.

We are not in political theater right now. What is happening in public life is not theater at all. It is fraught with imitation—true. It is fraught with design—true. But it is not theater at all. It is a series of commercial breaks. And it's hard to hang on to those breaks.

ARIANNA HUFFINGTON

COLUMNIST, COMMENTATOR

"Grace"

It occurred to me in the course of writing *After Reason*
that we, we had looked at human nature in a very
again, shrunken way, to use the—a term I've used before
in terms of three instincts
as a survivor
sex, and the instinct for—to assert ourselves
power
the ego instincts.
And that we had missed out on what I call the fourth instinct
which was the spiritual instinct.
And I call it an instinct because I believe that it is genetically
encoded in us

and that if we don't honor it we pay a heavy price.
We pay a heavy price as individuals and we pay a heavy price as
    a culture.
And, interestingly enough
when I was writing that book
After Reason, I—the one question I kept asking myself
and I had no answers [was]
but how do you—how do you honor it?
How do you get people to make it part of their lives because you
    can't tell people
"It would be a good idea if you believed in God."
[Laughter]
I mean it's grace.
You can't make yourself believe in something.
So, that's when for me it's come full circle now
with the work I'm doing now
getting all of us to be involved in service
because I believe that that's something that we can do and that can
    get us to God.
That we can't sort of get from here to God directly.
Sometimes we have to really serve his children and get to him
    indirectly.
And this—and the question of how do we get to the critical mass
is, is a constant preoccupation of mine
and it's hard sometimes to do it through prose.
You have to get it
because what we are talking about is not just rational.
So, when you do it through poetry and through the theater
you can get to a part of us that is not as barricaded as if you do it
    through columns or speeches.
You know
people in a, in a dark theater are more vulnerable in a positive
    way
and a lot of politics is performance in the negative sense.
It's interesting that we have—we have now taken performance to
    mean something very different than, say, when in *Hamlet*
you have "The play is the thing"

you know, through the play you get to the consciousness in a way
    that you can't do it through
ah, preaching or prose or this or that.
But now performance has come to mean something that is a lie
in the same way that the word *myth*
has come to mean something that is a lie.
And, you know
and myth is something which is so profound because it's beyond
    what we can express in rational terms.
It expresses deeper truths.
And, yet, what does it mean today?
It means a lie.
That's part of the, of the modern tragedy
of thinking that we can understand and live everything through our
    minds.
Shrunken humanity
shrunken view of nature.
It's like it's desiccated
and we don't even know we're not wise because we're so smart.

PERFORMING FOR THE
PRESIDENT

ELECTION DAY, 1996

THE CAMPAIGN WOUND TO A HALT, AND AT SOMETHING LIKE 4:00 A.M.
we, who were on that last mad swing to eight cities in two days, pulled
into Little Rock, Arkansas. We piled into an Arkansas hotel. I wouldn't
have to be awake early in the morning. In fact, I wouldn't have to get on a
press plane anymore. And that was it. I was exhausted. Richard Ben
Cramer had been right. You had to be in good shape to make it through.

In less than ten days, I was going to have to be onstage, playing, in a
two-thousand-seat house, my one-woman show *Twilight: Los Angeles,
1992*. It's about the Los Angeles riots, and in it I play forty-six characters.
It takes a lot of stamina. I'd be leaving Arkansas after the election results
were announced and heading to a spa.

I was glad for a bed with clean sheets, and the possibility of lying
down flat. I had spent several madcap days sitting up straight between
journalists on an airplane. Two male journalists, one of them a photographer, almost got into a knock-down-drag-out fight in the aisle. I was extremely tense myself from being around this less than happy bunch of
people. But a couple of levelheaded people broke the fight up, and everyone went back to naps on the plane, or to clicking away on a laptop.

When I woke up and went outside, Little Rock looked like it was set
up for a carnival. People could buy alcohol right out on the street.

I was hoping to find some kind of way to be near Clinton as the vote was coming in, but I knew there would be no such luck. Two of my friends, Diana Walker, a photographer for *Time,* and Karen Breslau, a correspondent for *Newsweek,* had figured out how to get behind the scenes. I knew from watching them that this required a very special skill in relationships, to go, as it were, behind the lines.

I learned that my friend the opera singer Jessye Norman was in town, and left word for her that I was too. We made a plan to meet. I was in the thick of the crowd at the Excelsior Hotel. People were getting drunker and drunker, and the human sea was getting denser and denser. I was to meet Ms. Norman by the elevator. There was no space to move. She got off the elevator with a friend, and they both immediately registered the impossibility of the situation on their faces. How, without an escort, would she ever get to where she needed to be, behind an outdoor stage? In the thick of this crowd appeared Vernon Jordan.

She asked him what she should do. He looked around the crowd, beckoned, and men came forward, almost like out of the woodwork. There were several aides to the president who looked as if they were just part of the crowd. Quickly one of them was assigned to Ms. Norman by Vernon Jordan, who just happened to be passing by.

The aide told us to hold hands and began to lead us through the crowd. A black woman in her early twenties passed by with friends. She suddenly blurted out to Ms. Norman, "Hey, ain't you somebody?"

Hey—ain't—you—somebody?

You get the feeling that people cruise these situations just to see who they can see. And that would be something to call home about.

Ms. Norman was taken to a big, old house that had almost no furniture. It had the look of a house that had once been wonderful, and then was turned over for an army headquarters of some sort. She went upstairs to prepare to sing. The room looked like an abandoned office. Strange to see a diva placed in such a spot to prepare to sing for the president and the nation.

I sat downstairs in another empty room, with a man who was watching the returns. It was over for Dole. We waited to see the concession speech. The room was very red, and disorderly.

I walked out back, behind the stage, and watched Jessye Norman sing. I watched the crowd who were cordoned off, and watched from behind as the president and Mrs. Clinton came out to wave at the crowd in the president's moment of victory. His second victory.

There was an anticlimactic feel to the event.

INAUGURATION EVE, 1997

We were told that it was going to be very, very cold on inauguration day. I got there the night before and went to the pre-inauguration celebration. This was followed by a party at the Jockey Club. I was shocked at how small the restaurant was at the Jockey Club and at the condensed mixture of movie stars and political folks. It reminded me of the small outdoor departure area at the old Martha's Vineyard airport the summers that Clinton was there. I suppose people in that circle could easily believe that there really are only two people in the world. The crowd was almost identical to the post–Academy Awards crowd at Mortons.

I had come to the party with a costume designer who was working with me on my play. She did research. We spent most of the evening standing at the bar, talking to the model Lauren Hutton about everything from politics to crocodiles. At one point, my designer turned to me and said, "You have no idea how much plastic surgery is in this room." I took a look around, and she was right. You could probably redo all of the nation's schools with the money reflected there in jewelry, cosmetic surgery, clothing, and appearance in general.

INAUGURATION DAY

I was in a group with Kevin Costner.

We were trying to get to our seats and were walking through the Capitol. The area was restricted—we weren't really supposed to walk through the building—but one of the guards noticed Kevin Costner. Security restrictions do not apply for movie stars.

The ceremony itself went without event. Ruth Bader Ginsburg said, "Every good wish," to Al Gore. To Clinton, she merely said, "Good luck."

We were leaving. A group of soldiers in formal dress and in formation were marching by. One of them noticed Kevin Costner and broke out of formation, gesturing wildly, pointing, and mouthing, "That's Kevin Costner!"

This soldier, and the guard who let us walk through a high-security area in the Capitol, are both supposed to be performing an important service for the president and the country. Yet celebrity caused them to leave their posts.

That night I was talking to Sidney Blumenthal. "It's form over content," he said, "everything is form over content." Clearly not the case for those soldiers. They abandoned form to recognize a movie star.

1997

WHEN CLINTON CAME TO SEE ME PERFORM

FORD'S THEATER

THE WATERGATE HOTEL

Soon after the inauguration, I was scheduled to perform *Twilight: Los Angeles, 1992,* at Ford's Theater. The show was a success and played to sold-out crowds.

On the Saturday before my last performance, I had only an evening show. No matinee. I was in my room at the Watergate Hotel, and the phone rang. It was the theater. They had just gotten word that President Clinton, Mrs. Clinton, and Al Gore were going to come to the last show. I was with my best friend of twenty-five years, a friend I see only once every five, sometimes ten, years.

I was not immediately ecstatic about the president coming. In fact, my reaction was the opposite. That certain dread hit me. That dread that I knew so well. It was the first-day-of-school dread magnified. It was the dread on the three days or so that the critics are coming to a show. It was the dread about performance. There's the thrill, but there's also the dread. The dread comes because there's a part of you, no matter how calm you try to be, that believes that performance—the taking on of personalities, of other personalities, and of staying in that state for nearly three hours, alone onstage—is a feeling of life and death.

It's an intense state of aloneness. Although the audience is there, what goes on inside is an intense aloneness. You fear you could lose your lines, lose your moments. But you have to go through till the end, and you never understand *really* how you get through. And no one can really help you except to say, "You're going to be fine." I always feel before a big performance, an opening, or a performance such as the one I was about to face with the president, that I am in the hospital, and that friends backstage are visitors at a hospital bed.

I also feel a big responsibility to the people I am portraying in the play. They are real, their words are real, and I have a responsibility to live up to their words. I am never as critical of the people I am performing as the audience thinks.

"What if I get stage fright?" I said to Jane.

We couldn't dwell on it. I had to perform that night. When I got home from the show, I got a call from Jane. "How are you feeling?"

"I'm worried I'll get stage fright."

Stage fright is not just nerves. It's much worse. I am told that Sir Laurence Olivier had such bad episodes of stage fright that he would have to have someone standing in the wings that he could see. I don't usually get a bad case of stage fright, but when I do it's memorable.

"You have to think of the thrill," she said. "The thrill of it. It's all an adventure. It's like going through the jungle. The thrill that anything can happen is what you have to think of."

In a way I felt like I were preparing for a big boxing match. It doesn't matter how many times you perform. The only thing that matters is your ability to be in the moment of the doing. It takes a tremendous amount of concentration and spiritual energy. The most important thing to have intact is your will to communicate, your lust to tell the story, as if every moment could fail, or every moment could soar. It's hard.

"You never know about these things. I could go through all this preparation, and he could cancel."

"What are you doing right now?" she said.

"I'm writing a recommendation for a student."

The night before I performed for the president of the United States I was sitting in bed in the Watergate Hotel, with my laptop, writing a recommendation for a student to get into graduate school.

1997

FORD'S THEATER

On Sunday morning I went to a spinning class, swam a mile, had a massage, and headed to the theater for the matinee. When I approached

Ford's Theater, I could see police cars and security tents. It looked like the president was coming after all.

When I got to the backstage entrance, my stage manager came out to meet me. He was a redhead with peachlike skin that was now flushed. His pace was swift. "The place is crawling with security," he said. "You're not going to believe this."

He took my bags and we entered the stage door.

There was a human wall. On both sides, against both walls, all the way down the hall, and all the way up the staircase, there were Secret Service. My stage manager and I recall that they seemed to be standing elbow to elbow. On both sides. Literally, there was a human wall. There were both men and women Secret Service. The women were very ordinary looking. When we got to my dressing room, there were Secret Service outside of it.

My press rep was waiting in a dressing room next to mine. He is from Los Angeles, but by coincidence he was there.

"You okay?"

"Yeah."

"The president will want to see you afterward."

"Okay."

"Need anything?"

By another coincidence, my mother, who lives in Baltimore, and who had seen the show several times already, had come with a busload of friends. I mentioned this as an afterthought.

"Your mother is here?" He paused.

I nodded.

"I'll take care of it." He went off to organize having my mother meet the president too.

I went in to work with my vocal coach, warmed up, and waited for the delayed curtain to finally rise. The theater had to move thirty people out of their seats, so the president could be surrounded by thirty selected, known people.

As I stepped onto the stage I was supremely aware that I was performing where Lincoln was shot, April 14, 1865.

The play is about the tragedy of the Los Angeles riots.

The audience was different that afternoon. They were almost raucous. Almost bouncing off the walls. But there is quite a lot of humor.

When they laughed, they really laughed. They often applauded inside the acts. It was wild. It was a very wild feeling, like being in a coliseum. I looked up often at Lincoln's box.

One of the characters in the play is Professor Cornel West. He is a very hard character to portray. He speaks a very complex English, with a lot of words, constructed, designed like an intricate musical score. It was the hardest thing I ever had to learn, and among the hardest to speak. You can't really go back and get a word in if you miss it because the construction is so tight. It takes a tremendous amount of concentration, and for that reason I put it at the top of the second act, so that I could prepare for it during intermission. I usually lie on the floor during intermission and breathe, or meditate, in preparation.

I went out to begin the second act. There are slides that announce the characters. When Cornel West's slide came up, a very vocal black woman in the audience yelled something out. I added a line to the show: "Don't rush me now." I had learned that from Reverend Weaver. "Don't let them rush the spirit."

Then it hit me. The audience was so wild because *they* were performing for the president too. They wanted him to know what they thought about these people, all of whom were saying racially charged things. This audience was the exact opposite of the audience who passively observes. This audience was proving itself to be a thoughtful citizenry. In its way.

The president's presence can convene a civic dialogue. In that way, I wish I could perform for the president all the time.

After the show, I was taken under the theater, through the museum, with its gory evidence of the assassination of Lincoln, and up the stairs to a holding area to meet the president. Just as I came up, I saw the first lady. She was leaning on a counter. She looked like a teenager who was waiting for her parents. When she saw me, she stood up and congratulated me.

After a while the door opened and the president burst in—with my mother on his arm. He had walked her up the aisle. There was a burst of energy when he came through. He was smiling, and wearing a blue shirt and a yellow tie.

Then my entire family arrived. I hadn't expected my sisters and brothers and their mates as well as my mother, so it was rather overwhelming. The president, the first lady, Al Gore, his son, and their entourage were all crowded around. We were bunched into a crowd, and several photographs were taken.

Finally the crowd began to dwindle. I stood at the door as people took off for the motorcade. I felt like I was saying good-bye at the end of a party at my own house. I was only a visitor at Ford's Theater. Yet theater has the possibility of providing a "house" in the course of two hours, and it was with that feeling that I saw them off.

The president and I had a few exchanges about his upcoming race initiative. He said slowly, "I . . . think the country is ready to do something about it." I was surprised that he wasn't more optimistic.

I turned to go. Someone from the theater said, "Don't go through that door!" Behind the door was the entire audience. They had been waiting for about half an hour—unable to move because the president was still in the theater. As I was taken another way, I could hear the explosion of people being released.

Afterward, the stage manager told me that a member of the SWAT team with a machine gun stood behind him in the small booth the entire time he called the show.

SPRING 1997
NEW YORK CITY

On Monday I was in New York. An article about the president's presence at my show came over my fax machine. I don't read reviews, and everyone who works with me knows that. Since it's unlikely that anyone would send me a review, I didn't expect the article to be a review. It wasn't, but there was a line in it that went something like this: "Her show, which was laced with profanity, brought a standing ovation at the end. The president laughed often." *Which was laced with profanity.*

I was absolutely amazed. This is a show about a tragedy in our country. It has forty-six Americans who testify, witness, expound on what happened to them in that tragedy. It represents a variety of cultures and social classes. Audiences laugh and cry. Sometimes people who are laughing will notice that the person to their left or right is crying at the same thing they found humorous. The language of these people, which is all verbatim, is in its way a gorgeous libretto of their American experience. To reduce it to "laced with profanity"? I was speechless.

1997
A FEW WEEKS LATER

The president was in New York. I had requested an interview. I was told it "might" happen. It was obvious I would be "on call." It's like being in a movie. You arrive in the morning and get ready for the scene. There's a chance that you won't get to the scene. Something could happen, so you're just held, possibly for nothing.

The rule was, the president would meet with me off the record.

He was at the Waldorf. Because I was working in New York at the time, I had taken an apartment on the West Side. I was working on the East Side, but I knew that there was no way I could get home to the West Side and change before meeting with the president. Traffic is impossible when he is in town. It was also clear that I was going to be "slipped in." This meant that I had to be very nearby when I got the go-ahead.

The logistical solution was that I got a hotel room right across the street from the Waldorf, and got dressed and even asked someone to help with my hair and makeup. This was really like being in a movie.

I waited, and at a specific time I called a special number. The man on the other end of the phone told me he would call back. I could look out the window at the Waldorf. The phone rang.

"I'll meet you on the Lexington Avenue side." He described what he looked like.

I went across the street immediately. The rendezvous was successful. I was taken up to the president's suite. I waited in another room, which had been turned into headquarters for the Secret Service. Everything was put to some sort of functional use. There were cables and wires every-where. The room itself was a mess. The "hotelness" of it was gone; it looked like a movie set or a combat headquarters.

I was called in to see the president. I met with him and with Sylvia Mathews, his deputy chief of staff. She sat quietly with a pen and pad. I was told that I could take nothing into the room.

The president spoke about his experiences with the press, because my play was going to be in part about the relationship of the press to the president. "Well, I'm only talking to you because I thought I perhaps I could be useful, by telling you what this is really like. I thought I could give you a feel for it."

The conversation was off the record. He talked for about an hour.

He walked me to the door.

"You were very lithe when you took your bow. Do you practice that a lot?" he asked.

"My bow?" I said. Did he actually mean my bow at the end of the show, as in "take a bow"?

"Yes, I was wondering if you practice that."

I didn't know how to answer that. "Uh, yes."

I said good-bye to the president and told him how grateful I was that he had seen the show and that he had met with me.

Do I practice my *bow*? I thought, as I stood at the elevator. What a *strange* remark. And then I realized that I did have to learn how to bow. Arthur Mitchell, the director of Dance Theatre of Harlem, taught me how to take a bow. It was a simple lesson.

"Watch me," Arthur Mitchell had said. "Bring everything together like this." He stood perfectly straight with his feet perfectly together, his body centered, and his torso tall.

"That's it," he said. "Bring everything together, because you're ending the evening, closing it down." Then he said, "Now, would you like a standing ovation?"

"Sure," I said.

"Then do this." He bent forward, and when he raised his torso, he lifted both of his arms out to the sides with his hands turned up. "You see," he said. "Try it."

I tried.

"That's right, you lift your hands up, you *instruct* them to stand," he said. "And they will."

I had an impulse to go back and tell the president how to take a bow. I couldn't have gotten back in. I also realized, Presidents don't really bow, they wave.

And there we have it. Presidents are not *performers*. Performers bow, and subjects bow. Performers bow because we understand that we are *subjects* of the audience. We do not, as performers, really *rule* the audience. It's a dance, but deep down we *have* to bow, because the audience demand that of us. They understand that, in some kind of odd way, we are speaking only with their permission. Presidents don't bow. They wave, and make victory signs. The presidency has so much to do with winning, and staying in the "win" position. I would imagine it's difficult to find the subject position. Of course, a president can be forced into a subject position by those on the other side who are very interested in turning him into a loser. So where does service happen?

Performers are not winning and losing. We are serving an idea. We are serving a feeling. We are bowing in recognition of those few special moments when we actually touch or feel humanity in its varied aspects. The audience, ideally, is a witness and a participant.

GEORGE STEPHANOPOULOS

FORMER AIDE TO PRESIDENT CLINTON

"Celebrity in Chief"

We're a celebrity culture
and the president is the celebrity in chief
and also there's this *weird* thing with the press
which was *not* true as much before
but this deathwatch has gone out of control
you know the idea that they have to be with him every moment
every second of every day
just in case something happens.
I think the only private time a president has
is when he's in the oval
and he walks from the oval
to either his private study or his private bathroom
that's it.
Once he's in the residence he can move between rooms
but there's still some servants around.
As far as officially, the only truly private time he has is
within that small

sweep
which is one
[he counts]
it's four rooms plus a terrace and one of those rooms is a
    bathroom.
He's sitting at a desk with one of the best views in Washington
certainly the best morning light I've ever seen in my life
but it's got glass this thick
that can't be touched
you've got a s——
two secretaries on the outside,
and two Secret Service people between them,
as you move across the hall in the oval
there's another room to where
there's a tiny little pantry and there's another Secret Service agent
    there
and then you get to my office—
And every door
is wired.
Like if I
moved in the back door
between my office and the oval—
the Secret Service would know because it was wired.
And
I've never thought of it this way before
either.
What happens? When you juxtapose incredible, immense, power
but the price—
I mean it's a different
um.
It's a different devil's choice
The price is
transparency.
Everything you do is known.
You can be the most powerful person in the world.
You're going to uh
have every privilege known to man.

Every whim! Is going to be catered to.
[he's chewing something]
The *deal* is
you can do whatever you want.
The price is that everybody is going to know *everything* you do!
It's beautiful!
And actually I've never thought of it before
but that's it!
A corollary to the rule
everything will be known—
but all that will be remembered in the short term is the bad.
They all feel that none of their good is acknowledged and that all
    of their
bad is exaggerated.
And,
and every one of them would do it again.
You have more power in
a second to help people
you could have never
thought of helping
than most people will have—
not most people—
than most
countries will have in twenty years.
The less noble things are—
I mean all that power
and you'll never be forgotten
at some level.
Not a bad gamble if you're in the position to accept it
if it was a locked deal.
[Pause]
I would be scared to death
To know there's no such thing as a private moment in my life . . .

CULTURE WARS AND

DOMESTIC BEATINGS

THE CULTURE WARS ARE NOT NEW. ANY OF US CAN GET CAUGHT IN the middle of them. If you are moving in the middle of the war zone, you might get hit. Be prepared.

CIRCA 1850
IN ABRAHAM LINCOLN'S TIME

I learned a lesson from Elizabeth Keckley, who was the dressmaker for Mary Todd Lincoln. She wrote an autobiography called *Behind the Scenes, or, Thirty Years a Slave and Four Years in the White House.* A large part of the book is about her taking care of Mrs. Lincoln after the death of Abraham Lincoln. Mrs. Lincoln was nearly penniless, so Mrs. Keckley accompanied her to New York to sell some of her dresses. There were those who felt that she took advantage of her closeness to Mrs. Lincoln in writing the book.

There was a takeoff, or burlesque, written about Mrs. Keckley's autobiography. It was called "Behind the Seams: by a Nigger Woman Who Took in Work for Mrs. Lincoln and Mrs. Davis." The work did not list an author, and it was signed with an X, said to be the mark of Betsy Keckley. It was published in a newspaper.

I read both Mrs. Keckley's autobiography and the takeoff. I was amazed at the time spent on the takeoff. It was a vulgar translation, word for word, of the original. For example, Mrs. Keckley's book begins, "My name is Elizabeth Keckley, my life has been an eventful one. I was born a slave, was a child of slave parents. The twelve hundred dollars with which I purchased the freedom of myself and son, I consented to accept only as a loan."

And the burlesque begins, "My name is Betsey Kickly, and I am a most extraordinary nigger. As this is the case and as a large number of people who know me have often requested me to write my life for the benefit from a pecuniary point of view, as I am hard up, and the pension of eight dollars a month does not suffice to pay my board, I am going to try an experiment and see if I can't make more money by writing a book than by taking in sewing."

We have talk shows and late-night comedy shows to take the place of such newspaper burlesques but, from as far back as Jefferson's time, in respected papers, we find forms of these burlesques in the attitudes that journalists have toward their subjects.

It may be that public life simply cannot have civility. I noticed a strong similarity between the narratives of slave beatings and the narratives of political beatings. Compare the following account of a beating from Elizabeth Keckley's narrative, and the story of former governor of Texas Ann Richards, who endured a political beating.

It was Saturday evening, and while I was bending over the bed, watching the baby that I had just hushed into slumber, Mr. Bingham came to the door and asked me to go with him to his study. Wondering what he meant by his strange request, I followed him, and when we had entered the study he closed the door, and in his blunt way remarked: "Lizzie, I am going to flog you."

"Whip me, Mr. Bingham! What for?"

"No matter," he replied. "I am going to whip you, so take down your dress this instant."

Recollect, I was eighteen years of age, was a woman fully developed, and yet this man coolly bade me take down my dress. I drew myself up proudly, firmly and said, "No, Mr. Bingham, I shall not take down my dress before you. Moreover, you shall not whip me unless you prove the stronger."

He seized a rope, caught me roughly, tried to tie me. I resisted with all my strength, but he was the stronger of the two, and after a hard struggle succeeded in binding my hands and tearing my dress from my back. Then he picked up a rawhide and began to ply it freely over my shoulders. With steady hand and practised eye he would raise the instrument of torture, nerve himself for a blow, and with fearful force the rawhide descended upon the quivering flesh. It cut the skin, raised great welts, and the warm blood trickled down my back. Oh God! I can feel the torture now—the terrible, excruciating agony of those moments. I did not scream: I was too proud to let my tormentor know what I was suffering. On the Friday following the Saturday which I was so savagely beaten, Mr. Bingham again directed me to come to his study. On entering the room I found him prepared with a new rope and a new cowhide. I told him that I was ready to die, but that he could not conquer me. In struggling with him, I bit his finger severely, when he seized a heavy stick and beat me with it in a shameful manner. Again I went home sore and bleeding. The following Thursday Mr. Bingham again tried to conquer me, but in vain. We struggled, and he struck me many savage blows. As I stood bleeding before him, nearly exhausted with his efforts, he burst into tears, and declared that it would be a sin to beat me more.

JUNE 1997

RESTAURANT NORA

WASHINGTON, D.C.

I was having dinner with Ann Richards and one of her previous campaign organizers, Jane Hickie. The subject got around to her campaign for governor. Her opponents did all manner of things—they brought up the fact that she had been treated for alcoholism, and accused her of drug addiction. She was toughened by the time she met this opponent by her campaign for treasurer, during which she was accused of being mentally ill, and of beating her children. So she had learned how to fight back.

ANN RICHARDS: Well, I remember them telling me what I had to do. I remember that—the campaign saying, Okay, you've got to go in there and you've got to let these guys have it. In honesty, I think that they thought each other was the opponent. I don't think they thought I had a hoot in Hades' chance of winning, and as a consequence, when they discovered that, really, I was the one they had to beat, they were both kind of tacky. But the campaign told me I had to go out there and I had to let them have it. And I can't even remember what all—I can't remember what all I said. All I know is that I felt very very cool. I was very self-possessed. I was very cool. I was very cool. In fact, I can still feel the power of it. It was real—because I know that's what I know how to do. I know how to, I know how to walk out and communicate. I mean that's really what I do best. So going out to a press conference and cleaning somebody's clock is no challenge.

JANE HICKIE: There were people packed in that room and you couldn't move. It was a full-scale—you know they're talking about the wrong thing, and "what's important here is"—I mean, she took charge. She used the attack on her as leverage.

ANN RICHARDS: I changed the focus of the campaign.

JANE HICKIE: And I mean there were people hanging out. You couldn't get in the doors. You couldn't get in the room. We were in the campaign headquarters, and Ann walked out, and I mean there were—it was just like this, and nobody was breathing. And she hit it and she was on it, and she was in charge, and they hadn't beat her. She beat them. And it was—everybody knew it. I mean, it was just—the place blew up.

The dialogue of campaigning is the dialogue of beatings. It is perhaps naïve of us, in the general public, to believe that civic discourse can take place while a beating is going on. As it turns out, these beatings can go on after a candidate has won. If there is no room for us to talk while they are beating each other, when shall our discourse occur? We have to carve out other spaces. People say that we fight because we are at peace. We give lip service to the need to make use of peacetime to get further ahead in making domestic life more civil in all ways. The danger of trying to find a way to talk to each other in the atmosphere of culture wars is that, inevitably, the fight "they" are having takes all the attention. But their fight is half performance, half bluster, half an adrenaline rush. We end up as mere spectators. There's a price to our spectatorship too.

PAULETTE JENKINS

INMATE,

MARYLAND CORRECTIONAL INSTITUTE FOR WOMEN

"Mirror to Her Mouth"

This is like when you bein abused you know and you don't tell?
Then somebody tell?
Then somebody
tell.
[she laughs]
I think he's a damned good president
how he conducts his job is one thing
it's just like
someone can have on two hats.
In some homes you would never think
that father abused that child
because look how well
dressed the child is
look how
the home is and
know what I'm sayin?
He got a good job,
but
you never know.
And that's how it start
that's exactly how it start.
When he becomes jealous
and want to be with you all the time.
You know.
And want to know why you're not doing this.
And why the children are making so much noise.
And can you keep 'em quiet?

And it began to escalate.
And it escalated.
I began to learn how to cover it up.
Because I didn't want nobody to know that this was happening in
    my home.
Ya know
I wanted everyone to think that we were a normal family,
and I mean
we had all the materialistic things.
But that didn't make my children pain any less.
I ran out of excuses about how we got black eyes,
and busted lips and bruises.
Me and the kids.
I didn't have no more excuses.
But it didn't change the fact that it was a nightmare,
for my children
it was a nightmare.
And I failed them,
dramatically.
Because I allowed it to continue on and on and on.
And the night that she got killed—
and the intensity just grew and grew and grew.
Until one night,
we came home,
from getting drugs,
and he got angry with Myeshia,
and he started beating her,
and he just continued to beat her.
He had a belt he would use a belt.
Because he had this warped perverted thing that Myeshia
was
having sex with her little brother
or
they was fondling each other.
That would be his reason.
I'm just speaking of the particular night that she died.
And he beat her.

And he put her in the bathtub.
And I was in the bedroom.
But before all this happened—
four months before she died—
I thought I could really fix this man.
So I had a baby by him.
Insane?
Thinking that
if I give him his own kid
he'll leave mine alone.
But the night that Myeshia died,
I stayed in the room with the baby
and I heard him
just beating her
just beating her
like I said he had her in the bathtub
and every time he would hit her—
she would fall.
And she would hit her head on the tub.
I could hear it.
It happened continuously,
repeatedly.
[whispering]
And I dared not to move.
I didn't move.
I didn't even go see what was happening.
I just sat there and listened.
And then later
[she sucks her teeth]
he sat her in the hallway
and
told her just set there.
And she set there for bout
four to five hours.
And then he told her to get up,
[crying]
and when she got up she said she couldn't see.

[whispering, crying]
Her face was bruised.
And she had a black eye.
All around her head was just swollen.
Her head looked like it was two sizes of its own size.
I told him let her go to sleep, and he let her go to sleep.
[whispering]
The next morning she was dead.
He went in and checked on her for school.
And he got very excited.
And he said
"She won't breathe."
I knew immediately that she was dead.
Cause I went in—
I didn't even want to accept the fact that she was dead.
So I went and took a mirror to her mouth.
There
was no-thing, coming out of her mouth.
Nothing.
He said
"We cannot let nobody know about this,
so you got to help me."
And we got the baby
and we drove like out to
[hear her getting the slightest bit tired here]
I-95.
I was so petrified
and so numb
all I could look
was in the rearview mirror.
And he just laid her right on the shoulder of the highway.
My own chile.
I let that happen too.

"THAT'S NOT MY JOB"

DIANA WALKER, THE PHOTOGRAPHER FOR *TIME* MAGAZINE WHOM I had met on the '96 campaign trail, gave me a small dinner party at her house. I was seated between Art Buchwald and a correspondent from *Time*.

I struck up a conversation with the *Time* correspondent. I asked him if he liked the president. He said, "That's not my job." That was during the first course.

He said that liking the president wasn't the point. You don't like the man, in fact you try to stay as far away from the man as you can. You're trying to look at the man in the office and at the degree to which he lives up to the office. He was very expressive when he talked, moving his head a lot. He said that my questions were as discreet as my answers.

I suddenly saw the president and the presidency as a man and a shadow, the shadow being the office. What's odd about shadows is that they change according to where the sun is at any given time of the day. Ann Lewis had talked to me about the president as wearing a "cloak." The cloak is the presidency. So there's a difference between the president and the presidency.

I offered up that you don't just look at a movie star as who she or he is. You are always looking at the movie star against the backdrop of something called movie star–ness. I gave an example of a movie star. He didn't agree that my example was really a movie star and offered up his idea of a real movie star—Holly Hunter. People—including journalists—have very personal reactions, very nonobjective reactions to presidents, movie stars, and more. Objective as they claim to be, I found journalists to be among the most opinionated people I have met—more opinionated than academics.

The correspondent then said that Washington was a city of fear. I told him that John Lahr had once described L.A. as a city of envy. Fear and envy, each in a capital of the nation's discourse. Then another guest said from across the table that Washington is a city where you delight in other people's failures. The conversation held little optimism.

When we were eating dessert, the same woman asked me, "Do you like the president?"

Taking a deep breath, I said, "That's not my job."

I said, "I hate to use a four-letter word here, but I'm an actress. My job is to love the character, to love the president."

The actor's love, of course, is a kind of greed, a greed to be the other, to know the other by being the other. The journalist, it seems, knows the other, in part by being skeptical of the other. Neither way of knowing is necessarily a "nice" way. In both cases you are crossing a threshold, invading, occupying an area where, in reality, you don't belong. Caution, perhaps, is the best approach.

TALKING TO THE
PRESIDENT

FALL 1997
THE WHITE HOUSE
WASHINGTON, D.C.

HAD BEEN TRYING TO GET AN ON-THE-RECORD INTERVIEW WITH THE president since 1995. This had entailed going to a variety of events where I had twenty-second interactions with him, getting him to my show *Twilight,* and having had an hour off-the-record conversation with him.

I was in rehearsal at the Arena Stage for the first workshop version of *House Arrest.* This was all pre–Monica Lewinsky.

The call came. This meant that everything else I was doing had to stop.

I was told that I should come to the press conference that Clinton was doing with the president of China. I was instructed to arrive about an hour before the conference began. When I arrived, no one was there except the photographers, who always arrive early to stake out their positions. I was taken to a seat near the side door. I was told that just before the president was finished with the press conference, I would be escorted to where he was, and, depending on a cue from Mike McCurry, if all systems were go, I could speak to the president for about five minutes, while he was in a kind of holding pattern. I was warned that this could all change, but that this was what we would aim for.

I sat on the side of the room during the press conference. The president seemed very calm throughout, and less expressive than usual. As the press conference was coming to an end, one of Mike McCurry's assistants beckoned to me from outside a door that led into the hallway of the

Old Executive Office Building. I gathered my tape-recording equipment and followed her. The president was just coming out. Mike McCurry met me. "We'll walk with him and see what's going to happen."

Everything was in motion, and it was not what I expected. I had imagined I would be in a small holding area for a few moments. This was moving. I had never been with the president when he was "moving." I knew what it was supposed to feel like from scenes I had been in in *The American President*. The blocking was the same, but there were lots more people, and real Secret Service up the ante in a way that anchors can't. It felt like I was on a kind of moving sidewalk—or a bit like when I was on-stage with the Alvin Ailey Dance Company. You have no choice but to move with them, it's amazing the first time you do it.

McCurry did a kind of a narrative as we walked along, sort of explaining to me what was happening. The way he talked was a striking counterpoint to the ambience of what was happening. His manner was very low-key, whereas the activities around me were extremely high-powered. The president was walking in front of a small crowd with the president of China. There were Secret Service behind him and all around him. It was like a small parade.

"Let's walk with the president," McCurry said at one point. So we moved just a little ahead, and I found myself standing right next to the president, with McCurry on my other side.

He said, "Mr. President, remember, we were talking about maybe you would talk with Anna for a few moments. You think that will be okay?"

"Sure," he said.

I was stunned at how this sounded. It was as if they were making this decision on the spur of the moment, when really, my ending up next to the president had taken several phone calls, security clearances, and four years' worth of other efforts. "Thanks a lot," I said. "I really appreciate it."

Although I wasn't acting, it had the feel of saying your lines onstage or in a movie when it's your first time. And I had spoken to the president on a few occasions now, but this time he was flanked by all his "motion." When you're acting with a big movie star, or in front of the camera for the first time—you are prepared, and you know your lines, but there's still something that feels very staged. The simplest line causes you tension.

The president was walking alongside the president of China. He did an introduction. "This is Anna Deavere Smith," he said to the president of China. "She is a great actress and a wise woman."

When I listen to the lines of this conversation on tape, my language sounds very "fake"—something that a director would make me redo. Yet I wasn't acting. I was simply being me in a very unusual experience, in fact, in a "bigger than life" experience. That's how some people would define acting. I actually think it's not enough to "just be you" in a bigger than life experience. In life and onstage, I think you have to rise to those occasions.

McCurry, somehow, very smoothly veered us away from the president, and we walked behind him as he continued to talk to the president of China. I now found myself walking between Madeleine Albright and Erskine Bowles.

"Anna, do you know Erskine?" McCurry said, as though we were all on a first-name basis.

I said how glad I was to meet him, and I smiled at Madeleine Albright.

McCurry continued to me, "I'm not sure exactly where you'll talk with him, but we'll just follow."

It was like being on a small ship. There was the sound of all the feet moving down the hallway of the Old Executive Office Building. I kept waiting for someone to call "cut."

We followed the president out of the building. He said a public good-bye to the president of China and went into the side door of the White House. The two presidents had a further about thirty-second conversation. And that was it. The president of China took off.

We went into the White House, which from that entrance in particular has no grandeur at all. The offices are sort of tacky. It would remind you of a side entrance to any suburban home—like entering a house through the den, or the most used part, a recreation room, for example.

McCurry said, "I think maybe you're going to do this in the Oval. I'm not sure."

We kept walking, and I found myself standing in the middle of the Oval Office. The president disappeared for a moment.

I had been in the Oval Office before, after one of the president's radio addresses. I had my picture taken with the president and the vice president. Having been in the movie *The American President* also took some of the once-in-a-lifetime feeling out of the event. The set design had been so accurate that I felt as though I had spent a lot of time in this room already. The scenes I shot in the Oval Office on a soundstage in Los Angeles are merged with my sitting with the president in the real Oval Office.

For a second, I flashed on a conversation I'd had with Nell Painter, a biographer of Sojourner Truth, in which she described Sojourner's visit with President Lincoln. She described the effort it took to get Sojourner Truth there, and pointed out that although she made it sound as if it were a wonderful meeting, in actuality Lincoln had kept her waiting for a long time, while he talked with some white male visitors, and addressed her as Auntie, which was a diminutive way of referring to black women. My interaction with Clinton was quite different from Sojourner Truth's interaction with Lincoln.

Clinton sat down, leaned over in his chair as if he were speaking to an old pal, and, sounding like a black woman really—a "girlfriend"—said, "How you doin', girl?"

One of the White House photographers snapped a couple of pictures. One of the aides said, "Mr. President, what do you think? About ten minutes?" He said yes, they shut the door and left.

It was just me, the president, and my tape recorder. I was later told that this was unusual. He is seldom left unstaffed, and they normally also do their own tape recording if he is being recorded.

Since I was to have only ten minutes, I jumped straight to questions I thought would get him to really speak. I began by asking him if he felt he was being treated like a common criminal. This was four months before the Monica Lewinsky story broke, but he had already been through the wringer.

He paused, and said thoughtfully, "I think George Washington said that. I don't know about that. No, I wouldn't say that."

He then took off on a jazzlike riff on how unfriendly his relationships with the press were. "I think that the political press has this image that the presidency is so all-powerful that none of the presumptions should apply, no presumption of innocence, no presumption that some techniques and things are off balance."

He is a very expressive man.

"I mean, it's really chilling when you think about what happened.

When Hillary's legal, uh, bills were found, Oh! It was all over the papers, right? She had to go talk to the grand jury. *First lady,* going to the grand jury . . . *big* pictures." He was sitting on the edge of his seat.

I had also met with George Bush, and with Jimmy Carter. Clinton was playing a whole different kind of music. Carter, sitting in his chair at the Carter Center, was very relaxed and comfortable for the entire interview. He was warm and gracious, but, although he was out of office, he seemed significantly careful, watching every word. Bush and I had met across the street from the White House in the summer of '97, on a sweltering day. It was so hot that nobody could move. Bush was upstairs in an elegant room with a table. He had taken his jacket off, loosened his tie. He drank Orange Crush soda on ice and ate two huge chocolate chip cookies, which had been made especially for him by the White House chef. He spoke very informally, with long, easy tones, and with a surprising irreverence for the press. He hadn't appreciated the way they tried to make him look as though he were without guts—and talked about how he'd just jumped out of an airplane. He made it sound easy, and had a sense of humor about some of the things that had happened. His sounds were those of "Oh it's all right, it'll be all right."

Bush gave what for me was a memorable warning when I said, "Some people say maybe we don't need a president."

"As long as we're fat, dumb, and happy, that may be right. Long as the economy is good, people say, 'Get the government out of my life, we don't need it.' Economy goes down, people get thrown out of work, that'll change. But as long as the economy is good and people are happy, you're not gonna have any great worrying about the White House."

He said all this as he easily broke off a chunk of chocolate chip cookie and took a swig of Orange Crush. He was perfectly happy to pass the time and do someone a favor. He had nothing to lose. Dana Carvey had imitated him already.

Nora and I and all the interns working on the project had thought of several questions to ask Clinton. His dossier was understandably pretty hefty. Yet I didn't have to ask very many questions. He held forth nonstop. "Today you have all the power in the world, and you can do everything but protect yourself. And the people you love."

People would come in to try to stop the meeting. "Uh, Mr. President, you're supposed to be speaking tonight, and I want to make sure every-thing's okay, you should rest your voice."

"I'm fine."

The door shut. Exit.

He spoke as though he had everything to lose, but they were trying to take it all from him anyway, so what the hell, let it rip. It was nearly ab-surd at this point. "It's like *Darkness at Noon,* Koestler's book, the Stalinist show trials. They decided what the truth was and told people to tell it."

Clinton's sounds were jagged, even sharp; sometimes he was barely getting his breath. There was an urgency—even though it was just he and I.

Someone abruptly opened the door, took a look, and left.

"There are elements in the press that believe that the only way that people who talk about politics matter is if the president's being weak-ened, shown up to be a bad guy. Somehow you have to prove yourself in-nocent, and if you can't it's your fault."

He laughed for a moment, and sat back. "But the country's done well. It seems for some of 'em, the better the country does the madder they get. The more they want—" He was laughing. The laugh had a squeak to it, and the sounds he made would have concerned a good vocal coach. He was getting very hoarse. I was surprised to hear the door open exactly at that moment, the moment he was laughing.

This time a slender white woman with a southern accent walked in. "You really ought to rest your voice. It's really, I'm sorry," she said, with a very concerned look on her face.

The president did not turn around to look at her. He merely said, "Okay. Go 'head. I'll be right there."

She held her ground. "But you're really straining it, and Mike had said five minutes and I've let it go about ten now."

The president didn't even look in the direction of the door. He waved her away. "Okay. Bye."

She left. The door shut.

He was on a roll. He had a wider range of expression than most of the people I had interviewed.

When I was in rehearsal, preparing to perform some of the people I had interviewed, my vocal coach listened to the tapes of interviews. She was struck, as I was, that the incarcerated women were oddly freer vo-cally than the press people I had interviewed, and the people who worked in the White House. Whereas the voices of the Washington insiders tended to be constrained in one place or another, the prisoners had full range, and especially full use of the lower parts of their bodies. Perhaps the inner workings of the voice are a rare place to find freedom when you are bound. African Americans have explored that area in song and in oratory during times of restraint.

As I watched the president I marveled at how uninhibited he was in the ironically small space he had. We're told that the only space he has is the Oval Office and a few rooms surrounding it. During the interview he sat in his yellow chair, but he moved forward, he moved back, he moved to the side, he gestured, he came all the way to the tip of the chair, and then sat all the way back. Only very expressive people do this. How could this be? Wouldn't the most observed person be the most inhibited?

People say that Clinton performs, that he is very aware of the picture he is making. In this case, that did not seem to be so. He was being led by his passion. He was telling me about what happened to Mrs. Clinton when, during Whitewater, they found her legal bills. Very exasperated, he said, "We said, 'We're glad they turned up because they support her story.' " He moved forward in his chair, gesturing expansively. *"Why would we cover up records that support her story?* That's what we said, that was down in . . . paragraph ten here."

Then he talked about how a Republican law firm had spent $4 million looking into all the documents of the savings and loan investigation. "You know what it said? No basis for criminal action! No basis for a civil suit! The records—support—Hillary's account!" He stopped short, as if he barely had the breath to finish. Then he leaned forward, whispering intensely. "Did all those people who [here he raised his volume] *blared* the record discovery, who *blared* the grand jury testimony bother—to—tell—the—American—people—that—that's—what—this—report—done—by—a—Republican—law firm, after they spent almost four—million—dollars, said?"

And then he bounced forward further, like Ali out of the rope-a-dope. *"No!"*

And he made a very raspy sound. "Little bitty notice made!"

Little bitty notice made? When people start talking like that is when I normally say in an interview, "Now you're talking." By *now* you're talking—I mean, now you are past language as information. I don't need information, I only need you to come out of the confines of presentable sentence structure, to bust right out of grammar to show me who you are.

It was jazz. Clinton was in a class by himself. Yet, I wondered why he was so aggravated. I wondered why his voice was so raspy, beyond allergies, beyond overuse.

Whatever it was, I'm not a judge. I'm not a jury. I'm not the IRS. I'm not the press. I'm not a special prosecutor. I don't think any of those perspectives would get me any closer to the heart of America or its soul. What I'm looking for is not what is right or wrong, I'm looking for what is right *and* wrong, and more than the sum of both.

I wasn't there to indict the man. I wasn't there to expose him. I was there to listen to him, and to try to get him to talk to me with "litty bitty notice made." My mind catapulted back quickly to that linguist who had given me the three questions at the beginning of my work on language.

The president was answering, without my asking him, one of the three questions. He was speaking as if he were answering "Have you ever been accused of something that you did not do?" Sometimes we find ourselves in a position where we speak as though we are always answering one of those three questions, as if one of those three questions is the very foundation of who we are.

"I think the thing is totally—out of . . . whack!" he said and sat back on "whack!"

Then a pause, and then out again. "I mean it's really *chilling* when you think about what happened! I was stupid enough to believe 'em when they said if we were honest, and forthright, it would clear the air!"

I had to do a very intense kind of listening to absorb it all. My tape recorder would never absorb this. Technology makes flat renderings, and it requires that we deliver a flat performance. You don't want to be too big for television. Television diminishes the humanness of our presidents, of our actors—of all our public figures, who by nature are *bigger* than life. Television, by its nature, likes people who are *smaller* than life. It's a little screen. It is intimate. Just you and me in your living room. It would be healthier to create technology that allows us to be as big, as heroic as we are.

After about thirty-five minutes, the door opened for the last time. Rahm Emmanuel walked right into the center of the room, around and in front of the president, and said, "I'm gonna do one thing. He's got to do a toast tonight. And I don't want im ta lose his voice."

I said thank you, shook hands with the president, and left.

GOT BACK TO REHEARSAL. SOME OF THE ACTORS OF COURSE WERE dying to know. "How was it?"

"It was fine," was all I said.

I couldn't have been back in the rehearsal hall for more than fifteen minutes when an intern came over to me and said, with alarm in her eyes, "It's the White House!"

I went to the phone. It was Mike McCurry. "What did he *say* in there?" he asked.

I gave a general summation.

"He was worried that he might have gone too far."

I tried to allay Mike's fears.

As I hung up the phone, I thought to myself, There is no going too far, if all you're listening for is rhythm and music. In fact, I wish more people would go further.

BILL NELSON

LEGAL SCHOLAR

NEW YORK UNIVERSITY SCHOOL OF LAW

"These People Rich and Those People Poor"

They [the press]
are enormously valuable, effective uh and I think important in
     bringing to light certain key scandals
such as Watergate,
I mean uh
the idea that we have to fear the press more than we have to fear
     government is absurd.

I think we have to fear the government immensely and uh
I think the uh, the uh, the opportunities and incentives for corruption
    in government are
huge, and the opportunities
and incentives for corruption on the part of the press are relatively
    small.
Uh the
uh uh
I think people who want to maintain private lives do not have much
    difficulty
maintaining private lives
and I think the press is indeed
I've never felt
I
I've never felt the press
of reporters upon me.
I'm sort of constantly battling the handful of real graduate students
    around this place who take Foucault seriously.
I understand that there are a lot of mechanisms creating culture
and it's important what those mechanisms creating culture are.
But the ability of government to come in and take your money
and to do it through the withholding tax
and then the ability of government to decide how to spend that
    money
and then it's my understanding that anyone who has ever made big
    money in the United States has done it as a result of receiving
    government subsidies in one form or another.
I'm,
there are exceptions
but I mean
the decision of government to let the money go this way rather than
    that
has an extraordinary tendency to make these people rich
and those people poor.
They certainly create the mind-set
uh
but they don't interfere with people's lives

the way that government does.
Uh the
I mean one has the uh
you know
occasional things come to mind
like there was this gay magazine outing people a while ago.
That seems to me
uh
very intrusive,
but I suspect the uh
the New York City Police Department outed a lot more gay people
    than that magazine
ever did.
I think the move away from fearing government
the move away from appreciating how much harm government can
    do
and how much good government can do
uh
has diverted people's attention from politics and from elections and
    has produced a lot of
the worst elections that we you know
uh uh
has produced
and God knows what it'll produce in the year 2000.

THE DEATH DRIVE:

IT'S THE MAD HATTER'S

TEA PARTY AND

TOM DeLAY IS POURING

WINTER, SPRING 1998
WASHINGTON, NEW YORK, LOS ANGELES,
SAN FRANCISCO, PALO ALTO

THERE WAS A TUMBLE OF TALK. I WAS REVISING MY PLAY *HOUSE ARREST*. It had had a "work in progress" performance in Washington. The idea was, I would revise it for a second performance scheduled for spring '98 in Los Angeles. I was on a plane from New York to San Francisco. The beginning of the story of Monica Lewinsky was in *The New York Times*.

Rather than going right to my computer when I got home, as planned, I went right to my tape recorder and plugged it into my telephone. I began immediately doing interviews over the phone. It was like starting all over again. Yet at that point no one was sure how far this would go, or not go. It went, as you know, very far. Too far.

SPRING 1998

Was Clinton lying? The press could not deal with it. I'm not saying they should have. They seemed significantly more distressed about it than the rest of the nation.

In the midst of this I began to wonder when we, as human beings, begin to learn about truths and lies. I called my sister, whose little girl was two at the time.

"She does know what it means to tell the truth."

"Does she know what a lie is?"

"I don't think she understands fully what a lie is. She makes up stories. She doesn't tell the full truth about some things. For instance she might hide her shoes somewhere and when I ask her where they are she says she doesn't know and will say that her daddy hid them or she'll blame things on Jessica you know the cat."

SUMMER 1998

Monica Lewinsky's semen-stained blue dress was found and displayed to the world. The DNA labs had gotten hold of it and showed that the president had not told the truth. I did another rewrite. The day we performed that rewrite turned out to be the day that Monica Lewinsky went before the grand jury for the first time.

Then, on August 17, 1998, Clinton confessed to the nation. I was on Martha's Vineyard at the time and soon saw the president at a party. He looked, as they say, "terrible." Yet I marveled at how he and the first lady had the stamina to show up in public at all. Every conversation had such an enormous subtext. The president caught my eye and said, "Let's go listen to the music." It meant nothing, but carried the weight of his reality. The first lady and I talked about the lack of women of color on the faculty at Stanford, where Chelsea was at school. Anything she talked about would seem to be an avoidance of the circumstances. But did any of us think that she or the president would talk about the real circumstances? Of course not.

The next morning I went to the president's radio address held in a school library. A young woman stood in front of a microphone, like a human clock, saying steadily, "The president's radio address will begin in exactly ten minutes from your mark. Mark. The president's radio address will begin in exactly nine minutes from your mark. Mark." I thought I was in a shooting gallery, or on an archery field—somewhere where there was a target. The president appeared, did the radio address, and had his picture taken with everyone who wanted a photo. We all had to fill out index cards with our addresses. The president looked tired, many of us said knowingly. But what did we know, other than the obvious.

I wrote another draft in September. I was waiting for FedEx to come pick it up, and television was broadcasting nonstop coverage on Congress's vote on whether or not to release the Starr Report. The draft went via FedEx. I took a flight to New York the next day. Everybody on the plane had *The New York Times* wide open reading the excerpts. Never had I seen such a flood of open newspapers on a plane trip.

This was a very difficult time to do theater, which likes to have nailed down, finished stories. The theater is not designed, just on the level of logistics, to keep up with real life. Perhaps theater is meant to be a more leisurely assessment of life as it goes by. I have been trying to create theater that reflects my time, as I live it. The story of the president was a marathon.

Even my classroom at Stanford held surprises.

FALL 1998

STANFORD UNIVERSITY, PALO ALTO, CALIFORNIA

It was the first day of class. I asked my students to do an exercise in which they portrayed one another's dreams. One dream was very strange. I asked the student for an explanation. She explained that the dream was about Chris Rock accusing her father of all kinds of things on the radio. She went on to say that Chris Rock in reality had accused her father of things on the radio. There was whispering in the class. "Who's her father?"

As I left the classroom I saw two grown men dressed in slacks and golf shirts just outside the door. The department administrator was there too, with revised class lists.

I took the lists and said, "Starr? Is . . ."

"I should have told you," he said.

Yes, he should have. Caroline Starr, Kenneth Starr's daughter, was in my class. Chelsea Clinton and Caroline Starr were at Stanford. Caroline stayed in the class for the semester. And the federal agents stood outside all semester.

To teach acting with something as dramatic as the Starr Report permeating our culture was an interesting predicament. I did not discuss the report or my work in class because of who was in my class. Caroline volunteered to keep attendance and a record of who was late for class when no one else would. She was also very well prepared all of the time. And although she was a freshman in a class of mostly upperclassmen, to some extent she "ran" the room. Celebrity power. No one ever contested her views or opinions. The class was strikingly apolitical.

The other class I taught was reading the writings of Konstantin Stanislavsky, the "father" of the acting "method." He was the main force behind what we know acting to be today. He brought naturalism to acting technique. One of my students came to office hours flushed in the face.

"I can't believe this book!" she said, speaking of Stanislavsky's text *An Actor Prepares,* which was written in Russia in the nineteenth century. "I am a student of Russian history, and this book is written as if he has no idea what is going on in the world around him!"

I understood his predicament. Sometimes it is impossible to get art to catch up with life. Then again, some of us don't try to get it to catch up. I taught simple, basic acting with no reference to the odd theater of our time. But then again, acting is not about truth and lies in the ordinary sense of truth and lies. Acting is not reality, but sometimes it is more about reality than reality.

FALL 1998

MY APARTMENT

SAN FRANCISCO

Suddenly history was no more stable than the present. A retired scientist named Eugene Foster did DNA testing and came up with further evidence that it was most likely the case that Thomas Jefferson was the father of Sally Hemings's children.

The people at Monticello were giddy with talk. The black descendants of Sally Hemings and Thomas Jefferson were on *The Oprah Winfrey Show.* There was a flurry of talk. The scientist, of course, could not get some of the finer points across.

"I have emphasized strongly, and in a loud voice, in many statements to the press that we would not be able to prove anything either positively or negatively with a hundred percent certainty."

I asked him what he thought the public believed.

"I think the general public has come to believe that we proved the relationship. We absolutely cannot say that!"

He was stuck on the idea of probability. Which is fundamental to science, but nobody cared about that. "They want to know, well, is it or isn't it?"

The press and everybody else, including Monticello, was off and running. The debate about Sally Hemings and Thomas Jefferson had been a part of the play. Now it looked as though there was no debate.

I visited the DNA lab at Stanford, which does some of the best work in the world on the human genome project. For all the seriousness of the work, I found the place to be refreshingly lighthearted, perhaps because it's all about evidence. As I entered, I remarked, "This place smells like egg salad."

"That's Ralph's hair," the postdoc who was my guide said, alluding to his wiry colleague.

They were in the process of "spinning" DNA. Literally.

My guide took me to a blackboard and showed me a complicated equation of X and Y chromosomes that displayed the relationship between Jefferson's DNA and that of his presumed sons.

After an intense hour in the lab, I thought back on the equation and said, "Now, wait a minute. All of this information is about Sally Hemings's *sons,* is that right?"

"Right."

"So, if she had had only daughters, we wouldn't be here, is that right?"

"Right."

Even in science—that which is thought to be real truth, real fact—the patriarchy reigned again.

Knowledge itself is so dependent on human achievement. Inherent in knowledge is ignorance. What, then, are "facts"? Temporary truths?

I was reminded of something David Broder had said at breakfast during my first year in Washington. "Instead of the *New York Times* thing about all the news that's fit to print, we would say to the people on the front page every day, 'This is a partial, hasty, compressed, necessarily distorted version of some of the news yesterday. We'll be back tomorrow and try to improve on the quality of the information we're giving you.' Because that's the truth."

FEBRUARY 1999
POST MONICA LEWINSKY
THE ZUNI CAFÉ
SAN FRANCISCO

The Zuni Café sits on a sunny corner on Market Street in San Francisco. It has gourmet food, often organically grown, always correctly served. I'm told the shoestring potatoes are terrific. There's an oyster bar. I know the owner, and there are a couple of pocketed tables that are perfect for tape-recorded interviews. I was interviewing Judith Butler, scholar of rhetoric.

"This was the second thing that interested me about the transcript. Is the sexual ambivalence. Why he could pursue pleasure to a certain degree and then he couldn't really uh let her—"

I chimed in. "But we weren't actually there ourselves. So this is according to Monica Lewinsky. According to *her.*"

I regretted saying that. I couldn't stop myself from thinking of things as though I were going to "play" Clinton. In which case I would have to try to see things in his best interest.

In the course of the past four years, I had interviewed Butler about eight times. She was always, for all her black-leather-jacketed, sometimes tough exterior, very gracious.

"Well, according to *her.* That's right," she conceded. "He pursued it to a certain degree. He maybe once or twice allowed her to bring him to a climax, but otherwise he didn't allow that to happen. We assumed he either gave himself that satisfaction or went without it. I do think there was a certain moral moment. 'I can't go that far.' 'I'll get addicted to you.' 'I won't be able to stop . . .' " Her voice was reaching a singsong.

We had known about Monica Lewinsky for a full year. At Christmastime Clinton had bombed Iraq. I was in San Francisco, holed up in its rainy season, working on the seventh or eighth draft of *House Arrest*. Butler continued:

". . . And I gather it's part of southern white baptism that a whole lot of those young boys grew up thinking you can do a whole lot of things with a girl but it's not sex until you've actually had intercourse. And of course I have a problem with that because it means no gay sex is ever sex. I mean that's so ridiculous."

To me there was nothing ridiculous about any single inch of this saga. Nor was it a farce, or a burlesque, or any of the many things that some of the smartest people I knew were calling it. To me, the whole thing felt like a funeral.

DECEMBER 1998
THE CONGRESSIONAL CHRISTMAS BALL
THE WHITE HOUSE

Amo and Priscilla had invited me to the Congressional Christmas Ball at the White House again this year. I have now two or three sets of pictures of going to that ball—pictures of me with Clinton and the Houghtons (two different Christmases), pictures of me and Priscilla in front of the White House Christmas tree, pictures of all of us dressed in our black-tie finest on P Street lining up to go. I have a veritable gallery of photos of myself with the president because somehow the president's presence is connected to a camera the way a car key is connected to a car. I also have a few wonderful photographs of the president "behind the scenes," courtesy of Diana Walker at *Time,* who manages, miraculously, to capture one of the most photographed men in the world "candidly." This year was an entirely different matter. Christmas in the White House on the eve of a possible impeachment.

We gathered in the living room on P Street with the Houghtons' other houseguests, then Senator Michael Castle of Delaware and his wife. Spirits were low.

Amo and the senator struggled with what they were going to do. They didn't know, they said, how they were going to vote. Senator Castle was most likely going to vote for impeachment. His constituency wouldn't have it otherwise.

"This is going to be some party," Amo said in his generously volumed voice.

"A lot of people aren't even coming," Senator Castle said.

"I think it's just *terrible,*" Priscilla exclaimed.

Both Amo and the senator were in cummerbunds and suspenders, not yet having donned their tuxedo jackets. Amo was holding a folded piece of paper in both his hands. It was an op-ed. The rest of us were holding drinks—varying from Perrier to Scotch.

"Amo. Read your op-ed for Anna," Priscilla instructed.

"Well . . ."

"It's *wonderful*."

"Well Idunnoaboutall *that*."

"*Amo,*" she insisted. "Amo has written the most wonderful piece for the *Times,* and he's *got* to send it."

"Is there a problem?" I asked.

"*Well,* I dunno," Amo continued.

"You *have* to," said Priscilla with urgency, making quick eye contact with each of us.

The senator seemed to understand Amo's predicament, and so did his wife. It was Priscilla who was showing that she was from a long line of Bostonian abolitionists, and was pulling out all the stops to insist that Amo stand up for what, at least in her mind, was right. She was possibly the most liberal of the bunch.

Finally, Amo read his op-ed aloud to us. He was asking his colleagues to think of Christmas as the spirit of forgiveness, and to avoid impeachment. That doesn't sound outrageously progressive, but it was considered so among Republicans who felt that "forgiveness" was out of the question. The stakes were high for Amo, a Republican, given the fact that this vote was expected to be a completely partisan affair.

Throughout the evening, Priscilla would enumerate the reasons why he needed to send the piece to the *Times*.

"Time tago," Amo called out.

The men rose and put on their jackets. Amo stuffed his op-ed in his breast pocket.

Amo and Priscilla are not ostentatious. Amo had a driver who drove a simple American economy car. We piled in. When we got to the White House, we left David, who had driven us, smoking his pipe in the little bit of snowfall that there was. As we approached the walk to the White House, we met an assemblage of young women and men with notebooks to check our names.

"Anna Deavere Smith," I said, for the umpteenth time upon reaching the White House.

"Spell that?"

"D-e-a-v-e-r-e. Sometimes they leave the *a* out," I said, by rote now. "You might want to check under Smith."

"I'm sorry, ma'am . . . I don't . . ."

"It's Anna Deavere Smith," Amo chimed in.

"Oh, here it is under Smith. Okay, that's easy. Welcome to the White House."

This was almost like doing your combination lock at the gym. I would imagine that, even if you entered the White House with the president himself, you'd be checked for clearance. As we came to the door we were greeted by Marines in full-dress uniforms.

FEBRUARY 1999
THE ZUNI CAFÉ (continued)

Judith Butler is more agitated than I've ever seen her. These are not the vocal tones of someone who finds a bit of humor here and there, who left philosophy for rhetoric because she was too expressive for her philosophy colleagues. This is not the Judith Butler who looked at me with pity when I said I believed in an "authentic voice." There is absolutely not a grain of nonchalance in her voice. She was on a verbal mission.

"He produces a certain mental story for himself where he's not quite acting, not quite fucking, he's not quite taking his pleasure. Cuts himself short, undermines his own constituency."

A waiter, prepared to perform, stands at the table with his palms together at his torso as if he were going to sing an aria. He stands with yet another version of our society's "studied nonchalance." The waiter's "studied nonchalance."

The waiters at Zuni are noticeably pulled up from the abdomen, pulled up from the torso. It's a nice line to look at. Our waiter recites the specials: ". . . and that's topped off with beet juice and truffle oil. What kind of water may I bring you?"

I gesture to Butler. She shrugs.

"Will you be drinking wine?" he asks.

I extend my hand to Butler, who shakes her head no. I shake my head no to the waiter; he sweeps up the wineglasses and leaves.

She launches again:

"He's devastated welfare! He's reneged on gays in the military! He's done a lot of horrible things. But I heard people who I've never heard before say, 'I've never been able to support what they've been doing in the last fifteen years, but this time I'm going to write to my congressman and say, "Don't impeach him," ' so he's got massive leftist support."

I sit up totally straight, to give myself plenty of room to absorb the punch line, which I know is coming any second. "At the very moment in which he has that, for the first time, the first time we've seen that in this country for fifteen years, twenty years, he starts bombing Iraq!"

I strike the table with my hand. "Now you're talking," I mumble. My utterance is not meant to applaud her *opinion* (which is what happens on a talk show). I applaud her linguistic achievement.

Usually when Butler gets an entire thought out—and they are long but clear thoughts—she giggles at her own linguistic achievement. This time she did not giggle.

DECEMBER 1998
THE WHITE HOUSE CONGRESSMAN'S CHRISTMAS BALL
(continued)

Normally, Priscilla, who is a great enthusiast, would say, as we entered the White House, "Doesn't the White House look *wonderful?*" This time she said, "There don't seem to be as many decorations. Amo, I was just saying to Anna, there seem to be less decorations."

"There's Barney Frank!" Amo said.

Amo scurried us over to Barney Frank and introduced me.

As I looked around the hallway of the White House, I was filled with a sudden anxiety. First of all, there's something about the place that makes it feel like a part of the National Park Service, or a bit like a museum, but not a very nice museum. Some of the furnishings seem almost shabby. There's a certain coldness to the place, and under the circumstances, it seemed particularly cold. I was looking at the portraits of presidents who had come before Clinton. I empathized immediately with what it would feel like to fail, big. To be dismantled from that powerful assembly and, in fact, to have never really fit in. Total, flat-out failure. What would it be like to wake up the morning after? It would be like having a leg amputated.

As before, we stood in a line of people to meet Clinton. In the few years I had been on the project, I had stood in those lines many times. They were always created with velvet ropes. The president meets his guests all in the activity of taking photographs. Young women staffers in pearls and Papagallos and carrying white file cards would come along to get our names and addresses, so that copies of the pictures taken with the president would reach our homes.

I never understood what would cause people, nearly all of whom were winners in a big way, to stand on line like this. Most of them had "made it" in business, politics, art, or intellectual life. Many of them are the kinds of people who would steal a cab right from under your nose in New York, and who metaphorically have gone to the head of most lines in their lives. This was easy to tell, just by their posture, the confidence they had. Many of the "members"—congressmen—brought their daughters to these balls rather than their wives. The daughters were girls of about thirteen or fourteen, in braces and dressed, no doubt, in their first evening gowns, usually red or teal blue velvet. When you reached the president, you would exchange a few words. This was meant to be a conversation, and, whether it was truly a conversation or not, it would undoubtedly be quoted—exactly what the president said, and how Mrs. Clinton looked, and what she said.

This year the line was rife with another kind of anticipation.

A woman at a free-standing mike with cards in her hand, announces: "Congressman Amory and Mrs. Priscilla Houghton." "Anna Deavere Smith."

We step up to the president and Mrs. Clinton.

I couldn't think of anyplace I would less rather be than in his shoes at that moment. I usually have a very clear memory of every time I have interacted with the president. He didn't seem to be present this time, and it was almost as if he were not there. Mrs. Clinton was more alive. He's a dyin' man, I thought, echoing an interview I had done with a member of FDR's press corps, who told me about Roosevelt's last days.

As we left, one among us whispered, "He looked awful, don't you think?"

And then the expected: "Hillary looked great."

One among us disagreed: "I could see the strain."

And another: "Looks like he's put on weight."

I remembered a cancer surgeon telling me, "When you tell people they've got cancer, the first thing they want to know is, 'Will I lose my hair?' And here they are—dying." We are a society obsessed with looks to the point of absurdity.

Senator Castle remarked that it was "a shame to bring all these people here to eat your food and drink your booze and tomorrow they're gonna stab you in the back." We could hear the music of one of the many bands playing that night and moved upstairs to the party.

FEBRUARY 1999
THE ZUNI CAFÉ (continued)

"You know the French call orgasm *le petit mort*," Butler was saying.

"The little death?"

"The little death. And I think the idea is that orgasmic pleasure can be a kind of self-loss. It can, it can be a moment in which you lose yourself, when you no longer have a sense of who you are and you lose your sense of individuality and you can have a sense of losing yourself and it can be quite terrifying in the sense that it can threaten you with a sense of obliteration. I mean, Freud developed the death drive . . ."

DECEMBER 1998
THE WHITE HOUSE CONGRESSMAN'S CHRISTMAS BALL
(continued)

We had now gone upstairs.

There was a huge table with food—never enough, however. People stood in line to get a plate and wait for food. If there was food, there were no plates. I did think that given that this was the "home" of the most powerful man in the world, the food part could feel a little less like cattle grazing.

"I'm just *starving*," said Priscilla. "Aren't *you*? Amo could care less about food! We'll have to fend for ourselves."

Amo had taken someone by the elbow and was obviously telling a joke. I saw him give that person a punch in the arm and burst into peals of laughter. I marveled at how he could do that, with what he had on his mind.

"I always tease Amo," Priscilla once said to me. "I think he's had that tuxedo for thirty years. They don't even make them like that anymore!"

"How many women can say that their husbands can still *fit* in a suit that's thirty years old?" I asked.

"Well, that's true," she conceded.

Amo's father had been, among other things, the ambassador to France, and his mother apparently could manage to know everyone at a party by the end of the night. She had passed on her charm and gregarious spirit to Amo, who was moving around the room in a way that was certainly "working" the party, but it didn't look like work. He was used to holding up his end of a conversation and doing a little soft shoe with it. It was like watching Fred Astaire, watching him move around that huge room.

Once when we were driving home from another one of those parties, he had quietly said, "When I was a kid . . . we—had—to—wear—a suit and tie, ta dinner every night."

FEBRUARY 1999
SAN FRANCISCO
ON THE PHONE AT MY STONE-TOP DESK

I was talking to Patricia Williams, who is a legal scholar. She also writes for *The Nation* magazine. She has a little boy named Peter, who was seven at the time. She told me about the time that a friend of his was over, and suddenly one of them called out, "Let's go play Monica and Bill." With that they whizzed by Patricia and her mother, who was visiting. They went into Peter's bedroom and slammed the door.

Patricia was stunned and horrified. Her mind immediately went many directions about what would or would not be good parenting under the circumstances. She didn't know what to do.

Her mother rose without a word and went to the door. She knocked. "Boys, boys? What's going on?"

Then they heard the boys making the sounds of war: "Kerblash, kerboom!" It turned out, Monica and Bill was a game of "bombing the Monica."

They had conflated various parts of the news into one thought. They had heard talk of Monica and Bill, and they had heard language about bombing. The Monica to them was a ship of some sort, or an area of land. Another riff on Freud's "death drive," from a seven-year-old.

FEBRUARY 1999
THE ZUNI CAFÉ (continued)

Butler is eating salad. Her face is full of expression as we proceed. Her eyes seem to be moving to read her own thought as the thought comes out of her mouth.

"Actually, Freud developed the notion of the death drive when he started asking why people repeat some of the same patterns in life. And at first he thought, oh, they repeat them because they're just trying to do them differently? Right?"

"Okay."

"So they keep getting involved with the same kind of people or they keep producing the same kind of problems on the job because they are looking for satisfaction they can't quite have."

"Okay."

"And finally he decided, well, there are certain kinds of compulsive repetition that don't seem to be about finding satisfaction at all, they seem to be about repeating traumatic events where there, there's no possibility of achieving satisfaction."

"I understand."

"And that's where he decided that there were certain people actually in the grips of something much more self-destructive, and he decided that, in addition to libido or sexuality as a primary desire of humans, there's also the death drive."

"That's a dreary thought, to say the least."

"And they can work together. One has to ask about Clinton. I don't think that Clinton is the only one with the death drive. I think his colleagues certainly revealed the depth of their own death drives."

I told Judith about Patricia Williams's son "bombing the Monica." "My God!" she exclaimed, with a mouth full of salad. "Oh, my God! There you go, there you go! You don't even need to read Freud." The "death drive," is seems, is pretty basic.

DECEMBER 1998
THE WHITE HOUSE CONGRESSMAN'S CHRISTMAS BALL
(continued)

Amo was chatting away. Priscilla was eating a "finger food" dessert. I perused the room. I stopped at the Clinton staff who were camped out on one side. No matter how dressed up they were, they always looked like they were working.

In fact, everyone at that party was working. It didn't matter what they had on, the fact of their work, their politicking work, was ingrained in every vessel. They could have been wearing Chanel, Armani, it didn't matter, the work seeped through.

I wandered over to the periphery, where members of Clinton's staff, each year, were stationed. I approached Sidney Blumenthal. "How are things?"

"Keep your eyes open for the next few days," he said. "It's going to get worse. Stop by." I never did. Maybe the whole thing was just too deadly.

I moved on to Ann Lewis. "How are things?"

Looking straight ahead at the party, with a huge smile on her face, she said, "It's Alice in Wonderland. It's the Mad Hatter's tea party, and Tom DeLay is pouring."

I wandered off and connected up with Amo. "Let's go hear the jazz band," he said, taking me by the arm. We went to where the music was, and found it a near-empty room.

"Look!" Amo pointed in the direction of the band. "Strom Thurmond is dancing!"

SPRING 1999
LOS ANGELES

We gave up, finally, on the idea of a traditional play and decided in fact to leave room for the expression of a possible theater of our time. In the end, when *House Arrest* was produced in 1999, we played one act as in a play and left the second act completely open for audience discussion of what was happening in our country. According to a *Los Angeles Times* critic, the audience is said to have been more engaged than it had been for a long time at that theater. At least it was a more truthful way to engage. If engagement is the goal. And I believe it is.

MAGGIE WILLIAMS

FORMER CHIEF OF STAFF TO THE FIRST LADY

"Lie Detector Test"

I don't know if you've ever taken one.
Well
you know
it's like going to the electric chair.
[she laughs]
I mean
they strap you
in
and put things all over you
little wires that are connected to
your arms
like a blood pressure thing
and uh
you sit there and uh
I mean I kept thinking you know the whole time
when I was taking the lie detector test—I thought this was it
then they wanted me to take one that was given I guess by the FBI,
I don't know, Justice, I'm totally mixed up on this—
and you sit in a chair and you think—
Now what did I do in my life to get to the place
where I'm taking a lie detector test?
This is also the first time I was
ever fingerprinted
when I went to the FBI Building
uh
ya know

I just
I just
ya know you just feel like a common criminal
(she laughs)
is what you feel like
is like a common criminal.
But the uh
the test itself was horrible
and I thought once I had taken it
Well there
people will have to see
they'll have to see that
I'm telling the truth
and then of course by the time I had taken the second one and
      passed it
I said, Well you know this is you know a hands-down situation.
I actually do think it was at the lie—
the two detector tests
where you know nothing changed according to the
questioning and the treatment
in fact it got harsher.
What they care about is making a kind of a political point
and then they really didn't care about me
I was just in the way.
I mean I switched it from being so intent
on trying to remember things
and get ready
for these things
to just reading the Bible
because it was clear that they didn't care about anything that I had
      to say.
[I ask: "Did you think I was coming to Washington to fight?]
Oh no.
Oh no.
I wasn't going to Washington to fight.
I was going to Washington
and I was going to work for the first lady

because
I had just, I mean
my experience in having worked with her before
was—
you know, we had worked on I thought the most important issues
there were—
We worked on children and family issues.
And,
if she was going to keep doing that—
which I was sure that she was—
to me it seemed like
you know the most important thing I could do.
And she gave me such great hope
quite frankly.
And that's what I thought I would be doing.
And,
uhm,
I didn't think that I would
be having to
defend my
integrity
and—
Also the idea
that you have people chipping away—
at you know
this person that—
you and
your mother and your father
and all these other people have worked so hard to help
create.
And in an instant
they can
uhm—
I didn't think
that I would be wasting so much
time.

EVERYBODY'S TALKING

MONICA LEWINSKY

1998–1999
WASHINGTON, NEW YORK, SAN FRANCISCO,
LOS ANGELES, BOSTON

At any rate, everybody was talking. The tones of studied nonchalance were lifting. I heard trochees, I heard original breathing, I heard original language, and the moving rhythms and spontaneous pitches were even allowing me to hear music in the voices. As usual, when people start talking, finally, I ask myself which of the three questions I learned in the late seventies are being answered. Metaphorically, that is.

"Do you know the circumstances of your birth?" That wasn't the metaphor. "Have you ever been accused of something that you did not do?" That wasn't the metaphor. It was for the president but not for those who were watching him. "Have you ever come close to death?" That may have been the metaphor.

I took my tape recorder here and there, and plugged it into my phone. It took Monica Lewinsky to bring interesting language out of Washington. Why is that? I was reminded of a woman I interviewed who was dying of AIDS. She had been a prostitute, a drug addict, and an alcoholic. She has decided now, at age forty-nine, and in the midst of a full-blown disease, that she wanted to live. "Why did I have to come to this, to come this far to know this?" she said, as she burst into tears.

Why does it so often take extreme circumstances to get us to that which is original about us? There must be other ways of coming forward, of coming out of complacent language, of looking for more, of taking risks, of questioning the status quo.

BEN BRADLEE

FORMER EDITOR, *THE WASHINGTON POST*

"Lying"

Well, all right, sure.
Kennedy did it.
That is apparently true.
He apparently did it,
but the best
eh I can learn
there were no lawsuits.
There were no charges
of uh
rape.
There were no charges of uh
sexual misbehavior of any kind.
The rules were different
no question about it.
I mean people uh—
If there was discretion
and nobody got
hurt.
I'm in a jam because I didn't know about it
but uhm
I heard the stories certainly.
Well the times are different
and there have been several suits,
several accusations
in the current
uhm
incident.
Not to talk about lying.

Which I think is the most interesting part of this.
This is not the first lie.
This is not the first big lie.
Look
Vietnam certainly produced a, a uhm atmosphere where lying
was routine
routine by the government.
The counterculture examined—
they'd had it with churches,
schools,
institutions of all kinds,
businesses uh
colleges,
establishments.
It was very antiestablishment.
That's one of the things they were yelling about
McNamara!
Numero uno.

A MEDLEY

DAVID KENDALL

COUNSEL TO THE PRESIDENT

"Dream"

Boy.
[Exhales sharply]
I di——, I had a lotta dreams,
and I don't write them down.
I dream a lot.
I had dr——, yeah, I had dreams of peril.
And, uh, I can't say more.
I mean, a couple times I was awakened.
They weren't nightmares, but they were, uh, they were avala——
uh, one was an avalanche dream.
Because, I'd wanted to go skiing,
you know, I, I like to ski.
And, um, and I was skiing and there was an avalanche.
And there was one that I wanna say was,
wanted to go to the, uh, aaahhhh, the exhibit of, ah,

Edo art in the East Wing, which started in, like, November.
And, uh, friends had gone and my wife had gone and other
    people.
And there is a Hokusai print,
a very famous print,
showing the waves,
showing Mt. Fuji in the background,
but waves breaking over a boat.
And there was a dream I had about a tidal wave,
which combined the final scene in *Deep Impact*
with this Hokusai print, I think.
Those are the only two I remember.
And I can't remember, I c——, can't remember when——
they were always kind of near when I was gonna be up . . .

CHRIS VLASTO

INVESTIGATIVE REPORTER
ABC NEWS

"Chasing Me"

Even the first day,
even when we put [the Monica Lewinsky story] out on the radio,
and I flew.
I actually was in New York
so I hadda fly,
I was in New York—
and I flew down on the first shuttle.
And I remember the sun was comin up
and I knew that day that there were about—
Oh no actually I called my mother
and I said
"Oh, Mom, there's a big story, I broke a big story."

And she said
"Oh no."
She got very nervous,
and she got very nervous
and [whispering, urgent, sitting forward]
"Don't tell me these things."
And then I, when I saw
the sun
in Washington
I knew that everyone was going to wake up
that morning and start chasing
me.

PETER BAKER

THE WASHINGTON POST

"Netanyahu"

And if you remember, and I'm sure you do,
that was the day
uhm, uh Netanyahu was in town.
And he
was meeting with Clinton and their meeting during the day had
    been unproductive
but they decided to meet again, you know spontaneously, in the
    evening
So there was the President of the United States
meeting late into the night
with Bibi Netanyahu
trying desperately to put the Middle East peace process back on
    track.
And so the White House was already lit up with the late candles
    with people working late

and then suddenly from their perspective this kind of comes and hits
    them.
It was a scary story to put into the paper because it was so
    unpredictable and unimaginable
and uh, uh you know the very next day of course George
    Stephanopoulos goes on the air, the very first thing he says, he
    was talking about impeachment.

CHERYL MILLS

COUNSEL TO PRESIDENT CLINTON

Well, see
I don't think the law is necessarily about rightness and wrongness.
I mean, I think that's a large part of what the law tries to capture.
But it also tries to capture obligations and responsibilities,
or weed out obligations and responsibilities.
So, you know, it's that terrible paradigm of,
you see a baby facedown in the water, you don't turn it over, did
    you commit
murder?
No, our—our—our law says, we're going to preserve that level of
    space for
you and say, you have no, uh, affirmative duty in this particular
    instance.
Um, even though it would have taken you nothing—
and some states don't buy that, and have passed good samaritan
    laws, and
others haven't,
and they struggle with how to deal with that.
I think the law tries to do right and wrong,
but it also tries to preserve and protect certain freedoms,
and even the freedom not to do as much as we might think in a
    moral sense.

Because we all can't agree on the morality of that
and to the extent that a large number of us can, we might have
　　made a choice
not to impose it on someone else.

MAXINE WATERS

CONGRESSWOMAN, CALIFORNIA

"How They Keep Everybody In Line"

When the Congressional Black Caucus
had a Democratic caucus
where we tried to convince our members not to vote with the
　　Republicans
to release [the Ken Starr] material
when it hadn't been examined.
And they were all at that time basically
knew that they were going to vote to dump it out.
They were disgusted with the president.
They saw him as going down and they weren't going with him
and we made that argument within the Democratic caucus.
And it was silence you could hear a pin drop
and we changed a few minds.
And even with Dick Gephardt, he didn't get it.
The argument was
out there in Missouri
where people were
sick and tired of the discussion—
it was a sleazy affair between the president and a young lady
that kind of thing.
Rumor had it [Gephardt] was prepared to go to
the White House and ask him to resign with press in tow.
But the Congressional Black Caucus

representing
the most impoverished,
the most needy the most maligned the most everything
ended up on the point
to save a president based on principle.
I mean you see yourself
in terms of what your forefathers were doing with slavery.
You know what I'm saying?
The slaves who had made it to the house
had to still fight for the slaves
in the field.
I guess that's kind of our—
ya know?
Yeah,
ya know.
And I've thought about this thing
I tell you I was consumed
with thought about all aspects
and my own feelings
and I was on the Judiciary Committee and we were reviewing the
     appropriations for the next budget
and we had to look at the civil rights portion of the budget
and the same members of the Judiciary Committee
who led the fight, those thirteen managers were the ones who were
     all opposed to any
increases in the civil rights budget,
ya know the Canadys and the Barrs and the—
I just said
I mean I went way beyond where members are expected to go
I said, "No
I want a discussion on civil rights now!"
I said [she laughs]
"We've got police abuse cases
you've got gays who are being lynched and burned.
Don't you all have anything to say?"
And they sat there. And Barney Frank
[she laughs]

Barney said you know he wished it had been recorded because it
    told the story
of who these guys really are
Mr. Hyde said
"this is not the time or the place"
And it really pissed me off.
Because now we have two gays on that committee
we have one and a woman who's come on
I said "With all of the gays and the women and the blacks on this
    committee this is not the time?
To talk about civil rights?"
I said "When *is* the time, Mr. Chairman?"
But the relationships around here transcend the issues.
That's how they keep everybody in line.

MIKE ISIKOFF

NEWSWEEK

"Persistence"

You have to be persistent.
I mean
people hang up on you
people slam doors in your face.
One thing you do have to have that's important
particularly on this stuff—
I don't know
you have to have a really thick skin.
Now you're putting me on the couch and I don't wanna go there.
I don't know, I was less concerned about—
I don't know—
not so much in the slamming doors in your face
although it's not especially pleasant.
You knock on a door you know "I'd like to—"

I remember the trooper's wife in Arkansas
I went to Danny Ferguson's home
and, and ya know I was waiting for him to go home.
Then I figured out he was home.
I knocked on the door.
I was in a car outside
oh I don't know maybe an hour.
His wife came to the door
and I tried to you
know, and she said "No way, no how
get out of here
and leave us alone"
And I go away
I'm not a stalker.

CHRIS VLASTO

"Dirt"

There's tons of [dirt]
there's a lot of stuff that wouldn't air.
I mean, I mean the same that's what Mike, Mike Isikoff and I
I mean they killed the story on Saturday.
I had it
we had it nailed.
I called down to Cuba that night
and [they] killed it.
On, on January 20 the whole date would have changed
They didn't want to run it!
And then we put it out on the radio at 12:30.
I talked to the senior vice president,
whoever was down there at the time
I told him "Look I've got the story!"
[He's banging his hand on the table]

"We, we've got it we've got it nailed we've got to put it on
because I hear *The Washington Post* is gonna do it. We've got to
    do it now we've got to do it now!"
And then he goes "Okay we'll get back to you."
And then David Weston, who's the president, called back and said
    "We need a third source"
or a fourth source, or whatever source we had and um
we went and got it.
And I called back
about a half hour later an hour later and said "We have it this it, it,
    this is, I mean you've got to do this story." And they had some
    conference
which I would love to have been in on
down in Cuba
where I think Ted and Tom
killed it
said "Well we're down here . . ."

MIKE ISIKOFF

But for this story go back to the war room.
It was the shame card that they use.
"Serious journalists don't ask questions about stuff
like this you're telling me you're a tabloid reporter
you're asking me sleazy questions."
Look at the way Mike McCurry describes me to Howie Kurtz in
    Spin Cycle
That sleazy in the Kathleen Willey thing
this other new sleazy charge being promoted by another bimbo
    beat reporter Mike Isikoff
who goes around chasin sex stories
how cheap and tawdry
scum
they'll think you're scum

they'll make fun of you
you're a bimbo beat tabloid reporter
that's the way they use this to keep people off of
this stuff.
There's a tawdry element to this stuff
I just thought it was gonna be
it was a story
I thought that Clinton's private conduct was reckless
and for the most part most of these women were telling
the truth
and in that sense
they were lying
the Clinton people were lying and the women were telling the truth.

CHRIS VLASTO

"Running"

But when we found the dress—
well, well, well
I ran!
I literally was running in the streets of Washington.
And I run into
Jackie's office
I said
"Jackie
sit down . . .
it exists."
And she died.
She almost fell out of the chair when I told her.
And that's a great
that's a great story.

MIKE ISIKOFF

"You Use Me I Use You"

It doesn't mean that people weren't promoting this stuff
the kind of people you wouldn't want to invite to your
  home for dinner
but
there's a lot in my book that will provide ammunition to
  all sides of this.
There's probably nobody to like in this story.
It is the nature of reporting you know
that when you're talking to people and trying to get them
  to tell you shit
you like, you know, sound and act sympathetic.
I mean that's what we do.
I mean that's the way you do your job.
I mean you know
I tried to use them
they tried to use me.
This is the way the world works.
This is the way we operate.
This is the way journalism operates.
This is the way Washington works for that matter.
There was a lot of it that was hilarious.
I hope that
if you read the book
you'll find a lot entertaining.
There's a lot of funny stories.

JACKIE JUDD

ABC NEWS

The day that Monica turned the dress over was a,
    was a huge day for us
not only because of the significance that the dress
    played in the story
but the dress had become emblematic of all of our reporting
and because the dress had never been turned over
it never existed
for
those who were critical of our work
and it colored how all of our reporting was seen
and—
So once the dress was turned over
it suddenly lent credibility not only to our initial report that she had
    claimed that such a dress existed.
But to all of our reporting—it all became more credible because of
    that single act of her turning the dress over.
That's all I wanted to say.

CHRIS VLASTO

"Semen"

The—blue—dress.
Oh I knew about it the first day and nobody wanted to touch it
before
before we broke it.
I had known that she—
I had heard that she had sent up a dress

that had semen on it
and
with all the gifts
to her mother in New York
and I thought it should have been mentioned the very first day
but
Oh
we can't bring that up.
Oh come on Chris shut up.
You cannot talk—
We don't want to talk about semen
oh no.
And they're goin on and on
You can't talk about semen
go away.

BARNEY FRANK

CONGRESSMAN, MASSACHUSETTS

"Oral Sex"

What did the president touch and when did he touch it?
I mean,
that was the big account of perjury
was that Bill Clinton acknowledged that she had performed oral
    sex on him but he denied that he touched her breasts or
    vagina.
To impeach the president of the United States because he admitted
    that the woman sucked him, but he denied that he touched her.
At one point I said to Maxine,
[Congresswoman Maxine Waters] was standing with her full back
    to the committee room chatting with me,
and I said "I don't know, Max.
What's all this nonsense about?"

I said "I don't, I guess I don't understand why everybody gets so
    excited about whether
he touched her breasts.
I mean touching a woman's breast is no big deal as far as I can
    see."
She grabbed my hand and said "Well you want me to show you?"
I said "No, no."
And the last thing I think was, I think, and I with this, I think—
was on censure.
I think it would have been better for the House to have done
    censure and not gone to the Senate.
And one of their arguments was censure doesn't mean anything.
It's just a slap on the wrist.
Two it's a bad precedent because it'll cripple the president if he can
    be censured on a regular basis.
Well it can't be both—it can't be too little and then too much.
I reminded people that I myself had been reprimanded [because of
    involvement with a male prostitute].
And what I said was "Look,
you all, some of you are saying this doesn't mean anything.
I know it means something.
I was reprimanded, I know what it meant to me.
And I don't see how anybody who ever served here can say a
    reprimand from this place doesn't mean anything.
It memorializes the fact that you behaved very badly."
Formally in the House, a censure, you have to stand in the well of
    the House while it's read.
It's a vote, it's a resolution voted by the House.
"The House hereby reprimands you for bad conduct."
You know it's forever in the records.
"We hereby resolve that you are a, an embarrassment and you
    behaved very badly."
I mean, I, you don't, if you're totally indifferent to the expressed
    formal
opinion of the United States House of Representatives,
it's hard for me to think you'd run for Congress.
(Pause)

[I asked: "Did you have any dreams you'd be willing tell me?"]
Yes and no.
Yes I had dreams, no I won't tell you about them.
I mean I was uncomfortable really,
and there was this period but on August 17,
I went to Provincetown for vacation on Sunday the sixteenth,
I was going to stay for three or four days.
And then this hit the fan and
I found myself on Monday night doing CNN, Fox, ABC, CBS, and
    NBC.
I did them all by remote in response to the Clinton piece.
Now why was I getting all five networks? Nobody else wanted to
    do it.
I was the only one willing to defend Clinton.
I may have had a dream or two about being up there, relatively
    isolated, defending Clinton. Um, and you know, there were
    some other Democrats who were sort of distancing.
So somebody said "Gee I, that's kind of brave, you're out there all
    alone defending Clinton."
And I said "Frankly, being in Provincetown and defending oral sex
is not a hard position."

A REMINISCENCE
BILL BARBEAU

FIREMAN, VIETNAM VET

"You Get All Your Dogs Together"

I was gonna stay wid my dog
I was gonna stay wid him
I mean I wanted to stay wid him.
It was him and I.
But you had local
animals

and the enemy
used to use
a local dog
from the village
that either ran out of
or come passin through
they'd feed the dog and the dog ed follow 'em
and the dog ed go out
and of course the dog wants to walk first on a trail
and if he stepped on a mine, so what.
But I took care of [Satan].
Thirteen months we ate
we ate out of the same plate.
We drank the same water
the same canteen cup.
We were like
tied together.
The end of that five-foot leash was the dog
that was him and I
and I'm not alone
it was all dog handlers were like that
all us scout dog handlers were like that
those of us that lived through it were close to your dog.
That's how your dog—
Sometimes the circumstances happen
that
you're gonna get killed
or the dog's gonna get shot.
Ya can't avoid that
but
you take care of that dog
the dog'll take care of you.
He kept me a-alive.
I kept that dog perfect
clean
fed.
We used to have um

circle jerks
for the dogs
for the male dogs.
You get four or five guys together and we bring our dogs in and
    you have circle jerks
and what it did was it kept your dog from
chasing
bitches in heat.
You get four or five dogs together and you jerk your dogs off.
I'm alive.
It's got its practical side.

ED BRADLEY

60 MINUTES HOST

"Captives"

Both are captives.
Um
I think the press is
individually and collectively a captive
of the White House.
[He puts a spoonful of yogurt in his mouth, and scrapes the cup]
In that
you go there every day.
And you stay there
Ehmm,
You, you don't leave because you have to look at these
photo ops.
As they're called.
That the president does during the course of the day.
And
[He scrapes the yogurt cup]
where there's an opportunity to throw a

question at him to which he doesn't always respond.
For example
a cabinet meeting.
A meeting with
some foreign leader
a meeting with congressional leaders
uhm
in which the press is ushered in—
for
a specific period of time—
a minute two minutes—
so they can get a picture—
they stand there with notes and pads—
eh—
"Mr. President, what about Bosnia?"
scream at him.
If he wants.
if he has something he wants to *say* then he'll use that opportunity
he'll take advantage of it.
If he doesn't
most of the time he'll ignore you.
Sometimes the president will say something when he has no
    intention of saying
something—
when it's not thought out,
and you get a free—
something.
But it's really a very limited exchange.
He's a captive
because
he's there.
Uhm
it's a very
controlled existence.
Uh
there's no freedom.
You can't just pick up and go,

uh
you can
rarely.
Uhm
without an announcement
that
the president is moving.
And the president moving
is not like you moving.
[He clears his throat]
You can't—
you can walk out here today and decide
"Well let me run over to Barney's I need to pick this thing up."
The president to do that has gotta take an entourage—
Somebody's gotta go there with dogs
and uh, eh—
ya know it just becomes uh, you, you
you are a captive of the White House!
True you have a lot of power and there's a lot you can do with it.
But you are a captive.
And the press
is very much a captive.
Because
[Hits his hand on the desk along with the next line in rhythm]
If he moves, we move.
If he sits, we sit.
[Hits the desk again]
And people don't like to say it
but everybody
particularly in those situations
and given the climate and the world we live in today
everybody's on the deathwatch.

PLAYING CLINTON

Perhaps Clinton's downfall was that he was too expressive in a time when studied nonchalance is the status quo. I don't know if that's Clinton's downfall, or the downfall of where we are as a society. People say that he should have had the moral courage to tell the truth when first confronted about Monica Lewinsky. I won't pretend to know what would have happened had he done that. I won't pretend to know if any of the people who have said what he should do would have done that had they been in his shoes.

The creation of language is the creation of a fiction. The minute we speak we are in that fiction. It's a fiction designed, we hope, to reveal a truth. There is no "pure" language. The only "pure language" is the initial sounds of a baby. All of us lose that purity, and as we get more "of" the world, we even lose sometimes the capacity to keep that breath moving in our language.

Our ability to create reality, by creating fictions with language, should not be abused. The abuse is called lying. Perhaps we understand the precariousness of our situation. We as linguistic animals. At the very least language is currency as we create "reality." To abuse language, to lie, is to fray reality, to tatter it. Those in public life who create our values are especially asked not to "lie." Yet most of us *say*, at least, that we believe we are often being lied to.

I am not satisfied to accept words at their face value. I don't really know what they mean, and I watch breakdowns of communication the way the morning helicopter looks for traffic delays. I assume them as a reality.

I take the words I can get and try to occupy them. Using the idea that my grandfather gave me—"If you say a word often enough it becomes you"—I borrow people for a moment, by borrowing their words. I borrow them for a moment to understand something about them, and to understand something about us. By "us," I mean humans.

In the course of occupying Clinton's words, I have learned only a few things so far. His idea was clear: The system is contentious. The press is aligned with power, and the pairing of the press with those who want power is bad for America—

"I told you what that Republican senator told me
and you can use this.
He said,
'Before you got elected
we were stupid enough to think the press was liberal
and then we realized
that they are liberal in the sense that most of 'em vote Democrat.'
He said 'They vote with you but they think like us.'
And I asked him what he meant and he said
"You're a Democrat
you come here thinkin you can do good.
You wanna use the power of the gubment to make good things happen,
improve people's lives."
He said "Republicans are suspicious
of the ability to make anybody's life better."
He said "We like this because we want power
and the press
they want power
so let 'em vote with you, they think like us.
When you're in they get power and we get power the same way.
We hurt you
so never mind what the truth is.
Hit the target!"

But Clinton is much more than that idea, and much more than his argument that "We really have to ask ourselves, Do we want to put our public officials in a position of having to bankrupt themselves just to survive in office?"

He is more than his confession "Now. I'm just like one those ol' Baby Huey dolls you had when you were a kid. You punch 'em and they come back up. So I'm fine."

And more than his warning

"But it's bad for the country.
It's bad
when the burden of proof is on the accused
and you're supposed to disprove all conceivable ac——
accusations
present
or future
and if you don't!
There's somethin wrong with ya.
That's bad."

I performed Clinton before the Monica Lewinsky scandal and after. It was harder to play it after. I was working against the disbelief of the audience. By my last performance of *House Arrest* in New York, I had learned something, in part because of the lighting designer. Lighting can do a lot to create a president, as Michael Deavere discovered when he brought lighting and the photo op into the White House.

My lighting designer had created an environment that made me look very far away from the audience. He wanted to show the power of the president. I decided that I should work with the image of power on the one hand but the feeling of powerlessness on the other. It was from that feeling of powerlessness, on an empty stage, in front of an audience that was predisposed *not* to believe me, that my work began.

In acting school we are told to play the play as if it were the first time. When I played Clinton, and ultimately when I played the entire play *House Arrest,* I began to play it as if it were the *last* time I would ever speak in public again. It was from that place that I began to get a feeling of what is at stake in the very powerful position of president of the United States.

It was my only way in. As an African American woman, I am actually not predisposed to know much about power. I am predisposed to identify with, and know a lot about, powerlessness. I was, from the outset, more comfortable playing an incarcerated child murderer, one who would be considered the lowest of the low, than I was playing the president of the United States.

So there I was, at the Public Theater in New York, every night. When it came time to be Clinton, I was looking out in the dark. And from out of the dark, I found a determination to find somebody out there in the darkness to talk to. I was going to find someone who would listen, someone who would hear my case. I was going to make my case. Whether I made my case or not was not the point, it was the activity of finding an ear upon which to rest my case. And my case was not really about the Republicans, and not really about the press, and not really about what they had done to Hillary and what they had done to me. My case was "I'm just like one those ol' Baby Huey dolls you had when you were a kid. You punch 'em and they come back up."

Inevitably someone, and sometimes many people, would laugh. Sometimes they would applaud. He had made his case. And he would continue with "So I'm fine." And again "I'm fine."

STUDS TERKEL

AMERICANIST

"Clowns"

Ya know when it gets back to as far as guys
presidents with dames.
My God!
Ya know
Kennedy my God
it wasn't so much Addison's disease
he suffered from satyriasis probably
In fact he said it.

So what?
And my favorite president
the one,
the one president of the century,
major league
FDR of course.
Well FDR is said to have had a fling with a socialite
and he had polio.
I said My God the man has polio
this might be very good therapy!
Long before McCarthy there was New Salem
I think Hillary has a point
about it being a right-wing—
[but]
that's too simple.
Well of course they're out to get him.
That's not what the issue is to me
the issue is
What the hell have we learned?
Where are we?
I was born in 1912
the year the *Titanic*
sank.
The greatest ship ever built!
It hits the tip of an iceberg and bam! It went down.
It went down
and I came up.
Wow some century!
But it's not this.
This almost becomes not the crowning touch
but the clowning touch!
It's the clowning touch!
It ends with a fright wig
putty nose
with baggy pants
and this is it!
It's not just Clinton and Monica

we all are wearing the fright wig and putty nose and baggy pants
we're all demeaned
by that I mean
all of us are clowns and that's what it's all about.
Instead of a new century
with all the discoveries made
in medicine
perhaps more to come.
And yet with fewer and fewer people controlling
more and more and more.
And the more and more and more feeling more and more and
     more
helpless.
And who runs the means of communication that condition these
     people to vote as they vote and think as they think?
We got Lewinsky-ism and Monica-ism
instead of what the hell we been doing to all these countries and to
     the have-nots in this country?
So we're wearing baggy pants putty nose
fright wigs.
We've been conditioned to wear them
by this time.
[Pause]
We've got to question official truth.
The thing that was so great about Mark Twain—
We honor Mark Twain ya know
and we don't read 'im.
We may read *Huck Finn,*
even Huck of course was tremendous.
Remember what Huck did?
That great scene on the raft you know
when Huck—
See
you have to
question official truth—
So truth—is the law was:
a black man is property, is a thing

and he's [Huck's] on with a property named Jim
a slave, see
on the raft.
And he heard that Jim says he's going to do a terrible thing.
And Huck is thirteen, twelve
and Jim said he's going to look for his wife and kids.
And he's gonna steal them
from the woman
or person who owns them.
And Huck says "That woman never did me any harm"
[Whispering]
I'm—
he's gonna steal!
In, in Huck's own mind—
Huck Finn is what it's all about.
The goodness of Huck you see.
He's an illiterate kid right
he's had no schoolin
but there's something in . . .
[Whispering, expressive, urgent]
and he says "Oh it's a terrible thing wow what an awful thing he's
    gonna steal."
And just then two slavers caught up—
the guys chasing the slaves,
looking for Jim
ya know.
And they come up "Anybody on that raft with ya?"
[Pause]
And Huck yeah (dibdebi) . . .
They know there's somebody there.
[Pause]
"Is he white or black?"
And Huck says
(Pause)
"White."
and they go off—
"Oh my God my conscience"

I lied!
Ya know
I lied
and he's gonna—
but if—
"I did a terrible thing"
(Pause)
"Why do I feel so good?"
There ya got it
in Huck
ya captured the human species.
That stuff that Huck is there
that part's been buried!
We're all demeaned.
We're all under the bed.
Who's under the bed?
The clowns are under the bed.
Clowns.
We're burlesque comics
the ringmasters
who is a ringmaster?
The guys who run the conglomerates whoever they are.
These ringmasters themselves are clowns too
except they happen to have power.
But they're also faceless.
The irony is most of these guys are faceless.
The ringmasters
in the old days
you knew in the old days,
this clown this brute
this—
But they're all there,
but they're faceless.
So there you have it!
So okay kid!
I've got to scram! I've got to go see my cardiologist!

ABOUT THE AUTHOR

ANNA DEAVERE SMITH is an actor, a teacher, a playwright, and the creator of an acclaimed series of one-woman plays based on her interviews with diverse voices from communities in crisis. She is the founder and director of The Institute on the Arts and Civic Dialogue at Harvard University, and is the Ann O'Day Maples Professor of the Arts at Stanford University. Her works include *Twilight: Los Angeles, 1992* and *Fires in the Mirror,* and she has written for *Newsweek* and *The New Yorker,* among other publications. She lives in San Francisco.

ABOUT THE TYPE

This book was set in Monotype Dante, a typeface designed by
Giovanni Mardersteig (1892–1977). Conceived as a private type for
the Officina Bodoni in Verona, Italy, the Monotype Corporation's
version of Dante followed in 1957.